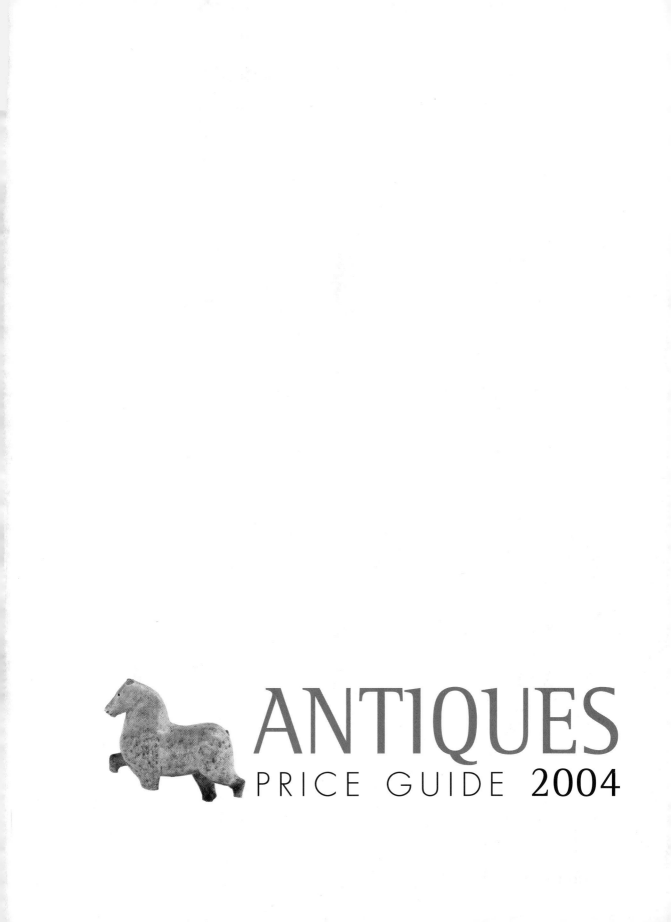

ANTIQUES
PRICE GUIDE 2004

ANTIQUES
PRICE GUIDE 2004

Judith Miller

DK

DK PUBLISHING

LONDON, NEW YORK, MELBOURNE,
MUNICH, and DELHI

A joint production from DORLING KINDERSLEY
and THE PRICE GUIDE COMPANY

THE PRICE GUIDE COMPANY LIMITED

Publisher Judith Miller

Publishing Manager Julie Brooke

Antiques Editor Silas Currie

European Consultant Martina Franke

Managing Editor Claire Smith

Editor Carolyn Wilmot

Assistant Editors Megan Watson,
Sara Sturgess, Christine Allinger

Digital Image Co-ordinator Cara Miller

Editorial Assistants Sandra Lange, Dan
Dunlavey, Katie Lamble, Kirsty Miller,
Alex Higham, Emily Crane, Lucie Baird

Design and DTP Tim Scrivens, TJ Graphics

Photographers Graham Rae, Bruce
Boyajian, John McKenzie, Byron Slater,
Steve Tanner, Elizabeth Field, Dave
Pincott, Ellen McDermott, Martin
Spillane, Mike Molloy

Advertising and Marketing Consultants
Richard Tidsall, Nisia Studzinska

Indexer Hilary Bird

Workflow Consultant Edward MacDermott

Publishing Advisor Nick Croydon

DORLING KINDERSLEY LIMITED

Category Publisher Jackie Douglas

Designers Martin Dieguez, Kelly Meyer,
Mandy Earey

Managing Art Editor Heather McCarry

Managing Editor Julie Oughton

DTP Designer Mike Grigoletti

Production Controller Joanna Bull

Production Manager Sarah Coltman

First American edition, 2003
00 01 02 03 04 05 10 9 8 7 6 5 4 3 2 1

Published in the United States by
DK Publishing, Inc.
375 Hudson Street
New York, New York 10014

The Price Guide Company Ltd
info@thepriceguidecompany.com

A CIP catalog record for this book is available from the Library of Congress.

ISBN 0-7894-9550-3

Colour reproduction by Colourscan, Singapore
Printed and bound by MOHN media and Mohndruck GmbH, Germany

Discover more at
www.dk.com

CONTENTS

INTRODUCTION

IT IS VERY EXCITING to be putting together my second full-color annual *Antiques Price Guide* with DK. During the year my team and I have been doing photography from Idaho to Philadelphia and gathering in around 10,000 new photographs, over 8,000 of which are featured in *Antiques Price Guide 2004*.

In a time when many other areas of investment have been shaky, the art and antiques market has been buoyant. As always, good, rare, desirable things are at a premium, with record prices a weekly phenomenon but the whole market has seen a steady improvement with solid growth being the key word.

The question I am always asked is how do we arrive at our price ranges. As we all know, the price of an antique is what a willing buyer will give to a willing seller. But that does beg a lot of questions. To feel more confident in buying antiques we need to have a "ball park" figure, an idea of what we would pay for a similar object. If the piece is damaged it will be substantially less; if it is in superb original condition, it will be substantially more. What this price guide gives you is some idea of where to begin. It tells you that something is

roughly $200–300, $2,000–3,000, or $20,000–30,000. As an object becomes more rare, more desired by serious collectors and dealers, the price guide will be wider. Record prices always astonish us, particularly if we happen to be the under bidder at an auction, or the person at an antiques fair who turned an object down, only to find it snapped up by someone who did not think the price outrageous.

As we change every image every year it is possible for us to reflect the marketplace. This year we have focused on the Decorative Arts section and Modern Classics from the 1950s onwards, as these are becoming increasingly popular.

Collecting is a wonderful hobby and what makes it more fascinating is being able to browse through thousands of relevant color photographs of goods that are in the marketplace and then to check out the price ranges. I was once asked why I produced the *Antiques Price Guide* and I admitted it was because I needed it! I trust you will use it as much as I do.

Enjoy!

Judith Miller.

LIST OF CONSULTANTS

CERAMICS

Jill Fenichell
305 East 61st Street
New York, NY 10021

18TH- AND 19TH-CENTURY FURNITURE

Paul Roberts
Lee Young
Freeman's, 1808 Chestnut Street
Philadelphia PA 19103

AMERICAN FURNITURE & AMERICANA

Lynda Cain
Freeman's
1808 Chestnut Street
Philadelphia PA 19103

AMERICAN ARTS & CRAFTS

David Rago
Craftsman Auctions
333 North Main Street
Lambertville NJ 08530

LALIQUE

Nicholas M. Dawes
333 Auctions
333 North Main Street
Lambertville
NJ 08530

AMERICAN GLASS

Dudley Browne
James D Julia Inc
PO Box 830
Fairfield
Maine 04937

AMERICAN PAINTINGS

Alasdair Nichol
Freeman's
1808 Chestnut Street
Philadelphia PA 19103

MODERN

David Rago
Rago Modern Auctions
333 North Main Street
Lambertville NJ 08530

We would also like to thank our many friends who give us so much of their time and expertise: Anne Rogers Haley and M.L. Coolidge at North East Auctions; Glenn Hart and Mitch Michener at Bucks County Antiques Center; and Victor Weiner and Sylvia Leonard Wolf of the Appraisers Association of America.

HOW TO USE THIS BOOK

Page tab – This device appears on every spread and identifies the main category heading as indicated in the Contents List on pp.5–6.

The Introduction – The key facts about a factory, maker, or style are given, along with stylistic identification points, value tips, and advice on fakes.

Caption – The description of the item illustrated, including, when relevant, the period, the maker or factory, medium, the year it was made, dimensions, and condition. Many captions have **footnotes** which explain terminology or give identification or valuation information.

Running head – Indicates the sub-category of the main heading.

A Closer Look At – Does exactly that. This is where we show identifying aspects of a factory or maker, point out rare colors or shapes, and explain why a particular piece is so desirable.

An early Lowestoft shell-shaped sweetmeat dish.
c1765   5.75in (14.5cm) high
$3,500-4,500   TBk

The object – The antiques are shown in full color. This is a vital aid to identification and valuation. In many areas of antiques, a slight color variation can signify a large price differential.

The source code – Every item in *Antiques Price Guide 2004* has been specially photographed at an auction house, a dealer's shop, an antiques market, or a private collection. These are credited by the code at the end of the caption, and can be checked against the Key to Illustrations on pp.724–8.

The price ranges – These give a ball-park figure of what you should pay for a similar item. The great joy of antiques is that there is not a recommended retail price. The price guides in this book are based on actual prices, either the amount a dealer will accept or the full auction price. They are expressed in US$ (even for the Canadian antiques shown). Canadian readers should refer to latest currency conversion rates at *http://finance.yahoo.com/*

CERAMICS

THE TERM 'CERAMICS' COVERS A RANGE OF ITEMS, from functional pottery to exquisite porcelain pieces, offering the collector a wide choice of collecting areas.

Household and decorative pottery was produced at affordable prices and items remain so now, thanks to their extensive production. Porcelain is usually more expensive, although the value of a piece depends on condition, rarity, aesthetic appeal and age. Pieces were often marked by the manufacturer but collectors should

be aware that factories often copied each others' styles and marks to make their own pieces more appealing.

At present the ceramics market is subdued, so common patterns are not selling well. Transfer-printed pieces have to be either rare or precisely printed to be valuable. However, rare items are still highly desirable.

The ascendancy of the Internet has meant that collecting habits, trends and prices are increasingly influenced by global rather than local interest.

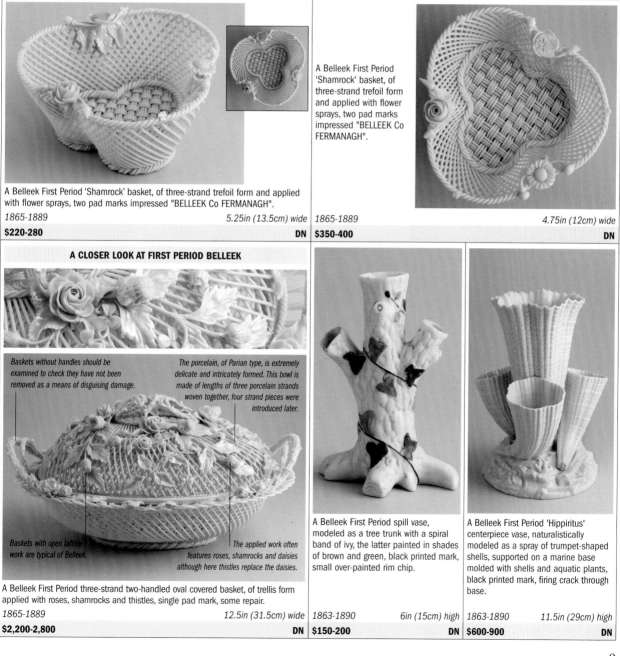

A Belleek First Period 'Shamrock' basket, of three-strand trefoil form and applied with flower sprays, two pad marks impressed "BELLEEK Co FERMANAGH".

1865-1889   *5.25in (13.5cm) wide*

$220-280   **DN**

A Belleek First Period 'Shamrock' basket, of three-strand trefoil form and applied with flower sprays, two pad marks impressed "BELLEEK Co FERMANAGH".

1865-1889   *4.75in (12cm) wide*

$350-400   **DN**

A CLOSER LOOK AT FIRST PERIOD BELLEEK

Baskets without handles should be examined to check they have not been removed as a means of disguising damage.

The porcelain, of Parian type, is extremely delicate and intricately formed. This bowl is made of lengths of three porcelain strands woven together, four strand pieces were introduced later.

Baskets with open lattice work are typical of Belleek.

The applied work often features roses, shamrocks and daisies although here thistles replace the daisies.

A Belleek First Period three-strand two-handled oval covered basket, of trellis form applied with roses, shamrocks and thistles, single pad mark, some repair.

1865-1889   *12.5in (31.5cm) wide*

$2,200-2,800   **DN**

A Belleek First Period spill vase, modeled as a tree trunk with a spiral band of ivy, the latter painted in shades of brown and green, black printed mark, small over-painted rim chip.

1863-1890   *6in (15cm) high*

$150-200   **DN**

A Belleek First Period 'Hippiritus' centerpiece vase, naturalistically modeled as a spray of trumpet-shaped shells, supported on a marine base molded with shells and aquatic plants, black printed mark, firing crack through base.

1863-1890   *11.5in (29cm) high*

$600-900   **DN**

American Belleek

American Belleek is the term given to late 19th and early 20th century US porcelain that was inspired by Irish Belleek or, more usually, contemporary Royal Worcester art porcelain. The name 'Belleek' was used as a trademark and is often printed on the wares of the Ott & Brewer porcelain factory, of Trenton, New Jersey, its successor, the Lenox Porcelain Co. and the Willets factory, also of Trenton, and Knowles, Taylor and Knowles, Liverpool, Ohio.

An American Belleek squat pitcher, by Knowles, Taylor & Knowles, with fishnet marking.

$500-800   **JF**

An American Belleek vase, by the Ceramic Art Co. which became the Lenox factory, Trenton NJ.

c1900   4.5in (11.5cm) high

$2,500-3,000   **JF**

An American Belleek Lotus ware potpourri vase and cover, by Knowles, Taylor & Knowles, double walled with reticulated body, reglued.

c1892   6.5in (16.5cm) high

$3,000-4,000   **JF**

An American Belleek Lotus ware cylindrical vase, by Knowles, Taylor & Knowles, Liverpool, Ohio, with gilt and applied floral decoration, on ball feet.

c1892   7.75in (20cm) high

$1,500-2,000   **JF**

An American Belleek large jar vase.

c1910

$2,000-2,500   **JF**

An American Belleek vase, by the Ceramic Art Co. which became the Lenox Factory, Trenton NJ, artist's monogram "K.E. Fox", probably for Katherine Fox who stayed on and worked at the Lenox factory.

11in (28cm) high

$1,200-1,800   **JF**

An American Belleek Ott & Brewer coffee pot, made in Trenton NJ, with fishscale decoration.

c1890   9in (23cm) high

$800-1,200   **JF**

An American Belleek shell-shaped cup and saucer, made by Ott & Brewer for the New Orleans exposition, very fine and transculcent porcelain.

1885   Saucer 5.5in (14cm) diam

$1,200-1,800   **JF**

A rare American Belleek vase, by Ott & Brewer, painted with gilded nasturtium on a cobalt ground, with gilded filigree handles, red "O&B Belleek" stamp with crown, minor wear to gilding at rim.

10in (25.5cm) high

$4,000-6,000   **DRA**

An American Belleek scalloped dish, by Ott & Brewer, painted with gilded leaves mounted on delicate branch base, red "Belleek O&B" crown mark, touch-up to minute fleck under rim.

8in (20.5cm) wide

$500-800   **DRA**

Two Berlin topographical cabinet cups and one saucer, the cup and saucer set with snakehead and unnamed view, the cup with a view of Egerne.

c1830s

$1,800-2,200 cup and saucer, $1,500-2,000 cup JF

A KPM, Berlin conical cup, depicting a statue of Gutenberg, with elevated scroll handle with ram's head, blue scepter mark, red orb mark.

c1835   *3.75in (9.5cm) high*

$400-600   BMN

A KPM, Berlin gilded cylindrical paw cup, the reserve depicting 'A Moonlit Scene', above three paws, handle with relief rosette, blue scepter mark "KPM".

c1837-44   *5.25in (13.5cm) high*

$300-400   BMN

A KPM, Berlin pictorial paw cup and saucer, the concave-sided cup with a gilt ground, decorated with pearl relief, the rectangular front reserve showing grotesque-style painting of 'A Girl with a Cat in a Garden under a Bird's Nest', with elevated handle and three paw feet, one paw slightly damaged, the large saucer with a smooth gold rim, red orb mark and blue scepter marks.

c1820-37   *Saucer 7.5in (19cm) diam*

$600-900   BMN

A tall KPM, Berlin campana-form vase, designed by Johann Carl Friedrich Riese in 1799, front reserve depicting 'Sanssouci Castle near Potsdam', on square plinth, blue scepter mark, red orb mark, painter mark "RS", press marks with year letter, handles restored.

1941   *17.25in (44cm) high*

$1,200-1,800   BMN

Two KPM, Berlin picture vases, campana form, design by Karl Friedrich Schinkel, nonidentical decoration, both sides with reserves of Berlin scenes: 'Opera House', 'Museum', 'New Ward', 'Long Bridge and City Castle', blue scepter mark, red orb mark, damaged.

c1832-1837   *12.25in (31cm) high*

$4,000-6,000   BMN

A pair of Berlin large porcelain urns, each campana form, the surfaces gilt except for a polychrome floral spray on each side of the body, surrounded by polychrome butterflies, factory mark under foot, light abrasion to top of rim of both.

16.25in (41.5cm) high

$700-1,000   FRE

A tall KPM, Berlin French-form vase, both sides with paintings in gilt reserves with shell and rocaille borders, showing 'The Manor in Gingst on the Island of Rügen', with gilt handles on a square plinth, blue mark with scepter.

c1850   *19.25in (49cm) high*

$3,000-4,000   BMN

A pair of large KPM, Berlin 'French vase' form vases, with gilt-edged cartouches of Babelsberg Castle, blue ground with gilt leaves, blue scepter mark on base, penny mark for 1847-49 and red scepter mark for KPM.

c1850   *19.25in (49cm) high*

$8,000-12,000   HMN

A KPM, Berlin vase, both sides with gilt-framed reserves depicting polychrome scenes from Tannhäuser, signed 'H. Krause, Dresden', acanthus bronze handles, glazed base with blue scepter mark, blue painter's mark, neck glued.

c1880-90   *29.75in (75.5cm) high*

$3,000-4,000   LPZ

A KPM, Berlin small amphora, 'French Vase' form, both sides painted with 'Bouquet of Flowers', blue scepter mark, red orb mark, letter mark for year.

c1905   *6in (15cm) high*

$300-400   BMN

Bow

The Bow factory was in production from c1744 to 1776. Situated in the parish of West Ham in Essex, England, it was founded by Thomas Fry from West Ham and Edward Heylyn from Bow.

It was the first factory to introduce 'bone china', with the addition of animal bone ash, which gave further strength to the body during firing. The early items consisted predominantly of tableware and many of the pieces copied the fashionable Japanese and Chinese styles. Later items included figures and more decorative pieces.

A distinctive feature of Bow porcelain is its thickness, probably as a result of under-firing to stop the wares from warping. When held up to the light, Bow tends to appear translucent only at the edges. Bow marks include a dagger, a longbow and an anchor. The early cream-colored porcelain may have a waxlike glaze and is subject to firing cracks, some of which may be superficial in appearance. Later Bow tends to show a more blue glaze.

The Bow factory had a remarkable output despite being in production for just thirty years.

A Bow white glazed figure depicting Winter, in the form of an old man in a cloak huddled over a brazier, carrying a stick, on shaped plinth with sticks.

c1750   5in (13cm) high

$600-900   L&T

A Bow white glazed figure of Spring, in the form of a young lady with baskets of flowers and a bee skep, with a square hole for a candle sconce.

c1750   5in (13cm) high

$600-900   L&T

A Bow figure group of two stout birds on a tree stump, with rocky base and a small dog, with a metal support for the candle sconce.

c1750   8.75in (22.5cm) high

$1,500-2,000   L&T

A Bow figure of birds and branches, depicting two stout birds on a tree stump with a small dog below, with appliquéd flowers and a round hole for a candlestick.

c1752   6.5in (16.5cm) high

$700-1,000   L&T

A pair of Bow white glazed figures of Fall and Winter, Fall sits on his basket of grapes while Winter warms his hands over a brazier, minor damage.

c1755-1760   5.25in (13.5cm) high

$1,000-1,500   WW

A CLOSER LOOK AT A BOW FIGURE

Enamel colors are often used in decoration, as are powder blue grounds. Coloring tends to be bold. Puce is a popular color on these later figures.

The Bow factory produced a range of figures, representing actors, actresses, statesmen, generals and mythological characters.

Check all extremities – fingers, plume and flowers, for signs of restoration.

This figure is in excellent condition, with finely molded details.

Look out for a square hole in the back of a Bow figure. This is sometimes a feature and was probably intended to support a metal candle bracket.

A Bow figure of Minerva, with plumed helmet with pink and gold armor and flowered and striped cloak, on a base with an owl.

c1760   12.5in (32cm) high

$1,500-2,000   L&T

A Bow figure of Minerva, with plumed helmet and loose drapery on high scalloped and scroll-cast plinth, with additional feet for balance.

c1755 *14in (36cm) high*

$2,200-2,800 **L&T**

A Bow candlestick, flanked by figures in the form of Cupid with a basket of flowers on his head and Venus, scantily clad clutching flowers, on scrolling plinth, lacking sconce.

c1760 *8.5in (22cm) high*

$1,200-1,800 **L&T**

A Bow figure of a shepherdess, modeled standing contraposto, a recumbent lamb at her feet, painted in colored enamels with iron-red and yellow-lined coatee and puce skirt with gilt flower-heads, on a flower-encrusted base, the base has been glued.

c1760 *6in (15cm) high*

$400-600 **DN**

A Bow polychrome painted figure of Minerva, with tall plumed helmet, plum-colored chain mail and flowered cloak, on plinth with a small owl, repaired arm at wrong angle.

c1760 *14.5in (37cm) high*

$400-600 **L&T**

A Bow figure of Juno and the Eagle, representing Air, after the statue by Etienne Le Hongre, she holds up a green and puce cloak and wears and floral dress, raised on a high scroll base, red anchor and dagger mark, old restoration to her wrist.

c1765 *10in (25.5cm) high*

$400-600 **WW**

A set of Bow figures, representing the Four Seasons, typically modeled with attributes, on gilt rocaille bases, three with anchor and dagger marks, minor damage and restoration.

c1765 *6.75in (17.5cm) high*

$3,000-5,000 **DN**

A rare Bow flowerpot, painted in colored enamels with flowers and leaves, and containing a tall arrangement of brightly colored flowers, some damage.

c1760 *8.25in (21cm) high*

$500-700 **LFA**

A Bow coffee cup, with loop handle, boldly painted in famille rose palette with peony and prunus and an insect in flight, decorator's mark "B" in brown.

c1753 *2.5in (6.5cm) high*

$300-400 **LFA**

Caughley

Thomas Turner took over the pottery at Caughley in 1772, after training at the Worcester factory. Caughley transfer-printed porcelain came to be known as Salopian, from the Roman name for Shropshire in which Caughley is situated. Most of Caughley wares are table services, including butter tubs, eggcups, asparagus servers, custard cups and candlesticks. The pieces were largely blue and white, in the Oriental style.

Caughley porcelain has many similarities to that of the Worcester factory. If you hold porcelain from either factory up to the light, the early examples have a green tinge. Later wares show an orange tinge, suggesting that both factories were using raw materials from the same source.

In 1799, the lease of the Caughley factory was sold to John Rose, whose factory was at Coalport. With it went the stock of unglazed goods, molds and copper-plates. Rose finally closed the factory in 1812.

A tea bowl, painted in underglaze blue, beneath a blue line rim, area glued.

The prints on this tea bowl relate to the early Caughley fruit prints (1775-80), although this bowl appears to be later.

c1785-90   3.25in (8.5cm) diam

$70-100   **LFA**

A Caughley blue and white slop bowl and a sugar bowl, the slop bowl printed with a vignette of the 'Mother and Child' pattern, the reverse with a vignette of Chinese figures with urns issuing flowers, with a blue "S" mark, slight scratches, foot-rim chips.

c1780   Larger 6.25in (16cm) diam

$400-600   **DN**

A Caughley 'Full Napkin' pattern lobed round plate, printed in underglaze blue, within a cell diaper band and landscape paneled scroll, flower and diaper border.

c1780-85   9.5in (24cm) diam

$100-150   **LFA**

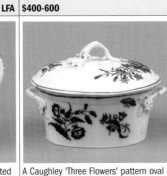

A rare Caughley 'Pagoda' pattern fluted baluster-shaped sparrow beak milk jug, with scale-molded loop handle, printed in underglaze blue, the scale, diaper and butterfly border picked out in gilt, blue printed "S" mark.

c1780-85   4.5in (11cm) high

$500-700   **LFA**

A Caughley 'Three Flowers' pattern oval butter tub and cover, the two twig handles and knop with applied flower-head terminals, printed in underglaze blue, within blue line borders, one terminal to knop restored.

c1780   6.25in (16cm) high

$220-280   **LFA**

A Caughley 'Fisherman and Cormorant' pattern mask jug, blue and cabbage leaf-molded with small chip to spout.

c1785   7.25in (18.5cm) high

$400-600   **DN**

A Caughley 'Cottage' pattern custard cup and cover, with loop handle and ball knop, printed in underglaze blue, beneath a cell diaper band, cover with small rim chip.

c1780-85   2.75in (7cm) high

$400-600   **LFA**

Chelsea

The Chelsea factory was the first successful British porcelain works and was founded in 1744 at Chelsea by Nicholas Sprimont, a Huguenot silversmith. Many of the designs at Chelsea were influenced by British silverware shapes. There are three distinct periods at Chelsea which are named after marks used at the time. The period (c1744-1749) is known as the Triangle period. These early wares are characterized by glassy white porcelain with minimal decoration and were influenced by British Rococo silver shapes. Popular items were cream-jugs, beakers and teapots.

The second phase at Chelsea is known as the Raised Anchor period (1749-52). These wares were more robust, and had tin oxide added to the glaze to opacify it. Decoration was increasingly styled on Kakiemon porcelain and landscapes in the manner of those on Meissen wares. Scenes from Aesop's fables became a Chelsea speciality. Birds and figures were also produced, but these are rare.

The next phase was the Red Anchor period (1752-1756). This period was famous for dessert table services, in particular tureens in the shape of fruit, vegetables, animals, birds, and fish. Botanical decoration became popular as well as figures.

The final phase at Chelsea was the Gold Anchor period (1756-1769). These later wares were influenced by the colored grounds and the Rococo shapes of the French wares of Vincennes and Sèvres. The Chelsea anchor mark was now painted in gold rather than red, and gilding became a popular form of decoration. These pieces were more elaborate and were intended to be purchased as luxury items.

The Chelsea factory was bought by John Heath and William Duebury, owners of the Derby factory, in 1769. Wares from this period are often referred to as Chelsea-Derby. The failing factory finally closed in 1784.

A Chelsea dish, molded in relief with flowers and painted in the Kakiemon style with a central 'ho ho' bird and flower sprays to the border, a brown line rim, a faint hairline and a small rim chip.

c1750   9.5in (24cm) diam

$400-600   **WW**

A Chelsea plate, with scenes from the Japanese legend of the Hob in the Well, red anchor mark.

c1752   9.25in (23.5cm) diam

$4,000-6,000   **TBk**

A Chelsea 'Botanical' plate, painted with a large flowering branch, a flowering convolvulus stem, a large butterfly and three insects, brown line rim, red anchor mark, a rim section well restored.

c1755   8.25in (21cm) diam

$1,500-2,000   **WW**

A Chelsea plate, boldly painted in colored enamels in the Hans Sloane style, with a turnip, two butterflies, flowers, a leaf and an insect, within a brown line rim, red anchor mark and number "2", riveted crack.

Painted botanical decoration at Chelsea was named after Sir Hans Sloane, an eminent scientist and patron of the Physic Garden, a botanical garden at Chelsea.

c1755   9.5in (24cm) diam

$800-1,200   **LFA**

A small Chelsea ashet, painted with Deutsche Blumen, the border relief decorated with scroll and diaper panel, painted red anchor mark.

13in (33cm) wide

$700-1,000   **L&T**

A Chelsea peony dish, molded with a large flower-head and leaves, the stalk handle issuing a flower bud, brightly enameled in iron-red, puce, green, yellow, and brown, red anchor mark.

c1755   8.75in (22cm) diam

$2,000-2,500   **WW**

PORCELAIN

A CLOSER LOOK AT A CHELSEA BOWL

Waste bowls were made in various sizes from early times until the 20thC.

The delicate work of the Japanese potter Kakiemon, with stylized paintings on porcelain with blossoms or a flowering tree, a bird or legendary animal, were highly popular with European ceramic factories.

The Chelsea factory was proud of the pure white appearance of its porcelain, and painted decoration was therefore kept to a minimum.

This bowl is a handsome and unusual octagonal shape, making this piece more desirable.

An early Chelsea 'Turtle in the Overcoat' pattern waste bowl, in the Kakiemon style.

c1750   *7.25in diam*

$6,000-9,000   **TBk**

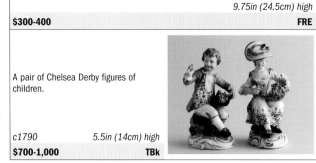

A late 19thC pair of European figures after Chelsea originals.

9.75in (24.5cm) high

$300-400   **FRE**

A pair of Chelsea Derby figures of children.

c1790   *5.5in (14cm) high*

$700-1,000   **TBk**

A Chelsea circular pierced basket, painted with central panel of Deutsche Blumen, including roses and lilies, faint painted red anchor mark, crack to rim.

1752-1756   *6.75in (17cm) diam*

$700-1,000   **L&T**

A matched pair of Chelsea-Derby circular fluted bowls, with pink and blue guilloche frieze.

7.75in (20cm) high

$400-600   **L&T**

A matched pair of Chelsea figures, depicting a sportsman and his companion, both wearing maroon jackets and the lady carrying a basket of fruit, the man with gun and powder flask, on rococo plinths each with a dog and scroll feet, both with painted gold anchor marks.

1756-1769   *9.5in (24cm) high*

$4,000-6,000   **L&T**

17

Coalport

The Coalport factory was founded by John Rose in 1796. Early pieces of Coalport are generally unmarked and are often difficult to identify. There is also a profusion of different patterns and styles of painting. This was because John Rose realized that there were several porcelain painters working independently who needed a regular supply of plain white porcelain to decorate. As a result of these different painters, such as Thomas Baxter, in London and George Sparks in Worcester, there is a great variety of decoration on Coalport porcelain.

Coalport wares include tea and dinner services and flower-encrusted ornamental wares. Early Coalport tended to follow Neo-Classical and 'Japan' patterns. After c1815 the fashion for French floral decoration was reflected in the Coalport style. The Rococo Revival of the 1830s was also a source of inspiration and wares were influenced by those at the Meissen factory near Dresden, Germany, and became known as 'English Dresden'. Wares from this period are typically encrusted with brightly colored modeled flowers and include jardinières, vases, baskets and inkstands. By the mid-19thC, Coalport employed many painters and no longer relied on independent artists. The Coalport factory is still in production today.

A CLOSER LOOK AT COALPORT TEAPOT

Always check the lid, knop, spout and handle for chips, as they are prone to damage.

Check gilding for signs of rubbing as this will affect the value.

The painting and gilding are exceptionally fine, in particular note the beautiful detailing of the butterflies, which gives them a three-dimensional quality.

The striking yellow color on this piece is both unusual and magnificent.

This shape is typical of teapots made at Coalport.

A rare late 18thC Coalport teapot.

6.25in (16cm) high

$2,200-2,800　　　　　**TBk**

A Coalport dessert plate, the outside decorated in colored enamels with flowers and leaves, on a shaded ground, within gilt bands, the dark green ground decorated in white with a stiff leaf border.

c1800-1810　　8.5in (21.5cm) diam

$120-180　　　　　**LFA**

A Coalport two-handled sauce tureen and cover, with ball knop, painted in colored enamels with flowers, on an iron-red and gilt geometrically paneled ground.

c1800-1810

$400-600　　　　　**LFA**

A Coalport John Rose 'Japan' pattern part tea service, painted and gilded in the Kakiemon style, with shrubs issuing flowers and baluster panels with C-scroll borders, comprising a teapot, cover and stand, a slop bowl, two sandwich plates, a milk jug, a sugar box and cover, and six teacups, saucers and coffee cans, minor wear, one can with restored handle.

c1800

$1,800-2,200　　　　　**DN**

An early 19thC John Rose Coalport teapot and cover, the rims of the oval sectioned bodies with wavy bands of vines with green leaves and red acorn-shaped flowers between gilt lines, bears Huxley-Robinson collection label.

$40-60　　　　　**Chef**

A pair of mid-19thC Coalport porcelain ewers, with gilding and applied flowers, the spreading feet gilded with grapes and leaves.

Provenance: *The Society of the Cincinnati.*

11in (28.5cm) high

$1,500-2,000   SI

A mid-19thC Coalport dessert plate, the rim with six strawberry vignettes separated by waisted turquoise shapes with gilt foliate edges, "55" impressed.

9.5in (24cm) diam

$40-60   **Chef**

A pair of mid-19thC Staffordshire chambersticks and snuffers, probably Coalport, the short column with relief and painted floral decoration on flower-encrusted circular base with gilt scroll handle, the conical snuffers with butterfly handles, fitting integral stands.

3.25in (8.5cm) diam

$1,500-2,000   **L&T**

A John Rose and Co. oval-shaped bough pot, with polychrome hand-painted flowers and rococo handles in blue and gilt.

1851-1861   *9.5in (24cm) long*

$80-120   D

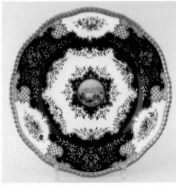

One of a set of 14 early 20thC Coalport plates, each painted with the 'X2592' pattern with central landscape roundel enclosed by three fruit and flower vignettes on a gilt royal blue ground within the gilt gadrooned rims, printed marks, some damage.

9in (23cm) diam

$1,800-2,200 (set)   **Chef**

A Coalport round two-handled sucrier and cover, with pointed knop, printed and painted with flowers and leaves, within gilt cartouches, on a blue ground, beneath a gilt gadrooned rim, printed mark in green.

c1920   *4.5in (11.5in) high*

$180-220   **LFA**

A 19thC Coalport plate, painted with a view of Carmel Valley, California, signed "P.H. Simpson", all within a raised gilt and rose decorated border with a gadrooned rim, titled and printed marks.

10.5in (26.5cm) diam

$400-600   **WW**

A 19thC Coalport bowl, the interior and exterior painted with rural view vignettes reserved within pale yellow foliate half-cartouches on a solid royal blue ground, enriched in gilt.

9in (23cm) diam

$320-380   **LC**

Derby

The Derby factory was in production from c1750, and has seen many changes of ownership. The works were established largely as a result of the business management of William Duesbury, a porcelain decorator, André Planché, a china maker, and John Heath, a copatron.

The early period was influenced by English silver shapes. Derby porcelain is often known as 'dry-edge', because the glaze was wiped away from the edge of the bases before firing. The factory was also heavily influenced by Meissen, and wares were aimed at the London market. Wares included tureens, tea wares and baskets, as well as leaf-shaped dishes and figures. Early figures typically portrayed mid-18th century subjects, such as Chinese or allegorical figures and pastoral themes. Derby porcelain is unmarked from before 1770. After this, a model number was often scratched into the base.

In 1770, Duesbury bought the ailing Chelsea factory and ran it until 1784 along with the Derby works. In 1797, Duesbury died and the factory went into a steady decline, eventually closing in 1848. Other factories were later established at Derby, including the Derby Crown Porcelain Co. (est. 1870), which became Royal Crown Derby in 1890.

A Derby shell-shaped creamboat of Dolphin Ewer type, with C-scroll handle, molded with two dolphins beneath the lip, and picked out in underglaze blue, small rim chip glued.

c1765	4in (10cm) high
$180-220	**LFA**

A Derby asparagus server, painted in dry blue with flower sprays, within blue line borders.

c1775	3in (7.5cm) long
$300-400	**LFA**

A Derby asparagus server, painted in underglaze blue with a Chinese river landscape, beneath a cell diaper band.

c1775	3in (7.5cm) long
$400-600	**LFA**

A rare Derby triple shell-shaped pickle dish, with central shell-molded finial, painted in underglaze blue with flowers, leaves and insects, within a geometric cell-paneled border, the shell and coral-molded base picked out in blue, incised beneath "78", one shell dish chipped.

There has only been one other Derby pickle dish ever recorded.

1778	6.5in (16.5cm) wide
$1,500-2,000	**LFA**

A Derby quatrefoil section teapot and a cover, painted in various colours with two Chinese figures beside a table with precious objects, the reverse with a man gesturing towards a butterfly, the fluted spout with a puce-painted shell motif terminal, applied with scroll handle, handle glued, the cover is an unassociated replacement.

c1756	
$450-550	**DN**

A pair of Derby flower-encrusted baluster pot pourri vases and covers, painted in colored enamels with bouquets of flowers, small chips to flowers.

c1760	7.75in (20cm) high
$700-1,000	**DN**

A pair of Derby flower-encrusted baluster pot pourri vases and covers, painted in colored enamels with bouquets of flowers, small chips to flowers.

c1760	7.75in (20cm) high
$700-1,000	**DN**

An unusual Derby small barrel-shaped teapot and cover, with loop handle and flower knop, modeled in relief with flowering branches, the scroll-molded borders picked out in gilt, tip of spout restored.

c1765   *4.25in (11cm) high*

$300-400   **LFA**

A CLOSER LOOK AT A DERBY MUG

This is an early Derby piece with very little damage, which increases its value.

This type of handle is known as a 'Chinese' handle.

The delicate painting on this piece is typical of early Derby, with a spray of flowers with a fine stem.

Early Derby's porcelain body meant that its tea wares were prone to cracking during use, and examples are rare.

A Derby barrel-shaped mug, minute chips.

c1765   *4.75in (12cm) high*

$1,200-1,800   **TBk**

A large Derby mask jug, with a flared rim and foot, painted with flower sprays, restored rim chip and crack.

c1760-1770   *9.5in (24cm) high*

$500-600   **WW**

A Derby square section vase and cover, applied overall with may blossom and berried branches, and picked out in colored enamels, within gilt line borders, foot-rim chip, minor chips to applied decoration.

c1770   *8.25in (21cm) high*

$180-220   **LFA**

A Derby shell-shaped cream boat.

c1770   *3.5in (9in) high*

$400-600   **TBk**

A Derby cabbage-leaf sauce boat.

c1780   *7in (18cm) long*

$400-600   **TBk**

A Derby ovoid vase and cover, with scroll handles, the body molded and applied with many small flower-heads on a turquoise ground, with gilded details, small chips.

c1770   *10.25in (26cm) high*

$400-600   **WW**

A pair of Derby leaf-molded small oval sauceboats, each with stalk loop handle, painted in puce monochrome with scattered flowers and leaves, and picked out in gilt, some restoration.

c1780   *5.25in (13.5cm) long*

$700-1,000   **LFA**

An unusual Derby plate, painted in green and black with a flowering branch, the spirally fluted border with green and gilt bands, crowned crossed batons mark in puce and pattern number "161".

c1785   *9in (23cm) diam*

$150-200   **LFA**

A rare Derby round sucrier and cover, with ring knop, decorated in purple monochrome with simple leaf garlands, suspended from flower-head and dash paneled bands, crowned crossed batons mark in puce and pattern number "83".

c1785   *5.5in (14cm) high*

$400-600   **LFA**

PORCELAIN

A pair of early Derby figures, with very distinctive early bases, unrestored.

c1760   8.25in (21cm) high

$5,000-7,000   **TBk**

A Derby figure of a rustic man, modeled walking with a pole supporting a small keg over his shoulder, on a scroll-molded base, painted in various colors and gilt, restored.

c1775   7.75in (19.5cm) high

$300-400   **DN**

A pair of Derby figures, one of a young man sacrificing a goat, the other of a young woman kneeling and holding a magpie, each incised "14".

c1780   5.75in (14.5cm) high

$500-700   **WW**

A pair of Derby table salts, in the form of a young boy and girl, each standing, holding a basket, decorated in colored enamels, and flanked by floral bocage, the scroll-molded bases picked out in turquoise and gilt, some damage.

c1780   5in (13cm) high

$300-400   **LFA**

A Derby biscuit porcelain group of a gardener and companion, leaning against a tree, incised model number "N68", gardener lacks the right hand, other small chips.

c1785   9in (23cm) high

$220-280   **DN**

A Derby biscuit group, 'The Antique Seasons,' four figures around a tree, rockwork base decorated with flowers and granite, incised, crowned crossed batons mark, no. "248", restoration.

c1785   10.75in (27cm) high

$500-700   **LFA**

A Derby figure of a putto, emblematic of Summer, standing holding a garland of flowers beside a basket of flowers on a pedestal, decorated in colored enamels, and picked out in gilt, on molded base, incised no. "64", minor chips.

c1790   5.5in (14cm) high

$400-600   **LFA**

A late 18thC Derby figure, of 'Neptune' beside a dolphin on shell encrusted rocky base, trident lacking and other losses.

8.5in (21.5cm) high

$400-600   **D**

A late 18thC Derby figure of 'Leda and the Swan,' with green cloak and flowered dress, with outstretched arm around swan's neck, on tall reed-decorated plinth.

11.75in (29.5cm) high

$3,000-4,000   **L&T**

A Dresden porcelain figural group, of a classical maiden with amorini.

6.75in (17cm) high

$150-200 Clv

A Dresden lidded vase, by Carl Thieme, Saxony, 1880, after an 18thC Meissen model, with 'Scenes from Watteau' and period scenes, branches, flowers and bird in relief, blue swords mark.

c1880 *13in (33cm) high*

$600-900 BMN

A 19thC Dresden vase, with reserve showing 'A View of Dresden from the New Town', coat-of-arms of Count von Sulkowski 'en camaïeu' on reverse, golden rose-mark on lid, title on base.

c1900 *21in (53.5cm) high*

$1,500-2,000 BMN

A Dresden urn, in Greek classical style, with three lion's paw supports, cylindrical body, decorated with a frieze of classical figures, with a detachable open cover, formal gilt borders.

c1890 *14.5in (37cm) high*

$600-900 FRE

A Dresden sucrier, from the Potschappel factory, with ornamental gilding, four reserves on sides and lid with flowers on cobalt-blue ground and couples in landscapes, the molded lid decorated with floral knop, blue mark to base.

3.5in (9cm) high

$120-180 BMN

One of a pair of late 19thC European Empire-style porcelain écuelles, covers and stands, probably Dresden, of tapered cylindrical form and painted with figures of rustics in landscapes, painted blue Nyon-style 'fish' marks.

$400-600 (pair) DN

A Dresden two-handled cup with saucer, model by Helena Wolfsohn, painted with birds and insects, gilt border, quatre-lobed shape with alternating flower and butterfly pattern, blue "AR" mark.

c1890

$400-600 BMN

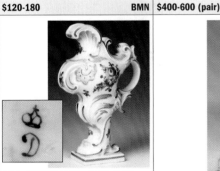

A late 19thC Dresden miniature jug, model by Helena Wolfsohn, baluster shape with rocaille and scroll decorations on a rectangular base, painted with flowers, gilt decorations, blue crowned painter's mark "D".

4.75in (12cm) high

$70-100 BMN

A Dresden figure bowl, from the Potschappel factory, floral polychrome painting, color and gilt decorations, the bowl resting on three figural angels, with undulating rim and relief flowers, blue swords mark, painter's mark, slightly damaged.

c1905 *8.25in (21cm) diam*

$180-220 BMN

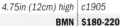

A 19thC Dresden Four Seasons mantel clock, with a striking 8-day movement, a flower-encrusted, open trelliswork case surmounted by a cherub, rococo scroll base flanked by three further cherubs.

19in (48cm) high

$2,200-2,800 FRE

Liverpool

There were several small porcelain factories in Liverpool in the second half of the 18thC, but there are so few records that it is often impossible to attribute pieces to specific factories. Wares are unmarked except for a few spurious Worcester crescents. The main factories were: Richard Chaffer 1754-65, Philip Christian 1765-76, Samuel Gilbody c1754-61, William Reid and others c.1755-70, John and Jane Pennington c1770-94, Seth Pennington and John Part 1778-1803.

Most of the factories used a soaprock porcelain, like that used at Worcester and Caughley. The greyish appearance of most Liverpool porcelain is very similar to that produced by Worcester, but the potting is variable and it can suffer from 'peppering', or small speckles to the glaze. Figures are rare, the most popular products being blue and white and coffee services. Decorators also used enamels decoratively, either in a style similar to Worcester or else in a harsh famille-rose palette. Collectors should be careful not to confuse it with New Hall or even Lowestoft.

An 18thC Pennington's Liverpool coffee cup, painted with coral and trefoil bands in blue above rinceau vine and wrythen molding.

2.75in (7cm) high

$150-200 — **Chef**

A Liverpool coffee can, with notched loop handle, painted in underglaze blue with trailing flowers and leaves, beneath a looped band.

c1775 — *2.5in (6.5cm) high*

$400-600 — **LFA**

A Penningtons Liverpool porcelain mug, scroll handle, painted flowers in underglaze blue beneath a blue diaper, possible old egg white hairline restoration.

c1780 — *4.75in (11cm) high*

$150-200 — **OACC**

A rare Liverpool plate, printed in underglaze blue with a spray of flowers and leaves, and scattered flowers, within a key fret, flower and cell diaper border, John and Jane Pennington's Factory.

c1780 — *8in (20.5cm) diam*

$400-600 — **LFA**

An 18thC English blue and white dish, attributed to Samuel Gilbody, painted in the Chinese taste with central peony and willow within diamond diaper and six vignettes on the cavetto and two scalloped bands on the rim, each scallop cradling a C-scroll, bears Mortlock label, faint star crack and nick to the rim.

Samuel Gilbody made blue and white porcelain in Liverpool from 1754 to 1760 but without much success, so the porcelain is quite rare.

11in (28cm) diam

$1,500-2,000 — **Chef**

A Chaffer's Liverpool blue and white chinoiserie waste bowl.

c1765 — *6.25in (16cm) diam*

$700-1,000 — **TBk**

A Liverpool coffee cup, with loop handle and indented rim, painted in Kakiemon style with flowers and leaves, alternating with orange and gilt diaper panels, decorated in iron red with mons, Richard Chaffers Factory.

c1758 — *2.5in (6.5cm) high*

$300-400 — **LFA**

A Liverpool globular teapot and cover, with pointed knop, painted in colored enamels, with exotic birds in branches, within simple iron red border.

c1770-75 — *6.25in (16cm) high*

$300-350 — **LFA**

A rare Chaffer's Liverpool cream jug, with a small spout and loop handle, the body painted with flower sprays and sprigs, no mark.

c1760 — *3.25in (8cm) high*

$1,200-1,800 — **WW**

A rare Pennington's Liverpool porcelain spoon tray, lozenge shape with a fluted edge, painted in polychrome with flower sprays and with an iron-red border design, unmarked.

c1785 — *6.25in (8cm) high*

$500-700 — **WW**

Longton Hall

The first of the famous Staffordshire factories was founded at Longton Hall in 1749 by saltglaze manufacturer, William Littler (1724-84). During its short life, the factory made eccentric and slightly crudely modeled wares and figures, often in shapes which showed the influence of saltglaze stoneware. The wares are heavy and translucent with numerous faults both in potting and glazing. In 1760, financial problems forced Littler to close Longton Hall and sell out to William Duesbury of Derby. Littler moved to Scotland where he started the West Pans factory (1764-77).

A Longton Hall blue painted sauce boat, with stiff leaf grooved sides and foot, painted on the exterior with chinoiserie figure panels, the interior with flower sprays.

8.5in (21.5cm) wide

$700-1,000   **L&T**

A rare Longton Hall miniature baluster shaped vase, painted in underglaze blue with trailing flowers and leaves, and an insect, short rim crack and associated chip.

c1754   2.75in (7cm) high

$700-1,000   **LFA**

A rare Longton Hall flared round flower pot, with turned-over rim, painted in underglaze blue with trailing flowers and leaves.

c1755   3in (7.5cm) high

$3,000-4,000   **LFA**

A Longton Hall turkey hen candlestick, figure of snowman type.

c1758

$4,000-6,000   **JF**

A Longton Hall mug, with sprung handle.

3.75in (9.5cm) high

$2,500-3,000   **TBk**

A rare Longton Hall tea bowl, finely printed in famille verte palette with two geese, in a Chinese landscape, with flowering trees and rockwork, the interior with a flower spray,, faint crack, small rim chip.

c1757   2.75in (7cm) diam

$800-1,200   **LFA**

A Longton Hall tea bowl and saucer.

c1755

$3,000-4,000   **JF**

A Longton Hall octagonal saucer, painted in famille rose palette with a bird on rockwork, and an insect in flight, flanked by flowering branches.

c1756   4.5in (11.5cm) wide

$600-900   **LFA**

A Longton Hall strawberry leaf plate, with raised decoration of strawberries and leaves, and loose painted floral sprays.

9in (23cm) diam

$2,200-2,800   **L&T**

A Longton Hall strawberry leaf molded dessert plate.

c1765   9.25in (23.5cm) diam

$3,000-4,000   **JF**

Lowestoft

The Lowestoft factory was founded in 1757 by Robert Browne and three partners. Wares produced at Lowestoft between 1757 and 1760 were all decorated with distinctive underglaze blue patterns and the foot-rims are often marked with a numeral. Between 1760 and 1765, the volume of production increased as the remote Suffolk factory established its reputation. In 1765, overglaze colors were used for the first time. After 1770, painted numeral marks were seldom used, shapes and patterns were simplified and the quality of potting declines. However, many shapes and patterns remain unique to the factory and these are the best indicators to look for when identifying Lowestoft.

A CLOSER LOOK AT THE LOWESTOFT ROBERT BROWNE PATTERN

This pattern is named after the first manager of the factory who was also the founding partner.

The identification of Lowestoft wares relies on knowledge of patterns and shapes, this pear shape is typical.

The use of powder blue is quite rare in Lowestoft, making this piece special.

The kick-back terminal on the lower joint of the handle and the tall domed cover are classic features of this pattern.

A Lowestoft powder blue 'Robert Browne' pattern coffee pot.
From the Stanley Fisher collection, illustrated in Fisher's book.

c1765   9.25in (23.5cm) high

$8,000-12,000   **TBk**

A Lowestoft blue and white coffee pot and cover, decorated with figures in a pagoda landscape.

c1770-80   8.75in (22.5cm) high

$1,500-2,000   **WW**

A 18thC Lowestoft porcelain sparrow beak cream jug, with scroll handle and Oriental style landscape decoration.

3.5in (9cm) high

$400-600   **Clv**

A Lowestoft feeding cup, transfer printed.

c1775   3in (7.5cm) high

$1,800-2,200   **TBk**

A Lowestoft sauceboat, with molded ground.

c1765   4in (10cm) high

$800-1,200   **TBk**

A Lowestoft butter boat, with acanthus molding.

c1775   2.25in (5.5cm) high

$700-1000   **TBk**

A Lowestoft bell-shaped mug.

c1765   4.5in (11.5cm) high

$3,000-4,000   **TBk**

Two views of a Lowestoft pilgrim flask, dated and initialed.

1787   4.75in (12cm) diam

$5,000-7,000   **TBk**

A Lowestoft octagonal tea caddy, with cover.

c1760-65   3.75in (9.5cm) high

$3,000-4,000   **TBk**

An early Lowestoft shell-shaped sweetmeat dish.

c1765   5.75in (14.5cm) high

$3,500-4,500   **TBk**

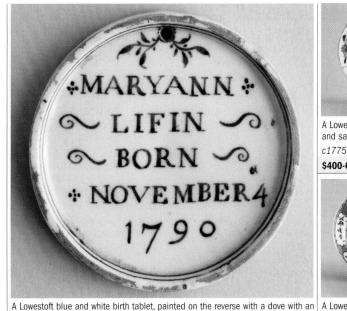

A Lowestoft blue and white birth tablet, painted on the reverse with a dove with an olive branch.

c1790   *3in (7.5cm) diam*

$12,000-18,000   **TBk**

A Lowestoft 'Jodrell' pattern tea bowl and saucer.

c1775   *4.75in (12cm) diam*

$400-600   **TBk**

A Lowestoft trio, painted with flowers in the Curtis style.

c1780-1785   *5in (12.5cm) diam*

$600-900   **TBk**

A Lowestoft tea bowl and saucer, painted with mandarin figures.

c1785-90   *Saucer 4.75in (12cm) diam*

$600-900   **TBk**

A Lowestoft 'Blackbird in the Tree' pattern tea bowl and saucer.

c1785-90   *4.5in (11.5cm) diam*

$400-600   **TBk**

A Lowestoft coffee cup, decoration by the 'Tulip' painter.

c1775   *2.5in (6cm) high*

$400-600   **TBk**

A Lowestoft coffee cup, with loop handle, painted in famille rose palette with figures in a garden, the iron red scroll border with a panel of flowers, and a damaged Lowestoft saucer, similarly decorated.

2.25in (6cm) high

$400-600   **LFA**

A pair of Lowestoft baluster-shaped vases, with covers.

c1785   *9in (23cm) high*

$5,000-7,000   **TBk**

A pair of Lowestoft Chinese-style bottle vases.

c1785   *6in (15cm) high*

$5,000-7,000   **TBk**

A Lowestoft trumpet-shaped vase, small crack.

c1785   *6.5in (16.5cm) high*

$2,200-2,800   **TBk**

PORCELAIN

Ludwigsburg

Ludwigsburg was one of the many porcelain factories to emulate Meissen wares. The factory was founded in Württemberg in 1758 by Duke Karl Eugen, starting in a barracks but later moving to a small castle. Its first director was Joseph Jakob Ringler, who remained there until 1802.

Ringler had stolen the secret formula from his previous employer, the Vienna factory, and went on to sell it to Höchst, Strasbourg and Nymphenburg. Ringler brought with him Gottlieb Friedrich Riedel, who had been director of painting at Frankenthal. Riedel's influence led to the creation of some of Ludwigsburg's finest wares, the Rococo figures.

Some of the best Rococo pieces were modelled by Johann Christian Wilhelm Beyer. Beyer, with fellow modeler Jean-Jacob Louis, was famed for his range of miniatures of the stalls and sideshows at the annual Württemberg-Venetian fair, figures of the Court Ballet and musicians. Although these miniatures are less than 4in (9cm) high, they are much livelier and brighter than the larger figures. Despite the input of Neoclassical sculptor Johann Heinrich von Dannecker in the 1790s, and a brief revival at the turn of the century, the factory went into decline and shut in 1824.

Although many wares are in Meissen style, a collector can spot Ludwigsburg by the smoky grey-brown tinge to the body of a piece. On areas of a figure that have been left white, this greyish glaze lends it the look of marble. The figures are crisply modeled but tend to lack the movement of Meissen, appearing rather stiff with bland faces. Wares were decorated in subtle pastel shades which complimented the smoky tone of the Ludwigsburg glaze. The key colors are greyish pinks, blues and greens with yellow, iron-red, black and gilding. Ludwigsburg bases vary widely from simple, mottled green-brown grass or rockwork mounds and slabs, to rich Rococo forms, with gilded highlights.

A large Ludwigsburg kettle, depicting birds-of-paradise, with gilt lambrequins, blue underglaze crowned "CC" mark, painter's mark "D", press marks.

c1765   9.5in (24cm) high

$7,000-10,000   NAG

A Ludwigsburg dish, painted in famille-rose colors, decorated with gilded herons, crowned "CC" mark, press mark "19", engraved mark, restored crack.

c1765   9in (22.5cm) diam

$1,500-2,000   LPZ

A Ludwigsburg rectangular tea canister, painted with figures beside a statue in a landscape, with a crowned crossed "C" mark.

c1770   4in (10.5cm) high

$600-900   WW

A Ludwigsburg rectangular tea canister and cover, painted in the manner of Johann William Stoll.

c1775   5.25in (13.5cm) high

$700-1,000   WW

A late 18thC Ludwigsburg porcelain teapot and cover, scrolled handle, leaf-moulded spout, circular foot-rim, underglaze blue monogram mark.

7.5in (19cm) long

$220-280   HamG

A Ludwigsburg oval charger, depicting poultry in a landscape, with raised edges and cut handles, gold border decoration, red "FR" mark.

c1810   16.25in (41.5cm) long

$1,500-2,000   NAG

A rare Ludwigsburg 'Print Seller' figure, modeled by J.J. Louis.

c1766   6in (15cm) high

$4,000-6,000   TBk

A Ludwigsburg figure, 'Meleagre killing a Boar,' painter's mark, restored.

c1770   11.5in (29cm) high

$3,000-4,000   LPZ

A Ludwigsburg group of figures, 'The Garland Winder', modeled by J. J. Louis in 1767, showing a lady-gardener standing and male gardener kneeling by a column crowned with a flame, painted in color, with gold decoration, domed base decorated with fruit, blue "CC" mark, crown glued.

c1775   10in (25.5cm) high

$700-1,000   BMN

A Ludwigsburg group of putti, 'The Garland-Winder with Amphora', modeled c1780, painted in color, with gold decoration, stepped rectangular base, no marks.

c1780   6.25in (16cm) high

$400-600   BMN

Meissen

The Meissen factory was famed throughout Europe in the 18thC for the artistic skill of its craftsmen and for the beauty and technical sophistication of its pieces.

Meissen was the first European factory to produce 'hard-paste' porcelain, a process which the Chinese had kept a secret for many years. In 1710, the first factory was founded in Dresden, later moving to Meissen. Johann Friedrich Böttger the alchemist who had helped to discover the process, organized the workshop.

Initially, the Meissen factory produced red stoneware, cut by Bohemian glass-cutters to resemble Oriental stoneware. By the time Böttger died in 1719, Meissen was making a yellowish porcelain but the discovery of kaolin nearby allowed the new director Höroldt to develop a pure white porcelain and consequently to experiment with ground colors to great effect.

The factory started to produce figures in 1731, when artist J.J. Kändler arrived. The fashion in the courts of 18thC Europe had

been to decorate dining tables with exquisite spun-sugar figures but when Count Brühl commissioned the 'Swan Service', a new fashion for porcelain decorative figures was born. Kändler modeled figures on Commedia dell'Arte, Chinoiserie and rustic characters, as well as the famous 'Monkey Band'.

By 1814, the factory was responding to European competition by producing Neoclassical pieces and then porcelain copies of famous paintings. Towards the end of the 19thC, Meissen was exporting to America and had perfected the pâte-sur-pâte technique, improving yet again on the quality of its wares. The Art Nouveau period from 1890 provided new inspiration and wares included figures by Paul Scheurich and plates by Henry van der Velde. The factory still makes Kändler figures today.

Collectors should be aware that Meissen's designs were copied by many other factories and the famous crossed swords mark was also emulated to increase the desirability of a piece.

A Meissen Böttger teapot with lid, depicting scenes from merchant life, decoration attributed to Augsburg or Breslau, no mark, restored.

c1720   *4.75in (12cm) high*

$15,000-20,000   **LPZ**

A Meissen teapot and lid, decorated with Chinoiserie paintings and Indianische Blumen, blue swords mark and "K.P.M", gold painter's mark "44".

c1723-24   *5in (12.5cm) high*

$12,000-18,000   **LPZ**

A Meissen Böttger porcelain pot with protruding lid, decorated with a river landscape and gold filigree, unmarked.

c1725   *8in (20.5cm) high*

$12,000-18,000   **NAG**

A Meissen Augsburg-Böttger porcelain coffee pot and cover, depicting a gold-decorated hunting scene, with Augsburg silver mounting, wear to gold.

c1720-30   *8.5in (22cm) high*

$7,000-10,000   **NAG**

A Meissen coffee pot with lid, depicting a landscape in enamel colors, Indian flower-sprays, broad gilt decoration, continuous merchant-life scene on lid.

c1725   *8in (20.5cm) high*

$15,000-20,000   **LPZ**

A Meissen teapot, with Dutch river landscapes painted in black 'en camaïeu' within gold cartouches, gold rims, blue swords mark with accented hilts, gold painter's mark "V" to lid and base, tip of spout restored, chip between handle mountings.

c1725   *4in (10.5cm) high*

$12,000-18,000   **LPZ**

A Meissen teapot, lid and body with 'merchant scene' paintings within gilt-edged borders on lilac background, coral and gold decoration, animal-head spout and scrolled handle, flat lid with pine cone knop, blue swords mark, lid repaired, burn to handle.

c1740   *4in (10cm) high*

$2,200-2,800   **BMN**

A Meissen coffee pot and lid, depicting garden and 'merchant' scenes, blue swords mark, gold painter's mark "46" on lid and base, press mark.

c1745   *8.5in (22cm) high*

$1,200-1,800   **LPZ**

A mid-18thC Meissen pot, with 'Scenes by Watteau of a Harlequin' on body and lid, gilded, pear-shaped body and colorfully painted mask-head spout, domed lid, blue swords mark.

6.25in (16cm) high

$1,800-2,200   **BMN**

A kettle, attributed to Meissen, with continuous floral decorations in purple, colored and gold decorations, flat lid with bud knop, movable handle with bronze mounting, unglazed base, not marked, restored.

c1750   *Body 5.75in (14.5cm) high*

$1,200-1,800   **BMN**

A Meissen cup and saucer, with colorful floral decoration in quatrelobe reserves on yellow ground, cup with gilded scrolled handle, molded saucer, smooth brown edges, blue swords mark.

c1760

$600-900   **BMN**

A Meissen cup and saucer, with floral decoration in quatrelobe reserves on purple ground, flower spray on handle, molded saucer, gilt-edged rims, blue swords mark, saucer restored.

c1760

$400-600   **BMN**

An early 19thC Meissen conical picture cup and saucer, in Biedermeier style, reserve with painting over transfer-print of 'A View of Pillnitz', molded saucer, blue swords mark, black title.

$1,000-1,500   **BMN**

A pair of 19thC Meissen ogee-shaped chocolate cups, covers and stands, each with flower knop, painted in enamels with figures and animals in wooded landscapes, within gilt scroll borders, marks in blue, some damage.

$800-1,000   **LFA**

A mid-19thC Meissen cup and saucer, with Indianische Blumen painted decoration and gold edging, the bulbous cup has a raised swan-shaped handle, the deep saucer has smooth edges, with blue sword mark.

$220-280   **BMN**

A Meissen yellow cup and saucer, with a painting of figures in a park in four gold reserves, gold floral decoration and gold pointed border, bunches of flowers on the saucer and reverse of cup, blue sword mark, partially restored.

c1860

$400-600   **BMN**

A Meissen plate, with lambrequin decoration, elevated border and undulating rim, decorated with Indianische Blumen, the border decorated with underglaze blue panels, gilded, blue swords mark with accented hilts and curved blades.

c1731   *8in (20.5cm) diam*

$1,500-2,000   **LPZ**

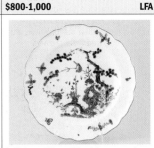

A Meissen 'Three Friends' pattern plate, painted in the Kakiemon palette, depicting a bird on a branch, and another in flight, with pine, bamboo and prunus, the indented rim with scattered flowers, and gilt line border, blue mark.

c1740   *9.25in (23.5cm) diam*

$1,000-1,500   **LFA**

A Meissen plate, in the famille-verte palette, depicting a large peony, a flying bird and insects, brocade border with butterfly reserves and gilded, wicker-relief undulating edges, blue swords mark, iron-red painter's mark "S", press mark "21".

c1740   *10in (25.5cm) diam*

$2,200-2,800   **LPZ**

A Meissen octagonal plate, with scenes by Watteau of a court garden landscape, within a gilt cartouche, blue swords mark, press mark "22".

c1745   *9.5in (24cm) diam*

$2,200-2,800   **LPZ**

An 18thC Meissen dish, the center painted with a jay and a bullfinch, the ozier-molded border decorated with insects, crossed swords mark and press mark "19".

11.75in (30cm) diam

$400-600   **WW**

A Meissen Hausmaler plate, painted by Franz Ferdinand Mayer-Pressnitz, showing a 'Comedy Scene' with a bagpipe player, dancer, dog and antique bust on plinth in front of a draped curtain in a landscape, within a large gilt border with flower bouquets, smooth edges, blue swords mark, border restored.

c1750   *8.5in (22cm) diam*

$1,200-1,800   **BMN**

A mid-18thC Meissen group of figures, design attributed to Friedrich Elias Meyer, representing 'The Four Continents', painted with gold edging on a vaulted rocaille stand, blue sword mark on unglazed base, restored.

9 in (22.5 cm) high

$20,000-30,000   **BMN**

A mid-18thC Meissen figure of 'A Girl Standing with Grapes', modeled by J.J. Kändler, painted with gold edges, round rocaille base, base unglazed, press mark "24", blue swords mark on stand, partially restored.

5.5in (13.5cm) high

$1,200-1,800   **BMN**

A Meissen figure of Chinese woman with child, standing on square flat plinth, carrying child on her back, unglazed base, blue swords mark at back of plinth, hat and neck restored.

c1750   *4.75in (12cm) high*

$2,200-2,800   **LPZ**

A Meissen group of figures, presumably modeled by Michel Victor Acier, 'Summer' from a cycle of 'The Four Seasons', four figures painted and gilt decorated, oval rococo base, blue swords mark, restored.

c1860   *5.75in (15 cm) high*

$3,000-4,000   **BMN**

JOHANN JOACHIM KÄNDLER

Johann Joachim Kändler was one of the most talented and creative designers at Meissen and was responsible for some of the finest figures and groups the factory ever produced.

After his apprenticeship at Dresden, Kändler entered the porcelain factory in Meissen under Kirchner in 1731 and soon became the head designer, a position he held for most of his life.

At Meissen, Kändler developed as a varied and creative designer. The famous big white animal sculptures, which were up to 12in (30cm) high, were one of his early designs. These were made for the 'Japanese' Palace of Augustus The Strong, Elector of Saxony, in Dresden.

Even though the huge animal sculptures were famous because of their naturalistic shapes, the production was very complicated and expensive. Consequently, Kändler moved on and designed smaller figures which were easier to produce. These were often based upon characters from the Italian Comedia dell'arte. The most desirable figures were shepherds, hunters, the famous 'Monkey Band' and actors, although he also created numerous allegories on love, faith, and the Four Seasons.

A Meissen group of figures 'The Wine Tasting', model probably by Johann Joachim Kändler, of a painted group of wine-growers standing on a rock with a barrel of wine, round rocaille base, blue sword mark with dot, base restored.

c1763-74   *7.75in (19.5cm) high*

$3,000-4,000   **BMN**

A Meissen figure of a girl, probably by Michel Victor Acier c1775, model no. E 58 'Sleeping Girl with Love Letter in Décolleté', blue swords mark.

7.5in (19 cm) high

$1,500-2,000   **BMN**

A Meissen biscuit porcelain group of figures, probably designed by Christian Jüchtzer c1780, model no. H24, 'Love and Time', press mark, damage.

c1774-1814   *10.5in (27.5cm) high*

$400-600   **BMN**

Minton

Thomas Minton (1765-1836) founded his factory in c1796 in Stoke-on-Trent, England. Under him, the factory's staple products consisted of useful and unpretentious tableware, painted or printed earthenware or bone china, following the typical shapes and decorative patterns of the period. Figures and ornamental porcelains were made increasingly from the 1820s. The factory was famous for cream-colored and blue-printed earthenware, majolica, bone china and Parian porcelain.

When Herbert Minton succeeded his father in 1836, he enlisted the services of artists and skilled artisans, which lead to the development of the Minton reputation as a high-quality producer, renowned for its 'art' porcelains. Minton was the only English china factory of the 19thC to employ a Sèvres process called 'pâte-sur-pâte' where layers of white slip – a mixture of clay and water – are built up on a colored ground then carved to create decoration with a striking effect of depth. In the 19thC, the Minton factory was the most popular source of made-to-order dinnerware for embassies and heads of state.

A Minton globular bowl and cover, with two entwined handles, finely painted in colored enamels with flowers and leaves, and applied with brightly colored flowers, on a gilt scroll ground, blue crossed swords mark, some restoration.

c1830-40   6.75in (17cm) high

$400-600   **LFA**

A Minton baluster shaped 'Chelsea' vase, with two entwined scroll handles, and fluted rim, applied in bold relief with brightly colored flowers and leaves, and painted with insects, on scroll molded foot, blue crossed swords mark, rim restored.

c1830-35   10in (25.5cm) high

$300-400   **LFA**

A pair of Minton candlesticks, each in the form of a young boy or girl seated beside a flower-applied tree stump, and decorated in colored enamels, the oval scroll bordered base picked out in gilt, crossed swords marks and incised "no. 8".

c1835-40   5.5in (14cm) high

$700-1,000   **LFA**

A Minton miniature basket, encrusted with flowers.

c1850   4.75in (12cm) long

$500-600   **TBk**

A pair of mid-19thC Minton plates, painted in the Sèvres style.

9.25in (23.5cm) diam

$600-900   **DN**

A pair of mid-19thC Minton plates, painted by J. Rouse, one depicting three children in the countryside, the other of an interior with children, both within reticulated and gilded borders and turquoise bands, one signed and titled "Kind Sisters".

9.25in (23.5cm) diam

$1,200-1,800   **WW**

A mid-19thC Minton porcelain part dinner service, comprising twelve dinner plates and twelve soup plates, printed and painted with insects, grasses and floral stems, impressed "MINTON" and "MINTONS" with date cyphers enameled in black and red "5839".

10.25in (26cm) diam

$400-600   **SI**

A Minton cabinet plate, painted by A. Boullemier, the center with a vignette of a woman in Regency dress standing before a plinth in a garden setting, within a pierced gilt fret border, printed and impressed marks, date code.

1893   *9.5in (24cm) diam*

$700-1,200   **DN**

A Minton pâte-sur-pâte plate, decorated by Albion Birks, the central grey-ground reserve carved in low relief with Venus and Cupid, signed lower right, within a gilt border of floral lappets, printed and impressed marks, date code.

1911   *9.25in (23.5cm) diam*

$3,000-4,000   **DN**

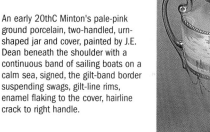

A Minton 'Celadon' and white porcelain figural posy holder, modeled as a girl with a large basket on her back, impressed marks, date code.

1868   *8.75in (22cm) high*

$220-280   **DN**

A Minton baluster-shaped vase, in Chinese style, finely painted in colored enamels with European flowers and leaves, within tooled gilt bands, on pierced brown glazed base, picked out in gilt, small chips to base.

c1870   *12.75in (32.5cm) high*

$220-280   **LFA**

An early 20thC Minton's pale-pink ground porcelain, two-handled, urn-shaped jar and cover, painted by J.E. Dean beneath the shoulder with a continuous band of sailing boats on a calm sea, signed, the gilt-band border suspending swags, gilt-line rims, enamel flaking to the cover, hairline crack to right handle.

7in (18cm) high

$300-400   **DN**

A Minton porcelain two-handled urn and cover, painted with pink roses and floral swags, with a turquoise border and gilding.

11in (28cm) high

$400-600   **GorL**

A Minton porcelain 'Rococo revival' pale-yellow ground part tea service, gilt with borders of scrolling foliage, comprising a teapot and cover, a sugar bowl and cover, a milk jug, a slop bowl, a pair of square shaped serving dishes, a sandwich plate, ten teacups and saucers, and nine coffee cups, iron-red painted pattern "no.5648", minor damage.

$300-400   **DN**

An English bone china model of a shepherdess, possibly Minton, painted with colored enamels.

c1830   *5.25in (13.5cm) high*

$400-600   **DN**

A pair of Minton candlestick figures, each holding flowers and raised on flower encrusted scrolling circular bases enriched with gilding, minor repairs.

c1835   *8.75in (22.5cm) high*

$1,000-1,500   **WW**

Nymphenburg

The Nymphenburg factory was founded in 1747 by the Elector Maximilian III, Joseph of Bavaria in Neudeck on Au. After fourteen years he moved the factory to the castle Nymphenburg in Munich, where it continues to operate today.

When Napoleon crowned Joseph of Bavaria King, the name of the factory changed to the Royal Porcelain Factory Nymphenburg. After the abdication of the last Bavarian king, it became the State-owned Porcelain-Factory Nymphenburg. It was taken over by the Wittelsbach family in 1975.

The Nymphenburg Factory became famous thanks to the designs of the Swiss modeler, Franz Anton Bustelli, who worked there between 1754 and 1763. The famous classical pearl service that was designed at the end of the 18th century by Dominikus Auliczek, was reserved by the Bavarian royal house until the last century.

When the Frankenthal factory closed 1799, some of its workers and its molds went to Nymphenburg and the factory began to flourish, combining traditional pieces with modern designs.

A Nymphenburg plate, painted with flowers, relief edge with cornucopia, gold-rubbed, press mark.

c1760-65   9in (23cm) diam

$600-900   **BMN**

An early 19thC Nymphenburg Empire-style cup and saucer, probably by Anton Auer, press, diamond and "P" marks.

$800-1,200   **BMN**

Wittelsbacherpalais

A Nymphenburg picture plate, with a painting of the 'Wittelsbach Palais', the floral gold-leaf border with purple background, press mark with star, black title, scratch marks, base slightly rubbed.

c1850-62   8.25in (21cm) diam

$1,800-2,200   **BMN**

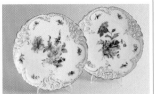

A pair of late 19thC Nymphenburg floral dessert plates, pierced gilded rims, underglaze blue printed marks.

8.25in (21cm) diam

$120-180   **Chef**

A Nymphenburg pictorial plate, showing 'Nymphenburg Castle', rocaille relief, gilt edge, green base mark.

c1900   14.75in (37.5cm) long

$1,000-1,500   **BMN**

A Nymphenburg rococo figure, based on a Frankenthal model by Johann Friedrich Lück, 'The Dancing Gentleman', painted in color, blue and gilded, on a round base, marked, blue "CT" mark, one arm restored.

c1760   8.25in (21cm) high

$150-200   **BMN**

A Nymphenburg figure of a child, based on a Frankenthal model by Johann Peter Melchior, 'Girl Playing Hand Organ', painted, gilted, press mark, blue crowned "CT" mark and "Melchior", slight damage.

c1920   5in (12.5cm) high

$150-200   **BMN**

A Nymphenburg figure of a lady, designed by Eugen Napoleon Neureuther, c1850, model no. 207, 'Traditional Middle-class Munich Woman' in long traditional dress, with prayer book, gold decorations, round base, press marks.

c1890   5.25in (13.5cm) high

$800-1,200   **BMN**

A Nymphenburg figure of a 'Minstrel', model no. 337, with string instrument, painted in color, flat oval base, green base mark, press marks, restored.

c1905   8in (20.5cm) high

$500-700   **BMN**

Parian

Parian is a creamy-white, slightly translucent porcelain designed to look like the fine marble from the island of Paros, which was used in the Classical period for high quality statues. The first firms to produce Parian, in around 1844, used a soft-paste or 'frit' composition which produced a beautiful, silky sheen. Minton produced some of the finest examples of Parian, which was used most successfully for sculptural pieces. Scaled-down models of larger pieces by contemporary and past sculptors were also produced, and sometimes the material was used in combination with glazed and painted bone china for display pieces.

Later a hard-paste form of Parian (known as 'nonfrit') was produced. It was cheaper and easier to mould but was coarser and lacked the silky sheen. Non-frit Parian was used by lesser makers to mass produce poor reproductions of the fine pieces produced in frit Parian by the quality manufacturers.

A mid-19thC Parian group of three Graces after Canova, they stand on the oval base naked but for a drape held by one.

12.25in (31cm) high

$700-1,000 Chef

A mid-19thC Parian figure, possibly of Susannah, she sits on a rock by a stream looking over her shoulder and holding her shoulder strap.

9.5in (24cm) high

$220-280 Chef

A 19thC Parian figure of a naked woman, standing contraposto by a draped column.

19.25in (49cm) high

$700-1,000 L&T

A 19thC Parianware figure of a goddess.

13in (33cm) high

$120-180 Clv

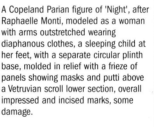

A Copeland Parian figure of 'Night', after Raphaelle Monti, modeled as a woman with arms outstretched wearing diaphanous clothes, a sleeping child at her feet, with a separate circular plinth base, molded in relief with a frieze of panels showing masks and putti above a Vetruvian scroll lower section, overall impressed and incised marks, some damage.

c1862 *26in (66cm) high*

$2,200-2,800 DN

A Parian figure of a seated classical maiden, possibly Minton, realistically modeled, shown seated on a rocky base, apparently unmarked.

c1860 *16in (41cm) high*

$1,800-2,200 FRE

A mid-Victorian Parian bust of Clytie, the classically dressed maiden held in a flower-head from the sternum upwards, a socle below.

9.5in (24cm) high

$220-280 Chef

A pair of Worcester Parian figures, representing young ladies before and after the storm, the one holding her drapes around her with neatly dressed hair, the other windswept, impressed rosette marks.

c1880 *11in (28cm) high*

$400-600 Chef

A Parian bust of Princess Alexandra, after M. Thornycroft, the three-quarter bust impressed with "Art Union London, Mary Thornycroft sc", complete with Parian socle.

15.25in (39cm) high

$300-400 FRE

PORCELAIN

Paris

An early 19thC Paris porcelain campana vase, painted with a panel of three figures smoking and drinking, on a gilt ground, decorated with flowers and Gothic tracery, red printed mark for Darte.

14in (35.5cm) high

$700-1,000   **WW**

A Paris porcelain campana vase, finely painted with fruit, floral and bird decorations, reserved on a sky blue ground with raised gilt decoration, the handles with ram's head terminals.

c1830   *13in (33.5cm) high*

$600-900   **SI**

A pair of Paris vases, some repairs.

c1830   *8in (20.5cm) high*

$1,200-1,800   **TBk**

A Paris porcelain concave-sided square two-handled tray, painted in colored enamels with four panels of flowers, within gilt cartouches, on a bright blue ground.

c1850   *12in (30.5cm) wide*

$120-180   **LFA**

A pair of Paris potpourri vases, by P.D. Honoré of Petite Rue Saint Gilles, restoration to covers.

c1860   *9in (22.5cm) high*

$3,500-4,500   **TBk**

Three late 19thC Paris porcelain purple ground cups and saucers, the first painted with beetles within gilt stylized foliate borders, the second and third painted with berried vines and leafage within gilt borders, all three monogrammed "AH", printed "CH. PILLVUYT & Cie./Paris".

$300-400   **SI**

A pair of mid-19thC Paris porcelain figures of a man and woman in Renaissance dress, painted in colors and gilt on scroll-molded bases, some chips and losses.

15.25in (39cm) high

$500-700   **DN**

Sèvres

A pair of Sèvres lobed oval sucriers and covers, the porcelain 18thC, the decoration later, each with entwined knop, finely painted in colored enamels with putti, and exotic birds in wooded landscapes, within gilt cartouches, on a bleu celeste ground, and with finely cast ormolu mounts as potpourri bowls, each with a pierced band and two C-scroll handles, surmounted by dragons, on pierced C-scroll base.

11.5in (29cm) wide

$6,000-9,000   **LFA**

A pair of Sèvres Seaux-à-Liquers, of oval form, each with two pierced leaf-scroll handles, painted in colored enamels with flowers, fruits and leaves, within tooled and gilt leaf-scroll, diaper and flower cartouches, on a bleu celeste ground, marks in blue for 1768 and decorator's marks for Jean-Jacques Pière.

12.25in (31cm) wide

$10,000-15,000   **LFA**

A Sèvres plate, later decorated in enamels with birds in a landscape, gilt molded border, painted mark in blue.

9.5in (24cm) diam

$300-400   **LFA**

A Sèvres two-handled vase, painted with landscapes, dated.

1793   *4.5in (11.5cm) high*

$2,500-3,000   **TBk**

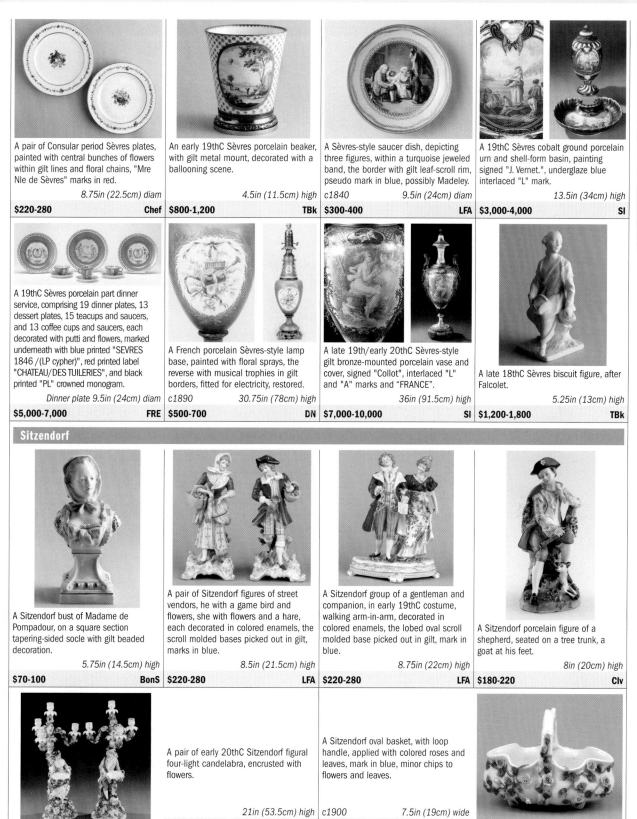

A pair of Consular period Sèvres plates, painted with central bunches of flowers within gilt lines and floral chains, "Mre Nle de Sèvres" marks in red.

8.75in (22.5cm) diam

$220-280   **Chef**

An early 19thC Sèvres porcelain beaker, with gilt metal mount, decorated with a ballooning scene.

4.5in (11.5cm) high

$800-1,200   **TBk**

A Sèvres-style saucer dish, depicting three figures, within a turquoise jeweled band, the border with gilt leaf-scroll rim, pseudo mark in blue, possibly Madeley.

c1840   *9.5in (24cm) diam*

$300-400   **LFA**

A 19thC Sèvres cobalt ground porcelain urn and shell-form basin, painting signed "J. Vernet.", underglaze blue interlaced "L" mark.

13.5in (34cm) high

$3,000-4,000   **SI**

A 19thC Sèvres porcelain part dinner service, comprising 19 dinner plates, 13 dessert plates, 15 teacups and saucers, and 13 coffee cups and saucers, each decorated with putti and flowers, marked underneath with blue printed "SEVRES 1846 /(LP cypher)", red printed label "CHATEAU/DES TUILERIES", and black printed "PL" crowned monogram.

Dinner plate 9.5in (24cm) diam

$5,000-7,000   **FRE**

A French porcelain Sèvres-style lamp base, painted with floral sprays, the reverse with musical trophies in gilt borders, fitted for electricity, restored.

c1890   *30.75in (78cm) high*

$500-700   **DN**

A late 19th/early 20thC Sèvres-style gilt bronze-mounted porcelain vase and cover, signed "Collot", interlaced "L" and "A" marks and "FRANCE".

36in (91.5cm) high

$7,000-10,000   **SI**

A late 18thC Sèvres biscuit figure, after Falcolet.

5.25in (13cm) high

$1,200-1,800   **TBk**

Sitzendorf

A Sitzendorf bust of Madame de Pompadour, on a square section tapering-sided socle with gilt beaded decoration.

5.75in (14.5cm) high

$70-100   **BonS**

A pair of Sitzendorf figures of street vendors, he with a game bird and flowers, she with flowers and a hare, each decorated in colored enamels, the scroll molded bases picked out in gilt, marks in blue.

8.5in (21.5cm) high

$220-280   **LFA**

A Sitzendorf group of a gentleman and companion, in early 19thC costume, walking arm-in-arm, decorated in colored enamels, the lobed oval scroll molded base picked out in gilt, mark in blue.

8.75in (22cm) high

$220-280   **LFA**

A Sitzendorf porcelain figure of a shepherd, seated on a tree trunk, a goat at his feet.

8in (20cm) high

$180-220   **Clv**

A pair of early 20thC Sitzendorf figural four-light candelabra, encrusted with flowers.

21in (53.5cm) high

$700-1,000   **SI**

A Sitzendorf oval basket, with loop handle, applied with colored roses and leaves, mark in blue, minor chips to flowers and leaves.

c1900   *7.5in (19cm) wide*

$70-100   **LFA**

Spode

Founded by Josiah Spode (1733-97) in 1776, the Spode factory at Stoke-on-Trent in Staffordshire, Englan, is still in operation today, although now merged with Worcester. It probably developed the first formula for English bone china c1800. It is pure white in appearance with a smooth, white, thin glaze. Before 1830, the mark was usually a hand-painted "SPODE" but by 1820 the mark was also being printed: for fine porcelain between 1815 and 1830 this is a circular mark bearing the company name and a ring of flowers. After 1833, when Copeland and T. Garrett bought out the founder's son Josiah II, "COPELAND & GARRETT" appears in a circle with "LATE SPODE" in the middle. The pattern numbers are usually painted in red. Until c1850, the majority of the table and ornamental wares were influenced by Roman or Etruscan designs; Imari designs were also popular and were meticulously painted. Spode-Copeland was the first factory to develop Parian and, from 1844, leading sculptors used this to produce busts and figures.

A composite Spode fruit service, with deep scalloped gilt scroll border, with rust and green leaf scroll border with pendants, central gilt base, rust painted mark, comprising oval twin-handled footed bowl, six smaller similar bowls, three scalloped, shaped bowls and 13 circular plates, with rust-printed Derby mark.

c1810   *Footed bowl 14in (36cm) wide*

$700-1,000 set   **L&T**

A Spode brown earthenware campana shaped vase, on knopped stem and round base, drilled, re-attached to base.
Spode also produced this in porcelain.

c1810   *8in (20.5cm) high*

$150-200   **LFA**

A Spode flared beaker vase, finely painted in colored enamels with three exotic birds in a tree, in an extensive landscape, within gilt line borders, on round base.

c1815-20   *6in (15.2cm) high*

$300-350   **LFA**

A pair of Spode flared beaker vases, each decorated in famille rose palette with flowers, leaves and rockwork, beneath a leaf and emblem paneled flower and iron red scroll ground band, pattern number 868 in red.

c1815   *5.25in (13.5cm) high*

$600-900   **LFA**

An early 19thC Spode Imari plate, painted with the 1495 pattern of central basket of flowers by a fence and within four bird vignettes on the gilt rim band, marks in red.

8.25in (21cm) diam

$60-90   **Chef**

A pair of Spode porcelain two-handled violet baskets and pierced covers, pattern no. 1139, painted with bouquets of flowers reserved on a gilt-scale ground, iron-red painted pattern numbers.

c1815

$4,000-6,000   **DN**

A Spode slender campana-shaped vase, finely painted in colored enamels with flowers and leaves, on a gilt ground, on round base, script mark in red and pattern number "711", cover lacking.

c1815   *6.25in (16cm) high*

$700-1,000   **LFA**

A Vienna-du Paquier pot, painted Indian-style in colors with iron-red, sea-green, enamel-blue, mosaic border on rim, scrolled handle, domed lid with baluster knop, no marks, restored.

c1720-30   *4.75in (12cm) high*

$1,200-1,800   **BMN**

A Vienna-du Paquier bowl, painted in iron-red, sea-green, brown and purple, depicting a Chinese man, ornamental border, resting on foot ring, damaged, unmarked.

c1720-30   *4.75in (12cm) diam*

$500-700   **BMN**

A set of six Vienna 'Neuozier' dinner plates, painted with colored flowers, gold decoration, undulating edges, blue shield mark, red painter's mark, cracks and restorations.

c1760   *4.75in (12cm) diam*

$300-400   **BMN**

A Vienna coffee pot, painting probably by P.E. Schindler Jr., 'en camaïeu'-painting in sepia of 'Architectural Landscapes', gold-leaf border, blue shield mark, knop restored.

c1760-70   *7in (18cm) high*

$700-1,000   **BMN**

A pair of Vienna cream pots, with colored 'straw flower' decor and cobalt-blue decoration, bulbous shape with ear-shaped handle and lid with bud-shaped knop, unglazed base, blue shield mark, press mark.

c1794   *4in (10cm) high*

$400-600   **BMN**

A Vienna baluster-shaped custard cup and cover, with scroll handle and flower knop, painted in colored enamels with figures, flowers and leaves, within gilt line borders, mark in blue.

3.25in (8cm) high

$400-600   **LFA**

A Vienna milk pot, the baluster-shaped body decorated with floral sprigs, with pointed spout and scroll handle on molded base, dome lid, knop broken off, blue shield mark, press mark.

c1813   *7in (18cm) high*

$30-40   **BMN**

A Vienna porcelain cachepot on stand, cachepot with underglaze blue shield mark and dated, the flaring cylindrical vessel on paw feet and a square base finely painted with a continuous frieze of flowers.

c1821-33   *9.5in (24cm) high*

$700-1,000   **SI**

A Vienna 'Digitalis alba' cup and saucer, with a purple ground and painted with colored flowers, border of saucer with floral gold decoration, conical cup with everted lip and raised rocaille handle, smooth edges, shield press mark on saucer, blue shield mark on cup, black title and year on base, restored.

1825

$300-400   **BMN**

A Vienna plate, decorated in colored enamels with 'Raub and Sabinerin', signed "Opitz", the blue ground border decorated in raised paste gilding and 'jeweled' with birds, flowers and leaf scrolls, painted mark in blue and titled verso.

c1900   *9.25in (23.5cm) diam*

$220-280   **LFA**

A Vienna plate, decorated in colored enamels with a classical figure and a putto, the puce and yellow ground border decorated in raised paste gilding and flower heads with leaf scrolls, mark in blue.

c1900   *9.75in (25cm) diam*

$150-200   **LFA**

A Vienna plate, decorated in colored enamels with 'Venus and Adonis', signed "Opitz", the blue ground border decorated in raised paste gilding and 'jeweled' with birds, flowers and leaf scrolls, painted mark in blue and titled verso, faint body crack.

c1900   *9.25in (23.5cm) diam*

$220-280   **LFA**

A Worcester feather-molded plate, with floral pattern.

c1763

$700-1,000　　　　**JF**

A Worcester round junket dish, molded with a flower-head, medallion and scallop shells, painted in underglaze blue with sprays of flowers and leaves.

c1760-65　　　9.75in (25cm) diam

$400-600　　　　**LFA**

A Worcester plate, with a shaped edge and printed with pine cones and flower sprays, crescent mark.

c1780　　　9in (23cm) diam

$300-350　　　　**WW**

A Worcester plate, with the 'Pine Cone' pattern printed in underglaze blue, within a flower and diaper border.

c1780　　　8.75in (22cm) diam

$220-280　　　　**LFA**

A Worcester cabbage leaf dish, printed in underglaze blue with the 'Wispy Chrysanthemum' pattern, blue crescent mark, rim chip.

c1770　　　10.25in (26cm) long

$220-280　　　　**LFA**

A Worcester 'Picklevine' pattern leaf dish.

c1760　　　3.5in (9cm) wide

$500-700　　　　**JF**

A Worcester flared round potting pot, painted in underglaze blue with the 'Prunus Fence' pattern, workman's mark, small rim chip restored.

c1755　　　6.75in (17cm) diam

$400-600　　　　**LFA**

A rare Worcester round bowl, painted in underglaze blue with the 'Weeping Willow' pattern, the interior with flowers and a flowering branch, workman's mark.

c1755　　　6in (15cm) diam

$1,200-1,800　　　　**LFA**

Two views of an early Worcester First Period Dr. Wall bowl, decorated with the 'Tambourine Player' pattern in underglaze blue.

c1751-74　　　4.75in (12cm) diam

$1,000-1,500　　　　**TBk**

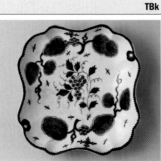

A Worcester concave-sided square dish, painted in underglaze blue with the 'Rubber Tree Plant' pattern, four-character Chinese style mark, faint crack.

c1770-1775　　　7.75in (19.5cm) wide

$220-280　　　　**LFA**

A first period Worcester blue and white bowl, painted with Chinese pavilions on islands, the interior rim with diamond diaper band.

c1775　　　8in (20.5cm) diam

$150-200　　　　**Chef**

A Worcester pierced oval basket, the two ropetwist loop handles with applied flower and leaf terminals, printed in underglaze blue with the 'Gilliflower' pattern, beneath a blue line rim, the exterior applied with flower-heads and picked out in blue, hatched crescent mark, foot-rim firing chips.

Provenance: Bayley Collection, number 12.

c1775   8.25in (21cm) long

$400-600   **LFA**

A Worcester blue and white pierced circular basket of interlaced ovals, the well printed with the 'Pine Cone' pattern, blue crescent mark.

c1780   7in (18cm) diam

$600-900   **DN**

An oval Worcester dish or stand, with a reticulated border applied with flower-heads, the center decorated with flower and leaf sprays, rim section repaired.

c1770-80   9.75in (25cm) diam

$400-600   **WW**

A pair of Worcester blue and white pierced circular baskets of interlaced ovals, the wells printed with the 'Pine Cone' pattern, blue crescent marks, one with a small crack through rim.

c1780   5in (13cm) diam

$700-1,000   **DN**

A Worcester butterdish, stand and cover, rose centered spray groups and rose and running border pattern.

$1,200-1,800   **JF**

An early Worcester tea bowl and saucer, painted with the 'Eloping Bride' pattern.

c1760   Saucer 4in (10cm) diam

$3,000-4,000   **TBk**

A pair of Worcester blue and white tea bowls and saucers, printed with the 'Fence' pattern, blue crescent marks.

c1780

$280-320   **DN**

A Worcester fluted coffee can, with lobed everted rim and "C" scroll handle, finely painted in underglaze blue, with the 'Prunus Root' pattern, workman's mark.

c1754-55   2.25in (5.8cm) high

$1,500-2,000   **LFA**

A Worcester hand-painted blue and white teacup, in 'The Tambourine pattern', workman's mark, damaged.

c1755   2.5in (6cm) high

$280-320   **PC**

A Worcester coffee cup, with notched loop handle, printed in underglaze blue with the 'Fisherman' pattern, the interior with a spearhead and cell diaper border, and picked out in gilt, hatched crescent mark, and another, similarly printed, disguised numeral mark.

c1775-80   2.5in (6cm) high

$150-200   **LFA**

Two first period Worcester blue and white tea bowls, one printed with Chinese islands, and the other with the 'Dairymaid' pattern, workman's and crescent marks, some damage.

Left $50-70, Right $150-200   **Chef**

A small globular First Period Worcester teapot and cover, the lid with knop finial and opposed printed panels of a figure in a pagoda by a fir and a figure in a houseboat.

Provenance: Betty Reed collection.

c1775   4.75in (12cm) high

$300-400   **L&T**

A Worcester 'Mansfield' pattern baluster coffee pot and cover, feather-molded, with an insect and meandering foliage, workman's mark, hairline crack to pot, small chip to spout, finial glued.

c1760   7.75in (20cm) high

$600-900   **DN**

A Worcester large fluted oval sauceboat, with angular loop handle, painted in underglaze blue with the 'Fringed Tree' pattern, the interior with a pavilion on an island, within a diaper and trailing flower border, workman's mark beneath the handle, two small rim chips.

c1756-58   8.5in (12.5cm) long

$400-600   **LFA**

A rare Worcester spirally molded cornucopia-shaped wall picket, painted in underglaze blue with the 'Cornucopia Daisy' pattern.

c1758   11.25in (28.5cm) high

$3,000-4,000   **LFA**

Worcester - Polychrome

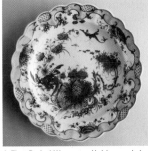

A First Period Worcester 'Jabberwocky' pattern plate.

c1751-74   8.5in (21.5cm) diam

$1,500-2,000   **TBk**

A Worcester saucer dish, painted in colored enamels with spotted fruit and insects, within a gilt C-scroll border, on an apple green ground.

c1770   7.25in (18.5cm) diam

$400-600   **LFA**

A Worcester plate, with fluted rim, painted in colored enamels with the 'Marchioness of Huntley' pattern of trailing flowers and leaves, within a gilt C-scroll cartouche and apple green border.

c1770-75   7.5in (19cm) diam

$300-400   **LFA**

A Worcester large oval dish, in the form of two overlapping cabbage leaves, finely painted in Kakiemon palette with birds, flowering branches and rockwork, within gilt cartouches, on a blue scale and gilt cailloute ground, blue fret mark.

c1770   12.5in (31.5cm) long

$700-1,000   **LFA**

A pair of First Period Worcester dessert plate, decorated with panels of flowering foliage on a dark blue scale ground, within gilt borders, underglaze blue Chinese seal mark, and label from the Harvey collection #114/84, chip to side.

c1770

$700-1,000   **FRE**

A Worcester heart-shaped dish, decorated in the London atelier of James Giles with a classical urn containing flowers, within a gilt anthemion band, the powder blue ground decorated in gilt with scrolling vines, blue crescent mark.

c1772   10.75in (26cm) wide

$400-600   **LFA**

A CLOSER LOOK AT FIRST PERIOD WORCESTER

The painting of Chinoiserie and flower decorations became more confident in the late 1760s.

The Rococo, honey-gilded frames are set against bold ground colors, such as the 'wet blue' used here.

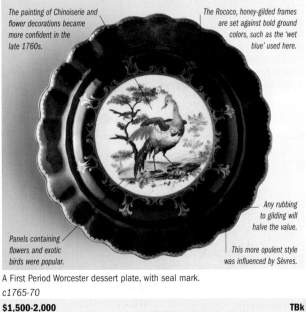

Panels containing flowers and exotic birds were popular.

Any rubbing to gilding will halve the value.

This more opulent style was influenced by Sèvres.

A First Period Worcester dessert plate, with seal mark.

c1765-70

$1,500-2,000   **TBk**

A CLOSER LOOK AT A BOOTHS WORCESTER COPY

Booths used fine earthenware which appears brown.

The sparrow-beak jug is out of proportion, the top half should be narrower.

The transfer printed designs appear dull and lifeless.

Booths pieces are inscribed with the company mark but these have often been removed.

A Booths baluster shaped sparrow-beak jug, in Worcester style, printed in colors with exotic birds and insects, within gilt cartouches, on a blue scale ground.

3.75in (9.5cm) high

$60-90　　　　　　　　　　　　　　　　**LFA**

A Worcester Barr, Flight & Barr plate, printed with a view of Port Mahon in Menorca, with armorial feature, impressed mark and script marks.

c1804-1813　　*8.75in (22cm) diam*

$1,500-2,000　　　　　　　　　**TBk**

A Worcester Flight Period spirally fluted globular teapot, the domed lid with knop finial, painted with sprigs of fuchsia and other flowers in crimson and gilt, the large body similarly painted with six opposed flower sprays with applied loop handle and scroll spout.

6.75in (17.5cm) high

$220-280　　　　　　　　　　　　　**L&T**

A Barr, Flight & Barr inkwell, with Sir Robert Burns related decoration, includes a stanza from Tam O' Shanter and pictures of his birthplace, Ravenschurch, and the friary where he worked.

c1810

$15,000-20,000　　　　　　　　**JF**

Worcester - Flight

Flight 1783-1792

When Thomas Flight bought the Worcester factory in 1783, he handed the running of the business over to his sons, John and Joseph. The brothers faced setbacks when their supervisor, Chamberlain, left the factory, but these problems were eased when John Flight went to France to train in the art of decoration.

Flight & Barr 1792-1804

When John Flight died, Joseph teamed up with Martin Barr. This stage was highly successful for Worcester and its work was compared favorably with the best in French porcelain.

Barr, Flight & Barr 1804-1813

In 1804, Martin Barr's son, Martin Junior, joined the company which was now producing an extremely popular range of wares featuring landscape scenes and botanical pictures. Commissions were also taken for copies of Chinese porcelain bearing the coats of arms of the country's aristocratic families.

Flight, Barr & Barr 1813-1840

When Martin Barr Senior died, Flight became the major shareholder so the name changed again. He worked with George and Martin Barr Junior, and was also joined by talented artist Thomas Baxter. When the demand for rich classical porcelain declined in this period, the company was slow to adapt to new styles and, finally, was forced to merge with Chamberlain in 1840.

A Flight Worcester armorial plate, from the Duke of Clarence service, richly decorated with the Duke's coat of arms, flanked by oak and laurel branches within a border of blue and green ribbons, crowned "Flight" and with the crescent mark.

Provenance: This plate is from the dessert service ordered in 1789 by Prince William who later became William IV.

1789　　　　　　*9.75in (24.5cm) diam*

$4,000-6,000　　　　　　　　　　**WW**

A CLOSER LOOK AT WORCESTER'S NEO-CLASSICAL STYLE

Popular in the late 18thC/early 19thC, this style leaves much of the surface white, with simple decoration and some gilding.

The teapot has fluting around the shoulders and shape similar to a Classical urn.

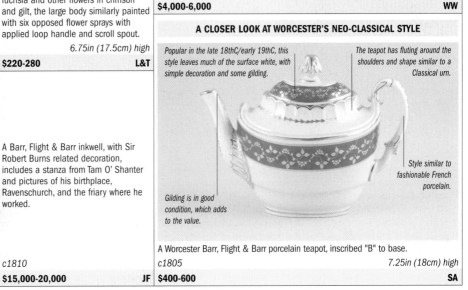

Gilding is in good condition, which adds to the value.

Style similar to fashionable French porcelain.

A Worcester Barr, Flight & Barr porcelain teapot, inscribed "B" to base.

c1805　　　　　　　　*7.25in (18cm) high*

$400-600　　　　　　　　　　　　　**SA**

A Worcester Flight, Barr & Barr inkwell, painted with a panoramic landscape and three figures, the gentleman carrying dead game, the well gilded with palmettes and seaweed, handle with mask terminal, painted mark, Coventry Street address, two chips.

c1813-40   5.5in (14cm) diam

$2,200-2,800   **GorL**

A Flight, Barr & Barr 12-piece part dessert service, decorated with a family crest within a gilded panel, in an apple green ground, with waved, gadrooned border, comprising a shaped circular bowl, three shaped oval dishes, a twin handled sucrier and cover and six dessert plates.

Bowl 12.75in (32.5cm) diam

$2,200-2,800   **FRE**

A pair of Worcester Flight, Barr & Barr vases, with continuous landscapes, one is a view in the Isle of Wight, the other is a view at Clifton.

c1820   6.5in (16.5cm) high

$5,000-7,000   **TBk**

A Worcester Flight, Barr & Barr cup and saucer, impressed mark.

c1820   Saucer 5in (13cm) diam

$400-600   **TBk**

A Worcester Flight, Barr & Barr period sugarbowl, painted with a band of gilt scrolling vine and brown leaves below the oval rim and about the handles, incised "B" mark.

7.25in (18.5cm) wide

$70-100   **Chef**

Worcester - Chamberlains

Robert Chamberlain (1736-98) left Dr. Wall at Worcester in 1789 to start his own business, which would remain connected with his family until 1851. Chamberlain produced extremely high quality hand-painted wares and in 1807 he was granted the royal warrant. His work ranged from cabinet pieces bearing popular views and details from well-known paintings to entire services. It could take years to produce some of the large, very expensive services made for his wealthy clientele. When the company merged with Flight, Barr & Barr in 1840, it kept the name Chamberlain & Company. The last in the line of Chamberlains – Walter – retired in 1851. In 1852, Richard William Binns (1819-1900) and William Henry Kerr (1823-1879) took over and began modernising the factory. They set it on its path to becoming part of Royal Worcester.

An early 19thC Chamberlain's Worcester soup plate, centrally painted with a basket of fruit roundel within royal blue rim gilt with S-scrolls and pendants within the dog-tooth rim band.

9.75in (24.5cm) diam

$100-150   **Chef**

A Chamberlain's Worcester jug/pitcher/ewer, with enriched 'Queen's' pattern.

c1790

$1,500-2,000   JF

A late 18thC Chamberlain's Worcester coffee pot and cover, painted with bands and sprigs of flowers and with gilt details, painted mark, pattern no.12, the knop restored.

9.5in (24cm) high

$300-400   WW

A rare Chamberlain's Worcester oval shell-molded basket, script mark in brown, and 63 Piccadilly address, small chip restored.

c1815   5.25in (13cm) wide

$400-600   LFA

A Chamberlain's Worcester flared beaker, finely painted in colored enamels with a named view of Croome, within a gilt rectangular S-scroll border, the puce ground with initials "SF" in gilt, within a lobed cartouche, beneath a gilt flower-head paneled band, titled in gilt beneath the panel and script London address mark in iron red.

Croome, in the Malvern Hills, is the site of a mid-18thC landscape park designed by Capability Brown. Chamberlain decorated a number of his wares with topographical scenes from Malvern – these were extremely popular and so he also produced framed plaques with these scenes.

c1840   4.5in (11.5cm) high

$700-1,000   LFA

Worcester - Grainger

Thomas Grainger (1783-1839) started his porcelain factory in 1801. He and his partner, John Wood, had trained as apprentices with Chamberlain at the Worcester factory. Grainger and Wood developed a good reputation for their ornamental wares, which were often painted with the fashionable rich Imari pattern or with flower and landscape scenes. In 1839, Thomas Grainger died and

his son George took over, backing the successful increased production of Neo-Rococo decorative wares as well as a more diversified range, which included tiles and door furniture. When George died in 1889, the factory was sold to Royal Worcester and many of the workforce transferred to the Royal Worcester factory in 1902.

A pair of G. Grainger Worcester porcelain jugs, with elongated pentagonal spouts, the globular-shaped bodies with gilded thistle decoration, scroll handles and each decorated with a landscape panel of Malvern Abbey and a view of Worcester City with river in foreground, puce printed marks.

$400-600   Clv

An early 19thC Grainger and Co. Worcester jug, painted with a fox and dead lamb by rocks within gilt canted rectangular frame below a gilt band of double anthemion motifs alternating with stars on the neck, painted marks.

5.25in (13.5cm) high

$300-400   Chef

A Grainger & Co. Worcester two handled cup, decorated on a pink ground with two views of Worcester from the river and from the cathedral.

5.75in (14.5cm) high

$400-600   BonS

A Grainger's Worcester part tea service, painted with bouquets of flowers within gilt gadrooned borders, comprising a teapot with cover and stand, a two-handled sugar box and cover, eight cups and saucers, a milk jug and a pair of sandwich plates, painted pattern "No. 1410", some staining and cracks.

c1830

$700-1,000   DN

PORCELAIN

A Swansea cup, with a flared rim and gilt handle, painted with a chamfered square panel with colorful flowers and with elaborate gilt border designs, marked "Swansea" in red script, a tiny chip where the top of handle meets the rim.

3.75in (9.5cm) high

$1,500-2,000　　　　**WW**

A late 19thC European porcelain Naples-style two-handled cabinet cup, cover and stand, molded 'con basso relievo istoriato' to one side with Aurora and chariot, to the other with figures and a chariot drawn by winged mythical beasts, the cover with Bacchic scenes, surmounted with a Bacchic putto finial, the saucer with floral swags, blue crowned "N" marks, chip to cover, one handle restored.

$150-200　　　　**DN**

A late 19thC to early 20thC Musterschutz porcelain tankard, modeled as an elderly gentleman with drooping full moustache, possibly Bismarck, the pewter mounted hinged lid modeled as a turnip top.

6.75in (17cm) high

$120-180　　　　**Chef**

A framed hand-painted porcelain plate, silvered ground with parakeets and wisteria, scratches.

Provenance: *Note with plate details purchase at Philadelphia Exposition 1876.*

1876　　　*9.5in (25cm) diam*

$600-900　　　　**FRE**

A Philadelphia Exposition china plate, with a polychrome transfer print scene of Memorial Hall and figures.

1876　　　*8.5in (21.5cm) diam*

$70-100　　　　**FRE**

A Fischer & Mieg, Pirkinhammer porcelain coffee set, designed by Dagobert Perche, comprising an oviform teapot and cover, a milk jug and cover, a sugar bowl and cover, five cups and six saucers, each piece decorated in alternating panels with colored floral sprays, marked on the bases with the factory device in a circle and "Oepiag", some also with "NeuWien".

Teapot 8.25in (21cm) high

$700-1,000　　　　**DN**

A late 19thC European porcelain part service, painted with a lake scene on a bleu celeste ground, comprising 15 cups, seven saucers and a waste bowl.

Cup 3in (7.5cm) high

$700-1,000　　　　**SI**

A pair of early 20thC European porcelain figures, modeled as a boy and girl in 18thC-style dress, the girl holding a bird on a lead and the boy depicted with a seated dog, underglazed blue crossed swords and star mark.

4.25in (11cm) high

$400-600　　　　**SI**

A pair of late 19thC French figures of a shepherd and shepherdess, painted in iron-red 'France' and with double-crossed scepter, each depicted in 18thC costume, standing on a floral encrusted and scroll-molded base, the male holding flowers and with a dog at his feet, the female holding a basket of flowers in one hand, a few blossoms in the other hand and with a lamb by her side.

12.5in (32cm) high

$1,800-2,200　　　　**SI**

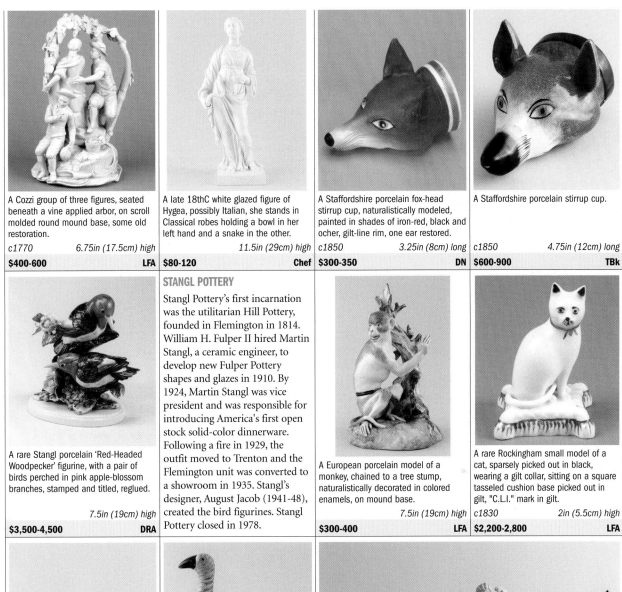

A Cozzi group of three figures, seated beneath a vine applied arbor, on scroll molded round mound base, some old restoration.

c1770   *6.75in (17.5cm) high*

$400-600   LFA

A late 18thC white glazed figure of Hygea, possibly Italian, she stands in Classical robes holding a bowl in her left hand and a snake in the other.

11.5in (29cm) high

$80-120   Chef

A Staffordshire porcelain fox-head stirrup cup, naturalistically modeled, painted in shades of iron-red, black and ocher, gilt-line rim, one ear restored.

c1850   *3.25in (8cm) long*

$300-350   DN

A Staffordshire porcelain stirrup cup.

c1850   *4.75in (12cm) long*

$600-900   TBk

A rare Stangl porcelain 'Red-Headed Woodpecker' figurine, with a pair of birds perched in pink apple-blossom branches, stamped and titled, reglued.

7.5in (19cm) high

$3,500-4,500   DRA

STANGL POTTERY

Stangl Pottery's first incarnation was the utilitarian Hill Pottery, founded in Flemington in 1814. William H. Fulper II hired Martin Stangl, a ceramic engineer, to develop new Fulper Pottery shapes and glazes in 1910. By 1924, Martin Stangl was vice president and was responsible for introducing America's first open stock solid-color dinnerware. Following a fire in 1929, the outfit moved to Trenton and the Flemington unit was converted to a showroom in 1935. Stangl's designer, August Jacob (1941-48), created the bird figurines. Stangl Pottery closed in 1978.

A European porcelain model of a monkey, chained to a tree stump, naturalistically decorated in colored enamels, on mound base.

7.5in (19cm) high

$300-400   LFA

A rare Rockingham small model of a cat, sparsely picked out in black, wearing a gilt collar, sitting on a square tasseled cushion base picked out in gilt, "C.L.I." mark in gilt.

c1830   *2in (5.5cm) high*

$2,200-2,800   LFA

A 20thC German porcelain swan bowl, the white bird with black and yellow feet and beak, the bowl within its wings.

6in (15cm) high

$30-50   Chef

An unusual Staffordshire porcelain model of a pigeon, naturalistically decorated in black, on shaped oval mound base, with a gilt band.

c1840-50   *5.25in (13.5cm) high*

$700-1,000   LFA

A late 19thC German porcelain composite part monkey band, modeled after the Meissen original, comprising two oboists, a bagpiper, a violinist, two cellists, a conductor, a horn player, a fife and drummer and another figure, damage and losses.

Conductor 5.5in (15cm) high

$700-1,000   DN

PORCELAIN

A New Hall serpentine-sided teapot and flat cover, painted in famille rose palette with flowers and leaves, within flower and pink ribbon bands, pattern number "186", crack at base of handle.

c1785   5.5in (14cm) high

$180-220   **LFA**

A Mason's bone china 'London' shape teapot, cover and stand, painted in colors with a band of flowers including rose and convolvulus, within gilt-line borders and a sugar box and cover, minor wear.

c1815

$700-1,000   **DN**

A rare Staffordshire porcelain faceted large ovoid jug, probably New Hall, with scroll handle, printed and painted in Chinese famille rose style with the 'Boy and the Butterfly' pattern, beneath a simple iron-red border, the handle picked out in puce.

This form of jug appears to be unrecorded.

c1810   6.5in (16.5cm) high

$600-900   **LFA**

A pair of 19thC French porcelain covered vases, each swirling lobed body decorated with polychrome floral swags, gilt diaper work and pink rocaille motifs, the whole highlighted with gilt, the covers similarly decorated, mounted as lamps.

17in (43cm) high

$1,500-2,000   **SI**

A pair of Samson famille rose armorial octagonal section baluster vases, each with complex oval armorial device amidst peony scrolls, rust painted mark "M Paris".

13in (33cm) high

$400-600   **L&T**

A 19thC English porcelain cobalt blue ground three-piece garniture, comprising three vases, each ovoid with waisted neck on square pedestal foot and applied with griffin handles, painted with floral baskets and sprays reserved on a cobalt blue ground with gilt highlights.

Tallest 11in (28cm) high

$400-600   **SI**

A pair of Alcock vases, with landscapes.

c1835-1840   9.75in (25cm) high

$1,500-2,000   **JF**

A pair of late 19thC Samson porcelain pink ground, two handled vases and covers, painted with reserves of exotic birds, heightened in gilt, gilt anchor pseudo mark.

15in (38cm) high

$1,500-2,000   **SI**

A pair of late 19thC gilt bronze-mounted porcelain vases, painted with classical battle scenes on a russet ground.

15in (38cm) high

$1,800-2,200   **SI**

A pair of late 19thC European porcelain chartreuse ground vases, each ovoid vessel with flaring neck, finely painted with a figural reserve on a puce and chartreuse ground heightened with gilt decoration.

13.25in (33.5cm) high

$1,800-2,200   **SI**

A late 19thC German porcelain iron-red ground vase, decorated in the manner of Berlin lacquered pieces, with raised gilt and cream Chinese figures at a table in a garden, flanked by birds in branches, on a foliate-cast ormolu base, impressed crowned shield and "ABT" mark.

30in (76cm) high

$1,800-2,200   **SI**

A pair of cornucopia vases, encrusted with colorful flowers and raised on Rococo bases, enriched with green enamel and gilding, no marks, some damage.

6in (15.5cm) high

$180-220 WW

A pair of late 19thC European porcelain purple ground cornucopia, each scrolling foliate cornucopia on a scroll-molded rectangular base, painted with reserves of fruit on a green ground and with birds perched on gilt scrolling foliage, underglaze blue "MA" mark.

9in (23cm) high

$800-1,200 SI

A pair of late 19thC Samson pink ground porcelain potpourri jars, each boat form vessel molded with lion's masks and rocaille borders and painted with a cartouche of Cupid, on a scrolling base, each pierced tapering cover molded with scales and ropework, with spiral pennant and ball finial, underglaze blue faux Sèvres mark, incised "M".

14.5in (37cm) high

$3,000-3,500 SI

A New Hall faceted cylindrical tea canister and cover, with a pineapple finial, decorated with gilt lines.

c1790　*5in (12.5cm) high*

$700-1,000 WW

A Pinxton faceted oval sucrier and cover, with two fixed ring handles and loop knop, painted in colored enamels with bands of scrolling flowers and leaves, within gilt line borders, cover with shallow rim chip.

c1810　*5.5in (14cm) high*

$600-900 LFA

A large German porcelain ozier-molded globular tureen and cover, painted in colors with sprays of flowers, birds and insects, the cover with sliced lemon finial, Berlin-style scepter mark, some rubbing to the gilding.

11.5in (29cm) diam

$400-600 DN

A Pinxton oval sucrier and cover, with two fixed ring handles and pointed knop, painted in green and gilt with flower-head, and leaf scroll bands, pattern number "312" in gilt.

c1810　*5.25in (14cm) high*

$500-700 LFA

A pair of 19thC English porcelain cobalt blue-ground sauce tureens, oval shaped with round rosette handles and a palmette finial, painted on colorful floral reserves and gilt highlights, one repaired.

7.75in (19.5cm) wide

$400-600 SI

A Swansea sucrier, cover and stand, and a matching plate decorated in the Japanese Imari style with flowers and panels, the stand and plate marked "Swansea" in red, pattern number "194".

c1820　*8.25in (21cm) high*

$1,500-2,000 WW

A rare Rockingham miniature flared oval basket, with loop handle, molded with leaves and decorated in gilt with seaweed, on lobed base, number "C.1.4" in red.

c1835　*3.75in (7cm) high*

$1,500-2,000 LFA

A Carl Thieme Rococo-style wall bracket, molded with foliage, painted with a romantic scene and applied with an amorino, chipped.

9.5in (24cm) high

$300-400 BonS

A Jacob Petit-style porcelain stacking teapot, formed as a floral encrusted three-storey house, blue enamel "J.P." mark.

12in (30.5cm) high

$600-900 SI

POTTERY

THE ART OF MAKING POTTERY FROM CLAY WAS DEVELOPED IN C6000BC IN THE ANCIENT NEAR EAST. By c2000BC pottery was used throughout ancient Mesopotamia and techniques such as using a wheel and turntable and lead glazes had been developed. These methods had spread to Greece by 600BC and to China during the Han Dynasty (206BC-AD220). It was not until the Middle Ages that pottery became a widespread medium in northern Europe. The process of adding tin oxide to the basic lead glaze to a form of tin-glazed earthenware, brought by Moorish invaders to Spain, resulted in the production of Hispano-Moresque wares and then Italian maiolica, French faience, German faience and, by the mid-16th C, Dutch and British delftware.

Pottery has a coarser texture than porcelain and there are two main types, porous earthenware and nonporous stoneware. This difference is created by the temperature at which wares are fired. Earthenware is fired to 2200°F (1200°C) and stoneware to 2500°F (1400°C). Stoneware is stronger and harder wearing than earthenware and sometimes has a slightly translucent appearance.

In order to make earthenware nonporous, it must be coated with a glaze but glazes are also used to decorate stoneware. Glaze types include lead, tin, and salt. Lead glaze has a glassy, transparent appearance and is used on most European wares. Tin glaze contains tin oxide and has an opaque-white finish. Salt glaze is created by throwing salt into the kiln during firing. The salt combines with the silicates in the ceramic body to form a thick, glassy glaze.

Commemorative Ceramics

A creamware cylindrical mug, flared towards the base and printed with the scene of the 'Tithe Pig' above a rhyme, an applied molded handle, a chip to the foot-rim and a body crack to one side.

c1780   *5in (12.5cm) high*

$800-1,200   **WW**

A late 18thC creamware cylindrical mug, printed with a scene of the execution of Louis XVI, the inscription giving details of the event, signed "J. Aynsley, Lane End", haircracks and slight staining.

4.75in (12cm) high

$1,800-2,200   **WW**

A late 18thC creamware cylindrical mug, transfer printed and painted in colored enamels with Corporal Cartouche teaching Miss Camp-Love her manual exercise, after John Collet's painting, brown line rims, together with documents and a pamphlet about the subject.

5.25in (13cm) high

$1,500-2,000   **WW**

A late 18thC creamware cylindrical mug, decorated with a scene entitled 'British Slavery' and inscribed "Ah cursed Ministry, they'll ruin us with their damn'd Taxes! Why zounds they're making slaves of us all and starving us to Death", a body crack and staining.

5.5in (14cm) high

$1,000-1,500   **WW**

Commemorative ceramics were made to celebrate incidents of historical, royal, sociological, political, theatrical, and topographical interest. The occasion being commemorated was painted, printed or molded into the body of the ceramic wares. The invention of transfer-printing in the mid-18thC meant that these pieces could be mass-produced easily and cheaply, and it is from this period onwards that commemorative wares became really popular.

There is a lot of scope for collectors in this area because there are so many different subjects to choose from. Some people collect purely royalty-related items or areas such as political, war related, foreign or sporting commemoratives. Wares include cups and saucers, mugs, plates, figures, and busts.

A late 18thC creamware jug, printed in black with a scene entitled 'Old Women Ground Young', the reverse a view of a courting couple inscribed "Oh Dear Jack be still - you shall not have your will", tiny rim chips and a few very faint body cracks.

5.5in (14cm) high

$700-1,000   **WW**

A pearlware commemorative jug, painted in a Pratt-type palette with sprays of flowers and inscribed "Samuel Spencer London", dated, cracked and repaired.

1806   *9in (25cm) high*

$400-600   **DN**

An early 19thC small creamware political satire mug, printed and painted with a scene titled "Narrow Escape of Boney through a Window", repaired.

3.5in (8.5cm) high

$400-600   **WW**

An early 19thC Orange Order cylindrical mug, printed in black and decorated with Masonic emblems, a pink luster rim, a restored rim chip.

4.75in (12cm) high

$400-600   **WW**

A CLOSER LOOK AT A COMMEMORATIVE MUG

A circular wall plaque, commemorating John Wesley, possibly by Dixon & Co. of Sunderland, printed in black with an untitled portrait inscribed "Follow after, he cries, as he mounts to the skies, Follow after your friend, to the blissful enjoyments that never shall end", the molded rim colored black and yellow, unmarked, small chip to rim.

c1820-30   *5.75in (16cm) diam*

$400-600   **DN**

This mug has an interesting subject which makes it of historical importance. This increases its value. Humor against Britain's old enemy also helps.

This mug commands a high price despite slight damage. This bears testimony to its historical and aesthetic appeal. There are many collectors who specialize in anything Napoleonic.

The coloring on this mug has remained vibrant. Excessive rubbing will reduce the value by one third.

The inscription says "How do you do Mr Boney." This is reference to the period of 1803-1805, when Napoleon seemed to be about to invade the British Isles. Propaganda in Britain depicted Napoleon as the devil incarnate and called him Boney, which eventually became corrupted to Bogey and Bogeyman.

A creamware political satire mug, printed and painted with Napoleon, two hair cracks and a chip to the foot-rim.

c1810   *4.75in (12cm) high*

$3,000-5,000   **WW**

A pearlware molded jug, commemorating Lord Wellington and General Hill, each with impressed title beneath a waist-length portrait flanked by flags, colored overglaze with red, brown, ocher, black and blue enamels, with silver luster lining to rim and foot, unmarked, small chip to rim, luster worn.

c1810-1815   *5in (13.5cm) high*

$220-280   **DN**

A pearlware cylindrical mug, printed in purple with a view of the entrance of the Liverpool and Manchester Railway, unmarked, minor damage.

c1830   *2.75in (7cm) high*

$400-600   **WW**

A Reform Bill mug, printed in puce and inscribed "Royal Assent to the Reform Bill 7 June 1832", the reverse with portraits of Lord Althorp, Earl Grey, Lord John Russell and Lord Brougham, mark for Machin & Thomas Burslem, minor damage.

c1832   *4in (10cm) high*

$400-600   **WW**

A Queen Victoria coronation commemorative salt glaze flask, by G. Wilson, Half Moon, Gracechurch Street, molded on each side with a portrait of the Queen after Hayter, the gadrooned shoulders of darker brown hue.

c1837   7.5in (19cm) high

$300-400   **Chef**

An Orange Order commemorative mug, of cylindrical form with turned foot and simple strap handle, printed in black and crudely colored with enamels, bearing three Orange Order prints, "Let Brotherly Love Continue" with initials "GR", "Protestant Ascendancy - Holiness to the Lord", and an equestrian portrait of King William III, unmarked, stained, cracks in body.

c1830-50   5.5in (15cm) high

$220-280   **DN**

A large black-printed mug, depicting 'The Miners' New Offices, Barnsley' with different size versions of the same view on the two sides and an internal grapevine border, black-printed mark for Robinson & Hollinshead of Burslem, some staining.

The offices were opened in 1874 and still survive at 2 Huddersfield Road, Barnsley.

c1874   4.75in (13cm) high

$220-280   **DN**

A 19thC Staffordshire transfer-printed pitcher, ovoid form, printed with a minstrel show, the spout printed with theater curtain, the inscription "I Wish I Was in Dixay" and "Sally is the Girl for Me" below figures.

The design for the jug was registered by the firm of Beech, Unwin & Co. of Green Dock Works, Longton, Staffordshire, July 27.

c1870   7in (17.5cm) high

$800-1,200   **FRE**

A Staffordshire mug commemorating the Battle of Inkerman, printed and painted with the battle scene and titled 'Sergent Thomas defending the colors at Inkerman'.

c1855   4.25in (10.5cm) high

$400-600   **WW**

A Wedgwood jug, commemorating the death of Benjamin Disraeli, of Dutch shape printed in black and enameled in colors, one side with a portrait, the reverse with "Beaconsfield, died April 19, 1881" and a long quote from the novel "Coningsby", and the neck with a floral and ribbon border listing eight of his novels, impressed mark and black-printed registration diamond for May 16, 1881, some rubbing to spout.

1881   6in (16.5cm) high

$150-200   **DN**

A commemorative mug, entitled 'Success to the Ship Canal', of tapering tankard form with angular handle, printed in black with the inscription on the front, a sailing ship on one side, and a portrait of 'Mr. Daniel Adamson, C.E.' on the other, with a simple rope border inside the rim and on the handle, unmarked, cracks, chips to foot.

Daniel Adamson was chairman of the Manchester Ship Canal committee; the canal was completed in 1893 and officially opened by Queen Victoria on January 1, 1894.

c1893-94   4.25in (11.5cm) high

$150-200   **DN**

A Liverpool creamware baluster jug, transfer-printed with a three-masted gunship in full sail in black monochrome, the obverse with 'An East View of Liverpool Light House and Signals on Bidston Hill,' indexed and enameled, pouring lip repaired, base hair cracked.

7.25in (18.5cm) diam

$700-1,000   **Gorl**

A Doulton and Lambeth earthenware jug, made to commemorate the Diamond Jubilee of Queen Victoria.

This jug was the largest of three sizes.

c1897	9.25in (23.5cm) high
$300-400	**H&G**

An earthenware plate, made to commemorate the Diamond Jubilee of Queen Victoria, showing scenes from different sports.

c1897	9.25in (23cm) diam
$150-200	**H&G**

A small earthenware transfer plate, made to commemorate the Diamond Jubilee of Queen Victoria.

c1897	6.25in (16cm) diam
$70-100	**H&G**

A Black Jackfield teapot, made for Tower Tea, to commemorate the Diamond Jubilee of Queen Victoria.

c1897	6in (15.5cm) high
$180-220	**H&G**

A small Doulton bone china vase, in memoriam to Queen Victoria.

c1901	5in (13cm) high
$400-600	**H&G**

A Royal Doulton & Lambeth stoneware jug, made to commemorate the coronation of Edward VII.

c1902	7.75in (20cm) high
$180-220	**H&G**

A Royal Doulton earthenware beaker, made to commemorate the coronation of Edward VII, made for sale in Simon's Town, South Africa.

c1902	2.5in (9.5cm) high
$100-150	**H&G**

A Royal Doulton bone china beaker, made to commemorate the coronation of Edward VII.

c1902	2.5in (9.5cm) high
$150-200	**H&G**

A pair of Royal Doulton bone china plates, made to commemorate the coronation of Edward VII and Alexandra.

c1902	8in (20.5cm) diam
$300-500 pair	**H&G**

An Aynsly for William Whitely bone china tea plate, made to commemorate the coronation of Edward VII.

c1902	6.75in (17cm) diam
$70-100	**H&G**

A European bone china ribbon plate, made to commemorate the coronation of Edward VII, a similar one was made showing Queen Victoria.

c1902	8.5in (21.5cm) diam
$70-100	**H&G**

A Hammersley bone china mug, made to commemorate the Silver Jubilee of King George V and Queen Mary.

c1935 3.75in (9.5cm) high

$100-150 H&G

A Paragon china plate, made to commemorate the Silver Jubilee of King George V and Queen Mary.

c1935 11in (28cm) diam

$150-200 H&G

A Carltonware earthenware beaker, made to commemorate generals of the Boer War.

c1900 4in (10cm) high

$220-280 H&G

A Royal Worcester bone china plate, made to commemorate Baden Powell and the relief of Mafeking.

c1900 9.25in (23.5cm) diam

$180-220 H&G

A Grimwades earthenware bowl, made to commemorate World War I.

c1916 5in (12cm) diam

$100-150 H&G

A Royal Winton earthenware 'Old Bill' plate, made to commemorate World War I.

c1916 8.5in (22cm) diam.

$150-200 H&G

A bone china plate, made to commemorate World War I.

c1918 8in (20.5cm) diam

$80-120 H&G

A Chelson China bone china mug, made to commemorate the signing of peace after World War I.

c1919 3in (7.5cm) high

$100-150 H&G

An earthenware mug, made to commemorate peace after World War I.

c1919 3in (8cm) high

$60-90 H&G

An earthenware child's daisy plate, supporting the repeal of the corn laws.

c1845 6in (15cm) diam

$150-200 H&G

A Wedgwood earthenware jug, made to commemorate the death of Alfred, Lord Tennyson.

c1892 8in (20.5cm) high

$300-400 H&G

A bone china mug, in memoriam to William Gladstone, with transfer of Hawarden Castle.

c1898 3.25in (8cm) high

$120-180 H&G

A Ridgways earthenware plate, made to commemorate Joseph Chamberlain.

c1904 10in (25.5cm) diam

$100-150 H&G

A biscuit stoneware bust of Benjamin Franklin, probably French.

c1824-1830 5in (13cm) high

$2,000-3,000 JF

A small European bisque bust of General Booth Salvation Army, probably made for his death in 1912.

c1912 4.25in (11cm) high

$60-90 H&G

A Russian parian bust of Lenin.

c1935 9.5in (24cm) high

$300-400 H&G

Creamware

Creamware is a refined, cream-colored earthenware with a transparent ivory-tinted lead glaze. Enoch Booth of Tunstall in the 1740s, Josiah Wedgwood (1730-1795), and Thomas Astbury (1686-1743) are all attributed with its invention. It was sophisticated enough to become a substitute for porcelain and was less prone to chipping. By the 1760s, it had caught the interest of Queen Charlotte, who ordered a creamware tea service in 1765. Consequently creamware is sometimes known as 'Queen's ware'.

Over the next hundred years creamware remained the standard pottery body in Britain and throughout much of Europe and North America. British production was centered in Staffordshire, Leeds, Liverpool, Bristol and Swansea.

The body of creamware is close-grained and composed of Devon clay mixed with flint and covered in a smooth lead glaze. It could be finely molded or cut and was also a good medium for decoration with underglaze blue, overglaze enameling and transfer-printing. Wares included tablewares, ornamental wares and sophisticated pierced wares.

Only Wedgwood and a few other companies marked their creamware, otherwise it can be difficult to attribute.

A creamware octagonal plate, of Whieldon-type, the border molded in relief with leaf-scrolls reserved on a diaper, painted in typical glazes, slight surface scratches.

c1760   8.25in (21cm) wide

$400-600   **DN**

A pair of Liverpool-printed creamware armorial plates, probably Wedgwood, printed in black with a central armorial with a shield supported by two lions and surmounted with a coronet, within floral swag borders, one with hairline crack.

c1780   9.75in (25cm) diam

$400-600   **DN**

A Leeds Pottery creamware oviform barber's bowl, with 'feuille de chou' border and shaped rim, impressed mark, some small rim chips.

c1780   11.25in (31cm) wide

$400-600   **DN**

A Leeds Creamware charger, with yellow and green splotches on a mottled brown ground.

c1785-1800   18.75in (47.5cm) long

$400-600   **Pook**

A Swansea creamware dessert plate, painted by Thomas Pardoe.

c1805

$800-1,200   **JF**

A Liverpool creamware ship plate, of circular shape, printed in black with a view of a British three-masted sailing ship and six vignettes of birds around the rim, the sea enameled in green, some restoration.

Provenance: Bears label for the Grant-Davidson collection, number E595.

c1795-1815   9.75in (25cm) diam

$220-280   **DN**

A Herculaneum creamware ship plate, with shaped rim, printed in black with a view of an American three-masted sailing ship and six flower sprays around the rim, impressed "HERCULANEUM".

c1800-10   10in (25.5cm) diam

$180-220   **DN**

A black-printed creamware ship plate, decorated with a view of a three-masted sailing ship within a simple black-lined border, unidentified impressed initial mark "S & W".

The initials S & W do not appear to be recorded in existing mark books; the only Staffordshire firm of appropriate date would appear to be Simpson & Wright who are listed at Shelton in a directory of 1802.

c1795-1815   9.75in (25cm) diam

$220-280   **DN**

A pair of 19thC French creamware plates, printed in black with riddles using words and pictures within floral borders, impressed marks.

8in (20.5cm) diam

$220-280   **WW**

A Minton creamware plate, finely painted in colored enamels by Antoine Boullemier, with a young child holding a gun, a hare running at his feet, within a basket molded border, and pierced arcaded rim, signed, impressed marks.

c1880   *9in (23cm) diam*

$350-400   **LFA**

A large group of assorted late 18thC/early 19thC Herculaneum and Wedgwood creamware table items, various forms including a large ovoid platter, two deep oval servicing bowls, a monteith, chop plate, seven shaped servicing dishes, a soup plate, five plates of varying sizes, two covered sauce boats, and extra covers, most decorated in a brown sprig pattern, others in leafy vine or grape, marked, imperfections.

Provenance: Possibly used at Wakefield, the Fisher family home in Germantown. Wakefield was built by Thomas Fisher in 1799, on property inherited by Fisher's first wife Sarah Logan. The Fishers and their descendants occupied the home until the 1970s.

$1,800-2,200   **FRE**

A black-printed creamware bowl, probably decorated at Liverpool, the inside with a three-masted sailing ship surrounded by small border vignettes of exotic birds, and around the outside with four prints including "Jemmy's Return", a sailing ship, "Jemmy's Farewell", and "The Waterman", unmarked, worn, haircracks, chips to foot-rim.

c1795-1810   *12in (30.5cm) high*

$300-400   **DN**

A creamware baluster coffee pot and cover, Staffordshire or Yorkshire, painted in colored enamels with floral bouquets, minor damage and wear.

c1780   *11in (28cm) high*

$400-600   **DN**

A late 18thC Wesley commemorative creamware teapot, possibly Wedgwood, printed by Green of Liverpool, a portrait of the preacher below three angels' heads on the cover, the reverse with a verse taken from 'Watt's Hymns.'

$4,000-6,000   **Chef**

A Staffordshire creamware teapot and cover, with a crabstock handle, and raised on three feet, the body applied with a scrolling vine and decorated with a mottled manganese glaze.

c1755-65   *6.75in (17cm) long*

$400-600   **WW**

A creamware baluster-shaped jug and oval basin, the feather-molded borders picked out in green, basin with rim crack.

c1780-1800   *10.25in (26cm) high*

$800-1,200   **LFA**

A creamware part service, comprising a teapot and cover, a slop bowl, a milk jug, a tea canister and cover and five tea bowls and saucers, painted in green enamel with scattered sprays of flowers and a swag band, some damage.

c1790

$2,200-2,800   **DN**

A creamware mottled-brown glazed miniature mug, of Whieldon-type, molded in relief with a trailed flowering vine, applied with a rope-twist handle and painted in shades of brown, ocher and green glazes.

c1760   *1.5in (4cm) high*

$220-280   **DN**

A late 18thC creamware cylindrical mug, with a loop handle decorated with combed colored slip between green reeded bands, an old restored crack.

6.25in (15.6cm) high

$2,200-2,800 **WW**

A late 18thC creamware cylindrical mug, printed and painted with 'The Landlord's Caution with Honest John Barley Corn', iron red borders, old over sprayed haircracks.

4.75in (12cm) high

$280-320 **WW**

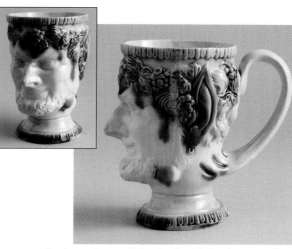

A creamware Bacchus mask mug, with loop handle, picked out in green, on fluted round base, foot-rim crack and small chips.

c1780-1800 *4.5in (11.5cm) high*

$220-280 **LFA**

A creamware group of 'Christ's Agony', of Obadiah Sherratt type, with Christ modeled kneeling in prayer, at his side a cherub proffering the Blessed Sacrement.

c1830 *7.75in (20cm) high*

$700-1,000 **DN**

A Yorkshire creamware cylindrical mug, decorated with brown slip and concentric bands, small chips to the foot-rim.

c1800 *6.25in (16cm) high*

$300-400 **WW**

A CLOSER LOOK AT A CREAMWARE CAT

Animals are always a popular area for collecting, making this piece very desirable.

This piece commands a high price despite being small in size. This is because these pieces are much sought after.

The sponged decoration is hand-painted, and although crude, possesses undeniable rustic charm.

There is very little damage on this piece, helping it to retain its value.

A creamware model of a seated cat, sponged in brown, yellow, ocher, and green on an oval mound base, small foot-rim chips.

c1800-1810 *3.75in (9.5cm) high*

$700-1,000 **LFA**

A creamware figure of a shepherdess, of Ralph Wood type, modeled standing holding a lamb, partially painted in colored glazes in shades of brown, green and ocher, with a restored neck.

c1780 *9.5in (24cm) high*

$700-1,000 **DN**

Two creamware figures of a gardener and companion, of Ralph Wood type, the gardener modeled standing beside a plinth holding a pot containing a pineapple, resting on a spade held in the other hand, his companion holding a flower, painted with colored glazes, repaired.

c1790

$700-1,000 **DN**

An early 19thC creamware cow creamer and cover.

7.25in (18.5cm) long

$500-700 WW

A Staffordshire creamware model of a recumbent leopard.

c1800 *2.5in (6.5cm) high*

$500-700 LFA

A Staffordshire creamware tea canister, naturally molded and colored as a cauliflower, probably Wedgwood.

c1760-65 *4.75in (12cm) high*

$700-1,000 WW

A William Greatbatch creamware tea canister, the rectangular body molded with osier and fruiting branches.

c1770-80 *4.25in (11cm) high*

$100-150 WW

A CLOSER LOOK AT A CREAMWARE JELLY MOULD

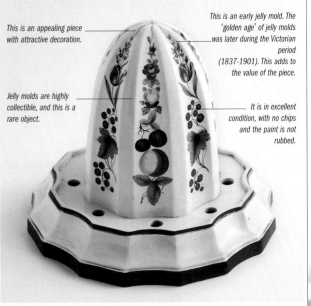

This is an appealing piece with attractive decoration.

Jelly molds are highly collectible, and this is a rare object.

This is an early jelly mold. The 'golden age' of jelly molds was later during the Victorian period (1837-1901). This adds to the value of the piece.

It is in excellent condition, with no chips and the paint is not rubbed.

A rare Wilson creamware jelly mold, the octagonal section dome painted on each face with fruit, flowers and leaves in bright polychrome enamels, the multisided base decorated with blue borders, impressed "Wilson".

c1790-1800 *7.75in (20cm) high*

$4,000-6,000 WW

A creamware rectangular tea canister, possibly Swansea, each side molded with a garland beneath a shell border, the details picked out in blue.

c1785 *5in (12.5cm) high*

$400-600 WW

A creamware spittoon, possibly Staffordshire or Yorkshire, of typical form with globular body and inverted rim, painted in shades of green, iron-red and blue with sprays of scattered cornflowers, slight wear to rim.

c1790 *4in (10cm) high*

$300-600 DN

A creamware navette-shaped sauce boat, painted with a band of blue flower-head bosses reserved on a yellow-ground band, within black-line borders, lacks cover.

c1790 *7.5in (19cm) wide*

$150-200 DN

Dutch Delft

The Netherlands became a center of production for tin-glazed earthenware from c1500, when immigrant Italian craftsmen settled in Antwerp. This new method of making pottery involved making extremely fine, soft and usually thinly potted wares with a thick, white glaze. These new techniques spread north during the 16thC and potteries were established at Haarlem, Amsterdam and Rotterdam, although it was the town of Delft that was really at the forefront of production, hence the term 'Delft ware'.

Early wares were influenced by Italian pottery and these pieces are known as 'Italian-Antwerp'. These were usually decorated with pine cone motifs, geometric patterns, strapwork and half-shaded petal borders. Decoration was usually in blue but also in polychrome, with designs in copper-green, yellow and ocher.

From the beginning of the 17thC, Delft ware was heavily influenced by the blue and white porcelain brought to Europe from the Orient by the Dutch East India Company. Within a few years the Italian maiolica colors were replaced by a palette of blue and white. In c1645, imports from China were stopped because the kilns in Jingdezhen had been destroyed by the invading Manchus. This meant that there was a huge increase in production of Dutch Delft ware. Wares included drug jars, tiles, dishes, flower holders and ewers. The most influential factories were The Metal Pot, The Rose, The Axe, The White Star, The Greek A, and The Peacock.

In c1683, Chinese porcelain started being imported again. This led Delft potters to experiment with a polychrome palette, with wares in famille verte and famille rose styles. By the 19thC, the popularity of English creamware led to a decline in the production of Dutch Delft ware, although it is still produced today.

A Dutch Delft fluted round dish, with central boss, painted in blue with an allover design of flowers and leaves, blue line rim, faint rim cracks.

c1700 · 10in (25.5cm) diam · $150-200 · LFA

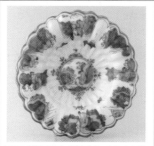

A late 17th/early 18thC Frankfurt delft dish, the sides molded with two bands of lobes about a central boss, each painted in washes of lavender blue with a Chinaman leaning against rocks, some damage.

12.75in (32.5cm) diam · $400-600 · Chef

A late 17th/early 18thC delft plate, possibly German, the octafoil rim painted in blue with alternating panels of flowers and Chinese figures in mountain retreats, the center with a figure by a river, some damage.

13in (33cm) diam · $300-400 · Chef

A mid-18thC Dutch Delft polychrome plate, painted with an exotic bird perched on a leafy branch and with rockwork and flowers.

8.75in (22.5cm) diam · $400-600 · WW

A late 18thC Delft portrait plate, printed in blue with a bust portrait of a naval lieutenant, titled 'J.C.J. Van Speyk', within a dentil band border and ocher rim, rim chip.

9in (23cm) diam · $100-150 · DN

A mid-18thC Dutch Delft blue and white charger, the central floral roundel within diamond diaper and alternating flower vignette rim band.

13.75in (35cm) diam · $400-600 · Chef

A mid-18thC blue and white Dutch Delft charger, centrally painted with a chinoiserie roundel of pavilions, rocks and a pine tree within a fruit and foliage border.

14in (36cm) diam · $400-600 · Chef

An early 18thC Dutch Delft blue and white basin, with a wavy rim, boldly painted in blue with a central design of fruit, flowers and leaves within a leaf scroll border.

10.75in (27.5cm) diam · $1,000-1,500 · WW

A second half 18thC Dutch Delft bowl, the interior blue and white with a central flower spray, the exterior painted in polychrome with a fence, flowers and foliage, small chips.

10.5in (27cm) high · $700-1,000 · WW

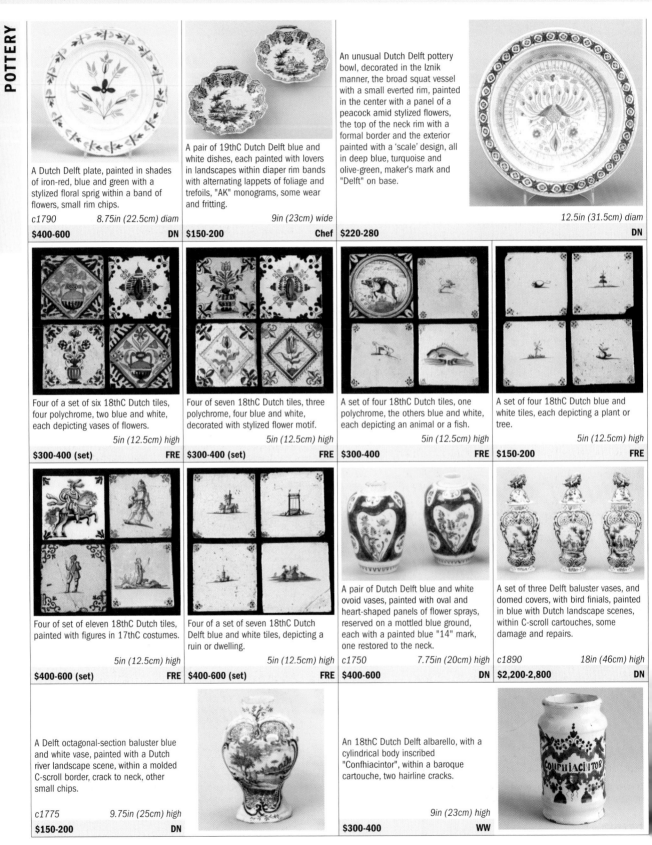

A Dutch Delft plate, painted in shades of iron-red, blue and green with a stylized floral sprig within a band of flowers, small rim chips.

c1790   8.75in (22.5cm) diam

$400-600   **DN**

A pair of 19thC Dutch Delft blue and white dishes, each painted with lovers in landscapes within diaper rim bands with alternating lappets of foliage and trefoils, "AK" monograms, some wear and fritting.

9in (23cm) wide

$150-200   **Chef**

An unusual Dutch Delft pottery bowl, decorated in the Iznik manner, the broad squat vessel with a small everted rim, painted in the center with a panel of a peacock amid stylized flowers, the top of the neck rim with a formal border and the exterior painted with a 'scale' design, all in deep blue, turquoise and olive-green, maker's mark and "Delft" on base.

$220-280

12.5in (31.5cm) diam

DN

Four of a set of six 18thC Dutch tiles, four polychrome, two blue and white, each depicting vases of flowers.

5in (12.5cm) high

$300-400 (set)   **FRE**

Four of seven 18thC Dutch tiles, three polychrome, four blue and white, decorated with stylized flower motif.

5in (12.5cm) high

$300-400 (set)   **FRE**

A set of four 18thC Dutch tiles, one polychrome, the others blue and white, each depicting an animal or a fish.

5in (12.5cm) high

$300-400   **FRE**

A set of four 18thC Dutch blue and white tiles, each depicting a plant or tree.

5in (12.5cm) high

$150-200   **FRE**

Four of set of eleven 18thC Dutch tiles, painted with figures in 17thC costumes.

5in (12.5cm) high

$400-600 (set)   **FRE**

Four of a set of seven 18thC Dutch Delft blue and white tiles, depicting a ruin or dwelling.

5in (12.5cm) high

$400-600 (set)   **FRE**

A pair of Dutch Delft blue and white ovoid vases, painted with oval and heart-shaped panels of flower sprays, reserved on a mottled blue ground, each with a painted blue "14" mark, one restored to the neck.

c1750   7.75in (20cm) high

$400-600   **DN**

A set of three Delft baluster vases, and domed covers, with bird finials, painted in blue with Dutch landscape scenes, within C-scroll cartouches, some damage and repairs.

c1890   18in (46cm) high

$2,200-2,800   **DN**

A Delft octagonal-section baluster blue and white vase, painted with a Dutch river landscape scene, within a molded C-scroll border, crack to neck, other small chips.

c1775   9.75in (25cm) high

$150-200   **DN**

An 18thC Dutch Delft albarello, with a cylindrical body inscribed "Confhiacintor", within a baroque cartouche, two hairline cracks.

9in (23cm) high

$300-400   **WW**

A Dutch Delft polychrome cow, standing four square above three frogs on the rectangular base, the girth and neck of its blue spotted body bedecked with flowers, some damage.

6in (15cm) high

$600-900   **Chef**

A pair of second half 18thC Dutch Delft polychrome models of recumbent horned cows, facing left and right and painted with sprays of flowers, some restoration.

$350-400   **DN**

A pair of Dutch Delft butter-dishes, on molded stands with painted foliate decoration.

8in (20cm) wide

$100-150   **Clv**

A 19thC Delft blue and white book flask, painted with a yacht between islands on one side and with flowers on the other cover, some wear and fritting.

4in (10cm) high

$100-150   **Chef**

An early 20thC Belgian delft kettle, burner and stand, by Boch Keramic, the fluted and rococo-molded bodies painted with flowers on a powder blue ground, "BK" monogram in blue.

13.5in (34cm) high

$50-80   **Chef**

British Delftware

British delftware, a tin-glazed earthenware, was manufactured from the mid-16thC. Potteries were established at Aldgate in east London by two Dutch potters, Jaspar Andries and Jacob Jansen, who were fleeing persecution in Antwerp. British delftware is coarser and harder than Dutch Delft ware and the glaze is generally smoother with a pinkish or bluish tinge. The decoration on British pieces is cruder than on those from the Netherlands, with designs including monarchs, oak leaves, bold flowers and chinoiseries.

British delftware from the 18thC tends to be distinctive, with more delicate decoration. Wares include punchbowls, plates, wine bottles, wall pockets, puzzle jugs and, rarely, tea and coffee pieces. It is very unusual for British delft to be marked, but dates and inscriptions are common forms of decoration and these will dramatically increase the value of a piece.

The most important areas of production for delftware were Southwark, Aldgate, and Lambeth in London and Bristol, Norwich, Liverpool, and Glasgow. Like Dutch Delft, the competition from creamware forced the British tin-glazed earthenware industry into decline, and manufacture had virtually ceased by the end of the 18thC.

A CLOSER LOOK AT A DELFTWARE PLATE

The style of the painting on this charger is distinctly English.

The design is simple yet lively, with good coloring, all of which increase the value.

Monarchs were frequently used on delftware chargers. Other motifs included tulips, oak leaves, geometric patterns and biblical themes.

Rare specimens of 17thC delftware in good condition will fetch vast sums at auctions.

A late 17thC commemorative polychrome delft dish, painted in yellow, blue, green, and manganese with King William III, flanked by trees, "WR" either side of his crowned head within the blue-dashed and yellow-lined rim, some damage.

The term 'blue dash' is used to denote a polychrome dish on which the rim is emphasized with a band of sloping blue dashes. These were very popular in the 17thC.

13.75in (35cm) diam

$20,000-30,000   **Chef**

A Bristol delft 'Farmyard' plate, painted in shades of iron-red, ocher and blue with a peacock between manganese sponge-decorated trees, wear to the glaze of the leading edge of the rim.

c1730   *7.75in (20cm) diam*

$6,000-9,000   **DN**

An early 18thC polychrome English delft dish, painted with Cupid drawing his bow in a landscape flanked by blue trees with sponged foliage and walking on green grassy mounds within blue and yellow lines on the blue dashed rim, some damage.

13.5in (34cm) diam

$15,000-20,000   **Chef**

An English delft plate, painted in blue, green, and iron-red with a flower spray, within a blue and iron red leaf scroll border.

c1740   *8.75in (22cm) diam*

$280-320   **LFA**

A mid-18thC English delft polychrome plate, painted with manganese tree trunks sprouting faint red foliage, with a bird, a butterfly and flower in the center.

9in (23cm) diam

$320-380   **Chef**

A mid-18thC English delft blue and white charger, centrally painted with bamboo and peonies growing by a fence, the rim with florette band.

14.5in (37cm) diam

$150-200   **Chef**

A mid-18thC English delft blue and white dish, centrally painted with an insect flying from bamboo and flowers within four scrolling flower stems on the rim, some wear and fritting.

13.5in (34cm) diam

$220-280   **Chef**

A mid-18thC English delft plate, the central iron-red rosette inside five blue circles, red star-like flower-heads and green leaves, some wear and fritting.

9.25in (23.5cm) diam

$600-900   **Chef**

A mid-18thC English blue and white delft dish, painted with two European travelers seated below a flowering shrub feeding a swan, the brown-lined edge enclosing six scrolling sprigs of cut flowers, some damage.

12in (30.5cm) diam

$300-600   **Chef**

A London delft plate, painted in blue in Chinese-style with a crane, flowering trees and rockwork, in a fenced garden, within a flower-paneled trellis band, the rim with four sprays of flowers and leaves, two minor rim chips.

c1760   *9in (23cm) diam*

$100-150   **LFA**

A pair of mid-18thC Bristol delft chargers, with chinoiserie-style decoration of birds and flowers.

14.5in (37cm) diam

$1,500-2,000   **Clv**

A pair of English delft plates, probably London or Liverpool, painted in shades of blue, manganese, ocher, and green with a bird and an insect in a stylized garden, one restored.

c1760   *8.75in (22.5cm) diam*

$400-600   **DN**

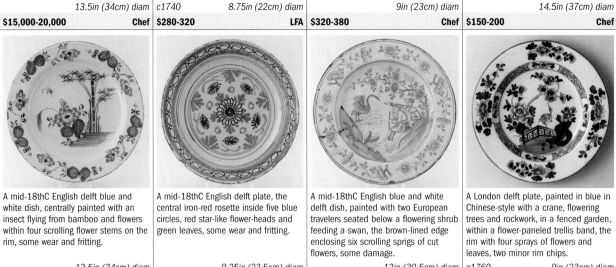

A London delft blue and white chinoiserie dish, painted with houses in a Chinese landscape, within a border of alternate panels of diaper sections and flowers, some rim chips.

c1770   *11.75in (30cm) diam*

$280-320   **DN**

An English delft plate, polychrome-painted with flowers within a border of trailing flowers and fruit.

·9.25in (23.5cm) diam

$300-600　**BonS**

An English delft octagonal plate, finely painted in blue, green, yellow, and manganese with flowering trees, a fence and rockwork, restored.

c1770　8.75in (22.2cm) diam

$150-200　**LFA**

An English delft dish, painted in blue, green, yellow, and manganese with flowering trees, bamboo, and rockwork, the rim with trailing flowers and leaves, some restoration.

c1770　13.25in (33.5cm) diam

$350-400　**LFA**

A first half 18thC English delft blue and white deep bowl, raised on a high foot, painted with a flower to the center within a dashed and scroll border, the exterior with panels of stylized flowers, a small rim chip.

10in (25.5cm) diam

$1,000-1,500　**WW**

A London delft bowl, the center with a blue flower-head, the exterior with Oriental huts among trees and stylized rockwork, a body crack and small chips.

c1780　10.5in (27cm) high

$600-900　**WW**

An English delft punch bowl, probably Bristol, painted in blue with panels of vases issuing flowers, within foliate scroll borders, cracks.

c1730　9in (25cm) diam

$400-600　**DN**

An English delft punch bowl, probably London or Liverpool, painted in shades of green, blue, manganese, and ocher with chinoiserie vignettes of buildings and distant birds in formation, hairline crack and rim chips.

c1770　9.5in (26cm) diam

$600-900　**DN**

A mid-18thC English delft ware puzzle jug, possibly Lambeth, painted in blue with a dash-rimmed floral pierced gallery above a globular body, painted with verse, flanked by flowers.

7.5in (19cm) high

$800-1,200　**Chef**

Two mid-18thC Liverpool delft square tiles, painted in polychrome with exotic birds and with leafy borders, one cracked.

5in (13cm) wide

$400-600　**WW**

An 18thC large English delft posset pot and cover, the cylindrical body with two scroll handles and short spout, painted in polychrome with peacocks, other birds, flowers and foliage, some restoration to the rim of the cover.

11.5in (29cm) wide

$4,000-6,000　**WW**

An early 18thC blue and white English delft mug, the cylindrical sides painted above the flared foot with a squirrel by a trellis of grapes, some damage.

6.75in (17cm) high

$4,000-6,000　**Chef**

A 17thC Bristol delft posset pot, with a domed cover decorated with chinoiserie style figures in landscape.

9.75in (25cm) high

$4,000-6,000　**Clv**

Earthenware

A pair of earthenware plates, each boldly printed in colored enamels with an exotic bird in a wooded landscape, the fluted and basket-molded border picked out in gilt, pseudo red anchor marks.

c1900   9.75in (25cm) diam

$180-220   LFA

A black-printed ship plate, entitled "East Indiaman Taking a Pilot on Board," decorated with the titled view of a three-masted sailing ship within a simple black-lined border, unmarked.

c1815-1830   8.75in (22.5cm) diam

$180-220   DN

A black-printed ship plate, entitled "East Indiaman Sailing from the Downs," decorated with the titled view of a three-masted sailing ship within a simple black-lined border, unmarked.

c1815-1830   9in (22.5cm) diam

$220-280   DN

A black-printed ship plate, entitled "Frigate Setting Sail," decorated with the titled view of a three-masted sailing ship within a simple black-lined border, unmarked.

c1815-1830   9in (23cm) diam

$220-280   DN

A black-printed earthenware jug, of squat shape with molded handle, decorated with an untitled view, usually found with title "Frigate Setting Sail" with black-lining around rim and on handle, unmarked, restored.

c1820-35   5.75in (14.5cm) high

$180-220   DN

A black-printed earthenware jug, entitled "East Indiaman Sailing from the Downs" and "Frigate Setting Sail," of ovoid shape with simple strap handle, decorated with the titled views of three-masted sailing ships with black lining around the foot and rim, unmarked, hair crack across base of handle.

Provenance: bears label for the Williams-Wood collection (suggesting Swansea and Thomas Rothwell).

c1815-30   7.75in (19.5cm) high

$400-600   DN

An 18thC tin-glazed earthenware chamfered rectangular tureen and cover, after a Chinese shape, with a scroll knop and animal handles, painted in blue with flowers.

12.25in (31cm) long

$400-600   WW

An 18thC tin-glazed model of a lion, sitting on his haunches and decorated with manganese and blue, raised on a chamfered rectangular base.

5.25in (13.5cm) high

$400-600   WW

An earthenware model of a bird, perched on rockwork, after a Chinese original, decorated in cream slip with flowers and leaves, area of base restored.

5.5in (14cm) high

$150-200   LFA

An earthenware model of a bird, in Whieldon style, splashed in brown and green, on rectangular mound base, beak restored.

6in (15cm) high

$150-200   LFA

Faience

An 18thC German faience tankard, with a hinged pewter lid, the body painted in blue with buildings between sponged trees, the handle decorated with blue dashes.

6in (15.5cm) high

$400-600   **WW**

Two views of an 18thC German faience tankard, with a hinged pewter lid, the cylindrical body painted in blue with a figure and a horse with a castle beyond, the base marked "K4".

9in (23cm) high

$600-900   **WW**

A 19thC French faience miniature tall-case clock, the porcelain clock face set in a foliate scroll and shell-molded case, painted with an 18thC couple playing on a swing and with riverscapes, reserved on a floral, insect and scroll-painted ground, underglaze "VP" mark, possibly Marseille.

19.75in (50cm) high

$700-1,000   **SI**

A mid-18thC French faience demi-lune bough pot, or bouquetier, of flared and fluted form, painted in shades of blue, green, ocher and iron-red with stylized floral sprays, some chips.

8.25in (21cm) wide

$150-200   **DN**

A mid-to late 18thC North Italian faience polychrome chinoiserie soup plate, painted and gilt, with flowering shrubs, within a border of flower-heads and shaped panels, cracked and chipped.

8.5in (21.5cm) diam

$80-120   **DN**

Quimper

Quimper ware (pronounced 'Compere') is a rustic French faience ware that was being produced from the late 17thC in the Breton town of Quimper. Wares were painted in bright colors, often with local flora and fauna, figures in Breton costume and artefacts of rural Britanny. Items include numerous individual vases, bowls and jugs, and a vast range of tablewares (including services for beverages such as coffee, chocolate, cider and liqueurs). Inkstands, candlesticks, book-ends, tobacco boxes, baby-feeders, chess sets, figurines and busts of religious and peasant figures were also popular pieces. Pierre-Paul Causey ran the factory from 1743 to 1782. In 1853 Antoine de la Hubaudière took over and pieces from this period are marked "HB".

Quimper faced great competition as creamware became popular and flooded the market at the beginning of the 19thC, almost causing faience production in France to cease. However, the Quimper factory persisted and is still in production today.

A Quimper fan vase, marked "Alfred Pourquier".

c1875   *4.75in (12cm) high*

$600-900   **CamA**

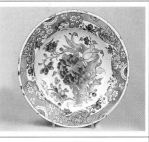

A pair of Quimper perfume bottles, marked "Henriot".

3in (8cm) high

$1,200-1,800   **CamA**

A Quimper Rouen-style centerpiece, marked "Desvres".

17.5in (44.5cm) long

$1,000-1,500   **CamA**

A pair of Quimper comports, marked "AP".

c1875-1900

$600-900   **CamA**

A Quimper vase, marked "Desvres".

c1900   *9.5in (24.5cm) high*

$1,200-1,800   **CamA**

A Quimper push-up candle holder, marked "Henriot".

c1925   *6.5in (16.5cm) long*

$320-380   **CamA**

A Quimper doughnut teapot, marked "Henriot".
This is a rare shape for a teapot.
c1900-1910   8.75in (22.5cm) high
$600-900   **CamA**

A Quimper shaving bowl, marked "Henriot".
c1890-1910   11.25 (29cm) wide
$400-600   **CamA**

A Quimper shoe-shaped wallpocket, marked "Henriot".
c1910-1925   10.5in (29cm) long
$220-280   **CamA**

A pair of Quimper figural hand-painted earthenware bookends, each inscribed "BOUVIER HB QUIMPER".
7in (18cm) high
$300-400   **FRE**

A Quimper butter-dish, decorated with the embroidery pattern, marked "HB".
7in (18cm) diam
$220-280   **CamA**

A Quimper bagpipe-shaped wall pocket, marked "HB".
c1890   9in (23cm) long
$400-600   **CamA**

A Quimper bagpipe-shaped cheese dish, marked "Henriot Quimper".
c1920   11in (28cm) long
$500-700   **CamA**

A Quimper bagpipe-shaped cheese dish, marked "Henriot Quimper".
c1920   9in (23cm) long
$400-600   **CamA**

A Quimper fish platter, marked "Henriot Quimper".
c1925   23.5in (60cm) long
$1,200-1,800   **CamA**

A Quimper Odetta pitcher, marked "HB Quimper".
c1900-1925
$600-900   **CamA**

A Quimper plate, marked "Henriot Quimper".
c1925   19in (48.5cm) wide
$400-600   **CamA**

A Quimper bagpipe-shaped snuff bottle, by Henriot Quimper.

3in (8cm) high

$320-380 CamA

A Quimper double salt, marked "Henriot" and "C. Maillard".

7.5in (19cm) long

$500-800 CamA

A Quimper knife rest, shaped as a sleeping Bretonne, marked "C. Maillard".

4.5in (11.5cm) long

$220-280 CamA

A Quimper trinket box, with a decor riche border, marked "Henriot Quimper".

c1925 *7in (18cm) long*

$400-600 CamA

A Quimper vase, marked "Henriot Quimper".

c1910 *12in (30.5cm) high*

$700-1,000 CamA

A Quimper centerpiece, decorated with Bretons on one side and flowers on the other, marked "Henriot Quimper".

c1910 *18in (46cm) long*

$2,200-2,800 CamA

A Quimper inkwell, marked "HR".

4in (10.5cm) wide

$300-400 CamA

IRONSTONE

An unusual Mason's Ironstone plate, centrally decorated in blue and gilt with a dragon head crest, the scroll-molded border painted in colored enamels with sprays of flowers and leaves, impressed strip mark.

c1815-20 *9.5in (24cm) diam*

$150-200 LFA

A Mason's Patent Ironstone China shaped rectangular well-and-tree meat dish, printed in black and painted in colored enamels and gilt with a chrysanthemum spray and other Oriental flowers with gilt-lining to the rim, puce-printed crown and drape mark, some surface wear.

c1840 *22.5in (57cm) wide*

$350-400 DN

A 19thC Staffordshire meat dish, with transfer and tinted decoration in the Imari-style.

19in (48cm) wide

$300-400 Clv

A pair of 19thC Minton & Boyle ironstone plates, with chinoiserie-style painted and printed decoration.

10.25in (26cm) diam

$120-180 Clv

A Spode stone china soup tureen, cover and stand, with Mosaic border and Willis center, outline printed in brown and enameled in iron red, blue, green, yellow and puce and with gilt highlights, pattern number 2647, brown printed seal marks, star-type crack within main body.

14.5in (37cm) long

$400-600 DN

An extensive ironstone dinner service, by Francis Morley & Co., printed and painted in the chinoiserie style with a bird amidst peony blossom, with continuous floral and shaped scroll panel border, comprising three graduated ashets, two twin-handled vegetable tureens and one cover and stand with dolphin-cast handles, two sauce tureen stands and one cover, 17 meat plates, 17 fish plates, 10 soup plates and 10 side plates.

$1,500-2,000   L&T

A pair of 19th/20thC ironstone chinoiserie vases and covers, the paneled baluster-form vessel mounted with dragon handles and floral vines, the cover with dragon finial, cobalt and green ground with gilt highlights and colorful decoration.

25in (63.5cm) high

$2,500-3,000   SI

A mid-19thC Elsmore and Forster ironstone novelty two-handled mug, the interior with three molded frogs, luster highlights.

5in (12.5cm) high

$120-180   SI

A CLOSER LOOK AT A PAIR OF MASON'S IRONSTONE VASES

The lavish gilding on these pineapple finials is typical of Mason's Ironstone. Expect to see some wear on areas that will have been regularly handled.

These hexagonal vases have been brightly painted with a flamboyant allover pattern. As such they are very desirable objects.

This pair are in excellent condition. It is rare to find Mason's Ironstone without at least a chip or two because they were intended for everyday use in the home.

The standard pattern wares at Mason's were produced in great numbers by many different artists of varying skill, so occasionally the painting is a little haphazard. However, this is all part of the charm of Mason's Ironstone.

A pair of early 19thC Mason's Ironstone vases and covers, with alternating panels on the hexagonal sides with fine textile molding and painted overall in Imari palette with lotus flowers, pink pomegranates and blue and green leaves, the covers with gilt pineapple finials, impressed marks on the covers.

12.25in (31cm) high

$4,000-6,000   Chef

A Mason's Ironstone small round chamber candlestick, with ring handle, decorated in Imari-style with flowering trees, a fence and rockwork, picked out in gilt, within a beaded band, small rim chip.

c1815-20   *3.25in (8cm) diam*

$400-600   LFA

A Mason's Patent Ironstone China jug, possibly from the Ashworth period, of flattened ovoid shape with scroll-molded handle, decorated with oval reserves of Chinese motifs surrounded by a cobalt blue ground gilded with leaves and flower-heads, all enameled in colors, puce-printed crown and drape mark, with all lettering obliterated.

c1840-70   *9.25in (23.5cm) high*

$280-320   DN

A pair of early 19thC Mason's Ironstone miniature orange tubs, the gilt wavy rims above basket-molded sides painted with flowers on a blue ground above four gilt feet to each, impressed marks.

2.5in (6.5cm) high

$400-600   Chef

Lusterware

A Sunderland luster jug, printed with the 'Mariner's Arms', a figure of Hope and a verse, of Dutch shape with simple strap handle, printed in purple and enamel colors, on one side with the pseudo 'Mariner's Arms', beneath the spout with a figure of Hope by an anchor and on the other side with a verse "When this you see remember me...", all in oval frames of pink luster with further luster splashed around the spout and neck, unmarked, restored.

c1825-50

$220-280   DN

A Sunderland luster jug printed with a sailing ship and a verse, of Dutch shape with simple strap handle, printed in black on one side with a three-masted ship inscribed "May Peace and Plenty on our Nation Smile..." and on the other with a verse "The men doom'd to sail with the blast of the gale...", both in oval frames of splashed pink luster around the spout and neck, unmarked, chips to spout.

c1830-50   *6in (15cm) high*

$180-220   DN

A pink luster jug, printed with the sailing ship 'Columbus' and a verse, possibly from Newcastle rather than Sunderland, of Dutch shape with simple strap handle, printed in black on one side with the ship inscribed "Columbus, the largest ship ever built", and on the other with a verse "Whene'er I see thy lovely face...", both highlighted with red, green and yellow enamels and in oval frames of pink luster with further dragged luster around the neck, unmarked.

c1830-50   *5.75in (14.5cm) high*

$400-600   DN

A small Sunderland luster jug, printed with 'A West View of the Cast-iron Bridge over the River Wear', of Dutch shape with simple strap handle, printed beneath spout in black with the inscribed view in an oval frame of splashed pink luster which extends up the spout and around the neck, unmarked, crack in spout.

c1830-50   *3.5in (9cm) high*

$220-280   DN

A Sunderland luster wash jug, printed with 'A West View of the cast-iron Bridge over the River Wear', of typical ewer shape with wide flaring spout and loop handle, printed in black on one side with the inscribed bridge view and on the other side with a verse "Thou noble bark of brightest fame", both in oval frames of splashed pink luster which also extends around the shoulder, rim and spout, unmarked.

c1835-60   *8in (21cm) high*

$400-600   DN

A Crimean War Sunderland luster jug, of Dutch shape with simple strap handle, printed in black and enamel colored on one side with a scene titles 'Sailors Farewell', on the front with a verse "I envy no one's birth or fame", and on the other side with a pseudo armorial "Crimea" surmounted with a ribbon "May They Ever Be United", all surrounded by pink luster squiggles with luster lining around the spout, neck and foot, unmarked, restoration to handle, star crack in base.

c1854-56   *7.25in (18.5cm) high*

$400-600   DN

An early 19thC Sunderland pink luster bowl, printed with the bridge on one side and with an armorial on the other for the 'Manchester Unity Independent Order of Odd Fellows', with strap handles.

5in (12.5cm) diam

$70-100   Chef

An early 19thC Sunderland pink luster bowl, printed in black with the Sunderland bridge and 'Tynemouth haven'.

5.25in (13.5cm) diam

$70-100   Chef

A Sunderland luster mug, printed with a sailing ship and a verse, of cylindrical shape slightly flared towards the foot with simple strap handle, printed in black and enamel colored on one side with an unnamed three-masted sailing ship and on the other with religious verse "Fear not my soul...", the body covered with splashed pink luster, unmarked, star crack in base.

c1820-40

$150-200   DN

A Dixon, Philips & Co. Sunderland luster plaque, entitled "Northumberland 74", of typical ornate picture frame shape, the center printed in black with the title print of a three-masted sailing ship, the border decorated with splashed pink luster and copper luster edging, impressed mark, small chip behind one corner.

c1830-50   *8.5in (21.5cm) wide*

$280-320   DN

A Dixon, Phillips & Co. Sunderland luster plaque, entitled "May Peace & Plenty...", of typical ornate picture frame shape, the center printed in black with a three-masted sailing ship above the framed inscription "May Peace and Plenty on our Nation smile, and Trade with Commerce Bless the British Isle", the border decorated with splashed pink luster and copper luster and copper luster edging.

c1830-50   8.5in (22cm) wide

$280-320   **DN**

A Sunderland luster plaque, 'Duke of Wellington - 131 Guns,' of typical ornate picture frame shape, center printed in black, enameled in colors with named naval ship, splashed pink luster and copper luster border, unmarked.
Provenance: Bears the label for Oliver Sutton Antiques.

c1845-60   9.5in (24cm) wide

$220-280   **DN**

A Crimean War Sunderland luster plaque, entitled "May They Ever be United", of typical ornate picture frame shape, the center printed in black and enameled in colors with sailors holding British and French flags, the border decorated with splashed pink luster edging, unmarked, restoration to top section of border.

c1854-56   8.75in (22.5cm) wide

$180-220   **DN**

A Scott of Southwick Sunderland luster plate, entitled "La Breyagne - 140 Guns", of 14-sided shape, the center printed in black and enameled in colors with the named naval ship, the border lined in brick red, the rim with pink luster, impressed "SCOTT".

c1840-60   9.25in (23.5cm) wide

$180-220   **DN**

A mid-19thC orange luster jug, printed and painted with a ship 'The Unfortunate London' on one side and with a verse on the other within ochre luster ovals, damage.

5.75in (14.5cm) high

$120-180   **Chef**

A Sunderland orange luster jug, printed with a sailing ship and a verse, of Dutch shape with simple strap handle, printed in black and enamel colored on one side with an unnamed three-masted, steam-assisted sailing ship and on the other with a verse "Now safe returned from dangers past...", both in oval frames of orange luster around the spout and neck, unmarked.

c1850-80   5in (12.5cm) high

$70-100   **DN**

A Sunderland luster plaque, entitled "Duke of Wellington - 131 Guns", of rounded rectangular shape with leaf-molded border and rope edging, the center printed in black and enameled in colors with the named naval ship, the border decorated with orange luster, unmarked.

c1830-1850   9in (23cm) wide

$220-280   **DN**

An early 19thC silver lusterware jug, with a mask molded to the spout, one side printed in iron-red with harvesters, the reverse with a rural scene all on a buff-colored ground.

5.5in (14cm) high

$280-320   **WW**

A Staffordshire copper luster and transfer-printed creamer, of baluster-form, black transfer-printed with portrait of Andrew Jackson and inscribed, "General Jackson the Hero of New Orleans" on both sides, the portraits enclosed by canary yellow reserves.

c1830   4in (10cm) high

$4,000-6,000   **FRE**

A silver lusterware political satire jug, painted and printed, titled 'Murat Reviewing the Grand Army' to one side and 'Boney tird of War's Alarms, Flies for Safty to his darlings Arms' to the other, minor damage.

c1810   5.75in (14.5cm) high

$600-900   **WW**

A silver lusterware molded jug, each side decorated with colorful vases of flowers.

c1820   5.5in (14cm) high

$600-900   **WW**

A pair of copper luster models of seated greyhounds, each on an oval base.

c1850   5.5in (14cm) high

$220-280   **LFA**

Maiolica

An Albissola maiolica two-handled vase, beneath a lighthouse symbol, of baluster-shape, the handles formed as coiled serpents with mask terminals, painted in blue with a milkmaid, cowherd and animals, damage and repair to handle, dated.

1734   *13.25in (34cm) high*

$300-400   **BonS**

A mid-18thC Italian maiolica jar, probably Abbruzzi, of waisted cylindrical form with everted rim, painted in blue with a view of a hill town, with lined border.

10in (25.5cm) high

$400-600   **BonS**

A late 19thC Cantagalli blue and white flask, the sides of ribbed square section painted with flowers and ancient buildings, cockerel mark.

5.5in (14cm) high

$60-90   **Chef**

A pair of late 19thC Italian maiolica Castelli-style bottle vases, painted with scenes of putti in an Italianate landscape, beneath slender cylindrical necks painted with a yellow and blue scale ground, one has glued repair to the neck.

10.5in (27cm) high

$800-1,200   **DN**

A 19thC maiolica dish, painted with a cherub encircled by scrolling grotesques, marked "Fock Mazzarella".

9.75in (25cm) high

$300-600   **WW**

A 19thC Italian maiolica charger, entitled "Death of Callisto" depicting men and dogs attacking a wolf, within a border of masks and foliage, enameled artist's mark, baring label of S.R.Twigg.

15.5in (39.5cm) diam

$700-1,000   **SI**

A late 19thC Cantagalli bowl, the oval rim with crimped edge above flowering vines and central floral roundel all on a pale yellow ground, cockerel mark.

11in (28cm) wide

$80-120   **Chef**

A 19thC maiolica lusterware jug, with a circular body and angled handle, decorated with a band of scrolling leaves in blue and yellow, inscribed "VE Gubbio".

8.5in (22cm) wide

$150-200   **WW**

A late 19thC Italian maiolica vase, the rococo-molded shape with ocher handle to one side and painted with a man talking to a lady doing her washing in the country, crowned "M" mark.

10in (25cm) wide

$70-100   **Chef**

A pair of Moustier-style wine coolers, with twist side handles, painted in green, yellow, manganese and blue, with figures, birds and flowers, "LC" marks, some restoration.

12.25in (31cm) wide

$500-700 (pair)   **WW**

A 19thC Spanish maiolica flask, the ring molding on the ovoid body defining bands of figures an animals, a green lizard forming the handle.

10.25in (26cm) high

$60-90   **Chef**

A 19thC rectangular maiolica tile, decorated in polychrome with a figure of a risen Christ before Roman soldiers, faint hairline crack.

10in (25.5cm) long

$100-150   **WW**

A late 19th/early 20thC Italian maiolica footed jardinière, of boat form on four paw feet, crowned "S" mark, minor losses to feet.

19in (48.5cm) long

$300-600   **BonS**

Pearlware

Pearlware was introduced in c1779 by Wedgwood. It was a variation on creamware but included more white clay, flint and the addition of cobalt oxide, giving it a slightly bluish appearance. It was widely used by manufacturers from the late 18thC well into the 19thC.

A lot of pearlware was decorated in underglaze blue by painting or, later, by transfer-printing. One of the most common designs was a version of the 'Willow' pattern. Other popular forms of decoration were chinoiserie subjects, Classical designs and English landscapes. Forms included ornamental Neoclassical wares, tablewares and, more rarely, figures.

A pearlware figure of Flora, the goddess modeled standing wearing classical robes, a lamb and a hound at her feet, on a titled square plinth base, the frieze molded in relief with an acanthus leaf band, the base inscribed "FIORO", some chips and losses.

c1800   *13in (33cm) high*

$600-900   **DN**

A pearlware bust of a man, in the classical style, possibly Sir Walter Scott (1771-1832), undecorated, with firing cracks and glaze chips.

c1830   *13.5in (34cm) high*

$400-600   **DN**

A pearlware figure of Neptune, of Enoch Wood type, typically modeled standing, on leg raised and supported by a dolphin, painted with colored enamels, glued repair to neck, trident missing.

c1825   *9.25in (23.5cm) high*

$300-400   **DN**

A pearlware figural candlestick of Cupid, perhaps Neale & Co., Cupid modeled standing with flared sconce, on a stepped square base, painted in colored enamels, chip to rear of sconce.

c1790   *9.25in (23.5cm) high*

$400-600   **DN**

A pearlware figure of Cybele, modeled standing, wearing flowing robes and holding a cornucopia of flowers, painted in various colors on a square brown-line base, old damage and repairs.

c1810   *10.25in (26cm) high*

$220-280   **DN**

A pearlware figure of a gardener's companion, modeled standing before bocage, wearing rustic dress holding a flower, on a square brown-line base, painted in various colors, chips and losses to bocage.

9in (23cm) high

$300-400   **DN**

An unusual pearlware figure of a standing Turk, decorated in blue, green, yellow, and ocher, the rectangular base incised "The Grand Turk", some restoration.

c1800   *6in (15cm) high*

$180-220   **LFA**

An early 19thC Wood and Caldwell pearlware model of a youth, seated on a green and brown stump and holding a yellow cup, raised on a pink and green rectangular base, impressed mark.

8in (20.5cm) high

$300-400   **WW**

A pair of Staffordshire pearlware figures, emblematic of Fall and Winter, having square bases with maroon line around.

c1820   *7.5in (19cm) high*

$120-180   **D**

A Staffordshire first quarter 19thC pearlware figure of a shipwrecked sailor, modeled washed up on rocks, a stricken vessel in the surf beyond, painted allover with colored enamels, losses.

6.5in (18cm) long,

$300-400   **DN**

A Staffordshire pearlware group of two dandies, standing, arm in arm, picked out in blue, green, yellow, brown and ocher, on shell-molded mound base, chips to brim of hat.

c1810   4in (10cm) high

$150-200   **LFA**

An early 19thC Staffordshire pearlware bucolic spill vase group, modeled with a ewe and lamb seated before a gnarled tree trunk, an owl perched in its branches, the sheep painted with ocher patches, the tree painted allover with a green glaze, minor chips and restoration.

7.25in (20cm) high

$320-380   **DN**

A pearlware spill vase group, modeled with a boy before a three-vase tree looking at a squirrel on a branch, painted with colored enamels, damage, repairs and losses.

c1820

$400-600   **DN**

A pearlware 'Tithe Pig' group, typically modeled with the vicar and his parishioners standing before a tree, some damage and losses.

c1820   6.25in (16cm) high

$400-600   **DN**

A pearlware 'Savoyard' group, of Sherratt-type, the Savoyard wearing exotic Eastern dress, modeled standing beside a central bocage, a lion and a performing bear, painted with colored enamels, some damage and repairs.

c1820   8.75in (22cm) high

$2,500-3,000   **DN**

A pearlware 'Songsters' group, modeled with a central tree-trunk spill vase supported on mound sections, to each side a man and companion playing musical instruments, painted in colors, some small areas of damage and repair.

c1825   11.75in (30cm) high

$2,500-3,000   **DN**

A 19thC Staffordshire pearlware pastoral group, with a man and a woman sitting beneath a gnarled tree-stump with two lambs and an owl, some damage.

7.75in (20cm) high

$300-400   **WW**

An early 19thC Pratt-type buccholic pearlware spill vase group, modeled with a shepherd leaning against a tree playing a flute, three recumbent sheep at his feet, painted in a typical palette, some small areas of restoration.

8.75in (22cm) high

$600-900   **DN**

A pair of first quarter 19thC Staffordshire pearlware groups of the 'Sailor's Departure' and the 'Sailor's Return,' each group typically modeled in a fond embrace and painted with colored enamels, the shaped iron-red bases titled "Departure" and "Return", some enamel flaking, overpainting and small chips and repairs.

8.75in (24cm) high

$400-600 (pair)   **DN**

A Staffordshire pearlware model of a shoe salesman, with a lady wearing a blue dress trying on shoes before a leafy tree, all on a green rustic base, restoration to tree and her hand.

9.5in (24cm) high

$320-380   **WW**

A first quarter 19thC Staffordshire pearlware Pratt-type watch-holder, probably Yorkshire, modeled as a longcase clock between two figures, restored.

8.75in (24cm) high

$700-1,000   **DN**

POTTERY

An early 19thC Staffordshire pearlware cow creamer and cover, typically modeled standing and being milked by an attendant milkmaid, painted in shades of manganese and ocher, restored horns, chipped cover.

6.25in (16cm) long

$700-1,000　　　　　　**DN**

A pearlware cow creamer, naturalistically modeled and painted with black and iron-red trefoil patches, tail restored.

c1825　　　6.25in (16cm) wide

$700-1,000　　　　　　**DN**

A pearlware model of a cow, the head turned and standing before bocage, on a scroll-molded mound base, painted with colored enamels, the cow with iron-red patches, flaking and losses.

c1835　　　6in (15cm) long

$600-900　　　　　　**DN**

A CLOSER LOOK AT A STAFFORDSHIRE COW CREAMER

Cow creamers are a form of milk jug. The cow's mouth is the spout, the tail functions as the handle, and the cover is in the center of the back.

Check that the cover is not missing as this will decrease the value.

A good indication of quality is a hole in an anatomically correct place. This helped to allow the cream to pour.

This creamer has charming features, which increase its value.

Following a typhoid epidemic in the 1850s, cow creamers lost their popularity because they were considered unhygienic.

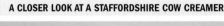

An early 19thC Staffordshire pearlware cow creamer and cover, typically modeled standing on a shaped rectangular green-glazed base, the cow partially painted with brown hooves and horns and mottled manganese patches, restored to ears and horns.

7.75in (19.5cm) long

$600-900　　　　　　**DN**

An early 19thC Staffordshire pearlware cow creamer, typically modeled standing on a shaped base with attendant milkmaid milking into a bucket, painted with mottled ocher patches and green-glazed base, replacement cover, restored to tips of horns.

6.75in (17cm) long

$700-1,000　　　　　　**DN**

A Staffordshire early 19thC pearlware cow creamer and cover, typically modeled standing on a shaped rectangular green-glazed base, the cow partially painted with mottled patches in shades of black and ocher, restored.

7in (18cm) long

$220-280　　　　　　**DN**

A first quarter 19thC Staffordshire pearlware cow creamer, modeled standing on on a stepped and shaped rectangular base with canted corners, with attendant maid milking the cow, painted in shades of brown and ocher mottled glazes, the base with mottled blue frieze, replacement cover.

7in (18cm) long

$700-1,000　　　　　　**DN**

A first quarter 19thC Staffordshire pearlware group of a cow, attendant and recumbent hound, of Yorkshire type, applied to a stepped rectangular base, painted in shades of blue, ocher, black and manganese, restored tips of horns.

7in (18cm) long

$1,500-2,000　　　　　　**DN**

A pearlware model of a recumbent ewe, the base painted in shades of ocher, green and brown, restored.

c1790

$400-600　　　　　　**DN**

A Staffordshire pearlware ewe and lamb group, modeled standing side by side on a shaped base, the ewe painted with pale ocher glazes, the green base with blue-line frieze, lamb has a restored ear.

c1800　　　4.75in (12cm) long

$700-1,000　　　　　　**DN**

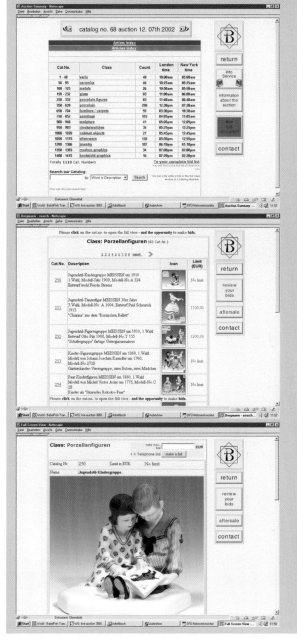

An early 19thC Staffordshire pearlware model of a sheep, set before a flowering tree with a lamb to the base, painted with colored enamels, the sheep's back inscribed "SH".

5.5in (13.5cm) high

$400-600   **WW**

A first quarter 19thC pearlware giant sheep and shepherdess group, of Yorkshire type, the shepherdess modeled standing before a large sheep, a pair of recumbent lambs at their feet, on a shaped rectangular base, painted in shades of ocher, black, blue and green, restored.

6.25in (16cm) high

$700-1,000   **DN**

A pearlware bocage model of a fallow stag, modeled with its head turned before flowering bocage, the mound base molded with flowers, painted in colored enamels, lacks tail, other chips and losses.

c1820   7.75in (19.5cm) high

$400-600   **DN**

A pearlware model of a lion, standing before flowering bocage on a scroll-molded base, modeled in the manner of a Medici lion, one paw resting on a ball and wearing a girth painted with colored enamels, chips and repair to bocage, some flaking.

c1825   5.75in (14.5cm) high

$1,800-2,200   **DN**

An early 19thC pearlware model of a bird, brightly colored and raised on a rocky base.

3in (7.5cm) high

$220-280   **WW**

A first half 19thC Staffordshire pearlware model of a dog, sniffing the ground and standing before a flowering tree on a green rustic base, impressed "15", the tail restored, the green enamel retouched.

6in (15cm) long

$700-1,000   **WW**

A Staffordshire pearlware model of a cat, possibly Scottish, modeled seated on its haunches, painted with colored enamels in shades of iron-red, ocher, black and green, on a shaped rectangular base, small overpainted chip to base.

c1830   4.5in (11.5cm) high

$600-900   **DN**

A pearlware baluster coffee pot and cover, painted in the Chinese Export-style with sprays of roses within diaper band borders, damage to the cover.

c1790   10.75in (27cm) high

$220-280   **DN**

A pearlware baluster coffee pot and domed cover, with an acorn finial, each section with a thin brown chequer band reserved on a mottled brown ground and within a border of flutes, some chips.

c1790   9.25in (23.5cm) high

$400-600   **DN**

A pearlware oviform jug, with cylindrical neck and auricular handle, painted with two panels of landscape views, reserved on yellow ground, the neck with black-bordered iron-red stripes, areas of old restoration to the neck and spout.

c1800   7.5in (20.5cm) high

$320-380   **DN**

An early 19thC silver or platinum luster jug with leaf band on the rim.

6in (15cm) high

$70-100   **Chef**

A rare pearlware 'Mocha' jug, of barrel-shaped form, painted with a central light-brown band mottled with dark-brown splashes, within pale blue and brown bands and two pale green bands molded with lozenges, strap handle, chip to foot-rim.

c1810

$1,500-2,000   **DN**

An early 19thC pearlware Royal commemorative jug, each side molded with a portrait bust and inscribed "Success to Queen Caroline", pink luster borders, small cracks and chips.

6.5in (16.5cm) high

$400-600 WW

A pearlware lozenge-shaped milk jug, with leaf-molded loop handle, painted in blue, green, brown and ocher with flowers and leaves, within oval panels, on a fluted blue and ocher ground.

c1810 *4.25in (11cm) high*

$220-280 LFA

A Swansea pearlware political satire jug, printed and painted and inscribed "Peace and Plenty", faint haircracks and wear.

c1814 *5.5in (13.7cm) high*

$400-600 WW

A pearlware ovoid jug, with straight neck and loop handle, printed and painted with dogs, gamebirds and sportsman, picked out in iron-red, green and brown on a yellow ground.

c1815 *4.75in (12cm) high*

$400-600 LFA

A CLOSER LOOK AT A PEARLWARE PUZZLE JUG

It is only possible to drink from one spout and all the other spouts must be covered and a hidden hole under the top of the handle must also be covered. They were intended as novelty or joke items to challenge the drinker.

The term 'pearlware' is misleading because it suggests that the wares have an iridescent appearance. The addition of cobalt oxide to the glaze actually gives it a bluish-white cast.

This piece is beautifully painted with an attractive flower design, which adds to its value.

The body is a white flinty earthenware and is characteristic of pearlware.

A Bristol pearlware ovoid puzzle jug, with loop handle, the pierced rim with three mask nozzles, finely painted in colored enamels with two sprays of flowers and leaves, and with monogram, within brown borders, one nozzle restored.

c1820 *5.75in (14.5cm) high*

$600-900 LFA

A pearlware sauceboat, naturalistically modeled as a duck, painted in shades of blue and ocher.

c1825 *6in (15cm) long*

$400-600 DN

A pearlware duck-shaped sauceboat, picked out in blue, brown, yellow and ocher, some restoration.

c1800-10 *6.25in (16cm) long*

$400-600 LFA

A Dutch pearlware marriage plate, printed in colored enamels with clasped hands, heart-shaped panels and inscriptions, black line borders, impressed "Whitening", dated, front rim crack.

1815 *9.75in (25cm) diam*

$320-380 LFA

A Swansea pearlware botanical plate, finely painted in colored enamels with a branch toadflax, the indented border with gilt line rim, impressed mark and titled in black verso, faint rim cracks, a small chip to underside of rim restored.

c1815-20 *7.25in (18.5cm) diam*

$300-400 LFA

A pearlware botanical plate, painted in colored enamels with a foxglove, within a brown line rim, titled in iron red verso and impressed number "13", rim crack.

c1815-20 *7.25in (18.5cm) diam*

$220-280 LFA

A John Rogers pearlware lobed oval meat dish, printed in brown with figures before a temple, in a Chinese river landscape, within a broad band of flowers and leaves and gadrooned rim, impressed mark and 'Chinese Porcelain' mark.

c1820 *21.25in (54cm) wide*

$350-400 LFA

Two pearlware circular plaques, one molded with a framed border, painted with a blue titmouse perched on the handle of a basket of flowers, the other with a vase of flowers, both cracked.

c1820   Larger 6.25in (16cm) diam

$400-600   DN

A pearlware oval plaque, molded in relief with two recumbent lions, painted in shades of brown, blue, green and ocher, minor rim chips.

c1825   11in (28cm) wide

$2,200-2,800   DN

A early to mid-19thC English polychrome pearlware plate, molded and sprigged with flowers, repairs to rim.

9.5in (24cm) diam

$300-400   FRE

Various pieces of Yorkshire printed pearlware, probably Ferrybridge, printed and painted in colors in a typical palette, comprising a two-handled jardinière with two fallow stags in a landscape, a pair of teacups and saucers, minor damage.

c1810

$700-1,000   DN

A Wedgwood pearlware volute krater pot-pourri vase, cover and liner, decorated with mottled pink luster, impressed mark, cracked.

c1810   13.5in (34cm) wide

$1,500-2,000   DN

A pearlware model of a cradle, printed in purple with figures and castles, the borders and turned finials picked out in purple luster.

c1830-40   8.25in (21cm) long

$700-1,000   LFA

One of a trio of Staffordshire pearlware demi-lune bough pots, with pierced liners, each gilded with a shield-shaped device within floral sprays.

c1800   8.75in (22cm) high

$1,000-1,500 (trio)   DN

A Liverpool pearlware small round bowl, printed in black with cattle and figures in wooded landscapes, the interior with a roundel of a sheep and a ram, within diaper and pendant leaf bands, rim chips.

c1790   4.75in (12cm) diam

$100-150   LFA

A pearlware serpentine-sided rectangular tea canister, painted in underglaze blue and yellow with flowers and leaves, the fluted borders picked out in blue, with metal cover.

c1790   4.75in (12cm) high

$400-600   LFA

A Bristol pearlware spirit barrel, decorated in the manner of William Fifield, painted in colored enamels with a central band of flowers between horizontal brown and green bands, molded in relief with a spigot hole.

c1830   4.25in (11cm) high

$300-400   DN

A Bristol pearlware spirit barrel, decorated in the manner of William Fifield, painted in colored enamels with a central band of flowers with monogram "FAW", between horizontal blue and pink bands, molded in relief with a spigot hole.

c1830   4.25in (11cm) high

$300-400   DN

Prattware

Prattware was developed in the late 18thC and is associated with the Pratt family from Lane Delph in Staffordshire, although it was also made by several other factories. It is similar to pearlware in color and weight, but is distinguished by a strong, high temperature palette that comprises yellow-ocher, green, blue and muddy brown. These colors were used to heighten areas of relief decoration and wares include molded teapots, jugs and figures.

A Pratt-type spill vase group, of a shepherd and companion, modeled seated with sheep before a tree, painted in typical palette, damage and losses.

c1790   7in (18cm) high

$400-600   **DN**

A Pratt-type group of Venus and Cupid, painted in shades of ocher, brown, and green, repaired base.

c1800   7in (18cm) high

$150-200   **DN**

A pair of figures representing Spring and Fall, attributable to the 'Garrison' Pottery, Dixon, Austin & Co., Sunderland, from a series of 'The Four Seasons,' modeled as classical maidens, Spring holding a cornucopia of flowers, Fall holding a sheaf of corn and a sickle, painted in a Pratt-type palette, Spring is restored to the base.

c1820   8.75in (22cm) high

$400-600   **DN**

An early 19thC Prattware figure, depicting Plenty standing on a square plinth with a cornucopia at her side, decorated in blue, green, ocher and brown.

10in (25.5cm) high

$400-600   **WW**

An early 19thC Prattware bust of William Shakespeare, decorated in blue, brown and ocher, small chips.

9.5in (24.5cm) high

$1,000-1,500   **WW**

A rare Prattware model of a seated pug dog, decorated with brown and ocher spots and a green base.

c1790   3in (8cm) high

$220-280   **WW**

A rare pair of late 18thC Staffordshire models of lions, recumbent on rectangular bases decorated with Pratt colors, the bases sponged blue, green and ocher, one with a small chip and fire cracks to the base.

8.5in (21.5cm) long

$7,000-10,000   **WW**

A Pratt-type model of a recumbent hound, on a green-glazed base and painted with brown and ocher spots, two small rim chips.

c1800   3.5in (9cm) long

$400-600   **DN**

A Prattware dolphin sauceboat, the scale-molded body decorated in green and ocher, minor repairs.

c1800   6in (15.5cm) long

$400-600   **WW**

A Pratt-type cow creamer, the cow sponged in shades of ocher and manganese, modeled standing and being milked by an attendant maid, replacement cover, restored section to base.

c1810   7in (18cm) long

$700-1,000   **DN**

A Pratt-type cow creamer and a cover, perhaps Newcastle-Upon-Tyne, typically modeled, a recumbent calf beneath, sponged with pale green patches and painted with ocher leaves, on a rectangular blue-line base.

c1810

$1,000-1,500   **DN**

Salt-glazed

A mid-18thC white salt-glazed stoneware dish, with a shaped and pierced rim and molded with scroll-edged panels of diaper designs, faint body crack.

10.5in (27cm) diam

$220-280 WW

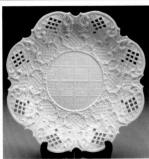

An early 19thC English salt-glazed plate, molded and pierced with diaper work and tracery.

11.25in (28.5cm) diam

$220-280 FRE

A salt-glazed stoneware two-handled oval tureen and cover, molded with diaper panels with foliate scroll borders and reserved on an ozier ground, supported on three mythical beast mask-and-paw feet, large foot-rim chip.

c1760 *11.5in (32cm) wide*

$400-600 DN

A small Staffordshire salt-glazed stoneware rectangular canister, molded with the 'Domino' pattern to each face.

c1750 *3.75in (9.5cm) high*

$600-900 WW

An English white salt-glazed stoneware teapot and cover, polychrome painted with a flautist to one side and a courting couple to the reverse between flowers, restoration to the cover.

c1760 *7in (18cm) high*

$1,000-1,500 WW

A rare Staffordshire salt-glazed teapot and cover, polychrome decorated with a portrait and inscribed "Semper Sublimis", all on an ermine ground.

c1765 *7.25in (18.5cm) long*

$800-1,200 WW

A 19thC brown salt-glazed stoneware gin flask, modeled as a man seated on a barrel and inscribed "Ale round my bar, good customers I see", the reverse inscribed "B Stringer Robin Hood Mill Bank St Westminster", tiny chips.

8.5in (22cm) high

$300-400 WW

A rare pair of 19thC salt-glazed stoneware gin flasks, modeled as Mr. Punch and Judy, each on an oval base.

7.75in (20cm) high

$700-1,000 WW

An unusual Staffordshire salt-glazed stoneware octagonal plate, printed in purple with the fable of a fox and a goat at a well, and in black and iron-red with flower sprays, the cartouche and diaper-molded border with brown line rim, one cover with old restoration, body cracks.

c1760 *8.5in (21.5cm) wide*

$400-600 LFA

Staffordshire Potteries

By the 17thC, Staffordshire was the center of the British ceramics industry. This was partly due to the abundance of local clay supplies and coal deposits. Slipware was the first true regional pottery in Britain and was produced in Staffordshire from the early 17thC. Salt-glazed stoneware was also manufactured in Staffordshire in great quantities throughout the 18thC.

There were a large number of potteries that rose to prominence in Staffordshire in the late 18thC and the 19thC. Important figures included Thomas Whieldon at Fenton Low, who produced redwares, polychrome wares and creamwares, and Josiah Wedgwood who developed jasper ware and black basalt at his factory at Burslem from c1769.

Based around the town of Stoke-on-Trent, the principal pottery towns were Burslem, Cobridge, Hanley, Fenton, Lane Delph, Lane End, Tunstall, Longton, Longport, Shelton and Newcastle-under-Lyme.

Staffordshire has become famed for its pottery figures, which are highly collectable today. During the 19thC, dozens of small potteries began producing cheap imitations of the much sought-after, but expensive, porcelain figures that had been made at Chelsea and Derby. These Victorian Staffordshire figures were often portraits of famous and infamous people, including members of the royal family, politicians, soldiers and sailors, actors and actresses and sports personalities. However, there are many reproductions on the market, so look closely for clumsily executed details, which are a feature of fakes. Also check for scratches in places that you would not normally expect to find wear. These may have been added to give the appearance of age.

A pair of early to mid-19thC Staffordshire figures, with a maiden with flowers and a gentleman with horn standing before a floral bocage, on blue, white and gilt base, minor losses.

10.75in (27.5cm) high

$600-900 **FRE**

A pair of early 19thC Staffordshire musician groups, he plays a trumpet while she plays a lute, both set before flowering bocage, and raised on rectangular bases, minor damage.

6.75in (17cm) high

$800-1,2000 **WW**

A mid-19thC Staffordshire figure, entitled 'The Harvest Festival', modeled with figures and animals standing beside a tree, on a terrain base, with wheat sheaves, minor chips.

7.75in (19.5cm) high

$500-700 **FRE**

A Staffordshire pottery group of two dandies, standing, arm in arm, flanked by bocage, and decorated in colored enamels, on red bordered oval mound base, minor chips to bocage.

6.25in (16cm) high

$600-900 **LFA**

A 19thC Staffordshire group, with a couple seated beside a stump and verse below, small chip.

12.5in (31.5cm) high

$180-220 **FRE**

A pair of Staffordshire figures of a gardener and companion, in Highland dress, each standing beside a tub of flowers, above a stream, and decorated in colored enamels, the oval base with a gilt band.

c1860-70 *14.75in (37.5cm) high*

$400-600 **LFA**

A pair of Staffordshire figures, modeled as a Scottish lad and lass, losses to both.

$300-400 **FRE**

A 19thC Staffordshire group, modeled as a Scottish lad and lass beside a green stump.

9.5in (24.5cm) high

$180-220 **FRE**

A Staffordshire pearlware figure of a young girl, seated reading a book, before bocage, and decorated in colored enamels, the square bordered green-glazed mound base applied with flowers and leaves, some damage.

c1820   9in (23cm) high

$150-200   LFA

An early 19thC Staffordshire figure of a lady, standing by an urn on a plinth and rectangular base.

                  9.25in (23.5cm) high

$150-200   Chef

Victorian Staffordshire

A 'Vicar and Moses' group, of Ralph Wood type, typically modelled with the vicar asleep, seated above his curate, the pew impressed "THE VICAR AND MOSES", painted in blue and brown glazes, impressed "62" to the base, chip to vicar's prayer book.

c1795   9.5in (24cm) high

$1,000-1,500   DN

A Staffordshire Crimean figure of Admiral Sir Deans Dundas, modelled standing next to a cannon, partially coloured and gilt on a titled base.

c1854   15.25in (39cm) high

$400-500   DN

A CLOSER LOOK AT A STAFFORDSHIRE FIGURE GROUP

This is a bold and striking group with clearly delineated features, making it highly desirable.

When checking for fakes, a useful tip is that reproductions tend to weigh less than the originals.

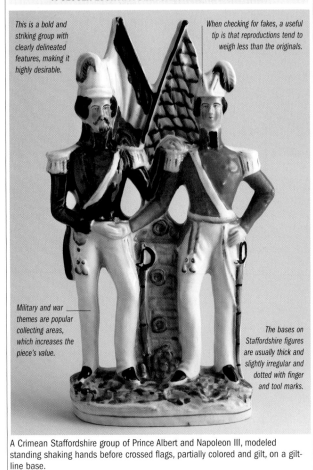

Military and war themes are popular collecting areas, which increases the piece's value.

The bases on Staffordshire figures are usually thick and slightly irregular and dotted with finger and tool marks.

A Crimean Staffordshire group of Prince Albert and Napoleon III, modeled standing shaking hands before crossed flags, partially colored and gilt, on a gilt-line base.

c1854   12.25in (31cm) high

$700-1,000   DN

A Staffordshire Crimean figure of Admiral Sir Deans Dundas, modeled standing beside a flag, leaning on a cannon, the gilt-line base inscribed "DUNDAS".

c1854   13in (33cm) high

$300-400   DN

A Staffordshire Crimean 'Wounded Soldier' group, modeled with a cavalryman supported by a sailor, the base with gilt title "THE WOUNDED SOLDIER", small areas of overpainting.

c1855   13in (33cm) high

$320-380   DN

A Staffordshire figure of Admiral Sir Charles Napier, modeled standing beside a canon, sparsely colored and gilt.

c1854   11in (28cm) high

$150-200   DN

A Staffordshire Thomas Parr equestrian group of Giuseppe Garibaldi, typically modeled leaning on his mount's withers, fully colored in a pale palette, restored.

c1861   9.5in (24cm) high

$300-400   DN

A Staffordshire Crimean 'The Victory' group, modeled with a British sailor seated on a gun carriage between a French and Turkish soldier holding flags, mostly colored and gilt, the base with gilt title "THE VICTORY", tops of flags restored.

c1856   12.75in (35cm) high

$2,200-2,800   **DN**

A mid-19thC Staffordshire group of the 'Sailor's Return', modeled with the mariner waving his hat, arm in arm with his sweetheart, partially colored and gilt, on a titled rectangular base.

12.5in (31.5cm) high

$300-400   **DN**

A mid-19thC Staffordshire figure of a Greenwich Hospital pensioner, modeled seated with a glass and jug and with a wooden leg, mostly colored and gilt, on a plain gilt-line base, chip to figure's cup.

8.25in (21cm) high

$300-400   **DN**

A mid-19thC Staffordshire 'Death of Nelson' group, the Admiral modeled supported between two officers, mostly colored and gilt, on a base titled in gilding, some wear.

8in (22cm) high

$300-400   **DN**

A pair of Staffordshire figures of a sailor and his companion, each modeled standing holding flags, on gilt-line bases, mostly colored and gilt, tip of sailor's flag restored.

c1854   9.5in (24cm) high

$300-400   **DN**

A Staffordshire Thomas Parr figure of Prince Alfred, modeled standing wearing a sailor suit and leaning on an anchor, small restored chip to anchor.

c1860   12.25in (31cm) high

$300-400   **DN**

A 19thC Staffordshire figure of William Wallace, painted in gilt and colors on a white ground, the naturalistic base with molded inscription "WALLACE".

17.25in (44cm) high

$150-200   **L&T**

A Victorian Staffordshire 'Highland Dancers' clock group.

13.75in (35cm) high

$150-200   **BonS**

A Staffordshire figure of Ben Franklin, in a blue frock coat standing on a plinth and inscribed "Franklin".

14.25in (36cm) high

$2,200-2,800   **Pook**

A large 19thC Staffordshire figure of a man standing beside a clock and holding a mandolin, chipped.

16in (40.5cm) high

$280-320   **FRE**

A mid-19thC Staffordshire figure, with a parrot, possibly the theatrical character Paul from 'Paul et Virginie', partially colored and gilt.

13.75in (35cm) high

$150-200   **DN**

A Staffordshire figural group, realistically modeled and titled 'Eva gaily laughing was hanging a wreath of roses 'round Tom's neck', Eva's left foot has been repaired.

8in (20.5cm) high

$70-100   **FRE**

A mid-19thC Staffordshire pair of figures of Milton and Shakespeare, typically modeled leaning on plinths, gilt titled bases, sparsely colored and gilt, minor rubbing to gilding.

10.25in (28cm) high

$220-280   **DN**

A Staffordshire porcelain flatback of a spaniel.

Although more common in pottery, these figures were also made in porcelain.

c1835   *6in (15.5cm) wide*

$600-900   **JF**

A Staffordshire porcelain poodle, with bird in mouth on cushion.

c1835   *4in (10cm) high*

$300-400   **JF**

A 19thC small Staffordshire model of a seated dog, decorated with black markings wearing a red collar and raised on a green rectangular base.

2.75in (7cm) high

$300-400   **WW**

A 19thC Staffordshire group of a dog and a girl.

13.5in (34.5cm) high

$400-600   **SI**

A pair of mid-19thC Staffordshire King Charles spaniels, the seated dogs with gilt details and padlocked collars, their muzzles and eyes in colors.

13in (33cm) high

$120-180   **Chef**

A pair of Staffordshire pottery inkwells, each in the form of a recumbent greyhound.

c1850-60   *7.5in (19cm) long*

$300-400   **LFA**

A pair of mid-19thC Staffordshire children and hound groups, the children modeled seated on the backs of large hounds, probably Newfoundlands, the hounds seated on their haunches, partially colored and gilt.

7in (18cm) high

$400-600   **DN**

A pair of Staffordshire pottery models of seated spaniels, each picked out in brown, and wearing a gilt collar, a basket of brightly colored fruits at its feet, on oval blue-glazed base, with a gilt band, minor chips.

c1860   *6.25in (16cm) high*

$1,500-2,000   **LFA**

A Victorian Staffordshire figure of a Dalmatian, standing on an oblong naturalistic base.

c1870   6.25in (15.5cm) high

$220-280   **BonS**

A pair of late 19thC Staffordshire pottery models of seated Dalmations, each decorated in black, and wearing a silvered collar, the oval blue-glazed bases with a silvered band.

5.25in (13.5cm) high

$350-400   **LFA**

A late 19thC Staffordshire model of a seated Dalmatian, raised on an oval blue base, some flaking to his spots.

5in (13cm) high

$220-280   **WW**

A late 19thC Staffordshire pair of models of spaniels, facing left and right, seated on their haunches, painted with with copper-luster patches.

10in (27cm) high

$150-200   **DN**

A pair of Staffordshire models of Pekinese dogs, possibly Bo'ness, modeled standing facing left and right, painted in shades of orange-brown and with blue ribbands.

c1900   8.75in (22cm) long

$120-180   **DN**

An early 19thC small Staffordshire model of a cow, decorated with black markings and raised on a green base.

2.5in (6.5cm) long

$400-600   **WW**

A first quarter 19thC Staffordshire pale-brown pottery group of a cow, attendant and recumbent hound, of Yorkshire type, applied to a stepped rectangular base, painted in shades of blue, black, green and manganese, restored tips of horns and teats.

6.25in (16cm) high

$800-1,200   **DN**

A Staffordshire pearlware spill vase, in the form of a cow and a calf, before a tree stump, decorated in colored enamels, and with granitic decoration, on mound base, some restoration.

c1825   4.5in (11.5cm) high

$400-600   **LFA**

An Obadiah Sherratt-type bull baiting group, modeled with the tethered bull tossing a terrier while another attacks his snout, beside his tail a man stands with outstretched arms, all on a rectangular table base applied with two oval plaques impressed "Bull Beating" and "Now Captin Lad".

c1830   15in (38cm) long

$3,000-4,000   **WW**

A 19thC Staffordshire earthenware group of a cow and a calf.

5.5in (14cm) long

$220-280   **SI**

A Staffordshire pearlware model of a recumbent deer, before bocage.

c1820   5.25in (13.5cm) high

$180-220   **LFA**

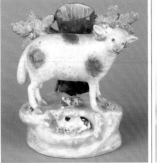

A Staffordshire pearlware spill vase, in the form of a ram and a lamb, before a tree stump, with bocage, decoration in colored enamels, on mound base.

c1825   4.75in (12cm) high

$220-280   LFA

A pair of Staffordshire figures, composed of a ram and yew, each with a lamb below and with bocage behind.

6.25in (15.5cm) high

$700-1,000   FRE

A pair of early 19thC Staffordshire figures, each modeled as a buck and doe beside a bocage.

9in (22.5cm) high

$220-280   FRE

A 19thC small Staffordshire figural spill vase, modeled with beige horse beside a green stump.

6in (15.5cm) high

$300-400   FRE

A Staffordshire pottery spill vase, in the form of a horse and a cow, drinking at a trough, before two birds in a tree, decorated in colored enamels, and with granitic decoration, the base with a gilt band, foot-rim chip glued.

c1860   10.5in (26.5cm) high

$180-220   LFA

A pair of Staffordshire pearlware small models of parrots, each picked out in colored enamels, on green-glazed oval mound base.

c1820   3.25in (8cm) high

$300-500   LFA

A Staffordshire pottery small model of a crouching rabbit, sponged in black, the oval base with green and black bands.

c1840-50   3.25in (8cm) wide

$300-500   LFA

A pottery hen tureen cover and base, modeled as a chicken sitting on its eggs, the lower section ozier molded, some small chips.

c1900   8.75in (22cm) high

$400-600   DN

A Staffordshire figure of a seated cat, sponged in black, with gilt detail.

c1840   1.5in (4cm) high

$500-700   JF

A Whieldon-type plate, with a shaped rim and border molded with basket work and diaper designs, all beneath a mottled glaze.

c1760   9.5in (24cm) diam

$300-500   WW

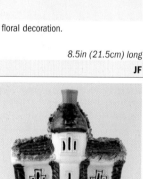

A Whieldon-type teapot and cover, with a bird finial and crabstock handle and spout, decorated with dappled brown and indigo glazes, a few very minor repairs.

c1760   6.75in (17cm) long

$600-900   WW

A Staffordshire model of a parrot, brightly colored and perched upon a stump on a circular base, a small reglued chip to the crest.

c1900   9in (23cm) high

$180-220   WW

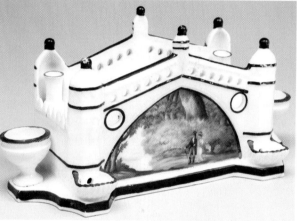

A Staffordshire inkwell, with landscape and floral decoration.

c1825   8.5in (21.5cm) long

$2,200-2,800   JF

A pair of Staffordshire flower encrusted vases.

c1830

$700-1,000   JF

A 19thC Staffordshire gaudy Dutch plate, decorated with flower blossoms, enclosed by decorative borders in blue, red, green and yellow, surface wear.

8.25in (21cm) diam

$180-220   FRE

A mid-19thC Staffordshire lavender-ground pastille burner, in the form of a cottage with a chimney, decorated with encrusted flowers and foliage, the front porch removable to reveal hollow interior and the base forming a small garden.

4.75in (12cm) high

$500-700   L&T

A Staffordshire pottery model of a cottage, with blue-glazed roof and colored granitic decoration, the door flanked by two swans.

c1860   6in (15cm) high

$100-150   LFA

A Staffordshire salt-glazed stoneware bear-baiting jug and cover, applied with clay chippings to simulate fur, his snout pierced with two chain links, details to the eyes, collar, paws and dog's head picked out in brown, the head with two hair cracks, the rim with a faint hair crack.

c1760   *10in (25.5cm) high*

$5,000-7,000   **WW**

A late 17thC Rhenish stoneware bellarmine, applied at the neck with a bearded mask and with and oval lion medallion to the side.

8in (20.5cm) high

$350-400   **WW**

A late 17thC Rhenish stoneware bellarmine, with a mask applied to the neck and a lion medallion to the side.

8.25in (21cm) high

$400-600   **WW**

A 19thC German salt-glazed bellied bellarmine jug, with applied long handle decorated with stylized mask and oval star impressed roundel.

13in (33cm) high

$400-600   **L&T**

A 20thC Renaissance-style English silver-mounted salt-glazed stoneware jug, the globular vessel with mottled brown glaze, mounted with a silver foot and hinged cover chased with fruit and lions' masks.

10.5in (26.5cm) high

$700-1,000   **SI**

A stoneware wine flagon, inscribed "Cantell's Stores, Buckingham, Brackley, Aylesbury & Winslow", printed to shoulders.

11in (28cm) high

$70-100   **D**

A large salt-glazed stoneware cylindrical mug, inscribed "John Skeat 1731" applied with a panel of Hogarth's 'Midnight Modern Conversation', with a hunting scene, chips and cracks, dated.

1731   *8.5in (21.5cm) high*

$700-1,000   **WW**

A Nottingham brown salt-glazed stoneware cylindrical mug, inscribed "William Bomer 1723", incised with two bands of scrolling flowers, dated, rim chips.

c1723   *4.5in (11.5cm) high*

$3,500-4,500   **WW**

A pair of Davenport stoneware mugs, each molded with the huntsmen pattern between chocolate bands and below gilt rims, one with impressed marks, some damage.

5.25in (13.5cm) high

$150-200   **Chef**

A Minton grey stoneware compressed round teapot and cover, applied in white with prunus, applied mark and number "59".

c1840   *2.75in (7cm) high*

$120-180   **LFA**

A stoneware drum-shaped two-handled sucrier and cover, with ball knop, applied in white with Classical figures, on oval green ground panels, on a bright blue ground, small rim chips.

4.5in (11.5cm) diam

$220-280   **LFA**

Toby Jugs

Toby jugs were first made in the 1760s and were instantly popular. They were first made by Ralph Wood and were based on the celebrated drinker Harry Elwes, nicknamed Toby Philpots. The Wood family, Ralph Wood I (1715-1772), and his son Ralph II (1748-1795), from Burslem in Staffordshire, England, made a series of earthenware jugs from c1760. The so-called 'Ralph Wood' Toby jugs are the most popular but Ralph II Toby jugs are considered better quality than Ralph I and are the most valuable.

The jugs were probably inspired by an engraving of Toby Philpot, showing him sitting down holding a mug of foaming ale in one hand and a glass or a pipe in the other. They were imitated throughout Staffordshire and elsewhere in England, from the 18thC, and are still being made today.

There are many variations, including the Thin Man, the Squire, Martha Gunn, the Brighton Bathing Machine Lady, Admiral Howe, Rodney's Sailor and the Snuff Taker. The most popular figure is the Toper or drinker.

Toby jugs are an extremely popular area for collecting. When buying look for sharply delineated, subtle enamel colors. Impressed marks will enhance the value. Also, check that the Toby jug's tricorn hat is present and in good condition, because without this the value will be dramatically decreased.

A rare creamware Admiral Lord Howe Toby jug, of Ralph Wood type, conventionally modeled and seated on a brown barrel, "63" impressed.

c1790	9.75in (25cm) high
$4,000-6,000	**WW**

A Pratt-type Toby jug and cover, typically modeled seated, holding a foaming jug of ale, painted in a typical palette, some old damage and repairs.

c1800	9.75in (25cm) high
$700-1,000	**DN**

A creamware Toby jug, typically modeled seated with foaming mug of ale, undecorated, repairs to hat, lacks cover.

c1800	10.25in (26cm) high
$220-280	**DN**

An early 19thC pearlware Toby jug and cover, sitting with foaming jug of ale and a pipe, wearing purple coat and yellow britches, the canted square base marbled.

	10.25in (26cm) high
$700-1,000	**Chef**

A Davenport pottery Toby jug, typically modeled seated with a foaming mug of ale, painted with colored glazes and with mottled base, impressed marks, hat repaired.

c1835	9.75in (25cm) high
$320-380	**DN**

An early 19thC pearlware 'Hearty Good Fellow' Toby jug, standing holding a beer jug and painted with enamels.

	11.5in (29.5cm) high
$400-500	**WW**

A Staffordshire Davenport pottery Toby jug, typically modeled seated with a foaming mug of ale, painted with colored glazes and with mottled base, impressed marks.

c1835	10in (25cm) high
$400-600	**DN**

A 19thC pearlware Toby jug, sitting holding his beer jug decorated with Pratt colors.

	9.5in (24cm) high
$700-1,000	**WW**

Transfer-printed Pottery

The invention of transfer-printing transformed the ceramics industry in the mid-18th century. Prior to this wares were hand-painted and this was time consuming, making ceramics an expensive commodity. This new process involved engraving a design onto a copper plate which was used to make a print onto a sheet of strong tissue paper. This printed paper was then pressed with the ink facing downwards onto the ceramic body. The ware and the paper were covered in cold water. The warm oily ink would stiffen on contact with the water and the design would remain on the surface of the ware.

At first blue was the only color that stayed stable in the furnace, and so this was used on all the wares. The first designs took their inspiration from Chinese ceramics. These early pieces, from the period 1780-1800, were often blurred and dark because too much ink was used on the copper plates. Also, dinner plates and dishes were generally made without a foot-rim and the glazes tended to be rippled and slightly uneven.

The introduction of stipple engraving in c1807, meant that areas of light and shade could be delineated more easily and European motifs started to be incorporated into the Chinese designs.

The period from c1815-1835 saw a vast increase in production of blue and white transfer-printed pottery. There were potteries all over Britain, especially in Staffordshire, Leeds, Swansea, Tyne-and-Wear and Scotland. The patterns from this period were mainly floral and framed in border decorating the rims of dinner services.

Advances in techniques meant that by c1835 the glazes used were smooth and several colors could be used, including sepia, mulberry and green. Common designs were the 'Willow' pattern and the 'Asiatic Pheasants' design.

By the second half of the 19th century the blue and white transfer-printed pottery industry was in decline. This was due to lack of demand as tastes changed and the market sought white services with decorative borders rather than dense, allover printed patterns.

A Copeland & Garrett plate, printed in underglaze blue with a view from the Caramanion Series, within a continuous band of figures of animals, impressed and printed marks.

c1840	9.75in (25cm) diam
$120-180	**LFA**

A Copeland late Spode 'Jasmine' pattern nursery plate.

c1850	5in (12.5cm) diam
$120-180	**GN**

A Copeland & Garrett 'Tower' pattern dog trough, restoration to feet.

1833-1847	10.5in (26.5cm) wide
$1,800-2,200	**GN**

A Davenport 'Bamboo and Peony' pattern vegetable tureen, firing fault to base restored.

c1815	10in (25.5cm) wide
$320-380	**GN**

A Copeland & Garrett ironstone twin-handled footbath, the slightly flared neck and inner neck decorated in underglaze blue and overglaze green, rust and gilt with chinoiserie peony and prunus sprays, the neck and foot with four continuous rouge de fer barbed friezes, painted pattern number in rust "6982" and printed green factory mark.

	22.75in (58cm) wide
$400-600	**L&T**

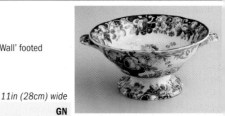

A Davenport 'Vase on Wall' footed comport, in puce.

c1830	11in (28cm) wide
$400-600	**GN**

A set of Davenport 'Fruit and Flower' pattern assorted miniatures.

c1830   *Largest 5.75in (14.5cm) wide*

$300-400   **GN**

A Godwin 'View of London' pattern platter.

c1820   *18.5in (47cm) wide*

$2,200-2,800   **GN**

A T. & T. Godwin 'View of London' pattern soup tureen, lid chip restored.

c1820   *14in (35.5cm) wide*

$1,200-1,800   **GN**

A Benjamin Godwin 'Chintz' pattern jug.

c1835   *8in (20.5cm) high*

$280-320   **GN**

A Minton 'Lace Border' pattern bourdaloue.

c1830

$600-900   **GN**

A Minton 'Florentine' pattern footbath.

c1825   *18.5in (47cm) wide*

$2,200-2,800   **GN**

A Minton 'Royal Persian' pattern part dinner service, comprising one dish, 14 dinner plates, six soup plates, two dessert plates and ten dished cereal plates, all printed in blue with the 'Floral' pattern and border, printed title marks and some items with impressed "Improved Stone China" seal marks, some minor rim chips.

1825-1840

$320-380   **DN**

A Minton blue-printed ironstone type 'Trellis and Plants' pattern footbath, the interior decorated on the base with dahlia and lily, the flared neck decorated on the outside and inside with continuous trellis and meandering flower frieze, relief cast scroll handles, over bellied sides with four scroll sprays of passion flowers and granny's bonnet, the base with narrow trellis frieze, printed pattern mark to base with pattern name within cartouche and script "M" below, impressed cypher mark.

c1857   *20in (51cm) wide*

$1,000-1,500   **L&T**

A Spode 'Dagger First' pattern dished plate.

c1800   *9in (23cm) diam*

$120-180   **GN**

A Spode 'Two Figures' pattern dished plate.

c1800   *9.5in (24cm) diam*

$150-200   **GN**

A Spode 'Buddleia' pattern dessert comport.

c1800 9.25in (23.5cm) diam

$280-320 **GN**

A rare Spode 'Gloucester' pattern segment dish.

c1810 12.5in (32cm) diam

$220-280 **GN**

A Spode 'Castle' pattern turkey platter.

c1815 21in (53.5cm) wide

$600-900 **GN**

A Spode 'India' pattern dessert dish.

c1815 7.25in (18.5cm) diam

$280-320 **GN**

A Spode 'Greek' pattern footed comport, with overglaze clobbering.

c1815 12in (30.5cm) wide

$400-600 **GN**

A Spode 'Greek' pattern lidded supper dish.

1815-20 13in (33cm) wide

$400-600 **GN**

A Spode 'Rome' or 'Tiber' pattern rectangular tray, printed in blue with the 'Italian Scene' and narrow stringing border, printed maker's mark.

1811-1825 10.5in (26.5cm) long

$350-400 **DN**

A Spode 'Tower' pattern pierced plate.

c1820 7.5in (19cm) diam

$280-320 **GN**

A Spode 'Group' pattern cheese plate.

c1820 8.25in (21cm) diam

$120-180 **GN**

A Spode 'Group' pattern cusped dish.

c1820 10.5in (26.5cm) diam

$280-320 **GN**

A Spode 'Italian' pattern shell comport.

c1820 9in (23cm) wide

$350-400 **GN**

A Spode 'Tower' pattern shell comport.

c1820 9in (23cm) diam

$280-320 **GN**

A Spode 'Forest Landscape' pattern cheese stand.

c1820 11in (28cm) wide

$400-600 **GN**

A Spode 'Tower' pattern plate warmer.

c1820   *11in (28cm) wide*

$400-600   **GN**

A Spode 'Group' pattern pickle dish.

c1820   *5.75in (14.5cm) wide*

$280-320   **GN**

A Spode 'Blue Rose' pattern plate.

c1825   *10in (25.5cm) diam*

$150-200   **GN**

A Spode 'Filigree' pattern pickle dish.

c1825   *5.25in (13.5cm) wide*

$280-320   **GN**

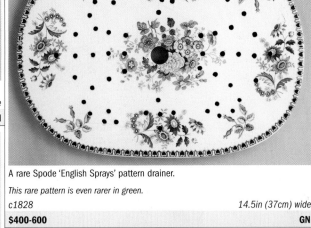

A rare Spode 'English Sprays' pattern drainer.

This rare pattern is even rarer in green.

c1828   *14.5in (37cm) wide*

$400-600   **GN**

A Spode 'Floral' pattern plate.

c1830   *9.75in (25cm) diam*

$180-220   **GN**

A Spode 'Flying Pennant' pattern basket and stand.

c1820   *Plate 9.5in (24cm) wide*

$700-1,000   **GN**

A Spode 'British Flowers' pattern vegetable tureen.

c1825   *11in (27.5cm) wide*

$400-600   **GN**

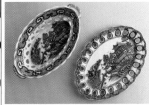

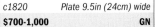

A Spode 'Castle' pattern spittoon.

c1820

$1,000-1,500   **GN**

A small Spode 'Tower' blue pattern oval section footbath, with twin lug handles and horizontal ribbed decoration printed with fishermen by a bridge in a rustic scene, continuous flower-head frieze to inner rim and foot, impressed and printed Spode marks.

16.5in (42cm) long

$2,200-2,800   **L&T**

Spode 'Filigree' pattern egg cruet set.

c1825   *7.5in (19cm) wide*

$700-1,000   **GN**

A Spode 'Girl at the Well' pattern footbath, of typical hooped form with molded handles, printed in blue with the rustic scene pattern and usual Union Wreath border, printed and impressed upper-case marks, impressed mark with large crown, repaired cracks in base.

1822-33   *17.25in (47cm) long*

$400-600   **DN**

A 'Temple with Panel' pattern jug, of ovoid shape with looped strap handle, printed in blue with a version of the chinoiserie scene featuring a diamond-shaped panel on the temple, with a typical chinoiserie border outside the neck and a nankin-type border with superimposed flowers inside the rim, unmarked, staining, small repair to spout.

c1790-1810   *8.5in (23cm) high*

$180-220   **DN**

A 19thC helmet-shaped water jug, with decoration depicting figures beside classical buildings.

9.5in (24cm) high

$150-200   **Clv**

A Don Pottery 'Vermicelli' pattern teapot, with scroll-molded loop knop to the cover, printed with two oval-framed rural scenes within the vermicelli ground, unmarked, restoration to tip of spout and faint hairline crack.

c1820-30   *11in (18cm) long*

$320-380   **DN**

A Staffordshire Enoch Wood & Sons coffee pot, printed in black with a house, urn and bird in a landscape with floral borders, the spout printed with a harp and sheet music laying by a flowering urn, the border at the shoulder and on the cover printed upside down, printed "HARP" and "EW&S".

c1830   *11in (28cm) high*

$350-400   **SI**

A 'Willow' pattern quart ale measure.

c1900   *6.5in (16.5cm) high*

$280-320   **BS**

An unusual pearlware bottle-shaped carafe, printed in underglaze blue with figures before buildings and flowers and fruits on a table, rim reduced.

c1830   *8in (20.5cm) high*

$300-400   **LFA**

A J. & M. P. Bell & Co. 'Triumphal Car' pattern blue and white oval drainer, printed with the romantic classical scene within a narrow version of the border of small flower-heads, impressed bell containing initials "JB".

c1842-1860   *12.25in (31cm) long*

$320-380   **DN**

A Brameld 'Castle Rochefort, South of France' plate.

c1820   *10in (25.5cm) diam*

$150-200   **GN**

A Clew 'Windsor Castle' plate, from the 'Foliage Border' series.

c1820   *9.75in (25cm) diam*

$350-400   **GN**

A Windsor 'Grapevine Border' series platter.

c1820   *18.5in (47cm) wide*

$1,500-2,000   **GN**

A 19thC open vegetable dish, by E. Wood, Burslem, printed with view of a small port with ships, peasants, and a castle, in a tree-filled setting.

11.5in (29.25cm) long

$400-600   **FRE**

A pearlware oblong dish, printed in underglaze blue with an allover design of flower-heads and leaf scrolls, within a blue line border.

c1815   *11.75in (30cm) wide*

$120-180   **LFA**

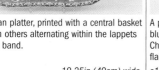

An early Victorian platter, printed with a central basket of flowers within others alternating within the lappets of the floral rim band.

19.25in (49cm) wide

$120-180   **Chef**

A pearlware canted rectangular meat dish, printed in blue with two figures in a boat, in an extensive Chinese landscape and scroll paneled border, glaze flaking to underside.

c1820   *21in (53.5cm) wide*

$220-280   **LFA**

A 'Piping Shepherd' pattern blue and white meat dish, printed with the genre scene of a shepherd playing to his lady beneath a gnarled tree, within a border of flowers and ivy, unmarked.

c1820-30   *19.75in (50cm) diam*

$400-600   **DN**

A 'Chinese Gardener' plate, unknown maker.

c1820   *9.75in (25cm) diam*

$120-180   **GN**

A 'Lovick' pattern plate, unknown maker.

c1830   *9.75in (25cm) diam*

$150-200   **GN**

Transfer-Printed

Following the American Revolution and War of Independence in 1812, English Staffordshire potters were keen to regain their American customers (although they had continued to supply some wares during the wars). Consequently, ironstone ceramics decorated with transfer-prints were made for the American market. They featured national heroes and patriotic images including Washington, Jefferson and Franklin.

The transfer-printed wares included dinner services, tea sets and other crockery. They proved extremely popular with American market from c1820 to c1860, reaching their peak of demand in c1845. The English potters responded by decorating the wares with more varied American images, such as buildings, locations and scenic landscapes. Later decoration included transportation images such as railroads, canals and boats powered by both steam and sail.

An Elkins & Co. Irish Scenery series dish, printed with an unidentified scene showing a tall country house across an estuary with sailing boats on the water, all within the usual series border of foliate scrolls, printed royal arms mark with maker's name and series title together with a printed wreath containing the name "Warren".

c1822-1830   14.75in (37.5cm) long

$300-400   DN

A John and William Ridgway pearlware vegetable dish, printed in medium blue underglaze with scalloped rose-leaf border enclosing a view of Mt. Vernon Near Washington, maker and view identification printed in underglaze blue, some imperfections.

c1825   11.75in (30cm) long

$700-800   SI

A dark-blue Staffordshire 'Peace and plenty' pattern platter, by James & Ralph Clews, impressed factory mark.

17in (43cm) long

$1,700-2,300   NA

A dark blue Staffordshire 'Lake George: State of New York' pattern platter, by Enoch Wood & Sons, impressed factory mark, printed title, eagle, shield and banner mark in underglaze-blue.

16.5in (42cm) long

$1,700-2,300   NA

A dark-blue Staffordshire 'Castle Garden Battery: New York' platter, by Enoch Wood & Sons, impressed 'Wood/18', printed title, eagle, shield and banner mark in underglaze-blue.

18.75in (47.5cm) long

$2,500-2,300   NA

A dark-blue Staffordshire 'Columbus' pattern platter, by Neff Wanton, Louisville, printed title and 'Columbus' in under glaze-blue.

14.25in (36cm) long

$2,300-2,800   NA

A medium-blue Staffordshire 'Boston State House' pattern platter, by John Rogers & Son, impressed "Rogers/16".

16.74in (42.5cm) long

$2,000-2,500   NA

A medium-blue Staffordshire 'Beauties of America Series: Almshouse, New York' pattern platter, by John & William Ridgway, printed title in underglaze-blue.

16.75in (42.5cm) long

$1,200-1,700   NA

A dark-blue Staffordshire 'Loading of General Lafayette at Castle Garden, New York, 16th August 1824' pattern platter, by James & Ralph Clews, impressed factory mark.

17in (43cm) long

$2,500-3,000 NA

A dark-blue Staffordshire 'Arms of the American States: New York' plate, by Thomas Mayer, impressed factory mark, printed eagle, shield and banner mark in underglaze-blue.

10in (25.5cm) diam

$950-1,250 NA

Two of set of 12 Staffordshire plates, including seven blue and white, the others polychrome, variously decorated with San Francisco bay, City Hall Portland, City Hall Massachusetts, Bermuda, a log cabin, Detroit, Asbury Park, New Jersey, City Hall, Detroit, The Myles Standish Monument, views of the Mayflower, Robert Burns, Memorial Hall, and State House, two cracked.

10.25in (26cm) diam

$350-450 (set) WW

Two of a set of ten Staffordshire plates, printed with Brooklyn Bridge, Canal Street, New Orleans, New Bedford, Fort Frederick, Old Albany, City Hall, Grand Rapids, Temple Square, Salt Lake, City Hall, Philadelphia, Old Brick Row, Yale, City Hall, St Louis, and City Hall, Cincinnati, various printed marks.

10in (25.5cm) diam

$550-650 (set) WW

An American 'Eagle and Urn' pattern cup and saucer, by James & Ralph Clew, printed with a pagoda within a floral and urn border, the urn decorated with a variation of the Great Seal of the United States, impressed factory mark beneath saucer.

Saucer 6.75in (17cm) diam

$380-430 NA

A transfer-printed pearlware cup and saucer, by Enoch Wood, each piece printed in dark underglaze depicting 'Lafayette at the Tomb of Franklin' within a floral border, impressed mark.

c1830 *5.75in (14.5cm) diam*

$400-500 SI

A dark-blue Staffordshire 'Landing of General Lafayette at Castle Garden, New York, 16th August 1824' pattern pitcher, by James & Ralph Clews, impressed factory mark.

17in (43cm) long

$2,400-2,800 NA

A medium-blue Staffordshire 'Famous Naval heroes: Washington, Independence, Truxtum' pitcher, unknown maker.

6.25in (16cm) high

$1,000-1,500 NA

A dark-blue Staffordshire 'Lafayette at Franklin's Tomb' pattern coffee pot, by Enoch Wood & Sons.

11in (28cm) high

$1,800-2,300 NA

Wedgwood

IN 1759 JOSIAH WEDGWOOD (1730-95) FOUNDED A POTTERY FACTORY at Burslem in Staffordshire. Cauliflower and pineapple wares were the first products made there and they continued to be made after the new factory, Etruria, was established in 1768.

One of the first improvements at the new factory were the changes made to black earthenware, which Josiah called black basalt ware. This was used to make imitation Greek vases. The factory also made Jasperware, for which it has become famous. This contained barium sulphate in the form of a Derbyshire mineral called 'cawk', and was perfected in 1774-75. Items made from 'jasper' ware include tableware, cameos, beads and buttons.

Josiah Wedgwood died in 1795, and the factory continued under his nephew, Thomas Byersley, and then Josiah Wedgwood II, until 1841. After Byersley's death in 1810, the pottery revived old styles of the 18thC but this changed in the 19thC when luster decoration began to be used, as well as Chinese-style painting on black basalts.

The 20thC saw many innovative designs at Wedgwood as well as a continuation of traditional ware, including jasper ware copies of 18thC originals. In 1989, Wedgwood merged with Waterford Glass to form the Waterford-Wedgwood Group, which is still producing pottery today.

A 19thC Wedgwood black basalt oval plaque, applied in relief with a male classical figure, impressed mark.

7.5in (19cm) high

$320-380   **LFA**

An 18thC Wedgwood black basalt oval bas-relief medallion, decorated with Hercules wrestling a lion.

5.5in (14cm) wide

$320-380   **Clv**

A pair of 19thC Wedgwood white-on-black plaques, each with raised white figures of classical maidens holding hands and dancing.

18in (45.5cm) long

$2,200-2,800   **FRE**

A Wedgwood black basalt bust of Minerva, the black and socle impressed "Wedgwood, made in England".

c1920   *20in (50cm) high*

$2,200-2,800   **FRE**

A Wedgwood black basalt bust of Mercury, the back and socle impressed "Wedgwood, city".

c1900   *18in (45.5cm) high*

$1,500-2,000   **FRE**

A second half 19thC Wedgwood blue 'jasper' ware dip taper tobacco jar and cover, decorated with white base reliefs of classical subjects, impressed marks.

6in (15.5cm) high

$400-600   **WW**

An early 20thC Chester silver-mounted Wedgwood blue 'jasper' ware bowl, the sides sprigged with Roman soldiers, horses and chariots below fruiting vines, impressed marks.

9in (23cm) diam

$60-90   **Che**

A Wedgwood 'jasper' ware canopic vase and cover, the cover molded as a pharaoh's head, the body applied with Egyptian motifs and bands of flower-heads, impressed "Wedgwood" and "1796" incised, a tiny restored rim flake.

1796   *9.75in (24.5cm) high*

$6,000-9,000   WW

A rare Wedgwood solid blue 'jasper' ware vase, with a lift-out lid and three laurel leaf bulb holders, the body decorated with Apollo and the nine Muses above a band of trophies raised on a spreading foot, impressed "Wedgwood V".

c1785-95   *8.75in (22.5cm) high*

$3,000-4,000   WW

A Wedgwood three-colored 'jasper' spill vase, with mauve cupid ovals alternating with harps between rams' heads holding floral swags on a green ground, impressed marks, date letter.

1870   *2.5in (6.5cm) high*

$60-90   Chef

A Wedgwood 'Queensware' Liverpool-printed oval tureen and cover, of two-handled gadrooned form, printed in black with an oak leaf swag-band above two oval panels of bucolic scenes and two similar vignettes beneath the handles, the cover with similar swag-band and surmounted with a flower-bud finial, impressed marks, minute chips to finial.

c1780   *12.75in (35cm) wide*

$700-1,000   DN

An early to mid-19thC Wedgwood part service, with Imari-style decoration and gold edges, including three hexagonal dishes, three oblong dishes, a compote, and 12 individual circular plates.

$1,500-2,000   FRE

A Wedgwood three-color 'jasper' ware vase, the tapering body with oval patera and floral swags hung from fluted pilasters, "Wedgwood" impressed.

c1794-1800   *5in (12.5cm) high*

$400-600   WW

Wemyss

Wemyss ware pottery was first made from the Fife pottery in Kirkcaldy, Scotland, in c1882. The distinctive underglaze patterns of Wemyss ware have remained highly popular and they are a growing collector's field.

Wares include jug-and-basin sets, large pig doorstops, tablewares, candlesticks and inkstands. Pieces are hand-painted with fruit, cabbage roses, birds, cats and many other subjects.

Robert Methven Heron inherited the business from his father and ran it from 1833-1906, during its main period of production. Karel Nekola was the principle painter, and made some commemorative pieces for Queen Victoria's Diamond jubilee in 1897. Thomas Goode and Co. were the main distributors in England and many pieces carry their mark.

In 1930 the rights were sold to the Bovey Tracey pottery in Devon. Nekola's son Joseph continued to paint Wemyss ware until he died in 1942.

A Wemyss ware preserve jar, of cylindrical form and decorated with apples, painted mark, lid missing.

5in (12.5cm) high

$180-220 **L&T**

A Wemyss ware shouldered vase, with cylindrical rim, decorated with apples, impressed "R. H. & S." mark.

6.25in (16cm) high

$300-400 **L&T**

An unusual Wemyss ware medium-sized loving-cup, decorated with cocks and hens, painted by Karel Nekola.

c1890-1900 *8in (20cm) high*

$2,200-2,800 **RdeR**

A large Wemyss ware porringer, decorated with black cockerels.

c1900 *6in (15cm) diam*

$600-900 **RdeR**

A Wemyss ware crocus mug, restored.

c1890 *5.75in (14.5cm) high*

$400-600 **RdeR**

A rare Wemyss ware medium-sized loving cup, decorated with forget-me-nots, some restoration.

If this piece were in good condition it would be worth $300 more.

c1900

$1,500-2,000 **RdeR**

A Wemyss ware square 'Honey Box' tray, decorated with honey bees and hive with grassy foreground and green edging, marked "Wemyss".

7.5in (19cm) diam

$320-380 **D**

A Wemyss ware honeycomb box, cover and stand, of square form painted with bees and hives, painted and impressed marks.

7.5in (19cm) wide

$700-1,000 **L&T**

A Wemyss ware quaich, decorated with yellow irises, retailed by Thomas Goode.

10.75in (27.5cm) diam

$400-600 **RdeR**

A Wemyss ware 'Jazzy' ovoid vase, with frilled rim, painted in colors, painted marks "No. 213".

5in (13cm) high

$150-200 **L&T**

A large Wemyss ware goblet vase, the tapered body painted with water lilies on a blue ground, the whole raised on a tapered stem support, impressed mark, printed Thomas Goode mark.

11.75in (29.5cm) high

$400-600 **L&T**

A small Wemyss ware plate, pheasant decoration, retailed by Thomas Goode.

c1900 *5in (12.5cm) diam*

$350-400 **RdeR**

A Wemyss ware preserve jar and cover, decorated with plums, impressed "R. H. & S." mark.

6.75in (17cm) high

$250-300 **L&T**

A Wemyss ware comb tray, painted with plums, "R. H. & S." mark.

c1900 *10in (25.5cm) wide*

$400-600 **RdeR**

A rare Wemyss ware pomade pot, decorated with plums, impressed mark.

c1900 *4in (10cm) diam*

$500-800 **RdeR**

No Rose without a thorn.

A Wemyss ware plaque, painted with a single rose.

c1920 *6in (15cm) wide*

$350-400 **RdeR**

A rare Wemyss ware muffin dish, painted with roses, restored.

c1900 *9in (23cm) diam*

$400-600 **RdeR**

A tall Wemyss ware candlestick, painted with roses.

c1900 *12in (30.5cm) high*

$300-500 **RdeR**

A Wemyss ware cat, painted with roses with glass eyes.

12in (30.5cm) high

$3,000-5,000 **RdeR**

"Nekola Pinxt."

A 1930s small Wemyss ware pig money box, painted with roses, signed "Nekola Pinxt".

6in (15cm) long

$300-500 **RdeR**

CERAMICS

CERAMICS - Bennington Pottery

Pottery has been made in Bennington, Vermont, since 1785 when Captain John Norton began to produce utilitarian earthenware and stoneware.

In 1849 Christopher Fenton patented a flint enamel glaze of mottled yellow, orange, blue and brown- an elaboration on the existing plainer 'Rockingham' mottled brown glaze. As well as producing every day household ware the factory also manufactured decorative ornaments such as Toby jugs caricaturing notable figures of the day and stylised animals. From 1847 the firm was known as The United States Pottery Company.

Lit R.C.Barret, "Bennington Pottery and Porcelain", 1958.

A rare Bennington flint-enamel four quart book flask, impressed "Bennington Battle" on the spine.

11in (28cm) high

$3,000-4,000   **NA**

A Bennington flint-enamel two quart book flask, impressed "Bennington Battle" on the spine.

8in (20.5cm) high

$1,000-1,500   **NA**

A Bennington flint-enamel one pint book flask, impressed "Bennington Battle" on the spine.

5.5in (14cm) high

$800-1,200   **NA**

A Bennington flint-enamel two-quart book flask, impressed "Spirits for Bennington" on the spine, Barret 411B.

8in (20.5cm) high

$1,200-1,800   **NA**

A rare Bennington flint-enamel two quart book flask, impressed "Kossuth" on the spine, Barret 411B.

Louis Kossuth (1802-1894) was actively involved in the Revolution of 1848 championing Hungary's independence from Austria. He toured the United States, 1851-52.

7.75in (20cm) high

$1,800-2,200   **NA**

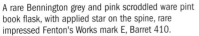

A rare Bennington grey and pink scroddled ware pint book flask, with applied star on the spine, rare impressed Fenton's Works mark E, Barret 410.

'Scroddled' is a term used to describe pottery made from an amalgam of different colored clay scraps.

5.75in (14.5cm) high

$5,000-7,000   **NA**

A rare Bennington flint-enamel book flask with elongated neck, impressed "Psalms" and "L.F. & Co. Patent" on the spine, Barret 411.

According to George Abraham and Gilbert May the "L. F. & Co" impressed mark for the Bennington firm of Luman, Fenton and Company is extremely rare and possibly unique.

6.25in (16cm) high

$3,000-4,000   **NA**

Left: Two Bennington flint-enamel book flasks, each impressed "Departed Spirits" on the spine, the first two quarts, the second one pint.

Tallest 8in (20.5cm) high

$1,500-2,000   **NA**

Right: Another set of two book flasks, of similar form but different color glazes.

Tallest 8in (20.5cm) high

$600-900   **NA**

A Bennington flint-enamel mottled olive-green and brown single candlestick, of cylindrical form surrounded by molded rings, unmarked.

6.5in (16.5cm) high

$700-1,000   **NA**

A Bennington flint-enamel coachman bottle, molded with a mustache, wearing tassels and holding a mug, clear impressed "1849 mark A", Barret C.

11in (28cm) high

$320-380   **NA**

A Bennington flint-enamel coachman barrel bottle, wearing tassels and holding a mug, clear impressed "1849 mark A", Barret G.

11in (28cm) high

$1,800-2,200   **NA**

A Bennington flint-enamel coachman bottle, molded with a mustache, wearing tassels and holding a mug, impressed "1849 mark A", Barret 421.

10.75in (27.5cm) high

$1,200-1,800   **NA**

A Bennington flint-enamel sitting toby pitcher, with grapevine handle, impressed "1849 mark A", Barret 416 E.

6.75in (17cm) high

$400-600   **NA**

A Bennington flint-enamel sitting toby pitcher, with grapevine handle, impressed "1849 mark A", Barret 416 E.

6.75in (17cm) high

$700-1,000   **NA**

A Bennington flint-enamel sitting toby pitcher with grapevine handle, impressed "1849 mark A", Barret 416 E.

6.75in (17cm) high

$400-600   **NA**

A rare Bennington green flint-enamel toby snuff jar and cover, faint impressed "1849 mark A", Barret 417C.

4.25in (11cm) high

$2,500-3,000   **NA**

A Bennington flint-enamel toby snuff jar and cover, impressed "1849 mark A", Barret 417E.

4.25in (11cm) high

$500-700   **NA**

A Bennington flint-enamel toby snuff jar and cover, impressed "1849 mark A", Barret 417B.

4.25in (11cm) high

$700-1,000   **NA**

A Bennington Rockingham toby snuff jar and cover, impressed "1849 mark A", Barret 417.

4.25in (11cm) high

$400-600   NA

A rare Bennington flint-enamel standing lion, facing right, modeled with one paw raised on a ball, with coleslaw mane and lowered tongue, Barret 377.

7.5in (19cm) high

$10,000-15,000   NA

A rare Bennington flint-enamel standing lion, facing right, modeled with one paw raised on a ball and set on a base, with coleslaw mane and lowered tongue, Barret 376.

11in (28cm) high

$15,000-20,000   NA

A rare Bennington flint-enamel standing lion, facing left, modeled with one paw raised on a ball and set on a base, with coleslaw mane and lowered tongue, on a brown and blue base, Barret 377.

10in (25.5cm) high

$15,000-20,000   NA

A matched pair of Bennington parian poodles, each carrying a basket and with a top-knot, one with mustache, Barret 371 and 372.

c1850-58 Tallest 9.25in (23.5cm) high

$4,000-6,000   NA

A late 19thC Bennington cow creamer.

c1870   7in (18cm) long

$200-250   BCAC

A rare Bennington flint-enamel spill vase, in the form of a recumbent deer, facing left, Barret 366.

8.5in (21.5cm) high

$4,000-6,000   NA

A Bennington flint-enamel alternate rib pattern pitcher and washbowl set, each rim edge molded with scrolls, each impressed with "1849 mark A", Barret 169.

Pitcher 25in (36cm) high

$2,200-2,800   NA

A rare Bennington scroddled ware pitcher and washbowl set, the pitcher molded in the diamond pattern, the bowl with twelve-sided edge, the pitcher impressed with "U.S.P. oval mark H" for the United States Pottery Company, Barret 170.

Pitcher 11.5in (29cm) high

$1,500-2,000   NA

Chalkware

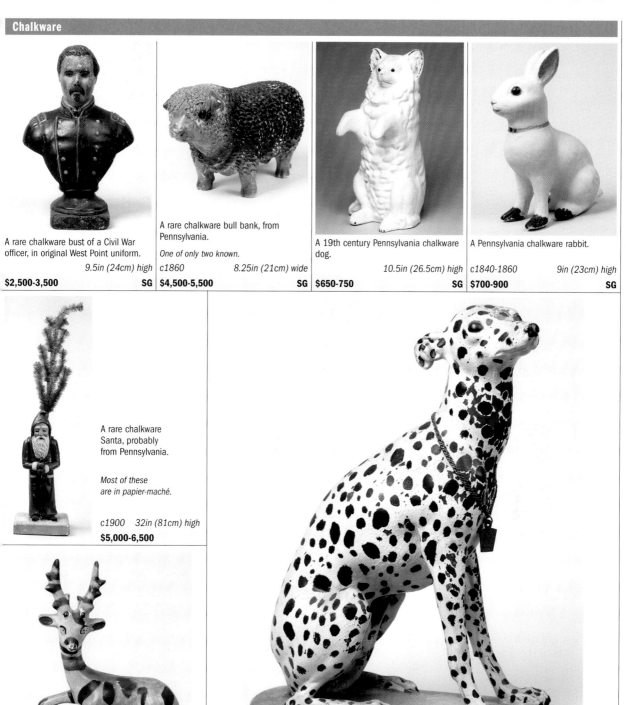

A rare chalkware bust of a Civil War officer, in original West Point uniform.

9.5in (24cm) high

$2,500-3,500　　**SG**

A rare chalkware bull bank, from Pennsylvania.

One of only two known.

c1860　　*8.25in (21cm) wide*

$4,500-5,500　　**SG**

A 19th century Pennsylvania chalkware dog.

10.5in (26.5cm) high

$650-750　　**SG**

A Pennsylvania chalkware rabbit.

c1840-1860　　*9in (23cm) high*

$700-900　　**SG**

A rare chalkware Santa, probably from Pennsylvania.

Most of these are in papier-maché.

c1900　　*32in (81cm) high*

$5,000-6,500

A Pennsylvania chalkware deer, with fine painted decoration .

c1820-1840　　*10in (25.5cm) high*

$1,200-1,800　　**SG**

A rare chalkware dalmation, possibly unique in form and size, origin unknown.

c1850　　*18in (46cm) high*

$7,500-9,500　　**SG**

FOLK ART

Redware

The majority of North American glazed red earthenware was made before 1840 by craftsmen who had brought their skills with them from Northern Europe. After 1840 finer, denser, clays were found in Pennsylvania and production in the state moved from redware to stoneware. However, the earlier redware was produced in greater quantities and with more varied decoration. With the limited range of methods of production, the emphasis was in the decoration, trailed and combed slip and sgraffito. Potters did other seasonal agricultural jobs and made pots with the help of their families or neighbors. They supplied the local community and rarely sold to people outside it.

A rare Moravian redware bowl, attributed to the workshop of Auston Christ, Salem, North Carolina, with typical cream and black 'seed pod' clusters inside cream and green bands on an orange slip base, hairline, flake.

Provenance: William Wiltshire. For information on Salem potters see "The Moravian Potters in North Carolina" by Bivins

c1800

$8,000-10,000

5in (12.5cm) diam

Pook

An early redware bowl.

10in (25.5cm) diam

$100-150   **BCAC**

A 19thC redware slip-decorated bowl.

8.25in (21cm) wide

$180-220   **BCAC**

A mid-19thC Pennsylvania redware loaf dish, with overall yellow dot and dash slip decoration, chips.

14in (35.5cm) long

$2,000-2,500   **Pook**

A large early 19thC Pennsylvania redware loaf dish, with four-line and dot slip decoration, chips.

18.25in (46.5cm) long

$2,200-2,800   **Pook**

A Canadian Cap Rouge redware bowl, from the outskirts of Quebec City, with some restoration.

c1820   *16.25in (41cm) wide*

$350-450   **BP**

An American redware plate, with slip decoration.

c1880   *11.5in (29cm) diam*

$800-1,200   **BCAC**

An American redware crock, with cream slip glaze.

c1880   *7.5in (19cm) high*

$80-120   **BCAC**

A two-handled Albany slip glazed redware jar, the base impressed and painted with '16-29', chips to base, some roughness to glaze.

c1865   *16.5in (cm) high*

$120-180   **FRE**

A redware 'football' flask.

c1880   *4in (10cm) wide*

$80-120   **BCAC**

A rare late 19thC redware bird rattle, possibly Shenandoah Valley, Virginia, with overall mottled green and brown glazed bird resting on an orange glazed oval plinth with inscribed circles.

3in (7.5cm) high

$2,500-3,000   **Pook**

A Pennsylvania redware footed fat lamp, with an open reservoir, strap handle and dished circular base.

c1800	3.5in (9cm) high
$1,000-1,500	**Pook**

A rare Pennsylvania redware bird whistle, in the form of a chicken, with overall mottled orange glazing.

c1800	3in (7.5cm) high
$500-700	**Pook**

A late 18thC American redware muffin pan, with scalloped and serpentine rim, for 14 muffins.

19in (48cm) wide

$1,500-2,000 **BP**

An early 19thC Pennsylvania redware whistle, in the form of a whale with two yellow dots on overall orange glazing.

	4.5in (11.5cm) long
$500-700	**Pook**

A pair of Pennsylvania redware figures, one of a cobbler seated with his tools and the other of his wife reading the Bible, both resting on plinths, minor chips.

c1880	8.25in (21cm) high
$5,000-7,000	**Pook**

An extremely rare 19thC American redware bank, in the form of a beetle with wings, eight legs and protruding eyes and snout, with overall black manganese splash decoration on an orange glazed body resting on a round plinth, found in Shepardstown, West Virginia.

This bank is probably a unique form of folk art sculpture.

6.5in (16.5cm) wide

$8,000-12,000 **Pook**

A late 19thC redware wall pocket, Strasburg, Virginia, attributed to the workshop of S. Bell & Son, with overall cream, brown and green glazing.

6.25in (16cm) high

$7,000-9,000 **Pook**

Slipware

A late 18thC Moravian redware rundlet, possibly Salem, North Carolina, of typical barrel form, with an orange glazed body decorated with incised circles and yellow and black flowers, with outward radiating black slip lines, missing spout rim.

	7.75in (20cm) high
$1,200-1,800	**Pook**

A rare Asa Smith Pottery, Norwalk CT slip-decorated plate, bearing the name "Elennor".

c1820	11in (28cm) diam
$7,500-8,500	**SG**

A Matawan Pottery, New Jersey slip-decorated plate, with bird decoration and inscribed "snipe".

This is one of the very few known examples of slipware with bird motif decoration.

c1830-1840	
$7,500-8,500	**SG**

A slipware plate, yellow on red iron oxide glaze, pie crust edge.

c1810	9.75in (24.5cm) diam
$1,500-2,000	**RAA**

CERAMICS

A Philadelphia slip-decorated charger, with six slip-trailed criss-cross lines and scattered drops of green.

The use of green slip is rare in Pennsylvania because it was created using copper oxide glaze which was expensive and therefore used sparingly.

c1790   13.5in diam

$7,500-9,500   **SG**

An Asa Smith Pottery, Norwalk, CT slip-decorated plate, bearing the name "Lafayette".

c1820   11.25in (28.5cm) wide

$7,500-8,500   **SG**

An Asa Smith Pottery, Norwalk, CT slip-decorated plate, bearing the name "Emily".

$5,200-6,200   **SG**

A slip-decorated pie plate, with sgraffito slip decoration, possibly by Jacob Mumbauer, Bucks County, Pennsylvania.

c1820   11.75in (30cm) diam

$7,500-8,500   **SG**

A slip-decorated loaf dish, with elaborate decoration, probably from New York State.

c1820-30

$5,500-6,500   **SG**

A Singer Pottery, Bucks County, Pennsylvania slip-decorated plate, for "Elli" or "Ehli".

c1880   12.5in (31.5cm) diam

$4,500-5,000   **SG**

Spatterware

The term refers to American and English pottery made between 1800-1850 and decorated with spattered or sponged patterns. It was developed in the late 18thC by Josiah Wedgwood in Burslem, Staffordshire, England. Between 1800-1820 the Wedgwood factory produced spatterware for the American market and it became its most popular export. The technique was copied by American potteries and some continue to make imitation spatterware today.

The technique involves spattering the surface of the china either with hundreds of small hand-painted dots or with the application of glazes with a sponge through a stencil. The decoration could be supplemented with hand painted animals, houses and other Folk art illustrations. The most collectible spatterware dates from c1850 and collectors look for the rarer patterns such as Christmas balls and unusual color mixes.

A rare vibrant five-color, red, green, blue, black and yellow spatter pitcher and bowl.

Pitcher 13in (33cm) high

$25,000-30,000   **Pook**

A red spatter coffee pot, with blue, green and red peafowl.

8.5in (21.5cm) high

$1,500-2,000   **Pook**

A blue spatter teapot, with double-sided blue, yellow and red peafowl.

5.5in (14cm) high

$1,500-2,000   **Pook**

A yellow spatter thistle cup and saucer.

$1,000-1,500   **Pook**

A fine and rare yellow, blue, red and green rainbow swirl pattern cup and saucer.

$20,000-25,000   **Pook**

A red spatter cup and saucer, with rare red and blue fort pattern.

$3,500-4,500   **Pook**

A red spatter cup and saucer, with yellow, blue, red and green peafowl on a bar.

$1,500-2,000   **Pook**

An unusual reddish purple spatter cup and saucer, with red thistle decoration.

$600-900   **Pook**

A miniature blue spatter cup and saucer, with fort pattern.

$300-400   **Pook**

A green drape spatter miniature cup and saucer, with red and yellow Christmas ball decoration.

$7,000-9,000   **Pook**

A red and blue rainbow spatter cup and saucer, with dahlia.

$1,200-1,800   **Pook**

A rare miniature red, blue, green and yellow rainbow spatter cup and saucer, in drape pattern.

$15,000-18,000   **Pook**

A rare four-color, purple, red, blue and green rainbow plaid cup and saucer.

$5,000-7,000   **Pook**

A red and yellow rainbow spatter cup and saucer, with red thistle.

$1,800-2,200   **Pook**

A vibrant purple and black rainbow octagonal platter.

This is a record price for an octagonal platter.

18in (45.5cm) long

$15,000-18,000   **Pook**

A red and green rainbow plate, with circular central design and radiating border.

9.5in (24cm) diam

$3,000-4,000   **Pook**

A blue and red rainbow spatter bull's-eye plate.

8.25in (21cm) diam

$7,000-9,000   **Pook**

A purple and black rainbow spatter bull's-eye toddy plate.

5in (12.5cm) diam

$2,500-3,000   **Pook**

CERAMICS

A red spatter plate, with blue, yellow and green peafowl.

9.25in (23.5cm) diam

$500-700 **Pook**

A green spatter plate, with purple, green and red peafowl.

8.25in (21cm) diam

$800-1,200 **Pook**

A red spatter plate, with green, red and blue peafowl.

8.5in (21.5cm) diam

$1,200-1,800 **Pook**

An unusual green, brown, yellow and red rainbow swirl plate.

This is a world record price for a single spatter plate.

8.25in (21cm) diam

$20,000-25,000 **Pook**

A red spatter plate, with red schoolhouse, brown and green spatter lawn and tree.

10.25in (26cm) diam

$3,000-4,000 **Pook**

A blue spatter paneled plate, with fort pattern.

8.75in (22.5cm) diam

$800-1,200 **Pook**

A red spatter plate, with blue schoolhouse, brown lawn and green tree.

8in (20cm) diam

$1,800-2,200 **Pook**

A red spatter shallow bowl, with blue, red and green star.

8.5in (21.5cm) diam

$1,800-2,200 **Pook**

A blue spatter paneled plate, with red, blue and green star.

9.25in (23.5cm) diam

$1,000-1,500 **Pook**

A red and blue rainbow plate, with central criss-cross design.

9.75in (25cm) diam

$2,000-2,500 **Pook**

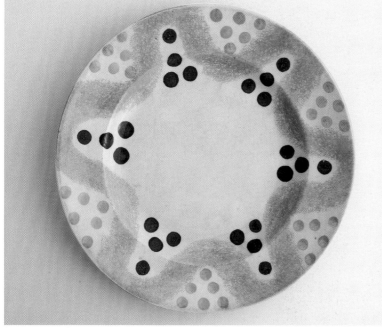

A green spatter plate, with red and yellow Christmas balls.

The 'Christmas Balls' pattern is very popular with collectors and prices have risen substantially over the last 15 years. In 1990 a similar plate sold for $880.

9.5in (24cm) diam

$8,000-10,000 **Pook**

A yellow spatter paneled plate, with red thistle.

9.75in (25cm) diam

$4,500-5,500 **Pook**

A blue spatter paneled toddy plate, with dahlia.

6.25in (16cm) diam

$500-700 **Pook**

A green and red spatter clover plate.

9.5in (24cm) diam

$5,500-7,000 **Pook**

A red spatter paneled plate, with purple primrose.

9.25in (23.5cm) diam

$1,800-2,200 **Pook**

A blue sponge spatter paneled plate, with plum decoration.

9.25in (23.5cm) diam

$400-500 **Pook**

A blue spatter plate, with four small brown acorns and green leaves.

8.25in (21cm) diam

$4,500-5,500 **Pook**

A blue and red rainbow spatter drape plate, with sprig.

8.25in (21cm) diam

$6,000-7,000 **Pook**

CERAMICS

Stoneware

A stoneware wine cooler.

c1880   10in (25.5cm) diam

$200-300   **BCAC**

A stoneware crock, with blue decoration.

c1880   8in (20cm) diam

$80-120   **BCAC**

A stoneware butter crock.

c1880   9in (23cm) diam

$150-200   **BCAC**

A stoneware crock, with stenciled decoration.

`   10in (25.5cm) high

$280-320   **BCAC**

A Brandy & Ryan, Ellenville NY stoneware crock, with bird decoration.

c1870   11.5in (29cm) diam

$650-750   **BCAC**

An early 19thC ovoid stoneware crock, with blue decoration.

11in (28cm) high

$180-220   **BCAC**

A late 19thC M & T. Miller, Newport, PA four gallon stoneware crock, impressed maker's mark, with a large cobalt flower.

12.75in (32.5cm) high

$1,200-1,800   **Pook**

A mid-19thC Hamilton & Jones, Greensboro Greene Co., PA five gallon stoneware crock, stenciled maker's mark, with free-hand cobalt floral and leaf decoration, hairline.

16.5in (42cm) high

$1,000-1,500   **Pook**

A Gillespie and Mace, St. Johns, C.E Quebec stoneware crock, impressed maker's mark, buff-glaze with hand-painted cobalt floral decoration.

c1857   10.25in (26cm) high

$800-1,200   RTC

An A. K. Ballard, Burlington, Vermont stoneware crock, impressed maker's mark, buff glaze with cobalt grape and vine decoration.

c1855   16.75in (42.5cm) high

$600-800   RTC

A C. W. Underwood, Fort Edward N.Y four-gallon stoneware crock, impressed maker's mark, decorated with a leafy spray, firing imperfections.

c1865   16in (40.5cm) high

$200-250   FRE

A 19thC stoneware jar, with multiple bands of incised 'roulette' decoration.

10in (25.5cm) high

$120-180   BCAC

An E.L. Farrat, Iberville, Quebec stoneware crock, impressed maker's mark, buff glaze with hand-painted cobalt floral decoration.

c1855   10.25in (26cm) high

$180-220   RTC

An E.F. and G.W. Farrat, St Johns and Montreal stoneware crock, impressed maker's mark, buff-glazed with hand-painted cobalt floral decoration.

c1857   11.25in (29cm) high

$350-450   RTC

A Fairy Milton, S J Baker, joined set of four 1/4 gallon stoneware bottles, marked "Faith", "Hope", "Glory" and "Comfort".

c1860   8.5in (21.5cm) high

$2,200-2,800   BCAC

A stoneware mug with blue slip decoration.

c1880   4.5in (11.5cm) high

$70-100   **BCAC**

An E. & L.P. Norton, Bennington VT stoneware jug, with blue slip decoration.

c1870   11in (28cm) high

$250-350   **BCAC**

A stoneware jug, with blue slip decoration.

c1880   9in (23cm) high

$100-150   **BCAC**

A stoneware jug-shaped money bank, or jug bank, with blue decoration.

c1920   4.5in (11.5cm) high

$80-120   **BCAC**

A stoneware jug bank.

c1900   4.25in (11cm) high

$200-300   **BCAC**

A 19thC New York stoneware jug, with cobalt floral decoration, inscribed "White Utica".

17in (43cm) high

$600-800   **Pook**

A Ballard, Cornwall, C. W Ontario stoneware jug, impressed maker's mark, buff-glazed with hand-painted cobalt floral decoration.

14.5in (37cm) high

$600-800   **RTC**

An Orrin L. Ballard, St. Johns C.E Quebec stoneware jug, impressed maker's mark, buff glaze and hand-painted cobalt floral decoration.

c1858   12.25in (31cm) high

$200-300   **RTC**

An E.L. Farrar, St Johns C.E, Quebec stoneware jug, impressed maker's mark, buff glaze with cobalt floral decoration.

c1855   14.5in (37cm) high

$250-350   **RTC**

An E. L. and M. Farrar, St Johns C.E stoneware jug, impressed maker's mark, buff glaze with hand-painted cobalt bud decoration.

c1855   14.75in (37.5cm) high

$120-180   **RTC**

A W. E. Welding, Bradford, Ontario brown-glazed earthenware covered pot, impressed maker's mark, and an H. Schuler, Paris, Ontario ovoid fruit jar.

Jar 10.75in (27cm) high

$80-120 each　　　　　　　　　　**RTC**

Two 19thC St Johns Quebec stoneware jugs, impressed, with grey-brown glaze and hand-painted cobalt floral decoration.

Tallest 11.25in (29cm) high

$180-220 each

　　　　　　　　　　　　　　　RTC

A 19thC White-Foley Pottery, Saint John stoneware jug, and another similar but lacking swag band.

Tallest 8.25in (21cm) high

$120-180 each　　　　　　　**RTC**

An early 19thC Farrar's Pottery, Fairfax, Vermont stoneware jug, impressed maker's mark, buff-glazed with hand-painted cobalt floral decoration.

15in (38cm) high

$280-320　　　　　　**RTC**

A mid-19thC Remmey-type stoneware pitcher, with blue floral and leaf decoration.

7in (18cm) high

$700-1,000　　　　**Pook**

A spongeware pitcher, possibly from Ohio, Pennsylvania or New England, unusual blue on white circular decoration.

c1850　　　　　9in (23cm) high

$400-500　　　　　　**SG**

A stoneware salt, with stenciled decoration.

c1880　　　　6in (15cm) diam

$50-70　　　　　　**BCAC**

An early 20thC American yellow ware bowl, with blue banded decoration.

5.25in (13.5cm) diam

$50-70　　　　　　**BCAC**

Three Rockingham-glazed food moulds, in mottled brown, comprising a circular swirl cake mould, a circular fluted cake mould and an oval pudding mould impressed with a wheat sheaf.

largest 7.75in (19.5cm) diam

$120-180 each NA

A Canadian pottery frog dish, painted by Carl Pearson, aged 10 with help from Emily Carr.
See Pearson, Carol 'Emily Carr As I Knew Her'. Toronto: Clarke, Irwin & Company Limited, 1954.

c1918 2.25in (9cm) wide

$1,500-2,000 BP

A mid-18thC Bucks County, Pennsylvania pottery crock, with bird and flower decoration, lid missing.

c1750 8in (20cm) high

$7,500-9,500 SG

A late 18thC Bucks County, Pennsylvania pottery crock, with Pennsylvania tulip decoration.

c1790 7in (17.5cm) diam

$15,000-18,000 S(

A rare Pennsylvania piggy bank, with unusual manganese slip decoration.
c1820-1830 9.5in (24cm) wide
$10,000-12,000 SG

A pair of flint-enamel candlesticks, of slightly flared and waisted form raised on a domed base, unmarked.

8.5in (21.5cm) high

$800-1,200 NA

A Lay Pottery cat, probably North Carolina or Georgia, earthenware with a clear slick glaze.

c1850-1875 9.5in (24cm) wide

$2,000-2,500 S(

A Jacob Mediger, Limerick, Pennsylvania large flower pot, with sgraffito decorated eagle and brown and clear slip glaze.

This is one of two known examples in this form. Jacob Mediger was one of the last great Pennsylvania potters and his pottery followed in the tradition of his father and grandfather who were also potters.

c1930 12in (30.5cm) high

$5,000-7,000 SG

A Canadian James Black, F***** Pottery, Quebec pottery tobacco jar, with applied relief foliage and pipes.
c1880-1908 8.75in (22cm) high
$550-650 BP

A Samuel Bell & Son, Strasberg, Virginia three-color multiglaze pitcher, stamped marks .

7.25in (18.5cm) high

$4,500-5,500 S(

A group of five pottery fruit banks, including two pears, one orange, one apple, one peach, with various color-glazed surfaces.

$250-450 each

SG

A small three-color multiglaze milk pitcher, attributed to Jacob Eberly of Strasburg, Virginia.

c1880   6.5in (16.5cm) high

$2,500-3,500

SG

A pottery watering can, with exceptional multi-glaze and slip decoration, possibly from Bucks County Pennsylvania, inscribed "JW 1843".

10in (25.5cm) high

$2,500-3,500

SG

A John Bell Pottery, Waynesboro, Pennsylvania rare graduated set of green-glazed flower pots.

c1860   Largest 8.25in (21cm) diam

$10,000-11,000

SG

$80-100 each

NA

Five Rockingham-glazed pitchers, of flattened form, the first molded on each side with a spray of tulips and a star beneath the spout, the second probably Ohio, applied with a moulded handle continuing to leafy vines, the remaining three of plain form.

Tallest 9.5in (25cm) high

NA

A flint-enamel coffee pot and cover, of paneled baluster form, applied with a shaped angular handle, the domed cover with conical finial, glazed overall in mottled brown and cream with each raised rib heightened in rich orange to deep brown, unmarked.

10in (25.5cm) high

$3,000-4,000

NA

CERAMICS

Canadian Earthenware

A Portneuf floral pattern pitcher.

8.25in (21cm) high

$700-1,000 **WAD**

A Stewiacke, Nova Scotia pitcher and basin, inscribed "J.W. Jennex 1886".

$400-600 **WAD**

An Ontario earthenware jug, Waterloo County, pear-shaped jug with dark brown spatter decoration, red body.

c1860 *8.25in (21cm) high*

$2,000-3,000 **RTC**

A late19thC Western Ontario earthenware jug, pear shaped with brown spatter, red-brown body.

9.25in (23.5cm) high

$1,500-2,000 **RTC**

A late 19thC Ontario earthenware jug, ovoid with dark brown spatter, red-brown body.

9.25in (23.5cm) high

$1,000-1,500 **RTC**

A mid-19thC Canadian earthenware fruit jar, possibly Waterloo County, ovoid jar with mottled reddish brown and dark brown glazes, red body.

8in (20.5cm) high

$120-180 **RTC**

A 19thC Quebec earthenware jug, wide-mouthed baluster jug with streaky brown glazes, red body.

8.5in (21.5cm) high

$220-280 **RTC**

A Canadian yellow ware jug, possibly Cap Rouge, Quebec, pear-shaped jug with branch handle, relief-moulded beaver on log and maple leaf design, vertically ribbed body.

c1862 *9in (23cm) high*

$1,200-1,800 **RTC**

Three Canadian ironstone jugs, St. Johns Stone Chinaware Co., St. Johns, Quebec, printed maker's mark, each of tapered cylindrical with branch handle and relief-moulded fern design, comprising one large and one medium white jug and one medium blue jug.

c1880 *Largest 7.75in (19.5cm) high*

$700-1,000 each **RTC**

A late 19thC Simon Thomas, Humberstone, North York earthenware vase, mottled green and yellow glazes, buff body.

9.75in (25cm) high

$700-1,000   RTC

A Dion Pottery, L'Ancienne-Lorette, Quebec tobacco jar, cylindrical, with relief-molded dancers and musicians, glazed brown, with red body, lacks lid and stand.

c1880-1890   *5.25in (13cm) high*

$80-120   RTC

A James Black, Farrar Pottery, Quebec tobacco jar, barrel-shaped earthenware jar with applied relief foliage and pipes, lid with cylindrical finial, glazed dark brown.

c1880-1908   *8.5in (21.5cm) high*

$350-400   RTC

A 19thC Canadian earthenware bowl, with exterior glazed reddish brown, interior with buff slip and brown dendritic decoration.

14.5in (37cm) diam

$500-700   RTC

A 19thC Quebec earthenware bowl, oblong with everted rim, with dark brown spatter glazes, red body.

11.75in (29.5cm) wide

$320-380   RTC

A St Johns Stone Chinaware Co. ironstone hotelware slop jar, printed maker's mark, made for Thomas Connor's Windsor Hotel, Cobourg, pear-shaped with foliate scroll handles and domed cover, decorated with mint green and gilded bands, transfer hotel logo worn.

c1873-1878   *15in (38cm) high*

$1,500-2,000   RTC

A St. Johns Stone Chinaware Co. ironstone bread tray, relief-molded wheat sheaf design, ribbon lettered "Waste Not Want Not" and white sprigged floral monogram decoration.

c1880   *13in (33cm) wide*

$2,000-3,000   RTC

A George Beech, Brantford, Ontario pottery picture frame, incised mark, "Made by G. Beech April 1862", oval frame glazed red-brown, with scalloped border and oval band decoration.

8.75in (22cm) high

$3,500-4,500   RTC

A rare pair of J. Marx, Paris, Ontario pottery picture frames, incised mark "J. Marx, Paris, 1863 Potter", each oval, glazed mottled blue-green, with scalloped border and oval band decoration.

1863   *11.25in (28.5cm) high*

$15,000-20,000   **RTC**

An Anthony Smith, Paris, Ontario terracotta picture frame, impressed and incised maker's mark, oval frame with scrolling edge and overall impressed eight-point star decoration.

1867   *13in (33cm) high*

$1,500-2,000   **RTC**

An Ontario redware picture frame, in a red and black spattered glaze, maker's mark "Jacob Weber" and dated "December 15th, 1871".

1871

$3,000-4,000   **WAD**

A pair of 19thC Ontario earthenware spitoons, attributed to Waterloo County, Ontario, each cylindrical, with brown and yellow spattered glazes.

Largest 5.25in (13.5cm) diam

$400-600 (pair)   **RTC**

A 19thC Quebec earthenware flower pot, attributed to Dion pottery, L'Ancienne-Lorette, Quebec, with ruffled rim and base, dark brown streaky glaze, red body.

7.75in (20cm) diam

$280-320   **RTC**

A pottery flower pot, with brown slip spatter on beige, possibly made by Weber of Egmondville, Ontario.

c1873-1897   *6in (15cm) high*

$220-280   **BP**

A late 19thC James W. Foley and Co., St Johns earthenware covered pot, impressed maker's mark and a late 19thC flower pot, possibly Maritimes.

Flower pot 6.5in (16.5cm) high

$80-120 each   **RTC**

Three various Portneuf bowls, each with floral band and sprig decoration.

Portneuf pottery was produced in Scotland for the Canadian market in the second half of the 19thC.

$150-250 each   **WAD**

Three various Portneuf bowls, with bird decoration.

Largest 3.75in (9.5cm) high

$150-250 each   **WAD**

A mid-19thC James Bailey, Bowmanville, Ontario pottery spaniel figurine, impressed maker's mark, glazed terracotta seated spaniel on oval base, minor restoration.

6.75in (17cm) high

$1,800-2,200   **RTC**

A J. and W.O. Brown and Co., Toronto, Ontario pottery spaniel penny bank, patent date 1859, impressed maker's mark, with mottled brown glazes.

13.75in (35cm) high

$3,000-4,000   **RTC**

A D. Orth, Campden, Ontario pottery spaniel, incised maker's mark, with mottled brown, orange and green glazes, incised decoration.

c1892   *9.25in (23.5cm) high*

$2,200-2,800   **RTC**

A Canadian pottery spaniel, incised script initials probably DS, earthenware, with mottled brown, orange and green glazes, incised decoration.

c1896   *9.25in (23.5cm) high*

$800-1,200   **RTC**

A Canadian pottery spaniel, signature indistinct, earthenware with mottled brown and orange glazes, incised decoration.

c1897   *9.5in (24cm) high*

$1,000-1,500   **RTC**

A late 19thC Canadian pottery spaniel, earthenware with mottled brown glaze.

4.5in (11.5cm) high

$800-1,200   **RTC**

Fraktur

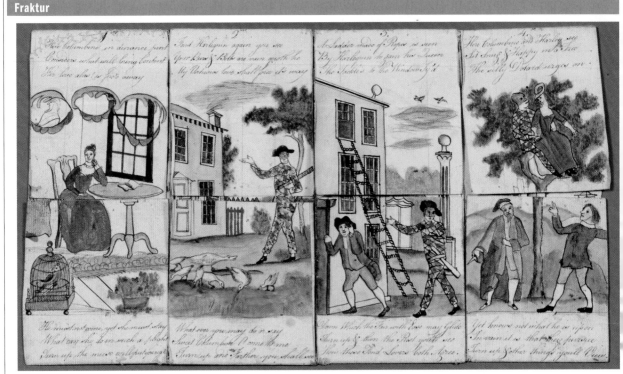

A late 18thC Metamorphosis, probably English, 'The Amorous Adventures of Columbine and Harlequin', described and illustrated in four panels, watercolor and ink on paper, some discoloration, old mends.

A Metamorphosis is an item designed to change in form or function.

12.5in (32cm) wide

$4,000-6,000 **FRE**

Johann Henrich Otto, attributed (Southeastern, Pennsylvania, active 1762-1797), watercolor and ink on paper fraktur, dated, Cumberland County, with central cartouche enclosing script surrounded by stylized floral trees arising from hearts, stars, winged head in blue, red, green and brown, some loss.

1793 *15in (38cm) wide*
$1,800-2,200 **Pook**

A printed fraktur, 'Geberts und Taufschein' or birth and christening certificate, by J. Stover, Lebanon Co., Pennsylvania, dated, the heart-shaped reserve enclosed by floral vines, hand-colored in shades of ochre and pumpkin, framed, some discoloration and staining.

1797 *15in (38cm) wide*
$800-1,200 **FRE**

Blowsy Angel Artist, (Southeastern, Pennsylvania, active 1780-1811), watercolor and ink on paper birth certificate with typical central round cartouche enclosed script, surmounted by a stylized swan and flanked by floral trees, birds and flying angels, some loss at fold line.

16in (40.5cm) wide
$2,000-2,500 **Pook**

A CLOSER LOOK AT A FRAKTUR

Fraktur is a term used for a variety of illustrated texts from the Pennsylvania German families. Their roots are in the religious certificates of Germanic Europe, such as scriptural and hymnal texts. In America they were essentially secular records. 'Geburts und taufschein', or birth and baptism records, were one of the most common texts.

Fraktur' is the name given to a particular form of Gothic style lettering, or typeface, that originated in Germany in the 15thC.

Whilst floral decorations are common on fraktur, the hex signs punctuating the vine and tulip borders are stylistic motifs particular to Minian's work.

John Van Minian is one of the better known and most commercial artists and the portraits of people in profile in oval cartouches in the corners are typical of his work.

John Van Minian, (Southeastern, Pennsylvania active 1800-1842), watercolor and ink on paper fraktur birth certificate, dated, for Suzanna Seidelman, with central cartouche enclosing script, the corners with oval profile portraits with elaborate red diamond borders, all surrounded by vines, tulips, hex signs and sun faces, some edge loss.

1801   15.5in (39.5cm) high

$20,000-25,000   **Pook**

Blowsy Angel Artist, (Southeastern, Pennsylvania, active 1780-1811), watercolor and ink on paper birth certificate with central elaborate round cartouche enclosed script surrounded by flying angels, floral trees and birds.

16in (40.5cm) wide

$3,000-4,000   **Pook**

A Berks County, Pennsylvania watercolor and ink on paper geburts und taufschein, dated, Maxatanny Township, with central script enclosed by a ring of stylized flowers, flanked by stylized trees arising from stars and tulips.

1823   15in (38cm) wide

$1,000-1,500   **Pook**

A hand-coloured printed taufschein for Margaret Elizabeth Labere, printed by C. G. Peters, Harrisburg, light stained and discoloration at edges.

c1837   15.5in (32cm) wide

$250-350   **FRE**

A vivid early 19thC Pennsylvania watercolor on paper fraktur drawing, with a central yellow urn with flowering orange and green tulip flanked by lovebirds and small branches of berries, minor foxing.

9in (23cm) high

$2,500-3,000   **Pook**

A Pennsylvania watercolour and ink on paper fraktur birth certificate for Adam Boyer, Montgomery County, dated, with central cartouche enclosed script surrounded by trailing vines, tulips and birds, some loss.

1818   12in (30.5cm) wide

$1,000-1,500   **Pook**

Martin Brechall, (Southeastern, Pennsylvania, active 1783-1830), watercolor and ink on paper fraktur with typical central cartouche surrounded by red, yellow and blue hearts, tulips and stylized flowers, losses.

15.75in (40cm) wide

$1,500-2,000   **Pook**

Friederich Krebs, (Southeastern, Pennsylvania, active 1784-1812), watercolor and printed geburts und taufschein, for Joseph Kemmel, with a central heart enclosing script flanked by typical vines, flowers and hearts.

15.25in (38.5cm) wide

$400-600   **Pook**

A Pennsylvania watercolor and ink on paper vorschrift, with yellow and red script and flower tree inscribed "Salomon Weber", minor edge loss.

12in (30.5cm) wide

$1,000-1,500

Pook

A diary of Sarah Logan Fisher (1806-1891), entries for 1816 and 1824, the small-format diary in stiff period wrapper with fold-out astrological chart, the entries begin in 1816 with Sarah as a school girl at 10 years of age, a number of empty pages follow and the entries resume when she is 18 years old in September 1824, recording the visit of Lafayette to Philadelphia.

Sarah Logan Fisher was the daughter of Quaker industrialist and merchant William Logan Fisher and his first wife Mary Rodman. She grew up at the Fisher home, Wakefield.

1816-1824

5.25in (13.5cm) high

$2,500-3,000

FRE

A hand-colored printed taufschein, Lyn Township, Lehigh County, Pennsylvania, Blumer and Busch, Allentown, Pennsylvania, in a bird's-eye maple frame, some discoloration.

For a related example see Pennsylvania German Fraktur of the Free Library of Philadelphia.

1848

17in (43cm) high

$400-600

FRE

A fraktur Bookplate, Lancaster imprint containing hand-painted bookplate dated 1891, decorated with flowers and striped border, initials, "JBE".

1891

$150-200

AAC

Weathervanes

A Canadian carved and light brown painted wood weathervane, in the form of a beaver, found in Quebec City.

c1825 21.25in (54cm) long

$800-1,200 BP

A fine late 19thC Quebec hollow sheet metal beaver weathervane, with original nine faceted sphere, pole and arrow, mounted on a later wooden base.

The beaver is a national symbol for Canada, symbolising industriousness and perseverance. See Blake McKendry 'Folk Art, Primitive and Naive Art in Canada', page 229.

32.25in (82cm) high

$3,000-4,000 BP

A 19thC Nova Scotia carved and painted folk art weathervane, in the form of the silhouette of a dove.

13in (33cm) long

$1,500-2,000 BP

A cast and sheet iron rooster weathervane, made at Gilmanton Ironworks, Rochester, New Hampshire. *This was made in three sizes, this is the middle size.*

23in (58.5cm) high

$8,000-12,000 SG

A cast zinc eagle weathervane on ball and arrow, old white paint.

c1900-1920

$1,800-2,200 BCAC

An eagle and arrow weathervane, with original surface with gilt and blend of verdigris copper, attributed to Fiske & Co, New York City.

c1870

$5,500-6,500 SG

A metal eagle weather vane, stand later.

10.25in (26cm) high

$650-750 BCAC

A sheet iron weathervane, folk art design of swordfish and seahorses.

$380-420 AAC

A rare and large late 19thC horse and rider jockey weathervane, gilded copper, with zinc head, totally original surface.

c1865-75 33in (84cm) long

$28,000-32,000 SG

A 20thC copper horse and sulky weathervane, with directionals.

46in (117cm) high

$300-400 SI

A rare rabbit-shaped miniature imitation weathervane, maker unknown.

This small size of miniature weather vane is fairly uncommon, and rabbits are a rare form. Provenance: Private collection Edith Gregor Halpert.

c1890-1900

$4,000-5,000 SG

A full-bodied leaping stag painted copper weathervane, in taupe and white colors.

44.5in (113cm) overall length

$30,000-35,000 NA

An axe, made heart in hand, for the fraternal organization, original handle.

$700-1,000 BCAC

An ash and metal clam basket, Maine, branded "J. G. S." and "S.S." on handle.

From the summer home in Sullivan Maine, of Mrs John (Julia) C. Spring, a pioneer collector of Americana.

$300-500 FRE

An early 20thC squirrel shooting gallery iron figure.

10in (25.5cm) wide

$500-700 SG

An American Queen Anne rushlight and candle holder, hand-forged iron, tri-legged, penny feet.

c1740 *12in (30.5cm) high*

$2,500-3,000 RAA

A mid-19thC hog scraper candlestick, sheet iron, complete with hook and lift.

c1855 *5.25in (13.5cm) high*

$150-200 RAA

A brass whale oil lamp.

c1880 *8.5in (21.5cm) high*

$220-280 BCAC

A Canadian automobile metal plaque, for the National Parks Board of Saskatchewan.

c1935 *4.75in (12cm) wide*

$50-70 BP

A George Washington cast-iron polychrome painted wall plaque, the profile portrait within a frame with red, white and blue ribbons, crossed laurel leaves below.

39in (99cm) high

$4,000-6,000 NA

A late 19thC bronze architectural element, representing the Seal of the City of New York, with spread winged eagle (symbol of the state of New York), above a sailor (representing early settlement) and an Indian (representing Native Americans), flanking a crest with a beaver (symbol of Dutch East India Co.), and windmill, barrel and flower above the date "1664", and banner inscribed "SIGILLUM. CIVITATIS.NOVI.EBORACI".

46in (117cm) high

$7,000-9,000 Pook

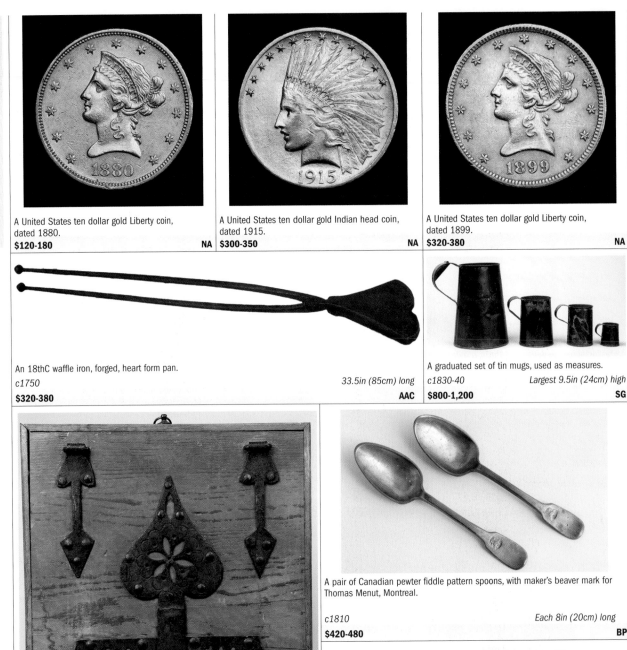

A United States ten dollar gold Liberty coin, dated 1880.

$120-180 NA

A United States ten dollar gold Indian head coin, dated 1915.

$300-350 NA

A United States ten dollar gold Liberty coin, dated 1899.

$320-380 NA

An 18thC waffle iron, forged, heart form pan.

c1750   *33.5in (85cm) long*

$320-380 AAC

A graduated set of tin mugs, used as measures.

c1830-40   *Largest 9.5in (24cm) high*

$800-1,200 SG

A pair of Canadian pewter fiddle pattern spoons, with maker's beaver mark for Thomas Menut, Montreal.

c1810   *Each 8in (20cm) long*

$420-480 BP

An early 19thC iron hasp, made for a Conestoga wagon tool box, decorated with heart and pinwheel motifs, one of the largest known of this type.

$4,000-5,000 SG

An early 19thC Pennsylvania punched tin coffee pot, with decoration of potted tulip flanked by birds, stars and trailing vines.

11.5in (29cm) high

$2,000-2,500 Pook

A pewter coffee pot, Ashbil Griswold, Meriden, Connecticut, the turned bulbous body on a low foot.

1840

10.5 in (27cm) high

$400-600   FRE

A rare 19thC painted tôleware pitcher, with original paint.

6.5in (16.5cm) high

$350-400   BCAC

A tôleware document box, with yellow swag and floral decoration.

c1830   9.75in (25cm) wide

$1,000-1,500   Pook

Two 19thC Pennsylvania paint-decorated tôleware tea caddies, the first with asphaltum ground decorated with white, green and red band of leaf and berries and yellow flourishes, the second with red ground decorated with black and white flower blossom heightened with yellow and green flourishes, paint loss, surface abrasions.

5.5in (14cm) high

$1,000-1,500 (for the two)   FRE

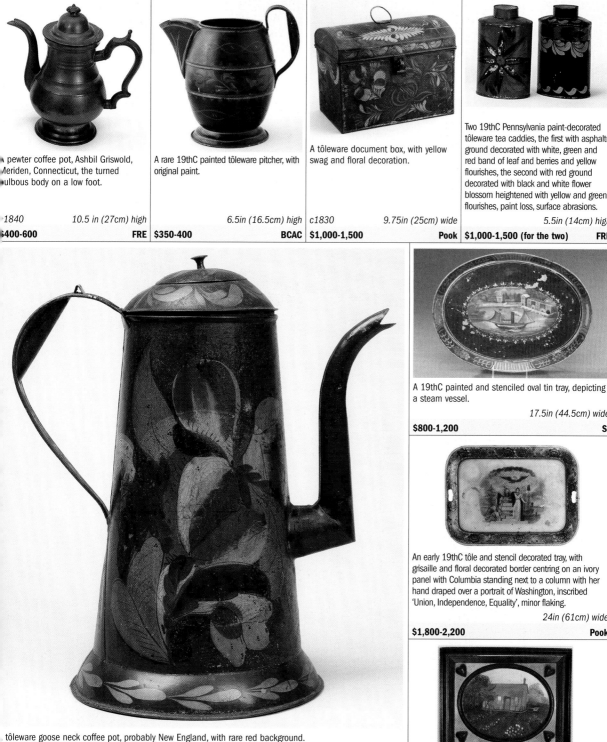

A tôleware goose neck coffee pot, probably New England, with rare red background.

tôleware usually has a black background. In good condition, a black pot such as this would be worth up to $10,000. Yellow tôleware is even rarer than red- a yellow coffee pot could be worth $75,000-100,000.

10.25in (26cm) high

$18,000-20,000   SG

A 19thC painted and stenciled oval tin tray, depicting a steam vessel.

17.5in (44.5cm) wide

$800-1,200   SI

An early 19thC tôle and stencil decorated tray, with grisaille and floral decorated border centring on an ivory panel with Columbia standing next to a column with her hand draped over a portrait of Washington, inscribed 'Union, Independence, Equality', minor flaking.

24in (61cm) wide

$1,800-2,200   Pook

A 19thC Canadian School oval painted tôle tray, central cartouche with painted homestead.

23.5in (60cm) wide

$800-1,200   WAD

FOLK ART

Rugs

A 19thC mounted hooked rug, central panel with three dogs within zig-zag border.

45.25in (115cm) long

$2,000-3,000   **BCAC**

A hooked rug, with a cat design.

36.5in (93cm) long

$1,000-1,500   **BCAC**

An early 20thC hooked rug, with resting cat design.

c1920-30   *38.5in (98cm) long*

$500-800   **BCAC**

A 19thC Canadian hooked 'beaver' motif rug, the central figure within an open maple leaf and log border, losses.

53in (135cm) wide

$300-400   **WA**

A 19thC pictorial hooked rug, with amusing stylized folk art dog, on a checkered background.

51in (129.5cm) wide

$3,500-4,500   **FRE**

A 19thC pictorial hooked rug, with central spread winged eagle, with blue and white striped wings perched atop American flag and shield within a red, green and blue rose and vine border and red stripes.

49in (124.5cm) wide

$2,500-3,000   **Pool**

A hooked rug, depicting a hunt scene with five dogs and planes flying overhead, worked in polychrome novelty weave wool and tweed fabrics on a burlap ground, backed with ticking.

c1935   *48in (122cm) wide*

$300-500   **FRE**

An early 20thC Canadian folk art hooked rug, a pictorial view of a farm worked in polychrome colors.

51.25in (130cm) wide

$3,000-4,000   **WA**

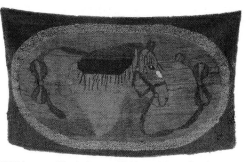

An early 20thC horse motif hooked rug, oval field containing profile of a tethered horse.

40in (101cm) wide

$500-700   **WAD**

A pictorial hooked rug, with two red and black roosters on striped ground with in-scrolling black border on brown ground.

44in (112cm) wide

$3,000-4,000   **Pook**

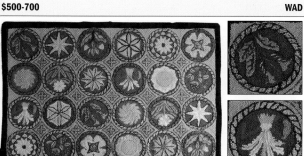

A New Jersey hand-hooked rag rug, of freeform design.

c1910   *43in (109cm) long*

$800-1,200   **RAA**

A hooked Rug, six red hearts in striped blocks, presented as wallhanging, signed'"J. E".

35in (58.5cm) wide

$700-1,000   **AAC**

Wood

An early 20thC Canadian geometrical hooked rug, worked in brown, green and purple squares giving a parquet effect.

72in (182cm) wide

$500-700   **WAD**

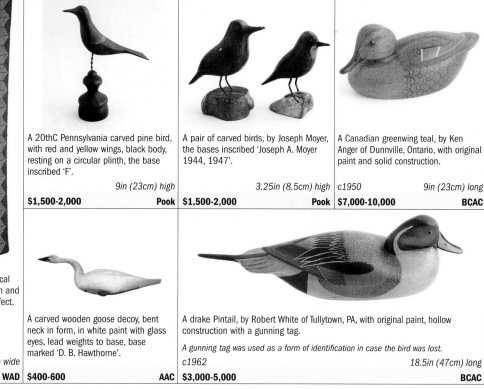

A 20thC Pennsylvania carved pine bird, with red and yellow wings, black body, resting on a circular plinth, the base inscribed 'F'.

9in (23cm) high

$1,500-2,000   **Pook**

A pair of carved birds, by Joseph Moyer, the bases inscribed 'Joseph A. Moyer 1944, 1947'.

3.25in (8.5cm) high

$1,500-2,000   **Pook**

A Canadian greenwing teal, by Ken Anger of Dunnville, Ontario, with original paint and solid construction.

c1950   *9in (23cm) long*

$7,000-10,000   **BCAC**

A carved wooden goose decoy, bent neck in form, in white paint with glass eyes, lead weights to base, base marked 'D. B. Hawthorne'.

$400-600   **AAC**

A drake Pintail, by Robert White of Tullytown, PA, with original paint, hollow construction with a gunning tag.

A gunning tag was used as a form of identification in case the bird was lost.

c1962   *18.5in (47cm) long*

$3,000-5,000   **BCAC**

A carved wooden horse with glass eyes, horse hair tail, painted brown.

16in (40.5cm) high

$250-350   **AAC**

A large 19thC turned wooden bowl, possibly maple, with original salmon painted exterior.

23in (58.5cm) diam

$600-800   **BCAC**

An early 19thC burlwood bowl.

20in (50cm) diam

$3,000-3,500   **BCAC**

A late 19thC burlwood bowl, with traces of red paint.

14.5in (37cm) wide

$700-900   **BCAC**

A finely turned 19thC American burlwood bowl.

9.75in (25cm) diam

$1,800-2,200   **Pook**

An early 20thC splint basket with open work handles.

19in (48cm) diam

$100-150   **BCAC**

A 19thC apple basket with wood bottom and bail handle.

$100-150   **BCAC**

A Canadian country melon basket, from the Bolton, Ontario area, with fair point lashing.

14.5in (37cm) wide

$200-250   **BP**

A two-finger pantry box with original green paint.

c1810   *5.5in (13.5cm) wide*

$750-850   **RAA**

A rare nest of six Nantucket baskets with swing handles, each stencilled 'H. A. Polhamus, New Rochelle', on underside.

It is very rare to find a complete 'nest', or graduated set, of named Nantucket baskets in fine original condition.

Largest 11in (28cm) diam

$20,000-25,000   **NA**

A stenciled and painted wood, rope and hide drum, decorated with the American eagle and scrolling foliate borders.

16in (40.5cm) diam

$300-500   **S**

A cherry wood flatware chest, or cutlery box, dovetailed construction.

$200-300   **BCAC**

A maple wood schoolgirl's penwork box, Philadelphia school, signed "Margaret Clarke" on the bottom edge.

c1820-30   *10in (25.5cm) wide*

$380-420   **BCAC**

A Tramp art lift-top box, with incised decorated and lined with pink Chinese silk.

c1910-20   *9in (23cm) wide*

$280-320   **BCAC**

An early 19thC decorated bentwood bride's box, with overall blue, yellow and ivory floral decoration on a salmon ground.

11.5in (29cm) wide

$400-600   **Pook**

A New England pine document box, with rosewood grained panels, yellow pinstriping and green borders.

c1820   *13.75in (35cm) wide*

$400-600   **Pook**

An 18thC Friesland chip carved storage box, with incised stars and sawtooth border, retaining a green painted surface.

11in (28cm) wide

$350-400   **Pook**

A decorated slide lid trinket box, dated, with polychrome tulip, pinwheel, and heart decoration on an ivory ground.

c1794   *7.75in (19.5cm) wide*

$2,200-2,800   **Pook**

A New England storage box, with brilliant yellow flower decoration against a black and brown grained background, with yellow and lime green on the perimeter.

28.5in (72.5cm) wide

$6,500-7,500   **SG**

A soft wood candle box, dove-tailed and with molded base and slide lid with raised panel and carved tulip design.

12in (30.5cm) high

$150-200   **AAC**

A late 19thc/early 20thC chip-carved and painted tramp art box, lift lid above single drawer, ornamented with layers of geometric and foliate decoration, painted brown, missing hinges to lid.

8.5in (21.5cm) high

$600-900   **FRE**

A Pennsylvania painted candle box, rectangular sliding lid on conforming case decorated with vase of leafy flowers, the sides decorated with flowerheads, in yellow, green, red and copper on a black ground, replaced lid.

c1840   *7.25in (18cm) wide*

$1,800-2,200   **FRE**

A 19thC sailor's scrimshaw bean canteen, depicting harbors and cities in great detail.

5in (12.5cm) diam

$400-500   **BCAC**

A heart-shaped box, covered with wall paper and lined with German language newspaper, from Pennsylvania, the newspaper dated.

1874

$400-450   **SG**

A 19thC green-painted wooden lantern, rectangular form with cotter-pin hinged access door, squared molded base, age crack to base.

14.25in (36cm) high

$1,200-1,800   **FRE**

A homeopathic set in mahogany box by F.E. Boericke, Philadelphia, the fitted set comprising ninety-six glass vials and six bottles, all numbered and with identification in the lid, minor losses.

10.5in (27cm) high

$400-600   **FRE**

A wooden flagon, dated.

1810   *13in (33cm) high*

$300-350   **BCAC**

A CLOSER LOOK AT A JOSEPH LEHN PAINTED BUCKET

Joseph Long Lehn (1798-1892)was a farmer who supplemented his income making finely-turned and paint decorated wooden items. A prolific craftsman, he is best known for his egg cups, covered saffron boxes, small footed bowls and more rarely larger items such as this.

Since his ware was produced for every day use, many have been damaged over the years. Collectors will pay a premium for examples such as this. The exceptional condition of the paint decoration makes this one of the finest examples of Mr. Lehn's work

His buckets show fine quality construction and this is a typical example, the sides consisting of 11 tapering oak staves held in place by three thin sheet-iron rivetted straps, the plank bases made from tulip poplar. The sides are decorated with a salmon pink ground brushed with a darker red wash, combed or figured in vertical diagonal bands

The iron straps are painted with trailing vines - also typical of his workshop

An important mid-19thC painted bucket by Joseph Lehn, Elizabethtown Township, Lancaster County, with overall vibrant salmon and orange graining, the iron bands with typical trailing vine design.

10.5in (26.5cm) diam

$8,000-12,000   **Pook**

A mid-19thC covered sugar bucket by Joseph Lehn, Elizabethtown Township, Lancaster County, the lid with incised concentric circles and running vines on a red ground encircling a five point star, over a base with three iron bands with similar vine decoration.

9.75in (25cm) high

$2,500-3,000   **Pook**

A mid-19thC egg cup by Joseph Lehn, Elizabethtown Township, Lancaster County, with strawberry vines on a tan ground with a red rim and trailing vine decoration.

PROVENANCE: *James Glazer, 1977.*

3.5in (9cm) high

$800-1,200   **Pook**

A mid-19thC footed bowl by Joseph Lehn, Elizabethtown Township, Lancaster County, with strawberry vines on a salmon ground above a red, green and black pedestal and base.

3in (7.5cm) high

$1,200-1,800   **Pook**

A mid-19thC lidded cup by Joseph Lehn, Elizabethtown Township, Lancaster County, with strawberry vine on a salmon ground with green and red banding, minor flaking.

4in (10cm) high

$1,200-1,800   **Pook**

A mid-19thC saffron box by Joseph Lehn, Elizabethtown Township, Lancaster County, with strawberry vines on a salmon ground, black finial and base.

5.52in (13.5cm) high

$500-700   **Pook**

A mid-19thC saffron box by Joseph Lehn, Elizabethtown Township, Lancaster County, with a foliate design on a tan ground with red, yellow and green bands, flaking to lid.

PROVENANCE: *Philip Bradley, 1982.*

$500-700   **Pook**

A mid-19thC footed saffron box by Joseph Lehn, Elizabethtown Township, Lancaster County, with a black finial above a strawberry vine on a salmon ground with red, green and black base, repaired crack to base.

PROVENANCE: *Lindsey Grigsby.*

5in (12.5cm) high

$600-900   **Pook**

A mid-19thC lidded saffron cup by Joseph Lehn, Elizabethtown Township, Lancaster County, with strawberry vine on a salmon ground with red and green bands, repaired crack to base.

5.5in (14cm) high

$1,000-1,500   **Pook**

A child-size walnut jelly cupboard, in original condition.

c1850   *21.25in (54cm) wide*

$1,500-2,000   **BCAC**

A miniature grain-painted dry sink, York Country PA, original condition.

c1870   *16in (40.5cm) wide*

$1,000-1,500   **BCAC**

A late 19thC miniature chest of drawers, with original finish.

9in (23cm) wide

$100-150   **BCAC**

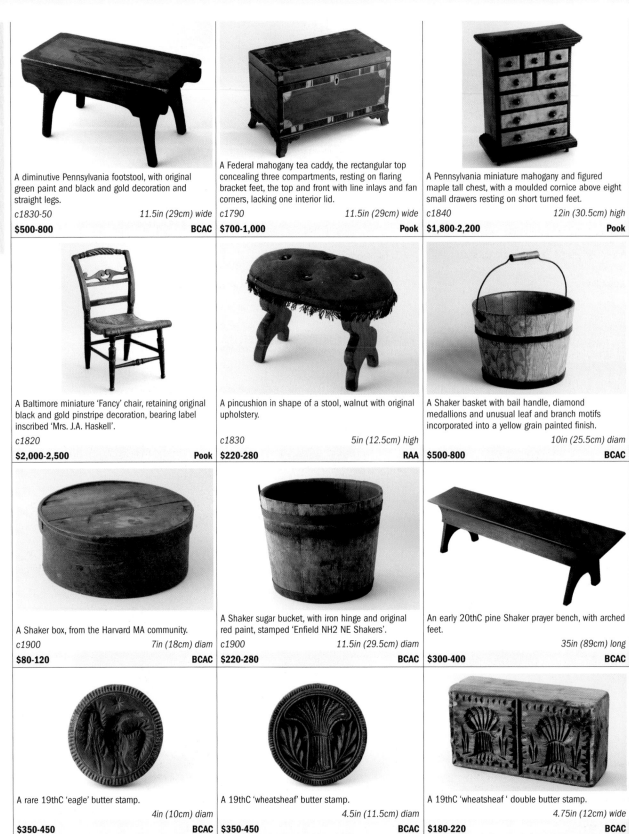

A diminutive Pennsylvania footstool, with original green paint and black and gold decoration and straight legs.

c1830-50   *11.5in (29cm) wide*

$500-800   **BCAC**

A Federal mahogany tea caddy, the rectangular top concealing three compartments, resting on flaring bracket feet, the top and front with line inlays and fan corners, lacking one interior lid.

c1790   *11.5in (29cm) wide*

$700-1,000   **Pook**

A Pennsylvania miniature mahogany and figured maple tall chest, with a moulded cornice above eight small drawers resting on short turned feet.

c1840   *12in (30.5cm) high*

$1,800-2,200   **Pook**

A Baltimore miniature 'Fancy' chair, retaining original black and gold pinstripe decoration, bearing label inscribed 'Mrs. J.A. Haskell'.

c1820

$2,000-2,500   **Pook**

A pincushion in shape of a stool, walnut with original upholstery.

c1830   *5in (12.5cm) high*

$220-280   **RAA**

A Shaker basket with bail handle, diamond medallions and unusual leaf and branch motifs incorporated into a yellow grain painted finish.

10in (25.5cm) diam

$500-800   **BCAC**

A Shaker box, from the Harvard MA community.

c1900   *7in (18cm) diam*

$80-120   **BCAC**

A Shaker sugar bucket, with iron hinge and original red paint, stamped 'Enfield NH2 NE Shakers'.

c1900   *11.5in (29.5cm) diam*

$220-280   **BCAC**

An early 20thC pine Shaker prayer bench, with arched feet.

35in (89cm) long

$300-400   **BCAC**

A rare 19thC 'eagle' butter stamp.

4in (10cm) diam

$350-450   **BCAC**

A 19thC 'wheatsheaf' butter stamp.

4.5in (11.5cm) diam

$350-450   **BCAC**

A 19thC 'wheatsheaf ' double butter stamp.

4.75in (12cm) wide

$180-220   **BCAC**

rare early 19thC painted pine and tin candlemold, th the name "J. Walker" stenciled on the side and calloped skirt, retains original red painted surface.

13in (33cm) wide

3,500-4,500 **Pook**

A combination butter paddle and print with deeply incised geometric flowers.

11.5in (29cm) high

$500-700 **Pook**

A late 18thC Pennsylvania walnut 'lollipop' double-sided butter print, each side with concentric stars.

10.75in (27.5cm) high

$700-1,000 **Pook**

rare late 18thC Pennsylvania carved maple 'double llipop' butterprint, each end double-sided with star ecoration.

12in (30.5cm) high

2,000-2,500 **Pook**

An 18thC Pennsylvania double-sided butterprint, one side with a deep cut pinwheel, the other with a stylized tulip.

4.5in (11.5cm) diam

$400-600 **Pook**

A Philadelphia wooden trade sign, painted with a two-masted steamship in open waters, the double-sided sign bound with wrought iron frame, weathered surface paint loss.

c1900 *54in (137cm) wide*

$2,200-2,800 **FRE**

hand-painted wooden trade sign for "Sked Bros. oultry Farm", double-sided sign featuring "Baby hicks" on one and "Fresh Eggs" on the other,, eathered surface with minor loss to frame.

34in (86.5cm)

1,500-2,000 **AAC**

A painted wooden shovel.

$150-200 **BCAC**

A New England maple busk, dated "Sept. 1, 1837", with the initials "L.K." with polychrome heart and trailing vine decoration.

14in (35.5cm) high

$400-600 **Pook**

A Quebec carved wood pine and square nail salt and candle box, from the Eastern Townships.

There is an identical box in the 'Musee de Civilization' in Quebec City.

c1880   17.25in (44cm) high

$700-1,000   BP

A Quebec pine box, with square nails and rim on hinge to hold lid open vertically.

c1820   6.75in (17.5cm) high

$400-600   BP

An Ontario 19thC pine knife box, from the Markham area.

21.75in (55.5cm) high

$400-600   BP

A 19thC Ontario gold painted turned treenware eggcup.

2.25in (15.5cm) high

$40-60   BP

An Ottawa chip carved fruitwood prayer box, in the form of a book, signed "Mrs James S. L. Cole, Ottawa, Ontario".

9in (22cm) wide

$350-400   WAD

A rare historical 'Rebellion Box', from the rebellion of 1837 instigated at Montgomery's Tavern on Yonge Street by W.L. MacKenzie, carved in the Toronto 'gaol' by prisoner William Alves in 1838.

2.25in (9cm) wide

$5,000-7,000   BP

A rare Quebec carved wood sugar mold, with cross and three leaves, from Ile D'Orleans.

c1850   15.25in (38.5cm) wide

$1,000-1,500   BP

A Quebec square carved maple wood butter mold, in the form of flowers, from the Eastern Townships.

c1890   6in (15.5cm) wide

$150-200   BP

A Quebec well carved and rare patriotic sugar mould.

c1860   8.75in (22cm) high

$1,800-2,200   BP

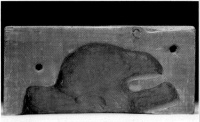

A 19thC pine maple-sugar mould, of beaver form.

12in (31cm) wide

$60-80   WAD

A 'dog' brick, probably from the Flamboro Brickworks of Ontario.

c1900   8.25in (21cm) wide

$200-250   BP

A 19thC wooden sugar mold, in the form of a beaver, found in North Hatley, Quebec.

8.75in (22cm) wide

$280-320   BP

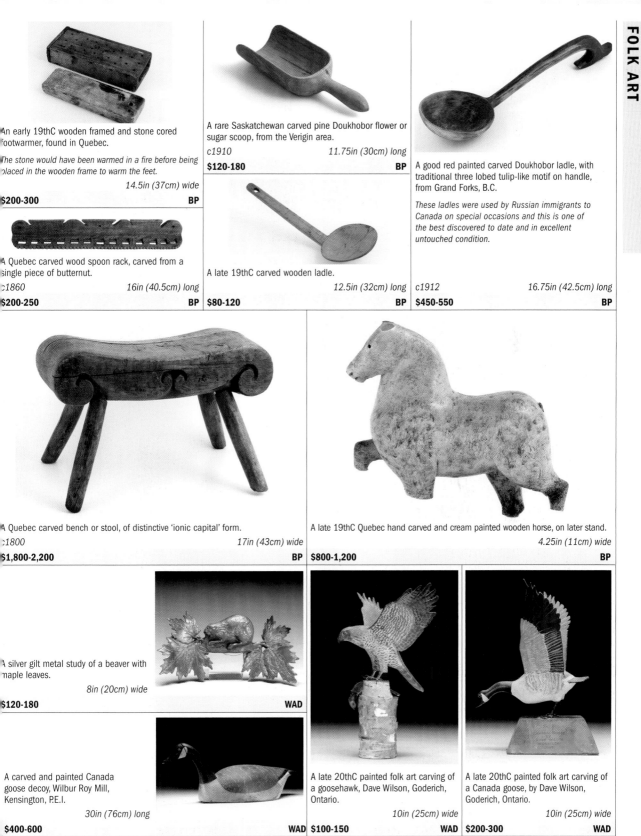

An early 19thC wooden framed and stone cored footwarmer, found in Quebec.

The stone would have been warmed in a fire before being placed in the wooden frame to warm the feet.

14.5in (37cm) wide

$200-300 **BP**

A Quebec carved wood spoon rack, carved from a single piece of butternut.

c1860 16in (40.5cm) long

$200-250 **BP**

A rare Saskatchewan carved pine Doukhobor flower or sugar scoop, from the Verigin area.

c1910 11.75in (30cm) long

$120-180 **BP**

A late 19thC carved wooden ladle.

12.5in (32cm) long

$80-120 **BP**

A good red painted carved Doukhobor ladle, with traditional three lobed tulip-like motif on handle, from Grand Forks, B.C.

These ladles were used by Russian immigrants to Canada on special occasions and this is one of the best discovered to date and in excellent untouched condition.

c1912 16.75in (42.5cm) long

$450-550 **BP**

A Quebec carved bench or stool, of distinctive 'ionic capital' form.

c1800 17in (43cm) wide

$1,800-2,200 **BP**

A late 19thC Quebec hand carved and cream painted wooden horse, on later stand.

4.25in (11cm) wide

$800-1,200 **BP**

A silver gilt metal study of a beaver with maple leaves.

8in (20cm) wide

$120-180 **WAD**

A carved and painted Canada goose decoy, Wilbur Roy Mill, Kensington, P.E.I.

30in (76cm) long

$400-600 **WAD**

A late 20thC painted folk art carving of a goosehawk, Dave Wilson, Goderich, Ontario.

10in (25cm) wide

$100-150 **WAD**

A late 20thC painted folk art carving of a Canada goose, by Dave Wilson, Goderich, Ontario.

10in (25cm) wide

$200-300 **WAD**

A 19thC ivory and glass box, decorated with a painting of cherubs inset into the glass lid, lined with blue velvet.

2.25in (5.5cm) diam

$80-100 BCAC

A 19thC bell jar with four stuffed birds, including song and hummingbirds mounted on twigs, turned wood base.

11in (28cm) high

$220-280 FRE

A wax flower arrangement in woven willow basket, under glass dome, in good condition with some discoloration and deterioration of flowers.

c1890 19in (48.5cm) high

$180-220 TWC

A late 19thC caged canary squeak toy.

7.5in (19cm) high

$500-700 Pool

A cement lawn jockey with original painted surface

c1930-40

$250-350 BCAC

A stone pheasant doorstop, with elaborate painted decoration.

c1900 9.5in (24cm) long

$700-1,000 SG

A 19thC Great Lakes inlaid pipe bowl, Ojibwa region, red and black pipe stone inlaid with lead.

7.5in (19cm) long

$600-900 FRE

A Diploma of the Society of the Cincinnati for Frederick Frye, and an enameled Gold Society of the Cincinnati Insignia, the diploma signed by George Washington and Henry Knox, dated "May 5, 1784", the parchment diploma was engraved by Jacque Le Veau (1729-1786) Paris, the text by Robert Scot (1744-1823), Philadelphia, and presented to Frederick Frye at the meeting of the Cincinnati in Philadelphia.

An original member of the Society of the Cincinnati, Frederick Frye was the son of Col. James and Sarah Robey Frye, born in Andover, Massachusetts, June 9, 1760. He eventually became Commandant of the Military post on Governor's Island in New York Harbor and served with the rank of Captain during the War of 1812.

$8,000-12,000 FRE

A note signed by Abraham Lincoln, inscribed "Allow the bearer Matthew H Read Jr to pass from Montreal in Canada to Albany New York and then remain in XXXX until further order from me, Dec 23 1864 A.Lincoln.", mounted in a frame with photograph of Lincoln.

Note 3.25in (8cm) wide

$6,000-9,000 BP

A set of three 19thC carved and painted pine figures of the Presidents Abraham Lincoln, Andrew Johnson and Ulysses S. Grant, each figure with carved face and hands, painted hair and glass bead eyes, wearing handmade clothing of period wool, silk and cotton, some wear to clothing, Lincoln's carved hat has old repair to brim.

Tallest 13.5in (34.5cm) high

$5,000-7,000 FRE

An embossed leather photo album with a fragment of Martha Washington's wedding dress, album dates to the 1860s, the album containing thirty-seven carte de visite photos, many subjects identified, and a piece of gold silk damask inserted into oval photograph sleeve, identified with the inscription, "A piece of Martha Washington's wedding dress. Presented by her great-granddaughter, Mrs. Kennon of Georgetown, D.C".

PROVENANCE: The silk fragment in this album matches a number of examples of the wedding gown in the collections of Mt. Vernon and the Huntington Library. Purchased from the Walter Knott Collection, 1965

1860   *6.25in (16cm) high*

$2,500-3,000   **FRE**

A log book of the whaling ship 'Waverly' of New Bedford, under Master Ephraim W. Kempton, log book of whaling voyage to the Pacific leaving New Bedford on 23 July 1849, returning on 25 April 1851. Later, in 1865, the rebel cruiser 'Shenandoa' burned and sank the 'Waverly' in the North Pacific, log contains several entries per page with illustrations.

$3,000-4,000   **NA**

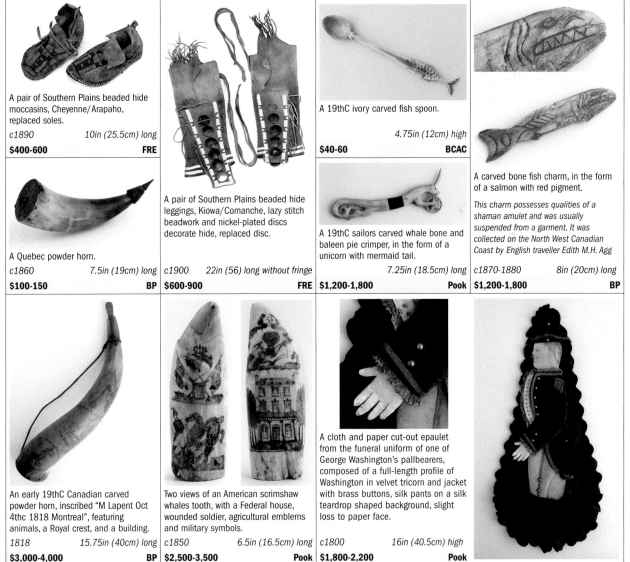

A pair of Southern Plains beaded hide moccasins, Cheyenne/Arapaho, replaced soles.

c1890   *10in (25.5cm) long*

$400-600   **FRE**

A pair of Southern Plains beaded hide leggings, Kiowa/Comanche, lazy stitch beadwork and nickel-plated discs decorate hide, replaced disc.

c1900   *22in (56) long without fringe*

$600-900   **FRE**

A 19thC ivory carved fish spoon.

4.75in (12cm) high

$40-60   **BCAC**

A 19thC sailors carved whale bone and baleen pie crimper, in the form of a unicorn with mermaid tail.

7.25in (18.5cm) long

$1,200-1,800   **Pook**

A carved bone fish charm, in the form of a salmon with red pigment.

This charm possesses qualities of a shaman amulet and was usually suspended from a garment. It was collected on the North West Canadian Coast by English traveller Edith M.H. Agg

c1870-1880   *8in (20cm) long*

$1,200-1,800   **BP**

A Quebec powder horn.

c1860   *7.5in (19cm) long*

$100-150   **BP**

An early 19thC Canadian carved powder horn, inscribed "M Lapent Oct 4thc 1818 Montreal", featuring animals, a Royal crest, and a building.

1818   *15.75in (40cm) long*

$3,000-4,000   **BP**

Two views of an American scrimshaw whales tooth, with a Federal house, wounded soldier, agricultural emblems and military symbols.

c1850   *6.5in (16.5cm) long*

$2,500-3,500   **Pook**

A cloth and paper cut-out epaulet from the funeral uniform of one of George Washington's pallbearers, composed of a full-length profile of Washington in velvet tricorn and jacket with brass buttons, silk pants on a silk teardrop shaped background, slight loss to paper face.

c1800   *16in (40.5cm) high*

$1,800-2,200   **Pook**

CERAMICS

Ancient Chinese

A Chinese Neolithic small pot.
4500-1000 BC   *6.75in (17cm) diam*
$220-280   **BAntC**

A Chinese Neolithic one-handled pot.
4500-1000 BC   *4in (10cm) high*
$220-280   **BAntC**

A Chinese Neolithic pot, with original paint work.
4500-1000 BC   *7.5in (19cm) high*
$220-280   **BAntC**

A Chinese Neolithic pot.
4500-1000 BC   *9.5in (25cm) high*
$500-700   **BAntC**

A Western Zhou Dynasty pottery cup.
1100-771 BC   *5in (12.5cm) wide*
$320-380   **BAntC**

A Han Dynasty pot, with chicken design.
206 BC-AD 220   *6.5in (16.5cm) wide*
$300-400   **BAntC**

A Chinese Neolithic pot.
4500-1000 BC   *14in (35.5cm) high*
$800-1,200   **BAntC**

A Han Dynasty two-handled jar.
206 BC-AD 220   *7in (17.5cm) high*
$220-280   **BAntC**

A Han Dynasty two-handled jar.
206 BC-AD 220   *5.5in (14cm) high*
$220-280   **BAntC**

A Han Dynasty two-handled jar.
206 BC-AD 220   *12.5in (31.5cm) high*
$800-1,200   **BAntC**

A Han Dynasty wine ewer, in the form of a tiger.
206 BC-AD 220   *6in (15cm) wide*
$220-280   **BAntC**

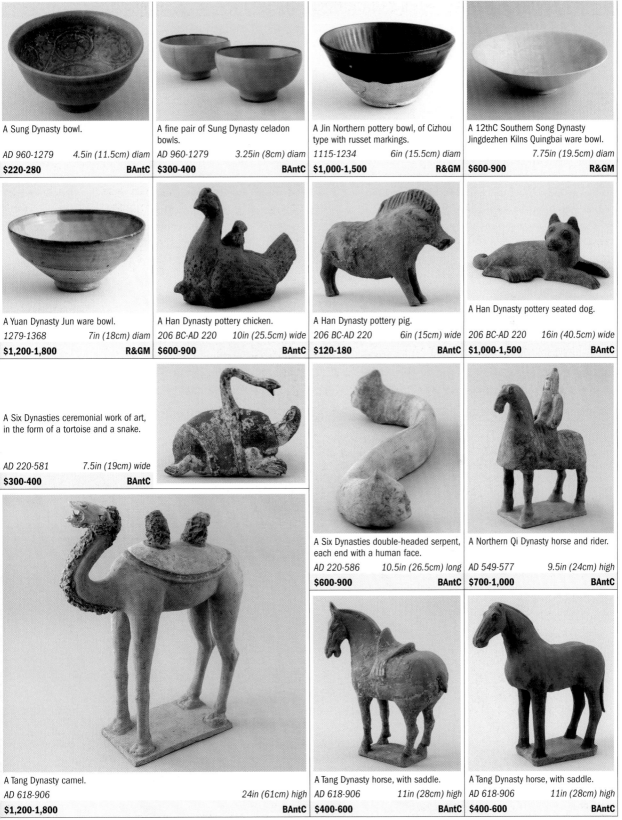

A Sung Dynasty bowl.

AD 960-1279   4.5in (11.5cm) diam
$220-280   **BAntC**

A fine pair of Sung Dynasty celadon bowls.

AD 960-1279   3.25in (8cm) diam
$300-400   **BAntC**

A Jin Northern pottery bowl, of Cizhou type with russet markings.

1115-1234   6in (15.5cm) diam
$1,000-1,500   **R&GM**

A 12thC Southern Song Dynasty Jingdezhen Kilns Quingbai ware bowl.

7.75in (19.5cm) diam
$600-900   **R&GM**

A Yuan Dynasty Jun ware bowl.

1279-1368   7in (18cm) diam
$1,200-1,800   **R&GM**

A Han Dynasty pottery chicken.

206 BC-AD 220   10in (25.5cm) wide
$600-900   **BAntC**

A Han Dynasty pottery pig.

206 BC-AD 220   6in (15cm) wide
$120-180   **BAntC**

A Han Dynasty pottery seated dog.

206 BC-AD 220   16in (40.5cm) wide
$1,000-1,500   **BAntC**

A Six Dynasties ceremonial work of art, in the form of a tortoise and a snake.

AD 220-581   7.5in (19cm) wide
$300-400   **BAntC**

A Six Dynasties double-headed serpent, each end with a human face.

AD 220-586   10.5in (26.5cm) long
$600-900   **BAntC**

A Northern Qi Dynasty horse and rider.

AD 549-577   9.5in (24cm) high
$700-1,000   **BAntC**

A Tang Dynasty camel.

AD 618-906   24in (61cm) high
$1,200-1,800   **BAntC**

A Tang Dynasty horse, with saddle.

AD 618-906   11in (28cm) high
$400-600   **BAntC**

A Tang Dynasty horse, with saddle.

AD 618-906   11in (28cm) high
$400-600   **BAntC**

SHIPWRECK CARGOES

Advances in deep-sea diving and underwater archaeology have made it easier to reach wrecks long sunk at the bottom of the sea. Each wreck is an important archaeological find and often reveals previously unseen ceramics. Shipwreck cargoes are of particular interest to collectors because they are inextricably bound up with intriguing past events, and present a host of questions and mysteries. For example, what caused the ship to sink? What was its destination? For some collectors, the shipwreck cargoes have opened up a world of Oriental ceramics that they would otherwise never have encountered.

The ships often contained hundreds of thousands of ceramic pieces as well as tons of tea, spices and silk, although the latter could not withstand the centuries under the sea. Each ship that sunk would have been a major human and economic disaster.

It is often difficult to date these Oriental ceramics because inventories are rare, although some ships, such as The Geldermalsen (the Nanking Cargo c1752), was a registered Dutch ship, and so it can be given a more accurate date. Many of the cargoes have revealed previously unseen wares, and it is interesting to wonder whether if these ships had reached their intended destination, they might have changed fashions and so ceramic history.

The longer a cargo has been on the market, the more it will have been sold on and therefore the rarer pieces will have become. Therefore wares from the Hatcher Cargo, the first to come on the market, as well as the Vung Tau and Diana Cargoes, are becoming increasingly rare. A Nanking cup and saucer originally sold at Christie's, in 1986, for around $120. Today they fetch in the region of $300. However, this will be the case eventually with all the cargoes, which makes them all highly collectible. One of the most attractive features of the shipwreck cargoes is their accessibility and affordability. Items go through a considerable price range, from $70 to thousands of dollars. Blue and white pieces are always popular, and items encrusted with coral and limpets are becoming increasingly valued for their aesthetic appeal. Always visit a specialist or a reputable auction when buying shipwreck cargoes, to ensure that pieces have been accurately valued.

Hoi An Hoard

The Hoi An Hoard was a Vietnamese cargo and is the oldest to have come onto the market, dating from c1450 to 1500. It sank in the depths of the South China Sea, off the Vietnamese coast near Hoi An. The ship was around 98.5 feet (30 meters) long and carried an estimated 250,000 ceramic items, although many were not recovered when it was brought to the surface in 1987. Vietnamese ceramics have been attracting increasing interest in recent years, and this is partly due to the recovery of the Hoi An Hoard, which has underlined their importance and beauty.

The ceramics were made of a hard, heavy pottery in the region of Chu Dou, 3.75 miles (6 kilometers) from Hai Dong, which was the largest center of ceramic production in medieval Vietnam. The majority of items were decorated with underglaze cobalt blue, and have remained in excellent condition, retaining their lustrous glaze despite centuries underwater. This is testimony to the high standard of production of the Vietnamese kilns.

A Hoi An Hoard bowl, painted with a fish and scrolling flowers.

c1450-1500   9in (23cm) diam

$1,200-1,800   **R&GM**

A Hoi An Hoard dish, with fish design.

c1450-1500   9in (23cm) diam

$700-1,000   **R&GM**

A Hoi An Hoard bowl, painted with a fish and scrolling flowers.

c1450-1500   9in (23cm) diam

$700-1,000   **R&GM**

A Hoi An Hoard bowl, painted with a fish and scrolling flowers.

c1450-1500   9in (23cm) diam

$500-700   **R&GM**

A Hoi An Hoard bowl, painted with a fish and scrolling flowers.

c1450-1500   9in (23cm) diam

$800-1,200   **R&GM**

A Hoi An Hoard serving dish, with scattered plant border and plant design, the glaze wiped clear of the edges.

c1450-1500   9.5in (24cm) wide

$220-280   **R&GM**

A Hoi An Hoard dish, with water plant design.

c1450-1500   8.75in (22.5cm) diam

$220-280   **R&GM**

A Hoi An Hoard shallow bowl, of compressed baluster form on shallow wide foot, the sides decorated with petals drawn in a simple line style, a border of ruyi or diaper below the unglazed rims.

These are described as bowls because no lids were recovered. However, they could be jars.

c1450-1500   3.75in (9.5cm) wide

$70-100   **R&GM**

A Hoi An Hoard bowl, of deep form, standing on a high foot, formal stiff lappets with a band of prunus scrolling below the rim, the inner rim with a crosshatched diaper border, the well with an open branch of flowering prunus.

c1450-1500   6in (15cm) diam

$250-300   **R&GM**

A Hoi An Hoard jar and cover.

c1450-1500   5in (12.5cm) high

$3,000-5,000   **R&GM**

A Hoi An Hoard small jar, of shallow baluster form decorated with scrolling flowers.

c1450-1500   1.25in (3.5cm) high

$70-100   **R&GM**

A Hoi An Hoard box and cover, with lotus flower motif.

c1450-1500   1.75in (4.5cm) wide

$150-200   **R&GM**

Three Hoi An Hoard miniature jars, of globular form, some with incised lines under the glaze, decorated with various stiff leaf lappets or ruyi-heads to neck, the bodies decorated with grasses and ruyi-shaped clouds or birds.

c1450-1500   1.25in (3.5cm) high

$60-90 each   **R&GM**

The Hatcher Cargo

The Hatcher cargo dates from c1643, and came on to the market in 1984. The ship was probably a Chinese junk with wares to be divided between the European (probably Dutch) market and the South East Asian markets. 25,000 pieces of ceramic were recovered, and the majority were blue and white from Jingdezhen, with some Swatow and blanc-de-Chine items. Jingdezhen was the Chinese capital of ceramic production and is situated on the on the eastern bank of the Yangtse River.

The ceramics on this ship were produced at a time of upheaval and unrest in China and so there is little historical evidence of ceramic production from this era. This cargo was key in the breakthrough to understanding ceramic manufacture at the end of the Ming dynasty (1644).

Two Hatcher Cargo wine cups, the straight side with sharply waisted base with a small thin foot rim, one with flower heads and leaves and a line border, the other similar with a diaper border.

c1643   2.75in (7cm) wide

$300-500 each   **R&GM**

Two Hatcher Cargo wine cups, of thinly potted shape, each decorated with a dragon chasing a flaming pearl around the cup exterior.

1.75in (4.5cm) wide

$300-400 each   **R&GM**

A Hatcher Cargo stem cup.

c1643   3in (7.5cm) high

$220-280   **PC**

A pair of Hatcher Cargo small cups.

c1643   1.5in (4cm) high

$180-220   **PC**

A Hatcher Cargo hand-painted blue and white box and cover, with liner, glaze on exterior of box affected by sea water.

c1643   3in (8cm) diam

$300-400   **PC**

A small Hatcher Cargo mustard pot and cover, slight chip to lid.

c1643   1.5in (4cm) high

$300-400   **PC**

A Hatcher Cargo small box and cover, with landscape scene on lid.

c1643   2in (5cm) diam

$220-280   **PC**

A Hatcher Cargo tall vase, with painted decoration including a rabbit and grasshoppers, chip to rim.

c1643   9.25in (23.5cm) high

$600-900   **PC**

A Hatcher Cargo box and cover, with rounded cover and painted blue on blue.

Similar examples were found on the Vung Tau Cargo despite a time gap of 50 years.

c1643   1.25in (3.5cm) wide

$300-400   **R&GM**

A Hatcher Cargo kraak kendi, of typical squat form decorated with kraak type panels of cranes and precious objects.

c1643   5.25in (13.5cm) high

$1,200-1,800   **R&GM**

A Hatcher Cargo teapot, lacking lid.

c1643   4.25in (11cm) high

$600-900   **PC**

Vung Tau Cargo

The Vung Tau cargo was Chinese and is dated c1690-1700. It was rescued in 1990 when 48,000 pieces of porcelain and other artefacts were found. It consisted of mostly Kangxi blue and white as well as an impressive selection of white wares and provincial wares. The junk was bound for Batavia (present day Jakarta in Java), a major trading center where it would have been bought by the Dutch East India Company who would have reshipped approximately 70% of it to Holland. The rest would have been for the Islamic market.

The Chinese manufacturers were clearly catering for the specific tastes of the European market. The cargo contained fashionable decorative vases, to fit into the baroque styles of the period. Other wares found included famille verte pieces and blanc-de-Chine items as well as goblets, wine and hot chocolate cups. The latter had become highly fashionable with the upper classes. The vases painted with Dutch canal houses were probably also intended for Dutch clientele.

A Vung Tau Cargo baluster vase, with domed cover, with figures in a rocky landscape with trees and the sea below.

The Vung Tau Cargo was one of the only cargoes that carried ornamental pieces such as vases. Other cargoes carried predominantly domestic wares.

c1690	4.5in (11.5cm) high
$400-600	**RB**

A Vung Tau Cargo vase and cover, of slender baluster form and molded with panels filled with cartouches of urns of flowers.

c1690	6in (15cm) high
$500-700	**R&GM**

A Vung Tau Cargo vase and cover, slightly blurred.

c1690	6in (15cm) high
$400-600	**R&GM**

A Vung Tau Cargo vase and cover, of baluster form with a complex waisted base, decorated with a bird on a rock with flowers, the inner rim unglazed, the cover with flowers.

c1690	6.75in (17cm) high
$400-600	**R&GM**

A Vung Tau Cargo vase and cover, some chips.

c1690	5.75in (14.5cm) high
$400-600	**R&GM**

A Vung Tau Cargo vase, small chips.

c1690	5.5in (14cm) high
$500-700	**R&GM**

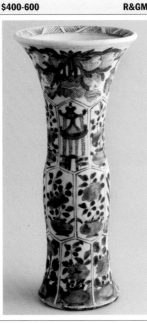

Two views of a Vung Tau Cargo Canal House vase, decorated with Dutch canal houses among baroque swags.

The Canal House vases were produced as a special order for rich Dutch clients.

c1690	10.25in (26cm) high
$700-1,000	**R&GM**

A Vung Tau Cargo Canal House vase cover, of domed form, the finial blue and waisted.

These covers were made for massive vases 19.75in (50cm) high.

c1690	6.25in (16cm) wide
$120-180	**R&GM**

A CLOSER LOOK AT A CANAL HOUSE VASE

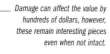

This pattern is unrecorded before this cargo, and only a few were recovered from the Vung Tau wreck. As such, it is a rare and highly desirable item.

Damage can affect the value by hundreds of dollars, however, these remain interesting pieces even when not intact.

This piece is decorated with Dutch canal houses among baroque swags. The detailing is quite crude and was possibly based on a rough sketch by a Dutch merchant.

The reverse of the vase shows a different pattern, in more traditional style, so the vase could be turned if the canal design was not liked.

A Vung Tau Cargo Canal House vase, decorated with Dutch canal houses among baroque swags, with domed cover.

c1690   13.25in (34cm) high

$1,000-1,500   **R&GM**

A Vung Tau Cargo selection of doll's house vases, made for export to be put in European doll's houses.

An example of one of these is at Haden Hall in Norfolk in the Queen Anne Doll's house. They were made for the European market and can still be found today in English stately homes.

c1690   2in (5.5cm) high

$100-150 each   **RB**

A Vung Tau Cargo beaker, decorated with 'penciled' decoration in the style of European engraving with lots of cross-hatching.

c1690   2.75in (7cm) high

$300-400   **R&GM**

A Vung Tau Cargo tazza.

c1690   5.5in (14cm) high

$1,200-1,800   **R&GM**

A Vung Tau Cargo teabowl, cover and saucer, with birds perched on peony sprays, divided into eight segments.

c1690   5in (12.5cm) diam

$500-700   **RB**

A Vung Tau Cargo small octagonal teabowl and saucer, painted with panels of peony sprays.

c1690   3.75in (9.5cm) diam

$500-700   **RB**

A Vung Tau Cargo large size octagonal tea bowl and saucer.

c1690   5in (13cm) diam

$400-600   **RB**

A Vung Tau Cargo beaker, cover and saucer, thinly potted with almost straight, slightly flaring beaker, the cover has underglazed under-rims, fungus marks to base.

These were probably made for coffee, or possibly hot chocolate.

c1690   Saucer 4.75in (12cm) wide

$220-280   **R&GM**

ORIENTAL

Four Vung Tau Cargo provincial bowls, with slightly flared edges, some with character marks on them.

c1690   *4.75in (12cm) diam*

$70-100 each   **RB**

A Vung Tau Cargo provincial bowl, in deep white-green-blue glaze with frit to foot, with an iron oxide dressed rim.

c1690   *6in (15cm) diam*

$50-70   **R&GM**

Six Vung Tau Cargo blanc-de-Chine bowls.

c1690   *1in (3cm) high*

$20-30 each   **R&GM**

The Nanking Cargo

The Nanking Cargo ship was called the Geldermalsen and belonged to the Dutch East India Company. The Geldermalsen was built in 1746 and was 150 feet (380 meters) long. It was carrying a valuable cargo of tea, Chinese silk, gold and ceramics. The latter made up only five percent of the value of the load, of which there were over 128,000 pieces. The Geldermalsen sunk on January 3, 1752 when it hit a reef. The survivors climbed onto a long boat and arrived at Batavia after eight days at sea, but 80 seamen lost their lives.

The Nanking Cargo became the most famous cargo when it sold at Christie's in Amsterdam in 1986, attracting worldwide media attention. However, for many the Nanking Cargo is not as interesting as wares from the Hoi An Hoard, Vung Tau and Hatcher. The ceramics from the Nanking were made during a period when shapes had become more standardized and designs were made for the European market with fewer purely decorative items. The cargo included 171 dinner services and numerous tea and coffee services. The majority of pieces were decorated with landscapes in blue and white as well as many pieces with Imari designs. A lot of the wares with Imari patterns were badly damaged by the seawater as the red and gold decoration was painted over the underglaze blue, which has survived the test of time.

From a historians viewpoint the Nanking Cargo has not revealed much new information because we already have an abundance of historical evidence from this period. However, the detailed ship's records have left a vivid account of the crew, cargo and ship itself. It is perhaps for this reason that the Nanking Cargo has retained its popularity, and wares from this cargo are highly collectible.

A Nanking Cargo 'Lattice Fence' pattern dish, the borders with three clusters of flowering branches.

This is the largest plate of this type.

c1750   *16.5in (42cm) diam*

$5,000-7,000   **RB**

A Nanking Cargo 'Willow Terrace' pattern soup dish.

c1750   *9in (23cm) diam*

$500-700   **RB**

A Nanking Cargo plate, decorated with a central scene of a pagoda building on a terrace next to a willow tree, with a large pine to the right and a smaller piece of land on the left, in one of the most popular patterns from the cargo.

c1750   *9in (23cm) wide*

$280-320   **R&GM**

A Nanking Cargo 'Three Pavilions' pattern plate, in blue and gold, the gold has been rubbed away.

c1750   *14in (36cm) diam*

$2,000-3,000   **RB**

A Nanking Cargo Imari plate, the sea has left only a ghostly, disjointed scene of a house on a promontory, removing most of the original design, chips, cracks.

c1750   *9in (23cm) wide*

$100-150   **R&GM**

A Nanking Cargo large size 'Blue Pine Tree' pattern tea bowl and saucer.

c1750   *4.5in (11.5cm) diam*

$300-400   **RB**

A Nanking Cargo 'Pagoda Riverscape' pattern tea bowl and saucer.

The blue decoration would have been glazed, and then the Imari enameling would have been painted over the top. The Imari enameling on this piece has been worn away. The blue has remained intact because it had the protection of the glaze.

c1750   4.75in (12cm) diam

$300-400   **RB**

An Nanking Cargo 'Peony Rock' pattern blue and white and enameled tea bowl and saucer.

5.25in (13.5cm) diam

$300-400   **RB**

A Nanking Cargo Batavian 'Bamboo and Peony' pattern tea bowl and saucer.

The Batavia area of porcelain trading gave its name to this style of ceramic which has a brown color on the underside.

c1750   4.5in (11.5cm) diam

$300-400   **RB**

A Nanking Cargo teacup and saucer.

The pattern has been lost because it was painted over glaze.

c1750   5in (13cm) diam

$70-100   **RB**

A Nanking Cargo blue and white Imari 'Pine Tree' pattern saucer and tea bowl.

4.5in (11.5cm) diam

$400-600   **RB**

A Nanking Cargo 'Pagoda Riverscape' pattern tea bowl and saucer.

Thousands of pieces were made in the 'Pagoda Riverscape' pattern and now epitomize the Nanking Cargo. The paper label must be intact to retain the value of the piece.

c1750   Saucer 3in (7.5cm) diam

$300-400   **RB**

A Nanking Cargo 'Pagoda Riverscape' pattern saucer.

c1750   4in (10cm) diam

$120-180   **RB**

A Nanking Cargo large size 'Scholar on the Bridge' pattern bowl.

c1750   7.5in (19cm) diam

$400-600   **RB**

A Nanking Cargo 'Peony Rock' pattern bowl.

c1750   6in (15cm) diam

$220-280   **RB**

A Nanking Cargo Imari bowl.

c1750   6in (15cm) wide

$220-280   **R&GM**

A Nanking Cargo blue and white 'Trellis' pattern sauceboat, of European silver-shape, painted with pine, peony, chrysanthemums, bamboo and a fence decorated with long life symbols on the exterior, and a chrysanthemum spray on the centre of the interior below border of 'Trellis' pattern.

c1750   *8.25in (21cm) wide*

$3,000-4,000   **RB**

A Nanking Cargo tureen, with pomegranate finial and shallow domed covers, delicately painted in a linear-style with areas filled in a paler blue wash with a broad river landscape.

c1750   *9.25in (23.5cm) wide*

$7,000-10,000   **RB**

A CLOSER LOOK AT A NANKING CARGO BUTTER TUB

These were made in imitation of wooden milk tubs with loops for a carrying cord.

These unusual objects were sometimes included in dinner services and similar examples were made at Delft and Meissen.

Round and oval butter tubs were recovered from the Geldermalsen in seven different shapes.

This tub is in excellent condition with extremely fine paint work.

A Nanking Cargo butter tub, of circular form with two raised flanges with holes, the covers flat with gently sloping edges, a rectangle has been left on either side to accommodate the flanges, the central low handle painted blue.

c1750   *4.5in (11.5cm) wide*

$700-1,000   **R&GM**

A Nanking Cargo cylindrical condiment jar, with shallow domed covers and a loop handle at the side.

Pieces from the Nanking Cargo tend to be shinier than pieces from other cargos, because of the quality of the porcelain.

c1750   *4.5in (11.5cm) wide*

$3,000-4,000   **RB**

A Nanking Cargo blue and white Imari beer mug.

The Chinese did not use beer mugs so these would have been made to order for the European market.

c1750   *5.25in (13.5cm) high*

$700-1,000   **RB**

A Nanking Cargo pair of salt stands, of a shallow-type.

These are of interest because they are shallow as they were used for rock salt rather than ground salt which requires deeper salt stands. They are typical of this period.

c1750   *3.25in (8.5cm) wide*

$4,000-6,000 pair   **RB**

Diana Cargo

The Diana was a 350 tonne wooden cargo ship - some 27 yards (30 meters) in length. It was an English ship, built in Calcutta in 1812, and was licensed to trade between India and the Far East. The Diana was on its way to Madras when it sunk near the Malacca Straits, West Singapore, on March 4, 1817.

In 1994 more than 24,000 pieces of porcelain were salvaged, including bowls, cups, saucers and baskets. Many of the shapes were designed specially for elaborate Western-style dining. The buyers would have been members of wealthy Madras society. Originally the cargo would also have included sugar, green tea, camphor and silk.

A Diana Cargo 'Diving Birds' pattern bowl and saucer, with trees and a pagoda.

c1817   6.25in (16cm) diam

$350-400   RB

A selection of Diana Cargo small painted porcelain toys.

c1817   2in (5.5cm) high

$120-180 each   RB

Three Diana Cargo covers.

The ceramics from the Diana Cargo, like all Cargos give a snap shot of the trade at the time. European, especially English factories were producing ceramics that undercut the Chinese, using factory production methods. Economy was the essence of trade at this Napoleonic period, so most of this Cargo is of poor quality.

c1817   3in (8cm) diam

$30-40 each   R&GM

A Diana Cargo small storage jar, for dried fruits and spices.

c1817   6in (15cm) high

$300-500   RB

A Diana Cargo large storage jar.

c1817   24in (61cm) high

$1,800-2,200   RB

A Diana Cargo glass wine bottle, with some encrustation.

c1817   9.5in (24cm) high

$220-280   RB

Tek Sing Cargo

Captain Michael Hatcher recovered the Tek Sing Cargo in 1986. It was the largest and most varied ever salvaged. The Tek Sing (meaning True Star), was bound from Amoy Harbour, China, to Batavia (today Jakarta). The cargo included 350,000 pieces of porcelain, large amounts of black and green tea, silk, furniture, mother-of-pearl, and herbs. There were 2,000 people on board including 1,600 passengers. 1,800 lives were lost on February 5, 1822 when the ship ran onto the Belvidere Reef, north of Java, and sank.

The cargo would have been intended primarily for the wealthy Chinese market in Batavia in Java, although some would probably have been purchased there by Dutch, English and French merchants for export to Europe. The porcelain was mostly bowls and dishes as well as pouring vessels and decorative objects. The ceramics in this cargo have created great interest because of the vast variety of shapes and style, many of which had not been seen before. The wares exhibit a high standard of painting and some are rare and valuable because of the block-print technique used to decorate them. There are also some monochrome wares, white and crackled-celadon bowls, and olive-glazed bowls.

Common motifs on the ware include flowering plants growing from rocks, peony (symbolizing wealth and status), prunus (symbolizing perseverance), magnolia (symbolizing purity) and bamboo (symbolizing fidelity and humility), chrysanthemums (meaning longevity) and pomegranate (representing fertility).

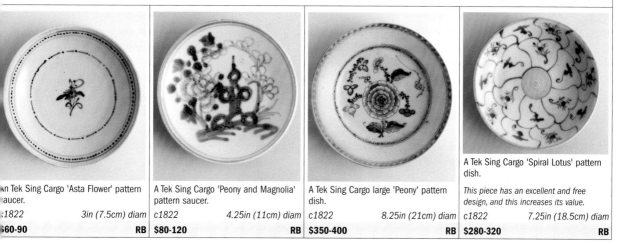

A Tek Sing Cargo 'Spiral Lotus' pattern dish.

A Tek Sing Cargo 'Asta Flower' pattern saucer.

c1822   3in (7.5cm) diam

$60-90   RB

A Tek Sing Cargo 'Peony and Magnolia' pattern saucer.

c1822   4.25in (11cm) diam

$80-120   RB

A Tek Sing Cargo large 'Peony' pattern dish.

c1822   8.25in (21cm) diam

$350-400   RB

This piece has an excellent and free design, and this increases its value.

c1822   7.25in (18.5cm) diam

$280-320   RB

A Tek Sing Cargo orchid leaf dish, with poetic inscription.
c1822   7.75in (20cm) diam
$400-600   **RB**

A Tek Sing Cargo basket of flowers dish.
c1822   6in (15cm) diam
$150-200   **RB**

A Tek Sing Cargo 'Magnolia' pattern dish.
c1822
$400-600   **RB**

A Tek Sing Cargo dish, with chrysanthemum design.
c1822   7in (18cm) diam
$400-600   **RB**

A Tek Sing Cargo dish, with chrysanthemum design, beside rockwork, with poem.
c1822   7.75in (19.5cm) diam
$400-600   **RB**

A Tek Sing Cargo shallow dish.
c1822   3.25in (8.5cm) diam
$60-90   **R&GM**

A Tek Sing Cargo tea bowl and saucer, with aster flower.

Aster flower pattern saucers are a good example of pieces from the Tek Sing Cargo that are affordable. Every one has been painted individually so they are all different.
c1822   Saucer 4.75in (12cm) diam
$120-180   **RB**

A Tek Sing Cargo tea bowl and saucer.
c1822   Saucer 4.75in (12cm) diam
$70-100   **R&GM**

A Tek Sing Cargo 'Hare' pattern ogee-shaped bowl.
c1822   6.75in (17cm) diam
$220-280   **RB**

A Tek Sing Cargo block-printed large bowl.
c1822
10in (25.5cm) diam
$1,500-2,000   **RB**

A Tek Sing Cargo 'Boy' pattern bowl, with a boy holding a lotus bloom standing in front of a garden fence.
c1822   6.75in (17.5cm) diam
$300-400   **RB**

A Tek Sing Cargo bowl, with a scholar standing beside a fence.
c1822   6.75in (17cm) diam
$300-400   **RE**

A Tek Sing Cargo bowl.
c1822   4.25in (11cm) diam
$50-80   **R&GM**

A Tek Sing Cargo set of sake cups.
c1822   1.25in (3.5cm) high
$70-100 each   **RB**

A Tek Sing Cargo small tea bowl, blurred.

c1822   1.5in (4cm) high
$50-80   **R&GM**

A Tek Sing Cargo hexagonal box and cover, pencil drawn with a peony flower head.
c1822   2.75in (7cm) diam
$700-1,000   **RB**

Two Tek Sing Cargo circular boxes, painted with a double ring, flowers and a banana leaf.
c1822   3in (8cm) diam
$300-400 each   **RB**

Three Tek Sing Cargo spoons.
c1822   4in (10cm) long
$20-30 each   **R&GM**

A Tek Sing Cargo spoon.
c1822   4.5in (11.5cm) long
$50-80   **R&GM**

A Tek Sing Cargo olive glaze circular bowl, of bombé form with horizontal ridge at the mouth, the matching cover with fish knop.
c1822   5.25in (13.5cm) high
$1,000-1,500   **RB**

A Tek Sing Cargo encrusted storage jar.
c1822   8.25in (21cm) high
$600-900   **RB**

Three Yongzheng/early Qianlong period models of boys, modeled wearing an apron tied up at the front, from an unrecorded wreck.

These figures were recorded in two wrecks, the Nanking Cargo (c1752) and the Tek Sing Cargo (c1822). Some experts believe that this means that, in 1822, old (i.e. made in 1752) ceramics were still shipped. An alternative explanation may be that the Chinese continued to make popular shapes for export to give their customers what they wanted. The large group of boys from the Tek Sing were identical and if they had been 'antique' it would have been very difficult to get such a large matching group together at one time, because they would have been sold on. Therefore it is more likely that these boys were popular from at least the 1730s to the 1820s, and were not antiques being transported.

A Tek Sing Cargo seated boy.
c1822   3in (7.5cm) high
$1,500-2,000   **RB**

c1730   3in (8cm) high
$400-600 each   **R&GM**

A Tek Sing Cargo encrusted storage jar.
c1822   8.25in (21cm) high
$700-1,000   **RB**

Chinese Blue and White

A Chinese blue and white porcelain Guan, painted to depict a dragon chasing the flaming pearl of wisdom, Yuan Dynasty.

6in (15cm) high

$1,000-1,500 SI

A 15thC Chinese blue and white porcelain stem cup, with figures amongst flowering trees, Ming Dynasty.

4.5in (11.5cm) diam

$1,500-2,000 SI

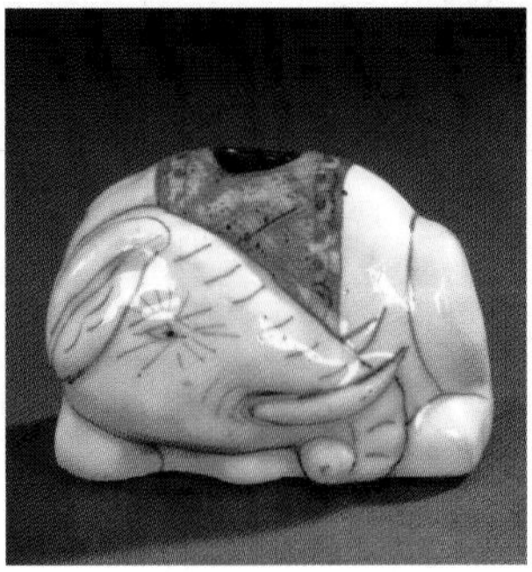

A Chinese blue and white porcelain brush washer in the form of an elephant, Jiajing mark and period.

3.5in (9cm) long

$400-600 SI

A Jiajing blue and white Ming dish, cracked.

c1522-1566   *12.5in (31.5cm) diam*

$400-600 R&GM

A Chinese blue and white Kraak plate, Wanli period.

$400-600 GG

A Chinese blue and white porcelain deep bowl, decorated with a continuous scene of dragons and other animals in a landscape, the interior with a confronting five-clawed dragon, six character Wanli mark.

1573-1619   *6.25in (16cm) diam*

$10,000-15,000 WW

A deer design dish, Ming Dynasty.

c1600   *8.25in (21cm) diam*

$180-220 R&GM

A Chinese Kraaksporselein bottle vase, decorated in underglaze blue with pendant panels of flowers and precious objects, with key fret, clouds and ropes of pearls to the neck, Wanli period, neck cracked.

12.25in (31cm) high

$700-1,000 DN

An early 17thC Chinese porcelain Kendi, or wine flask, with globular body and long shaft, with brass-mounted spout, painted with paneled foliage in under-glaze blue.

c1610   *8in (20.5cm) high*

$700-1,000 GorL

A Chinese Wanli period Kraak porcelain charger, centrally decorated with a dragon amongst clouds within a border of alternating panels showing precious objects and fruit sprays, the reverse with stylized foliage, cracked.

$2,500-3,000 DN

A Chinese porcelain Meiping vase, of slender baluster shape, with everted rim and decorated in underglaze blue, with a band of figures within cloud and decorative bands, a six character Wanli mark of the period, neck restored.

13in (33cm) high

$700-1,000 DN

A large Chinese Wanli Kraak circular charger, the central painted panel depicting two birds amidst blossom, with wide basket weave and geometric motif panels, the flared border with fan-shaped panels of flowers alternating with stylized fish scale panels, the underside sparsely decorated.

19.25in (49cm) diam

$1,500-2,000   **L&T**

A Chinese blue and white porcelain tripod incense burner, with figures under a pine tree, Ming Dynasty.

6in (15cm) diam

$1,500-2,000   **SI**

A Chinese Kraak porcelain dish, painted with a central panel of geese beside a pond, encircled by eight smaller panels, cracked.

c1620-40   14.25in (36cm) high

$500-700   **WW**

A Chinese Kraak porcelain dish, painted with a central of birds, flowers and foliage, encircled by eight smaller panels.

c1620-40   14.25in(36cm) diam

$1,000-1,500   **WW**

A Chinese blue and white porcelain bowl, Ming Dynasty with Changhua mark.

6in (15.2cm) diam

$220-280   **SI**

A Chinese Kraak porcelain blue and white bowl, decorated inside and out with panels of figures and flowers, a small rim chip and very faint 1in (2cm) hairline.

c1640   *13.5in (34cm) wide*

$5,000-7,000   **WW**

A Chinese blue and white tea bowl and saucer, Kangxi period.

1662-1722

$300-400   **GG**

A blue and white stem cup, with shaped rim, splayed foot decorated with panels of flowers, Kangxi period.

1662-1722   5in (12.5cm)

$1,200-1,800   **GG**

A rare Kangxi blue and white octagonal lobed ewer, with tall phoenix head spout, the panels painted with peony, lotus and other flowers, missing cover.

8.75in (3.5cm) high

$6,000-9,000   **GorL**

A rare Kangxi blue and white reticulated teapot and cover painted with flowers, fritted.

7in (17.75cm) wide

$3,000-4,000   **GorL**

A rare Kangxi blue and white candlestick with octagonal base, Salomonic base stem, barely twist, and square holder painted with emblems and flowers, crack to base.

6.25in (16cm) high

$3,000-4,000   **GorL**

A Kangxi blue and white candlestick, with domed octagonal base and knopped stem, painted with flowers.

6in (15.25cm) high

$1,800-2,200   **GorL**

A Kangxi blue and white tall stem cup with spiral fluted panels, drilled, and three Kang Hsi blue and white lobed oviform vases with slender neck and stems.

5in (12.75cm) high

$500-700   **GorL**

A Kangxi tea bowl and saucer.

c1662-1722   *3.75in (9.5cm) diam*

$300-400   **R&GM**

A Kangxi tea bowl and saucer.

c1662-1722 Saucer 5in (12.5cm) diam

$80-120   **R&GM**

A 17thC Chinese jar, of squat form with slightly flared sides and decorated in underglaze blue, with panels decorated with a musician, a scholar and a lady, beneath a Y-diaper border, leaf mark.

7in (18cm) high

$500-700   **DN**

A 17thC Chinese ovoid jar, decorated in underglaze blue with a continuous band of scholars and attendants.

7.75in (20cm) high

$320-380   **DN**

A Kangxi blanc-de-Chine vase, with applied decoration.

c1662-1772   *9.5in (24cm) high*

$3,000-4,000   **R&GM**

A Kangxi blue and white vase, with tall cylindrical neck, painted with bamboo sprays above seated figures drinking on a fenced terrace, Chengua mark, rim chip.

8.75in (22.25cm) high

$3,000-4,000   **GorL**

A Chinese Kangxi period slender bottle vase, with trumpet neck and applied with foliate and pierced handles, decorated in underglaze blue with a band of birds in flowering branches and the body with flower sprays.

9.75in (24.5cm) high

$3,000-4,000   **DN**

A Kangxi blue and white oviform jar, painted with mythical beasts on rockwork above breaking waves, with wooden stand.

9.25in (23.5cm) high

$1,800-2,200   **GorL**

A large Chinese Kangxi blue painted 'yan yan' vase, with flared trumpet neck decorated with two continuous landscape friezes showing figures and landscapes.

18in (46cm) high

$2,800-3,200   **L&T**

A Kangxi European subject 'charity' tea bowl and saucer, depicting the Virgin Mary and Child.

c1700   *5.5in (14cm) diam*

$500-700   **R&GM**

A Chinese blue and white porcelain Yen Yen vase, with shaped reserves enclosing figural decoration on brocade ground, Kangxi.

c1700   17.75in (45cm) high

$1,800-2,200   **SI**

A pair of Chinese blue and white porcelain vases, painted to depict immortals, late Ming/early Qing Dynasty.

10in (25.5cm) high

$1,500-2,000   **SI**

A Chinese Kangxi blue painted oviform vase, painted with prunus on a 'cracked ice' ground, with relief carved prunus decorated wood lid, encircled four character Kangxi mark and printed paper label.

10.25in (26cm) high

$500-700   **L&T**

A Chinese Kangxi blue painted oviform jar, with carved and pierced prunus decorated cover, the ground painted in the 'cracked ice' pattern, with three quatrefoil shaped panels enclosing precious objects.

8.5in (21.5cm) high

$300-400   **L&T**

A Chinese tea bowl and saucer.

c1720-50   5.25in (13.5cm) diam

$80-120   **R&GM**

A pair of Kangxi ormolu-mounted blue and white cylindrical jars and covers, variously painted with foliage, one cover badly cracked, one base star cracked.

Tallest 4.75in (12cm) high

$500-700   **GorL**

A mid 18thC Chinese blue and white chamfered rectangular dish, with a molded border, the center decorated with a large insect perched on a flowering chrysanthemum spray, within a complex floral border.

12.25in (31cm) high

$400-600   **WW**

An unusual 18thC blue and white dish, with a short flared rim, painted in the Japanese style, with a fan shaped panel of flowers and leaves and with lozenge and prunus motifs, the reverse with three flowering branches, kin mark.

8.5in (21.5cm) diam

$600-900   **WW**

An 18thC blue and white tripod cylindrical censer on short feet, painted with two four-clawed dragons contesting a flaming pearl.

3.5in (9cm) high

$220-280   **GorL**

An 18thC Chinese export blue and white porcelain barber's bowl, centrally painted with garden scene of willows, flowers and rock work, within diaper work and blossoming branches.

12.5in (31.5cm) diam

$800-1,200   **SI**

A 19thC Chinese blue and white tea or wine pot, with short neck and downswept shoulders to the ovoid body, painted on one side with two figures in an interior and on the other by an inlet, artemesia leaf mark, some damage.

6.5in (16.5cm) high

$220-280   **Chef**

A pair of Chinese Qianlong period octagonal blue and white salts, decorated with a landscape scene with a pagoda and boats.

3.5in (8.5cm) long

$700-1,000   **GG**

A Qianlong blue and white bulbous vase, decorated with gourds.

5.5in (14cm) high

$1,200-1,800   **GorL**

A pair of late 19thC Chinese blue and white jars and covers, depicting a garden scene with two gentlemen smoking pipes under trees, additional figure of an attendant holding a parasol, with bullocks tethered to a branch, a fenced pavilion with a woman looking out of a window.

11.75in (30cm) high

$700-1,000 **BonS**

A 19thC Chinese celadon and blue porcelain jar, of ovoid form, with blue and white calligraphy on a celadon ground, Qianlong mark.

8.75in (22cm) high

$320-380 **SI**

A pair of late 19thC Chinese blue and white porcelain stem cups, each painted with mountainous riverscape, Qing Dynasty.

3.25in (8cm) diam

$300-400 **SI**

A 19thC Chinese blue and white porcelain bulb vase, molded with a cylindrical neck, a garlic mouth ending in a star-form rim above five mouths on the shoulder, painted with birds perched on flowering branches, Qing Dynasty.

9.5in (24cm) high

$400-600 **SI**

A late 19thC Chinese blue and white lobed round tulip vase, with slender neck, painted with figures, on a prunus and cracked ice ground.

9.5in (24cm) high

$120-180 **LFA**

A late 19thC Chinese white and blue porcelain dish, the interior with flowering tree decoration, the exterior with children at play, fence and pavilion, Guangxu mark.

7in (18cm) diam

$220-280 **SI**

A 19thC Chinese blue and white large ginger jar, mounted as a table lamp.

24in (61cm) high

$2,200-2,800 **SI**

An early 20thC large copper-red and underglaze blue vase, of Meiping form, boldly painted with a group of cockerels with plumed tails, standing beneath a pomegranate tree, the copper-red of intense tone with greenish streaking.

20.75in (52.5cm) high

$3,000-4,000 **DN**

A large Oriental late Ming-style jar, decorated in underglaze blue with scaly beasts in a landscape.

16.25in (41cm) high

$320-380 **DN**

A 19thC Chinese blue and white porcelain vase and cover, of baluster form with a conical neck, painted overall with floral decoration and scrolling foliage decoration.

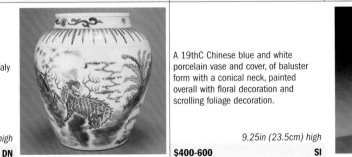

9.25in (23.5cm) high

$400-600 **SI**

Chinese Celadon

A Chinese Song Dynasty Qingbai porcelain saucer, very finely molded in relief with two fish swimming amongst water weeds within an inner dragon-skin border, unglazed edge, minute chip and frit to rim.

c960-1280   4.5in (11cm) diam

$600-900   **GG**

A 12thC Korean Koryo Dynasty green celadon bowl, of slightly lobed form, the interior incised with with scrolls, perfect condition.

7.5in (19 cm) diam

$700-1,000   **GG**

A 15thC Ming Longquan celadon bowl.

6.75in (17.5cm) diam

$700-1,000   **R&GM**

An 18thC green celadon pear-shaped vase, with wavy everted rim and fluted body, base and foot crack.

6.in (15.5cm) high

$80-120   **GorL**

A Chinese celadon covered porcelain vase, molded with shaped cartouches enclosing precious objects on a brocade ground, Qianlong molded seal mark.

12in (30.5cm) high

$800-1,200   **SI**

A 19thC Chinese Celadon porcelain charger.

13.5in (34cm) diam

$220-280   **SI**

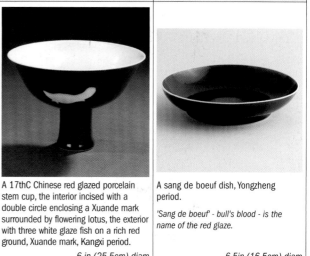

A 17thC Chinese red glazed porcelain stem cup, the interior incised with a double circle enclosing a Xuande mark surrounded by flowering lotus, the exterior with three white glaze fish on a rich red ground, Xuande mark, Kangxi period.

6.in (25.5cm) diam

$600-900   **SI**

A sang de boeuf dish, Yongzheng period.

'Sang de boeuf' - bull's blood - is the name of the red glaze.

6.5in (16.5cm) diam

$700-1,000   **TBk**

A Chinese red glazed porcelain dish, Daoguang mark and period.

7.25in (18.5cm) diam

$400-600   **SI**

A Chinese blanc-de-Chine porcelain libation cup, molded with a flowering prunus branch, Kangxi period.

3.5in (9cm) high

$320-380   **SI**

A mid 19thC pair of Chinese blanc-de-Chine porcelain figures of Fu lions, each seated on a rectangular plinth.

13.75in (35cm) high

$800-1,200   **SI**

A 19thC Chinese white porcelain vase and cover of baluster form.

8.5in (21.5cm) high

$400-600   **SI**

Chinese Famille Verte

A small famille verte bowl, with a phoenix, mythical beast, bamboo and plants, Kangxi period.

4.5in (11cm) diam

$300-400 GG

A famille verte octagonal pedestal dish, painted with a deer.

$350-400

6.75in (17cm) high

GorL

A Chinese famille verte porcelain basket, of oval outline, the center with a court scene, reticulated sides and brocade border with four cartouches enclosing flowerheads, Qing Dynasty.

10.5in (27cm) long

$220-280 S

A 19thC Chinese famille verte porcelain bowl, the exterior painted to depict a man on horseback with two attendants and calligraphy.

7.5in (19.5cm) diam

$400-600 SI

A 19thC Chinese famille verte porcelain bowl, painted to depict three medallions enclosing a riverscape decoration on a powder blue ground.

8in (20cm) diam

$280-320 SI

A famille verte square vase with rounded shoulders, painted with panels of chrysanthemum, peony, lotus, and prunus, within key-pattern borders, neck cut down, drilled to side, Kangxi period.

10.5in (26.5cm) diam

$400-600 GorL

A famille verte cylindrical brush pot, painted with a long-tailed bird on rockwork issuing prunus, rim frits, Kangxi period.

5.5in (14cm) high

$800-1,200 GorL

Two views of a Chinese Kangxi period famille verte caddy, with a silver cover, of hexagonal form, each panel painted with ladies by a fence, with flowers growing from a rock and precious objects with a vase.

c1662-1722

7.25in (18.5cm) high

$1,200-1,800 GG

A Chinese famille verte porcelain cachepot, Kangxi period.

c1710 *10.75in (27cm) high*

$1,200-1,800 SI

A pair of Chinese famille verte vases, with ormolu mounted rims, some wear, Kangxi period.

11.75in (30cm) high

$2,500-3,000 Chef

A late 19thC Chinese famille verte porcelain covered jar, of baluster form, painted with figural decoration, electrified.

9in (23cm) high

$150-200 S

A 19thC Chinese famille verte porcelain jar, of ovoid form, painted with two dragons chasing the flaming pearl of wisdom on a crackled beige ground, Qianlong mark.

8in (20cm) high

$300-400   **SI**

A Chinese ovoid jar and cover, with gilded temple dog finial, the body decorated with famille verte reserve panels of flowers and utensils on a royal blue ground.

c1662-1722

$220-280   **Clv**

A large Kangxi period famille verte dish, depicting figures making offerings in a fenced garden with pine trees, beyond pagodas covered in clouds, the rim with precious objects in cartouches, hairline crack from rim and across center and rim chip restored.

13.75in (35cm) diam

$2,500-3,000   **GG**

A Chinese Tianqi period famille verte small hexagonal dish, painted with peony and crysanthemum issuing from incised rock-work, the base marked in underglaze blue with "T'ien hsia t'ai p'ing" ("Peace throughout the empire"), minute rim chip.

c1621-1627   *5.5in (14cm) diam*

$800-1,200   **GG**

A 19thC Chinese famille verte porcelain teapot, with silver cover and handle, decorated with a flower-filled vase, with age crack, Qianlong period.

6in (15cm) high

$300-400   **SI**

A pair of 19thC Chinese famille verte porcelain figures of fu dogs, marked Qing Dynasty.

9in (23cm) high

$320-380   **SI**

Chinese Famille Rose

A Chinese famille rose octagonal plate, the center decorated with four bats around a central 'shou' character on a yellow ground.

c1730-1740   *8.5in (21.5cm) diam*

$600-900   **WW**

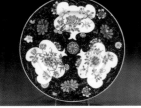

One of a pair of Chinese famille rose porcelain chargers, with three shaped reserves enclosing floral decoration on green ground, Yongzheng period.

c1730   *15in (38cm) diam*

$300-400 (pair)   **SI**

A Qianlong period porcelain charger, painted with sprays of peonies and birds in famille rose enamels.

15in (38cm) high

$300-400   **GorL**

An 18thC Chinese export porcelain serving plate, of octagonal shape, painted with peonies and scrolls in famille rose enamels.

c1750   *16in (40.5cm) high*

$800-1,200   **GorL**

A Chinese famille rose barrel-shaped mug, with scroll handle, painted with flower sprays and inscribed oval cartouche under a garlanded diaper border, Qianlong period.

5in (12.5cm) high

$180-220 OACC

A Chinese famille rose coffee cup, with arms of Foster, Qianlong period.

c1787

$220-280 GorL

Two Chinese famille rose porcelain mugs, with floral decoration, Qianlong period.

5.75in (14.5cm) high

$100-150 each SI

A pair of Chinese famille rose tankards, the tall, finely potted sides with strap handles and flared at the base, decorated with a crest of a dove pecking a sheaf of corn, probably for Dandy of Suffolk, and scattered flowers beneath a spearhead border, one with minor rim bruise, the other with crack to base of handle and chip on base, Qianlong period.

6.25in (16cm) high

$800-1,200 DN

A Chinese famille rose coffee cup, with the arms of Balderstone, Qianlong period.

c1795

$150-200 GorL

A Chinese famille rose coffee cup, decorated with a dove holding a garland crest over a shield with floral sprig, Qianlong period.

c1795

$70-100 GorL

A mid 19thC Canton famille rose part tea set, the flared cup with angular handle, densely painted with continuous frieze of figures on a terrace, with narrow painted inner border, the saucer with similar roundel panel, old ownership label with monogram, comprising six cups, six saucers and three bread plates.

$700-1,000 L&T

A Yongzheng famille-rose teapot.

c1725

$700-1,000 GG

A Chinese famille rose globular teapot and cover, with molded lotus base, painted with panels of figures in sampans on a black and green scrolling foliage ground, fitted, spout chip, Yongzheng period.

6in (15.5cm) wide

$600-900 GorL

A Chinese famille rose cream jug and cover, painted with a roundel of figures by a wall near plantain, Qianlong period.

$800-1,200 GorL

A late 19thC Chinese Cadogan famille rose porcelain teapot, with cockerel and floral decoration.

6in (15cm) high

$280-320 S

Two 19thC Chinese famille rose porcelain teapots, with floral decoration.

6.25in (16cm) high

$100-150 (each) SI

A Chinese famille rose oviform tea caddy and cover, painted with a leaf shaped panel of cockerel reserved on a gilt ground, base drilled, neck chip, Yongzheng period.

4.75in (12cm) high

$500-700 **GorL**

A Chinese famille rose trumpet-shaped beaker vase, painted with butterflies and peony, Qianlong period.

9.5in (24.5cm) high

$600-900 **GorL**

A Chinese famille rose porcelain bottle vase, with bird and floral decoration, Qing Dynasty.

16.5in (42cm) high

$320-380 **SI**

A late 19thC Chinese porcelain famille rose bottle vase and cover, painted with figural and floral reserves, top and base probably associated.

16.5in (42cm) high

$600-900 **SI**

A famille rose brushpot, molded in the form of a lotus leaf, together with a brushpot molded with cabbages, and a famille rose brushpot with a lady resting under a willow tree, all with wooden stands.

5in (12.5cm) high

$800-1,200 **DN**

A Chinese famille rose porcelain vase, of ovoid form, with floral decoration on a blue ground, green fu-dog form handles, electrified.

14.75in (37.5cm) high

$220-280 **SI**

A pair of Chinese famille rose porcelain vases, of lozenge form with a qilin amongst flowering branches decoration, early Republic period.

1911-1930 *12.75in (32.5cm) high*

$180-220 **SI**

A Hongxian period eggshell famille rose vase, enameled on one side with Shou Lao and two boys carrying an enormous peach, the reverse with a poem.

7.5in (19cm) high

$600-900 **DN**

One of a pair of Hongxian period famille rose vases, each of ovoid form with a trumpet neck, painted with a pair of quails on rockwork with issuing flowers.

9.25in (25cm) high

$400-600 (pair) **DN**

A grisaille and gilt-decorated vase, of large baluster form, painted with a standing dignitary and three attendants in a terraced garden scene, mark of Liqingshan Fang, crack.

13.75in (35cm) high

$600-900 **DN**

A Hongxian period famille rose vase, of slightly tapering ovoid form with a broad flared rim, painted with scattered butterflies, with a wooden stand.

8.25in (21cm) high

$300-400 **DN**

A large famille rose vase, the tall ovoid body painted with three drunken deities laughing and playing beside a prunus tree, mark of Juren Tang, haircrack.

13.75in (35cm) high

$350-400 **DN**

A 19thC Chinese export porcelain tureen, cover and stand in famille rose colors, octagonal form with dome top and boar's-head handle, decorated in blue, pink, yellow, and green, with conforming undertray, platter repaired.

Platter 14.75in (37.5cm) long

$2,500-3,000　　　　　**FRE**

A late 19thC Canton circular famille rose punch-bowl, the exterior densely painted in polychrome enamels with three repeated figural panels and three blossom, bird and butterfly panels below continuous deep floral frieze, the interior decorated with central roundel incorporating four repeat panels.

14.5in (37cm) diam

$700-1,000　　　　　**L&T**

A famille rose plaque, depicting Buddha standing under a pine tree, framed and glazed.

7in (18cm) high

$300-400　　　　　**DN**

A framed Hongxian period famille rose table screen, of rectangular section, painted with figures in a landscape.

14.25in (36cm) high

$600-900　　　　　**DN**

A Chinese famille rose porcelain figure of a Guanyin, standing wearing long robes, jewelry and a veil, holding a vase, early Republic period.

1911-1930　　　13in (33cm) high

$320-380　　　　　**SI**

Chinese Export

A Chinese Qianlong period Mandarin bowl, decorated with a European hunting scene, with figures on horseback and hounds in a landscape, rivets and hairline cracks restored to a high standard.

c1770　　　11in (28cm) diam

$800-1,200　　　　　**GG**

An 18thC Chinese export porcelain punch-bowl, painted with figures in pleasure boats and waterside buildings, reserved against a diaper ground, restored.

13in (33cm) high

$600-900　　　　　**GorL**

A late 18thC Chinese export porcelain square centerbowl, painted with flowers and insects.

11.5in (29cm) wide

$500-700　　　　　**SI**

A pair of oval export porcelain reticulated fruit stands and underplates, decorated with peach and brown banding and floral swags, the initial "C" enclosed by draped shields.

c1800　　　10in (25cm) wide

$1,200-1,800　　　　　**FRE**

A Chinese export porcelain orange Fitzhugh scalloped and fluted monteith, with American eagle decoration, the exterior with two polychrome enameled spreadwing eagles bearing American shields and ribbons reading 'E. Pluribus Unum', the interior with a central floral spray.

10.75in (27.5cm) diam

$20,000-30,000　　　　　**NA**

A pair of Chinese Kangxi blanc-de-Chine flared cups, each molded with three prunus sprays, one with small rim chips.

c1662-1772   3.25in (8.5cm) high

$600-900   **WW**

A Yongzheng en grisaille tea bowl and saucer, with the arms and portrait of "Petrus Boudaan, Ecclesiastes Amstelodamensis", gilt scroll border.

Saucer 4.5in (11.5cm) diam

$500-700   **GorL**

A Qianlong tea bowl, with the arms of Holburne of Menstrie, Baronets of Nova Scotia, spearhead border.

c1745

$180-220   **GorL**

A Qianlong coffee cup, with the arms of Wallace of Scotland.

c1745

$320-380   **GorL**

A pair of mid-18thC Chinese export tea bowls and saucers, finely decorated with initials "ISC" within a shell and C-scroll cartouche and a border of C-scrolls and flowers, cracks.

$300-400   **DN**

A Qianlong coffee cup, with the arms of Parsons impaling Windygate, spearhead border and motto "Arte salutari".

c1750

$350-400   **GorL**

A Qianlong coffee cup, decorated en grisaille with the arms of Board of Bordhill and Lindfield in Sussex.

c1750

$150-200   **GorL**

A Qianlong coffee cup, with the arms of Allen spearhead border.

c1760

$220-280   **GorL**

An 18thC export porcelain Chinese coffee cup.

c1760   3in (8cm) high

$100-150   **AD**

A Qianlong coffee cup, with the arms of Jenkins, spearhead border.

c1755

$300-400   **GorL**

A Qianlong coffee cup, with the arms of Hare, spearhead border.

c1755

$320-380   **GorL**

c1760

$280-320

A Qianlong tea cup, with the arms of Dawes of Stapleton, Co. Leicester, chain border.

GorL

A Qianlong tea bowl, with the arms of Poyntz with Courtenay in pretense.

William Poyntz married in 1763, the service by descent is now at Althorp in Northamptonshire, England.

c1765

$280-320   GorL

A Qianlong en grisaille coffee cup, with the arms of Wilson.

c1765

$280-320   GorL

A Qianlong coffee cup, with arms of Pollock, diaper border.

c1765

$300-350   GorL

A Qianlong coffee cup, apparently with the arms of French of Frenchlands, or Lunsford of Sussex, Fitzhugh border.

c1770

$220-280   GorL

A Qianlong coffee cup, decorated with the Arms of Liberty, depicting John Wilkes and his opponent Lord Mansfield.

c1770

$1,200-1,800   GorL

A Qianlong two-handled chocolate cup, with arm and dagger crest and initials W.E.P. in a cartouche.

c1770

$120-180   GorL

A Qianlong beaker cup, with the arms of Shepherd.

c1770

$300-350   GorL

A Qianlong coffee cup, with arms per fesse, monogram, vineous crest and border.

c1780

$320-380   GorL

A Qianlong cup and saucer, with the arms of Rev. William Crichton.

c1780   *Saucer 5.5in (14cm) diam*

$300-400   GorL

A Qianlong coffee cup, decorated with the initials J.R.M. within a sunburst surround, later bands and line border.

c1785

$100-150   GorL

A Qianlong coffee cup, with the arms of Cure, later diaper, trellis and scale border.

c1790

$280-320   GorL

A Qianlong coffee cup, with the arms of Bedford, probably Captain William Bedford of the East India Company.

c1790

$180-220   GorL

A Chinese export porcelain cider jug, the bulbous body painted with a blue floral band at the rim and with an oval landscape vignette on each side, all variously gilt, the domed cover similarly decorated and with a crouching foo dog finial, cover repaired, cracks to spout and rim.

11.5in (29.5cm) high

$1,000-1,500   **FRE**

A Chinese export large tapering-sided mug, with notched loop handle, and silver mounted-rim, carved overall with peony and lotus, above an underglaze blue ruji headband, handle glued, Kangxi period.

8.75in (22cm) high

$400-600   **LFA**

A Qianlong cylindrical mug, with the arms of Newland impaling Hutchinson, vine border, lacks handle.

c1738   *5.25in (13.5cm) high*

$320-380   **GorL**

An 19thC Chinese export porcelain bulbous-shaped cream jug, with enameled bird and insect decoration, damaged.

3.5in (9cm) high

$120-180   **Clv**

A rare large sepia, blue enamel and gilt cylindrical mug, with double strap handle headed by grapes, painted with a sepia oval roundel of a European house, Pencarrow, Cornwall, below a blue enamel floral rim with pendant husks forming swags around the body.

6.25in (16cm) high

$2,800-3,200   **GorL**

A Ming aubergine and turquoise glazed tile maker's figure of a fish above waves, on a semicylindrical base.

13.5in (34.25cm) high

$700-1,000   **GorL**

A Kang Hsi green, aubergine, and yellow-glazed biscuit group of the Laughing Twins, Hehe Erxian, one holding money on pierced rockwork base, chips, wood stand.

5.5in (14cm) high

$400-600   **GorL**

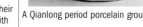

A good pair of Chinese porcelain models of cockerels, standing with their heads turned, the rockwork bases with a blue glaze, Qianlong period.

Provenance: *Viscount Astor, Cliveden sale, 1967.*

c1760   *15.25in (39cm) high*

$10,000-15,000   **WW**

A Qianlong period porcelain group.

c1780   *6in (15cm) high*

$7,000-10,000   **TBk**

A Qianlong export iron-red seated hound, wearing a green collar and gilt belt, restored leg and ear, mouth chips.

6.75in (17.25cm) high

$1,500-2,000   **GorL**

A pair of 18thC Chinese Sancai porcelain figures of Fu dogs.

Sancai means 'three colors'.

3.75in (9.5cm) high

$400-600   **SI**

An 18thC Chinese turquoise porcelain figure of a fu dog.

5in (13cm) high

$180-220 SI

A pair of Chinese pottery figures of Fu dogs, Qing Dynasty.

11.75in (30cm) high

$400-600 SI

A Chinese gilt and brown porcelain figure, of Li Po seated on a rock-form base with a robin's-egg glaze, Qing Dynasty.

6.75in (17cm) high

$320-380 SI

A Chinese porcelain figure of Kuei Hsin standing on a carp, Qing Dynasty.

9in (23cm) high

$600-900 SI

An early 20thC Chinese Sancai figure of a Guanyin, seated on a throne, holding a child.

10.5in (26.5cm) high

$280-320 SI

A pair of 18thC Chinese Armorial soup plates, the borders decorated with shields and the motto "Hazard Zit Eordward" and with floral festoons and sprigs.

8.75in (22cm) diam

$700-1,000 WW

One of a set of 14 Chinese Qianlong period porcelain plates, each decorated with a miller, wife and child outside a cottage, the underglaze blue diaper border paneled with Imari-type panels of flowers and birds, some chips.

9.75in (24.5cm) diam

$3,000-4,000 set DN

A Chinese Qianlong period circular charger, painted in enamels and gilt with bamboo and flowering shrubs, the border with conforming decoration.

13.75in (35.5cm) high

$150-200 BonS

A Chinese export porcelain orange Fitzhugh rectangular serving dish, with American eagle decoration, with inverted curved sides and notched corners, the center painted with a polychrome enameled spreadwing eagle bearing an American shield and ribbon reading "E. Pluribus Unum".

8in (20cm) long

$10,000-15,000 NA

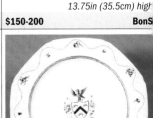

A Chinese export porcelain famille rose decorated dinner plate, with the Sargent family coat-of-arms and motto, en suite with the plate on the right.

Provenance of both Sargent plates:
Ignatius Sargetn family of Gloucester, MA.

$5,000-7,000 NA

A Chinese export porcelain famille rose decorated dinner plate, with the Sargent family coat-of-arms and motto, en suite with the plate on the left.

$6,000-9,000 NA

A Chinese wucai porcelain vase, painted to depict medallions with figural decoration amongst flying cranes, flowers and scrolling foliage, with Jiajing underglazed blue, six-character mark.

20.75in (52.5cm) high

$2,500-3,000   SI

A Chinese Chongzhen period wucai vase, decorated with phoenix amongst scrolling poenies above lapets, the shoulders with a band of scrolling peonies below a neck band of flaming pearls, three restored hair-line cracks and piece put back in the rim, three chips restored on cover.

1623-1643   *13in (33cm) high*

$1,800-2,200   GG

A pair of 18thC Chinese vases and one cover, the blue and white baluster bodies of barbed section, the lappet-shaped reserves of vases of flowers alternating with island views, all with later European over-painting in Imari colors, the cover damaged.

11.75in (30cm) high

$700-1,000   Chef

A large 19thC Chinese Transitional-style jar, decorated in underglaze blue with figures, rocks and plantains.

15.5in (39cm) high

$1,500-2,000   DN

19thC Chinese grisaille and white porcelain vase, of ovoid form, with waisted neck and flowering branch motif, Qing Dynasty.

9in (23cm) high

220-280   SI

A 19thC Cantonese vase, the baluster body painted with four reserves of dignitaries by pavilions on a ground of fruit, flowers, birds and Buddhist objects, mythical beasts applied to the shoulders below the playful shi-shi handles.

24.5in (62cm) high

$320-380   Chef

A large Oriental export ovoid vase and cover, enameled in colors with panels of flowers on an iron-red ground, scattered with fans, gilt metal finial, restored.

25.25in (64cm) high

$700-1,000   DN

A Chinese aubergine and turquoise glazed porcelain vase, of ovoid form with a waisted neck, decorated with calligraphy, ruji head and floral sprays.

9.5in (24cm) high

$280-320   SI

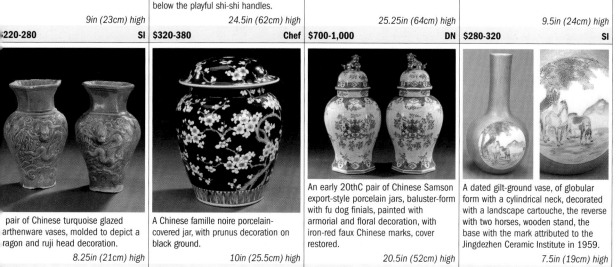

pair of Chinese turquoise glazed earthenware vases, molded to depict a dragon and ruji head decoration.

8.25in (21cm) high

150-200   SI

A Chinese famille noire porcelain-covered jar, with prunus decoration on black ground.

10in (25.5cm) high

$280-320   SI

An early 20thC pair of Chinese Samson export-style porcelain jars, baluster-form with fu dog finials, painted with armorial and floral decoration, with iron-red faux Chinese marks, cover restored.

20.5in (52cm) high

$400-600   SI

A dated gilt-ground vase, of globular form with a cylindrical neck, decorated with a landscape cartouche, the reverse with two horses, wooden stand, the base with the mark attributed to the Jingdezhen Ceramic Institute in 1959.

7.5in (19cm) high

$600-900   DN

ORIENTAL

A Showa period Satsuma earthenware vase, painted to depict three geisha under a flowering tree.

7.5in (19cm) high

$400-600   SI

A large Satsuma baluster vase and cover, the domed cover with large finial in the form of a crouching Buddhistic lion with scalloped border, painted with four cartouche panels of wise men, on wide foo with gilt continuous flowerhead decoration.

33in (84cm) hig

$1,500-2,000   L&

A late 19thC large Satsuma floor vase, the slender ovoid form mounted on either side of the neck with lion's head and ring handles, enameled and gilt-decorated with immortals below a lappet band on the interior and exterior of the rim, wear to gilding.

33in (84cm) high

$800-1,200   FRE

A 19thC Meiji period Satsuma earthenware vase, of ovoid form with shaped everted mouth, the shoulders with a gilt bow raised in high relief above figures in a landscape.

13.25in (33.5cm) hig

$400-600   S

A Satsuma vase, by Ryuzan, decorated with cranes beneath a full moon on rocks with crashing waves and a rocky coastal landscape, both panels on a black ground decorated in gilt, signed "dai nihon, kyoto, ryuzan sei zo", some rubbing.

12.5in (32cm) high

$2,000-3,000   DN

A Meiji period Satsuma earthenware vase, of ovoid form, with ribbed body with immortals and geisha decoration.

10in (25.5cm) high

$600-900   SI

A pair of Satsuma ovoid vases, with lion mask handles, each decorated with figures on a terrace in a river landscape, the neck with a band of flowers, signed, wood stands.

6.75in (17cm) high

$600-900   DN

A pair of Satsuma earthenware vases, each of ovoid form painted to depict pagoda amongst flowering branches.

c1900   *6.5in (16.5cm) high*

$320-380   SI

An early 20thC Satsuma koro, painted with two panels of figures sitting in gardens enjoying literary pursuits, elephant mask handles to the globular body, with dark blue ground.

6.25in (16cm) hig

$80-120   Che

A Satsuma cylindrical teapot and cover, decorated in polychrome and gilt with domestic scenes, wisteria and brocade bands, lid broken.

5.5in (14cm) high

$120-180 GorL

A Satsuma small bowl, depicting butterflies inside and outside a gilt net, the center with iron red drawstring, oblong gilt and black mark.

4.75in (12cm) diam

$150-200 BonS

A Satsuma potteries canted rectangular tray, finely decorated with figures in a ship-shaped carriage within a brocade border, the base with a branch of flowering prunus, signed.

7in (18cm) wide

$3,000-4,000 DN

A small Satsuma fluted bowl with scalloped rim, painted and gilt with Lohan and Ratan within a figural and brocade border, the exterior with shaped panels of figural groups, signed Hattori.

5.25in (13.5cm) diam

$150-200 BonE

A small Imperial Satsuma fluted bowl with foliate rim, painted and gilt to the center with floral roundels, the exterior with floral sprays, signed probably "Shiroyama ga...".

4.75in (12cm) diam

$400-600 BonE

A Meiji period Satsuma figural group, signed and molded to depict two figures on a cloud-form base, wearing robes with a 'brocade' decoration.

13.5in (34cm) high

$700-1,000 SI

An early 20thC Satsuma plate, by Taizan, centrally gilt and painted in red blue and ocher with a phoenix mon on a sun yellow ground, the rim with floral mon, black painted and impressed marks.

7.25in (18.5cm) diam

$120-180 Chef

A Meiji period blue and white porcelain charger, with a mountainous landscape under a pine tree and flying crane border.

19.5in (49.5cm) diam

$700-1,000 SI

A Meiji period blue and white porcelain charger, painted to depict a riverscape.

22in (56cm) diam

$600-900 SI

A pair of Japanese blue and white chargers, each painted with a mountainous landscape, within a flowerhead trellis band.

c1880 *14.75in (37.5cm) diam*

$120-180 (pair) LFA

A Meiji period blue and white porcelain charger, painted with a prunus tree issuing from rockery above, figures seated on a low table.

18.5in (47cm) diam

$150-200 SI

CERAMICS

A 19thC blue and white porcelain bowl.

10in (25cm) diam

$150-200 SI

A late 19thC Hirado group of playful Buddhist lions, one biting the back of the other, their manes and tails detailed in blue, some damage.

6in (15cm) high

$150-200 Chef

A Meiji period Hirado blue and white porcelain reticulated double gourd netsuke, with gilt metal attachment, slight damage.

$350-400 GorL

A Taisho period Nabashima iron-red and blue porcelain vase, of ovoid form with floral decoration.

5in (13cm) high

$220-280 SI

A Japanese Arita vase, of archaistic bronze form, with a flared hexagonal section neck, molded handles, the sides molded with panels and on a flared, lobed, lozenge-shaped foot, the surface molded in shallow relief with chrysanthemum to the neck and chrysanthemum, rocks and waves to the main panels, all picked out in iron-red, blue and green and painted with waves to the foot, old firing cracks and some restoration, with paper labels "Burleigh (sic) House" and "Read 8", and a paper label for Red Cross Exhibition, wrongly numbered "49a".

Provenance: *Probably Burghley House, Sir C. Hercules Read, Gerald Mere Collection.*

Much of the collection at Burghley House was amassed during the tenure of John, the fifth Earl of Exeter and his wife Anne, in the latter third of the 17thC. Great patrons and connoisseurs of the fine and decorative arts, the Earl and Countess traveled extensively throughout Europe, acquiring paintings, sculpture, tapestries, furniture, jewelry and object d'art on their four (recorded) tours between 1679 and 1699.

c1660-1680 *6.75in (17cm) high*

$15,000-20,000 DN

A CLOSER LOOK AT AN ARITA VASE

This piece is of early Arita enameled porcelain.

The vase is composed of a greyish paste and the body is dressed in a thin off-white glaze.

It is decorated in thick and irregular saturated enamels characteristic of the earliest phase of Arita export ware between c1660 and 1680: a rich, almost blood red; deep cerulean, turquoise and a little black detailing.

It has remained in good condition, which adds to its value.

An Arita vase, in the form of a lady holding a basket and standing by a naturalistically modeled stump of a pine tree, with a flower at her feet, picked out in iron-red and blue, inscribed in pen, probably by Culpepper Tanner, with letters and numerals, paper label printed "Burghley House" and paper label inscribed "Read 7", paper label for Red Cross exhibition wrongly numbered "49".

Provenance: *Burghley House, Sir C. Hercules Read, Gerald Mere Collection.*

c1660-1680 *7.25in (18.5cm) high*

$15,000-20,000 DN

A late 17thC Arita flared barbed round bowl, the interior painted in underglaze blue with a figure in a river landscape, within a scale and dragon paneled band, the exterior with bats and emblems with brown line rim.

7.75in (19.5cm) diam

$700-1,000 LFA

A rare Arita tokuri, of square section decorated overall with karakuza scrolls, incised Johaneeum number "N:47", from the Japanese Palace, Dresden.

c1700 *7in (18cm) high*

$2,200-2,800 WW

A late 18thC Imari porcelain bowl, of deep circular form, ribbed sides, scalloped rim, the interior with four gilt chrysanthemum within a shaped medallion decorated with cranes amongst flowering trees beneath alternating vertical brocade bands, the exterior with a similar decoration, on high circular foot with a blue and white brocade motif.

18.75in (47.5cm) diam

$15,000-20,000 SI

A late 19thC Japanese Imari fluted circular bowl, painted and gilt with panels of birds amidst foliage.

10.75in (27.5cm) high

$300-400 BonS

A Meiji period Imari porcelain plate, with fan-shaped reserves enclosing floral and brocade decoration.

9.25in (23.5cm) diam

$150-200 SI

A Meiji period Imari porcelain charger, painted with a central medallion with a floral spray, with radiating panels enclosing floral, crane, and fence motifs on a brocade ground.

18in (46cm) diam

$400-600 SI

A Meiji period Imari porcelain charger, with figures under a prunus tree and birds.

24.5in (62cm) diam

$400-600 SI

An early 20thC Imari bowl, the fluted sides painted with fan shape reserves of gardens alternating with three red rosettes on a blue ground.

12.5in (32cm) diam

$300-500 Chef

A pair of late 19thC Meiji period Kutani porcelain double vases, attributed to Nanri Kaju, having a wavy flared rim with red and gold band about the neck, open circles on outer vase surrounded with red, gold-edged hexagonal bands on circular flaring base, both the top and bottom are decorated with floral reserves on red and gold field, one vase extensively repaired.

24.75in (63cm) high

$1,000-1,500 FRE

An early 20thC Kutani bowl, painted with sages eating al fresco, the exterior with cranes, Kutani marks, some damage.

44.5in (17.5cm) diam

$50-80 Chef

A late 17thC Kakiemon square section flask, with short straight neck, painted with panels of birds and waterplants, alternating with panels of figures, two body cracks to base.

8.75in (22cm) high

$1,000-1,500 LFA

A large porcelain charger, the brown ground decorated with song-birds amongst bamboo and blossom.

19in (48.5cm) diam

$600-900 GorL

One of a pair of octagonal bowls, finely decorated with peony, pomegranates and wisteria, within a turquoise ground band of flowers and leaves, impressed marks.

11.5in (29cm) wide

$300-400 (pair) LFA

A pair of polychrome porcelain vases, of flattened ovoid form, with floral decoration.

c1930 *7.25in (18.5cm) high*

$100-150 SI

Snuff Bottles

A 19thC glass, seal type snuff bottle with red overlay, carved with figures, bats and a dog, with stopper.

2.25in (5.5cm) high

$6,000-9,000 GorL

A 19thC glass seal type snuff bottle, with a five-color overlay carved with a bird, butterfly, flowers and foliage, mask ring handles, with stopper.

2.25in (5.5cm) high

$1,200-1,800 GorL

A 19thC snowstorm-ground, pear-shaped snuff bottle, with four-color overlay and four 'chilong' dragons, with green jadeite stopper.

2.25in (5.5cm) high

$2,200-2,800 GorL

A 19th/20thC white-ground glass, disc-shaped snuff bottle, with four-color overlay depicting upright rose sprays, with stopper.

2.25in (5.5cm) high

$600-900 GorL

A 19th/20thC white-ground glass oviform snuff bottle with green overlay depicting two dragons, with stopper and red leather case.

2.5in (6.5cm) high

$70-100 GorL

A 19th/20thC large white-ground glass, tapering rectangular snuff bottle, with blue overlay, upright flower sprays, with stopper.

3.5in (9cm) high

$180-220 GorL

A 19th/20thC pink-ground globular snuff bottle, with turquoise overlay depicting birds amongst foliage, with stopper.

2.25in (5.5cm) high

$70-100 GorL

A 20thC snowstorm-ground, glass, disc-shaped snuff bottle, with red overlay depicting two coiled dragons, lion mask ring handles, with stopper.

2.5in (6.5cm) high

$180-220 GorL

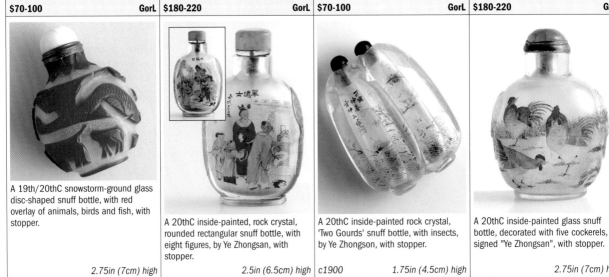

A 19th/20thC snowstorm-ground glass disc-shaped snuff bottle, with red overlay of animals, birds and fish, with stopper.

2.75in (7cm) high

$50-80 GorL

A 20thC inside-painted, rock crystal, rounded rectangular snuff bottle, with eight figures, by Ye Zhongsan, with stopper.

2.5in (6.5cm) high

$1,500-2,000 GorL

A 20thC inside-painted rock crystal, 'Two Gourds' snuff bottle, with insects, by Ye Zhongson, with stopper.

c1900 *1.75in (4.5cm) high*

$1,800-2,200 GorL

A 20thC inside-painted glass snuff bottle, decorated with five cockerels, signed "Ye Zhongsan", with stopper.

2.75in (7cm) high

$600-900 GorL

20thC ivory polychrome snuff bottle, carved in relief with a lotus pond, with matching stopper.

1900   *2.5in (6.5cm) high*

220-280   **GorL**

A painted ivory baluster snuff bottle, deeply carved with figures in pavilion landscapes, with ivory stopper.

3.5in (9cm) high

$700-1,000   **GorL**

A mother-of-pearl snuff bottle, carved with Shoulao holding a staff and large peach, rocks and fruit on the reverse, with matching stopper.

2.5in (6.5cm) high

$150-200   **GorL**

An early 19thC famille rose Canton enamel disc-shaped snuff bottle, with birds and peony, with gilt metal stopper.

2in (5cm) high

$700-1,000   **GorL**

19thC enameled milk-white ground glass disc-shaped snuff bottle, with pairs of chickens and ducks, with stopper.

2.5in (6.5cm) high

500-700   **GorL**

A 19thC famille rose turquoise ground snuff bottle, decorated with panels of flowers, small rouge-de-fer panels of riverscapes on each side, with matching stopper.

3.25in (8.5cm) high

$300-400   **GorL**

A 19thC large polychrome, molded, porcelain snuff bottle, decorated with two dragons chasing a sacred pearl among clouds above waves, with stopper.

3.5in (9cm) high

$280-320   **GorL**

A 19thC green and egg-plant glazed, molded, porcelain snuff bottle, of a curled lotus leaf and buds, with stopper.

2.75in (7cm) high

$150-200   **GorL**

late 19thC enameled porcelain, rounded rectangular snuff bottle, with key deer, gilt details, with stopper.

2.5in (6.5cm) high

120-180   **GorL**

A pair of 19th/20thC famille rose molded porcelain snuff bottles, decorated with panels of boys, Qianlong iron-red seal marks, with stoppers.

1.75in (4.5cm) high

$600-900   **GorL**

An 18th/19thC large white jade finger citrus snuff bottle, with stopper.

3.5in (9cm) high

$1,800-2,200   **GorL**

A mottled green, brown, and celadon jadeite, gourd-shaped snuff bottle, with relief tendrils, bat and fox, with stopper.

c1900 *2.75in (7cm) high*

$600-900 GorL

A 19th/20thC jadeite snuff bottle, carved as Lui Hai's three-legged toad, with stopper.

2.25in (5.5cm) high

$300-400 GorL

A mottled celadon and brown jade triangular cylindrical snuff bottle, relief carved with boys, foliage and rocks, with stopper.

2.25in (5.5cm) high

$280-320 GorL

A 19thC agate irregular snuff bottle, with butterfly and flower sprays from the white skin, with stopper.

2.5in (6.5cm) high

$1,200-1,800 GorL

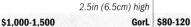

A 19th/20thC embelished jade snuff bottle, decorated with flowers and foliage, with stopper.

2.5in (6.5cm) high

$1,000-1,500 GorL

A mottled white and spinach jade flattened baluster snuff bottle, incised with shou roundels, lion mask ring handles, with jadeite stopper.

2in (5cm) hig

$80-120 Go

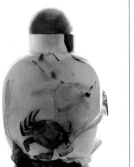

A 19thC agate snuff bottle, carved with a crab and a bird among rocks, small chip, with stopper.

2.5in (6.5cm) high

$350-400 GorL

A late 19thC agate or jasper rounded square snuff bottle, carved from the brownish skin with Chung Kuei, bat an pine, with stopper.

2.25in (5.5cm) hig

$300-400 Go

A 19th/20thC agate fruit-form snuff bottle, carved in relief with three figures in a leafy boat, with carved coral stopper.

2in (5cm) high

$3,000-4,000 GorL

A grey agate rounded square snuff bottle, with flautist seated on buffalo, with stopper.

2.5in (6.5cm) high

$180-220 GorL

A grey agate rounded square snuff bottle, relief carved with a monkey, dee and bird, with stopper.

2.25in (5.5cm) hig

$180-220 Go

An unusual 19th/20thC reddish brown lacquered metal snuff bottle, embelished with a lady accompanied by five children, with stopper.

2in (5cm) high

$400-600 GorL

A 19thC red lacquer disc-shaped snuff bottle, carved with figures amongst pavilions, with stopper.

2.75in (7cm) high

$600-900 GorL

late 19thC embelished wood arched rectangular flattened snuff bottle, with hree figures and a cluster of foliage, Qianlong mark, with stopper.

2.75in (7cm) high

1,800-2,200 GorL

A 19thC clear amber irregular snuff bottle, carved as a cluster of fruit, with stopper.

2.25in (5.5cm) high

$320-380 GorL

A 19thC turquoise matrix large snuff bottle, carved as an upright fish on wave base, with matching stopper and carved wooden stand.

4.5in (11.5cm) high

$600-900 GorL

Chinese Metalware

An unusual 18thC Chinese bronze incense burner, modeled as a horse, well cast with its head lowered.

6.25in (16cm) high

$600-900 WW

A 19thC Chinese white metal model of a junk, on a carved wood base, some damage.

c1850

$80-120 DN

Ming bronze Buddha seated in hyanasana, the hands of Mudra, wearing a finely incised floral and hequer-patterned loose robe tied at is waist and a swastika at his chest, is hair in tight curls.

8.75in (22.25cm) high

1,500-2,000 GorL

Two Chinese gilt bronze figures of attendants, one with joined hands, the other holding an offering in front of his chest, Ming Dynasty.

Larger 6in (15cm) high

$60-90 SI

A 19thC Chinese bronze figure of Buddha, seated in vajrasana, the left hand held in vitarka mudra, the other hand in bhumisparsa mudra, the hair arranged in rows with an usnisa above an urna between the downcast eyes, wearing a voluminous outer robe fastened around the waist with a bow.

14in (35.5cm) high

$1,000-1,500 SI

A Chinese archaistic bronze vessel, with a loop handle and a fu lion form spout.

9in (23cm) diam

$220-280　　SI

A Chinese bronze and champlevé tripod censor, with stylized floral and foliate design, lid cast with leaf-form finial.

4.75in (12cm) high

$120-180　　SI

A Chinese bronze urn, cast with a phoenix and a dragon.

8.5in (21.5cm) high

$180-220　　S

A Chinese circular cake basket, the scrolled rim with a wide, finely hammered band containing pierced prunus vignettes, with a swing handle, together with a butter-dish, cover and stand decorated with chrysanthemum, and a jampot, similarly decorated.

Basket 10.75in (27cm) diam

$400-600　　BonS

A Chinese archaistic bronze jue, the deep U-shaped body supported on three blade-shaped legs, cast with a broad band of taotie masks with raised bosses forming eyes and flanking a loop handle, the rim surmounted by two finials with circular caps decorated with whorls.

7.5in (19cm) high

$350-400　　SI

A Chinese Yixing pottery pewter-mounted tea set, comprising a teapot, bowl and cover, pitcher and water pot, together with a black lacquered tray.

Tray 22in (56cm) wide

$220-280　　SI

A pair of Chinese bronze urns, cast with birds and dragons.

5in (13cm) high

$150-200　　SI

A Chinese silver spoon, chased and applied with chrysanthemum decoration.

7in (17.5cm) long

$320-380　　SI

A Chinese four-trumpet épergne, pierced and chased with chrysanthemum, with waved rims, on a carved rosewood stand.

10.75in (27cm) high

$400-600　　Bon

Japanese Metalware

A Japanese bronze koro, cast to depict a lobster, Meiji period.

A koro is a Japanese incense burner.

12in (30.5cm) long

$600-900　　SI

A Japanese bronze koro, signed, cast to depict three tortoises, Meiji period.

10in (25.5cm) long

$600-900　　SI

A pair of Japanese Shibuichi figures of pheasants, with black lacquered stand, Meiji period.

Shibuichi is a form of Japanese metalwork.

Larger 17in (43cm) high

$3,000-3,500　　SI

A Japanese figural koro, shell form incense burner, Meiji period.

12in (30.5cm) high

$600-900　　SI

A Japanese bronze figure of a Geisha, bears a signature, late Meiji period.

14in (36cm) high

$220-280　　Bon

A Japanese bronze vase, cast to depict a carp, Meiji period.

11in (28cm) long

$400-600   **SI**

A pair of Japanese bronze figures of striding elephants, each beast naturalistically modeled and with trunks curled, signed possibly Kane Yasunga Chu.

17in (43cm) long

$1,500-2,000   **DN**

An 18th/19thC Japanese cast iron mask of Okame, mounted on a pine board.

8.75in (22cm) high

$500-700   **WW**

A 19thC Japanese iron circular plaque, cast in relief with Kwannon, a faint seal mark.

Kwannon is a Buddhist goddess of mercy.

13.5in (34cm) diam

$180-220   **WW**

A pair of Japanese mixed metal vases, each of square baluster outline, waisted neck, with two cicada-form handles on the shoulders, the body with two shaped cartouches enclosing flying birds above flowering peonies, signed, Meiji period.

13.25in (34cm) high

$15,000-20,000   **SI**

A Japanese mixed metal basket, with insect decoration, Meiji period.

9.75in (23cm) high

$1,800-2,200   **SI**

A Japanese bronze vase, with applied insects, signed, Meiji period.

6.5in (16.5cm) high

$800-1,200   **SI**

A Japanese bronze koro, signed, with shi-shi finial, Meiji period.

4.75in (12cm) high

$400-600   **SI**

A large Japanese bronze vase, of ovoid form, cast with shaped cartouches with flying cranes in high relief, the foot with a dragon chasing the flaming pearl of wisdom, bird head-form handles, Meiji period.

45in (104.5cm) high

$600-900   **SI**

A pair of Japanese bronze square censers, each heavily cast in low relief with a band of key fret decoration on the rim above calligraphy, with bamboo and ring-form handles, raised on three short feet, Meiji period.

9.75in (25cm) wide

$320-380   **SI**

A Japanese bronze vase, signed, of double gourd form, Meiji period.

10.75in (27.5cm) high

$400-600   **SI**

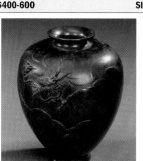

A Japanese bronze vase, of ovoid form with raised dragon chasing the flaming pearl of wisdom decoration, signed, Meiji period.

8in (20.5cm) high

$280-320   **SI**

ORIENTAL

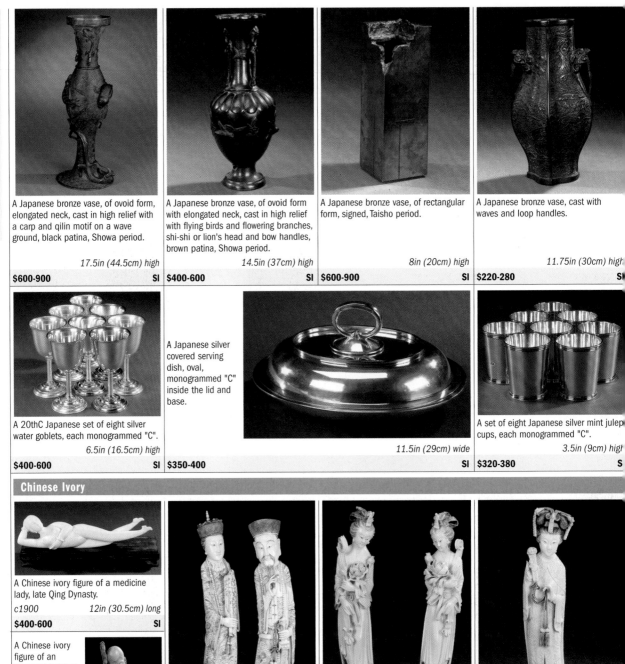

A Japanese bronze vase, of ovoid form, elongated neck, cast in high relief with a carp and qilin motif on a wave ground, black patina, Showa period.

17.5in (44.5cm) high

$600-900 SI

A Japanese bronze vase, of ovoid form with elongated neck, cast in high relief with flying birds and flowering branches, shi-shi or lion's head and bow handles, brown patina, Showa period.

14.5in (37cm) high

$400-600 SI

A Japanese bronze vase, of rectangular form, signed, Taisho period.

8in (20cm) high

$600-900 SI

A Japanese bronze vase, cast with waves and loop handles.

11.75in (30cm) high

$220-280 SI

A 20thC Japanese set of eight silver water goblets, each monogrammed "C".

6.5in (16.5cm) high

$400-600 SI

A Japanese silver covered serving dish, oval, monogrammed "C" inside the lid and base.

11.5in (29cm) wide

$350-400 SI

A set of eight Japanese silver mint julep cups, each monogrammed "C".

3.5in (9cm) high

$320-380 S

Chinese Ivory

A Chinese ivory figure of a medicine lady, late Qing Dynasty.

c1900 *12in (30.5cm) long*

$400-600 SI

A Chinese ivory figure of an immortal holding a flowering branch and a staff, late Qing Dynasty.

Provenance: *With a bill of sale from Chao Ming Chen, Baltimore, November 14, 1933.*

c1900 *5.5in (14cm) high*

$280-320 SI

A pair of early 20thC Chinese large ivory emperor and empress figures, each standing, wearing a long robe and holding a fan.

26in (66cm) high

$2,800-3,200 SI

An early 20thC pair of Chinese ivory meirin, each standing, wearing a long robe and high chignon, holding a flowering branch.

11.75in (30cm) high

$800-1,200 SI

An early 20thC Chinese ivory figure of a meirin, standing, wearing a long robe and high chignon, holding a ruji scepter.

12in (30.5cm) high

$500-700 S

An early 20thC Chinese ivory figure of a bodhisattva, seated on a lotus throne, radiating arms with attributes.

11.75in (30cm) high

$700-1,000 SI

An early 20thC pair of Chinese ivory emperor and empress figures, each seated on an elaborate throne, wearing a long robe carved with dragon decoration, long necklaces and headdress.

8in (20cm) high

$1,200-1,800 SI

Eight 20thC Chinese polychrome ivory horses, each standing, mounted with a polychrome saddle and pleated saddle blanket, festooned with foliate trappings suspended from applied harness straps.

2.75in (6.5cm) high

$1,000-1,500 SI

A Chinese ivory brushpot, carved to depict figures under trees, Qing Dynasty.

c1900 *5.25in (14.5cm) high*

$600-900 SI

A lightly stained Japanese ivory okimono-style netsuke, of a group of street vendors and entertainers in a large sakazuki, Meiji period.

c1868-1912 *2.25in (6.5cm) diam*

$600-900 GorL

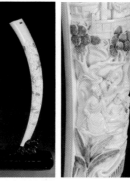

An early 20thC Chinese large ivory tusk, with carved detail of a garden with pagoda and figures.

37.5in (95cm) long

$1,500-2,000 SI

An early 20thC Chinese ivory incense burner, carved with a dragon chasing the flaming pearl of wisdom in low relief, raised on three fu-lion mask and paw feet, with a fu-lion finial.

9in (23cm) high

$600-900 SI

An early 20thC pair of Chinese ivory vases, each of ovoid form with a cylindrical neck, carved with a pagoda in a garden with pine trees and figures, above a band of elephants.

10in (25.5cm) high

$500-700 SI

JAPANESE IVORY

A Japanese carved ivory figure of a Bijin holding her hat before her face, supported on an integral oval base, signature to base, Meiji period.

7.25in (18.5cm) high

$500-700 BonS

A Japanese ivory carving of a peasant, standing by and also holding a basket with frogs, on rockwork base, signed, bleached.

c1900 *4.75in (12cm) high*

$700-1,000 DN

A pair of Chinese ivory figures, depicting a figure of a Guanyin and a man, together with a Japanese figure of a Hotei, late Qing Dynasty/early Republic period.

c1900 *5in (13.5cm) high*

$180-220 SI

Ten Japanese ivory netsuke, carved as an actor, a woman with a scroll, a man with a fan, a man, and a child with a fan, a man holding a double-gourd vessel, a man carving, a man and child holding a fan behind his back, a man wearing a hat and a sack, and two immortals, Taisho period.

$400-600   **SI**

A Japanese ivory okimono, carved as three musicians wearing short costumes with brocade decoration, together with the figure of an immortal, Taisho period.

Largest 4.5in (11.5cm) high

$280-320   **SI**

A early 20thC Japanese large ivory figure of Jurojin, the standing figure wearing priest's robes and the base with red lacquer seal mark.

Jurojin is the Japanese god of longevity.

c1910   *21.25in (54cm) high*

$3,500-4,500   **DN**

A Japanese ivory figure of an egg-seller, the crouching figure holding an egg up to her eye, a basket of eggs by her side, signed, minor chips.

3.75in (9.5cm) high

$1,500-2,000   **DN**

A Japanese carved ivory figure of a farm laborer, holding a sheaf of corn over his shoulder, signed.

5.5in (14cm) high

$150-200   **DN**

A late 19thC Japanese ivory table screen or 'tsuitate', carved with children picking pomegranates on both sides.

6.5in (16.5cm) high

$1,200-1,800   **GorL**

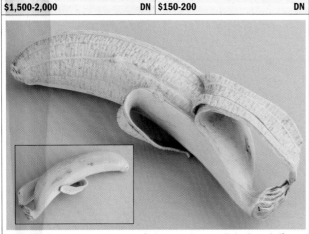

A late 19thC Japanese ivory carving of a banana, the naturalistic pieces half peeled, some chips.

6.75in (17cm) high

$700-1,000   **DN**

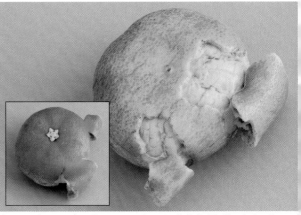

A Japanese ivory carving of a satsuma, the naturalistic fruit half peeled and brightly stained orange.

c1900   *2.5in (6.5cm) diam*

$800-1,200   **DN**

Lacquer

red lacquer cylindrical box and cover
arved with lychee and foliage, some
ld damage, Ming Dynasty.

3in (7.75cm) diam

$2,800-3,200 **GorL**

A red lacquer cylindrical box and cover,
with deeply carved fruit and foliage,
restored, Qing Dynasty.

2.25in (5.75cm) diam

$500-700 **GorL**

Three pieces of Chinese red lacquer,
comprising two wooden containers with
gooseneck-form handles and one tub
with an inverted cover, Qing Dynasty.

c1870   Largest 15.5in (39.5cm) high

$300-400 **SI**

Two Chinese polychrome lacquered
baskets, Qing Dynasty.

c1870   12in (30.5cm) high

$280-320 **SI**

hree Chinese polychrome lacquered
wooden trays, each of rectangular
utline, one painted to depict children
t play, one to depict figures in a
arden and one to depict scholarly
bjects, Qing Dynasty.

1860   Largest 23.75in (60cm) wide

$220-280 **SI**

Four Chinese red lacquered food
containers, of various forms and
decoration, Qing Dynasty.

c1870   11.75in (30cm) high

$280-320 **SI**

Two Chinese red lacquered containers,
with figural and floral decoration, Qing
Dynasty.

c1890   20in (51cm) high

$280-320 **SI**

A red lacquer tripod globular censer
with mask-headed cylindrical legs,
carved on the body with Shoulou, other
immortals and attendants on a terrace
divided by gilt bronze loose ring-mask
handles, the stepped domed cover with
emblems below a gilt bronze seated
lion finial, probably Qianlong.

$700-1,000 **GorL**

A late 19th/early 20thC
Chinese gilt and iron red
lacquered wood figure of a
warrior, standing on a
circular cloud-form plinth
with an emerging dragon,
wearing armor and a hat.

24.5in (62cm) high

$300-400 **SI**

Two late 19th/early20thC Chinese gilt and
iron red lacquered wood figures of
dignitaries, one standing, one seated, each
wearing long robes and a headdress.

Larger 18.5in (47cm) high

$150-200 **SI**

A Tibetan polychrome lacquered wood
table, of rectangular form, with folding
legs, painted with dragon and floral
motifs.

c1860   35.25in (89.5cm) wide

$220-280 **SI**

A Japanese red and black lacquer bow,
together with ten arrows and quiver with
moon decoration.

Bow 86in (218.5cm) long

$220-280 **SI**

Textiles

A Chinese dark blue gauze coat, with two civilian second rank golden pheasant badges, each badge with an appliquéd bird, couched metallic thread, late Qing Dynasty.

c1900

$1,200-1,800   SI

A Japanese black silk kimono, depicting forest vignettes on a black ground, with gold threads, together with a blue silk kimono and a black and grey kimono, Showa period.

$120-180   SI

A pair of late 19thC Manchu lady's shoes, the red silk slippers mounted on natural cotton platforms embroidered in silver thread with stylized squirrels, bound in black.

$300-400   BonK

Attributed to Tei Ling (Chinese, 18thC), 'Birds on Flowering Branches', ink and color on silk, framed.

39.5in (99cm) high

$400-600   S

Chinese 19thC School, landscape in ink and color on a silk scroll, framed.

68.5in (174cm) wide

$280-320   SI

A late 18thC Chinese panel, embroidered in colored silks and metal threads on Imperial yellow and green silk roundels, reserved against a floral sprig and bat ground, within a similar border, some damage.

$400-600   BonK

A late 19thC Japanese panel, embroidered in predominantly blue, white, ocher, grey, brown, and black silks on a cream silk satin ground with cockerels and chickens in a landscape, with exotic birds and butterflies in a blossoming tree, also bearing character marks, mounted, glazed and framed.

23.5in (60cm) wide

$280-320   Bonk

A late 19thC watercolor and block print on silk, depicting oriental figures within a garden landscape, on an ocher ground, mounted in a peach silk border, glazed and framed.

74.75in (190cm) wide

$400-500   BonK

A late 19th/early 20thC Chinese wall hanging, embroidered in colored silks and metal threads on a green silk ground with spot motifs and characters, depicting storks, deer, flowering jardinières, and a censer, some discoloration and fading, mounted, glazed and framed.

69.75in (177cm) wide

$180-220   BonK

A Chinese silk panel, embroidered in satin stitch, depicting a meirin with a phoenix and bat.

59in (150cm) high

$150-200   SI

An Oriental Eau de Nil silk satin panel, embroidered in colored silks and metal with a peacock and butterflies amidst floral and foliate ground, mounted, glazed and framed.

22.5in (57cm) high

$280-320   Bonk

Japanese Drawings

Hisashi Otsuka (Japanese, 20thC), 'Lady Mieko Spring', print, pencil signed and sealed, numbered "223/300", framed.

38in (96.5cm) high

$1,500-2,000 SI

Hisashi Otsuka (Japanese, 20thC) 'Kiss of the Black Swan', print, pencil signed and sealed, numbered "225/300", framed.

37in (94cm) wide

$1,200-1,800 SI

Hisashi Otsuka (Japanese, 20thC), 'Kabuki Warrior', print, pencil signed and sealed, numbered "225/300", framed.

39in (99cm) high

$600-900 SI

Hisashi Otsuka (Japanese, 20thC), 'Lady Floating Blossom', print, signed and sealed, numbered "225/300", framed.

27in (68.5cm) high

$400-600 SI

Yoshida Hiroshi (Japanese, 1876-1950), 'Sea of Clouds', color woodcut, signed in brush in Japanese, pencil signed in Roman script "Hiroshi Yoshida".

c1928   32.5in (82.5cm) wide

$3,200-3,800 SI

Yoshida Hiroshi (Japanese, 1876-1950), 'Rapids', color woodcut, signed in brush in Japanese, pencil-signed in Roman script "Hiroshi Yoshida", jizuri seal.

c1928   32.5in (82.5cm) wide

$3,200-3,800 SI

Yoshida Hiroshi (Japanese, 1876-1950), 'Deer in Kasuga', color woodcut, signed in brush in Japanese, pencil-signed in Roman "Hiroshi Yoshida", jizuri seal.

c1928   20in (51cm) high

$1,200-1,800 SI

Yoshida Hiroshi (Japanese 1876-1950), 'Gion Shrine Gate', color woodcut, signed and sealed, together with 'Hirakawa Bridge' color woodcut from the series 'Twelve Scenes of Tokyo', signed and sealed.

14.75in (37.5cm) high

$400-600 SI

Ito Shinsui (Japanese, 1898-1972), 'Morning After Snow', color woodcut, signed and sealed.

c1939   51.25in (130cm) high

$800-1,200 SI

Shigeki Kuroda (Japanese, 1953-), 'Big Wall', watercolor on paper, pencil signed.

29.75in (75.5cm) wide

$300-400 SI

CLOISONNÉ

A 16thC Chinese cloisonné small arrow vase, decorated with flowerheads on a turquoise ground, Ming Dynasty, dents to the foot.

5in (13cm) high

$800-1,200   **WW**

An early 18thC cloisonné bottle vase, with stylized scrolling lotus on a turquoise ground, gilt bronze rim and foot.

6in (15.25cm) high

$800-1,200   **GorL**

A Chinese cloisonné covered jar, of ovoid form and domed cover, overall with scrolling floral sprays on reddish-brown ground, electrified.

10in (25.5cm) high

$320-380   **SI**

Two Japanese cloisonné vases, of ovoid form with floral decoration on a blue ground, electrified, Meiji period.

9.5in (25cm) hig

$280-320   **S**

A pair of Japanese cloisonné vases, of ribbed ovoid form, with floral and butterfly decoration on black and blue ground, signed, Meiji period.

8in (20.5cm) high

$280-320   **SI**

Six Chinese cloisonné cups and saucers, with floral decoration on a blue ground, late Qing Dynasty-early Republic period.

c1910   Saucers 5.25in (13.5cm) diam

$150-200   **SI**

A late 19thC Japanese cloisonné plaque, finely decorated with cranes perched in flowering branches on a pink ground. *c1890*

19.75in (50cm) hig.

$1,800-2,200   **DN**

A Chinese cloisonné garniture, comprising a pair of covered jars and a pair of vases with floral decoration on black background, late Qing Dynasty.

c1910   *8in (20cm) high*

$150-200   **SI**

A pair of 19thC Chinese cloisonné censers, in the form of red-capped cranes, each standing on a green enameled tree trunk.

9.5in (24cm) high

$800-1,200   **WW**

Wood

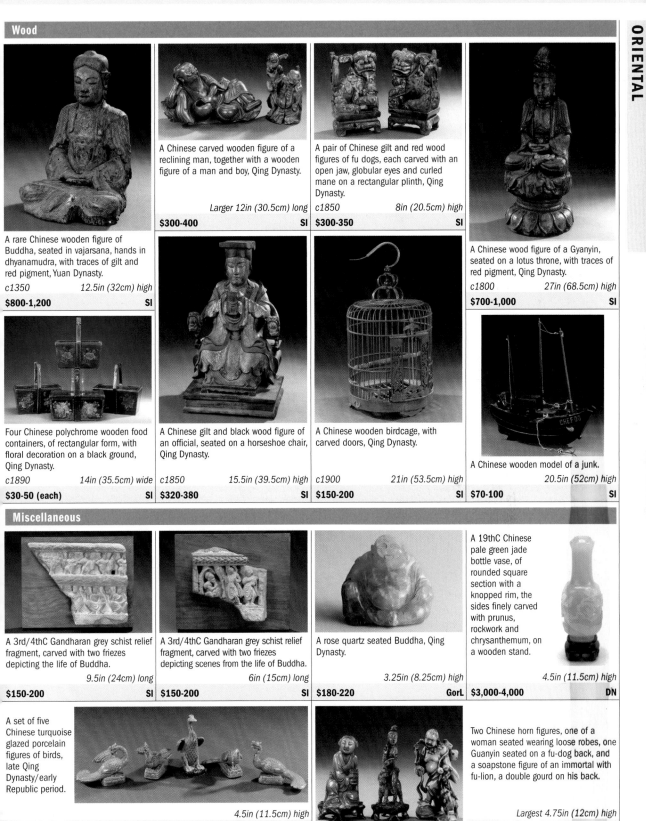

A rare Chinese wooden figure of Buddha, seated in vajarsana, hands in dhyanamudra, with traces of gilt and red pigment, Yuan Dynasty.

c1350   12.5in (32cm) high

$800-1,200   **SI**

A Chinese carved wooden figure of a reclining man, together with a wooden figure of a man and boy, Qing Dynasty.

Larger 12in (30.5cm) long

$300-400   **SI**

A pair of Chinese gilt and red wood figures of fu dogs, each carved with an open jaw, globular eyes and curled mane on a rectangular plinth, Qing Dynasty.

c1850   8in (20.5cm) high

$300-350   **SI**

A Chinese wood figure of a Gyanyin, seated on a lotus throne, with traces of red pigment, Qing Dynasty.

c1800   27in (68.5cm) high

$700-1,000   **SI**

Four Chinese polychrome wooden food containers, of rectangular form, with floral decoration on a black ground, Qing Dynasty.

c1890   14in (35.5cm) wide

$30-50 (each)   **SI**

A Chinese gilt and black wood figure of an official, seated on a horseshoe chair, Qing Dynasty.

c1850   15.5in (39.5cm) high

$320-380   **SI**

A Chinese wooden birdcage, with carved doors, Qing Dynasty.

c1900   21in (53.5cm) high

$150-200   **SI**

A Chinese wooden model of a junk.

20.5in (52cm) high

$70-100   **SI**

Miscellaneous

A 3rd/4thC Gandharan grey schist relief fragment, carved with two friezes depicting the life of Buddha.

9.5in (24cm) long

$150-200   **SI**

A 3rd/4thC Gandharan grey schist relief fragment, carved with two friezes depicting scenes from the life of Buddha.

6in (15cm) long

$150-200   **SI**

A rose quartz seated Buddha, Qing Dynasty.

3.25in (8.25cm) high

$180-220   **GorL**

A 19thC Chinese pale green jade bottle vase, of rounded square section with a knopped rim, the sides finely carved with prunus, rockwork and chrysanthemum, on a wooden stand.

4.5in (11.5cm) high

$3,000-4,000   **DN**

A set of five Chinese turquoise glazed porcelain figures of birds, late Qing Dynasty/early Republic period.

4.5in (11.5cm) high

$280-320   **SI**

Two Chinese horn figures, one of a woman seated wearing loose robes, one Guanyin seated on a fu-dog back, and a soapstone figure of an immortal with fu-lion, a double gourd on his back.

Largest 4.75in (12cm) high

$70-100   **SI**

ASIAN WORKS OF ART

ORIENTAL

Asian Works of Art - Indian

A 3rd-4thC Gandharan grey schist figure of Buddha.

16in (40.5cm) high

$1,800-2,200   **SI**

An ivory miniature of Suraj Ud Daula, Delhi, India.

c1830   *2.5in (6.5cm) high*

$400-600   **AM**

An ivory miniature of Amir Akbar Khan, Delhi, India.

c1840   *2.5in (6.5cm) high*

$400-600   **AM**

An ivory miniature of the procession of Akbar II, Delhi, India.

c1840   *2.5in (6.5cm) wide*

$400-600   **AM**

An ivory miniature of a princess, Delhi, India.

c1840   *2.25in (5.5cm) long*

$350-400   **AM**

An ivory miniature of the Durbar of Akbar II, Delhi, India.

c1840   *2.5in (6cm) wide*

$350-400   **AM**

An ivory miniature of Amir Rhman Khan, Delhi, India.

c1850

$400-600   **AM**

An ivory miniature of Amir Dost Mohamed, Delhi, India.

c1850   *2.75in (7cm) high*

$400-600   **AM**

Three 19thC Indian bronze figures of deities, comprising a figure of Buddha, seated in vajrasana on a lotus base, his right hand in varadamudra, a figure of a four-armed deity standing in samapada on a lotus throne, primary left hand resting on his hip, primary right hand in varadamudra, and a figure of a Bodhisattva, seated in vajrasana.

Largest 6in (15cm) high

$60-90 each   **SI**

A north Indian gold, gem stone and enamel hinged bangle or Kara, probably Jaipur, the front designed as two opposing tigers' heads decorated in golden yellow enamel with colored detail, each set with a small rose diamond, the hollow round section hoop decorated in various colored enamels and set with rose-cut diamonds and cabochon rubies.

$2,200-2,800   **DN**

Islamic

An Iron Age Iranian grey earthenware jug, of globular form with a loop handle.

c1,400-800BC   *10in (25.5cm) high*

$400-600   **SI**

An Iznik circular pottery bowl, painted in blue, black and turquoise, overlaid with sealing wax red with a serrated leaf and stylized tulip and carnation sprays, the border decorated with spirals, bears paper label "Morris and Company, 17 George Street, Hanover Square", "R1186 Rhodian Dish CPYY £13".

c1600

$3,500-4,000   **L&T**

An early 19thC Persian bowl, decorated in pastel shades of blue, yellow and green, with arabesques and panels of flowers.

21.75in (55cm) diam

$600-900   **FRE**

A 19thC large Persian faience tile with floral decoration on a cobalt blue and white ground, framed.

16in (41cm) long

$400-600 SI

A late 19thC/early 20thC Moorish luster faience jar, underglazed blue and luster, with calligraphy and animals.

30in (76cm) high

$3,500-4,000 SI

An 18thC Persian faience tile, depicting a man on horseback.

9in (22.5cm) high

$700-1,000 SI

An Ottoman silver ewer and basin, marked with the tugra of Abdulhamid Han bin Mecidel El-Muzaffer Ayar 90.

A tugra is an Islamic authentication monogram.

1876-1909 *18in (46cm) high*

$15,000-20,000 SI

Thai

An Ottoman silver hookah, marked with the tugra of Abdulmec id Han bin Mahmudel Muzaffer Daima Ayar 90, maker's mark for Papadopulos, Izmir.

1839-1861 *19in (48cm) high*

$12,000-18,000 SI

A Thai bronze figure of Buddha, his right hand raised in abhaya mudra, wearing a long robe with central sash, the face with downcast expression, Ayutthaya style, Bangkok period.

17in (43cm) high

$220-280 SI

A Thai lacquered and gilt bronze figure of a disciple, his hands in anjali mudra, wearing a dhoti draped across his left shoulder, his face with serene expression, Bangkok period.

28.25in (71.5cm) high

$2,200-2,800 SI

A Thai storage jar, from Swankhalok Thailand, top repaired.

c1350-1500 *9.75in (25cm) high*

$70-100 R&GM

Three Thai gilt bronze figures of Buddha, two figures seated in vajrasana on a three-tier pedestal, the right hand in bhumisparshamudra, the left on his lap, one figure holding an attribute in his lap, Bangkok period.

Largest 8.25in (21cm) high

$60-90 each SI

A Thai gilt bronze figure of a musician, Bangkok period.

15.75in (39.5cm) high

$700-1,000 SI

A Thai bronze head of Buddha, his face with serene expression, aquiline nose, smiling lips, elongated earlobes, curled hair and usnisa, Ayutthaya period.

5in (13cm) high

$220-280 SI

A Thai gilt bronze figure of Buddha, standing on a four-tier throne, his hands raised in abhaya mudra and wearing a long cape-like sanghati, Bangkok period.

23in (58.5cm) high

$500-700 SI

Boxes

An early 18thC small Chinese red lacquer chest, of rectangular outline, hinged cover, the back panel painted with a gilt flowering branch, Ming Dynasty.

17in (43cm) wide

$400-600 SI

Two mid 19thC small Chinese polychrome chests, each of rectangular form with two side drawers, one painted with figural decoration, the other with fruit and figural decoration, Qing Dynasty.

c1860 *16in (40.5cm) wide*

$100-150 SI

A Chinese black and red lacquered elm trunk, of square outline, opening to an interior with two sections, Qing Dynasty.

29in (73.5cm) wide

$180-220 SI

A set of three Chinese polychrome pig skin trunks, decorated with scenes of geisha in pagoda and landscape settings.

Provenance: *Acquired in Japan in the 1940s.*

Largest 28in (71cm) wide

$500-700 SI

A pair of Chinese polychrome wood rice containers, of barrel form, painted with pagoda and floral decoration on an ocher ground.

12in (30.5cm) high

$180-220 SI

A late 19th pair of Chinese polychrome wood rice containers, of barrel form, painted with pagoda and floral decoration, Qing Dynasty.

c1870 *17.75in (45cm)*

$300-400 SI

A Middle Eastern rosewood, ivory, tortoiseshell and mother-of-pearl box, decorated in typical geometric manner, the sliding lid enclosing a later fitted interior, with leather lift out tray above A-Z sectioned filing system, marked for "Leuchars & Son, 35-39 Piccadilly, London and 2 Rue de la Paix, Paris".

20in (51cm) wide

$350-400 L&T

An early 19thC Tibetan polychrome wood chest, painted floral decoration.

c1830 *30in (76cm) wide*

$350-400 SI

A mid 19thC small Tibetan polychrome box, of rectangular form, with floral and scrolling foliate decoration.

c1850 *16.75in (42.5cm) wide*

$300-400 SI

An early 19thC small Tibetan polychrome wood trunk, of rectangular outline, painted with dragon and foliate decoration.

c1830 *23in (58.5cm) wide*

$400-600 SI

A near pair of late 19thC Tibetan polychrome wood rice containers, of square form, painted with floral decoration.

c1880 *12.5in (32cm) high*

$350-400 SI

Two Tibetan polychrome boxes, each of circular form, painted to depict precious objects.

c1880 *Largest 15in (38cm) diam*

$600-900 SI

Cabinets

An 18thC Chinese camphor 'tresor' cabinet, Beijing, of rectangular outline, with a graduated arrangement of shelves, above a frieze of two drawers and a pair of panel doors, on square section legs, decorated overall with carved relief of stylized confronting dragons and tendrils.

39.5in (100cm) wide

$1,200-1,800   SI

An 18thC Chinese elm cabinet, Fukien Province, of rectangular outline, with open slat and panel doors opening to an interior with two shelves and two drawers, above a recessed panel and wide apron, on square section legs, decorated overall in carved relief of scrolling foliage and precious objects.

42in (106.5cm) wide

$1,500-2,000   SI

An 18thC Chinese lacquered namu cabinet, Fukien Province, of rectangular outline in two sections, the top section with a pair of panel doors over a frieze of two drawers, the bottom section with one large drawer above a pair of panel doors above a wide apron with scrolling foliate carving, on square section legs.

40.5in (103cm) wide

$1,200-1,800   SI

A 19thC Chinese red and gold lacquered wood marriage cabinet, Fukien Province, the top section with a pair of panel doors carved with figures dancing, opening to an interior with one shelf and two drawers above a frieze with two drawers; the bottom with a pair of doors flanked by two small drawers.

36.5in (93cm) wide

$1,500-2,000   SI

A Chinese red lacquered elm cabinet, Qing Dynasty.

c1850   *39in (99cm) wide*

$600-900   SI

A Chinese red lacquered elm cabinet, all over gilst decoration, Qing Dynasty.

c1850   *47in (119cm) wide*

$700-700   SI

A 19thC Chinese jumu cabinet, Shangxi Province, both sections with 'cracked ice' open work panels and doors, the top opening to an interior with two shelves.

49.25in (125cm) wide

$1,500-2,000   SI

A Chinese elm cabinet, pair of doors with pierced broken ice work panels, stile supports, Qing Dynasty.

c1890   *43.75in (111cm) wide*

$700-1,000   SI

A 19thC Chinese hardwood secrétaire bookcase, the top with dentil cornice above two glazed doors enclosing shelves, the base with a paneled fall front drawer enclosing a fitted interior above two short and two long drawers with brass handles, on bracket feet.

41.25in (105cm) wide

$1,500-2,000   DN

A Chinese gilt and black elm medicine cabinet, 32 small drawers each with calligraphic inscriptions, Qing Dynasty.

c1850   *33.75in (86cm) wide*

$600-900   SI

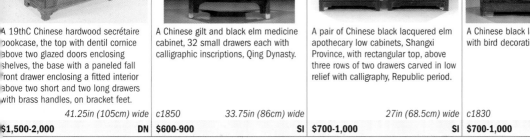

A pair of Chinese black lacquered elm apothecary low cabinets, Shangxi Province, with rectangular top, above three rows of two drawers carved in low relief with calligraphy, Republic period.

27in (68.5cm) wide

$700-1,000   SI

A Chinese black lacquered elm cabinet, with bird decoration, Qing Dynasty.

c1830   *32.5in (82.5cm) wide*

$700-1,000   SI

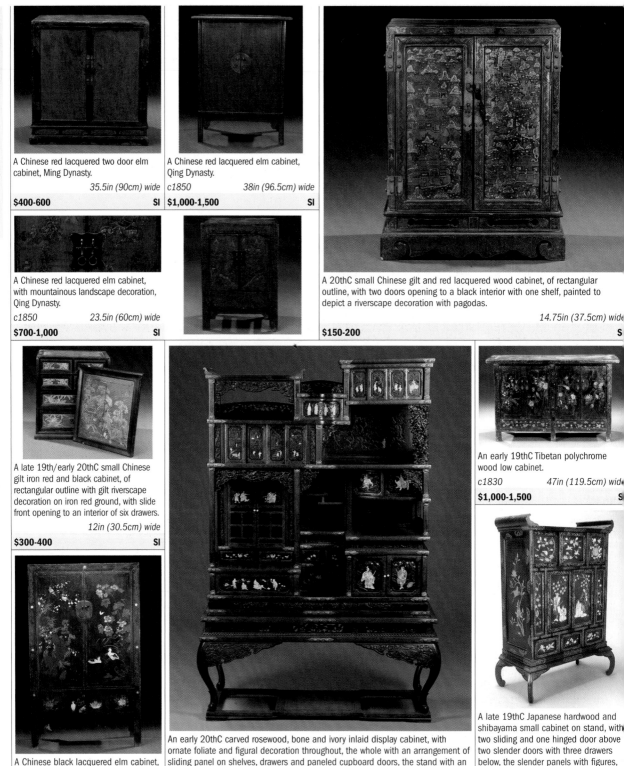

A Chinese red lacquered two door elm cabinet, Ming Dynasty.

35.5in (90cm) wide

$400-600   **SI**

A Chinese red lacquered elm cabinet, Qing Dynasty.

c1850   38in (96.5cm) wide

$1,000-1,500   **SI**

A Chinese red lacquered elm cabinet, with mountainous landscape decoration, Qing Dynasty.

c1850   23.5in (60cm) wide

$700-1,000   **SI**

A 20thC small Chinese gilt and red lacquered wood cabinet, of rectangular outline, with two doors opening to a black interior with one shelf, painted to depict a riverscape decoration with pagodas.

14.75in (37.5cm) wide

$150-200   **S**

A late 19th/early 20thC small Chinese gilt iron red and black cabinet, of rectangular outline with gilt riverscape decoration on iron red ground, with slide front opening to an interior of six drawers.

12in (30.5cm) wide

$300-400   **SI**

An early 19thC Tibetan polychrome wood low cabinet.

c1830   47in (119.5cm) wide

$1,000-1,500   **S**

An early 20thC carved rosewood, bone and ivory inlaid display cabinet, with ornate foliate and figural decoration throughout, the whole with an arrangement of sliding panel on shelves, drawers and paneled cupboard doors, the stand with an open work frieze on cabriole legs, carved with exotic birds and united by an under tier.

45in (114.5cm) wide

$3,000-4,000   **SI**

A Chinese black lacquered elm cabinet, of rectangular outline, with two doors, Qing Dynasty.

c1860   45.5in (115.5cm) wide

$700-1,000   **SI**

A late 19thC Japanese hardwood and shibayama small cabinet on stand, with two sliding and one hinged door above two slender doors with three drawers below, the slender panels with figures, the others with flowers and birds, the sides and top lacquered in gilt.

20.75in (53cm) hig

$400-600   **DI**

Screens

An ebonized Japanese four-fold screen, each fold with leaf carved frame and pierced cresting enclosing lacquered panel with projecting ivory flower each old.

45.25in (115cm) high

$300-400   **L&T**

A Chinese red lacquered elm four-panel screen, of rectangular outline, reticulated to depict birds, animals and scrolling foliage, Qing Dynasty.

c1800   *82.5in (210cm) high*

$600-900   **SI**

A mid 20thC porcelain mounted four-fold screen, each panel consisting of three rectangular plaques inset into a Chinese hardwood frame, the top one painted with flowers, the middle and bottom plaque with figures, the bottom plaques by Liu Xiren and with a seal of the artist, the reverse in red lacquer with inscriptions.

Born in Baimamiao in Nanchang, Liu Xiren (1906-1967) and his brother Lu Xiyu ran their own workshop in Nanchang. He was the most influential porcelain painter of his time in Nanchang.

74.5in (189cm) high

$8,000-12,000   **DN**

A Chinese black lacquered hardstone inset four panel screen, on black ground with inlaid hardstones.

72in (183cm) high

$400-600   **SI**

A pair of 19thC Chinese camphor window panels, Shangxi Province, of rectangular outline, carved open work with bats and flower heads in circular and quatrefoil reserves.

32.5in (82.5cm) wide

$400-600   **SI**

Stands

A late 19thC/early 20thC Chinese polychrome lacquered stand.

19in (48cm) high

$150-200   **SI**

A 20thC near pair of Chinese rosewood plant stands, with marble inset tops, on shaped legs, headed by mask motifs.

$280-320   **SI**

A late 19thC Burmese carved hardwood four tier corner whatnot, the four serpentine graduated tiers with ornate foliate pierced aprons and similarly carved scrolled upright supports surmounted by an Eagle cresting.

23in (58.5cm) wide

$1,000-1,500   **SI**

A Chinese huang huali wood stick stand with four divisions, the sides carved with stylized clouds.

11.75in (30cm) wide

$800-1,200   **DN**

A 20thC Chinese rosewood two tier jardiniere stand, with ornate foliate carved decoration throughout, the undulating circular top with inset marble, on cabriole legs headed by grotesque masks.

31.5in (80cm) diam

$300-400   **SI**

A Chinese hardwood stand, profusely carved, the circular top with inset marble slab above frieze and pierced apron on scrolling legs joined by pierced circular under tray.

31.75in (81cm) high

$300-600   **L&T**

ORIENTAL

Chairs

An 18thC Chinese elm armchair, Shangxi Province, with an arched crestrail and rectangular splat, hard cane seat, legs framed by beaded apron and long flange brackets.

$600-900 SI

An 18thC Chinese elm official's hat chair, with shaped crest rail, slightly curved back splat with carved cartouche above a beaded apron.

$280-320 SI

A pair of 19thC Chinese lacquered elm armchairs, Shangxi Province, each with a scrolling crestrail with paneled splat carved with an animal and objects, with a panel seat and outscrolled arms.

$400-600 SI

A mid 19thC pair of Chinese elm elbow chairs, in the 18thC style, Qing Dynasty.

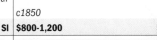
c1850

$800-1,200 S

An early 19thC pair of Chinese official's hat chairs, Qing Dynasty.
c1820

$3,000-4,000 SI

An early 20thC Chinese carved rosewood rocking chair, the arched square back ornately carved with rampant dragons and open work scrolls, the serpentine arms joined by a paneled seat above a conforming carved apron, on splayed legs united by rockers.

$300-400 SI

A 20thC Chinese rosewood corner chair the scroll arms with open work bamboo leaf carved splats joined by a shaped paneled seat on simulated bamboo turned legs, joined by an X-shaped stretcher.

$300-400 S

A 20thC Chinese stained hardwood elbow chair, the curved back carved with dragons chasing pearls with a solid serpentine seat, with a stylized cloud seat rail and cabriole legs.

$500-700 DN

A 20thC Chinese rosewood corner chair, with ornate foliate carved decoration throughout, the square back joined by a paneled seat on simulated bamboo splayed legs joined by stretchers and ending hoof feet.

$300-400 SI

A 20thC Chinese carved softwood three piece parlor suite, upholstered in gold fabric with foliage and birds, the foliate pierced shaped backs surmounted by rampant dragons, the settee with conforming arms on cabriole legs with claw and ball feet joined by ornate scroll carved aprons.

$1,000-1,500 SI

A 20thC Burmese spoon-back carved hard wood nursing chair, with ornate pierced carved decoration throughout, the shaped back and padded drop in seat on cabriole legs molded as rampant lions.

$400-600 S

Stools

A pair of Chinese elm stools, each of square form, Qing Dynasty.

c1880   18in (46cm) wide

$120-180   SI

A pair of Chinese low wood stools, Qing Dynasty.

c1830   10.75in (27.5cm) wide

$220-280   SI

A pair of Chinese wood stools, each of square form, Qing Dynasty.

c1850   21in (53.5cm) high

$100-150   SI

A Chinese elm daybed, Qing Dynasty.

c1850   64in (162.5cm) long

$250-300   SI

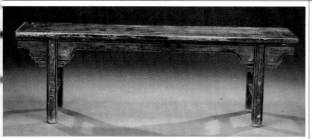

A Chinese elm bench, Qing Dynasty.

c1850   67in (170cm) wide

$400-600   SI

A pair of Chinese wood benches, Qing Dynasty.

c1850   50.25in (127.5cm) long

$280-320   SI

Side Tables

An 18thC Chinese red lacquered elm altar table, Beijing, of rectangular solid top with everted ends, above a frieze of two drawers and scrolling apron with relief carved foliate design, on cabriole legs.

45in (114cm) wide

$1,000-1,500   SI

An 18thC Chinese Nanmu altar table, Fukien Province, with a rectangular top above pierced scrolling apron with spandrels, on square section legs joined by a low stretcher.

37.5in (95cm) wide

$600-900   SI

An 18thC Chinese walnut altar table, Shangxi Province, with beaded scrolling apron carved in relief with confronted dragons and tendrils, supported on square section legs, with a small drawer above a recessed panel on each side.

68.5in (174cm) wide

$1,200-1,800   SI

A late 18th/early 19thC Chinese walnut two drawer side table, Shangxi Province, with rectangular top above a frieze of two drawers, supported on square section legs joined by low stretcher.

33in (84cm) wide

$400-600   SI

A late 18th/early 19thC Chinese lacquered elm wine table, Shangxi Province, the rectangular top above a pierced waist of recessed lozenges and beaded apron, supported on square section legs ending in hoof feet.

37.75in (96cm) wide

$400-600   SI

An early 19thC Chinese elm side table, Qing Dynasty.

c1810   48in (122cm) wide

$1,000-1,500   SI

A Chinese elm painting table, Qing Dynasty.

c1810   67in (170cm) wide

$700-1,000   SI

An early 19thC pair of Chinese elm side tables, Qing Dynasty.

c1820   39in (99cm) wide

$800-1,200   SI

Low Tables

A 20thC Chinese hexagonal low side table, with foliate carved decoration throughout, the dished top on three splayed legs united by a gallery under tier.

28.5in (72.5cm) wide

$300-400 SI

An 18thC Chinese red lacquered elm low table, Shandong Province, of rectangular top, above apron with key fret decoration, with nail-head decoration corner brackets, on rectangular legs ending with feet with scrolled toes.

34in (86.5cm) wide

$500-700 SI

A Chinese black lacquered wood low table, of rectangular outline, with inlaid mother-of-pearl and hard stones depicting scenes with a pavilion and figures within a walled garden on black ground, supported on cabriole legs.

31in (79cm) wide

$250-300 SI

A Chinese elm low table, Qing Dynasty.

c1850 *27in (68.5cm) wide*

$250-300 SI

An early 19thC Mongolian polychrome painted wood low table.

c1810 *25.25in (64cm) wide*

$600-900 SI

A Chinese huali huali wood rectangular low table, the cleated top above a frieze carved with stylized scrolls, on straight legs with angular scroll carved terminals, some repair to frieze.

35.5in (90.5cm) wide

$600-900 DN

A nest of four Chinese hardwood tables, each with tray top and pierced apron, shaped legs with stretchers.

Largest 28in (71cm) high

$280-320 L&T

A Chinese elm low table, Qing Dynasty.

c1810 *28.5in (72.5cm) wide*

$280-320 SI

A Chinese hardwood low table, with four drawers, Qing Dynasty.

c1860 *34in (84.5cm) wide*

$400-600 SI

A nest of four Chinese carved hard wood tables.

Largest 27in (65.8cm) high

$280-320 S

Chairs & Settles

An 18thC box settle, with paneled back and bracket feet.

61in (155cm) wide

$1,500-2,000   **FRE**

An early George III oak settle, with ogee field panel carved back, scrolled arms and cabriole legs with hooved feet.

73in (185.5cm) wide

$1,800-2,400   **FRE**

A mid-18thC oak settle, with a paneled back, shaped arms and a squab seat on cabriole legs with pad feet.

71.75in (182cm) wide

$1,000-1,500   **DN**

A late 19thC French carved oak monk's bench, with foliate carved and linenfold paneled back, centerd by mask motifs, the scroll arms and lifting seat above a conforming linenfold paneled apron.

55.5in (141cm) wide

$2,200-2,800   **FRE**

A 19thC French carved oak and walnut bench, with some earlier elements, the galleried back with carved panels depicting dragons, figures and cherubs, with square arms above a solid seat, on spiral turned legs.

54.5in (138.5cm) wide

$1,500-2,000   **FRE**

An oak reclining wing armchair, in the late 17thC style, with wrought iron fittings, damask upholstered arms and seat, the supports, legs and stretchers of turned form with brass terminals and casters.

$350-450   **DN**

A Scandinavian oak elbow chair, probably Norwegian, the back carved with geometric panels of stylized plant-forms flanked by geometric banding that extends to the arm-rests which are supported on formalized horse's heads, the solid seat similarly carved, on carved supports united by stretchers.

$450-550   **DN**

An early 18thC oak open armchair, the arched top above molded frame and solid splat, the curved arms above baluster turned uprights and solid seat above cabriole legs linked by a shaped stretcher, restorations.

$450-550   **L&T**

A 17thC oak side chair, the leaf carved and caned back between barley twist uprights, corresponding seat and front rail, barley twist turned and block legs joined by corresponding H-stretcher.

$250-350   **L&T**

A 17thC oak side chair, the back carved with pierced crowns and scroll work, the barley twist uprights with acorn finials, paneled board seat with corresponding front rails and H-stretcher.

$220-280   **L&T**

A 17thC oak Derbyshire side chair, the arched paneled back carved with stylized plants, the uprights with bobbin turned pilasters and royalist masks, board seat, legs joined by stretchers.

$1,500-2,000   **L&T**

A 17thC style oak side chair, the Yorkshire pattern back with two lobed and carved rails with acorn pendants above paneled seat, turned and block legs joined by stretcher.

$150-200   **L&T**

An 18thC oak armchair, the solid leaf carved back with stylized foliate panel above board seat and arms with scroll terminals and turned supports on turned and block front legs.

$1,200-1,800　　　　**L&T**

A Victorian oak rocking chair, Elizabethan style, the back carved with crest and date 1587 and name "Dorothy Manners nee Vernor" and incorporating older panel of Flight of Egypt, panel seat, bobbin turned legs.

$1,200-1,800　　　　**L&T**

Two of a set of four George IV provincial ash and elm side chairs, the square spindle backs, shaped seats, square tapered legs joined by stretchers.

Possibly Norfolk 'Hepplewhite' provincial chairs.

$350-450 (set)　　　　**SI**

A pair of French mid-19thC walnut and rush seat country chairs, with ladder backs and scroll arms above serpentine-shaped seats, on turned legs with foliate carved wavy aprons.

$1,200-1,800　　　　**SI**

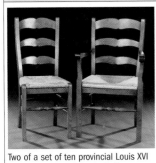

Two of a set of ten provincial Louis XVI style oak dining chairs, including two armchairs, ladder backs and rush seats, on legs joined by turned stretchers.

$1,500-2,000 (set)　　　　**SI**

Two of a set of eight ash and elm windsor chairs, in the 19thC style, spindle back with hoop mid-rail, saddle seat, legs with crinolin stretchers.

$3,500-4,500 (set)　　　　**SI**

A mid-19thC yew wood and elm high back windsor chair, with a hoop back with a pierced shaped splat, turned legs joined by a crinoline stretcher.

Stylistically this chair is very similar to examples published and made by the Allsop firm in Worksop, Nottinghamshire.

$1,000-1,500　　　　**FRE**

A mid-19thC ash and elm windsor chair, North Nottinghamshire, with a hoop shaped spindle back with a pierced splat and outswept scroll arms, above a solid seat on baluster turned legs, joined by stretchers.

$750-850　　　　**FRE**

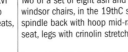

A 19thC oak Orkney chair, with shaped rush back and paneled arms, board seat above box base with chamfered fielded panels, brass caps and casters.

$1,800-2,800　　　　**L&T**

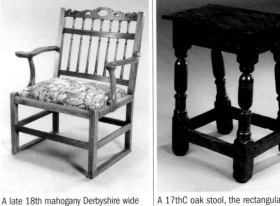

A late 18th mahogany Derbyshire wide chair, with pierced crest rail and spindle back, shaped arms and a drop-in seat.

$350-450　　　　**DN**

A 17thC oak stool, the rectangular top above molded frieze, the turned spreading legs joined by stretchers.

$1,500-2,000　　　　**L&T**

Windsors

...pair of birdcage Windsor side chairs, ...even spindle backs.

200-300	BCAC

...child's Windsor high chair, rectangular ...est rail supported by turned stiles with ...rowback center post, plank seat ending in ...layed legs, original green over black paint.

1850-70	35.5in (90cm) high
1,000-1,500	BCAC

A fine Philadelphia comb-back Windsor armchair, with original red paint, with carved ears and fully carved spade feet, excellent condition.

This is a rare example of one of the earliest forms of Windsor chair. All too often the original painted surface was removed in the early 20thC.

c1760-70

$30,000-40,000	SG

A Philadelphia Windsor arm chair, crest rail with butterfly over a seven-spindle back, bamboo turnings.

$200-300	AAC

An early 19thC set of eight New England rod back Windsor side chairs, with bamboo turnings, retaining old black painted surface, one dated 1809 and another initialed "LM".

c1810

$4,000-6,000	Pook

...late 19thC/early 20thC century painted ...eech six spindle Salem rocker.

400-600	BCAC

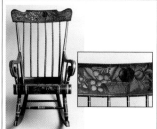

A rocking chair with 'Boston' style seat, original paint and stenciling, probably Lancaster county, PA, signed illegibly on bottom.

c1830

$600-900	BCAC

A Kingston Ontario rod back Windsor Rocking Chair, comb piece above a shaped splat with scrolled arms, impressed mark "J.R. Hunt, Maker".

c1830

$600-700	WAD

A New England painted rod back Windsor rocking chair, with a seven spindle back over scrolled arms, retains red and black grain decoration with yellow floral highlights.

$2,200-2,800	Pook

...18thC Bucks County ladderback ...mchair, found in Newton PA, mid-19thC ...aint and leather upholstery.

...1770

5,000-7,000	BCAC

A late 18thC Delaware Valley ladderback chair, with leather seat added April 3, 1847.

$600-900	BCAC

A mid 19thC child's chair, with ring-turned finials above the top slat, turned and incised arm rests and four box stretchers.

c1850-60   22in (56cm) high

$500-700	BCAC

A late19thC grain-painted ladder back rocking chair, rosewood graining heightened with yellow and green pinstriping, rush seat.

c1875   44.5in (113cm) high

$220-280	FRE

FURNITURE

A mid-19thC Quebec mixed hardwood ladder-back armchair, the back carved "Maria 1853" with straight outstretched arms above a solid seat raised on tapering legs joined by stretchers.

$300-400   **WAD**

A mid-19thC child's grain painted side chair, arrowback shaped crest rail, rabbit ears, shaped and incised seat, turned legs, labeled "Joel Pratt Jr Sterling Mass".

c1835-50

$800-1,200   **BCAC**

A Canadian Louis XV birch armchair, with three salamander-shaped slats flanked by block and urn turned stiles over a rush seat resting on similarly turned legs joined by stretchers, front stretchers restored.

$3,000-4,000   **Pook**

An 18thC Quebec oak armchair in the Louis XV manner, the back with three shaped splats and outstretched arms above a reeded seat on square section legs joined by stretcher, extended legs.

$180-220   **WAD**

An 18thC Quebec rustic painted pine armchair, rectangular back with turned stiles and downswept arms above a plank seat raised on square section supports joined by stretchers.

$2,500-3,000   **WA**

A 19thC child's 'arrowback' arm chair, with rush seat.

$150-200   **SI**

A set of three Mid-Atlantic States Classical tiger maple rush-seat side chairs, damage to rush seats.

c1825   *33.25in (84.5cm) high*

$700-1,000   **FRE**

A pair of Baltimore green-painted and gilt-decorated cane-seat side chairs, the crest rail decorated with clasped hands, old paint and repairs.

c1825   *29.5in (75cm) high*

$700-1,000   **FRE**

An early 19thC set of eight maple and rush seated dining chairs, six single and two arm chairs, refinished and old repairs, probably New England.

c1830   *34in (86cm) high*

$800-1,200 (set)   **S**

A set of six Pennsylvania painted and stencil-decorated plank seat side chairs, painted gold and stenciled, paint wear.

c1845

$800-1,200   **FRE**

A Windsor writing chair, all original.

$1,500-2,000   **BCAC**

A pair of late 19thC Canadian carved and painted children's chairs in the popular 17thC British style.

21.75in (55.5cm) high

$500-700 (pair)   **BP**

A Canadian child's potty training chair, with original red paint.

c1880   *25.5in (65cm) hig*

$250-350   **B**

A pair of 19thC Spanish pine and oak benches, on twin shaped end supports with cast iron scroll stretchers.

91in (231cm) wide

$750-850 **SI**

An early 20thC near pair of Charles II style oak joint stools.

17.5in (44cm) wide

$300-400 **SI**

A George III oak press, the molded cornice above two cupboard doors with ogee arched fielded panels, separated by a central circled panel, enclosing a pegged interior, the lower section with three fielded panels above three drawers, on block feet.

61in (155cm) wide

$5,000-6,000 **L&T**

An early 19thC oak secretaire corner cupboard, the ogee cornice above two paneled doors enclosing shelves, above a fall front drawer with fittings, and two paneled doors, flanked by pilasters, on a plinth base.

54.75in (139cm) wide

$2,200-2,800 **DN**

An 18thC and later French provincial carved oak press cupboard, with foliate carved decoration throughout, the molded cornice above a palmette frieze and two paneled cupboard doors, opening to reveal shelves, the lower section with two further cupboard doors on stile feet.

53.5in (136cm) wide

$3,000-4,000 **FRE**

A 19thC oak Gothic side cabinet, the molded cornice above pair of carved doors with arched panels incorporating saints flanking central boss, single door and further panels below, above open shelf, flanked by similar canted sides, on molded plinth.

62.25in (158cm) wide

$2,200-2,800 **L&T**

An early 18thC oak corner cupboard, with one paneled door enclosing shelves.

30in (76cm) wide

$450-550 **DN**

A pair of Flemish oak and ebony side cabinets, each with a molded cornice and foliate carved frieze above a quarter-paneled door, opening to reveal a shelf, on stile feet with pierced aprons.

38.5in (98cm) wide

$1,500-2,000 **FRE**

A mid-18thC French provincial oak hanging cupboard, probably from Normandy, the arch-molded top above a paneled door carved with a flowering urn, opening to reveal a later shelf, below is one drawer and a galleried late shelf.

28in (71cm) wide

$600-800 **FRE**

A late 19thC provincial carved oak hall cupboard, Brittany, France, with a carved acanthus and dentil cornice above a galleried frieze and one cupboard door, centerd by a carved panel, below an apron drawer, raised on bun feet.

29.5in (75cm) wide

$1,000-1,500 **FRE**

An 18thC style oak chest on stand, the rectangular top with molded edge above two short and three dummy fronted long drawers, on stand with shaped apron and turned and blocked legs joined by stretchers, incorporating earlier elements.

36.25in (92cm) wide

$1,200-1,800 **L&T**

A late George III oak bureau cabinet, the top section with a cornice above two paneled doors enclosing fittings, the fall with similar fittings, above four long graduated drawers with later brass handles and escutcheons, on later bracket feet.

34.5in (87.5cm) wide

$1,000-1,500 **DN**

FURNITURE

A Pennsylvania white painted corner cupboard, the upper case with molded cornice above two paneled doors, the lower case with single paneled door, imperfections.

c1800   63in (160cm) wide

$1,500-2,000   **FRE**

A south-western Ontario bird's eye maple and tiger maple corner cabinet, the upper section with stepped molded cornice above a glazed door flanked by glazed panels, the lower with a bipanel door raised on geometrical bracket feet.

31.5in (80cm) wide

$2,000-3,000   **WAD**

A Lancaster County painted poplar corner wall cupboard, with a molded cornice over a glazed door with rattail hinges, scalloped skirt supported by cut out straight bracket feet, retains original red-painted surface with blue, yellow, ivory and green highlights.

48in (122cm) wide

$15,000-20,000   **Pook**

A 19thC Ontario painted glazed china cabinet, Wilno area of Renfrew County, scrolling crest flanked by finials above a pair of glass doors enclosing shelves with three short drawers and a pair of cupboard doors below, bracket feet.

49in (124cm) wide

$2,000-3,000   **WAD**

A rare early 19thC Quebec painted pine armoire in the Louis XV manner, stepped cornice with fluted decoration above a pair of shaped fielded panel doors raised on stile feet.

53in (135cm) wide

$20,000-25,000   **WAD**

A late 18thC Canadian pine two door armoire, with molded cornice above double panel doors enclosing shelves, bracket feet.

55in (140cm) wide

$2,500-3,500   **WAD**

An early 19thC Pennsylvania 'Pewter' cupboard, original paint, 'picture frame' moldings all around, paneled doors.

44in (111.5cm) wide

$7,000-10,000   **BCAC**

An 18thC Canadian carved and painted pine buffet, the top above fielded panel sides and a pair of drawers and lozenge carved doors, stile feet.

54in (137cm) wide

$8,000-12,000   **WAD**

An 18thC Quebec painted pine armoire, stepped molded cornice above a pair of fielded panel doors enclosing shelves, stile feet.

54in (137cm) wide

$5,000-7,000   **WAD**

A mid-19thC New England painted pine apothecary cupboard, with 64 small numbered drawers, above three larger drawers, retains overall ocher grain decoration.

43in (109cm) wide

$10,000-15,000   **Pook**

A rare 18thC Quebec painted two door low buffet, rectangular top with molded edge with panel sides, long panel drawer above two fielded panel doors carved with the cross of St. Andrew, stile feet.

53.5in (136cm) wide

$14,000-18,000 **WAD**

A Canadian 18thC carved pine side cabinet, with a rectangular top above a pair of lozenge carved short drawers and a pair of heavily carved doors all with wrought iron pulls.

32in (81cm) wide

$1,000-1,500 **WAD**

A Canadian 18thC small rustic painted pine single door side cabinet, the three-quarter galleried top above a fielded panel door, plinth base.

28.25in (72cm) wide

$1,100-1,500 **WAD**

An early 19thC Quebec carved pine jam cupboard, molded cornice above a single fielded panel door enclosing shelves, stile feet.

c1800   *27in (68cm) wide*

$700-900 **WAD**

A 19thC Ontario grained painted drysink, carved backboard and sunken well top above a pair of central cupboard doors flanked by square drawers, bracket feet.

51.25in (130cm) wide

$3,500-4,500 **WAD**

A George III oak bureau, the fall enclosing interior fittings, above two short and three long drawers with later brass handles and escutcheons, on bracket feet.

37.5in (95cm) wide

$1,800-2,200 **DN**

A Charles II oak, walnut and snakewood chest, in two parts, the rectangular top above four long mitre-molded drawers, centered by two further secret drawers, on stile feet.

50.5in (128cm) wide

$5,000-7,000 **FRE**

An early 18thC oak chest in two parts, with two short and three long drawers with geometric moldings and later brass drop handles, on bun feet, restorations.

38in (97cm) wide

$2,000-3,000 **DN**

A mid-17thC oak coffer, later plank top above shield and foliage carved front, shaped brackets and feet, with some later carved decoration.

41in (104cm) wide

$400-600 **SI**

A 17thC oak style chest, the hinged plank top with molded edge above scrolling serpent carved frieze with initials "A. P." and dated above three stylized floral panels.

1668   *59in (150cm) wide*

$1,200-1,800 **L&T**

A late 17thC Italian walnut and marquetry cassone, the boarded hinged top enclosing a void interior above a crossbanded, paneled block front, inlaid with scrolling foliage, raised on shaped bracket feet with an ogee molded apron.

68.5in (174cm) wide

$3,000-4,000 **FRE**

A Charles II carved oak bible box on later stand, the hinged lid enclosing a compartmented interior above foliate scroll and lunette carved sides, the later stand with bobbin turned supports and conforming stretchers.

22in (56cm) wide

$400-600 **FRE**

A 17thC oak cupboard, the rectangular top with molded edge above paneled front and sides with carved central door on turned and block legs joined by stretchers.

34.25in (87cm) wide

$2,200-2,800 **L&T**

An 18thC oak dresser base, the projecting rectangular top above three molded drawers and shaped solid trestle ends on sled feet.

68in (173cm) wide

$1,500-2,000 **L&T**

Blanket Chests

A New England William and Mary blanket chest, with a lift-over lid over a case with three panels and molded stiles above a single long-molded drawer, resting on stile feet, top restored.

43.5in (110.5cm) wide

$4,000-6,000   **Pook**

A late 18thC Pennsylvania walnut blanket chest with drawers, rectangular molded hinged lid on case with three drawers, bracket feet and original hardware.

51.5in (130cm) wide

$2,500-3,500   **FRE**

An 18thC and later polychrome painted blanket chest, signed "G.W. Yeagley, '50", the rectangular molded top opening to a well with a till on conforming case with a molded base, decorated with rectangular and shaped reserves enclosing urns with flowers and birds, the top inscribed with the initials "H.W.F." and "P.E.K." and the backboard inscribed with decorator's signature.

42in (106.5cm) wide

$1,800-2,200   **FRE**

A CLOSER LOOK AT A BLANKET/DOWER CHEST

The majority of the Pennsylvanian German settlers came from the upper Rhine valley region of southern Germany and neighboring Switzerland. Escaping religious oppression and lured by the promise of a better life they emigrated to America in ever increasing numbers bringing with them their own religious beliefs, cultural identity and distinctive methods of furniture manufacture and decoration. Chests are the most common form of Pennsylvania German furniture. Fathers would give them to their sons and daughters on their 14th birthday. They retained them throughout their lives and girls would take them to their new households after their marriages. They are often known as 'dower' or 'dowry' chest but this is misleading as men would own chests as well.

The relief molded arcade front design is characteristic of chests produced in the Lancaster area. The arcade is derived from Baroque and Medieval furniture and architectural design.

The painted decoration includes the motifs that collectors cherish: an early date, tulips that the immigrants had brought with them to Pennsylvania and compass or 'hex' signs. The 'hex' signs have no mystical or supernatural significance. The Pennsylvania Germans used special nail configurations not hex signs to protect their barns and houses from evil spirits.

A Pennsylvania German polychrome pine dower chest, probably Lancaster County, the rectangular molded top over a case, with the date "1782" painted above an architecturally carved front, with three arched panels painted with tulips, compasses and various folk symbols, each panel separated by carved and painted columns, on a step-molded base and bracket feet.

50.75in (129cm) wide

$15,000-20,000   **FRE**

A Maryland painted dower chest, dated the front with a faded salmon ground, a central stylized tulip with date and the initials "P.S", flanked by six tulips, trailing vines and diamonds, all within a black and yellow saw tooth border, over a base molding resting on straight bracket feet, loss to left rear foot.

Provenance: *Removed from an Arlington, MD home.*

1791   *48in (122cm) wide*

$5,000-7,000   **Pook**

An 18thC Canadian carved and painted blanket chest, St. Isidore, Dorchester County, Quebec, with hinged plank top with molded edge enclosing a storage compartment and candle box above a carved serpentine apron raised on peg feet.

48.5in (123cm) wide

$3,500-4,500   **WAD**

A Pennsylvania pine dovetailed blanket chest, on bracket feet, original forged iron hinges, remains of paint on an alligatored surface, some loss to feet, patch on base, tin patch on edge, missing crab lock.

53in (134.5cm) wide

$350-450 **AAC**

A grain painted pine blanket chest, possibly Bucks Co., PA, dovetailed construction, interior glove box, on turned feet.

38.5in (98cm) wide

$400-600 **AAC**

An early 19thC New England painted pine blanket chest, the rectangular top over a nailed case resting on later bracket feet, retains overall green and black sponge decoration with black pin striping and floral highlights, initialed "E.B.F."

41.5in (105.5cm) wide

$800-1,200 **Pook**

A Lebanon County Pennsylvania decorated dower chest, attributed to the Seltzer School, the front decorated with two ivory tombstone panels, with pots of tulips all on a red ground supported by straight bracket feet, restorations.

c1810 *47in (119cm) wide*

$1,200-1,800 **Pook**

A 19thC inlaid cherry blanket chest, the rectangular hinged lid inlaid with a compass star opening to well with till, the conforming case inlaid with the initials "A.Z.", raised on bracket feet, refinished, old scratches and discolorations to lid.

19.5in (50cm) wide

$800-1,200 **FRE**

A Pennsylvania painted pine blanket chest, with a lift lid over two short drawers resting on turned feet.

c1820 *39in (99cm) wide*

$2,200-2,800 **Pook**

A Montgomery County Pennsylvania painted blanket chest, with a rectangular top over a dovetailed case with three short drawers retaining the original brass pulls, resting on ogee bracket feet, retains original salmon and ocher grained surface.

c1820 *48in (122cm) wide*

$5,000-7,000 **Pook**

A Pennsylvania paint decorated poplar blanket chest, with a rectangular lift top over a paneled case resting on turned feet in overall vibrant red and black grain decoration.

c1820 *39in (99cm) wide*

$3,000-4,000 **Pook**

An early to mid-19thC grain-painted blanket chest, the rectangular hinged lid opening to a well with a till, on a conforming case with molded base and bracket feet.

43.5in (110.5cm) wide

$800-1,200 **FRE**

A 19thC/20thC small, grain-painted and paint-decorated blanket chest, rectangular top with molded edge on conforming case, with bracket feet, the front and sides decorated with shaped reserves enclosing stylized urns with flowers, paint loss.

33in (84cm) wide

$1,500-2,000 **FRE**

FURNITURE

Dressers

A George III oak dresser, with an open shelved superstructure with an egg and dart molded cornice, the lower section with three frieze drawers above two smaller apron drawers, raised on turned legs united by an undertier.

61.5in (156cm) wide

$6,000-8,000   **FRE**

A 19thC oak dresser, the open shelved back raised on base with three long drawers and cabriole front legs.

81.5in (207cm) wide

$3,000-4,000   **L&T**

An oak dresser, by Winstanley, Ashburn, with spirally turned columns, three-drawer base and cabriole legs, with intergral 8-day movement clock, with anchor escapement striking on a bell, the brass dial signed, date aperture.

73.25in (186cm) wide

$2,700-3,200   **DN**

A Continental mahogany plate rack with drop carved cornice, lion mask carved brackets and two shelves above a floral marquetry frieze, some splits.

47in (119.5cm) wide

$300-400   **DN**

Tables

A late 17thC oak refectory table, with some later components, the cleated rectangular top above a knurled frieze, raised on carved baluster turned legs, joined by a peripheral stretcher.

109in (277cm) long

$4,500-5,500   **SI**

A 17thC Continental oak refectory table, the solid top, probably associated, raised on scrolled trestle supports with flat base joined by stretcher.

88.5in (225cm) long

$1,500-2,000   **L&T**

An 18thC Catalan refectory table, the planked top raised on splayed trestle ends joined by H-stretcher and secondary supports, extensive restoration.

86.5in (220cm) long

$1,800-2,400   **L&T**

A mid-17thC oak dais table, the deep frieze carved with diaper work incorporating a Tudor rose, also carved with the initials E.S. above I.S. and further stamped E.S, on typical cup and cover supports terminating in chamfered block feet, with reeded cross stretchers, the later four plank top with cut corners and with wrought iron retaining nuts and bolts.

119in (302cm) long

$6,000-8,000   **FRE**

A late 19thC French Louis XV style provincial walnut center table, wavy frieze on cabriole legs united by X-stretcher.

62in (157.5cm) wide

$1,000-1,500   **SI**

A 17thC oak gateleg table.

26.5in (68cm) wide

$600-800   **LC**

A late 17thC oak gateleg oval dropleaf table, turned twin end supports.

25.5in (65cm) wide

$500-600   **FRE**

A late 17thC style oak gateleg table, oval top on turned supports, flattened bun feet.

51.5in (131cm) wide

$1,000-1,500   **SI**

A mid-18thC oak and fruitwood rectangular side table, with a frieze drawer above a shaped apron, on turned tapering legs with pad feet, some repairs, including a spliced leg.

27.25in (69.5 cm) high

$600-800   **DN**

Tables

An 18thC Pennsylvanian painted pine tavern table, scrubbed three-board top on red-painted base with two drawers, turned legs ending in replaced pad feet.

1780 *62in (157.5cm) wide*

$2,000-3,000   **FRE**

A pine doughbox table, rectangular top with breadboard ends, on turned leg base, minor repairs.

48in (122cm) wide

$300-500   **AAC**

An 18thC Quebec painted pine work table, scrubbed rectangular top with rounded corners raised on octagonal carved legs joined by bowed stretchers with carved foliate decorative brackets, original red pigment.

54.5in (139cm) wide

$3,500-4,500   **WAD**

An early 18thC Canadian painted pine table in the Louis XVI manner, rectangular top above two short drawers, on turned supports joined by block and turned stretchers with three finials.

34in (86cm) wide

$1,800-2,200   **WAD**

An Ontario painted tiger maple and cherry work table, scrubbed finish top with bread board ends above two short drawers, on tapering square section legs with splayed feet.

c1840 *30in (76cm) high*

$5,000-7,000   **WAD**

A Canadian Regency painted pedestal table, with rectangular top with molded edge above scroll bracket supports and single drawer, on turned pedestal base and curving cabriole legs on casters.

28in (71cm) wide

$2,000-2,500   **WAD**

A pine demi-lune table, on three tapered square legs, pinned construction.

34.5in (87.5cm) wide

$400-500   **AAC**

A Federal rustic blue painted serving table, rectangular overhanging top with rounded front corners above a straight skirt and tapering square section legs.

36.25in (92cm) wide

$1,000-1,500   **SI**

A mid-19thC rustic painted double-tiered dressing table, in maple and pine wood, with three drawers, with yellow and green paint and black stencil decoration, original hardware.

c1840 *3.5in (9cm) wide*

$5,000-7,000   **SG**

Miscellaneous

An early 19thC Pennsylvania painted pine cradle, paneled tapering ends pierced with heart devices, curved runners.

32in (81cm) wide

$400-600   **SI**

A New England painted stool, decorated with flower motif, probably maple wood.

c1840   *7.5in (19cm) high*

$600-900   **SG**

A wood and rush stool, with green foliage decoration and nicely turned stretchers, probably from New England.

c1840   *7in (17.5cm) high*

$700-1,000   **SG**

A late 19thC Canadian primitive green painted stool, with hole in center.

8in (20cm) high

$40-60   **BI**

A Pennsylvania pine school master's desk, slant top with six drawer interior, on fluted tapered legs, repair to back leg.

33.5in (85cm) wide

$600-900   **AAC**

A Pennsylvania painted and stencil-decorated settee, scrolled crest above back rests supported by turned spindles flanked by downswept arms on plank seat and turned legs joined by stretchers, painted green and decorated in copper, gold and yellow stenciled arrangements of fruit, age cracks, paint wear.

c1830   *69.5in (175cm) wide*

$1,500-2,000   **FRE**

A late19thc/early20thC painted and carved settee, rectangular seat frame with openwork rail, spiral turned legs.

48in (122cm) wide

$1,200-1,800   **FRE**

A New England chair table, pine and poplar, round top pinned to chair base with stretcher, replaced top.

48in (122cm) diam

$700-1,000   **AAC**

A 19thC Quebec carved folk art wall bracket, pinwheel finial sprouting flowers and doves, with cast brackets.

39.5in (100cm) wide

$800-1,200   **WAD**

A 19thC Quebec tiger maple letter box, with diamond point panel, hinged top and internal tray.

15.5in (39cm) wide

$500-700   **WAD**

A late 18thC Canadian carved pine wall shelf, roundel and groove carved frieze with dentil stepped molded cornice.

50in (127cm) wide

$700-1,000   **WAD**

An 18thC Quebec carved and painted pine clock shelf, rectangular back with scroll carved crest and carved molded edge with step molded shelf.

39.5in (100cm) high

$800-1,200   **WAD**

A 19thC mixed hardwood spinning wheel, signed "F. Young".

34.25in (87cm) high

$300-400   **WAD**

THE FURNITURE MARKET

Against a background of sliding stocks and shares and the turbulent international political scene, the American furniture market shows continued signs of a slow but steady recovery. The strongest demand is for pieces of good original color and condition by respected cabinetmakers. As work by the finest late 18thC makers becomes ever more expensive, items by 'lesser' makers and high quality but anonymous pieces have noticeably risen in value.

Dealers at the larger antique trade fairs have also reported a growth in the number of overseas dealers and private collectors coming to buy at the middle to upper end of the market. Smaller decorative pieces, in more exotic veneers such as satinwood and olivewood, continue to do well.

The market for Regional furniture remains buoyant with a premium being paid for the earlier Windsor chairs and items retaining untouched painted decoration. Alongside this, interior designers have stimulated the demand for lighter painted Swedish Gustavian and French country furniture and the richer golden veneers of Biedermeier.

Montgomery County, Pennsylvania walnut schrank, with a stepped cornice above a frieze inlaid "Geo. R. 1765" [George Rahn), in two herringbone cartouches above a base with two drawers, all supported by bold bun feet, [tered.

urchased from the Rahn family at a eorge Merril sale, Maine 1987.

59in (150cm) wide

10,000-15,000   **Pook**

A mid 18thC Lancaster County, Pennsylvania walnut kas, with a stepped ogee cornice above two doors each with recessed panels flanked and centering fluted stiles over a base with two drawers flanked by plinths, retains original Gothic hardware, lacking turned feet.

c1750   *71in (180.5cm) wide*

$5,500-6,500   **Pook**

An early American Pennsylvania walnut kas, the wide molded cornice above a case with a twin astragal raised panel doors alternating with recessed panel stiles, the base with an arrangement of three drawers on molding with bracket feet.

86in (218.5cm) wide

$14,000-18,000   **NA**

A New York William and Mary walnut kas, the top with deep bolection molding above a case with two paneled and molded long doors; the lower section with a long drawer above a molded base on frontal ball feet.

70in (178cm) wide

$2,800-3,200   **NA**

Classical mahogany linen press, eeded cornice above two paneled oors and reeded doors opening to ull-out trays above four drawers, raised n ring-turned feet, the blue paper label s engraved "John Needles Manufacturer f Cabinet Furniture/54 Hanover Street, altimore", altered from original form.

1825   *43.5in (110.5cm) wide*

3,000-5,000   **FRE**

A Pennsylvania Federal mahogany secretary linen press, the upper section with a molded cornice over two cupboard doors, the lower section with pull out desk with fitted interior over two cupboard doors resting on French feet.

42.75in wide

$3,000-5,000   **Pook**

A New England Federal mahogany and mahogany veneer linen press, the cornice with three turned urn finials above frieze, the middle section with two recessed paneled doors opening to four sliding shelves, the lower section with a slide over two long drawers on French feet joined by a shaped skirt, the underside of base inscribed in black paint: "T. F. Gadsen, Mt. Pleasant, near Charleston, S.C.", the backboard marked "Miss Trapier, Washington, D.C.",

c1800   *49.5in (126cm) wide*

$18,000-22,000   **SL**

A George III mahogany wardrobe, the top with a molded cornice above two paneled doors, the base with two false drawers and one long drawer, on ogee bracket feet.

52.75in (134cm) wide

$1,000-1,500   **DN**

An early 19thC German painted shrank, or cupboard, the door with painted cartouches of children, foliage and mottos, opening to reveal shelves.

48.5in (123cm) wide

$2,000-3,000   **SI**

An early 19thC mahogany linen press, with molded cornice and two paneled doors above two short and two long drawers on splayed feet, lacking sliding trays.

53.5in (136cm) wide

$1,800-2,200   **DN**

A George IV mahogany and ebony gentleman's linen press, the cupboard doors enclosing sliding trays.

45.5in (115.5cm) wic

$2,000-3,000   **S**

A CLOSER LOOK AT A REGENCY LINEN PRESS

Smarter examples of linen presses are to day placed in sitting rooms and halls, as well as the more conventional bedroom setting. The attractive proportions of this example are reminiscent of examples produced by the Lancaster firm of Gillows.

The feet should always be checked for signs of later replacements as they are often the first area to be damaged on such a piece, either by damp rot from standing on stone floors or by vacuum cleaners when standing on carpets.

Distinctive cut brass and ebony decorative detail to the frieze indicate that this was made by a good Regency cabinetmaker such as George Oakley.

The doors are made from solid panels of a more expensive cut of timber known as 'Flame' figured mahogany. Unbleached by sunlight, they retain good original color.

A late Regency mahogany linen press, the frieze with brass and ebony panels, above two paneled doors enclosing ash-lined sliding trays, the base with two short and two long drawers with original brass handles, on splayed feet.

52.75in (134cm) wide

$5,000-7,000   **DN**

A William IV mahogany clothes press, the angular cornice above two doors with arched panels, the base with two short and two long drawers on turned feet.

50in (127cm) wide

$800-1,200   **DN**

A 19thC mahogany wardrobe, the molded concave cornice above two triple paneled doors, on bracket feet.

50.25in (127.5cm) wic

$3,000-4,000   **D**

A Victorian mahogany, amboyna, oak and ebonized wardrobe, by Lamb of Manchester, the molded cornice inset with roundels above two paneled doors enclosing recesses and two short and two long drawers, on plinth base, reduced in width and restored.

49.5in (126cm) wide

$500-700   **DN**

A 19thC French oak armoire, the molded arched cornice above relief carved frieze centered by a basket of flowers, pair of doors with shaped scrolling panels , flanked by fluted angles on scroll feet.

57.5in (146cm) wide

$1,500-2,000   **L&T**

A late 19thC mahogany and satinwood banded wardrobe, with boxwood, ebor and checker stringing, the concave cornice above two astragal-glazed doo with silk hangings, above panels, on a plinth base, possibly reduced in depth

55.5in (141cm) wic

$1,800-2,200   **D**

An early 20thC Louis XVI-style walnut, marqueterie and gilt metal mounted armoire, the arched top above one mirrored panel and two further doors enclosing hanging space, on turned legs with brass cappings.

65.5in (166.5cm) wide

$1,200-1,800   **SI**

A mahogany wardrobe, the cornice above two double-paneled and crossbanded flame veneered doors, on bracket feet.

52.75in (134cm) wide

$800-1,200   **DN**

A Heal's mahogany wardrobe, with ivory maker's plaque, with a dentil cornice and a flame veneered frieze, the double paneled doors above two drawers, on ogee bracket feet.

55.25in (140.5cm) wide

$1,500-2,000   **DN**

A late George III mahogany breakfront wardrobe, the concave cornice above two paneled doors, two short and two long drawers flanked by double-paneled doors, some elements lacking.

105.5in (268cm) wide

$800-1,200   **DN**

A Regency mahogany compactum, the recessed central section with pair of paneled doors, five long graduated drawers, flanked by paneled cupboards with rosettes and arched crestings above plain cornice, plinth base.

$1,500-2,000   **L&T**

An early 19thC mahogany reverse breakfront wardrobe, the stepped cornice above four paneled doors enclosing hanging space and sliding trays on plinth base.

95in (241cm) wide

$2,500-3,000   **L&T**

An early Victorian mahogany inverted break-front wardrobe, with a molded cornice above seven long drawers with turned wood handles flanked by two mirrored doors on plinth base.

87.5in (222cm) wide

$800-1,200   **DN**

A Victorian mahogany break-front wardrobe, the molded cornice with an arched center and a scroll-carved panel, above two paneled doors flanked by mirrored doors with scroll arched panels, on a plinth base.

111.5in (283cm) wide

$1,500-2,000   **DN**

A CLOSER LOOK AT A VICTORIAN WARDROBE

Wardrobes are typically made using mahogany or walnut, it is much rarer to find an example in satinwood.

The maker's stamp is that of the renowned firm of London cabinetmakers, Johnstone Jeanes & Co who exhibited to acclaim at the Great Exhibition at the Crystal Palace in 1851.

The sheer weight of the doors on wardrobes can mean that, over time, they warp and damage the retaining hinges. It is best to check that doors open and close tightly as repairs are often expensive and time-consuming.

A gentleman's wardrobe is characterized by the exterior arrangement of drawers to either side of the central hanging space.

A mid-Victorian satinwood gentleman's wardrobe by Johnston Jeanes & Co., 67 New Bond Street, London, the shaped rectangular top above two hinged paneled cupboard doors enclosing four long slides over a long drawer, flanked by eight graduated drawers with turned knobs and on a low conforming base, one panel lacking element of molding, minor scratches, stamped "#10829".

94.5in (240cm) wide

$5,000-7,000   **FRE**

FURNITURE

Bookcases - Cabinets

A Federal mahogany china cupboard, in two parts, the upper half with molded and dentil cornice above two glazed doors opening to two shelves, the lower half with two raised panel doors and molded base.

$4,000-6,000   **FRE**

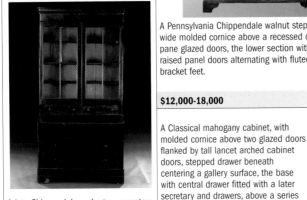

A Pennsylvania Chippendale walnut stepback cupboard, the upper section with wide molded cornice above a recessed case with fluted pilasters and twin nine-pane glazed doors, the lower section with a frieze of four drawers over a pair of raised panel doors alternating with fluted stiles on base molding with drop on bracket feet.

88.5in (225cm) wide

$12,000-18,000   **NA**

A Canadian Ontario cherrywood two piece china cabinet, the upper section with a stepped molded cornice above two glazed panel doors, the lower with three short drawers above two panel cupboard doors with a carved serpentine apron below raised on bracket feet.

53.5in (136cm) wide

$3,000-3,500   **WAD**

A late Chippendale mahogany secretary bookcase, drawer with inkwells and an inset writing surface.

42in (107cm) wide

$1,200-1,800   **SI**

A Classical mahogany cabinet, with molded cornice above two glazed doors flanked by tall lancet arched cabinet doors, stepped drawer beneath centering a gallery surface, the base with central drawer fitted with a later secretary and drawers, above a series of lancet arched cupboard doors and turned beehive feet.

c1812-20   *60in (152.5cm) wide*

$8,000-12,000   **FRE**

An early 19thC Federal mahogany secretary, astragal glazed upper section above fitted secretary, bun feet, alterations.

Provenance: *The drawers bear the signatures "W. Hill" and "Charles MacMahon, January 1832".*

42.5in (108cm) wide

$4,000-6,000   **FRE**

An early 19thC cherry and walnut fall front secretary bookcase, three long graduated drawers below, the whole within reeded quarter columns, on ogee bracket feet.

41in (104cm) wide

$7,000-9,000   **NA**

A New England Sheraton secretary desk, the upper section with central gilded eagle finial, over two doors above a middle section with three doors opening to a fitted interior, on turned and reeded legs, feet restored.

c1820   *40in (101.5cm) wide*

$3,000-4,000   **Pook**

An American 19thC Chippendale style carved mahogany oxbow slope front desk, upper paneled case above associated base with slant-front opening to serpentine interior, on ogee bracket feet.

$8,000-12,000   **FRE**

A Pennsylvania Federal walnut secretary, the associated upper section with a broken arch bonnet over two lattice mullioned doors, four graduated drawers, on flaring ogee feet.

c1800   *37.25in (94.5cm) wide*

$5,000-8,000   **Pook**

A 20thC red lacquer bureau bookcase in Queen Anne style, with chinoiserie decoration, mirrored doors enclosing fitted interior with pigeon-holes, drawers and cupboard doors, the lower section with fall front, concealing stepped interior with a covered well, on bun feet.

38in (96.5cm) wide

$4,000-6,000   **SI**

A pair of mahogany bookcases in the George I style, each with broken pediment above egg-and-dart cornice and door with shaped glazed panels flanked by fluted pilasters, conforming sides, enclosing adjustable shelves, deeper base with pair of doors with brass wire panels and rosettes, on shaped bracket feet.

31.75in (81cm) wide

$6,000-9,000   **L&T**

A CLOSER LOOK AT A WALNUT BUREAU BOOKCASE

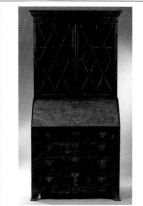

The 'broken arch' pediment is unusual to find. It is more conventional to see plain domed and triangular forms.

The small proportions increase the range of houses and flats this can be placed into, making it more desirable.

This sliding section is known as a candle slide, a lit candle placed on it would reflect off the mirrored cabinet section and illuminate not only the desk below but the room as well.

The good quality of the walnut veneers suggest that they may have been stripped off an original piece of early 18thC furniture.

A burr walnut and feather-banded bureau cabinet in George I style, the domed architectural pediment with an ogee molding, above a shaped door with a beveled mirror enclosing adjustable shelves and drawers, above a slide, the base with a fall enclosing pigeon-holes, drawers and an inset, above three long drawers, on bracket feet, possibly using early veneers.

Original, unrestored examples of early 18thC walnut furniture are appearing less and less at auctions and dealers. Good quality later 'copies' have risen steeply in value as buyers seek to recreate the look without having to spend large sums of money. If this had been a genuine example it would have realized up to five times this price.

26in (66cm) wide

$10,000-15,000   **DN**

A mahogany bureau bookcase, in the mid-18thC style, the architectural cornice above two doors with arched panels above two candle slides, the base with a fall above two short and three long graduated drawers on ogee bracket feet, 18thC and later.

40.25in (102cm) wide

$2,000-2,500   **DN**

A Louis XV walnut cabinet bookcase, with a C-scroll molded, arched top with a foliate scroll surmount, glazed panel doors, with a shelved interior, later fall front modeled as two drawers, lower section with conforming drawers, molded cabriole legs, wavy apron.

49in (124.5cm) wide

$4,000-6,000   **FRE**

A George III mahogany bureau bookcase, the molded cornice above two astragal-glazed doors enclosing adjustable shelves, the associated base with a fall enclosing drawers, above two short and three long graduated drawers on ogee bracket feet, some damage.

43in (109cm) wide

$1,200-1,800   **DN**

A mahogany bureau bookcase, the dentil cornice above two astragal-glazed doors enclosing adjustable shelves, the associated George III base with a fall above four long graduated drawers with turned handles and bracket feet.

42in (106.5cm) wide

$1,200-1,800   **DN**

A George III mahogany bureau bookcase, with satinwood crossbanding and boxwood stringing, the associated later bookcase with blind fret frieze, part-astragal glazed doors enclosing shelves, bureau fall above drawers and lopers, on ogee bracket feet.

45.25in (115cm) wide

$6,000-9,000   **L&T**

A George III mahogany bureau bookcase, the projecting cornice above two astragal doors enclosing adjustable shelves, the sloping fall enclosing fitted interior above four long graduated drawers, on splayed bracket feet.

41.75in (106cm) wide

$2,200-2,800   **L&T**

A Maine or New Hampshire Sheraton mahogany and figured birch secretary, probably Kittery or Portsmouth, upper case fitted with a cornice with foliate carved panels, above bird's-eye maple frieze panels and a pair of twin doors with eglomise panels over clear glass fronting a fitted interior, the lower section with hinged fall-front with banded edge over three drawers with flanking bottle drawers, the arched apron with beaded edge on ring turned legs.

Property from the Wadsworth Atheneum Museum of Art, sold to benefit the Acquisitions Fund.

40in (101.5cm) wide

$10,000-15,000   **NA**

A New England Federal inlaid mahogany and tiger maple tambour desk, upper section with rectangular cross banded top above two tambour doors and prospect door, all opening to fitted interior and flanked by inlaid pilasters, the lower section with fold-out writing surface above three cross banded drawers, all raised on reeded tapering legs ending in peg feet, old veneer patches, veneer losses.

North Shore or Portsmouth Hepplewhite figured mahogany and bird's-eye maple veneer secretary, original bill of sale, the crest of twin arches centered by plinth with scrolled brackets with eagle and urn finials, upper case fronted by twin-framed doors with diamond mullions over bird's-eye maple crossbanded bordered panels, fitted desk interior and adjustable shelves, above drawers on tapered legs with pointed feet.

The original bill of sale accompanies this piece and reads "Mr. Joseph Atwood/Bought of Wm. Simpson/1 Bookcase and Secretary/$37.00/July17th 1811/Rec'd Payment in full". The maker is up to now unrecorded but the evidence of a superior master-craftsman of a North Shore or Portsmouth center of a New England Hepplewhite secretary-desk adds a hitherto unrecorded maker to the list of important New England craftsmen.

1811   *39.75in(101cm) wide*

80,000-100,000   **NA**

c1800   *36in (91.5cm) wide*

$3,500-4,500   **FRE**

An early 19thC satinwood open bookcase, fitted with two shelves flanked by classical pilasters.

66in (167.75cm) wide

1,500-2,000   **FRE**

A pair of Victorian walnut open bookcases, each with projecting top above six shelves, plinth base.

$10,000-12,000   **AH**

English Bureaux

A William and Mary walnut kneehole bureau, the rectangular top with mahogany crossbanding above fall front with feather-banding and matched veneers enclosing a fitted interior with a well, the plain frieze with lopers above waist-molding and arched kneehole flanked to either side by three feather-banded graduated drawers, on shaped bracket feet, restorations.

31.5in (80cm) wide

$4,000-6,000   **L&T**

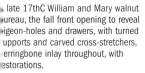

late 17thC William and Mary walnut bureau, the fall front opening to reveal pigeon-holes and drawers, with turned supports and carved cross-stretchers, herringbone inlay throughout, with restorations.

6,000-8,000   **FRE**

A William and Mary-style small walnut bureau, the fall front enclosing a fitted interior with pigeon holes and drawers.

20in (51cm) wide

$1,000-1,500   **SI**

Slant-lid Desks

A Connecticut Chippendale cherry wood slant-lid desk, the case with four long graduated drawers on bandy cabriole legs with ball and claw feet, the center drop with carved pinwheel.

38in (96.5cm) wide

$15,000-20,000　　　　**NA**

A CLOSER LOOK AT A NEWPORT CHIPPENDALE DESK

Although this desk is not labeled it displays various stylistic characteristics that suggest the work of one of the finer Rhode Island cabinetmakers such as John Townsend. The interior is almost identical to a secretary-desk ascribed to Townsend and illustrated in "The New Fine Points Of Furniture" by Albert Sack, published 1993 Crown Publishers.

This is a rare and good commercial example of a Newport desk despite the relatively poor condition with the stress damage to the drawer intersections, age splits and bruising.

The case drawers and the short drawers to the interior are all annotated with sequential graphite lettering. Again this is a feature found in authenticated pieces by Townsend.

The turned wooden knobs look to be later additions. It is likely that this desk was made with brass batwing mounts with bail handles that would have matched the larger handles to the sides. Always inspect the inside of the drawers and look for signs of empty screw holes that will indicate the original setting for the hardware.

A Newport Chippendale carved mahogany slant-lid desk, with block and shell carved interior, attributed to John Townsend, th[e] dovetailed top and sloped lid above interior centered by a concave blocked prospect door headed by a six-lobed shell flanked on each side by three pigeon-holes, each crested by a small drawer fronted by a scooped concave dome and flanke[d] by three concave blocked drawers, the top one shell carved, the case with four long graduated drawers, each with thumb molded edges, on base molding with ogee bracket feet, the sides with brass carrying handles.

c1760-80　　　　　　　　　　　　　　　　　*38.5in (98cm) wid[e]*

$50,000-60,000　　　　　　　　　　　　　　**N[A]**

A Hartford area Chippendale cherry slant-lid desk, attributed school of George Belden, the dovetailed top over a sloped lid opening to interior with drawers and cubbyholes, the case with four long graduated drawers, each thumb molded on base molding with ogee bracket feet.

44in (112cm) wide

$3,500-4,500　　　**NA**

A Massachusetts or New Hampshire Queen Anne carved tiger maple slant-lid desk, School of Peter Bartlett (1788-1838), Salisbury, New Hampshire, the dovetailed top with sloping thumbmolded lid opening to a curved compartment interior with a stack of four concave blocked prospect drawers with flanking document drawers faced with half column, further flanked by valanced drawers over cubbyholes and drawers, the case with four long graduated thumb molded drawers on base molding with bandy cabriole legs and shaped returns on pad feet.

36in (91.5cm) wide

$30,000-40,000　　　　　　　　　　**NA**

A late 18thC Massachusetts Chippendale mahogany serpentine fron[t] slant-front desk, the slant top opens to a fitted interior with six drawers and fou[r] pigeon-holes.

43in (109cm) wid[e]

$3,500-4,500　　　**S[I]**

A late 18thC Chippendale mahogany serpentine slant-front desk, the fitted interior with six drawers and four pigeon-holes, and flanked prospect door over four graduated drawers on a molded base on ball and claw feet.

This desk was part of the collection of John C. Toland (d. 1835), of Baltimore. Many pieces of Toland's collection were illustrated in "American Antique Furniture," published by the Baltimore Museum of Art in 1947.

42in (106.5cm) wide

$6,000-8,000　　　　**SI**

A Massachusetts Chippendale mahogany oxbow slant-lid desk, probably Newburyport, School of Abner Toppan, with elaborate stepback interior with top row serpentine and blocked, the blocked concave fan-carved drawers at the center and each end with fluted document drawers over a frieze of drawers, the case with four oxbow long graduated drawers, the top one compartmented, on ball and claw feet.

$10,000-15,000　　　　**N[A]**

41in (104cm) wid[e]

late 18thC Philadelphia Chippendale alnut slant-front desk, fitted interior bove case with four graduated thumb-olded drawers, ogee bracket feet, nperfections.

39in (99cm) wide

3,000-5,000   **FRE**

A late 19thC Newport Chippendale style mahogany blockfront kneehole desk, elaborately carved.

39.75in (101cm) wide

$3,500-4,500   **FRE**

Chippendale walnut slant-front desk, ith fitted interior with pigeon-holes nd drawers with conforming center ection, over four graduated lipped rawers, on ogee bracket feet, eplacements, repairs.

38in (96.5cm) wide

2,500-3,500   **AAC**

A Boston, Massachusetts, Chippendale mahogany slant-front desk, the blocked lid with central fan carving enclosing a fitted interior with an arched and raised panel prospect door flanked by document drawers with fluted columns, pigeon-holes and drawers, above a blocked case with four graduated drawers above a scalloped shell drop, resting on short cabriole legs and ball and claw feet, carving on interior drawers possibly 19thC.

c1770   *40in (101.5cm) wide*

$20,000-30,000   **Pook**

New England Federal inlaid mahogany desk, rectangular top with reeded edge bove arrangement of five drawers, arched skirt, tapering reeded legs on casters, ome restoration.

1820   *35.75in (91cm) wide*

4,000-6,000   **FRE**

A Hepplewhite slant-front cherry desk, over base with four graduated lipped drawers on bracket feet, with inscription "This Desk Belonged to General Dixon, Camden Del.", dated 1889.

41in (104cm) wide

$2,000-3,000   **AAC**

A Hepplewhite walnut slant-front desk, with fitted interior over four graduated cock beaded drawers, mahogany drawer fronts, on French bracket feet, replacements.

42in (106cm) wide

$1,500-2,000   **AAC**

A Hepplewhite mahogany campaign desk, rectangular form, fitted interior with storage compartment and three drawers, green felt writing surface with two lift lids, on base with single cock beaded drawer, brass handles on sides for carrying, on tapered legs.

c1820   *30in (76cm) wide*

$3,000-4,000   **AAC**

A Napoleon III ebonized and brass inlaid side cabinet, with gilt-metal mounts, the white marble top with outset corners above a paneled cupboard door inlaid with flowering urns, scrolls and griffins, enclosing a shelved interior, on a plinth base.

29.5in (75cm) wide

$700-1,000   **SI**

A mid-19thC Dutch ebonized marqueterie and parquetry inlaid side cabinet, the cupboard door enclosing shelves, flanked by spiral twist columns, flattened bun feet.

33in (84cm) wide

$3,000-4,000   **SI**

A 19thC walnut and marqueterie inlaid meuble d'appui, rectangular marble top, paneled door, profuse marqueterie inlaid with flowers and foliage, with silvered strapwork and leaf cast motifs, flanked by silvered leaf cast and exotic fish brackets, on cast bracket feet.

30.75in (78cm) wide

$4,000-6,000   **L&T**

A Victorian walnut and tulipwood-banded side cabinet, with gilt metal and porcelain mounts, the grey marble top above a glazed door enclosing a velvet lined interior, on plinth base with bun feet.

29.5in (75cm) wide

$600-900   **D**

A late Regency mahogany collector's cabinet, the molded rectangular top above an open cupboard frame with bobbin molding enclosing nine drawers, on turned and gadrooned feet.

19.25in (49cm) wide

$1,500-2,000   **L&T**

A mid-19thC mahogany rectangular cabinet, the molded top above two paneled doors enclosing shelves on turned feet.

24.5in (64.5cm) wide

$700-1,000   **DN**

A rosewood side cabinet, the top with a nulled edge above two short drawers and two doors with brass grilles enclosing adjustable shelves, on a plinth base, constructed from 19thC timber.

38.75in (98.5cm) wide

$1,200-1,800   **DN**

An early Victorian mahogany cupboard with two paneled doors enclosing sliding trays on turned feet.

50in (127cm) wide

$700-1,000   **D**

A George IV rosewood break-front cabinet, the black St Anne marble top above a central frieze drawer, the pilasters with later giltwood capitals flanked by four brass grille doors backed with pleated silk, enclosing shelves, on a plinth base, restored.

53.5in (135.5cm) wide

$1,200-1,800   **DN**

A good late Regency rosewood and brass strung cabinet, the upper portion fitted with a galleried shelf with scroll supports above four drawers with four gilt brass lattice-work cupboard doors below, on six beaded tapered feet.

48in (122cm) wide

$15,000-20,000   **FRE**

A Napoleon III boulle and ebonized mirrored back credenza of break-front form, inlaid with scrolling brasswork on a red tortoiseshell ground, serpentine-shaped top above three glazed panel doors, lower section with three glazed doors, bracket feet, shaped apron.

76in (193cm) wide

$1,200-1,800   **SI**

A mid-Victorian figured walnut and marqueterie serpentine credenza, with gilt metal mounts, the foliate inlaid frieze above a conformingly inlaid cupboard door flanked by simulated fluted pilasters and two further glass panel doors, on a shaped plinth base.

59.5in (151cm) wide

$5,000-7,000

An early 19thC Italian gilt wood and painted table cabinet, the glazed panel with serpentine arch before a velvet-lined interior and enclosed within molded frame with leaf and flower cresting and with husk swags to the angles, the sides painted with faux marble panels, the whole raised on paw feet.

13.25in (33.5cm) high

$1,200-1,800 **L&T**

A 20thC burr walnut and marqueterie table cabinet, probably Austrian, the hinged door depicting the standing figure of a young woman holding a flower, a male admirer kneeling before her, the side panels and drawer with inlaid foliate motifs, the interior with a series of drawers with further foliate inlay.

13.25in (33.5cm) high

$1,000-1,500 **DN**

Chiffoniers

A small Regency rosewood and brass inlaid chiffonier, the rectangular top with mirror-backed shelf on brass column supports with pierced three-quarter gallery, brass inlaid frieze and doors with ogee panels on saber feet.

26.5in (67cm) wide

$4,000-6,000 **L&T**

A Regency rosewood and brass inlaid chiffonier, the rectangular mirror back with ledge top above a base with two frieze drawers and pair of mirrored cupboard drawers, flanked by consoles, on scrolled feet.

44.75in (114cm) wide

$3,000-4,000 **L&T**

A Regency rosewood and brass inlaid chiffonier, the raised back with two shelves and pierced brass gallery sides, turned supports and a mirrored back, the inverted break-front base with a drawer and two paneled drawers, on ebonized turned feet, adapted and restored.

36.5in (93cm) wide

$3,000-4,000 **DN**

A Regency rosewood and brass chiffonier, the raised back with a pierced brass three-quarter gallery and a shelf on slender brass supports, the frieze with nulled borders, above two grille doors lined with pleated silk, flanked by turned columns, on a plinth base with outset corners.

36.5in (92.5cm) wide

$1,500-2,000 **DN**

A William IV rosewood chiffonier, the rectangular top with panel back and open shelf with turned and lappeted supports and pediment ledge back centered by scrolling leaf-carved cartouche, the base with glazed doors flanked by corresponding columns enclosing sliding trays with shaped rosewood fronts, on plinth base.

57in (100cm) wide

$4,000-6,000 **L&T**

A George IV mahogany chiffonier, the raised back with two shelves and slender ring-turned and lappet-carved supports, above two frieze drawers with later brass handles and two later glazed doors, on bracket feet.

38in (96.5cm) wide

$1,200-1,800 **DN**

An early Victorian mahogany chiffonier, the raised back with a three-quarter gallery on spindle supports, the base with a felt-lined adjustable writing slope above two short drawers and two arched, fabric-lined doors flanked by reeded pilasters on turned tapering feet, the back possibly of a later date.

37.25in (94.5cm) wide

$2,200-2,800 **DN**

A mid-19thC Burmese carved hardwood chiffonier, open shelves above cupboard doors enclosing shelved interior, with ornate open work carving throughout depicting exotic birds, foliage and grotesque masks.

60in (152.5cm) wide

$700-1,000 **SI**

An early Victorian mahogany chiffonier bookcase, the rectangular top with shelf on scrolled console supports, above open adjustable shelves, flanked by molded consoles, on plinth base.

36.25in (92cm) wide

$2,000-3,000 **L&T**

Bedside Cabinets

A George III mahogany night stand, the tray top with pierced carrying handles over a pair of covered doors and one deep drawer modeled as two, raised on molded square legs, alterations.

19in (48cm) wide

$700-1,000   **SI**

A George III mahogany tray top bedside commode, the wavy gallery with pierced handles, above a crossbanded and ebony strung door simulating two doors, above a pull-out base on straight legs.

20.75in (53cm) wide

$2,000-3,000   **DN**

A George III mahogany tray top commode, the rectangular top with shaped gallery and pierced carry handles above pair of crossbanded doors and later pair of doors below, on square section legs, adapted.

22in (56cm) wide

$1,200-1,800   **L&T**

A George III mahogany pot cupboard, the rectangular tray top with three-quarter gallery and pierced carry handles above door and square section chamfered legs.

22.75in (36cm) wide

$500-700   **L&T**

A George III mahogany and boxwood strung bedside table, the raised shaped back with one shelf above a tambour door with brass handle, on square tapering legs.

16in (41cm) wide

$4,000-6,000   **DN**

A George III mahogany pot cupboard, the raised back with side handles, above two doors on square chamfered legs.

30in (76cm) wide

$800-1,200   **DN**

A late George III mahogany tray top pot cupboard, with pierced handles and a door on square tapering legs and a flat cross-stretcher.

14in (87cm) wide

$700-1,000   **DN**

A George IV mahogany bedside cupboard/table, the rectangular top with rounded corners and two drop leaves, above a fall frieze simulating two drawers, veneered similarly to the back, on reeded turned tapering legs, with brass terminals and casters stamped "COPE COLLINSON PATENT STRONG", lacking a small section of molding.

32.75in (83cm) wide (extended)

$2,000-3,000   **DN**

A late 19thC French rosewood and inlaid pot cupboard, of tapered form, the grey marble top above a dummy drawer and one cupboard drawer on a plinth base and bracket feet.

13in (33cm) wide

$700-1,000   **SI**

A pair of late 19thC Louis XV-style kingwood and gilt metal mounted bedside cabinets, the green marble tops above a frieze drawer and a cupboard door, on slender square cabriole legs headed by caryatids and ending in sabots.

17in (43cm) wide

$3,000-4,000   **SI**

A CLOSER LOOK AT A BEDSIDE CABINET

Fine quality, decorative cabinets such as this fetch a premium at auction. Although separated from the rest of the bedroom suite, its small size means it can now be used in almost any room.

Cabinetmakers Edwards and Roberts were established in London in 1845, specializing in selling 18thC furniture with added marqueterie and copies of earlier decorative pieces.

Sometimes these cabinets are 'created' by chopping up a larger and less commercial piece, such as a large dressing table. Always check the interior and underside for imperfect, rough or messy construction. Edwards and Roberts were sticklers for detail and even the unseen areas on such a piece will be finished to a very high standard.

A late 19thC mahogany bedside cabinet, stamped "Edwards and Roberts", with satinwood banding, reeded bands, the paneled door centered with a marqueterie urn, with a turned handle, enclosing a shelf, on a plinth base.

16in (40.5cm) wide

$3,000-4,000   **DN**

Corner Cupboards

A Mid-Atlantic or Southern States Federal cherry corner cupboard, with a single glazed and hinged door, with two short drawers and a pair of recessed paneled doors below, on shaped bracket feet, refinished and some restoration.

c1800   46in (117cm) wide

$5,000-7,000   **SI**

A Pennsylvania Chippendale walnut corner cupboard, the wide projecting molded cornice above a case with a pair of beaded cupboard doors opening to shelves, over another pair of doors opening to shelves, on base molding.

41in (104cm) wide

$3,800-4,200   **NA**

A Federal cherry corner cupboard, probably Pennsylvania, with a single glazed door opening to three shelves, with two recessed paneled doors below on a shaped skirt with bracket feet, refinished, alterations.

43in (109cm) wide

$2,200-2,800   **SL**

A New England barrel back pine corner cupboard, open top with shell carved hood and butterfly shelves, over a raised panel door base flanked by reeded stiles, replacements.

33in (84cm) wide

$600-800   **AAC**

An early 18thC New York yellow pine corner cupboard, with dentil frieze over a pair of glazed doors opening to interior, a pair of recessed panel doors below, on straight bracket feet, refinished.

48in (122cm) wide

$2,000-3,000   **FRE**

A Centennial Chippendale mahogany corner cupboard, broken arch pediment, ball and claw feet, reeded quarter columns, shell carved doors.

22in (56cm) wide

$4,000-5,000   **AAC**

A CLOSER LOOK AT A FEDERAL CORNER CUPBOARD

It is more common to find standing corner cupboards with flat top or straight cornices. The scrolling swan neck pediment with the gentle slope down to the corners and the inlaid pinwheel terminals are attractive features.

Whenever a piece has glazed doors they should be examined for signs of alteration or replacement. The doors can be whole scale replacements for less desirable solid doors. The frames and glazing bars should have the same colour depth, wear and quality of wood as the surrounding frame. This particular arched architectural design is unusual and a comparable example from Frederick County is illustrated, fig 118.6 in the catalogue for 'The Colonial Williamsburg Collection' (pub 1997).

High style Federal corner cupboards are rare and even the more sophisticated examples have relatively little inlay. It is worth looking for the best examples such as this with a highly attractive inlaid meandering vine.

The use of line and spandrel inlay to the panel doors together with the unusual feature of the integrated swan neck pediment are features more typically found on tallcase clocks of the period. It is possible that the cabinet maker responsible for this cabinet was also a good clock case maker.

A Southern Federal inlaid walnut corner cupboard, possibly Virginia, with swan's-neck molded crest with inlaid pinwheel terminals, the tympanum with oval foliate medallion and inlaid meander vine, the twin arched glazed doors enclosing shelves, the projecting lower case with a frieze of three drawers, the pair of recess panel doors with line inlay and corner spandrels centering an oval medallion, on molded base with shaped bracket feet.

Provenance: property from the Wadsworth Atheneum Museum of Art, sold to benefit the Acquisitions Fund

51.5in (129.5cm) wide

$28,000-32,000   **NA**

A George III oak corner cupboard, the upper and lower sections with paneled doors enclosing shelves, bracket feet.

30in (76cm) wide

$1,000-1,500 SI

A George III mahogany corner cabinet, the molded and inlaid cornice above a frieze inlaid with a central patera flanked by shells, the paneled cupboard doors enclosing a shelf, on block feet.

49.75in (126cm) wide

$1,200-1,800 L&T

A 19thC painted corner cabinet in the early George III style, the broken pediment above molded cornice with bolection frieze and pair of astragal-glazed doors enclosing shaped shelves, on base with pair of four panel doors and plinth.

46.5in (118cm) wide

$3,000-4,000 L&T

A Victorian giltwood and gesso three-tier hanging corner shelf, the arched top with a shell and foliate surmount above three graduated tiers with mirrored paneled backs and flanked by fluted pilasters.

17.5in (44.5cm) wide

$1,500-2,000 SI

A late Victorian satinwood and marqueterie corner cupboard, labeled "C. Trollope & Sons", the frieze drawer inlaid with ribbon-tied drapery above a glazed panel door enclosing shelves, flanked by velvet-lined open shelves, raised on square tapered legs with spade feet.

29.5in (75cm) wide

$1,500-2,000 SI

An Edwardian mahogany corner cabinet in the Chippendale style, the carved swan neck pediment and fluted pedestal above astragal-glazed doors enclosing velvet-lined shelves, pair of cupboard doors with shaped panels, stop-fluted pilasters, blind fret panels, on molded cabriole legs with ball and claw feet.

39.75in (101cm) wide

$4,000-6,000 L&T

An Edwardian rosewood bow-front corner cabinet, with boxwood and ivory inlay, the upper section with glazed door enclosing velvet-lined and mirror-backed shelved interior, an open mirror back shelf raised on square section tapering legs joined by shaped undershelf with balustraded brass gallery.

68in (173cm) wide

$1,800-2,200 L&T

An early 20thC mahogany and crossbanded display cabinet, the cornice centered with an architectural pediment above an astragal-glazed door and canted sides, the base with fiddle back mahogany and satinwood lozenges to the door and canted sides.

37.5in (95cm) wide

$1,200-1,800 DN

Display Cabinets

A late 19thC Dutch mahogany, marqueterie, tulipwood crossbanded and boxwood strung display cabinet, the checker-banded raised gallery above a part-glazed and inlaid door flanked by canted corners.

23in (58cm) wide

$1,200-1,800 DN

A late 19thC rosewood display cabinet in the George II style, molded cornice, glazed panel doors enclosing shaped shelves and lined interior, with a fall front, on squat shell-carved cabriole legs joined by a wavy apron.

33in (84cm) wide

$6,000-9,000 SI

A late 19thC red painted and parcel gilt vitrine, in the Louis XV style, with a shelved plushed fitted interior, small cabriole legs.

39in (99cm) wide

$1,000-1,500 SI

A pair of Louis XV-style kingwood vitrines, with gilt metal mounts, each with glazed cabinet with scrolling pediment, door with beveled glass enclosing glass shelves, on shaped apron base, cabriole legs.

33.5in (85cm) wide

$7,000-10,000 L&T

A CLOSER LOOK AT A CABINET ON STAND

...e combination of painted marble and ...rtoiseshell is characteristically European. ...e combination of ripple-molded ebonized ...rips and tortoiseshell is also found in ...utch furniture and mirrors.

Such cabinets were often termed 'a Cabinet of Curiosities'. The drawers to the interior would often have been filled with medals, coins, interesting dried animals, birds' eggs, and mineralogical specimens.

The later British stand is probably not a replacement but a specific commission for the cabinet by the owner upon his return from Europe.

...ne quality exotic cabinets such as this ...re often brought back as souvenirs by ...ealthy noblemen who had been on The ...and Tour of Europe.

An 18thC Spanish tortoiseshell and marble mounted cabinet on a Regency stand, the rectangular cabinet with ripple-molded ebony banding, stringing, gilt plaster and stamped metal moldings, the drawers with marble panels painted with buildings in a landscape, the pair of central doors surrounded by drawers and enclosing trompe l'oeil interior, the mahogany base with ebonized scrolling acanthus and palmette moldings, central hinged door centered by a carved crest and flanked by sliding doors, on plinth and leaf carved paw feet.

Provenance: *Blair House, Ayrshire.*

60.75in (154cm) wide

L&T

...2,000-18,000

Cellarets & Wine Coolers

...George III mahogany and brass-...ound oval wine cooler, with lion's mask ...de carrying handles and tin liner, ...sed on square chamfered legs with ...erced angle brackets and leather ...sters.

...e difference between a wine cooler and ...cellaret is that a cellaret is designed ...th fitted compartments for storing ...ttles dry, close to the dining table, ...ereas a cooler has a lead or tin liner ...th draining hole for chilled water or ice ... actually cooling the bottles.

23.5in (60cm) wide

...,500-3,000 **SI**

A George III mahogany and brass bound wine cooler, the hexagonal body with lead lined honeycombed interior and drainer, on a base with fluted frieze with square section molded legs and leather casters.

19in (48cm) wide

$4,000-6,000 **L&T**

A Regency mahogany cellaret, of sarcophagus form, the hinged lid surmounted by a fruiting vine, opening to reveal a now-plush fitted interior on paw feet.

29in (74cm) wide

$3,000-4,000 **SI**

A George IV mahogany cellaret, of sarcophagus form, the hinged lid enclosing a void interior on a later plinth base.

32in (81cm) wide

$2,000-3,000 **SI**

...William IV mahogany sarcophagus ...aped cellaret, the hinged top with a ...ncave edge, on tapering paneled sides ...d paw and scroll carved feet with ...cessed casters.

28.75in (73cm) high

...,000-4,000 **DN**

An early 19thC mahogany and boxwood strung bow-front cellaret, the hinged lid enclosing a baize-lined interior on square tapering legs with spade feet.

20in (51cm) wide

$1,500-2,000 **DN**

An early 19thC mahogany and brass bound oval wine cooler/jardinière, with a zinc liner, brass lion's mask handles on later square tapering legs and block feet.

26in (66cm) wide

$800-1,200 **DN**

A walnut oval and brass bound wine cooler/jardinière with a metal liner and four outswept legs.

24.5in (62cm) wide

$700-1,000 **DN**

Open Armchairs

A New England Queen Anne maple rush-seat armchair, yoked crest and shaped stile centering a vasiform splat, the rush seat raised on vase-and-block turned legs, ending in Spanish feet.

40.75in (103.5cm) high

$1,800-2,200   FRE

A Philadelphia Queen Anne walnut arm chair, attributed to William Savery (1721-1787), serpentine crest rail above a vasiform splat, cabriole front legs joined by flattened stretchers.

40in (101cm) high

$18,000-22,000   FRE

A CLOSER LOOK AT A PHILADELPHIA QUEEN ANNE ARMCHAIR

A useful aid to dating a chair like this one is to pick it up and feel the weight. Mid-18thC timber tends to be much denser than later wood and original examples are surprisingly heavy.

Two manuscript copie of the Philadelphia pric lists of 1772 survive. walnut cabriole leg cha such as this would hav been a third les expensive than mahogany versio

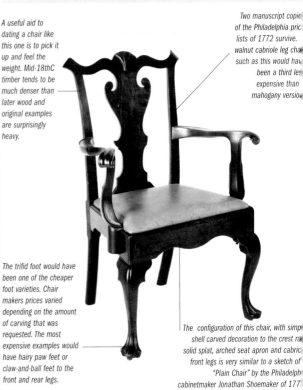

The trifid foot would have been one of the cheaper foot varieties. Chair makers prices varied depending on the amount of carving that was requested. The most expensive examples would have hairy paw feet or claw-and-ball feet to the front and rear legs.

The configuration of this chair, with simp shell carved decoration to the crest ra solid splat, arched seat apron and cabrio front legs is very similar to a sketch of "Plain Chair" by the Philadelph cabinetmaker Jonathan Shoemaker of 177

A Philadelphia Chippendale mixed wood armchair, having a serpentine crest rail, solid urn-shaped splat, curved and flaring arms with scrolled knuckles, straight seat rail with a slip seat on plain cabriole legs, pad feet, restorations.

$5,000-7,000   FRE

A George I walnut open armchair, the waisted back with shaped burr walnut veneered splat and scrolling arms, eagles head terminals, drop-in seat on cabriole legs with hairy paw feet.

$18,000-22,000   L&T

A Philadelphia Queen Anne walnut armchair, the serpentine crest with a carved shell over vasiform splat, carved outward scrolling arms terminating in voluted handholds, over a trapezoidal seat frame, shaped skirt, and cabriole legs terminating in trifid feet.

Provenance: *Pioneer Philadelphia collector and author.*

c1775

$45,000-50,000   Poo

A late 19thC/early 20thC mahogany library elbow chair, in the George II style, the inverted serpentine back and seat within shaped arms with bird terminals, on bird and foliate carved cabriole legs with claw and ball feet.

$3,000-4,000   DN

A mid-19thC walnut arm chair, George II style, tapestry and needlepoint upholstered back with decoration of handmaidens washing the maidens feet, scrolling arms, carved apron above honey suckle carved cabriole legs, bold claw-and-ball feet.

$5,000-6,000   SI

A George III mahogany Gainsborough chair, the arched back, padded scroll arms and stuffed over seat above a blind fret carved frieze, on waisted square tapered legs carved with trailing bellflowers and ending with block feet.

$10,000-15,000   SI

A George II mahogany armchair, the paper scrolled back with vertically pierced and scrolled splat, open arms with out scrolled terminals, stuff-over seat and acanthus carved cabriole fro and rear legs with claw-and-ball feet.

$18,000-22,000   L&

vo of a set of four giltwood elbow
hairs, each with flower carved crest,
pholstered back, arms and serpentine
onted seat, on cabriole legs, probably
0thC in the 18thC manner.

2,700-3,000 (set)   DN

A pair of mahogany elbow chairs, each
with a lobed crest above a pierced and
carved splat, with shaped arms
terminating with carved patera, a drop-
in seat and straight chamfered and
molded legs, late George III and
adapted.

$450-550   DN

A George III mahogany child's open
ladder back armchair, with stuff over
seat on square section legs.

$750-850   FRE

A George III mahogany elbow chair, the
shaped crest above a pierced splat with a
drop-in seat, shaped sides and straight
chamfered legs, formerly a commode chair.

$300-400   DN

George III mahogany country elbow
hair, with pierced ladder back, shaped
rms, padded seat and straight legs
th H-stretchers.

600-800   DN

A pair of George III painted open armchairs, each decorated in the neo-Classical
style on a sage green ground, the back with painted panel of putti, downswept
arms and caned seat on square section tapering legs.

Provenance: Blair House, Ayrshire.

$10,000-12,000   L&T

An 18thC and adapted Dutch walnut and
floral marquetry elbow chair, with a shell
carved crest and knees, a solid vase-
shaped splat, shepherds crook-style
arms, a drop-in seat and cabriole legs
with ball-and-claw-feet, some worm,
some damage including the seat rail.

$3,000-4,000   DN

early 20thC French painted and
ded open armchair, in late 18thC
yle, the oval back with a ribbon crest,
th scrolled arms and supports,
added back, arms and seat on turned
bering fluted legs.

600-800   DN

A pair of 20thC Italian carved giltwood and
upholstered armchairs, in the 18thC style,
the padded backs surmounted by a coat
of arms, flanked by rampant lions above
scroll arms modelled as dolphins, stuff over
seats raised on foliate-carved X-frame
supports, centered by mask motifs and
ending in claw feet.

$6,000-8,000   SI

A pair of Edwardian mahogany
Hepplewhite style armchairs, with
guilloche carved molded frames, each
with shield back with five leaf carved
spars, downswept open arms, stuff-over
seat and turned tapering leaf carved
reeded legs with toupie feet.

$3,000-4,000   L&T

A Regency mahogany carver, the paneled
bar back with reeded top above pierced
and leaf-carved mid rail, scrolling arms,
drop-in seat and saber legs.

$220-280   L&T

A pair of late 19thC mahogany Gainsborough chairs, in the George III style, downswept arms and stuff-over seats covered in blue fabric, cabriole legs.

$4,000-6,000   SI

A 20thC ebonised and parcel gilt open armchair, in the Regency style, covered in foliate pattern and striped fabric, the square back with ball finials and scroll arms, stuff-over seat, on saber legs.

$400-600   SI

A French Empire mahogany and upholstered fauteuil, rectangular padded back above scroll over arms with rosette roundel decoration, square tapering legs.

$1,000-1,500   S

A pair of French ebonised and parcel gilt open armchairs, in the early 19thC style, each with reeded frame, back rail with flower head roundels, padded back, arms and buttoned seat on reeded turned legs and brass casters.

$1,200-1,800   DN

A William IV mahogany elbow chair, carved with stylized scrolls and foliage, with scrolling arms and drop-in seat.

$400-600   DN

An early Victorian mahogany library armchair, the buttoned back with console supports, stuff-over seat and turned and carved front legs with casters.

$2,000-3,000   L&T

A Victorian oak armchair, constructed in 1847 from original timber of the Maxwell Seaton Sluice of 1784, with a rope-twist carved hoop back, the crest inscribed and initialled "D", with a padded back, seat and arms supported by dolphins with a chain carved seat rail on massive scroll carved legs.

44.5in (113cm) hig

$6,000-8,000   D

A pair of mid-19thC Louis XVI style carved giltwood fauteuils, with ornate drapery and foliate carved decoration, the backs, padded scroll arms and stuff-over serpentine seats in pink and green fabric, on Doric column style tapering legs.

$4,000-6,000   SI

c1865

$600-1,000   FR

A Louis XVI style ormolu-mounted walnut open armchair, attributed to A. and H. LeJambre, Philadelphia, shaped and upholstered back with carved pendant enclosed by downswept beaded arms, the shaped seat rail with rosettes on tapering fluted legs ending in ball feet, casters, old breaks, losses.

Provenance: *A photocopy of a receipt to reupholster chair from A. and H. LeJambre, 1206 Walnut Street, dated 1882, accompanies this lot.*

A pair of 19thC French painted open armchairs, each with a flower carved crest and apron, a padded back, arms and serpentine seat on cabriole legs, formerly gilt, some worm damage.

$900-1,100 DN

A Victorian rosewood open armchair, the crest carved with flower heads, with button upholstered padded back, arms and seat on leaf-carved cabriole legs, with brass casters.

$1,200-1,400 DN

A mid-19thC pair of Italian carved walnut throne chairs, with tapestry upholstered back and seat within richly carved frame decorated with seated putti, lion monopodia legs.

$6,000-8,000 SI

A late Victorian oak tub shaped library chair, by James Shoolbred & Co, with red morocco leather buttoned back, arms and seat, on turned legs stamped "D5250" and ceramic casters.

A Victorian mahogany open armchair, with scrolled button back, padded arms and seat on shell and scroll-carved cabriole legs and ceramic casters.

A Victorian walnut framed gentleman's easy chair, the morocco leather buttoned back and seat with studded decoration and open arms raised on turned front legs and casters.

A late 19thC Italian carved giltwood and upholstered open armchair, in the 18thC style, the arched square back, padded scroll arms and stuff-over seat on square tapered legs ending on gadrooned block feet joined by a wavy H-stretcher.

$1,000-1,200 DN   **$3,000-4,000** L&T   **$4,500-5,500** DN   **$1,200-1,500** SI

A late 19thC Continental and upholstered open armchair, the square padded back surmounted by a pair of cherubs and a flowering urn, the arms with lion terminals, on fluted turned tapered legs joined by an H-stretcher.

A pair of late 19thC Continental walnut and upholstered open armchairs, the arched paneled backs carved with doric pilasters and surmounted by angels, the arms with figural terminals above a solid seat, on square tapered legs joined by H-stretchers.

A pair of late 19thC Italian giltwood and upholstered chairs, in the 18thC style, the arched square backs and stuff-over seats on reeded acanthus scrolled arms, molded square tapered legs with block feet joined by wavy X-stretchers.

$3,000-4,000 SI   **$1,500-2,000** SI   **$4,500-5,500** SI

Armchairs

A Pennsylvania Chippendale mahogany easy chair, the arched upholstered back flanked by ogival wings and outscrolled arms above upholstered seat with loose cushion, molded square legs joined by stretchers.

43.5in (110.5cm) high

$4,000-6,000   **FRE**

A Massachusetts Chippendale carved mahogany wing chair, the canted back with serpentine crest joining shaped wings with rolled arms on frontal cabriole legs with a turned recessed stretcher.

$6,000-10,000   **NA**

A Philadelphia Chippendale mahogany easy chair, with serpentine crest, outward flaring arms and straight molded legs joined by stretchers.

$4,000-6,000   **Pook**

A George III mahogany wing back armchair, upholstered in damask with brass studding, on cabriole legs, paw feet, possibly Irish, some restoration.

$10,000-12,000   **DN**

A late George III wing back armchair, with sectional upholstery, tapering legs with brass terminals and casters, one back leg repaired.

$1,800-2,200   **DN**

A William IV rosewood armchair, with leather upholstery, turned and lappet carved legs headed by paterae with brass terminals and casters.

$2,200-2,800   **DN**

A pair of George IV mahogany framed library armchairs, in the manner of Gillows, the upholstered tub backs with carved decoration, on turned and reeded legs with brass casters, one chair now with brass studs to the arm, one leg replaced.

$15,000-20,000   **DN**

A Victorian mahogany gentleman's armchair, with padded back, arms and seat, cabriole legs with brass casters.

$1,000-1,500   **DN**

A Victorian walnut armchair, with padded button design, carved cabriole legs with scroll feet and lignum casters.

$600-800   **DN**

A Victorian oak and upholstered tub chair, covered in a buttoned brown leather, the curved galleried back above a stuff-over seat, on fluted turned and tapered legs ending in casters.

$1,200-1,500 SI

An Edwardian mahogany framed tub armchair, with buttoned leather upholstery, the front uprights carved with lion's head terminals and strap work decoration, raised on legs with paw feet.

$2,700-3,000 L&T

A Victorian walnut framed gentleman's easy chair, stamped "Jas. Shoolbred & Co", the morocco leather buttoned back and seat with studded decoration and outscrolled arms, raised on turned front legs and casters.

$3,000-4,000 L&T

A Victorian walnut framed gentleman's easy chair, morocco leather buttoned back and seat, open arms on turned front legs and casters.

$3,500-4,500 L&T

An early 20thC armchair by Howard & Sons, upholstered in red morocco leather with a buttoned back, on mahogany turned legs with brass terminals and casters.

This chair retains its original morocco leather upholstery and is therefore more desirable than a re-upholstered one.

$6,000-8,000 DN

A pair of Louis XV style walnut and tapestry upholstered fauteuils, each with the shaped back and loose cushion seat raised on molded cabriole legs.

$3,000-4,000 FRE

A late 19thC burr walnut chair, in the French Empire style, the shaped back, padded arms and stuff-over seat on square cabriole legs ending in brass paw feet.

$450-550 SI

Two of a set of four 20thC burr walnut and upholstered chairs, in the French Empire style, with gilt metal mounts, the arched backs, padded arms and stuff-over seats on cabriole legs headed by anthemion and ending in paw feet.

$1,800-2,400 (set) SI

A Louis XVI style carved walnut bergère, the arched back with a ribbon-carved crest, continuing into downswept arms with scroll terminals, the bow front loose cushion seat with conforming rails raised on turned tapering fluted legs.

$450-550 SI

A late 19th/early 20thC giltwood wing armchair, with upholstered back, sides and seat, the frame carved with scrolls, cabriole legs.

$1,200-1,800 DN

An early 20thC wing armchair, the upholstered shaped back, wings and outscrolled arms with squab seat above mahogany cabriole front legs with pad feet.

$1,200-1,800 L&T

FURNITURE

A George III mahogany dining chair, with a vase shaped splat, on square chamfered legs joined by an H-stretcher.

$450-550   **SI**

A pair of George III mahogany dining chairs, with pierced Gothic form splats above drop-in seats, raised on square chamfered legs, joined by H-stretchers.

$1,500-2,000   **FRE**

Two of a set of six 18thC late Directoire elm dining chairs, including two armchairs, with paneled top rails, dart carved spindle backs and stuff-over seats, gold foliate patterned fabric, on square tapered legs.

$6,000-8,000 (set)   **SI**

Two of a set of four late George III mahogany dining chairs, each with an arched back with vertical slats, padded seat on molded square tapering legs with H-stretcher, the seat rails renewed.

$600-800 (set)   **DN**

Two of a set of six George III mahogany dining chairs, each with a slatted back, woolwork upholstered seat, square tapering legs and H-stretcher, one elbow chair.

$1,000-1,500 (set)   **DN**

Two of a set of six early 19thC Sheraton style mahogany dining chairs, each with top rail centered by ribbon-tied and husk carved panel and roundel terminals, turned and reeded uprights and lattice splat stuff-over seat and square section tapered legs with spade feet.

$4,500-5,500 (set)   **L&T**

Two of a set of six George III style mahogany dining chairs, including two carvers, each with arched top rail above pierced splat, drop-in needlework seat and square section tapered legs joined by H-stretcher.

£1,000-1,500 (set)   **L&T**

Two of a set of six late George III mahogany dining chairs, each with a serpentine back and pierced splat with a beaded band, drop-in seat, on molded square tapering legs with an H-stretcher, some repairs.

$1,500-2,000 (set)   **DN**

Two of a set of six late George III mahogany dining chairs, each with a serpentine crest and stylized pierced splat, padded seat, tapering legs and an H-stretcher.

$3,000-4,000 (set)   **DN**

Two of a set of six late George III mahogany dining chairs each with a serpentine crest, later carved with patera and trailing foliage, pierced splat, drop-in seat and straight chamfered legs with H-stretchers.

$1,200-1,800 (set)   **DN**

Two of a set of four late George III mahogany dining chairs, each with a lancet shaped back and pierced splat carved with a ribbon and wheat ears, with an upholstered serpentine seat, on molded square tapering legs.

$350-450 (set)   **DN**

Two of a set of four George III mahogany dining chairs, each with a shaped crest, a pierced vase-shaped splat with drop-in seat on square tapering legs with H-stretcher.

$1,800-2,400 (set)   **DN**

Two of a set of six mahogany dining chairs in George III style, each with a serpentine crest and pierced splat carved with wheat ears, an urn and patterae, drop-in seat on straight molded legs with H-stretcher, largely 19thC but repaired.

$1,200-1,800 DN

A pair of late 19thC mahogany side chairs, in 18thC style, each with a vase shaped pierced splat and scroll-carved top rail, drop-in seats and square tapering legs.

$700-1,000 FRE

vo of a set of eight late 19thC mahogany Hepplewhite style dining chairs, each ith molded shield back centered by pierced splat with fan inlaid foliate patterns, drop-in seat and molded square section legs with spade feet and H-stretcher.

6,000-8,000 (set) L&T

Two of a harlequin set of six 19thC mahogany dining chairs, each with a serpentine crest, pierced splat, drop-in seat and square tapering legs with an H-stretcher.

$1,000-1,500 (set) DN

Two of a set of eight early 20thC Sheraton-style mahogany dining chairs, including two carvers, each with lattice back and husk carved tablet to toprail, stuff-over seat and molded tapering legs, one chair a modern copy.

$4,500-5,500 (set) L&T

vo of a set of six 19thC mahogany ning chairs, pierced splats above rop-in seats, square section legs.

1,200-1,800 (set) SI

Two of a set of six 19thC mahogany dining chairs, each with a shield-shaped back with husk carved slats, a drop-in serpentine seat, on molded square tapering legs with H-stretchers.

$4,500-5,500 (set) DN

Two of a set of seven Regency mahogany dining chairs, each with roundel carved top rail above roundel mounted twin mid-rails, caned seat on saber legs, one chair with a damaged back.

$1,800-2,200 (set) SI

vo of a set of six Regency mahogany ning chairs, including two carvers, ach with paneled bar backs with eded cresting, drop-in seat and olded saber legs, carvers with down-crolled open arms.

2,500-3,000 (set) L&T

Two of a set of ten Regency mahogany dining chairs, including one carver, the top rail with molded edge above interwoven back lower rail with turned boss, stuff-over seats, square tapering legs, spade feet.

$4,500-5,500 (set) L&T

Two of a set of six late George III mahogany dining chairs, each with a paneled crest rail, a rope-twist back and a padded seat on turned tapering legs.

$3,000-4,000 (set) DN

Two of a set of six Regency simulated rosewood dining chairs, each with a shallow outscrolled incised yoke back above two mid-rails and diagonally reeded uprights with carved capitals, the drop-in seat on saber legs.

$1,500-2,000 (set) L&T

233

Chairs

A set of six New England country Queen Anne side chairs on Spanish feet, each with molded crest with arched shoulders, with volutes above a vasiform splat with flanking spooned stiles, a trapezoidal rush seat on block and vase turned legs joined by double stretchers.

$20,000-30,000 (set)   **NA**

A set of four 20thC Queen Anne style side chairs, painted dark red with rush seats.

41in (104cm) high

$1,800-2,200   **FRE**

A pair of Massachusetts Queen Anne walnut side chairs, each with yoked crest and curved shoulders above a vasiform splat and trapezoidal slip seat, the conforming rail with scallop on cabriole legs with pad feet on platforms, joined by recessed arrow-turned box stretcher.

$10,000-15,000   **NA**

A rare early pair of Philadelphia Queen Anne walnut dining chairs, each with carved yolk crest over a vasiform splat above a trapezoidal seat frame, supported by cabriole legs terminating in stockinged feet joined by flat serpentine stretchers.

$20,000-25,000   **Poo**

A Boston, Massachusetts Queen Anne walnut side chair, on cabriole legs terminating in pad feet joined by block and ring turned stretchers, retains silver plaque on rear seat rail.

c1740

$3,000-4,000   **Pook**

A Delaware Valley Queen Anne walnut side chair, with a shell carved crest rail flanked by bold backward scrolling ears over a pierced splat above a slip seat resting on a shaped apron and cabriole legs terminating in trifid feet.

c1760

$5,000-7,000   **Pook**

A CLOSER LOOK AT A PAIR OF CHIPPENDALE CHAIRS

The provenance in the catalog records these chairs as having come from a pioneer Philadelphia collect and author. As with other pieces in the same sale, they had been documented with photographs taken *1926 and had belonged to Mrs Marion Carson who had cowritten Hornor's "Blue Book" in 1935.*

The serpentine crest rail wi the central relief carv scallop shell is typical of me 18thC Philadelp chairs. The carv volutes that flank th shell are attracti details that lift the chairs above oth exampl

These are characterized as Chippendale because of the pierced splat and projecting corners, or ears, of the top rail. An earlier Queen Anne chair would have had a solid splat and arched curving toprail.

The deep seat rails and shell carved cabriole leg are common to Philadelphia chairs but the skillf workmanship of the craftsman is evident in the pleasing serpentine line of the rail to the knee block and the bold claw and ball feet.

A fine pair of Delaware Valley Chippendale walnut dining chairs, each with a carved crest with central shell, pieced splat, drop-in seat on cabriole legs and carved knees terminating in ball and claw feet.

c1770

$30,000-40,000   **Poo**

A Delaware Valley Queen Anne walnut dining chair, with carved shell and serpentine crest ending in scrolled ears over a vasiform splat above a trapezoidal seat, on stockinged feet.

c1765

$15,000-20,000   **Pook**

A Philadelphia Federal carved mahogany sidechair, the molded and rope-carved shield back above a serpentine seat on reeded tapering legs with reverse stop fluting and joined by a serpentine stretcher, restoration.

c1790   *38.5in (98cm) high*

$1,000-1,500   **FRE**

A set of three mid-to-late 18thC New England turned maple rush-seat side chairs, each with arched cresting with raked ears above a pierced splat, trapezoidal seat, block-and-vase turned legs ending in Spanish feet.

39.5in (100.5cm) high

$1,800-2,200   **FRE**

set of ten Federal mahogany dining chairs, including a pair of armchairs, each ith a serpentine crest, curved stiles enclosing a baluster form slat, molded seat ail on square legs and stretchers, on casters, old breaks and repairs, loss of eight.

rovenance: This set of chairs descended in the Moore Family of Sandy Springs, Maryland. They may have been acquired at the time of the marriage of Esther Hallett to oseph Townsend of Chester County, Pennsylvania, at Pearl Friends, New York in 1803.

40.25in (102cm) high

10,000-15,000   FRE

A Baltimore Hepplewhite mahogany side chair, with a rounded shield crest over a serpentine apron resting on square incised legs joined by an H-stretcher.

c1810

$800-1,200   Pook

A Hepplewhite mahogany side chair, with a shield back over a serpentine apron resting on square molded tapering legs joined by an H-stretcher.

$400-600   Pook

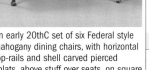

ne of a pair of Classical carved nahogany side chairs, arched crest rail bove fruit basket carved mid-rail, on aber legs with paw feet.

1815   33in (84cm) high

1,800-2,200 (pair)   FRE

An early 20thC set of six Federal style mahogany dining chairs, with horizontal top-rails and shell carved pierced splats, above stuff over seats, on square tapered legs and block feet.

£1,800-2,200 (set)   SI

A set of six late Federal inlaid mahogany chairs, including two armchairs, scrolled stiles enclose rectangular crest and back rails, upholstered trapezoidal seats, turned tapering front legs.

32.25in (82cm) high

$2,000-3,000 (set)   FRE

A late 19thC harlequin set of six mahogany and satinwood inlaid dining chairs in the 'Sheraton' style, including two arm chairs, some chairs bear paper label "Di Salvo Bros, New York".

$1,000-1,500 (set)   SI

n early 19thC set of six rosewood ining chairs, with acanthus carved top ils and triple splat backs, above stuff-ver seats covered in striped fabric, on rned and reeded legs.

3,500-4,500 (set)   SI

A pair of mid-19thC laminated rosewood sidechairs, each with a shaped, molded back enclosing scrolling devices centering a medallion on circular upholstered seats and conforming glower-carved rail, cabriole legs, old breaks and losses.

c1850

$1,500-2,000   FRE

A mid-19thC carved and turned chair in the Gothic Revival manner, possibly New York, tracery pierced back within turned uprights, distressed seat, turned legs.

46in (117cm) high

$500-700   SI

A mid-19thC carved mahogany hall chair, the urn shaped back carved with ribbon tied drapery, festoons and rams mask motif, above a solid seat an acanthus carved turned legs.

$800-1,200   SI

235

Two of a set of four late 19thC Italian painted and parcel gilt dining chairs, the shield shaped backs and serpentine stuff-over seats covered in patterned green fabric raised on molded square tapered legs.

$600-900 (set) SI

Two of a set of six late 19thC Continental walnut dining chairs, each with a foliate scroll carved crest, oval padded back and seat, on cabriole legs.

$700-1,000 (set) DN

Two of a set of eight late Victorian walnut dining chairs, each with a tartan buttoned back and seat, the oval back flanked by fluted columns, on turned tapering legs.

$1,800-2,200 (set) DN

A set of eight late Victorian mahogany dining chairs, by Lamb of Manchester, each with a scroll crest and turned finials, a rectangular leather upholstered back and seat, on cabriole legs with pad feet and ceramic casters, stamped "LAMB, MANCHESTER".

$1,500-2,000 (set) DN

Two of a set of seven Victorian walnut dining chairs, stamped "Gillow & Co.", with ebonised ring turning and fluting, each with square maroon leather back, stuff-over seat and baluster turned and blocked front legs joined by corresponding H-stretcher.

$4,500-5,500 (set) L&T

Two of a set of twelve oak dining chairs, each with lion mask finials, a padded back and seat on spirally fluted and turned legs and H-stretcher, some damage.

$700-1,000 (set) DN

Two of a set of four Italian Neo-classical satinwood dining chairs, each with paneled leather back and stuff-over seat on turned front legs.

$1,000-1,500 (set) L&T

Two of a set of twenty six Edwardian oak dining chairs, including two larger carvers, each with incised decoration, spoon back with central splat above stuff-over bow front seat and turned tapering front legs with casters.

$6,500-7,500 (set) L&T

A set of eleven Edwardian mahogany dining chairs, each with curved toprail above pierced vase shaped splat, the close nailed leatherette upholstered seat on acanthus carved and fluted turned tapering legs with toupie feet.

$4,500-5,500 (set) L&T

Two of a set of six Edwardian mahogany dining chairs, each with molded square back, the carved top rail raised at the center and three pierced vertical splats, stuff-over nailed leather seat and molded square section tapered front legs with spade feet.

$3,000-4,000 (set) L&T

Two of a set of eight late 19thC mahogany dining chairs, each with a boxwood strung curved crest rail, reeded spindles and a reeded frame, padded seat and square tapering legs with spade feet, some restoration.

$4,500-5,500 (set) DN

A set of sixteen early 20thC mahogany dining armchairs, in the Adam Revival manner, each with carved serpentine top rail above pierced and carved waisted splat and stuff-over leather seat, molded seat rail and paneled square section tapered legs with spade feet, two chairs modern copies.

$12,000-15,000 (set) L&

Hall chairs

A near pair of late 19thC Italian carved walnut hall chairs, the open work tapered backs carved with grotesque masks and caryatids above padded seats and similarly carved supports.

$600-900   **SI**

A pair of George III mahogany hall chairs, each with waisted back with arched molded top rail and central painted oval with a heraldic horse's head, above shaped circular seat and turned tapering front legs.

$2,200-2,800   **L&T**

A pair of early 19thC mahogany hall chairs, each with reeded oval back centered by a shell on waisted support, rounded seat on ring turned front legs.

$700-1,000   **L&T**

A George IV mahogany hall chair, the cartouche shaped back with a reeded swag and scroll crest, a solid seat and turned tapering legs.

$400-600   **DN**

A George IV mahogany hall chair, the oval back on C-scroll supports, with a solid seat, on lappet carved and turned tapering legs.

$250-350   **DN**

Two of a set of six early Victorian mahogany hall chairs, each with a shield shaped back with central painted crest, a solid serpentine seat on turned tapering legs.

$2,500-3,500 (set)   **DN**

A Victorian oak hall chair, the round back carved with three fish on turned supports with lobed finials, padded seat, the seat rail with turned pendant finials on turned legs.

$320-380   **DN**

Side chairs

A William and Mary style walnut side chair, the tall caned back with bird's head cresting, spreading shaped seat above carved and turned front legs, hoop stretcher and turned and blocked back legs.

$700-1,000   **L&T**

A George I walnut side chair, with a vase-shaped splat and drop-in seat, on molded cabriole legs ending in pad feet.

$1,200-1,800   **FRE**

A late 19thC Dutch walnut and floral marquetry side chair, in the early 18thc style, with a solid vase shaped splat, drop-in seat and cabriole legs with claw-and-ball feet.

$400-600   **DN**

A pair of Louis XV walnut side chairs, each with shell and rocaille carved frame about padded back and stuff-over seat, cabriole legs scroll feet, with extensive restorations.

$400-600   **SI**

A pair of George III elm side chairs, stuff-over back and seat raised on drapery carved cabriole legs, ending in pad feet, restored.

$4,500-5,500   **FRE**

Two of a set of four George III mahogany side chairs, each with upholstered back with serpentine top rail, stuff-over seat and Chinese lattice blind fret seat rails and front legs with pierced brackets and molded feet with casters, joined by pierced fretwork H-stretcher, restorations.

$12,000-15,000 (set)   **L&T**

A George III mahogany provincial side chair, wavy top rail above pierced interlaced splat, with tapestry drop-in seat, molded square section legs.

$600-900   **SI**

A George III mahogany speaker's chair, the chair with thistle-carved tablet and fluted frieze top rail, upholstered close-nailed leather back, armrests and seat, with reeded frame and legs, on similarly reeded trolley with solid shaped footrest, with a baize-lined folding writing slope flanked by D-shaped shelves supported on two uprights to the front, the whole on brass casters.

63in (160cm) long

$3,000-4,000   **L&T**

An Edwardian satinwood and painted bergère, in the Sheraton style, with caned square back, paneled arms, legs with brass cappings and casters

$1,800-2,200   **SI**

An early 19thC mahogany bergère, with reeded frame and caned back, arms and seat on square tapering legs with brass casters.

$1,200-1,800   **DN**

Two of a set of six Regency ebonised side chairs, each with a reeded crest and X back rail with brass mounts, caned seat on saber legs.

$2,000-3,000 (set)   **DN**

An Edwardian Sheraton style painted satinwood side chair, the caned shield-shaped back surmounted by a medallion depicting a female figure, the serpentine seat raised on square tapered legs and spade feet.

$400-600   **SI**

Two of a set of four early 19thC French mahogany side chairs, with bar backs and foliate tapestry padded seats, raised on square saber legs.

$600-900 (set)   **SI**

A pair of George IV mahogany side chairs, each with a rope-twist crest rail and reeded supports and back rail centered with a roundel, a drop-in wool work seat on reeded legs with turned cross stretchers, possibly Scottish.

$300-400   **DN**

Two of a set of six 19thC Italian walnut side chairs, spindle balustrade backs above drop-in seats, roundel headed turned tapering legs.

$600-900 (set)   **SI**

Two of a set of three early 19thC Dutch mahogany side chairs, each rail back with rosewood and boxwood bands, with a woolwork padded seat on square tapering legs with floral marquetry.

$300-400 (set)   **DN**

A pair of early Victorian papier mâché chairs, with chinoiserie decoration on a black and gilt ground, each with lobed and waisted pierced back, cane seat and cabriole front legs joined by turned stretchers.

$600-900   **L&T**

A pair of Charles X rosewood and inlaid side chairs, the buttoned backs and stuff-over seats covered in brown silk fabric, on carved cabriole legs.

$900-1,200   **SI**

One of a set of eight rare mid-19thC French chairs in the Louis XVI style, the white painted and parcel gilt-mounted frames carved with ribbon twists, each with a padded cartouche shaped back and rounded seat, upholstered in Aubusson style tapestry, on fluted turned tapering legs, some seat rails painted with numbers.

$15,000-18,000 (set)   **DN**

Two of a set of six 19thC Continental side chairs, in 17thC style, each with satinwood inlaid mahogany ladder-backs with giltwood scroll-carved ears, stuff-over seats, the legs and stretchers conforming in design.

$1,500-2,500 (set)   **FRE**

Two of a set of four mid-19thC German fruitwood side chairs, each with an openwork top rail and splat carved with a stag hunting scene, rushed seats.

$400-600 (set)   **FRE**

Two of a matched set of eight French Empire style beech and marquetry side chairs, inlaid throughout with scrolling foliage, urns, swags and exotic birds, the square backs with downswept sides above drop-in seats, on saber legs.

$1,500-2,500 (set)   **FRE**

A Victorian walnut chair, with Gothic needlework upholstery, the tall back framed by barleytwist columns, above spreading seat and corresponding tapering legs.

$400-600   **L&T**

A set of four Victorian rosewood parlour chairs, bearing label of J. Kendell & Co and workman's name "Illingworth", each with waisted molded open back containing asymmetric C-scrolls, buttoned stuff-over serpentine seat on molded cabriole legs with scroll toes.

Kendell & Co were a Leeds firm of cabinetmakers who were subsequently taken over by the notable firm of Marsh and Jones.

$700-1,000 (set)   **L&T**

A Victorian walnut salon chair, the waisted button back with molded and carved frame flanked by turned and blocked fluted uprights, stuff-over bow front seat on turned and fluted tapering legs and ceramic casters.

$400-600   **L&T**

FURNITURE

An Edwardian walnut settee in the Queen Anne style, the arched back, scroll arms and stuffed over seat covered in harvest pattern green fabric, on shell-carved cabriole legs ending in hoof feet.

56in (142cm) wide

$1,200-1,800   SI

An early 19thC mahogany sofa, with boxwood stringing, the square back above downswept square fronted arms, glazed cotton plaid upholstery with seat squab and cushions, seat rail centered by tablet on square section tapering legs with brass caps and casters.

74in (188cm) wide

$1,200-1,800   L&T

An early 19thC French Empire mahogany settee, the padded back and stuff over seat covered in pink tapestry fabric decorated with urns, with scroll arms and saber legs.

44.5in (113cm) wide

$1,200-1,800   SI

A European walnut sofa in early 19thC style, with an architectural crest flanked by carved scrolling brackets, with padded back, sides and seat on outswept legs with paw feet.

76in (193cm) wide

$600-900   DN

An early Victorian oak sofa, with upholstered back, arms and seat, the arm facings carved in deep relief with leaves and acorns, on octagonal tapering legs with brass casters.

84.25in (214cm) wide

$1,500-2,000   DN

An early Victorian carved rosewood framed sofa, on scroll carved cabriole legs with ceramic casters.

72in (183cm) wide

$1,000-1,500   DN

An early Victorian rosewood framed sofa, with two rounded ends, the low back with spirally fluted supports with scroll arms, upholstered in green raised fabric on carved cabriole legs with ceramic casters.

71.25in (181cm) wide

$800-1,200   DN

A 19thC French Empire mahogany sofa, with gilt metal mounts, the molded back applied with paterae, the scroll carved arms with leaf cast bands, with padded back and seat on cabriole legs.

99.5in (253cm) wide

$6,000-9,000   DN

A Victorian walnut settee, with buttoned back, padded arms and seat, molded frieze, square tapering legs and brass paw terminals and ceramic casters with Victorian registration marks, the rear legs replaced.

52.75in (134cm) wide

$300-400   DN

A Victorian upholstered day bed, on turned and fluted legs with brass casters.

62.25in (158cm) long

$500-700   DN

A Victorian upholstered conversation suite, comprising four independent buttoned sections, two long and two ends, on simulated rosewood scrolling feet and casters.

$5,000-7,000   L&T

Sofas

Sofas tend to be overstuffed, with padding and upholstery wrapped around the supporting frame. Consequently, with less carved wood on show, there are fewer visual clues that allow one to determine the age and origin of a sofa as opposed to a chair. The best indicators are the overall outline and the shape and details of the legs. The exceptions to this are mid-18thC open chair-back settees which are extremely rare and are seldom seen outside of museums and important private collections. It is unusual to find sofas that retain their original upholstery. This was often changed to fit in with the changing color schemes of the rooms they stood in.

A late 18thC Chippendale mahogany settee, English or American, serpentine back with scrolling arms, shaped seat and square fluted legs.

70in (178cm) wide
$6,000-8,000   FRE

A Classical mahogany sofa, with serpentine crest rail carved with central leaf and floral motif, the scrolled arms with roundel terminals and scribed to the skirt with leaf-carved panels above downswept legs carved with oak leaves and ending in brass caps and casters.

c1818   82in (208cm) wide
$15,000-20,000   FRE

A Salem Hepplewhite mahogany cabriole sofa of small size, arched molded crest rail continuing to down curved arms with rosette terminals, frontal square tapering legs with spade feet, the frame upholstered.

Provenance: The Peirce Mansion, Portsmouth.

63in (160cm) wide
$18,000-22,000   NA

A New York Sheraton carved mahogany sofa, by Duncan Phyfe, the tripartite crest with bowknot and thunderbolts centering a panel with swagged drapery with bowknot and tassles above downsloped reeded arms on flaring reeded supports, on frontal tapering reeded, on brass casters, the back, sides and seat upholstered.

77.5in (197cm) wide
$15,000-20,000   NA

A Hepplewhite mahogany settee, the rectangular crest with figured veneer panels centering a triple reeded panel, upholstered back flanked by downswept arms with roundel terminals on carved urn and ball supports, the rectangular frame on turned and reeded legs ending in brass casters.

c1805   53.5in (136cm) wide
$30,000-40,000   FRE

A CLOSER LOOK AT A NEW ENGLAND SOFA

This sofa is almost identical to an example from the Winterthur Museum which was illustrated and discussed in Charles F. Montgomery's "Federal Furniture", pp. 308-309, plate 274.

The term 'Sheraton' refers to furniture influenced by the London cabinetmaker Thomas Sheraton and his book "The Cabinet-Maker And Upholsterer's Drawing-Book", published between 1791-1793.

One of the most commercial aspects to this sofa is its diminutive size. The length is at least 12in (30.5cm) less than comparable examples from the same period.

Sofas, such as this, would often be moved around to allow changes in room layout and for cleaning the floor underneath. The process of moving can put strain onto the legs and it is advisable to carefully examine the juncture of the leg and seat frame for evidence of damage.

A New England Sheraton inlaid mahogany and flame birch sofa of small size, Rhode Island or Massachusetts, the sloping crest rail with central raised tablet with contrasting ellipse within inlaid outline and the edge capped with reeding continuing on the downsloped arms, each above a reeded baluster support, on tapering reeded legs, headed by inlaid panels and ending in spade feet.

63in (160cm) wide
$18,000-22,000   NA

A pair of late 19thC Empire style settees, in the style of Duncan Phyfe, each with ribbon and foliate relief carved frame above turned arms and turned tapering legs.

$2,500-3,000 (pair)   SI

A Classical mahogany sofa, with plain bowed crest rail and scrolled arms, scribed and having carved floral terminals, the skirt beneath with ormolu mounted panels above scrolled legs with oakleaf carving ending in floral rosettes on turned ball feet.

c1815-1820   81in (206cm) wide
$7,000-10,000   FRE

A Philadelphia late Federal carved mahogany sofa, the downswept back above outscrolled arms continuing to an acanthus-carved seat rail on tapering leaf-carved legs ending in brass casters.

Provenance: The sofa descended in the Richard Willing family and was probably used in his 105 South Third Street, Society Hill home.

c1820   74in (188cm) wide
$1,000-1,500   FR

A late 19thC/early 20thC mahogany and upholstered settee, in the Classical style.

78in (198cm) wide
$700-1,000   SI

A Classical carved mahogany sofa, the upholstered back with carved rail above rectangular seat with reeded scrolled ends on leaf and feather carved legs and paw feet.

c1825   88in (224cm) wide
$1,800-2,200   FRE

A Mid-Atlantic States Classical carved mahogany sofa, shaped upholstered back, with scrolled and carved rail above rectangular seat with caved and upholstered ends, carved legs with paw feet.

Provenance: The Sedgeley Club, Philadelphia

c1825   86in (218cm) wide
$1,200-1,800   FR

An early 19thC Empire mahogany settee, bold scroll over arms and cabriole legs with animal feet richly carved with foliage.

64in (162.5cm) wide
$2,500-3,500   SI

A Mid-Atlantic States late Classical carved mahogany sofa, the scrolled crest rail flanked by eagle heads above waterleaf-carved scrolled arms and plain seat rail, all raised on cornucopia and leaf carved legs ending in paw feet, the upholstery tufted at back and arms, losses, old repairs.

c1830   83.5in (212cm) wide
$1,800-2,200   FRE

A late 19thC Gothic Revival mixed wood bench, in the manner of Frank Furness, surface wear.

53in (135cm) wide
$800-1,200   FR

A Louis XVI style giltwood salon suite, comprising settee and pair of fauteuils, each with rope twist frame about Aubusson style upholstered backs and seats.

400-600 SI

A Louis XVI style giltwood salon suite, comprising settee and pair of fauteuils, each with guilloche frame about Aubusson style upholstered back and seat.

$500-700 SI

A French beech settee, with flower carved crest, the frame carved with leaves and bead and reed border and canted back and seat on fluted turned tapering legs.

43in (109cm) wide

$1,000-1,500 DN

Window Seats

late 19thC Louis XVI style giltwood and caned window seat, the arched arms and cane seat above a rope-twist frieze, on fluted turned tapered legs.

32in (81cm) wide

600-900 SI

An Edwardian Sheraton style painted satinwood window seat, the open work raised back decorated with foliate swags and a central cherub motif, the caned seat raised on square splayed legs.

37in (94cm) wide

$1,500-2,000 SI

A 19thC giltwood window seat, with leaf carved and turned side supports, a rectangular padded seat on turned tapering legs headed by paterae.

23.75in (60.5cm) wide

$600-900 DN

An early 20thC mahogany window seat, carved with acanthus, with an upholstered back, outswept sides and seat, on scroll legs with paw feet.

49.5in (126cm) wide

$1,200-1,800 DN

Stools

pair of American Classical mahogany upholstered stools, old repairs, losses.

22in (56cm) wide

1,800-2,200 FRE

A George II walnut footstool with a drop-in seat, cabriole legs and pad feet, possible restorations.

18in (45.5cm) wide

$1,500-2,000 SI

A George II mahogany foot stool, the rectangular padded seat on acanthus carved cabriole legs ending in scroll feet.

28in 971cm) wide

$3,000-4,000 SI

An early Victorian box ottoman, the hinged square padded woolwork top above silk upholstered sides, on a rosewood plinth with bun feet.

30in (76cm) wide

$600-900 DN

FURNITURE

A late 18thC Queen Anne highboy, Massachusetts or Rhode Island, broken swan's-neck pediment above seven thumb-molded drawers, on cabriole legs, restoration.

c1780   40in (101.5cm) wide

$20,000-30,000   **FRE**

A Connecticut Chippendale cherry and inlaid highboy, fan carved and compass inlaid, cabriole legs with ball-and-claw feet, altered.

43.75in (111cm) wide

$20,000-30,000   **Pook**

A late 19thC Philadelphia Chippendale style carved mahogany bonnet-top highboy, mid section with arrangement of eight drawers, on cabriole legs.

97.5in (248cm) high

$7,000-10,000   **FRE**

A late 19thC Chippendale style mahogany highboy, lower half with three drawers enclosing shell-carved drawer, on cabriole legs and ball-and-claw feet

A late 19thC Chippendale style mahogany highboy, lower half with three drawers enclosing shell-carved drawer, on cabriole legs and ball-and-claw feet

$3,500-4,500   **FR**

A CLOSER LOOK AT A HIGHBOY

This highboy illustrates many features associated with Connecticut furniture. It is made of cherry wood on a pine carcase but has an unusual layout and displays an individualistic interpretation of embellishments.

The arrangement of drawers in both the upper and lower cases is atypical for this region. The more common arrangement is three short drawers above four graduated long drawers to the top, and one long drawer above three short drawers to the stand.

The cabinetmaker signed his name in chalk on the bottom drawer of the upper case. He made at least one other piece a matching dressing table, now in the collection of the Henry Ford Museum.

The cabriole legs have a carved projecting diamond or heart at the 'ankle'. This may be a stylistic reference to the pierced motifs of the Connecticut 'heart-and-crown' chairs of 1730-1750.

The Spanish feet are double molded, creating almost a foot above a foot. The more conventional form is the molded pad foot or the claw and ball foot.

A Connecticut Queen Anne carved maple flat-top highboy, signed "Hu(dson)" or "Hu(chins)", the upper case with coved molding and an arrangement of a five short over three long drawers, the lower section of six short drawers, the whole flanked by chamfered fluting with lamb's tongue, above cabriole legs terminating in Spanish feet.

39in (99cm) wide

$35,000-45,000   **NA**

A North Shore of Massachusetts Queen Anne figured maple highboy, five graduated drawers above single drawer and three short drawers, the center one with finely carved fan, on cabriole legs.

38.25in (97cm) wide

$50,000-60,000   **NA**

A New England Queen Anne carved maple highboy, two short and three graduated long drawers, three short drawers below, cabriole legs with pad feet.

37in (94cm) wic

$6,000-8,000   **N/**

A New York Queen Anne walnut highboy, Long Island, split drawer and three long drawers above base with three short drawers, cabriole legs with pad feet.

41in (104cm) wide

$5,000-7,000   **NA**

A mid-18thC Pennsylvania walnut highboy, plain cove molded cornice above five small and three graduated drawers, base with one long and three varisized drawers, plain cabriole legs.

40.25in (102cm) wi

$30,000-40,000   **FR**

Tall Chests

A Pennsylvania Chippendale walnut tall chest, having flat plain cove molded cresting, two small and four graduated wide lip molded drawers, fluted chamfered corners on tall ogival bracket feet with pads below, old oval brasses.

c1780   39.5in (100.5cm) wide
$4,000-6,000   **FRE**

A Pennsylvania, Maryland or Virginia Federal walnut high chest, with molded cornice above an arrangement of three short drawers over six graduated long drawers, shaped skirt raised on French bracket feet, paper label inscribed in ink, "this belongs to Nancy Cope Hazard."

c1800   41.25in (104.5cm) wide
$6,000-9,000   **SI**

A walnut Hepplewhite tall chest, dovetailed case having three over two over four scratch beaded drawers, on bracket feet, replaced hardware, facing crack on foot.

39in (99cm) wide
$3,000-4,000   **AAC**

A late 18thC Pennsylvania Chippendale walnut tall chest of drawers, molded cornice above nine drawers flanked by fluted quarter-columns on a molded base with ogee bracket feet, refinished.

46in (117cm) wide
$5,000-7,000   **FRE**

A Mid-Atlantic States Chippendale walnut tall chest of drawers, the projecting molded cornice and dovetailed top projecting above a case with a frieze of drawers, the base molding with ogee bracket feet with scrolled returns.

39in (99cm) wide
$6,000-9,000   **NA**

A Pennsylvania Chippendale walnut high chest, with a stepped cornice above three over three short drawers above four graduated long drawers flanked by fluted quarter columns on ogee feet with shaped returns.

c1780   40in (102cm) wide
$10,000-15,000   **Pook**

A CLOSER LOOK AT A CHEST-ON-CHEST

The straight top is the plainest of the cornice types. More elaborate examples include scrolling swan necks or broken triangular forms.

The overall form of the piece is plain with none of the carved ornament that was found on comparable examples from the same period. However the bold flowing ogee bracket feet, with the sharp curved tooth to the spandrel, suggest that this is a restrained creation by a cabinetmaker capable of much grander designs.

The pull out brushing slide would have served two purposes. As the name suggests it would be used as a firm surface on which to brush off dirt from clothes. It could also be used as a writing surface.

Just as with chairs of this period it is more usual to find plain back legs/feet. The customer would have paid a little more to have these back feet as ornamented as the front ones.

A late 18thC Mid-Atlantic States Chippendale mahogany chest-on-chest, the upper case with molded cornice above an arrangement of eight drawers, the lower half with a molded waist above brushing slide and three graduated long drawers, all flanked by canted fluted corners, raised on ogee molded bracket feet, refinished, age splits, old repairs to molding.

43.75in (111cm) wide
$70,000-100,000   **FRE**

A Pennsylvania Chippendale walnut tall chest, with a cove and reeded cornice over nine drawers flanked by fluted quarter columns resting on ogee bracket feet, feet restored.

c1780   41in (104cm) wide
$5,000-7,000   **Pook**

A New England Chippendale cherry bonnet-top chest-on-chest, the upper section with molded swan's-neck crest above case with three short drawers, the centre one fan carved, over four long graduated drawers, lower section with four long graduated drawers on base molding with bracket feet.

39.5in (100cm) wide

$28,000-32,000   **NA**

A Massachusetts Chippendale cherrywood bonnet top chest-on-chest, the upper section with molded broken swan's-neck pediment above fan carved drawer centered by two short drawers and four graduated long drawers, enclosed by fluted pilasters, the lower section with four graduated long drawers on a molded base with bracket feet, appears to retain original hardware, old breaks.

c1775   *42.5in (108cm) wide*

$50,000-70,000   **FRE**

A George III chest-on-chest, with dentil molded cornice and blind fret frieze, two short and three long drawers, the lower section with a brushing slide above three long drawers, raised on splayed feet.

42in (107cm) high

$5,000-7,000   **SI**

A George III mahogany chest-on-chest, the molded cornice with blind fret frieze above two short and three long drawers flanked by fretted canted angles, the base with three long graduated drawers and shaped bracket feet, cast brass swan neck handles.

71.25in (181cm) high

$3,000-4,000   **L&T**

A CLOSER LOOK AT A PENNSYLVANIA WALNUT CHEST-ON-CHEST

Minor details, such as the particular twist form on finials, are useful guides to determining the origin of furniture. On an urn and flame finial from a comparable Newport piece, the urn will tend to be fluted and the flame smaller with a 'cork-screw' twist.

On grander examples of Pennsylvania chest-on-chests the top centre small drawer often has richly carved shell, scroll and floral decoration. This drawer is uncarved and allows the colour and figuring of the wood to act as the sole decoration.

This is a restrained example of its type, lacking the richness of carving and stylistic motifs that collectors tend to look for. However the combination of original finish, good condition, attractive color and pleasing proportions make it a good commercial object.

It is more common to see chest-on-chests of this time with canted corner angles decorated with fluted strips or quarter columns. As this piece does not have this decorative detail it reduces the width by 2-3 inches (5-7.5cm) compared to other examples.

A Pennsylvanian Chippendale walnut chest-on-chest, the molded swan's-neck crest over a case with three over two short drawers above three long graduated drawers, the lower case with mid-molding and three long graduated drawers on base molding with ogee bracket feet with shaped returns.

40.5in (103cm) wide

$70,000-90,000   **NA**

An early George III mahogany chest, the molded top above four long graduated drawers on bracket feet, poor condition.

31.75in (81cm) wide

$1,800-2,200   DN

A mid-18thC European mahogany and crossbanded chest, the quarter veneered top with molded edge above two short and two long drawers with brass handles and escutcheons on bracket feet.

34.5in (88cm) wide

$2,500-3,000   DN

An 18thC oak and crossbanded chest, the molded top above two short and three long drawers with later brass handles, on later bracket feet, possibly originally the top to a chest on stand.

37.5in (95cm) high

$600-900   DN

A mid-18thC walnut, boxwood and ebony strung chest, the canted rectangular top with quarter veneers and crossbanding, above two short and three long drawers with later brass handles and escutcheons, on bracket feet, the sides pine, top possibly associated.

36.5in (92cm) wide

$1,800-2,200   DN

An early George III mahogany mule chest, the hinged top above two short and one long drawer with brass handles, escutcheons and carrying handles, on ogee bracket feet, lacking the base to the bracket feet.

50.5in (128.5cm) wide

$1,200-1,800   DN

An early George III mahogany chest, of small proportions, the rectangular caddy top above two short and three long graduated drawers, on shaped bracket feet.

30.75in (78cm) wide

$2,500-3,000   L&T

A mid-18thC walnut gentleman's fitted dressing chest of bow front form, possibly North German, the shaped top cross-banded with mahogany and with satinwood banding, serpentine sides, the fitted drawer with brushed slide, opening to reveal compartments and pigeon-holes, above three further long graduated drawers, on scroll carved bracket feet.

44in (111.75cm) wide

$10,000-15,000   FRE

A CLOSER LOOK AT A GEORGE III CHEST

This is a nice example of a small George III chest of good color and original untouched condition and will always command considerable interest. However, as with other types of furniture, demand for smaller chests has risen in inverse proportion to the drop-in demand for larger examples. To satisfy this demand, larger less commercial chests are cut down and adapted.

A useful tip is to remove the drawers and examine the internal surfaces. Adapted pieces have screw holes, marks and modern timber.

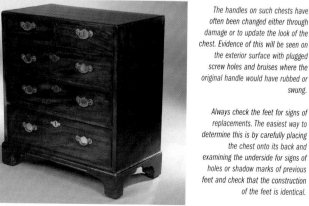

The handles on such chests have often been changed either through damage or to update the look of the chest. Evidence of this will be seen on the exterior surface with plugged screw holes and bruises where the original handle would have rubbed or swung.

Always check the feet for signs of replacements. The easiest way to determine this is by carefully placing the chest onto its back and examining the underside for signs of holes or shadow marks of previous feet and check that the construction of the feet is identical.

An early George III mahogany 'caddy top' chest, the rectangular top above two short and three graduated long drawers on shaped bracket feet.

30.5in (77cm) wide

$5,000-7,000   L&T

A George III mahogany chest, the top with a molded edge above four long drawers with original brass handles on bracket feet.

27.5in (70cm) wide

$5,000-7,000   DN

FURNITURE

A George III mahogany and satinwood banded chest of drawers, two short and three graduated long drawers raised on bracket feet.

40in (101.5cm) wide

$1,200-1,800 SI

A George III mahogany chest, the top with a molded edge above two short and three long drawers with brass handles on bracket feet.

39.75in (101cm) wide

$1,200-1,800 DN

A George III mahogany chest, the top with a molded edge above a slide and four long graduated drawers with later brass handles and escutcheons flanked by canted blind fretwork corners, on ogee bracket feet.

34.75in (88cm) wide

$1,500-2,000 DN

A George III mahogany chest, the top with molded edge above two short and three long drawers with brass handles, on bracket feet.

36.25in (92cm) wide

$1,200-1,800 DN

A George III mahogany chest, the walnut crossbanded and checker strung top above a crossbanded and baize inset slide and four long graduated drawers with brass handles, flanked by reeded quarter pilasters on bracket feet, the walnut crossbanding and chequer stringing of a later date.

Embellishments such as this later inlay were often added in the 19thC and 20thC to lift an earlier piece out of the ordinary and therefore enhance its value. Today's buyers will sometimes overlook later decoration when the end result is attractive.

37.25in (94.5cm) wide

$1,800-2,200 DN

A George III oak and mahogany crossbanded chest, with two short and three long drawers flanked by reeded pilasters on bracket feet, the top part of a chest on chest.

43.75in (111cm) wide

$700-1,000 DN

A George III mahogany chest, the top with a molded edge above two short and three long drawers with later brass handles on bracket feet.

39.75in (101cm) wide

$1,200-1,800 DN

A George III mahogany chest, the molded top above two short and three long drawers with brass handles and bracket feet.

39.75in (101cm) wide

$1,200-1,800 DN

A George III mahogany chest, the top with a molded edge above two short and three long drawers with later brass handles on bracket feet.

37.5in (95cm) wide

$700-1,000 DN

A George III mahogany chest, the top with a molded edge above a fitted drawer with a leather inset slide, and three long drawers with later brass handles and escutcheons on bracket feet, the top of a later date and the height possibly reduced.

35.75in (91cm) wide

$1,500-2,000 DN

Chests

A Massachusetts Chippendale mahogany oxbow chest of drawers, probably North Shore, Newburyport, the rectangular top with serpentine front and molded edge above a case with four long graduated drawers with beaded dividers, on base molding with center drop with demi-lune shell and cabriole legs on ball and claw feet.

34.5in (87.5cm) wide

30,000-40,000   **NA**

A Salem Chippendale birch oxbow chest of drawers, the top with serpentine front and molded edge projecting above a conforming case with four long graduated drawers with double arch dividers, the base molding with center drop with volute carved ends and central demi-lune shell, on bandy cabriole legs and ball and claw feet.

36in (91.5cm) wide

$18,000-22,000   **NA**

A CLOSER LOOK AT A CHIPPENDALE CHEST

The attribution to Thomas Affleck is partly based on the history of the chest as it may have been one of the items William Logan commissioned for his daughter Sarah's marriage to Thomas Fisher in 1772. Thomas Fisher and his brothers were Thomas Affleck's closest friends in Philadelphia.

Affleck furniture is characterized by rich elegant carving of scroll work and shells which elegantly accentuate and ornament the surrounding case. This chest's commercial appeal comes through the well drawn compact proportions, 3 feet wide and 2 3/4 feet high (92cm by 84cm).

A Providence Chippendale mahogany chest, with Joseph Rawson label, the rectangular moulded top projecting above a case with four long drawers on ogee bracket feet, the top drawer with printed label.

9in (99cm) wide

4,000-6,000   **NA**

Scottish-born Thomas Affleck (1740-1795) was one of pre-revolutionary Philadelphia's most prestigious cabinetmakers. A documented chest-on-chest commissioned from Affleck by William Logan is now in the Collection of the Metropolitan Museum.

The shape and placing of the hardware, with the escutcheon plates creeping over the lip molding of the drawers is almost identical to a highboy on display in the American Museum in Claverton Manor, Bath, Britain.

A Philadelphia Chippendale mahogany four drawer chest, possibly by Thomas Affleck (1740-1795), with a rectangular lip-molded top with notched corners, graduated wide lip-molded drawers with large willow mount brasses, the interior of the top drawer compartmented, quarter-round fluted corners on vigorous ogival bracket feet.

c1770   *36.25in (92cm) wide*

$140,000-160,000   **FRE**

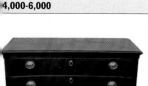

A Chippendale walnut chest of drawers, four graduated lipped drawers flanked by quarter columns on ogee bracket feet, losses to drawer lips and foot pad, warped drawer front.

40in (101.5cm) wide

500-700   **AAC**

A Chippendale walnut chest of drawers, four graduated lipped drawers, bracket feet, replaced hardware.

38in (96.5cm) wide

$2,500-3,500   **AAC**

A late 18thC Philadelphia Chippendale walnut chest of drawers, the rectangular top with molded edge above four thumb-molded graduated drawers enclosed by fluted quarter columns on molded base with ogee bracket feet, refinished.

c1790   *37.5in (95cm) wide*

$10,000-15,000   **FRE**

A late 18thC Philadelphia Chippendale mahogany chest of drawers, rectangular top with molded edge above four thumb-molded drawers flanked by fluted quarter-columns, raised on ogee bracket feet, restoration.

c1790   *41in (104cm) wide*

$2,000-3,000   **FRE**

FURNITURE

A New England Chippendale birch chest of drawers, the rectangular top with molded edge projecting above a case with four long drawers, on bracket base with shaped returns, appears to retain original bail brasses.

$3,000-4,000   NA

A Connecticut Chippendale cherry chest of drawers, the rectangular top with wide molded edge above a case with concave scooped corners and four long graduated drawers with scratch beaded outline on base molding with ogee bracket feet.

38.5in (98cm) wide

$5,000-7,000   NA

A New England Chippendale cherry chest of drawers, the rectangular top with serpentine front projecting above a case with four long graduated drawers, separated by beaded dividers, the base molding with shaped bracket feet and drop with stylized leafage.

39in (99cm) wide

$4,000-6,000   NA

A Federal inlaid bow front chest of drawers, the top with inlaid banding over four drawers, each with bird's-eye maple panels centering a Brazilian rosewood panel, on flaring bracket feet, replaced foot facing.

c1800   *44.25in (112.5cm) wide*

$15,000-20,000   FRE

A Southern States Federal inlaid mahogany bow front chest, the bowed top with a line inlaid edge above conforming case with four graduated drawers, each draw front with exotic wood tablets, the central tablet with a swag, shaped apron continues to French feet.

c1810   *41.5in (105.5cm) wide*

$10,000-15,000   FRE

A Massachusetts Chippendale figured mahogany serpentine chest of drawers, possibly Salem, the rectangular top with molded edge and serpentine front projecting above a case with four conforming long graduated drawers, each beaded on conforming base molding and ogee feet.

38.25in (97cm) wide

$10,000-15,000   NA

A Federal style mahogany inlaid serpentine front chest, the conforming rectangular top with notched corners over case with canted stiles enclosing five drawers with shield shaped escutcheons.

41.5in (105.5cm) wide

$1,800-2,200   S

A New England mahogany bow front chest of drawers, with four long graduated drawers above a wavy apron, raised on splayed bracket feet.

c1810   *41in (104.5cm) wide*

$3,000-4,000   SI

A Federal mahogany and inlaid chest of drawers, the shaped top above four long graduated drawers, raised on splayed bracket feet.

c1810   *44.5in (113cm) wide*

$1,500-2,000   SI

A Federal mahogany and line inlaid chest of drawers, raised on later feet.

c1800   *42.5in (108cm) wide*

$1,000-1,500   SI

A Sheraton mahogany chest of drawers bow front, four graduated cock beaded drawers, turned feet, split top repaired, replaced feet.

39in (99cm) wid

$600-900   AA

A Hepplewhite bow front chest of drawers, having four graduated cock beaded drawers, French bracket feet, minor repairs, replacements.

42in (107cm) wide

2,500-3,500   AAC

A Sheraton cherry chest of drawers, with bird's-eye maple facings, having four graduated cock beaded drawers, paneled sides, on turned feet, replaced hardware.

43in (109cm) wide

$1,500-2,000   AAC

A Hepplewhite walnut chest of drawers, four graduated cock beaded drawers over a shaped skirt and French bracket feet, losses to trim and feet, crack in top.

41in (104cm) wide

$800-1,200   AAC

An early 19thC New England Federal mahogany chest of drawers, four conforming long drawers flanked by turned and reeded stiles continuing to legs, age cracks, refinished.

22in (56cm) wide

$2,500-3,000   FRE

Pennsylvania Federal tiger maple chest of drawers, with a rectangular top over a case with four graduated drawers flanked by chamfered stiles, over a shaped skirt resting on flaring French feet.

36in (91.5cm) wide

3,500-4,500   Pook

A Federal inlaid mahogany chest of drawers, the rectangular top with applied inlaid edge above a case with four long graduated drawers each with crossbanding, stringing and beaded edge, on base molding with straight bracket feet.

39.75in (101cm) wide

$4,000-6,000   NA

A New England Hepplewhite inlaid mahogany bow front chest, with inlaid edge projecting above four long graduated drawers, each with contrasting banding, the shaped skirt with banding on French feet, the oval eagle brasses later.

41in (104cm) wide

$5,000-7,000   NA

Massachusetts Federal inlaid mahogany bow front chest of drawers, the D-form top edged with contrasting banding with zigzag motif above a case with four long conforming graduated drawers with beading and stringing, the shaped skirt with similar banding, raised on French feet, the silvered brasses marked on the bails, "H & B".

39.25in (100cm) wide

5,000-8,000   NA

An early 19thC Federal chest of drawers, rectangular top over four graduated drawers, the shaped skirt continuing into tapering bracket feet, replaced hardware, refinished.

42.5in (108cm) high

$1,500-2,000   SI

An early 19thC New England Federal inlaid mahogany chest of drawers, rectangular top with line inlay over four graduated drawers, shaped apron, with French feet.

40in (101.5cm) wide

$500-700   FRE

A New England pine chest of drawers, two over three graduated drawers, on bracket feet, replaced feet.

38in (96.5cm) long

$500-700 AAC

A late Federal cherrywood and mahogany chest of drawers, the rectangular reeded top above four graduated drawers flanked by reeded pilasters and raised on turned legs with button feet.

c1810 40in (101.5cm) wide

$2,000-3,000 FRE

A late Federal cherrywood chest, the rectangular top with reeded and cockbeaded edge above four graduated drawers, turned legs, ball and peg feet.

c1810 42in (106.5cm) wide

$2,000-3,000 FRE

A late Federal cherry chest of drawers, possibly Pennsylvania, the top over case with four graduated cock-beaded drawers raised on baluster turned feet.

41.5in (105.5cm) wide

$1,000-1,500 S

A Biedermeier chest of drawers, veneered three drawer chest with line inlaid top and arched panel design on front.

38in (96.5cm) wide

$3,000-4,000 AAC

A CLOSER LOOK AT A SOAP HOLLOW CHEST

Connoisseurs and collectors of American decorative arts place a high value on furniture made by some Amish and Mennonite craftsmen. This chest is attributed to Peter K. Thomas (1838-1907) who was one of the foremost furniture makers in the small town of Soap Hollow in Conemaugh, near Johnstown, PA.

Soap Hollow furniture is often, as here, painted red with black and gold trim. Some examples have a yellow ground with tan, brown and bright green decoration.

The decorative design probably originate from the Swiss homeland o the Mennonites

The designs, dates and inscriptions on Soap Hollow furniture are usually stenciled and not applied freehand

The meaning of the inscription "Mary Miller is unclear. It may be that she was a descendant of th original owner and that the "M" inscribed on th back board stands fo Mille

A late Classical mahogany chest, with rectangular backboard over two short drawers and projecting top supported by columnar stiles enclosing four drawers, all raised on turnip-turned feet.

c1840 43.25in (110cm) wide

$400-600 SI

A mid-19thC grain-painted and stenciled chest of drawers, attributed to Peter K. Thomas, Soap Hollow, Somerset County, Pennsylvania, dated, the scrolled backboard painted dark green and devices and the initials "A" and "M" in gold and copper, the chest grain-painted in ocher and yellow, the six drawers edged in yellow and stenciled with scrolled and geometric devices and flanked by stenciled trailing roses on posts, raised on green-painted turned feet, a faint inscription on side in pencil: "Mary Miller", old mended break to backboard scroll.

1863 39in (99cm) wid

$30,000-40,000 FR

Commodes

A Louis XV provincial walnut serpentine commode, Bordeaux region, two short and three long drawers, in-scrolled legs, with shaped paneled sides.

49in (124.5cm) wide

$5,000-7,000   **SI**

A good mid-18thC Italian olivewood and parquetry serpentine commode, with a crossbanded and quarter veneered shaped top above three long drawers with later brass handles and escutcheons, on splayed feet.

60in (152cm) wide

$10,000-15,000   **DN**

A mid-18thC Italian walnut and crossbanded serpentine commode, the molded top above three long drawers, on bracket feet joined by a wavy apron and ending in later casters.

32in (81cm) wide

$4,000-6,000   **SI**

An 18thC style Gustavian kingwood and marqueterie commode, marble top above gilt metal guilloche frieze, cabriole legs with gilt-metal mounts.

38in (96.5cm) wide

$800-1,200   **SI**

A Louis XVI walnut breakfront commode, the molded top above three short and two long drawers, flanked by stop-fluted canted corners, on conforming square tapered legs.

51in (129.5cm) wide

$5,000-7,000   **SI**

A Louis XV provincial walnut serpentine commode, two drawers with brass drop handles, floral relief carved frieze, short cabriole legs, restorations.

47.5in (120.5cm) wide

$3,500-4,500   **SI**

A Louis XV provincial walnut serpentine commode, three long drawers, pierced apron, hoof feet, restorations.

48.5in (123cm) wide

$4,000-6,000   **SI**

A French Transitional kingwood and rosewood banded breakfront commode, with canted corners, three short drawers above two long drawers, tapering square section legs.

46in (117cm) wide

$2,500-3,000   **SI**

A late 18thC French Transitional kingwood, tulipwood, rosewood, marqueterie and parquetry breakfront commode, white marble top, cabriole legs with sabots, one sabot missing.

51.5in (131cm) wide

$4,000-6,000   **FRE**

A late 18thC Italian walnut and parquetry commode, the later marble top above two long drawers with geometric inlay, centered by ribbon tied laurel wreaths, on square tapered legs.

40in (101.5cm) wide

$2,500-3,000   **SI**

A 19thC French Louis XVI style kingwood three drawer commode, the marble top with pierced brass gallery on slender fluted supports.

26in (66cm) wide

$1,200-1,800   **FRE**

A late 18thC Dutch mahogany commode, of serpentine form, with later gilt brass pierced gallery, above two doors with serpentine corners and a shaped apron enclosing a shelf, on outswept bracket feet, some later staining and restoration, lacking mounts.

50.5in (128.5cm) wide

$10,000-15,000   **DN**

FURNITURE

A Victorian mahogany escritoire, the raised back with a gallery and molded cornice above a triple paneled fall front enclosing pigeon-holes, drawers and a leather inset, the base with a concealed frieze drawer above two paneled doors enclosing six drawers flanking a kneehole.

49.5in (126cm) wide

$700-1,000 DN

A late 19thC Sheraton Revival rosewood and floral marqueterie desk, the raised back with a gilt metal three-quarter gallery and four drawers flanking a mirror, the leather inset top with a bowfronted central section, above seven drawers on square tapering legs with spade feet, brass terminals and ceramic casters, the simulated rosewood feet possibly of a later date.

44.5in (113cm) wide

$2,000-3,000 DN

A pair of late 19thC Sheraton Revival satinwood bonheurs du jour, crossbanded, checker banded and boxwood and ebony strung, each with three-quarter gallery and Tunbridgeware band above a door centered with a marqueterie fan and flanked by two vertical and six short drawers, the outset front folding to enclose a leather inset above one long and two short drawers, on square tapering legs.

31in (78.5cm) wide

$7,000-10,000 DN

A Louis XV style kingwood and parquetry bonheur du jour of serpentine outline, with a shaped raised back centered by a clock, with white enamel dial and striking eight-day movement, flanked by two cupboard doors modeled as leather-bound bookends, below are three small drawers and a leather inset writing surface, the apron with five drawers around the kneehole, raised on square cabriole legs ending in paw-cast sabots.

44in (112cm) wide

$2,500-3,000 FRE

An Edwardian rosewood lady's writing desk, by Maple & Co., the superstructure with central mirror flanked by galleried piers fitted with drawers, the shaped top with inset leather skiver above an arrangement of three drawers each inlaid with black marqueterie raised on slender square section cabriole legs and casters, stamped to right hand drawer.

42in (107cm) wide

$2,500-3,000 L&T

An Edwardian lady's writing desk, with boxwood stringing and satinwood banding, the superstructure with pierced brass rail above open shelves and stationary drawers, the shaped top with inset skiver above an arrangement of five drawers on square section tapering legs.

40in (102cm) wide

$2,500-3,000 L&T

An early 20thC French walnut and tulipwood parquetry bonheur du jour, of curved form with gilt metal mounts, the raised back with a central brass gallery and marble top above two drawers, flanked by shaped shelves, above a pull-out leather inset and a frieze drawer, on slender cabriole legs, the back veneered.

30in (76cm) wide

$800-1,200 DN

An Edwardian painted satinwood writing desk, the superstructure with astragal glazed panel flanked by angled doors painted with Classical verses and containing pigeon-holes above crossbanded drawers, the top with canted angles and tool skiver, above a single drawer on square section tapering legs linked by stretchers supporting decorative curved brackets.

42in (107cm) wide

$1,200-1,800 L&T

An Edwardian satinwood writing desk, with boxwood and ebony stringing, the superstructure with waved surmount above central open shelf enclosed by serpentine drawers, the whole raised above square section tapering legs united by stretchers and terminating in silvered caps and casters.

42.4in (108cm) wide

$3,000-4,000 L&T

An Edwardian Louis XV style kingwood and parquetry kidney shaped writing table, with gilt brass mounts, the shaped top above frieze drawer on tapering cabriole legs.

34.25in (87cm) wide

$6,000-9,000 L&T

An Edwardian plum pudding mahogany kidney shape ladies writing desk, in the Sheraton style, three frieze drawers, square tapering legs and spade feet.

36.5in (93cm) high

$700-1,000 SI

A late 19thC French mahogany writing desk, the molded serpentine top with an inset leather writing surface, below are three frieze drawers with foliate-carved decoration, on square tapered legs ending in brass cappings.

58.5in (148.5cm) wide

$700-1,000 S

An 18thC Italian giltwood overmantel, the central rectangular beveled plate below a mirrored crest and surround, the frame carved with C-scrolls and foliage, some damage and repair.

39.75in (101cm) wide

$7,000-10,000   **DN**

An 18thC Italian giltwood wall mirror, the rectangular frame carved with foliate scrolls, the beveled plate is a later addition, some damage.

32in (81cm) wide

$2,500-3,000   **DN**

A George II style giltwood wall mirror, the beveled rectangular plate within molded frame with shallow broke pediment, drapery sides and shaped apron centered by a shell.

45.25in (115cm) long

$1,200-1,800   **L&T**

A pair of walnut and giltwood wall mirrors, in the George II style, each with shaped rectangular plates with leaf carved and gilded slips within shaped frames with broken swan neck pediments centered by an eagle with outstretched wings.

24.5in (62cm) wide

$3,000-4,000   **L&T**

A late 20thC George II style walnut and parcel gilt pier glass, the rectangular plate with rounded corners, the fluted swan-neck pediment centered by a flaming urn, the skirt applied with scrolling acanthus foliage.

54in (137cm) high

$400-600   **SI**

A walnut fret work wall mirror, pierced cresting above gilt relief decoration, rectangular plate within molded slip.

16in (40cm) wide

$1,000-1,500   **SI**

A George III style walnut and parcel-gilt wall mirror, the rectangular plate with re-entrant upper corners, the molded conforming frame with a pierced and fretted foliate crest centered by a hoho bird, the fretted skirt similar.

19in (48cm) wide

$600-900   **SI**

A George III oval giltwood mirror, the frame with a pierced foliate scroll crest, and a gadrooned border.

25.5in (65cm) wide

$6,000-9,000   **DN**

A George III oval giltwood wall mirror, oval plate glass within beaded border applied with ribbon tied husks.

19in (48cm) wide

$400-600   **FRE**

An early 19thC ebonized and gilt overmantel mirror, the inverted breakfront cornice above a verre eglomise panel painted with floral swags, flanked by cluster columns with stiff leaf capitals, some paintwork of a later date.

20.75in (52.5cm) wide

$500-700   **DN**

An early 19thC gilt overmantel mirror, the inverted breakfront cornice above a band of gilt spheres and a maritime trophy, flanked by cluster columns with leaf carved capitals, probably regilded.

20.75in (53cm) wide

$500-700   **DN**

An early 19thC Northern European giltwood pier mirror, rectangular with a shaped scroll carved crest, the molded edges with strapwork and floral relief, wear to gilt surfaces, mirror replaced.

30in (76cm) wide

$3,000-4,000   **FRE**

American Mirrors

A late 18thC Chippendale mahogany mirror, with label of John Elliott (1713-1791), scrolling pediment over molded frame enclosing mirror plate, corresponding pendant below, losses, replaced mirror plate.

$1,200-1,800   **FRE**

A 19thC Chippendale style tiger maple and parcel-gilt looking glass, scrolled crest pierced with giltwood bird above molded glass surrounded, a similarly scrolled pendant below.

41in (104cm) high

$1,500-2,000   **SI**

A CLOSER LOOK AT A PAIR OF CHIPPENDALE MIRRORS

These mirrors would have been hung flanking either a door or a window. Their substantial size would tend to indicate a large and important setting.

The phoenix surmoun is one of many motifs suggested by Thomas Chippendale in his book "The Gentleman and Cabinetmaker's Director", 1754. Othe designs included Asia figures in amoungs oriental pavilions an gliding swans

The most delicate and fragile elements of this type of mirror are the surmount and trailing branches to the sides. They are frequently damaged when moved or cleaned and small repairs are only to be expected.

It is uncommo for pairs of mirror to stay togethe over time as the are often spl between differen members of th family. A pair ca realise up to thre times the price (a single example

A Chippendale parcel-gilt mahogany looking glass, scrolling pediment pierced with a carved and gilded foliate device above molded frame and mirror plate, probably American, no backboard, old repairs.

26.5in (67cm) high

$600-900   **FRE**

A Chippendale walnut and parcel-gilt mirror, the deep shaped crest with pierced gilt shell within open circle with incised trailing tendrils and scrolled ears above a rectangular molded frame with inner gilded molding.

44.75in (114cm) high

$3,000-4,000   **NA**

One of a pair of American Chippendale walnut and parcel-gilt mirrors, each with central phoenix, facing right and left, within a gilded swan's-neck crest with rosettes with foliage above a frame with outset square upper corners with straight sides and flanking gilt leaf fillets enclosing gilded slip molding and mirror plate, scalloped pendant apron.

55.75in (141cm) high

$30,000-40,000 (pair)   **NA**

A Queen Anne walnut cushion molded two-part beveled mirror, the rectangular frame with ogival top and applied molded edge, the mirror plates conforming.

50in (127cm) high

$2,500-3,000   **NA**

A 19thC Queen Anne style walnut mirror, shaped, molded frame enclosing two part beveled edge mirror plate.

20in (51cm) wide

$1,200-1,800   **SI**

A Classical giltwood looking glass, the molded shaped cornice over tablet with carved spray or roses and mirror plate enclosed by rope-turned colonettes.

26.5in (67cm) wide

$1,200-1,800   **SI**

A Federal giltwood looking glass, molded cornice above a wreath and acanthus molded frieze, flanked by rope-turned colonnettes, spherules and molded base below.

c1800   *30.25in (77cm) wid*

$2,500-3,000   **S**

A Classical giltwood pier glass, attributed to Joseph Barry, of rectangular form with molded edge and blocked floral rosettes to the corners and molded acanthus leaf decoration.

c1820   37.5in (95cm) wide

$15,000-20,000   FRE

A Federal tiger maple ogee mirror, step down molded frame.

35in (90cm) high

$1,500-2,000   AAC

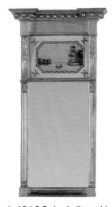

An early 19thC Federal giltwood looking glass, stepped cornice hung with spherules above eglomize panel and mirror plate flanked by colonnettes, restored.

38.5in (98cm) high

$800-1,200   FRE

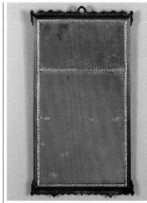

A Chippendale mahogany and giltwood two-part mirror, the frame with openwork shallow crest and with gilded and molded slip enclosing two mirror plates.

Provenance: *Collection of Barbara Streisand.*

20in (51cm) wide

$5,000-7,000   NA

A Federal bird's-eye maple mirror, rectangular molded frame with ebonized accents.

34in (86.5cm) high

$280-320   AAC

A Classical carved giltwood girondole mirror, the crest with a recumbent stag on a rocky plinth flanked by serpents and acanthus carved appliqués, over an acanthus and acorn carved frame enclosing a convex glass, above a shell carved pendant.

52in (132cm) high

$12,000-18,000   Pook

A Classical carved giltwood and part ebonized four light girandole, eagle surmount with outspread wings, above a shaped support flanked by scrolling leafage, the circular carved frame enclosing a reeded slip and convex mirror plate, the frame mounted with four curved candle arms, a leafy pendant below, repairs, missing candle cups, gilt loss.

c1825   52in (132cm) high

$10,000-15,000   FRE

A Classical giltwood and part-bronzed convex two-light girandole, the convex mirror within a reeded collar and frame applied with spherules, surmounted by a displayed eagle above a plinth and suspending a chartreuse beaded swag, issuing two scrolled candlearms, fitted with clear bobeches hung with chartreuse prisms, over pendant foliage.

34in (86cm) high

$15,000-20,000   NA

Cheval Mirrors

A George III mahogany cheval mirror, in the manner of Gillows, the double baluster turned top rail above rectangular mirror plate flanked by turned supports and similar stretcher, on splayed reeded legs with brass caps and casters.

26.25in (67cm) wide

$1,200-1,800   **L&T**

A George IV mahogany and crossbanded rectangular cheval mirror, the rising and adjustable mirror flanked by acorn finials, plain end supports and stretchers on downswept square tapering legs with brass terminals and casters.

25.25in (64cm) wide

$800-1,200   **DN**

A George IV mahogany cheval mirror, the rectangular plate with a crossbanded frame with turned finials, supports and stretchers and outswept square tapering legs, the gilt metal terminals cast with foliage on brass casters.

26in (66cm) wide

$1,500-2,000   **DN**

A late 19thC Sheraton Revival mahogany marqueterie, boxwood and ebony strung cheval mirror, the rectangular plate on straight supports with urn finials and splayed legs, with brass terminals and casters.

31in (78.5cm) wide

$700-1,000   **DN**

A CLOSER LOOK AT A CHEVAL MIRROR

Cheval or standing dressing mirrors were first recorded in Paris at the court of Louis XVI in the mid-18thC.

English examples of cheval mirrors tend to be relatively restrained both in terms of form and decoration. Typically they're found in mahogany and rosewood with the decorative embellishments limited to stringing, marqueterie and gilt metal detailing.

The more sophisticated the design, the more commercial the cheval mirror will tend to be. Attractive features to look for include adjustable angle and height, and fittings for candles, collars, studs and in a few rare instances ash-tray holders.

This mirror is decorated in what is known as the Empire Revival manner which emulates the French style of the first quarter of the 19thC. It is characterized by the use of iconography symbolic of ancient Rome and imagery derived from contemporary archaeological exploration executed in an opulent mix of rich woods, gilt bronze mounts and expensive marbles.

A French Empire style walnut, ebony strung, ebonized and parcel gilt cheval mirror, with architectural pediment and ball and leaf finials, the crossbanded rectangular plate flanked by leaf-capped columns, on sphinx plinth end supports with a turned stretcher.

69.25in (176cm) high

$2,200-2,800   **DN**

A late 19thC mahogany and satinwood crossbanded cheval mirror, the dentil cornice above a boxwood and ebony strung frame and supports, on downswept feet with brass casters.

30in (76cm) wide

$500-600   **DN**

An Edwardian Sheraton revival mahogany and inlaid cheval mirror, the blind fret carved broken swan neck pediment flanked by urn finials, the rectangular adjustable mirror with square upright supports, inlaid with fans and trailing bellflowers, on saber legs ending in hairy paw caps and casters.

29.5in (75cm) wide

$1,200-1,800   **$**

Screens

A European three fold leather screen in the 17thC style, with embossed decoration simulating nine panels, painted with buildings, figures in landscapes, flowers and insects in polychrome on a gilt ground, with studded borders.

57.25in (144.5cm) wide overall

$2,500-3,000   **DN**

An early 19thC embossed leather four fold screen, each fold painted in gilt and colors with baskets of fruit, flowers and perching birds.

93in (236cm) wide overall

$4,000-6,000   L&T

A Victorian three fold scrap/découpage screen with giltwood borders, arches and brass hinges, decorated to both sides.

72.75in (184.5cm) wide overall

$1,800-2,200   DN

An early Victorian embossed leather four fold screen, painted with foliate scrolls and flowers to one side, some splits and repairs.

72.5in (184cm) wide overall

$1,500-2,000   DN

A 19thC European walnut three fold glazed screen, the central arched leaf carved with a scroll and floral crest, flanked by rectangular leaves, with brass double hinges on bracket feet.

72in (183cm) wide overall

$400-600   DN

A late 19thC French carved giltwood three fold screen, the graduated arched folds with pierced foliate carved surmount above glazed and fabric covered panels on scroll feet.

58.5in (148.5cm) wide overall

$1,500-2,000   SI

A late 19thC French three fold painted and parcel gilt screen, each fold with a ribbon tied surmount above astragal glazed panels and foliate pattern fabric covered panels.

57.75in (146.5cm) wide overall

$1,200-1,800   SI

An Edwardian mahogany three fold screen, each fold with astragal glazed panels and bellflower carved decoration above green fabric covered panels.

54.75in (139cm) wide overall

$800-1,200   SI

A Victorian rosewood firescreen, the molded rectangular frame with applied shelf, enclosing a glazed silkwork sliding panel raised on a trestle base linked by a turned stretcher.

15.5in (39cm) wide

$400-600   L&T

A late 19thC ebonized rectangular firescreen, with a reeded frame and a European fabric backed oil painting, above a fretwork panel and turned stretcher on splayed end supports.

21.75in (55cm) wide

$800-1,200   DN

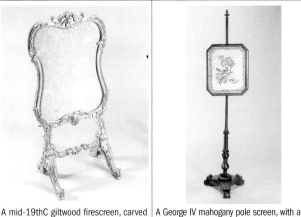

A mid-19thC giltwood firescreen, carved overall with flowers, scrolls and leaves, the cartouche-shaped banners on end supports united by a stretcher and outswept scroll legs.

17.5in (44cm) wide

$320-380   DN

A George IV mahogany pole screen, with a turned finial, the woolwork canted rectangular rosewood framed banner on a turned column and concave sided triform applied with roundels on scroll feet.

56.75in (144cm) high

$220-280   DN

FURNITURE

A George III Scottish mahogany stage back sideboard, the stepped raised back with two side drawers above three drawers with brass handles around an arched recess on square tapering channeled legs.

66.25in (168cm) wide

$1,500-2,000   **DN**

A George III Scottish mahogany sideboard, with box stringing, the shaped top with corresponding raised stage incorporating sliding doors, above single false front frieze drawer flanked by deeper serpentine drawer and cupboard, raised on square section tapered legs with spade feet.

71.25in (181cm) wide

$2,200-2,800   **L&T**

A George III mahogany and inlaid bow front sideboard, the central frieze drawer within two further deep drawerswith dummy two drawer fronts, one a cellaret, flanked by two conforming cupboard doors with pot compartment to the side, raised on reeded square tapered legs.

79.5in (202cm) wide

$3,500-4,500   **FRE**

A George III mahogany serpentine sideboard, with ebony stringing, the shaped top above frieze drawer with tambour fronted cupboard below flanked by deep and shallow drawers, false fronted to right, on square section tapered legs with spade feet.

60in (152cm) wide

$2,200-2,800   **L&**

A George III serpentine sideboard, fitted with a long frieze drawer above two deep drawers, each fitted for cutlery on six reeded tapering legs, satinwood crossbanded throughout, brass rail detached, screw holes filled.

42in (107cm) wide

$3,000-4,000   **FRE**

A George III style mahogany serpentine sideboard, with boxwood stringing, the shaped top above pair of drawers flanked by deeper cupboards on square section tapered legs with spade feet.

72.5in (184cm) wide

$1,500-2,000   **L&T**

A George III mahogany serpentine sideboard, the shaped top with brass rail above central door and arched kneehole flanked by shallow and deep drawers on square section tapered legs with spade feet.

72in (183cm) wide

$2,500-3,000   **L&T**

A small George III style mahogany sideboard, with boxwood stringing, the rectangular top with satinwood crossbanding and central bow above central drawer and brackets flanked by two short and one deep false fronted drawer, on square section tapered legs.

51.25in (130cm) wid

$1,000-1,500   **L&**

A 19thC mahogany bowfront sideboard in the George III style, of small proportions, the shaped top above central drawer flanked by a deep drawer and deep cupboard and raised on square tapering legs terminating in spade feet.

42in (107cm) wide

$700-1,000   **L&T**

A mahogany bowfront sideboard, the top with a molded edge above an arrangement of seven drawers around a central arched recess, on square tapering legs, in part late George III but adapted, repolished.

56.75in (144cm) wide

$600-900   **DN**

An early 19thC mahogany and ebony strung bow front sideboard, with two deep drawers flanking two further drawers with later brass handles on square tapering legs and spade feet.

65in (165cm) wide

$2,500-3,000   **DN**

A late George III mahogany and ebony strung bow front sideboard, the crossbanded and ebony strung top above an outset central drawer flanked by a deep drawer and a door both simulating two short drawers, on square tapering legs with reeded bands.

54.25in (137.5cm) wid

$7,000-10,000   **D**

Sideboards

A CLOSER LOOK AT A HEPPLEWHITE SIDEBOARD

The term 'Hepplewhite' refers to furniture inspired by the designs of the English cabinetmaker George Hepplewhite in his book "The Cabinetmaker and Upholsterer's Guide". The book was published two years after his death in 1788 by his widow Alice, and was widely used in Britain, America and all over the world.

The 'Bottle' Drawer is sometimes also known as a 'cellaret' drawer. As the name suggests it would be used for storing wine and spirits for the meal and would have a protective zinc lining.

A Salem late Federal mahogany sideboard, the rectangular top with outset rounded corners edged with banding and stringing, above a case with center stack of three drawers, flanked by a short drawer over a bottle drawer, further flanked by cupboard doors alternating with half-round reeded columns continuing to swelled cylindrical legs with rings tapering to feet, the pressed brass rosettes with ring pulls.

68in (173cm) wide

$10,000-15,000   **NA**

This sideboard would have probably been built as part of an entire dining room interior scheme. The chairs and dining table would have had conforming decorative inlay.

The dot above pointed arch stringing motif is peculiar to Scottish cabinetmakers. Its presence on a New York piece would suggest a cabinetmaker who has worked in Scotland.

A New England Federal mahogany and bird's-eye maple sideboard, the rectangular swell-front top with outset corners above conforming case with four drawers flanked by reeded and ring-turned tapering legs ending in ball feet, repairs, veneer loss.

A New York Hepplewhite mahogany sideboard, the rectangular top with wide inset corners and inlaid edges above a conforming case with center drawer of a pair of serpentine cupboard doors, flanked by a bowed drawer over a bottle drawer, all with rope twist geometric inlay, the stiles with diamond-over-oval stringing continuing to square tapering legs with line inlay and cuffs.

73.25in (186cm) wide

$20,000-30,000   **NA**

c1815   *41.25in (105cm) wide*

$15,000-20,000   **FRE**

A Classical carved mahogany sideboard, rectangular stepped top above conforming frieze with drawers and molded reserves supported by figural engaged colunns in the form of bearded, turbaned men, flanking lancet arch panel doors, all raised on turned beehive feet, losses to veneer and figures,

92.5in (242.5cm) wide

$10,000-15,000   **FRE**

A Federal mahogany sideboard, rectangular top on case with three doors above two hinged doors flanking recessed section with pair of swell-fronted doors, on turned feet, veneer patches, age cracks, replaced hardware.

c1820   *61in (155cm) wide*

$1,500-2,000   **FRE**

An early 19thC Classical mahogany pedestal sideboard, the top with rectangular surface over three drawers resting on a pair of cabinets, each with turned and reeded columns flanking a cupboard door with inlaid lancet arch, on a molded base and carved hairy paw feet, original stamped brass lion head handles.

72.25in (183.5cm) wide

$8,000-12,000   **FRE**

A Boston Classical ormolu mounted mahogany pedestal sideboard, the rectangular top with conforming splashboard above a case with frieze with three drawers on twin pedestals with ormolu mounted columns.

69in (175cm) wide

$5,000-7,000   **NA**

A late George III mahogany and ebony strung bow front sideboard, three small drawers and one deep cellaret drawer with later brass handles around a central arch on ring turned, tapering legs.

54.25in (138cm) wide

$2,500-3,500   DN

An English early 19thC mahogany bow front mahogany sideboard, rectangular top above central drawer and recessed arched drawer flanked by deeper drawers, on ring turned legs with toupie feet.

66in (168cm) wide

$3,500-4,500   L&T

A Regency mahogany inverted breakfront sideboard, with ebony stringing, the shaped top above frieze with central projecting tablet flanked by drawers and bow-front pedestals with deep drawers raised on ring turned tapering legs.

62.5in (159cm) wide

$2,500-3,500   L&T

A Regency mahogany pedestal sideboard, with ebony stringing, the central rectangular section with ledge back and single frieze drawer flanked by taller pedestals with tapering bodies and crossbanded paneled doors enclosing shelves, on bold carved paw feet.

90in (229cm) wide

$5,000-7,000   L&T

A Scottish late Regency mahogany pedestal sideboard, the central stepped bow front section with three frieze drawers, the centre one panel fronted, the panel back with scrolling leaf carved surmount, flanked by pedestals, each with raised platform top with gadrooned edge above two drawers, the upper one false fronted, and cupboard with arched paneled door flanked by scrolled consoles, on plinth base.

107in (272cm) wide

$800-1,200   L&T

A Classical mahogany pedestal sideboard, shaped backboard densely carved with leafage on a stepped rectangular top above conforming ogee-molded frieze fitted with drawers, raised on pair of pedestals, each with columnar supports on plinth bases.

c1840   *72.25in (183.5cm) wide*

$3,000-5,000   FRE

A Classical carved mahogany and marble sideboard, Philadelphia or Baltimore, mirrored back flanked by scrolled carved supports above end sections with carved drawer fronts on columnar supports enclosing swell-front doors and centering mid section with marble top, slide, drawer and paneled doors, all raised on paw feet, veneer losses, age cracks.

c1840   *74in (188cm) wide*

$3,000-3,500   FRE

A Mid-Atlantic States Empire carved mahogany sideboard, backboard with twin turned and reeded galleries on a rectangular top above a reeded and floral-carved overhanging frieze, with three beaded edge drawers supported by baluster and reed pilasters enclosing four recessed panel doors, ring and ball turned feet.

c1845   *67in (170cm) wide*

$1,600-2,000   FRE

Stands

A Rhode Island Queen Anne maple dish-top candlestand, with old surface, the circular top with a double molded edge above a flaring pedestal with cup turning and tripod exaggerated cabriole legs with slipper feet.

28.25in (71.5cm) high

$10,000-15,000   **NA**

A Connecticut, New London Queen Anne black painted cherry dish-top candlestand, flaring pedestal with urn turning on tripod arched legs with slipper feet.

27.75in (70.5cm) high

$15,000-20,000   **NA**

A Massachusetts Queen Anne mahogany tilt-top candlestand, probably Newburyport, flaring pedestal on arched tripod cabriole legs with ridged pointed slipper feet on pads.

27.5in (70cm) high

$3,000-4,000   **NA**

A Philadelphia Queen Anne walnut candlestand, a birdcage support above turned suppressed ball standard supported by cabriole legs terminating in pad feet.

c1765   *27.25in (69cm) high*

$20,000-30,000   **Pook**

A Chippendale mahogany tilt-top birdcage candlestand, circular dished top on turned tapering support with compressed ball, triparite base with cabriole legs ending in slipper feet, no ring or key.

20.25in (51.5cm) diam

$7,000-9,000   **FRE**

A late 18thC Philadelphia Chippendale walnut tilt-top birdcage candlestand, circular dished top above baluster-turned support and cabriole legs ending in slipper feet.

17in (43cm) diam

$5,000-7,000   **FRE**

A CLOSER LOOK AT A MUSIC STAND

Small multipurpose tables such as this were very popular in the late 18thC. Although this is often known as a "music" stand it would also have been used as a reading table. There are examples where the rest is removable and the table can also function as a stand for ornaments.

Whilst many late 18thC tea and supper tilt-top tables have survived unscathed by constant use, fire and periodic wars, music stands such as this are relatively uncommon. The main reason is that there are many elements that can get damaged very easily.

The reading surface is hinged and supported on strut ratchets. If someone is clumsy either when opening or closing it both the hinges and the ratchets can be severely damaged.

The birdcage support is an attractive feature on a table and allows the upper section to rotate.

These candle holders are attached to the frame using a single swivelling joint. The application of too much downward pressure will snap the joint and tear the holders off leaving an untidy tear to the wood of the frame.

A Pennsylvania Federal walnut tilt top candlestand, the round top inlaid with a spread winged eagle with shielded breast holding olive branch and arrows, supported by a turned shaft and three downcurving legs.

c1790   *29.25in (74cm) high*

$1,500-2,000   **Pook**

A Federal red stained candlestand, turned stem and tripod base.

26in (66cm) high

$350-450   **SI**

A rare Philadelphia mahogany music stand, the adjustable reading surface with ledge above two retractable round candleholders, supported by a birdcage over a suppressed ball pedestal, resting on cabriole legs terminating in bold pad feet.

c1770   *32in (81cm) high*

$12,000-18,000   **Pook**

FURNITURE

An early 19thC New England Federal maple candlestand, rectangular top on baluster-turned support with arched legs, discoloration to the top.

16in (40.5cm) wide

$600-900　　　　　　**FRE**

A Windsor candlestand, with circular top and three turned, splayed legs joined by stretchers supporting a central dished shelf, retains original red painted surface.

c1800　　　*28in (71cm) high*

$600-900　　　　　　**Pook**

A 19thC turned maple candlestand, adjustable candle cups and dished tray on a threaded shaft and cylindrical support on X-form base.

47in (119cm) tall

$400-600　　　　　　**SI**

A 19thC Gothic Revival stand.

29.5in (75cm) high

$700-1,000　　　　　**TDG**

A Sheraton mahogany two drawer stand, banded top on turned legs.

19.5in (49.5cm) wide

$500-700　　　　　　**AAC**

A Sheraton mahogany two drawer stand, on turned legs.

20in (51cm) wide

$400-600　　　　　　**AAC**

A Sheraton two drawer cherry stand, with mahogany veneer facings, on turned legs.

20in (51cm) wide

$300-400　　　　　　**AAC**

A New England Federal inlaid pine stand, with single inlaid drawer, imperfections.

c1810　　　*28in (71cm) high*

$800-1,200　　　　　**FRE**

A Federal inlaid single drawer stand, shaped top inlaid with geometric device above single drawer on square tapering legs, imperfections.

28.5in (72.5cm) high

$600-900　　　　　　**FRE**

A New England Federal maple one-drawer stand, the rectangular top above straight frieze with drawer on squared tapering legs, discoloration to top.

c1800　　　*28in (71cm) high*

$350-450　　　　　　**FRE**

A Hepplewhite pine stand, single dovetailed drawer, tapered legs.

23.5in (60cm) wide

$200-300　　　　　　**AAC**

A Hepplewhite style tiger maple stand, square top on tapered splay leg base.

17.5in (44.5cm) wide

$400-600　　　　　　**AAC**

A New England pine stand, top with molded edge, over a single drawer supported by tapered square legs.

26in (66cm) high

$120-180　　　　　　**AAC**

A red painted pine stand, rectangular top above chamfered drawer with glass knob and turned tapering legs ending in peg feet.

c1810　　　*20.25in (51.5cm) wide*

$1,500-2,000　　　　**FRE**

A late 19thC George III style mahogany drum table with alternating real and dummy drawers, tripod base with carved leaf work decoration.

44in (112cm) diam

$2,500-3,000   **SI**

An early 19thC Dutch mahogany and marqueterie oval center table, inlaid throughout with scrolling foliage, the top centered by a flowering urn, raised on slender square tapered legs with brass bun feet.

38in (96.5cm) wide

$2,200-2,800   **FRE**

An early 19thC Empire rosewood and marble topped center table, the dished grey marble top with a tapered square column support carved with C-scrolls and acanthus, on a shaped platform base ending in scroll feet and casters.

60.5in (154cm) diam

$7,000-10,000   **SI**

A William IV plum pudding mahogany center table, the circular tilt top with plain frieze raised on turned pedestal with lotus leaf clasps and corresponding saucer with ball molding, concave triform base with lobed bun feet.

48in (122cm) diam

$2,500-3,000   **L&T**

An early Victorian walnut octagonal center table, the tilt top with satinwood panel and elaborate marqueterie and specimen wood decoration, on triangular pedestal with carved and turned columns and strapwork decoration on corresponding tripod base with molded cabriole legs and scroll toes with casters.

48.25in (123cm) wide

$7,000-10,000   **L&T**

A Victorian ebonized center table, the elongated octagonal top with ebony crossbanding and boxwood inlaid panel at center raised on four turned and carved supports with gilt fluting joined by rectangular and pierced collar with four corresponding square section cabriole legs, modern brass casters.

51.25in (130cm) wide

$3,000-4,000   **L&T**

A mid-19thC Austrian or French figured walnut oval center table, with a crossbanded oval top, raised on an openwork, foliate carved, X-form base.

44in (75cm) wide

$600-900   **FRE**

A mid-Victorian rosewood center table, the shaped oval top with molded edge above a single frieze drawer raised on a turned and leaf carved column on quadruped base with C-scroll and rocaille work legs terminating in wooden casters.

50.75in (129cm)

$700-1,000   **L&T**

A mid-19thC mahogany octagonal center table, the revolving top above shallow paneled frieze with alternate drawers, raised on tapering square pedestal with canted scroll consoles and concave quadriform plinth, facetted bun feet with sunken casters.

54.25in (138cm) diam

$2,200-2,800   **L&T**

FURNITURE

A George IV mahogany breakfast table, the rectangular top with rounded corners and a reeded edge, on turned column and four reeded outswept legs with brass terminals and casters, the top repaired and fixed in place.

54.25in (138cm) wide

$700-1,000   **DN**

A mahogany rectangular tilt top breakfast table, the rosewood crossbanded top on turned column with four reeded splayed legs, the base early 19thC, the top of a later date.

52in (132.5cm)

$300-500   **DN**

A Regency mahogany breakfast table, the rectangular crossbanded top raised on turned pedestal and four reeded saber legs with brass caps and casters.

54.75in (139cm) wide

$2,200-2,800   **L&T**

A Regency mahogany breakfast table, the rectangular top with rounded angles and burr yew banding, the reeded edge above ring turned tapering column on quadruped base with curved legs, inlaid with bands of stained mahogany and terminating in cast paw caps and casters.

56in (142cm) wide

$1,200-1,800   **L&T**

A George IV mahogany breakfast table, the rectangular tilt-top with a molded edge on a turned column and four lappet-carved and channeled splayed legs with brass paw terminals and casters.

59in (150cm) wide

$700-1,000   **DN**

An early Victorian rosewood and simulated rosewood breakfast table, the round tilt top on a turned column and concave sided triform with reeded bun feet and recessed casters.

49.75in (126.5cm) diam

$1,500-2,000   **DN**

An early Victorian mahogany breakfast table, the round tilt top with a molded edge on a lappet carved column and collar, a platform and paw feet.

51.5in (131cm) diam

$800-1,200   **DN**

A mid-19thC French rosewood and marqueterie tilt top breakfast table, the circular top inlaid with a central foliate motif, raised on a facetted baluster column support and ending in a triform base.

44in (112cm) diam

$1,800-2,200   **S**

A mid-Victorian walnut and marqueterie oval breakfast table, the molded top inlaid with scrolling foliage, raised on a turned column supports and ending in four foliate carved cabriole legs and casters.

52.5in (133.5cm) wide

$1,800-2,700   **SI**

A Victorian walnut oval breakfast table, the quarter veneered burr walnut top with marqueterie and a molded edge, on a turned and carved column and four cabriole legs with scroll feet and ceramic casters.

53in (135cm) wide

$800-1,000   **DN**

A Victorian figured walnut and ebony banded breakfast table, quarter veneered oval tilt top on four out splayed legs with casters.

46.5in (118cm) wide

$800-1,200   **SI**

A Victorian mahogany breakfast table, the round tilt-top with a molded edge, on a tapering triangular section column with a gadrooned collar, a concave sided platform and scroll feet with recessed casters.

48in (122cm) diam

$1,500-2,000   **DN**

Drop-leaf tables

A Queen Anne walnut drop-leaf table, rounded drop leaf top on base with scalloped skirt on cabriole legs with stocking drake feet, minor repairs.

52in (132cm) wide

$800-1,200   **AAC**

A Rhode Island Chippendale mahogany drop-leaf table, rectangular top with conforming hinged leaves on squared top-fluted legs, surface scratches, losses to sides of legs.

44in (112cm) wide

$8,000-12,000   **FRE**

A New York Classical carved mahogany drop-leaf table, each drawer with a lion's-head pull, on columnar supports and shaped platform, acanthus and paw carved feet, on casters.

c1815

$1,500-2,000   **FRE**

A Classical mahogany drop-leaf table, the rectangular top with hinged leaves above a frieze with single drawer and turned legs ending in baluster and ball feet.

$600-900   **SI**

A CLOSER LOOK AT A DROP-LEAF TABLE

Although this table was found in Chester County it is probable that it was made in Philadelphia. The high-arched skirt and large single-board leaves are indicative of a Philadelphia origin.

The connection point of the flaps to the hinges is one of the weakest points on such a table. The best way of determining whether damage or repairs have occurred is to turn the table upside down and to examine the underside.

It is often the small details that distinguish the finer pieces of furniture. On this table it is the large and imposing claw and ball feet with well observed carving of the webs between the claws and the pointed talons.

A Chippendale walnut drop-leaf table, the rectangular top supporting two drop leaves over a frame with a scalloped skirt supported by cabriole legs terminating in bold ball and claw feet.

48in (122cm) wide

$15,000-20,000   **Pook**

A Mid-Atlantic States Classical carved mahogany drop-leaf table, the rectangular top with conforming leaves with notched corners above a carved concave frieze, on a waterleaf carved pedestal, shaped platform and molded down curving legs ending in paw feet, on casters.

c1825   *28.75in (73cm) high*

$2,000-3,000   **FRE**

A mid-18thC Pennsylvania Queen Anne walnut drop-leaf table, the rectangular top with conforming leaves and notched corners on a shaped and molded apron, and cabriole legs ending in pad feet.

50.5in (128.5cm) wide

$1,800-2,200   **FRE**

A late 18thC Chippendale walnut drop-leaf table, the rectangular top with hinged leaves raised on cabriole legs ending in ball-and-claw feet impressed "McLean #7", one leaf replaced.

46.5in (118cm) wide

$2,200-2,800   **SI**

A Classical mahogany drop-leaf breakfast table, attributed to Jenkins Family of Cabinetmakers, Baltimore, Maryland, on swept reeded legs.

c1825   *43.75in (111cm) wide*

$2,200-2,800   **SI**

A Classical carved mahogany drop-leaf table, rectangular top with shaped leaves on leaf-carved legs ending in turned feet.

c1825   *19.5in (49.5cm) long*

$600-900   **FRE**

TABLES

Dining Tables

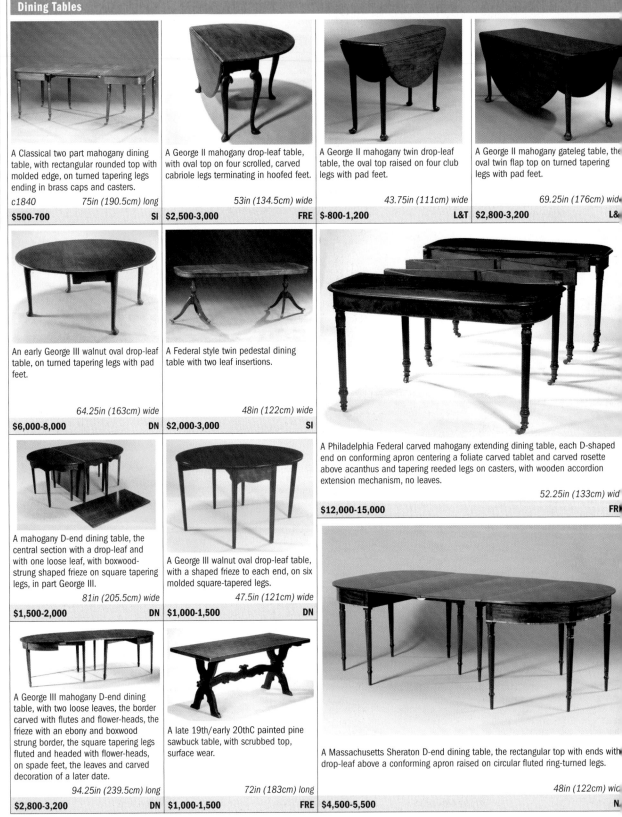

A Classical two part mahogany dining table, with rectangular rounded top with molded edge, on turned tapering legs ending in brass caps and casters.

c1840   *75in (190.5cm) long*

$500-700   **SI**

A George II mahogany drop-leaf table, with oval top on four scrolled, carved cabriole legs terminating in hoofed feet.

53in (134.5cm) wide

$2,500-3,000   **FRE**

A George II mahogany twin drop-leaf table, the oval top raised on four club legs with pad feet.

43.75in (111cm) wide

$-800-1,200   **L&T**

A George II mahogany gateleg table, the oval twin flap top on turned tapering legs with pad feet.

69.25in (176cm) wide

$2,800-3,200   **L&**

An early George III walnut oval drop-leaf table, on turned tapering legs with pad feet.

64.25in (163cm) wide

$6,000-8,000   **DN**

A Federal style twin pedestal dining table with two leaf insertions.

48in (122cm) wide

$2,000-3,000   **SI**

A Philadelphia Federal carved mahogany extending dining table, each D-shaped end on conforming apron centering a foliate carved tablet and carved rosette above acanthus and tapering reeded legs on casters, with wooden accordion extension mechanism, no leaves.

52.25in (133cm) wid

$12,000-15,000   **FR**

A mahogany D-end dining table, the central section with a drop-leaf and with one loose leaf, with boxwood-strung shaped frieze on square tapering legs, in part George III.

81in (205.5cm) wide

$1,500-2,000   **DN**

A George III walnut oval drop-leaf table, with a shaped frieze to each end, on six molded square-tapered legs.

47.5in (121cm) wide

$1,000-1,500   **DN**

A George III mahogany D-end dining table, with two loose leaves, the border carved with flutes and flower-heads, the frieze with an ebony and boxwood strung border, the square tapering legs fluted and headed with flower-heads, on spade feet, the leaves and carved decoration of a later date.

94.25in (239.5cm) long

$2,800-3,200   **DN**

A late 19th/early 20thC painted pine sawbuck table, with scrubbed top, surface wear.

72in (183cm) long

$1,000-1,500   **FRE**

A Massachusetts Sheraton D-end dining table, the rectangular top with ends with drop-leaf above a conforming apron raised on circular fluted ring-turned legs.

48in (122cm) wi

$4,500-5,500   **N.**

A mahogany D-end dining table in George III style with one loose leaf and a plain frieze, on tapering legs with spade feet, the legs retipped.

62.25in (158cm) long

$500-700 DN

A George III-style mahogany and cross banded D-end dining table, with two leaf insertions, the rounded rectangular top with reeded edge, raised on twin tripod-end supports terminating in brass cappings and casters.

120in (305cm) long

$1,800-2,200 SI

A CLOSER LOOK AT A REGENCY DINING TABLE

This is a fine example of one of the most commercial forms of early 19thC dining tables. In 1805, Richard Gillow had patented a design for the 'Imperial Extending Dining Table' which could be enlarged, reduced or moved with ease. The leaves are supported on what Mr Gillow termed "lazy tongs," a concertina-action x-frame.

It is unusual to find a table of this type that retains all its original leaves. All too often they are mislaid in house moves or warped by being left in the damp. To check the originality of the leaves look for the same pattern of grain and figuring to run through the entire length of the table. Variations in color are almost inevitable as some leaves will have been more exposed to sunlight than others.

A mahogany, satinwood-banded, boxwood and ebony strung, D-end dining table, comprising pair of ends and a drop-leaf center section on square tapering legs, early 19thC but adapted.

116.5in (296cm) long

$1,500-2,000 DN

A mahogany D-end dining table with two loose leaves and a central drop-leaf section, with a plain frieze on straight chamfered legs, in part George III, adapted.

41.75in (106cm) long

$1,200-1,800 DN

A mahogany and ebony strung extending D-end dining table, with two loose leaves, the rectangular top with rounded corners above a plain frieze on square tapering legs, in part George III but adapted.

87.75in (223cm) long

$2,200-2,800 DN

When considering whether to buy a dining table, always try sitting at it. Some dining tables have deep friezes which, whilst they would have been no problem for our more diminutive ancestors, can be very uncomfortable for us today. Always check that your dining room will comfortably take the dimensions of your intended table and that there is adequate access through the house to get the table in.

The strong, thick, reeded design of these particular legs means that there is unlikely to be much damage or wear to them. On extending dining tables, it is the legs that tend to take the most punishment when the table is opened and closed. Stress fractures are not uncommon and there can be problems at the joints between the top of the legs and the main table frame.

A Regency mahogany telescopic dining table, with five leaves, the rounded rectangular top and molded edge raised on eight turned and reeded tapering legs with ebonised rings and brass caps and casters.

145.75in (370cm) long (extended)

$40,000-60,000 L&T

A Regency mahogany extending dining table, the rectangular top with rounded angles and reeded edge, raised on ring-turned reeded legs with brass caps and casters, the central section turning through 90° and extending with draw action, two leaves.

136.25in (346cm) long (extended)

$15,000-20,000 L&T

An early 19thC mahogany D-end triple pedestal dining table, the top with a reeded edge and drop-leaves, with adjustable leaf supports linked to the folding splayed and reeded legs with brass terminals and casters, lacking one leaf.

Provenance: *From The Hon. Mrs Daisy Fellowes collection.*

143.5in (364.5cm) long (extended)

$20,000-30,000 DN

A mahogany and ebony strung rectangular three-pillar dining table, the top crossbanded and with brass inlay, the central section with two drop leaves and two frieze drawers all on square tapering columns and outswept legs with brass paw terminals and casters, early 19thC but adapted.

88.5in (224.5cm) long

$2,500-3,000 DN

A mahogany triple pedestal dining table in the Regency style with two loose leaves, the top with rounded corners and a reeded edge, on turned columns each with three splayed legs and brass paw terminals and casters, stamped "S & H Jewell".

104.75in (266cm) long

$3,000-4,000 DN

A George II-style walnut card table, the crossbanded folding top with outset corners enclosing a baize-lined interior and counter wells above a shaped frieze on shell-carved cabriole legs, on ball and claw feet.

37in (90.5cm) wide

$4,000-6,000　　　　　　　**DN**

An early George III mahogany demi-lune games table, with a fold-over top enclosing a baize playing surface with counter wells, a void interior with inkwell, plain frieze raised on turned tapered legs, ending in pad feet.

32.75in (83cm) wide

$2,200-2,800　　　　　　　**FRE**

A mahogany card table, the rectangular top with outset corners folding to enclose a baize lining and counter wells above a drawer on scroll-carved cabriole legs and ball and claw feet, largely mid-18thC, but adapted.

18.25in (46.5cm) wide

$1,200-1,800　　　　　　　**DN**

A George III carved mahogany fold-over card table, hinged fold-over top with entrelac-carved edge above frieze drawer, molded square section legs, later alterations.

31in (79cm) wide

$1,000-1,500　　　　　　　**SI**

A George III mahogany demi-lune card table, the hinged top enclosing a later leather inset interior, on molded square tapering legs headed by carved ovals.

36.25in (92cm) wide

$700-1,000　　　　　　　**DN**

A George III mahogany triple fold-over games/tea table, hinged top opening to reveal polished and baize playing surfaces, plain frieze above square chamfered legs with pierced angle brackets.

32in (81.5cm) wide

$2,500-3,000　　　　　　　**FRE**

A pair of George III satinwood and tulipwood crossbanded serpentine tables, one a card table, the other a tea table, each with fan and floral marqueterie, boxwood stringing, hinged tops enclosing a baize and satinwood interior respectively, frieze corners inlaid to simulate flutes on straight tapering legs with brass terminals stamped "Cope's patent" and casters, wear and restoration.

38.25in (97cm) wide

$20,000-30,000　　　　　　　**DN**

A George III mahogany, boxwood and ebony strung card table, the rectangular crossbanded folding top with rounded corners enclosing a baize lining, on square tapering legs.

36.25in (92cm) wide

$2,200-2,800　　　　　　　**DN**

A George III satinwood, boxwood and ebony strung card table, the rectangular rosewood crossbanded hinged top with rounded corners above a frieze with a central tablet on square tapering legs with collars.

36.25in (92cm) wide

$2,500-3,000　　　　　　　**DN**

A late Regency mahogany, box and ebony strung card table, the figured mahogany and tulipwood crossbanded rectangular top with canted corners folding to enclose a baize-lined interior on square tapering legs, some damage, the top warped.

36in (91.5cm) wide

$1,200-1,800　　　　　　　**DN**

A Regency mahogany and crossbanded games table, the fold-over top enclosing a baize playing surface, spiral twist turned tapering legs, brass cappings and casters.

36in (91.5cm) wide

$1,200-1,800　　　　　　　**S**

Card-Games Tables

A Chippendale carved mahogany card table of narrow size, the rectangular hinged top with square outset corners above a conforming apron with drawer, on cabriole legs with carved knees and ball-and-claw feet.

32.5in (82.5cm) wide

$7,000-10,000 NA

A Pennsylvania Chippendale mahogany card table, with a molded rectangular top over a frame with a single drawer supported by square tapering legs ending in Marlborough feet.

c1790   34.5in (88cm) wide

$700-1,000 Pook

A Massachusetts Sheraton inlaid mahogany and bird's-eye maple card table with rosewood crossbanding, the hinged serpentine top with turret ends above a three panel apron, the center one with oval panel in mitred frame, the flanking panels rectangular, the spool turned stiles continuing to tapering reeded legs.

29in (73.5cm) wide

$2,800-3,200 NA

A New England inlaid mahogany serpentine front card table, the serpentine front hinged top with turret corners, edged with contrasting sawtooth inlay, the apron with tripartite satinwood veneer panels, the center one bird's-eye maple with zebrawood oval, the ringed stiles above tapering reeded legs with swelled cuffs.

29.25in (74cm) wide

$14,000-18,000 NA

A Massachusetts Sheraton carved mahogany card table, McIntire School, the serpentine hinged top over a conforming apron with carved basket of fruit joining turned and reeded legs with floral and leaf carving.

37in (94cm) wide

$3,500-4,500 NA

A mahogany Hepplewhite card table, oxbow shaped top on tapered legs, with gateleg support.

35.5in (90cm) wide

$500-700 AAC

A good pair of Federal inlaid mahogany card tables, each with a serpentine folding top above a conforming frieze with inlaid dies centering a bold maple panel, the whole on square tapered legs.

c1800   35.5in (90cm) wide

$30,000-40,000 FRE

A Federal inlaid mahogany and mahogany veneer card table, probably New York, the hinged, lobed top over conforming frieze with contrasting veneered tablets, tapering reeded legs ending in brass caps and casters, veneer losses throughout.

30.75in (78cm) wide

$1,000-1,500 SI

A Boston Classical mahogany and ormolu mounted lyre base card table, the rectangular swivelling hinged top with bowed center section, lyre-form pedestal with brass 'strings', on four part ebonized outsplayed legs and brass paw caps and casters.

36in (91.5cm) wide

$3,000-5,000 NA

A CLOSER LOOK AT A CLASSICAL CARD TABLE

This table came from the collection of Mr Robert T Trump. A noted and highly regarded figure in the field of Classical furniture he wrote two articles about Joseph B Barry for the "Antiques Magazine". Though this table is not labeled he proved through stylistic comparison that it was probably Barry's work.

The carefully chosen 'pie-cut' mahogany veneers to the top are unusual and distinctive. A lesser cabinetmaker would have used a single unsegmented piece.

This table relates to one attributed to Barry in the Telfair Museum, Savannah, Georgia. The leaf carving relates to the labeled Barry pier table at the Metropolitan Museum of Art.

The giltwood medallion is copied from an English ormolu mount of the type forbidden from importation to America during the War of 1812. The presence of this unusual feature gives a good indication of the date of manufacture.

A Classical carved mahogany card table, with hinged octagonal top inlaid in pie sections and rotating to reveal a compartment, above a cylindrical shaft with turned ring and carved with feathers and acanthus leaves above a similarly carved ring, resting on a rectangular plinth with carved giltwood medallion on four splayed legs ending in brass paw feet and casters.

c1812   36in (91.5cm) wide

$15,000-20,000 FRE

A Regency brass-inlaid rosewood card table, the fold-over rectangular top with rounded angles above a frieze centered by a tablet on stepped square-section tapered pedestal and four saber legs with cast brass paw feet.

35.75in (91cm) wide

$4,000-6,000　　　　**L&T**

A Regency rosewood and brass marquetry card table, the rectangular top with rounded corners and a baize lining, on a shaped column, concave-sided platform and four splayed legs with brass paw terminals and casters.

35.5in (90.5cm) wide

$1,800-2,200　　　　**DN**

A New England Classical mahogany card table, with fold-over top.
c1825　　　　*35.5in (90cm) wide*

$600-800　　　　**SI**

A Classical mahogany card table, attributed to Anthony Jenkins (active 1832-1857), Baltimore, Maryland, rectangular top with reeded edge on a baluster and ring-turned support raised on downswept reeded legs ending in brass claw caps on casters.

For a related card table see "Classical Maryland 1815-1845 Fine and Decorative Arts from the Golden Age", Maryland Historical Society (1993) Fig 153, plate 126.

39in (99cm) wide

$5,500-6,500　　　　**FRE**

A late Regency mahogany card table, the rectangular hinged top with rounded corners above a paneled and beaded frieze with scrolled brackets, on a ring turned column with platform base and four reeded scrolled legs with brass terminals and casters.

36in (91.5cm) wide

$1,500-2,000　　　　**DN**

A George IV rosewood and simulated rosewood card table, the rectangular top with brass stringing and inlay and rounded corners, folding to enclose a baize lining, the frieze with a central tablet on a turned column and four outswept feet with brass paw terminals and casters.

36in (91.5cm) wide

$2,000-3,000　　　　**DN**

A William IV rosewood card table, the rectangular folding top enclosing a baize lining, with a tablet frieze flanked by scroll brackets, on a square tapering column, a concave-sided platform and scroll and paw feet with recessed casters.

35.75in (91cm) wide

$1,000-1,500　　　　**DN**

A Victorian mahogany card table, the rectangular top with rounded corners and a swivel baize-lined folding top above a recess, on a turned column and four scroll and leaf carved cabriole legs, lacking casters.

36in (91.5cm) wide

$600-900　　　　**DN**

A Classical carved mahogany card table, rectangular top with canted corners above of cove-molded frieze centering a carved tablet, baluster turned, carved and reeded support on a shaped platform raised on paw feet on casters.

37.5in (94cm) wide

$2,000-3,000　　　　**FRE**

A CLOSER LOOK AT A TEA TABLE

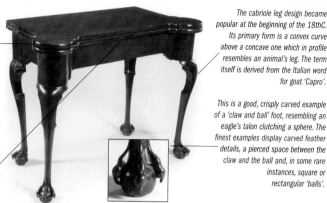

This table would originally have been one of a pair with a matching card or games table. This is reflected in the unusual design of the top with its bold, outset corners. The card table would probably have had sunken wells at the interior corners to store gaming chips. The tea table has no need for such internal features but mimics the outline shape.

Whilst the card table interior would have been baize-lined, this is plain mahogany. The hinged fold-over top rests on a concertina-action, twin leg support with folding cross stretcher.

The cabriole leg design became popular at the beginning of the 18thC. Its primary form is a convex curve above a concave one which in profile resembles an animal's leg. The term itself is derived from the Italian word for goat 'Capro'.

This is a good, crisply carved example of a 'claw and ball' foot, resembling an eagle's talon clutching a sphere. The finest examples display carved feather details, a pierced space between the claw and the ball and, in some rare instances, square or rectangular 'balls'.

A George II mahogany concertina-action tea table, the hinged top with rounded outset corners and frieze, on cabriole legs and ball and claw feet.

37.75in (96cm) wide

$4,000-6,000 | DN

A George III mahogany, ebony banded and boxwood strung tea table, the rectangular hinged top with inset re-entrant corners enclosing a plum pudding mahogany interior, on turned tapering legs, inlaid with satinwood flutes and headed by lozenges.

35.75in (91cm) wide

$1,500-2,000 | DN

A Queen Anne maple tea table, probably from Rhode Island, the oval top above a shaped apron and tapering turned legs ending in pad feet, age splits, discoloration to top, losses to one foot.

32.5in (82.5cm) wide

$2,000-3,000 | FRE

A New England Queen Anne maple tea table, with black painted base over old blue, the rectangular top with molded edge projecting over a shaped skirt fitted with a drawer on cabriole legs and pad feet.

27.5in (70cm) high

$14,000-16,000 | NA

Boston Chippendale walnut tilt-top tea table, the square top with molded edge and notched corners tilting above a fluted pillar over a swirling cup on tripod cabriole legs with leaf carved knees and ball and claw feet.

28in (71cm) high

$10,000-15,000 | NA

A George IV mahogany tea table, the rectangular folding top with rounded corners, the flame veneered frieze with a nulled border, on an acanthus-carved baluster column and four outswept molded legs with brass leaf-cased terminals and casters.

36.25in (92cm) wide

$1,500-2,000 | DN

A mid 18thC walnut tilt-top table, on a birdcage and baluster turned column and three squat cabriole legs with stylized ball and claw feet, possibly American, lacking casters.

32.25in (82cm) diam

$1,000-1,500 | DN

Worktables

A Regency mahogany drop-leaf work table, having a rectangular top with two drawers, one being fitted with a writing slide and one with a wool basket, square tapering legs with spade feet with casters.

36in (91.5cm) wide

$4,000-5,000   **FRE**

A George IV mahogany and rosewood crossbanded work table, the boxwood strung canted rectangular top with two drop leaves above two drawers and a sliding wool bag, opposing false drawer fronts on turned tapering legs, with brass terminals and casters.

29.5in (75cm) wide

$2,500-3,000   **DN**

A Sheraton mahogany sewing table, bears the paper label of Jacob Forster (1764-1838), Charlestown, Massachusetts and dated in ink, the rectangular molded top above a stack of two compartmented drawers, the bag drawer on the side with lock above stop-fluted stiles continuing to tapering reeded legs with ringed cuffs, with original brass knobs.

Provenance: Carswell Rush Berlin; Nathan Benn. A similar one-drawer stand with label is illustrated in "American Antiques from Israel Sack Collection", vol 10 p 272.

1814   *20in (51cm) wide*

$20,000-25,000   **NA**

A mid-Atlantic States late Federal figured mahogany workstand, rectangular shaped top supported by half-round colonettes enclosing two bolection drawers on rounded, tapering, ring turned legs ending in ball feet.

c1820   *28in (71cm) high*

$1,000-1,500   **FRE**

A late Federal mahogany work table, the square top with outset corners above two drawers, raised on reeded turned and tapered legs united by a galleried undertier.

c1810   *28.5in (72.5cm) high*

$1,800-2,200   **SI**

A Classical figured-mahogany work table, probably Philadelphia, rectangular top on a projecting frieze with drawer supported on turned colonettes centering two drawers, tapering cylindrical support, shaped platform base on scrolled feet.

c1825   *21in (53.5cm) wide*

$500-700   **FRE**

An American late Classical figured mahogany drop leaf workstand, with three bolection drawers, the third drawer opening to a deep cylindrical well, on double scroll uprights and feet.

c1830   *28in (71cm) high*

$800-1,000   **FR**

A Federal mahogany and bird's-eye maple two-drawer work table, octagonal top above conforming frieze with two drawers, ring-turned supports continuing to tapering reeded legs ending in peg feet, refinished, surfaced scratches.

Illustrated on page 1102 fig 3906 in "American Antiques from the Israel Sack Collection Vol IV", 1974.

17.75in (45cm) wide

$10,000-15,000   **FRE**

A Classical carved mahogany and mahogany veneered two drawer work table, turned column and leaf carved cabriole legs, paw feet.

c1835   *21in (53cm) wide*

$550-650   **SI**

Pembroke tables

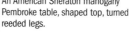

A mid-Atlantic States Federal inlaid mahogany Pembroke table, oblong top with hinged D-shape leaves on bowed frieze with inlaid lily of the valley and single drawer, on square tapering legs, drawer with label of "David Stockwell, Wilmington, Delaware".

c1800		32in (81.5cm) wide
$2,000-3,000		**FRE**

A Pennsylvania Chippendale inlaid-cherry Pembroke table, the rectangular hinged top with conforming leaves, inlaid with hearts and a tulip above a frieze with a single molded drawer, raised on molded and chamfered square legs ending in Marlborough feet, joined by a cross-stretcher, some restoration.

c1800		33in (84cm) wide
$800-1,200		**FRE**

An American Sheraton mahogany Pembroke table, shaped top, turned reeded legs.

	22in (55.75cm) wide
$800-1,200	**AAC**

An American Classical mahogany Pembroke table.

c1830	29in (73.5cm) wide
$500-800	**SI**

A 19thC New England cherry and tiger maple small Pembroke table.

$1,800-2,200	**BCAC**

A Massachusetts Sheraton inlaid mahogany Pembroke table, the rectangular top with square drop leaves above an apron with single drawer joining turned and reeded legs.

	36in (91.5cm) wide
$5,000-7,000	**NA**

A George III-style mahogany Pembroke table, the rectangular top with rounded edge and chamfered legs joined by turned and blocked H-stretcher.

	38.5in (98cm) wide
$1,500-2,000	**L&T**

An early 19thC mahogany Pembroke table, the rectangular top with reeded edge above two graduated drawers and opposing dummies, raised on ring turned legs with toupie feet.

	26.75in (68cm) wide
$700-1,000	**L&T**

A late George III mahogany Pembroke table, the rectangular top with a molded edge, with a frieze drawer opposing a false drawer on square tapering legs with brass terminals and casters.

	38.25in (97cm) wide
$400-600	**DN**

A Regency mahogany Pembroke table, the rosewood crossbanded top with reeded edge, above a frieze drawer with later brass handles, a false drawer on ring turned column, saber legs with brass paw terminals and casters.

	47.25in (120cm) wide
$800-1,200	**DN**

A William IV mahogany Pembroke table, the top with rounded corners above a frieze drawer with turned handles to each end, on a turned tapering column, concave-sided platform base and massive paw feet with casters.

	44.75in (114cm) wide
$600-900	**DN**

Sofa Tables

A Regency mahogany sofa table, the rounded rectangular top above two real and two opposing dummy frieze drawers, raised on twin lyre supports, ending in reeded saber legs with brass cappings and casters.

57.5in (146cm) wide (extended)

$5,000-7,000 | **SI**

A Regency mahogany sofa table, the canted rectangular drop-leaf top above a paneled frieze with two drawers on a stepped gadrooned column support ending in four saber legs with hairy paw caps and casters.

58.5in (148cm) wide

$2,500-3,000 | **SI**

A Regency mahogany sofa table, with purplewood stringing, the rectangular top with drop flaps and rounded angles above opposing frieze and dummy drawers raised on paired, turned, blocked and reeded supports joined by corresponding stretcher on downscrolled square section reeded legs with brass caps and casters.

58.25in (148cm) wide

$6,000-9,000 | **L&T**

A Regency rosewood and brass strung sofa table, the rounded rectangular top with three-quarter trellis pierced gallery, twin frieze drawers, anthemion contre-partie decoration to the corners, on twin lyre supports terminating in paw feet, with central turned stretcher.

40in (101.5cm) wide

$12,000-18,000 | **FRE**

A small Regency mahogany sofa table, the rounded rectangular top with a reeded edge, the frieze with two real and two opposing dummy drawers, raised on pierced twin end supports and acanthus-carved saber legs, joined by a turned stretcher and terminating in brass casters.

20.75in (52.5cm) wide

$3,000-4,000 | **FRE**

An early 20thC Regency style mahogany and satinwood banded sofa table, the rounded rectangular top with a reeded edge above two real and two opposing dummy frieze drawers, the twin end supports ending in downswept legs, joined by a cross stretcher and terminating in brass hairy paw caps and casters.

33in (84cm) wide

$700-1,000 | **SI**

A Regency rosewood sofa table, inlaid with boxwood stringing, the rounded rectangular twin-flap top above two frieze doors, on two vase-shaped trestle supports and concave quadripartite base with splayed arrow inlaid legs terminating in brass lion's paw caps and casters.

36.25in (92cm) wide

$3,000-4,000 | **L&T**

A George IV mahogany and ebony strung sofa table, the rectangular top with rounded corners above two frieze drawers with turned handles, opposing false drawers on plain end supports, with a high stretcher, reeded outswept legs, brass terminals and casters, the top repolished, repairs.

58.25in (148cm) wide

$700-1,000 | **DN**

A William IV mahogany sofa table, top with a molded edge, above two frieze drawers opposing false drawers, turned stretcher, plinths with roundels and quarter roundels.

50.25in (127.5cm) wide

$4,000-6,000 | **DN**

Console-Pier Tables

A demi-lune console table, painted overall in Neoclassical style with a fan, ribbons and foliage on a cream ground with meandering floral borders on a ground simulating timber, on square tapering legs with collars, the table possibly 18thC, the paintwork of a later date.

39.5in (100.5cm) wide

$6,000-9,000 | **DN**

A George III satinwood, rosewood crossbanded, ebony and boxwood strung demi-lune pier table, top with a marqueterie fan and paneled frieze.

56.25in (133cm) wide

$4,000-6,000 | **DN**

A CLOSER LOOK AT A CLASSICAL PIER TABLE

...his table is attributed to the ...abinetmaker Joseph B Barry (1757-...838). he was born in Ireland, trained ... London and worked as a ...abinetmaker in Philadelphia and ...avannah.

...arry's will listed a 'wine cooler and ...ier table,' possibly identifying this ...ype of pier table. It is probable that ...he oval recess at the undertier was ...esigned to accommodate an oval ...ine cooler.

The American Classical style derives its name from its revival of Classical decorative motifs. It was based on archeological discoveries from Italy, Egypt and Greece.

The distinctive winged paw foot design is inspired from designs by Thomas Hope and "A Collection of Ornamental Designs after the Antique" by George Smith, 1812.

...fine Classical mahogany pier table, attributed to Joseph B Barry, with rectangular white marble slab on molded frieze with ...arved giltwood scrolls and supported on turned columns with brass caps, a framed mirror behind and oval niche beneath ...nset with marble, the whole on carved giltwood winged paw feet.

...1815

39.5in (100cm) wide

20,000-30,000 | **FRE**

A pair of satinwood and marquetry semi-elliptical pier tables, in the George III Neo-classical style, with rosewood and cross banding, each with radiating veneers centered with a fan, ribbons, foliage and anthemion, with simulated fluting to the frieze, on square tapering legs headed with paterae and with rounded inlaid collars.

48.75in (124cm) wide

£12,000-18,000 | **DN**

...pair of Classical mahogany marble-top pier tables, each with rectangular ogee ...olded top on conforming apron above scrolled supports painted with acanthus ...eafage and ornamented with applied giltwood gadrooning, and rectangular base ...ith sloping gadrooned skirt, mirror back, all raised on claw feet, the tables ...scribed "H.H." in pencil, refinished, corner of one marble top chipped.

43.5in (110.5cm) wide

22,000-28,000 | **FRE**

A Chippendale style mahogany and pine marble top table, two frieze drawers over a shaped skirt, cabriole legs with carved knees with ball and claw front feet and rear pad feet, alterations.

45in (114cm) wide

$2,400-2,800 | **SI**

A walnut console table, of canted rectangular form, with Sainte-Anne-des-Pyrenees type marble top, the base with a crossbanded frieze and central pendant carving, the cabriole legs topped with volutes, carved with scrolls and foliage, on scroll feet, possibly adapted from a George II Irish card table, the marble damaged.

Although this piece of furniture is possibly altered, the quality of carving and colour ensures desirability and value.

22.5in (57cm) wide

£3,500-4,500 | **DN**

...n early 19thC walnut console table, ...ith boxwood stringing, the grey marble ...op with rounded angles to the front ...bove a single frieze drawer over two ...crolling consoles with supports to the ...ear, raised on a shaped platform base ...ith curved brackets above carved paw ...eet to the front.

49.75in (126cm) wide

3,000-4,000 | **L&T**

A matched pair of Anglo-Indian rosewood pier tables, the white marble tops above ogee-molded gadrooned friezes, raised on two reeded scroll supports, with mirrored, paneled backs, ending on shaped plinth bases with carved scroll feet.

44.5in (113cm) wide

£8,000-12,000 | **SI**

A Federal style inlaid mahogany demi-lune console table with marble top, the skirt inlaid with eagle and shield and paterae joined by stringing raised on molded tapering lags.

29in (73.5cm) high

$800-1,200 | **SI**

A CLOSER LOOK AT A GEORGE III SIDE TABLE

This exceptional table came from a collection formed by the Hon. Daisy Fellowes and stood in the Small Dining Room in Donnington Grove from 1945-1991. It had been purchased by her in the early 20thC but was sold to her without any record of where it originally came from or who had designed it.

Provenance such as this is sometimes very important when it comes to determining the commercial value of a piece. In this instance, however, the sheer quality, originality and grandeur ensured substantial domestic and international interest when this table came up for auction.

The slabs and the bases of such tables are relatively fragile and it is not uncommon to find that the marble has been broken or the top and bottom are a later marriage. In this instance the good proportions and the flowing outline from top to base indicate that the two sections started life together. The specimen top would have been made in Italy, possibly in Florence or Rome, and is a rich collection of over 100 different varieties of marble and semiprecious hard stones including porphyry and lapis lazuli. A detail that lifts this top from other similar examples is the finely carved repeating flower-head motif that runs the length of the edge.

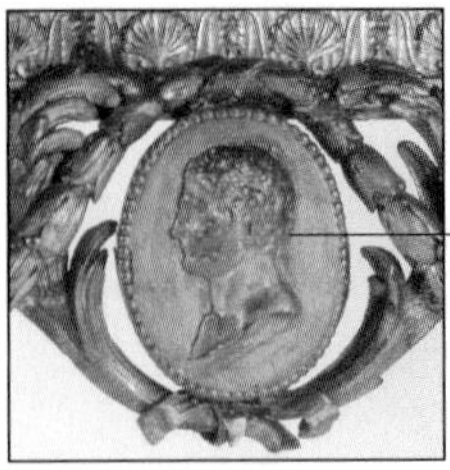

The carved and gilt wood base would hav been made in England in the 1760s. It is fine example of the Neoclassical style in th manner of Robert Adam (1728-1792) an Sir William Chambers (1723-1796) wh drew inspiration from the rediscovery an excavation of the Roman cities of Pompe and Herculaneum. This frieze notably include at its center a relief portrait medallion of Roman man, possibly an Emperor. The fa this is the sole asymmetrical detail in a otherwise wholly symmetric piece would ten to indicate that this table would original have been one of a pair of tables. Th matching table would have stood to the le with a similar central profile portra medallion, possibly of a woman, looking t the righ

The base was created by applying a th layer of gold leaf onto a layer of gesso whic covers the carved wood frame. It uncommon to find gilded or painted furnitu which retains its original color scheme. Th rooms in which they stand are subject changes of interior decoration and th furniture is sometimes repainted or regilde to bring it 'up to date', so tables like this ca have up to six different color layer

An early and rare George III gilt wood rectangular side table, the trellised specimen marble top on a white marble field above a flower-head carved and molded border, the base with a stiff leaf and bead bordered frieze with anthemion, S-scrolls and husks, above carved and pierced swags centered with an oval portrait medallion of a Roman Emperor, on six square tapering legs headed by palmettes in laurel wreaths, the legs with trailing floral swags hung from roundels, on block feet.

66.5in (169cm) wid

$600,000-900,000 **D**

A George III mahogany side table, the molded rectangular top above a frieze with central tablet and gadrooned molding, on fluted square chamfered legs.

53.5in (136cm) wide

$2,000-3,000 **L&T**

A George III mahogany side table, the rectangular verde antico marble top raised on base with Greek key frieze and cabriole legs with acanthus carving and claw and ball feet, alterations.

52.75in (134cm) wide

$7,000-10,000 **L&T**

A George III mahogany bowfront side table, with rosewood banding and boxwood stringing, drawers to the front, raised on square section tapering legs.

45.25in (115cm) wide

$2,000-2,500 **L&T**

An early 19thC mahogany side table, the two drawers with later ebonized turned handles, flanking a concave anc arched recess, on square tapering legs

44.75in (114cm) wic

$600-900 **D**

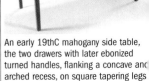

Lowboys

An American Queen Anne walnut cherry dressing table or low boy, having a rectangular top with notched corners and lip molding, one wide and three small drawers in case, the centermost of the smaller drawers fan carved, with shaped apron and two inverted acorn turned finials, cabriole legs on pad feet.

19.75in (50cm) wide

$9,000-11,000   **FRE**

A fine Queen Anne carved mahogany dressing table, the rectangular molded top with notched front corners above one long and three short drawers, flanked by fluted chamfered corners above a shaped skirt with central wavy shell pendant, the cabriole legs with acanthus-leaf carving on ball and claw feet.

c1750   *34.5in (87.5cm) wide*

$60,000-80,000   **FRE**

A New England Queen Anne walnut-veneered dressing table, quarter-veneered rectangular top above one long drawer with a fitted interior and three short drawers, a shaped apron below with pendant finials on cabriole legs ending in chamfered feet, back bears inscribed name, possibly "S. B. Warner", and printed celluloid label of "B. Altman & Co., New York", refinished, veneer repairs, replaced brasses.

32.5in (82.5cm) wide

A mahogany lowboy, the rectangular top with re-entrant front corners above three frieze drawers and a shaped apron on angular cabriole legs with pointed feet, in part mid-18thC but adapted.

31.5in (81cm) wide

$700-1,000   **DN**   **$17,000-20,000**   **FRE**

A Pennsylvanian Queen Anne walnut lowboy, the rectangular top with molded edge and notched frontal corners projecting above a case with fluted corners and a long over three short thumbmolded drawers, the shaped skirt on cabriole legs with shell carved knees and trifid feet.

36in (91.5cm) wide

$5,500-6,500   **NA**

A Delaware Valley Queen Anne walnut dressing table, the oblong top with rounded corners over a case with 4 short drawers retaining the original chased brasses, over a skirt with a central drop, supported by cabriole legs terminating in Spanish feet.

c1760   *30in (76cm) wide*

$22,000-28,000   **Pook**

A Napoleon III ebonized and gilt metal dressing table, three drawers inset with porcelain panels depicting putti, with fluted tapering legs.

43.5in (110.5cm) wide

$3,000-4,000   **SI**

A late 19thC Louis XV style kidney-shaped kingwood and parquetry combined dressing, writing and reading table, with a ratchet adjustable reading stand and a dressing mirror above a brushing slide with inset leather writing surface.

42.5in (108cm) wide

$3,000-4,000   **SI**

A Virginia Chippendale walnut dressing table, with a molded rectangular top over a frame with a single drawer supported by square beaded edge legs.

32.5in (82.5cm) wide

$3,500-4,500   **Pook**

Occasional Tables

A George III mahogany spider leg Sutherland table, the slender legs ring turned and terminating in baluster feet.

30.25in (77cm) long

$3,500-4,500   **FRE**

A Victorian walnut octagonal table, the top with a parquetry stylized star and a molded edge, on three turned supports with a central finial and three carved outswept legs with ceramic casters.

21.75in (55cm) diam

$600-800   **DN**

A Victorian walnut Sutherland table, the oval drop-leaf top on slender turned legs ending in casters.

29.5in (75cm) wide

$700-1,000   **SI**

A late 19thC French kingwood and parquetry bijouterie table, the hinged top opening to reveal a mirrored and velvet lined interior, with shaped frieze and slender cabriole legs.

15.75in (40cm) wide

$1,500-2,000   **FRE**

A Federal walnut dressing table, cheval mirror top over a two drawer over two drawer case, sulphide knobs, supported by a turned stretcher leg base.

36in (91.5cm) wide

$350-450   **AAC**

An Edwardian mahogany, satinwood crossbanded and boxwood strung rectangular bijouterie table, with a hinged glazed top and glazed sides on square tapering legs with an X-stretcher and spade feet.

18in (46cm) wide

$600-900   **DN**

A late 19thC Sheraton Revival satinwood table, the rectangular top with a raised border, and painted with tools and flowers, on square tapering legs with a shaped undertier.

16.25in (41cm) wide

$700-1,000   **DN**

A George III mahogany tripod table, the tilt-top on a baluster turned column, three cabriole legs and pad feet.

35.5in (90cm) diam

$700-1,000   **DN**

A George III mahogany tilt-top tripod table, turned column and tripod base.

20in (51cm) diam

$800-1,200   **SI**

A mahogany tripod table, dished tilt-top on a baluster turned column, cabriole legs, George III and later.

27in (69cm) wide

$300-400   **DN**

An early 19thC Empire mahogany and brass inlaid occasional table, top with inset marble and pierced brass gallery.

14.25in (36cm) diam

$700-1,000   **SI**

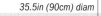

An early 19thC French provincial mahogany and oak tripod table, rounded rectangular top on slender stem and outswept base.

14in (35.5cm) wide

$500-700   **SI**

A George III-style tapestry inset tilt-top tripod table, top and base associated, alterations.

21in (53cm) wide

$300-400   **SI**

A George IV elm and fruitwood tripod table, turned stem on in swept tripod base.

24in (61cm) diam

$800-1,200   **SI**

A 19thC Ceylonese rosewood occasional table, profusely inlaid, the circular top centered by monogram "CPH", raised on turned and spirally reeded pedestal and three carved scrolling legs.

30in (76cm) diam

$1,500-2,000   **L&T**

A Victorian satin birch table, the round top with a molded edge, inlaid with a central star in specimen timbers, on a turned column and a triform base with bun feet.

17.5in (44cm) diam

$800-1,200   **DN**

A pair of Victorian mahogany wine tables, each with thumbnail rim and circular top above ring turned pedestal with spirally fluted knop and tripod base with carved cabriole legs terminating in ball and claw feet.

27.25in (69cm) diam

$3,000-4,000   **L&T**

An adjustable Victorian mahogany and iron occasional table, the circular top with molded edge raised on cast iron base with spirally reeded column and four scrolling feet with paw terminals and casters.

The proportions of this piece of furniture would suggest that it may be a marriage as the top is clearly too small for the base and the combination of wrought iron and mahogany in this configuration is incongruous.

19.75in (50cm) diam

$400-600   **L&T**

A late 19thC giltwood and porcelain occasional table, the top inset with a porcelain panel depicting a romantic scene of angels, the acanthus carved column support on conforming cabriole scroll legs.

20in (51cm) diam

$2,500-3,000   **SI**

A pair of 19thC European walnut octagonal occasional tables, the radiating veneered tops raised on faceted column supports, ending in four hipped saber legs.

30in (76cm) high

$1,200-1,800 SI

Writing-Library Tables

A late George III mahogany fireside writing table, with leather inset top and silk upholstered face screen, fitted with a single frieze drawer on square tapering legs with brass casters.

29in (43.5cm) wide

$2,500-3,000 FRE

A Regency bird's-eye maple and ebony strung writing box on stand, hinged slope with a leather inset, a cedar-lined side drawer with a brass inset handle, C-scroll stretcher and splayed feet.

15in (38cm) wide

$2,200-2,800 DN

A George IV rosewood rectangular writing table, the slope top with an inset skiver and rounded corners, the frieze with two side drawers and bead and reel borders, on an adjustable spirally reeded baluster column and four reeded and stiff leaf carved outswept legs with casters, lacking the book rest.

19.75in (50cm) wide

$4,000-6,000 DN

A good George IV rosewood and brass strung and inlaid library table, the rectangular top crossbanded in rosewood and yew, with rounded corners, above two cedar lined frieze drawers opposing false drawers and paneled sides all with nulled borders, with plain end supports and a straight stretcher, on outswept leaf carved legs with gilt metal terminals cast with a shell and stylized leaves and casters, the embossed brass border to the frieze of a later date, lacking some brass inlay.

54in (137cm) wide

$10,000-15,000 DN

A George IV rosewood writing table, the rectangular top with rounded corners, leather insets and central adjustable writing slope, above three frieze drawers and tapering end supports with pierced panels, brackets, roundels and a turned stretcher, on plinth ends and bun feet.

34in (86.5cm) wide

$1,000-1,500 DN

A William IV oak and pollard oak rectangular table, the top with rounded corners and a plain frieze on end supports and a stretcher with stylized flower-heads, plinth bases and scroll feet.

41.5in (105.5cm) wide

$1,800-2,200 DN

A Victorian mahogany library table, the rounded rectangular top with leather writing surface above two drawers and two false drawers, on vase-shaped end supports, joined by a turned stretcher, on bar bases with bun feet fitted with casters.

57.75in (147cm) wide

$700-1,000 L&T

A George IV mahogany writing table, the top with a reeded edge and rounded corners above two short drawers on ring turned tapering legs with brass terminals and casters.

40.5in (103cm) wide

$2,500-3,000 DN

An early Victorian mahogany rectangular writing table, the crossbanded top with molded border and leather inset above two frieze drawers opposing false drawers on turned tapering legs with brass terminals and casters.

53.25in (135cm) wide

$1,500-2,000 DN

A 19thC mahogany library desk, the rectangular top with molded edge and rounded angles, inset modern skiver above six opposing paneled drawers, on turned tapering legs with brass caps and casters.

59.75in (152cm) wide

$2,500-3,000 L&T

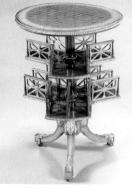

A late 19thC French mahogany book stand, with gilt metal mounts, the round top with cross-hatched inlay and kingwood bands, above two revolving tiers with pierced divisions on a tripod base, with leaf cast terminals.

17.75in (45cm) diam

$3,000-3,500   **DN**

A Victorian amboyna, ebony and ebonised jardinière, of rectangular form with rounded ends, the cover enclosing a metal liner with a concave molded edge above a frieze, set with green jasper type round plaques with classical figures on fluted turned tapering legs with ceramic casters and a shaped X-stretcher.

35.5in (90cm) wide

$2,500-3000   **DN**

A late 19thC French rosewood, beech and tulipwood jardinière, with gilt metal mounts, the oval cover with lattice inlay and two handles, the base with a pierced gallery on cabriole legs with a shaped undertier.

21.25in (54cm) wide

$600-900   **DN**

An Edwardian mahogany cocktail cabinet, the divided hinged rectangular top enclosing rising interior with crystal decanters and glasses, and cigarette box, on square section tapered legs with brass caps and casters.

23.25in (59cm) wide

$800-1,200   **L&T**

Washstands

A George III mahogany and boxwood strung bow-front corner washstand, the top with central hole flanked by two sunken saucers and arched splashbacks, above shelf with central drawer flanked by false drawers, the splayed square section legs joined by shaped stretcher.

24in (61cm) wide

$450-550   **L&T**

A Mid-Atlantic States Federal mahogany inlaid washstand, squared cover with reeded edge lifts to reveal a conforming top fitted with an opening for a bowl and two removable shallow mahogany cups, on squared legs joined by a medial shelf with an inlaid drawer.

c1800   *14in (35.5cm) wide*

$350-450   **FRE**

An American Classical tiger maple washstand.

c1830   *32.5in (82.5cm) wide*

$1,500-2,000   **SI**

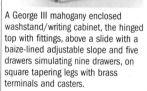

A George III mahogany enclosed washstand/writing cabinet, the hinged top with fittings, above a slide with a baize-lined adjustable slope and five drawers simulating nine drawers, on square tapering legs with brass terminals and casters.

28in (71cm) wide

$800-1,200   **DN**

A Regency mahogany washstand, in the manner of Gillows, the marble top with three-quarter mahogany gallery, above three frieze drawers on reeded tapering legs ending in brass caps and casters.

$1,800-2,200   **L&T**

A William IV mahogany washstand, the shaped three-quarter gallery with roundels above a marble top, the two frieze drawers with turned handles on turned and reeded tapering legs.

45.25in (115cm) wide

37in (94cm) wide

$400-600   **DN**

An early 19thC mahogany washstand, the rectangular top with deep three-quarter splashback incorporating shelf, above deep frieze and turned tapering legs joined by shaped undershelf.

30in (76cm) wide

$700-1,000   **L&T**

Miniature Furniture

A mahogany miniature highboy, having a flat molded crest rail, four graduated wide drawers above, base with wide drawer on square cabriole legs and square pad feet.

18.5in (47cm) high

$450-550   **FRE**

A New England miniature slope-front desk, in Chippendale style, the case with a hinged lid opening to fitted interior, above three graduated drawers with molded edges over bracket feet, the case with extensive repairs, restorations and replacements.

21.5in (54.5cm) wide

$1,900-2,100   **FRE**

A Classical style miniature mahogany open armchair, bears label to the underside, "James B.... Washington, DC".

500-800   S

A miniature Sheraton mahogany chest of drawers, four graduated drawers, paneled sides, turned legs, original hardware, veneer loss.

15.5in (39.5cm) wide

$1,800-2,200   **AAC**

A miniature Chippendale walnut chest, molded top over two short and three long drawers, flanked by columns resting on spurred ogee bracket feet.

12in (30.5cm) wide

$1,500-2,000   **AAC**

A 19thC miniature cabinet chest, pair of glazed doors above an arrangement of five drawers, raised on bun feet.

15.25in (38.5cm) wide

$350-450   S

A miniature inlaid walnut chest of drawers, the molded top on case with three drawers, each with string inlay on a shaped bracket foot, some restoration.

14in (35.5cm) wide

$220-280   **SI**

A miniature birds-eye maple chest with bamboo turnings and marble top.

8in (20cm) high

$300-400   **SI**

An early 19thC Mid-Atlantic States inlaid walnut watch stand, in the form of a miniature tallcase clock, the upper section surmounted by arched pediment and the lower section with a drawer, raised on ball feet.

15in (38cm) high

$1,500-2,000   **SI**

A Louis XV style miniature vitrine, green painted with flowers, single bevelled glass door with mirror back glass shelves, rich gilt metal mounts.

14.25in (36cm) high

$800-1,200   **FR**

A set of mahogany chemist's drawers, comprising four rows of seven drawers with black-on-gilt mirrored labels and faceted glass handles.

78in (198cm) wide

$2,200-2,800   **L&T**

An American 19thC inlaid and painted walnut sailor's box, the cover inlaid with a compass star and roses painted in green and pink, the sides inlaid with reserves depicting Neptune, the front with an eagle escutcheon and a fan, the interior fitted with compartments, one with the cover inscribed "From WW.H.K TO K.A.S", on a later table base.

16in (40.5cm) wide

$1,100-1,500   **SI**

A New England Hepplewhite birch pencil post bedstead in red paint, the chamfered posts on square tapering legs, the flat headboard with half-moon cut-out sides.

52.5in (133.5cm) wide

$6,000-8,000   **NA**

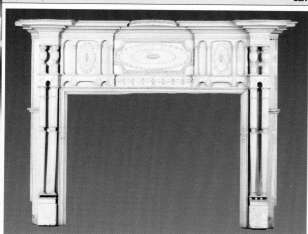

A New York Federal carved and white painted mantel surround, the shaped shelf above fireplace surround with carved elliptical paterae and drapery swag.

63in (160cm) high

$7,500-8,500   **NA**

An American Sheraton mahogany and rosewood veneer pianoforte with ormolu mounts, the lid above a five octave ivory keyboard, the case with rosewood banding and embossed brass band with rosettes, on cylindrical tapering ribbed legs with brass collars and ferrules with casters.

68in (172cm) wide

$4,000-6,000   **NA**

An Edwardian mahogany and boxwood strung and inlaid oval tray, with a shaped border and brass handles, now converted to a low table.

26.75in (68cm) wide

$400-600   **DN**

A mahogany butler's tray on stand, in George III style, three-quarter gallery back with pierced carrying handles on frame base.

37in (94cm) wide

$400-600   **SI**

A Victorian 'tole peint' tray, painted overall with exotic birds and scrolls around an urn of flowers on a bronzed ground.

21.25in (54cm) wide

$600-900   **DN**

A Victorian papier mâché tea tray, of typical form, with later stylized bamboo stand, some repairs to tray.

25in (63.5cm) wide

$600-900   **FRE**

An unusual mid- to late 19thC French painted tin and ormolu bread basket, the tray painted with figures fishing in a river landscape, the bronze stand with reeded decoration and supported on hoofed feet.

17.5in (44.5cm) wide

$700-1,000   **FRE**

Candlesticks

A late 17thC pair of English brass trumpet candlesticks, with circular bases and mid-drip pans, repairs.

8in (20cm) high

$3,000-4,000   **Pook**

A mid-17thC English brass trumpet candlestick, with a wide dome base, sausage-turned shaft and round top.

6.25in (16cm) high

$2,500-3,000   **Pook**

A mid-17thC English brass trumpet candlestick, with a raised circular base, sausage-turned shaft with mid-drip pan and circular top.

7.5in (19cm) high

$3,500-4,500   **Pook**

A pair of French champlevé-enameled candlesticks, by Barbedienne, signed on edge of base "F. Barbedienne".

8in (20cm) high

$500-700   **DN**

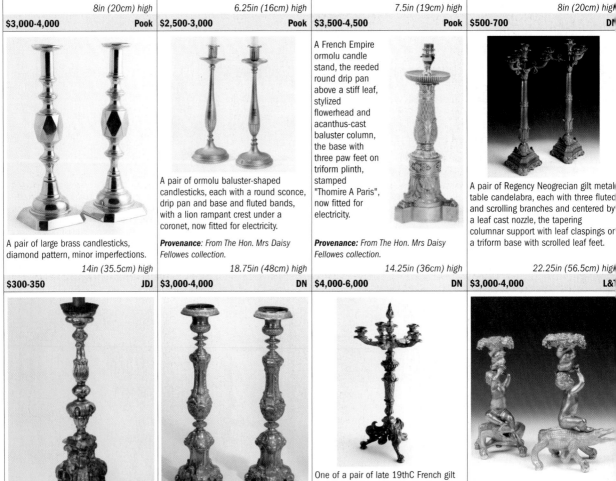

A pair of large brass candlesticks, diamond pattern, minor imperfections.

14in (35.5cm) high

$300-350   **JDJ**

A pair of ormolu baluster-shaped candlesticks, each with a round sconce, drip pan and base and fluted bands, with a lion rampant crest under a coronet, now fitted for electricity.

Provenance: From The Hon. Mrs Daisy Fellowes collection.

18.75in (48cm) high

$3,000-4,000   **DN**

A French Empire ormolu candle stand, the reeded round drip pan above a stiff leaf, stylized flowerhead and acanthus-cast baluster column, the base with three paw feet on triform plinth, stamped "Thomire A Paris", now fitted for electricity.

Provenance: From The Hon. Mrs Daisy Fellowes collection.

14.25in (36cm) high

$4,000-6,000   **DN**

A pair of Regency Neogrecian gilt metal table candelabra, each with three fluted and scrolling branches and centered by a leaf cast nozzle, the tapering columnar support with leaf claspings on a triform base with scrolled leaf feet.

22.25in (56.5cm) high

$3,000-4,000   **L&T**

An 18thC Italian silvered wood altar-type candlestick, with carved detail and triform base, now fitted for electricity, some damage.

23in (58cm) high

$350-400   **DN**

A pair of 19thC Italian brass pricket candlesticks, with embossed acanthus and shell decoration, raised on triform bases with scroll feet.

36in (91.5cm) high

$1,500-2,000   **FRE**

One of a pair of late 19thC French gilt metal six-light candelabra, the branches and knopped stems cast with stylized foliage, on tripod legs with conforming decoration and lion masks suspending shells, claw feet, removable flame finials.

c1890   20.75in (53cm) high

$400-600 (pair)   **BonS**

A pair of gilt brass candelabra, each with a putto supporting a sconce in the form of a cornucopia, and resting on a crocodile.

8.5in (22cm) high

$300-400   **L&T**

A bronzed and gilt metal colza-type light fitting, of triform with flame finial, reservoir, masks anthemion and a leaf pendant finial, with suspension chains and leaf boss.

16.25in (41cm) wide

$4,000-6,000 — DN

A 19thC Rococo-style ormolu chandelier, cast overall with acanthus scrolls, with a central baluster column, vine-scrolling branches and a pendant husk.

25.5in (65cm) high

$4,000-6,000 — DN

A Regency-style gilt and patinated candelabra, the body of flattened saucer form, eight branches formed as swans each with single nozzle and drip tray, link chains and ceiling boss.

23.5in (60cm) high

$1,000-1,500 — L&T

A 20thC porcelain-mounted gilt metal five-light chandelier, modeled as a basket issuing flowering branches.

20in (51cm) diam

$700-1,000 — SI

A pair of 20thC silver-plated four-light small chandeliers, baluster-form standard and scrolling candle arms.

12in (30.5cm) high

$700-1,000 (pair) — SI

An Italian 18thC-style carved giltwood six-branch chandelier, the triform support carved with drapery, terminating in six S-scroll molded branches, with an acorn finial below.

35in (89cm) high

$2,200-2,800 — SI

A Gothic leaded-glass hall light, the tall conical top with foliate motifs and fluted vents, leaded panes of amber and white frosted glass, wrought strapwork and pierced banding.

27.25in (69cm) high

$350-400 — DN

A cutglass and gilt metal mounted ceiling light, with an anthemion pierced band and rams' masks, above reeded bands and hobnail-cut decoration, with a pendant finial.

21.25in (54cm) high

$4,000-6,000 — DN

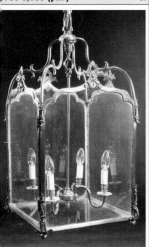

A brass hall lantern, the four branches within glazed and arched sides with cartouche crests, suspended by brass scrolls.

31.5in (80cm) high

$5,000-7,000 — DN

Wall Lamps

One of a set of four giltwood wall lights, each with a foliate and urn crest and two scrolling wall branches, fitted for electricity.

16.5in (42cm) high

$2,200-2,800 (set) — DN

Two of a set of four Louis XVI-style ormolu wall sconces, each with swagged urn with flame finial, two scrolled branches suspending cloth cast swags, with urn sconces, on tapering pierced back plate with leafy terminal.

18.5in (47cm) high

$5,000-7,000 (set) — L&T

A set of four giltwood and ebonized two-branch wall lights, each with a floral crest, foliate scroll and fluted branches, and a lobed and oak leaf pendant finial.

13.5in (34.5cm) high

$1,200-1,800 (set) — DN

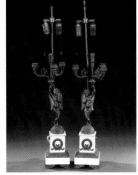

A pair of early 19thC French Empire gilt-bronze and onyx three-light candelabra, mounted as table lamps.

23.25in (59cm) high

$3,000-4,000 SI

A pair of French Sienna marble and bronze table lamps, each with triform base, tapering column, four sconces.

c1920 *36in (91.5cm) high*

$2,500-3,000 FRE

A small Victorian Corinthian column oil lamp, by Frederick Bradford McCrea, detachable silver part-fluted reservoir.

c1896 *19.75in (50cm) high*

$1,500-2,000 DN

A pair of brass lamp bases, each as two leaf-capped fluted columns, on a green marble base, fitted for electricity.

11in (28cm) hig[h]

$600-900 D[N]

A pair of European gilt metal-mounted table lamps, each with a Corinthian capital and octagonal tapering column, on a stepped square star-cut base.

17.5in (44cm) high

$3,000-4,000 DN

A 20thC French bronze and crystal lamp, the vase-form cut crystal standard with bronze borders and scroll handles, a square pedestal base with crystal rosettes, molded foot-rim.

15.75in (40cm) high

$600-900 FRE

A pair of brass, marble and glass lamps, the first, a sinumbra lamp, the second a solar lamp, each with a baluster-form etched and cutglass shade and lusters, marble base.

c1830 *33.5in (85cm) high*

$3,000-4,000 FRE

A kerosene pull-down library or dining room lamp, brass frame, decorated shade ring, milk glass shade with enameled flowers, brass smoke bell, restoration.

12in (30.5cm) diar[n]

$300-400 JD[J]

A pair of late 19thC Chinese famille rose porcelain and gilt bronze five-light candelabra, each with four foliate scroll arms terminating in urn-form candle cups, mounted as table lamps.

22.5in (57cm) high

$3,000-4,000 SI

A porcelain banquet lamp base, hand decorated with applied flowers, painted flowers and gold trim, base marked with blue crossed arrows, minor damage, lamp converted for electricity.

20in (51cm) high

$200-300 JDJ

A cut overlay lamp base, the white cut to cranberry body rests on a brass stem with marble base, probably made originally as an electric lamp, collar replaced, marked "5-66397".

13in (33cm) high

$1,500-2,000 JDJ

A brass fire trumpet now mounted as a lamp, sold with a hand-colored lithographic appointment to Fire Department of City of New York.

c1863

$700-1,000 S[I]

A 20thC gilt bronze Bouillotte lamp, with red tole shade.

23.75in (60cm) high

$1,000-1,500 SI

Two of a set of four Regency silvered metal colza lamps, each with ovoid reservoir with leaf cast covers and applied Grecian masks to the sides, with twin projecting burners, raised above a turned socle on cylindrical green marbled collars on turned and faceted marble plinths.

11in (28cm) hig[h]

$4,000-6,000 (set) L&

BOXES

BOXES HAVE ALWAYS BEEN A POPULAR COLLECTING AREA, simply because of the range and diversity offered. A variety of materials were used including wood, tortoiseshell, mother-of-pearl, gold and silver. They were made for various purposes such as containers for perfume bottles, vanity boxes, tea caddies, decanter boxes and writing boxes.

Tea was first introduced to England from China in the mid-17thC and became popular during the late 18thC. It was an expensive commodity and so tea caddies were made to keep the leaves fresh. They are generally shaped like small chests and contain three metal canisters. The earliest examples were fashioned in walnut, although these are rare and it is more common to find those made in mahogany. It is unusual to find a caddy complete with its original canisters, and these will be of more value.

Writing boxes are an appealing area for collecting because they can actually be used for their original purpose. They open to reveal a removable compartment for inkwells, pens, sand, seals and wax, and a bottom compartment for storing paper. They are generally rectangular in shape and have a folded surface for writing which would have been covered in felt, velvet or leather.

Key things to look for when buying an antique box are good patination and original fittings. Also carved details and nice decoration will increase the value. Damage to veneers, inlay and hinges will decrease value.

Tea Caddies

An 18thC burr-walnut tea caddy, with feather-banded decoration, the domed hinged lid with swan-neck carrying handle enclosing a divided interior, some losses, above plain sides.

10.25in (26cm) wide

$4,500-5,500　　　　**L&T**

A George III satinwood two-compartment tea caddy, oblong with kingwood edge bandings and box line inlay, the top, four sides and interior marqueterie-inlaid with fan medallions and leaves.

c1790　　　　　　　*8in (20cm) wide*

$2,200-2,800　　　　**BonS**

A late 18thC Sheraton-style two-sectional tea caddy, the top set with two sets of circular fan inlay, burr wood corners and cross banding.

7in (18cm) wide

$300-400　　　　**D**

A George III boxwood-strung and rosewood-inlaid tea caddy of rectangular box form, the interior with two lidded canisters flanking a cut glass mixing bowl.

c1790　　　　　　*14in (36cm) wide*

$400-600　　　　**BonS**

A late 18thC two-sectional tea caddy, the top with quarter veneers of walnut and having central burr wood medallion to center with thin line chequering to edge, the pattern repeated to front, sides and back, base metal handle and escutcheon to front, the lid opening to reveal two sections inside, lids missing.

7in (17.5cm) wide

$300-400　　　　**D**

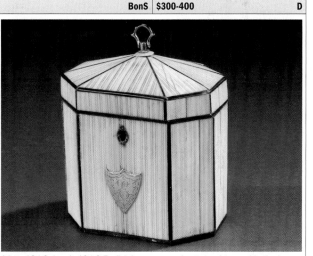

A late 18thC / early 19thC English ivory-veneered octagonal tea caddy, the ivory carved with reeding, with tortoiseshell stringing and a monogrammed shield-form reserve.

Provenance: *Property of a Virginia Estate.*

5in (12.5cm) wide

$1,800-2,000　　　　**SI**

A mahogany sarcophagus-shaped tea caddy, converted to hold letters.

c1810

$120-180   BonS

An early 19thC mother-of-pearl serpentine-fronted two-sectional tea caddy, of castle form, the top opening to reveal ivory facings with carved finials of mother-of-pearl encrusted lids, those lifting to reveal zinc-lined interior, some mother-of-pearl missing.

8in (20cm) wide

$1,000-1,500   D

An early 19thC tortoiseshell and mother-of-pearl tea caddy, the hinged pagoda lid enclosing a divided interior with two lids, above paneled front and spreading base, with squat bun feet.

7.25in (18.5cm)

$1,200-1,800   L&T

An early 19thC Regency satin birch tea caddy, rectangular with ebony banding and metal mounts, enclosing two covered containers and a glass bowl.

11.75in (30cm) long

$600-900   SI

A William IV rosewood sarcophagus-shaped tea caddy, with fitted interior and glass mixing bowl.

$120-180   D

A first half 19thC Chinese carved ivory and silver-mounted tea caddy, the hinged lid enclosing two canisters and a spoon, the panels elaborately carved and pierced and set before red silk, minor faults.

6.5in (16.5cm) long

$6,000-8,000   WW

An early 19thC English ivory-mounted tortoiseshell-veneered tea caddy, with silvered-copper ball feet, escutcheon and monogrammed reserve, the interior with two covered compartments.

6.75in (17cm)

$1,800-2,200   SI

A 19thC satin birch tea caddy, with brass inset handle and fitted interior.

$220-280   D

A 19thC Chinese gilt-decorated brown lacquer tea caddy, the interior with two pewter canisters with covers.

9.5in (24cm) wide

$1,000-1,500   SI

A 19thC Chinese gilt decorated black lacquer tea caddy, octagonal on paw feet and painted with figural reserves, the interior with two pewter canisters with covers and bone finials.

Provenance: Property of a Virginia Estate.

7.75in (19.5cm) wide

$1,000-1,500   **SI**

A tortoiseshell-covered box, the mirrored tortoiseshell repeat-over lid and two sides having base metal lozenge to top opening to reveal two-sectional tea caddy with central mixing bowl within.

12in (30.5cm) wide

$300-400   **D**

Caskets

A Russian pierced and engraved ivory box, of rectangular form with a stepped lid, the wood box overlaid with ivory pierced work and panels, the whole incised with vines, floral and geometric patterns stained green and ochre, raised on four feet.

c1800   *8.75in (22.5cm) long*

$150-200   **SI**

A coromandel dome-top letter box, applied with a gilt metal 'cable', fretted escutcheon and spandrels, the top with a conforming panel inset with a Wedgwood-style plaque.

c1840   *8.75in (22cm) wide*

$400-600   **BonS**

A 19thC Georgian-style miniature casket, painted to the lid with the ruins of Dean Castle, the body with painted restication and brass clasps to the angles, on plinth with shaped bracket feet, the escutcheon engraved "Jas Boyd 1818", the interior painted with rhyme to the lid and fitted with trays.

11.5in (29cm) wide

$700-1,000   **L&T**

A 19thC brass-mounted mahogany chest with the brass reserve engraved "Harmonie de Charles D.", probably a travelling case for a musical instrument.

5.5in (64.5cm) wide

$800-1,200   **SI**

A fine Victorian burr walnut and brass-mounted casket, with silk-lined interior.

$300-350   **D**

A second half 19thC mother-of-pearl inlaid gilt and paint decorated papier-mâché box, the cover painted with two men, their horses and hounds returning from a stag hunt, opening to a compartmented interior.

Provenance: Property of a Virginia Estate.

$300-400   **SI**

A Continental ivory casket, with floral vine and black-enameled banded decoration, the hinge-top enclosing lift-out tray and multiple compartments.

13in (33cm) long

$1,200-1,800   **SI**

A Continental inlaid satinwood casket, decorated with scenic panels depicting Classical subjects.

12in (30.5cm) long

$3,500-4,500   **SI**

An Edwardian silver, enamel and watercolor presentation box, by Robinson &Co., Birmingham, the oblong box mounted with two enamel shields, an enamel banner inscribed "INTUS SI RECTE NE LABORA", and four watercolor miniatures of English institutions and scrolls on laurel branches, the conforming cover with a scrolling handle centring on the monogram "WHM", on an oak base and lined with purple silk.

1906   *13in (33cm) long*

$3,000-4,000   **SI**

A late 19thC Napoleon III gilt and silvered bronze and onyx casket, rectangular with tapering cover, with inset onyx panels and elaborate mounts including putti at the front corners, a grotesque mask escutcheon, scroll handle with putto head terminals and flowering cornucopia, the interior padded and lined in pink fabric.

14.5in (37cm) wide

$2,200-2,800   **SI**

An Austrian silver gilt Renaissance-style jewel casket, elaborately encrusted with cabochon garnets and turquoise with miniature sculptures of knights at each corner, the all-over chased floral design shows remnants of white and blue enamel, the jeweled handle features two knight's heads.

5in (12.5cm) wide

$4,000-6,000   **JDJ**

TUNBRIDGEWARE

Tunbridge Wells, a spa town in the South East of England, has become famous for its Tunbridgeware. It was first made by local woodworkers to sell as souvenirs to visitors to the wells. These small wooden domestic objects were decorated with patterns created from complicated mosaics of colored woods. The technique was first used from the late 17thC, but Tunbridgeware was predominantly produced from the 1830s until the end of the 19thC.

The Wise family (c1746-1876) and the Burrows family (from c1740) were two of the earliest specialists in making Tunbridgeware. James Burrows invented the tessellated mosaic technique in c1820, which is characterized by designs composed of minute square tesserae. Later manufacturers were William Fenner (1790-1840), Edmund Nye (1836-1851), Thomas Barton (1870-1903), Henry Hollamby (1842-1891), Boyce,

Brown & Kemp (1873-1923), and the Tunbridge Wells Manufacturing Company (1923-1926) which was the last company to produce this 300 year old art.

Tunbridgeware appealed to Victorian tastes and quickly grew in popularity, making it a very profitable industry. Decoration included bandings and panels of foliage, flowers, topographical views, geometric patterns, animals and figures. Articles included stamp boxes, sewing implements, workboxes, picture frames and tables.

When buying Tunbridgeware it is important to check for damage. Pieces are prone to warping and the mosaics occasionally lift, which will greatly decrease the value. Check for good bold coloring and interesting subjects. It is always a bonus if an item has its original label, particularly if it is attributed to one of the aforementioned manufacturers.

An early 19thC Tunbridgeware sarcophagus-shaped whitewood work box, the top with perspective cube and pen work crossbanding, the sides with boxwood strung rosewood panels.

7in (18cm) long

$300-400　　　　**B**

A Tunbridgeware rosewood tea caddie, probably by Burrows, the top with stylized flower and scroll panel within half square cross banding, the sides inlaid alternating bands of beetles and moths within checkered stringing, the interior with two half square mosaic lidded boxes in unrestored condition.

c1840　　　　*11.75in (30cm) long*

$1,200-1,800　　　　**B**

A 19thC walnut Tunbridgeware banded box, with fitted interior.

$70-100　　　　**D**

A 19thC walnut and Tunbridgeware banded stationary box, with interior tray and concealed writing slope.

$80-120　　　　**D**

A 19thC Tunbridgeware and parquetry-top workbox.

$180-220　　　　**D**

A 19thC semidomed top walnut and Tunbridgeware banded toiletry box, with internal compartments, tray and manicure items.

$300-400　　　　**D**

A 19thC Tunbridgeware and walnut ladies vanity case or writing box, with fitted interior.

$300-400　　　　**D**

A Victorian walnut Tunbridgeware stationery box, the domed top inlaid with a view of a ruined abbey within a mosaic border, the curved sides with a band of flowers and foliage.

c1870   8.25in (21.5cm) wide

$800-1,200   **BonS**

A Tunbridgeware rosewood tea caddie, the top inlaid with tesserae wood anemones within geometric tesserae crossbanding, possibly by Barton.

4.75in (12cm) high

$180-220   **B**

An early to mid-19thC Tunbridge-ware rosewood and sycamore banded glove box, possibly by Barton, locked.

10in (25cm) wide

$220-280   **B**

A Tunbridgeware maple stationary box, by Henry Hollamby, the cylindrical top with tesserae rose spray within tesserae crossbanding, the sides with broad rose and scroll border, the underside with rare Hollamby paper label, complete with key.

Henry Hollamby set up his own Tunbridgeware business in 1842. By about 1880 he was the largest manufacturer in Tunbridge Wells. He is famous for his large views of buildings such as Herstmonceux Castle and Shakespeare's birthplace.

6.25in (16cm) long

$1,000-1,500   **B**

A Tunbridgeware ebony cribbage box, possibly by Barton, the top with perspective cube tablet between cribbage markers, the sides with distinctive rose and scroll border banding.

Thomas Barton is the most famous manufacturer of Tunbridgeware. His work is easy to recognize because of the woods that he used. He used coromandel and ebony as a background and oak that had been stained green. His work is often labeled with his name or occasionally "Formerly of Nye". He took over the Nye workshop shortly before the death of Edmund Nye. In 1864 Barton was awarded first prize in the First Class for skilled manufacture at the Tunbridge Wells Industrial Exhibition. In 1903 he died and the business ended.

7.75in (20cm) long

$400-600   **B**

A Tunbridgeware rosewood box, by Thomas Barton, the cushion-shaped top with perspective cube panel within stylized tesserae crossbanding, the base with torn label, the maker's name and address clearly visible.

8.75in (22cm) long

$350-400   **B**

A Tunbridgeware circular snuff box, the lid with tesserae and half-square mosaic, part of lid rim missing.

3.25in (8cm) diam

$220-280   **B**

A Tunbridgeware rosewood stamp box, the lid with printed Queen Victoria half penny stamp, within tesserae crossbanding.

1.75in (4.5cm) long

$220-280   **B**

A Tunbridgeware rosewood handkerchief box, the pin hinged lid with tesserae panel of a standing stag, within stylized tesserae cross banding, with turned ivory handle.

6in (15.5cm) long

$300-400   **B**

A Tunbridgeware satin birch caddie, the top with perspective cube panel within geometric tesserae crossbanding, the sides with tesserae rose banding, the interior with lidded zinc-lined division, faults to lock.

5.25in (13.5cm) high

$150-200   **B**

A Tunbridgeware oak tea caddie, the domed cover inlaid rose bouquet within geometric tesserae crossbanding, the sides with scrolling leaf and berry banding, the interior with two lidded divisions, some faults.

8.5in (21.5cm) high

$300-400   **B**

A Tunbridgeware rosewood work box, the top with view of Eridge Castle within tesserae mosaic bands, the sides with broad Van Dyke bands, the interior complete with seven stickware cotton reels, a tape measure thimble and needle wallet, all standing on rosewood bun feet.

11.25in (28.5cm) long

$1,800-2,200   **B**

An early Tunbridgeware whitewood sewing clamp, the cylindrical body painted with stylized leaves and printed with a view of Brighton Pavilion.

7.5in (19cm) high

$400-600   **B**

A Tunbridgeware drum-shaped tape measure, with eight point star top.

1.5in (4cm) high

$180-220   **B**

A scarce novelty Tunbridgeware whitewood sewing companion, in the form of a Brighton Pavilion, the onion-shaped lid enclosing various fittings, the base penned with arcaded doors, the fish scale roof and circular stepped base split.

7.75in (19.5cm) high

$1,000-1,500   **B**

A Tunbridgeware cylindrical sewing companion, with stickware collars.

1.5in (4cm) high

$60-90   **B**

A novelty Tunbridgeware stickware pin wheel, modeled as a kettle with pin cushion cover and bone handle, the spout damaged, and the foot chipped.

1.75in (4.5cm) high

$180-220   **B**

A Tunbridgeware bird's-eye maple silk skein holder, the top with scrolling tesserae leaf panel, the sides with tesserae mosaic bands.

88.5in (225cm) long

$400-600   **B**

A Tunbridgeware stickware bottle case.

2.25in (5.5cm) high

$150-200   **B**

A Tunbridgeware view of the Pantiles, attributed to Henry Hollamby, in tesserae frame.

7in (18cm) x 9in (23cm)

$700-1,000   **B**

A Tunbridgeware photograph frame, with canted tesserae mosaic borders.

7.75in (19.5cm) long

$300-400   **B**

A late 19thC marqueterie and Tunbridgeware gilt-metal mounted jardinière, with tole liner.

16.5in (42cm) long

$400-600   **SI**

A CLOSER LOOK AT A TUNBRIDGEWARE TABLE

Larger Tunbridgeware commands a premium.

A perfect piece with little damage and a complicated design could be up to three times the value of a less impressive piece.

Damage will always severely affect the value because Tunbridgeware is extremely difficult to restore.

Any piece by one of the famous makers commands a premium. This piece may have been made by Wise. The Wise family began their business in the middle of the 18thC and subsequent generations produced various Tunbridgeware using traditional methods of turnery and scorched inlay.

A Tunbridgeware rosewood wine table, possibly by Wise, the rectangular top with marble, half square and Van Dyke borders damage in two corners due to the carcase moving, on octagonal stem and quatrefoil shaped base, with turned bun feet.

20in (51cm) square top

$3,000-4,000   **B**

A Tunbridgeware note book, one cover with perspective cube and the other with flowers, bound by a replacement pencil.

3.5in (8.5cm) long

$220-280   **B**

A Tunbridgeware ebony book cover, by Edmund Nye or Thomas Barton, the center rose spray on white sycamore ground within stylized cross and flower crossbanding, complete with spine.

11.5in (29cm) long

$400-600   **B**

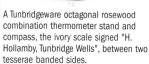

A Tunbridgeware octagonal rosewood combination thermometer stand and compass, the ivory scale signed "H. Hollamby, Tunbridge Wells", between two tesserae banded sides.

5in (12.5cm) high

$600-900   **B**

Bottles

A bottle, with unusual deep kick up.

6in (15.5cm) high

$800-1,200 CamA

An English squat onion bottle, of early form.

c1690 *5in (13cm) high*

$800-1,200 CamA

An English onion wine bottle.

c1700

$800-1,200 CamA

An onion wine bottle, found in Scots cellar.

c1715 *7.5in (19cm) high*

$600-900 CamA

An early English mallet bottle, transitional form.

c1725 *7in (18cm) high*

$400-600 CamA

An English mallet wine bottle.

c1730 *8in (20.5cm) high*

$400-600 CamA

A glass bottle, from an unknown wreck, probably Dutch.

c1730-1750 *7.75in (19.5cm) high*

$300-400 R&GM

An American mallet bottle.

c1740 *8in (20.5cm) high*

$400-600 CamA

A tall English cylinder bottle.

c1780 *10.25in (26cm) high*

$120-180 CamA

A green spirit bottle, with flute-cut body and pouring lip.

c1830 *14in (35.5cm) high*

$400-600 SvA

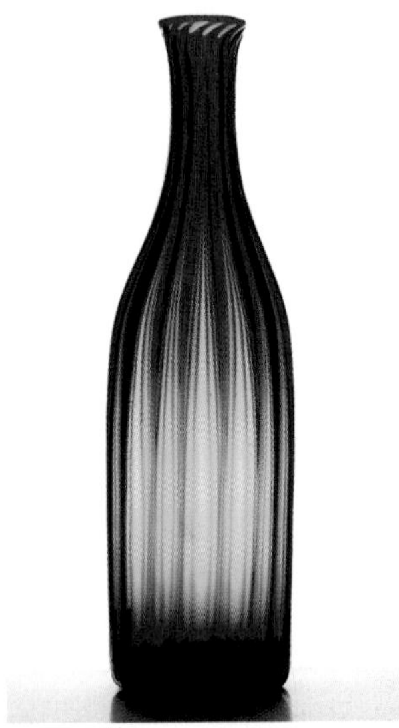

A blue glass vertically ribbed spirit bottle.

c1830 *9.5in (24cm) high*

$300-500 SvA

A pair of amethyst spirit bottles, with silver mounts and stoppers.

c1839

$1,000-1,500 SvA

A set of three spirit bottles, in amethyst, blue and green, with plated cork mounts in a silver plated trefoil stand.

c1840   *15.5in (39cm) high*

$1,000-1,500   **SvA**

A pair of Bristol blue bottles, silver mounted by TC, the tall slender shapes with grape cast mounts and stoppers, Birmingham hallmarks.

1842   *13.5in (34cm) high*

$300-400   **Chef**

A cylinder bottle, of unusual style, found in the Caribbean.

9.75in (25cm) high

$70-100   **CamA**

A Nailsea green glass jug, with white inclusions and loop handle.

c1810   *8.25in (21cm) high*

$500-800   **SvA**

An olive green Nailsea jug, with white marbled splashes.

c1810   *4.5in (11cm) high*

$400-600   **SvA**

A blue North Country baluster cream jug, with wrythen molded body.

c1810   *3.5in (9cm) high*

$200-300   **SvA**

A cut water jug, with base-cut flutes and a band of strawberry-cut diamonds above, with heavy strap handle.

c1820   *7.5in (19cm) high*

$500-800   **SvA**

A small cut cream jug, with diamond and prism cutting.

c1825   *2.75in (7cm) high*

$200-300   **SvA**

An unusually large baluster-shaped jug, with heavy strap handle, the body engraved "Mr. N. Player", above a wire cask and "Cooper's Tools" either side, marked underneath "P.O.K.H.S. July 1828".

1828   *8.25in (21cm) high*

$800-1,200   **SvA**

A baluster-shaped jug, engraved with roses.

c1845   *11.5in (29.5cm) high*

$600-900   **JH**

An acid-etched baluster water jug, with floral panels.

c1880   *8.5in (21.5cm) high*

$180-220   **JH**

Decanters

A shoulder decanter, engraved with wine label for white wine.

White wine is a rare label. Port and Madeira are more common.

c1765	11.5in (30cm) high
$700-1,000	**JH**

A large decanter, of club shape, engraved "Port" within a floral cartouche, with cut diamond stopper.

c1780	
$1,800-2,200	**SvA**

A square spirit decanter, with flute-cut body, engraved "Nectar for the God of War Victorius Nelson", within a round cartouche, cut mushroom stopper.

c1805	7in (17.5cm) high
$800-1,200	**SvA**

A George III four-bottle decanter frame, with tall, angular ring handle, molded collars on ball feet, containing four contemporary octagonal cut glass decanters, damaged.

c1810	10.5in (27cm) high
$300-500	**BonS**

A blue spirit decanter, with beveled lozenge stopper.

c1800	12in (30cm) high
$300-500	**SvA**

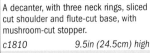

A decanter, with three neck rings, sliced cut shoulder and flute-cut base, with mushroom-cut stopper.

c1810	9.5in (24.5cm) high
$200-300	**JH**

One of a pair of 'Prussian' shape decanters, with broad flute cutting at base and cut mushroom stopper.

c1830	8.75in (22cm) high
$600-900 (pair)	**SvA**

A Yeoward sliced cut decanter, with step-cut neck and matching stopper.

c1830	9.5in (24.5cm) high
$200-300	**JH**

A decanter, lens cuts to body, with step-cut neck, hollow blown stopper.

c1835	10in (25.5cm) high
$200-250	**JH**

A decanter, cut with alternating panels, with diamonds and pillars, hollow blown stopper, one neck ring.

c1840	10.5in (26.5cm) high
$120-180	**JH**

A Victorian spirit decanter, finely engraved with fruiting vine, with ball stopper similarly engraved.

c1860	9.5in (24cm) high
$350-400	**SvA**

An opaque white carafe, with pink pull-up decoration and everted rim.

c1860	7.5in (19cm) high
$300-500	**SvA**

A Victorian decanter, with compressed ovoid body and engraved band.

c1820 10.5in (26cm) high

$100-150 SvA

A late 19thC Stuart decanter, with ribbed body, square section indentations, applied nipped trails.

10.5in (27cm) high

$220-280 JH

One of a pair of shaft and globe decanters, engraved with stars, hollow blown stopper.

c1890 10in (25.5cm) high

$200-250 (pair) JH

An American silver and cut glass decanter, by Tiffany & Co., the body cut with diamonds and fitted with a stopper chased with putti heads, flowers, a ribbon and a trumpet.

1875-1891 9in (23cm) high

$1,000-1,500 SI

A Victorian tantalus, with three crystal decanters.

$700-1,000 GS

A rare cranberry glass and ormolu decanter, in the form of a tufted duck, the cranberry glass body with folded clear glass handle and tail, with detailed ormolu head, neck and feet, the head lifting to reveal cork stopper to decanter.

9in (23cm) high

$1,200-1,800 D

Wine Glasses

An air twist wine glass, the ogee bowl with a hammered flute lower section, the stem with a seven-ply spiral thread, supported on a folded conical foot.

1740 6.5in (16.5cm) high

$1,000-1,500 DN

A wine glass, with bucket bowl, on a multiple spiral air twist stem and plain domed foot.

c1745 6.25in (16cm) high

$500-800 SvA

One of a pair of air twist wine glasses, the bell bowls on stems with shoulder knops and multiple spiral air twists, folded conical feet.

c1745 6.75in (17cm) high

$1,200-1,800 (pair) SvA

A wine glass, with a bucket shaped bowl on a stem with a multiple spiral air twist, plain conical foot.

c1745 6in (15.5cm) high

$2,200-2,800 SvA

A wine glass, the round funnel bowl on a stem with a double series air twist, plain conical foot.

c1745   *6in (15.5cm) high*

$600-900   SvA

A wine glass, with trumpet bowl, multiple spiral air twist drawn stem and folded conical foot.

c1745   *7.75in (19.5cm) high*

$600-900   SvA

A wine glass, with pan-top bowl and two-knopped multiple air twist stem, plain conical foot.

c1745

$700-1,000   SvA

A mercury air twist wine glass.

c1745   *5.5in (14cm) high*

$300-500   JH

A wine glass, with round funnel bowl, multi-spiral air twist, shoulder and center knops.

c1745

$500-800   JH

An air twist wine glass, the waisted bucket bowl supported on a stem enclosing a spiral gauze core, on a conical foot.

c1750   *6.25in (16cm) high*

$700-1,000   DN

An air twist wine glass, the bell bowl supported on a shoulder-knopped stem filled with spiral threads, on a conical foot, minute foot-rim chip.

c1750   *7.5in (19cm) high*

$600-900   DN

An air twist wine glass, the round funnel bowl supported on a double series stem and conical foot.

c1750

$180-220   DN

A pair of air twist wine glasses, the broad funnel bowls supported on a stem with a double mercury twist on conical feet.

c1750   *7in (18cm) high*

$1,000-1,500   DN

An air twist wine glass, the bowl with a honeycomb-molded lower section, the stem with gauze core within a pair of spiral threads.

c1750   *6in (15.5cm) high*

$600-900   DN

A wine glass, the trumpet bowl on a drawn multiple spiral air twist stem, the body engraved with the Jacobite rose, two buds, oak leaf and star, folded foot.

c1750

$3,000-4,000   SvA

An 18thC Lynn wine glass, the horizontally ribbed bowl on double helix opaque twist stem and circular foot.

5.5in (14.25cm) high

$1,200-1,800   Che

An engraved opaque twist wine glass, the ogee bowl with a bird in flight and a fruiting vine, on a double series stem and conical foot.

1770

300-500 | **DN**

A pair of engraved opaque twist wine glasses, the round funnel bowls with a bird in flight and fruiting vine, supported on double series stems and conical feet, one with a lightly polished foot.

c1770   6.75in (17cm) high

$700-1,000 | **DN**

A pair of engraved opaque twist wine glasses, of possible Jacobite significance, the bucket bowls engraved with a rose spray, the double series stems with a pair of entwined tapes within a multi-ply spiral.

c1770   6in (15.5cm) high

$2,000-2,500 | **DN**

An engraved opaque twist wine or ale glass, the ogee bowl with a hop sprig and ears of barley, supported on a double series stem and conical foot.

c1770   6.25in (16cm) high

$600-900 | **DN**

n opaque twist wine glass or cordial, e round funnel bowl supported on a ulti-ply corkscrew stem and a conical ot.

1770   6.25in (16cm) high

300-500 | **DN**

One of a pair of engraved opaque twist wine glasses, of Jacobite significance, with flowers and a bird, double series stem, some ingrained dirt on stems.

c1770   6in (15cm) high

$1,200-1,800 (pair) | **DN**

An opaque twist wine glass, the bell bowl with a solid lower section and tear inclusions, supported on a double series stem and conical foot.

c1770   7in (18cm) high

$600-900 | **DN**

A rare wine glass, the deceptive rounded bowl with basal flutes, on multi-spiral opaque twist stem, with ply bands outside a corkscrew.

c1770   5.75in (14.5cm) high

$3,000-4,000 | **LFA**

'Lynn' wine glass, the funnel-shaped bowl th five ribs, on multi-spiral opaque twist em, with a ply band outside two spiral bles.

1770   5.5in (14cm) high

1,200-1,800 | **LFA**

An engraved baluster wine glass, the bell bowl with a band of fruiting vine, supported on a knop above a cushion knop and true baluster stem, on a domed foot, possible small polished areas to foot-rim.

c1720   7in (18cm) high

$2,500-3,000 | **DN**

A baluster wine glass, the trumpet bowl on a drawn stem with inverted baluster knop, air tear and folded foot.

c1720   6.75in (17cm) high

$1,000-1,500 | **SvA**

A wine glass, with teared swelling beneath bowl, folded foot.

c1730   6in (15.5cm) high

$320-380   JH

A teared drawn trumpet wine glass, with folded foot.

c1730   5.5in (14cm) high

$200-300   JH

A wine glass, the bell bowl on a stem with a shoulder air-beaded knop above a cushion knop, plain section and base knop, conical foot.

c1745   6.75in (17cm) high

$1,200-1,800   SvA

A mid-18thC wine glass, the roundel conical bowl engraved with flowerheads framed by leaves alternating with diamond diaper vignettes, the hollow clear stem on ogee domed folded foot.

6.25in (16cm) hig

$700-1,000   Che

An Anglo-Venetian wine glass, with propeller stem.

c1680   5.5in (14cm) high

$700-1,000   SvA

An 18thC Dutch wine glass, the ogee bowl inscribed "HET WELVAAREN VAN DE WYNKOOPEREY" (Success of the wine coopers) and depicting a trader or merchant toasting a stand of barrels, within an engraved frame displaying elements of the wine and coopering trade, on composite stem of multi knop and white enamel spirals, on circular domed foot, with associated lid.

7.75in (20cm) high

$1,800-2,200   L&T

Two of a set of six fine green wine glasses, with conical fluted bowls and bladed knop stems.

c1830   5in (13cm) hig

$400-600 (set)   Sv

A green wine glass, with conical bowl, knopped stem and plain foot.

c1830   5in (13cm) high

$80-150   SvA

Two of a set of four light green wine glasses, with flute-cut bowls and knopped stems, plain feet.

c1860   5in (13cm) high

$200-300 (set)   SvA

A diamond-cut wine glass, with notched cut stem, star-cut foot, the underside engraved "Manchester Race Course Company Ltd".

c1900   5in (13cm) high

$80-120   JH

A ribbed wine glass, with intaglio engraving of flowers and leaves, with star-cut base, probably by Stevens and Williams.

c1910-20

$30-50   J

...goblet, the bucket bowl on a stem
...ith a multiple spiral air twist, plain
...onical foot.

1750   *6.75in (17.5cm) high*

600-900   **SvA**

A large conical beaker, engraved with
the Jacobite rose and one unopened
bud, the reverse shows a bird in flight
with a sprig in its beak.

c1750   *5in (12.5cm) high*

$1,800-2,200   **SvA**

A glass goblet, with ovoid bowl
engraved with swags and stars on a
facet stem, with plain conical foot.

c1775   *6in (15cm) high*

$700-1,000   **SvA**

A large green goblet, radially molded
with incised twist stem, conical foot.

c1800   *6in (15.5cm) high*

$1,200-1,800   **SvA**

...glass rummer, the bucket bowl finely engraved with stagecoach theme, the
...oach door marked "Newcastle, York, London", the reverse showing a view of a
...hurch spire, probably St. Marys, with initials "MBH" finely engraved.

1800   *6.25in (16cm) high*

1,800-2,200   **SvA**

A large goblet, finely engraved with
stagecoach theme, the stagecoach door
marked "Newcastle, York, London", the
reverse showing a view of a hamlet, the
rest of bowl engraved with fruiting vine.

c1820   *8.25in (21cm) high*

$1,000-1,500   **SvA**

A glass goblet, the round body star-cut,
on a plain square foot.

c1820   *6in (15cm) high*

$180-220   **SvA**

A rummer, the bucket bowl engraved
with the Sunderland bridge, the reverse
with initials "RD" within a square
cartouche and floral sprays, with
knopped stem and plain conical foot.

c1820   *5.5in (14cm) high*

$600-900   **SvA**

A Dutch-engraved light-baluster goblet,
the round funnel bowl engraved with
arms showing four lions-rampant
beneath a coronet and flanked by lion
supporters, supported on a bobbin-
knopped stem, the central knop filled
with bead inclusions, on a conical foot,
minute foot-rim chip.

Provenance: *Exhibited: 'Strange and Rare,
50th Anniversary of The Glass Circle' at
Broadfield House Glass Museum,
September 1987, No. 41, and thence to
The Pilkington Glass Museum, St. Helens,
Lancs., UK.*

c1750   *7.5in (19cm) high*

$3,500-4,500   **DN**

A Dutch-engraved pedestal-stemmed goblet, with broad vertical flutes and engraved with two mirror-monograms and vines, tapered hexagonal stem.

c1750   *6in (15cm) high*

$800–1,200   **DN**

A two-handled rummer, the funnel bowl molded with vertical flutes above a flattened knop, supported on a short stem with a conical foot.

c1790   *6in (15cm) high*

$1,000–1,500   **DN**

A rummer, with a lemon squeezer base.

c1790   *5in (13cm) high*

$120–180   **JH**

A petal-molded rummer, with capstan stem.

c1800   *5in (13cm) hig*

$80–120   **JH**

Miscellaneous Glasses

An early 19thC Masonic tumbler, with engraved pillars, set square and compass, with star on reverse.

3.5in (9cm) high

$180–220   **JH**

A bucket bowl rummer, with two panels, with Masonic symbols and initials.

c1830-40   *5.25in (13.5cm) high*

$280–320   **JH**

A toasting glass, the trumpet bowl with plain slender stem and plain foot.

c1740   *6.75in (17.5cm) high*

$300–500   **SvA**

A glass flute, with trumpet bowl and slender stem, mixed opaque and air twist, plain conical foot.

c1760   *7.5in (19cm) hig*

$1,000–1,500   **Sv**

A bonnet glass, the double ogee bowl diamond-molded on a plain foot.

c1750   *2.75in (7cm) high*

$60–90   **SvA**

A bonnet glass, the double ogee bowl diamond-molded, on a plain conical foot.

c1750

$50–80   **SvA**

An 18thC Ratafia glass, the slender conical bowl flute molded above double helix opaque twist stem and circular foot.

7in (18cm) high

$2,200–2,800   **Chef**

A George III pint mug, the rim molded with three ribs above a trailed girth to the baluster body fluted above a petal foot.

5.5in (14cm) hig

$400–600   **Che**

A cordial glass, the lipped ogee bowl engraved with a band of rose sprays, on a facet-cut stem with plain conical foot.

c1770	6.5in (16cm) high
$600-900	**SvA**

A rare blue bonnet glass, with diamond-molded ogee bowl, rudimentary foot.

c1840	3.5in (8.5cm) high
$500-800	**SvA**

A mid-18thC jelly glass, the panel molded bell bowl over air-beaded knop.

On a jelly glass a plain stem is desirable. If this glass had a plain stem it would be worth $500-600.

	3.5in (9cm) high
$180-220	**JH**

A cordial glass, probably Irish, with plain stem and folded foot.

c1740-1770	6.75in (17cm) high
$700-1,000	**JH**

A dram glass, the ribbed ovoid bowl over oversewn foot.

Oversewn foots are only a feature on dram glasses.

c1770	3in (7.5cm) high
$180-220	**JH**

A drawn trumpet liqueur glass, engraved with three panels of flowers including roses.

c1770	5in (13cm) high
$40-60	**JH**

A tulip bowl hollow stem champagne glass, with diamond cut stem.

A set of six would be worth $280-320.

c1875	
$40-60	**JH**

A late 19thC hollow stem champagne glass, with slice cutting.

$30-40	**JH**

Ale Glasses

A hops and barley engraved ale glass, with plain stem and folded foot.

c1740	6.5in (16.5cm) high
$280-320	**JH**

An air twist ale flute, the flared bowl supported on a stem filled with spiral threads, on a conical foot.

c1750	7.75in (20cm) high
$200-300	**DN**

An 18thC ale glass, the conical bowl with flammiform fluting, the short stem on folded foot.

	5in (12.5cm) high
$200-300	**Chef**

An ale glass, engraved with hops and barley, with double series opaque twist stem and plain conical foot.

c1760	7in (17.5cm) high
$700-1,000	**SvA**

An opaque twist firing glass, the ogee bowl supported on a double series stem and substantial circular foot.

c1770	5in (12.5cm) high
$1,000-1,500	**DN**

An engraved opaque twist firing glass, the ogee bowl with a bird in flight and a flowerhead, supported on a double series stem and a substantial conical foot.

c1770	4.5in (11.5cm) high
$700-1,000	**DN**

Sweetmeat

A baluster sweetmeat, the ogee bowl with pincered ornament to the lower section, supported on a double-knopped stem with bead inclusion and a domed foot, which is possibly trimmed.

c1740	
$600-900	**DN**

A sweetmeat glass, with double ogee bowl and knopped stem with center ball knop, plain domed foot.

c1750	6in (15.5cm) high
$300-500	**SvA**

A sweetmeat glass, with double ogee body, eight sided pedestal stem and plain domed foot.

c1750	7in (17.5cm) high
$320-380	**SvA**

A sweetmeat glass, with a lipped ogee bowl, petal-cut body and rim, the stem with upper and lower collars, domed radially molded foot.

c1760	6.5in (16cm) high
$500-800	**SvA**

An early George III sweetmeat glass, the ogee bowl worked with eight ribs ending in diamonds above the Silesian stem and domed folded foot.

	6.5in (17cm) high
$800-1,000	**Chef**

A cut pedestal bowl with turnover rim, the rim cut with three fluted bands, the bowl with a central three-strand lozenge band, on a waisted stem and square 'lemon squeezer' foot, minute foot-rim chips.

c1790	8.25in (21cm) wide
$1,000-1,500	**DN**

Bowls

A double lipped wine glass cooler, marked underneath "Francis Collins Dublin".

1790-1800	
$2,200-2,800	**SvA**

An Irish canoe bowl on molded pedestal base, scalloped rim.

c1800	10in (25.5cm) high
$1,200-1,800	**JH**

A fruit bowl, with fan-cut rim above star-cut diamonds.

c1820	10in (25.5cm) high
$120-180	**JH**

A pair of early 19thC Boulton style cut glass and gilt metal campana wine coolers, each applied with egg and dart borders, reeded handles and Bacchanalian masks, with stiff leaf bands and a round base, the glass cut with strawberry diamonds and with a gadrooned lower section.

	7.75in (20cm) high
$4,000-6,000	**DN**

A large heavy Irish oval fruit bowl, with diamond and prism-cut decoration.

c1825

$1,800-2,200   SvA

A late 19thC engraved finger bowl, with everted rim, engraved with a border of flowering foliage, the lower section cut with stylized flowerheads above flutes.

3.75in (9.5cm) diam

$500-700   DN

A pair of Varnish & Co. pale-green, silver-cased pedestal bowls or sweetmeat dishes, the round bowls with flared and notched rims, on waist-knopped stems and conical feet, each set with a patent inset disc.

Varnish & Co. London (1849-52) were retailers and Patentees of double-walled silvered glass, which may have been manufactured for them by James Powell & Sons. The company was founded by Edward Varnish and Frederick Hale Thompson.

c1850   5.75in (14.5cm) high

$1,000-1,500   DN

A Victorian enameled and ruffled cranberry glass compote.

10.5in (27cm) diam

$180-220   CamA

Jars

An Irish piggin, with diamond-cut bowl, serrated rim with fan-cut stave, star-cut base.

c1810   5in (12.5cm) high

$1,000-1,500   SvA

An Irish pickle jar, with diamond-cut body and round radially molded foot, the domed cover with associated cutting.

c1815   7in (17.5cm) high

$600-900   SvA

A matched pair of cut-glass urns and covers, each with ovoid bowls and bell-shaped covers, etched with friezes of deer running and scrolled foliage with strawberry cut borders on square cut plinths.

13.75in (35cm) high

$2,200-2,800   L&T

A cut preserve jar and cover, with globular body and a band of strawberry diamonds between prismatic bands, the body with upturned fluted rim and cover, the cover similarly decorated, with mushroom finial, short stem and disc-shaped conical foot.

c1815   6in (15.5cm) high

$600-900   SvA

A pair of Low Countries cut-footed urns and domed spire covers, with ovoid bodies and domed feet, cut with a shaped diamond band, stars and circles, the feet and covers with vertical flutes.

29.5in (75cm) high

$1,200-1,800   DN

Bohemian

A ruby-flashed ewer, English or Bohemian, oviform with a flattened shoulder beneath cylindrical neck and trefoil spout, engraved with a fruiting vine and a crest of a flightless bird holding a horseshoe in its beak, perhaps the arms of Coke or Cooke.

c1840   13.5in (34cm) high

$700-1,000   **DN**

A Bohemian clear and intaglio-engraved goblet, engraved and polished with a domestic scene of parents seated at a table in a garden with their child, supported on a faceted and knopped stem and scalloped-edge foot.

c1840   6.5in (16.5cm) high

$400-600   **DN**

A pair of mid-19thC Bohemian glass lustres, each with baluster-form stem, scalloped rim and circular foot, each painted with ruby, gilt and white decoration, one repaired.

10in (25.5cm) high

$700-1,000   **SI**

A mid- to late 19thC Bohemian ruby-flashed goblet, the fluted, thistle-shaped bowl supported on a knopped stem cut with fine diamonds, above a fluted pedestal foot, minute foot-rim chip.

9.75in (24.5cm) high

$700-1,000   **DN**

A late 19thC Bohemian enameled glass large vase, painted with a pair of Victorian ladies in a landscape, the base applied with bosses and painted with floral vines.

18.75in (48cm) high

$800-1,200   **SI**

A mid- to late 19thC Bohemian opaque-white overlay and green vase, the middle section painted with colored enamels, the neck and domed foot fluted and gilded, some wear to gilding.

16.25in (41cm) high

$600-900   **DN**

An opalescent engraved ewer and goblet, by J. & L. Lobmeyr, engraved and gilded, 'jeweled' with opaque white dots, each with monogram mark, the foot of the ewer cracked and chipped.

c1880   Ewer 9.75in (25cm) high

$600-900   **DN**

Two of a set of ten late 19thC Bohemian faceted green-and-gilt wine glasses, each fluted ovoid bowl with a foliate band suspending swags, on a faceted stem and conical foot, some rubbing to gilding, some small chips.

5.5in (14cm) high

$600-900 (set)   **DN**

A late 19thC Bohemian ruby-flashed trumpet vase, engraved with a continuous scene of deer in a forest landscape, between a scalloped rim and two fluted knops, supported on a domed and fluted foot, the lower section with a floral band, occasional minute chips and scratches.

c1890   18in (46cm) high

$1,800-2,200   **DN**

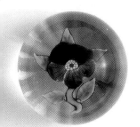

A Baccarat pansy weight, with three green leaves and two further leaves to he stalk, star cut base.

2in (5cm) diam

200-250   **GorL**

A Baccarat pansy weight, of conventional type, on a star cut base.

1845-50   *2.75in (7cm) diam*

$400-600   **GorL**

A Baccarat patterned millefiori weight, with two interlocking trefoil garlands of arrows, head canes and stardust canes.

1845-50   *2.75in (7cm) diam*

$1,000-1,500   **GorL**

A rare Baccarat magnum close-packed millefiori paperweight, "B1847" and date on diamond-cut base.

1847   *4in (10cm) diam*

$18,000-22,000   **LHS**

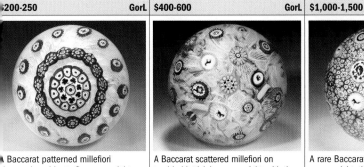

A Baccarat patterned millefiori hamrock and butterfly paperweight, containing four rows of complex canes round a central claret-colored cog cane.

1845-50   *3in (7.5cm) diam*

5,500-7,500   **LHS**

A Baccarat scattered millefiori on tumbled latticinio paperweight, with the Gridel silhouettes of a animals, in a bed of latticinio and colored filigree, "B1847" signature/date.

1847   *3in (7.5cm) diam*

$3,500-4,500   **LHS**

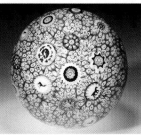

A rare Baccarat red carpet ground paperweight, the Gridel canes depicting animals and shamrocks, signed and dated "B1848" in blue and red lettering.

1848   *3in (7.5cm) diam*

$18,000-22,000   **LHS**

A Baccarat butterfly and white flower paperweight, the butterfly with multi-coloured millefiori wings, the double-tiered white flower with complex cane centre, on clear star-cut ground.

1845-50   *2.75in (7cm) diam*

$3,500-4,500   **LHS**

A Baccarat garlanded large butterfly paperweight, with star-cut base.

1845-50   *3in (7cm) diam*

3,000-4,000   **LHS**

A Baccarat clematis buds paperweight, containing five, pale-blue, clematis buds, with green sepals, on stems with emerald leaves, the star-cut ground in a crystal dome.

1845-50   *2.75in (7cm) diam*

$1,800-2,200   **LHS**

A Baccarat faceted rock paperweight, three upright spires of sandy ground flecked with green glass, and six and one faceting, wear around the top window and side facets.

3.25in (8.25cm) diam

$180-220   **LHS**

A Clichy miniature concentric millefiori weight, in shades of pale pink, white, green and deep mauve about a central green set up.

1845-50   *1.75in (4.5cm) diam*

$400-600   **GorL**

A Clichy faceted miniature concentric millefiori weight, the central cane surrounded by five blue canes within a circle of pink and green at the periphery, cut with a window and five rinties.

1.75in (4.5cm) diam

320-380   **GorL**

A rare Clichy spaced millefiori newel post, with 80 well-defined canes, including five Clichy roses, two white and three pink, pastry mold, starburst, edelweiss, complex star and cog canes, all on clear ground, set in the original brass fitting, minor bruises and scratches.

1845-50   *4.25in (11cm) diam*

$6,000-9,000   **LHS**

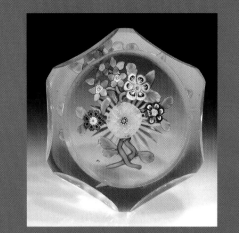
Miscellaneous

A clear rolling pin, with faint pale blue pull up.

c1850   14.5in (37cm) long

$200-250   SvA

A colored glass rolling pin, with splashed red and blue decoration.

c1850   16in (41cm) long

$90-120   SvA

TOP: An early brown and clear looped glass rolling pin, with rough pontil at one end and opening at the other end.

15in (38cm) long

$80-120   JDJ

BOTTOM: An early black and white spatter glass rolling pin, with rough pontil and closed at the opposite end, some roughness to the closed end.

15.5in (39.5cm) long

$80-120   JDJ

A Sandwich deep amethyst master salt, blown in the mold in a six-sided urn-shape with polished pontil, some roughness and chips to the top corners of the panel.

3.75in (9.5cm) high

$300-400   JDJ

An early 20thC American overlaid glass bottle and six shot glasses, the rectangular bottle molded "I.W. Harper" with hexagonal stopper and each cylindrical glass overlaid with Japanese-inspired blossoms. bottle

9.75in (25cm) high

$380-430   SI

A 19thC American blown multi-coloured witch's ball.

4.5in (11.5cm) diam

$40-50   SI

An American arched window frame, with stained and painted glass panels including one with George Washington bust portrait, including spouting dolphin and spewing dragon decorated panels, five-point stars and central pendant portrait medallion.

54in (137cm) high

$1,500-2,000   NA

SILVER

The MARKET FOR SILVER IS CURRENTLY FOCUSED ON TOP-END PIECES with good marks and makers, and crisp, clean lines. Good quality silver is becoming an investment buy for those looking to spend at least $7,000 to $9,000, and it is expected that a profit may be made over a ten year period. Provincial hallmarks such as Aberdeen, Inverness and Dublin have rocketed in price, with the rarer provincial marks doing especially well. Boxes are currently very popular and span the price range from $50 to $30,000, and are therefore much sought after by gift-buyers and collectors alike.

There has been a decline in the sale of a number of items which are associated with formal dining, such as tea sets and entrée dishes. Changes in our general lifestyle and in the way we entertain have meant that food and drink are presented in a much more informal way than they once were and there has been a corresponding shift in the market. However, good quality canteens continue to be popular and many collectors look to add to their existing sets with additional items such as fish servers and ladles. Particularly rare items, such as soup tureens, are also still desirable.

Tea, Coffee Pots & Tea Sets

A George III silver coffee pot, by Benjamin Gignac, domed hinged lid with a gadrooned edge and flame finial, with a scrolled fruitwood handle and a cast, chased ribbed and leafage-capped spout, with low molded foot, a gadrooned edge, marked under rim, the body later engraved with garland reserves and a crest on each side, maker's mark for London 1733, worn.

c1733   11.75in (30cm) high
$2,200-2,800   FRE

An English silver coffee pot, by Francis Crump, with a domed hinged lid and flame finial, scroll- and leafage-chased spout and a wooden handle, with low spreading step-molded foot, marked on the side and with maker's mark under base, London 1763, later initials on side, handle replaced, dents.

c1763   11.5in (29cm) high
$2,200-2,800   FRE

A CLOSER LOOK AT A SILVER COFFEE POT

Extensive decoration is unusual prior to the Victorian period, but this high quality chasing adds to the desirability of the piece. Over-polishing should be avoided to prevent damage to the chasing and patina.

The spout is in the form of a bird's beak, which is a decorative feature, but also makes it less susceptible to damage.

Damaged handles should be repaired where possible as it takes some time for new ones to blend in with the piece.

Late 18thC coffee pots are generally baluster or pear shaped and stand on a spreading foot.

A late George II pear-shaped coffee pot, by Thomas Moore II, embossed with flowers and scrolls and engraved with a cartouche, domed cover, cast spout and wood handle, London hallmarks.

c1758   10.5in (26.5cm) high
$1,200-1,800   DN

A George II silver coffee pot, possibly by Thomas Parr, engraved with a coat of arms, mounted with a wooden handle, the spout capped with leafage, London hallmarks for 1747 or 1748.

9in (23cm) high
$1,500-2,000   SI

An early George III silver Argyle, by William and Aaron Lestourgeon, with monogrammed round body, slim spout and wooden handle, base with hinged reservoir cover, domed cover with flame finial, London hallmarks.

c1769   6.75in (17cm) high
$1,800-2,200   DN

A George III vase-shaped Argyle, by Peter & William Bateman, London, with reeded borders, on a pedestal foot, with a spool shaped cover and ball finial, the interior with a cone-shaped section and a detachable cover.

c1806   8in (20cm) high
$1,800-2,200   WW

A silver coffee pot, by Thomas Fletcher, Philadelphia, the ovoid form body chased and applied with scroll, leafage and blossoms around two vacant reserves and below a slightly ribbed neck with an alternating band of leaves and anthemions, marked under base "[T]FLETCHER/PHILAD initials removed from reserves.

c1838   *11in (28cm) high*

$3,000-3,500   **FRE**

A café-au-lait pot, of tapering circular form, engraved monogram and dated "1908", Sheffield 1904.

$180-220   **L&T**

A café-au-lait set, in the Georgian style, tapering slight baluster body, acorn finial, acanthus-clasped spout, disc foot, London 1929, 22oz.

$400-600   **L&**

A silver coffee pot, by Willian Gale & Son of New York NY, the cast double-scroll handle and swan neck spout decorated with foliage, the step-domed hinged lid ending in a seed finial, the body and foot chased with floral and/or scroll decoration, the foot and lid with bead decoration, and the shoulder with shield and dart molding above engraved latticework, mono "C", finial slightly slanted.

1856   *13.75in (38cm) high*

$1,500-2,000   **IHB**

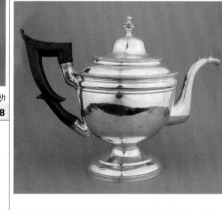

A silver tea pot, of oval form with conforming molded base, the domed and hinged cover with urn finial, several gadroon bands near top, the swanneck spout with grape and leaf appliqué, nicely carved scroll handle, marked by Christian Wiltberger of Philadelphia PA (1793-1817), no monogram, spout tip recently repaired.

11in (30cm) high

A George III oval teapot, by Peter and Ann Bateman, the plain body with reeded borders, straight tapered spout and wood handle.

c1778

$600-900   **BonS**

$2,300-2,800   **IHB**

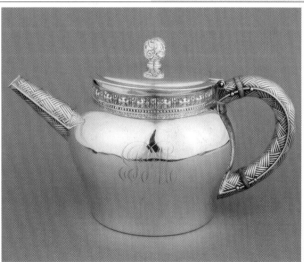

An silver tea pot, by Tiffany & Co. of New York NY, mono "JdePM", of circular reverse pear-form on shallow ring foot, the slightly domed hinged cover with foliate ball finial, the C-scroll handle and short tapering cylindrical spout stamped with woven reed decoration (4676M7341).

c1877-1891   *3.75in (10cm) high*

$650-750   **IHB**

An Empire-style silver tea pot made by Samuel Kirk and struck with the fifth period Baltimore City assay marks used by Samuel Steel, mono "JAH".

c1835-1843   *10in (27.5cm) high*

$2,000-2,500   **IHB**

A silver-plate hot water kettle, by Charles W. Hamill & Co Baltimore, chased floral repoussé decoration, no monogram, plate worn, stand and burner removed.

1876-1884   *11in (30cm) high*

$320-380   **IHB**

An English silver teapot and stand, by Solomon Hougham, engraved, the lid with an ebony finial, conforming stand, fully marked, reserves on both with late initials, damage to rim of lid, repair to hinge, wear to all engraving.

c1797   *6.25in (16cm) high*

$1,200-1,800   **FRE**

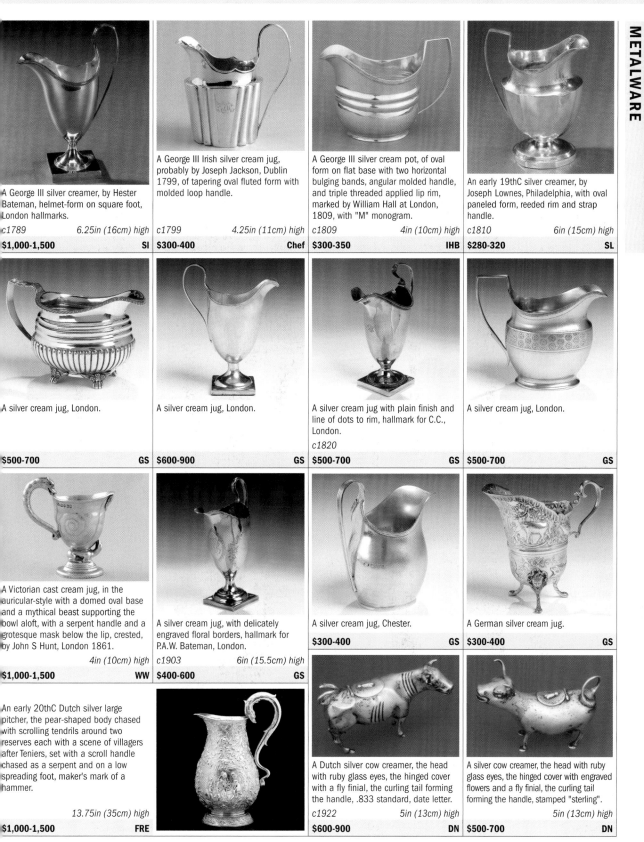

A George III silver creamer, by Hester Bateman, helmet-form on square foot, London hallmarks.

c1789   6.25in (16cm) high

$1,000-1,500   SI

A George III Irish silver cream jug, probably by Joseph Jackson, Dublin 1799, of tapering oval fluted form with molded loop handle.

c1799   4.25in (11cm) high

$300-400   Chef

A George III silver cream pot, of oval form on flat base with two horizontal bulging bands, angular molded handle, and triple threaded applied lip rim, marked by William Hall at London, 1809, with "M" monogram.

c1809   4in (10cm) high

$300-350   IHB

An early 19thC silver creamer, by Joseph Lownes, Philadelphia, with oval paneled form, reeded rim and strap handle.

c1810   6in (15cm) high

$280-320   SL

A silver cream jug, London.

$500-700   GS

A silver cream jug, London.

$600-900   GS

A silver cream jug with plain finish and line of dots to rim, hallmark for C.C., London.

c1820

$500-700   GS

A silver cream jug, London.

$500-700   GS

A Victorian cast cream jug, in the auricular-style with a domed oval base and a mythical beast supporting the bowl aloft, with a serpent handle and a grotesque mask below the lip, crested, by John S Hunt, London 1861.

4in (10cm) high

$1,000-1,500   WW

A silver cream jug, with delicately engraved floral borders, hallmark for P.A.W. Bateman, London.

c1903   6in (15.5cm) high

$400-600   GS

A silver cream jug, Chester.

$300-400   GS

A German silver cream jug.

$300-400   GS

An early 20thC Dutch silver large pitcher, the pear-shaped body chased with scrolling tendrils around two reserves each with a scene of villagers after Teniers, set with a scroll handle chased as a serpent and on a low spreading foot, maker's mark of a hammer.

13.75in (35cm) high

$1,000-1,500   FRE

A Dutch silver cow creamer, the head with ruby glass eyes, the hinged cover with a fly finial, the curling tail forming the handle, .833 standard, date letter.

c1922   5in (13cm) high

$600-900   DN

A silver cow creamer, the head with ruby glass eyes, the hinged cover with engraved flowers and a fly finial, the curling tail forming the handle, stamped "sterling".

5in (13cm) high

$500-700   DN

A silver cream pot, of helmet form on squat pedestal foot, the body and foot chased all-over with floral and scroll repoussé decoration, cast angular scroll handle with floral and ram's head decoration, marked by Samuel Kirk and struck with the Baltimore assay marks used by Samuel Steele, small rim crack at upper handle joint.

c1835-43   7.75in (21cm) high

$850-1,250   **IHB**

A silver cream pitcher, of pear-form with die-rolled ring foot and lip with plain S-scroll handle, the body decorated with a scroll and floral repoussé reserve and a little additional floral chasing, sold by Robert Brown & Son of Baltimore MD, monogram removed.

c1850   5.25in (14.5cm) high

$3,500-4000   **IHB**

A silver repoussé pitcher, by S. Kirk & Son, Baltimore, the ovoid body with a loop handle and a spout cast with a mask, chased in high relief with floral vines on a stippled ground, engraved "Chas A. Whitney/ from/ W.H.A./ Novr 1893".

          8.5in (22cm) high

$1,500-2,000   **SI**

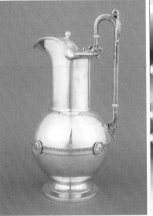

A silver hot milk jug, by the Gorham Mfg Co of Providence RI and retailed by Geo W. Webb & Co. of Baltimore MD, the globular body on spreading foot, the long cylindrical neck topped with hinged offset domed cover, the scroll handle and applied midrib decorated with a total of five different classical portrait medallions (211/3), engraved "M&B Wisesenfeld Feby 23d. 1868 .JF', restored with later insulators.

1868   10in (27.5cm) high

$1,500-2,000 I   **HB**

A Renaissance Revival-style silver cream pot, by the Gorham MFg Co. of providence RI, retailed by the unknown "C&M", with tapering circular body on four cast legs and with applied handle, no monogram.

1869   4.75in (13cm) high

$280-330   **IHB**

A colonial revival silver cream pot and sugar bowl, by Gorham Mfg Co Providence RI, with plain pear-shaped bodies, 4 cast scroll feet, cast double scroll handles, mono "MDF".

1889   4in (10cm) high

$100-140   **IHB**

A silver-mounted claret pitcher, by the Gorham Mfg Co of Providence RI, the fancy cut glass pear-form body on short foot with C-scroll handle, bead-decorated silver collar and spout fitted with spring-loaded hinged cover operated by cast foliate scroll thumbpiece (S3106), no monogram, repair to silver, some chips and cloudiness to interior.

1897   10.5in (26cm) high

$500-600   **IHB**

A silver water pitcher, of vase form on low pedestal base, by the Gorham Mfg Co of Providence RI and retailed by Spaulding & Co. of Chicago IL, the foot rim and lip applied with thread edge, foliate scroll handle (NO2487A), monogram "SJL".

1909   8.75in (24cm) high

$550-650   **IHB**

A silver cream pot and sugar bowl, of bulbous circular form on ring foor, floral decorated strap handles, the bodies chased with floral repoussée decoration (No26/30), made by the Stieff Co. of Baltimore MD, monogram "K".

1915-1917   3.5in (9.5cm) high

$550-650   **IHB**

A silver pitcher, by Chicago Silver Co., of baluster form with angular handle and applied reeded foliate rim, monogram "B".

c1925-50   9in (23cm) high

$600-700   **SI**

A silver water pitcher, by Dominicle & Waff.

1938

$650-750   **IHB**

A silver water pitcher, by Reed & Barton, monogram "JHH".

1950   8in (20cm) high

$200-300   **SI**

A silver cream pot and sugar bowl, of plain form with short spreading foot scroll, strap handles.

c1970-1975   3.75in (9.5cm) high

$30-40   **IHB**

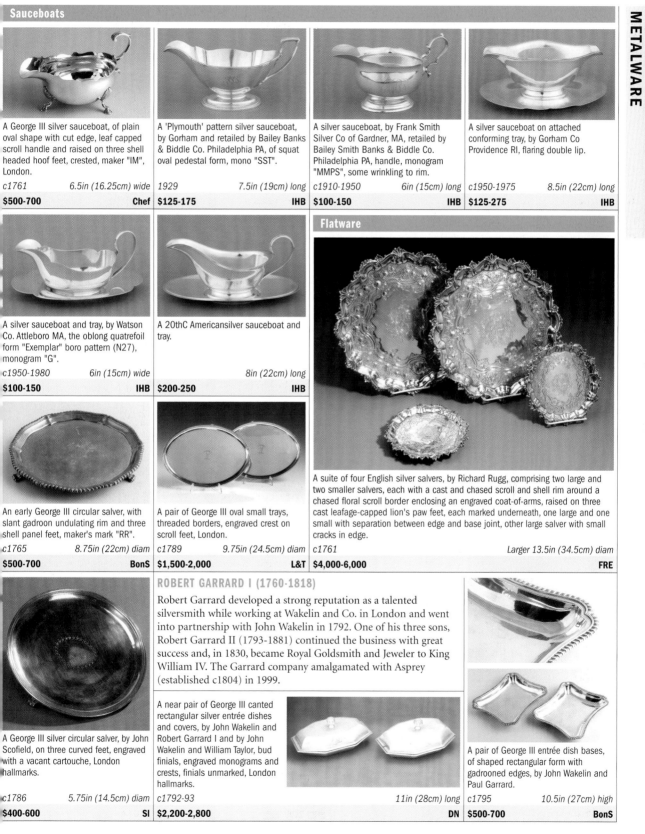

Sauceboats

A George III silver sauceboat, of plain oval shape with cut edge, leaf capped scroll handle and raised on three shell headed hoof feet, crested, maker "IM", London.

c1761   6.5in (16.25cm) wide
$500-700   Chef

A 'Plymouth' pattern silver sauceboat, by Gorham and retailed by Bailey Banks & Biddle Co. Philadelphia PA, of squat oval pedestal form, mono "SST".

1929   7.5in (19cm) long
$125-175   IHB

A silver sauceboat, by Frank Smith Silver Co of Gardner, MA, retailed by Bailey Smith Banks & Biddle Co. Philadelphia PA, handle, monogram "MMPS", some wrinkling to rim.

c1910-1950   6in (15cm) long
$100-150   IHB

A silver sauceboat on attached conforming tray, by Gorham Co Providence RI, flaring double lip.

c1950-1975   8.5in (22cm) long
$125-275   IHB

A silver sauceboat and tray, by Watson Co. Attleboro MA, the oblong quatrefoil form "Exemplar" boro pattern (N27), monogram "G".

c1950-1980   6in (15cm) wide
$100-150   IHB

A 20thC Americansilver sauceboat and tray.

8in (22cm) long
$200-250   IHB

Flatware

A suite of four English silver salvers, by Richard Rugg, comprising two large and two smaller salvers, each with a cast and chased scroll and shell rim around a chased floral scroll border enclosing an engraved coat-of-arms, raised on three cast leafage-capped lion's paw feet, each marked underneath, one large and one small with separation between edge and base joint, other large salver with small cracks in edge.

c1761   Larger 13.5in (34.5cm) diam
$4,000-6,000   FRE

An early George III circular salver, with slant gadroon undulating rim and three shell panel feet, maker's mark "RR".

c1765   8.75in (22cm) diam
$500-700   BonS

A pair of George III oval small trays, threaded borders, engraved crest on scroll feet, London.

c1789   9.75in (24.5cm) diam
$1,500-2,000   L&T

ROBERT GARRARD I (1760-1818)

Robert Garrard developed a strong reputation as a talented silversmith while working at Wakelin and Co. in London and went into partnership with John Wakelin in 1792. One of his three sons, Robert Garrard II (1793-1881) continued the business with great success and, in 1830, became Royal Goldsmith and Jeweler to King William IV. The Garrard company amalgamated with Asprey (established c1804) in 1999.

A George III silver circular salver, by John Scofield, on three curved feet, engraved with a vacant cartouche, London hallmarks.

c1786   5.75in (14.5cm) diam
$400-600   SI

A near pair of George III canted rectangular silver entrée dishes and covers, by John Wakelin and Robert Garrard I and by John Wakelin and William Taylor, bud finials, engraved monograms and crests, finials unmarked, London hallmarks.

c1792-93   11in (28cm) long
$2,200-2,800   DN

A pair of George III entrée dish bases, of shaped rectangular form with gadrooned edges, by John Wakelin and Paul Garrard.

c1795   10.5in (27cm) high
$500-700   BonS

A silver bonbon dish, by Dominick & Haff, New York NY, retailed by Bailey, Banks & Biddle & Co. of Philadelphia PA, of shaped oval form with lobed sides and rim, the rim applied with pierced foliate scroll decoration, monogram "MDeHM".

1889   9in (25.5cm) long

$150-200   **IHB**

A silver pin tray, made by Hamilton & Diesinger of Philadelphia PA, with embossed floral and scroll decorated rim, ornate monogram "CMU".

c1885-1899   5.5in (15cm) long

$80-100   **IHB**

A pair of silver fruit stands, by S. Kirk & Son of Baltimore MD, the shaped rectangular dish on four spreading feet, the sides of the dish and the feet chased with floral repoussée decoration (2656), engraved "SBSF" on top and "NOV 28th 1894" beneath rim.

7.5in (19cm) wide

$2,500-3,500   **IHB**

A silver bowl, by Tiffany & Co., New York NY, of shaped cylindrical form with slightly domed base, the steeply sloping sides flaring out to a rim applied with clover decoration, no monogram.

c1891-1902   10.25 (28cm) diam

$750-850   **IHB**

A silver butterdish, by Lebkuecher & Co., Newark NJ, of plain circular form, beaded edge, pierced liner, monogram "HSL".

c1895-1915   6in (16.5cm) diam

$60-80   **IHB**

A silver compote, by Redlich & Co NY, retailed by Bailey Banks & Biddle Co. of Philadelphia PA, with enclosed and pierced floral and latticework decoration, monogram "MdeHM".

c1890-1915   8in (22cm) diam

$300-400   **IHB**

A silver bread tray, by Merdien Britannia Co. Meriden CT, with shaped well, applied sausage and ring edge, monogram "CML".

1890-1920   13.5in (37cm) long

$100-150   **IHB**

A silver cake basket, by the Baltimore Silversmiths Mfg Co. (later Schofield Co.), the sides chased with floral repoussée decoration with an applied cast foliate edge, monogram "DJF".

c1905 14.5in (39.5cm) long

$1,300-1800   **IHB**

A silver waiter, with three cast claw and ball feet, embossed festoon border with gadroon edge, engraved chain motif, armorial and motto, maker unknown, mono "T.Co", recent repair.

c1895-1925   12in (33cm) diam

$250-350   **IHB**

A pair of silver compotes, of shaped circular form on trumpet foot, the foot and dish chased with repousé floral decoration inside an applied foliate edge (No. 70), made by the S. Kirk & Son Co. of Baltimore MD, mono "CLR".

c1900-1925   8.25 (22.5cm) diam

$1,800-2300   **IHB**

A silver large sandwich plate, made by the S. Kirk & Son Co. of Baltimore MD, the rim chased with floral repoussée decoration inside an applied foliate edge (No.194), ribbon monogram, surface scratches from knife cuts.

c1900-1925   12in (33cm) diam

$850-950   **IHB**

A silver strawberry dish, by Tuttle Silver Co Boston MA, retailed by Bailey Banks & Biddle, Irish reproduction 'Dublin' pattern, monogram "MRC".

1929   8.25in (23cm) diam

$100-150   **IHB**

An American silver open butterdish, by S. Kirk & Son Inc, Baltimore MS, with molded edge and pierced liner, monogram "MFJS".

c1925-1950 6.5in (18cm) diam

$100-150   **IHB**

A silver sandwich plate, by Randahl Shop of Chicago IL, with two Art Deco handles, some scratches.

c1920-1950   11.5in (31cm) wide

$80-130   **IHB**

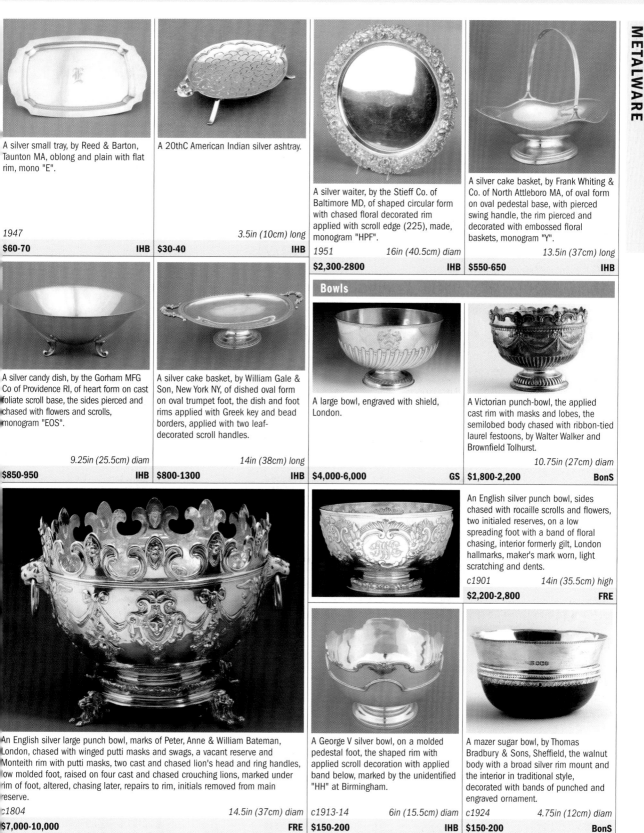

A silver small tray, by Reed & Barton, Taunton MA, oblong and plain with flat rim, mono "E".

1947

$60-70   IHB

A 20thC American Indian silver ashtray.

3.5in (10cm) long

$30-40   IHB

A silver waiter, by the Stieff Co. of Baltimore MD, of shaped circular form with chased floral decorated rim applied with scroll edge (225), made, monogram "HPF".

1951   16in (40.5cm) diam

$2,300-2800   IHB

A silver cake basket, by Frank Whiting & Co. of North Attleboro MA, of oval form on oval pedestal base, with pierced swing handle, the rim pierced and decorated with embossed floral baskets, monogram "Y".

13.5in (37cm) long

$550-650   IHB

A silver candy dish, by the Gorham MFG Co of Providence RI, of heart form on cast foliate scroll base, the sides pierced and chased with flowers and scrolls, monogram "EOS".

9.25in (25.5cm) diam

$850-950   IHB

A silver cake basket, by William Gale & Son, New York NY, of dished oval form on oval trumpet foot, the dish and foot rims applied with Greek key and bead borders, applied with two leaf-decorated scroll handles.

14in (38cm) long

$800-1300   IHB

Bowls

A large bowl, engraved with shield, London.

$4,000-6,000   GS

A Victorian punch-bowl, the applied cast rim with masks and lobes, the semilobed body chased with ribbon-tied laurel festoons, by Walter Walker and Brownfield Tolhurst.

10.75in (27cm) diam

$1,800-2,200   BonS

An English silver large punch bowl, marks of Peter, Anne & William Bateman, London, chased with winged putti masks and swags, a vacant reserve and Monteith rim with putti masks, two cast and chased lion's head and ring handles, low molded foot, raised on four cast and chased crouching lions, marked under rim of foot, altered, chasing later, repairs to rim, initials removed from main reserve.

c1804   14.5in (37cm) diam

$7,000-10,000   FRE

An English silver punch bowl, sides chased with rocaille scrolls and flowers, two initialed reserves, on a low spreading foot with a band of floral chasing, interior formerly gilt, London hallmarks, maker's mark worn, light scratching and dents.

c1901   14in (35.5cm) high

$2,200-2,800   FRE

A George V silver bowl, on a molded pedestal foot, the shaped rim with applied scroll decoration with applied band below, marked by the unidentified "HH" at Birmingham.

c1913-14   6in (15.5cm) diam

$150-200   IHB

A mazer sugar bowl, by Thomas Bradbury & Sons, Sheffield, the walnut body with a broad silver rim mount and the interior in traditional style, decorated with bands of punched and engraved ornament.

c1924   4.75in (12cm) diam

$150-200   BonS

A pair of silver salt cellars, by Charters, Cann & Dunn and retailed by John & James Cox, both of New York NY, the trefoil bowls on three cast and chased headed scroll feet, applied molded rim, mono "GHL".

c1848-1853   *3in (8cm) diam*

$400-500   IHB

A pair of silver salt cellars, by Edward Moore for Tiffany & Co., New York, of bulbous circular bowl form on spreading foot, worn engraved "HAB to EBF", worn and one foot rotates.

c1858-1865   *2.5in (7cm) diam*

$150-200   IHB

A pair of silver salt cellars, by Wood & Hughes of New York NY, of plain circular pedestal form on stepped foot, the broad rim with two applied masque handles, no monogram, recently repaired.

c1860-1870   *4in (11cm) wide*

$200-250   IHB

Four silver salt cellars, of bulbous circular bowl form with flaring rippled rim, the surface chased with foliate arabesque decoration, marked by "WH" at London, probably by William Harrison of Harrison Bros & Howson or William Hunter, no monogram.

c1881-1882   *2.5in (7cm) diam*

$200-250   IHB

A pair of silver individual salts, by Gorham Mfg Co., Providence RI, of round bowl form with flat base, sloping sides and horizontally reeded shoulder in-curved to vertically reeded rim, monogram "EAW", worn gilt interiors.

1882   *1.5in (4cm) diam*

$30-40   IHB

A silver dresser jar, by the Whiting Mfg Co. of New York NY, of plain circular form, the slip-on cover embossed with foliate scroll rim (No. 3905), monogram "P".

c1890-1915   *3in (8cm) diam*

$200-250   IHB

A silver candy dish, by the Gorham Mfg Co., Providence RI, of heart form on three ball feet, the sides embossed and pierced with floral and scroll decoration (4310), no monogram.

1896   *8in (22cm) wide*

$180-230   IHB

A silver hair receiver, by the Baltimore Sterling Silver Co. (Stieff Co. predecessor), the body of bulbous form with slip-on domed cover, the body and cover chased with floral repousse decoration, monogram "CS".

c1895-1905   *3.25in (9cm) high*

$500-600   IHB

A silver porringer, by Towle Mfg Co., of Newburyport MA, of modern form, the saucepan-style shallow bowl with molded lip, the pierced handle with scroll decoration, monogram "AEY".

c1910-1940   *7.25in (20cm) long*

$150-200   IHB

A silver punch bowl, of plain circular form on molded spreading foot, molded applied horizontal mid-rib, narrow brim with applied foliate and floral rim (3601), made by S. Kirk & Son Inc of Baltimore MD, engraved unicorn head opposite the mongramo "B" / "B*K".

c1925-1930   *10.25in (28cm) diam*

$800-1,100   IHB

A silver wine taster, by Currier & Roby, New York NY, of typical shallow circular form with large and small embossed mounds decorating the sides, looped wire handle with curved oval thumbpiece on top (1529).

c1920-1950   *4.25in (11.5cm) wide*

$130-180   IBH

A silver porringer, made by Watson Co., Attleboro MA and retailed by J.E. Caldwell & Co., of Philadelphia PA, of typical keyhole form (D35), monogram "B W*P".

c1920-1960   *6.5in (18cm) diam*

$60-80   IHB

An 'Irish-style' silver bowl, by Webster Co., N Attleboro MA, on short stepped pedestal foot, lobed sides frame and lip, monogram "SST", foot damaged.

c1930-1970   *6.5in (18cm) diam*

$100-150   IHB

A silver-covered glass dresser jar, made by the Alvin-Beiderhase Co., Sag Harbor, New York, and retailed by Theo A. Kohn & Son, New York NY, the bulbous but glass jar with slip-on floral embossed cover.

3.25in (9cm) diam

$100-150   IHB

A Victorian silver mounted porringer, by William Hutton & Sons, London, the body formed from ivory, fitted with two handles.

c1895   3.5in (9cm) diam

$150-200   **Chef**

An 18thC Irish silver two-handled cup, only Hibernia and Dublin mark legible, of plain bell shape, with two leaf capped scroll handles, the body with molded girdle.

5.25in (13.5cm) high

$400-600   **Chef**

A Russian silver covered sugar bowl, of Classical vase form on trumpet foot on square base, leaf decoration on body and domed, finialed slip cover, reeded ear-form strap handles, marked by "I Yemikov", Moscow, damage and repairs.

c1790-1814   7.5in (19cm) high

$600-900   **IHB**

An Edwardian Scottish silver centerpiece bowl, the boat-shaped body with high scrolled acanthus terminals and fret-pierced rim, the lower body and pedestal foot semilobed, by Hamilton and Inches, Edinburgh.

c1909   13.75in (35cm) high

$2,200-2,500   **BonS**

Baskets

A George III silver sugar basket, by Hester Bateman, engraved and pierced floral and foliate decoration, with cobalt glass liner, London hallmarks.

c1787   7in (17.5cm) wide

$1,000-1,500   **SI**

A CLOSER LOOK AT A SILVER BASKET

Baskets were used to hold bread, fruit, cakes or sweets as table centerpieces. They were popular, decorative items and were made in large numbers, despite their high price.

London makers command higher prices and baskets should be checked for marks both on the handle and the main body.

This simple piercing decoration is typical of the late 18thC when designs became less ornate.

Pierced apron supports were used in this period and should be checked for damage.

A George II silver oval bread basket, by Gabriel Sleath and Francis Crump, London, decorated with pierced lattice-work centered by an engraved coat-of-arms featuring a pair of lambs' heads inside a shield surrounded by a tied bouquet, the hinged scroll lattice-work handle terminating in acanthus leaves.

c1787   13.5in (34cm) wide

$6,000-9,000   **SI**

A George III silver sugar basket, by Peter, Ann and William Bateman, navette-form, engraved floral swags, reeded edge, London hallmarks.

1800   5.75in (14.5cm) wide

$500-700   **SI**

A George III silver centerpiece, the pierced sides cast with bellflowers and two bow-tied monogrammed reserves, below a guilloche rim and above a leaftip border, with two ram's head and ring handles, on ball feet, the interior engraved with a coat of arms, London, maker's mark "IS", possibly Joseph Scammell.

Provenance: Property from the Estate of Robert M. Gottschalk.

1795   12.5in (32cm) wide

3,500-4,000   **SI**

A Victorian silver basket, by Rob and David Henell, London.

$3,500-4,000   **GS**

A George V silver basket, by Maple & Co. Ltd., Sheffield, oval on four curved legs with trifid feet, pierced with scrolling foliage and swags and applied with a serpentine foliate rim.

c1911   9.25in (23.5cm) long

$400-600   **SI**

A Dutch silver punch-bowl, of hemispherical form on four cast floral and trellis feet, the pierced sides engraved with floral foliate and bird decoration, applied floral garlands descending from the applied scroll and shell rim, two scroll and floral handles, clear glass liner, marked by B. Dijkstra (Fa. Gebr Niekerk) at Groningen 1902-1927, defaced date mark may be 1914, also struck with pseudo-hallmarks and French import marks.

13in (33cm) wide

$2,200-2,800   **IHB**

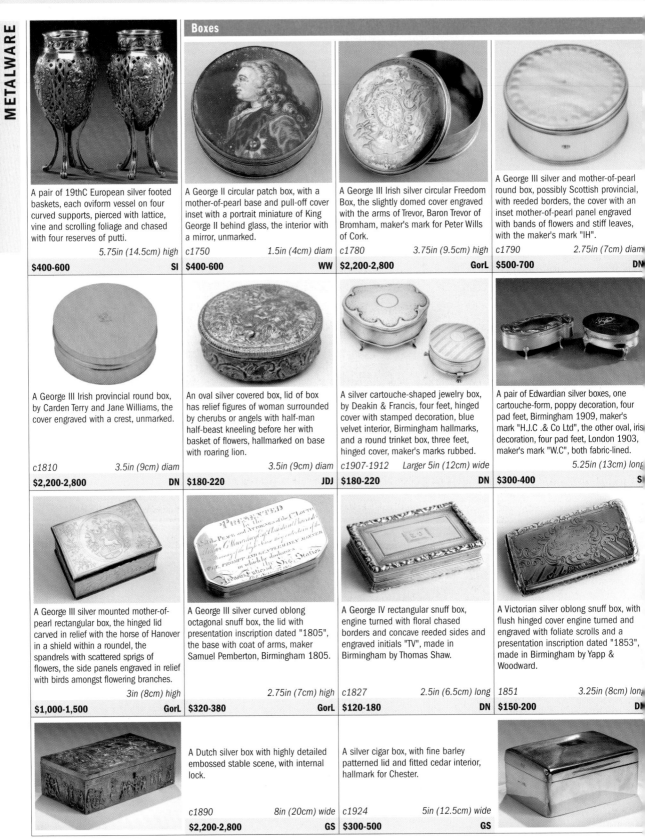

Boxes

A pair of 19thC European silver footed baskets, each oviform vessel on four curved supports, pierced with lattice, vine and scrolling foliage and chased with four reserves of putti.

5.75in (14.5cm) high

$400-600 SI

A George II circular patch box, with a mother-of-pearl base and pull-off cover inset with a portrait miniature of King George II behind glass, the interior with a mirror, unmarked.

c1750 *1.5in (4cm) diam*

$400-600 WW

A George III Irish silver circular Freedom Box, the slightly domed cover engraved with the arms of Trevor, Baron Trevor of Bromham, maker's mark for Peter Wills of Cork.

c1780 *3.75in (9.5cm) high*

$2,200-2,800 GorL

A George III silver and mother-of-pearl round box, possibly Scottish provincial, with reeded borders, the cover with an inset mother-of-pearl panel engraved with bands of flowers and stiff leaves, with the maker's mark "IH".

c1790 *2.75in (7cm) diam*

$500-700 DN

A George III Irish provincial round box, by Carden Terry and Jane Williams, the cover engraved with a crest, unmarked.

c1810 *3.5in (9cm) diam*

$2,200-2,800 DN

An oval silver covered box, lid of box has relief figures of woman surrounded by cherubs or angels with half-man half-beast kneeling before her with basket of flowers, hallmarked on base with roaring lion.

3.5in (9cm) diam

$180-220 JDJ

A silver cartouche-shaped jewelry box, by Deakin & Francis, four feet, hinged cover with stamped decoration, blue velvet interior, Birmingham hallmarks, and a round trinket box, three feet, hinged cover, maker's marks rubbed.

c1907-1912 *Larger 5in (12cm) wide*

$180-220 DN

A pair of Edwardian silver boxes, one cartouche-form, poppy decoration, four pad feet, Birmingham 1909, maker's mark "H.J.C .& Co Ltd", the other oval, iris decoration, four pad feet, London 1903, maker's mark "W.C", both fabric-lined.

5.25in (13cm) long

$300-400 SI

A George III silver mounted mother-of-pearl rectangular box, the hinged lid carved in relief with the horse of Hanover in a shield within a roundel, the spandrels with scattered sprigs of flowers, the side panels engraved in relief with birds amongst flowering branches.

3in (8cm) high

$1,000-1,500 GorL

A George III silver curved oblong octagonal snuff box, the lid with presentation inscription dated "1805", the base with coat of arms, maker Samuel Pemberton, Birmingham 1805.

2.75in (7cm) high

$320-380 GorL

A George IV rectangular snuff box, engine turned with floral chased borders and concave reeded sides and engraved initials "TV", made in Birmingham by Thomas Shaw.

c1827 *2.5in (6.5cm) long*

$120-180 DN

A Victorian silver oblong snuff box, with flush hinged cover engine turned and engraved with foliate scrolls and a presentation inscription dated "1853", made in Birmingham by Yapp & Woodward.

1851 *3.25in (8cm) long*

$150-200 D

A Dutch silver box with highly detailed embossed stable scene, with internal lock.

c1890 *8in (20cm) wide*

$2,200-2,800 GS

A silver cigar box, with fine barley patterned lid and fitted cedar interior, hallmark for Chester.

c1924 *5in (12.5cm) wide*

$300-500 GS

A Victorian engraved scent bottle, by S. Mordan & Co. Ltd., London, of square section with a hinged cover and glass stopper, initialed "G", with lined and fitted case with retailer's mark of Gibson & Co., Belfast.

c1890	2.25in (5.5cm) high
$600-900	**WW**

A German silver 'jeweled' casket, with Old Testament scenes.

	4.75in (12cm) high
$1,000-1,500	**SI**

Caddies

A George III tea caddie, oval, with a rising domed cover surmounted by an ivory knop finial, the body engraved with a lower band of foliage and an upper frieze of flowering foliage on a rayed ground, with pricked borders, initialed within a wreath cartouche and complete with lock and key, maker's mark mis-struck, "?S", London 1807.

	6.5in (16.5cm) high
$2,200-2,800	**WW**

A George III silver tea caddie, of bombe form on pierced foliate feet with floral finial, chased with pastoral figures and landscapes and rocaille decoration, maker's mark illegible, London hallmarks.

c1766	5.5in (14cm) high
$1,500-2,000	**SI**

A silver-covered perfume bottle, by Gorham Mfg Co., with silver gilt cover hinged to a neck collar and small enameled portrait minature beaded edge border, no monogram.

1896	4in (11cm) high
$500-700	**IHB**

An S. Kirk and Son silver tea caddie, Baltimore, the ovoid vessel and cylindrical cover chased with flowers and foliage on a stippled ground.

1896-1925	4in (10cm) high
$600-900	**SI**

A silver dresser jar, by Gorham Mfg Co., of plain circular apple form with slip-on mushroom lid, monogram "DL".

c1900-1930	6in (16.5cm) wide
$250-350	**IHB**

An American silver repoussée tea caddie, by S. Kirk & Son Co., Baltimore, the ovoid vessel with cylindrical cover chased with flowers and foliage on a stippled ground, monogram "MGB".

1896-1925	3.75in (9.5cm) high
$600-900	**SI**

A 20thC Argentinian silver pineapple, realistically modeled by Juan C. Pallarols.

	12in (30cm) high
$400-500	**SI**

Vinaigrettes

A George III rectangular vinaigrette, the hinged cover engraved with a vacant oval cartouche with sprays of foliage and banded, the gilt interior with a pierced fret-hinged grille engraved with a lion in a roundel and sprays of foliage, by Thomas Brough, London 1800.

	1.5in (3.5cm) high
$300-400	**WW**

A pair of George II silver candlesticks, by William Cafe, each with a baluster form standard, shaped cylindrical nozzle and removable drip pan, all on a domed shaped circular base, and cast and chased with blossoms and leaves among scrolls, each base with a later-engraved crest in a small scroll reserve, marked on inside rim of base, one slightly uneven.

c1758   11.5in (29cm) high

$10,000-15,000   **FRE**

A pair of early George III silver candlesticks, by William Cafe, the stop-fluted columns with pierced Corinthian capitals and square gadrooned nozzles, the domed bases embossed with flutes and leaves with gadrooned borders and engraved with crests, London hallmarks.

c1763   12.25in (31cm) high

$2,200-2,800   **DN**

A set of four telescopic candlesticks, with foliate knops and vertical fluting, on shaped circular feet with conforming decoration.

c1810

$600-900   **BonS**

A set of four candlesticks, Sheffield.

c1820

$4,000-6,000   **GS**

A set of four William IV shaped square raised candlesticks, by John Settle and Henry Williamson, with shell and leaf-chased capitals and nozzles, fluted knopped stems on acanthus and C-scroll chased bases, Sheffield hallmarks.

c1830   9.5in (24cm) high

$3,000-4,000   **DN**

A pair of William IV round silver candlesticks, by John Green & Co., the vase-shaped capitals, baluster stems and round bases with reeded borders and embossed with ferns, later drilled for electricity and one with an associated nozzle, Sheffield hallmarks.

c1834   12in (30cm) high

$3,000-3,500   **DN**

A set of four William IV candlesticks, with lobed columns and petal-shaped bases engraved with a shield, probably for Bague, Sheffield, by Henry Wilkinson & Co.

1835-36   11.5in (19cm) high

$1,500-2,000   **DN**

A Victorian taper stick, by Charles Reily and George Storer, with octagonal vase-shaped capital and baluster stem on a round base, London hallmarks.

c1838   3.75in (9.5cm) high

$300-400   **DN**

A pair of German silver candlesticks, of circular form on four applied hollow grapevine feet, the pyroform shafts engraved with Greek key bands, struck with an unidentified maker's mark and the Berlin bear mark with "M" assay letter, repaired.

c1870   12.25in (31cm) high

$600-900   **IHB**

A pair of Victorian short candlesticks, by Horace Woodward, with plain round columns and square bases, with initials "LR" and a baron's coronet, London hallmarks.

c1875   3.75in (9.5cm) high

$800-1,200   **DN**

A silver-plated chamberstick, of circular form, gadrooned rim and bobeche, removable extinguisher and scroll handle, monogram "WMW", by Gotham Mfg Co, Providence RI.

c1880-1908   7in (18cm) wide

$80-110   **IHB**

Four silver candlesticks, made by Currier & Roby of New York NY, quality reproductions of 1706 octagonal form assembled from castings and turnings, no mono.

c1920-1950   7in (19cm) high

$2,000-3,000   **IHB**

An 18thC silver beaker, the slightly tapering cylindrical body with plain rims engraved underneath "P*L", unmarked.

3.5in (9cm) high

$150-200   FRE

A silver beaker, by R. & W. Wilson, Philadelphia, cylindrical, the tapering sides between molded lip and foot-rims, uninitialed, marked under base "R.&W.WILSON/PHILADA", dents and scratches to sides and foot-rim.

c1840   3.75in (9.5cm) high

$300-350   FRE

A Southern silver beaker, by Megede, Lexington, Kentucky, cylindrical, the tapering sides between molded beaded lip and foot-rims, the front engraved "Julia Goddbar Walker./ 43" and on the reverse "LA& MA", marked under base "MEGEDE LEXINGTON/ COIN", dents and scratches to sides and rims.

c1850   3.25in (8.5cm) high

$600-700   FRE

A silver water goblet, of typical form on trumpet foor, molded bead foot and lip rims, the body and foot chased with grapevine decoration, gilt interior, unmarked, mono "ECC".

c1840-1870   6in (16.5cm) high

$600-700   IHB

A silver water goblet, by Tiffany & Co. of New York NY, the inverted pear-form cup on a trumpet foot (18659), etched mono "PRC".

1914-1925   6in (16.5cm) high

$300-400 IHB

Two silver cocktail goblets, made by the Whiting Mfg Co. of Bridgeport CT, of typical wide mouthed form on trumpet foot, the bowl and foot both all-over hammered, block mono "E".

1923   5.5in (15cm) high

$80-110   IHB

A silver water goblet, of typical form with molded rims, by William R. Elbers Co New York NY, no monogram, polished.

c1930-1940

$80-100   IHB

A set of twelve silver wine cups, made by the Schofield Co. of Baltimore MD, the plain bowl of tulip form with flaring lip, sitting on a narrow and tall cylindrical stem on a wide spreading shallow foot, mono "ALS".

c1925-1950

$380-420 (set)   IHB

set of four silver julep cups, each monogrammed "R.D.W." and dated.

957   3.75in (9.5cm) high

300-400   SI

A pair of silver water goblets, by Stieff Co. Baltimore MD, the plain inverted bell-shaped bowl on trumpet foot (No. 0801), no monogram.

1960   6.5in (18cm) high

$180-230   IHB

A pair of silver water goblets, in a typical plain pattern on trumpet foot (no. 72), S. Kirk & Son Inc Baltimore, mono "T"/"J*A".

c1950-1975   6.5in (18cm) high

$180-200   IHB

A silver presentation cup, by Stieff Co., Baltimore MD, with two angular strap handles, engraved "Paint and Powder Club Presidents Cup, Nicholas J. Kohlerman M.D. 1968-1969".

c1969   5.75in (16cm) high

$80-100   IHB

Mugs

An 18thC Irish silver half-pint beer mug, Hibernia and Dublin Town mark only, of plain baluster shape with heavy molded edge, scroll handle, inscribed.

4.25in (10.5cm) high

$400-600   **Chef**

A George III baluster-shaped silver pint mug, by Fuller White, with leaf-capped double scroll handle on a spreading foot, later embossed with a hunting scene, with London hallmarks.

c1762   *5in (12.5cm) high*

$700-1,000   **DN**

A silver youth cup, of plain pear form with applied hollow handle, made by the Graff, Washbourne & Dunn of New York NY, engraved "EEL Jr 1907", repaired and polished.

2.75in (7.5cm) high

$80-100   **IHB**

A silver baby cup, made by S. Kirk & Son Inc of Baltimore MD, of plain cylindrical form with molded lip, molded strap scroll handle (222), mono removed.

c1950-1980   *2.5in (7cm) high*

$70-90   **IHB**

A silver youth cup, made by Frank Smith Silver Co., Gardner MA, retailed by Black, Starr & Frost, New York NY, of octagonal baluster form, on short pedestal base with cast double scroll handle, engraved "From his God Father TT Dec. 16, 1897", recently restored.

1897   *4in (10cm) high*

$150-200   **IHB**

A silver youth cup, of short tapering cylindrical form with tucked in base on molded ring foot, cast and chased foliate scroll handle, the body chased with floral repoussé decoration, marked sterling only, presumably Baltimore MD, mono removed.

c1880-1915   *3in (8cm) high*

$380-430   **IHB**

A silver youth cup, the bell-shaped bowl on short spreading pedestal foot, applied bead foot and lip rims, the bowl engraved with foliate decoration, hollow S-scroll handle, marked by Bailey & Co., of Philadelphia PA, engraved "Edith from her Uncle Sam.", small crack at upper handle joint.

1848-1878   *4.5in (12cm) high*

$650-750   **IHB**

A silver cup, of bell form on spreading foot, the ring and scroll handle with applied medallion portrait, the body engraved with engine-turned decoration, gilt interior, made by Albert Coles & Co. of New York, old English monogram "E.Mc.C".

c1860-1877   *3.5in (9.5cm) high*

$500-600   **IHB**

A silver punch cup and saucer, of plain circular form with applied Greek Key lip, handle and saucer border, the cup on a spreading pedestal foot, made by the Gorham Mfg Co of Providence RI, engraved on cup "Anna P. Dorr 1858".

1858   *5.5in (15cm) diam*

$250-350   **IHB**

A silver youth cup, made by the Gorham Mfg Co. of Providence RI, of tapering cylindrical form with angular C-scroll handle and gilt interior, engraved "BTJ to CW Ross 1869".

1868   *3.5in (10cm) high*

$150-200   **IHB**

A large silver cup, made by the Whiting Mfg Co., New York, retailed by J.E. Caldwell & Co., Philadelphia PA, of reel form with undulating applied floral and foliate footrim, sinuous foliate-decorated scroll handle (3918-Pat.1892), engraved with large foliate scroll mono "WND" on front and presentation "From David S. Bispham Christmas 1893" on base.

1893   *5in (13.5cm) high*

$650-750   **IHB**

Victorian silver youth cup, of cylindrical form with hollow D-scroll handle, the body engraved with floral and foliate scroll decoration, marked "HA" for Atkin Bros at Sheffield, engraved "Dorothy Kate Thomas from her Aunt Kate 8th Novr 1889".

1889-1890	.75in (9.5cm) high
$300-400	**IHB**

A silver pint mug, by William Hutton & Sons Ltd, the straight tapering sides with a tucked-under base on a domed round foot, with a molded border and scroll handle, engraved beneath with a presentation inscription, Sheffield hallmarks.

c1932	4.75in (12cm) high
$280-320	**DN**

A 20thC Mexican silver covered cup, of plain cylindrical form with scroll-formed wire handle, slightly domed, tight fitting cover and unusual sipping spout, marked "Taller Contreras".

	3in (8cm) high
$120-180	**IHB**

A George I Britannia standard two handled loving cup, plain, engraved group of three initials, threaded band to center, simple scroll handles, stepped pedestal foot, Seth Lofthouse, London.

1715	5in (13cm) high
$1,200-1,800	**L&T**

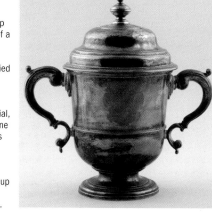

George I silver cup, the cylindrical body with molded rim over a chased, padrooned midband and scroll reserve engraved with a coat-of-arms, the sides set with two hollow scroll-form handles, marked under rim, repairs to lobed chasing, foot, and one handle joint, marks worn, light dents and scratches.

1726	6in (15cm) high
$3,000-3,500	**FRE**

An extremely rare early 18thC silvered brass cup and cover, in the form of a silver example of the period with two double scroll handles and applied girdle and a spreading circular foot, the cover with two rising domed sections and a knop finial, the body engraved on one side with a coat-of-arms and struck on the other side below the rim with pseudo marks (D? and two stylized lions), the cup rests on a later turned wooden plinth inscribed.

c1735-45	11in (28cm) high
$7,000-10,000	**WW**

A George III two-handled loving cup, by Dorothy Langlands, Newcastle, scroll handles, pedestal foot.

1811	
$400-600	**L&T**

Ewers & Decanters

George III Irish silver tumbler cup, by Gustavus Byrne, engraved with foliate scrolls, pendants and ribbon-tied swags round an oval reserve with a monogram, Dublin hallmarks.

1795	3.25in (8.5cm) diam
$1,800-2,200	**DN**

A George IV silver beaker, of cylindrical form with applied molded lip, marked "WE" for William Eaton at London, engraved crest of a greaved arm.

c1823-1824	3.5in (9cm) high
$400-600	**IHB**

A Victorian silver ewer, of baluster form with hinged cover and scroll handle, engraved with scrolling foliage, the handle with a female mask terminal, the cover with a berry finial.

c1846	12.5in (32cm) high
$1,200-1,800	**SI**

A Victorian baluster-shaped ewer, guilloche rim, fluted scroll spout above panels and borders, hinged cover with floral medallions, arched handle, maker's mark "R and S", Sheffield.

c1857	
$600-900	**BonS**

An English silver claret jug, the faceted clear glass ovoid body cut with leaves and fruit and mounted with a scroll and floral chased collar with satyr-head masks, on a low foot with rocaille scroll and cabochon chasing, fully marked foot "London, C.E.", worn.

c1891   13in (33cm) high

$2,800-3,200   **FRE**

A pair of European silver-mounted small decanters, with a faceted knob stopper, the base of the decanter fitting into a silver holder with shallow embossed garden scenery, struck with pseudomarks, probably by a German manufacturer, and then imported into England by Thomas Glaser in London.

c1890-1891   7.5in (19cm) high

$300-400   **IHB**

A Victorian silver-mounted glass claret jug, by Finley and Taylor, the clear glass bottle-shaped body with a star-cut base, a scroll handle and hinged cover with oval thumb-piece, London hallmarks.

c1893   11.75in (29.5cm) high

$1,200-1,800   **DN**

A late 19th/early 20thC German silver-mounted glass decanter, the hexagonal tapering vessel mounted with an angular handle and ribbon-tied reeded neck, acorn finial.

                    10.5in (26.5cm) high

$600-800   **S**

A silver two bottle tantalus stand, by TG Hawkes & Co. of Corning NY, comprising two circular bases joined by a tubular shaft leading to a sliding horizontal handle which locks the toppers of the diamond-decorated cut glass "Scotch" and "Rye" decanters, monogram "IJE" on handle.

c1910-1940

$800-1,200   **IHB**

Wine Labels

A George II escutcheon wine label, incised "PORT" by Sandilands Drinkwater, London, lion passant and maker's mark only.

c1745

$300-400   **WW**

A George III kidney-shaped wine label, with a feather edge, incised "HOCK", maker's mark and lion passant only, by Margaret Binley, London.

c1770

$220-280   **WW**

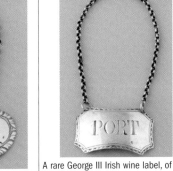

A rare George III Irish wine label, of waisted, canted oblong outline with a bright cut border, incised "PORT" by Andrew Goodwin, Dublin, maker's mark only "AG" with mullet between.

c1775

$300-400   **WW**

A George III scroll wine label, with an oval cartouche surmount, an engraved ropework border and chased bunches of grapes, crested and incised "SHERRY" by William Cattell, London, maker's mark and lion passant only.

c1780

$220-280   **WW**

A George III heraldic wine label, in the form of a gryphon passant crest, above a scroll filled area, incised "PORT", unmarked, probably last quarter of the 18thC.

$400-600   **WW**

A George III wine label, in the form of a scroll with an openwork surmount of foliate festoons and an oval cartouche, initialed and incised "GIN" by T. Phipps & E. Robinson, London, maker's mark only, struck twice.

c1785

$400-600   **WW**

A rare George III ascribed North Country provincial wine label, of oblong outline with a wavy top edge and a bright cut border, incised "SWEET WINE" by Richard Clark, York, maker's mark, lion passant and duty mark only.

c1790

$700-1,000   **WW**

A George III navette-shaped wine label, with a reeded border, incised "BRANDY" by Susanna Barker, London, no date letter.

c1790

$220-280 WW

A pair of George III silver-gilt wine labels, of canted oblong outline, with a cartouche and scroll surmount and reeded borders, pierced "PORT" and "CLARET" by Henry Chawner, London, no date letter.

c1790

$600-900 WW

A George III wine label, in the form of a 12-pointed star with bright engraving and a plain center, incised "SHERRY" by William Allen (II) London, no date letter.

c1790

$600-900 WW

A George III wine label, of canted oblong form with a reeded border, incised "HERMITAGE", by Robert Barker, London.

c1793

$320-380 WW

A rare George III reeded wine label, of canted oblong outline incised "WIGHT" by Peter & Ann Bateman, London.

c1793

$700-1,000 WW

A CLOSER LOOK AT A SILVER WINE LABEL

The labels were hung around the neck of the bottle by chains – they are not essential for sale but their absence will detract from the price.

Wine labels were first produced in 1740 to identify the bottles of new wines and drinks that were becoming more commonly available, but were not properly labeled.

Watch for alterations to the wording on the label where the original piercing has been replaced with a rarer name.

Rare names are more collectible. The name 'Mountain' refers to a popular 18thC variety of Malaga wine using mountain grapes. Another rare name is 'Vidonia', a white wine from the Canary Islands.

A George III wine label, in the form of a 12-pointed star with bright engraving and a plain center incised "MOUNTAIN" by Thomas Morley, London 1793.

$1,500-2,000 WW

A George III wine label, in the form of a crescent with a 'batswing' outline and reeded border incised "RUM" by Peter & Ann Bateman, London 1797.

$300-400 WW

A George III gorget-shaped wine label, incised "HOLLANDS" by Peter & Ann Bateman, London.

c1799

$220-280 WW

A rare George III Irish wine label, of canted oblong form with a bright cut border, incised and filled "MADEIRA" by George Nangle, Dublin, no date letter.

c1800

$400-600 WW

A matched set of three wine labels, of rounded oblong form with gadrooned borders, incised "SWEET WINE", "CLARET" and "HOCK" by William Bateman, London 1817-18.

$320-380 WW

A near pair of William IV vine leaf wine labels, pierced "PORT" and "SHERRY", probably by William Knight (II).

$220-280 WW

A silver sommelier's cup, liqueur label and a George II caddy spoon, the cup is by Lalaounis, the label is inscribed "RYE" and the spoon, "London 1798" with bright cut engraving.

$150-200 SI

An early 19thC Dutch corkscrew, with a curved handle, initialed, a wire helix and a baluster body with an intaglio seal terminal which unscrews to reveal a toothpick, struck only with a 19thC Dutch duty mark.

3in (8cm) long

$600-900 WW

A silver mounted brass folding corkscrew, the silver tapering cylindrical case of hammered form engraved with a monogram and retailed by J.C. Vickery, 181-183 Regent Street W, made in London by Charles Dumenil.

c1904 *3.5in (9cm) long*

$300-400 DN

An Edward VII silver pocket flask, with slip-off bottom forming a cup, mushroom form screw cap and body engraved all over with floral and foliate scroll decoration, interior screw cap, the body marked by Arthur & John Zimmerman at Birmingham in 1906/1907, the outer cap marked by Thomas Jones Watson at London in 1906/1907, one shoulder corner dented.

4in (10.5cm) high

$300-400 IHB

An Edwardian mounted glass spirit flask, of rounded oblong form, with a leather clad upper body and a pull-off cup, by James Dixon & Sons, Sheffield.

1908 *6in (15cm) high*

$500-700 WW

A George III ascribed West Country brandy saucepan and cover, with a turned wooden handle, crested twice, by Richard Ferris, Exeter, maker's mark, lion passant and duty mark only.

c1800 *3in (8cm) diam*

$700-1,000 WW

A French silver wine bucket, retailed by Tiffany & Co. Paris.

10in (25cm) high

$1,500-2,000 SI

A silver George II baluster-shaped caster, by Samuel Wood, with a molded girdle and border, the pierced cover with knopped finial, London hallmarks.

c1744 *6in (15cm) high*

$400-600 DN

A George III pepper caster, with writhen finial and baluster body by John Delmester.

c1764 *5.5in (14cm) high*

$220-280 BonS

A George III silver caster, maker's mark "RP" centered by a leaf, London hallmarks.

c1768 *6in (15cm) high*

$400-600 SI

A George III silver covered sugar urn, on square foot with fluted boarders, the cover with a circular flower-head surmounted by a ball finial, engraved with a coat of arms on either side of the body and on the cover, London, by Daniel Smith and Robert Sharp.

c1787 *6in (15cm) high*

$1,000-1,500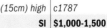

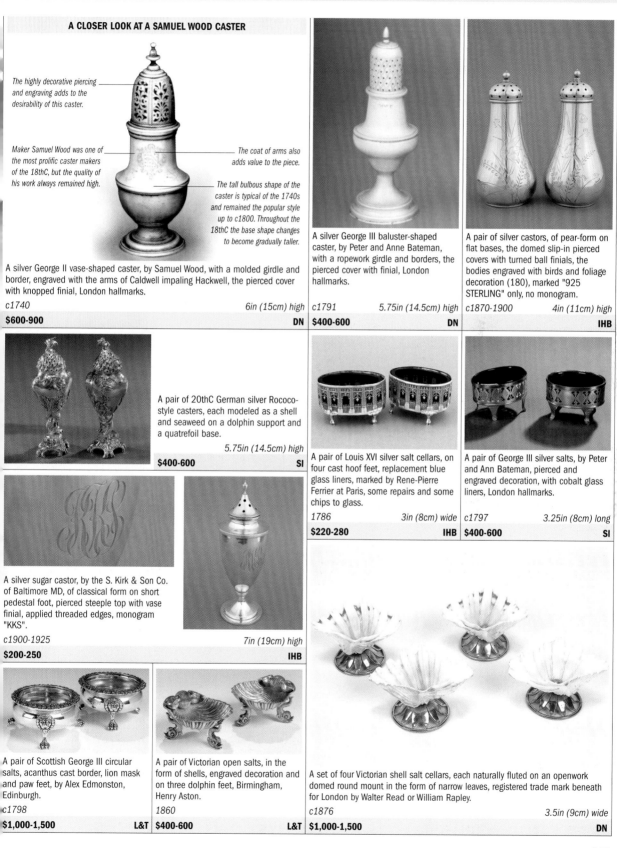

A CLOSER LOOK AT A SAMUEL WOOD CASTER

The highly decorative piercing and engraving adds to the desirability of this caster.

Maker Samuel Wood was one of the most prolific caster makers of the 18thC, but the quality of his work always remained high.

The coat of arms also adds value to the piece.

The tall bulbous shape of the caster is typical of the 1740s and remained the popular style up to c1800. Throughout the 18thC the base shape changes to become gradually taller.

A silver George II vase-shaped caster, by Samuel Wood, with a molded girdle and border, engraved with the arms of Caldwell impaling Hackwell, the pierced cover with knopped finial, London hallmarks.

c1740　　　　　　　*6in (15cm) high*

$600-900　　　　　　　　　　**DN**

A silver George III baluster-shaped caster, by Peter and Anne Bateman, with a ropework girdle and borders, the pierced cover with finial, London hallmarks.

c1791　　　*5.75in (14.5cm) high*

$400-600　　　　　　　　　**DN**

A pair of silver castors, of pear-form on flat bases, the domed slip-in pierced covers with turned ball finials, the bodies engraved with birds and foliage decoration (180), marked "925 STERLING" only, no monogram.

c1870-1900　　　*4in (11cm) high*

IHB

A pair of 20thC German silver Rococo-style casters, each modeled as a shell and seaweed on a dolphin support and a quatrefoil base.

5.75in (14.5cm) high

$400-600　　　　　　　　　**SI**

A pair of Louis XVI silver salt cellars, on four cast hoof feet, replacement blue glass liners, marked by Rene-Pierre Ferrier at Paris, some repairs and some chips to glass.

1786　　　　　*3in (8cm) wide*

$220-280　　　　　　　**IHB**

A pair of George III silver salts, by Peter and Ann Bateman, pierced and engraved decoration, with cobalt glass liners, London hallmarks.

c1797　　　*3.25in (8cm) long*

$400-600　　　　　　　　　**SI**

A silver sugar castor, by the S. Kirk & Son Co. of Baltimore MD, of classical form on short pedestal foot, pierced steeple top with vase finial, applied threaded edges, monogram "KKS".

c1900-1925　　　　*7in (19cm) high*

$200-250　　　　　　　　　**IHB**

A pair of Scottish George III circular salts, acanthus cast border, lion mask and paw feet, by Alex Edmonston, Edinburgh.

c1798

$1,000-1,500　　　　　　**L&T**

A pair of Victorian open salts, in the form of shells, engraved decoration and on three dolphin feet, Birmingham, Henry Aston.

1860

$400-600　　　　　　　　**L&T**

A set of four Victorian shell salt cellars, each naturally fluted on an openwork domed round mount in the form of narrow leaves, registered trade mark beneath for London by Walter Read or William Rapley.

c1876　　　　　*3.5in (9cm) wide*

$1,000-1,500　　　　　　　**DN**

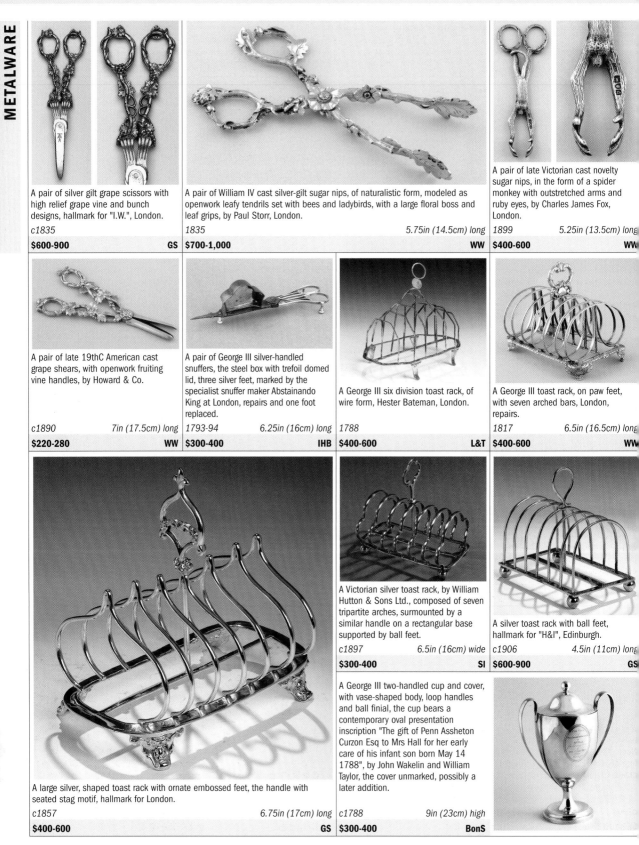

A pair of silver gilt grape scissors with high relief grape vine and bunch designs, hallmark for "I.W.", London.

c1835

$600-900 GS

A pair of William IV cast silver-gilt sugar nips, of naturalistic form, modeled as openwork leafy tendrils set with bees and ladybirds, with a large floral boss and leaf grips, by Paul Storr, London.

1835 5.75in (14.5cm) long

$700-1,000 WW

A pair of late Victorian cast novelty sugar nips, in the form of a spider monkey with outstretched arms and ruby eyes, by Charles James Fox, London.

1899 5.25in (13.5cm) long

$400-600 WW

A pair of late 19thC American cast grape shears, with openwork fruiting vine handles, by Howard & Co.

c1890 7in (17.5cm) long

$220-280 WW

A pair of George III silver-handled snuffers, the steel box with trefoil domed lid, three silver feet, marked by the specialist snuffer maker Abstainando King at London, repairs and one foot replaced.

1793-94 6.25in (16cm) long

$300-400 IHB

A George III six division toast rack, of wire form, Hester Bateman, London.

1788

$400-600 L&T

A George III toast rack, on paw feet, with seven arched bars, London, repairs.

1817 6.5in (16.5cm) long

$400-600 WW

A Victorian silver toast rack, by William Hutton & Sons Ltd., composed of seven tripartite arches, surmounted by a similar handle on a rectangular base supported by ball feet.

c1897 6.5in (16cm) wide

$300-400 SI

A silver toast rack with ball feet, hallmark for "H&I", Edinburgh.

c1906 4.5in (11cm) long

$600-900 GS

A large silver, shaped toast rack with ornate embossed feet, the handle with seated stag motif, hallmark for London.

c1857 6.75in (17cm) long

$400-600 GS

A George III two-handled cup and cover, with vase-shaped body, loop handles and ball finial, the cup bears a contemporary oval presentation inscription "The gift of Penn Assheton Curzon Esq to Mrs Hall for her early care of his infant son born May 14 1788", by John Wakelin and William Taylor, the cover unmarked, possibly a later addition.

c1788 9in (23cm) high

$300-400 BonS

A George III syphon tube, in the form of an S-shaped straw with a hinged and pierced section for cleaning access and a plain tang, initialed and unscrewing in the middle for storage purposes.

9.5in (24.5cm) long

$400-600 WW

A George III oblong silver kitchen nutmeg grater, by Thomas Phipps and Edward Robinson II, with a gadroon, shell and foliate border and hinged cover, London hallmarks.

c1810   4.75in (12.5cm) high

$1,800-2,200 DN

A rare George III hair comb, by James Perchard & William Brooks (II), London.

1808   7in (25.5cm) long

$400-600 WW

An early 19thC rare pastry cutter, with crimped wheel at one end and a lozenge-shaped marker at the other, unmarked.

5.25in (13.5cm) long

$400-600 WW

A pair of silver-plate fish servers, marked by the J. Russell Co. of Southbridge MA, in the 'Antique' pattern with fish decorated blade and tines, monogram "MCB".

c1887-1900   11in (28cm) long

$40-50 IHB

A silver saucepan, by Goodnow & Jenks, Boston, the reel-shaped stand with bud finial, turned wood handle, probably adaptation of copper or brass design, no monogram.

c1893-1905   7in (17.5cm) high

$250-350 IHB

A silver-mounted glass inkwell, by Tiffany & Co. of New York NY, the square body cut in a vertical ribbed design, the silver gilt cover with spiral-lobed decoration and screw lockiing mechanism, with patent date, monogram "ESW", silvergilt worn.

1885   2.75in (7cm) wide

$750-850 IHB

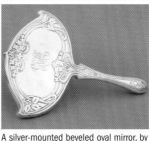

A silver-mounted beveled oval mirror, by Theodore Hoster & Bros, Providence RI, mono "GWJ", with Art Nouveau floral and scroll decoration, no. 2978, minor spotting to re-silvered mirror.

c1895-1915   11in (30cm) long

$80-100 IHB

A silver tea bell of typical form, by Frank M. Whiting & Co of N. Attleboro MA, retailed by Bailey, Banks & Biddle Co. of Philadelphia P/A, with ribbed handle, bulge at bottom of bell, made some dents.

c1900-1930   4.5in (11.5cm) high

$30-40 IHB

A pair of silver-handled military brushes, by R. Blackinton & Co. of North Attleboro MA, of shaped obling form with lion decorated silcer handles, mono "LHB", some dents.

c1904   4.5in (12cm) high

$80-100 IHB

A five-piece silver silver dresser set, by Reed & Barton of Taunton MA, consisting of hand mirror, comb, hair, cloth and hat brushes all embossed with high relief floral decoration against a hammered background (120A), mono "NAF".

c1890-1915   9.5in (26cm) long

$600-700 IHB

A silver mesh purse, hinged frame with link chain, some engraved decoration on side, struck with the butterfly trademark used by Ernst Gideon Bek Inc. of Pforzheim, Germany, and distributed by Binder Bors Inc., New York.

c1900-1925   5.5in (14cm) long

$100-150 IHB

A George V silver ashtray and lighter, the ashtray of clover form with cigarette rest, the stacking lighter of conforming shape, marked by E.J. Greenberg at Birmingham.

1929-30   4in (10.5cm) wide

$50-80 IHB

Silverplate

An English silverplated entrée dish and cover, applied with foliate borders, handles and feet, the top handle cast as two lion pelts and branches, further engraved decoration and crest, maker's mark "M.H. and Co."

14.25in (36cm) long

$300-400 SI

A 19thC Sheffield silverplate dish cover, of typical form, the oblong body with a chased branch handle above scrolling oak leaves and acorns, the unengraved sides over gadroon and shell borders and a broad concave rim, together with a Gorham silver-plate well-and-tree platter, the cover marked under handle plate "IB".

Platter 21in (53.5cm) long

$320-380 FRE

An English silver-plated oval breakfast dish, retailed by Hardy Bros., Sydney, Australia, of typical form, the oval body with a retracting lid opening to a removable strainer supported on four reeded tapering legs with claw-and-ball feet, wear to plating.

14.5in (37cm) long

$300-400 FRE

A pair of silver-plated standard lamps, each with a Corinthian capital, a fluted column, a square plinth with applied wreaths to each side, on a stepped square base and scroll-and-paw feet.

53.5in (136cm) high

$3,000-4,000 DN

A set of four early 19thC Sheffield silver plate telescopic candlesticks, removable drip pans with egg-and-dart edge above a vase sconce with acanthus base, on a knopped baluster column and a reeded acanthus collar, on circular bases.

c1825 *10.5in (26.5cm) high*

$700-1,000 BonS

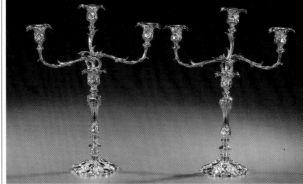

A pair of silverplated three-light candelabra, the serpentine floral and leaf form arms molded with acanthus leaves and terminating in candlecups.

20in (50cm) high

$2,800-3,200 SI

A pair of Victorian silver-plated wine coolers, by Elkington & Co. Ltd, Birmingham, of campana form on a raised circular base below molded leaf and vines, the undulating everted rim with beaded edges.

1880 *11.25in (28cm) high*

$3,000-4,000 S

An early 19thC Sheffield silver plate part-fluted round tea urn, engraved with an armorial, with two leaf-chased handles and nulled borders, the tap with a chased spigot, on a square base with leaf-capped paw feet, the domed cover with a flower finial, engraved with a crest of the arms of Hill of Kent and Linarce, and also Lanacre of Yorkshire.

14.5in (37cm) high

$600-900 DN

A French silverplated wine cradle, by Liezard Pere et Fils, with a bottle cradle and ivory-knopped crank below a chased vine handle and supported on a circular base with vines and leaves on a matted surface and four scroll feet, marked on crank mechanism "Liezard Pere et Fils/Brevetes S.G.O.C.", light wear to plating.

c1900 *14in (35.5cm) high*

$3,000-4,000 FRE

A pair of heavy silverplated wine coasters with vine leaf cast borders, turn wood base.

8.25in (21cm) diam

$300-400 L&T

Animals

A bronze, entitled 'Cheval' by Antoine-Louis Barye, inscribed "Barye", with brown patina.

1796-1875   *5.5in (17cm) high*

$5,000-7,000   **SI**

A pair of bronze Marly horses, signed "Coustou", each rearing horse being held by a male attendant, on naturalistic bases.

22.5in (57cm) high

$1,800-2,200   **L&T**

A pair of Marly horses, after Nicolas Coustou, patinated bronze, mounted as table lamps.

16in (40.5cm) high

$700-1,000   **SI**

A pair of Austrian bronze bookends, each cast in the form of a young boy astride a donkey, playing the flute, each stamped "AUSTRIA", minor dents.

c1890   *5in (12.5cm) high*

$700-1,000   **FRE**

A rare Vienna bronze cold-painted horse's head.

c1900   *4.25in (11cm) high*

$1,500-2,000   **RdeR**

A 19th/20thC bronze, entitled 'Mule' by Etha Richter, inscribed "Etha Richer" and "C. A. Bierling" with brown patina.

5.75in (14.6cm) high

$500-700   **SI**

A gilt bronze Marly horse, after Coustou, signed "Coustou". *Although signed, this piece is a later reproduction.*

1950   *15in (38cm) high*

$500-700   **SI**

A bronze horse with dark brown patina, by Russian actress Nathalie de Golejewski and inscribed "N de golejevski".

19in (48cm) high

$1,800-2,200   **FRE**

A 19thC gilt bronze sculpture, by T. Pavtrot, of two birds, one with a beetle, on an oval plinth and oval rouge marble stand.

6.5in (16.5cm) high

$700-1,000   **FRE**

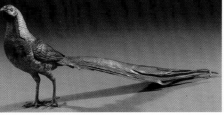

An Austrian cold-painted bronze figure of a pheasant, by Bergmann, impressed marks, tail repaired.

19in (48.5cm) long

$500-700   **SI**

A pair of 'Bird and Bee' exquisite bronze casts, by Ferdinand Pautrot, with exceptional detail.

c1870   *6.75in (17cm) high*

$3,000-3,500   **RGA**

A Vienna bronze cold-painted owl, with Geschutz mark.

c1900   *4in (10cm) high*

$700-1,000   **RdeR**

A Vienna bronze painted African grey parrot, with Geschutz mark.

c1900

$1,500-2,000   **RdeR**

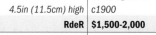

A Vienna bronze cold-painted European jay, with "B" mark.

c1900   *4.5in (11.5cm) high*

$1,500-2,000   **RdeR**

A Vienna bronze cold-painted great dane, signed "B" for Bergmann.

c1900   *5.5in (14cm) long*

$1,500-2,000   **RdeR**

A 20thC Vienna bronze cold-painted cock pheasant.

12in (30.5cm) high

$700-1,000   **RdeR**

A 19thC bronze group, entitled 'Chasse à la Perdrix à Pointer and Setter Flushing Game', by Pierre Jules Mêne, inscribed "P. J. Mêne", brown patina.

8.75in (22cm) high

$2,200-2,800   **SI**

A bronze sculpture, after P.J. Mêne, of a standing whippet, on an oval rouge marble plinth, signed "P. J. Mêne".

$500-700   **FRE**

A 19thC bronze group, entitled 'Chien de Chasse et Trophees' by Pierre Jules Mêne, inscribed "P. J. Mêne" with dark brown patina, with golden brown highlights.

12in (30.5cm) high

$3,000-4,000   **SI**

A Vienna bronze cold-painted gun dog/spaniel.

c1900   *6.25in (16cm)*

$500-700   **RdeR**

Left: A bronze inkwell, after the antique, the circular lid depicting a putti wrestling with a serpent on a lion skin, the drum base fitted with ceramic well, cast with frieze of warriors on paw feet and red and black turned marble base.

7.5in (19cm) high

$500-700   **L&T**

Right: A 19thC small cast bronze figure of a greyhound, on rectangular plinth.

6.25in (16cm) wide

$700-1,000   **L&T**

A pair of bronzed metal whippets, each seated on an ogee-molded base.

32in (81.5cm) high

$1,500-2,000   **SI**

Left: A 19th-20thC bronze entitled 'Bulldog', inscribed "E.E. Codman" and stamped "Gorham Co. Q (?) 40", with brown and green patinas on marble base.

4.5in (11.5cm) high

Right: A 19thC bronze group entitled 'Stag and Hind', by Alfred Dubucand, inscribed "Dubucand", with golden brown and brown patinas.

5.75in (14.5cm) high

$600-900 (each)   **SI**

A Hagenaur small bronze model of a cat, with highly stylized features and curved rod-like tail, sitting on a circular base, marked with "wHw".

2.25in (5.5cm) high

$100-150   **DN**

An ashtray with a gilt bronze model of a cat, by K. Heynen-Dumont, the cat sits on its haunches and toys with a ball, resting on a curved base mounted on one edge of the circular marble, signed.

4.25in (10.5cm) high

$500-700   **DN**

A 19thC bronze group, entitled 'A Cow and Calf', by Pierre Jules Mêne, inscribed "P. J. Mêne" and stamped "Mêne" on side of base with brown patina, on black slate base.

9.25in (23.5cm) high

$700-1,000   **SI**

A 19thC bronze, entitled 'Four Bulls', by Peter Paul Prince Troubetzkoy, inscribed "Troubetzkoy" with dark rich brown patina, the present model is a late casting.

9in (23cm) high

$1,800-2,200   **SI**

A 19thC bronze entitled 'Gazelle', by Antoine-Louis Barye, inscribed "Barye" and stamped "AN6E" under base, with brown patina.

3.75in (96cm) high

$500-700   **SI**

A Vienna bronze cold-painted royal stag.

c1900   *6.5in (16.5cm) high*

$700-1,000   **RdeR**

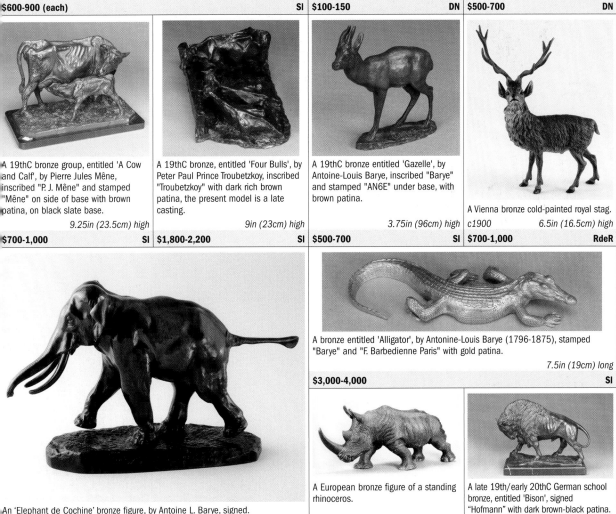

A bronze entitled 'Alligator', by Antonine-Louis Barye (1796-1875), stamped "Barye" and "F. Barbedienne Paris" with gold patina.

7.5in (19cm) long

$3,000-4,000   **SI**

An 'Elephant de Cochine' bronze figure, by Antoine L. Barye, signed.

c1860   *6in (15cm) high*

$6,000- 9,000   **RGA**

A European bronze figure of a standing rhinoceros.

30.25in (77cm) long

$2,200-2,800   **DN**

A late 19th/early 20thC German school bronze, entitled 'Bison', signed "Hofmann" with dark brown-black patina.

15.5in (39.5cm) high

$3,000-3,500   **SI**

A late 20thC bronze figure of a Native American Chief, signed "C. Kauba", figure standing with full headdress holding rifle, golden brown and silver painted finish, mounted on green marble disk base.

27in (28.5cm) high

$600-900   **TWC**

A 19thC bronze figure, modeled as an urchin warming his hands over a cauldron, signed "J. Cardona", chocolate brown patination, illuminated from inside, with bronze foundry mark and serial number "66988", later wiring for electricity.

13.5in (34.5cm) high

$400-600   **FRE**

A bronze figure, modeled as an infant standing on a stool, holding a shoe, mid-brown patination, some wear, unmarked.

c1900   *13.5in (34.5cm) high*

$600-900   **FRE**

A French bronze figure, entitled 'Leçon de Flute', after Guadez, with "Medaille d'Or" foundry mark, dated, the young man shown seated and playing the flute, mid-brown patination, wear to patination.

c1900   *19in (48.5cm) high*

$1,500-2,000   **FRE**

An early 20thC recast French bronze figure, entitled "Little Red Riding Hood", after Auguste Moreau, dark brown and chocolate brown patination, no foundry mark but with an applied copyright mark on the base.

27in (68.5cm) high

$800-1,200   **FRE**

A Neoclassical style bronze statue, depicting a mother and her child with two playful cherubs.

64in (162.5cm) high

$3,000-4,000   **SI**

A late 19thC gilt bronze familial group, after Moreau, signed "Moreau".

17in (43cm) high

$1,500-2,000   **SI**

A patinated bronze group of a Classical lady and gentleman, signed "Bodendick".

19.5in (50cm) high

$1,000-1,500   **SI**

An Edward S. Hoffman III 20thC American bronze, entitled "Reclining Nudes", with cast date, edition 3/3 and signature.

1968   *10in (25.5cm) high*

$600-900   **FRE**

Four 19thC silvered bronze figures of the Four Seasons.

6.75in (17cm) high

$700-1,000   **SI**

A late 19th/early 20thC pair of patinated bronze figures, entitled "King Arthur and Hercules", mounted as table lamps.

22in (56cm) high

$3,000-4,000   **SI**

An Albert Ernest Carrier Belleuse (1824-1887) bronze bust, entitled "Raphael", brown patina, on socle, inscribed "A. Carrier".

8.25in (21cm) high

$500-700   **SI**

A bronze bust of Edward VII on a square socle and plinth, incised "Sydney Church SC, Elkington & Co, London 1901, Copyright".

c1901

$300-400   **DN**

Joe Beeler, CAA, 'Chief Goes to Washington', bronze edition of 35.

This sculptor received the Best of Show and Gold medal at the Cowboy Artists of America Annual Exhibition in 1990.

19in (48cm) high

$20,000-30,000   **Alt**

George Carlson, AOA, NAWA, 'Basque Sheepherder', bronze edition of 9.

28in (71cm) high

$4,000-6,000   **Alt**

Juan Dell, TAPA, 'Following the Bison', bronze edition of 30.

13in high (33cm) high

$2,000-3,000   **Alt**

Fred Fellows, CAA, 'No Easy Way Out', bronze edition of 50.

Without plinth 42in (107cm) high

$30,000-40,000   **Alt**

Herbert Haseltine, 'Shire Stallion: Harboro'Nulli Secondus', in partially gilded bronze, cast and patinated by Valsuani in Paris, mounted on a marble base, with letter from H. Haseltine.

13.5in (34cm) high

$30,000-40,000   **RENO**

G. Harvey, 'Those that Plunder', bronze edition of 30.

17in (43cm) high

$4,000-5,000   **Alt**

Doug Hyde and Bill Prokopiof, 'Standing Indian Woman', top portion stone, bottom portion bronze.

65in (165cm) high

$20,000-30,000   **Alt**

Harry Jackson, CAA, NAWA, NSS, 'Two Champs II', bronze polychrome edition of 50.

23.5in (60cm) high

$12,000-18,000   **Alt**

Harry Jackson, CAA, NAWA, NSS, 'Iroquois Guide II', bronze polychrome edition of 350.

14in (35.5cm) high

$2,000-3,000   **Alt**

Harry Jackson, CAA, NAWA, NSS, 'Sacagawea II', bronze polychrome edition of 350.

17in (43cm) high

$3,000-4,000   **Alt**

Harry Jackson, CAA, NAWA, NSS, 'The Marshal', bronze polychrome, edition of 20.

In 1969 Time Magazine commissioned Jackson to sculpt John Wayne as Rooster Cogburn from the film 'True Grit' for their August 8 cover, which subsequently appeared on the cover of Time and Saturday Evening Post, making it the most widely recognized western sculpture by a living artist.

29.5in (75cm) high

$40,000-60,000   **Alt**

Harry Jackson, CAA, NAWA, NSS, 'Dog Soldier', bronze polychrome edition of 20.

25in (63.5cm) high

$30,000-40,000   **Alt**

James Nathan Muir, 'Rescue under Fire', bronze.

22in (56cm) high

$20,000-30,000   **RENO**

James Nathan Muir 'Saving the Flag', bronze edition of 24.

$15,000-20,000   **Alt**

Charles M. Russell, 'The Medicine Man', bronze, stamped "Roman Works, N.Y".

Nancy Russell left a description of the Medicine Man, identifying the figure as Sleeping Thunder, the artist's fictional character. She wrote: 'when a Medicine Man went to a sick lodge to help drive away the bad spirits, he had his pipe and his medicine with him, he sits on his robe, cross-legged, facing the lodge door where the sick person is to be healed.

7in (18in) high

$60,000-90,000   **RENO**

Charles M. Russell, 'Counting Coup', bronze, modeled 1905, cast mid-1920s, stamped "Roman Bronze Works N.Y.".

This piece is the second documented sculpture in Russell's oeuvre, a powerful composition in three dimensions.

$200,000-250,000   **RENO**

Charles Schreyvogel (1861-1912), 'The Last Drop', bronze with base stamped 'copyright 1903 by Charles Schreyvogel, Roman Bronze Works, NY.

1903

$50,000-70,000   **RENO**

Robert Scriver (1914-1999), 'Too Late for the Hawken', bronze edition of 50.

22in (56cm) high

$6,000-9,000   **Alt**

Henry Shrady, ANA, NSS, NIAL, 'An Empty Saddle', bronze.

Shrady's first sculpture was a complex grouping of men, horses and a canon, which Gorham Silver Company cast.

11in (28cm) high

$50,000-60,000   **Alt**

Melvin Warren, CAA, 'Words of Wisdom', bronze edition of 100.

10in (25.5cm) high

$3,000-4,000   **Alt**

Melvin Warren, CAA, 'The Drifter', bronze edition of 20.

9.5in (24cm) high

$3,500-4,500   **Alt**

Melvin Warren, CAA, 'Commander', bronze edition of 60.

9.75in (25cm) high

$2,500-3,000   **Alt**

Fritz White, AOA, CAA, 'In Search of the Snow Goose', bronze edition of 16.

34in (86cm) high

$8,000-12,000   **Alt**

Olaf Wieghorst, 'The Navajo Madonna', bronze edition of 10.

23in (58.5cm) high

$20,000-30,000   **Alt**

Tallcases

Tallcases were made in the usa and in europe but they have been especially popular in Britain since the mid-17thc, where they are known as 'longcase clocks'.

The cases were often made by cabinetmakers and so reflect period furniture style. The best tallcases of the 17thC have marqueterie decoration. Later 17thC pieces often have a lenticle, or small glass window, which reveals the pendulum.

The earliest dials were square with narrow chapter rings. After 1715, break-arches became popular as they allowed more elements to be displayed on the face. Round dials were common in the 19thC, especially in France. The dial material can help to date a piece too: brass dials with applied chapter rings are the earliest type, European dials began to be made of painted wood in the 18thC, with painted metal becoming more common in the 19thC. Brass dials fetch higher values.

The main factors to consider when assessing a clock are: originality, proportions and size, case material, color or patination, quality of original work and of restoration, date and name of maker. The value of a clock can be reduced by as much

as three-quarters if it shows unsympathetic restoration or abnormal signs of ageing. Special features, such as a 'strike-silent', add value, as do 8-day movements, which allow the piece to be wound once a week.

Genuine tallcases can be difficult to buy because they comprise so many different elements – cases, dials, movements, weights and pendulums. All of these elements may become mixed up, altered or replaced. Previously this may have happened during storage or removal but more recently financial gain is often the reason for mismatched elements so it is important to buy from someone who understands clocks and whom you trust.

It is harder to buy a clock with a good case than a good movement. If a tallcase has been stored in unsuitable conditions, only the movement will have survived. Beware of 'marriages' where the dial or movement has been replaced, as this substantially reduces the value of a clock as an investment. If the clock fulfills these criteria, it will be a good purchase and a great pleasure.

Roy Clements

A month duration, marqueterie tallcase, by Brouncker Watts, Fleet Street, London.	A walnut tallcase, by John Wise, London, with brass dial, showing calendar aperture.	An 18thC oak, 8-day, arched-dial tallcase clock, with well-patinated cabinet.	An 8-day tallcase clock, with allover floral marqueterie, with caddie pediment, the brass dial with a calendar.	An early 18thC oak 8-day tallcase clock, by John Atkinson, Isle of Man, the twin train movement with anchor escapement striking on a bell, date aperture, base with molded plinth.
			This is a fine example of early 18thC marqueterie.	
c1693 77in (195.5cm) high	c1700		c1700	78in (198cm) high
$60,000-90,000 **Pen**	$30,000-50,000 **Pen**	$8,000-12,000 **Pen**	$50,000-70,000 **Pen**	$1,500-2,000 **L&T**

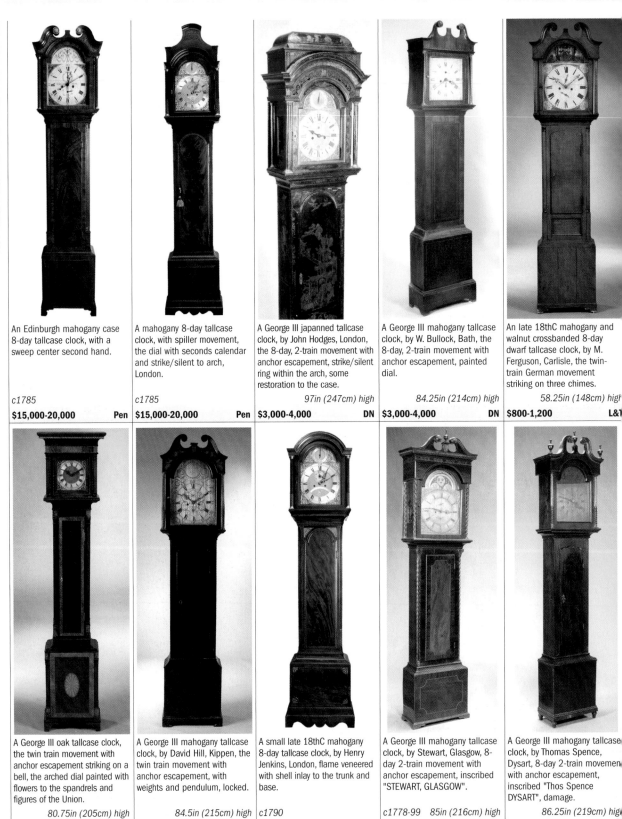

An Edinburgh mahogany case 8-day tallcase clock, with a sweep center second hand.

c1785

$15,000-20,000   **Pen**

A mahogany 8-day tallcase clock, with spiller movement, the dial with seconds calendar and strike/silent to arch, London.

c1785

$15,000-20,000   **Pen**

A George III japanned tallcase clock, by John Hodges, London, the 8-day, 2-train movement with anchor escapement, strike/silent ring within the arch, some restoration to the case.

97in (247cm) high

$3,000-4,000   **DN**

A George III mahogany tallcase clock, by W. Bullock, Bath, the 8-day, 2-train movement with anchor escapement, painted dial.

84.25in (214cm) high

$3,000-4,000   **DN**

An late 18thC mahogany and walnut crossbanded 8-day dwarf tallcase clock, by M. Ferguson, Carlisle, the twin-train German movement striking on three chimes.

58.25in (148cm) high

$800-1,200   **L&T**

A George III oak tallcase clock, the twin train movement with anchor escapement striking on a bell, the arched dial painted with flowers to the spandrels and figures of the Union.

80.75in (205cm) high

$1,200-1,800   **L&T**

A George III mahogany tallcase clock, by David Hill, Kippen, the twin train movement with anchor escapement, with weights and pendulum, locked.

84.5in (215cm) high

$1,800-2,200   **L&T**

A small late 18thC mahogany 8-day tallcase clock, by Henry Jenkins, London, flame veneered with shell inlay to the trunk and base.

c1790

$20,000-30,000   **Pen**

A George III mahogany tallcase clock, by Stewart, Glasgow, 8-day 2-train movement with anchor escapement, inscribed "STEWART, GLASGOW".

c1778-99   85in (216cm) high

$2,200-2,800   **DN**

A George III mahogany tallcase clock, by Thomas Spence, Dysart, 8-day 2-train movement with anchor escapement, inscribed "Thos Spence DYSART", damage.

86.25in (219cm) high

$1,500-2,000   **DN**

A Massachusetts Queen Anne tallcase clock, by David Blasdel of Amesbury, the dome-top hood with astragal glazed door opening to a brass pewter dial with maker's name above a waisted case with two raised panels and a glazed bull's-eye on a plinth base.

84in (213.5cm) high

$6,000-8,000 NA

A Pennsylvania Chippendale walnut 30 hour tallcase clock, by Adam Brandt, Hanover, arched brass and steel face with spandrels of figures, leaves and birds, maker's nameplate to arch, lip-molded waist door within quarter-fluted angles, on later ogival bracket feet.

c1750 *93in (236cm) high*

$15,000-18,000 FRE

A Chippendale walnut tallcase clock, enamel face with Roman numerals, gilt embellished spandrels, moon phase dial and subsidiary calendar and seconds, waisted case with long double arched door above plinth base on plain feet.

91in (231cm) high

$4,000-6,000 NA

A late 18thC Pennsylvania walnut tallcase clock, by Jacob Gorgas (1728-1789), Ephrata, arched painted face with moon, sun and earth, waisted case with canted fluted corners enclosing a shaped door, over paneled base and bracket feet.

c1780 *93in (236cm) high*

$8,000-12,000 FRE

A late 18thC Pennsylvania Chippendale tallcase clock, broken swan's neck pediment with rosettes, painted metal face with moon phases, on waisted case with a shaped door, base box with a shaped panel, both with fluted quarter-columns, molded base, minor losses.

c1790 *93in (236cm) high*

$6,000-9,000 FRE

A Pennsylvania Chippendale cherry tallcase clock, white painted face bearing the name "Solomon Yeakle", the case with arched panel door flanked by canted and fluted stiles over a rectangular base on ogee bracket feet.

c1790 *96.5in (245cm) high*

$8,000-12,000 Pook

A Federal inlaid walnut tallcase clock, English bright-cut face with painted moonphase, engraved "Thurstan Lassel, Toxteth Park", the case beneath with inlaid chamfered corners flanking an inlaid and figured door, on later bracketed feet, restorations to clock face.

c1800 *96.5in (245cm) high*

$12,000-15,000 FRE

A Federal inlaid mahogany tallcase clock, painted face and moonphase, the case beneath with striped-inlaid frieze above an inlaid and figured door within fluted quarter columns, on straight bracket feet, some repainting to dial.

c1800 *94in (238.5cm) high*

$10,000-15,000 FRE

A Federal cherry and inlaid tallcase clock, signed "John Kimball, Jr., Boston, Massachusetts", with striking eight-day movement, painted dial, waisted trunk.

By repute, the clock case was made by Roswell Adasuu of Vermont and was brought to West Norfolk, Connecticut in the 1870s when the Connecticut Western Railroad was built.

c1800 *88.5in (225cm) high*

$5,000-7,000 SI

A Boston Federal mahogany tallcase clock, by Aaron Willard, dated "August 9 1812", dial with maker's name below a demi-lune panel with boy fishing, the spandrels with crosshatching and scalloped florettes in red and gilt, the waisted case with inset reeded and gilded quarter-columns, rectangular door with crossbanding and gilt molded edge opening to the label, the box base with painted gilt line faux-inlay on French feet.

95in (241cm) high
$40,000-50,000 NA

A Federal inlaid cherry tallcase clock, imported enameled dial with moon phase mechanism, waisted case with inlaid rectangular door within chamfered angles inlaid with meander vine, shaped bracket feet.

98in (250cm) high
$6,000-9,000 NA

A Philadelphia walnut tallcase clock, by Thomas Parker (1761-1833), painted metal face with moon phases, tulip and rose decorated spandrels, on waisted case with an arched door, rectangular plinth, molded base and bracket feet.

86in (218.5cm) high
$8,000-12,000 FRE

A Delaware Federal cherry tallcase clock, with a broken arch bonnet enclosing a white face dial, signed "Evan Evans, New Castle" over a case with raised paneled door, rectangular base and bracket feet.

93.5in (237.5cm) high
$4,000-6,000 Pook

A Connecticut Federal mahogany tallcase clock, by Riley Whiting, Winchester, painted and decorated face inscribed with name "R. Whiting, Winchester", flowers at spandrels, above a shaped waisted door flanked by fluted quarter columns, the squared plinth raised on bracket feet.

c1810   84in (213cm) high
$2,500-3,500 SI

A New York or Philadelphia Federal inlaid mahogany tallcase clock, attributed to John Clarke, dial with Arabic numerals and floral painted corner spandrels below arch with stylized pine cone, waisted case with shaped door within inlaid quarter-columns, on shaped apron and French feet.

98in (249cm) high
$5,000-8,000 NA

A Pennsylvania Chippendale mahogany tallcase clock, dial attributed to Spencer Nolen and Samuel Curtis, painted with eagle, Liberty cap, crossed flags and military trophies and arch with depiction of the naval engagement of the Enterprize & Boxer, waisted case with fluted inset quarter-columns, ogee feet.

c1818   100in (254cm) high
$8,000-10,000 NA

A Connecticut Federal painted and decorated tallcase clock, by Riley Whiting, Winchester, dial with maker's name below demi-lune panel with floral urn, waisted case with rectangular door with Greek key border on cut out feet, with faux graining overall.

85.5in (217cm) high
$18,000-22,000 NA

A Maine Federal cherry inlaid tallcase clock, by James Cary, Jr. (1806-1850), Brunswick, arched painted face with a rocking ship movement and floral spandrels, rectangular lip-molded waist door within quarter-fluted corners, on later ogival bracket feet.

94.25in (239.5cm) high
$7,000-10,000 FRE

An early 19thC mahogany tallcase clock, 8-day 2-train movement with rack-strike on a bell, wear to dial.

82.75in (210cm) high

$2,200-2,800   **DN**

A Regency mahogany tallcase clock, the 8-day 2-train movement with anchor escapement and rack-strike on a bell, the dial with subsidiary seconds dial, the plain case with gilt-metal fittings, the hood with circular brass bezel and surmounted with three various ball finials, restored.

78in (198cm) high

$700-1,000   **DN**

An early 19thC oak and mahogany crossbanded tallcase clock, by G. Healer, Wantage, with 30-hour movement striking on a bell.

600-900

$600-900   **DN**

A George IV mahogany tallcase clock, by William Roberts, Bath, the 8-day 2-train movement with anchor escapement and rack-strike on a bell, the dial with date aperture and subsidiary seconds dial.

c1825.   89in (226cm) high

$3,000-4,000   **DN**

A George IV mahogany tallcase clock, the 8-day 2-train movement with anchor escapement and rack-strike on a bell, the dial with subsidiary date and seconds dial, painted with spandrels of figures representing the continents, the arch with a moonphase automaton.

8.5in (225cm) high

$3,500-4,500   **DN**

A Canadian painted pine tallcase clock, by J & R Twiss, Montreal, the hood with broken arch pediment enclosing a hand-painted gilt enameled face, with serpentine carved base with bracket feet.

82.5in (209cm) high

$1,500-2,000   **WAD**

An early Victorian mahogany regulator, by W.W. Kent, the single-train movement with deadbeat anchor escapement, inscribed and dated "W W KENT 1837", with single brass-cased weight and bob pendulum.

73.25in (186cm) high

$4,000-6,000   **DN**

A 19thC mahogany tallcase clock, by Samuel Hart, Devizes, the 8-day 2-train movement with anchor escapement and rack strike on a bell, the dial with subsidiary seconds dial and date aperture, the arch painted with a bucholic scene, broken pediment and eagle finial.

c1846   87.5in (222cm) high

$2,200-2,800   **DN**

A 19thC oak and mahogany tallcase clock, the 30-hour movement with anchor escapement, the arch painted with a shooting scene, some damage and repairs to the hood.

81.75in (208cm) high

$1,000-1,500   **DN**

A mahogany tallcase clock, the 8-day, 2-train movement with anchor escapement, arched dial inscribed "Edm. Wills, Salisbury", 19thC plain case, the hood with a broken pediment.

92in (234cm) high

$2,200-2,800   **DN**

A 19thC oak tallcase clock, the 8-day movement with anchor escapement, inscribed within the arch "ROSS EPWORTH", the hood with broken pediment and lacking a glazed door.

84.25in (214cm) high

$1,200-1,800　　　　DN

A 19thC oak 8-day clock, by Jon Wallace, Leven, the twin train movement with anchor escapement, the arched dial painted with batswing spandrels and mechanical sailing ship.

84.25in (214cm) high

$2,500-3,000　　　　L&T

A 19thC mahogany 8-day tallcase clock, by Tho. Johnston, Paisley, the twin train movement with anchor escapement, plinth base with later bracket feet.

84.25in (214cm) high

$1,200-1,800　　　　L&T

A 19thC mahogany regulator, the single train movement with anchor escapement, enameled dial, molded drum hood and glazed door.

78.75in (200cm) high

$1,200-1,800　　　　L&T

A 19thC oak and mahogany 8-day tallcase clock, by Telford, Maryport, the twin train movement with anchor escapement striking on a bell, with false plate, moon phase dial to the arch.

90.5in (230cm) high

$1,800-2,200　　　　L&T

A George III mahogany 8-day tallcase clock, by James Hendrie, Falkirk, the twin train movement with anchor escapement, striking on a bell, with arched brass dial.

84.25in (214cm) high

$2,500-3,000　　　　L&T

A 19thC mahogany 8-day tallcase clock, by C. Robertson, Blairgowrie, the twin track movement with anchor escapement, striking on a bell, the arched dial painted with the seasons and lady of the lake.

83.5in (212cm) high

$2,500-3,000　　　　L&T

A 19thC 8-day tallcase clock, by Drysdale, Edinburgh, the twin train, converted to single train, movement with anchor escapement, with false plate "Walker & Hughes, Birmingham", strike removed.

85.75in (218cm) high

$800-1,200　　　　L&T

An early 19thC mahogany 8-day tallcase clock, the twin train movement with anchor escapement, the trunk with lancet door and panel base, splay feet.

83.25in (211.5cm) high

$1,200-1,800　　　　L&T

An early 19thC mahogany 8-day tallcase clock, by P.R. Keir, Falkirk, the twin train movement with anchor escapement, painted dial.

89in (226cm) high

$1,500-2,000　　　　L&T

An early 20thC inlaid mahogany tallcase clock, 8-day 3-train movement with anchor escapement, dial with retailer's stamp for "Yoell, Retford", arch with 'chime/silent' dial, broken pediment.

99.5in (235cm) high

$4,000-6,000   **DN**

A carved oak tallcase clock, the five pillar, 8-day, 2-train movement with anchor escapement, brass dial set with a silvered plaque inscribed "Geo Tyler London", the 1930s case heavily carved.

81in (206cm) high

$2,200-2,800   **DN**

A 20thC mahogany and inlaid tallcase clock, of so-called 'Grandmother' type, the 8-day 2-train German movement with anchor escapement, striking on a gong, the dial inscribed "Garrard Hale NORWICH".

69.25in (176cm) high

$1,000-1,500   **DN**

A mahogany tallcase clock, the 8-day, two-train movement with rack strike on a bell, the chapter ring inscribed "Smorthwait Colchester", lancet door inlaid with a shell motif.

83.75in (213cm) high

$1,200-1,800   **DN**

A mahogany tallcase clock, the 8-day 2-train movement with anchor escapement and rack-strike on a bell, dial assembled, crack through lower section of case.

97.25in (247cm) high

$1,800-2,200   **DN**

An oak tallcase clock, the Dutch wall clock 30-hour movement striking on a bell, plain case and hood with flat pediment with dentil rim, damage and losses to the case.

76.75in (195cm) high

$700-1,000   **DN**

A pine tallcase clock, the 30-hour movement with anchor escapement and outside countwheel strike on a bell, gilt foliate spandrels and inscribed "JOSH. MILES SHASTON", above a house by the sea.

78.75in (200cm) high

$800-1,200   **DN**

An oak and mahogany inlaid tallcase clock, the 8-day 2-train movement with anchor escapement and rack-strike on a bell, the arch with a sunburst boss inscribed "Samuel, Austin Rumsey Fecit".

85.5in (217cm) high

$1,000-1,500   **DN**

An oak tallcase clock, the 8-day 2-train movement with anchor escapement and rack-strike on a bell, arch with a silvered bell inscribed "Patrick Hardie. Morpeth", restored.

87in (221cm) high

$1,500-2,000   **DN**

A George III mahogany bracket clock, Eardley Norton, London, 8-day 2-train movement with anchor escapement, half-hour pass-strike, 'Strike/Silent' dial, beneath a demi-lune band inscribed "EARDLEY NORTON LONDON".

c1760-94   *21.75in (55cm) high*

$7,000-10,000   DN

A fruitwood bracket clock, the 8-day 2-train fusee movement with verge escapement and striking on a bell, the dial inscribed "Cannon London", some restored/replacement sections to the case, previously ebonized.

c1790   *20in (50.5cm) high*

$3,500-4,500   DN

An anchor escapement 8-day bracket clock, with convex white dial, the mahogany case with fretted decoration and decorative backplate, by W. Alexander, Parliament Street, London.

c1800   *15.5in high (39cm) high*

$7,000-10,000   Pen

A William IV oak bracket clock, by William Johnson, London, the backplate inscribed "Wm. Johnson, 50 Strand, London".

21.25in (54cm) high

$3,000-4,000   L&T

A Regency mahogany and brass-inlaid bracket clock, by John Butler, Reading, the 2-train fusee movement with anchor escapement and striking on a bell, the back-plate inscribed "John Butler, READING", the dial inscribed "JNo: Butler No. 3 Broad Street READING".

18.5in (47cm) high

$2,200-2,800   DN

A Regency mahogany bracket clock, the 8-day 2-train movement with anchor escapement and striking on a bell, some damage and lost inlay to the case.

24in (61cm) high

$1,500-2,000   DN

A fine Regency rosewood 8-day bracket clock, with pull repeat, the finely patinated case-brass strung with delicate brass inlaid decoration, with five-pillar movement, strike/silent, by Desbois & Wheeler, London.

c1820   *19in (48cm) high*

$7,000-10,000   Pen

A very small mahogany 8-day bracket clock, with architectural top, with cast-decorated bezel, with porcelain dial.

c1820   *9.75in (25cm) high*

$4,000-6,000   Pen

A French lacquered case bracket clock, the 8-day 2-train movement striking and chiming on two bells the hours and the half-hour, the backplate stamped "DL JACOPIN", the case 19thC and a bracket ensuite, some damage, not striking.

20in (51cm) high

$1,500-2,000   DN

A Regency mahogany and brass inlaid bracket clock, by James Milne, Montrose, inscribed "Milne, Montrose", flanked by inlaid columns, above inlaid frieze with bobbin molding, on plinth base.

22in (56cm) high

$1,500-2,000   L&T

A late 19thC Louis XV provincial-style painted wood bracket clock, cartouche-form on scroll feet and a bracket shelf, painted ocher with blue and red flowers.

32in (81.5cm) high

$700-1,000   SI

A 20thC Louis XIV style tortoiseshell veneered and gilt bronze bracket clock, Tiffany & Co., New York, movement stamped "TIFFANY & CO./NEW YORK" and with "Medaille d'Argent", porcelain reserve on front inscribed "Tiffany & Co./New York", angel finial.

21in (56cm) high

$1,000-1,500   S

A late Victorian tortoiseshell and silver-mounted carriage timepiece, by Drew & Sons, Piccadilly Circus, London W, French 8-day movement with platform lever escapement, London hallmarks for Drew & Drew.

c1899   2.75in (7cm) high

$1,000-1,500   DN

A French carriage timepiece, with circular enamel dial, the case with elaborate openwork foliate panels to three sides.

c1900   5in (13cm) high

$400-600   BonS

An early 20thC brass Corniche-cased carriage clock, the 8-day 2-train movement with detached lever escapement, one glass chipped.

7.5in (19cm) high

$500-700   DN

A 20thC French gorge brass-cased and alarmed carriage clock, by L' Epee (Frederic & Cie), the 8-day 3-train movement with detached lever escapement striking hours and with half-hour pass-strike on a coiled gong.

7in (18cm) high

$400-600   DN

A miniature sterling silver carriage clock, enameled with black and white vertical stripes, marked on the face "ZENITH" and signed on the bottom "ARGENT .925 sterling silver", housed in its own leather bound carrying case with some fraying to lining.

Clock 2in (5cm) high

$1,000-1,500   JDJ

A French carriage clock, the ogee-molded case with circular white enamel dial set in an engine-turned frame, original leather traveling case.

5.5in (14cm) high

$500-700   BonS

Mantle Clocks

A burr walnut cased mantle chronometer, by Thomas Mercer, St. Albans, the dial with subsidiary seconds and wind dials inscribed "Thomas Mercer, No. 1231, St Albans, England".

Mercer was one of the finest makers of timepieces working in the English tradition in the second half of the 19thC.

9.5in (24cm) high

$6,000-9,000   L&T

A George III quarter-chiming musical table clock, by James McCabe, the 8-day 3-train fusee movement with anchor escapement, chiming on 12 bells with pull repeat, arch with three subsidiary dials, "Chime/Silent", "Fast/Slow", seven tunes, plaque inscribed "James McCabe London".

25.5in (65cm) high

$12,000-18,000   DN

A Regency period rosewood and brass inlaid mantle timepiece, the drum dial with Roman numerals and a single fusee movement, on a rectangular plinth base.

c1810   15.75in (40cm) high

$400-600   BonS

An early 19thC French gilt bronze mantle clock, cracked white enamel dial, the movement with silk suspension and outside count wheel striking on a bell, the case cast as an allegorical figure of Victory, some damage.

10in (25.5cm) high

$400-600   FRE

An early Victorian mahogany mantle clock, the 8-day 2-movement with anchor escapement and striking on a bell, the case with convex glass and brass bezel, the domed top with leaf-molded pediment.

16.25in (41.5cm) high

$700-1,000   DN

A 19thC black slate cased mantle clock, the circular dial with gilt numerals and visible escapement, the case with Greek style gilt metal mask heads, 8-day striking movement.

16in (40.5cm) wide

$150-200   Clv

A late 19thC brass and ceramic paneled mantle clock, movement by Japy Frères, stamped for G. Fontaine, numbered "279" at the rear of the case, set with six blue and white panels, the twin train movement with rack striking on a bell, minute hand repaired.

c1890   14.75in (37.5cm) high

$600-900   **BonS**

A late 19thC French gilt metal mantle clock, in the form of a kneeling boy suspending the drum-cased movement from linenfold, on a white marble plinth applied with floral swags.

c1890   10.5in (26.5cm) high

$600-900   **BonS**

A late 19thC French marble mantle clock, applied with a gilt metal figural finial in the form of a Classical woman seated on a turtle, the plinth with a formal leaf border and bracket feet, striking movement.

20.5in (52cm) high

$600-900   **BonS**

A late 19thC Louis XV boulle-style mantle clock, the brass inlaid faux tortoiseshell case mounted with gilt bronze.

30in (76cm) high

$1,500-2,000   **SI**

A late 19thC French porcelain mantle clock, decorated in Rococo-style with encrusted flowers to cobalt, white and gilt body, clock face marked "Paris".

12.5in (31.5cm) high

$700-1,000   **D**

A late 19thC French red-marble clock base, surmounted with a spelter model of a stallion with a hound, the 8-day 2-train movement striking on a bell, the rectangular base with a gilt-metal frieze of Classical figures.

Largest 20in (51cm) wide

$400-600   **DN**

A late 19thC French gilt-metal and porcelain-mounted mantle clock, the 8-day 2-train movement striking on a bell, case set with Sèvres-style porcelain plaques, backplate, case and pendulum stamped "18367".

12.25in (31cm) high

$1,500-2,000   **DN**

A late 19thC French gilt-metal and porcelain mounted mantle clock, the 8-day 2-train movement with outside countwheel strike on a bell, the case surmounted with putto, mounted with porcelain plaques painted with putti.

14.25in (36cm) high

$600-900   **DN**

An Art Nouveau 8-day balloon clock, the mahogany case inlaid with boxwood and exotic hoods, with white porcelain dial, with French movement.

c1890-1900

$700-1,000   **Pen**

An Edwardian mahogany and pale wood-banded lancet mantle clock, the 8-day 2-train movement striking on gongs, the banded case with a pair of fluted pilasters with brass Ionic capitals, some wear to the dial.

15in (38cm) high

$600-900   **DN**

An Edwardian mahogany mantle clock, inlaid with ribbon-tied swags and stringing, circular white enamel dial, on bracket feet.

7.75in (19.5cm) high

$220-280   **BonS**

An Edwardian walnut-cased 8-day mantle clock, with domed pediment above brass dial flanked by carved columns on stepped plinth base.

$180-220

An early 20thC French gilt metal clock, movement by Marti & Ciethe, elaborately cast rectangular case surmounted by a finial, the cream enamel dial with a cast boss to the center, the twin train movement with rack striking on a gong.

c1910   *15.75in (40cm) high*
$450-550   **BonS**

An early 20thC French gilt brass and Champlevé enamel, four-glass portico mantle clock, lacking hands, the movement with mercury pendulum, feather damaged, retailed by Bailey Banks & Biddle, Philadelphia.

20.5in (52cm) high
$1,500-2,000   **FRE**

An American eight-day half hour strike cathedral gong anniversary clock, with an eight-day movement, housed within an oak case.

$200-300   **D**

An Eli Terry pillar and scroll clock, mahogany case, painted tablet, brass finials, painted dial, wooden works, repainted face, minor repairs, replaced finials.

17.5in (44.5cm) long
$2,000-2,500   **AAC**

A 1940s walnut cased mantle clock, having 8-days and Whittington & Westminster chimes.

$50-80   **D**

A Paris mantle clock, decorated with gilt decorations on a blue ground, separate finial with a man and a woman in exotic 16thC costume, the enamel dial signed "L Ainei Paris", probably Jacob Petit, incised cross and four bar marks.

19in (48cm) high
$450-550   **BonS**

A late Federal stencil-decorated mahogany shelf clock, labeled "Eli Terry, Plymouth, CT.", the door with reverse-painted glass panel depicting stately buildings.

Provenance: *The Society of the Cincinnati*

c1835, 17in (42.5cm) w.
$3,000-3,500 SI.

A Massachusetts Federal mahogany and eglomise shelf clock, by Joseph Morse of Walpole, the bonnet with scrolled crest above an eglomise door with maker's inscription opening to a dished dial, the lower section with eglomise panel on a moulded base with gilt paw feet.

32in (81cm) high
$15,000-20,000   **NA**

A late 29thC French Sèvres-style gilt-metal mantle clock, 8-day 2-train movement striking the hours on a bell with half-hour pass-strike, dial with a Watteauesque scene, handle for case door lacking, wear to gilding.

13.75in (35cm) high

$600-900   **DN**

A French red tortoiseshell boulle mantle clock, the balloon-shaped case with cast brass foliate mounts with cut brass reserves to the front.

14.25in (36cm) high

$700-1,000   **BonS**

A Neoclassical cast brass and ormolu mounted mantle clock for American market, by Jean Baptiste Dubac, Paris, with figure of George Washington, inscribed "Dubac Ave Michele-6-Comte-No 33 A Paris" and "Washington, The First in War, First in Peace, and in His Countrymen's Hearts", eagle is of a later date.

Several variations of this clock are known, some with a different figure and others with varying inscriptions.

$12,000-18,000   **Pook**

A French white marble and gilt brass-mounted mantle clock, signed "Bryson & Sons, Edinburgh", the twin train movement with circular dial and applied Roman chapters, enclosed within drum case.

21.5in (54.5cm) wide

$3,000-4,000   **L&T**

A gilt brass mantle clock, in the Louis XVI style, the twin train movement striking on bell, the elaborate case with Sèvres style dial, panel and finial, on concave shaped and molded plinth with velvet base.

17.5in (44cm) high

$600-900   **L&T**

An ormulu mantle clock, with porcelain dial reading "Deniere FANT de Bronzes Paris".

24in (61cm) high

$1,800-2,200   **ET**

A 19thC polished steel and gilt metal clock garniture, comprising a clock with twin train movement, the laurel cast base set with three seated hounds, linked by chains, the whole raised on hoof feet, and two attendant candelabra cast with oak leaves on Rococo bases.

Clock 17.5in (44.5cm) high

$4,000-6,000   **L&T**

A late 19thC French patinated, parcel gilt bronze and onyx three-piece clock garniture, the clock surmounted by figure of Charlemagne mounted on horseback and with military trophies, each six-light candelabra mounted with busts of Charlemagne, military trophies.

24in (61cm) high

$4,000-6,000   **SI**

A late 19thC French gilt bronze and rouge marble three-piece mantle garniture, central plinth fitted with a Mougin clock, each two-light candelabra in the form of a putto, lacking sculpture from central plinth.

Candelabra 14in (35.5cm) high

$1,500-2,000   **SI**

A late 19thC French bronze and slate three-piece clock garniture, clock by Japy Frères, surmounted by a sculpture of two Classical ladies reading a letter, with a pair of six-light candelabra, each modeled as a Classical lady holding aloft candle branches, bronze signed "Dubois".

Clock 30in (76.5cm) high

$10,000-15,000   **SI**

A late 19thC Louis XVI-style gilt metal-mounted onyx three-piece clock garniture, the portico clock mounted with floral swag and urn finial, flanked by conforming urn-form garniture, dial inscribed "Pillon Ginestet/Beziers".

Clock 16.5in (42cm) high

$450-550   **SI**

A late 19thC French gilt metal-mounted three-piece clock garniture, movement by Japy Frères & Cie, painted porcelain dial, the ceramic case painted with figures in pastoral landscapes reserved on a cobalt ground, flanked by similarly painted five-light candelabra.

Candelabra 16.75in (42.5cm) high

$1,500-2,000   **SI**

A late 19thC gilt-metal and porcelain mounted clock garniture, 8-day 2-train movement striking on a bell, case mounted with Sèvres-style panels painted in the manner of Boucher, and a pair of similar urns on plinth bases, losses.

18.5in (47cm) high

$3,500-4,500   **DN**

A late 19thC/early 20thC monumental German porcelain three-piece clock garniture, comprising a clock, dial signed "Maple & Co.", mounted with a female figure, flanked by a pair of six-light candelabra modelled as figures, one figure with underglaze blue crossed mark.

41.75in (106cm) high

$4,500-5,500   **SI**

Wall Clocks

A banjo clock, by E. Howard & Co., painted dial with Roman numerals, signed "E. Howard & Co., Boston", Eglomise tablet and throat with oak leaf and acorn decoration, refinished, repainted tablets.

44in (112cm) long

$800-1,000   **AAC**

A late Victorian rosewood and white metal-inlaid drop-dial wall clock, the 2 train movement striking on a bell and with painted dial, the access door with glass panel inscribed in gilding with "CHAMPION REGULATOR", reserved on a painted blue ground.

28in (71cm) high

$250-350   **DN**

A late 19thC German walnut veneer and ebonised wall timepiece, in the Vienna regulator-style, the 8-day single train movement with deadbeat escapement, the dial with subsidiary seconds dial, in a rectangular architectural case, lacks case fittings top and bottom.

32in (81cm) high

$450-550   **DN**

An English fusée dial clock, with mahogany case.

c1860   *Dial 16in (40.5cm) diam*

£1,500-2,000   **Pen**

An Act of Parliament clock, with lacquer work and trunk, by William Allam, London.

c1770   *57in (145cm) high*

$15,000-20,000   **Pen**

A rosewood Beidermieir period 8-day wall regulator, with 2-piece porcelain dial with piecrust bezel.

c1840

$8,000-10,000   **Pen**

Barometers

A Louis XVI giltwood barometer, circular painted dial with drapery pendant and a crest carved as a dove within a wreath above wheat and farming implements.

c1800   *35in (89cm) high*

$1,800-2,200   **SI**

A Regency satinwood and line inlaid wheel barometer, by J. Predary, Manchester, silvered dial, hygrometer, thermometer and spirit level, inscribed "J Predary, Manchester".

41in (104cm) high

$2,500-3,000   **DN**

An early 19thC mahogany stick barometer, by Adie & Son, Edinburgh, the engraved brass vernier with arched top, wooden cover to tube, reeded rectangular reservoir.

34.25in (87cm) high

$3,500-4,500   **L&T**

A mid-19thC mahogany and inlaid wheel barometer, by B. Molinari, Oxford, with silvered dial beneath a thermometer with silvered register, the case inlaid with shell motifs.

38.5in (98cm) high

$800-1,200   **DN**

A mid-19thC rosewood-veneer, mother-of-pearl wheel barometer, by C.A. Canti, London, with thermometer, register, timepiece, inscribed "C.A. CANTI... HIGH HOLBORN."

49.5in (126cm) high

$1,000-1,500   **DN**

A mid-19thC mahogany wheel barometer, by Valbine, Northleach, hygrometer, thermometer, convex mirror and spirit level, mirror damaged.

39in (99cm) high

$400-600   **DN**

A mid-19thC mahogany and inlaid wheel barometer, by S. Gatward, Hemel Hempstead, silvered dial inscribed "S Gatward, Hemel Hempstead, Warranted", and thermometer.

38.5in (98cm) high

$1,000-1,500   **DN**

A mid-19thC mahogany and inlaid wheel barometer, by J. Aprile, Sudbury, silvered dial inscribed "J. Aprile, Sudbury, Warranted", thermometer with silvered register.

39.25in (100cm) high

$800-1,200   **DN**

A mid-19thC mahogany and line-inlaid wheel barometer, by Porri, Nottingham, silvered dial inscribed "PORRI, Nottingham", and thermometer with silvered register.

39.25in (100cm) high

$800-1,200   **DN**

A mid-19thC mahogany, line-inlaid wheel barometer, silvered dial, hygrometer, thermometer, mirror, spirit level, inscribed "A Payne... Clerkenwell".

38.25in (97cm) high

$400-600   **DN**

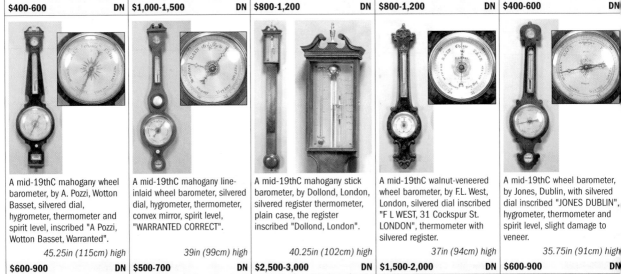

A mid-19thC mahogany wheel barometer, by A. Pozzi, Wotton Basset, silvered dial, hygrometer, thermometer and spirit level, inscribed "A Pozzi, Wotton Basset, Warranted".

45.25in (115cm) high

$600-900   **DN**

A mid-19thC mahogany line-inlaid wheel barometer, silvered dial, hygrometer, thermometer, convex mirror, spirit level, "WARRANTED CORRECT".

39in (99cm) high

$500-700   **DN**

A mid-19thC mahogany stick barometer, by Dollond, London, silvered register thermometer, plain case, the register inscribed "Dollond, London".

40.25in (102cm) high

$2,500-3,000   **DN**

A mid-19thC walnut-veneered wheel barometer, by F.L. West, London, silvered dial inscribed "F L WEST, 31 Cockspur St. LONDON", thermometer with silvered register.

37in (94cm) high

$1,500-2,000   **DN**

A mid-19thC wheel barometer, by Jones, Dublin, with silvered dial inscribed "JONES DUBLIN", hygrometer, thermometer and spirit level, slight damage to veneer.

35.75in (91cm) high

$600-900   **DN**

A mid-19thC mahogany plain case wheel barometer, with hygrometer, thermometer, mirror, spirit level inscribed "WARRANTED CORRECT".

37.5in (95cm) high

$500-700   **DN**

A mid-19thC mahogany and line-inlaid wheel barometer, by Webb & Son, Newbury, hygrometer, thermometer, convex mirror, inscribed "Webb & Son Newbury", losses.

38.25in (97cm) high

$400-600   **DN**

A late 18thC mahogany and inlaid wheel barometer, by F. Pelegrino, with silvered dial beneath a large thermometer with silvered register, the dial inscribed "F Pelegrino Fecit".

37.75in (96cm) high

$2,200-2,800   **DN**

A late 19thC mahogany wheel barometer, by Row, Alton, with silvered dial inscribed "ROW, ALTON", and with center sweep hand beneath a thermometer, the case applied with foliate carving.

38.5in (98cm) high

$500-700   **DN**

An English Art Nouveau barometer, scalloped oak case inlaid with copper whiplash motifs and mother-of-pearl floral buds, the works signed "Aitchinson & Co, London".

c1900   *34in (86.5cm) high*

$400-600   **FRE**

Watches

A gentleman's 14ct yellow gold wristwatch, dial set with subsidiary seconds, day and month dials, attached to a black alligator style band, clasp is not gold.

$400-600   **SI**

A lady's Swiss gold cocktail watch, by Binesa, two-piece case with capped lugs on an integral gaspipe link bracelet, stamped '0750', Invicta Ltd., Swiss 15-jewel incabloc movement.

c1950

$180-220   **DN**

A Breguet quarter repeating full hunter pocket watch, in 18ct rose gold.

When triggered the watch chimes hours and quarters.

c1900

$10,000-15,000   **Som**

An 18ct gold Cartier lady's pendant watch, with translucent enamel and diamond-set back and crown, on original matching enamel, gold and pearl chain.

c1915

$15,000-20,000   **Som**

A Cartier diamond dress watch, with diamond-set bezel, black Roman numeral dial and signed "Cartier Paris".

1920s

$15,000-20,000   **Som**

A platinum case Cartier Paris wristwatch, complete with original diamond-set deployant buckle.

1920s

$50,000-70,000   **Som**

A 1920s Cartier 18ct yellow gold 'Knife Edge' dress pocket watch, in full hunter case.

'Knife Edge' watches were so called because the movement is so slim. As such they are one of the most popular Cartier watches.

$12,000-18,000   **Som**

A 1920s Cartier Calibre 101 cocktail watch, platinum, diamond and ruby-set case, back wind, European Watch and Clock movement.

$30,000-40,000   **Som**

A rare platinum diamond-set Cartier bracelet cocktail watch, with brilliant-cut and baguette-cut diamonds in bracelet, back wind and 104 movement.

It is rare to find Cartier bracelet cocktail watches in such good condition.

c1930

$40,000-60,000   **Som**

An early Cartier Paris 18ct yellow gold dress pocket watch, with enameled Egyptian huntsmen scene.

Cartier produced various enamel scened pocket watches and they are very collectible.

c1920s

$7,000-10,000　　　　Som

A Cartier 18ct yellow gold 'Le Grand Tank' watch, curved rectangular case and classic Roman numeral dial, EWC (European Watch and Clock) movement.

'Grand Tank' also called 'American Tank'.

c1930

$20,000-30,000　　　　Som

A 1930s Cartier 'Tank' 18ct gold wristwatch, manual wind with brushed finish case and "France" printed on dial.

The Cartier 'Tank' is so called because it has a similar shape to a Sherman tank. It is still produced in a similar style today. Cartier produced watches from London, New York and Paris, with each different factory producing a slightly different look or theme.

$15,000-20,000　　　　Som

A Cartier 'Reverso' wristwatch, with two slim-line mechanical movements cased back-to-back, with a brushed-gold colored dial on one side, and white with black Roman numeral dial on the other.

These watches were produced in the 1960s in limited numbers and were popular with people traveling because the reverso element allows two different time zones.

c1960s

$30,000-40,000　　　　Som

A Cartier 'Bamboo' wristwatch, with bamboo-shape case.

During the 1960s-70s Cartier produced wristwatches with unusual cases, which are now popular with collectors looking for style pieces from those eras.

$7,000-10,000　　　　Som

A gentleman's Swiss 14ct gold bracelet watch, by Creation, Geneve, the brushed gold dial with baton numerals and hands, with date aperture, two-piece rectangular case on integral block bracelet, Swiss quartz seven-jewel movement Cal. ETA 956.

c1970

$400-600　　　　DN

A Hamiltons lady's platinum and diamond wristwatch, with black 'feuille' hands surrounded by collet and bead-set circular-cut diamonds, on a white gold and diamond-set link bracelet, dial and movement signed, in Hamilton box, diamonds 1.5cts.

$1,000-1,500　　　　SI

A gentleman's 18K gold wristwatch and 14K gold band, by International Watch Company, Schaffhausen Deluxe, the dial with center seconds sweep hands.

$700-1,000　　　　FRE

A gentleman's 18K gold wristwatch with 18K gold band, by Juvenia, the 17-jewel movement no. 785, the back of the case inscribed and dated.

1975

$600-900　　　　FRE

A repeating 18ct yellow gold automatic pocket watch, by 'Le Roy' of Paris, quarter repeating and key-wound.

Everything was key-wound until c1855 when crown-wound watches were introduced.

c1820

$10,000-15,000　　　　Som

A lady's Swiss 18ct gold bracelet watch, by Omega, silvered dial, two-piece case with faceted glass, on woven bracelet, Omega 17-jewel oblong movement, Cal. 483, signed.

c1955

$220-280　　　　DN

A lady's Swiss 18ct white gold and diamond square bracelet watch, by Omega, silvered dial, square two-piece case with eight-cut diamond 32-stone bezel, integral woven bracelet, Omega 17-jewel oblong movement Cal.484, case, dial and movement signed.

c1960

$500-700　　　　DN

An 18ct rose gold Parmigiani Fleurier split-second chronograph, no. 6 from a limited edition of 10, modern case with 1940s Venus movement.

Face 1.5in (3.5cm) wide

$30,000-40,000　　　　WG

A gentleman's 18ct yellow gold and diamond wristwatch, signed "Piaget", with a black dial, diamond accents and gold colored 'Dauphin' hands, with a textured interwoven band, signed on dial and band.

$2,500-3,000 SI

A Patek Phillipe 14ct yellow gold full hunter pocket watch, with white enamel dial and black Roman numerals.

'Full hunter' pocket watches are covered and were designed for gentleman on horseback.

c1910

$6,000-9,000 Som

An early Patek Phillipe 18ct gold cushion case wristwatch, enamel dial, and luminescent Arabic numerals.

These watches are getting harder to find with the dials intact because the enamel is fragile and tends to break easily.

c1920

$15,000-20,000 Som

A platinum-cased Patek Phillipe dress pocket watch, with unusual diamond-set dial.

c1940

$10,000-15,000 Som

A Patek Phillipe platinum cased tonneau wristwatch, with two-tone dial.

c1920

$20,000-30,000 Som

A Patek Phillipe 18ct gold open-faced pocket watch, with split second chronograph and minute repeat silvered dial with gold applied numerals.

c1920

$30,000-40,000 Som

A Patek Phillipe platinum cased lady's cocktail watch.

c1930

$15,000-20,000 Som

A Patek Phillipe chronograph wristwatch, in 18ct gold, complete with certificate, originally sold on June 26, 1939.

$30,000-40,000 Som

A Patek Phillipe stainless steel 'Calatrava' wristwatch, with two-tone dial.

This piece has an indirect center seconds where Calatrava are usually associated with subsidiary seconds dials.

1940s

$10,000-15,000 Som

A 1940s Patek Phillipe wristwatch, ref. 1593, commissioned by Tiffany & Co. from Patek Phillipe, in 18ct yellow gold.

This watch is available as standard but having Tiffany & Co on the dial (part of a limited edition) makes it more desirable.

$20,000-30,000 Som

A Patek Phillipe 'Calatrava' wristwatch, in 18ct gold with Breguet numeral dial and subsidiary seconds.

The Calatrava is the most popular watch that Patek Phillipe have ever produced.

c1945

$7,000-10,000 Som

A Patek Phillipe lady's covered dial bracelet watch, in 18ct gold.

1950s

$10,000-15,000 Som

A late 1950s Patek Phillipe ref: 2526 wristwatch, with enamel dial.

This was the first automatic watch by Patek Phillipe. Manufacture started in 1953.

$20,000-30,000 Som

A gentleman's 18ct yellow gold wristwatch, signed "Beuche Girod", featuring a 1904 Statue of Liberty gold coin dial, on a light textured gold band.

$1,200-1,800 SI

A silver-cased Rolex Prince 'Jump Hour' wristwatch.

Few Jump Hours were made and now are difficult to find in good condition.

$15,000-20,000 Som

An early cushion-case 9ct yellow gold Rolex Oyster wristwatch, enamel dial.

Introduced in 1914, Rolex Oyster watches were the first waterproof watches.

$4,000-6,000 Som

An 18ct Rolex Prince wristwatch, in yellow and white gold, the two-tone dial, engraved on the case.

The engraving on this piece makes it very rare.

c1930

$20,000-30,000   Som

An 18ct Rolex Prince wristwatch, with yellow-gold flared case.

These are also known as 'The Doctor's Watch' because the large dial helped doctors to time heart rates.

c1935

$15,000-20,000   Som

A 9ct Rolex Prince 'Stripe' wristwatch, in white and yellow gold with two-tone dial.

c1935

$15,000-20,000   Som

A 1940s Rolex 'Bubble back' 18ct gold wristwatch, with three-quarter Arabic numeral dial and thunderbird bezel.

This was so named because of the revolutionary shape of the convex back made to house the movement.

$7,000-10,000   Som

A stainless steel Rolex 'Bubble back' wristwatch, with polished bezel and illuminised Arabic numerals, silvered dial and subsidiary seconds.

c1940

$4,000-6,000   Som

A stainless steel Rolex 'Bubble back' wristwatch, with quarter Arabic dial and thunderbird bezel.

1940s

$3,000-5,000   Som

A hooded 18ct Rolex 'Bubble Back' wristwatch, in rose gold and stainless steel, with curved case.

c1940

$10,000-15,000   Som

An 18ct yellow gold lady's Rolex 'Buckle watch', with silver dial and diamond-set bezel.

c1950s

$6,000-9,000   Som

A 1950s Rolex chronograph, with rare small sub dials and orginal green aged patina, in Oyster case.

Face 1.5in (3.5cm) wide

$20,000-30,000   WG

A Tiffany & Co platinum-cased pavé diamond-set lady's fob watch, with matching diamond-set bow.

c1910

$15,000-20,000   Som

A gentleman's 14K gold wristwatch, by Tiffany, the dial with seconds subsidiary, the 19-jewel movement no. M94455, the back of the case inscribed and dated.

1948

$300-400   FRE

A Vacheron Constantin square-cased lady's cocktail watch, with enamel and diamond-set bezel.

c1915

$15,000-20,000   Som

A Verge 18ct gold and enamel pocket watch, with elaborate case and unusual design.

c1820

$6,000-9,000   Som

A Waltham lady's silver open-faced pocketwatch and fob chain, with white dial, blue metallic 'diamond' hands, integral sterling link chain, signed.

Chain 21in (53.5cm) long

$120-180   SI

An 18ct yellow gold diamond and enamel set fob watch, with enamel dial and subsidiary seconds.

c1890

$4,000-6,000   Som

SCIENTIFIC INSTRUMENTS - Optical

A 'Gloria' magic lantern, with original wooden box, twelve lantern slides of English fairytales and two moving slides.

c1900

$220-280 ATK

Six hand-colored "The Magic Circle" phenakistiscope discs, by G. Tregear, London, marked.

10.25in (26cm) diam

$600-900 ATK

A rare English 'M'Leans Optical Illusions' or 'Magic Panorama' game, with holder and four hand-colored lithographed discs in original folder.

The phenakistocope was invented in 1832 based on the principle of 'persistence of vision' where a series of drawings seen through a slit on a spinning disc gave the impression of movement. Unsurprisingly these 'optical toys', which were expensive in their day, are now rare as the card was easily damaged when being spun.

c1850 *Discs 9.25in (23.5cm) diam*

$1,000-1,500 ATK

A painted German magic lantern, unknown maker, lacks burner and mirror.

c1860 *6.5in high*

$350-400 ATK

A French anamorphy set, by Walter Frères, Paris, with twenty-one anamorphes on French royalty, original folder and replaced cylinder mirror.

c1850 *4.25in (11cm) high*

$1,200-1,800 ATK

A rare mahogany and brass magic lantern, by J.T. Chapman, Manchester, with slide carrier and gas light burner, Dr. Auer system.

21in (53.5cm) high

$700-1,000 ATK

A large zoetrope, with a quantity of card cartoon strips.

c1870

$600-900 ATK

A rare "Lanterna de Orient: 1001 Nacht" magic lantern, by Jean Schoenner, Nuremberg, with burner.

Novelty shaped painted tinplate magic lanterns are extremely rare and highly desirable to collectors. Their fragile, thin metal bodies and colorful finishes were easily damaged and only a very few were made in complex novelty shapes, which were expensive at the time.

c1896 *13.5in (34.5cm) high*

$12,000-18,000 ATK

A professional biunnial magic lantern, unmarked, lacks burner.

21in (81cm) high

$500-800 ATK

An early brass megascope, by J. Dubosq, Paris, possibly restored.

c1870 *53cm high*

$1,500-2,000 ATK

A "Megalétoscopia Privilegiata" megalithoscope, by Carlo Ponti, together with an original 'Carnaval de Venise' photograph.

1862

$4,000-6,000 ATK

An extremely rare mahogany and brass triunnial magic lantern, by John Wrench & Son, London, marked "J.W., London Made, Established 1816", converted to halogen lighting, together with two additional sets of lenses.

As well as being impressive visually, triunnial magic lanterns were impressive functionally, allowing up to three different lantern slides to be faded in and out. This gave added life and movement to a magic lantern story.

c1890 *31.5in (80cm) high*

$20,000-30,000 ATK

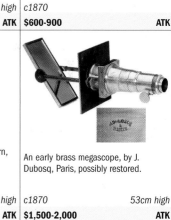

An American kaleidoscope, on a wooden stand.

Tube 12in (30.5cm) wide

$800-1,200 BA

SCIENTIFIC INSTRUMENTS

Surveying

A brass theodolite, by Cook, Troughton & Simms, in fitted wooden case.
11.75in (30cm) wide
$500-700 BA

A polished brass half-circle theodolite, in fitted wooden case.
Case 11.5in (29cm) wide
$700-1,000 BA

A rare lacquered brass theodolite, by Carl Zeiss, Jena.
c1925
$700-1,000 ATK

A brass transit.
15.5in (39.5cm) high
$1,200-1,800 BA

A brass sextant with compass, marked "Stella", possibly by Heath, in fitted mahogany case.
Case 11.5in (29cm) high
$700-1,000 BA

A massive 19thC lacquered brass surveyor's level, by Simms of London, with 2in (5cm) telescope with restricted view field, with later base.

This example is rare due to its large size. The restricted field of view was used for work on canals or mountain contours.
$1,200-1,800 ET

A lacquered brass pantograph, by William Harris, London, in original mahogany case with manufacturer's label.
c1780   *27.5in (70cm) long*
$500-700 ATK

A cased wooden compass.
2.75in (7cm) wide
$300-500 BA

A brass sundial, by Dolland, London.
10in (25.5cm) diam
$600-900 BA

Microscopes

Baker, Henry, "The Microscope Made Easy", London, second edition, 311 pages plus index with 14 numbered copper plate engravings plus one unnumbered, contemporary calf, rebacked with original label relaid.
1743
$1,000-1,500 ATK

A lacquered brass traveling microscope, by Watkins, London, in fitted mahogany case.
c1770   *14.25in (36cm) high*
$800-1,200 ATK

A lacquered brass Cuff-type microscope, by McIntosh, London, on a mahogany base, with five objectives and accessories, in fitted mahogany case.
c1780   *17.25in (44cm) high*
$3,000-4,000 ATK

An early English lacquered brass traveling microscope, with complete objective set, in fitted mahogany case.

c1810　　　*10.5in (27cm) high*

$500-700　　　**ATK**

An brass Culpepper-type microscope, by Bate of London, in fitted mahogany case.

c1820　　　*Case 12in (30.5cm) high*

$1,800-2,200　　　**BA**

A 19thC brass binocular microscope, by Baker, in fitted mahogany case.

Case 19in (48.5cm) high

$1,200-1,800　　　**BA**

A mid-to-late 19thC brass 'Improved Compound' microscope, by Carpenter & Westley, in fitted mahogany case.

Case 16.75in (42.5cm) high

$2,200-2,800　　　**BA**

Medical

A surgeon's set, by Brady & Martin, Newcastle-on-Tyne, in fitted mahogany case.

Surgeon's sets should be carefully examined for completeness, consistency of maker (whose name will be marked on the instruments) and condition, with rust and damage lowering value.

16.5in (42cm) wide

$1,000-1,500　　　**BA**

A presentation post-mortem set, various makers.

9.75in (25cm) wide

$700-1,000　　　**BA**

A French cupping set, in fitted mahogany case.

Case 10.75in (27.5cm) wide

$1,000-1,500　　　**BA**

A cupping set, by T. Eddington, Manchester.

Bloodletting was a common medical practice during the first half of the 19thC and was said to cure by relieving 'vascular tension'. A sharp lancet or scarificator cut into a blood vessel and a glass cup was placed over the cut. A syringe in the top of the cup produced a vacuum inside the cup to help the blood on its way out. It wasn't uncommon for up to one-sixth of the average body's blood to be removed in one session!

9in (23cm) wide

A cased apothecary's set.

8.5in (21.5cm) high

$700-1,000　　　**BA**

A mahogany 'Garden City' dentist's chair, with adjustable seat and headrest, upholstered in red velvet.

c1887

$700-1,000　　　**ATK**

An oak and iron collapsible U.S. Army dentist's chair, with adjustable seat, headrest and footrest, seat restored.

c1890

$2,200-2,800　　　**ATK**

$1,500-2,000　　　**BA**

Telescopes

A late 18thC lacquered brass refracting telescope on a stand, by Adams, London, with rack and pinion focusing, the stand unscrewing with folding legs, in a fitted mahogany case, signed.

Telescope 30in (76cm) long

$1,200-1,800　　　**ET**

A 19thC leather bound silver handheld reflecting telescope, signed and engraved, objective lens with sliding ray shade and cap, mahogany case with label.

Case 21.75in (55cm) long

$2,200-2,800　　　**ET**

A lacquered brass pocket telescope on folding stand, by Gregory Gilbert No.6 London, outer tube with inscription reading "ADMIRAL DE WYNTER", with screw-on lens cap, eyepiece with wheel of apertures.

7in (18cm) high

$2,500-3,000　　　**ET**

MISCELLANEOUS

Miscellaneous

A Geographical terrestrial globe.

12in (30.5cm) diam

$600-900   **BA**

A star globe, by Kelvin Hughes, dated.

1940   *10.25in (26cm) wide*

$1,000-1,500   **BA**

A brass Parkes & Hadley's orrery.

13in (33cm) wide

$2,500-3,000   **BA**

A German oak-cased brass barograph.

c1920   *13.75in (35cm) long*

$500-700   **ATK**

A silver cased pocket aneroid barometer, by Negretti & Zambra, London, engraved with the crest of the Campbell family, the case with London hallmark.

1927

2.25in (5.5cm) wide

$600-900   **ET**

A mahogany cased barograph, by Smart & Mason.

14in (35.5cm) wide

$600-900   **BA**

An Enigma type A cipher machine.

The Enigma machine was the German code machine used for military and reconnaissance communications during World War II. The highly complex encryption system used a series of up to three moving rotors and a plugboard that 'remapped' a letter between seven and nine times. It was the talented team based at Bletchley Park and including Alan Turing who managed to crack the code eventually.

c1941

$20,000-30,000   **ATK**

A Malling Hansen writing ball, with 54 spring-driven hemispherical typebars.

The first commercially available typewriter was invented by Danish pastor Malling Hansen (1835-1890), who was a director and teacher at an institution for the deaf and dumb in Copenhagen. It was a commercial success, with owners including philosopher Friedrich Nietzsche. It also won a number of awards in the 1870s. Due to its slow printing speed, it was soon eclipsed by the Sholes & Glidden Type Writer, introduced in 1874 by E. Remington & Sons. Today, very few writing balls survive, making them highly desirable.

c1867

$100,000-150,000   **ATK**

A Victorian en tremblant butterfly brooch, with diamond sapphires and ruby flower stem.

c1840   *4.75in (12cm) long*

$7,000-10,000   **NBlm**

A 19th English bee brooch, set with rubies and diamonds and with opal eyes.

$7,000-10,000   **JP**

A 19thC Dutch lyre brooch, set with diamonds.

$12,000-18,000   **JP**

A rams head stick pin, signed "Pierret, Paris".

c1860

$12,000-18,000   **JP**

A Victorian S-shaped lizard brooch, with turq-set spine.

2.25in (6cm) long

$1,000-1,500   **NBlm**

A mid-to late 19thC French brooch, with a bee intaglio in amethyst and decorated with natural pearls and diamonds.

$6,000-9,000   **JP**

An onyx brooch set with a micromosaic of the Colosseum in Rome, with a mother of pearl back and gold mount.

Such pieces were made as expensive souvenirs for wealthy tourists during the 19thC.

c1880   *1.75in (4cm) wide*

$800-1,200   **GS**

A late 19thC American three-leaf brooch, set with colored tourmalines.

$6,000-9,000   **JP**

A gold brooch, in the shape of a childs head, signed "E. Vernier".

c1900

$1,200-1,800   **JP**

An American 14ct gold brooch, in the shape of a dove.

c1900

$800-1,200   **JP**

A French gold brooch, in the shape of a zeppelin, set with diamonds, sapphires and rubies.

c1900

$3,500-4,500   **JP**

An English butterfly brooch, set with diamonds, emeralds and rubies.

c1910

$3,000-4,000   **JP**

A platinum double-ring 'love' brooch, engraved and set with sapphires and diamonds.

c1910

$8,000-12,000   **JP**

An Austrian 14ct white gold bakelite kingfisher pin, with diamonds and sapphires and synthetic sapphires, by Arthur Tuschak.

1911-1922   *1.25in (3cm) wide*

$3,000-4,000   **NBlm**

A 1920s German platinum dragonfly brooch, set with blue, yellow and pink colored diamonds.

$15,000-20,000   **JP**

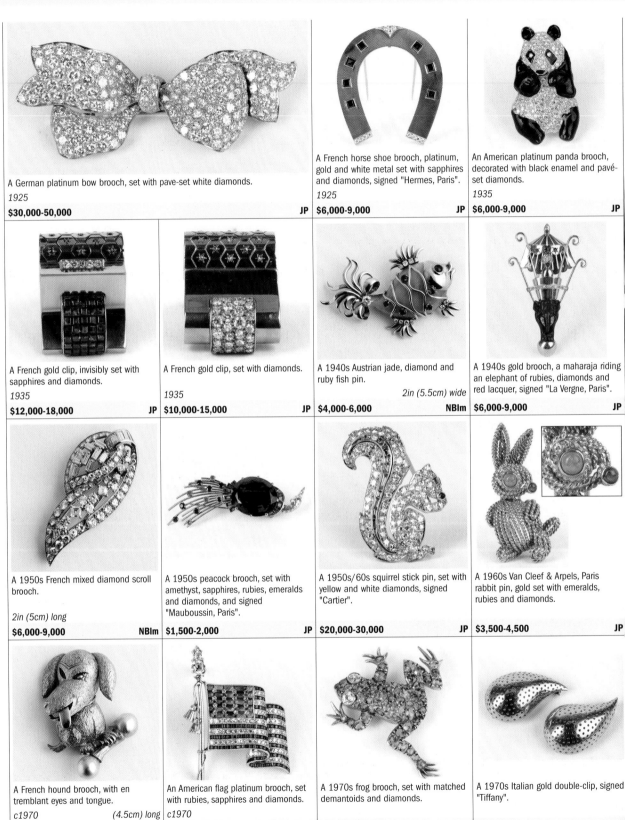

A German platinum bow brooch, set with pave-set white diamonds.

1925

$30,000-50,000   **JP**

A French horse shoe brooch, platinum, gold and white metal set with sapphires and diamonds, signed "Hermes, Paris".

1925

$6,000-9,000   **JP**

An American platinum panda brooch, decorated with black enamel and pavé-set diamonds.

1935

$6,000-9,000   **JP**

A French gold clip, invisibly set with sapphires and diamonds.

1935

$12,000-18,000   **JP**

A French gold clip, set with diamonds.

1935

$10,000-15,000   **JP**

A 1940s Austrian jade, diamond and ruby fish pin.

2in (5.5cm) wide

$4,000-6,000   **NBlm**

A 1940s gold brooch, a maharaja riding an elephant of rubies, diamonds and red lacquer, signed "La Vergne, Paris".

$6,000-9,000   **JP**

A 1950s French mixed diamond scroll brooch.

2in (5cm) long

$6,000-9,000   **NBlm**

A 1950s peacock brooch, set with amethyst, sapphires, rubies, emeralds and diamonds, and signed "Mauboussin, Paris".

$1,500-2,000   **JP**

A 1950s/60s squirrel stick pin, set with yellow and white diamonds, signed "Cartier".

$20,000-30,000   **JP**

A 1960s Van Cleef & Arpels, Paris rabbit pin, gold set with emeralds, rubies and diamonds.

$3,500-4,500   **JP**

A French hound brooch, with en tremblant eyes and tongue.

c1970   *(4.5cm) long*

$800-1,200   **NBlm**

An American flag platinum brooch, set with rubies, sapphires and diamonds.

c1970

$15,000-20,000   **JP**

A 1970s frog brooch, set with matched demantoids and diamonds.

$15,000-20,000   **JP**

A 1970s Italian gold double-clip, signed "Tiffany".

$10,000-15,000   **JP**

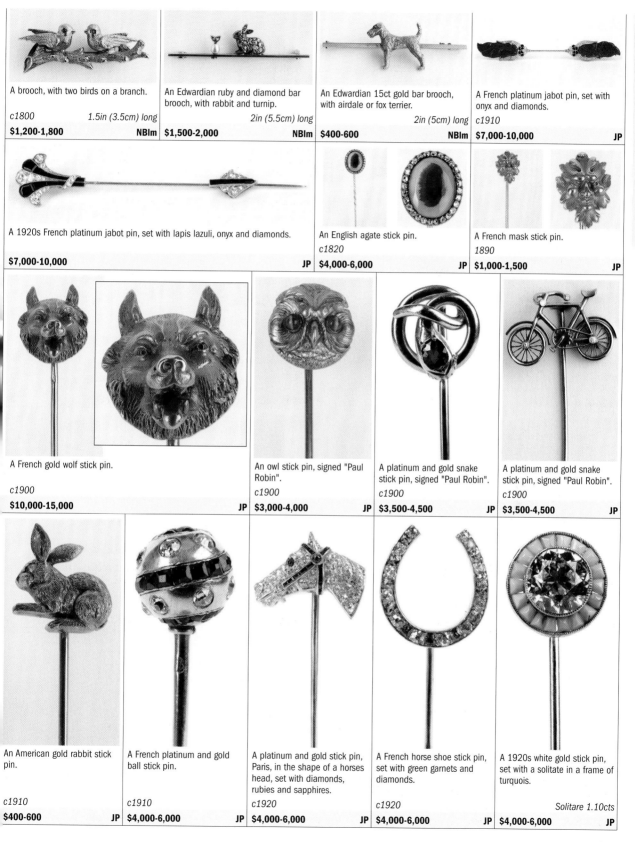

A brooch, with two birds on a branch.

c1800 1.5in (3.5cm) long
$1,200-1,800 NBlm

An Edwardian ruby and diamond bar brooch, with rabbit and turnip.

2in (5.5cm) long
$1,500-2,000 NBlm

An Edwardian 15ct gold bar brooch, with airdale or fox terrier.

2in (5cm) long
$400-600 NBlm

A French platinum jabot pin, set with onyx and diamonds.

c1910
$7,000-10,000 JP

A 1920s French platinum jabot pin, set with lapis lazuli, onyx and diamonds.

$7,000-10,000 JP

An English agate stick pin.

c1820
$4,000-6,000 JP

A French mask stick pin.

1890
$1,000-1,500 JP

A French gold wolf stick pin.

c1900
$10,000-15,000 JP

An owl stick pin, signed "Paul Robin".

c1900
$3,000-4,000 JP

A platinum and gold snake stick pin, signed "Paul Robin".

c1900
$3,500-4,500 JP

A platinum and gold snake stick pin, signed "Paul Robin".

c1900
$3,500-4,500 JP

An American gold rabbit stick pin.

c1910
$400-600 JP

A French platinum and gold ball stick pin.

c1910
$4,000-6,000 JP

A platinum and gold stick pin, Paris, in the shape of a horses head, set with diamonds, rubies and sapphires.

c1920
$4,000-6,000 JP

A French horse shoe stick pin, set with green garnets and diamonds.

c1920
$4,000-6,000 JP

A 1920s white gold stick pin, set with a solitate in a frame of turquois.

Solitare 1.10cts
$4,000-6,000 JP

Necklaces/Pendants

A Victorian turq and pearl locket.

1.5in (4cm) high

$1,500-2,000 — NBlm

A Victorian emerald, diamond and pearl necklace, the centerpiece with emerald-cut emerald of approx. 3.70cts.

$20,000-30,000 — DN

A necklet, with five swallows and rose diamond set wing edges.

This necklet is said to have belonged to Princess Caroline, niece of Napoleon III

c1875   *15in (38cm) long*

$4,000-6,000 — NBlm

A mid-to late 19thC French pendant, of bully Bristol glass with a reverse-engraved picture of pug dog, and engraved with "Chole", set in a gold horse shoe.

$20,000-30,000 — JP

A group of gold-filled and malachite panel jewelry, in case marked "Francis Peck Ltd., Nassau".

$1,500-2,000 — FRE

A Liberty blue pliqué-à-jour enamel necklace.

c1900   *15in (38cm) long*

$4,000-6,000 — NBlm

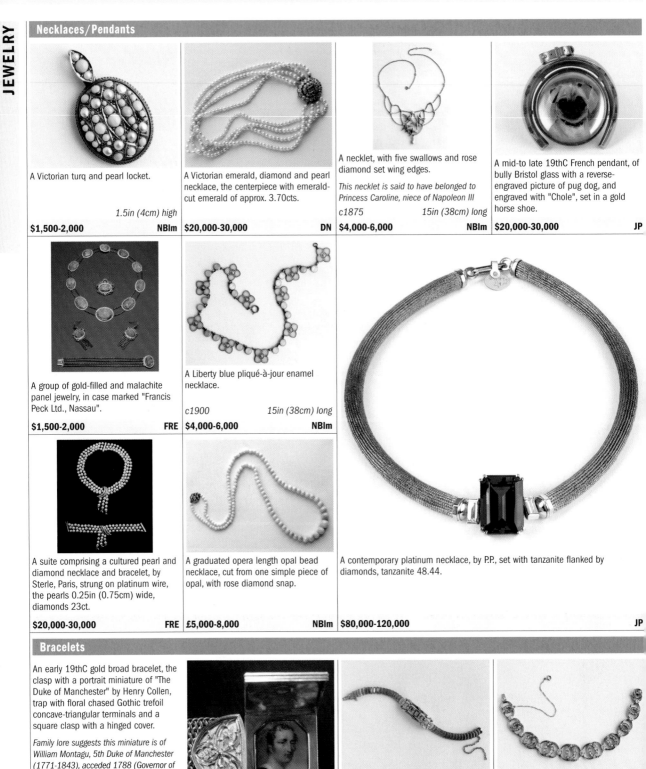

A suite comprising a cultured pearl and diamond necklace and bracelet, by Sterle, Paris, strung on platinum wire, the pearls 0.25in (0.75cm) wide, diamonds 23ct.

$20,000-30,000 — FRE

A graduated opera length opal bead necklace, cut from one simple piece of opal, with rose diamond snap.

£5,000-8,000 — NBlm

A contemporary platinum necklace, by P.P., set with tanzanite flanked by diamonds, tanzanite 48.44.

$80,000-120,000 — JP

Bracelets

An early 19thC gold broad bracelet, the clasp with a portrait miniature of "The Duke of Manchester" by Henry Collen, trap with floral chased Gothic trefoil concave-triangular terminals and a square clasp with a hinged cover.

Family lore suggests this miniature is of William Montagu, 5th Duke of Manchester (1771-1843), acceded 1788 (Governor of Jamaica from 1807 to 1828). However, this may be the 6th Duke, as Collen would probably not have been active before 1815.

Miniature 1in (2.75cm) high

$3,000-4,000 — DN

A rectangular emerald, diamond and gold bracelet.

c1880   *9.5in (24cm) long*

$10,000-15,000 — NBlm

A diamond, silver and gold graduated interlocking crescents bracelet.

c1900   *8.75in (22cm) long*

$10,000-15,000 — NBlm

An Edwardian diamond platinum briolette.
15.25in (40cm) long
$7,000-10,000 NBlm

A French platinum bracelet, set with diamonds and sapphires in a floral design.
1910
$30,000-50,000 JP

A French platinum line bracelet, set with sapphires and diamonds.
1920 Sapphires 13cts
$50,000-60,000 JP

A French platinum bracelet, set with diamonds and two borders of emeralds.
1920 Diamonds 40cts
$70,000-100,000 JP

An early 1920s French platinum bracelet, set with diamonds, onyx and natural pearls.
$7,000-10,000 JP

A platinum bracelet, set with emeralds and diamonds, signed "E. Goldschmidt, Köln".
1925
$30,000-50,000 JP

A platinum bracelet, set with fine sapphires and diamonds.
1925
$5,000-7,000 JP

An American 18ct gold and platinum bracelet, set with fine star ruby cabouchons.
1930
$4,000-6,000 JP

An American bracelet, set with diamonds.
Diamonds 11cts
$20,000-30,000 JP

A pair of gold bracelets, which combine to form a necklace, by Boucheron, Paris.
c1950
$15,000-20,000 JP

An American platinum bracelet, set with peridots and emerald-cut diamonds.
1960
$12,000-18,000 JP

A Swiss 18ct gold bracelet, set with six rare pink-ish jade cabouchons.
1970
$30,000-50,000 JP

Earrings

A pair of 1930s platinum and diamond set scroll fan ear clips, est. 6ct, by Trabert & Hoeffer Maubossin.
1.25in (3cm) long
$12,000-18,000 NBlm

A pair of 1940s gem set rose ear clips, by Boucheron.
0.75in (2cm) wide
$3,000-4,000 NBlm

A pair of 1940s stylized calibré ruby ear clips.
1.5in (3.5cm) wide
$3,000-4,000 NBlm

JEWELRY

A pair of cabochon-cut Ceylon sapphire and diamond earrings, sapphires 10ct, diamonds 3.4ct.

c1950

$7,000-10,000   **FRE**

A pair of emerald and diamond set leaf ear clips, est. 2.3ct, by Fred.

c1970   *1in (2.5cm) long*

$6,000-9,000   **NBlm**

A 1970s pair of half-hoop chrysoprase and diamond ear clips, by Van Cleef and Arpels.

1in (2.5cm) wide

$6,000-9,000   **NBlm**

A pair of 1970s bow ear clips, est. 5.5ct, by Van Cleef Arpels.

1in (2.5cm) long

$12,000-18,000   **NBlm**

A pair of 1970s Tiffany Schlumberger diamond and gold earrings.

1.25in (3cm) long

$12,000-18,000   **NBlm**

A 1980s Italian pair of multi-gem set 18ct gold comet ear clips.

3.25in (8cm) long

$3,000-4,000   **NBlm**

A contemporary pair of earrings, by P.P., set with Bakelite and diamonds.

Diamonds 2ct.

$7,000-10,000   **JL**

Rings

A 17thC agate cameo of Socrates, on 19thC mount.

1in (2.5cm) wide

$1,500-2,000   **NBlm**

An oval opal and diamond cluster ring.

c1900   *0.75in (2cm) diam*

$4,000-6,000   **NBlm**

An Edwardian gold, ruby and 21 diamond oval cluster ring, mixed-cut ruby approx. 4.7octs.

$6,000-9,000   **DN**

An intaglio ring, with a nicolo intaglio of the Escudo family, in diamond surround.

c1920   *1in (2.5cm) wide*

$2,500-3,000   **NBlm**

A platinum ring, set with diamonds, rubies and sapphires.

1925

$20,000-25,000   **JL**

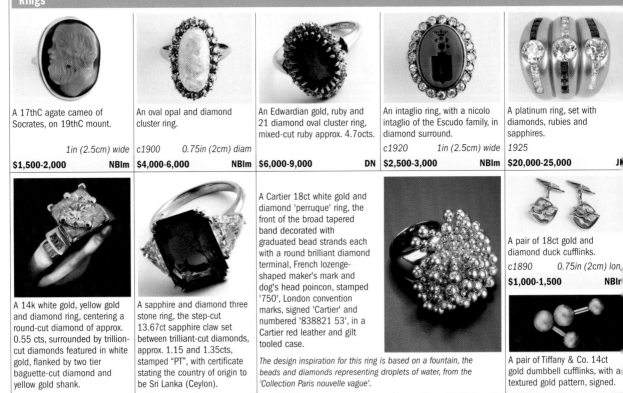

A 14k white gold, yellow gold and diamond ring, centering a round-cut diamond of approx. 0.55 cts, surrounded by trillion-cut diamonds featured in white gold, flanked by two tier baguette-cut diamond and yellow gold shank.

$400-600   **SI**

A sapphire and diamond three stone ring, the step-cut 13.67ct sapphire claw set between trilliant-cut diamonds, approx. 1.15 and 1.35cts, stamped "PT", with certificate stating the country of origin to be Sri Lanka (Ceylon).

$15,000-20,000   **DN**

A Cartier 18ct white gold and diamond 'perruque' ring, the front of the broad tapered band decorated with graduated bead strands each with a round brilliant diamond terminal, French lozenge-shaped maker's mark and dog's head poincon, stamped '750', London convention marks, signed 'Cartier' and numbered '838821 53', in a Cartier red leather and gilt tooled case.

The design inspiration for this ring is based on a fountain, the beads and diamonds representing droplets of water, from the 'Collection Paris nouvelle vague'.

$3,000-4,000   **DN**

A pair of 18ct gold and diamond duck cufflinks.

c1890   *0.75in (2cm) lon*

$1,000-1,500   **NBl**

A pair of Tiffany & Co. 14ct gold dumbbell cufflinks, with a textured gold pattern, signed.

$350-400   **S**

COSTUME JEWELRY

IT IS EASY TO SEE WHY COSTUME JEWELRY IS SUCH A POPULAR AREA TO COLLECT. The field is so broad, with numerous categories including couture, Art Deco, patriotic, holiday themes, and many more. The attraction lies in the possibility of owning a piece of the glamor and glitz of bygone eras without paying through the nose.

The technical process of making a fine piece of costume jewelry is lengthy and complicated. The first step is for the designer to create a drawing and then skilled workers make a model from the original design. Then white metal is hand-cast into a mold to replicate the model. The piece is then hand-polished before a three-part plating process is enacted, whereby copper is applied as a sealer, nickel to create a hard surface before gold or rhodium is electroplated. The crystal stones are then hand-set.

Notable names to look out for are Coco Chanel, Stanley Hagler, Joseff of Hollywood, Trifari, Schiaparelli, Miriam Haskell, Christian Dior, Coro (craft), Boucher et Cie, Weiss and Hattie Carnegie.

The Internet has made an enormous difference to the costume jewelry market, drastically changing accessibility. Also be aware that as fashions change, many previously neglected manufacturers may become more collectible, so as well as following trends it is important to simply buy what you like.

Stanley Hagler

A CLOSER LOOK AT STANLEY HAGLER PIN

The design is embellished by small metal roses, which are further enhanced by setting a diamanté stone in the center.

Seed pearls are hand-wired to create the petal shapes and then assembled to make flowers. They are a frequent feature of Hagler's designs.

The three-dimensional design is a signature of Stanley Hagler's work.

The simple ivory-colored cameo is set off by the extravagant floral frame.

A 1960s Stanley Hagler floral cameo pin, with carved ivory cameo, butter glass and jonquil rhinestones, hand-wired to a filigree gold-plated frame.

3in (8cm) wide

$150-200   Cris

STANLEY HAGLER

Stanley Hagler started designing jewelry in 1951 when he decided to make a bracelet for the Duchess of Windsor. It was a great hit with the staff of Vogue magazine who asked for copies. Two years later he went into business with Edward Nakles and set up a workshop in Greenwich Village, New York.

Hagler's extravagant creations won him eleven "Great Designs in Jewelry" prizes. In 1968 he described his design philosophy, "The point of creating exaggerated objects is that in order to be successful, you must underline your own point of view. If the average necklace reaches the middle of the bust, bring yours down to the navel. You certainly won't look like the average woman. It is an extreme fashion, which, when it reaches its highest point, establishes a trend."

Halger's jewelry was often multipurpose: a clasp might also be a brooch, a necklace worn doubled as a bracelet, and earrings had components which could be removed for a different look.

Nakles left the company in 1968 and Hagler moved to Hollywood where he ran the company alone. He died in 1996.

A 1960s Stanley Hagler vase of flowers pin, with carved shell leaves, mother-of-pearl petals and clear crystal rhinestone highlights.

3.5in (8.5cm) high

$220-280   Cris

A 1960s Stanley Hagler orchid flower pin, with beige composite and smoked topaz rhinestones hand-wired to a rose gold frame.

3in (7.5cm) high

$220-280   Cris

A 1960s Stanley Hagler flower pin, with turquois and powder blue glass, clear crystal rhinestones, gold-plated leaves, hand-wired to a filigree gold-plated frame.

2.5in (6cm) high

$80-120   Cris

An early 1980s Stanley Hagler vase of flowers pin, with pastel blue, green and pink glass petals and pastel pink and blue beads, hand-wired to a filigree gold-plated frame.

2.75in (7cm) high

$180-220   Cris

A late 1980s Stanley Hagler pandas, flowers and foliage pin, with carved ivory pandas, amethyst and green glass beads and jonquil crystal rhinestones hand-wired to a filigree gold-plated frame.

2.5in (6.5cm) wide

$300-350   Cris

A late 1980s Stanley Hagler flowers, leaves and butterflies pin, with colored glass beads, lucite and red cabouchons and hand-wired to a filigree, gold-plated frame.

5in (12.5cm) long

$320-380   Cris

A late 1980s Stanley Hagler flower pin, with grey glass beads and carved jade stones hand-wired to a filigree gold-plated frame.

3.75in (9.5cm) diam

$300-350   Cris

A pair of late 1980s Stanley Hagler earrings and a pin, pearls, seed pearls and diamanté hand-wired onto gold plated backing, marked "Stanley Hagler N.Y.C".

Pin 3in (8cm) long

$220-280   PC

A 1960s Stanley Hagler bees bib necklace, with topaz octagon crystal rhinestones, amber glass beads and hand-wired with gold-plated wire.

Necklace 14.5in (36cm) circ

$600-900   Cris

A 1960s Stanley Hagler Buddha pendant and floral motif necklace, with ivory Buddha and petals and French jet beads hand-wired to a filigree gold-plated frame.

Necklace 19in (48cm) long

$600-900   Cris

A CLOSER LOOK AT STANLEY HAGLER NECKLACE

Multiple beaded strands blended into extravagant compositions are a feature of Stanley Hagler's work.

The beaded areas are built up until they are three-dimensional.

The beads are hand-wired onto filigree gilt metal backings.

Hagler's designs were crafted so that they fit perfectly around the neck and lay in a flattering way.

Elaborate, pierced and signed filigree backings are classic Stanley Hagler.

An early 1980s Stanley Hagler hearts and flowers pendant necklace and earrings with faux coral glass beads and cabouchons hand-wired to filigree gold-plated bases.

Necklace 15.75in (40cm) circ

$600-900   Cris

A late 1980s Stanley Hagler floral motifs pendant necklace and earrings, with amethyst Murano glass beads and drops and amethyst rhinestones, hand-wired to filigree gold-plated frames.

Necklace 15.75in (40cm) circ

$700-1,000   Cris

A late 1980s Stanley Hagler floral motif necklace and earrings, with faux coral glass beads, woven faux coral petals and clear crystal rhinestones hand-wired to filigree gold-plated frames.

Necklace 17.75in (45cm) circ

$400-600   Cris

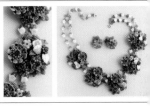

A late 1980s Stanley Hagler floral motif necklace and earrings, with small green glass beads and Murano green glass petals hand-wired to a filigree gold-plated frame.

Necklace 30in (76cm) circ

$500-700   Cris

Christian Dior

Christian Dior's 'new look' revolutionized fashion in 1947 by returning femininity after the war. Many pieces of costume jewelry made from then until his death in 1957 were designed by Dior himself. In 1955 the company signed a licensing agreement with Henkel & Grosse, a German company renowned for its high quality costume jewelry. All Henkel & Grosse for Dior pieces are marked with the Christian Dior name and year of manufacture. Dior jewelry was also made by Kramer, Maer and Schreiner. Today, Paris designer Robert Goossens – known for his work with Chanel – works with John Galliano to create couture and production jewelry for the House of Dior. Necklaces and earrings made before 1960 are popular with collectors for their classic, wearable style. However, later pieces are also collected as they represent good value for money.

A CLOSER LOOK AT CHRISTIAN DIOR PIN

The flowerheads are jointed, allowing them to move with the wearer.

This is a couture piece designed by Francis Winter.

The white metal is set with rhinestones.

These early pieces were made by artists for a small number of customers - some were one-offs, others part of a limited number made. Later pieces were made in greater numbers to be sold in shops and boutiques.

A rare late 1940s Christian Dior lily of the valley pin.

4.25in (11cm) long

Wain

A rare Mitchell Maer for Christian Dior articulated flower pin, with rhinestones in a yellow metal setting.

Hooks on the back of the setting allow the wearer to arrange the articulated sections.

1950-52   *7in (18cm) long*

$1,000-1,500   **Wain**

A Mitchell Maer for Christian Dior parure, consisting of a necklace, bracelet and earrings, pale and dark blue glass stones in a white metal setting.

1950-52   *16.5in (42cm) long*

$1,200-1,800   **Wain**

$800-1,200

A Mitchell Maer for Christian Dior Empire-style pin, earrings and necklace, with 'festoon'-style flattened gold plated and enameled metal chains set with clear paste stones.

1950-52   *16.5in (42cm) circ*

$1,800-2,200   **Wain**

A Mitchell Maer for Christian Dior pin, in the form of a bird holding a 'diamond' in its beak, in white metal set with paste.

1950-52

$500-700   **Wain**

A rare Christian Dior snail on a leaf pin, with sterling silver set with clear and red paste, date mark.

1958

$1,000-1,500   **Wain**

A rare Christian Dior bird pin, with en tremblant wings, sterling silver set with clear paste, faux pearls and enamel, date mark.

1958

$1,500-2,000   **Wain**

A Mitchell Maer for Christian Dior pin, with white metal set with paste and faux pearls.

1950-52

$2,200-2,800   **Wain**

A Christian Dior floral necklace, gold-plated, green and red crystal rhinestones and faux pearls, date mark.

1958   *14.5in (37cm) circ*

$500-700   **Cris**

COSTUME JEWELRY

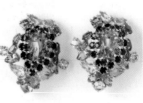

A late 1950s Christian Dior 'eye' pin, the rhodium-plated back set with pearl drops, blue cabouchons, clear navette crystal rhinestones and faux pearl.

2.5in (6cm) wide

$300-350 Cris

A pair of Christian Dior earrings, yellow metal set with red, green and clear crystals, date mark.

1959 *1.5in (4cm) long*

$60-90 PC

A pair of Christian Dior earrings, white metal set with pale and dark blue crystals, date mark.

1959 *1.5in (4cm) long*

$80-120 PC

A Christian Dior necklace and earrings, with white metal set with faux diamonds, rubies and moonstones, date mark.

1959

$800-1,200 Wain

A Christian Dior necklace and earrings, with white metal set with clear paste and faux pearls, date mark.

Yves Saint Laurant took over at Christian Dior in 1958. By 1959 his style was evident in Christian Dior's designs.

1959

$800-1,200 Wain

A Christian Dior necklace, with white metal set with paste pearls, iridescent, topaz and hearmatite stones, dated.

1959

$600-900 Wain

A rare Christian Dior three leaf clover pin, with sterling silver set with clear and red paste, date mark.

1959

$1,000-1,500 Wain

A Henkel and Grosse for Christian Dior brooch, with white metal set with yellow and green paste and glass pearls, date mark.

1962 *2.75in (7cm) long*

$300-350 Wain

A Henkel and Grosse for Christian Dior pin, with white metal set with clear paste and glass pearls, date mark.

1960 *3in (8cm) long*

$400-600 Wain

A Henkel and Grosse for Christian Dior necklace, with japanned metal set with smokey quartz paste stones, date mark.

Japanned metal has been blanked using lacquer or another process. It was originally used for mourning jewelry, and later for its decorative effect.

1962

$700-1,000 Wain

A Christian Dior fish pin, with yellow metal set with pavé diamanté and glass leaf fins, date mark.

1968 *3.25in (8.5cm) long*

$400-600 Wain

A Christian Dior necklace, with gold plated metal set with paste turquois stones, date mark.

1970 *22in (56cm) circ*

$700-1,000 Wain

Trifari

Trifari and Krussman was founded in 1918 by Gustavo Trifari and Leo F. Krussman, in New York. In 1925 Carl Fishel joined and the company became Trifari, Krussman and Fishel (TKF). In 1929 designer Alfred Philippe joined and during his 40 years with the company created some of its most sought-after designs. From the 1930s through to the 1960s Trifari created one-off pieces for Broadway productions. Trifari produced patriotic jewelry during World War II and other popular designs include 'fruit salad', 'jelly bellies' and 'pearl bellies'.

A 1930s Trifari necklace, with blue flowers, red berries and green leaves.

Flower 0.75in (2cm) diam

$400-600   **Rox**

A 1940s Trifari necklace and earrings, pearl, gold and diamanté.

Earrings 1in (3cm) long

$220-280   **Rox**

A 1930s Trifari necklace and bracelet, with blue and diamanté beads.

Bracelet 7in (18cm) long

$400-600   **Rox**

A Trifari necklace and bracelet, from the Princess Eugene series.

c1940   *Bracelet 7in (18cm) long*

$400-600   **Rox**

A 1940s Trifari necklace, set with pastel 'fruit salad' stones.

3in (7.5cm) long

$220-280   **Rox**

A 1940s Trifari necklace and earrings, with pink carved glass leaves and rhinestones, designed by Alfred Philippe.

Necklace 15.5in (39.5cm) circ

$220-280   **RG**

A 1950s Trifari necklace, bracelet and earrings demi-parure, with faux pearls, emeralds and diamonds, from an original design for Mamie Eisenhower.

Necklace 15in (38cm) circ

$400-600   **Cris**

A 1950s Trifari necklace and earrings.

Earrings 2in (5cm) long

$50-70   **TR**

A 1950s Trifari floral motif necklace and earrings, with faux pearls and small black crystal rhinestones on gold-plated castings.

Necklace 15in (38cm) circ

$700-1,000   **Cris**

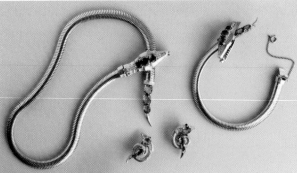

A late 1950s Trifari 'coral, pearls and fish' chatelaine pin, gold-plated with faux pearls and light blue enamel.

Coral 1.2in (3cm) long

$80-120   **Cris**

A 1960s Trifari snake necklace, bracelet and earrings.

Earrings 1in (3cm) long

$400-600   **Rox**

A 1960s Trifari pink necklace, bracelet and earrings.

Earrings 3.5in (9cm) long

$320-380   **Rox**

A 1930s Trifari pin flower pin, with white metal set with faux moonstones, pavé rhinestones and enamel.

3.5in (9cm) long

$400-600   **TR**

A 1930s Trifari pin, with red, gold and diamanté.

3.25in (8cm) long

$300-350   **TR**

A 1940s Trifari 'fruit salad' pin.

3.5in (9cm) long

$150-200   **TR**

A 1940s Trifari fur clip, two-tone yellow and rose gold-plated silver set with faux rubies and diamonds.

3.5in (9cm) long

$400-600   **Cris**

A large mid-1940s Trifari crown pin with red and blue cabouchons, green baguettes and clear crystal rhinestones on sterling silver.

1.75in (4.5cm) high

$180-220   **Cris**

A 1940s Trifari heart-shaped brooch and earrings, in green, gold, blue, and clear Lucite on gold-plated casing with pear drop sapphire crystals.

Brooch 2in (5.5cm) long

$300-350   **Cris**

A 1960s Trifari pin, two pairs earrings.

Pin 2.25in (6cm) long

$80-120   **Rox**

A 1940s Trifari bracelet.

7.5in (19cm) long

$180-220   **Rox**

Fahrner

Seeger and Fahrner was founded in 1855. In 1895 Theodor Fahrner became the sole proprietor. He was one of the most influential German manufacturers of costume jewelry and nonprecious ornamental objects. In 1900 he participated in the Paris Exposition, winning a silver medal. His philosophy was that the artistic merit of a piece was more important than the value of the materials used to make it. The company was based in Pforzheim in Germany and was successful despite fierce competition. In 1902 there were 602 costume jewelry factories in the town. Fahrner funded his artistic lines with mass-produced ones, which are usually unmarked. These unmarked ones are worth a fraction of the price of marked pieces. The company closed in 1979. Early pieces are very collectible and valuable, but there are a number of very good reproductions about and it can be difficult to tell the difference.

A Fahrner pin, with rock crystal set with turquois stones in a silver mount.

1.5in (4cm) long

$1,200-1,800 TR

A 1930s Fahrner brooch, in silver set with onyx and marcasite.

1.75in (4.5cm) long

$3,000-4,000 TR

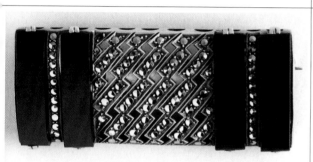

A 1930s Fahrner black and diamanté brooch.

2in (5.5cm) long

$3,500-4,500 TR

A Fahrner brooch, in silver set with chalcedony, amonizite and marcasite.

2in (5.5cm) wide

$1,000-1,500 TR

A 1930s Fahrner brooch, in silver set with enamel and marcasite.

2in (5cm) wide

$700-1,000 TR

A 1930s Fahrner brooch, in silver set with pale blue stone and marcasite.

2.5in (6cm) wide

$500-700 TR

A Fahrner pendant on a cord, in silver set with enamel and rose quartz.

Pendant 2in (5cm) long

$2,200-2,800 TR

A 1930s Fahrner pendant, in silver set with enamel, marcasite and amonizite.

2in (5cm) long

$350-400 TR

Chanel

A Chanel frog pin, with green, black and red enamel on a lead casting, with clear crystal rhinestone eyes and feet.

c1927   *2.4in (6cm) wide*

$2,200-2,800   **Cris**

A 1950s French Chanel couture bracelet, with poured glass set in a gilded metal frame.

6.75in (17cm) long

$2,200-2,800   **Wain**

A CLOSER LOOK AT A CHANEL PIN

The detailing on the leaves is superb.

This is an amusing and vibrant piece.

The designer has created an exaggerated sense of perspective. The house at the base is tiny, making the larger than life Mexican jump out at you.

Chanel often took inspiration from foreign imagery, as in this Mexican palm tree. In particular she was fond of Africa and India.

A 1930s American Chanel pin, in the form of a Mexican in a palm tree with house at the base, in gilded metal, enamel and paste.

$1,000-1,500   **Wain**

A rare 1930s Chanel star pin, in gold plated metal.

This is an early French piece.

4.25in (11cm) long

$1,000-1,500   **Wain**

A 1950s French Chanel Moghul-style couture necklace, poured glass set in a gilded metal frame.

16.5in (42cm) long

$2,200-2,800   **Wain**

A 1980s Chanel faux pearl necklace, marked "Chanel", made in France.

32in (81.5cm) long

$120-180   **RG**

A late 1990s Histoire de Verre (H. de V.) floral motif necklace and earrings, with ruby poured glass and clear crystal rhinestones on brass wire frames.

Necklace 20in (51cm) circ

$1,000-1,500   **Cris**

A late 1990s Histoire de Verre (H. de V.) leaves-and-berries motif necklace and earrings, with aubergine and green poured glass on brass frames.

Necklace 20.5in (52cm) circ

$1,000-1,500   **Cris**

A late 1990s Histoire de Verre (H. de V.) necklace, with red, topaz, amethyst and amber poured glass beads on a brass wire frame.

19in (48cm) circ

$220-280   **Cris**

A late 1990s Histoire de Verre (H. de V.) floral necklace and earrings, with amethyst and jonquil poured glass on brass frames.

Necklace 21.25in (54cm) circ

$1,000-1,500   **Cris**

A late 1990s Histoire de Verre (H. de V.) flower pin, with sapphire-blue and green poured glass and clear crystal rhinestones, and gold-plated stem and border, on a brass frame.

3.3in (8.5cm) long

$280-320 **Cris**

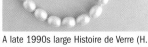

A late 1990s large Histoire de Verre (H. de V.) single-strand pearl necklace, with baroque pearls and gold-plated filigree spacers.

32.25in (82cm) circ

$220-280 **Cris**

An early 1990s Iradj Moini frog pin, with large 1950s textured jade-green stones, clear crystal rhinestone highlights and red cabouchon eyes.

Iradj Moini designs jewelry using his own mark and makes couture pieces for Oscar de la Renta.

3.75in (9.5cm) wide

$500-700 **Cris**

An early 1990s Iradj Moini red apple pin, the fruit of red cabouchons, the leaves of green octagon stones, the stalk of clear crystal rhinestones.

4.3in (11cm) high

$500-700 **Cris**

A late 1990s Iradj Moini flower pin, with mother-of-pearl petals and clear crystal rhinestones on a Ruthinium-plated frame.

5.5in (14cm) high

$700-1,000 **Cris**

An early 1990s Iradj Moini bouquet-of-flowers pin and earrings, with red, olivine and amber French hand-blown glass petals, carved jade leaves and clear crystal rhinestone highlights.

Pin 4in (10cm) high

$800-1,200 **Cris**

A mid-1990s Iradj Moini 'trembler' flower pin, with prong-set clear crystal rhinestones.

5in (13cm) high

$1,000-1,500 **Cris**

A pair of Joseff of Hollywood earrings, marked "Joseff".

c1940 *2.5in (6.5cm) long*

$120-180 **PC**

A Joseff of Hollywood Sun God pin, marked "Joseff".

c1940 *3in (8cm) diam*

$150-200 **PC**

A Joseff of Hollywood Moon God with ruff pin, marked "Joseff".

c1940　　　　　　*3in (8cm) diam*

$400-600　　　　　　**PC**

A very rare 1940s Joseff of Hollywood Russian gold plated 'C-cutter' pin.

　　　　　　6in (15.5cm) high

$700-1,000　　　　　　**Cris**

A 1960s Miriam Haskell necklace, from the 'Shooting Star' collection, with three strands of baroque pearls meeting in two ears of wheat in gilded metal set with roses montées and oblong faux pearls, ending with faux baroque pearl tassels each ending with a drop pearl.

　　　　　　21.75in (55cm) long

$1,200-1,800　　　　　　**Wair**

A Miriam Haskell necklace.

c1940　　　　　*2.5in (6cm) deep*

$500-700　　　　　　**TR**

A Miriam Haskell pin and earrings.

　　　　　　

$150-200　　　　　　**PC**

A 1930s Marcel Boucher ear of wheat brooch, rhodium plated, signed with Marcel Boucher logo.

Marcel Boucher designed for Cartier in the late 1920s. After the Wall Street Crash he opened a costume jewelry business with a small range of ten to twelve designs per season - to ensure quality. He designed with his wife Sandra who had worked for Tiffany. When he died in 1964 she carried on designing for five years. Many jewelers started making costume jewelry after the Wall Street Crash because the market for precious jewelry had declined.

　　　　　　4.5in (11.5cm) long

$300-400　　　　　　**RG**

A 1950s Marcel Boucher bracelet, gold-plated with red, green and blue cabouchons, and edged with clear rhinestones.

　　　　　　7in (18cm) circ

$300-400　　　　　　**Cris**

An early 1950s Marcel Boucher necklace, bracelet and earrings demi-parure, with sapphire blue and clear crystal rhinestones on Rhodium plating.

　14in (35.5cm) long

$600-900　　　　　　**Cris**

A 1940s Coro plume pin, emerald green glass stones with clear crystal rhinestone highlights on a gold-plated frame.

The name Coro is a contraction of an earlier trade name: Cohn & Rosenberger, a company founded in New York City in 1902. Coro Inc was founded in 1919, and produced affordable costume jewelry. During the 1930s the company built a factory in Providence, Rhode Island, and was the first to establish the viability of mass produced costume jewelry. The company's most expensive pieces were produced under the Corocraft name in the 1940s. This line was succeeded by Vendome in 1944. By creating a number of lines and marks Coro was able to produce jewelry in a wide variety of styles and price ranges which would be affordable to most buyers. Today Coro is the largest American costume jewelry manufacturer, employing over 2,000 people.

　　　　　　4.75in (12cm) long

$300-350　　　　　　**Cris**

A very rare mid-1940s Coro Duette 'brave and squaw' pin, rose-gold-plated over a sterling silver casting, with red and green enamel and ruby and clear rhinestone highlights.

1.75in (4.5cm) high

$800-1,200   Cris

A mid-1940s Coro Duette owls pin, with blue enamel and large aquamarine and clear crystal rhinestones over a sterling silver casting.

1.5in (4cm) high

$180-220   Cris

An early 1940s Elsa Schiaparelli necklace, gold-plated with pink enamel stones and clear crystal rhinestones.

15in (38cm) circ

$600-900   Cris

An 1950s Elsa Schiaparelli bracelet, pin and earrings demi-parure, silver-plated with baby blue cabouchons.

Elsa Schiaparelli (1890-1973) was born in Rome and studied in England before moving to America and becoming a scriptwriter. In the late 1920s she moved to Paris and opened a boutique selling her own designs. Her dresses and suits – inspired by artistic movements such as Surrealism and Dadaism – revolutionized fashion. Schiaparelli expanded production to include jewelry and in the late 1930s and early 1940s Jean Schlumberger designed some unsigned pieces for her. She spent the duration of WWII in New York, but on her return to Paris found her designs were out of favor. Schiaparelli returned to New York where she started to mass-produce her clothing and jewelry. As a result, post-war pieces are more common and affordable than Schiaparelli's prewar designs. Her postwar jewelry features aurora borealis and frosted glass stones. This is a good area for new collectors.

Bracelet 7.25in (18.5cm) circ

$700-1,000   Cris

A 1950s Elsa Schiaparelli pin and earrings, with prong-set blue cabouchons and blue and green crystal rhinestones.

Pin 2.5in (6cm) diam

$300-350   Cris

A 1950s Henry Schreiner pin, set with faux moonstones and inverted crystals.

The Schreiner Company often set stones upside down because it allowed the stone to pick up the color of the fabric it sat on and look like to was made specifically for that garment.

2.75in (7cm) long

$120-180   Cris

A 1950s Henry Schreiner necklace and earrings, gold-plated with aquamarine, jonquil and aurora borealis crystal rhinestones.

German-born Henry Schreiner worked as a blacksmith before emigrating to America in 1923. There was little work for blacksmiths in New York, and so he took other jobs, before joining the Better Shoe Buckle Company in 1926. By 1939 he was running his own costume jewelry business. Schreiner jewelry was never made commercially or mass-produced. The company used unusual stones specially made in Czechoslovakia and Germany, to create its signature combinations of unusual colors and cuts. It closed in the late 1970s.

Necklace 17.4in (44cm) circ

$1,000-1,500   Cris

A 1950s Henry Schreiner necklace and earrings, silver-plated with ruby red glass drops and clear crystal rhinestones.

Necklace 15in (38cm) circ

$600-900   Cris

A late 1990s Larry Vrba bow pin, Ruthinium-plated with clear crystal rhinestones.

4in (10cm) wide

$150-200   Cris

A late 1990s large Larry Vrba flower pin, with abalone shell, faux pearls, glass beads and clear crystal rhinestones on a Ruthinium-plated back.

Larry (Lawrence) Vrba started working for Miriam Haskell in accounts in 1969. He developed a passion for costume jewelry and later became head designer.

7.75in (20cm) long

$220-280   Cris

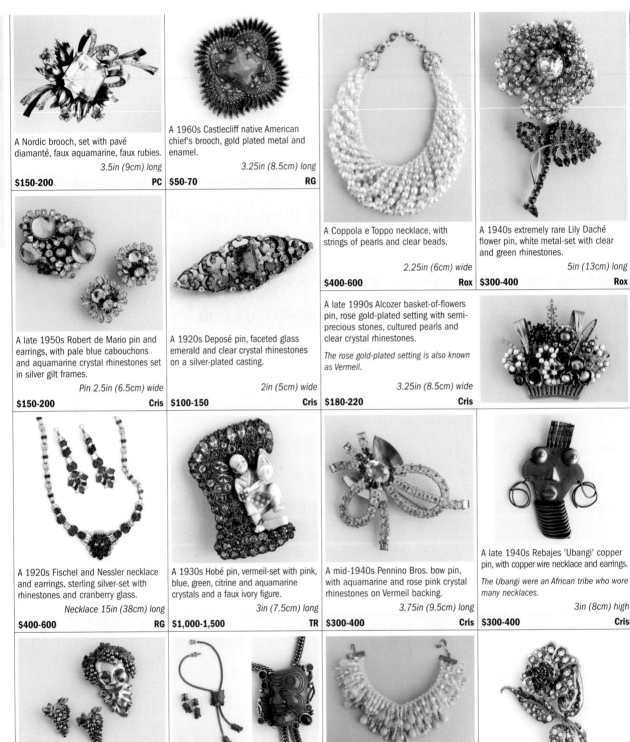

A Nordic brooch, set with pavé diamanté, faux aquamarine, faux rubies.

3.5in (9cm) long

$150-200   **PC**

A 1960s Castlecliff native American chief's brooch, gold plated metal and enamel.

3.25in (8.5cm) long

$50-70   **RG**

A Coppola e Toppo necklace, with strings of pearls and clear beads.

2.25in (6cm) wide

$400-600   **Rox**

A 1940s extremely rare Lily Daché flower pin, white metal-set with clear and green rhinestones.

5in (13cm) long

$300-400   **Rox**

A late 1950s Robert de Mario pin and earrings, with pale blue cabouchons and aquamarine crystal rhinestones set in silver gilt frames.

Pin 2.5in (6.5cm) wide

$150-200   **Cris**

A 1920s Deposé pin, faceted glass emerald and clear crystal rhinestones on a silver-plated casting.

2in (5cm) wide

$100-150   **Cris**

A late 1990s Alcozer basket-of-flowers pin, rose gold-plated setting with semi-precious stones, cultured pearls and clear crystal rhinestones.

The rose gold-plated setting is also known as Vermeil.

3.25in (8.5cm) wide

$180-220   **Cris**

A 1920s Fischel and Nessler necklace and earrings, sterling silver-set with rhinestones and cranberry glass.

Necklace 15in (38cm) long

$400-600   **RG**

A 1930s Hobé pin, vermeil-set with pink, blue, green, citrine and aquamarine crystals and a faux ivory figure.

3in (7.5cm) long

$1,000-1,500   **TR**

A mid-1940s Pennino Bros. bow pin, with aquamarine and rose pink crystal rhinestones on Vermeil backing.

3.75in (9.5cm) long

$300-400   **Cris**

A late 1940s Rebajes 'Ubangi' copper pin, with copper wire necklace and earrings.

The Ubangi were an African tribe who wore many necklaces.

3in (8cm) high

$300-400   **Cris**

A mid-1940s Reja 'Bacchanalian' mask pin and earrings, with sterling silver mask, rose-gold-plated grapes and green enameled leaves.

Pin 3in (7.5cm) high

$700-1,000   **Cris**

A late 1950s Selro Oriental heads-bolero pendant necklace and earrings, with red lucite and silver-plated chain.

Earrings 1in (2.5cm) long

$150-200   **Cris**

A late 1990s Ian St. Gielar necklace, with a clear crystal woven collar and aquamarine and clear glass drops.

12.5in (32cm) long

$300-400   **Cris**

A 1920s English silver and paste floral brooch, marked "sterling silver".

2in (5cm) long

$70-100   **RG**

An early 1920s French 'fruit salad' hanging-basket-of-flowers pin, with primary color cabouchons and crystal rhinestones and clear crystal rhinestones, on a sterling silver casting.

1.5in (4cm) wide

$150-200　　　　　　　　　　**Cris**

A 1930s European silver and paste basket brooch, marked "835".

This is a good shape, a popular subject and a good quality piece.

2in (5cm) long

$300-350　　**RG**

A 1930s English brooch, silver-set with paste, onyx and pearls, unmarked.

2.25in (5.5cm) long

$180-220　　**RG**

An unmarked fur clip, in white metal with copper wash, set with clear and red rhinestones.

c1930　　*2.5in (6.5cm) long*

$60-90　　**PC**

A 1940s American sterling silver brooch and earrings.

Brooch 3.25in (8.5cm) long

$80-120　　**RG**

A pair of English silver, marcasite and coral colored glass drop earrings, marked "silver".

3in (7.5cm) long

$120-180　　**RG**

A 1920s pair of French paste earrings, white metal set with clear glass and faux aquamarine stones.

2in (5.5cm) long

$2,200-2,800　　**TR**

A 1920s French necklace, with yellow metal chain interspersed with faux pearls, decorated with yellow metal leaves and red and green glass and faux pearl drops.

1.5in (4cm) deep

$800-1,200　　**TR**

A 1920s silver and carved glass bracelet, probably French, unmarked.

$180-220　　**RG**

A German enameled pendant, unmarked.

c1930　　*1.75in (4.5cm) long*

$300-400　　**TR**

A 1930s unmarked bracelet, pin and earrings, yellow metal set with multicolored glass stones.

Earrings 1in (3cm) long

$1,200-1,800　　**Rox**

ENAMEL BOXES

Enamel boxes were first produced in Europe in the early 18th century. They were predominantly used as containers for snuff or patches (beauty spots), as well as bonbonnières, étuis, and tokens of love or 'souvenir de l'amitié'. They were perceived as an essential fashion accessory for the 18th century aristocracy who were charmed by their beauty and delicacy. The amount and quality of boxes owned was a sign of a person's position and standing in society.

Early enamels were hand-painted. However, the introduction of transfer-printing in England c1750 led to an increase in production, and both hand-painted and transfer printed boxes were widely produced until c1840. Factories producing enamels included Battersea,

Birmingham, Bilston and many in south Staffordshire. The Battersea factory is often credited with being the most prolific, however, it closed in 1756 after just three years, whereas the other factories existed at various times for over a century. By the 1830s the English enameling industry was in decline. The Industrial Revolution meant that it could not compete with the profusion of ceramic, glass and metal goods on the market, and artistic standards began to deteriorate. The last recorded enameler ceased trading in 1840.

The majority of enamels are on a copper base, which was more accessible and affordable than gold or silver. English enamels are generally unmarked, and only occasionally bear the artist's signature.

Bilston Enamels

A Bilston enamel 'faux montre' (fake watch), decorated with embossed flowers against a pale yellow ground.

c1740   1.5in (4cm) diam

$1,000-1,500   HD

A Bilston enamel box, with raised flowers on a blue and turquois ground.

c1760   2in (5cm) long

$700-1,000   HD

A Bilston enamel bonbonnière, in the form of a brown and red bird with yellow markings, on a flower-painted base, some restoration.

c1760   1.75in (4.5cm) long

$1,500-2,000   HD

A Bilston enamel bonbonnière, in the form of a bird on a sgraffito ground, the base with birds and a waterfall.

Bonbonnières were used to hold cachous to freshen the breath, as lack of dental hygiene in the 18thC meant that halitosis was a problem. Bilston produced many different bonbonnières in bird and animal shapes, inspired by objects made in porcelain at Meissen and Chelsea.

c1770   2.5in (6.5cm) high

$1,800-2,200   HD

A Bilston enamel patch-box, in the form of a basket of flowers, with original steel mirror.

c1770   1.5in (4cm) high

$6,000-9,000   HD

A Bilston enamel bonbonnière, of a black and white King Charles spaniel on a pink base, the lid inscribed "I give it to you", restored.

c1770   1.25in (3.5cm) diam

$1,800-2,200   HD

A cartouche-shaped Birmingham enamel snuff box, depicting children playing, the sides with rococo scrolls and flowers.

c1755   *2.5in (6.5cm) long*

$2,200-2,800   **HD**

A Birmingham enamel snuff box, with a portrait of William, Lord Blakeney, after an engraving by James McArdell from a portrait by Sir E. Chalmers.

c1756-61   *2.25in (6cm) diam*

$4,000-6,000   **HD**

A rare Birmingham enamel box, the lid depicting the 'Round' game, after a painting by Lancret, the sides with flowers of Deutsche Blumen after Meissen.

c1760   *5in (12.5cm) long*

$8,000-12,000   **HD**

A Birmingham enamel tea caddie, with mythological scenes depicting 'Pyramus and Thisbe', 'Persius and Andromeda' and scenes from 'The Ladies Amusement'.

c1760   *3.25in (8.5cm) long*

$6,000-9,000   **HD**

A Birmingham snuff box, depicting The Forum in Rome with Trajan's Column and the Colosseum, the base depicting classical landscapes, old chip to base.

c1760   *2.75in (7cm) long*

$3,000-6,000   **HD**

A Birmingham enamel snuff box, made to commemorate the death of George II, the lid depicting Britannia weeping at his tomb.

c1760   *2.5in (6.5cm) long*

$1,500-2,000   **HD**

An English enamel snuff box, on a Sheffield plate base, the lid transfer-printed with Masonic symbols, probably Birmingham.

c1760   *2.5in (6.5cm) long*

$1,500-2,000   **HD**

A Birmingham enamel snuff box, depicting Britannia mourning George II, on a black ground, with a skull and crossbones, old restoration.

It is rare to find black used as the ground color.

Exhibited at Necessary Extravagances 1993.

c1760   *2.25in (6cm) long*

$1,500-2,000   **HD**

A Birmingham enamel tôle casket, with a scene of an Italian town, after the style of Piranesi.

The enamel plaque is set into the casket, which is applied with gilt strap and arabesque work on a black japanned ground. Japanning is the process of coating objects with layers of colored varnish to imitate true Chinese and Japanese lacquer. This industry flourished in Birmingham, Wolverhampton, Pontypool, and London. These japanned caskets and toilet boxes were set with Birmingham enamel plaques, often with grand Classical and Mediterranean port scenes. The caskets were sometimes fitted with a set of four toilette boxes, painted in a similar style but with different scenes.

c1755   *9.75in (25cm) long*

$12,000-18,000   **HD**

A South Staffordshire enamel egg-shaped bonbonnière, depicting floral riguettes on a rare purple ground within gilt scrolls, some restoration to lid.

c1770   2.25in (6cm) high
$3,000-4,000   **HD**

A South Staffordshire blue gingham scent bottle case, depicting children and flowers with gilt decoration, some restoration.

c1775   2.25in (6cm) high
£1,000-1,500   **HD**

A very rare South Staffordshire enamel snuff box, depicting 'The Siege of Gibraltar'.

c1780   2.5in (6.5cm) long
$3,500-4,000   **HD**

A fine South Staffordshire enamel snuff box, depicting 'Birds with an Overturned Basket of Fruit', after Robert Hancock, on a blue ground, the interior with 'La Cascade', after Watteau, some restoration.

c1770   2.75in (7cm) long
$8,000-12,000   **HD**

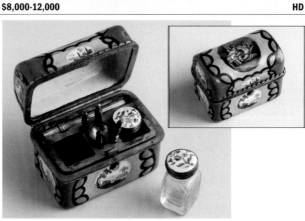

A South Staffordshire enamel writing nécessaire, depicting putti and pastoral scenes within blue borders on a green and purple ground, the interior fully fitted with writing accoutrements.

c1775   2.5in (6.5cm) long
$7,000-10,000   **HD**

A large South Staffordshire enamel étui with répoussé flowers against a pale yellow ground with a gilt trellis pattern, fully fitted.

c1775   4in (10cm) lon
$4,000-6,000   **H**

A South Staffordshire enamel patch-box, with Masonic symbols against a lilac ground, original cracked glass mirror, some restoration.

c1775   2in (5cm) diar
$1,500-2,000   **H**

A South Staffordshire pink egg, with whit and gold dot decoration, and floral sprays inscribed "Long May You Live".

c1780   1.75in (4.5cm) lon
$700-1,000   **H**

European Enamels

French, Austrian, German, Italian, Dutch, Hungarian and Spanish artists manufactured elaborate enamel-painted copper-based objects from the 15th century. During the 18th century in Europe, snuffboxes and other items were widely produced in enamel on a gold base. They typified the affluence and ostentation that was particularly prevalent in France until the Revolution, when the Swiss took over the market, producing richly decorated souvenirs and snuffboxes.

German and Austrian enamelers also produced gold-based boxes. However, a large proportion of their output was copper-based, and similar to those being produced in England. In Germany, The House of Fromery, founded by the goldsmith Pierre Fromery, was perhaps the most renowned enameling company, making boxes on a white enamel ground with raised gold or silver decoration. Dresden was the heart of porcelain production in Germany but it also became a center for enameling. The same artist's painting can sometimes be found on both enamel and porcelain.

A German silver-mounted enamel box, the lid and sides painted with pastoral scenes, the base and interior lid with landscapes painted in puce.

c1770   3in (8cm) long
$1,500-2,000   **HD**

A rare German enamel box, painted with floral sprays and insects, the interior lid with a symbolic portrait of a aristocratic lady, small chips to edges.

c1790   3.25in (8.5cm) lon
$3,000-4,000   **H**

A CLOSER LOOK AT A TABLE SNUFF BOX

The enameling on this box is so fine that it has the appearance of painted porcelain. In many instances the same artist's work can be found on porcelain and enamels.

Intricate subjects with highlights and shading are more desirable.

The interior lid of this box is even more finely painted than the exterior. This is because these boxes were intended to be used and opened. The inside decoration was just as important as that on the outside.

A rare South Staffordshire enamel snuff box with 'Les Poussins' after Boucher, on a powder blue ground.

Ex. Ionides collection.

c1770   3in (8cm) long
$6,000-9,000   HD

This box is in perfect condition, damage will halve the value.

Enamel boxes were frequently inspired by the works of famous Italian and French artists such as Jean Antoine Watteau (1684-1721). The delicately painted scene on this box would have provided a talking point about the artist's work.

A South Staffordshire enamel table snuff box, with figures from Watteau's 'La Cascade', with gold scrolls, turquois ground, the interior lid depicting Diana and Actaon.

c1770   3in (8cm) long
$12,000-18,000   HD

A South Staffordshire enamel snuff box, depicting 'Caffe' after Nilson.

c1770   3in (7.5cm) long
$3,000-4,000   HD

An extremely rare South Staffordshire double-lidded enamel snuff box, with pastoral and fishing scenes, within raised gilt scrolls, against a deep pink ground, with floral vignettes, slight wear to lids, some restoration.

c1770   3.5in (9cm) long
$4,000-6,000   HD

A large South Staffordshire enamel étui, depicting a portrait of Lady Fenhoulet, after Reynolds, the lid with floral cartouches.

c1760   4.25in (11cm) long
$4,000-6,000   HD

A South Staffordshire double-lidded boar's head enamel bonbonnière, the outer lid with a hunter spearing a boar, small chips repaired.

This box has a double-lid to conceal the 'erotic' scene of a gentleman assisting a lady with her shoe on the inner lid.

c1770   3.25in (8.5cm) long
$7,000-10,000   HD

A South Staffordshire enamel étui.

An étui is a small box containing various articles such as scissors, tweezers, a miniature spoon, pencil and ivory memorandum slip.

c1770   3.5in (9cm) long
$1,500-2,000   HD

A South Staffordshire enamel scent bottle and bonbonnière combined, painted with scenes after Watteau.

c1770   4in (10.5cm) high
$2,500-3,000   HD

A rare South Staffordshire enamel snuff box, with a pierced lid, decorated with a basket of flowers, the base painted with floral vignettes against a pink ground.

c1770   2in (5cm) long
$2,500-3,000   HD

A South Staffordshire enamel snuff box, with figures after Watteau, the interior lid painted with a portrait of Mrs. Brooks, the base with 'La Caffe' and 'The Stag Hunt'.

c1770   3.25in (8.5cm) log
$6,000-9,000   HD

A silk-lined gold-mounted European enamel aide-mèmoire, depicting architectural scenes, the interior with an ivory slip and colored engravings of figures.

c1775   *4in (10.5cm) long*

$1,000-1,500   **HD**

A very fine small Vienna enamel egg-shaped vinaigrette, depicting courting couples in a landscape, hallmarked Simon Grunewald.

c1870   *1in (2.5cm) high*

$1,000-1,500   **HD**

Contemporary Enamels

Many antiquated methods of manufacture have been eclipsed by modern developments and machinery. For the last 130 years the enameling craft has remained predominantly dormant, despite short-lived revivals. Halcyon Days, based in London, began reviving the art of 18th century enameling in 1970.

The firing and chemistry of the enameling ingredients remains the same. The only change is the use of modern lithographic and silk-screen processes for transfer-printing. With the help of a manufacturing firm in Bilston, one of the leading centers for the production of enamels in Georgian times, they design and market contemporary enamel boxes, inspired by those made a century earlier.

A contemporary enamel box, the 28th in a series of dated year boxes, made by Halcyon Days, dated.

2003   *2in (5.5cm) long*

$140   **HD**

A contemporary enamel box, made to commemorate the Golden Jubilee of Her Majesty Elizabeth II, limited edition of 500, made by Halcyon Days.

2002   *3.25in (8.5cm) long*

$400   **HD**

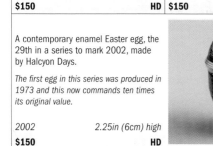

A contemporary enamel box, made to mark the 5th anniversary of the death of Diana Princess of Wales, in 24ct gold on a deep purple ground, made by Halcyon Days.

2in (5cm) long

$150   **HD**

A contemporary enamel box, depicting a recumbent fox, by Graham Rust for Halcyon Days.

2.25in (5.5cm) long

$150   **HD**

A contemporary enamel Easter egg, the 29th in a series to mark 2002, made by Halcyon Days.

The first egg in this series was produced in 1973 and this now commands ten times its original value.

2002   *2.25in (6cm) high*

$150   **HD**

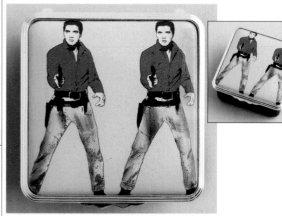

A contemporary enamel box, depicting Elvis Presley, after Andy Warhol, issued to mark the 25th anniversary of Elvis Presley's death in 1977, limited edition of 500, made by Halcyon Days.

2002   *2in (5.5cm) long*

$150   **HD**

A CLOSER LOOK AT A CARD CASE

Card cases that feature well-known buildings are highly collectible.

The decorative scrollwork is particularly attractive.

The design on the front is deeply embossed and the piece is in good condition.

This case is attributed to Nathaniel Mills, a well-known Birmingham silversmith. Pieces by him are particularly desirable.

A silver 'castle top' card case, of shaped outline, the front chased with a view of Worcester Cathedral between leaves and 'C' scrolls, the back embossed with foliate scrolls on a matt ground and a cartouche with 'Mary Stevenson', made in Birmingham by Nathaniel Mills.

1845   *4in (10cm) long*

$3,500-4,500   **DN**

A silver 'castle top' card case, of shaped outline, chased with a view of Christchurch, Oxford, within a surround of foliate scrolls, the back embossed with foliate scrolls and cartouche, made in Birmingham by Nathaniel Mills.

1849   *4in (10cm) long*

$7,000-10,000   **DN**

A Scottish silver card case, engraved with a view of Dunegan Castle, Skye, within a surround of foliate scrolls and turrets, the back engine turned and engraved with exotic birds, made in Edinburgh by James Nasmyth & Co.

1850   *3.75in (9.5cm) long*

$2,200-2,800   **DN**

A Victorian silver card case, of shaped outline, the front engraved with a view of the Crystal Palace, within a scroll panel and engine turning, the back similarly engine turned and with a monogrammed cartouche, made in Birmingham by Nathaniel Mills.

1850   *4in (10cm) long*

$400-600   **DN**

A Victorian silver card case, of shaped outline, centrally engraved with round reserves with either a bust of Shakespeare or a crest within borders of geometric patterns and foliate scrolls, marked "Birmingham by Edward Smith".

1856   *4in (10cm) long*

$220-280   **DN**

An embossed silver card case, the front depicting a minstrel serenading two ladies in a wooded glade within flower and leaf borders, the back depicting a peacock in a formal garden, made in Birmingham, maker's mark "H & A".

1900   *4in (10cm) long*

$300-400   **DN**

A silver small oblong card case, with a flat hinged end-cover and a serrated thumb-piece, engraved with flowers and scrolling leaves, matt panels and a cartouche with initials, "Birmingham 1903 by W H Sparrow".

1903   *3.25in (8.5cm)*

$100-150   **DN**

An embossed silver card case, the front with a panel depicting a stag and deer in a highland landscape within a leaf and C-scroll surround and a cartouche with initials, the back embossed with flowers, scrolls, diaper and a cartouche, made in Birmingham by Crisford & Norris.

1911   *4in (10cm) long*

$300-400   **DN**

A 19thC Indian white metal card case, chased and embossed with flowers and leaf scrolls on a matt ground, the front with a shield, unmarked.

     3.5 (9cm) long

$120-180   **DN**

A Canton white metal and gilt filigree card case, set with central panels of a bird and objects, the border enameled in cloisons in blue and green enamel.

4in (10.5cm) high

$150-200   **GorL**

A tortoiseshell covered card case with mother-of-pearl inlay and an ivory edged lid.

c1835

$220-280 **GS**

A tortoiseshell overlaid card case, with mother-of-pearl inlay.

c1835

$220-280 **GS**

A Victorian tortoiseshell and mother-of-pearl card case, one side depicting a view of the Crystal Palace, the back a beehive within a floral surround.

4in (10cm) long

$400-600 **DN**

A Victorian ivory-veneered card case, the front engraved with a full-rigged sailing ship, the back inscribed "Presented to Capt. A. Wilford from the crew of the 'Evelyn', Poole 1882".

3.25in (8.5cm) long

$120-180 **DN**

A mother-of-pearl and abalone shell covered card case.

c1890

$120-180 **GS**

A rectangular snuff box, with shaped and foliate engraved sides and base and a leaf and scroll chased hinged cover with inscription "Edward Terru from his beloved wife", made in Birmingham by David Pettifer.

3.25in (8cm) long

$350-400 **DN**

A George III rectangular tortoiseshell snuff box, with gilt metal mounts, the lid with a raised portrait bust of Socrates.

c1765 *3in (8cm) long*

$700-1,000 **HD**

A 19thC gold and moss agate oblong vinaigrette, engine-turned with a moss agate cover and a pierced grille, unmarked.

1.5in (3.5cm) long

$600-900 **DN**

A Fabergé Karelian birch cigarette case, with match compartment and cabochon ruby thumb piece, by work master Feodor Afanassiev.

4in (10.5cm) long

$4,000-6,000 **NBlm**

A French two-colour gold oval snuff box, by Gabriel-Raoul Morel, Paris.

1809-1819

$6,000-9,000 **NBlm**

A 19thC French gold box, all over machine-finished with chased edge and ivory enamel bands to lid, the lid set with a miniature painting on ivory, six rose diamonds above.

3.25in (8.5cm) long

$3,000-4,000 **FRE**

A silver gilt aide memoire, decorated in Aesthetic taste with exotic birds and bamboo, the blue silk and red leather lined interior with a pencil and an ivory panel, made in Birmingham.

1886 *4in (10cm) long*

$400-600 **DN**

A Fabergé-style jade, rose quartz and pink enamel table clock, the globe-form clock supported by three monkeys in the hear, speak and see no evil postures, on a trefoil base with disk feet, in a fitted leather case, by Geneva Clock Co. Switzerland.

5in (13cm) high

$7,000-10,000   **SI**

A Stuart Devlin silver gilt Easter egg, the brushed body opening to reveal an interior with hedgehog and flowering plant on a green enameled ground, stamped marks, hallmarked for London and dated.

1978   *2.75in (7cm) diam*

$300-400   **L&T**

A bloodstone egg-shaped bonbonnière, mounted à cage, chased and embossed with putti and flowers, with rose-cut diamond button, the hinged cover with guilloché green enamel band inscribed "Dieu Vous Benit".

c1830   *1.75in (4.5cm) high*

$3,000-4,000   **HD**

An Italian silver and enamel comb and a lipstick case, the comb with a silver and green enamel top and conforming case with a polychrome scene of figures in a landscape, the reverse with engraved scrolls of foliage, the rectangular lipstick case with a hinged mirrored top, similarly decorated, both marked "800", the lipstick case marked "Italy", wear and dents to both, comb missing five teeth.

Comb 4.5in (11.5cm) long

$120-180   **FRE**

A Gorham gilt metal and enamel mounted opaque turquois glass ornament, the blue bowl with a bouquet of enamel flowers, on a square base with paw feet, designed by Jane Hutchinson.

7.5in (19cm) high

$300-400   **SI**

A late 19thC Dutch silver miniature tall case clock, the circular clock face enameled with an orange tree, within the arched case surmounted by three figural finials, the door with putti above the bombé base with a pastoral scene on foliate feet, inscribed "Vivat Oranje".

10.25in (26cm) high

$1,500-2,000   **SI**

Sewing Accessories

An early Victorian pin cushion, in the form of a recumbent cow, made in Sheffield by Hawkesworth, Eyre & Co.

1847   *2.5in (6.5cm) high*

$700-1,000   **DN**

A novelty pin cushion, in the form of a lady's shoe with a high heel and a tied ribbon bow, loaded and stuffed, by C. Saunders & F. Shepherd, Birmingham.

1891   *4.5in (11cm) long*

$300-400   **WW**

A novelty pin cushion, in the form of a lady's high heeled shoe with a buckle, stuffed and loaded, by Adie & Lovekin Ltd, Birmingham.

1894   *2.5in (6.5cm) long*

$300-400   **WW**

A mounted hat pin cushion, circular with fine bead borders and pierced tapering sides, lined and loaded, by William Comyns, London.

1898   *3.25in (8.5cm) diam*

$300-350   **WW**

A pin cushion, in the form of a camel standing four square, made in Birmingham by Adie & Lovekin Ltd.

1905   *2.75 in (7cm) high*

$700-1,000   **DN**

A pin cushion, in the form of a donkey standing four square, made in Birmingham by Levi & Salaman.

3.25in (8.25cm) high

£800-1,000   DN

A pin cushion, in the form of a pig, standing four square, made in Birmingham by Adie & Lovekin Ltd.

1905   2.25in (5.75cm) high

$350-400   DN

A novelty frog pin cushion, loaded and stuffed, by Adie & Lovekin, Birmingham, marks worn.

c1907   2.5in (6.5cm) long

$400-600   WW

A pin cushion, in the form of an ostrich walking on a textured oval base, made in Birmingham by Adie & Lovekin Ltd.

1907   2in (5cm) high

$1,000-1,500   DN

An Edwardian novelty pin cushion, in the form of a hatching chick, stuffed and loaded, by Sampson Mordan & Co, Chester.

c1909   1.25in (3cm) high

$180-220   WW

A pair of Edwardian novelty condiments, in the form of fledgling chicks, with screw-off bases, by Sampson Mordan & Co, Chester 1909.

1.5in (4cm) high

$220-280   WW

A pin cushion, in the form of an elephant standing four square, made in Birmingham by Adie & Lovekin Ltd.

1909   2in (5cm) high

$220-280   DN

A pin cushion, in the form of a fish, made in Chester 1909 by Sampson Mordan & Co, Rd.53100.

1.75in (4.5cm) high

$1,000-1,500   DN

A pin cushion, in the form of a rabbit crouching, with small glass eyes, made in Birmingham by Adie & Lovekin Ltd.

1911   2.25in (6cm) high

$600-900   DN

A modern pin cushion, in the form of a swan, made in Birmingham, convention mark.

2in (5.5cm) high

$40-60   DN

A Victorian sterling silver and wood glove darner.

4.25in (11cm) long

$120-180   BCAC

A silver needle case, with engraved foliate and line decoration, marked 'SP' for Samuel Pemberton.

c1790   3.5in (9cm) long

$350-400   JSC

A Dutch silver needle case, with low relief design of people in a forest scene, with Dutch control marks.

c1762   4in (10cm) long

$400-600   JSC

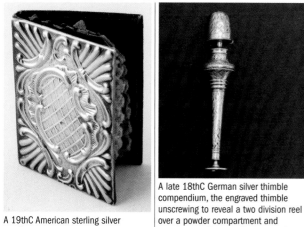

A 19thC American sterling silver needlecase.

2in (5cm) high

$120-180   **BCAC**

A late 18thC German silver thimble compendium, the engraved thimble unscrewing to reveal a two division reel over a powder compartment and tapering needle case, the base with circular seal.

4in (10cm) high

$800-1,200   **KBon**

$300-350

A tortoiseshell octagonal thimble case, with original thimble.

c1820

RdeR

A tortoiseshell needlecase, with ivory compartments for needles.

c1820

$300-400   **RdeR**

$800-1,200   **CBe**

An early 19thC tortoiseshell overlaid sewing kit, with star-shaped pique inlay, ivory bands, fitted compartments lined with red plush, containing a thimble, a mother-of-pearl pocket knife, scissors, Mordan pencil, fabric needle and packet holder.

4in (10cm)

CBe

$220-280

A late Victorian tortoiseshell and mother-of-pearl needle box, in the form of a slope front stationery box, marked inside "Lund, Fleet St, London".

2.25in (5.5cm) high

DN

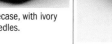

$300-350   **CBe**

A small blonde tortoiseshell needle packet holder, with ivory band to hinged lid, and bone internal dividers in the plush lined interior.

2in (5cm) high

A late 17thC early 18thC Flemish carved oak figural needle case.

4in (10cm) high

$800-1,200   **JSC**

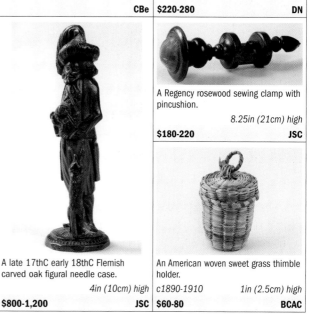

A Regency rosewood sewing clamp with pincushion.

8.25in (21cm) high

$180-220   **JSC**

An American woven sweet grass thimble holder.

c1890-1910   *1in (2.5cm) high*

$60-80   **BCAC**

A turned wood needle case.

c1930   3in (7.5cm) high

$70-100   BCAC

An early 20thC turned wood 'The Voyage Sewing Necessaire' sewing kit, with Sheffield folding scissors, patented.

1896   2.5in (6.5cm) high

$120-180   BCAC

A 19thC turned wood needle case, with pin cushion on top.

c1900   3in (7.5cm) high

$150-200   BCAC

An 19thC American thimble holder, depicted as a monkey.

2.25in (5.5cm) high

$180-220   BCAC

A 19thC gilt metal chatelaine, with pierced clip and chains holding two oval hinged boxes, two oval tapering needlecases and a scissor case, each decorated with scrolls and figures on a frosted ground.

8.5in (22cm) long

$500-700   KBon

An oval étui, containing a needlecase, bodkin, thimble and propelling pencil by Mordan & Co., with pearl-mounted pocket knife and a pair of steel scissors, the case with hallmark for London.

1889   5.25in (13.5cm) long

$500-700   KBon

A late 19thC French leather-covered cased sewing kit, with fitted interior holding thimble, scissors and bodkin, scissors marked "RENAUD", retailed by J.M. Rozier of Lyon.

Case 5in (13cm) wide

$150-200   CBe

A beaded sewing emery, possibly Native American.

c1900   3in (7.5cm) long

$70-100   BCAC

A mid-19thC pair of scissors and holder, made for a chatelaine, the scissors in the holder resembling a sword in a scabard.

4.5in (11.5cm) high

$150-200   JSC

A late Victorian silver chatelaine, with a silver scissor sheath, a silver Mordan & Co propelling pencil, a silver notebook and a cylindrical tool, with hallmark for William Comyns, London.

1889   14.5in (37cm) long

$700-1,000   KBon

A tortoiseshell and enamel étui, with silver gilt tools.

c1820

$700-1,000   RdeR

A pressed brass Queen Victoria '1837-1897 Diamond Jubilee' commemorative needle case by W.Avery & Son, Redditch.

c1897   2.75in (7cm) high

$350-400   **CBe**

A pressed brass 'Victoria Needle Case' by H. Millward & Sons, with belt and buckle, stamped "Registered 12 April 1872".

c1872   3.25in (8.5cm) long

$300-400   **CBe**

A blonde tortoiseshell boite à cire pique sealing wax case, with gold stars and gold mounts.

c1790   5in (13cm) long

$1,500-2,000   **HD**

A silver-mounted horn beaker, depicting a lioness attacking an Exeter mail coach at Winterslow near Salisbury in 1816, with a silver plaque engraved with the initials "J.P".

c1816   3.25in (8.5cm) high

$1,200-1,800   **HD**

A CLOSER LOOK AT A PRISONER-OF-WAR SPINNING-JENNY

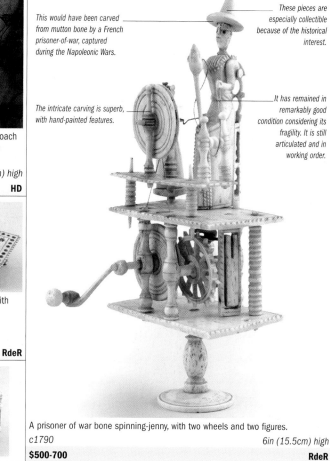

This would have been carved from mutton bone by a French prisoner-of-war, captured during the Napoleonic Wars.

The intricate carving is superb, with hand-painted features.

These pieces are especially collectible because of the historical interest.

It has remained in remarkably good condition considering its fragility. It is still articulated and in working order.

A late 19thC Russian gilt metal figure of a sprawling recumbent bear, on lapis lazuli rectangular base.

$3,000-4,000   **GorL**

A prisoner-of-war dominoes set, with paintings of the prison.

c1790

$400-600   **RdeR**

A prisoner-of-war casket, with mutton bone dominoes, one piece missing.

$400-600   **RdeR**

A prisoner of war bone spinning-jenny, with two wheels and two figures.

c1790   6in (15.5cm) high

$500-700   **RdeR**

MISCELLANEOUS

A rare 1830s ivory needle threader, by Gillet of Bristol.

The needle would be pushed into the large hole at the top of the metal plate. The larger hole on the other side would allow easier insertion of the thread into the needle eye.

3.25in (8.5cm) long

$120-180　　　　　　　　　　　　　　　　　**JSC**

A small Victorian puzzle pin cushion, with mourning pins.

3in (7.5cm) diam

$70-100　　　**BCAC**

A bronze and fabric sewing caddie, in the form of a hand and lace cuff.

4.5in (11.5cm) long

$400-600　　　**BCAC**

A sailor's valentine, in mahogany case.

Sailors were said to have made these for their sweethearts in England. In fact girls made them and sold them to the sailors.

c1840　　　　　　*9.25in (11.75cm) high*

$2,200-2,800　　　　　　　　　　　**RdeR**

An ormolu posy holder.

c1860　　　*4.75in (12cm) high*

$400-600　　　**RdeR**

A French opaline glass egg, sitting on a nest of gilt metal, used to hold miniature sewing tools.

c1870

$1,200-1,800　　　　　**BCAC**

A pair of serpentine-type green marble dogs, each seated on a rectangular base, carved to simulate paved stone with canted corners, some damage.

12.25in (31cm) high

$500-700　　　　　　　　　　　　　**DN**

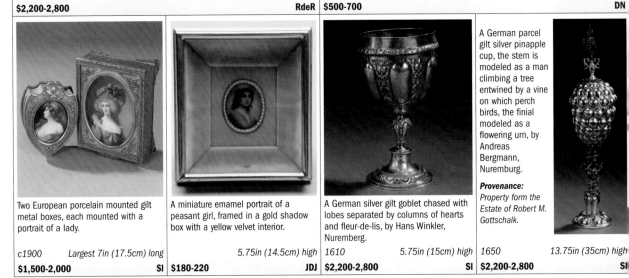

Two European porcelain mounted gilt metal boxes, each mounted with a portrait of a lady.

c1900　　*Largest 7in (17.5cm) long*

$1,500-2,000　　　　　　　　　**SI**

A miniature emamel portrait of a peasant girl, framed in a gold shadow box with a yellow velvet interior.

5.75in (14.5cm) high

$180-220　　　　　　　　　**JDJ**

A German silver gilt goblet chased with lobes separated by columns of hearts and fleur-de-lis, by Hans Winkler, Nuremberg.

1610　　　*5.75in (15cm) high*

$2,200-2,800　　　　　　**SI**

A German parcel gilt silver pinapple cup, the stem is modeled as a man climbing a tree entwined by a vine on which perch birds, the finial modeled as a flowering urn, by Andreas Bergmann, Nuremburg.

Provenance:
Property form the Estate of Robert M. Gottschalk.

1650　　*13.75in (35cm) high*

$2,200-2,800　　　　　　**SI**

A late 19thC Kazak rug, from South-west Caucasus.

78in (198cm) long

$3,500-4,500   SI

A Kazak cloud band rug, with three central medallions on a rust field with ivory borders.

c1900   98 x 62in (249 x 157cm)

$6,000-8,000   Pook

A Kazak rug, with three medallions on a blue field within an ivory border.

c1900   90 x 51in (229 x 129.5cm)

$4,500-5,000   Pook

A Kazak rug.

c1900   89 x 52in (226 x 132cm)

$600-900   AAC

A Caucasian Kazak rug, with graduated triple medallions in shades of teal, cobalt and ochre on a cinnabar ground.

c1910   123 x 56in (312 x 142cm)

$1,800-2,200   DRA

A Kazak rug, minor end loss, old patches of re-weaving.

c1910   80 x 58in (233.5 x 147.5cm)

$450-550   AAC

A Karachop Kazak rug, the green field bearing traditional geometric medallions and devices, within a principal ivory ground crab border.

92.25in (234cm) long

$2,200-2,800   DN

A Kazak Soumac rug, the mid-blue field bearing a triple eagle medallion pattern within a principal, ivory ground and geometric border.

126in (320cm) long

$400-600   DN

A Kazak rug, the tomato red field bearing a mid-blue medallion containing three latch-hook octagons, within a reciprocal ground geometric border.

83.5in (212cm) long

$400-600   DN

A Kazak rug, the variegated blue field with four octagonal figured medallions, within an octagonal figured principal border, with subsidiary borders.

87.5in (222cm) long

$180-220   DN

A late 19thC Kuba rug, from Northeast Caucasus, dated "13**".

65 x 38in (165 x 97cm)

$3,000-5,000   SI

A Kuba rug.

c1900   71 x 45in (180 x 114cm)

$1,000-1,500   AAC

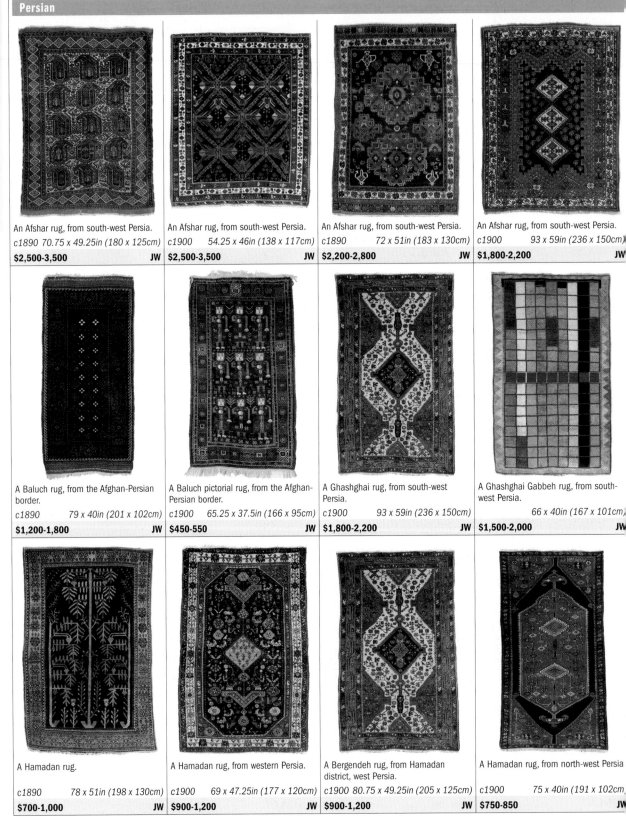

Persian

An Afshar rug, from south-west Persia.
c1890 70.75 x 49.25in (180 x 125cm)
$2,500-3,500   **JW**

An Afshar rug, from south-west Persia.
c1900   54.25 x 46in (138 x 117cm)
$2,500-3,500   **JW**

An Afshar rug, from south-west Persia.
c1890   72 x 51in (183 x 130cm)
$2,200-2,800   **JW**

An Afshar rug, from south-west Persia.
c1900   93 x 59in (236 x 150cm)
$1,800-2,200   **JW**

A Baluch rug, from the Afghan-Persian
border.
c1890   79 x 40in (201 x 102cm)
$1,200-1,800   **JW**

A Baluch pictorial rug, from the Afghan-
Persian border.
c1900   65.25 x 37.5in (166 x 95cm)
$450-550   **JW**

A Ghashghai rug, from south-west
Persia.
c1900   93 x 59in (236 x 150cm)
$1,800-2,200   **JW**

A Ghashghai Gabbeh rug, from south-
west Persia.
66 x 40in (167 x 101cm)
$1,500-2,000   **JW**

A Hamadan rug.

c1890   78 x 51in (198 x 130cm)
$700-1,000   **JW**

A Hamadan rug, from western Persia.

c1900   69 x 47.25in (177 x 120cm)
$900-1,200   **JW**

A Bergendeh rug, from Hamadan
district, west Persia.
c1900 80.75 x 49.25in (205 x 125cm)
$900-1,200   **JW**

A Hamadan rug, from north-west Persia

c1900   75 x 40in (191 x 102cm)
$750-850   **JW**

A Heriz rug, from south-west Persia.

c1880   *74 x 54in (188 x 137cm)*

$2,200-2,800   **JW**

An antique Heriz rug, minor end loss and wear.

c1890   *107 x 150in (272 x 381cm)*

$4,500-5,500   **AAC**

A Heriz rug.

c1910   *113 x 154in (287 x 391cm)*

$2,000-2,200   **AAC**

A Heriz carpet, from north-west Persia.

c1920   *116in (294.5cm) long*

$3,500-4,500   **FRE**

A Heriz rug, from north-west Persia.

c1920   *76.25 x 53.5in (194 x 136cm)*

$2,200-2,800   **JW**

A Heriz rug.

c1925   *103 x 153in (262 x 389cm)*

$2,500-3,500   **AAC**

A Heriz carpet, from north-west Persia.

c1930   *153 x 117in (388.5 x 297cm)*

$4,500-5,500   **SI**

A Heriz carpet, from north-west Persia.

c1930   *108.75 x 78.75in (276 x 200cm)*

$1,200-1,800   **JW**

A Heriz rug, patched, overall wear.

c1930 *108 x 145in (274.5 x 368.5cm)*

$900-1,200   **AAC**

A Heriz rug, north-west Persia.

51in (130cm) long c1940

$600-900   **SI**

A mid-20thC Heriz carpet, from north-west Persia.

147 x 112in (373 x 285cm)

$1,800-2,200   **SI**

A Heriz rug.

c1950   *142 x 106in (360.5 x 269cm)*

$450-550   **ACC**

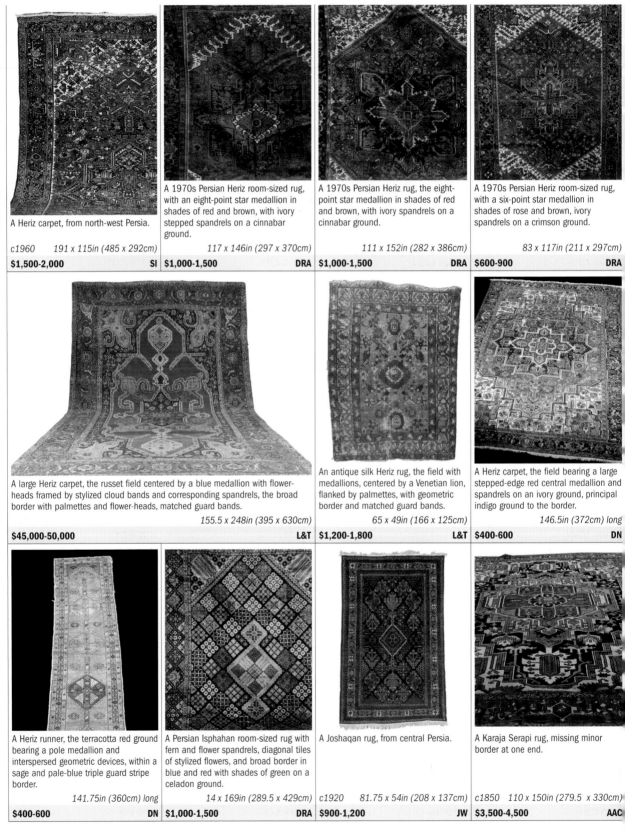

A Heriz carpet, from north-west Persia.

c1960   191 x 115in (485 x 292cm)

$1,500-2,000   **SI**

A 1970s Persian Heriz room-sized rug, with an eight-point star medallion in shades of red and brown, with ivory stepped spandrels on a cinnabar ground.

117 x 146in (297 x 370cm)

$1,000-1,500   **DRA**

A 1970s Persian Heriz rug, the eight-point star medallion in shades of red and brown, with ivory spandrels on a cinnabar ground.

111 x 152in (282 x 386cm)

$1,000-1,500   **DRA**

A 1970s Persian Heriz room-sized rug, with a six-point star medallion in shades of rose and brown, ivory spandrels on a crimson ground.

83 x 117in (211 x 297cm)

$600-900   **DRA**

A large Heriz carpet, the russet field centered by a blue medallion with flower-heads framed by stylized cloud bands and corresponding spandrels, the broad border with palmettes and flower-heads, matched guard bands.

155.5 x 248in (395 x 630cm)

$45,000-50,000   **L&T**

An antique silk Heriz rug, the field with medallions, centered by a Venetian lion, flanked by palmettes, with geometric border and matched guard bands.

65 x 49in (166 x 125cm)

$1,200-1,800   **L&T**

A Heriz carpet, the field bearing a large stepped-edge red central medallion and spandrels on an ivory ground, principal indigo ground to the border.

146.5in (372cm) long

$400-600   **DN**

A Heriz runner, the terracotta red ground bearing a pole medallion and interspersed geometric devices, within a sage and pale-blue triple guard stripe border.

141.75in (360cm) long

$400-600   **DN**

A Persian Isphahan room-sized rug with fern and flower spandrels, diagonal tiles of stylized flowers, and broad border in blue and red with shades of green on a celadon ground.

14 x 169in (289.5 x 429cm)

$1,000-1,500   **DRA**

A Joshaqan rug, from central Persia.

c1920   81.75 x 54in (208 x 137cm)

$900-1,200   **JW**

A Karaja Serapi rug, missing minor border at one end.

c1850   110 x 150in (279.5 x 330cm)

$3,500-4,500   **AAC**

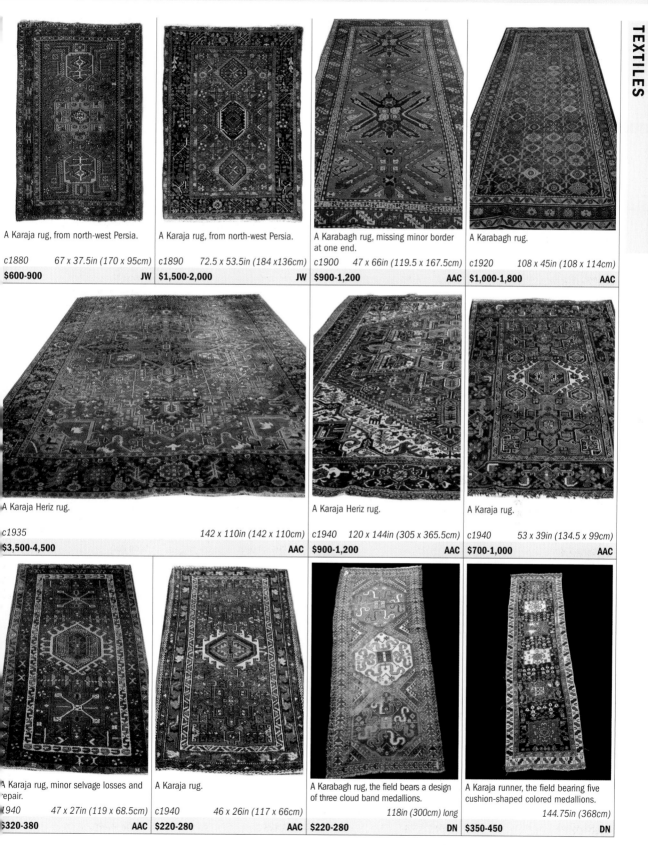

A Karaja rug, from north-west Persia.

c1880   67 x 37.5in (170 x 95cm)

$600-900   **JW**

A Karaja rug, from north-west Persia.

c1890   72.5 x 53.5in (184 x136cm)

$1,500-2,000   **JW**

A Karabagh rug, missing minor border at one end.

c1900   47 x 66in (119.5 x 167.5cm)

$900-1,200   **AAC**

A Karabagh rug.

c1920   108 x 45in (108 x 114cm)

$1,000-1,800   **AAC**

A Karaja Heriz rug.

c1935   142 x 110in (142 x 110cm)

$3,500-4,500   **AAC**

A Karaja Heriz rug.

c1940   120 x 144in (305 x 365.5cm)

$900-1,200   **AAC**

A Karaja rug.

c1940   53 x 39in (134.5 x 99cm)

$700-1,000   **AAC**

A Karaja rug, minor selvage losses and repair.

1940   47 x 27in (119 x 68.5cm)

$320-380   **AAC**

A Karaja rug.

c1940   46 x 26in (117 x 66cm)

$220-280   **AAC**

A Karabagh rug, the field bears a design of three cloud band medallions.

118in (300cm) long

$220-280   **DN**

A Karaja runner, the field bearing five cushion-shaped colored medallions.

144.75in (368cm)

$350-450   **DN**

A Mothtasham Kashan prayer rug, from central Persia.

Mothtasham was a designer from Kashan. His colors are softer and the rugs are generally better quality.

c1880   72 x 53in (183 x 135cm)

$4,500-5,500   JW

A Kashan rug, from central Persia.

c1920   32.75in x 26.25in (83 x 67cm)

$350-450   JW

A mid-20thC Kashan carpet, central Persia.

146in (371cm) long

$2,200-2,800   SI

A 1920s Persian Kashan area rug, with a geometric pattern overall in cobalt and brown on a crimson ground.

51 x 76in (129.5 x 193cm)

$1,000-1,500   DRA

A Khamseh rug, from south-west Persia.

c1890   72 x 60.5in (183 x 154cm)

$1,000-1,500   JW

A Khamseh rug.

114.25in (290cm) long

$350-450   DN

A fine Sarouk carpet, from central Persia.

c1890   150 x 107.75in (382 x 274cm)

$12,000-15,000   JW

A Sarouk rug, minor wear and moth damage.

c1930   118 x 156in (300 x 396cm)

$2,200-2,800   AAC

A Sarouk rug.

c1930   57 x 41in (144.5 x 104cm)

$600-900   AAC

A Sarouk rug, minor selvage loss.

c1930   56 x 31in (142 x 101.5cm)

$600-900   AAC

A Persian Sarouk rug.

c1940   78in (198cm) long

$1,800-2,200   FRE

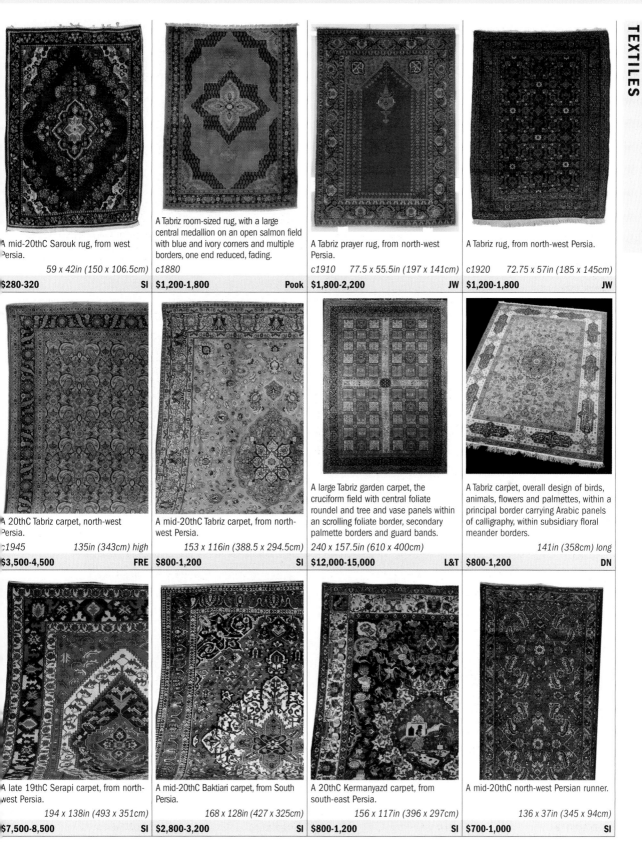

A mid-20thC Sarouk rug, from west Persia.

59 x 42in (150 x 106.5cm)

$280-320   **SI**

A Tabriz room-sized rug, with a large central medallion on an open salmon field with blue and ivory corners and multiple borders, one end reduced, fading. *c1880*

$1,200-1,800   **Pook**

A Tabriz prayer rug, from north-west Persia.

c1910   *77.5 x 55.5in (197 x 141cm)*

$1,800-2,200   **JW**

A Tabriz rug, from north-west Persia.

c1920   *72.75 x 57in (185 x 145cm)*

$1,200-1,800   **JW**

A 20thC Tabriz carpet, north-west Persia.

c1945   *135in (343cm) high*

$3,500-4,500   **FRE**

A mid-20thC Tabriz carpet, from north-west Persia.

153 x 116in (388.5 x 294.5cm)

$800-1,200   **SI**

A large Tabriz garden carpet, the cruciform field with central foliate roundel and tree and vase panels within an scrolling foliate border, secondary palmette borders and guard bands.

240 x 157.5in (610 x 400cm)

$12,000-15,000   **L&T**

A Tabriz carpet, overall design of birds, animals, flowers and palmettes, within a principal border carrying Arabic panels of calligraphy, within subsidiary floral meander borders.

141in (358cm) long

$800-1,200   **DN**

A late 19thC Serapi carpet, from north-west Persia.

194 x 138in (493 x 351cm)

$7,500-8,500   **SI**

A mid-20thC Baktiari carpet, from South Persia.

168 x 128in (427 x 325cm)

$2,800-3,200   **SI**

A 20thC Kermanyazd carpet, from south-east Persia.

156 x 117in (396 x 297cm)

$800-1,200   **SI**

A mid-20thC north-west Persian runner.

136 x 37in (345 x 94cm)

$700-1,000   **SI**

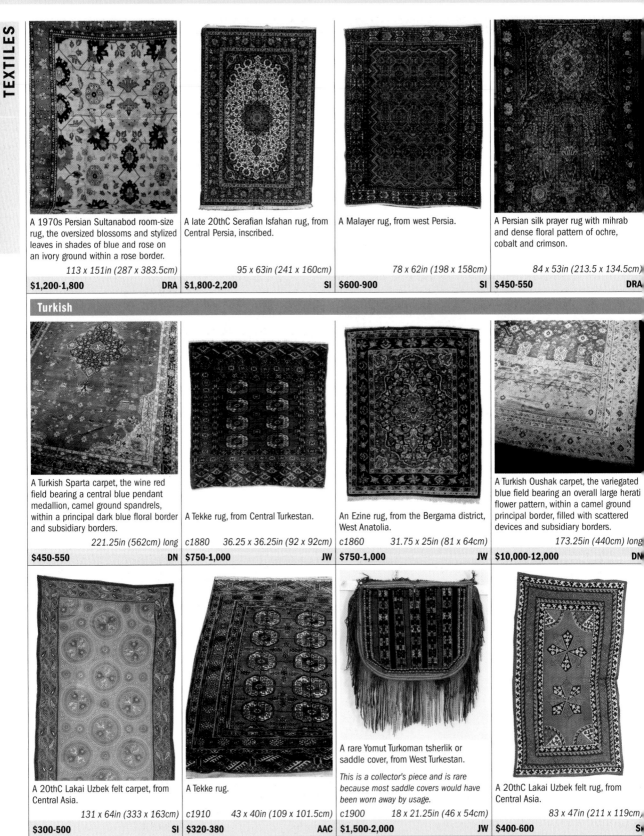

A 1970s Persian Sultanabod room-size rug, the oversized blossoms and stylized leaves in shades of blue and rose on an ivory ground within a rose border.

113 x 151in (287 x 383.5cm)

$1,200-1,800   DRA

A late 20thC Serafian Isfahan rug, from Central Persia, inscribed.

95 x 63in (241 x 160cm)

$1,800-2,200   SI

A Malayer rug, from west Persia.

78 x 62in (198 x 158cm)

$600-900   SI

A Persian silk prayer rug with mihrab and dense floral pattern of ochre, cobalt and crimson.

84 x 53in (213.5 x 134.5cm)

$450-550   DRA

Turkish

A Turkish Sparta carpet, the wine red field bearing a central blue pendant medallion, camel ground spandrels, within a principal dark blue floral border and subsidiary borders.

221.25in (562cm) long

$450-550   DN

A Tekke rug, from Central Turkestan.

c1880   *36.25 x 36.25in (92 x 92cm)*

$750-1,000   JW

An Ezine rug, from the Bergama district, West Anatolia.

c1860   *31.75 x 25in (81 x 64cm)*

$750-1,000   JW

A Turkish Oushak carpet, the variegated blue field bearing an overall large herati flower pattern, within a camel ground principal border, filled with scattered devices and subsidiary borders.

173.25in (440cm) long

$10,000-12,000   DN

A 20thC Lakai Uzbek felt carpet, from Central Asia.

131 x 64in (333 x 163cm)

$300-500   SI

A Tekke rug.

c1910   *43 x 40in (109 x 101.5cm)*

$320-380   AAC

A rare Yomut Turkoman tsherlik or saddle cover, from West Turkestan.

This is a collector's piece and is rare because most saddle covers would have been worn away by usage.

c1900   *18 x 21.25in (46 x 54cm)*

$1,500-2,000   JW

A 20thC Lakai Uzbek felt rug, from Central Asia.

83 x 47in (211 x 119cm)

$400-600   SI

Miscellaneous

A fine western Indian Peking silk and brocaded metal thread carpe.

The floral designs on this rug are rare. Motifs are more commonly dragons or Fo dogs.

c1890   107 x 71.25in (272 x 181cm)

$4,000-5,000   **JW**

A rare Agra Wagireh or sample rug, dated 1952.

These sample rugs were made in the jails of Agra in North India. The jails stopped making them in 1952.

70 x 48.75in (178 x 124cm)

$2,000-2,500   **JW**

An 18thC Flemish tapestry, of a courting scene.

113 x 100in (287 x 254cm)

$5,000-6,000   **SI**

A late 19th/early 20thC Continental tapestry, of a landscape with two birds.

82 x 91in (208 x 231cm)

$1,500-2,000   **SI**

A 20thC Kayseri prayer rug, from West Anatolia.

70 x 48in (178 x 122cm)

$300-400   **SI**

A Flemish verdure tapestry, woven with a deer in a wooded landscape, populated with rabbits and parrots, with floral blooms in the foreground and a castle amidst hills in the background.

69in (175cm) wide

$7,500-8,500   **L&T**

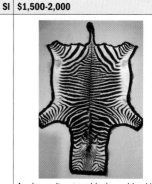

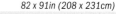

A zebra pelt rug, on black wool backing.

60 x 84in (152.5 x 213.5cm)

$800-900   **Fre**

A 1930s Austrian Oushak room-size rug, with overall floral pattern in teal, yellow and ivory on a cinnabar ground with teal border.

99 x 135in (251.5 x 343cm)

$1,500-2,000   **DRA**

A Navajo rug, brown, red, black and gray geometric pattern.

63in (160cm) wide

$450-550   **Fre**

A Navajo rug, red, pink, yellow and black geometric pattern on ivory field.

40in (101.5cm) wide

$150-200   **Fre**

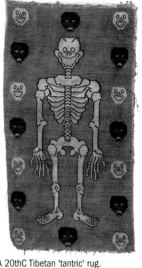

A 20thC Tibetan 'tantric' rug.

54in (137cm) long

$450-550   **SI**

Samplers

A band sampler, the upper section worked in colored silks with bands of trailing flowers, above Vitruvian scrolls and alphabets, the lower section with white work, drawn-work, cutwork and needlepoint lace, worked by Elizabeth Willsonne and dated, mounted, framed and glazed, repairs and discoloration.

1671   *20.5in (52cm) high*

$4,500-5,500   **KBon**

A band sampler, signed and dated.

1675   *24in (61cm) high*

$2,200-2,800   **ATL**

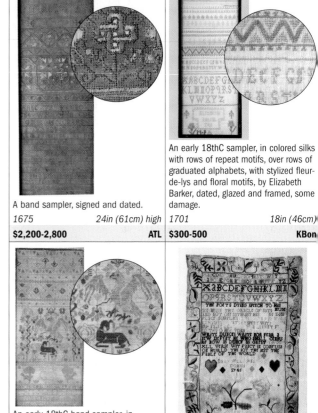

An early 18thC sampler, in colored silks with rows of repeat motifs, over rows of graduated alphabets, with stylized fleur-de-lys and floral motifs, by Elizabeth Barker, dated, glazed and framed, some damage.

1701   *18in (46cm)*

$300-500   **KBon**

An early 18thC band sampler, in colored silks with satin, cross, running and other stitches, worked by Elenor (Hines) and dated, within a glazed frame, discoloration.

1706   *17.25in (44cm) high*

$1,200-1,800   **KBon**

A mid-18thC embroidered sample, in frame.

c1745   *15in (38cm) high*

$1,200-1,800   **ATL**

An 18thC sampler, in colored silks with bands of repeat motifs and rows of alphabets, above indistinct verse over further spot motifs including flowering jardinières, dogs and crowns, possibly by Elizabeth Chaille, within a glazed frame.

20.75in (53cm)

$220-280   **KBon**

A George II sampler, in colored silks with graduated rows of alphabets and trailing floral bands, above verse and motifs, worked by Sarah Chamberlain, taught by Sarah Dawber, mounted, framed and glazed, some fading, dated.

1751   *15in (38cm) high*

$400-600   **KBon**

A George III sampler, in silks to a linen ground, with rows of alphabets and motifs above a central religious figure with arms outstretched, initialed indistinctly and dated, glazed, framed, some fading and discoloration.

1772   *18.5in (47cm) high*

$400-600   **KBon**

A George III sampler, worked in red silks with rows of alphabets and Vitruvian scrolls over various sayings, "Every plant and flower sets forth gods power, they can be wise that good counsel despise, learn to live as you would wish to die", worked by Elisabeth Brooks, aged 10 years and dated, some soiling and holes, within a glazed frame.

1774   *12in (30.5cm)*

$400-600   **KBon**

A George III map of England, Scotland and Wales sampler, entitled "An Accurate Map of England and Wales" and surmounted by a figure, depicting countries and part of surrounding countries, enclosed by a border with degrees, dated, mounted, glazed and framed.

1778   *19.75in (50cm) high*

$700-1,000   **KBon**

A George III sampler, in colored silks with rows of alphabets and trailing floral bands above verse: "Teach me to feel another's woe, to hide the faults I see, feel mercy I to others show, that mercy show too me", by Mary Fisher, dated, within a glazed frame, minor damage.

1780   *12.25in (31cm) high*

$450-550   **KBon**

An 18thC sampler, in colored silks with floral bands and rows of alphabets above verse: "Favour is deceitful and beauty is vain but a woman, that reareth the lord she shall be praired", by Susanna Chaille, July 19th 178*, within a glazed frame.

1784   *17.75in (45cm) high*

$600-900   **KBon**

A George III sampler, entitled "Map of England", in colored silks with black ink titles and two oval cartouches, "Map of England", 'By S. Roope of Bristol' and dated, mounted, glazed and framed.

1784   *17.75in (45cm) high*

$320-380   **KBon**

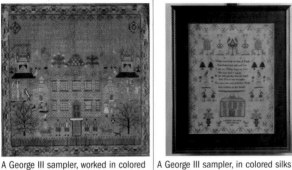

A George III sampler, worked in colored silks with rows of alphabets above a Georgian-style house flanked by flowering jardinières, a figure of a gentleman and a lady holding a sword and scales, by Mary Colton Hersam aged 11 years, dated, glazed frame, some dye movement.

1784   *17in (43cm) high*

$450-550   **KBon**

A George III sampler, worked in colored silks with verse above three flowering jardinères flanked by camels, figures and stylized castles above a central brickwork house flanked by further houses, trees and figures, later framed and glazed, some restoration.

17in (43cm) wide

$1,200-1,800   **KBon**

A George III sampler, in colored silks with a central verse, "When rising from the bed of death, overwhelmed with guilt and fear, I see my maker face to face, oh how shall I appear..." by Laetitia Millman, dated, some damage, mounted, glazed and framed.

1815   *15.25in (39cm) high*

$300-500   **KBon**

A George III oval sampler, entitled "A Map of Europe", with countries outlined in colored silks and text in black, also incorporating a compass and wreath cartouche and dated, all over surface discoloration and restorations, mounted, glazed and framed.

1790   *21.25in (54cm) high*

$220-380   **KBon**

A George III sampler, in colored silks with two central flowering jardiniéres between birds, figures and trees above "The Temple of Solomon" and verse, worked by Eliza Lavell and dated, within a border, mounted, framed and glazed, color running and some holes.

1792   *12.25in (31cm) high*

$450-550   **KBon**

A late 18th/early 19thC sampler, in colored silks and wools with rows of alphabets above initials "AD" and "AB" separated by a heart, within a glazed maple frame, with hand-written note verso, later backed, some holes.

12.5in (32cm) wide

$1,000-1,500   **KBon**

A George III oval sampler, a map of England and Wales, in colored silks depicting England and Wales, worked by C. Griffith, dated, glazed and framed.

1802   *19in (48cm) high*

$180-220   **KBon**

A George III sampler, in colored silks with a central flowering jardinière over Adam and Eve below the tree of life flanked by verse and floral motifs, worked by Elisabeth Crane, possibly aged 14 years, dated, discoloration and some soiling, within glazed frame.

1807   *17.75in (45cm)*

$1,200-1,800   **KBon**

A George III sampler, in colored silks on linen, with a row of trees and jardinières, above verse, above spot motifs including a bird in a tree, flowering jardinières, crowns, figures and a swan with a central tree of life, by Ann Carr, aged 15, within a trailing strawberry border, dated, glazed and framed.

1806   *15.25in (39cm) high*

$9,000-11,000   **KBon**

A George IV sampler, worked in brown silks, with rows of graduated alphabets, over verse entitled "True Dignity", worked by Elizabeth Parker, Glasgow, and dated June 7th 1821, within a trailing vitruvian border, within a glazed rosewood frame.

1821   *12.5in (31.5cm)*

$220-280   **KBon**

A George IV sampler, in red silks, with verse reserved against a ground worked in colored silks by Ann Rebecca Beck, aged 12 years, dated January 26th 1826, within a glazed maple frame, restorations and discoloration.

1826   *17.75in (45cm) high*

$320-380   **KBon**

A William IV sampler, in colored silks with a row of alphabets above a central flower jardinière surmounted by a bird and hearts, flanked by floral and foliate spot motifs, dogs and birds, by Elizabeth Ambridge, aged 9 years, dated, glazed and framed, all over holes.

1836   *13.5in (34cm) high*

$320-380   **KBon**

An early 19thC darning sampler, worked with darning techniques and embroidery in rust and green colored silks, initialed "D*W" above a central cross surrounded by rectangular patterns, within stylized trailing floral and foliate borders, mounted, framed and glazed, minor discoloration.

5.75in (14.5cm) wide

$800-1,200   **KBon**

A William IV sampler, worked in puce, yellow, pink and green silks with a pagoda flanked by birds and flowering jardinières over an Islamic-style house between trees, by Ann Sparling, within a trailing strawberry border, dated, mounted, glazed and framed, some discoloration and holes.

1832   *15in (38cm) wide*

$220-280   **KBon**

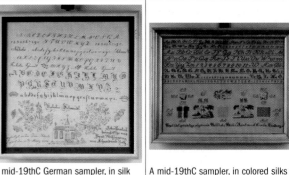

A mid-19thC German sampler, in silk on linen with rows of alphabets in Italic and Gothic script above a rural church, with Germanic text, by Natalie Schmidt and dated 28th March, mounted, glazed and framed.

1852   *14.5in (37cm) high*

$300-400   **KBon**

A sampler, inscribed "Be Faithful unto Death...", dated.

1818   *21.75in (55cm) high*

$1,000-1,500   **ATK**

A William IV sampler, in magenta and brown silks on linen, with a verse, "Teach me what I am by nature, How to lift my thoughts on high teach me o thou great creator, how to live and how to die', by Maria Goodman, taught by Mrs Starr Magdaleni, dated, within a glazed walnut frame.

1835   *6in (15cm) high*

$800-1,200   **KBon**

A mid-19thC sampler, in colored silks with rows of Italic and Germanic alphabets, by Emilie Lindberg, dated, within a glazed frame.

1854   *19.5in (49.5cm) wide*

$350-450   **KBon**

Quilts and Coverlets

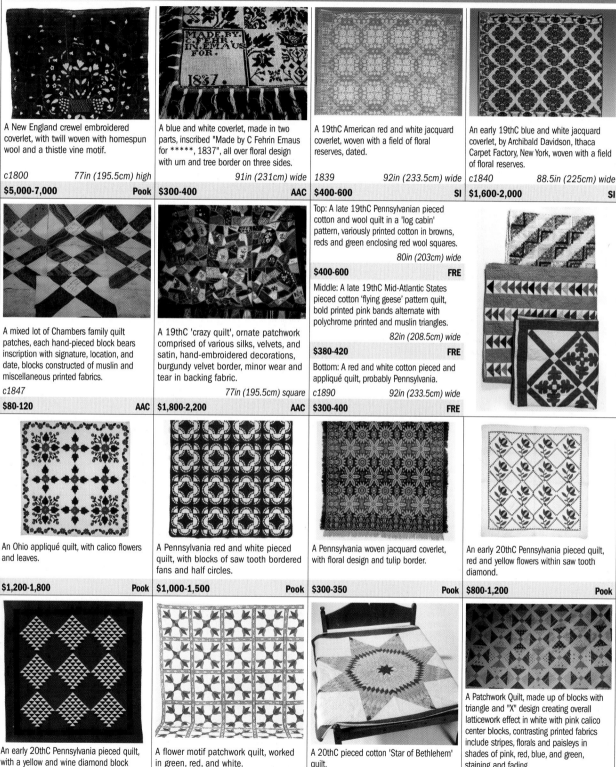

A New England crewel embroidered coverlet, with twill woven with homespun wool and a thistle vine motif.

c1800   77in (195.5cm) high

$5,000-7,000   Pook

A blue and white coverlet, made in two parts, inscribed "Made by C Fehrin Emaus for *****, 1837", all over floral design with urn and tree border on three sides.

91in (231cm) wide

$300-400   AAC

A 19thC American red and white jacquard coverlet, woven with a field of floral reserves, dated.

1839   92in (233.5cm) wide

$400-600   SI

An early 19thC blue and white jacquard coverlet, by Archibald Davidson, Ithaca Carpet Factory, New York, woven with a field of floral reserves.

c1840   88.5in (225cm) wide

$1,600-2,000   SI

A mixed lot of Chambers family quilt patches, each hand-pieced block bears inscription with signature, location, and date, blocks constructed of muslin and miscellaneous printed fabrics.

c1847

$80-120   AAC

A 19thC 'crazy quilt', ornate patchwork comprised of various silks, velvets, and satin, hand-embroidered decorations, burgundy velvet border, minor wear and tear in backing fabric.

77in (195.5cm) square

$1,800-2,200   AAC

Top: A late 19thC Pennsylvanian pieced cotton and wool quilt in a 'log cabin' pattern, variously printed cotton in browns, reds and green enclosing red wool squares.

80in (203cm) wide

$400-600   FRE

Middle: A late 19thC Mid-Atlantic States pieced cotton 'flying geese' pattern quilt, bold printed pink bands alternate with polychrome printed and muslin triangles.

82in (208.5cm) wide

$380-420   FRE

Bottom: A red and white cotton pieced and appliqué quilt, probably Pennsylvania.

c1890   92in (233.5cm) wide

$300-400   FRE

An Ohio appliqué quilt, with calico flowers and leaves.

$1,200-1,800   Pook

A Pennsylvania red and white pieced quilt, with blocks of saw tooth bordered fans and half circles.

$1,000-1,500   Pook

A Pennsylvania woven jacquard coverlet, with floral design and tulip border.

$300-350   Pook

An early 20thC Pennsylvania pieced quilt, red and yellow flowers within saw tooth diamond.

$800-1,200   Pook

An early 20thC Pennsylvania pieced quilt, with a yellow and wine diamond block pattern.

$700-1,000   Pook

A flower motif patchwork quilt, worked in green, red, and white.

98.5in (250cm) square

$600-900   WAD

A 20thC pieced cotton 'Star of Bethlehem' quilt.

82in (208.5cm) wide

$700-1,000   FRE

A Patchwork Quilt, made up of blocks with triangle and "X" design creating overall latticework effect in white with pink calico center blocks, contrasting printed fabrics include stripes, florals and paisleys in shades of pink, red, blue, and green, staining and fading.

91in (231cm) wide

$150-200   Pook

TEXTILES

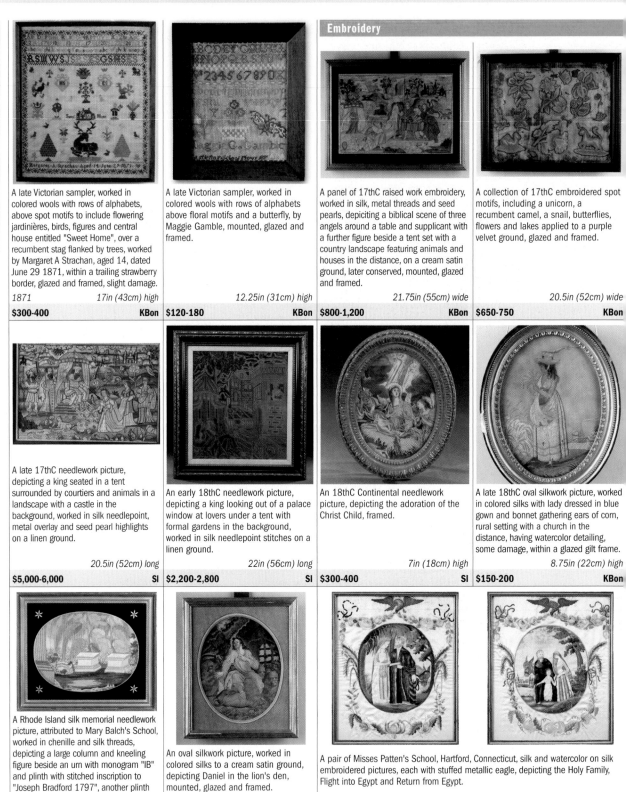

A late Victorian sampler, worked in colored wools with rows of alphabets, above spot motifs to include flowering jardinières, birds, figures and central house entitled "Sweet Home", over a recumbent stag flanked by trees, worked by Margaret A Strachan, aged 14, dated June 29 1871, within a trailing strawberry border, glazed and framed, slight damage.

1871   *17in (43cm) high*

$300-400   **KBon**

A late Victorian sampler, worked in colored wools with rows of alphabets above floral motifs and a butterfly, by Maggie Gamble, mounted, glazed and framed.

12.25in (31cm) high

$120-180   **KBon**

Embroidery

A panel of 17thC raised work embroidery, worked in silk, metal threads and seed pearls, depicting a biblical scene of three angels around a table and supplicant with a further figure beside a tent set with a country landscape featuring animals and houses in the distance, on a cream satin ground, later conserved, mounted, glazed and framed.

21.75in (55cm) wide

$800-1,200   **KBon**

A collection of 17thC embroidered spot motifs, including a unicorn, a recumbent camel, a snail, butterflies, flowers and lakes applied to a purple velvet ground, glazed and framed.

20.5in (52cm) wide

$650-750   **KBon**

A late 17thC needlework picture, depicting a king seated in a tent surrounded by courtiers and animals in a landscape with a castle in the background, worked in silk needlepoint, metal overlay and seed pearl highlights on a linen ground.

20.5in (52cm) long

$5,000-6,000   **SI**

An early 18thC needlework picture, depicting a king looking out of a palace window at lovers under a tent with formal gardens in the background, worked in silk needlepoint stitches on a linen ground.

22in (56cm) long

$2,200-2,800   **SI**

An 18thC Continental needlework picture, depicting the adoration of the Christ Child, framed.

7in (18cm) high

$300-400   **SI**

A late 18thC oval silkwork picture, worked in colored silks with lady dressed in blue gown and bonnet gathering ears of corn, rural setting with a church in the distance, having watercolor detailing, some damage, within a glazed gilt frame.

8.75in (22cm) high

$150-200   **KBon**

A Rhode Island silk memorial needlework picture, attributed to Mary Balch's School, worked in chenille and silk threads, depicting a large column and kneeling figure beside an urn with monogram "IB" and plinth with stitched inscription to "Joseph Bradford 1797", another plinth inscribed "Enoch Butts 1783".

19 x 26in (48 x 66cm) sight

$10,000-12,000   **NA**

An oval silkwork picture, worked in colored silks to a cream satin ground, depicting Daniel in the lion's den, mounted, glazed and framed.

c1800   *9.75in (25cm) high*

$350-450   **KBon**

A pair of Misses Patten's School, Hartford, Connecticut, silk and watercolor on silk embroidered pictures, each with stuffed metallic eagle, depicting the Holy Family, Flight into Egypt and Return from Egypt.

A note with the pictures says one of them was worked by Marietta Gridley c1805.

16.25in (41.5cm) high

$23,000-25,000   **NA**

An early 19thC Philadelphia Folwell School silk embroidered and painted oval needlework picture, depicting central young couple flanking a basket of fruit, with a young boy and girl binding sheaves of wheat and two other farmers harvesting fields in the landscape, all before a red farmhouse, willow and green fields.

23in (58.5cm) wide

$5,000-6,000   **Pook**

An early English 19thC circular silkwork picture, worked in colored threads, depicting a classical maiden, possibly Diana, laden with flowers at a river's edge, with a bow and sheath of arrows beside under a tree, with watercolor detailing to her arms, legs, face and skyline, within a glazed ebonized frame.

6.25in (16cm) diam

$250-350   **KBon**

An early 19thC Philadelphia silk and painted oval needlework picture, probably Folwell School, depicting allegorical garden scene with maiden holding garland, standing beside seated soldier napping under a tree within a reverse painted liner, inscribed "Ann G. Walpole Philadelphia, 1822".

19.5in (49.5cm) high

$10,000-15,000   **Pook**

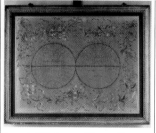

An early 19thC map of the world, entitled "The World with all the modern discoveries", detailing the eastern western hemispheres and countries in black ink, with silk thread and braid detailing, reserved against a naturalistic trailing floral border, worked in colored silks, to a silk ground, some splitting and discoloration, mounted, glazed and framed.

23.5in (60cm) wide

$700-800   **KBon**

An early 19thC woolwork picture, on a silk ground, depicting a farm laborer dressed in a smock holding a scythe, within a rural landscape, with watercolor detailing to face sky and hands, mounted, glazed and framed, some splitting to silk ground.

17.25in (44cm) high

$350-450   **KBon**

An early 19thC needlework picture, probably New England, depicting a young lady and two young gentlemen within an oval reserve, the inscription "Sweet Poll O", worked in long-stitch with silk threads directly over a print, the faces and hands of figures left unworked, framed, some loss.

10in (25cm) high

$4,000-6,000   **FRE**

An early 19thC oval silkwork picture, worked in colored chenilles depicting an infant holding onto its mother's apron, with a dog within a country setting, some staining to edges, within a glazed gilt frame.

8.5in (21.5cm) high

$350-450   **KBon**

An early 19thC Berlin work picture, in colored silks depicting Lot with two women and the burning of Sodom, with watercolor detailing with Latin title in black ink on paper to corner, some damage, within a glazed gilt frame.

14.75in (37.5cm) wide

$500-600   **KBon**

A 19thC embroidered, cut-paper and mirrored needlework collage, depicting houses and trees along a river, heightened with watercolor on a silk ground, some old repairs, breaks and stains to silk.

9.5in (24cm) wide

$800-1,000   **FRE**

A Canadian naïve cotton-on-linen embroidery, made by Edna O'Brien of Carillon, Quebec, when 16 years old.

c1900 9in (23cm) high

$850-950   **BP**

TEXTILES

A cutwork chalice cover, probably 17thC, with four tassels, one at each corner and bobbin lace edging with detached hoops.

8in (20cm) wide

$120-180   **KBon**

A mid-17thC needlework casket, the lid embroidered in colored silks depicting a central fountain surmounted by a cherub, with a woman playing a lute and her suitor within a garden setting, the lid opening to reveal compartments lined with pink satin, the door panels depicting a man and woman within a garden landscape opening to reveal a locking panel and a series of nine drawers and five further secret compartments, within a later glazed case, some wear.

11.5in (29.5cm) wide

$6,000-8,000   **KBon**

An 18thC silk fragment.

24.5in (62cm) long

$30-50   **ATL**

An ivory brocade, with colored silks.

c1750   *25in (64cm) long*

$80-120   **ATL**

A length of 18thC silk.

41in (104cm) long

$180-220   **ATL**

A length of 19thC exotic polychrome brocade, mint condition.

63.75in (162cm) long

$250-350   **ATL**

A green silk sample.

c1860   *52.75in (134cm) long*

$220-280   **ATL**

An early 19thC quilt.

85in (216cm) wide

$600-900   **ATL**

An early 19thC strip silk quilt.

85in (216cm) long

$650-850   **ATL**

A fine green patchwork quilt.

c1840-50   *(150cm) wide*

$500-700   **ATL**

A 19thC American Carolina 'Lily' quilt.

78.75in (200cm) wide

$800-1,200   **ATL**

A red velvet 'crazy' quilt.

52.75in (134cm) wide

$350-450   **ATL**

A Kashmiri hand-woven paisley shawl.

c1820-30   *126in (320cm) wide*

$1,800-2,200   **ATL**

A fine quality silk and wool double-sided shawl.

c1850   *63in (160cm) wide*

$500-700   **ATL**

A fine Scottish silk and wool paisley shawl, in perfect condition.

c1860   *126in (320cm) wide*

$1,000-1,500   **ATL**

Samplers

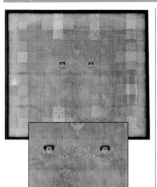

A late 18thC Dutch darning sampler.

c1785   *15in (38cm) wide*

$1,200-1,800   **BCAC**

An 18thC needlework sampler, alphabet, pious verse, potted flowers and birds in trees above a house flanked by couples within a sawtooth border enclosed by a wide meandering chain stylized floral outer border centering inscription, worked in silk threads in shades of pink, green, blue, yellow, and white on a linen ground, framed, some fading.

An almost identical needlework is illustrated in "Girlhood Embroidery, American Samplers and Pictorial Needlework 1650-1850", by Betty Ring, Volume 1 (1993) page 78, fig 76. Ring notes that versions of this sampler were worked from about 1790 to at least 1805, the majority of the makers of these needleworks came from communities surrounding Boston, West Cambridge, Lexington and Concord and attended a boarding school which has yet to be identified.

21in (53cm) high

$15,000-20,000   **FRE**

An early 19thC freeform sampler, by Charlotte Wills, dated Nov 1812.

16in (40.5cm) high

$1,000-1,500   **BCAC**

An early 19thC sampler, dated, alphabet text, bird and house spot motif decoration.

1813   *15.5in (39.5cm) high*

$1,500-2,000   **BCAC**

A mid-19thC sampler, by Susana Aibron, aged 16, dated Feb 1827, framed.

11.75in (30cm) high

$1,000-1,500   **BCAC**

A mid-19thC sampler, by Eliza Wright, alphabet text and floral decoration, framed.

1833   *17in (43cm) high*

$2,000-2,500   **BCAC**

An embroidered linen show towel, Susana Brubacker, Pennsylvania, alphabet and spot devices of flowers and crowns, worked in threads on linen ground, some discoloration.

53in (135cm) high

$600-800   **FRE**

A mid-19thC wool work sampler, New Jersey or Pennsylvania, alphabet and panel with bird and foliage worked in colorful yarns, framed, losses.

22 in (56cm) wide

$250-350   **FRE**

A Canadian framed needlework sampler by Margaret Hamilton, executed in a variety of blue, green, white, and yellow stitches on a linen ground, worked with an arrangement of floral studies and Soloman's Temple.

c1843   *19in (48cm) high*

$700-1,000   **WAD**

A Canadian framed needlework sampler by Margaret Hamilton, executed in a variety of blue, green, white, and yellow stitches on a linen consisting of an arrangement of floral studies.

c1850   *19in (48cm) high*

$400-600   **WAD**

A 19thC needlework sampler, Pennsylvania or New Jersey, alphabet and various spot devices including basket of flowers and birds, worked in silk threads, framed, imperfections.

c1890   *9.5in (24cm) wide*

$1,200-1,800   **FRE**

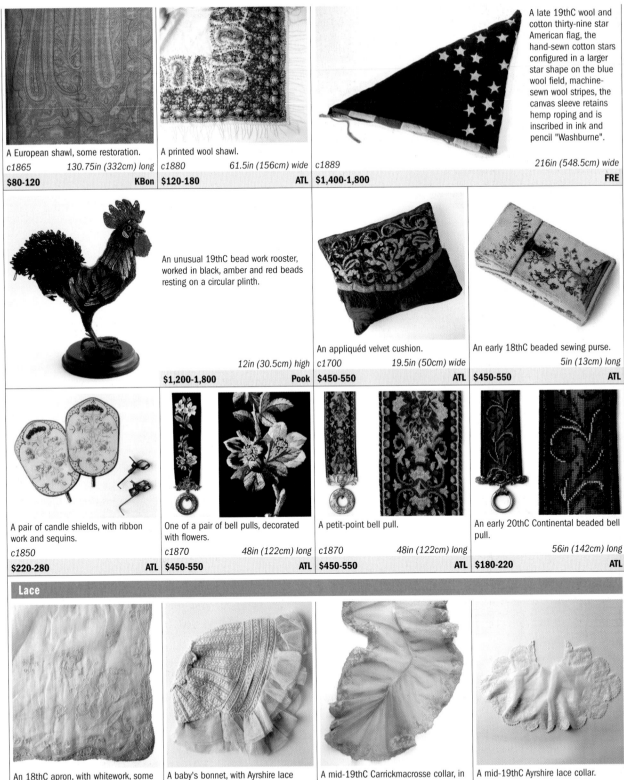

A European shawl, some restoration.

c1865   130.75in (332cm) long

$80-120   **KBon**

A printed wool shawl.

c1880   61.5in (156cm) wide

$120-180   **ATL**

A late 19thC wool and cotton thirty-nine star American flag, the hand-sewn cotton stars configured in a larger star shape on the blue wool field, machine-sewn wool stripes, the canvas sleeve retains hemp roping and is inscribed in ink and pencil "Washburne".

c1889   216in (548.5cm) wide

$1,400-1,800   **FRE**

An unusual 19thC bead work rooster, worked in black, amber and red beads resting on a circular plinth.

12in (30.5cm) high

$1,200-1,800   **Pook**

An appliquéd velvet cushion.

c1700   19.5in (50cm) wide

$450-550   **ATL**

An early 18thC beaded sewing purse.

5in (13cm) long

$450-550   **ATL**

A pair of candle shields, with ribbon work and sequins.

c1850

$220-280   **ATL**

One of a pair of bell pulls, decorated with flowers.

c1870   48in (122cm) long

$450-550   **ATL**

A petit-point bell pull.

c1870   48in (122cm) long

$450-550   **ATL**

An early 20thC Continental beaded bell pull.

56in (142cm) long

$180-220   **ATL**

Lace

An 18thC apron, with whitework, some restoration.

28.75in (73cm) wide

$180-220   **ATL**

A baby's bonnet, with Ayrshire lace work.

c1830   7.75in (20cm) wide

$50-80   **ATL**

A mid-19thC Carrickmacrosse collar, in dark cream.

c1850   32.25in (82cm) long

$100-150   **ATL**

A mid-19thC Ayrshire lace collar.

22in (56cm) wide

$30-50   **ATL**

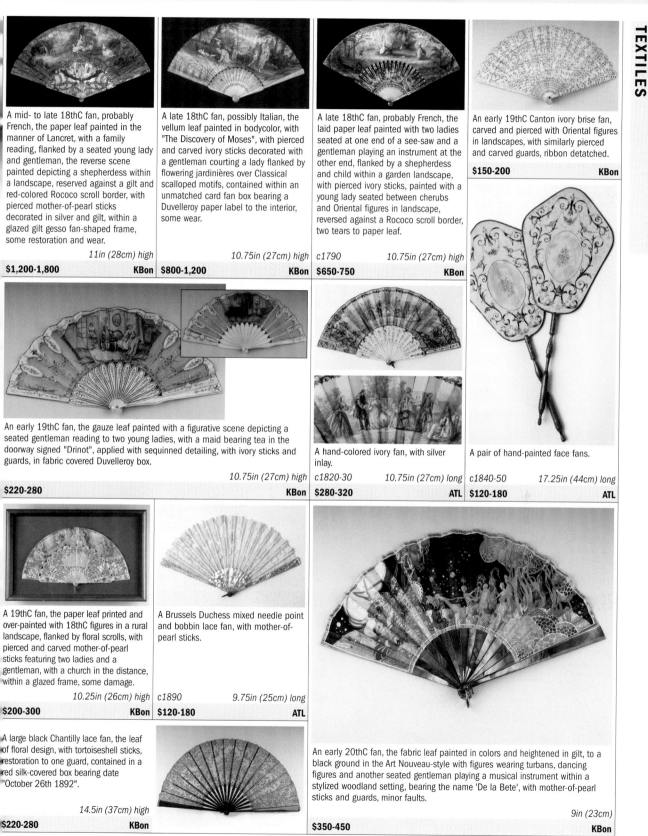

A mid- to late 18thC fan, probably French, the paper leaf painted in the manner of Lancret, with a family reading, flanked by a seated young lady and gentleman, the reverse scene painted depicting a shepherdess within a landscape, reserved against a gilt and red-colored Rococo scroll border, with pierced mother-of-pearl sticks decorated in silver and gilt, within a glazed gilt gesso fan-shaped frame, some restoration and wear.

11in (28cm) high

$1,200-1,800　　　　**KBon**

A late 18thC fan, possibly Italian, the vellum leaf painted in bodycolor, with "The Discovery of Moses", with pierced and carved ivory sticks decorated with a gentleman courting a lady flanked by flowering jardinières over Classical scalloped motifs, contained within an unmatched card fan box bearing a Duvelleroy paper label to the interior, some wear.

10.75in (27cm) high

$800-1,200　　　　**KBon**

A late 18thC fan, probably French, the laid paper leaf painted with two ladies seated at one end of a see-saw and a gentleman playing an instrument at the other end, flanked by a shepherdess and child within a garden landscape, with pierced ivory sticks, painted with a young lady seated between cherubs and Oriental figures in landscape, reversed against a Rococo scroll border, two tears to paper leaf.

c1790　　　*10.75in (27cm) high*

$650-750　　　　**KBon**

An early 19thC Canton ivory brise fan, carved and pierced with Oriental figures in landscapes, with similarly pierced and carved guards, ribbon detatched.

$150-200　　　　**KBon**

An early 19thC fan, the gauze leaf painted with a figurative scene depicting a seated gentleman reading to two young ladies, with a maid bearing tea in the doorway signed "Drinot", applied with sequinned detailing, with ivory sticks and guards, in fabric covered Duvelleroy box.

10.75in (27cm) high

$220-280　　　　**KBon**

A hand-colored ivory fan, with silver inlay.

c1820-30　　*10.75in (27cm) long*

$280-320　　　　**ATL**

A pair of hand-painted face fans.

c1840-50　　*17.25in (44cm) long*

$120-180　　　　**ATL**

A 19thC fan, the paper leaf printed and over-painted with 18thC figures in a rural landscape, flanked by floral scrolls, with pierced and carved mother-of-pearl sticks featuring two ladies and a gentleman, with a church in the distance, within a glazed frame, some damage.

10.25in (26cm) high

$200-300　　　　**KBon**

A Brussels Duchess mixed needle point and bobbin lace fan, with mother-of-pearl sticks.

c1890　　*9.75in (25cm) long*

$120-180　　　　**ATL**

A large black Chantilly lace fan, the leaf of floral design, with tortoiseshell sticks, restoration to one guard, contained in a red silk-covered box bearing date "October 26th 1892".

14.5in (37cm) high

$220-280　　　　**KBon**

An early 20thC fan, the fabric leaf painted in colors and heightened in gilt, to a black ground in the Art Nouveau-style with figures wearing turbans, dancing figures and another seated gentleman playing a musical instrument within a stylized woodland setting, bearing the name 'De la Bete', with mother-of-pearl sticks and guards, minor faults.

9in (23cm)

$350-450　　　　**KBon**

Bags

A Georgian card purse, with metallic embroidery.

c1770-80   6.25in (16cm) wide

$350-450   **ATL**

A late 18thC drawstring beaded purse.

5.5in (14cm) wide

$1,000-1,500   **ATL**

A late 18thC silk drawstring purse, lined with satin.

7.5in (19cm) wide

$350-450   **ATL**

An early 19thC beaded purse, with silver frame and decorated with birds and unusual palm or willow trees.

2.75in (7cm) wide

$120-180   **ATL**

A needle-weave net and silk purse.

c1820   10.5in (27cm) high

$300-400   **ATL**

A sovereign or miser's purse, with marcasite beads and net.

c1840   12.5in (32cm) wide

$30-50   **ATL**

A beaded purse, in a gilded marcasite frame.

c1850

$700-1,000   **ATL**

A native American Indian felt purse.

c1880   6in (15cm) wide

$180-220   **ATL**

A petit-point needlework purse, in a pearl frame.

c1900   6in (15cm) wide

$300-400   **ATL**

A native American Indian purse, made for export.

c1900   6.25in (16cm) wide

$120-180   **ATL**

An Art Deco metallic beaded purse.

7in (18cm) wide

$150-250   **ATL**

An Art Deco beaded purse, with faux tortoiseshell frame.

6.75in (17cm) wide

$100-150   **ATL**

A 1920s Austrian petit-point purse, in ormolu and marcasite frame.

$120-180   **ATL**

A beaded miser's purse, with roses and ormolu knops.

7.5in (19cm) wide

$100-150   **ATL**

A white net and lace dress.

c1915

$80-120　　　　　　　　**W**

A 1920s black tulle and sequinned evening dress.

$250-350　　　　　　　　**W**

A 1920s green and yellow net and silk dress and jacket.

$100-150　　　　　　　　**W**

A 1920s navy and gold lamé jacket.

$80-120　　　　　　　　**W**

An American wide brimmed black horsehair fashion hat, on a wire frame, black silk lining and trim with rhinestone clip.

c1910　　　　　15.25in (39cm) wide

$20-30　　　　　　　　**AAC**

A pair of American early 19thC black kid and velvet silk embroidered lace-up shoes with stacked heels.

9in (23cm) long

$50-80　　　　　　　　**AAC**

A pair of child's embroidered boots.

c1870　　　　　　5in (13cm) long

$120-180　　　　　　　　**ATL**

A 1930s navy crepe dress, with print bodice.

Size 12

$60-90　　　　　　　　**W**

A pair of late Victorian quilted silk child's booties.

5.5in (14cm) high

$100-150　　　　　　　　**ATL**

A pair of Inuit boots.

5in (13cm) long

$150-200　　　　　　　　**ATL**

A pair of American Indian boots.

4in (10cm) long

$180-220　　　　　　　　**ATL**

A late 19thC miniature matador's outfit, with chair.

6.25in (16cm) high

$200-300　　　　　　　　**ATL**

Jumeau

A Jumeau doll, early incised "size 8", this is a pre-Tete Jumeau period, 8-ball jointed fixed wrist body, original mohair wig, very pale bisque.

19.25in (49cm) high

$4,500-5,500　HB

A Jumeau doll, with closed mouth, with red stamp mark and marked "depose Tete Jumeau size 7", has original mohair wig and original clothes, with glass paperweight eyes and pierced ears.

c1880　18in (45.5cm) high

$3,200-3,800　HB

A Tete Jumeau doll, with original clothes and wig, blue paperweight eyes, mint condition, red stamp mark " Tete Jumeau", size 7.

c1880　18in (46cm) high

$4,500-5,500　HB

A Tete Jumeau doll, with blue eyes, red stamp, simple cotton typical miniature dress.

c1880　18in (46cm) high

$3,200-2,800　HB

A Jumeau closed mouth doll, with red stamp mark "Tete Jumeau", hairline crack.
One faint hairline crack halves the value of these dolls.

c1880　26.25in (67cm) high

$1,500-2,000　HB

A French Jumeau bisque head doll, with fixed glass eyes, open mouth, upper teeth, feather brows, pierced ears, mohair wig, on fully jointed composition body, hairline to back of head.

c1890　15in (38cm) high

$700-1,000　BonC

A Jumeau bisque head bébé, with glass eyes, open mouth and upper teeth, feather brows, pierced ears and wig, on a fully jointed composition body, wearing a velvet dress, wrong hands.

c1895　25in (64cm) high

$1,500-2,000　BonC

A doll made for the French market, the head by Simon & Halbig, put onto a French Jumeau body, dressed as French Bébé, original clothes and open mouth with teeth.

1900-1910　19in (48cm) high

$1,500-2,000　HB

A DEP head on Jumeau body doll, made for French market, open mouth and teeth, imported head.

c1910　29.25in (74cm) high

$1,500-2,000　HB

A 1920s SFBJ French character doll, often called 'Laughing Jumeau', well molded limbs.

16.25in (41cm) high

$700-1,000　HB

A very rare Jumeau portrait head doll, on a shoulder plate attached to a kid body.

28in (71cm) high

$9,000-11,000　HB

Kammer & Reinhardt

A Kämmer & Reinhardt 'Marie' character doll, original nurses uniform, incised "101", painted blue eyes, realistic expression.

c1900   14.25in (36cm) high

$3,200-3,800   **MP**

A Kämmer and Reinhardt 'Peter' doll, in original sailor suit, with painted brown eyes.

c1900   15in (38cm) high

$3,200-3,800   **MP**

A German Kämmer & Reinhardt 101 'Marie' bisque head character doll, painted intaglio eyes, wig, jointed composition body.

c1909   16.5in (42cm) high

$2,000-3,000   **BonC**

A rare German Kämmer & Reinhardt 101 mulatto bisque head character doll, painted eyes, original wig, jointed composition body.

c1910   19in (48cm) high

$3,000-4,000   **BonC**

A rare German Simon and Halbig/Kämmer & Reinhardt 117 bisque head character doll, with weighted blue eyes, real lashes, open mouth and four upper teeth, long mohair wig, on a fully jointed composition body, wearing a dress, underclothes and ballet shoes.

c1910   27in (69cm) high

$4,500-5,500   **BonC**

A '114' Kämmer & Reinhardt 'Gretchen' realistic character doll, 5-piece body, original clothes.

c1910   9in (23cm) high

$1,500-2,000   **MP**

A German Kammer & Reinhardt 117 'Mein Leibling' bisque head character doll, with jointed composition body.

c1911   21.5in (55cm) high

$4,500-5,500   **BonC**

Simon & Halbig

A Simon & Halbig doll, made for the French market, 'flirty eyed doll' with walking movement and voice box, blows kisses, elaborate original wig and clothes, with mohair eyelashes, original shoes and clothes.

c1870   22.5in (57cm)

$1,200-1,800   **HB**

A Simon & Halbig doll, on leather body, with swivel neck and original flannel dress.

c1870   21.25in (54cm) high

$1,200-1,800   **HB**

A Simon & Halbig doll, incised "S&H939", closed mouth, made for French market, fixed blue eyes, horsehair wig.

c1890   22.5in (57cm) high

$3,000-4,000   **HB**

A composition lady doll with cloth body, graceful lady hands molded stockings and shoes, in Edwardian clothes, possibly by Simon & Halbig.

c1910   16.75in (50cm) high

$1,200-1,800   **HB**

A Simon & Halbig bisque socket head doll, impressed "Simon Halbig K*R 23", reset stationary glass eyes, wig, stringing loose, jointed composition body, original finish.

c1910   9in (23cm) high

$500-800   **WHA**

A Simon & Halbig doll, with composition body, bisque head, open mouth with teeth.

c1915   33.75in (86cm) high

$900-1,100   **HB**

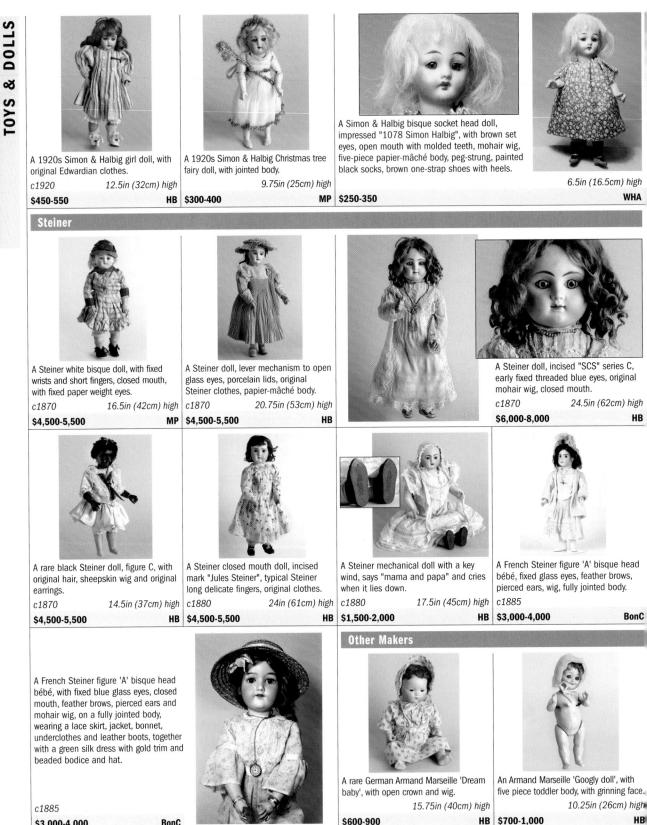

A 1920s Simon & Halbig girl doll, with original Edwardian clothes.

c1920 *12.5in (32cm) high*

$450-550 **HB**

A 1920s Simon & Halbig Christmas tree fairy doll, with jointed body.

9.75in (25cm) high

$300-400 **MP**

A Simon & Halbig bisque socket head doll, impressed "1078 Simon Halbig", with brown set eyes, open mouth with molded teeth, mohair wig, five-piece papier-mâché body, peg-strung, painted black socks, brown one-strap shoes with heels.

6.5in (16.5cm) high

$250-350 **WHA**

Steiner

A Steiner white bisque doll, with fixed wrists and short fingers, closed mouth, with fixed paper weight eyes.

c1870 *16.5in (42cm) high*

$4,500-5,500 **MP**

A Steiner doll, lever mechanism to open glass eyes, porcelain lids, original Steiner clothes, papier-mâché body.

c1870 *20.75in (53cm) high*

$4,500-5,500 **HB**

A Steiner doll, incised "SCS" series C, early fixed threaded blue eyes, original mohair wig, closed mouth.

c1870 *24.5in (62cm) high*

$6,000-8,000 **HB**

A rare black Steiner doll, figure C, with original hair, sheepskin wig and original earrings.

c1870 *14.5in (37cm) high*

$4,500-5,500 **HB**

A Steiner closed mouth doll, incised mark "Jules Steiner", typical Steiner long delicate fingers, original clothes.

c1880 *24in (61cm) high*

$4,500-5,500 **HB**

A Steiner mechanical doll with a key wind, says "mama and papa" and cries when it lies down.

c1880 *17.5in (45cm) high*

$1,500-2,000 **HB**

A French Steiner figure 'A' bisque head bébé, fixed glass eyes, feather brows, pierced ears, wig, fully jointed body.

c1885

$3,000-4,000 **BonC**

A French Steiner figure 'A' bisque head bébé, with fixed blue glass eyes, closed mouth, feather brows, pierced ears and mohair wig, on a fully jointed body, wearing a lace skirt, jacket, bonnet, underclothes and leather boots, together with a green silk dress with gold trim and beaded bodice and hat.

c1885

$3,000-4,000 **BonC**

Other Makers

A rare German Armand Marseille 'Dream baby', with open crown and wig.

15.75in (40cm) high

$600-900 **HB**

An Armand Marseille 'Googly doll', with five piece toddler body, with grinning face.

10.25in (26cm) high

$700-1,000 **HB**

A rare 1920-30s Armand Marseille doll, with a quality bisque face, varnished wooden body and contemporary clothes, " P. Sch" mark and "A.M" mark.

22in (56cm) high

$450-550   **HB**

A mint condition Bru doll, marked "0", closed mouth with leather body, plump realistic bisque hands, original clothes and shoes.

c1870   *24.75in (63cm) high*

$12,000-15,000   **HB**

A Bru Brevete doll, an all kid body, with swivel bisque head and shoulder plate, with blue eyes made from blue and brown glass, with realistically sculptured hands.

c1870   *15.25in (39cm) high*

$15,000-20,000   **HB**

An early Ferdinand Gaultier doll, on kid body, bisque lower arms, swivel head, bisque shoulder plate on leather body, with wig.

c1870   *20in (51cm) high*

$4,500-5,500   **HB**

A French fashion doll, possibly Gaultier, swivel neck on leather body.

c1870   *26.5in (67cm) high*

$3,000-4,000   **HB**

A Ferdinand Gaultier Bébé doll, early mark "F.G", (later marks are in cartouche), fixed wrists, 8-ball joints, paperweight eyes.

c1875-80   *22.5in (57cm) high*

$4,500-5,500   **HB**

A 1920s Heubach character doll with painted eyes, with molded hair and ribbon, they made a series of character dolls.

10.75in (27cm) high

$1,500-2,000   **HB**

A 1920s Heubach baby, rarer than a 'Dream baby'.

12.5in (32cm) high

$320-380   **HB**

An early Kestner bisque socket head doll, impressed "13", sleep eyes, slight bulge back of neck, early German 8-ball jointed body appropriate for early Kestner.

18in (45.5cm) high

$2,000-3,000   **WHA**

A German doll, attributed to Kestner, incised no. "247", open and closed mouth showing molded teeth, original wig, fixed wrist, early 8-ball jointed body with fixed wrist.

1875-80   13.75in (35cm) high

$1,500-2,000   **HB**

A Kestner child, impressed "Made in Germany 167", bisque socket head, sleep eyes, plaster pate, wig, articulated Kestner composition body, stamp in red "Germany".

16in (40.5cm) high

$450-550   **WHA**

A Kestner character child, bisque socket head, impressed "Made in Germany 143", sleep eyes, open mouth with molded teeth, replaced wig, appropriate Kestner body.

9in (23cm) high

$500-700   **WHA**

An SFBJ French doll.

c1915-20   9in (23cm) high

$150-200   **HB**

A small George III carved wooden doll, of gessoed head, enamelled eyes, cloth arms, wooden legs, right leg separated.

c1780

$3,800-4,200   **BonC**

A wooden articulated mannequin, possibly religious, from Italy or France, articulated at the waist.

c1800-10   *12.5in (32cm) high*

$600-800   **HB**

Nine of eleven early 19thC German dolls, the nine wooden dolls pictured with painted features, black hair and in original dress, some limbs missing, other dolls in the lot.

Average 3.5in (9cm) high

$1,500-2,000 (set)   **BonC**

A wax head doll, on cloth body, with turned in feet and original clothes.

c1820-30   *15.75in (40cm) high*

$700-1,000   **HB**

An all wood Grodnertal doll, with fine painted hairstyle and comb in her hair.

c1830   *12.5in (32cm) high*

$1,200-1,800   **HB**

An English wax pumpkin head doll, elaborate hair style with ribbon in her hair, with wooden legs and hands.

c1830   *14.25in (36cm) high*

$150-200   **HB**

A set of four miniature Grodnertal dolls, with painted faces.

c1830   *1.75in (4.5cm) high*

$450-550   **HB**

A typical early glazed china doll, with sloping shoulders and oval face, with a cloth body and lower wooden legs, arms and wig.

c1850   *13.25 (34cm) high*

$600-900   **HB**

A pale bisque head doll, with molded hair and blue hair band, attached blue glass earrings, with an elaborate hair style, bisque arms, missing dress.

c1850   *14.25in (36cm) high*

$700-1,000   **HB**

A French glass eyed china doll, in original clothes, china hands.

The doll was bought by George Routledge, Lord Lieutenant of Cumberland, England, publisher and founder of the Routledge publishing company for his youngest daughter Ada Maria Routledge. As a child Ada Maria remembered coming down after dinner to meet such guests as Dickens and Longfellow, whose books her father was publishing.

c1850

$4,500-5,500   **HB**

15in (38.25cm) high

An early black papier-mâché lady doll, with leather body.

c1850

$450-550   **HB**

A French papier-mâché 'Pauline' doll, on a kid leather body.

1850-60   *33.5in (85cm) long*

$3,000-4,000   **HB**

A wax over composition doll, with wax limbs.

c1860   20.5in (52cm) high

$450-550   **HB**

An early, rare waxed shoulder head doll with flirty glass eyes, original clothes, with wax limbs, elaborate boots and heels.

c1860   19in (48cm) high

$1,500-2,000   **HB**

An English 'Peddlar' doll, the basket contains miniature perfume bottles and scissors.

10.25in (26cm) high

$1,200-1,800   **HB**

A poured wax boy doll, a portrait of one of Queen Victoria's sons.

c1860   16.5in (42cm) high

$1,200-1,800   **HB**

A glazed china head doll, with glass eyes, possibly by Rhomer.

c1860-70   16.5in (42cm)

$1,200-1,800   **HB**

A Schmitt French bébé doll, marked "SCH" in a sheild size 3, marked on body, original clothes, with brown paperweight eyes.

c1879   20.5in (52cm) high

$6,000-8,000   **MP**

A French fashion doll, with all original clothes, complete with bustle, with original bonnet by early French doll maker Barrois, a closed mouth doll, made for the teenage market, original jewelry.

1870-80   17in (43cm) high

$3,000-4,000   **HB**

A wooden bodied '183' Belton head doll, fixed wrist, original shoes, closed mouth, pierced ears, made for French market, possibly German.

c1870   15.75in (40cm) high

$1,500-2,000   **HB**

A pair of female, shoulder plate German dolls, closed mouths and dressed in national peasant costume, wigs are missing.

c1880   13in (33cm) high

$900-1,100   **HB**

A Montanari poured wax baby doll, with inserted hair and poured wax limbs on a cloth body, made to celebrate the birth of Queen Victoria's children.

c1870   30.25in (77cm) high

$1,200-1,800   **HB**

A rare Bébé Mothereau character doll incised on back of head "BM", with closed mouth and threaded blue eyes, all original clothes.

1870-75

$6,000-8,000   **HB**

A French Paul Gerrard doll, early wooden body and 8-ball joints, blue paperweight eyes and open mouth with teeth.

c1880   19.25in (49cm) high

$1,200-1,800   **HB**

DOLLS

A Bruckner topsy-turvy doll.

$550-650 **BCAC**

An early 20thC American carved and painted figure of a woman, with a cloth body, dressed in cotton clothing.

13.5in (34cm)

$200-300 **FRE**

An American carved and painted figure of an African-American man, fully jointed, was originally a dancing toy dressed in printed cotton and flannel clothing and felt shoes, paper hat, wear to clothing.

c1900 *14.5in (37cm) high*

$1,000-1,500 **FRE**

A Jail House Carvers folk art carving of an Amish family.

5in (12.5cm) high

$500-600 **Pook**

A Deans native American doll, made for special exhibition of Deans toys.

1945-50 *31in (79cm) high*

$600-900 **HB**

A pair of 1940s Deans Dutch boy and girl dolls.

Boy 35.5in (79cm) high

$600-900 (pair) **HB**

Dolls cradles

A 19thC Pennsylvania painted pine and poplar doll cradle, with scrolled sides and cheese cutter rockers, retains old yellow paint.

22in (56cm) long

$200-300 **Pook**

An American painted pine doll cradle, with turned posts, scalloped headboard and rocker, retaining original ochre and salmon grained surface.

16in (40.5cm) long

$850-950 **Pook**

A Pennsylvania decorated pine doll cradle, with overall orange and brown graining, together with a patchwork doll quilt and a peg doll.

c1840 *13.75in (35cm) long*

$600-700 **Pook**

Dolls Houses

A mid-Victorian painted wooden dolls house, wooden base, slate pitch roof, opening in two wings to six rooms on three levels, each room with fireplace.

50in (127cm) high

$700-1,000 **BonC**

An English wooden dolls house 'Holme Lucy', black pitched tile roof, back opens in three sections, with original contents, minor damage to some furniture.

c1906 *28.5in (72cm) high*

$3,200-3,800 **BonC**

A set of doll's furniture by Thonet, including chair, table, rocking chair (all pictured) and a sofa.

c1895 *Table 12.5in (32cm) high*

$3,200-3,800 (set) **CA**

Dinky

A Dinky Honest John missile launcher (665), complete with missile instructions, boxed.

$150-200   W&W

A Dinky military recovery tractor (661), with Scammell six wheel breakdown vehicle, complete with hook and cord in working order, boxed, minor wear and rusting to winch handle.

$100-150   W&W

A Dinky missile erector vehicle, with corporate missile and launching platform (666), boxed with packing and paperwork, some rusting.

$300-400   W&W

A rare late Dinky 25 pounder field gun set, with tractor gun, limber with plastic wheelhubs, tractor with windows, in a rare picture box, some damp damage.

Box 8.25in (21cm) long

$150-200   W&W

A French Dinky Military Brockway bridge vehicle (884), with a 10 wheeled GMC truck with detachable roadway sections, two pump up boats and pontoons, complete with paperwork, boxed with packing, mint.

$300-400   W&W

A French Dinky Military M3 half track (822), complete with machine gun and rail, boxed, minor wear.

$100-150   W&W

A French Dinky AMX tank bridge laying vehicle (883), complete with paperwork, in original box.

$200-300   W&W

A French Dinky Military GMC tanker (823), finished in olive green with black cab top, decals to side and rear of tank, complete with accessory road sign and leaflet in original box with inner packaging, very minor mark to front of tank.

$500-700   W&W

A French Dinky Military GMC heavy duty break-down truck (808), in olive green with black canopy to cab, rear jib and supports, complete with hook and cord, boxed, minor wear to wheel hubs.

$300-400   W&W

A French Dinky military GMC 10 wheeled truck (809), in olive green with black cab top, with five-point star to cab sides and bonnet, original box with inner packaging and USA decal transfers.

$300-400   W&W

A French Dinky military Berliet breakdown wagon (826), in olive green, with original box complete with instructions, minor age wear to box.

$150-200   W&W

A French Dinky Toys Military DUKW amphibious vehicle (825), complete with driver, hatch cover and all accessories, boxed.

$120-180   W&W

A Dinky Toys French Dinky no. 827 Panhard FL10, in military green, with French flags to turret box and No. 813 Canon DE155, in military green with gray rubber tracks, damage to one rear stabiliser but still present.

$150-200   Vec

A rare Dinky Airspeed envoy 'The Kings Aeroplane' (62K), in red silver and blue livery, G-A EXX registration to top of wings, complete with paperwork and metal flying supports, boxed, minor wear.

c1939

$300-400   W&W

A rare Dinky Douglas DC3 air liner (60t), in silver livery with "PH-ALI" to wing tops, with gliding hook and paperwork instructions, minor wear to box, some working to paintwork.

$150-200   W&W

A scarce Dinky De Havilland Leopard Moth (60b), in mid-blue with "G-A CPT" to top of tin wings, with open windows and rolled tinplate wheels, complete with two bladed propeller, some chipping.

$150-200   W&W

A rare Dinky Percival Gull monoplane (60c), in mid-blue and silver, with "G-A DZO" registration on tin wings and open windows, with rolled tinplate wheels complete with twin bladed propeller, some chipping.

$120-180   **W&W**

A Dinky Messerschmitt BF 109E (726), in dessert camouflage livery, in bubble pack, mint condition.

$150-200   **W&W**

A Dinky Hawk Harrier (722), in metallic blue and green RAF camouflage livery, complete, boxed with packing and paperwork, minor wear.

$80-120   **W&W**

A Dinky A6M5 Zero Sen fighter (739), in metallic green with red Japanese markings, in bubble pack, minor wear.

$150-200   **W&W**

A Dinky Junkers JU 87B Stuka (721), in dark green and pale blue livery, complete with bomb, in an original first issue box with packing, minor wear.

$120-180   **W&W**

A Dinky Spitfire Mk II from the Battle of Britain film (719), in RAF camouflage livery in an original first issue box with packing, minor wear.

$150-200   **W&W**

A Dinky Foden 14 ton tanker Regent (942), in standard livery, boxed.

$450-550   **W&W**

A Dinky Pullmore car transporter (982), with mid-blue cab, light blue trailer and loading ramp, both boxed, minor wear.

$150-200   **W&W**

A CLOSER LOOK

This is the rare first type cab, produced in 1952 only.

It is in the rare maroon color, with a silver flash.

Both the model and the box are in near mint condition, which is extremely unusual, and is another reason for the high price.

This model was also produced in green with a green flash and hubs, which is still rare but less desirable, and would be worth around $1,500.

A Dinky Toys no. 505 Foden flat truck with chains, with first-type cab, maroon cab, chassis, back and ridged hubs, silver side flash, near mint including blue lift-off lid box.

This is an outstanding model.

$15,000-20,000   **Vec**

A Dinky Toys no. 350 Tinys Mini Moke vehicle, taken from TV Series 'The Enchanted House', cast wheels, inner pictorial stand and outer box, rear plastic cover is split, slight mark to box.

$320-380   **Vec**

A Dinky Toys No. 106 'The Prisoner' Mini-Moke vehicle, in white with flat spun hubs, with picture box, the decal on bonnet appears to be re-stuck and is grubby.

$320-380   **Vec**

A Dinky Toys pre-war pair of 28 Series delivery vans, including an repainted 'Ovaltine' van and a yellow van with black smooth hubs.

$250-350   **Vec**

A Dinky Toys pre-war no. 28 series 'Pickfords' van, in deep blue, missing windscreen pillar to right-hand side and slight crack to side of van.

$220-280   **Vec**

Corgi

A Corgi no. 426 'Chipperfields Circus' Smith's Karrier booking office, with flat spun hubs and box.

$450-550   Vec

A Corgi no. 511 'Chipperfields Circus' Chevrolet Impala, with cast wheels complete with Mary Chipperfield and dancing poodles, with window box.

$400-500   Vec

A Corgi no. GS23 'Chipperfields Circus' gift set, comprising a land rover, six wheel crane, Bedford giraffe transporter, elephant cage on trailer and two animal cages, with picture box.

$400-500   Vec

A Corgi no. GS21 'Chipperfields Circus' gift set, comprising Scammell crane with menagerie trailer, with cast wheels, three trailers and elephant cage, with window box and header card.

$1,500-2,000   Vec

A Corgi no. GS19 'Chipperfields Circus' gift set, comprising a land rover with tin canopy and elephant cage on trailer with spun hubs, with outer picture box.

$450-550   Vec

A Corgi 'James Bond' Aston Martin DB5 (261), first example in metallic gold, complete with men and packet, boxed with display insert.

$200-300   W&W

A 1980s Corgi 'James Bond' Aston Martin, with mainly non-functioning features, this was a Belgian Salesman's example, minor wear.

$120-180   W&W

A Corgi no. 811 'James Bond' Moonbuggy, taken from the film 'Diamonds Are Forever', in blue, white, yellow and red, cellophane replaced.

$450-550   Vec

A Corgi no. 261 'James Bond' Aston Martin DB5, from the film 'Goldfinger', with red interior, wire wheels, secret instruction pack, with box.

$350-450   Vec

A Corgi no. GS40 3-piece 'Batman' gift set, comprising a Batmobile, Batboat on trailer and Batcopter, slight surface corrosion to tow hook, with window box.

$500-700   Vec

A Corgi no. GS3 'Batman' 2-piece gift set, comprising a Batmobile and Batboat on trailer, slight color discoloration to tow hook and missing missiles, with window box.

$380-420   Vec

A Corgi no. 1360 'Batman' Twin-pack, with little and large Batmobiles, both are mint with missiles still attached, with window box.

$400-500   Vec

A Corgi 'Monkeemobile' (277), in red and white livery with yellow interior, complete with all four figures, boxed, minor wear to cellophane, vehicle mint.
1965

$220-280   W&W

A Corgi no. 277 'Monkeemobile', with white roof and cast wheels, with box.

$320-380   Vec

A Corgi no. 804 'Noddy's' car, with cast wheels, very minor marks, with window box.

$320-380   Vec

A Corgi no. 801 'Noddy's' car, complete with Big Ears and Gray Faced Golly, with cast wheels and in window box, slight mark.

$320-380   Vec

A Corgi no. GS14 'Daktari' gift set, with Bedford giraffe transporter, land rover and cattle truck, with figures, with picture box and picture header card, inner polystyrene packing is mint.

$450-550   Vec

A Corgi no. 497 'The Man From Uncle' Thrushbuster, with cast wheels and lamps, waverley ring and inner pictorial stand and packing, slight wear to front decal, with box.

$700-1,000   Vec

A Corgi no. 803 'The Beatles' Yellow Submarine, with red front and rear hatches, including inner plastic tray, window box has been re-cellophaned.

$320-380   Vec

A Corgi no. GS5 'Agricultural' gift set, comprising a land rover, plough, trailer, Massey Ferguson tractor, cattle truck, and other accessories, box slightly dirty, front and rear bumpers peeling.

$450-550   Vec

A Corgi no. GS5 'Agricultural' gift set, comprising a land rover, plough, tipping trailer, Massey Ferguson tractor, cattle truck, other animals and accessories, window box repaired in places.

$320-380   Vec

A Corgi no. GS47 'Farm Set', comprising tractor with working conveyor on trailer, with picture box.

$320-380   Vec

A Corgi no. 1111 Massey Ferguson 780 combine harvester, with front and rear plastic hubs and yellow plastic tines, with inner packing and outer blue and yellow box.

$300-400   Vec

A Corgi no. 268 'The Green Hornet' Black Beauty, with cast wheels and sealed secret instructions pack containing leaflet, missiles and spinners mint, minor marks to bonnet.

$700-1,000   Vec

A Corgi No. GS37 'Lotus Racing Team' gift set, comprising various vehicles, with window box, missing folding leaflet.

$320-380   Vec

A Corgi Ford Consul Cortina Super Estate Car (440), in metallic blue with 'wood' panels, with golfer, caddie, clubs and trolley, original box with display insert, minor damage, contents mint.

$150-200   W&W

A Corgi Major Decca mobile airfield radar (1106), in cream with orange stripes, boxed with packing, minor wear and chips.

$120-180   W&W

A group of three Corgis, a no. 236 Austin A60 Motor School Car, pale blue, spun hubs, a no. 252 Rover 2000 Saloon, steel blue with red interior, spun hubs and a no. 418 Austin Taxi, black with lemon interior and flat spun hubs, with boxes.

$320-380   Vec

A Corgi No. GS38 'Rally Monte Carlo' gift set, a Citroen DS19 in blue and white, a Rover 2000 in red and white and a Mini Cooper-S in red and white with racing number 52, slight wear.

$450-550   Vec

A Corgi set of three 'Co-op' gift sets, a Commer milk float, Commer van and Scammell truck and trailer, in blue and white, all are mint and in correct plain mail-away carded outer packaging.

$500-700   Vec

A Corgi no. 1110 Bedford S 'Mobil Gas' petrol tanker, with red, flat spun hubs, with box.

$200-300   Vec

A Corgi no. 1126 Ecurie Ecosse racing car transporter, in dark blue with yellow lettering, spun hubs, with box and folded leaflet.

$350-450   Vec

A large Corgi tinplate 'Corgi Toys' handing advertising sign, slight surface rust in places, slightly sunfaded on one side.

$450-550   Vec

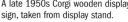

A late 1950s Corgi wooden display sign, taken from display stand.

$350-450   Vec

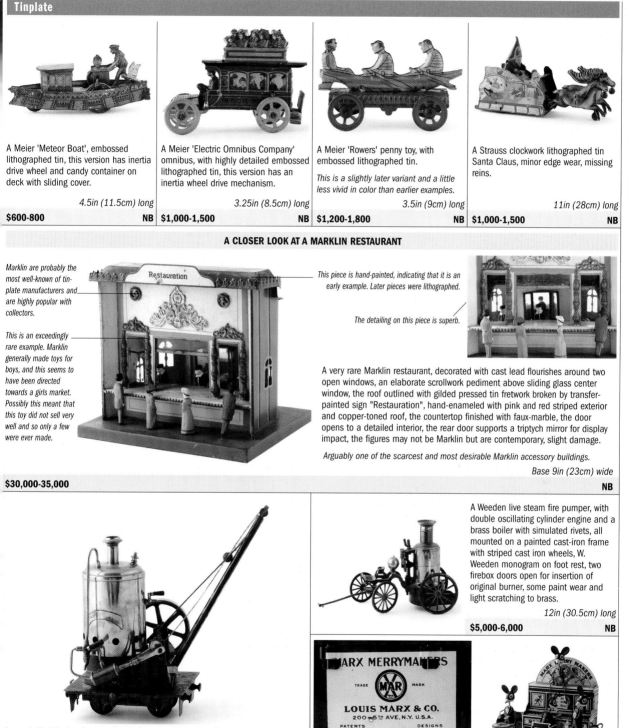

Tinplate

A Meier 'Meteor Boat', embossed lithographed tin, this version has inertia drive wheel and candy container on deck with sliding cover.

4.5in (11.5cm) long

$600-800   **NB**

A Meier 'Electric Omnibus Company' omnibus, with highly detailed embossed lithographed tin, this version has an inertia wheel drive mechanism.

3.25in (8.5cm) long

$1,000-1,500   **NB**

A Meier 'Rowers' penny toy, with embossed lithographed tin.

This is a slightly later variant and a little less vivid in color than earlier examples.

3.5in (9cm) long

$1,200-1,800   **NB**

A Strauss clockwork lithographed tin Santa Claus, minor edge wear, missing reins.

11in (28cm) long

$1,000-1,500   **NB**

A CLOSER LOOK AT A MARKLIN RESTAURANT

Marklin are probably the most well-known of tin-plate manufacturers and are highly popular with collectors.

This is an exceedingly rare example. Marklin generally made toys for boys, and this seems to have been directed towards a girls market. Possibly this meant that this toy did not sell very well and so only a few were ever made.

This piece is hand-painted, indicating that it is an early example. Later pieces were lithographed.

The detailing on this piece is superb.

A very rare Marklin restaurant, decorated with cast lead flourishes around two open windows, an elaborate scrollwork pediment above sliding glass center window, the roof outlined with gilded pressed tin fretwork broken by transfer-painted sign "Restauration", hand-enameled with pink and red striped exterior and copper-toned roof, the countertop finished with faux-marble, the door opens to a detailed interior, the rear door supports a triptych mirror for display impact, the figures may not be Marklin but are contemporary, slight damage.

Arguably one of the scarcest and most desirable Marklin accessory buildings.

Base 9in (23cm) wide

$30,000-35,000   **NB**

An early Marklin hand-enameled tin 1-gauge donkey car, live steam operated crane, with brass boiler, gears, drive rods, piston chamber caps, etc., with original burner, embossed label on boiler "W. Gamage Ltd., Holborn, London, Made in Germany", hand crank rotates the entire superstructure, base of steam plant is cast-iron, some paint loss.

9in (23cm) high

$30,000-35,000   **NB**

A Weeden live steam fire pumper, with double oscillating cylinder engine and a brass boiler with simulated rivets, all mounted on a painted cast-iron frame with striped cast iron wheels, W. Weeden monogram on foot rest, two firebox doors open for insertion of original burner, some paint wear and light scratching to brass.

12in (30.5cm) long

$5,000-6,000   **NB**

A Marx clockwork lithographed tin 'Merry Music Makers with Marquee', with violinist and arched marquee.

9.5in (23cm) high

$1,800-2,200   **NB**

Britains

A Britains 'Air Force Personnel', including four pilots in sidcot suits, four pilots in full flying kit, five US aircraftsmen, three in short coats, two in long and three US aviators in WWI flying suits.

$300-400   **Vec**

A Britains Set 334, including six US marching airmen in service dress with peak caps, brown belts and boots.

$320-380   **Vec**

A Britains line regiment color party, comprising two standard bearers with colors and an escort of four marching soldiers at the slope and early fixed arm mounted French officer.

$450-550   **Vec**

A Britains set 1914, comprising eight marching ARP wardens, in black suits with steel helmets, with "Armies of the World" label.

$800-1,200   **Vec**

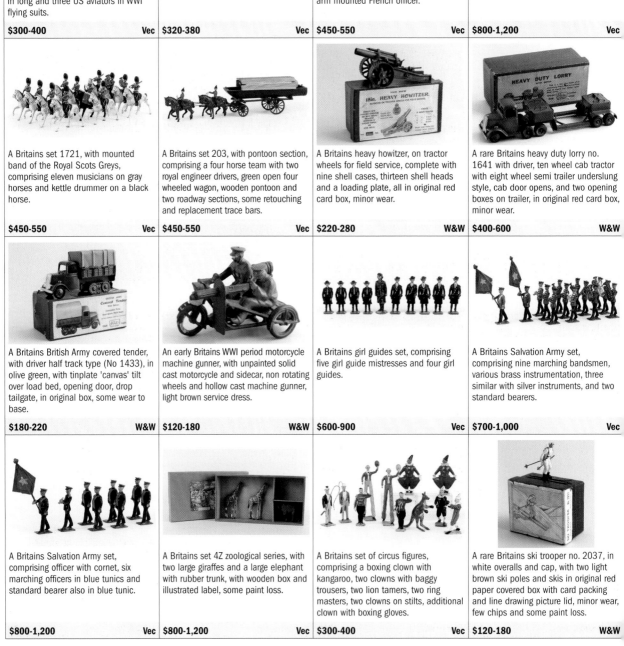

A Britains set 1721, with mounted band of the Royal Scots Greys, comprising eleven musicians on gray horses and kettle drummer on a black horse.

$450-550   **Vec**

A Britains set 203, with pontoon section, comprising a four horse team with two royal engineer drivers, green open four wheeled wagon, wooden pontoon and two roadway sections, some retouching and replacement trace bars.

$450-550   **Vec**

A Britains heavy howitzer, on tractor wheels for field service, complete with nine shell cases, thirteen shell heads and a loading plate, all in original red card box, minor wear.

$220-280   **W&W**

A rare Britains heavy duty lorry no. 1641 with driver, ten wheel cab tractor with eight wheel semi trailer underslung style, cab door opens, and two opening boxes on trailer, in original red card box, minor wear.

$400-600   **W&W**

A Britains British Army covered tender, with driver half track type (No 1433), in olive green, with tinplate 'canvas' tilt over load bed, opening door, drop tailgate, in original box, some wear to base.

$180-220   **W&W**

An early Britains WWI period motorcycle machine gunner, with unpainted solid cast motorcycle and sidecar, non rotating wheels and hollow cast machine gunner, light brown service dress.

$120-180   **W&W**

A Britains girl guides set, comprising five girl guide mistresses and four girl guides.

$600-900   **Vec**

A Britains Salvation Army set, comprising nine marching bandsmen, various brass instrumentation, three similar with silver instruments, and two standard bearers.

$700-1,000   **Vec**

A Britains Salvation Army set, comprising officer with cornet, six marching officers in blue tunics and standard bearer also in blue tunic.

$800-1,200   **Vec**

A Britains set 4Z zoological series, with two large giraffes and a large elephant with rubber trunk, with wooden box and illustrated label, some paint loss.

$800-1,200   **Vec**

A Britains set of circus figures, comprising a boxing clown with kangaroo, two clowns with baggy trousers, two lion tamers, two ring masters, two clowns on stilts, additional clown with boxing gloves.

$300-400   **Vec**

A rare Britains ski trooper no. 2037, in white overalls and cap, with two light brown ski poles and skis in original red paper covered box with card packing and line drawing picture lid, minor wear, few chips and some paint loss.

$120-180   **W&W**

Miscellaneous

A Charbens circus figures set, comprising trapeze artists on bars, unicyclist, ringmaster, clown on stilts, sealion with ball, podium man with Indian clubs and strongman with barbells, all good condition.

$700-1,000   **Vec**

A rare Charbens 'Soap Box Racer' comprising a yellow 'Soap Box' with red wheels, Scout Sittingood, Cub Scout pushing and Cub Scout throwing stone.

$500-700   **Vec**

A Salco 'Mickey and Minnie on the River', green boat, two seats, two oars, Mickey and Minnie, with box.

$800-1,200   **Vec**

A Salco Mickey and Donald's garden set, with blue wheelbarrow, spade and rake and Mickey and Donald, with box.

$700-1,000   **Vec**

A Salco Mickey and Minnie's barrel organ, with Mickey and Minnie and orange organ, in good illustrated box.

$700-1,000   **Vec**

A Phillip Segal 'Three Little Pigs', in yellow, blue and orange suits, with original box.

$1,000-1,500   **Vec**

A Benbros Robin Hood series, comprising Robin Hood, Little John, Will Scarlet, Mutch, Friar Tuck, Sheriff of Nottingham, Bishop, our men at arms, Maid Marian, two trees and two deer, with box and illustrated label, one base edge torn, one lid edge partially missing, old marks and stains.

$1,000-1,500   **Vec**

A Moko orange dairy cart, with black wheels, unpainted horse, seated milkman and five crates, old tape repairs, slightly creased.

$600-1,000   **Vec**

A Sacul Film related issue Rob Roy set, comprising Rob Roy in full highland tartan, raised sword as to attack and English Redcoat also with raised sword, illustrated box, no insert packaging, good condition.

$2,200-2,800   **Vec**

A Crescent Dan Dare set, comprising Dan Dare, Miss Peabody, Dan Dare in space suit, two Treens, one silver, one gold, rocket and rocket launcher with box.

$1,800-2,200   **Vec**

A rare Marx Fairyking series, with characters in book form from Disney films, divided into 21 individual compartments showing figures from all the stories including Mickey Mouse, Pluto, Donald Duck, Pinocchio, minor marks.

$700-1,000   **Vec**

A 1960s Japanese Linemar Toys battery-operated 'Camera Shooting Bear', mint and boxed.

11in (28cm) high

$600-800   **ATK**

A Japanese tinplate battery powered 'Attacking Martian' robot, by Hoikawa, the black tinplate body with bright tinplate ears, eyes and mouth, red boots containing travel wheels, green lenses on twin opening doors to abdomen and chest area, walks, swings arms, stops, doors open, guns come out and fire with flashing and sound, in original box, minor wear.

This is an early 1980s reissue. The first examples fetch in the region of $450-550.

$120-180   **W&W**

A painted, carved wooden figure of a waiter, thought to be from a jazz band group, wearing black trousers, striped yellow waistcoat, frilled shirt, black bow tie and bowler hat, some minor damage.

36.75in (93.5cm) high

$220-280   **DN**

Banks

An American cast-iron mechanical bank, in the form of an owl with a rotating head a top a log plinth.

7.5in (19cm) high

$950-1,250   **Pook**

A late 19thC American cast-iron mechanical bank, of Uncle Sam and his "U.S." treasury purse atop a plinth with an American eagle, crack to base.

11.5in (29cm) high

$1,000-1,500   **Pook**

An Ives palace bank, replacement key.

c1890   *8in (20.5cm) high*

$1,800-2200   **CamA**

Three late 19thC American painted cast-iron still banks, each in the form of a building, some paint loss.

c1890   *4.5in (11.5cm) high*

$140-180 each   **FRE**

Two late 19thC painted cast-iron still banks, each in the form of a bank building, with painted copper-colored detailing, one bears patent of "23 July 1895".

5.75in (14.5cm) high

$200-300 each   **FRE**

An early 20thC iron bank, shaped as a jockey on a horse, untouched original paint, some surface wear.

10.5in (26.5cm) wide

$1,200-1,500   **SG**

A Stevens 'Teddy and The Bear' mechanical bank, painted cast-iron, with copper highlights on base, lettering on base retains strong paint, some chipping on teddy's outfit.

10in (26cm) long

$3,500-4,500   **NB**

A Stevens painted cast-iron 'General Butler' still bank.

6.5in (16.5cm) high

$2,000-3,000   **NB**

A J. & E. Stevens cast-iron tammany mechanical bank, depicting Boss Tweed sitting in a chair.

c1890

$250-350   **SI**

A set of early building blocks, paper on wood.

$250-350   BCAC

A 19thC pull toy, of a monkey riding a cat, found in New England.

$2,200-2,400   SG

Dale Ford (b. 1934) 'Stage Coach', made of wood, metal, paint, fiber and leather.

24in (61cm) long

$5,500-6,500   ALT

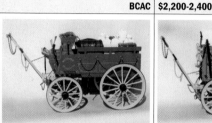

Dale Ford (b. 1934), 'Stage Coach', made of wood, metal, paint, fiber and leather in plexiglass.

23in (58.5cm) long

$6,000-7,000   ALT

Dale Ford (b. 1934), 'Stage Coach', made of wood, metal, paint, fiber and leather in plexi-glass case.

24in (61cm) long

$6,000-7,000   ALT

A late 19thC wooden toy wagon, with slated slides with old red paint, stenciling and paper labels.

19in (48.5cm) long

$300-400   BCAC

A Disney clockwork train.

12in (30.5cm) long

$450-550   BCAC

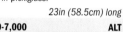

An L. & N.W.R.D. 'The Railway Guard' (or 'The Mail Train to the North') music sheet cover, depicting L.N.W. Guard on platform with 'Rugby' train awaiting departure, framed and glazed.

12.5in (32cm) high

$60-100   SAS

Teddies

A Steiff cinammon bear.

c1907   *14in (34cm) high*

$7,500-8,500   HGS

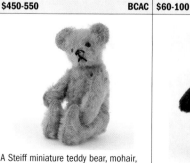

A Steiff miniature teddy bear, mohair, black bead eyes, stitch eyes and nose, swivel head, jointed shoulders and hips.

c1920   *3.5in (9cm) high*

$220-280   BonC

A Steiff bear.

8in (20.5cm) high

$2,200-2,800   HGS

An early mohair bear, probably Steiff, shoe button eyes, stitch nose, felt pads, button missing, voice box not working.

12in (30.5cm) high

$700-1,000   WHA

A 1920s Bing blond plush teddy bear.

28in (69cm) high

$7,500-8,500   HGS

Rocking Horses

A mid-Victorian velocipide, the bay horse with painted metal head and neck, having flared nostrils, pricked ears and glass eyes, galloping wooden body with original cloth saddle and blanket, three large spoked metal wheels with pedals and steering handle for front wheel, one eye broken.

32in (81cm) high

$450-550   **BonC**

An English carved wooden rocking horse, a gesso dapple gray horse, carved pricked ears, flared nostrils, baring teeth, original leather bridle with metal studs, saddle with leg rests for side saddle, red rosettes and metal stirrup, horsehair mane and tail, safety rocker, marked in transfer "Henry's, 22 Kings, Winchester".

c1880   *44in (122cm) high*

$800-1,200   **BonC**

A carved wooden rocking horse, the painted dark bay horse with gray socks, baring teeth, horse hair and mane, remains of leather saddle and bridle, wooden safety rockers, metal plaque to stand "A.W. Gamage lmt, Holborn, London, R.C.", some gesso peeling.

c1880   *48in (122cm) high*

$1,000-1,500   **BonC**

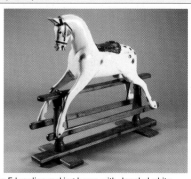

An American late 19thC carved and painted rocking horse, with glass eyes, horsehair mane and tail, saddle retains original fabric, hardware cast "Mallable/Unbreakable", worn.

36.25in (92cm) high

$700-1,000   **FRE**

An Ayres pony skin rocking horse, a large piebald horse, with clear glass eyes, horse hair mane and tail, original leather bridle, saddle and red cloth, metal stirrup, wooden safety rocker, plaque "Manufacturing by Ayres, London", minor bald patches.

c1900   *53in (135cm) high*

$800-1,200   **BonC**

An Edwardian rocking horse, with dappled white wooden body, stained pine safety stand, turned columns and three-bolt swinger brackets, with glass eyes, remnants of leathercloth saddle and leather tack, partly repainted, no mane, tail or stirrups.

Stand 52.25in (133cm) long

$800-1,200   **DN**

A small Edwardian rocking horse, with dappled dark gray-green wooden body on a green-painted safety stand with turned columns and three-bolt swinger brackets, the straight head with glass eyes, with horsehair tail and red leather tack and saddle and green felt saddlecloth, no mane or stirrups.

Stand 31.75in (81cm) long

$700-1,000   **DN**

An Edwardian rocking horse, entitled 'Patrick', with dapple gray wooden body on a stained pine safety stand with turned columns and four-bolt swinger brackets, with glass eyes, horsehair mane and tail, metal stirrups, replacement leather saddle and one replacement stirrup.

Stand 60.25in (133cm) long

$4,500-5,500   **DN**

A carved wood circus roundabout galloper, in the shape of a horse standing with front right leg raised and with integral shaped saddle, unpainted.

41.75in (106cm) long

$100-150   **DN**

TOYS & DOLLS

Chinese

A small ivory Cantonese Burmese-type chess set, in a Sedeli-work ivory, pewter and mother-of-pearl inlaid box of oblong shape.

c1840 *King 3in (7.5cm) high*
$450-550 CO

A 19thC Cantonese Staunton-pattern chess set, with Chinese influence knights.

King 3.25in (8cm) high
$220-280 CO

A 19thC Cantonese carved ivory Chinese export figural chess set.

King 4.75in (12cm) high
$800-1,200 CO

A 19thC ivory Burmese-type chess set, probably Cantonese.

King 3.75in (9.5cm) high
$700-1,000 CO

An ivory Macao-type `bust' chess set, probably Cantonese, in an inlaid wooden box with a hinged lid.

c1830 *King 4.5in (11.5cm) high*
$3,800-4,200 CO

A 20thC large Chinese ivory figural chess set, in fitted wooden presentation board/box.

King 6.25in (16cm) high
$1,000-1,500 CO

Indian

- Chess sets of this type usually date from the late 18thC to the mid 19thC. They tend to be in greens and reds and the pawns are often musicians or foot soldiers.
- This example is made from painted and lacquered ivory and represents opposing troops under the control of Indian princes in the period before the Indian mutiny.
- This ornamental set was a superior piece made for the British export market and is intended for display and curiosity rather than to be used. They are very popular with collectors and can realise prices between $7,500 to $22,000.
- A similar example is displayed at the British Museum in London.

An Indian Rajhasthan painted ivory figural chess set.

c1790 *5.5in (14cm) high*
$14,000-18,000 CO

A 20thC Indian Rajhasthan ivory figural chess set, in a fitted attaché case.

King 1.5in (4cm) high

$1,500-2,000   **CO**

A 20thC Indian metal figural chess set, one side with faint gilding.

King 2.25in (6cm) high

$900-1,100   **CO**

Miscellaneous

An ivory and hardwood 'tribal' chess set, possibly Kenyan.

c1920   *5in (13cm) high*

$700-1,000   **CO**

A 19thC Nuremberg bone Selenus chess set.

King 4.25in (10.5cm) high

$450-550   **CO**

A late 19thC Islamic rock crystal chess set, one side with red stained bases, the other with green stained bases, the pieces with floral gilt decoration.

King 2.25in (6cm) high

$3,800-4,200   **FRE**

A Scandinavian modern wooden figural set, the pieces of a stylized design, one side in a darker colored wood, kings and queen of Medieval form, bishops with crosses to the front, knights as horses' heads, rooks as turrets, pawns with shields, fitted in a wooden presentation box.

c1950   *King 4in (10cm) high*

$450-550   **FRE**

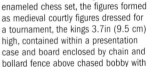

A Viennese white metal, gilt and enameled chess set, the figures formed as medieval courtly figures dressed for a tournament, the kings 3.7in (9.5 cm) high, contained within a presentation case and board enclosed by chain and bollard fence above chased bobby with enameled panels and strap work clasps and knights to the corners, on a molded mahogany plinth with cast and pierced bracket feet.

6.75in (17cm) high

$16,000-20,000   **L&T**

An Aelteste Volkstedter Porzellanfabrik figural set, orange one side and blue the other, the king wearing pantaloons, the queen cross-legged on a cushion, bishops as counsellors, knights as rearing horses, rooks as elephants with howdahs, pawns as cross-legged Chinese figures, the pieces marked on the underside.

King 4in (10cm) high

$1,500-2,000   **FRE**

A 20thC Meissen porcelain figural chess set, after a design by J.J. Kaendler, with Meissen crossed swords mark.

Johann Joachim Kaendler, the son of a Protestant pastor, began his work at Meissen in 1731, becoming Model Master in 1733. During his 43 years with the Meissen Porcelain Manufactory, Kaendler produced numerous successful models. He died in 1775.

King 2.5in (6.5cm) high

$10,000-15,000   **CO**

An Indonesian painted wood gilt decorated figural chess set.

c1920   *King 5in (9.5cm) high*

$450-550   **CO**

TRIBAL ART

TRIBAL ART APPEALS TO COLLECTORS ON SEVERAL LEVELS. Firstly, it is valued for its artistic sophistication, diversity and staggering beauty. Secondly, it is a point of reference for those interested in western art, which has been greatly enriched by the artistic contribution of Africa, Oceania, the Americas and Asia. From an archaeological perspective, tribal art provides a link to a past and present that is complex and diversified.

Tribal art is defined by westerners as items that have been used by the people as part of their own traditions and daily life, and where collectors prize it for its aesthetic value, the indigenous people consider the items as necessary ritual or domestic instruments. Pieces are usually concerned with major life events and transition, such as birth, life and death.

The majority of tribal art was exported during the colonial period of the second half of the 19th century,

and pieces older than this are rare and highly sought after. Colonization had a huge impact on former cultural practices and many craftsmen were prevented from using certain materials and subjects for their art.

The commercialization of tribal art during the 1920s has meant that good quality objects have become few and far between, and therefore outstanding pieces command high prices. Tribal art that has been made for the tourist trade is not considered genuine.

Over the last ten years tribal art has maintained its popularity both with collectors and with those who are just looking for a one-off original piece. In African art, Punu masks remain highly commercial, because of their clean lines and tangible beauty. Textiles are also very desirable. Oceanic art is becoming increasingly popular because of its vibrancy and color. Shields in particular are highly collectible.

Central Africa

Central Africa encompasses Chad, Cameroon, Gabon, Angola and Democratic Republic of Congo (D.R. Congo), formerly Zaire. It spans vast areas of rainforest and savannah and is home to an array of peoples and cultures. Despite the diversity, there are similarities between the socio-political, cultural and religious values of the various societies. The majority of groups within Central Africa rely on farming, including crops such as cereals and bananas, chickens goats and sheep, although few tend cattle. Hunting is of intrinsic importance and many pieces of tribal art are made from the durable parts of hunted animals, such as the skin, teeth and claws. Initiation rites form a central part in the lives of communities throughout the region and usually use tribal art works during the ceremonies. These rites are often compulsory for boys and include physical hardship and seclusion. Ceremonies and initiations are also held for marriage, kings and chiefs, healers and diviners and dancers and sculptors.

Images and art are also produced as teaching aids to instruct initiates in the knowledge and behaviour of the society. Statues and figures often embody religious beliefs and are used in practices including those concerned with ancestors, protection, healing, destiny, funerals, and the enhancement of fertility. Ancestor figures are one of the major forms of veneration and are believed to protect and maintain the family and ethnic group.

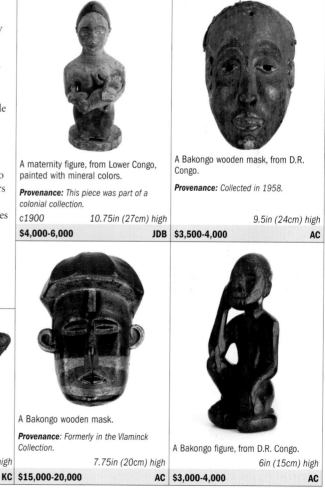

A maternity figure, from Lower Congo, painted with mineral colors.

Provenance: This piece was part of a colonial collection.

c1900   10.75in (27cm) high

$4,000-6,000   JDB

A Bakongo wooden mask, from D.R. Congo.

Provenance: Collected in 1958.

9.5in (24cm) high

$3,500-4,000   AC

A Bakongo wooden mask.

Provenance: Formerly in the Vlaminck Collection.

7.75in (20cm) high

$15,000-20,000   AC

An archaeological bronze torque, from Lower Angola.

6.75in (17.5cm) diam

$7,000-10,000   PC

A wicker shield, from Chad.

c1900   35in (89cm) high

$700-1,000   KC

A Bakongo figure, from D.R. Congo.

6in (15cm) high

$3,000-4,000   AC

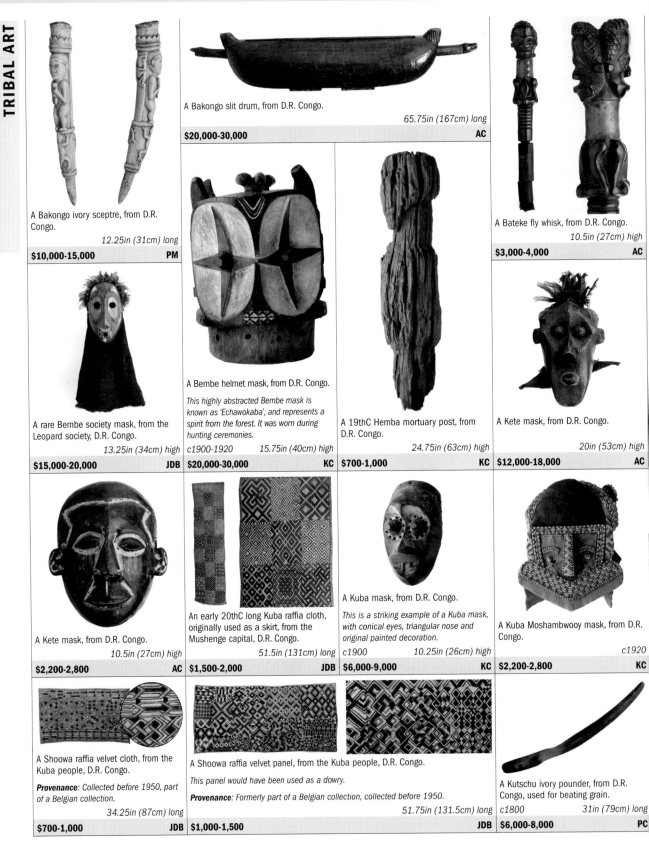

A Bakongo ivory sceptre, from D.R. Congo.

12.25in (31cm) long

$10,000-15,000 — **PM**

A Bakongo slit drum, from D.R. Congo.

65.75in (167cm) long

$20,000-30,000 — **AC**

A rare Bembe society mask, from the Leopard society, D.R. Congo.

13.25in (34cm) high

$15,000-20,000 — **JDB**

A Bembe helmet mask, from D.R. Congo.

This highly abstracted Bembe mask is known as 'Echawokaba', and represents a spirit from the forest. It was worn during hunting ceremonies.

c1900-1920   *15.75in (40cm) high*

$20,000-30,000 — **KC**

A 19thC Hemba mortuary post, from D.R. Congo.

24.75in (63cm) high

$700-1,000 — **KC**

A Bateke fly whisk, from D.R. Congo.

10.5in (27cm) high

$3,000-4,000 — **AC**

A Kete mask, from D.R. Congo.

20in (53cm) high

$12,000-18,000 — **AC**

A Kete mask, from D.R. Congo.

10.5in (27cm) high

$2,200-2,800 — **AC**

An early 20thC long Kuba raffia cloth, originally used as a skirt, from the Mushenge capital, D.R. Congo.

51.5in (131cm) long

$1,500-2,000 — **JDB**

A Kuba mask, from D.R. Congo.

This is a striking example of a Kuba mask, with conical eyes, triangular nose and original painted decoration.

c1900   *10.25in (26cm) high*

$6,000-9,000 — **KC**

A Kuba Moshambwooy mask, from D.R. Congo.

c1920

$2,200-2,800 — **KC**

A Shoowa raffia velvet cloth, from the Kuba people, D.R. Congo.

Provenance: Collected before 1950, part of a Belgian collection.

34.25in (87cm) long

$700-1,000 — **JDB**

A Shoowa raffia velvet panel, from the Kuba people, D.R. Congo.

This panel would have been used as a dowry.

Provenance: Formerly part of a Belgian collection, collected before 1950.

51.75in (131.5cm) long

$1,000-1,500 — **JDB**

A Kutschu ivory pounder, from D.R. Congo, used for beating grain.

c1800   *31in (79cm) long*

$6,000-8,000 — **PC**

A Pende house panel, from D.R. Congo.

c1930   *46in (117cm) long*

$4,000-6,000   **KC**

A Pygmy tapa cloth, originally used as a skirt, from D.R. Congo.

34.75in (88cm) long

$600-900   **JDB**

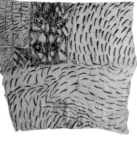

A Pygmy tapa cloth, from D.R. Congo.

33.5in (85cm) long

$700-1,000   **JDB**

A Salampasu mask, from D.R. Congo, made from wood and copper.

Masks were an intrinsic part of Salampasu society and boys had to rise through the ranks of this warrior society to earn the right to wear them. To acquire a mask, they had to carry out specific tasks and pay with food and livestock. The number of masks that a man owned indicated his wealth and knowledge.

22.5in (57cm) high

$2,200-2,800   **PC**

An early 20thC woven Salampasu dancing mask, from D.R. Congo, used in initiation rituals.

30.25in (77cm) high

$4,000-6,000   **JDB**

A Salampasu animal mask, from D.R. Congo.

Provenance: *Collected before 1950 by Kegel Konietski, Hamburg.*

22in (56cm) high

$4,000-6,000   **JDB**

A Songye knife, from D.R. Congo.

c1920   *11.75in (30cm) high*

$2,200-2,800   **KC**

A late 19thC/early 20thC Songye Kanyok fetish figure, from D.R. Congo.

12in (30.5cm) high

$3,000-4,000   **JDB**

A Songye magical figure, from D.R. Congo.

c1920   *7in (18cm) high*

$800-1,200   **JBB**

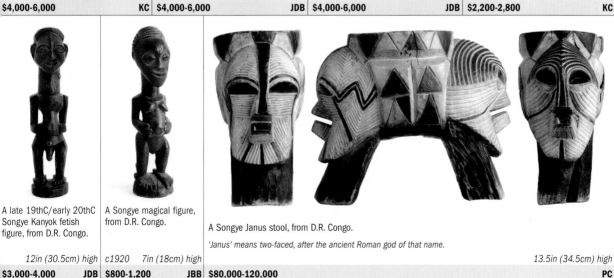

A Songye Janus stool, from D.R. Congo.

'Janus' means two-faced, after the ancient Roman god of that name.

13.5in (34.5cm) high

$80,000-120,000   **PC**

A male Songye Kifwebe society mask, from D.R. Congo, made from raffia.

Provenance: *Collected before 1952 by a Belgian colonial.*

20.5in (52cm) high

$1,500-2,000   **JDB**

A male Songye Kifwebe Kalebwe-style society mask.

Provenance: *Collected before 1950. Kalebwe means 'carved with a square chin'.*

24.5in (62cm) high

$6,000-8,000   **JDB**

A Songye Kifwebe mask, from D.R. Congo.

c1930   *16in (41cm) high*

$8,000-12,000   **KC**

A Suku or Holo Kakungu mask, from D.R. Congo.

17.75in (45cm) high

$5,000-7,000   **AC**

An early 20thC Songye Kifwebe mask, from D.R. Congo.

The Songye migrated from the southern part of D.R. Congo to the Lualaba river during the 16thC. They are a patriarchal society divided into several sub-groups, with strict laws forbidding drinking in public and showing grief. The Kifwebe secret society, within the Songye, wear these dramatic masks during ceremonies. Legend has it that these masks would have been worn by a king or chief who would take their most loyal slave, kill him and take out his heart, place the heart in the mouth of the mask and then pierce it. The soul of the good slave would then be absorbed by the mask. There are male and female masks: the male mask has a crest on the head, and often has red pigment; the female mask is usually without a crest. The masks are characteristically styled with linear markings and a square, protruding mouth.

25.5in (65cm) high

$30,000-50,000   **KC**

A Tabwa whistle, from D.R. Congo.

5in (13cm) high

$2,200-2,800   **PC**

A Tchokwe wooden chair, from D.R. Congo.

16.5in (42cm) high

$3,000-4,000   **AC**

A Tchokwe/Pende stool, from D.R. Congo.

14.5in (37cm) high

$7,000-10,000   **AC**

A Tchokwe Kassai baboon stool, from D.R. Congo.

16in (41cm) high

$3,500-4,000   **JDB**

A 19thC Ubangi zoomorphic slit drum, from D.R. Congo.

Wooden slit drums were associated with chiefs and leaders, and served as voices of authority.

72.75in (185cm) long

$12,000-18,000   **KC**

A Congo mirror fetish figure, from D.R. Congo.
c1890   9.25in (23.5cm) high
$1,500-2,000   JBB

A large Songye magical figure, from D.R. Congo.
c1880   28.25in (72cm) high
$15,000-20,000   JBB

A Legan mask, from D.R. Congo.
c1880
$12,000-18,000   JBB

A Mbala hunting whistle, from D.R. Congo.
c1880   6.25in (16cm) long
$1,200-1,800   JBB

A Ngbaka back rest, from D.R. Congo.
c1875   15.75in (40cm) l
$700-1,000   JBB

A Songye chief's emblema, from D.R. Congo.
c1920   20in (51cm) high
$600-900   BB

A Yaka cane-top figure, from D.R. Congo.
c1895   10.5in (26.5cm) h
$400-600   JBB

A Yaka fly whisk, from D.R. Congo, made with wood, horse hair and copper.
c1880   21.25in (54cm) long
$1,500-2,000   JBB

West africa

West Africa includes Senegal, Guinea, Ivory Coast, Ghana, Burkina Faso, Togo, Benin, Nigeria, Cameroon, Liberia and Sierra Leone. Inland West Africa includes Mauritania, Mali and Niger.

The masquerading tradition is prevalent throughout Western Africa, and masks are made from a variety of materials, including wood, textiles and metals. From a collector's point of view these masks are complete in their aesthetic appeal, but they were originally made as part of a performance. Each mask had a complex meaning and purpose, and would have been danced during important ceremonies. West African textiles were widely produced from cotton, wool, raffia and tapa, and the region is rich in sculpture.

A Fon fetish figure, from Benin, with cowrie shells.
25.5in (65cm) high
$2,200-2,800   AC

A Bobo figure, from Burkina Faso.
28in (71cm) high
$7,000-10,000   AC

A Bwa mask, from Burkina Faso.
21.75in (55cm) high
$2,200-2,800   AC

A 16th/17thC small terracotta Akan figure, from Ghana.

Provenance: Ex Rene de Woolf collection.

7in (18cm) high

$700-1,000   **JDB**

An Ashante terracotta pottery head, from Ghana.

Provenance: Ex Freddy Rollin collection.

11.75in (30cm) high

$1,500-2,000   **JDB**

An Ashante Aquaba fertility doll, from Ghana.

Aquaba dolls are female dolls with large stylized circular heads. Women carried them in the hope that they would make them conceive, and treated them like real children.

15in (38cm) high

$2,200-2,800   **PC**

Two views of a Fanti Aquaba figure, from Ghana.

11.75in (30cm) high

$3,000-4,000   **PC**

A rare Baule oil container, from the Ivory Coast.

c1870   9in (23cm) high

$10,000-15,000   **JBB**

A Baule bronze mask, from the Ivory Coast.

3in (7.5cm) high

$3,000-4,000   **PC**

A Baule portrait mask, from the Ivory Coast.

1900-1920   10.75in (27cm) high

$4,000-6,000   **KC**

A Baule figure, from the Ivory Coast.

14.25in (36.5cm) high

$7,000-10,000   **AC**

A Dan mask, from the Ivory Coast.

The Dan inhabit the western region of the Ivory Coast, and their masks typically have upturned noses, high foreheads and concave faces. They are usually covered in rich dark patinas. However, styles vary between the different societies within the Dan, and some have rougher patinas and more geometric features.

9.75in (24.5cm) high

$7,000-10,000   **PC**

A Dan or Mano mask, from the Ivory Coast.

7.5in (19cm) high

$7,000-10,000   **AC**

A Dan Bete warrior's mask, from the Ivory Coast.

Provenance: Ex Emerson Fowler collection.

11in (28cm) high

$7,000-10,000   **JDB**

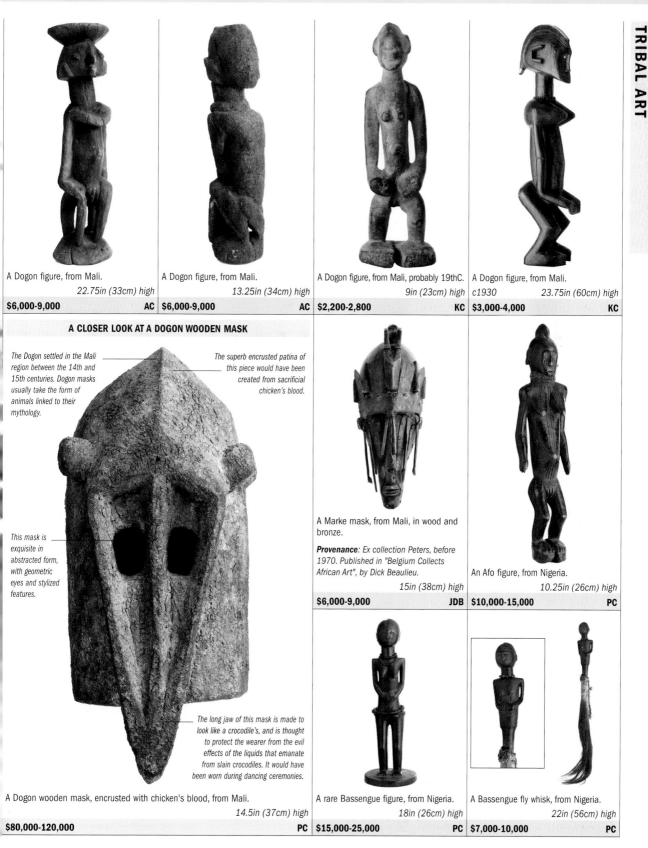

A Dogon figure, from Mali.

22.75in (33cm) high

$6,000-9,000 AC

A Dogon figure, from Mali.

13.25in (34cm) high

$6,000-9,000 AC

A Dogon figure, from Mali, probably 19thC.

9in (23cm) high

$2,200-2,800 KC

A Dogon figure, from Mali.

c1930 *23.75in (60cm) high*

$3,000-4,000 KC

A CLOSER LOOK AT A DOGON WOODEN MASK

The Dogon settled in the Mali region between the 14th and 15th centuries. Dogon masks usually take the form of animals linked to their mythology.

The superb encrusted patina of this piece would have been created from sacrificial chicken's blood.

This mask is exquisite in abstracted form, with geometric eyes and stylized features.

The long jaw of this mask is made to look like a crocodile's, and is thought to protect the wearer from the evil effects of the liquids that emanate from slain crocodiles. It would have been worn during dancing ceremonies.

A Dogon wooden mask, encrusted with chicken's blood, from Mali.

14.5in (37cm) high

$80,000-120,000 PC

A Marke mask, from Mali, in wood and bronze.

Provenance: *Ex collection Peters, before 1970. Published in "Belgium Collects African Art", by Dick Beaulieu.*

15in (38cm) high

$6,000-9,000 JDB

An Afo figure, from Nigeria.

10.25in (26cm) high

$10,000-15,000 PC

A rare Bassengue figure, from Nigeria.

18in (26cm) high

$15,000-25,000 PC

A Bassengue fly whisk, from Nigeria.

22in (56cm) high

$7,000-10,000 PC

A Yoruba bracelet, with a part-fish, part-ram's head and part-human motif, from Nigeria.

2.75in (7cm) wide

$5,000-7,000   **PC**

A late 19thC pair of Yoruba Ibeji figures, from Nigeria.

Ibeji dolls were made when twins were born and are believed to be magical. If one or both twins died, the doll would be taken in its place and treated like a living child. The blue pigment on these figures actually comes from the blue washing powder of the colonials. The tribes people thought it was magical and so put it on their dolls.

11.75in (30cm) high

$3,500-4,500   **JDB**

A pair of early 20thC Yoruba Ibeji figures, from Nigeria.

9.5in (24cm) high

$2,200-2,800   **JDB**

A Yoruba Ibeji figure, from Nigeria.

12.5in (31.5cm) high

$1,500-2,000   **AC**

An unusual first half 20thC Yoruba game bowl, from Nigeria.

6.75in (17cm) high

$1,500-2,000   **JDB**

A gorilla mask, from Nigeria.

9.75in (25cm) high

$3,500-4,500   **PC**

A Diola headdress, from Senegal, with raffia and antelope horns.

19.25in (49cm) high

$1,500-2,000   **JDB**

East Africa

The East African region includes Kenya, Tanzania, Uganda, Rwanda, Zambia, Malawi, Mozambique, Zanzibar, Somalia, Ethiopia, Sudan and Madagascar. Due to the climate and frequent drought conditions, many of the peoples in Eastern Africa are herdsmen, driving either cattle or camels. As a result, much of the tribal art from this region was intended for multifunctional, portable use, such as headrests and stools.

A 1960s headrest, from Ethiopia.

7in (18cm) high

$70-100   **JBB**

A 1960s headrest, from Ethiopia.

7.5in (19cm) high

$70-100   **JBB**

A 1950s Ethiopian wedding cup.

6.5in (6.5cm) high

$400-600   **JBB**

An Ethiopian neckrest.

Provenance: *Ex collection Alain Guisson.*

7.75in (20cm) high

£800-1,000   **JDB**

An Afaar headrest, from Ethiopia.

Head and neck rests were made to protect elaborate hairstyles from becoming disheveled during sleep. They were often buried with their owners, but in some cases they were kept as a way of contacting the late owner through the ancestral realm.

c1950   *5.5in (14cm) high*

$150-200   **JBB**

An Ethiopian granary storage vessel.

36.25in (92cm) high

$4,000-6,000   **KC**

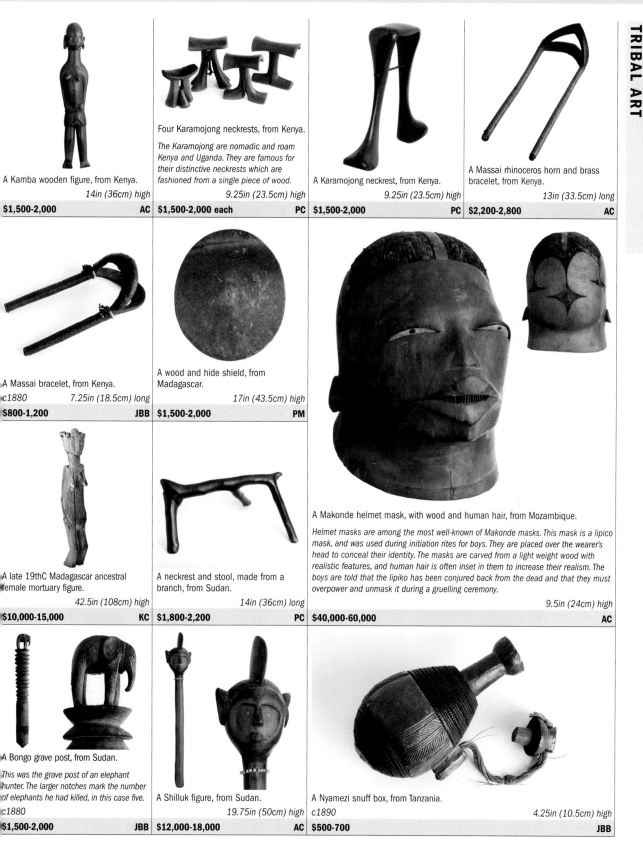

A Kamba wooden figure, from Kenya.

14in (36cm) high

$1,500-2,000   AC

Four Karamojong neckrests, from Kenya.

The Karamojong are nomadic and roam Kenya and Uganda. They are famous for their distinctive neckrests which are fashioned from a single piece of wood.

9.25in (23.5cm) high

$1,500-2,000 each   PC

A Karamojong neckrest, from Kenya.

9.25in (23.5cm) high

$1,500-2,000   PC

A Massai rhinoceros horn and brass bracelet, from Kenya.

13in (33.5cm) long

$2,200-2,800   AC

A Massai bracelet, from Kenya.

c1880   *7.25in (18.5cm) long*

$800-1,200   JBB

A wood and hide shield, from Madagascar.

17in (43.5cm) high

$1,500-2,000   PM

A late 19thC Madagascar ancestral female mortuary figure.

42.5in (108cm) high

$10,000-15,000   KC

A neckrest and stool, made from a branch, from Sudan.

14in (36cm) long

$1,800-2,200   PC

A Makonde helmet mask, with wood and human hair, from Mozambique.

Helmet masks are among the most well-known of Makonde masks. This mask is a lipico mask, and was used during initiation rites for boys. They are placed over the wearer's head to conceal their identity. The masks are carved from a light weight wood with realistic features, and human hair is often inset in them to increase their realism. The boys are told that the lipiko has been conjured back from the dead and that they must overpower and unmask it during a gruelling ceremony.

9.5in (24cm) high

$40,000-60,000   AC

A Bongo grave post, from Sudan.

This was the grave post of an elephant hunter. The larger notches mark the number of elephants he had killed, in this case five.

c1880

$1,500-2,000   JBB

A Shilluk figure, from Sudan.

19.75in (50cm) high

$12,000-18,000   AC

A Nyamezi snuff box, from Tanzania.

c1890   *4.25in (10.5cm) high*

$500-700   JBB

A Fipa mask, from Tanzania.

9.75in (25cm) high

$8,000-12,000   **AC**

A Barotze hare box, from East Africa.

12.5in (32cm) long

$800-1,200   **JDB**

A Barotze bowl, used for kneading dough (manjok) for bread, from East Africa.

15.25in (39cm) high

$1,200-1,800   **JDB**

A wooden vessel, from East Africa.

c1900

$150-200   **KC**

Southern Africa

Southern Africa includes the regions Namibia, Botswana, Zimbabwe, Mozambique, Swaziland, Lesotho and South Africa. The area is often considered to be less rich in tribal art than West or Central Africa, because of the comparable lack of masking traditions. Also ancestor figures were rarely carved for religious practices. However, there is an abundance of finely carved everyday objects, such as headrests and snuff bottles, which incorporate functionality, symbolism and aestheticism. There has been a growing interest in art from Southern Africa over the past 20 years, resulting in an appreciation and increased knowledge about pieces which had previously been neglected.

A Chopi cup, from South Africa.

c1900   *6.75in (17cm) high*

$220-280   **KC**

A Shangaan prestige staff, from South Africa.

c1880   *33.75in (86cm) high*

$7,000-10,000   **KC**

A wooden neckrest, from Swaziland.

17.75in (45cm) long

$1,800-2,200   **PC**

A Tsonga spoon, from South Africa.

c1900   *24.5in (62cm) long*

$1,000-1,500   **KC**

A Tswana spoon, from South Africa.

c1850   *11.5in (29cm) high*

$6,000-9,000   **KC**

A Shona neckrest, from Zimbabwe.

Shona neckrests typically curve upwards at the ends. They were used by men and would have been buried with them after their death.

c1880   *6in (15.5cm) high*

$1,200-1,800   **JBB**

A 19thC Xhosa pipe, from South Africa.

7in (18cm) long

$1,000-1,500   **KC**

A Shona wooden stool, from Swaziland.

8.5in (21.5cm) high

$2,200-2,800   **PC**

A Shona neckrest, from Zimbabwe.

c1880   *5in (13cm) high*

$2,200-2,800   **KC**

Oceania

The term 'Oceanic art' includes works from the South and North West Pacific, including Papua New Guinea, Irian Jaya, Melanesia, Polynesia, Indonesia, New Zealand and Australia.

The art works from these areas are deeply varied and differ from country to country. Items include wooden scrollwork carvings and ritual masks, basketry masks from the Sepik River people, from Papua New Guinea, drums, canoe prows, figures, spirit hooks and shields, and the beautifully fashioned, carved objects with mother-of-pearl that are characteristic of the Solomon Islands.

Pieces are often representations of a rich fabric of mythology that has been built up over thousands of years. It is from this region that artists such as Alberto Giacometti, Henry Moore and Max Ernst took inspiration, moved as they were by the vibrancy and form of Oceanic art.

Papua New Guinea

Papua New Guinea is a remote island to the north of Australia, lying just south of the equator. The first recorded sighting by Europeans was in 1512 by two Portuguese explorers. Dutch explorers followed and named it New Guinea because of similarities to Africa. There are a huge variety of cultures, with more than 800 indigenous languages being spoken. The crocodile, the cassowary (a large flightless bird), and pigs are important features of Papuan mythology, and are frequently represented in their art. Each piece has a very specific use and embodies an individual spirit, believed to protect the village and to ward off evil spirits. The cultures practice grand ceremonies that include vivid displays of body adornment, dance and ritual.

Due to the humidity of the climate and the proliferation of insects and fungi, much of the tribal art from this area has decayed. Also in the past, missionaries destroyed a lot of the pieces, believing them to be pornographic or idolatrous. Only items that have been removed from the jungle have any chance of being preserved. The Sepik River region in particular has produced a wide selection of artefacts, including masks, domestic implements and necklaces.

Two views of an Abelam ceremonial yam mask (baba mask), Papua New Guinea.

19.25in (49cm) high

$1,500-2,000 | **JYP**

An Abelam ceremonial yam mask (baba mask), Papua New Guinea.

8.75in (22cm) high

$1,000-1,500 | **JYP**

A gable mask, from Blackwater lakes, Papua New Guinea.

41.25in (105cm) high

$1,800-2,200 | **JYP**

A gable mask, from Blackwater lakes, Papua New Guinea.

32.75in (83cm) high

$1,800-2,200 | **JYP**

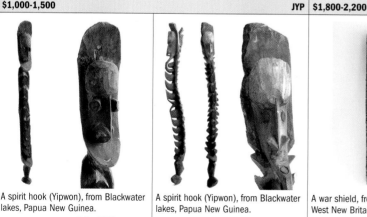

A spirit hook (Yipwon), from Blackwater lakes, Papua New Guinea.

51in (130cm) high

$2,500-3,000 | **JYP**

A spirit hook (Yipwon), from Blackwater lakes, Papua New Guinea.

59.75in (152cm) high

$1,800-2,200 | **JYP**

A war shield, from Kandrian village, West New Britain, Papua New Guinea.

49.25in (125cm) high

$1,500-2,000 | **JYP**

A spirit hook, from Karawari River, Papua New Guinea.

70.75in (78cm) high

$2,200-2,800 | **JYP**

A yam mask, from Maprik area, Papua New Guinea.

19in (48cm) high

$500-700   **JYP**

A fiber arm band, from Maprik area, Papua New Guinea. *c1900-1950*

$800-1,200   **KC**

A Baining fire dance mask, from East New Britain, Papua New Guinea.

The Baining people inhabit the Gazelle Peninsula of New Britain in Papua New Guinea. They are famous for their large masks made of bark cloth stretched over wickerwork frames. The masks are used in ceremonies and then usually destroyed.

33.5in (85cm) high

$1,200-1,800   **JYP**

A male totem figure, from Maprik area, Papua New Guinea.

41in (104cm) high

$1,500-2,000   **JYP**

A spirit hook, probably from May River, Papua New Guinea.

36.75in (93cm) high

$2,500-3,000   **JYP**

A Moka Kina Highlands shield, from Papua New Guinea.

c1950   *15in (38cm) high*

$400-600   **KC**

A basketry helmet mask, from Papuan Gulf, Papua New Guinea.

17.25in (44cm) high

$1,500-2,000   **JYP**

A Tatanua mask, from New Ireland, Papua New Guinea.

c1900   *16.5in (42cm) high*

$20,000-30,000   **KC**

A Kanipu mask, from Papuan Gulf, Papua New Guinea.

62in (90cm) high

$2,200-2,800   **JYP**

Two views of a Keveke mask, from Papuan Gulf, Papua New Guinea.

70in (178cm) high

$1,500-2,000　　　**JYP**

An ancestor board (gobi), from Papuan Gulf, Papua New Guinea.

Ancestor masks embody specific ancestors and draw the spirit of the dead into the village. These spirits then bring the positive aspects from their past lives to the community.

c1900　　　*39in (99cm) high*

$12,000-18,000　　　**KC**

An ancestor board (gobi), from Elema region, Papuan Gulf, Papua New Guinea.

Provenance: *Ex Busch collection, Melbourne, Australia.*

c1880　　　*39.25in (100cm) long*

$3,500-4,500　　　**KC**

A skull rack, from Babaguima village, Papuan Gulf, Papua New Guinea.

33.75in (86cm) high

$2,800-3,200　　　**JYP**

A spirit mask or spirit hook, from the Ramu River, Papua New Guinea.

Coloring a shield or carving is believed to increase its power and pieces are often redecorated before important ceremonies. Pigments are taken from charcoal, plants, burnt shells and minerals, mixed with tree sap, clay and water and then applied with feathers or plant stems.

56in (142cm) high

$2,200-2,800　　　**JYP**

A spirit mask or spirit hook, from Ramu River, Papua New Guinea.

53in (135cm) high

$1,500-2,000　　　**JYP**

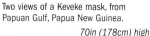

Two views of a Tambuan mask, from Ramu River, Papua New Guinea.

41.75in (106cm) high

$2,200-2,800　　　**JYP**

A spirit hook, from the Ramu River, Papua New Guinea.

27.5in (70cm) high

$1,000-1,500　　　**JYP**

Two views of a canoe prow, from Ramu River, Papua New Guinea.

65.25in (166cm) high

$1,500-2,000　　　**JYP**

A 19thC ancestor figure, from Sepik area, Papua New Guinea.

Provenance *Ex Webster collection, London 1897 and Pitt-Rivers Museum, Dorset.*

13.75in (35cm) high

$30,000-50,000　　　**KC**

A Sepik neckrest, from Papua New Guinea.

c1900   *6in (15cm) high*

$1,000-1,500   **KC**

Two views of an Arapesh sago utensil, from East Sepik, Papua New Guinea.

c1930   *24in (61cm) high*

$400-600   **KC**

A first half 20thC large tapa cloth, from East Sepik area, Papua New Guinea.

$3,500-4,500   **JDB**

A yam mask, from Wosera area, Papua New Guinea.

16in (41cm) high

$800-1,200   **JYP**

An ancestor figure, from Wosera village, East Sepik, Papua New Guinea.

43.25in (110cm) high

$3,000-4,000   **JYP**

A spirit mask, from Kandingai village, Sepik, Papua New Guinea.

13in (33cm) high

$350-400   **JYP**

An early 20thC Wewak 'mosquito' mask, from Kubalia village, Lower Sepik, Papua New Guinea.

17.25in (44cm) long

$3,500-4,500   **JDB**

An ancestor post, from Washkuk area, Middle Sepik, Papua New Guinea.

63in (160cm) high

$1,000-1,500   **JYP**

A house post fragment, from Middle Sepik, from Papua New Guinea.

48in (122cm) high

$6,000-9,000   **JYP**

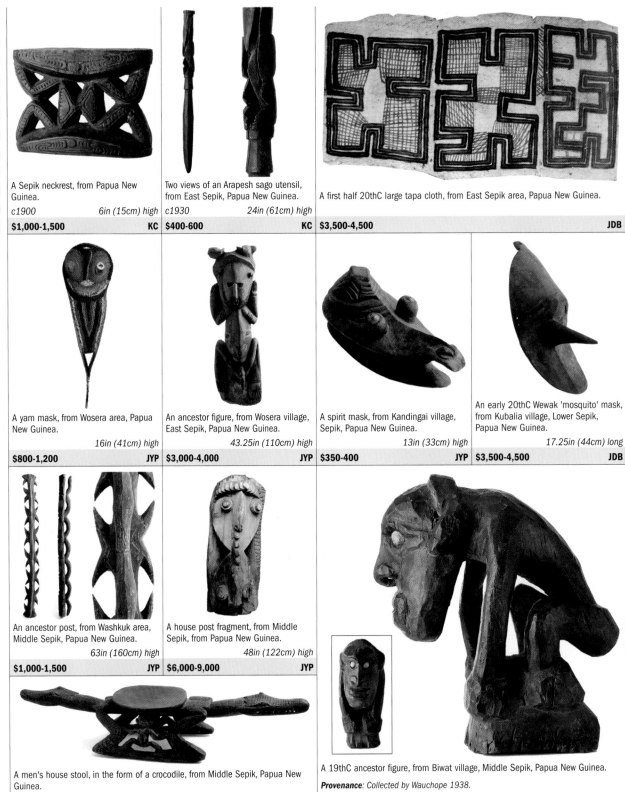

A men's house stool, in the form of a crocodile, from Middle Sepik, Papua New Guinea.

49.25in (125cm) long

$2,200-2,800   **JYP**

A 19thC ancestor figure, from Biwat village, Middle Sepik, Papua New Guinea.

Provenance*: Collected by Wauchope 1938.*

13.75in (35cm) high

$20,000-30,000   **KC**

A Minja yam cult head, from Washkuk area, Middle Sepik, Papua New Guinea.

21.25in (54cm) high

$700-1,000   **JYP**

A cult house post, from Kandingai village, Middle Sepik, Papua New Guinea.

84.25in (214cm) high

$5,000-7,000   **JYP**

A scarecrow bird figure, probably from Tambanum village, Middle Sepik, Papua New Guinea.

31.75in (81cm) high

$400-600   **JYP**

A yam cult head (Yena), from Washkuk area, Middle Sepik, Papua New Guinea.

44.75in (114cm) high

$2,200-2,800   **JYP**

An ancestor figure, from Washkuk area, Middle Sepik, Papua New Guinea.

39.25in (100cm) high

$1,000-1,500   **JYP**

A Yina figure, from Washkuk area, Middle Sepik, Papua New Guinea.

50.25in (128cm) high

$2,500-3,000   **JYP**

An ancestor figure, from Washkuk area, from Middle Sepik, Papua New Guinea.

63in (160cm) high

$1,500-2,000   **JYP**

A house pole, from Washkuk area, Middle Sepik, Papua New Guinea.

76.75in (195cm) high

$1,500-2,000   **JYP**

A food hook, from Sepik River, from Papua New Guinea.

Cult hooks, food hooks or suspension hooks are used to preserve food. They prevent animals getting to it and are believed to embody good spirits that are thought to increase the length of time before decay sets in.

c1925   *22in (56cm) long*

$1,000-1,500   **JBB**

A hand drum, from Sepik River, Papua New Guinea.

24.5in (62cm) high

$700-1,000   **JYP**

A hand drum, from Sepik River, Papua New Guinea.

24.75in (63cm) high

$800-1,200   **JYP**

Two views of an ancestor figure, from Sepik River, Papua New Guinea.

47.25in (120cm)

$1,200-1,800   **JYP**

A men's house decoration board, from Sepik River, Papua New Guinea.

60.75in (154cm) high

$1,200-1,800   **JYP**

A Sepik River figural hook.

Provenance: *Ex Erik Grate collection, Stockholm.*

c1900   *24.75in (63cm) high*

$25,000-30,000   **KC**

A wooden stool, in the form of a turtle, from Sepik River, Papua New Guinea.

22in (56cm) long

$300-400   **JYP**

A wooden stool, from Sepik River, Papua New Guinea.

19.25in (49cm) long

$400-600   **JYP**

A decoration board, from Upper Sepik River area, Papua New Guinea.

78.25in (199cm) high

$1,800-2,200   **JYP**

A basket doll, with cowrie shells, from Sepik River, Papua New Guinea.

9.5in (24cm) high

$400-600   **JYP**

An ancestor figure, from Sepik River, Papua New Guinea.

Provenance: *Ex Dr. Herman Finck collection.*

c1900   *11in (28cm) high*

$10,000-15,000   **KC**

Two views of a suspension hook, from Middle Sepik, Papua New Guinea.

24in (61cm) high

$2,000-3,000   **JYP**

A ceremonial basket hook, from Upper Sepik, Papua New Guinea.

35.75in (91cm) high

$1,800-2,200   **JYP**

A house doorboard, from Telefomin village, West Sepik, Papua New Guinea.

86.75in (220cm) high

$3,500-4,500   **JYP**

A bird stone figure, from Southern Highlands, Papua New Guinea.

7.5in (19cm) high

$3,000-4,000   **JYP**

A war shield, from Southern Highlands, Papua New Guinea.

63in (160cm) high

$2,200-2,800   **JYP**

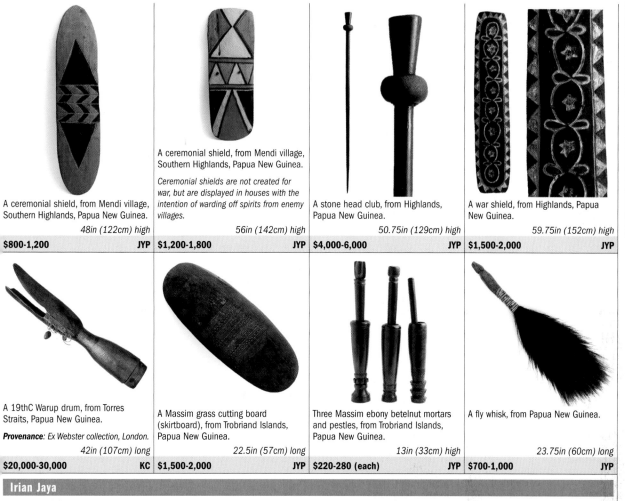

A ceremonial shield, from Mendi village, Southern Highlands, Papua New Guinea.

48in (122cm) high

$800-1,200 **JYP**

A ceremonial shield, from Mendi village, Southern Highlands, Papua New Guinea.

Ceremonial shields are not created for war, but are displayed in houses with the intention of warding off spirits from enemy villages.

56in (142cm) high

$1,200-1,800 **JYP**

A stone head club, from Highlands, Papua New Guinea.

50.75in (129cm) high

$4,000-6,000 **JYP**

A war shield, from Highlands, Papua New Guinea.

59.75in (152cm) high

$1,500-2,000 **JYP**

A 19thC Warup drum, from Torres Straits, Papua New Guinea.

Provenance: *Ex Webster collection, London.*

42in (107cm) long

$20,000-30,000 **KC**

A Massim grass cutting board (skirtboard), from Trobriand Islands, Papua New Guinea.

22.5in (57cm) long

$1,500-2,000 **JYP**

Three Massim ebony betelnut mortars and pestles, from Trobriand Islands, Papua New Guinea.

13in (33cm) high

$220-280 (each) **JYP**

A fly whisk, from Papua New Guinea.

23.75in (60cm) long

$700-1,000 **JYP**

Irian Jaya

Irian Jaya (also Papua) is an Indonesian province on the western half of the island of New Guinea. The eastern half is the mainland of the independent nation of Papua New Guinea. The Asmat people of Irian Jaya are famous for their elaborate carved objects and their distinctive 'praying mantis' treatment of the human form. They live in the tidal swamps of Irian Jaya as seminomadic hunters and gatherers.

An Asmat ceremonial initiation pole, from Jamas-Jeni village, North-western Asmat, Irian Jaya.

82.75in (210cm) high

$1,200-1,800 **JYP**

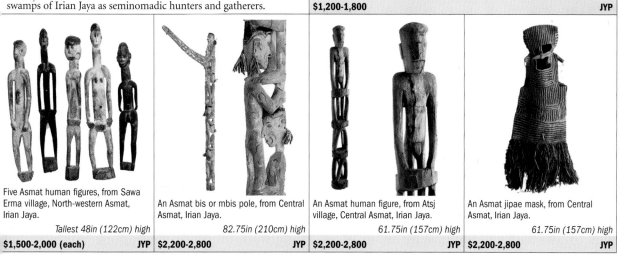

Five Asmat human figures, from Sawa Erma village, North-western Asmat, Irian Jaya.

Tallest 48in (122cm) high

$1,500-2,000 (each) **JYP**

An Asmat bis or mbis pole, from Central Asmat, Irian Jaya.

82.75in (210cm) high

$2,200-2,800 **JYP**

An Asmat human figure, from Atsj village, Central Asmat, Irian Jaya.

61.75in (157cm) high

$2,200-2,800 **JYP**

An Asmat jipae mask, from Central Asmat, Irian Jaya.

61.75in (157cm) high

$2,200-2,800 **JYP**

An Asmat war shield, from North-western Asmat, Irian Jaya.

50.75in (129cm) high

$1,000-1,500 | **JYP**

An Asmat war shield, from the Casuarina coast, Irian Jaya.

78.25in (199cm) high

$2,500-3,000 | **JYP**

An Asmat war shield, from Korowai area, Irian Jaya.

69.25in (176cm) high

$1,500-2,000 | **JYP**

An Asmat war shield, from North Citak area, Irian Jaya.

76.75in (195cm) high

$1,500-2,000 | **JYP**

An Asmat sago bowl, from Central Asmat, Irian Jaya.

25.5in (65cm) high

$1,000-1,500 | **JYP**

An Asmat sago plate, from Central Asmat, Irian Jaya.

The sago palm provides the staple food of the Asmat.

22.75in (58cm) high

$900-1,300 | **JYP**

A holy stone, from Korowai area, Irian Jaya.

11.5in (29cm) long

$3,000-4,000 | **JYP**

A house post finial, from Lake Sentani, Irian Jaya.

52.25in (133cm) high

$1,500-2,000 | **JYP**

The Philippines

The Philippines is situated between the Pacific Ocean and the South China seas.

The Ifugao people inhabit the Cordillera Central Mountains, in Northern Luzon. They are famous for their impressive rice terraces, built step by step from the bottom of valleys to 1,000 meters high. The Ifugao have a unique culture that is at least 3,000 years old and marked by exceptional creativity. To increase rice crops, the Ifugao carve wooden effigies that are said to embody rice deities who have the power to ensure a bountiful harvest.

An Ifugao figure, from the Philippines.

18.5in (47cm) high

$6,000-7,000 | **PC**

An Ifugao wooden spoon, from the Philippines.

9in (23cm) long

$3,500-4,500 | **PC**

An Ifugao wooden and brass spoon, from the Philippines.

7in (18cm) long

$12,00-15,000 | **PC**

A wooden spoon, from the Philippines.

7.5in (19cm) long

$4,000-5,000 | **PC**

A Solomon Islands canoe ornament.
c1900   11.75in (30cm) high
$6,000-9,000   KC

A 19thC Solomon Islands war shield.
32.75in (83cm) high
$3,500-4,500   KC

Two Batak canal paddles, from Sumatra.
Tallest 73.25in (186cm) high
$2,200-2,800 (each)   AC

Australia and New Zealand

A Tiwi Aborigine culture funeral Tunga
bark bag, from Melville Island, Australia.
21.25in (54cm) high
$600-900   JYP

A Tiwi Aborigine culture funeral Tunga
bark bag, from Melville Island, Australia.
31in (45cm) high
$600-900   JYP

An early 20thC Aborigine hat, from
Queensland, Australia.
18.5in (47cm) high
$600-900   KC

A Tiwi Aborigine Pukamani funeral pole,
from Melville Island, Australia.
72.5in (184cm) high
$3,000-4,000   JYP

An Aborigine wooden shield, from
Australia.
32.25in (82cm) high
$4,000-6,000   PC

A Maori meeting house panel, from New Zealand.
c1870-1880   71in (182cm) high
$40,000-50,000   KC

Pre-Columbian

Pre-Columbian works of art created in Central and South America before the arrival of Europeans in the 15th century are renowned for their high levels of artistic achievement. The Americas had been home to indigenous civilizations whose artefacts bear witness to an exceptional degree of technical advancement. Pottery was probably first developed in Columbia or Ecuador around 2000BC and was used to make containers. Throughout the region it is the most common surviving artefact. Pottery was fashioned by hand as well as molded. Typical decoration included incised designs, carving, painting, and polishing. It was usually painted in just one or two colors.

A Casa Grandes pottery effigy bowl, molded with two masks and painted with a geometric decoration.

Provenance: *Property from the Estate of Dr. and Mrs. Melvin Stich, Chevy Chase, Maryland.*

6.5in (16.5cm) high

$350-400   SI

A pair of Casa Grandes terracotta vessels, one of circular form, the interior painted with four circular cartouches on black ground, the other of globular form with loop handles on the shoulders, painted with brown geometric decoration.

7.75in (19.5cm) diam

$350-400   SI

A Chimu pottery figural vessel.

c AD1100-1400   8.5in (22cm) high

$150-200   SI

A Chimu silver beaker, repoussé with double facial features, hook nose, and large rimmed almond eyes, wearing a headdress with a jaguar head.

c AD1100-1400   8.25in (21cm) high

$1,200-1,800   SI

A Chimu blackware double-bodied avian vessel, with each chamber molded with bosses, the bird head with incised eyes.

c AD1100-1400   8.75in (22cm) high

$300-400   SI

A late Preclassic Chupicuaro pottery tripod bowl.

c300-100BC   8.25in (21cm) diam

$700-1,000   SI

A Chimu blackware stirrup spouted vessel, with globular molded body to depict coiled snakes.

The Chimu Kingdom occupied the region that today is Peru, from around AD1000 to 1470. Its artistic traditions were continued by the Incas, who conquered the Chimu in 1471. Most Chimu pottery was massproduced using molds and pots generally have tall, elegant spouts.

c AD1100-1400   9in (23cm) high

$220-280   SI

A set of four late Preclassic Chupicuaro terracotta vessels, two of tripod form, one painted with black and white vertical line decoration, the other with a band of black and beige geometric decoration encircling the body, one of circular form with reddish-brown, black and beige zigzag pattern, and one with conical foot and flaring bowl, the exterior painted in reddish-brown and beige zigzag pattern.

c300-100BC   9.5in (24cm) diam

$300-400   SI

A Proto-classic Colima terracotta gadrooned vessel, and a Nayarit terracotta vessel, the former is a broad fluted vessel supported on three short human-form legs with feet, the latter in the form of a pumpkin with white and burnt orange linear decoration.

c100BC-AD250   6.75in (17cm) high

$250-350   SI

A set of three Proto-classic Colima terracotta flutes, one in the form of a snake, one in the form of a stylized owl and one with face-form decoration.

c100BC-AD250   17.25in (44cm) long

$300-400   SI

A pair of late Preclassic early Proto-classic Colima pottery figures.

c300BC-AD250   7.75in (20cm) high

$300-400   SI

A set of seven Proto-classic Colima terracotta figures, comprising four figures of men, two standing with arms crossed across their stomachs, one with long nose and pointed head, one wearing an eagle headdress, and three figures of women, one standing with her arms crossed across her stomach, one with arms behind her head, and one with arms outstretched.

Colima is famous for its pottery, which is typically fashioned as representations of the human form as well as many representing dogs, which were believed to serve as a pathway from earth to paradise.

100BC-AD250   7.75in (20cm) high

$350-400   SI

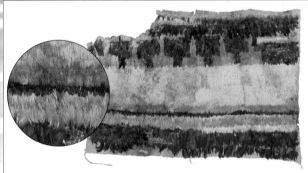

An Inca feather panel, composed of alternating bands of blue, yellow and orange feathers, each feather individually wrapped around a cotton string and attached in overlapping rows to the plain wave cotton backing, framed.

By the mid-15thC, the Inca Empire was the largest society in the New World and remained so until the arrival of the Europeans 100 years later. The Incas inhabited the highlands and coast of Peru, Ecuador, parts of Chile, Bolivia and Argentina.

c AD550-950   42in (106.5cm) long

$1,500-2,000   SI

A late Classic Mayan Yucatan/Northern Campethe vessel.

c AD550-950   3.75in (15cm) diam

$600-900   SI

Two late Classic Mayan polychrome terracotta vessels.

AD550-950   10.25in (26cm) high

$400-600   SI

A colonial wood kero, of flaring form painted with two panels depicting figures, flowers and geometric deisgns.

c1470-1560   5.25in (14cm) high

$350-400   SI

A Guanacaste zone Costa Rican jade axe God.

c300BC-AD300   3.5in (9cm) high

$350-400   SI

A Costa Rican jade axe God.

c AD200-600   4in (10cm) high

$350-400   SI

A Haida polychrome wood totem pole, signed 'Philip Thorn'.

24.75in (63cm) high

$700-1,000   SI

A Proto-classic Jalaisco figure of a female seated with her arms on her lap.

c100BC-AD250   9.25in (23.5cm) high

$400-600   SI

A pair of Proto-classic Jalisco polychrome terracotta figures of a man.

100BC-AD250   9.75in (25cm) high

$400-600   SI

A late Classic Mayan polychrome cylinder vessel.

The Mayans inhabited a region encompassing what is today Guatemala, Belize, Honduras and El Salvador, and parts of southern Mexico.

c AD550-950   9in (23cm) high

$700-1,000   SI

Four late Classic Mayan terracotta figures, comprising two figures of priests, one with arms crossed over his chest, one cradling a bowl, and one figure of a man seated wearing a necklace, ear spools and elaborate headdress, and a figure of a man.

c AD550-950   *9in (23cm) high*

$800-1,200   **SI**

A Mochica painted vessel painted on each side with a running warrior, the large fan wing trailing behind.

c AD200-500   *10.75in (27.5cm) high*

$800-1,200   **SI**

A Mochica figural erotic stirrup spout vessel, of rectangular form molded in high relief with an embraced couple.

c500-100BC   *7.5in (19cm) high*

$700-1,000   **SI**

Two early Postclassic Mixtec polychrome terracotta vessels, one of circular form with tripod foot, with a band encircling the rim painted in orange tones on a reddish-brown and black geometric decoration.

Largest 5.75in (14.5cm) diam

$220-280   **SI**

A Mochica painted vessel.

c AD800-1100   *11in (28cm) high*

$1,000-1,500   **SI**

Eight Preclassic figures, including a Mochica standing figure wearing a skirt, a Vercruz warrior, a Chupicuaro standing figure and five Preclassic figures.

c1150-500BC   *6.75in (17cm) high*

$400-600   **SI**

A Mochica double chamber vessel, molded to depict a conch shell and a clam, with remains of pigment.

cAD200-500   *6.75in (17cm) high*

$700-1,000   **SI**

Six Mochica terracotta fertility figures, with traces of pigment.

c300-100BC   *4.5in (11.5cm) high*

$350-400   **SI**

Two Proto-classic Nayarit terracotta figures, one of a woman seated, with arms on her stomach, one of a man standing, supported by three legs, one hand on his mouth, the other on his hip, one arm missing.

100BC-AD250   *Tallest 12in (30.5cm) h*

$220-280   **SI**

A Nayarit pottery figure of a man, seated cross-legged, holding a mirror and a bowl.

c AD800   *8in (20cm) high*

$400-600   **SI**

Two Nayarit terracotta figures of men, each seated with his arms on his hips.

100BC-AD250   *9.5in (24cm) high*
$220-280   **SI**

A Nazca polychrome pottery vessel, painted with a mystical flying figure together with a Nazca-Huari effigy vessel.

c AD300-600   *8in (22cm) high*
$350-400   **SI**

Two black pottery vessels, one of globular form, the other in the form of a bird with molded head and wings.

                  7.5in (19cm) high
$220-280   **SI**

A Sican gold mask, with continuous rectangular hammered sheet repoussé with a stylized human face.

c AD900-1100   *13in (33cm) long*
$4,000-6,000   **SI**

A late Preclassic/early Protoclassic Teotihuacan stone figure.

c300BC-AD200   *8in (20cm) high*
$700-1,000   **SI**

A Tiahuanaco pottery cup with stylized jaguar decoration.

c AD700-1000   *5.75in (14.5cm) high*
$300-500   **SI**

An early Preclassic Tlatilco figure.

c1150-550BC   *11.5in (29cm) high*
$300-500   **SI**

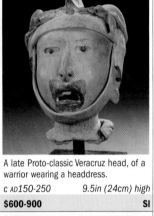

A late Proto-classic Veracruz head, of a warrior wearing a headdress.

c AD150-250   *9.5in (24cm) high*
$600-900   **SI**

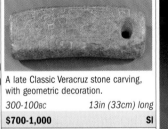

A late Classic Veracruz stone carving, with geometric decoration.

300-100BC   *13in (33cm) long*
$700-1,000   **SI**

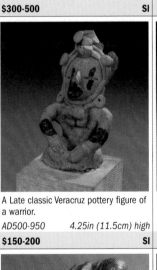

A Late classic Veracruz pottery figure of a warrior.

AD500-950   *4.25in (11.5cm) high*
$150-200   **SI**

A late Classic Veracruz pottery smiling head, wearing a plain headdress.

c AD550-950   *4.75in (12cm) high*
$100-150   **SI**

A late Proto-classic Veracruz pottery head, of a warrior.

c AD150-250   *10in (25cm) high*
$350-400   **SI**

Three Inuit stone carvings, comprising two soapstone carvings, one of a walrus and one of a seal, and a green stone carving of a muskox, with a carving of a polar bear.

The Inuit inhabit the seacoasts of the Arctic and sub-Arctic regions of North America and the north eastern tip of Siberia. Inuit means 'real people'.

11.5in (29cm) long
$300-400   **SI**

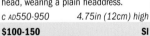

Two Inuit soapstone carvings, depicting a walrus and a seal, marked 'Povungnituk Q. Josie'.

5.75in (14.5cm) long
$220-280   **SI**

A Vicus double-bodied figural vessel, with each chamber painted with stylized feline.

c AD100-500   *7in (18cm) high*
$400-600   **SI**

A Kwaikul totem pole, from the North-west coast of America.

c1890   *33.75in (86cm) high*
$1,500-2,000   **JBB**

455

A late New Kingdom Egyptian upper part of a carved ushabti, with traces of painted decoration.

c1200-1100 BC   *5in (12.5cm) high*

$220-280   HG

A Late Period Egyptian turquoise faience ushabti, depicted mummiform, wearing a tripartite wig and a false beard, inscribed with hieroglyphic text.

c664-525 BC   *4in (10cm) high*

$220-280   SI

A Late Period Eygptian faience ushabti, depicted mummiform, wearing a tripartite wig and a false beard, inscribed with hieroglyphic text.

c664-525 BC   *4in (10cm) high*

$220-280   SI

A Late Period Egyptian turquoise faience ushabti, depicted mummiform, wearing a tripartite wig and a false beard, inscribed with hieroglyphic text.

c664-525 BC   *4in (10cm) high*

$500-700   SI

A Late Period Egyptian ushabti, depicted mummiform wearing a tripartite wig and false beard, inscribed with hieroglyphic text.

c664-525   *BC 4in (10cm) high*

$300-500   SI

Four Late Period Eygptian turquoise ushabti, the mummiform figures with arms crossed over the abdomen, wearing tripartite wigs and false beards.

c664-525 BC   *1.75in (4.5cm) high*

$380-420   SI

Two Late Period Egyptian white and turquoise faience ushabti, depicted mummiform, wearing tripartite wigs and false beards.

c664-525 BC   *3in (7.5cm) high*

$220-280   SI

A Late Period Egyptian green faience ushabti, depicted mummiform wearing a tripartite wig and a false beard, inscribed with hieroglyphic text.

c664-525 BC   *4in (10cm) high*

$300-500   SI

A Late Period Egyptian white and turquoise faience ushabti, depicted mummiform, wearing a tripartite wig and a false beard, inscribed with hieroglyphic text.

c664-525 BC   *5.25in (13.5cm) high*

$450-550   SI

A late Dynastic Period Egyptian light-green glazed faience ushabti, with two lines of hieroglyphs in a T-shape.

c730-332BC   *c4in (10cm) high*

$350-450   HG

A late Dynastic Period Egyptian blue-glazed ushabti.

c730-332BC   *4.25in (11cm) high*

$70-100   HG

A late Dynastic Period Egyptian light-blue glazed ushabti, inscribed in hieroglyphs 'Wa-Ib-Re, Controller of the Estates'.

c730-332 BC   *2.5in (6cm) high*

$300-500   HG

Greek

A Minoan gray steatite (soapstone) hemispherical vessel, with profuse incised geometric decoration.

c2400-2200 BC   *4in (10cm) diam*

$3,000-4,000   **HG**

A Mycean buff pottery stirrup vessel, with ochre painted decoration.

c1200 BC   *3.75in (9.5cm) high*

$600-900   **HG**

A Geometric period Greek bronze fibula, with sprial decoration.

8th-7thC   *BC 2in (5cm) diam*

$600-900   **HG**

A Greek pottery figure of a bull, with geometric features and painted decoration, from the Boeotia region.

7thC BC   *5in (12.5cm) high*

$800-1,200   **HG**

A Greek hollow-molded pottery head, in the Archaic style, possibly representing Achilles.

c600-550 BC   *4.5in (11.5cm) high*

$700-1,000   **HG**

A Greek Attic black-glazed lekythos (flask), stylized ray pattern to shoulder.

6thC BC   *4in (10cm) high*

$280-320   **HG**

A Greek South Italian colonial black glazed shallow pottery dish.

4thC BC   *5.5in (14cm) diam*

$220-280   **HG**

A Greek pottery plaque, representing the head of Demeter, probably a votive temple offering.

c550-500 BC   *4in (10cm) high*

$380-420   **HG**

A Hellenistic period Greek pottery draped figure, in the Tanagra style.

Tanagra was a town in the Boeotia region.

c1stC BC   *7in (18cm) high*

$1,000-1,500   **HG**

A Lucanian red figure oenochoe (wine jug), with disc foot and centrally ribbed handle, the body painted with a seated youth holding a palm branch in each hand, a palmette complex under the handle.

This is attributed to the Primato Painter.

c340 BC   *12in (30.5cm) high*

$4,500-5,500   **SI**

A Magna Graecia, Apulian red figure-ware pelike (storage jar), decorated with a seated youth and draped female and two draped youths.

c350BC   *17.25in (44cm) high*

$4,500-5,500   **AnA**

Miscellaneous

A Paleolithic Anatolian crude gray chert axe head.

c80,000-60,000 BC 6in (15.5cm) high

$70-100 HG

A Syrian carved limestone stylized eye idol, from Tell Brak.

c3400-3100 BC 2in (5cm) high

$600-900 HG

An Anatolian red stone stamp seal, decorated with an ibex.

c3400-3100 BC 2in (5cm) wide

$300-500 HG

An Anatolian stylized white marble idol, from Troy.

c3300-3100 BC 3in (7.5cm) high

$700-1,000 HG

A Sumerian marble furniture attachment, in the form of a stylized bull.

c3100-2800 BC 2.5in (6.5cm) high

$1,800-2,200 HG

An Early Bronze Age Cypriot red and black mottled burnished pottery vessel.

c2700-2200 BC 5.5in (14cm) diam

$700-1,000 HG

An early Bronze Age Cypriot small pottery vessel, with incised decoration.

c2700-2200 BC 3.5in (9cm) high

$180-220 HG

An early Bronze Age Cypriot small burnished pottery juglet.

c2700-2200 BC 2.25in (5.5cm) high

$70-100 HG

A late Bronze Age Cypriot small pottery juglet, with painted geometric decoration.

c1650-1050 BC 4in (10cm) high

$220-280 HG

An early Iron Age Cypriot geometric printed pottery chalice.

c1050-650 BC 4.25in (11cm) diam

$280-320 HG

An Luristan finely patinated bronze ceremonial finial, in the form of a master of ceremonies gripping two stylized creatures, from Western Iran.

c1000-800 BC 4.25in (10.5cm) high

$1,800-2,200 HG

A late 19thC cast-iron garden bench, cast by "John McLean Maker, N.Y. N.Y.", the three-part back cast, the medallions and scrolling devices above a pierced seat with Gothic openwork apron, shaped legs.

37.5in (95cm) high

$1,500-2,000 FRE

A late 19thC American cast-iron and wood garden bench, with shaped back of scroll and leaf devices above four board wood seat enclosed by scrolled arms continuing to form feet.

31.75in (80cm)

$650-950 FRE

A white painted cast iron garden seat.

58.5in (148.5cm) wide

$150-200 SI

A Victorian iron garden bench, cast overall with interlaced ferns, with a slatted wood seat on naturalistic legs.

47.25in (120cm) wide

$900-1,100 DN

An early 20thC American black iron garden bench, the seat and back with horizontal slats.

51in (130cm) long

$650-850 FRE

A 20thC cast-iron garden settee and side chair, the latter marked "Atlanta Stove Works, Atlanta, Georgia", the backs and legs cast with bunches of grapes and grapevines.

Bench 38in (96.5cm)

$250-350 FRE

A pair of unusual 20thC rustic glazed stoneware garden seats, modeled as entwined tree trunks with mottled glaze in green, blue and brown, one stamped "Hurlford, Fire Clay Works, Kilmarnock".

38in (96.5cm) high

$4,500-5,500 SI

A cast iron garden armchair, attributed to Karl Friedrich Schinkel.

c1820

$700-800 SI

A Dryad wicker garden chair, the curved back and arms, pierced to the sides above a seat with loose cushion and plain apron on turned feet, bears maker's label.

$250-300 L&T

Two of a set of six wirework and cut metal, white-painted garden chairs, each with an oval back and splayed legs with an X-stretcher, some rust.

$850-950 (set) DN

A pair of cast-iron garden urns, marked Kramer Bros., Dayton, Ohio and Walbridge & Co., Buffalo, New York, in three parts, the bowl cast with gadrooning and scrolling leafy devices and the similarly cast pedestal raised on a plain squared plinth, handles to bowl section missing.

30in (76cm) high

$900-1,100 FRE

A pair of late19thC American cast-iron garden urns, gadrooned rim on fluted bowl and pedestal, square plinth.

28in (71cm) high

$1,500-2,000 FRE

A late19thC American cast-iron garden urn.

22in (56cm) high

$900-1,200 FRE

A pair of early 19thC brass and wrought iron andirons, the brass urn finials on baluster shaped supports on arched legs with penny feet, bent fire dogs.

20in (50.75cm) high

$450-500   **FRE**

A pair of brass ball-top andirons, turned shafts with "spikes" on octagonal legs, ball feet.

c1815   *18in (45.75cm) high*

$550-650   **FRE**

An early 19thC pair of American Federal cast brass and wrought iron andirons, urn form finials on hexagonal plinth raised on arched spurred legs ending on ball feet.

19in (48cm) high

$550-600   **SI**

A 19thC pair of Victorian brass ball-top andirons.

19in (45.5cm) high

$250-300   **SI**

A pair of 19thC Louis XV-style gilt bronze chenet.

14.5in (37cm) high

$700-800   **SI**

A 19thC pair of Prussian soldiercast iron andirons, by Nowes/Boston, Boston.

20in (51cm) high

$650-750   **SI**

A 19thC pair of Neo-classical style brass andirons.

19in (48.5cm) high

$450-550   **SI**

A pair of 20thC Neo-classical style brass andirons, in the form of owls perched on entwined serpents, on molded bases.

21in (35.5cm) high

$700-800   **SI**

A pair of American Classical brass andirons.

c1835   *19.5in (49.5cm) high*

$600-700   **SI**

A pair of American late Classical large brass and wrought iron andirons, large urn-form with ball finials on a rounded plinth and squared base, with conforming brass urn-form element at end of brass-capped curved billet bars.

PROVENANCE: *From the Clarence Zantzinger home, Greenacre, Chestnut Hill, Philadelphia.*

c1840   *19.5in (49.5cm) high*

$4,000-5,000   **FRE**

A 19thC pair of Louis XV style gilt-metal chenet and fender.

45in (114.5cm) long

$800-1,000　　　**SI**

A gilt metal fender with foliate scrolls and fruit on bun feet.

44.5in (113cm) wide

$1,300-1,600　　　**DN**

A pair of 19thC brass pierced fenders, with rope-twist band and rounded ends on paw feet.

47.5in (121cm) wide

$300-400　　　**DN**

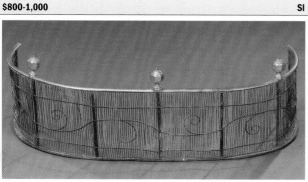

An early 19thC American brass and wire-work fire fender.

40in (101.5cm) long

$900-1,100　　　**SI**

A 19thC cast iron and gilt metal fender, with rail and fluted sides and front, each end with a figure of a sphinx with a strapwork saddle on a plinth, centerd with a classical portrait medallion, on chased turned feet. Provenance: From The Hon. Mrs Daisy Fellowes collection, President of the Society of London Fashion Designers in the 1940's.

79.5in (202cm) wide

$5,500-6,000　　　**DN**

A Samuel Yellin wrought iron door, by Samuel Yellin Workshop, Philadelphia, unmarked.

75in (190.5cm) high

$11,000-13,000　　　**FRE**

A pair of Samuel Yellin wrought iron and brass railings, by the Samuel Yellin Workshop, Philadelphia, each stamped "YELLIN".

Provenance: These railings came out of the (former) Church of the Savior at 3723 Chestnut Street, Philadelphia.

$2,500-3,500　　　**FRE**

An early 19thC cast iron and brass fire basket, the arched back centerd by a roundel, the serpentine front terminating in projecting turned and knopped baluster supports.

25in (64cm) wide

$1,300-1,600　　　**L&T**

A 19thC tôleware coal helmet, embossed with foliate panels and later painted in gilt with laurel swags on a cream ground, with integral coal shovel.

18in (46cm) long

$750-850　　　**L&T**

A 19thC reconstituted stone figure of a recumbent lion, on a rectangular plinth.

28.25in (72cm) wide

$450-550　　　**DN**

Portrait Miniatures

A James Tassie portrait medallion, white paste in mid relief, depicting Lord George Gordon (1751-93), agitator, signed "Tassie f.1781/ LORD GEO. GORDON", slate background, oval glazed ebonized pearwood frame.

1781   *3.25in (8.25cm) high*

$1,300-1,500   **GorL**

A James Tassie portrait medallion, white paste in mid relief, on papered glass, depicting Scottish judge Lord Methuen, inscribed "Tassie F./LORD METHUEN/ 1794", oval ebonized pearwood frame.

1794   *3.5in (9cm) high*

$1,300-1,500   **GorL**

JAMES TASSIE

James Tassie (1735-99) studied sculpture and modelling at the Academy of Fine Arts at the University of Glasgow. In 1766, Tassie moved to London and quickly became known for making replicas of classical gems and producing portrait medallions of eminent figures of the day. The portraits were modeled from life and were very detailed, with the subjects wearing either classical-style drapery or contemporary fashions. The figures depicted are from diverse backgrounds, including politics, medicine, the military and the arts. Many were Scottish, including professors at the Scottish universities. His nephew and heir, William Tassie (1777-1860), carried on the business when he died.

An Anne Mee watercolor on ivory portrait of the Countess of Antrim, inscribed verso and dated 1799, ormolu frame with inscription, the reverse with plaited hair.

At the age of 20, Anne Foldsone Mee (1770-1851) was employed by the Prince of Wales to paint at Windsor Castle. She was a pupil of George Romney and Richard Cosway and was an enormously successful miniaturist.

1799   *3in (7.75cm) high*

$1,000-1,500   **GorL**

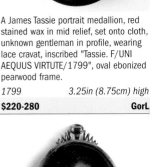

A James Tassie portrait medallion, white paste in mid relief, set onto glass, depicting Lord Daer, inscribed "Tassie F/LORD DAER/1794", oval ebonized pearwood frame.

1794   *3.5in (9cm) high*

$650-750   **GorL**

A James Tassie portrait medallion, red stained wax in mid relief, set onto cloth, unknown gentleman in profile, wearing lace cravat, inscribed "Tassie. F/UNI AEQUUS VIRTUTE/1799", oval ebonized pearwood frame.

1799   *3.25in (8.75cm) high*

$220-280   **GorL**

A School of Pieter Codde oil on canvas, laid on board portrait of a young man, bust length, in wide collar, brown coat, holding the stem of a pipe, inscribed on wood backing "1632 AE 19 Saveray".

The Dutch school of Pieter Codde operated between 1599 and 1678.

1632   *4in (10.25cm) high*

$280-320   **GorL**

A Nathaniel Hone watercolor on ivory, portrait of a gentleman, wearing a tricorn hat and gold braided blue coat, monogrammed and dated 1763, oval, mounted in a green, red and gold striped carton pierre snuff box, with tortoiseshell lining and scroll engraved gold mounts.

1763   *2.5in (6.5cm) diam*

$2,200-2,800   **GorL**

A 17thC English School oil on copper, portrait of a gentleman with long brown hair and wide collar, oval brass frame.

    2in (5cm) high

$1,000-1,500   **GorL**

An English School oil on copper, portrait of a gentleman, facing right, in armour with brown tunic and white cravat, oval silver gilt frame with spiral cresting.

c1670   *3in (7.75cm) high*

$900-1,200   **GorL**

An English School oil on copper panel portrait of James II, full face, in yellow-lined scarlet cloak, tied lace cravat and full bottomed wig, brass frame.

    4in (10.25cm) high

$1,200-1,800   **GorL**

An early 19thC portrait miniature of a lady, inscribed "M. James", in profile, looking to the left, in a square gilt bronze mounted leather frame.

    5.25in (13.5cm) high

$70-100   **SI**

A Samuel Haughton silhouette, painted on plaster, unknown young man, re-stuck label, ebonized pearwood frame.

c1790 3.5in (9cm) high

$500-700 GorL

A silhouette of a gentleman, attributed to Thomas Rider, painted on convex glass, plaster backed, ebonized frame.

c1790 3.75in (9.5cm) high

$70-100 GorL

A William Hamlet the Elder silhouette of an unknown lady, painted on convex glass, plaster backboard, trade label.

c1810 3in (7.75cm) high

$350-450 GorL

An A. W. Mason silhouette of the Duke of Sussex, painted on card, bronzed, inscribed verso, papier maché frame.

c1826 3.25in (8.25cm) high

$800-1,200 GorL

A cut silhouette by Augustin Edouart, full length study of a child playing with a ball, signed and dated 1827, foxed, shadow painted background, trade label "no. 5", ebonized frame.

Augustin Edouart (1789-1861) made some of the most sought-after silhouettes in the early- to mid-19thC. He was born in France but spent most of his life in England and also worked in America. Once, when returning from a trip to America, Edouart's boat was shipwrecked. He survived but many volumes of duplicates of his work – some 9,000 portraits in all – were lost. However, fourteen volumes were saved and provide an important collection commemorating the celebrities of his day. He also wrote a treatise on silhouettes, with many illustrations, which is now extremely rare.

c1827 5.75in (14.75cm) high

$1,500-2,000 GorL

A John Field silhouette, painted on plaster, bronzed, unknown gentleman, papier maché frame with rectangular ormolu mount.

c1772-1848 3.25in (8.25cm) high

$280-320 GorL

A set of three silhouettes, attributed to Frank Furness, dated 1889 and 1890, the subjects identified on reverse as Charles Stuart Wurts, Mary F. Tunis and Tom Tunis, matted.

Frank Furness (1839-1912), an architect from Philadelphia, cut silhouettes while visiting his brother. This group descended through the Wurts family.

1889/1890 6in (15.25cm) high

$220-280 FRE

A silhouette of a gentleman, attributed to Rembrant Peale, signed R. Peale, the hollow-cut bust length profile backed with black fabric, framed.

4.5in (11.5cm) high

$700-1,000 FRE

A painted silhouette of the Littlefield family, the four figures in a landscape and inscribed "Hon. Stephen Littlefield and Children", the children identified as George, Walter and Marion, framed, signed illegibly.

c1840 11in (28cm) wide

$500-700 SI

A paper silhouette, attributed to the Royal Victoria Gallery Cut, bronzed with painted background, unknown young woman, wearing a veiled peaked hat, half length in profile to sinister, papier maché acorn frame.

c1840 3.75in (9.5cm) high

$300-500 GorL

A set of late 18thC German School cut paper silhouettes, ten head and shoulder profiles of gentlemen, all named sitters and dated, presented in a green calf-bound album, in the form of a visitors book, now with the majority absent, slip cased.

$350-450 GorL

A set of nine early 19thC Philadelphian Peale Museum hollow-cut silhouettes, eight mounted on two sides of a scrap book page, sitters identified as Elizabeth and Samuel Rodman, William Rotch Jr., William Rotch, Sarah Rodman Morgan, and Anna or Eliza Rodman, and a gentleman, backed with fabric.

Most of the subjects in the silhouettes are related to or friends of the Fisher family.

$1,000-1,500 FRE

A pair of 19thC American silhouettes of a lady and a gentleman, the figures drawn in black ink and heightened with white and gold ink.

7in (17.75cm) high

$350-450 FRE

Waterman

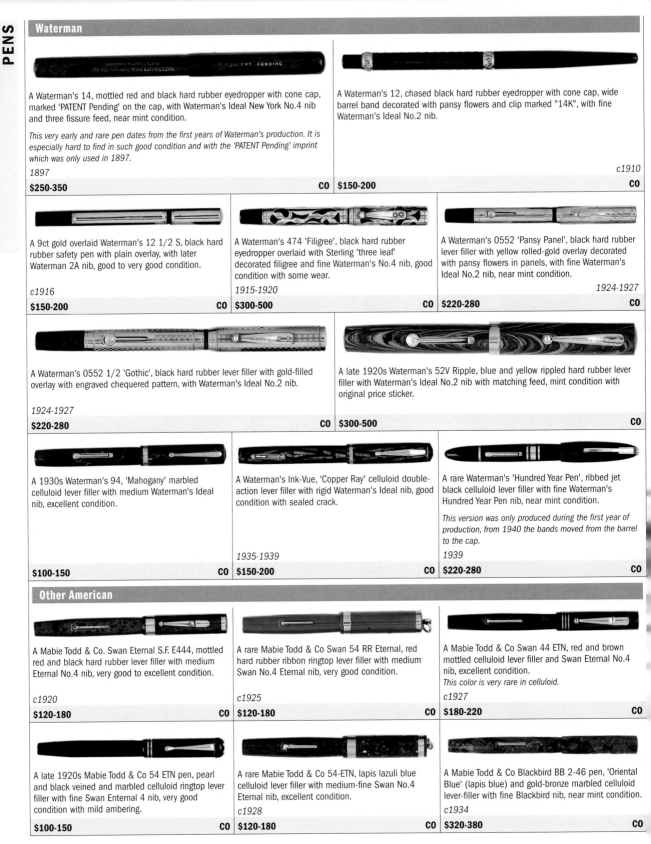

A Waterman's 14, mottled red and black hard rubber eyedropper with cone cap, marked 'PATENT Pending' on the cap, with Waterman's Ideal New York No.4 nib and three fissure feed, near mint condition.

This very early and rare pen dates from the first years of Waterman's production. It is especially hard to find in such good condition and with the 'PATENT Pending' imprint which was only used in 1897.

1897

$250-350 CO

A Waterman's 12, chased black hard rubber eyedropper with cone cap, wide barrel band decorated with pansy flowers and clip marked "14K", with fine Waterman's Ideal No.2 nib.

c1910

$150-200 CO

A 9ct gold overlaid Waterman's 12 1/2 S, black hard rubber safety pen with plain overlay, with later Waterman 2A nib, good to very good condition.

c1916

$150-200 CO

A Waterman's 474 'Filigree', black hard rubber eyedropper overlaid with Sterling 'three leaf' decorated filigree and fine Waterman's No.4 nib, good condition with some wear.

1915-1920

$300-500 CO

A Waterman's 0552 'Pansy Panel', black hard rubber lever filler with yellow rolled-gold overlay decorated with pansy flowers in panels, with fine Waterman's Ideal No.2 nib, near mint condition.

1924-1927

$220-280 CO

A Waterman's 0552 1/2 'Gothic', black hard rubber lever filler with gold-filled overlay with engraved chequered pattern, with Waterman's Ideal No.2 nib.

1924-1927

$220-280 CO

A late 1920s Waterman's 52V Ripple, blue and yellow rippled hard rubber lever filler with Waterman's Ideal No.2 nib with matching feed, mint condition with original price sticker.

$300-500 CO

A 1930s Waterman's 94, 'Mahogany' marbled celluloid lever filler with medium Waterman's Ideal nib, excellent condition.

$100-150 CO

A Waterman's Ink-Vue, 'Copper Ray' celluloid double-action lever filler with rigid Waterman's Ideal nib, good condition with sealed crack.

1935-1939

$150-200 CO

A rare Waterman's 'Hundred Year Pen', ribbed jet black celluloid lever filler with fine Waterman's Hundred Year Pen nib, near mint condition.

This version was only produced during the first year of production, from 1940 the bands moved from the barrel to the cap.

1939

$220-280 CO

Other American

A Mabie Todd & Co. Swan Eternal S.F. E444, mottled red and black hard rubber lever filler with medium Eternal No.4 nib, very good to excellent condition.

c1920

$120-180 CO

A rare Mabie Todd & Co Swan 54 RR Eternal, red hard rubber ribbon ringtop lever filler with medium Swan No.4 Eternal nib, very good condition.

c1925

$120-180 CO

A Mabie Todd & Co Swan 44 ETN, red and brown mottled celluloid lever filler and Swan Eternal No.4 nib, excellent condition.
This color is very rare in celluloid.

c1927

$180-220 CO

A late 1920s Mabie Todd & Co 54 ETN pen, pearl and black veined and marbled celluloid ringtop lever filler with fine Swan Enternal 4 nib, very good condition with mild ambering.

$100-150 CO

A rare Mabie Todd & Co 54-ETN, lapis lazuli blue celluloid lever filler with medium-fine Swan No.4 Eternal nib, excellent condition.

c1928

$120-180 CO

A Mabie Todd & Co Blackbird BB 2-46 pen, 'Oriental Blue' (lapis blue) and gold-bronze marbled celluloid lever-filler with fine Blackbird nib, near mint condition.

c1934

$320-380 CO

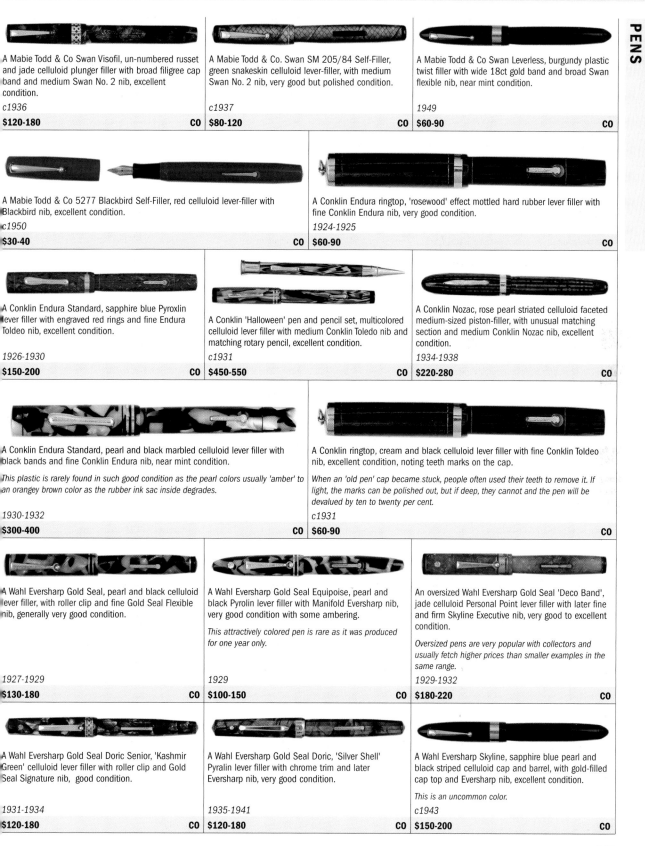

A Mabie Todd & Co Swan Visofil, un-numbered russet and jade celluloid plunger filler with broad filigree cap band and medium Swan No. 2 nib, excellent condition.

c1936

$120-180   CO

A Mabie Todd & Co. Swan SM 205/84 Self-Filler, green snakeskin celluloid lever-filler, with medium Swan No. 2 nib, very good but polished condition.

c1937

$80-120   CO

A Mabie Todd & Co Swan Leverless, burgundy plastic twist filler with wide 18ct gold band and broad Swan flexible nib, near mint condition.

1949

$60-90   CO

A Mabie Todd & Co 5277 Blackbird Self-Filler, red celluloid lever-filler with Blackbird nib, excellent condition.

c1950

$30-40   CO

A Conklin Endura ringtop, 'rosewood' effect mottled hard rubber lever filler with fine Conklin Endura nib, very good condition.

1924-1925

$60-90   CO

A Conklin Endura Standard, sapphire blue Pyroxlin lever filler with engraved red rings and fine Endura Toldeo nib, excellent condition.

1926-1930

$150-200   CO

A Conklin 'Halloween' pen and pencil set, multicolored celluloid lever filler with medium Conklin Toledo nib and matching rotary pencil, excellent condition.

c1931

$450-550   CO

A Conklin Nozac, rose pearl striated celluloid faceted medium-sized piston-filler, with unusual matching section and medium Conklin Nozac nib, excellent condition.

1934-1938

$220-280   CO

A Conklin Endura Standard, pearl and black marbled celluloid lever filler with black bands and fine Conklin Endura nib, near mint condition.

This plastic is rarely found in such good condition as the pearl colors usually 'amber' to an orangey brown color as the rubber ink sac inside degrades.

1930-1932

$300-400   CO

A Conklin ringtop, cream and black celluloid lever filler with fine Conklin Toldeo nib, excellent condition, noting teeth marks on the cap.

When an 'old pen' cap became stuck, people often used their teeth to remove it. If light, the marks can be polished out, but if deep, they cannot and the pen will be devalued by ten to twenty per cent.

c1931

$60-90   CO

A Wahl Eversharp Gold Seal, pearl and black celluloid lever filler, with roller clip and fine Gold Seal Flexible nib, generally very good condition.

1927-1929

$130-180   CO

A Wahl Eversharp Gold Seal Equipoise, pearl and black Pyrolin lever filler with Manifold Eversharp nib, very good condition with some ambering.

This attractively colored pen is rare as it was produced for one year only.

1929

$100-150   CO

An oversized Wahl Eversharp Gold Seal 'Deco Band', jade celluloid Personal Point lever filler with later fine and firm Skyline Executive nib, very good to excellent condition.

Oversized pens are very popular with collectors and usually fetch higher prices than smaller examples in the same range.

1929-1932

$180-220   CO

A Wahl Eversharp Gold Seal Doric Senior, 'Kashmir Green' celluloid lever filler with roller clip and Gold Seal Signature nib, good condition.

1931-1934

$120-180   CO

A Wahl Eversharp Gold Seal Doric, 'Silver Shell' Pyralin lever filler with chrome trim and later Eversharp nib, very good condition.

1935-1941

$120-180   CO

A Wahl Eversharp Skyline, sapphire blue pearl and black striped celluloid cap and barrel, with gold-filled cap top and Eversharp nib, excellent condition.

This is an uncommon color.

c1943

$150-200   CO

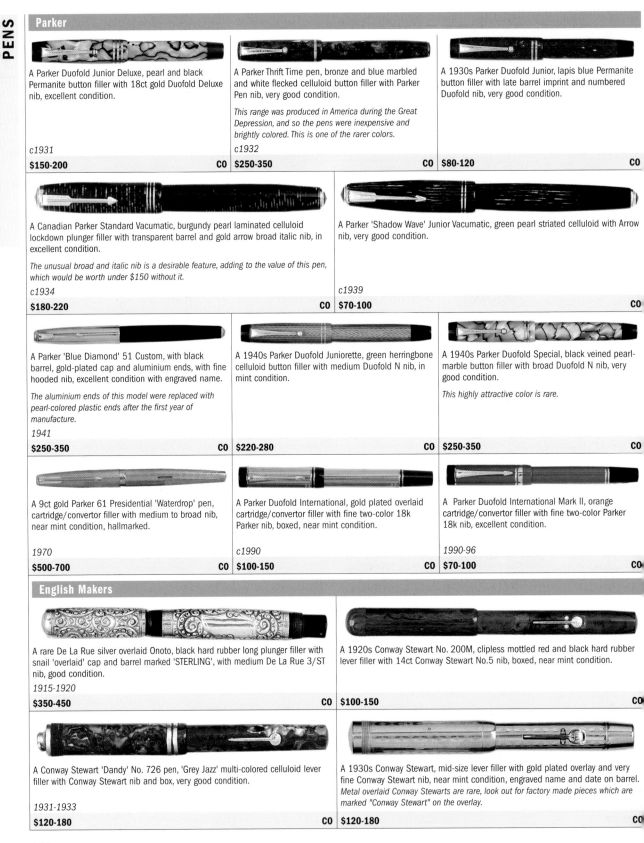

Parker

A Parker Duofold Junior Deluxe, pearl and black Permanite button filler with 18ct gold Duofold Deluxe nib, excellent condition.

c1931

$150-200　CO

A Parker Thrift Time pen, bronze and blue marbled and white flecked celluloid button filler with Parker Pen nib, very good condition.

This range was produced in America during the Great Depression, and so the pens were inexpensive and brightly colored. This is one of the rarer colors.

c1932

$250-350　CO

A 1930s Parker Duofold Junior, lapis blue Permanite button filler with late barrel imprint and numbered Duofold nib, very good condition.

$80-120　CO

A Canadian Parker Standard Vacumatic, burgundy pearl laminated celluloid lockdown plunger filler with transparent barrel and gold arrow broad italic nib, in excellent condition.

The unusual broad and italic nib is a desirable feature, adding to the value of this pen, which would be worth under $150 without it.

c1934

$180-220　CO

A Parker 'Shadow Wave' Junior Vacumatic, green pearl striated celluloid with Arrow nib, very good condition.

c1939

$70-100　CO

A Parker 'Blue Diamond' 51 Custom, with black barrel, gold-plated cap and aluminium ends, with fine hooded nib, excellent condition with engraved name.

The aluminium ends of this model were replaced with pearl-colored plastic ends after the first year of manufacture.

1941

$250-350　CO

A 1940s Parker Duofold Juniorette, green herringbone celluloid button filler with medium Duofold N nib, in mint condition.

$220-280　CO

A 1940s Parker Duofold Special, black veined pearl-marble button filler with broad Duofold N nib, very good condition.

This highly attractive color is rare.

$250-350　CO

A 9ct gold Parker 61 Presidential 'Waterdrop' pen, cartridge/convertor filler with medium to broad nib, near mint condition, hallmarked.

1970

$500-700　CO

A Parker Duofold International, gold plated overlaid cartridge/convertor filler with fine two-color 18k Parker nib, boxed, near mint condition.

c1990

$100-150　CO

A Parker Duofold International Mark II, orange cartridge/convertor filler with fine two-color Parker 18k nib, excellent condition.

1990-96

$70-100　CO

English Makers

A rare De La Rue silver overlaid Onoto, black hard rubber long plunger filler with snail 'overlaid' cap and barrel marked 'STERLING', with medium De La Rue 3/ST nib, good condition.

1915-1920

$350-450　CO

A 1920s Conway Stewart No. 200M, clipless mottled red and black hard rubber lever filler with 14ct Conway Stewart No.5 nib, boxed, near mint condition.

$100-150　CO

A Conway Stewart 'Dandy' No. 726 pen, 'Grey Jazz' multi-colored celluloid lever filler with Conway Stewart nib and box, very good condition.

1931-1933

$120-180　CO

A 1930s Conway Stewart, mid-size lever filler with gold plated overlay and very fine Conway Stewart nib, near mint condition, engraved name and date on barrel.
Metal overlaid Conway Stewarts are rare, look out for factory made pieces which are marked "Conway Stewart" on the overlay.

$120-180　CO

Montblanc

A Montblanc 132 OBB Meisterstück, black celluloid piston filler with medium two-color 4810 nib, excellent condition.

1938-1940

$250-350   CO

A Danish Montblanc Masterpiece, coral red celluloid push-knob filler with fine 4810 M nib, excellent condition.

1937-1947

$300-500   CO

A Montblanc 332 OB, black celluloid piston filler with four engraved cap bands, chrome-plated teardrop clip and broad oblique tin Montblanc nib, in very good condition.

The OB relates to the size of the nib - oblique and broad.

1943-1946

$80-120   CO

A Montblanc 134 Meisterstück, black celluloid piston filler with two-color 4810 nib, in good condition.

1947-1948

$100-150   CO

A Montblanc 242G, black celluloid piston filler with Montblanc nib.

1950-1954

$120-180   CO

A Montblanc 144 Meisterstück, black celluloid piston filler with two color 4810 nib, good condition, cap bands loose.

1949-1960

$100-150   CO

Other German Makers

A Pelikan 100, jade green celluloid barrel sleeve piston filler with fine oblique Pelikan 'star' nib, in good condition.

This rare, early Pelikan can be recognized by the color of the barrel, two pairs of air vents in the cap and the early filling knob at the bottom of the pen.

c1931

$150-200   CO

A late 1930s Pelikan 100, silver and black striated celluloid barrel sleeve piston filler with fine 14K Pelikan nib, excellent condition.

$220-280   CO

A 1940s Pelikan 100N, gray-black marbled celluloid barrel sleeve piston filler with rolled gold trim and medium Pelikan .585 nib, very good condition.

$180-220   CO

A 1940s Pelikan 100N, gray-black striated barrel sleeve piston filler, with chrome trim and fine oblique Pelikan nib, very good condition.

$220-280   CO

An early 1950s Pelikan 400, tortoiseshell and brown striated celluloid piston filler with medium Pelikan nib, excellent condition.

$80-120   CO

A Pelikan 400 'for red ink', tortoiseshell and brown striped celluloid piston filler with extra fine 14K Pelikan nib and cap with red celluloid Pelikan logo.

The red cap top is a scarce and unusual feature indicating this pen was used for red ink. Similar Pelikan 400s without it are worth less than half this value.

c1953

$220-280   CO

A rare Pelikan 520N, plastic piston-filler with guilloche decorated rolled gold cap and broad nib with Pelikan logo, near mint condition.

This pen is rare as it was produced for less than a year.

c1956

$120-180   CO

A Soennecken 120 BBS, black lined blue pearl celluloid button filler, with double broad, semi-oblique Soennecken nib, excellent condition.

c1947

$150-200   CO

A Soennecken 111 Extra, gray pearl herringbone celluloid piston filler, with medium nib.

c1954

$250-350   CO

A 1950s Soennecken 112, red pearl striated celluloid piston filler, with medium Soennecken nib, very good condition.

$60-90   CO

Percussion Pistols

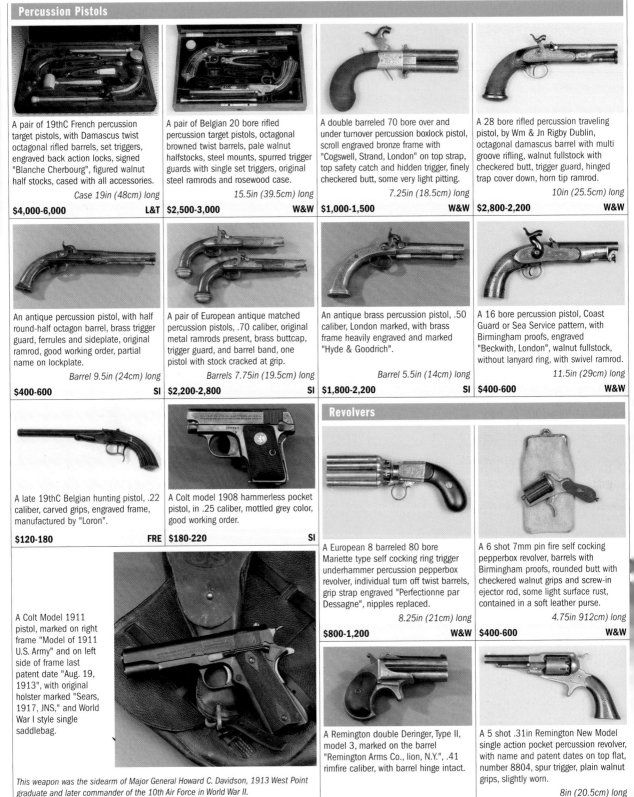

A pair of 19thC French percussion target pistols, with Damascus twist octagonal rifled barrels, set triggers, engraved back action locks, signed "Blanche Cherbourg", figured walnut half stocks, cased with all accessories.

Case 19in (48cm) long

$4,000-6,000   **L&T**

A pair of Belgian 20 bore rifled percussion target pistols, octagonal browned twist barrels, pale walnut halfstocks, steel mounts, spurred trigger guards with single set triggers, original steel ramrods and rosewood case.

15.5in (39.5cm) long

$2,500-3,000   **W&W**

A double barreled 70 bore over and under turnover percussion boxlock pistol, scroll engraved bronze frame with "Cogswell, Strand, London" on top strap, top safety catch and hidden trigger, finely checkered butt, some very light pitting.

7.25in (18.5cm) long

$1,000-1,500   **W&W**

A 28 bore rifled percussion traveling pistol, by Wm & Jn Rigby Dublin, octagonal damascus barrel with multi groove rifling, walnut fullstock with checkered butt, trigger guard, hinged trap cover down, horn tip ramrod.

10in (25.5cm) long

$2,800-2,200   **W&W**

An antique percussion pistol, with half round-half octagon barrel, brass trigger guard, ferrules and sideplate, original ramrod, good working order, partial name on lockplate.

Barrel 9.5in (24cm) long

$400-600   **SI**

A pair of European antique matched percussion pistols, .70 caliber, original metal ramrods present, brass buttcap, trigger guard, and barrel band, one pistol with stock cracked at grip.

Barrels 7.75in (19.5cm) long

$2,200-2,800   **SI**

An antique brass percussion pistol, .50 caliber, London marked, with brass frame heavily engraved and marked "Hyde & Goodrich".

Barrel 5.5in (14cm) long

$1,800-2,200   **SI**

A 16 bore percussion pistol, Coast Guard or Sea Service pattern, with Birmingham proofs, engraved "Beckwith, London", walnut fullstock, without lanyard ring, with swivel ramrod.

11.5in (29cm) long

$400-600   **W&W**

A late 19thC Belgian hunting pistol, .22 caliber, carved grips, engraved frame, manufactured by "Loron".

$120-180   **FRE**

A Colt model 1908 hammerless pocket pistol, in .25 caliber, mottled grey color, good working order.

$180-220   **SI**

Revolvers

A European 8 barreled 80 bore Mariette type self cocking ring trigger underhammer percussion pepperbox revolver, individual turn off twist barrels, grip strap engraved "Perfectionne par Dessagne", nipples replaced.

8.25in (21cm) long

$800-1,200   **W&W**

A 6 shot 7mm pin fire self cocking pepperbox revolver, barrels with Birmingham proofs, rounded butt with checkered walnut grips and screw-in ejector rod, some light surface rust, contained in a soft leather purse.

4.75in 912cm) long

$400-600   **W&W**

A Colt Model 1911 pistol, marked on right frame "Model of 1911 U.S. Army" and on left side of frame last patent date "Aug. 19, 1913", with original holster marked "Sears, 1917, JNS," and World War I style single saddlebag.

This weapon was the sidearm of Major General Howard C. Davidson, 1913 West Point graduate and later commander of the 10th Air Force in World War II.

$6,000-9,000   **SI**

A Remington double Deringer, Type II, model 3, marked on the barrel "Remington Arms Co., lion, N.Y.", .41 rimfire caliber, with barrel hinge intact.

$600-900   **SI**

A 5 shot .31in Remington New Model single action pocket percussion revolver, with name and patent dates on top flat, number 8804, spur trigger, plain walnut grips, slightly worn.

8in (20.5cm) long

$700-1,000   **W&W**

An antique Remington model 1875 Army revolver, in .44 caliber, bluing on loading lever, military proof marked, original grips show some wood shrinkage, with trace of cartouche.

$800-1,200   SI

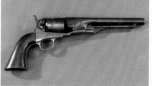

An antique Colt model 1860 Army revolver, with military proof marks, good scene on cylinder, one replaced screw in frame, some original blue on frame, original walnut grips with cartouche.

1862

$600-900   SI

A late 19thC Jacob Rupertus Spur trigger revolver, .22 caliber, seven shot revolving barrel, serial no. 2544.

$300-400   FRE

A Remington new model revolver, .44 caliber, lacquered overall.

$700-1,000   FRE

A cased 6 shot .44in rim fire Webley double action revolver, slightly tapered round barrel, engraved "Thomas Bissell, 75 Tooley Street, London", compound ejector lever on barrel, upper butt strap engraved "414".

9in (23cm) long

$1,200-1,800   W&W

A cased 5 shot 80 bore 2nd Model Tranter self cocking double trigger percussion revolver, barrel engraved "Veisey & Son", hinged rammer on left, checkered walnut butt, 80 percent of original finish.

9in (23cm) long

$2,500-3,000   W&W

A cased 5 shot 54 bore Adams Model 1851 self cocking percussion revolver, barrel engraved "Deane Adams & Deane, 30 King William St, London Bridge", engraved "Adams' Patent No 8717 R", checkered walnut butt.

11in (28cm) long

$3,000-4,000   W&W

A cased rare 5 shot 120 bore Tranter's Patent double action percussion revolver, engraved "Thos Williams, South Castle St, Liverpool" and "No 15957T", stamped "Tranter's Patent", trigger guard, rammer, checkered walnut butt.

8.5in (21.5cm) long

$3,000-4,000   W&W

A fine cased 6 shot 120 bore self cocking bar hammer percussion pepperbox revolver, color hardened barrels, butt strap engraved "J Dickson & Son, 60 Princes St, Edinburgh", plain walnut grips, mahogany case.

7in (18cm) long

$3,000-4,000   W&W

A fine cased 4 shot 46 bore self cocking bar hammer percussion pepperbox revolver, by Needler Hull, mirror blued barrels, color hardened frame, rounded checkered walnut butt, in mahogany case.

$3,000-4,000   W&W

A scarce 6 shot 7mm pin fire 'Apache' combined revolver/knuckleduster/dagger, folding wavy blade, the German silver frame stamped "L. Dolne, Invur", folding trigger, some wear to blade.

9in (22.75cm) long

$2,200-2,800   W&W

A Colt model 1901 New Army revolver, .38 calibre, wood grips show wear, barrel shows wear and abrasions.

Barrel 5in (12.5cm) long

$180-220   SI

A Webley mark VI revolver, .455 caliber, made in England, patent date 1918.

$150-200   SI

A German Luger, made by DWM, in 9mm caliber with original holster, safety marked Gesichert.

1921

$700-1,000   SI

A late 19thC military cadet hat and sword, each with "PMA" initials, Model 1860 field and staff sword with cast brass hilt, metal scabbard and etched blade, together with a large albumen photograph of cadet in uniform and two civilians, framed.

Initials "PMA" denote the Pennsylvania Military Academy, originally located in West Chester, PA, later moving to Chester to become the Pennsylvania Military College and eventually Widener University in the latter 20th century.

$600-800   **FRE**

A US Navy model 1852 officer's sword, made for Jacob Reed's Sons, Philadelphia, gilt brass hilt marked "U.S.N.", rayskin grips.

c1900   *37in (94cm) long*

$800-1,200   **FRE**

An Edward VIII Diplomat's dress sword, Wilkinson blade, etched and polished and crowned EVIIIR cipher, beaded hilt and scabbard mounts, leather scabbard.

32in (81cm) long

$400-600   **W&W**

French trophies of war, captured by Sir David Milne, comprising a senior French naval officer's saber and scabbard, with a decorated stirrup-hilt of ormolu, the hilt à l'allemande, a curved blade, having a clipped point and a false edge, 8.25in (21cm) long, in scabbard embossed in high relief with Classical and martial trophies, and a senior French naval officer's waist-belt, c1800.

Sabers with hilts of this style are derived from sabers carried by hussars in the army of the Austrian empire in the mid-18thC and as such are known as 'à l'allemande' in France. French naval officers of the period 1792-1814 were ordered to carry sabers when on board ship, reserving their épées for shore duties. It is likely that this saber was surrendered to Milne by a French ship's captain.

$18,000-22,000 (set)   **L&T**

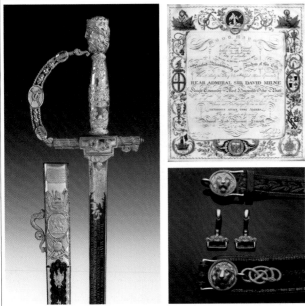

A George III presentation 100 guineas sword, belt and Freedom scroll, 1816, conferring the Freedom of the City of London, to Sir David Milne, the sword mounted in ormolu, the grip probably in gold, a straight bladed sword of spadroon type in an ormolu mounted scabbard with dark blue velvet panels, the polished grip bears, in relief, the Arms of the City of London and those of Sir David Milne, and having pendant from them the badges of the KCB and the Dutch Royal Military Order of William, by Richard Teed (1756-1816); the handwritten and illuminated vellum scroll conferring Freedom of the City of London, signed "J. Huxley Sculpt."

The sword and freedom of The City of London were presented to Rear Admiral Sir David Milne in September 1816 by the Guildhall of The City of London "in testimony of the esteem & gratitude of this court for the zeal bravery & talent display'd by him in the victorious attack upon Algiers by the fleet under the commd. of Adml. Lord Visct. Exmouth, on the 27th of August last".

Sword 31in (79cm) long

$120,000-150,000   **L&T**

A collection of Civil War militaria, comprising drumsticks and documents, relating to Henry R. Wentzel, musician in Captain Steele's Company H, 175 regiment, Pennsylvania Draft Militia, including a tin type showing Wentzel in his musician's frock, his drumsticks and manuscript material including his discharge papers dated August 1863 and a letter in which he describes his daily duties as a drummer.

Henry R. Wentzel was born in Montgomery County PA. A carpenter in private life, he served nine months in the Infantry.

$1,500-2,000   **FRE**

An officer's blue cloth peaked forage cap, of The 97th (Earl of Ulster's) Regiment.

$220-280 **W&W**

A scarce Officer's blue cloth peaked forage cap, of the Cambridgeshire Militia.

$400-600 **W&W**

An early style Officer's red cloth pill box hat, of the 15th (The King's) Hussars.

$300-400 **W&W**

A good Officer's blue cloth pill box hat, of the 7th (The Queen's Own Hussars), in gilt japanned tin case inscribed "William Paget-Tomkinson Esq.".

$400-600 **W&W**

A scarce Officer's scarlet cloth pill box hat, of the 10th (D of Cambridge's Own) Bengal Lancers.

$300-400 **W&W**

An Officer's American style grey cloth kepi, of the Norfolk Rifle Volunteers.

$350-400 **W&W**

An other Rank's American style grey cloth kepi, of the Norfolk Rifle Volunteers.

$300-400 **W&W**

A Croatian SS Fez.

$1,000-1,500 **W&W**

An interesting lightweight summer slouch hat, of the 1st Royal Guernsey Light Infantry Militia.

$220-280 **W&W**

Badges & Insignia

A collection of American militaria, including a boxed pair of gilt metal and gold bullion Civil War epaulettes, with the rosette of the 26th Infantry, a model 1860 Light Cavalry Saber, by Ames Co., Mtts, dated 1860; a carte de visite showing Andrew Jackson Ward in his cavalry canteen, with original strap inscribed with his name.

Provenance: Jackson Ward served in the 2nd Regiment, New York Veteran Cavalry.

$1,800-2,200 **FRE**

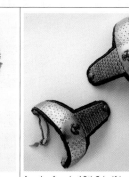

A pair of pre-1855 officer's full dress epaulettes of The 64th (2nd Staffordshire) Regiment.

$220-280 **W&W**

A pair of early 19thC half hoop Light Infantry officer's wings.

$300-400 **W&W**

A Victorian officer's pouch and belt, of The Prince of Wales's Own Bengal Lancers.

$350-400 **W&W**

A mid-Victorian officer's gilt waist belt, of the 2nd Madras Native Infantry.
c1850

$300-400 **W&W**

A pre-1881 officer's rectangular shoulder belt plate, of The 78th Highland Regiment (or Ross-Shire Buffs).

$700-1,000   **W&W**

A Victorian officer's gilt and silver plated helmet plate, of The York and Lancaster Regiment.

$300-400   **W&W**

A Victorian officer's gilt and silver plated rectangular belt plate, of The Highland Light Infantry.

$350-400   **W&W**

A late Victorian officer's silver plaid brooch, of The Gordon Highlanders, hallmarked for Edinburgh, 1881.

$700-1,000   **W&W**

An officer's gilt and silver-plated rectangular shoulder belt plate, of The Gordon Highlanders.

$300-400   **W&W**

A post 1902 gilt and silver plated rectangular shoulder belt plate, of the King's Own Scottish Borderers.

$700-1,000   **W&W**

Powder Flasks

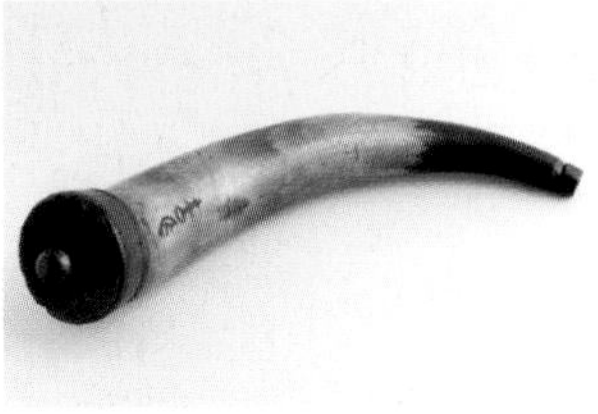

A scarce Danish gunner's cow horn powder flask, of King Christian Vth (1670-1699).

13.75in (35cm) long

$700-1,000   **W&W**

A gunner's powder horn.

13.75in (35cm) long

$300-400   **W&W**

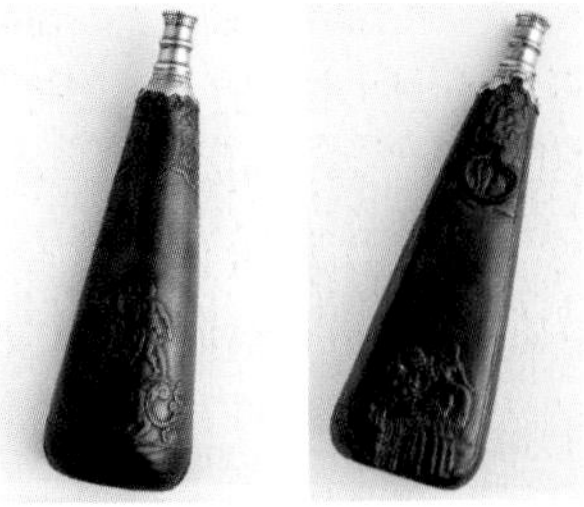

An 18thC European silver mounted carved horn powder flask, carved all over with figures, animals and shield.

7.75in (20cm) long

$300-400   **W&W**

A scarce European powder flask charger, japanned tin body with glazed port hole.

9in (23cm) long

$220-280   **W&W**

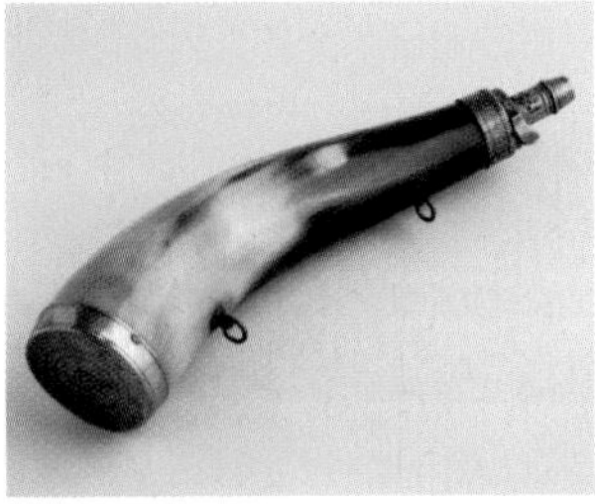

A European brass-mounted cow horn powder flask.

10in (25cm) long

$60-90   **W&W**

A European flattened cow horn powder flask.

8.25in (21cm) long

$60-90   **W&W**

A Danish cow horn military powder flask.

10.75in (27.5cm) long

$120-180   **W&W**

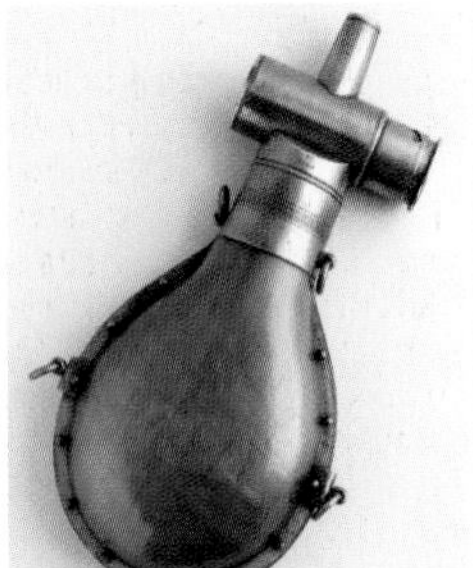

An Austrian pressed lanthorn powder flask.

8in (20.5cm) long

$120-180   **W&W**

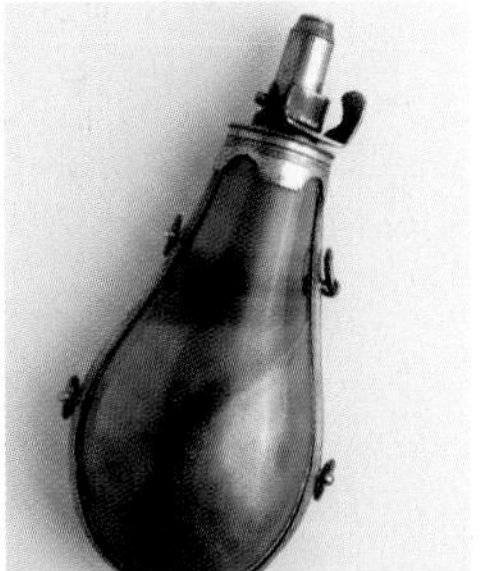

A European pressed lanthorn flask.

7.5in (19cm) long

$70-100   **W&W**

A French copper pistol powder flask.

4.75in (12cm) long

$400-600   **W&W**

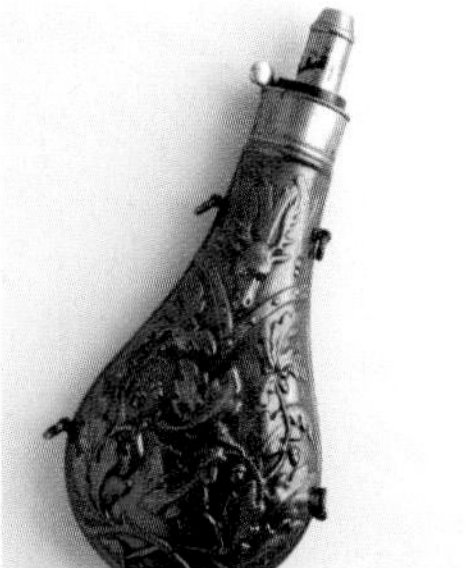

A large embossed copper powder flask.

9in (23cm) long

$150-200   **W&W**

Miscellaneous

An early 19thC stonebow 'prod', by W Adkin of Woodbridge (Suffolk), walnut stock, hinged loading lever, lock with signed cover, 'Pitch Fork' rearsight, engraved steel furniture, checkered grip, replaced cords.

c1800   30in (76.5cm) long

$1,000-1,500   **W&W**

A scarce Indian combined pistol and axe, probably 18thC, small steel head with thick peen, fixed pan for hand ignition, long rectangular section steel handle with bud shaped finial, good age patina overall.

15.5in (39.5cm) long

$350-400   **W&W**

An 18thC brass framed powder tester 'eprouvette', hand ignited with tall pan, wheel engraved as graduated one to twelve with brass pointer.

5.25in (13.5cm) long

$600-900   **W&W**

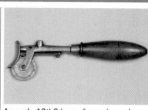

An early 19thC brass framed powder tester "eprouvette", hand ignited with tall pan, wheel engraved from one to seven and graduated in eighths, turned wooden handle.

8in (20.5cm) long

$350-400   **W&W**

A late 18thC European bronze barreled model cannon, barrel with swollen muzzle, chiseled dolphin lifting loops, baluster cascabel, on split trail with 8 spoked wheels, iron shod with iron mounts, traces of polychrome decoration overall to carriage.

Barrel 14.25in (36cm) long

$800-1,200   **W&W**

A late 18thC European bronze barreled model cannon, barrel 12.5in, with turned reinforces, swollen muzzle, chiseled dolphin lifting loops, baluster cascabel. On its split trail with 8 spoked wheels, iron shod with iron mounts, traces of polychrome decoration overall to carriage.

Barrel 12.5in (32cm) long

$1,200-1,800   **W&W**

A well made 1/6th scale model of an infantry three pounder field cannon, brass barrel on steel mounted wooden carriage with multi spoked steel shod wheels, capstan elevating screw, long trail stamped with Woolwich Rotunda arsenal inventory mark of a crown above "MA 6219".

19in (48.5cm) long

$1,800-2,200   **W&W**

A 19thC well made model of an Armstrong muzzle loading Coastal Defence gun, steel multi stage barrel, capstan elevating screw, on its fixed iron carriage, sliding on its inclined and traversing platform, on a pair of rails screwed to their mahogany base.

Barrel 17.5in (45cm) long

$1,800-2,200   **W&W**

A WWII Japanese military 'body flag', silk with handwritten characters around a red orb, together with a WWII period woollen French national flag.

$180-220 (for the two)   **FRE**

A National Guard cartridge box, with "Frazier's patent" stampings to inside, wooden cartridge block and brass "NG" plate for National Guard.

$150-220   **FRE**

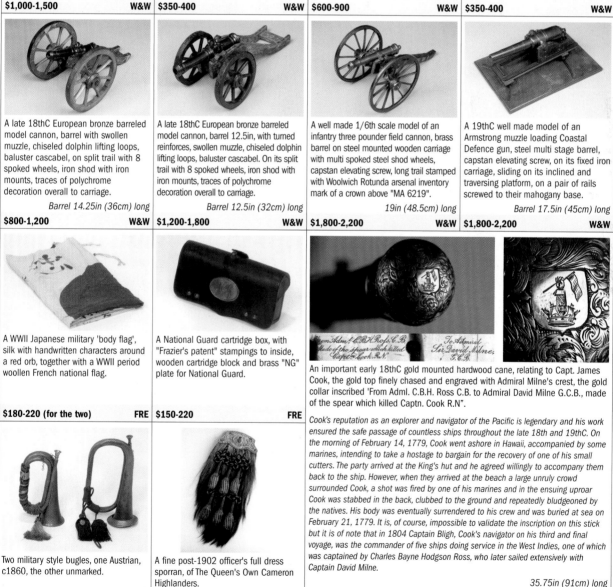

An important early 18thC gold mounted hardwood cane, relating to Capt. James Cook, the gold top finely chased and engraved with Admiral Milne's crest, the gold collar inscribed 'From Adml. C.B.H. Ross C.B. to Admiral David Milne G.C.B., made of the spear which killed Captn. Cook R.N'.

Cook's reputation as an explorer and navigator of the Pacific is legendary and his work ensured the safe passage of countless ships throughout the late 18th and 19thC. On the morning of February 14, 1779, Cook went ashore in Hawaii, accompanied by some marines, intending to take a hostage to bargain for the recovery of one of his small cutters. The party arrived at the King's hut and he agreed willingly to accompany them back to the ship. However, when they arrived at the beach a large unruly crowd surrounded Cook, a shot was fired by one of his marines and in the ensuing uproar Cook was stabbed in the back, clubbed to the ground and repeatedly bludgeoned by the natives. His body was eventually surrendered to his crew and was buried at sea on February 21, 1779. It is, of course, impossible to validate the inscription on this stick but it is of note that in 1804 Captain Bligh, Cook's navigator on his third and final voyage, was the commander of five ships doing service in the West Indies, one of which was captained by Charles Bayne Hodgson Ross, who later sailed extensively with Captain David Milne.

35.75in (91cm) long

Two military style bugles, one Austrian, c1860, the other unmarked.

$280-320 (for the two)   **FRE**

A fine post-1902 officer's full dress sporran, of The Queen's Own Cameron Highlanders.

$2,200-2,800   **W&W**

$200,000-300,000   **L&T**

474

Carltonware

A Carlton Ware 'Red Devil' bowl, pattern number "3765", printed, original paper label.

9.25in (23.5cm) high

$1,500-2,000　　　　　　**WW**

A Carlton Ware single-handled 'Red Devil' vase, pattern number printed mark "3765", remains of paper label.

7in (18cm) high

$3,500-4,000　　　　　　**WW**

A Carlton Ware 'Flower and Falling Leaf' bowl, pattern number "3948", printed and painted marks.

8in (20.5cm) diam

$700-1,000　　　　　　**WW**

A Carlton Ware glazed earthenware luster bowl, with transfer mark, few scrapes to glaze.

3.75in (9.5cm) high

$120-180　　　　　　**FRE**

A Carlton Ware 'Bell' vase, pattern number "3738", printed and painted marks.

4.75in (12cm) high

$800-1,200　　　　　　**WW**

A pair of Carlton Ware painted and glazed earthenware vases, transfer marks.

8in (20cm) high

$400-600　　　　　　**FRE**

A Carlton Ware 'Jagged Bouquet' vase, pattern number "3457", printed and painted marks.

6in (15.5cm) high

$500-700　　　　　　**WW**

A Carlton Ware 'Tutankhamen' tomb jar and cover, printed and enameled with hieroglyphics in gilt and enamels on a blue ground, printed Tutankhamen mark "2711".

12.5in (32cm) high

$5,000-6,000　　　　　　**WW**

A Carlton Ware lusterware 'Armand' vase, of tapering cylindrical form with canted angles, printed and painted in gilt and colors with exotic moths on a pale blue ground, printed and painted marks "2134/136".

7.75in (19.5cm) high

$220-280　　　　　　**L&T**

Clarice Cliff

Two views of a Clarice Cliff Bizarre Bonjour 'May Avenue' vase, printed mark, minor faint hairline to top rim.

$5,000-7,000　　　　　　**WW**

A Clarice Cliff 'Coral Firs' vase, pattern 613, printed mark, restored base.

8.25in (21cm) high

$1,500-2,000　　　　　　**WW**

A Clarice Cliff Bizarre 'Coral Firs' vase, pattern 565, printed marks.

6.25in (16cm) high

$700-1,000 WW

A Clarice Cliff Bizarre 'Daffodil Coral Firs' vase, pattern 450, printed mark.

13.25in (33.5cm) high

$800-1,200 WW

A Clarice Cliff 'Secrets' vase, pattern 358, unmarked.

8.25in (21cm) high

$700-1,000 WW

A Clarice Cliff Fantasque Bizarre 'Secrets' vase, 342, printed mark.

8in (20cm) high

$700-1,000 WW

A Clarice Cliff Bizarre 'Orange Secrets' vase, pattern 196, printed mark.

6.3in (16cm) high

$1,000-1,500 WW

A Clarice Cliff 'House and Bridge' pattern vase.

c1931-35   7in (18cm) diam

$3,000-4,000 SCG

A Clarice Cliff Fantasque Bizarre 'House and Bridge' goblet vase, pattern 363, printed mark, crack to rim.

6.25in (16cm) high

$700-1,000 WW

A Clarice Cliff Bizarre 'Windbells' pattern cylindrical vase, printed mark, Louis Meisel paper label.

9in (21cm) high

$400-600 WW

A Clarice Cliff Fantasque Bizarre single-handled Isis 'Windbells' vase, printed mark.

10in (25cm) high

$3,000-4,000 WW

A Clarice Cliff Tube 'Gloria Autumn' vase, variation on pattern 464, printed mark.

8.25in (21cm) high

$1,800-2,200 WW

A Clarice Cliff Bizarre 'Gloria Crocus' globe vase, 370, printed and painted mark.

6in (15.5cm) high

$1,200-1,800 WW

A Clarice Cliff Isis 'Anemone' vase, printed and molded mark.

10.25in (26cm) high

$320-380　　**L&T**

A Clarice Cliff Bizarre 'Applique Palermo' vase, 230, printed mark.

6in (15.5cm) high

$2,200-2,800　　**WW**

A Clarice Cliff 'Floreat' vase, Meiping shape.

c1929-30　　*12in (30.5cm) high*

$2,200-2,800　　**SCG**

A Clarice Cliff Fantasque Bizarre 'Gibraltar' vase, 195, printed mark.

8.75in (22cm) high

$1,500-2,000　　**WW**

A Clarice Cliff Bizarre Bonjour 'Green Japan' vase, printed mark, restored.

6.75in (17cm) high

$700-1,000　　**WW**

A Clarice Cliff Bizarre Isis single-handled 'Inspiration Hollyhocks' vase, printed and painted marks.

10in (25cm) high

$1,500-2,000　　**WW**

A Clarice Cliff 'Latona Tree' stepped vase, pattern 369A, painted "Latona" mark, Louis Meisel sale paper label.

7.75in (19.5cm) high

$1,200-1,800　　**WW**

A Clarice Cliff Fantasque Bizarre 'Lily' vase, pattern 362, printed mark.

8.25in (21cm) high

$700-1,000　　**WW**

A Clarice Cliff Fantasque Bizarre 'Moonlight' vase, pattern 366, printed mark and minor paint flakes.

6in (15.5cm) high

$2,200-2,800　　**WW**

A Clarice Cliff Fantasque Bizarre 'Pastel Autumn' vase, pattern 212, printed mark.

5.5in (14cm) high

$1,500-2,000　　**WW**

A Clarice Cliff Bizarre 'Sunray' vase, pattern 342, printed mark, restored.

8in (20cm) high

$1,800-2,200　　**WW**

A Clarice Cliff Fantasque 'Umbrellas and Rain' vase, pattern 186, printed mark, minor glaze loss.

8.5in (21.5cm) high

$600-900　　**WW**

A Clarice Cliff large Fantasque Bizarre Coronet 'Butterfly' pattern jug, printed mark.

8in (20cm) high

$1,800-2,200   WW

A rare Clarice Cliff Fantasque Bizarre 'Oranges and Lemons' pattern conical sugar sifter, printed and painted mark.

5.5in (14cm) high

$3,000-4,000   WW

A rare Clarice Cliff Fantasque Bizarre 'Solitude' pattern conical sugar sifter, printed marks.

5.5in (14cm) high

$2,200-2,800   WW

A Clarice Cliff Bizarre 'Moonlight' pattern conical sugar sifter, printed mark, tiny chip to base of rim.

5.5in (14cm) high

$1,200-1,800   WW

A Clarice Cliff Bizarre 'Secrets' pattern conical sugar sifter, printed mark.

5.5in (14cm) high

$1,200-1,800   WW

A Clarice Cliff Bizarre 'Coral Firs' pattern conical sugar sifter, printed mark.

5.5in (14cm) high

$1,200-1,800   WW

A Clarice Cliff 'Flower Tree' pattern conical sugar sifter, printed mark.

5.5in (14cm) high

$700-1,000   WW

A Clarice Cliff 'Forest Glen' pattern conical sugar sifter, printed mark, restored.

5.5in (14cm) high

$1,200-1,800   WW

A Clarice Cliff Bizarre 'Killarney' conical sugar sifter, printed mark.

5.5in (14cm) high

$1,500-2,000   WW

A Clarice Cliff 'Red Roofs' pattern conical sugar sifter, printed marks.

5.25in (13.5cm) high

$2,500-3,000   L&T

A Clarice Cliff Bizarre Bonjour 'Idyll' pattern sugar sifter, printed mark, minor restoration to vents.

5in (13cm) high

$700-1,000   WW

A rare Clarice Cliff Bizarre 'Devon' pattern plate, printed mark.

8.5in (21.5cm) diam

$700-1,000   WW

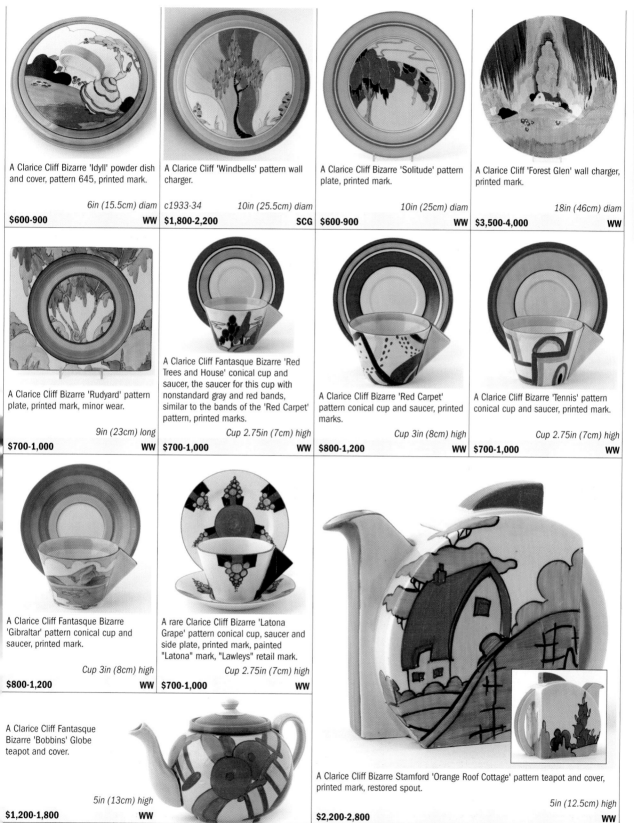

A Clarice Cliff Bizarre 'Idyll' powder dish and cover, pattern 645, printed mark.

6in (15.5cm) diam

$600-900   WW

A Clarice Cliff 'Windbells' pattern wall charger.

c1933-34   10in (25.5cm) diam

$1,800-2,200   SCG

A Clarice Cliff Bizarre 'Solitude' pattern plate, printed mark.

10in (25cm) diam

$600-900   WW

A Clarice Cliff 'Forest Glen' wall charger, printed mark.

18in (46cm) diam

$3,500-4,000   WW

A Clarice Cliff Bizarre 'Rudyard' pattern plate, printed mark, minor wear.

9in (23cm) long

$700-1,000   WW

A Clarice Cliff Fantasque Bizarre 'Red Trees and House' conical cup and saucer, the saucer for this cup with nonstandard gray and red bands, similar to the bands of the 'Red Carpet' pattern, printed marks.

Cup 2.75in (7cm) high

$700-1,000   WW

A Clarice Cliff Bizarre 'Red Carpet' pattern conical cup and saucer, printed marks.

Cup 3in (8cm) high

$800-1,200   WW

A Clarice Cliff Bizarre 'Tennis' pattern conical cup and saucer, printed mark.

Cup 2.75in (7cm) high

$700-1,000   WW

A Clarice Cliff Fantasque Bizarre 'Gibraltar' pattern conical cup and saucer, printed mark.

Cup 3in (8cm) high

$800-1,200   WW

A rare Clarice Cliff Bizarre 'Latona Grape' pattern conical cup, saucer and side plate, printed mark, painted "Latona" mark, "Lawleys" retail mark.

Cup 2.75in (7cm) high

$700-1,000   WW

A Clarice Cliff Fantasque Bizarre 'Bobbins' Globe teapot and cover.

5in (13cm) high

$1,200-1,800   WW

A Clarice Cliff Bizarre Stamford 'Orange Roof Cottage' pattern teapot and cover, printed mark, restored spout.

5in (12.5cm) high

$2,200-2,800   WW

A Clarice Cliff Fantasque Bizarre 'Umbrellas and Rain' pattern conical coffee pot and cover, printed mark, minor restoration to tip of spout.

7.5in (19cm) high

$400-600   **WW**

A Clarice Cliff export novelty 'Teepee' pattern teapot and cover, made for the Canadian market, printed mark, restored tip to spout, small chip to base rim.

3in (17.5cm) high

$400-600   **WW**

A Clarice Cliff Bizarre Cylindrical 'Orange Picasso Flower' pattern preserve pot and cover, printed mark, restored.

3.5in (9cm) high

$400-600   **WW**

A Clarice Cliff Fantasque Bizarre 'Windbells' pattern cylindrical preserve pot and cover, printed mark, small loss to base rim.

3.5in (9cm) high

$700-1,000   **WW**

A rare Clarice Cliff Bizarre Cube 'Green Firs' pattern candlestick, printed mark "6", restored.

2in (5cm) high

$1,200-1,800   **WW**

A Clarice Cliff Fantasque Bizarre Bonjour 'Orange Secrets' pattern biscuit barrel and cover, printed mark, tiny nick to rim of barrel.

6in (15.5cm) high

$1,200-1,800   **WW**

A Clarice Cliff Fantasque Bizarre Octagon 'Orange Trees and House' pattern candlestick, printed mark.

8in (20.5cm) high

$800-1,200   **WW**

A Clarice Cliff Bizarre octagon 'Lightning' pattern candlestick, printed mark.

8in (20.5cm) high

$1,200-1,800   **WW**

A pair of Clarice Cliff Fantasque Bizarre 'Autumn' bookends, pattern 405, marks, restored corner to one.

6in (15.5cm) high

$800-1,200   **WW**

A pair of Clarice Cliff Bizarre 'Blue Firs' candlesticks, pattern 331, printed marks.

3.25in (8.5cm) diam

$1,000-1,500   **WW**

A Clarice Cliff Bizarre 'Green Cowslip' English Basket flower brick, printed mark, base rim restored.

12in (31cm) high

$500-700   **WW**

A Clarice Cliff Bizarre 'Limberlost' pattern part table centerpiece, comprising two cube candlesticks and two troughs, pattern 659, printed marks.

Troughs 10in (25cm) long

   WW

$1,500-2,000

A pair of Royal Doulton stoneware vases, the baluster shapes decorated with wavy bands of husks on a brown band separating celadon above blue grounds on the shoulders and bodies, impressed marks.

11.5in (29cm) high

$180-220   **Chef**

A Doulton Lambeth jardinière, by Hannah B. Barlow, of broad oviform, decorated with blue and brown formal foliate borders, the central panel incised with a continuous band of cattle in a sparse landscape, impressed factory marks, dated, with incised artist's monogram "HBB" numbered "696", assistant's monogram for Lucy A. Barlow, numbered "731".

1884   *7.75in (19.5cm) high*

$1,000-1,500   **DN**

A Doulton Lambeth stoneware jardinière, by Hannah B. Barlow, incised scene, impressed factory marks, dated, incised artist's monogram "HBB", numbered "692" and assistant's monogram for Lucy A. Barlow.

1884   *8in (20cm) high*

$1,000-1,500   **DN**

A large Doulton Lambeth stoneware twin-handled jardinière, of shouldered ovoid form with applied scrolling flowering foliage on a streaked opaque, brown and green glaze, impressed mark.

23.25in (59cm) diam

$400-600   **L&T**

A Doulton Lambeth 'Silicon' ware jardinière, of ovoid form with three applied handles and three applied feet, pierced and decorated with applied foliate and rosette friezes, impressed marks.

7.75in (19.5cm) high

$100-150   **L&T**

A Doulton Lambeth 'hunting ware' three-handled tyg, the cylindrical body with applied hunting and tavern scenes in relief, the handles molded as hounds, impressed marks.

6.25in (16cm) high

$150-200   **L&T**

A Doulton Lambeth stoneware tobacco jar and cover, of ovoid form with decoration of applied molded flowers, leaves and rosettes, impressed marks.

5in (13cm) high

$220-280   **L&T**

A Doulton Lambeth tapering-sided jug, incised by Hannah Barlow, with loop handle, with four lions within incised stiff leaf bands, the rim with a silver band, impressed and incised marks for 1878, the rim London, faint base firing crack.

1878   *9.75in (25cm) high*

$1,000-1,500   **LFA**

A Doulton Lambeth stoneware jug, decorated by George Hugo Tabor, with incised flowers on white-slip textured ground, handle modeled as a branch with a bear on it, impressed factory marks, dated, artist's initials numbered "269" and marks for Eliza L. Hubert and Harry Barnard, restoration.

1879   *10.5in (27cm) high*

$700-1,000   **DN**

A Doulton globular ewer, with angular loop handle, incised and modeled with flower-heads, on a scale ground, picked out in blue and brown, impressed and incised marks for 1879.

1879   *5.75in (14.5cm) high*

$100-150   **LFA**

A large Doulton Lambeth stoneware 'Owl' jug, with dark brown glaze, the beak and neck rim applied with silver and with black and orange glass eyes, impressed factory marks, the silver mounts marked "CS FS" with London hallmarks and with retail mark for "Thornhill, Bond St., London".

1893　　　*12.5in (32cm) high*

$2,500-3,000　　　**DN**

A Doulton Lambeth stoneware jardinière on a stand, in the Renaissance style, the ovoid jardinière molded in high relief with cartouches of scrolling foliage and rocaille work and with twin carrying handles, glazed in shades of blue, brown, green and caramel, the base similarly molded with scrollwork capital and spreading fluted column on baluster base with circular plinth, both pieces with impressed factory marks.

47.25in (120cm) high

$2,200-2,800　　　**L&T**

A Royal Doulton stoneware jardinière and stand, the bowl of globular shape, applied with flowers and scrolls, band of florets on the neck-rim, the tall baluster stand decorated, impressed factory marks, some damage to top of stand.

41.25in (105cm) high

$500-700　　　**DN**

A Doulton Lambeth stoneware and brass oil lamp, by Mark V. Marshall, incised with panels of foliage, in a brass framework on scrolling legs and cruciform base, impressed factory marks, dated, with artist's initials "MvM" numbered "303" and Mary Starey as assistant, converted to electricity.

1884　　　*15.75in (40cm) high*

$700-1,000　　　**DN**

A Doulton Lambeth 'Faience' vase, of broad oviform sketchily painted in naturalistic colors with butterflies amid pendant foliage and gourds against an inky-blue ground, between formal borders, impressed factory mark and date, no evidence of the artist's identity.

1876　　　*12.25in (31cm) high*

$220-280　　　**DN**

A pair of rare Doulton Lambeth 'Carrara' vases, flared necks molded with dolphins, swags and vases resembling torchères laden with fruit, gilding, flat-painted with interwoven foliate scrolls, impressed factory marks, printed "Carrara" mark and script initials "L.R" possibly for modeler.

11in (28cm) high

$800-1,200　　　**DN**

A pair of Royal Doulton 'Barbotine' landscape vases, finely tube-lined in red, the wooded landscape scenes with blue trees and dark green trees with yellow balloon-like fruits in the foreground, against a pale-green textured ground, factory marks on bases and numbered "7525?".

8.75in (22.5cm) high

$700-1,000　　　**DN**

A Doulton & Co. red flambé glazed earthenware cabinet vase, hand-painted with "Doulton & Co LTD Burslem" sticker, stamped numbers to base.

4.5in (11.5cm) high

$220-280　　　**FRE**

A pair of Doulton Burslem baluster vases, each painted and printed in gilt and colors with poppies on a cream ground, printed, impressed and painted marks.

12in (30.5cm) high

$150-200　　　**L&T**

A pair of Doulton glazed earthenware moon flasks, each printed and painted in blue and gilt with a Japanoiserie design on a white ground, raised on four carved feet, gilt painted mark "9871" with monogram.

12in (30.5cm) high

$500-700 L&T

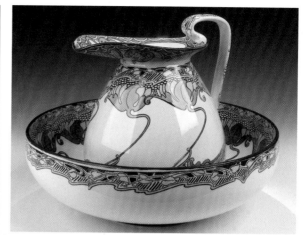

A Doulton Burslem 'Kelmscot' pattern ewer and basin set, printed and painted in shades of yellow, green and blue with stylized Art Nouveau plant forms.

10.25in (26cm) high

$400-600 L&T

A Doulton Burslem jug and basin, with blue-and-white transfer 'Virginia' pattern decoration.

Jug 11.5in (29cm) high

$220-280 Clv

A Royal Doulton jardinière on pedestal, painted in blue with a mother and child in landscapes, green printed "ROYAL DOULTON/ENGLAND" with a lion on a crown.

c1825 *32.5in (82.5cm) high*

$700-1,000 SI

A Royal Doulton figure of 'Biddy Pennyfarthing', "HN1843", printed marks.

9in (23cm) high

$150-200 Chef

A Royal Doulton figure of 'The Balloon Man', "HN1954", printed marks.

7.75in (19.5cm) high

$120-180 Chef

A Royal Doulton miniature figure of 'Polly Peachum', "M23", printed and painted marks in green.

2in (5cm) high

$120-180 LFA

A Royal Doulton 'St. George' figure, "HN2051", painted in colors, printed marks.

7.75in (20cm) high

$180-220 L&T

A Royal Doulton 'Parson's Daughter' figure, mounted on a turned ebonized base with lamp fitting.

9.75in (25cm) high

$320-380 L&T

A Royal Doulton 'Auld Mac' musical character jug, the Thorens movement playing "The Campbells are Coming", printed marks.

6.25in (16cm) high

$300-400 Chef

DECORATIVE ARTS

A CLOSER LOOK AT MAJOLICA

Majolica was developed from 1850 and is a vibrantly colored molded earthenware, decorated with thick lead glazes.

The glazes on the best pieces are hard and glossy - a dull patch may be a sign of restoration.

Quality pieces such as this by George Jones can be identified by the crisp application of the glazes - some lesser wares have blurred lines between the colors.

Elaborate novelty tableware such as strawberry dishes were very popular in the Victorian period and are highly collectible today.

A George Jones majolica strawberry dish, modeled as a trough with curved ends, with two detachable bowls, the handle formed as a network entwined with strawberry leaves, flowers and fruit upon which are perched two blue tits, impressed mark and molded registration mark, three wings chipped.

1875   15.25in (38.5cm) high

$5,000-7,000   **WW**

A mid-Victorian majolica jardinière, by George Jones, the cylindrical sides molded and painted with humming birds amongst orange blossom on a blue ground above four vine lappet feet, impressed marks.

11.5in (29cm) wide

$1,200-1,800   **Chef**

A pair of English majolica ewers, possibly George Jones, each with a flared neck with scroll handles above gadrooned shoulders, body with ram's head masks and floral swags, repaired handles and foot.

c1870   14.25in (36cm) high

$1,500-2,000   **DN**

A Minton majolica 'Tower' ewer and hinged cover, with crabstock handle and jester knop, molded in bold relief with figures merry making, and picked out in colors, within vine borders, impressed marks and shape number "1321".

12.5in (31.5cm) high

$1,000-1,500   **LFA**

A George Jones majolica dish and ladles, modeled with a thrush perched on a branch between two nests, the shaped dish molded in relief with blossom, with three ladles, one a sugar sifter, one a cream-ladle and the larger a serving spoon, impressed date registration lozenge, restored.

1870   10in (27.5cm) wide

$2,200-2,800   **DN**

A George Jones majolica oval strawberry dish and accessories, molded with flowering and fruiting strawberry plants, each end with a hole for the sugar bowl and cream jug, with leaf-molded serving spoon, sugar bowl and cream jug ensuite, indistinctly impressed date registration lozenge, probably 1872, restored.

c1872   13in (36cm) wide

$1,200-1,800   **DN**

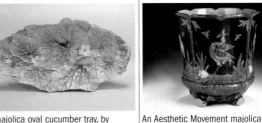

A majolica oval cucumber tray, by George Jones, molded in relief with flowering cucumber plants, painted with colored glazes in shades of green and ocher, lilac raised pad mark, some rim chips.

c1873   17in (43cm) wide

$1,200-1,800   **DN**

An Aesthetic Movement majolica jardinière, probably by George Jones, of slightly tapering cylindrical form molded with panels of storks hunting for fish within faux bamboo frames on a naturalistic base, restored.

15.75in (40cm) high

$500-700   **L&T**

A majolica faux bois oval bough pot and pierced liner, by George Jones, painted with colored glazes in shades of brown and green, the interior pale blue, the mottled green and brown base has a pale patch with painted numerals "228?", small rim chips to the pierced liner.

c1875   4.5in (11.5cm) wide

$700-1,000   **DN**

A Minton majolica jug, modeled with mermaids and a child, acanthus handle with mask terminal, rim restored.

c1873   11.5in (29cm) high

$150-200   **GorL**

A Minton majolica blue-ground mask jug, of globular form with flared neck, the body molded in relief with a band of berried holly, the neck with a band of mistletoe, applied with a branch handle, painted in colored glazes, impressed marks, date code, extensive riveted repairs to neck, foot-rim chip.

1867   6.75in (17cm) high
$320-380   **DN**

A Minton majolica monkey teapot and cover, formed with the ape clinging to a large coconut, his head as the cover, impressed factory marks and date code, the handle reglued and other minor damages.

1874   8.5in (21.5cm) long
$3,500-4,000   **WW**

A Minton majolica two-handled pedestal ovoid jar and cover, molded in relief with oak leaves and acorns, painted with colored glazes, date code, restored.

1856   11.5in (29cm) high
$1,000-1,500   **DN**

A 19thC Minton majolica vase, possibly designed by Christopher Dresser, of bottle form with slender neck slightly everted at the rim on an integral laquered hardwood stand, decorated with Isnic-style cartouches within wreaths in colored enamels and gilt on a turquois ground, printed mark.

          8in (20cm) high
$1,000-1,500   **BonS**

A Minton majolica jardinière, of squat baluster form and decorated with strapwork cast with lions' heads, the whole raised on paw feet, impressed marks, damage to base.

          18in (45cm) high
$400-600   **L&T**

A Minton majolica square section two-handled jardinière, probably painted by Emilie Lessore, with two panels of Bacchic putti, reserved on a dark-blue ground, with an impressed date code, the panels with an "LE" monogram, cracked.

1859   7.5in (19cm) high
$400-600   **DN**

A Minton majolica garden seat, molded and painted in colors to simulate a bamboo seat, with impressed marks and a date code, cracked and riveted.

1879   18.5in (47cm) high
$1,500-2,000   **DN**

A late 19thC Minton majolica figural vase, impressed "MINTONS/1761", signed "A. Carrier".

          27.5in (70cm) high
$5,000-7,000   **SI**

A Minton majolica nut-dish, modeled as a blue-titmouse perched on an oak-leaf applied with acorns, painted with colored glazes, impressed marks, date code, model number "1331", damage and repairs.

1868   7.35in (20cm) wide
$300-400   **DN**

A Wedgewood majolica plate with pierced border, the center decorated in low relief with a girl pushing a wheelbarrow, beneath a green glaze, within a scrolling band of ivy and a pierced border, with impressed marks and a date code, some light surfacing.

1867
$300-400   **DN**

A pair of Wedgwood majolica dessert plates, molded as a sunflower head, within an ozier-molded border, painted in shades of ocher and brown, with impressed marks and a date code.

1882   8.75in (22cm) diam
$300-400   **DN**

A pair of Wedgwood majolica octagonal plates, centers molded in low relief and painted in glaze with studies of putti, within brown-glazed borders molded in relief with foliate swags, impressed marks, date code.

1864   9in (23cm) diam
$300-400   **DN**

A Wedgewood majolica three-division strawberry dish, decorated with strawberries, leaves and flowers.

9.5in (24cm) wide

$600-900   GorL

A Wedgewood majolica jardinière, molded in relief in the Baroque manner, with band of oval panels suspending swags, painted in colored glazes, impressed marks and date code for December 1871, cracked, restored rim chip.

1871   6.75in (17cm) high

$150-200   DN

A rare Wedgewood majolica jardinière, decorated in deep relief, with a medallion on each side with an exotic parrot on a ring perch suspended with ribbons and bows, dark blue, cobalt, turquois interior with yellow rim, impressed marks to base.

$400-600   D

A Wedgewood majolica 'Caterer' jug, of typical form, painted with colored glazes in shades of blue and brown, impressed marks, date code for 1872, minute chip to spout.

1872   6.75in (17cm) high

$350-400   DN

A 19thC Holdcroft majolica bear pitcher, the seated figure with spoon design handle, blue glazed interior.

11.5in (29cm) high

$400-600   Clv

An English majolica figural comport, perhaps Joseph Holdcroft, modeled as a putto supporting a shallow dish, the dish is molded in relief with a frieze of flowers, hairline crack to dish, some small chips.

c1880   11.5in (29cm) high

$3,500-4,500   DN

A pair of Joseph Holdcroft majolica flower stands, modeled as a stork and a heron standing before tall vases molded with aquatic plants, painted with colored glazes, some restored sections, heron lacking tip of beak.

c1875   Heron 34.25in (87cm) high

$8,000-12,000   DN

JOSEPH HOLDCROFT

Like George Jones, Joseph Holdcroft was an employee of Minton who left to produce his own majolica. He was noted for his original designs, although he often copied earlier shapes. Minton storks and herons, inspired by the models of Meissen and J.J. Kändler, were reproduced by Holdcroft. These pieces are smaller and appear less lifelike than the Kändler models. As there are many unsigned pieces, look out for the familiar glaze of green or grey on the undersurface.

A pewter-mounted oval section jug and hinged cover, by Joseph Holdcroft, modeled as a tree trunk with a flowering branch handle, impressed "J_Holdcroft", restored.

c1880   Jug 9.5in (24cm) high

$180-220   DN

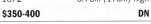

A mid-Victorian majolica swan planter, the glass-eyed bird glazed overall in turquois and with black feet.

12in (30.5cm) high

$150-200   Chef

A green glazed majolica ewer, in the form of a seated frog, impressed numbers "1996" and "51".

11.75in (30cm) high

$300-400 LFA

A late 19thC pair of English porcelaineous majolica figures of Ruth and Rebecca, Ruth holding a sheaf of corn and an oil pot, Rebecca standing beside a well with a ewer, painted with pale-colored glazes, Rebecca has a firing crack through base, hairline crack to Ruth.

Taller 19in (52.5cm) high

$3,000-4,000 DN

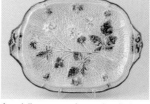

A majolica rectangular two-handled dish, molded in relief with blackberries and leaves, some restoration.

14.5in (36cm) wide

$150-200 LFA

Three mid to late 19thC majolica leaf-molded plates, each modeled with three-overlapping leaves on a stippled ground, in green, pink, yellow, brown, and white glazes.

8in (20.5cm) diam

$300-500 SI

A pair of late 19thC majolica three-branch candelabra, probably by Hugo Lonitz, each naturalistically modeled with a fox stalking a duck through long grass, before three branch stems modeled as an oak tree issuing leaves, painted with colored glazes, with impressed marks "J.R." and numerals "1291", some small areas of restoration.

c1890

$8,000-12,000 DN

An English majolica tray with four egg cups, modeled as a basket with ivy, with a carrying handle, impressed "GEORGE SKEV/WILNECOTE WORKS/TAMWORTH", and four fitted egg cups, one repaired, with conforming decoration, brown and green glaze.

7in (18cm) high

$220-280 SI

A late 19thC majolica spoon warmer, the conch shell with seaweed molded on its sides and resting on brown, green and ocher oval rocky base, indistinct impressed mark.

7in (18cm) wide

$400-600 Chef

A 19thC majolica basket-shaped bowl, with rustic design handle, the body molded with birds nest amongst leaves in yellow, brown, and green.

8in (20cm) high

$220-280 Clv

A 19thC French majolica asparagus plate.

9.5in (24.5cm) long

$400-600 CamA

A 19thC French majolica asparagus server.

15in (38.5cm) long

$400-600 CamA

A Portuguese majolica table centerpiece, modeled and decorated in colored enamels, restoration.

c1880   *14in (35.5cm) high*

$600-900 LFA

A 20thC majolica molded and glazed vase, with a small lion's mask, possibly German.

11.5in (29cm) high

$150-200 D

A 19thC European majolica asparagus basket and tray, the basket is on four foliate feet and tied with pink ribbon, the tray oval and printed with Anci Mouzin, Lecat & Cie factory mark and impressed "M".

Tray 12in (30.5cm) long

$400-600 SI

DECORATIVE ARTS

A Majolica oval 'Le Fecundite' dish, in 17thC style, picked out in colored enamels, the border molded with fruits and masks, foot-rim chips restored.

c1890 10in (25.5cm) wide
$150-200 LFA

A European majolica barrel-shaped jar, the cover molded with doleful dog peering out, beneath a mottled blue/green glaze, indistinct impressed mark, cover glued.

c1880 10.25in (26cm) high
$220-280 LFA

A late 19thC Sarreguemines majolica tobacco box, modeled as a monkey playing an upright piano, painted with colored glazes, impressed marks, lacks cover, monkey missing left hand.

9.5in (24cm) long
$700-1,000 DN

A Haviland and Company oyster plate.

c1885 9in (23cm) diam
$700-1,000 CamA

A Haviland and Company oyster plate.

c1890
$400-600 CamA

A Haviland and Company oyster plate.

c1890 8.25in (21cm) diam
$800-1,200 CamA

A Haviland and Company oyster plate.

c1910 9in (23cm) diam
$300-400 CamA

A Minton oyster plate, dated.

1857 10in (25.5cm) diam
$1,200-1,800 CamA

A mid-Victorian Minton majolica oyster plate, typically molded with nine turquois shell-shaped compartments divided by turret and mollusc shells outside cockle band and central marbled concave dishing, impressed mark.

10in (25.5cm) diam
$800-1,200 Chef

A Minton majolica oyster plate, with cracker well, dated.
1885 9in (23cm) diam
$1,500-2,000 CamA

A Minton malachite oyster plate.
c1876 9in (23cm) diam
$1,500-2,000 CamA

A Limoges oyster plate, marked "LS&S".
c1890 8.5in (22cm) diam
$220-280 CamA

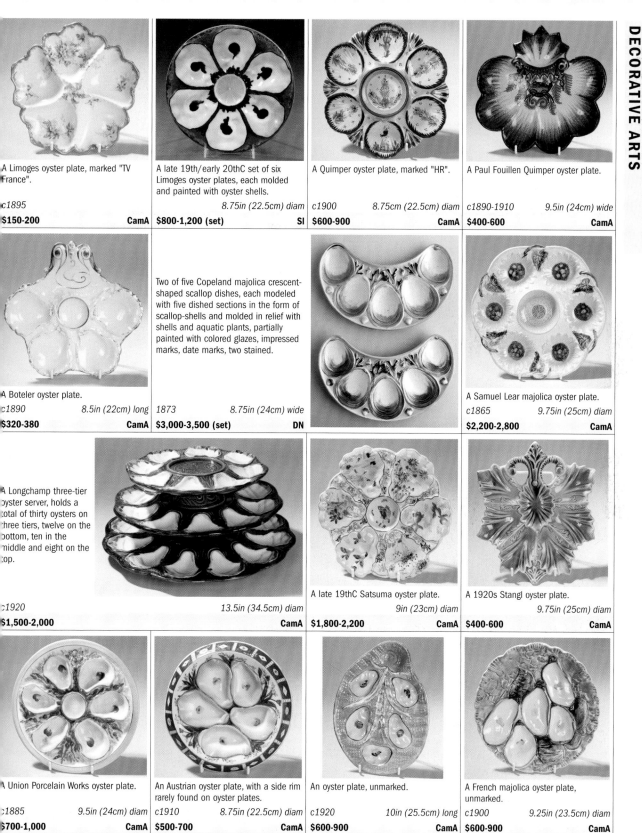

A Limoges oyster plate, marked "TV France".

c1895

$150-200 CamA

A late 19th/early 20thC set of six Limoges oyster plates, each molded and painted with oyster shells.

8.75in (22.5cm) diam

$800-1,200 (set) SI

A Quimper oyster plate, marked "HR".

c1900 8.75cm (22.5cm) diam

$600-900 CamA

A Paul Fouillen Quimper oyster plate.

c1890-1910 9.5in (24cm) wide

$400-600 CamA

A Boteler oyster plate.

c1890 8.5in (22cm) long

$320-380 CamA

Two of five Copeland majolica crescent-shaped scallop dishes, each modeled with five dished sections in the form of scallop-shells and molded in relief with shells and aquatic plants, partially painted with colored glazes, impressed marks, date marks, two stained.

1873 8.75in (24cm) wide

$3,000-3,500 (set) DN

A Samuel Lear majolica oyster plate.

c1865 9.75in (25cm) diam

$2,200-2,800 CamA

A Longchamp three-tier oyster server, holds a total of thirty oysters on three tiers, twelve on the bottom, ten in the middle and eight on the top.

c1920 13.5in (34.5cm) diam

$1,500-2,000 CamA

A late 19thC Satsuma oyster plate.

9in (23cm) diam

$1,800-2,200 CamA

A 1920s Stangl oyster plate.

9.75in (25cm) diam

$400-600 CamA

A Union Porcelain Works oyster plate.

c1885 9.5in (24cm) diam

$700-1,000 CamA

An Austrian oyster plate, with a side rim rarely found on oyster plates.

c1910 8.75in (22.5cm) diam

$500-700 CamA

An oyster plate, unmarked.

c1920 10in (25.5cm) long

$600-900 CamA

A French majolica oyster plate, unmarked.

c1900 9.25in (23.5cm) diam

$600-900 CamA

Martinware

A Martin Brothers stoneware vase, incised with a frieze of four grotesque birds, inscribed "5-1894 Martin Bros London & Southall".

8.75in (22cm) high

$7,000-10,000   **WW**

A Martin Brothers stoneware vase, incised with pomegranates and caterpillars, incised "9-1896 Martin Bros, London & Southall", Exhibition paper label.

10.5in (27cm) high

$7,000-10,000   **WW**

A Martin Brothers stoneware gourd vase, covered in a mottled brown ocher glaze, incised "R W Martin & Bros, Southall".

9in (23cm) high

$600-900   **WW**

An early Martin Brothers Celtic style stoneware jardinière, incised "Designed and carved by R. Wallace Martin, at Fulham Pottery, July 1873", "R. W. Martin Fecit..."

1873   *8.25in (21cm) high*

$700-1,000   **LFA**

A Martin Brothers stoneware dish, incised and colored floral decoration, incised "Martin Bros. London & Southall" and dated.

1892   *7in (18cm) diam*

$350-400   **DN**

A Martin Brothers stoneware cruet tray, glazed in shades blue, ocher and brown, marked "Martin Bros London & Southall 11-1909", small chips to rim.

5in (12.5cm) wide

$320-380   **WW**

A Martin Brothers Barrister Eagle jar and cover, a one-off silver-plated presentation piece.

$15,000-20,000   **SJH**

A Martin Brothers stoneware bird, with shaved head, incised to head rim and base rim "R W Martin & Bros, London & Southall 6-1907", minor frits to rim of body.

9.25in (23.5cm) high

$20,000-30,000   **WW**

A large Martin Brothers bird, in shades of blue, green and brown, on ebonized wood base, the neck with brass reinforcer incised "R W Martin & Brothers, London & Southall 11 1900", the base incised "R W Martin London & Southall 11 1900".

$50,000-60,000

A Martin Brothers stoneware bird, the broad beak with slightly tilted, sideways glance, incised to head rim and base rim "Martin Bros 5-1897 London & Southall", faint hairline to rim of body.

9.5in (23.5cm) high

$20,000-25,000   **WW**

14.5in (37cm) high

WW

Four rare Martin Brothers 'White King & Queen' and 'Brown King & Queen' chess pieces, each modeled as a medieval king or queen, glaze incised marks "R W Martin 1901", minor damage.

6in (15cm) high

$12,000-18,000   **WW**

A Martin Brothers stoneware vesta, wall-mounted square section, modeled as an ox head supporting a ball, in shades of ocher and blue, marked "R W Martin Southall", chips to rim.

8.5in (22cm) high

$1,200-1,800   **WW**

A Martin Brothers stoneware tile, incised with two grotesque fish and a jellyfish in shades of green, blue and ocher, in later wooden frame, unmarked, chips and minor damages to extremities.

5.5in (14cm) wide

$800-1,200   **WW**

Meissen

The first European hard-paste porcelain factory was established in 1710 in Dresden, Saxony but soon moved to Albrechtsburg Castle in Meissen. Johann Friedrich Böttger set up the enterprise by royal decree and organized the workshop.

Upon Böttger's death in 1719, Johan Gregor Höroldt (1696-1775) was made director and initiated the growth and great success of the company. Meissen struggled during the Seven Year War from 1756 to 1763, but regained its place in the market and survived, partly due to the arrival of Michel Victor Acier (1736-1799) in 1764. He brought fresh ideas to the factory with his

Rococo and Classical styles and chose designs of figures such as cupids, children, lovers and musicians that were to prove extremely successful in the 19thC. By the late 19thC exports to America were increasing and demand was strong for their high-quality wares which displayed their perfected pâte-sur-pâte technique. The Art Nouveau period from 1890 brought a new wave of designs and Meissen produced popular pieces with a number of designers including Henry Van de Velde (1863-1957) and Paul Scheurich (1883-1945). The factory remains in operation using the crossed swords mark.

A Meissen figure of a Hun on horseback, designed by Erich Hösel, partially restored, blue sword mark.

c1897   11.75in (30cm) high
$4,000-6,000   BMN

A Meissen Art Nouveau figure, of a child holding a doll in his hands, designed by Konrad Hentschel.

c1904   4.5in (11.5cm) high
$2,500-3,000   BMN

A Meissen child with paper hat riding on a wooden horse, designed by Konrad Hentschel, tail slightly restored, base unglazed, blue swords mark.

c1910   6.75in (17cm) high
$1,800-2,200   BMN

A Meissen standing child with doll in her hand, designed by Konrad Hentschel, head professionally reglued, blue swords mark.

c1910   6.5in (16.5cm) high
$2,200-2,800   BMN

A Meissen figure of a child, designed by Paul Helmig, girl with bag of sweets, painted in color, swords mark.

c1910   5.75in (14.5cm) high
$2,500-3,000   BMN

A Meissen figure group designed by Paul Scheurich, gilding, signed and dated, swords mark.

1919   11in (28cm) high
$3,000-4,000   BMN

A Meissen child with doll in a stroller, designed by Konrad Hentschel, hairline cracks on base, swords mark.

c1910   5.75in (13.5cm) high
$4,000-6,000   BMN

A Meissen sitting child with drinking dog, designed by Konrad Hentschel, colorfully painted, blue swords mark.

c1910   3.5in (9cm) high
$3,000-4,000   BMN

A Meissen Art Nouveau figure, designed by Walter Schott, gilded, slightly damaged, blue swords mark.

c1900   12in (30cm) high
$1,200-1,800   BMN

A Meissen girl with cap, a cat in her arms, designed by Konrad Hentschel, body of cat restored, swords mark.

c1910   4.75in (12cm) high
$2,200-2,800   BMN

A Meissen schoolboy with dog, designed by Erich Hösel, some damage, restoration, blue swords mark.

c1910   6.75in (17cm) high
$3,000-4,000   BMN

A Meissen teenager with ox-eye daisies, designed by Konrad Hentschel, flowers restored, hairline cracks, swords mark.

c1910   6.25in (16cm) wide
$7,000-10,000   BMN

CERAMICS

DECORATIVE ARTS

Minton

Four Minton Hollins & Co 'Eight-inch' Shakespearean tiles, by John Moyr Smith, transfer-printed with theatrical subjects, artist's name on fronts and molded maker's marks on reverse.

$600-900   DN

A set of five Minton tiles by John Moyr Smith, depicting "Cinderella", "Golden Locks", "Puss in Boots", "Six Swans", and "Rumpelstiltskin", each with monogram and molded factory mark.

6in (15.5cm) high

$400-600   L&T

A Minton 'Shakespearean' tile, designed by John Moyr Smith, showing Romeo and Juliet in black outline against white, molded "Minton China Works Stoke on Trent" and two other Minton tiles, also designed by Moyr Smith, showing in blue, scenes from 'King Lear'.

6in (15cm) wide

$100-150   DN

A Minton circular tile, by John Moyr Smith, depicting Mary, Joseph and Jesus, within a molded brass frame forming a kettle stand, on flattened bun feet, bears monogram.

7.75in (19.5cm) diam

$100-150   L&T

JOHN MOYR SMITH

Scotsman John Moyr Smith (1839-1912) was a prolific artist whose work is seen on more tiles than any other known artist. He worked with Minton and gained them the Grand Prize at the 1878 Paris International Exhibition. He also designed illustrations for books and greetings cards but was popluar in his time mainly for his illustrations and cartoons in the satirical magazine 'Punch'.

A early 20thC Minton shaped tray, painted by L. Boullemier, bleu celeste ground, gilt rim, puce globe mark, crack.

c1910   *13.75in (35cm) wide*

$1,800-2,200   DN

A Minton pâte-sur-pâte canteen, black background with white figures, signed on bottom "Minton" in a globe.

6in (15cm) high

$1,200-1,800   JDJ

A Minton charger decorated by Louis J. Rhead, painted with the profile of a young woman within a band of chrysanthemums, signed and dated, with impressed marks to the underside.

1880   *16.25in (41.5cm) diam*

$4,000-6,000   L&T

A Minton Art Pottery circular wall plate, painted in the manner of W.S. Coleman, in dark blue outline with the profile of a naked female child cautiously persuing a butterfly, all against a deep blue ground, marked "Minton's Art Pottery Studio, Kensington Gore" and impressed marks with date code.

1872   *13.5in (34cm) diam*

$800-1,200   DN

A pair of Minton Japonaiserie pink-ground vases, each with a tall cylindrical neck above a compressed globular body and brown and gilt bracket foot, the neck with a geometric band with flower-head boss and a band of stylized foliage, indistinct impressed marks, one has a chipped rim.

c1870   *8.25in (21cm) high*

$600-900   DN

A pair of Minton Secessionist baluster vases, each transfer-printed with panels of leaves flanked by tube-lined roses in musted pink tones with mauve centers, with tube-lined vertical stems against a shaded green ground, impressed "Mintons" with a date code.

1908   *10.5in (27cm) high*

$700-1,000   DN

A Minton's Secessionist twin-handled vase, of tall tapering form, decorated in tube-line with flowering blossom on a treacle ground, printed marks "no.34".

14.25in (36cm) high

$250-300   L&T

A large Bernard Moore punch bowl, of circular form painted to the interior with a dragon within a Celtic entwined band and to the exterior with Celtic panels, in red on a white ground, painted mark "Bernard Moore 1910" and monogram "AJ", impressed mark "Mintons".

c1910   *18in (45.5cm) diam*

$1,500-2,000   L&T

Moorcroft

After an initial association with Macintyre and Company, William Moorcroft (1872-1945) established his own pottery in 1913 at Cobridge near Burslem. The company was financed by Liberty's of London who then maintained control over the business. William died in 1945 and his son Walter (1917-2002) took over. He began to bring in new ideas, using designs of exotic plants as well as the native plants his father had favoured. The company enjoyed great success over the following decades and in 1959 Walter was joined by his brother John. The brothers worked hard to preserve the traditional techniques of hand-crafted wares. In 1962 the family bought out Liberty's. Walter remained design director until 1987, despite the company moved out of the family's control in the mid-1980s.

A pair of Moorcroft 'Florian Ware' vases, of baluster form each decorated with cornflowers and painted in shades of blue, printed marks, initialed in green, "M743".

11in (28cm) high

$1,500-2,000　　　　**L&T**

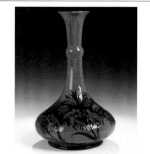

A Moorcroft ovoid vase, with slender neck and everted rim, decorated in the 'Blue Cornflower' pattern and painted in shades of blue and powder blue ground, impressed marks, signed in blue, restoration.

12.25in (31cm) high

$700-1,000　　　　**L&T**

Two MacIntyre Moorcroft Florian ware flared baluster-shaped jardinières, each tube-lined with growing anemones and leaves, picked out in blue and green, on a white ground, printed mark in brown, registration number "401753" and Moorcroft painted signature mark.

5in (13cm) high

$1,200-1,800 (each)　　　　**LFA**

A Moorcroft limited edition vase, decorated with "H. M. S. Syrius", impressed and painted marks, "30/150".

14.75in (37.5cm) high

$220-280　　　　**L&T**

Two Moorcroft hibiscus glazed earthenware cabinet vases.

Taller 4.25in (11cm) high

$300-400　　　　**FRE**

A Moorcroft baluster vase, decorated in the 'Alhambra' pattern and highlighted with gilt, printed Macintyre mark, painted mark "M2489".

11.75in (30cm) high

$600-900　　　　**L&T**

A twin-handled 'Cornflower' Macintyre vase, the shouldered tapering body with two small loop handles, printed mark and signed "W Moorcroft" in green.

8.75cm (22.5cm) high

$1,500-2,000　　　　**BonS**

A Moorcroft tall tapering vase, with everted rim, painted in the 'Flower Panels' pattern, impressed mark, signed in green, restored.

12.5in (31.5cm) high

$600-900　　　　**L&T**

A 1930s Moorcroft vase, the waisted cylindrical shape slip trailed with colored freesia-like flowers on a ground toning from olive at the rim to deep blue at the foot, impressed facsimile signature and "Potter to HM The Queen" and painted initials, some damage.

10.25in (26cm) high

$220-280　　　　**Chef**

A Moorcroft octagonal bowl, decorated in the late 'Florian' pattern, impressed mark and impressed facsimile signature, restoration.

9.75in (25cm) diam

$220-280　　　　**L&T**

A pair of Moorcroft round plates, each tubelined and painted with the 'Anemone' pattern, on a dark blue ground, impressed marks and painted initial marks.

10.25in (26cm) diam

$220-280 (pair)　　　　**LFA**

A large Moorcroft ovoid jardinière, decorated in the late 'Florian' pattern, impressed mark, signed in green.

7.75in (20cm) high

$800-1,200　　　　**L&T**

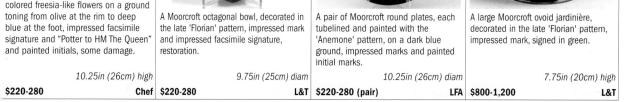

Pilkington's

The Pilkington's factory was founded in 1891 near Manchester, but was renamed Royal Lancastrian when given a Royal Warrant in 1913. Founded by the Pilkington brothers, the factory was originally established to produce architectural ceramics, but extended its range to make domestic pieces in around 1897 to show off the glazes it had produced for decorative tiles. The vessels have particularly distinctive glazes but production costs for luster ware were high and the pottery division ceased trading in 1938. The company still exists today producing tiles.

A Pilkington's 'Royal Lancastrian' oviform vase, by William Salter Mycock, decorated in dark tones with vertical leafy branches against a bright, shaded and mottled orange ground, impressed factory marks.

4.5in (11.5cm) high

$120-180   DN

A Pilkington's 'Royal Lancastarian' ribbed ovoid vase, designed by Gwladys Rogers, decorated with curving blue leaf fronds on a mottled grey ground, impressed marks.

c1935   7in (18cm) high

$220-280   WW

A Pilkington's 'Royal Lancastrian' Lapis Ware broad oviform vase, designed by Gwladys Rodgers, decorated in green, pale brown and mauve with stylized plant-forms against a grey ground, factory marks, artist's mark and incised "E.T.R" for Radford.

6.75in (17.5cm) high

$220-280   DN

A Pilkington's 'Royal Lancastrian' Lapis Ware oviform vase, designed by Gwladys Rodgers, decorated in pale blue and green with a broad band of stylized foliage against a mottled grey ground, impressed factory marks, artist's marks and incised "E.T.R." for Radford.

9in (23cm) high

$220-280   DN

A Pilkington's 'Royal Lancastrian' oviform vase, molded with broad overlapping leaves beneath an off-white glaze, impressed factory marks.

8in (20.5cm) high

$120-180   DN

A Pilkington's 'Royal Lancastrian' vase, the inverted mushroom shape grading from green on the neck to soufflé brown on the globular base, impressed marks.

6.25in (16cm) high

$120-180   Chef

A Pilkington's 'Royal Lancastrian' flared vase, by Gwladys Rodgers, painted on the inner surface with radiating petal forms in blue, green and brown against a buff-colored ground, impressed factory marks and artist's mark.

5.5in (14cm) high

$100-150   DN

A Pilkington's shouldered vase, of tapering cylindrical form, covered with a streaky turquois glaze with gold illusions to the shoulder, impressed marks, dated.

1909   13in (33cm) high

$400-600   L&T

A Pilkington's 'Royal Lancastrian' ovoid vase and cover, by Richard Joyce, with a fish knop, the body relief molded and decorated with silver and iridescent luster with carp swimming amidst waves on a green ground, painted and impressed marks, date code.

1913   9in (23cm) high

$4,000-6,000   WW

A Pilkington's plaque, painted in black with the Pilkington's Tile and Pottery Co. Ltd, framed.

From the May Craven collection. Craven was a glaze chemist at the Pilkington's factory.

7.75in (15cm) wide

$350-400   L&T

Royal Crown Derby

A Royal Crown Derby porcelain peach ground ewer, the bulbous vessel with scroll handle and elongated spout, decorated with an iris and a daisy, molded with scrolling floral vine and heightened in gilt, printed crowned mark under "ROYAL CROWN DERBY".

c1890   *6in (15cm) high*
$180-220   **SI**

A Crown Derby porcelain turquois ground vase, the bulbous base with flaring neck applied with two handles with mask terminals, decorated with gilt birds, insects and foliage, red printed crowned mark, retailed by Abram French, Boston.

c1880-90   *6in (15cm) high*
$220-280   **SI**

A Royal Crown Derby Sèvres-style urn and cover, painted by C. Harris, two-handled, of shouldered form, decorated with a gilt-line quatrefoil panel depicting an exotic bird in a landscape, reserved on a bleu de roi, turquois and gilt ground, iron-red printed marks, date code.

1896   *6.5in (16.5cm) wide*
$1,800-2,200   **DN**

A pair of Royal Crown Derby campana and covers, painted by C. Gresley, the front panels signed, the covers with flammiform finials, iron-red printed marks, date code for 1904, the covers with date codes for 1904 and 1933, one with later cover.

1904-1933   *10.25in (26cm) high*
$4,000-6,000   **DN**

A Royal Crown Derby baluster-shaped two-handled vase, decorated with cobalt blue ground with decorative gilding in floral swags having a central cartouche containing hand-painted floral arrangement, rim damaged and reglued.

    10in (25.5cm) high
$120-180   **D**

A pair of Royal Crown Derby vases, decorated with the Imari pattern number 1128, on the two-handled ovoid bodies, the socle feet short neck and cover joined by central rods through the bodies, date code, printed marks.

1968   *12.25in (31cm) high*
$700-1,000   **Chef**

A Royal Crown Derby shaped oval dish, painted with flowers and gilt scrollwork on a pink ground.

c1910
$120-180   **WW**

A Royal Crown Derby plate, impressed date, centrally painted with flowers within gilding, apple green band and gadrooned rim, red printed marks.

1910   *9in (23cm) diam*
$150-200   **Chef**

A Royal Crown Derby bone china loving cup, made to commemorate the 95th birthday of H.M. Queen Elizabeth the Queen Mother.

1995   *3.5in (9cm) high*
$180-220   **H&G**

A Royal Crown Derby square tray painted by Albert Gregory, signed beneath the bouquet lower left, iron-red marks, date code.

1911   *6in (15cm) high*
$4,000-5,000   **DN**

A pair of Royal Crown Derby square dishes, painted by Albert Gregory, with signed iron-red printed marks and date codes.

1906-08   *4.75in (12cm) diam*
$14,000-18,000   **DN**

CERAMICS

Royal Dux

A Royal Dux figure of a young woman, wearing a high feathered bonnet and holding a fan in her left hand, standing beside an urn raised on a tree stump, part gilt, pink and olive coloring, impressed number "993".

17.25in (44cm) high

$400-600 **BonS**

A Royal Dux figure of a country girl, standing beside a water pump to fill a pitcher, part gilt, pink and olive coloring, impressed number "25023".

17.25in (44cm) high

$350-400 **BonS**

A Dux-style large earthenware group, depicting a Greek potter and female companion, he is sitting on a rock, resting a vase on his knee, impressed numeral mark only.

22.5in (57cm) high

$350-400 **BonS**

A Royal Dux figure of a young woman carrying a basket on her head, a pitcher at her feet, applied pink triangle mark, impressed "651".

18.75in (47.5cm) high

$320-380 **BonS**

A Royal Dux figure of a young girl, carrying a basket of fish, standing on circular base, triangular pad with impressed mark, printed mark, impressed numeral "2292".

$280-320 **BonE**

A Royal Dux 'The Water Carrier' porcelain figure, number "1052".

16.25in (41cm) high

$320-380 **Clv**

A large Royal Dux figure, wearing a turban, sitting side saddle on a donkey on naturalistic rectangular plinth, with pink triangular mark and impressed number marks.

15.25in (39cm) high

$600-900 **L&T**

A Royal Dux Art Deco porcelain figure, an erotic dancer, scantily clad and raised on a lotus flower base, highlighted in gilt, applied pink triangle and printed and impressed marks.

15.75in (40cm) high

$400-600 **L&T**

A pair of large Royal Dux figures of a lady and a gentleman, both wearing elaborate, lacy costumes, the lady with a lute on her back the gentleman holding a guitar, both on flower encrusted bases, triangular pad with impressed mark.

34.5in (88cm) high

$4,000-6,000 **BonE**

A Royal Dux porcelain figure, 'The Seated Bather', pink triangle mark, "Made in Czechoslovakia", "P. Aichele".

19in (48cm) high

$800-1,200 **DN**

A Royal Dux Art Nouveau painted and glazed ceramic vase, stamped ink mark, chips to foot.

11in (28cm) high

$220-280 **FRE**

Royal Worcester

Initially established in 1751, the Worcester factory became known as the Worcester Royal Porcelain Company in 1862 and was to multiply ten times in size by 1900. The Victorian period was very successful for the company. Key designers included George Owen (1845-1917), who worked on imitating ivory pieces, and James Hadley (1837-1903), who was a great exponent of the fashionable Japonaiserie style in his figural designs. From 1901 much more everyday day ware was produced, but grander designs always remained an important part of the factory's work. The 1930s and 1940s brought a new wave of success as the Royal Worcester ceramic sculptures became extremely popular. The company merged with Spode in 1978 and continues today.

A pair of Royal Worcester amphora shaped porcelain vases, finely painted on a rose pompadour ground, with enameled beading and enriched in gilding, signed "Phillips", printed mark.

c1912   7in (18cm) high

$1,200-1,800   SI

A Royal Worcester ovoid vase, with slender neck and two scroll handles, painted in colored enamels by J.W. Sedgley with an iris, on shaded ground, within gilt line border, signed, printed mark in green, tiny foot-rim nick.

c1905   7.5in (19cm) high

$600-900   LFA

A Royal Worcester ovoid vase, with flared neck, painted in colored enamels by H.H. Price, with luscious fruit, on a shaded ground, signed, printed mark in puce for 1941 and shape number "2571".

8.25in (21.5cm) high

$700-1,000   LFA

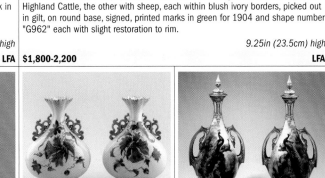

A pair of Royal Worcester ovoid vases and covers, each with two pierced scroll handles and turned knop, painted in colored enamels by John Stinton, one with Highland Cattle, the other with sheep, each within blush ivory borders, picked out in gilt, on round base, signed, printed marks in green for 1904 and shape number "G962" each with slight restoration to rim.

9.25in (23.5cm) high

$1,800-2,200   LFA

A Royal Worcester ivory-ground globular potpourri vase and pierced cover, with pierced neck, printed, painted and gilded with sprays of flowers, shape number '1018', green printed mark, date code, an associated liner.

1903   7.5in (19cm) high

$600-900   DN

A Royal Worcester two-handled globular vase, with a flared bucket neck, printed, painted and gilded with sprays of flowers, puce printed marks, shape number '1109', date code, slight rubbing to gilding.

1886   8.75in (22cm) high

$350-400   DN

A pair of Locke & Co. Worcester porcelain onion-shaped vases, with painted and gilded foliate decoration and having pierced scroll handles.

7.5in (19cm) high

$220-280   Clv

A pair of English Royal Worcester covered two-handled urns, by Frank Southell, each painted with peacocks, gilt borders, with covers, base marked with underglaze green Worcester mark, numbered "229D" and "H5074.20."

c1900   5in (12.5cm) high

$15,000-20,000   FRE

A Royal Worcester porcelain vase, egg-form vessel on a triple dolphin stem, rim pierced with masks and scrolling foliage, molded with stylized decoration, printed mark with crown flanked by six dots over "ROYAL WORCESTER ENGLAND".

c1897   8.75in (22cm) high

$300-400   SI

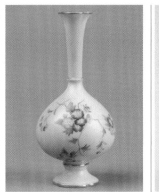

A Royal Worcester small bottle shaped vase, printed and painted with flowers on a blush ivory ground, printed mark in green and shape number "G789".

1902   *5in (12.8cm) high*

$60-90   **LFA**

A Royal Worcester jug, the neck and gilt handle modeled as an upturned root, the quatrefoil sectioned sides printed and painted with floral scrolls, printed marks, and date code.

1893   *7.25in (18.5cm) high*

$220-280   **Chef**

A small Royal Worcester porcelain Aesthetic vase, of compressed shape with cylindrical neck, painted and enameled, factory marks on the base.

5.75in (14.5cm) high

$70-100   **DN**

A Royal Worcester waisted beaker vase, painted in colored enamels by H. Ayrton with luscious fruit, within gilt line border, signed, printed mark in puce and shape number "G923".

c1926   *6in (15.5cm) high*

$350-400   **LFA**

A Royal Worcester tall waisted vase, painted by H. Chair, painted with 'shot' enamels, green printed mark, puce registration number "410714", model number "2286", partial date code.

c1900   *15in (38cm) high*

$1,500-2,000   **DN**

A rare mid- to late 19thC Worcester vase in the Japanese style, modeled in the form of a Shibayama vase, on a textured base, impressed mark and red Worcester mark, some wear to gilding.

7.75in (19.5cm) high

$1,500-2,000   **FRE**

A Royal Worcester 'Sabrina Ware' cylindrical vase, painted by A. Shuck, with a pair of storks wading by grasses in a woodland setting, factory marks on base with date code.

1909   *5in (13cm) high*

$280-320   **DN**

A Royal Worcester plate painted and signed "Rushton", with a woman feeding chickens beneath fruit trees with cottages beyond and a river to one side, an acid etched gilt rim inscribed "Apple Blossom Old Storrige Worcestershire".

c1935   *10.5in (27cm) diam*

$800-1,200   **WW**

A pair of Royal Worcester plates, painted with fruit, signed "H. Ayrton", within gilt gadrooned borders, black marks.

8.75in (22.5cm) diam

$700-1,000   **WW**

A pair of gold ground Royal Worcester plates, each painted with a central panel of fruit, signed "A. Telford", the gold ground acid etched with stylized foliage, gold marks.

9.25in (23.5cm) diam

$600-900   **WW**

A Royal Worcester lobed oval two-handled dish, painted in colored enamels by H. H. Price, with luscious fruit, on a shaded ground, within a gilt gadrooned rim, signed, printed mark in puce.

1937   *12.25in (31cm) wide*

$1,000-1,500   **LFA**

A Royal Worcester leaf form fruit tray, floral branches on a cream field.

c1890   *13.5in (34.5cm) high*

$300-400   **FRE**

A Royal Worcester peach ground dish, in the form of a shell, painted with floral sprigs, on whelk feet.

10.5in (27cm) high

$350-400   **BonS**

A Royal Worcester Aesthetic moon flask, with twin handles, molded with peony brambles and flying birds in the Japanese style and raised on scrolled feet, the whole flask covered in celadon glaze, impressed marks "542".

14in (35.5cm) high

$600-900   **L&T**

A Royal Worcester vase, of squat baluster form, embossed, sprigged and painted with flowers.

c1900   *7.5in (19cm) high*

$220-280   **FRE**

A Royal Worcester seated faun, modeled by James Hadley, seated on a separate rocky base, losses.

8in (22cm) high

$70-100   **DN**

A Royal Worcester figure of a Chinaman, modeled by James Hadley, painted with colored enamels, puce marks, date code and inscribed "Chink", model number "837".

1931   *6.35in (17cm) high*

$350-400   **DN**

A Royal Worcester figure of a girl with a basket, modeled by J. Hadley in the Kate Greenaway style, printed and impressed marks, date letter.

1884   *8in (22cm) high*

$220-280   **DN**

A rare Royal Worcester miniature figure of the 'Boy on Boar', modeled by Phoebe Stabler, decorated in colored enamels, printed and painted marks in puce and shape number "2882".

c1931   *3.5in (9cm) high*

$400-600   **LFA**

A Royal Worcester boxed coffee set, painted by C. Johnson, blue-scale ground with panels of exotic birds in the 18thC style, comprising a baluster coffee pot and cover, a milk jug, a sugar bowl, six cups and saucers, and six European silver-gilt and blue enameled coffee spoons, the porcelain with puce printed marks and date code, in a fitted case with hinged cover, some damage.

1927

$800-1,200   **DN**

A Royal Worcester part coffee set, designed by Scottie Wilson, comprising coffee pot and cover, a milk jug, a pair of plates, six side plates, a saucer, five bowls of varying size and a rectangular tray, transfer-printed in black against terracotta with stylized swans, birds on leafy branches and some with fish, factory marks and artist's facsimile signature.

Plates 8in (20.5cm) diam

$300-400 (set)   **DN**

A pair of Royal Worcester Hadley figural candlesticks, in the form of a boy and girl seated asleep on tree stumps, naturalistic stems, the sconces molded with oak leaves, impressed and printed marks "Rd No. 60364".

c1837-1903   *9.25in (23.5cm) high*

$600-900   **BonS**

A Royal Worcester porcelain green ground vase, modeled as an oil lamp with three dolphin-form flower holders and centering a tall flaring flower holder, heightened in gilt, printed mark with crown flanked by two dots and "ROYAL WORCESTER ENGLAND".

c1893   *11.75in (30cm) high*

$350-400   **SI**

CERAMICS

Wedgewood

A Wedgewood 'Matt Straw' vase, designed by Keith Murray, printed mark, facsimile signature.

23.5in (60cm) diam

$800-1,200   **WW**

A rare Wedgewood vase, designed and glazed by Norman Wilson covered in a robin's egg blue glaze, impressed marks, "NW" monogram.

Norman Wilson developed the glazes used by Keith Murray. Signed pieces by Wilson are rare and some experts expect to see his popularity growing to match that of Murray.

5cm (12.5cm) high

$300-400   **WW**

KEITH MURRAY

Keith Murray (1892-1981) was born in New Zealand and emigrated to England when he was 14. He trained as an architect and became one the key designers of the early 20thC working with ceramics, glass and silver. Between 1832 and 1948 he designed for a number of top companies including Stevens & Williams, Wedgewood and Mappin & Webb. Murray is known for bold clean shapes emphasized by horizontal banding and ceramics with matt and semimatt glazes.

A rare Wedgewood grey vase, designed by Keith Murray, various and impressed and incised marks, facsimile signature.

7.5in (19cm) high

$700-1,000   **WW**

A Wedgewood ovoid vase designed by Keith Murray, the ribbed body covered with a matt green glaze, printed marks.

9.5in (24cm) high

$400-600   **L&T**

A Wedgewood 'Matt Straw' vase designed by Keith Murray, impressed marks, printed facsimile signature.

6.25in (16cm) high

$600-900   **WW**

A Wedgewood 'Matt Straw' bowl designed by Keith Murray, impressed marks, printed "KM" monogram.

9in (22.5cm) high

$300-400   **WW**

A Wedgewood 'Matt Straw Top Hat' bowl, designed by Keith Murray, printed mark, facsimile signature.

13.75in (35cm) diam

$600-900   **WW**

A Wedgewood 'Moonstone' coffee service, designed by Keith Murray, each matt cream glazed piece with molded bands, comprising a coffee pot and cover, milk jug, sucrier, cover, four coffee cans and saucers, impressed and printed marks.

8.25in (21cm) high

$1,200-1,800 (set)   **WW**

A 20thC Wedgewood inkstand, designed by Keith Murray, the white rectangular stand with pen tray before the lidded box containing two inkwells, impressed marks and facsimile signature.

10in (25.5cm) wide

$400-600   **Chef**

A Wedgewood 'Moonstone' coffee set, designed by Keith Murray, comprising coffee pot and cover, milk and covered pot.

$280-320   **LFA**

A Wedgewood 'Dragon' luster bowl, of octagonal form, printed and painted to the exterior with dragons on a green ground and to the interior with dragon and inserts on an orange ground, printed mark.

8in (20.5cm) diam

$350-400   **L&T**

A Wedgewood 'Fairyland' luster bowl, designed by Daisy Makeig Jones, of octagonal form, printed and painted in colors to the exterior in the 'Castle on a Road' pattern and to the interior with 'Fairy in a Cage' pattern, printed and painted marks "Z3125".

9in (23cm) diam

$800-1,200   **L&T**

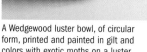

A Wedgewood luster bowl, of circular form, printed and painted in gilt and colors with exotic moths on a luster ground, printed and painted marks, "Z4832".

8.25in (21cm) diam

$400-600   **L&T**

A Wedgewood 'Taurus the Bull', designed by Arnold Machin, modeled in a simplified manner, decorated with transfer-printed signs of the Zodiac interspersed with stars, marked "Wedgewood Barlaston England".

16in (40.5cm) long

$400-600   **DN**

A Wedgewood model of Ferdinand the Bull, designed by Arnold Machin, a simplistically modeled creature, impressed "Wedgewood, Made in England", printed "Wedgewood Barlaston England".

12.25in (31cm) long

$400-600   **DN**

A Wedgewood figure of an exotic cow, with molded and incised floral design, painted in colors on a white ground, printed marks.

9.75in (25cm) long

$180-220   **L&T**

A Wedgewood lemonade jug (with four matching beakers, not shown), produced for Liberty's of London, designed by Professor Richard Guyatt.

1953   *7.5in (19cm) high*

$1,500-2,000 (set)   **REN**

A Wedgewood slender flared vase, decorated in colored enamels and gilt with butterflies, on a lustrous ground, on round base, printed mark in gilt and pattern number "Z4832", foot-rim chip glued.

6in (15.2cm) high

$150-200   **LFA**

A pair of Wedgewood 'Dragon Luster' vases, each of baluster form, printed in gilt with dragons on a mottled blue ground, printed and painted mark "Z4829".

8.25in (21cm) high

$400-600   **L&T**

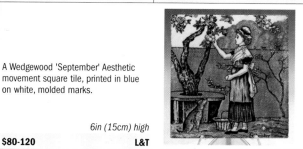

A Wedgewood 'September' Aesthetic movement square tile, printed in blue on white, molded marks.

6in (15cm) high

$80-120   **L&T**

Miscellaneous

A Rosenthal figure of a girl with bear, designed by Adolf Oppel, a marble base, golden base mark.

c1900   8.75in (22cm) high

$450-550   **BMN**

A Rosenthal figure group 'Musica', designed by Ferdinand Liebermann, allegorical figure of woman, flanked by putti, signed and marked.

c1921   14.5in (36.5cm) high

$1,800-2,200   **Qu**

A Rosenthal figure of a young girl, painted in color, standing on base wearing a summer dress, signed.

c1927   16.5in (41.5cm) high

$3,500-4,000   **HERR**

A Rosenthal figure of a sitting musician with guitar and dog, painted in color, signed.

c1915   14in (35cm) high

$1,000-1,500   **HERR**

A Rosenthal figure 'The robber', designed by Grete Zschäbitz, manufacturer's stamp.

c1926   5.75in (14.5cm) high

$1,000-1,500   **HERR**

A Rosenthal figure 'The Small Grumble', designed by Grete Zschäbitz, manufacturer's stamp.

c1926   6in (15.2cm) high

$750-850   **HERR**

A Rosenthal vase with lid, designed by Hans Schiffner, painted with dragons, manufacturer's stamp.

c1920   12.75in (32cm) high

$280-320   **HERR**

A Rosenthal figural group, 'Spring Love', designed by Richard Aigner, with green mark "K295/1".

c1920   10.5in (26.5cm) high

$350-450   **FIS**

A Rosenthal coffee pot, milk jug and sugar bowl, designed by Hans Günther Reinstein, from the Botticelli series, painted with blue underglaze, lid restored, manufacturer's stamp and artist's stamp.

c1903

Coffee pot 8.5in (21cm) high

$1,200-1,800   **HERR**

A glazed earthenware wine jug by Emile Gallé, with picture of a Dutch drinker, rim with dots of gold, signed, minor hairline cracks.

c1884   8.75in (22cm) high

$1,000-1,500   **Qu**

A coffee pot by Emile Gallé, in the shape of a calabash, spout with bird's head, branch-molded handle, leaf-molded lid, glazed, professionally restored, marks and stamps.

c1889   10.5in (26.5cm) high

$1,000-1,500   **Qu**

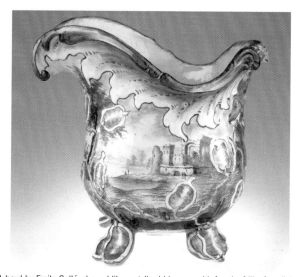

A bowl by Emile Gallé, shaped like a stylized blossom with four leaf-like feet, light blue pewter glaze, rocailles decoration, blue painting of a coast with ruins, signed, restored chips.

c1880   8.5in (21.5cm) high
$1,200-1,800   **Qu**

A Louis XVI jardinière with emblem of the city of Nancy, designed by Emile Gallé, made by Saint-Clément, white pewter glaze, blue glaze paintings, signed "Gallé Nancy St. Clément", single minor chips.

c1876   17in (43cm) wide
$1,000-1,500   **Qu**

A glazed earthenware Emile Gallé vase, depicting blooming branches on blue, green and brown dotted ground, base signed "EG Lothringer Kreuz Nancy déposé" and stamp "E... G... DEPOSE".

c1880   7in (17.7cm) high
$1,000-1,500   **Qu**

A William de Morgan circular charger, painted in red with lusters with a fantastical fish on a foliate ground, the reverse painted with concentric bands and a leafy band.

14.25in (36.5cm) diam
$3,000-4,000   **L&T**

A William de Morgan luster punch bowl, of deep circular form, painted to the exterior with leaves and flowers in ruby luster and to the interior with a central rosette on a ruby luster ground.

13in (33cm) diam
$500-700   **L&T**

A lion lighter by Emile Gallé, Nancy, a lion sitting on a base and looking to its right, white pewter glaze.

c1876   9.5in (23.5cm) high
$1,000-1,500   **Qu**

A late 19thC William de Morgan vase, with loop handles, the conical body decorated in red luster with mythical feline beasts on a floral ground, one handle damaged, some staining.

7.25in (18.5cm) high
$1,200-1,800   **WW**

A William De Morgan 'Iznik' vase and cover, painted by Jo Juster, with stylized flowers and leaves in blue on a pale ground, "W De Morgan Fulham J.J." painted in black.

c1890   10.75in (27.5cm) high
$6,500-7,500   **WW**

A William de Morgan glazed tile, of square form decorated in the 'Iznik' style with flowers and leaves, impressed Merton Abbey mark.

8in (20.5cm) wide
$1,000-1,500   **L&T**

A Schwarzburger figure by Otto Kramer, with exotically dressed dancer, hands restored, signed and stamped.

c1926   7in (17.5cm) high
$500-700   **HERR**

A Schwarzburger pair of figures by Gustav Oppel, painted in color, signed and stamped "GOPPEL".

c1924   5.5in (13.5cm) high
$450-550   **HERR**

DECORATIVE ARTS

A pair of Schwarzburger oriental dancing figures, by Gustav Oppel, painted in color, rim of trousers restored, signed and stamped.

c1919   13.5in (32.5cm) high
$1,000-1,500   **HERR**

A Schwarzburger lamp base, 'Ash Wednesday', by W. Schwartzkopf, slightly damaged, signed and stamped.

c1920   14in (35cm) high
$800-1,200   **HERR**

A Schwarzburger lamp base 'Hawk Hunter' by Mauritius Pfeiffer, horn functions as holder, stamped.

c1918   28.5in (72cm) high
$2,200-2,800   **HERR**

A Crown Devon Mattajade 'Fairy Castle' vase, pattern number 2406, printed and painted marks.

15in (38cm) high
$1,400-1,600   **WW**

A Crown Devon Mattajade 'Fairy Castle' vase, pattern number 2406, printed and painted marks.

6.5in (16cm) high
$1,000-1,500   **WW**

A Crown Devon 'Geometric Parrot' vase, pattern, printed mark.

9in (23cm) high
$1,000-1,500   **WW**

A Crown Devon vase, decorated with a bird of paradise among stylized flowers and foliage, printed mark.

11.5in (29.5cm) high
$1,000-1,500   **WW**

A pair of Christopher Dresser bottle vases, possibly Linthorpe, the necks treacle glazed at the rim and shading to turquoise, the compressed spherical bodies splashed and streaked with cream and pink, impressed signatures.

10.25in (26cm) high
$1,500-2,000   **Chef**

A large Ault jardinière, the design attributed to Christopher Dresser, of globular shape decorated with linear banding and fluted wing-like panels that extend to form short scroll handles, glazed olive-green shading to pinkish-red on the upper section, vase mark in relief on base with "Ault" and "England", star-crack on side.

12.75in (32.5cm) high
$220-280   **DN**

An Old Hall 'Persia' pattern plate, designed by Christopher Dresser, transfer-printed with highly stylized flowers and foliage, picked out with turquoise, pink, blue, red and lemon.

9in (23cm) wide
$80-120   **DN**

A Theodore Deck earthenware model of a duck, with a white band around its neck with violet feathers below, its wing plumage in turquoise, deep blue and speckled brown, the tail feathers in turquoise shading to black, impressed "TH. Deck" on base, losses to feet.

12.5in (32cm) long
$5,000-7,000   **DN**

A Theodore Deck enamel circular wall plate, painted by Ehrmann, depicting a naked Classical female figure, in naturalistic colors against a bright blue background, signed on edge "Ehrmann" and on reverse "TH D" monogram.

11.5in (29cm) diam
$1,500-2,000   **DN**

A Goldscheider figure of a stylish female dancer, from a model by Lorenzl, wearing a puce-colored top trimmed with yellow and black banding and a long floral-printed skirt, on a circular black base, marked on upper base "Lorenzl" and with factory marks on the underside of base.

19.75in (50cm) high

$3,500-4,500 **DN**

A late 19thC Goldscheider terracotta figure of a girl walking with baskets, by J. Caniroff, incised and impressed marks, some damage.

29.5in (75cm) high

$150-200 **Chef**

A ceramic table lamp by Walter and Marcell Goldscheider, three women holding hands, cracked.

c1905 *18in (46cm) high*

$6,000-8,000 **HERR**

A Poole Carter Stabler Adams Ltd. pottery vase, of cylindrical form, painted in green, gray and rust with flowers and foliage on crackle glaze white ground, impressed and painted marks.

12in (30.5cm) high

$150-200 **L&T**

A 1920s Poole blue bird vase, the three birds amongst flowers in a band on the shoulders below ocher and blue pecked neck and rim bands, "LA 575-PN" and other marks.

7.5in (19cm) high

$220-280 **Chef**

A Poole Carter Stabler Adams shouldered vase, shape no "966", pattern 'EP', painted by Mary Brown, impressed CSA mark, painted artist's cypher.

9.5in (24.5cm) high

$1,000-1,500 **WW**

One of a set of six mid-20thC Royal Copenhagen 'Flora Danica' soup plates, each decorated with a named plant, printed marks, wave and cancellation marks.

10in (25cm) diam

$1,000-1,500 (set) **DN**

A set of six Royal Copenhagen porcelain figures of children in regional costume, comprising a figure of Fyn numbered "12420", a figure of Esvig numbered "12417", a figure of Sjaelland numbered "12418", a figure of Faeroerne numbered "12416", a figure of Sjaelland numbered "12418" and a figure of Gronland numbered "12419", all but the first with original boxes.

Largest 4in (10cm) high

$1,800-2,200 **SI**

Four Royal Copenhagen porcelain figures of children in national costume, comprising a figure of Amager numbered "12412", a figure of Gronland numbered "12419", a figure of Fano numbered "12413" and a figure of Amager numbered "12414", each with original box.

Largest 6in (15cm) high

$1,200-1,800 **SI**

DECORATIVE ARTS

A monumental jasperware covered vase and pedestal, by J. Adams & Co., the baluster-form vase applied with two goats' heads joined by boldly molded oak leaf and acorn swags, the domed cover, neck and foot with oak leaf and acorn borders, the waisted pedestal with conforming decoration, impressed marks.

Jasperware is a hard, fine-grained colored stoneware developed in the 1770s by Wedgwood and then copied by other factories in the 19thC.

c1870   52in (132cm) high

$6,000-8,000   **SI**

An Allander shouldered ovoid vase, covered with a streaked blue and purple glaze on a mottled ground, incised mark "Allander Feb 1908".

2in (5cm) high

$220-280   **L&T**

A French Argilor porcelain nightlight, with the central figure of a female warrior, probably Diana the Huntress, horns missing, the wooden base incorporates a mirror, signed on back "Argilor Paris France".

9.5in (24cm) high

$150-200   **DN**

A Bailey Fulham Pottery stoneware oviform vase, with cylindrical neck, incise-decorated with birds and nests, pottery mark in oval, rebus for Kettle and dated "1895", and another similar vase, from the same pottery, signed "CJC Bailey", also with Kettle rebus.

Tallest 15.25in (38.5cm) high

$280-320 (both)   **DN**

A Boch Frères 'Gres Keramis' glazed stoneware vase, by Charles Catteau, stamped in dog mark with "KERAMIS MADE in BELGIUM Ch. Catteau. D.1242" and incised "Gres Keramis", stamped numbers "1057C".

7.5in (19cm) high

$1,300-1,500   **FRE**

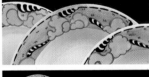

An extensive Bough part dinner service, painted by Richard Amour with a band of foliage, comprising 15 dinner plates, 15 soup plates, 13 fish plates, 14 dessert plates, 12 side plates and two vegetable tureens and covers, printed and painted marks.

$500-700   **L&T**

A Brannam pottery centerpiece, in the form of a grotesque bird-like vessel, incised "C.H.Brannam, Barum, 1901" with initials "R.P.", restoration to bird's head.

9.75in (25cm) long

$1,000-1,500   **DN**

A Brownfield and Son porcelain gilt-decorated vase, the peach-bodied bulbous vessel molded with maple leaves on a basket weave ground, printed double globe mark, impressed "BROWNFIELD".

c1871-92   4.5in (11.5cm) high

$120-180   **SI**

A 'Putto with flowers', by the Wiener Kunstkeramische Busch & Ludescher factory, pressmarks.

c1910-30   5.75in (14.5cm) high

$300-500   **BMN**

An Edouard Cazaux pottery sculpture, 'Baigneuse Nile Alongee', modeled as a naked young woman poised with her hands cupped over her crossed legs, all beneath a mottled green and golden glaze, signed on upper base "Cazaux".

10.5in (26.5cm) high

$1,500-2,000   **DN**

A Longwy ceramic glazed earthenware vase, designed by M. P. Chevallier, with stamped ink mark "SOCIETE DES FAIENCERIES LONGWY FRANCE" and "M. P. Chevallier", hairline crack.

10in (25.5cm) high

$450-550   **FRE**

A pair of French porcelain Aesthetic Movement vases, each square tapering vessel applied with strapwork handles, painted in underglaze blue on a silver ground with gilt highlights, depicting Asian figures, impressed "H.A. & Cie".

c1890   *12in (30cm) high*

$1,800-2,200   **SI**

A Craven Dunnill & Co. oviform luster vase, molded on base with "Craven Dunnill Jackfield Salop. England".

12.75in (32.5cm) high

$300-500   **DN**

A pair of 19th/20thC Copeland octagonal plates, each with a gilt rim with a jeweled cobalt border, the center decorated with an exotic bird in gold and small opal panels.

9.75in (25cm) diam

$500-700   **FRE**

A Crown Ducal dish, designed by Charlotte Rhead, with a band of slip trailed oranges between one, the green concentric rings on a buff ground, slip trailed signature.

12.5in (32cm) diam

$350-450   **Chef**

A French porcelain Art Deco figure of Columbine, modeled in a stylized manner, on a square base, signed on base "Dax".

13.25in (33.5cm) high

$450-550   **DN**

A Delphin Massier ceramic oviform vase, painted on base "Delphin Massier, Vallauris (A.M.)".

11.5in (29.5cm) high

$1,300-1,500   **DN**

A Dunmore style twin-handled vase, of ovoid form, molded and incised with naïve Classical scenes, with applied handles having mark terminals.

10in (25cm) high

$150-200   **L&T**

An Aesthetic Movement painted wall plate, naturalistically painted with the profile head and shoulders of a Classical maiden, signed on the reverse "Arthur Ellidgley" and dated "1888", on a German blank.

10in (25.5cm) high

$60-90   **DN**

A Sir Edmund Elton bottle-shaped vase, modeled with a flowering branch, on a trickled blue/brown ground, painted mark in black, firing fault.

c1900   *10.5in (2.5cm) high*

$150-200   **LFA**

An allegorical figure of a girl with long dress, by Wiener Emailfarbwerk Schauer & Co., posing as Spring, press marks and stamps, some chips to blossoms.

c1900   *25.5in (63.7cm) high*

$1,000-1,000   **Qu**

CERAMICS

An Etling porcelain nightlight, modeled as a man wearing a white turban with jeweled top, marked "Editions Etling Paris", "SEGB" in segmented oval, and "France", restoration to floral cover.

8in (20.5cm) high

$180-220   **DN**

A late 19thC Hungarian Fischer pottery bowl, with pierced borders and handles, painted in iron-red and gilt with a ground of scrolling foliage, within turquoise lappet borders, printed mark, minor rubbing to gilding.

14in (36cm) wide

$220-280   **DN**

A Hungarian pottery twin-handled flask, by Fischer of Budapest, flattened baluster shape, transfer-printed and painted, factory marks on base.

12.25in (31cm) high

$150-200   **DN**

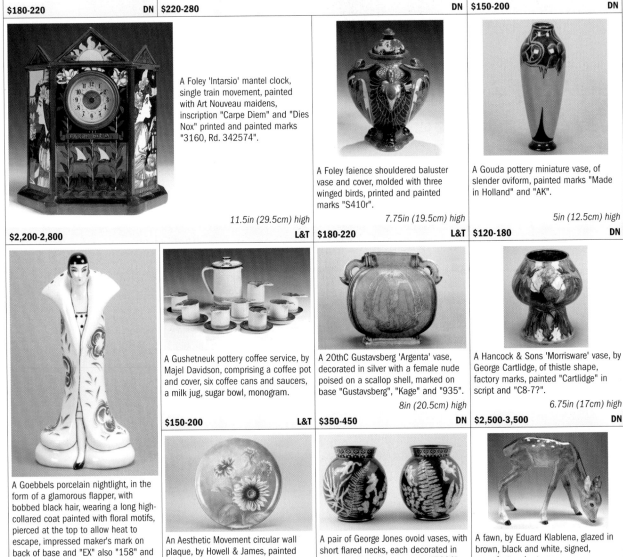

A Foley 'Intarsio' mantel clock, single train movement, painted with Art Nouveau maidens, inscription "Carpe Diem" and "Dies Nox" printed and painted marks "3160, Rd. 342574".

11.5in (29.5cm) high

$2,200-2,800   **L&T**

A Foley faience shouldered baluster vase and cover, molded with three winged birds, printed and painted marks "S410r".

7.75in (19.5cm) high

$180-220   **L&T**

A Gouda pottery miniature vase, of slender oviform, painted marks "Made in Holland" and "AK".

5in (12.5cm) high

$120-180   **DN**

A Goebbels porcelain nightlight, in the form of a glamorous flapper, with bobbed black hair, wearing a long high-collared coat painted with floral motifs, pierced at the top to allow heat to escape, impressed maker's mark on back of base and "EX" also "158" and "dep".

7.5in (19cm) high

$220-280   **DN**

A Gushetneuk pottery coffee service, by Majel Davidson, comprising a coffee pot and cover, six coffee cans and saucers, a milk jug, sugar bowl, monogram.

$150-200   **L&T**

An Aesthetic Movement circular wall plaque, by Howell & James, painted with monogram "MCR", exhibition label.

1883   *16.25in (41.5cm) diam*

$150-200   **DN**

A 20thC Gustavsberg 'Argenta' vase, decorated in silver with a female nude poised on a scallop shell, marked on base "Gustavsberg", "Kage" and "935".

8in (20.5cm) high

$350-450   **DN**

A pair of George Jones ovoid vases, with short flared necks, each decorated in pâte-sur-pâte, gilt pattern no. "5664".

c1880   *6in (15cm) high*

$600-900   **LFA**

A Hancock & Sons 'Morrisware' vase, by George Cartlidge, of thistle shape, factory marks, painted "Cartlidge" in script and "C8-7?".

6.75in (17cm) high

$2,500-3,500   **DN**

A fawn, by Eduard Klablena, glazed in brown, black and white, signed, manufacturer's stamp.

c1925   *12in (29.5cm) high*

$1,000-1,500   **Qu**

A plate by El Lissitzky, decorated in red geometric shapes, some wear, marked.

1923   12in (30.5cm) diam

$300-500   **HERR**

Two Maling cabinet plates, one decorated with a brightly colored rural scene of a watermill, flowers and trees the other with a brown sailing ship.

11in (28cm) diam

$300-500   **DN**

A French pottery vase, attributed to Paul Jean Milet, naturalistic colors against a golden foil ground, marked on the base "MP" and "Sèvres".

9.5in (24cm) high

$450-550   **DN**

A Moore owl and tree trunk vase, the white long-eared bird perched on a naturalistically colored tree trunk, impressed mark.

13in (32cm) high

$650-750   **Chef**

A Madonna by Michael Mörtl, white glaze and colorfully painted, incised signature on the inside "M. Mörtl".

c1910   14.5in (36cm) high

$1,000-1,500   **Qu**

A John Pearson earthenware cream bowl, painted to the interior with a pelican within bands of stylized foliage, painted marks.

9.5in (24cm) diam

$750-850   **L&T**

A Pirkenhammer porcelain figure, designed by Anton Klieber, modeled as a girl with golden locks and slippers on a sofa, impressed factory marks "F&M".

5.5in (14cm) high

$600-900   **DN**

A beer mug, by Richard Riemerschmid, Munich, depicting a dandelion, hairline crack on inside, marked.

1900

$750-850   **Qu**

A Riessner, Stellmacher & Kessel Art Nouveau oviform vase, makers' marks and "Made in Austria" on base.

13in (33cm) high

$2,500-3,000   **DN**

A Royal Bonn Art Nouveau vase, hand-painted with a portrait of a young woman, signed "T Stichers".

c1900   15.5in (39.5cm) high

$750-850   **FRE**

A Rye pottery tapered cylindrical vase and cover with decoration of glazed molded hops on a mottled ground.

11in (28cm) high

$220-280   **Clv**

A pair of Sarreguemines pottery 'Japanesque' large vases, converted to lamp bases, drilled for electricity.

16.25in (41cm) high

$1,200-1,800   **DN**

A J.V. Schwarz ceramic rectangular plaque, designed by C.S. Luber, molded to simulate tube-lining, in vivid colors, impressed on back "sc", "5049" and "R".

17.5in (44.5cm) wide

$1,200-1,800   **DN**

A Sèvres porcelain Art Nouveau oviform vase, with red mark "RF, Decore a Sèvres 1909, Manufacture Nationale" and blue painter's mark "P".

20in (50.5cm) high

$1,200-1,800   **DN**

A Shelley luster vase, by Walter Slater, with a fish swimming amongst waterweed, printed mark, facsimile signature.

10in (26cm) high

$1,500-2,000   **WW**

A Shelley luster ginger jar and cover, by Walter Slater decorated with an exotic bird amongst prunus, printed mark, facsimile signature.

9.25in (23.5cm) high

$3,000-4,000   **WW**

A Villeroy & Boch, Dresden vase, with stylized blossoms, incised on base and stamp.

c1915   12in (29.5cm) high

$300-500   **Qu**

A Volkstedt porcelain figure, from ENS workshops, of a girl in a harlequinesque costume, factory marks on base and indistinct modeller's signature, restored.

9.5in (24cm) high

$350-450   **DN**

A Charles Vyse figure, 'The Morning Ride', incised "Charles Vyse Chelsea", damage.

10.5in (27cm) high

$1,200-1,800   **WW**

A Wadeheath Musical Jug, in 'The Big Bad Wolf' pattern, cast in low relief, printed mark.

10.5in (26.5cm) high

$1,000-1,500   **WW**

An Art Nouveau ceramic wall plaque, by Ernst Wahliss, molded with lilies surrounding the head of a woman, stamped mark.

c1900   15in (38cm) diam

$500-700   **FRE**

An Ernest Wahliss Art Nouveau ewer, impressed marks "Made in Austria 4696" and painted "Alexandra Porcelain Works 4608, 410".

24.5in (62.5cm) high

$2,200-2,800   **L&T**

An earthenware bowl, by Helen Walton, with a pattern of honeysuckle and bees on a pale green ground, painted monogram and apple motif to base.

5.5in (14cm) diam

$1,000-1,500   **L&T**

A Ludwig Wessel biscuit barrel, Bonn, with glazed majolica flower design, knob re-glued, mark on base.

c1900   7in (18cm) high

$50-80   **BMN**

A Wileman & Co. Foley China Art Nouveau design two-handled tapered cylindrical vase, with stopper.

11.75in (30cm) high

$300-400   **Clv**

A WMF Art Deco ceramic tray, circular with hand-decorated flowers, metal frame stamped "WMF", diamond mark.

c1930   12in (30.5cm) diam

$220-280   **FRE**

A pair of early 20thC Zsolnay Pecs double gourd vases, decorated with blue Isnik flowers, printed marks.

6in (15.5cm) high

$180-220   **Chef**

A Zsolnay luster oviform vase, glazed, towers mark and "Made in Hungary" on base.

9.75in (24.5cm) high

$450-550   **DN**

An Austrian Art Nouveau amphora figural group, with a wave forming the vase, two dishes and a boy and girl, stamped marks, hairline crack to base.

c1900   12in (30.5cm) high

$500-700   **FRE**

An Austrian Art Nouveau figural dish, representing the birth of Venus, impressed "Made in Austria".

7in (18cm) high

$500-700   **Chef**

A Continental Art Deco porcelain figure, molded as a girl in a flowering floral gown and raised on an oval base, painted in colors, apparently unmarked.

8.25in (21cm) high

$220-280   **L&T**

An Italian ceramic group of a mother and child, in the manner of Goldscheider, signed on base "FMz" in a triangle and "Italy".

5.5in (14cm) high

$220-280   **DN**

Clifton

A Clifton Indian ware squat vessel, after the Homolobi tribe, painted and incised with geometric wave pattern in red and brown on terracotta ground, marked "Clifton/Homolobi".

10in (25.5cm) wide

$500-700 DRA

A Clifton Indian ware squat vessel after the Homolobi tribe, painted and incised with stylized birds in flight in brown and ivory on terracotta ground, glaze flakes, stamped "Clifton/ Homolobi/235".

9in (23cm) wide

$500-800 DRA

A Clifton Indian squat vessel, after the Homolobi tribe, incised and painted with brown stylized animals on terracotta ground, incised "Clifton/Homolobi/234".

8.5in (21.5cm) wide

$300-500 DRA

A large Clifton Indian squat vessel, after the Pueblo Viejo tribe of Arizona, painted and incised with a stylized Greek key band and geometric patterns, stamped "Clifton" and titled.

15.5in (39.5cm) wide

$600-900 DRA

A large Clifton Indian squat vessel, after the Pueblo Viejo, Upper Gila Valley, Arizona, incised and painted with a geometric design in black and ivory on a terracotta ground, two-inch bruise to inner rim, some flakes to glaze, incised "Clifton" with tribe, and "190".

15in (38cm) wide

$600-900 DRA

A Clifton Indian tapering vessel, "Four Mile Ruin, AZ", incised and painted with stylized Greek key decoration in brown on a terracotta ground, incised "236", stamped with tribe.

7.25in (18.5cm) wide

$350-400 DRA

A Clifton Indian ware gourd-shaped vase, after the Arkansas tribe, with geometric steps in ivory on red ground, several glaze flakes, marked "Clifton/205".

6.5in (16.5cm) wide

$300-500 DRA

A Clifton Indian ware bulbous vase, after the Four Mile Ruin, AZ tribe, with stylized eagles in black on a red ground, 5in crack from rim, marked "Clifton with tribe/192".

9.5in (24.5cm) high

$700-1,000 DRA

A large Clifton Indian bottle-shaped vase, after the Mississippi tribe, incised and painted with symbols around the neck and swirls on its base, in black and ivory on terra cotta ground, incised "Clifton/Mississippi/227".

12.25in (31cm) high

$500-800 DRA

A Clifton Indian ware gourd-shaped vessel, after the Middle Mississippi tribe, painted with petal forms in terra cotta and gray on a black and terra cotta ground, stamped "Clifton" with tribe, "231".

12.25in (31cm) high

$500-800 DRA

A Clifton Indian ware gourd-shaped vessel, after the Middle Mississippi tribe, painted with petal forms in two tones of terra cotta on a darker terra cotta ground, incised "Clifton/231".

12.25in (31cm) high

$500-700 DRA

A Clifton Tirrube blauster vase, painted with a single white rose with green foliage on a terracotta ground, incised "Clifton/153".

7.75in (19.5cm) high

$300-400 DRA

A Clifton Tirrube blauster vase, printed by A. Haubrich with a white heron and palm fronds on a terracotta ground, stamped "Clifton/257", incised "A.Haubrich".

12in (30.5cm) high

$1,200-1,800   DRA

A Clifton Tirrube vase, painted with white narcissus and green foliage on a terracotta ground, stamped "Clifton/281".

8.25in (21cm) high

$600-900   DRA

A Clifton Tirrube bottle-shaped vase, painted with ivory nasturtium and green leaves on a terracotta ground, stamped "Clifton/148".

9.25in (23.5cm) high

$400-600   DRA

A large Clifton Tirrube bottle-shaped vase, painted with white and grey tulips on terracotta ground, stamped "CLIFTON/254".

12in (30.5cm) high

$700-1,000   DRA

A large Clifton Tirrube squat vessel, painted with a single white rose with green foliage on a terracotta ground, stamped "Clifton/212".

6.5in (16.5cm) wide

$400-600   DRA

A Clifton Crystal Patina ovoid vase, with green and beige matte glaze dripping over a celadon microcrystalline ground, incised "Clifton/CAP/1906/154".

1906   8.5in (21.5cm) high

$500-800   DRA

A rare Clifton Crystal Patina bulbous vase, with silver-plated poppy overlay, incised "Clifton/CAP/1906/141", and stamped "Electrotytic/Trenton NJ".

1906   6.75in (17cm) high

$800-1,200   DRA

A Clifton Crystal Patina bulbous vase, with matte amber glaze dripping over a celadon microcrstalline ground, incised "Clifton/CAP/1906/141".

1906   6.5in (16.5cm) high

$400-600   DRA

A Clifton Crystal Patina vase, with flaring four-sided neck and squat base covered in a celadon and amber crystalline flambé glaze, incised "Clifton/1907".

1907   7.25in (18.5cm) high

$400-600   DRA

A Clifton Crystal Patina spherical vase, with a sunburst effect in matte yellow and chartreuse over a celadon ground, incised "Clifton/CAP/1906".

1906   7in (18cm) wide

$1,000-1,500   DRA

A Clifton Crystal Patina squat vessel, covered in celadon microcrystalline and matte green flambé glaze, minute fleck near rim, incised "Clifton/190?/160".

1907   7.75in (19.5cm) wide

$400-600   DRA

A Clifton Crystal Patina ovoid vase, with green and beige matte glaze dripping over a celadon microcrystalline ground, incised "Clifton/CAP/1906/154".

1906   8.5in (21.5cm) high

$500-800   DRA

A Clifton vase with four-sided flaring rim and squat base, covered in an ivory and taupe matte glaze, some glaze bubbles, incised "Clifton/1905/137".

1905   *7.25in (18.5cm) high*

$600-900   **DRA**

A Clifton cabinet vase, molded with fish and waves under a smooth matte green glaze, a couple of minute nicks to high points, incised "Clifton/CAP/1906/108".

1906   *3.5in (9cm) wide*

$1,200-1,800   **DRA**

Fulper

A Fulper corseted two-handled vase, covered in Copperdust crystalline to Flemington Green flambé glaze, vertical mark.

9.5in (24cm) high

$800-1,200   **DRA**

A Fulper gourd-shaped two-handled vase, covered in amber and sheer turquoise flambé glaze, vertical mark.

7.5in (19cm) high

$350-400   **DRA**

A large and rare Fulper buttressed vase, pierced with triangles around the neck, covered in a Flemington Green flambé glaze, restoration to rim and base, rectangular ink mark.

13.25in (33.5cm) high

$3,500-4,500   **DRA**

A large Fulper bulbous vessel, covered in a frothy blue crystalline matte-to-Chinese Blue crystalline flambé glaze, raised racetrack mark.

12in (30.5cm) high

$2,000-2,500   **DRA**

A Fulper spherical vessel, with closed-in rim, covered in a mirror black glaze, a few scratches, incised racetrack mark.

7in (18cm) wide

$300-400   **DRA**

A Fulper spherical vessel, with closed-in rim covered in a frothy mirrored glaze in black and gray, vertical mark.

7in (18cm) wide

$500-800   **DRA**

A large Fulper squat vase, covered in a superior frothy mirror black glaze over Chinese blue crystalline, restoration to drilled hole on bottom, restored incised vertical mark.

10in (25.5cm) wide

$1,000-1,500   **DRA**

A Fulper bulbous urn with collared rim and two angular handles, covered in mirror black glaze, some scratches and crazing, raised racetrack mark.

9in (23cm) high

$600-900   **DRA**

A large and rare Fulper bulbous and ribbed vase, of Oriental shape with floriform rim, covered in a Cat's Eye-like scratches, around the rim, raised racetrack mark.

11.5in (29cm) high

$2,500-3,000   **DRA**

A large Fulper bulbous vase, covered in a gunmetal and Chinese blue crstalline flambé glaze, raised racetrack mark.

12in (30.5cm) high

$3,500-4,500   **DRA**

A Fulper vase with flat shoulder, covered in a Wisteria matte glaze, ink racetrack mark.

7.5in (19cm)

$500-800   **DRA**

A Fulper large squat two-handled vessel with reticulated rim, covered in a frothy indigo and light blue microcrystalline glaze, stilt-pull and grinding chips, horizontal stamped mark.

10.5in (26.5cm) wide

$400-600   **DRA**

A Fulper corseted vase, covered in a frothy matt blue glaze, Flemington ink stamp.

7.5in (19cm) high

$250-300   **DRA**

A tall Fulper milk-can shaped vase, covered in Leopard Skin glaze, restoration to three stilt-pull chips and to several lines at rim, rectangular ink mark.

12in (30.5cm) high

$600-900   **DRA**

A Fulper footed centerbowl with two double-scroll handles, its interior covered in a flame pattern of Cat's Eye and mahogany glaze, its exterior in mottled mahogany over matte mustard, ink racetrack mark.

13in (33cm) wide

$800-1,200   **DRA**

Grueby

A Grueby vase, with floriform rim decorated by Gertrude Priest with tooled and applied buds alternating with broad leaves, covered in matte green glaze, chip and hairline from rim, circular pottery mark/artist's initials.

7in (18cm)

$1,800–2,200   **DRA**

A Grueby two-color vase, decorated with tooled and applied leaves alternating with yellow buds, and covered in a great feathered matte green glaze, touch-up to base fleck and restoration to rim chips, circular pottery mark.

9in (23cm) high

$6,000–9,000   **DRA**

A Grueby ovoid vase, with three tooled and applied full-height leaves under a leathery matte green glaze, a couple of minute flecks to leaf edge, circular pottery stamp.

7.5in (19cm) high

$3,000–4,000   **DRA**

A large Grueby barrel-shaped vase, by Wilhelmina Post, with tooled and applied short and tall leaves alternating under a matte green glaze, touch-ups to leaf edges, also 1"sq glaze miss, stamped "Grueby Pottery/WP".

8.5in (21.5cm) high

$2,500–3,000   **DRA**

A large Grueby vase, by Wilhelmina Post, with stovepipe neck and bulbous base decorated with tooled and applied leaves under a leathery matte green glaze, circular pottery mark "/WP".

16.5in (42cm) high

$10,000–15,000   **DRA**

A rare Grueby tear-shaped vase, with tooled and applied full-height triangular leaves under a frothy matte green glaze, circular pottery mark.

6.75in (17cm) high

$4,000–6,000   **DRA**

A Grueby four-sided bowl, by Wilhelmina Post, decorated with tooled and applied leaves under a leathery matte green glaze, with glossy interior, tight line from rim, circular pottery mark "WP".

6.25in (16cm) square

$3,500–4,500   **DRA**

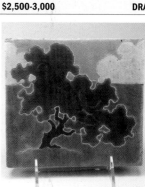

A Grueby tile, decorated in cuenca with an oak tree, the leaves in greenish-brown oatmealed matte glaze, minor chips to corners and edge, few minute flecks to cuenca walls, signed "EN".

6in (15cm) wide

$4,000–6,000   **DRA**

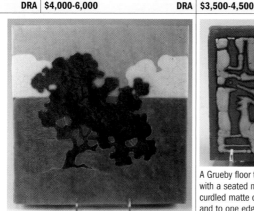

An exceptional and extremely rare Grueby tile design, by Addison LeBoutiller, decorated in cuenca with a large oak tree in dark green oatmealed glaze over green grass, puffy ivory clouds in blue sky, inscribed "MM".

12.25in (31cm) square

$40,000–50,000   **DRA**

A Grueby floor tile, of red clay decorated with a seated monk reading, against a curdled matte ochre glaze, chip to corner and to one edge, unmarked.

6in (15cm) square

$500–700   **DRA**

A Grueby tile, decorated in cuenca, with an indigo and ochre ship with ivory sails, on a dark teal blue ground, signed "GM".

8in (20.5cm) square

$1,800–2,200   **DRA**

Newcomb

A large Newcomb College bulbous vase, carved by Sadie Irvine, with branches of pink, blue, and yellow dogwood on a shaded pink and blue matte ground, "NC/SI/KG23/178/JM".

1915   *8.25in (21cm) high*
$8,000-12,000   **DRA**

A Newcomb College Transitional vase, carved by Sadie Irvine, with crocuses on a green ground, "NC/SI/HG34/186/JM".

1915   *8.5in (21.5cm) high*
$3,500-4,500   **DRA**

A Newcomb College tapering vase, carved by Sadie Irvine with Spanish moss, small area of abrasion near base from firing, "NC/SI/236/QP70".

1917   *6.5in (16.5cm) high*
$3,500-4,500   **DRA**

A Newcomb College squat four-handled vessel, carved by Sadie Irvine, with light blue trillium with yellow centers on a blue matte ground, interior spider lines, typical, underglaze firing lines to handles, "NC/SI/LN29/247/JM".

1921   *5.5in (14cm) wide*
$2,500-3,000   **DRA**

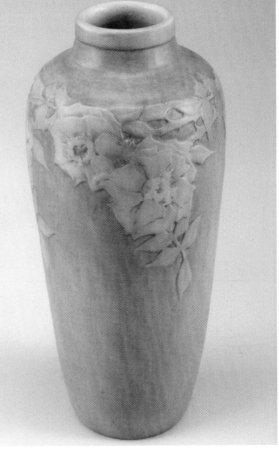

A Newcomb College bulbous vessel, carved by Sadie Irvine, with blue and yellow daffodils on a light blue matte ground, "NC/SI/LV64/46/JM".

1921   *4.75in (12cm) wide*
$2,000-2,500   **DRA**

A Newcomb College tapering bud vase, carved by Sadie Irvine, with sycamore leaves and red berries on a blue matte ground, "NC/SI/LT67/170/JM".

1921   *8in (20.5cm) high*
$2,000-2,500   **DRA**

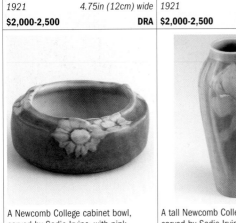

A Newcomb College cabinet bowl, carved by Sadie Irvine, with pink daisies with yellow centers around green rim, "NC/SI/OA89/10/JM".

1924   *3.75in (9.5cm) wide*
$1,200–1,800   **DRA**

A tall Newcomb College ovoid vase, carved by Sadie Irvine, with blue and yellow irises on green stems against a blue matte ground, "NC/SI/OM94/150/JM".

1925   *10.5in (26.5cm) high*
$5,000-8,000   **DRA**

A tall Newcomb College vase, carved by Sadie Irvine, with pink roses and yellow centers on green leaves, 3in Y-shaped line and bruise from rim, "NC/SI/MD16/151/JM".

1922   *11.75in (30cm) high*
$10,000-15,000   **DRA**

A Newcomb College ovoid vase, carved by Sadie Irvine, with branches of pink gladiola on a dark blue ground, "NC/SI/PE31/181/JM".

1926   *6in (15cm) high*

$3,000-5,000   **DRA**

A Newcomb College cylindrical vase, carved by Sadie Irvine, with pink blossoms on green stems against a blue ground, 2in line from rim and restoration to other side, "NC/SI/JH/329/RL/54".

1929   *5.75in (14.5cm) high*

$1,000-1,500   **DRA**

A Newcomb College ovoid vase, carved by Sadie Irvine, with live oaks and moon, "NC/SI/JH/236/TK99".

1931   *6.5in (16.5cm) high*

$3,500-4,500   **DRA**

A Newcomb College ovoid vase, carved by Sadie Irvine with live oaks, Spanish Moss, and a full moon on a blue matte ground, "NC/SI/HM/287/TS50".

1932   *6in (15cm) high*

$4,000-6,000   **DRA**

An unusual Newcomb College squat vessel, carved by Sadie Irvine, with stylized foliage under a pink, green, and blue matte glaze, 1in line from rim, "NC/SI/UM100/FF/JM".

1933   *4in (10cm) wide*

$2,000-2,500   **DRA**

A large Newcomb College Transitional vase, by A.F. Simpson, with sharply carved live-oak trees covered in Spanish moss, "NC/AFS,FZ79/184/JM/B".

1913   *8in (20.5cm) high*

$8,000-12,000   **DRA**

A Newcomb College Transitional squat bowl, carved by A.F. Simpson, with a band of white and yellow daisies on a pale blue ground, minute fleck to rim, "NC/AFS/GN6/157/84/JM".

1914   *5.25in (13.5cm) wide*

$2,000-2,500   **DRA**

A Newcomb College Transitional bowl, carved by A.F. Simpson with pink poppies on a blue-green ground, two short and tight lines to rim, "NC/AFS/HU21/33/JM".

1916   *6in (15cm) wide*

$1,000-1,500   **DRA**

A Newcomb College candlestick, carved by A.F. Simpson, with foliate ribs under a purple and blue glaze, "NC/AFS/IQ41/19/232".

1917   *7.5in (19cm) high*

$1,500-2,000   **DRA**

A Newcomb College squat two-handled vessel, carved by A.F. Simpson, with pink crocuses, on a purple-to-blue ground, minor stilt-pull nicks outside footring, "NC/AFS/ME87/254/JM".

1922   *4.75in (12cm) wide*

$1,800-2,200   **DRA**

A Newcomb College bud vase, carved by A.F. Simpson, with Spanish Moss and moon on a blue ground, short, dark crazing line to rim, does not go through, "NC/AFS/NO11/JM32".

1923   *6.5in (16.5cm) high*

$3,000-4,000   **DRA**

A Newcomb College ovoid vase, carved by A.F. Simpson, with pink narcissus and green leaves on a blue ground, "NC/NT71/182/AFS".

1924   *8.25in (21cm) high*

$3,000-4,000   **DRA**

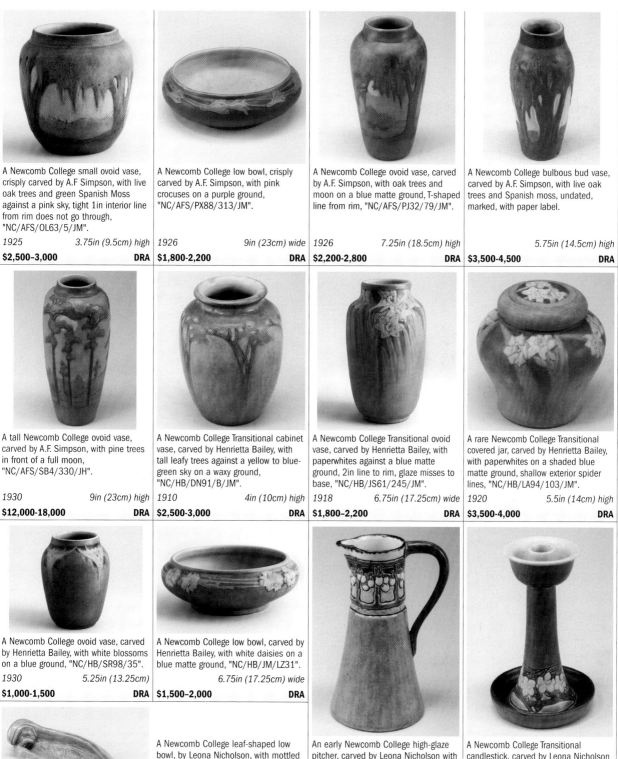

A Newcomb College small ovoid vase, crisply carved by A.F. Simpson, with live oak trees and green Spanish Moss against a pink sky, tight 1in interior line from rim does not go through, "NC/AFS/OL63/5/JM".

1925   *3.75in (9.5cm) high*
$2,500–3,000   **DRA**

A Newcomb College low bowl, crisply carved by A.F. Simpson, with pink crocuses on a purple ground, "NC/AFS/PX88/313/JM".

1926   *9in (23cm) wide*
$1,800-2,200   **DRA**

A Newcomb College ovoid vase, carved by A.F. Simpson, with oak trees and moon on a blue matte ground, T-shaped line from rim, "NC/AFS/PJ32/79/JM".

1926   *7.25in (18.5cm) high*
$2,200-2,800   **DRA**

A Newcomb College bulbous bud vase, carved by A.F. Simpson, with live oak trees and Spanish moss, undated, marked, with paper label.

5.75in (14.5cm) high
$3,500-4,500   **DRA**

A tall Newcomb College ovoid vase, carved by A.F. Simpson, with pine trees in front of a full moon, "NC/AFS/SB4/330/JH".

1930   *9in (23cm) high*
$12,000-18,000   **DRA**

A Newcomb College Transitional cabinet vase, carved by Henrietta Bailey, with tall leafy trees against a yellow to blue-green sky on a waxy ground, "NC/HB/DN91/B/JM".

1910   *4in (10cm) high*
$2,500-3,000   **DRA**

A Newcomb College Transitional ovoid vase, carved by Henrietta Bailey, with paperwhites against a blue matte ground, 2in line to rim, glaze misses to base, "NC/HB/JS61/245/JM".

1918   *6.75in (17.25cm) wide*
$1,800–2,200   **DRA**

A rare Newcomb College Transitional covered jar, carved by Henrietta Bailey, with paperwhites on a shaded blue matte ground, shallow exterior spider lines, "NC/HB/LA94/103/JM".

1920   *5.5in (14cm) high*
$3,500-4,000   **DRA**

A Newcomb College ovoid vase, carved by Henrietta Bailey, with white blossoms on a blue ground, "NC/HB/SR98/35".

1930   *5.25in (13.25cm)*
$1,000-1,500   **DRA**

A Newcomb College low bowl, carved by Henrietta Bailey, with white daisies on a blue matte ground, "NC/HB/JM/LZ31".

6.75in (17.25cm) wide
$1,500–2,000   **DRA**

A Newcomb College leaf-shaped low bowl, by Leona Nicholson, with mottled green, blue and brown glaze, incised "Leona Nicholson/1949".

1949   *13.25in (33.5cm) long*
$600-900   **DRA**

An early Newcomb College high-glaze pitcher, carved by Leona Nicholson with clusters of white flowers within panels around neck, on a medium blue ground, "NC/LN/BG68/JM".

1906   *7.5in (19cm) high*
$7,000-10,000   **DRA**

A Newcomb College Transitional candlestick, carved by Leona Nicholson with white blossoms and green leaves on a blue-green ground, restoration to small chip at rim, "NC/LN/FC26/B".

1912   *6.25 (16cm) high*
$2,000-2,500   **DRA**

A large Newcomb College Transitional ovoid vase, attributed to A.C. Arbo, carved with fleshy hibiscus blossoms in dark blue and blue-green matte glaze, "NC/ER13/JM/".

1911   *10.5in (26.5cm) high*

$7,000-10,000   **DRA**

A Newcomb College pitcher, carved by C.M. Chalaron, with pink Art Deco flowers against a purple and blue matte ground, "NC/CMC/230/MZ96/JM".

1923   *8in (20.5cm) high*

$2,500-3,000   **DRA**

A rare and early Newcomb College high-glaze ovoid vase, painted by Olive Webster Dodd with green artichoke blossoms, chip to base, "NC/P99/JM/Q/OWD".

1902   *9.5in (24cm) high*

$15,000-20,000   **DRA**

An early Newcomb College high-glaze chocolate pot, carved by Lucia Jordan, with a stylized landscape against a blue-green ground, "NC/LJ/JM/BN33/Q".

1907   *11in (28cm) high*

$20,000-30,000   **DRA**

An early Newcomb College high-glaze mug, painted by A.W. Lonnegan, with stylized artichokes on an ivory and light blue ground, restoration to fracture on handle, "NC/Lonnegan/R15/Q/JM".

1902   *5in (12.5cm) wide*

$1,200-1,800   **DRA**

A Newcomb College Transitional bulbous vase, carved by May S. Morel, with white bell-shaped flowers and green leaves on a denim blue ground, "NC/MM/DN66/JM/K".

1910   *5.5in (14cm) high*

$2,500-3,500   **DRA**

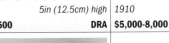

An early Newcomb College high-glaze mug, painted by Amelie Roman, with stylized pods on an ivory ground, tight line where rim meets handle, restored handle, "NC/AR/E18/X/Q/JM".

1901   *5in (12.5cm) high*

$1,000-1,500   **DRA**

A Newcomb College Transitional ovoid vase, carved with white lotus on a dark blue-green matte ground, "NC/illegible artist's mark/DY51/B/JM".

1910   *8in (20.5cm) high*

$5,000-8,000   **DRA**

A Newcomb College ovoid vase, with ribbed body, covered in a dripping green over olive glossy glaze, repair to chip at base, incised "NC", and "D".

5.25in (13.5cm)

$400-600   **DRA**

A Newcomb college hand-built gourd-shaped vase, covered in mirror black and turquoise glossy glaze, stilt-pull chip, "NC/HB".

5.75in (14.5cm) high

$700-1,000   **DRA**

A Newcomb College bulbous vase, with two buttressed handles covered in gunmetal, green and yellow glaze, small flake to corner to one handle, "NC/JM/FR".

9in (23cm) wide

$2,000-3,000   **DRA**

A Newcomb College ridged low bowl, covered in a blue-to-purple matte glaze, "NC/JM".

8.25in (21cm) wide

$800-1,200   **DRA**

George Ohr

A George Ohr bulbous vessel, with pinched and folded rim, and dimpled mid-section, one side covered in aventurine glaze, the other in mirror black, stamped "G.E. OHR/Biloxi, Miss".

4.75in (12cm) high

$10,000-15,000   **DRA**

A George Ohr ovoid vase, with a deep in-body twist under a folded rim, covered in mahogany and black flambé glaze, stamped "G.E. OHR, Biloxi, Miss".

4.75in (12cm) high

$8,000-12,000   **DRA**

A George Ohr vase, the top torn and folded, covered in a speckled dark green over amber glaze, restoration to hairlines at rim, stamped "G.E. OHR/Biloxi, Miss".

4.75in (12cm) high

$7,000-10,000   **DRA**

An early George Ohr footed vase, with ruffled rim covered in bottle green semi-matte glaze with clay powder deposits, firing lines and bursts, stamped "GEO. O. OHR/BILOXI".

4.75in (12cm) wide

$1,000-1,500   **DRA**

A George Ohr vase, with large asymetrical dimples to body and ruffled neck, the exterior covered in green and black speckled glaze on orange ground, the interior in sheer orange glaze, stamped "G.E. Ohr, Biloxi, Miss".

5in (12.5cm) wide

$12,000-18,000   **DRA**

An early George Ohr faceted pitcher, molded with a bouquet of flowers on one side, nude maidens and putti on the other, covered in a mirror brown glaze, several small chips, incised "G.E. OHR/Biloxi, Miss/1896".

1896   *7.75in (19.5cm) high*

$1,500-2,000   **DRA**

A George Ohr cinched mug, with two handles, one rectangular and one ear-shaped, covered in mirror green glaze with gunmetal flashes, repair to small chips at rim, script signature.

5in (12.5cm) high

$6,000-9,000   **DRA**

A large George Ohr crab plaque, covered in a dark green glaze, restoration to three claws and two tips, signed "Biloxi, Miss./1899" on reverse.

1899   *8.5in (21.5cm) high*

$3,000-3,500   **DRA**

A George Ohr panther head inkwell, covered in green and gunmetal glaze, fleck to corner, stamped on bottom with a "Biloxi" welcome.

4.25in (11cm) long

$1,200-1,800   **DRA**

A George Ohr bulbous vase, with in-body twist and torn rim, covered in mottled gunmetal and green glaze, minor nick to rim, script signature.

4.5in (11.5cm) high

$8,000-12,000   **DRA**

A George Ohr bulbous vase, with folded rim covered in a rare purple mottled glaze, stamped "G.E. OHR/Bloxi, Miss".

4in (10cm) high

$4,000-6,000   **DRA**

A rare George Ohr vessel, with pinched and folded rim and bulbous mid-section, covered in a mottled raspberry, indigo, and gray semi-matte glaze, minor flake to rim, stamped "G.E. Ohr/Biloxi, Miss".

4.5in (11.5cm) high

$8,000-12,000   **DRA**

A George Ohr tapered vase, with folded rim and dimpled body, covered in mottled amber glaze, stamped "G.E OHR/Biloxi, Miss".

4in (10cm) high

$3,000-4,000 DRA

A George Ohr cabinet vase, shaped as an oil lamp with two handles, covered in mottled brown and gunmetal glaze, several chips to rim and base, script signature.

3.5in (9cm) wide

$1,800-2,200 DRA

A George Ohr mug, with ear-shaped handle, the exterior covered matte rose glaze, the interior in mottled gunmetal brown, script signature.

5in (12.5cm) wide

$3,000-4,000 DRA

A rare George Ohr artist's palette inkwell, with two paint tubes, two brushes, and dipping vessel covered in mottled green and gunmetal glaze, restoration to both brushes and one tube, touch-up to rim of vessel, and a few minor nicks, stamped "G.E. OHR/BILOXI".

6.25in (16cm) high

$3,500-4,500 DRA

A George Ohr spherical vessel, with cupped rim and deep, asymmetrical in-body twist, the exterior covered in a tomato red and forest green speckled glossy glaze, with amber and green speckled interior, stamped "G.E. Ohr/Biloxi, Miss".

4.25in (11cm) wide

$30,000-40,000 DRA

A George Ohr bulbous vessel, with pinched rim and in-body twist, covered in a red, amber, and forest green mottled glossy glaze, stamped "G.E. Ohr/Biloxi, Miss".

5in (13cm) high

$15,000-20,000 DRA

A George Ohr vase, covered in a speckled raspberry and black glossy glaze, with green flashes at rim, small restoration to one lobe and scratches to two areas of body, minor nicks, stamped "BILOXI, MISS/GEO. E. OHR".

3.75in (9.5cm) high

$8,000-12,000 DRA

A George Ohr ashtray/pipe knocker, covered in speckled amber glossy glaze, glaze drip to bottom, kiln kiss to side, stamped "G.E. OHR/BILOXI, MISS".

5in (12.5cm) wide

$500-700 DRA

A George Ohr small teapot, covered in green speckled glossy glaze, minor restoration to spout, rim and lid, stamped "GEO E OHR/BILOXI, MISS".

6.5in (16.5cm) wide

$5,000-7,000 DRA

A George Ohr baluster cabinet vase, covered in blue, raspberry and green sponged-on glossy glaze, stamped "G.E OHR/Biloxi, Miss".

5in (12.5cm) high

$4,000-6,000 DRA

A large George Ohr bisque vase, a few small nicks to rim, incised on body, "Made in the presence of owner John Power/By his friend/G E Ohr/Biloxi 1-24-1903," and on bottom, "mary had a little Lamb & Ohr has a little Pottery".

1903   *9in (23cm) high*
$20,000-30,000   **DRA**

A George Ohr squat bisque vessel, with a deep, swirling twist around its shoulder, incised "mud from N.O. Street/G E Ohr/New Orleans/States/1905".

1905   *4.75in (12cm) wide*
$5,000-7,000   **DRA**

A George Ohr bisque flaring bowl, with folded closed-in rim, cracks and chips from firing, script signature.

7in (18cm) wide
$1,800-2,200   **DRA**

A George Ohr bisque vessel, pinched and dimpled with triple-lobed opening, minor chip to rim, script signature.

5.25in (13.5cm) wide
$4,000-6,000   **DRA**

A large George Ohr bisque corseted tyge with three different handles, script signature.

8.5in (21.5cm) high
$2,500-3,000   **DRA**

A George Ohr gourd-shaped bisque vessel, of pale clay with darker iron flashes, script signature.

4.75 (12cm) high
$2,000-2,500   **DRA**

A large George Ohr bulbous vase, with dimpled base and folded rim, covered in a rare blue, green, gray and lavender sponged glaze, stamped "G.E. OHR/Biloxi, Miss".

5.5in (14cm) high
$15,000-20,000   **DRA**

A George Ohr chamber pot, with brown and black sponged decoration to exterior, and interior 'contents', opposing short lines (one restored), stamped "G.E OHR/Biloxi, Miss".

2.25in (5.5cm) high
$1,000-1,500   **DRA**

A large George Ohr teapot, with exaggerated snake-like spout, with white, red, and pink glaze sponged on an amber ground, stamped "G.E. OHR/Biloxi, Miss".

12.5in (31.75cm) long
$50,000-70,000   **DRA**

A George Ohr log cabin inkwell, in white and red clay, the cabin glued to the base, stamped "G.E. OHR / BILOXI, MISS", with a "Biloxi Welcome" mark.

3in (7.5cm) high
$800-1,200   **DRA**

A George Ohr curio, with shell and curlicues on a notched back, covered in amber glaze, restoration to one side, small chip to edge on back, stamped "G.E OHR/BILOXI".

3.75in (9.5cm) high
$800-1,200   **DRA**

Rookwood

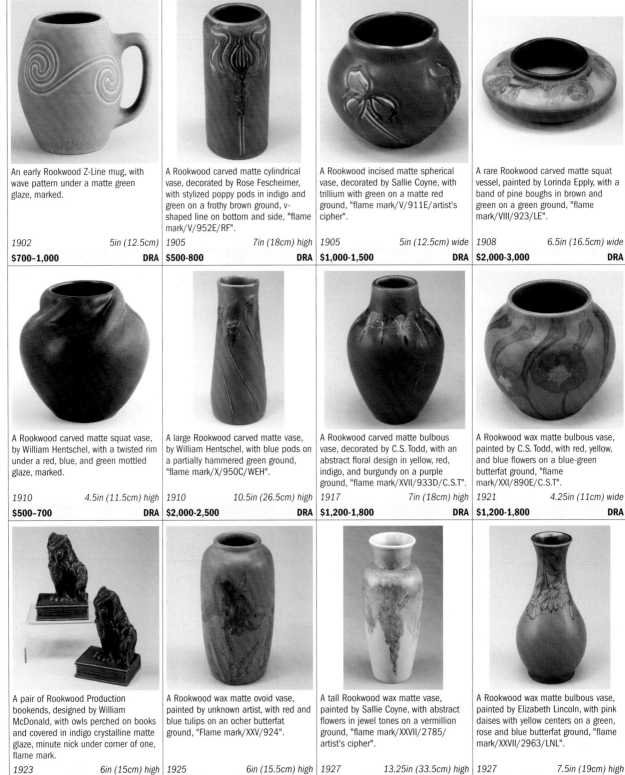

An early Rookwood Z-Line mug, with wave pattern under a matte green glaze, marked.

1902   5in (12.5cm)

$700–1,000   **DRA**

A Rookwood carved matte cylindrical vase, decorated by Rose Fescheimer, with stylized poppy pods in indigo and green on a frothy brown ground, v-shaped line on bottom and side, "flame mark/V/952E/RF".

1905   7in (18cm) high

$500–800   **DRA**

A Rookwood incised matte spherical vase, decorated by Sallie Coyne, with trillium with green on a matte red ground, "flame mark/V/911E/artist's cipher".

1905   5in (12.5cm) wide

$1,000–1,500   **DRA**

A rare Rookwood carved matte squat vessel, painted by Lorinda Epply, with a band of pine boughs in brown and green on a green ground, "flame mark/VIII/923/LE".

1908   6.5in (16.5cm) wide

$2,000–3,000   **DRA**

A Rookwood carved matte squat vase, by William Hentschel, with a twisted rim under a red, blue, and green mottled glaze, marked.

1910   4.5in (11.5cm) high

$500–700   **DRA**

A large Rookwood carved matte vase, by William Hentschel, with blue pods on a partially hammered green ground, "flame mark/X/950C/WEH".

1910   10.5in (26.5cm) high

$2,000–2,500   **DRA**

A Rookwood carved matte bulbous vase, decorated by C.S. Todd, with an abstract floral design in yellow, red, indigo, and burgundy on a purple ground, "flame mark/XVII/933D/C.S.T".

1917   7in (18cm) high

$1,200–1,800   **DRA**

A Rookwood wax matte bulbous vase, painted by C.S. Todd, with red, yellow, and blue flowers on a blue-green butterfat ground, "flame mark/XXI/890E/C.S.T".

1921   4.25in (11cm) wide

$1,200–1,800   **DRA**

A pair of Rookwood Production bookends, designed by William McDonald, with owls perched on books and covered in indigo crystalline matte glaze, minute nick under corner of one, flame mark.

1923   6in (15cm) high

$320–380   **DRA**

A Rookwood wax matte ovoid vase, painted by unknown artist, with red and blue tulips on an ocher butterfat ground, "Flame mark/XXV/924".

1925   6in (15.5cm) high

$1,200–1,800   **DRA**

A tall Rookwood wax matte vase, painted by Sallie Coyne, with abstract flowers in jewel tones on a vermillion ground, "flame mark/XXVII/2785/artist's cipher".

1927   13.25in (33.5cm) high

$2,000–3,000   **DRA**

A Rookwood wax matte bulbous vase, painted by Elizabeth Lincoln, with pink daisies with yellow centers on a green, rose and blue butterfat ground, "flame mark/XXVII/2963/LNL".

1927   7.5in (19cm) high

$1,200–1,800   **DRA**

A Rookwood wax matte flaring vase, painted by Elizabeth Lincoln, on an impressed pattern, with red, blue, and green flowers, marked.

9in (23cm) high

1929

$1,200-1,800　　　**DRA**

A Rookwood wax matte two-handled centerbowl, painted by Elizabeth Lincoln, with red chrysanthemums and pink flowers on a yellow butterfat ground, "flame mark/XXVIV/2951/LNL".

1929　　　*10in (25.4cm) wide*

$1,000-1,500　　　**DRA**

A Rookwood wax matte flaring vase, painted by Margaret MacDonald, with green, black, yellow, and red blossoms and leaves on a blue and yellow butterfat ground, a couple of shallow chips to foot, "flame mark/XXX/6200/E/MHM".

1930　　　*5.5in (14cm) high*

$600-900　　　**DRA**

A Rookwood Production barrel-shaped vase, embossed with waves under a light blue matte glaze, marked.

1932　　　*4.5in (11.5cm) high*

$300-400　　　**DRA**

A Rookwood scenic vellum plaque, 'A Lake in the Mountain', mounted in original dark-stained frame, flame mark.

1912　　　*Plaque 8in (20.5cm)*

$3,000-4,000　　　**DRA**

A Rookwood scenic vellum plaque, 'The Ravine', painted by Fred Rothenbush with a snowy landscape of a creek running through woods, mounted in original frame, a few flecks, "flame mark/XIII/V/FR".

1913　　　*Plaque 8in (20.5cm) high*

$4,000-6,000　　　**DRA**

An unusual Rookwood scenic vellum plaque, painted by Kate Van Horn, with islands and palm trees, overall crazing, mounted in original frame, "flame mark/XIV/K.V.H".

1914　　　*Plaque 8in (20.5cm) high*

$4,000-6,000　　　**DRA**

A large Rookwood scenic vellum plaque, painted by Lenore Ashbury, with a landscape of trees by a pond at dusk, mounted in new Arts & Crafts oak frame, "flame mark/XV", signed "L.A." on front.

1915　　　*Tile 12.5in (32cm) wide*

$8,000-12,000　　　**DRA**

A large Rookwood scenic vellum plaque, painted by Ed Diers, with trees and fall foliage by a river, mounted in a new Arts & Crafts oak frame, "flame mark/XVI", signed "E.D." on front.

1916　　　*Tile 12.5in (32cm) wide*

$7,000-10,000　　　**DRA**

A Rookwood scenic vellum plaque, painted by Sallie Coyne, with silhouetted trees in front of a river, in blues, greens, and yellows, uncrazed, mounted in original frame, paper label, artist signature.

11in (28cm) high

$4,000-6,000　　　**DRA**

A large and rare Rookwood fiance tile, decorated in cuenca, mounted in new Roycroft quarter-sawn oak frame, restoration to three corners of tile, no visible mark on tile, incised Roycroft logo on back of frame.

Tile 12in (30.5cm) square

$1,200-1,800　　　**DRA**

DECORATIVE ARTS

A Rookwood scenic vellum cylindrical vase, painted by E.T. Hurley, with birch trees by a lake, scaling and bruise at base, "flame mark/XV/952E/ETH".

1915   *7.75in (19.5cm) high*

$1,800-2,200   **DRA**

A Rookwood scenic vellum bulbous vase, painted by Fred Rothenbusch, with trees in a meadow, glaze blemish to tree, "flame mark/XIX/950E/FR".

1919   *7.5in (19cm) high*

$1,200-1,800   **DRA**

A Rookwood scenic vellum bottle-shaped vase, painted by Ed Diers, with trees in a meadow, "flame mark/XXI/732C/ED".

1921   *7.25in (18.5cm) high*

$1,800-2,200   **DRA**

A tall Rookwood scenic vellum ovoid vase, painted by Carl Schmidt with sailboats in a Venetian port, "flame mark/CS/XXII/295C/V".

1922   *11.5in (29cm) high*

$5,000-7,000   **DRA**

A Rookwood vellum vase, painted by Carl Schmidt, with blue and purple irises on a shaded apricot ground, fine crazing throughout, "flame mark/V/951D/CS".

1905   *8.25in (21cm) high*

$2,500-3,000   **DRA**

A Rookwood vellum vase, painted by Edith Noonan, with swimming trout on shaded pink, ivory and teal ground, "flame mark/VIII/911E/V/EN".

1908   *5in (12.5cm) wide*

$1,500-2,000   **DRA**

A Rookwood vellum ovoid vase, by Kate Van Horn, decorated with paperwhites on a shaded ivory and slate blue ground, extensive restoration to body, "flame mark/X/939D/V/K.V.H".

1910   *7.75in (19.5cm) high*

$280-320   **DRA**

A Rookwood vellum vase, painted by Ed Diers with pink begonias on a shaded grey ground, no seconded mark, "flame mark/XV/808/V/E.D".

1915   *8in (20.5cm) high*

$800-1,200   **DRA**

A Rookwood vellum squat vessel, painted by E.T. Hurley, with branches of cherry blossoms on a blue and lavendar ground, uncrazed, "flame mark/XXVIII/389/ETH".

1928   *6in (15cm) wide*

$1,000-1,500   **DRA**

A Rookwood jewel porcelain bulbous vase, painted by Kate Van Horn, with stylized blue flowers and blue-green leaves on a black ground, opposing lines from rim, "flame mark/XVII/2066/P/K.V.H".

1917   *7.25in (18.5cm) high*

$300–400   **DRA**

A Rookwood jewel porcelain vase, painted by Lorinda Epply, with a wreath of purple irises and curlicued leaves on an ivory ground, two short and shallow scaling lines to rim, "flame mark/XIX/1873/LE".

1919   *5.5in (14cm) high*

$500–800   **DRA**

A Rookwood jewel porcelain vase, painted by Jens Jensen, with white birds outlined in green on an indigo ground, "flame mark/XLIV/6315/artist's cipher".

1944   *6.5in (16.5cm) high*

$1,200-1,800   **DRA**

A large Rookwood jewel porcelain classically-shaped vase, painted by Arthur Conant, with peacocks perched on blooming apple branches and over paper whites, in jewel tones on a gray ground, "flame mark/XIX/2273/artist's cipher".

1919   *17.25in (44cm) high*

$12,000-18,000   DRA

An early Rookwood standard glaze light covered jar, painted by Sadie Markland, with an elf seated on a stump, 2in hairline to base, "flame mark/622/L".

1893   *4in (10cm) wide*

$600-900   DRA

A Rookwood standard glaze bulbous vase, painted by Constance Baker with orange poppies, marked "flame mark/846C/CAB".

1899   *10.5in (26.5cm) high*

$1,000-1,500   DRA

A Rookwood standard glaze tall pitcher, painted by Sallie Toohey, with orange tiger lillies, "flame mark/838/C/artist's cipher".

1899   *10in (25.5cm) high*

$1,000-1,500   DRA

A Rookwood standard glaze ovoid vase, painted by Clara Lindeman with clover blossoms and leaves, marked "flame mark/II/922D/C.C.L".

1902   *7in (18cm) high*

$400-600   DRA

A Rookwood Squeezebag vase, decorated by Elizabeth Barrett, with tall branches of leaves in blue and café-au-lait, minor fleck to top of branch, marked "flame mark/XXVIII/1779/EB".

1928   *75in (19.5cm) high*

$500-800   DRA

A Rookwood Squeezebag vase, decorated by William Hentschel, with stylized foliate design in blue and café-au-lait, marked "flame mark/XXXI/6149D/WEH".

1931   *6in (15cm) high*

$800-1,200   DRA

A Rookwood Squeezebag vase, decorated by Loretta Holtcamp, with black palm trees on an ivory ground, "flame mark/LIII/LH/S".

1953   *8in (20.5cm) high*

$1,000-1,500   DRA

A Rookwood iris glaze bulbous vase, painted by Irene Bishop, with branches of cherry blossoms on a black-to-peach ground, "flame mark/VII/942D/W/IB".

1907   *5.5in (14cm) high*

$1,000-1,500   DRA

An unusual Rookwood Goldstone ovoid vase, painted and incised by C.S. Todd, with flowers and foliage in bottle green under a gold rim, marked "flame mark/ XXI/2102/C.S.T".

1921 6.75in (17cm) high

$1,800-2,200 DRA

A Rookwood iris glaze ovoid vase, painted by Lorinda Epply, with branches of cherry blossoms on a lavender ground, seconded mark, possibly for very faint glaze inconsistency, marked "X'ed".

1911 2.75in (7cm) high

$1,000-1,500 DRA

A Rookwood production tall vase, embossed with stylized tulips under a pink and green butterfat ground, seconded mark for scaling to top and bottom, marked "X'ed".

1920 11in (28cm) high

$200-300 DRA

A Rookwood butterfat baluster vase, decorated by William Hentschel, with branches of leaves in robin's egg blue, white and brown, marked "flame mark/ XXVII/927D/WEH".

1929 9in (23cm) high

$1,200-1,800 DRA

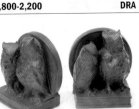

A pair of Rookwood owl bookends, designed by William McDonald, in glazed earthenware, flame mark, designer monogram.

1927 6.5in (16.5cm) high

$800-1,200 FRE

A Rookwood Shipware 17-piece tea set, comprising a lidded teapot, two creamers, two sugar bowls, two saucers, eight 8in plates, all decorated with blue ships on a white ground, nicks to all spouts, marked.

$400-600 DRA

Van Briggle

An early Van Briggle vase, embossed with poppies under matte chartreuse glaze, marked "AA/VAN BRIGGLE/ 1902/2d".

1902 8in (20.5cm) high

$3,000-5,000 DRA

An early Van Briggle gourd-shaped vase, with poppies under a touquoise and purple matte glaze, the clay showing through, several short firing lines to base, rim and shoulder, incised "AA/Van Briggle/1903/III/137".

1903 8.75in (22cm) high

$2,500-3,000 DRA

An early Van Briggle vase, crisply embossed with poppy pods and leaves under a green and pink mottled matte glaze, incised "AA/173/Van Briggle/ 1903/V".

1903 10in (25.5cm) high

$6,000-9,000 DRA

An early Van Briggle bulbous vase, embossed with leaves under a feathered matte turquoise glaze, "AA/VAN BRIGGLE/1904".

1904 5.5in (14cm) high

$1,200-1,800 DRA

An early Van Briggle bulbous vase, embossed with leaves under a good feathered matte turquoise glaze, marked "AA/VAN BRIGGLE/1904".

1904 5.5in (14cm) high

$1,200–1,800 DRA

An early Van Briggle two-handled squat vase, covered in a fine brown and green orange peel glaze, marked "AA/VAN BRIGGLE/1905/236".

1905 7.5in (19cm) wide

$800-1,200 DRA

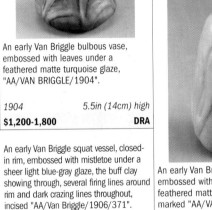

An early Van Briggle squat vessel, closed-in rim, embossed with mistletoe under a sheer light blue-gray glaze, the buff clay showing through, several firing lines around rim and dark crazing lines throughout, incised "AA/Van Briggle/1906/371".

1906 4.5in (11.5cm) wide

$400-600 DRA

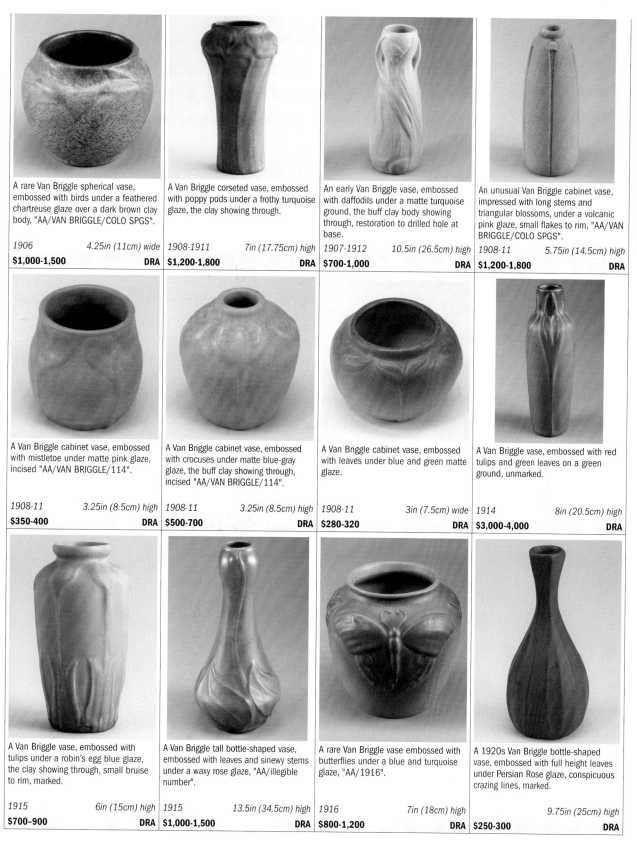

A rare Van Briggle spherical vase, embossed with birds under a feathered chartreuse glaze over a dark brown clay body, "AA/VAN BRIGGLE/COLO SPGS".

1906   *4.25in (11cm) wide*
$1,000-1,500   **DRA**

A Van Briggle corseted vase, embossed with poppy pods under a frothy turquoise glaze, the clay showing through.

1908-1911   *7in (17.75cm) high*
$1,200-1,800   **DRA**

An early Van Briggle vase, embossed with daffodils under a matte turquoise ground, the buff clay body showing through, restoration to drilled hole at base.

1907-1912   *10.5in (26.5cm) high*
$700-1,000   **DRA**

An unusual Van Briggle cabinet vase, impressed with long stems and triangular blossoms, under a volcanic pink glaze, small flakes to rim, "AA/VAN BRIGGLE/COLO SPGS".

1908-11   *5.75in (14.5cm) high*
$1,200-1,800   **DRA**

A Van Briggle cabinet vase, embossed with mistletoe under matte pink glaze, incised "AA/VAN BRIGGLE/114".

1908-11   *3.25in (8.5cm) high*
$350-400   **DRA**

A Van Briggle cabinet vase, embossed with crocuses under matte blue-gray glaze, the buff clay showing through, incised "AA/VAN BRIGGLE/114".

1908-11   *3.25in (8.5cm) high*
$500-700   **DRA**

A Van Briggle cabinet vase, embossed with leaves under blue and green matte glaze.

1908-11   *3in (7.5cm) wide*
$280-320   **DRA**

A Van Briggle vase, embossed with red tulips and green leaves on a green ground, unmarked.

1914   *8in (20.5cm) high*
$3,000-4,000   **DRA**

A Van Briggle vase, embossed with tulips under a robin's egg blue glaze, the clay showing through, small bruise to rim, marked.

1915   *6in (15cm) high*
$700-900   **DRA**

A Van Briggle tall bottle-shaped vase, embossed with leaves and sinewy stems under a waxy rose glaze, "AA/illegible number".

1915   *13.5in (34.5cm) high*
$1,000-1,500   **DRA**

A rare Van Briggle vase embossed with butterflies under a blue and turquoise glaze, "AA/1916".

1916   *7in (18cm) high*
$800-1,200   **DRA**

A 1920s Van Briggle bottle-shaped vase, embossed with full height leaves under Persian Rose glaze, conspicuous crazing lines, marked.

9.75in (25cm) high
$250-300   **DRA**

A Van Briggle vase, embossed with swirling leaves under Persian Rose glaze, small chip to base, incised "AA/Van Briggle/USA".

1925   7.25in (18.5cm) high

$200-300   DRA

A large Van Briggle bulbous vase, embossed with leaves and covered in Persian Rose glaze, nick to one leaf, incised "AA/Van Briggle/USA".

1925   15in (38cm) high

$500-750   DRA

A rare Van Briggle tile, decorated in cuenca, with a purple cardinal on a mustard and green leafy branch, mounted in period molding frame, two short tight lines from one edge, light wear to cuenca walls, unmarked.

6in (15cm) square

$2,200-2,800   DRA

Other Factories

A Walrath lemonade pitcher and six goblets, each painted with yellow lemons and green leaves on a brown matte ground, cracks to two goblets, 0.5in chip to other, forth as-is, incised "Walrath Pottery/1911".

$1,500-2,000   DRA

A Walrath flower bowl, with seated nude figure, the bowl carved with waves and covered in sheer mottled matte green and terracotta glaze, incised Walrath Pottery.

8.5in (21.5cm) high

$1,000-1,500   DRA

A Walrath flower bowl with kneeling nude figure, the interior covered in sheer matte mottled green glaze, the exterior in leathery deep matte green, small nick to finger, incised Walrath.

7.25in (18.5cm) wide

$800-1,200   DRA

A rare Walrath bulbous vase, matte-painted with stylized orange blossoms on brown and light green stems, aganst a speckled matte green glaze, incised Walrath Pottery.

6in (15cm) high

$4,000-6,000   DRA

A tall Marblehead cylindrical vase, covered in matte brown glaze.

10in (25.5cm) high

$1,800-2,200   DRA

An early Arthur Baggs at Marblehead experimental cylindrical cabinet vase, painted with indigo stylized blossoms on a matte grey background, incised "AB" and painted "B1".

in (5cm) high

$1,200-1,800   DRA

A Marblehead squat vessel covered in matte indigo glaze, with a glossy light blue interior, glaze misses to interior, hairline from rim, stamped ship mark.

6.25in (16cm) wide

$280-320   DRA

An early Roseville Velmoss bulbous vase, with pale green leaves on darker green ground, unmarked.

5.75in (14.5cm) high

$700-1,000   DRA

A Roseville green 'Baneda' jardinière, with a crisp mold and good color, unmarked.

11.5in (29cm) diam

$2,500-3,000 DRA

A Roseville center bowl.

$180-220 BCAC

An ivory porcelain vase, by John Bennett.

c1890   *6.5in (16.5cm) high*
$1,800-2,200 JF

An early 1880s squared vase, made by the Chelsea Keramic Art Works, Chelsea Mass., was lamped - probably meant to be.

8.75in (22.5cm) high
$800-1,200 JF

A Teco ovoid vase, with two buttressed handles covered in a smooth matte green glaze, stamped "Teco".

5.25in (13.5cm) high
$1,200-1,800 DRA

A Teco organically-shaped two-handled vase, covered in smooth matte green glaze, stamped "Teco".

8.5in (21.5cm) wide
$1,800-2,200 DRA

Two Copeland comports, with John Bennett decoration, marked with his address, parrot and parakeet (marked 'cross beak popa') decoration.

John Bennett brought Copeland blanks from England and taught decoration on Lexington Avenue. Decoration of this kind was the height of fashion amongst ladies at the time.

c1880

8.75in (22.5cm) high
$1,000-1,200 JF

A rare Chelsea Keramic Art Works vase, an amber glaze, glaze nick and bruise to rim, stamped "CHELSEA KERAMIC ART WORKS/ROBERTSON & SONS".

7in (18cm) high
$600-900 DRA

A rare Dedham experimental ovoid vase, by Hugh Robertson, covered in a matte green orange-peel glaze, firing lines to base, incised "Dedham Pottery/HCR".

7.5in (19cm) high
$1,800-2,200 DRA

A rare and unusual Denver White bulbous vase, painted by Skiff, with pine boughs in brown and green on natural ground, incised "Denver/W/Skiff".

5.75 (14.5cm) high
$500-800 DRA

A tall gourd-shaped vase, in the style of Hampshire, impressed with a Greek key pattern under matte green glaze, tight line from rim, unmarked.

12.5in (32cm) high
$400-600 DRA

A large Hampshire bulbous vase, covered in a great leathery green and blue matte glaze, incised" Hampshire Pottery" with number.

9.75in (25cm) wide

$2,500-3,000   **DRA**

A Jugtown vase, with flat shoulder, covered in white semimatte glaze, circular stamp.

3.75in (9.5cm) high

$180-220   **DRA**

A Jugtown vase, covered in a Chinese blue frothy matte glaze, circular stamp mark.

7in (18cm) wide

$700-1,000   **DRA**

A rare Losanti bulbous porcelain vessel, carved and modeled by Marie-Louise McLaughlin, with blossoms in grain-of-rice technique, under glossy white glaze with oxblood flashes, marked Losanti in ink, incised artist's cipher and "55".

4.75in (12cm) high

$20,000-30,000   **DRA**

A Marie-Louise McLaughlin Losanti ware squat porcelain vessel, incised with scrolled wreath in white against a mottled dark blue ground, two short hairlines from rim, signed "Losanti", incised "MCL" and "65".

4.25in (11cm) wide

$1,200-1,800   **DRA**

A Jerome Massier figural pitcher, with mermaid handle and head of Neptune embossed under the spout, covered in mottled turquoise crystalline glaze, stamped "Jerome Massier/Fils/Vallurais".

10in (25.5cm) high

$600-900   **DRA**

A rare Markham cabinet vase with dead-matte volcanic glaze, marked "Markham/6187".

4.25in (11cm) high

$700-1,000   **DRA**

A Saturday Evening Girls hemispherical bowl, decorated in cuerda seca with a band of Greek key in taupe and ivory on a white and brown semimatte ground, signed "SEG/10.12/FL".

6in (15cm) wide

$1,000-1,500   **DRA**

A Saturday Evening Girls dinner plate, decorated in cuerda seca with white lotus blossoms on a blue-gray ground, bruise to rim, three small chips to bottom ring, signed "SEG/AM/11-14".

10in (25.5cm) diam

$600-900   **DRA**

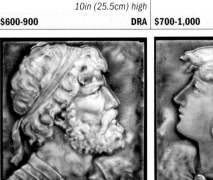

A pair of tiles, by the Trent Tile Co, Trenton NJ, probably part of fire surrounds, depict a man and woman in Hellenic god/goddess style.

c1900

6in (15.5cm) sq.

$800-1,200   **JF**

A Liberty cup and saucer, by Union Porcelain Works, Green Point Brooklyn, all motifs relate to America, a figure of Liberty and an American eagle on the handle, attributed to Karl L.H. Mueler.

1876

$1,200-1,800   **JF**

A University City three-footed porcelain dish, by Taxile Doat, embossed with a shell and painted with fish and sea plants on a white crackled ground, blue 'jewels' on bisque feet, several long firing lines, marked "UC/1914/TD".

1914   5.25in (13.5cm) wide

$800-1,200   DRA

A rare Arequipa bulbous vase, carved with an abstract design and covered in gunmetal black glaze, minor flat stilt-pull chip, incised "Arequipa Calirornia/AP", with tree.

4.75in (12cm) high

$3,500-4,500   DRA

A large Durant Kilns flaring bowl, of ridged texture, covered in Persian blue volcanic glaze, small chip to rim, incised "Durant/1915".

1915   6in (15cm) high

$500-700   DRA

A Franuntel (USA) vase, painted with trees on a cliff over the ocean with sailboats, outlined in gold on green, stamped mark.

6in (15cm) high

$400-600   DRA

A Jalanovich console set, with large faceted, fluted center bowl and pair of tall candlesticks covered in semi-matte with glaze, a few minor flecks, some dark crazing lines, and small minor bruise to one stick, incised "Jalan" with date.

1926   Bowl 15.5in (39.5cm) diam

$2,000-3,000   DRA

A rare Jervis two-handled planter, covered in a smooth matte green glaze, incised "Jervis/197".

11.5in (29cm) wide

$500-800   DRA

A North Dakota School of Mines faceted bowl, carved by Van Kamp with panels of flowers under a matt brown glaze, stamped and signed.

7in (18cm) wide

$350-400   DRA

A large Pierrefonds urn, with double spout and two full-height arched handles, covered in a frothy-blue and turquoise crystalline glaze, flat chip to footring, stamped "Pierrefonds".

13.5in (34.5cm) high

$350-400   DRA

A rare Strobl vase, embossed with stylized blooms on tall stems joined by a wreath of leaves, under a fine curdled matte green glaze, three small glaze flakes to high points, stamped "SP/767".

6.75in (17cm) high

$600-900   DRA

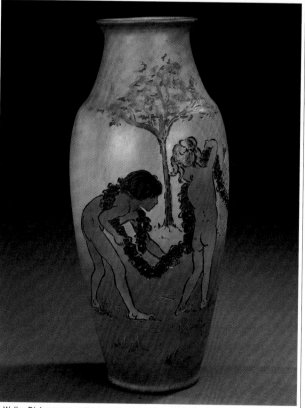

A Weller Dickensware pottery vase, stamped mark, incised and painted with three nude children and four ladies dancing in the background on a ground shading from blue to yellow to green.

The Weller Pottery in Zanesville, Ohio was operational from 1888-1948.

c1905   16in (40.5cm) high

$2,500-3,000   SI

GLASS

Daum Frères

In 1878, Jean Daum (1825-85) took over a glassworks near Nancy, France, in payment for a debt. The following year his lawyer son Auguste (1853-1909) joined him and in 1887, two years after their father had died, the younger brother Antonin (1864-1931), who was an engineer, also joined the firm. The brothers made a great success of the business, embracing the new Art Nouveau style and were greatly influenced by the master glass producer Emile Gallé. After Gallé's death in 1904, Daum Frères became the leading French glassmakers. Daum moved quickly to pick up new fashions in design and new generations at the glassworks initiated new directions for the business. Daum glass production can be split into four eras: Art Nouveau, Art Deco, Crystal and Nouveau Pâte-de-verre. All Daum art glass was signed, usually with '"Daum Nancy"' together with the cross of Lorraine. In 1962, it was renamed 'Cristallerie Daum' and the Daum factories are still in business, as a public company, today.

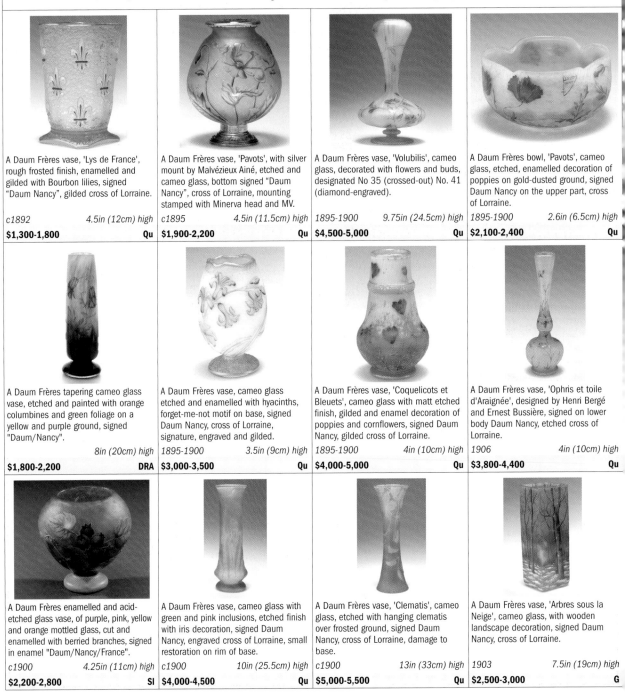

A Daum Frères vase, 'Lys de France', rough frosted finish, enamelled and gilded with Bourbon lilies, signed "Daum Nancy", gilded cross of Lorraine.

c1892   4.5in (12cm) high
$1,300-1,800   Qu

A Daum Frères vase, 'Pavots', with silver mount by Malvézieux Ainé, etched and cameo glass, bottom signed "Daum Nancy", cross of Lorraine, mounting stamped with Minerva head and MV.

c1895   4.5in (11.5cm) high
$1,900-2,200   Qu

A Daum Frères vase, 'Volubilis', cameo glass, decorated with flowers and buds, designated No 35 (crossed-out) No. 41 (diamond-engraved).

1895-1900   9.75in (24.5cm) high
$4,500-5,000   Qu

A Daum Frères bowl, 'Pavots', cameo glass, etched, enamelled decoration of poppies on gold-dusted ground, signed Daum Nancy on the upper part, cross of Lorraine.

1895-1900   2.6in (6.5cm) high
$2,100-2,400   Qu

A Daum Frères tapering cameo glass vase, etched and painted with orange columbines and green foliage on a yellow and purple ground, signed "Daum/Nancy".

8in (20cm) high
$1,800-2,200   DRA

A Daum Frères vase, cameo glass etched and enamelled with hyacinths, forget-me-not motif on base, signed Daum Nancy, cross of Lorraine, signature, engraved and gilded.

1895-1900   3.5in (9cm) high
$3,000-3,500   Qu

A Daum Frères vase, 'Coquelicots et Bleuets', cameo glass with matt etched finish, gilded and enamel decoration of poppies and cornflowers, signed Daum Nancy, gilded cross of Lorraine.

1895-1900   4in (10cm) high
$4,000-5,000   Qu

A Daum Frères vase, 'Ophris et toile d'Araignée', designed by Henri Bergé and Ernest Bussière, signed on lower body Daum Nancy, etched cross of Lorraine.

1906   4in (10cm) high
$3,800-4,400   Qu

A Daum Frères enamelled and acid-etched glass vase, of purple, pink, yellow and orange mottled glass, cut and enamelled with berried branches, signed in enamel "Daum/Nancy/France".

c1900   4.25in (11cm) high
$2,200-2,800   SI

A Daum Frères vase, cameo glass with green and pink inclusions, etched finish with iris decoration, signed Daum Nancy, engraved cross of Lorraine, small restoration on rim of base.

c1900   10in (25.5cm) high
$4,000-4,500   Qu

A Daum Frères vase, 'Clematis', cameo glass, etched with hanging clematis over frosted ground, signed Daum Nancy, cross of Lorraine, damage to base.

c1900   13in (33cm) high
$5,000-5,500   Qu

A Daum Frères vase, 'Arbres sous la Neige', cameo glass, with wooden landscape decoration, signed Daum Nancy, cross of Lorraine.

1903   7.5in (19cm) high
$2,500-3,000   G

A Daum Frères vase, 'Libellules et Renoncules', etched decoration of pond plants with flowers, two diving dragonflys on upper part, background partly worked with martelé, signed "Daum Nancy", engraved and gilded cross of Lorraine.

1904   9.5in (24cm) high

$30,000-35,000   **Qu**

A Daum Frères vase, etched decoration of dragonflies, flowers, buds and water rose petals, bottom signed "Daum Nancy" with engraved cross of Lorraine.

c1904   12in (30.5cm)high

$15,000-18,000   **FIS**

A Daum Frères vase, 'Ophris et Toile d'Araignée', designed by Henri Bergé and Ernest Bussière,signed "Daum Nancy", etched cross of Lorraine.

1906   4in (10cm) high

$2,500-3,000   **Qu**

A Daum Frères vase, with marine landscape and sailing boats, cameo glass with etched decoration, signed "Daum Nancy", cross of Lorraine.

c1910   3in (7.5cm) high

$1,500-1,800   **Qu**

A Daum Frères vase, with coastal landscape decoration, signed "Daum Nancy" on body, etched cross of Lorraine.

c1910   4.5in (11.5cm)

$1,500-1,800   **Qu**

A Daum Frères vase, 'Cinéraires Bleus', etched daisy decoration, signed "Daum Nancy" on base, cross of Lorraine.

1905-1908   16in (40.5cm) high

$17,000-20,000   **HERR**

A Daum Frères vase, 'Glycines', etched and enamelled floral decoration, signed "Daum Nancy" on body, etched cross of Lorraine cross.

c1910   8.1in (20.5cm) high

$2,500-3,000   **Qu**

A Daum Frères vase, 'Pois de Senteur', decorated with sweet-peas, signed "Daum Nancy", etched cross of Lorraine, painter's monogram WH.

1910   18.75in (47.5cm) high

$2,000-2,500   **Qu**

A vase by Daum Frères, 'Montbretias Rose', cameo glass with etched decoration, signed "Daum Nancy", etched cross of Lorraine, painter's mark.

1910   13.5in (34.5cm) high

$5,000-6,000   **Qu**

A Daum Frères night light, matt etched cameo glass on cast-iron mount, signed "Daum Nancy", engraved cross of Lorraine, converted for electricity.

c1910   6.5in (16.5cm) high

$1,000-1,400   **Qu**

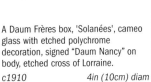

A Daum Frères box, 'Solanées', cameo glass with etched polychrome decoration, signed "Daum Nancy" on body, etched cross of Lorraine.

c1910   4in (10cm) diam

$1,500-2,000   **Qu**

A pair of Daum Frères beakers, cameo glass painted with flowers, signed "Daum Nancy", etched cross of Lorraine.

c1910   2.28in (6cm) high

$1,600-1,900   **Qu**

A Daum Frères vase, 'Coeurs de Jeanette' cameo glass decorated with bleeding hearts, signed "Daum Nancy", etched cross of Lorraine.

c1910   4.75in (12cm) high

$1,500-2,000   **Qu**

A Daum Frères vase, 'Roncier en Automne' part-etched decoration, signed "Daum Nancy" on body, etched cross of Lorraine.

c1910   4.75in (12cm) high

$1,700-2,000   **QU**

A Daum Frères vase, 'Chandelles et Dents de Lion', signed Daum, Nancy on stand, engraved cross of Lorraine.

c1910   17.75in (45cm) high

$13,000-15,000   **Qu**

A Daum Frères vase, clear glass mottled with purple and light blue, overlaid by green and dark purple powder, continuous etched decoration, bottom signed "Daum Nancy" with cross of Lorraine.

c1910   20in (50cm) high

$8,000-10,000   **FIS**

A Daum Frères vase, 'Berluze', clear glass with enamelled decoration, signed "Daum Nancy" and with etched cross of Lorraine.

c1910-15   14.5in (37cm) high

$900-1,200   **Qu**

A Daum Frères vase, cameo glass with streaked yellow inclusions, etched with flowering iris and painted in coloured enamels, cameo signature ""Daum Nancy"", with cross of Lorraine mark.

8.25in (21cm) high

$225-300   **L&T**

A Daum Frères cameo glass vase, the mottled lemon yellow and opaque body of swollen cylindrical form acid etched with cowslips and painted in colours, painted mark ""Daum Nancy" France".

5in (12.5cm) high

$600-800   **L&T**

A Daum Frères Art Deco bowl, cut glass, engraved ""Daum Nancy" FRANCE" to foot.

3.5in (9cm) high

$400-600   **FRE**

A Daum Frères vase, cameo glass with enamel etched decoration, signed "Daum Nancy" and with cross of Lorraine, slight fault on base.

c1912   37.5in (95.5cm) high

$1,000-1,400   **Qu**

A Daum Frères vase, 'Gentiane Cilié', etched decoration, signed "Daum Nancy", engraved cross of Lorraine.

c1912   9in (23cm) high

$6,000-8,000   **Qu**

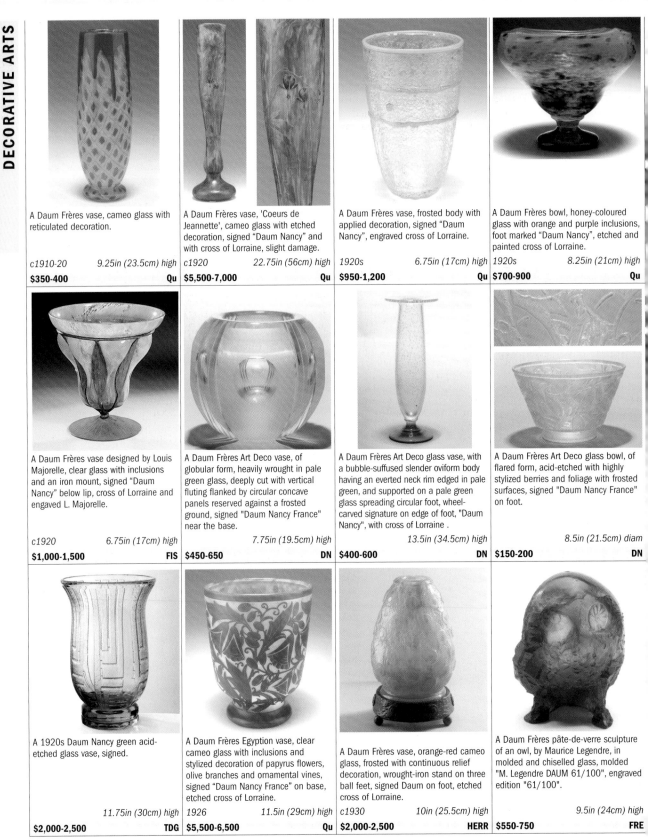

A Daum Frères vase, cameo glass with reticulated decoration.

c1910-20   9.25in (23.5cm) high

$350-400   Qu

A Daum Frères vase, 'Coeurs de Jeannette', cameo glass with etched decoration, signed "Daum Nancy" and with cross of Lorraine, slight damage.

c1920   22.75in (56cm) high

$5,500-7,000   Qu

A Daum Frères vase, frosted body with applied decoration, signed "Daum Nancy", engraved cross of Lorraine.

1920s   6.75in (17cm) high

$950-1,200   Qu

A Daum Frères bowl, honey-coloured glass with orange and purple inclusions, foot marked "Daum Nancy", etched and painted cross of Lorraine.

1920s   8.25in (21cm) high

$700-900   Qu

A Daum Frères vase designed by Louis Majorelle, clear glass with inclusions and an iron mount, signed "Daum Nancy" below lip, cross of Lorraine and engaved L. Majorelle.

c1920   6.75in (17cm) high

$1,000-1,500   FIS

A Daum Frères Art Deco vase, of globular form, heavily wrought in pale green glass, deeply cut with vertical fluting flanked by circular concave panels reserved against a frosted ground, signed "Daum Nancy France" near the base.

7.75in (19.5cm) high

$450-650   DN

A Daum Frères Art Deco glass vase, with a bubble-suffused slender oviform body having an everted neck rim edged in pale green, and supported on a pale green glass spreading circular foot, wheel-carved signature on edge of foot, "Daum Nancy", with cross of Lorraine .

13.5in (34.5cm) high

$400-600   DN

A Daum Frères Art Deco glass bowl, of flared form, acid-etched with highly stylized berries and foliage with frosted surfaces, signed "Daum Nancy France" on foot.

8.5in (21.5cm) diam

$150-200   DN

A 1920s Daum Nancy green acid-etched glass vase, signed.

11.75in (30cm) high

$2,000-2,500   TDG

A Daum Frères Egyption vase, clear cameo glass with inclusions and stylized decoration of papyrus flowers, olive branches and ornamental vines, signed "Daum Nancy France" on base, etched cross of Lorraine.

1926   11.5in (29cm) high

$5,500-6,500   Qu

A Daum Frères vase, orange-red cameo glass, frosted with continuous relief decoration, wrought-iron stand on three ball feet, signed Daum on foot, etched cross of Lorraine.

c1930   10in (25.5cm) high

$2,000-2,500   HERR

A Daum Frères pâte-de-verre sculpture of an owl, by Maurice Legendre, in molded and chiselled glass, molded "M. Legendre DAUM 61/100", engraved edition "61/100".

9.5in (24cm) high

$550-750   FRE

Emile Gallé

Emile Gallé (1846-1904) was born in Nancy, France, the son of a glass factory owner, and became recognised as the best master craftsman of his time. In 1874, after a period of travelling, studying and training in glass making, he returned to Nancy and founded his own workshop. Initially Gallé made glass in the traditional style, using Classical forms as the basis of his designs. He then began to take inspiration from the natural world, drawing on his botanical studies. He produced two types of glass, one became known as 'Industrial Gallé' which was produced to a budget, while the others were true works of art which were more costly to produce because of the time involved in their creation. The company went from strength to strength and by 1890 employed over 300 workmen. A large new Gallé glassworks was opened in 1894. Gallé also extended his work to include furniture production and he opened a carpentry shop specializing in marquetry, again drawing heavily from natural forms for his designs. After his death in 1904 his wife continued to run the factory until 1914, the pieces produced in this period have a star beside the word Gallé. The factory closed in 1914 and Gallé's son in law Paul Perdrizet continued the business from 1914 to 1936.

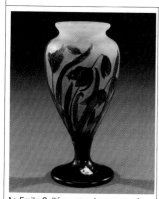

An Emile Gallé cameo glass vase, of yellow tinged grey glass, overlaid with purple and cut with bellflowers, signed in cameo "Gallé".

c1900   6.5in (16.5cm) high

$1,200-1,500   SI

An Emile Gallé vase, 'Colchiques', clear, pink, opalescent and purple cameo glass, foot covered with silver leaves, etched with flowering colchicums, etched "Gallé" mark, restoration to foot.

c1900   10in (25.5cm) high

$3,500-4,500   Qu

An Emile Gallé vase, cameo glass decorated with gladioli on a matt etched ground, signed Gallé on lower body
.

c1900-1904   (73 cm) high

$5,000-6,000   Qu

An Emile Gallé vase with Louis XVI-style gilded bronze mount, cameo glass with etched decoration of iris flowers, etched "Gallé" mark on body.

c1900-1904   11 in (28 cm) high

$2,000-2,400   Qu

An Emile Gallé lamp base, cameo glass, etched decoration of flowering clematis, etched "Gallé" mark on the foot and body.

1902-03   9in (23cm) high

$300-350   Qu

An Emile Gallé vase, cameo glass, decorated with purple flowers on a green ground, signed "Gallé".

20in (51cm) high

$3,000-4,000   DRA

An Emile Gallé vase, 'Glycines', cameo glass decorated with flowers, etched "Gallé" mark on foot.

1902-03   8.5in (21.5cm) high

$850-1,000   Qu

A Emile Gallé cabinet vase, cameo glass, etched decoration of branches on green and opaque-yellow ground, rubbed on rim, signed Gallé.

3.5in (9 cm) high

$300-400   DRA

An Emile Gallé vase, 'Colchiques', cameo glass, etched decoration of colchicums, one deep-cut flower, etched "Gallé" mark on lower body.

1902-1904   5.5in (14 cm) high

$2,000-2,500   Qu

A CLOSER LOOK AT A GALLÉ TABLE LAMP

The hanging shade – formed like a stylized hibiscus flower – is a typical naturalistic Art Nouveau motif.

The shade is made up of five slightly overlapping cameo glass petals and a smaller crown with etched decoration.

The patinated bronze base echoes the naturalistic form of the shade.

The cameo glass is a combination of milky light green, clear and olive brown glass.

An Emile Gallé table lamp, the upper area etched "Gallé" , bronze base.

c1903   15in (38cm) high

$12,000-14,000   **Qu**

An Emile Gallé vase, 'Soliflores Clématites', cameo glass, decorated with a clematis flower and buds, etched "Gallé" mark to side.

1902-1904   13in (33cm) high

$1,000-1,400   **Qu**

An Emile Gallé vase, cameo glass with etched lily decoration, etched "Gallé" mark to side.

c1905   12.4in (31.5 cm) high

$2,000-2,400   **HERR**

An Emile Gallé wall lamp, bronze arm in the form of a fairytale animal, hanging glass shade with etched and polished magnolia decoration, shade slightly scratched, etched "Gallé" mark.

c1905   16.5in (42cm) high

$2,000-2,500   **HERR**

An Emile Gallé vase, cameo glass decorated with purple and blue orchid flower sprays on yellow ground, signed "Gallé".

3in (8cm) high

$2,000-2,500   **DRA**

An Emile Gallé vase, cameo glass, decoration with of dark trees on yellow ground.

11in (28cm) high

$1,000-1,500   **DRA**

An Emile Gallé cabinet vase, cameo glass decorated with purple cherry branches on a yellow ground, slightly damaged rim, signed "Gallé".

4in (10cm) high

$550-750   **DRA**

An Emile Gallé vase, cameo glass with landscape decoration, etched "Gallé*" mark .

1904-1906   7.75in high

$1,500-2,000   **Qu**

An Emile Gallé vase, "Buleia", cameo glass with etched decoration consisting of blossoming branches of butterfly bush, etched "Gallé*" mark.

c1905   7.75in (19.5cm) high

$2,000-2,500   **Qu**

An Emile Gallé Easter egg jar with lid, cameo glass decorated with a wooded landscape, etched "Gallé*" mark.

c1904-1906   4in (10cm) high
$1,200-1,500   **Qu**

An Emile Gallé vase, clear glass cased with white and purple glass, etched iris decoration, fire polished, cut rim, etched "Gallé" mark.

c1906   11.25in (28.5 cm) high
$1,700-2,000   **HERR**

An Emile Gallé vase, cameo glass with etched leaf and flower decoration with interior painting, etched "Gallé" mark.

c1910   13in (33cm) high
$2,000-2,400   **HERR**

An Emile Gallé table lamp, etched landscape decoration, cast-iron mounting on heavy, rectangular base, etched "Gallé" mark.

c1910   7.5in high (19cm)
$2,000-2,500   **DN**

An Emile Gallé perfume bottle, red cherry decoration on mottled yellow ground, complete with silver disperser, rubbed on foot, glued on base, signed "Gallé".

c1910   18in (25.5cm) high
$450-650   **DRA**

An Emile Gallé cabinet vase, cameo glass, amber on purple and yellow ground, cherry decor, signed "Gallé", small crack on rim.

c1910   4in (10cm) high
$500-800   **DRA**

An Emile Gallé bottle-shaped vase, decoration of purple and green sweet peas on peach ground, minor rubbing, signed Gallé.

c1910   5.75in (14.5cm) high
$500-800   **DRA**

An Emile Gallé vase, cylindrical body on bun foot, cameo glass, decoration of green and purple dogwood on mottled peach ground, damage to neck, signed "Gallé".

12.75in (33cm) high
$1,000-1,400   **DRA**

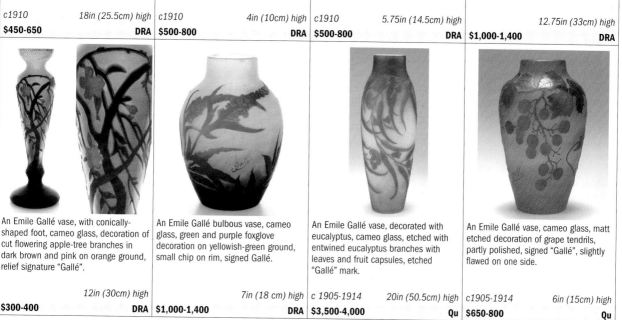

An Emile Gallé vase, with conically-shaped foot, cameo glass, decoration of cut flowering apple-tree branches in dark brown and pink on orange ground, relief signature "Gallé".

12in (30cm) high
$300-400   **DRA**

An Emile Gallé bulbous vase, cameo glass, green and purple foxglove decoration on yellowish-green ground, small chip on rim, signed Gallé.

7in (18 cm) high
$1,000-1,400   **DRA**

An Emile Gallé vase, decorated with eucalyptus, cameo glass, etched with entwined eucalyptus branches with leaves and fruit capsules, etched "Gallé" mark.

c 1905-1914   20in (50.5cm) high
$3,500-4,000   **Qu**

An Emile Gallé vase, cameo glass, matt etched decoration of grape tendrils, partly polished, signed "Gallé", slightly flawed on one side.

c1905-1914   6in (15cm) high
$650-800   **Qu**

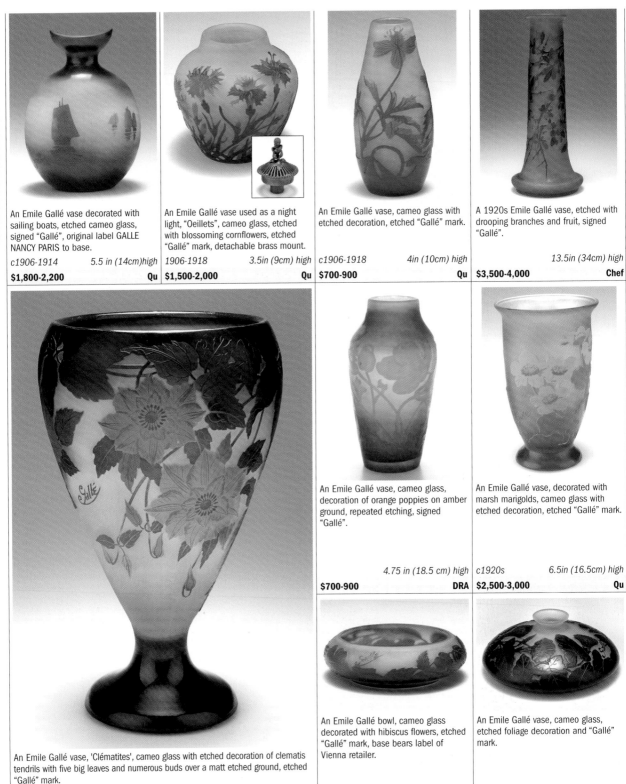

An Emile Gallé vase decorated with sailing boats, etched cameo glass, signed "Gallé", original label GALLE NANCY PARIS to base.

c1906-1914   *5.5 in (14cm)high*

$1,800-2,200   **Qu**

An Emile Gallé vase used as a night light, "Oeillets", cameo glass, etched with blossoming cornflowers, etched "Gallé" mark, detachable brass mount.

1906-1918   *3.5in (9cm) high*

$1,500-2,000   **Qu**

An Emile Gallé vase, cameo glass with etched decoration, etched "Gallé" mark.

c1906-1918   *4in (10cm) high*

$700-900   **Qu**

A 1920s Emile Gallé vase, etched with drooping branches and fruit, signed "Gallé".

13.5in (34cm) high

$3,500-4,000   **Chef**

An Emile Gallé vase, cameo glass, decoration of orange poppies on amber ground, repeated etching, signed "Gallé".

4.75 in (18.5 cm) high

$700-900   **DRA**

An Emile Gallé vase, decorated with marsh marigolds, cameo glass with etched decoration, etched "Gallé" mark.

c1920s   *6.5in (16.5cm) high*

$2,500-3,000   **Qu**

An Emile Gallé vase, 'Clématites', cameo glass with etched decoration of clematis tendrils with five big leaves and numerous buds over a matt etched ground, etched "Gallé" mark.

c1920s   *12.25 in (31cm) high*

$7,000-9,000   **Qu**

An Emile Gallé bowl, cameo glass decorated with hibiscus flowers, etched "Gallé" mark, base bears label of Vienna retailer.

c1920s   *4.25 in (11cm) diam*

$400-550   **Qu**

An Emile Gallé vase, cameo glass, etched foliage decoration and "Gallé" mark.

c1920s   *6in (15cm) high*

$1,800-2,200   **Qu**

An Emile Gallé vase, 'Cyclamen', cameo glass, etched cyclamen flowers decoration, etched "Gallé" mark.

c1920s   7.75 in (19.5cm) high
$2,500-3,000   Qu

An Emile Gallé vase, cameo glass decorated with green and purple dogwood on a mottled peach ground, damage to neck, signed "Gallé".

13in (33 cm) high
$1,000-1,500   DRA

An Emile Gallé vase, 'Aux Libelulles', designed by Eugène Kremer, etched, enamelled and gilded with dragonflies, signed "E. Gallé Nancy", flaw to foot.

c1884   5in (12.5cm) high
$2,500-3,500   FIS

An Emile Gallé vase, enamelled and gilded decoration of stylized elder branches with flowers and berries, signed "Emile Gallé à Nancy".

1885   9in (23cm) high
$1,600-2,000   Qu

An Emile Gallé bowl, clear glass with polychrome enamel decoration of flowering branches and Japanese ornamental images, engraved and gilded signature "E. Gallé à Nancy".

c1885-1890   8in (20.5cm) diam
$2,000-2,500   Qu

An Emile Gallé footed bowl, by Emile Gallé, Nancy, painted and gilded with flowers, ornamental rosettes, tendrils and spirals, signed "Emile Gallé à Nancy", minimal polished flaws at the top of one handle and the foot.

c1889   8in (20.5cm) high
$1,000-1,500   Qu

An Emile Gallé bowl, "Coupe aux Chardons", enamelled and gilded decoration of flowering thistles and a Lothringer cross, signed "Emile Gallé à Nancy" .

c1890-1894   4in (10Ccm) high
$1,000-1,500   Qu

An Emile Gallé carafe "Araignee et Feuilles d'Automone", cameo glass in Ludwig Rühle silver gilt mount, signed.

c1895   13in (33cm) high
$15,000-20,000   Qu

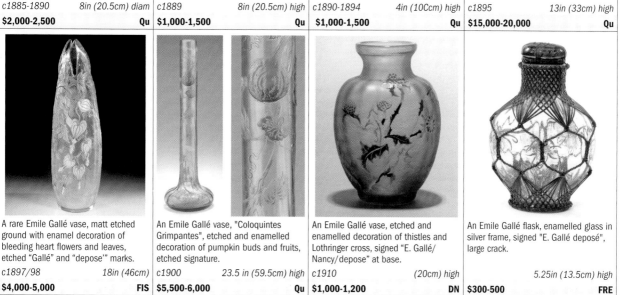

A rare Emile Gallé vase, matt etched ground with enamel decoration of bleeding heart flowers and leaves, etched "Gallé" and "depose'" marks.

c1897/98   18in (46cm)
$4,000-5,000   FIS

An Emile Gallé vase, "Coloquintes Grimpantes", etched and enamelled decoration of pumpkin buds and fruits, etched signature.

c1900   23.5 in (59.5cm) high
$5,500-6,000   Qu

An Emile Gallé vase, etched and enamelled decoration of thistles and Lothringer cross, signed "E. Gallé/ Nancy/depose" at base.

c1910   (20cm) high
$1,000-1,200   DN

An Emile Gallé flask, enamelled glass in silver frame, signed "E. Gallé deposé", large crack.

5.25in (13.5cm) high
$300-500   FRE

DECORATIVE ARTS

René Lalique

René Lalique (1862-1945) was born in Ay, Champagne, France. The year he was born, the family moved to the outskirts of Paris, and at 16 he began an apprenticeship with jeweller Louis Aucoc. Inspired by his initial training and already producing unique designs of his own, Lalique travelled, studied and worked at Boucheron and Cartier before setting up his own workshop in Paris in 1886. His reputation grew and Lalique received critical acclaim for his Art Nouveau work at the Paris Exposition in 1900. He had begun to experiment with glass in the mid 1890s and his glass work really took off with his production of perfume bottles for companies such as François Coty and Nina Ricci. Other glass designs included car mascots, ashtrays and lighting. In 1921 he designed interiors for the French liner 'Paris' and this was followed by further ocean liner commissions and work on the decoration of the train which became known as the Orient Express. By 1925 he was being praised for his contribution to Art Deco glassware. The company still exists today – pieces after his death are marked 'Lalique' instead of 'R. Lalique'.

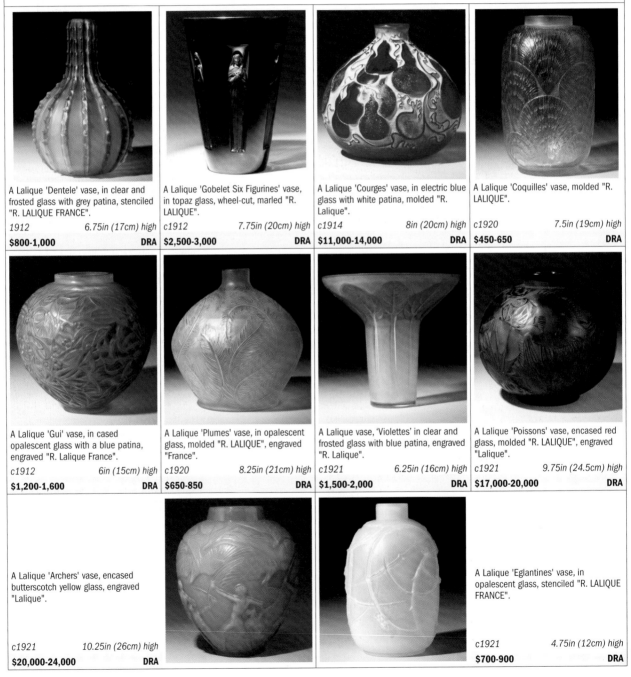

A Lalique 'Dentele' vase, in clear and frosted glass with grey patina, stenciled "R. LALIQUE FRANCE".

1912　　　　6.75in (17cm) high

$800-1,000　　　　DRA

A Lalique 'Gobelet Six Figurines' vase, in topaz glass, wheel-cut, marled "R. LALIQUE".

c1912　　　　7.75in (20cm) high

$2,500-3,000　　　　DRA

A Lalique 'Courges' vase, in electric blue glass with white patina, molded "R. Lalique".

c1914　　　　8in (20cm) high

$11,000-14,000　　　　DRA

A Lalique 'Coquilles' vase, molded "R. LALIQUE".

c1920　　　　7.5in (19cm) high

$450-650　　　　DRA

A Lalique 'Gui' vase, in cased opalescent glass with a blue patina, engraved "R. Lalique France".

c1912　　　　6in (15cm) high

$1,200-1,600　　　　DRA

A Lalique 'Plumes' vase, in opalescent glass, molded "R. LALIQUE", engraved "France".

c1920　　　　8.25in (21cm) high

$650-850　　　　DRA

A Lalique vase, 'Violettes' in clear and frosted glass with blue patina, engraved "R. Lalique".

c1921　　　　6.25in (16cm) high

$1,500-2,000　　　　DRA

A Lalique 'Poissons' vase, encased red glass, molded "R. LALIQUE", engraved "Lalique".

c1921　　　　9.75in (24.5cm) high

$17,000-20,000　　　　DRA

A Lalique 'Archers' vase, encased butterscotch yellow glass, engraved "Lalique".

c1921　　　　10.25in (26cm) high

$20,000-24,000　　　　DRA

A Lalique 'Eglantines' vase, in opalescent glass, stenciled "R. LALIQUE FRANCE".

c1921　　　　4.75in (12cm) high

$700-900　　　　DRA

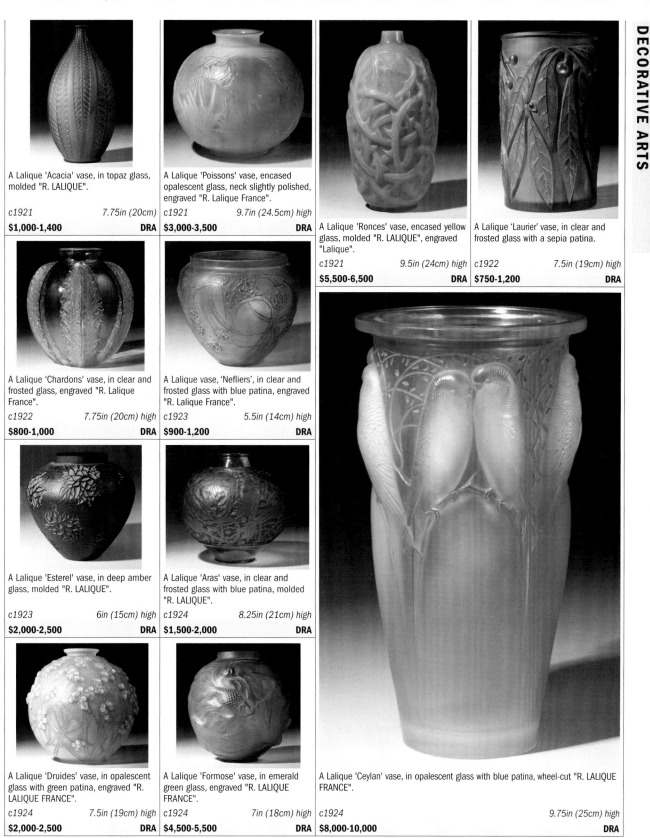

A Lalique 'Acacia' vase, in topaz glass, molded "R. LALIQUE".

c1921　　　　7.75in (20cm)

$1,000-1,400　　　　**DRA**

A Lalique 'Poissons' vase, encased opalescent glass, neck slightly polished, engraved "R. Lalique France".

c1921　　　　9.7in (24.5cm) high

$3,000-3,500　　　　**DRA**

A Lalique 'Ronces' vase, encased yellow glass, molded "R. LALIQUE", engraved "Lalique".

c1921　　　　9.5in (24cm) high

$5,500-6,500　　　　**DRA**

A Lalique 'Laurier' vase, in clear and frosted glass with a sepia patina.

c1922　　　　7.5in (19cm) high

$750-1,200　　　　**DRA**

A Lalique 'Chardons' vase, in clear and frosted glass, engraved "R. Lalique France".

c1922　　　　7.75in (20cm) high

$800-1,000　　　　**DRA**

A Lalique vase, 'Nefliers', in clear and frosted glass with blue patina, engraved "R. Lalique France".

c1923　　　　5.5in (14cm) high

$900-1,200　　　　**DRA**

A Lalique 'Esterel' vase, in deep amber glass, molded "R. LALIQUE".

c1923　　　　6in (15cm) high

$2,000-2,500　　　　**DRA**

A Lalique 'Aras' vase, in clear and frosted glass with blue patina, molded "R. LALIQUE".

c1924　　　　8.25in (21cm) high

$1,500-2,000　　　　**DRA**

A Lalique 'Druides' vase, in opalescent glass with green patina, engraved "R. LALIQUE FRANCE".

c1924　　　　7.5in (19cm) high

$2,000-2,500　　　　**DRA**

A Lalique 'Formose' vase, in emerald green glass, engraved "R. LALIQUE FRANCE".

c1924　　　　7in (18cm) high

$4,500-5,500　　　　**DRA**

A Lalique 'Ceylan' vase, in opalescent glass with blue patina, wheel-cut "R. LALIQUE FRANCE".

c1924　　　　9.75in (25cm) high

$8,000-10,000　　　　**DRA**

A Lalique 'Malines' vase, an opalescent glass, stenciled "R. LALIQUE", engraved "France".

1924   5in (13cm) high

$550-650   DRA

A Lalique 'Six Figurines et Masques' vase, in opalescent glass with blue patina, engraved "R. Lalique France".

1924   9.75in (25cm) high

$8,000-10,000   DRA

A Lalique 'Albert' vase, in topaz glass, wheel-cut "R. LALIQUE".

1925   6.75in (17cm) high

$2,000-2,500   DRA

A Lalique 'Perles' vase, in opalescent glass, molded "R. LALIQUE".

1925   4.75in (12cm) high

$1,000-1,300   DRA

A Lalique 'Dahlias' vase, in clear and frosted glass, with silver metal rim, gray patina and black enamel, molded "R. LALIQUE".

1925   5.5in (14cm) high

$2,000-2,500   DRA

A Lalique 'Montmorency' opalescent glass vase, of broad bucket form molded in high relief with four horizontal bands of cherries and stems heightened with blue staining, marked "R. Lalique France", having metal mount for use as a lamp.

1925   8in (20cm) high

$7,000-8,000   DN

A Lalique molded 'Charmilles' glass vase, with traces of pink patine, base cracked, inscribed "Lalique/France", model introduced 1926.

14in (35.5cm) high

$450-550   SI

A Lalique 'Domremy' vase, in opalescent glass with sepia patina, engraved "R. Lalique France", no979.

1926   8.75in (22cm) high

$1,200-1,600   DRA

A rare Lalique 'Koudour' vase, in clear glass with black enamel decoration, molded "R. LALIQUE", engraved "R. Lalique France".

1926   7in (18cm) high

$6,000-7,000   DRA

A Lalique 'Lagamar' vase, in clear and frosted glass with black enamel decoration, wheel-cut "R. LALIQUE".

1926   7.25in (18.5cm) high

$11,000-14,000   DRA

A Lalique 'Beliers' smoked glass twin-handled vase, the handles as rams, the ovoid body with footed stem, wheel etched mark "R. Lalique".

1926   7.5in (19cm) high

$2,000-2,500   L&T

A Lalique 'Oranges' vase, in clear and frosted glass with black enamel decoration, molded "R. LALIQUE".

1926   *11.5in (29cm) high*

$30,000-40,000   **DRA**

A Lalique 'Palissy' vase, in cased opalescent glass, engraved "R. Lalique France".

1926   *6.25in (16cm) high*

$2,000-3,000   **DRA**

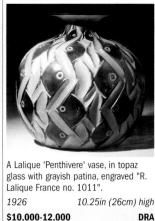

A Lalique 'Penthivere' vase, in topaz glass with grayish patina, engraved "R. Lalique France no. 1011".

1926   *10.25in (26cm) high*

$10,000-12,000   **DRA**

A Lalique 'Sarments' (Lave-Raisins) opalescent glass vase, of flared cylindrical shape, molded in relief with interwoven foliate stems, marked "R. Lalique France" on base.

1927   *5.75in (14.5cm) high*

$450-550   **DN**

A Lalique 'Avalon' vase, in clear and frosted glass, wheel-cut "R, LALIQUE FRANCE".

1927   *5.75in (15cm) high*

$1,400-1,800   **DRA**

A Lalique 'Ormeaux' vase, in cased opalescent glass, engraved "R. Lalique France".

1926   *6.5in (17cm) high*

$1,200-1,500   **DRA**

A Lalique 'Ornis' opalescent glass vase, wheel-cut "R. LALIQUE FRANCE".

1926   *8.75in (22cm) high*

$6,500-8,500   **DRA**

A Lalique 'Sophora' vase, in deep amber glass, now drilled and mounted as an electric table lamp, marks not visible.

1926   *10.25in (26cm) high*

$1,400-1,800   **DRA**

A Lalique 'Tournesol' vase, in clear and frosted glass with yellow patina, engraved "R. Lalique France".

1927   *4.75in (12cm) high*

$1,400-1,800   **DRA**

A Lalique 'Tourbillons' vase, molded "R. LALIQUE", engraved "France".

1926

$40,000-50,000   **DRA**

A Lalique 'Beautreillis' vase, in topaz glaze, wheel-cut "R. LALIQUE FRANCE".

1927   5.75in (14.5cm) high
$1,600-2,000   DRA

A Lalique 'Champagne' vase, in topaz glass, engraved "R. Lalique France".

1927   6in (15.5cm) high
$2,000-2,500   DRA

A Lalique 'Dordogne' vase, in white opalescent glass with sepia patina, molded "R. LALIQUE", engraved "R. Lalique France".

1927   7.25in (18cm) high
$6,000-7,000   DRA

A Lalique 'Espalion' vase, in opalescent glass with blue patina, molded "R. LALIQUE".

1927   7in (18cm) high
$1,400-1,800   DRA

A Lalique 'Malesherbes' vase, in deep amber glass with white patina, engraved "R. Lalique France".

1927   9in (23cm) high
$3,000-4,000   DRA

A Lalique 'Moissac' vase, in yellow glass, wheel-cut "R. LALIQUE FRANCE".

1927   5in (13cm) high
$1,800-2,200   DRA

A Lalique 'Oleron' vase, encased opalescent glass with green patina, engraved "R. Lalique France".

1927   3.5in (9cm)
$1,000-1,400   DRA

A Lalique 'Rampillon' vase, in yellow glass, stenciled "R. LALIQUE FRANCE".

1927   5in (13cm)
$1,500-2,000   DRA

A Lalique 'Camaret' vase, in cased opalescent glass, engraved "R. Lalique France".

1928   6.75in (17cm) high
$1,000-1,400   DRA

A Lalique 'Coq et Raisins' vase, in clear and frosted glass with blue-grey patina, stenciled "R. LALIQUE FRANCE".

1928   6in (15cm) high
$1,200-1,600   DRA

A Lalique 'Perigord' vase, in opalescent glass, engraved "R. Lalique France".

1928   6in (15cm) high
$2,000-2,500   DRA

A Lalique 'Raisins' vase, in clear and frosted glass with blue patina, wheel-cut "R. LALIQUE FRANCE".

1928   6in (15.5cm) high
$700-900   DRA

A Lalique 'Amiens' vase, in opalescent glass, wheel-cut "R LALIQUE".

1929   7in (18cm) high
$2,000-2,500   DRA

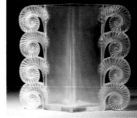

A Lalique 'Orly' clear glass vase, of inverted bullet shape supported on four semi-circular flanges, molded with radiating bands of beading, marked "R. Lalique France".

1930   6.75in (17cm) high
$2,000-2,400   DN

A Lalique 'Cerises' vase, in opalescent glass with blue patina, stenciled "R. LALIQUE FRANCE".

1930   *7.75in (20cm) high*

$3,500-4,000   **DRA**

A Lalique 'Fontainebleau' vase, in deep blue glass with greyish patina, engraved "R. Lalique France no. 1011".

1930   *7in (17.5cm) high*

$6,000-8,000   **DRA**

A Lalique 'Grenade' vase, in black glass with white patina, stenciled "R. LALIQUE".

1930   *4.75in (12cm) high*

$2,500-3,000   **DRA**

A Lalique 'Lierres' vase, in clear and frosted glass with blue-green patina, molded "R. LALIQUE".

1930   *3.75in (10cm) high*

$1,500-2,000   **DRA**

A Lalique 'Piriac' vase, in blue glass, stenciled "R. LALIQUE FRANCE".

1930   *7.25in (18.5cm) high*

$5,000-6,000   **DRA**

A Lalique 'Saint-Francois' vase, encased opalescent glass with blue patina, stenciled "R. LALIQUE FRANCE".

1930   *6.75in (17.5cm) high*

$3,000-4,000   **DRA**

A Lalique 'Formose' opalescent glass vase, molded overall with the interspersed bodies of tropical fish, signed on the foot "R. Lalique France".

1930   *6.75in (17cm) high*

$1,800-2,200   **DN**

A Lalique 'Tulipes' vase, in opalescent glass, engraved "R. Lalique France".

1930   *7.25in (18.5cm) high*

$2,500-3,000   **DRA**

A Lalique 'Chamois' vase, in clear and frosted glass with blue patina, stenciled "R. LALIQUE FRANCE".

1931   *5in (12.5cm) high*

$1,000-1,300   **DRA**

A Lalique 'Avallon' vase, clear opalescent and blue-stained glass vase, molded with birds perched on berried branches, wheel etched mark "R. Lalique France" and etched mark "No. 986".

1931   *5.75in (14.5cm) high*

$2,000-2,500   **L&T**

A Lalique 'Bagatelle' clear, frosted and sepia-stained glass vase, of swollen cylindrical form, molded with birds and leaves, etched mark "R. Lalique France".

1931   *6.75in (17cm) high*

$1,000-1,400   **L&T**

A Lalique 'Biches' frosted and grey-stained glass vase, of ovoid form, molded with deer among fruiting branches, etched mark "R. Lalique France".

1931   *6.75in (17cm) high*

$1,000-1,400   **L&T**

A Lalique 'Bacchantes' clear frosted and blue stained glass vase, of tapering cylindrical form, molded with a frieze of naked female figures, etched mark "R. Lalique, France".

9.75in (25cm) high

$8,000-10,000   L&T

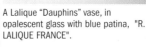

A Lalique 'Le Mans' vase, in amber glass with white patina, "R. LALIQUE FRANCE".

1931   *4in (10.5cm) high*

$2,500-3,000   DRA

A Lalique "Dauphins" vase, in opalescent glass with blue patina, "R. LALIQUE FRANCE".

1932   *6in (15cm) high*

$2,500-3,000   DRA

A Lalique 'Chamonix' vase, in opalescent glass, "R. LALIQUE FRANCE".

1933   *7in (18cm) high*

$900-1,200   DRA

A Lalique 'Chataignier' vase, stenciled "R. LALIQUE FRANCE".

1933   *5in (12.5cm)*

$450-650   DRA

A Lalique 'Acina' vase, in clear and frosted glass with blue patina, stenciled "R. LALIQUE FRANCE".

1934   *8.75in (22cm) high*

$1,500-2,000   DRA

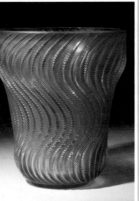

A Lalique Art Deco vase, vase, in clear glass, stenciled "R. LALIQUE FRANCE".

1935   *5.5in (14cm) high*

$2,000-2,500   DRA

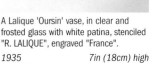

A Lalique 'Oursin' vase, in clear and frosted glass with white patina, stenciled "R. LALIQUE", engraved "France".

1935   *7in (18cm) high*

$1,500-2,000   DRA

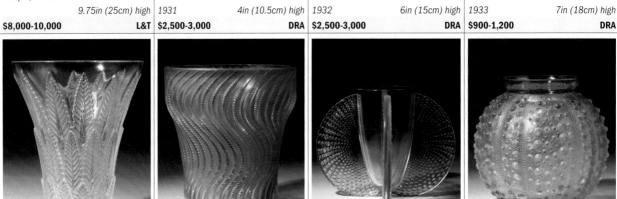

A Lalique 'Font-Romeau' vase, in clear and frosted glass, stenciled "R. LALIQUE FRANCE".

1936   *8.75in (22cm) high*

$1,800-2,200   DRA

A Lalique 'Pan' vase, modeled as the flutes of Pan, in clear and frosted glass with gray patina, stenciled "R. LALIQUE FRANCE".

1937   *12.5in (32cm) high.*

$6,000-8,000   DRA

A Lalique 'Saint Tropez' vase, in opalescent glass, stenciled "R. LALIQUE FRANCE".

1937   *7.5in (19cm) high*

$1,500-2,000   DRA

A Lalique 'Camargue' vase, in clear and frosted glass, engraved "Lalique France", base with large polished area.

1942   *11.5in (29.5cm)*

$2,500-3,000   **DRA**

Two Lalique 'Ceylan' frosted and opalescent glass vases, both molded with budgerigars, with blue staining and wheel etched mark "R. Lalique, France".

                    9in (23cm) high

$4,500-6,500 each   **L&T**

A Lalique bowl, in clear and frosted glass with sepia patina and black enamel, molded "R. LALIQUE.

1912   *11.5cm (4.5in) diam*

$800-1,000   **DRA**

A Lalique 'Lutteurs' frosted glass bowl, of ovoid form, with tapered base, molded with a frieze of naked male figures, etched mark "R. Lalique, France No. 890".

                    5.5in (14cm) high

$3,000-4,000   **L&T**

A Lalique Art Deco table light, the shades comprising two opposed "Coquilles" opalescent bowls, on a stepped oval brass base with disc feet, both shades with wheel etched mark "R. Lalique, France".

1920   *11.5in (29cm) high*

$600-800   **L&T**

A Lalique 'Ondines' bowl, in clear and frosted glass with blue patina, engraved "R. Lalique France".

1921   *8.25in (21cm) diam*

$800-1,000   **DRA**

A Lalique 'Gui' bowl, in clear and frosted glass with sepia patina, "R. LALIQUE FRANCE".

1921   *8in (20.5cm) diam*

$500-600   **DRA**

A Lalique 'Poissons' bowl, in opalescent glass.

1921   *9.5in (24cm) diam*

$850-1,000   **DRA**

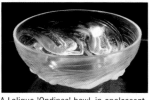

A Lalique 'Ondines' bowl, in opalescent glass, wheel-cut "R. LALIQUE FRANCE".

1921   *8.25in (21cm) high*

$1,500-2,000   **DRA**

A Lalique 'Chiens' bowl, in opalescent glass, molded "R. Lalique", engraved "France".

1921   *9.5in (24cm) diam*

$1,000-1,400   **DRA**

A Lalique 'Nemours' bowl, in clear and frosted glass with sepia patina and brown enamel highlights, molded "R. LALIQUE".

1921   *10in (25.5cm) diam*

$800-1,200   **DRA**

A Lalique 'Volubulis' bowl, in yellow opalescent glass, wheel-cut "R. LALIQUE FRANCE".

1921   *8.5in (21.5cm) diam*

$800-1,000   **DRA**

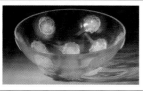

A Lalique 'Tournon' centerbowl, in opalescent glass, molded "R. LALIQUE FRANCE".

1928   *12in (30.5cm) diam*

$1,300-1,600   **DRA**

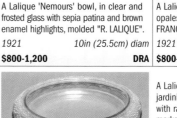

A Lalique 'Saint-Paul' clear glass oval jardinière, molded on the underside with radiating bands of beading, marked "R. Lalique France".

1931   *16.25in (41cm) wide*

$400-500   **DN**

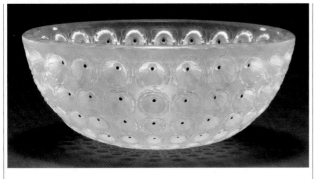

A Lalique 'Nemours' molded and painted crystal bowl, engraved "Lalique France".

10in (25.5cm) diam

$600-800   **FRE**

A Lalique 'Houppes' opalescent glass powder bowl, the cover molded on the inside with powder puffs, the base incised "R Lalique France, No. 29".

5.5in (14cm) diam

$750-950   **Chef**

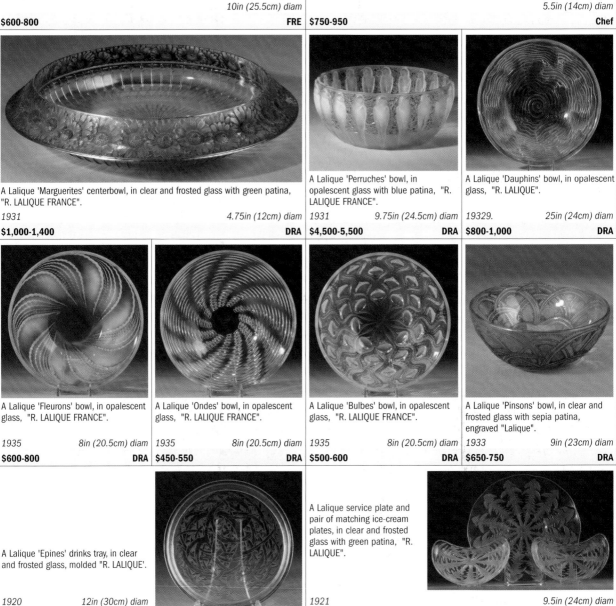

A Lalique 'Marguerites' centerbowl, in clear and frosted glass with green patina, "R. LALIQUE FRANCE".

1931   *4.75in (12cm) diam*

$1,000-1,400   **DRA**

A Lalique 'Perruches' bowl, in opalescent glass with blue patina, "R. LALIQUE FRANCE".

1931   *9.75in (24.5cm) diam*

$4,500-5,500   **DRA**

A Lalique 'Dauphins' bowl, in opalescent glass, "R. LALIQUE".

19329.   *25in (24cm) diam*

$800-1,000   **DRA**

A Lalique 'Fleurons' bowl, in opalescent glass, "R. LALIQUE FRANCE".

1935   *8in (20.5cm) diam*

$600-800   **DRA**

A Lalique 'Ondes' bowl, in opalescent glass, "R. LALIQUE FRANCE".

1935   *8in (20.5cm) diam*

$450-550   **DRA**

A Lalique 'Bulbes' bowl, in opalescent glass, "R. LALIQUE FRANCE".

1935   *8in (20.5cm) diam*

$500-600   **DRA**

A Lalique 'Pinsons' bowl, in clear and frosted glass with sepia patina, engraved "Lalique".

1933   *9in (23cm) diam*

$650-750   **DRA**

A Lalique 'Epines' drinks tray, in clear and frosted glass, molded "R. LALIQUE'.

1920   *12in (30cm) diam*

$400-600   **DRA**

A Lalique service plate and pair of matching ice-cream plates, in clear and frosted glass with green patina, "R. LALIQUE".

1921   *9.5in (24cm) diam*

$600-800   **DRA**

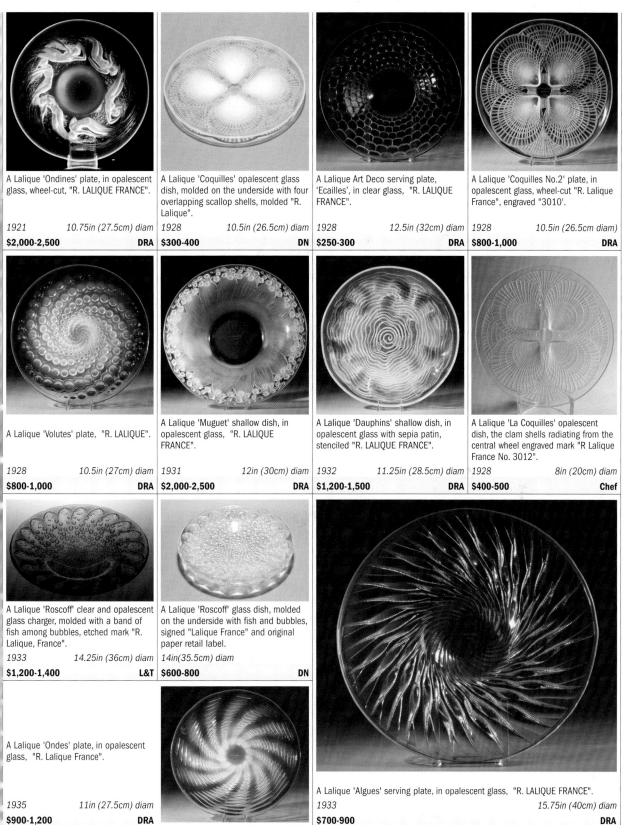

A Lalique 'Ondines' plate, in opalescent glass, wheel-cut, "R. LALIQUE FRANCE".

1921   *10.75in (27.5cm) diam*
$2,000-2,500   **DRA**

A Lalique 'Coquilles' opalescent glass dish, molded on the underside with four overlapping scallop shells, molded "R. Lalique".

1928   *10.5in (26.5cm) diam*
$300-400   **DN**

A Lalique Art Deco serving plate, 'Ecailles', in clear glass, "R. LALIQUE FRANCE".

1928   *12.5in (32cm) diam*
$250-300   **DRA**

A Lalique 'Coquilles No.2' plate, in opalescent glass, wheel-cut "R. Lalique France", engraved "3010'.

1928   *10.5in (26.5cm diam)*
$800-1,000   **DRA**

A Lalique 'Volutes' plate, "R. LALIQUE".

1928   *10.5in (27cm) diam*
$800-1,000   **DRA**

A Lalique 'Muguet' shallow dish, in opalescent glass, "R. LALIQUE FRANCE".

1931   *12in (30cm) diam*
$2,000-2,500   **DRA**

A Lalique 'Dauphins' shallow dish, in opalescent glass with sepia patin, stenciled "R. LALIQUE FRANCE".

1932   *11.25in (28.5cm) diam*
$1,200-1,500   **DRA**

A Lalique 'La Coquilles' opalescent dish, the clam shells radiating from the central wheel engraved mark "R Lalique France No. 3012".

1928   *8in (20cm) diam*
$400-500   **Chef**

A Lalique 'Roscoff' clear and opalescent glass charger, molded with a band of fish among bubbles, etched mark "R. Lalique, France".

1933   *14.25in (36cm) diam*
$1,200-1,400   **L&T**

A Lalique 'Roscoff' glass dish, molded on the underside with fish and bubbles, signed "Lalique France" and original paper retail label.

14in(35.5cm) diam
$600-800   **DN**

A Lalique 'Ondes' plate, in opalescent glass, "R. Lalique France".

1935   *11in (27.5cm) diam*
$900-1,200   **DRA**

A Lalique 'Algues' serving plate, in opalescent glass, "R. LALIQUE FRANCE".
1933   *15.75in (40cm) diam*
$700-900   **DRA**

553

A rare Lalique 'Hortense' cake tray, in clear and frosted glass with engraved decoration, molded "R. LALIQUE".

1942   *15.25in (39cm)*
$500-700   **DRA**

A Lalique 'Gros Bourdon' letter seal or door handle, in clear and frosted glass with charcoal patina, engraved "R. Lalique".

1910   *2.25in (6cm) high*
$3,500-4,000   **DRA**

A Lalique 'Tete D'Aigle' letter seal, in black, glass with whitish patina, engraved "R. Lalique".

c1911   *3in (8cm) high*
$1,800-2,200   **DRA**

A Lalique 'Aigle' letter seal, in clear and frosted glass with gray patina, engraved "Lalique".

1912   *3in (8cm) high.*
$2,000-2,500   **DRA**

A Lalique 'Sauterelles' letter seal, in electric blue glass, molded "LALIQUE".

1912   *1.75in (4.5cm) high*
$1,000-1,300   **DRA**

A Lalique 'Cigognes' letter seal, in clear and frosted glass with gray patina, molded LALIQUE.

1919   *2.75in (7cm) high*
$1,000-1,300   **DRA**

A rare Lailque 'Victoire' letter seal, in clear and frosted glass with sepia patina, molded "LALIQUE", engraved with intaglio monogram "YS?".

1920   *1.75in (4.5cm) high*
$1,500-2,000   **DRA**

A Lalique 'Statuette Drapee' letter seal, in clear and frosted glass with green patina, engraved "Lalique".

1912   *2.5in (6.5cm) high*
$3,500-4,000   **DRA**

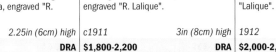

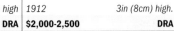

A Lalique 'Hirondelles' letter seal, clear and frosted glass, engraved "R. Lalique".

1919   *2.25in (5.5cm) high*
$550-750   **DRA**

A Lalique 'Lapin' letter seal, in topaz glass, engraved "R. Lalique France".

1925   *2.25in (6cm) high*
$600-900   **DRA**

A rare Lalique 'Deux Tourterelles' paperweight, in topaz glass, "R. LALIQUE FRANCE".

1925   *4.75in (12cm) high*
$2,500-3,000   **DRA**

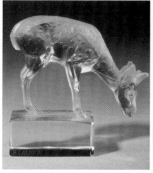

A Lalique 'Daim' paperweight, in clear and frosted glass, molded and "R. LALIQUE".

1929   *3.5in (8.5cm) high*

$700-900   **DRA**

A Lalique 'Antelope' paperweight, in clear and frosted glass, engraved "R. Lalique France".

1929   *3.25in (8.5cm)*

$700-900   **DRA**

A Lalique 'Moineau Hardi' paperweight, in clear and frosted glass, engraved "R. Lalique".

1929   *3.5in (9cm) high*

$400-600   **DRA**

A Lalique 'Moineau Moqueur' paperweight, in clear and frosted glass, "R. LALIQUE".

1930   *3.25in (8.5cm) high*

$400-600   **DRA**

A Lalique 'Toby' paperweight, in clear and frosted glass, "R. LALIQUE FRANCE".

1931   *3.25in (8.5cm) high*

$2,000-2,500   **DRA**

A Lalique 'Faucon' car mascot, in clear and frosted glass, molded "R. LALIQUE FRANCE", wheel-cut "FRANCE".

1925   *6in (15cm) high*

$3,000-4,000   **DRA**

A Lalique 'Faucon' car mascot, in clear and frosted glass, molded "R. LALIQUE FRANCE", wheel-cut "FRANCE".

1925   *6in (15cm) high*

$2,500-3,000   **DRA**

A Lalique 'Tête de Coq' car mascot, molded "LALIQUE FRANCE".

1928   *6.75in (17.5cm) high*

$1,000-1,500   **DRA**

A Lalique 'Coq Nain' car mascot, in clear and frosted glass, molded "R. LALIQUE".

1928   *8in (20.5cm) high*

$1,000-1,500   **DRA**

A Lalique 'Tête de Paon' car mascot, in clear and frosted glass, molded "R. LALIQUE FRANCE", comb missing.

1928   *4.75in (12cm) high*

$700-900   **DRA**

A Lalique 'Hirondelle' car mascot, in clear and frosted glass, molded "R. LALIQUE FRANCE".

1928   *6in (15cm) high*

$2,000-2,500   **DRA**

A Lalique 'Sainte-Christophe' car mascot, in clear and frosted glass, molded "R. LALIQUE FRANCE".

1928   *5in (13cm)*

$1,000-1,500   **DRA**

A Lalique 'Victoire' car mascot, in clear and frosted glass, molded "R. LALIQUE FRANCE". 26cm (10in) long together with an original Lalique wood display mount
1928

$25,000-30,000   **DRA**

A Lalique 'Tête D'Aigle' car mascot, in clear and frosted glass, engraved "Lalique France", now mounted as a bookend with metal collar and onyx base.

11cm (4.25in) high

$2,000-2,500   **DRA**

A Lalique 'Libellule' car mascot, in clear and frosted glass with pale amethyst tint, molded "R. LALIQUE FRANCE" and engraved "R. Lalique France".

This mascot is accompanied by a letter from the present owner authenticating the mascot as the one formerly used by Gary Cooper on his Duesenberg, and presented to her by Mr Cooper as a gift.

1928   *8.25in (21cm)*

$10,000-15,000   **DRA**

A Lalique 'Faucon' clear, frosted and amethyst tinted car mascot, molded as a falcon on a circular base, traces of grey staining, molded marks "R. Lalique", and wheel etched mark "France".

1925   *6.25in (15.75cm) high*

$2,300-2,800   **L&T**

A Lalique 'Sanglier' car mascot, in topaz glass, molded "R. LALIQUE" and "R. LALIQUE FRANCE".

1929   *3.75in (9.5cm) high*

$1,000-1,400   **DRA**

A Lalique molded and frosted crystal eagle head, engraved "Lalique France".

4.5in (11.5cm) high

$450-650   **FRE**

A Lalique 'Coq Nain' smoked clear and frosted glass car mascot, molded as a cockerel on a circular base, molded marks "R. Lalique France".

1928   *7.75in (20cm) high*

$2,300-2,800   **L&T**

A Lalique 'Archer' glass mascot, of circular disc shape intaglio molded with the kneeling naked figure of male archer, molded "R. Lalique" and engraved "France", also marked on base "No. 1126".

1929   *4.75in (12cm) high*

$2,000-2,400   **DN**

A Lalique perfume bottle 'Ambre' for D'Orsay, in black and white glass with patina, molded "LALIQUE".

1912   *5in (13cm) high*

$2,500-3,000   **DRA**

A Lalique 'Mystere' perfume bottle for D'Orsay, in black and white glass with patina, molded "LALIQUE".

1912   *3.75in (9.5cm) high*

$2,500-3,000   **DRA**

A Lalique 'Fleurettes' perfume bottle, in clear and frosted glass with blue patina, molded "LALIQUE" with extended "L".

1919   8.75in (16cm) high

$600-800   **DRA**

A Lalique perfume atomizer, 'Epines', with metal mount, in clear and frosted glass, "R. LALIQUE FRANCE".

1924   4in (10.5cm) high

$250-300   **DRA**

A Lalique 'Amphitrite' perfume bottle, in clear and frosted glass with blue patina, engraved "R. Lalique".

1920   3.75in (9.5cm)

$3,000-4,000   **DRA**

A Lalique 'Dans La Nuit' perfume display bottle for Worth, in clear and frosted glass with blue enamel, molded "R. LALIQUE", engraved "Lalique France".

1924   9.5in (24cm)

$1,500-2,000   **DRA**

A Lalique 'Gylcines' perfume bottle for Gabilla, in clear and frosted glass with blue patina, molded "R. LALIQUE PARIS FRANCE".

1925   4.25in (10.5cm) high

$1,800-2,200   **DRA**

A Lalique 'Helene' (Lotus) perfume bottle, in clear and frosted glass, "R. LALIQUE FRANCE".

1928   2.75in (7cm)

$2,000-2,500   **DRA**

A Lalique 'Le Parfum Des Anges' perfume bottle, for Oviatt of Los Angeles, in clear and frosted glass with sepia patina, molded "R. LALIQUE FRANCE".

1928   3.25in (8.5cm) high

$1,800-2,200   **DRA**

A Lalique 'Muguet' perfume bottle, in clear and frosted glass with green patina, "R. LALIQUE FRANCE".

1931   4in (10cm) high

$2,000-2,500   **DRA**

A Lalique 'Oree' perfume bottle for Claire, in clear and frosted glass with sepia patina, stopper molded "LALIQUE", base molded "FRANCE", with paper label from the Wannamaker Stores.

1930   3.25in (8cm) high

$3,000-3,500   **DRA**

A Lalique 'Requette' perfume bottle for Worth, in clear glass with blue enamel, unopened, complete with original contents and card display box, "LALIQUE FRANCE".

1949   6.25in (16cm) high

$1,200-1,600   **DRA**

A Lalique 'Chypre' clear, frosted and sepia stained perfume bottle and stopper, for Forvil, the cylindrical body molded with flowers, bearing inscription "Chypre Forvil", molded mark "R. Lalique Paris France".

4in (10.4cm) high

$550-750   **L&T**

A Lalique 'Roses' perfume bottle for Worth, Paris, molded all over with flowers, molded marks "R. Lalique French Bottle".

3.25in (8.5cm) high

$400-600   **L&T**

A Lalique 'Roses' perfume bottle for Worth, in clear and frosted glass with blue patina, molded "R. LALIQUE FRENCH BOTTLE".

5.25in (13cm) high

$700-900   **DRA**

A Lalique 'Louveciennes' box, in clear and frosted glass, molded "LALIQUE DEPOSE".

1910   *2.75in (7cm) diam*

$2,000-3,000   **DRA**

A Lalique 'Quatre Scarabees' box, in black glass with white patina, engraved "R. Lalique France".

1911   *3.25in (8.5cm) diam*

$3,000-4,000   **DRA**

A Lalique 'Quatres Scarabees' box, in black glass with white patina, engraved "R. Lalique France".

1911   *3.25in (8.5cm) diam*

$2,000-2,500   **DRA**

A Lalique 'Mesanges' box, in opalescent amber glass, molded "R. Lalique".

1921   *6.75in (17cm) diam*

$1,200-1,600   **DRA**

A Lalique 'Cigales' box, in opalescent glass, molded "R. Lalique", engraved "France".

1921   *6.75in (17cm) diam*

$1,000-1,300   **DRA**

A Lalique 'Cleones' box, in amber glass, molded "R. Lalique", engraved "France".

1921   *6.75in (17cm) diam*

$1,200-1,600   **DRA**

A Lalique 'Chrysantheme' molded blue glass powder jar, molded as a chrysanthemum, inscribed "R. Lalique".

3.5in (9cm) diam

$1,500-2,000   **SI**

A Lalique 'Georgette' box, in opalescent glass with satin and card base, molded "R. Lalique".

1922   *8.25in (21cm) diam*

$2,000-2,500   **DRA**

A Lalique 'Saint-Marc' box, in opalescent glass, molded "R. Lalique".

1922   *9.75in (25cm) diam*

$2,000-3,000   **DRA**

A rare Lalique 'Cerises' red celluloid box, molded "R. Lalique".

1923   *2in (5.5cm) diam*

$1,000-1,500   **DRA**

A Lalique 'Saint Nectaire' box, in clear and frosted glass with green patina, engraved "R. Lalique France".

1925   *3.25in (8.5cm) diam*

$600-800   **DRA**

A Lalique 'Eglantines' box, in clear and frosted glass with green patina, engraved "R. Lalique France".

1926   *5.25in (13.5cm) diam*

$700-900   **DRA**

A Lalique powder box and cover, for Coty, cover molded with maidens, molded marks.

3.25in (8.5cm) diam

$350-450   **DN**

A Lalique 'Primeveres' box, in opalescent glass, molded "R. Lalique".

1930   *7.75in (20cm) diam*

$1,000-1,300   **DRA**

A Lalique glass and diamond brooch, with four flower heads.

c1900   2in (5.5cm) long

$9,000-11,000   **NBlm**

A Lalique 'Meduse' green glass and gold ring, ring size 8, gold replaced.

1912

$700-1,000   **DRA**

A Lalique 'Femmes dans le Fleurs' brooch, in blue glass and metal with gray patina.

1913   2in (5cm) long

$2,500-3,000   **DRA**

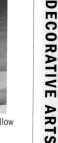

A Lalique 'Trefles' pendant, in yellow glass, molded Lalique.

1920   2.5in (6cm) long

$700-900   **DRA**

A Lalique 'Guepes' pendant, in deep amber glass with sepia patina on black silk cord, engraved "Lalique".

1920   2.25in (5.5cm) high

$800-1,200   **DRA**

A Lalique 'Mugue' lozenge-shaped pendant, in opalescent glass on original green silk cord, molded "R. Lalique".

1921   1.75in (4.5cm) long

$1,000-1,300   **DRA**

A Lalique 'Panier de Fruits' pendant, in frosted glass with blue patina, engraved "R. Lalique".

1922   1.5in (4cm) high

$400-600   **DRA**

A rare souvenir programme for the 'Journée de Sarah Bernhardt', features illustrations by Lalique, Georges Clairin and Rene Foy.

1893   33in (84cm) high

$3,000-4,000   **DRA**

A Lalique original design for a perfume bottle or veilleuse with 'Marguerites', design, pencil, ink and watercolour on 'BFK Rives' parchment paper.

1900-05   11in (28cm)

$2,500-3,000   **DRA**

A Lalique original design, "Chantecler", pencil, ink and watercolour.

1900-05

$2,500-3,000   **DRA**

An illustrated catalogue, "The Art of Rene Lalique", issued by Breves Lalique Galléries, London, and enclosing an additional supplement of Lalique mascots.

1928

$400-600   **L&T**

A Lalique 'Inseparables' clock frame, in clear and frosted glass, molded "R. LALIQUE".

1926   4.25in (11cm) high

$700-1,000   **DRA**

A pair of Lalique 'Raisin Muscat' menu plaques, in clear and frosted glass, both engraved "R. Lalique France".

1924   6in (15cm) high

$800-1,000   **DRA**

A pair of Lalique 'Pinsons' menu holders, in clear and frosted glass, both engraved "R. Lalique France".

1924   1.75in (4.5cm) high

$650-850   **DRA**

A Lalique 'Fauvettes A' illuminating table centrepiece, in clear and frosted glass with original nickel-plated metal illuminating base, wheel-cut "R. LALIQUE".

1930   *13.25in (33.5cm) high*

$13,000-16,000   **DRA**

A rare Lalique "Oeuvres de Lalique" display plaque.

1928   *3in (8cm) high*

$3,500-4,500   **DRA**

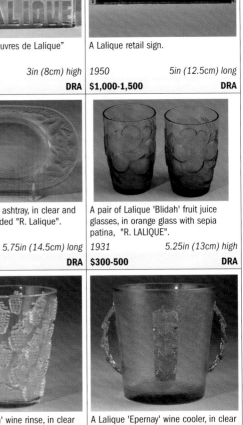

A Lalique retail sign.

1950   *5in (12.5cm) long*

$1,000-1,500   **DRA**

A Lalique 'Medici' ashtray, in clear and frosted glass, molded "R. Lalique".

1924   *5.75in (14.5cm) long*

$650-750   **DRA**

A pair of Lalique 'Blidah' fruit juice glasses, in orange glass with sepia patina, "R. LALIQUE".

1931   *5.25in (13cm) high*

$300-500   **DRA**

A pair of Lalique 'Bahia' fruit juice glasses, in orange glass with sepia patina, "R. LALIQUE".

1931   *5in (12.5cm) high*

$300-500   **DRA**

A Lalique 'Hesperides' pitcher and a 'Bahia' serving tray, in orange glass, both "R. LALIQUE".

1931   *8.75in (22cm) high*

$900-1,200   **DRA**

A Lalique 'Malaga' wine rinse, in clear and frosted glass, engraved "Lalique France".

1950   *5.75in (14.5cm) high*

$350-450   **DRA**

A Lalique 'Epernay' wine cooler, in clear and frosted glass, "R. LALIQUE FRANCE".

1938   *7.5in (20cm) high*

$1,500-2,000   **DRA**

A Lalique 'Vigne Strie' decanter and pair of wine glasses, in clear and frosted glass with sepia patina, molded "LALIQUE" on stopper.

1920   *Decanter 11.5in (29cm) high*

$2,000-2,500   **DRA**

A rare Lalique 'Satyr' carafe, engraved "R. Lalique pour Cusenier".

1923   *10.25in (6cm) high*

$3,000-3,500   **DRA**

A Lalique 'Selestat' decanter and stopper, in clear glass with applied black glass ring at the neck, molded "R. LALIQUE FRANCE.

1925   *10.5in (27cm) high*

$800-1,000   **DRA**

A Lalique 'Masques' carafe, in clear and frosted glass with sepia patina, engraved "R. Lalique France".

1913   *10in (25cm) high*

$2,000-2,500   **DRA**

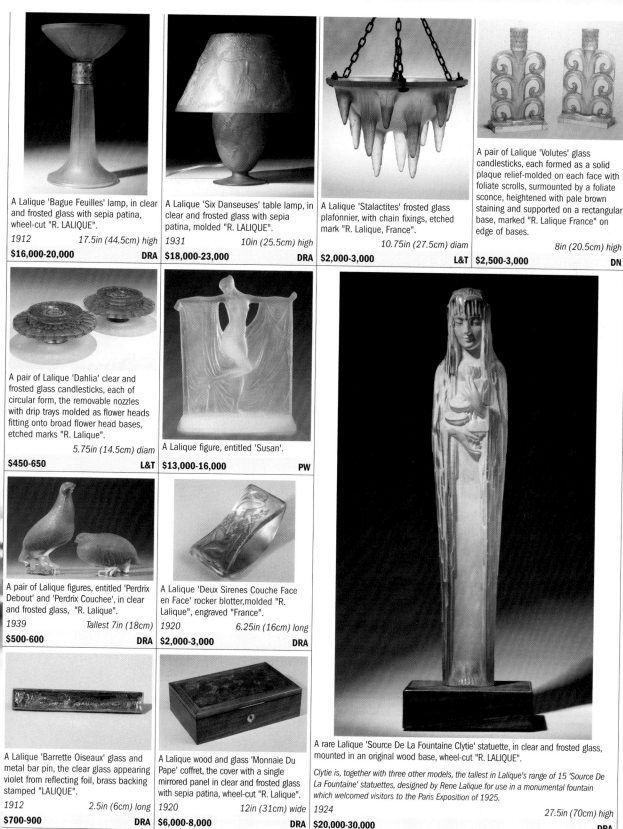

A Lalique 'Bague Feuilles' lamp, in clear and frosted glass with sepia patina, wheel-cut "R. LALIQUE".

1912   *17.5in (44.5cm) high*

$16,000-20,000   DRA

A Lalique 'Six Danseuses' table lamp, in clear and frosted glass with sepia patina, molded "R. LALIQUE".

1931   *10in (25.5cm) high*

$18,000-23,000   DRA

A Lalique 'Stalactites' frosted glass plafonnier, with chain fixings, etched mark "R. Lalique, France".

10.75in (27.5cm) diam

$2,000-3,000   L&T

A pair of Lalique 'Volutes' glass candlesticks, each formed as a solid plaque relief-molded on each face with foliate scrolls, surmounted by a foliate sconce, heightened with pale brown staining and supported on a rectangular base, marked "R. Lalique France" on edge of bases.

8in (20.5cm) high

$2,500-3,000   DN

A pair of Lalique 'Dahlia' clear and frosted glass candlesticks, each of circular form, the removable nozzles with drip trays molded as flower heads fitting onto broad flower head bases, etched marks "R. Lalique".

5.75in (14.5cm) diam

$450-650   L&T

A Lalique figure, entitled 'Susan'.

$13,000-16,000   PW

A pair of Lalique figures, entitled 'Perdrix Debout' and 'Perdrix Couchee', in clear and frosted glass, "R. Lalique".

1939   *Tallest 7in (18cm)*

$500-600   DRA

A Lalique 'Deux Sirenes Couche Face en Face' rocker blotter, molded "R. Lalique", engraved "France".

1920   *6.25in (16cm) long*

$2,000-3,000   DRA

A Lalique 'Barrette Oiseaux' glass and metal bar pin, the clear glass appearing violet from reflecting foil, brass backing stamped "LALIQUE".

1912   *2.5in (6cm) long*

$700-900   DRA

A Lalique wood and glass 'Monnaie Du Pape' coffret, the cover with a single mirrored panel in clear and frosted glass with sepia patina, wheel-cut "R. Lalique".

1920   *12in (31cm) wide*

$6,000-8,000   DRA

A rare Lalique 'Source De La Fountaine Clytie' statuette, in clear and frosted glass, mounted in an original wood base, wheel-cut "R. LALIQUE".

Clytie is, together with three other models, the tallest in Lalique's range of 15 'Source De La Fountaine' statuettes, designed by Rene Lalique for use in a monumental fountain which welcomed visitors to the Paris Exposition of 1925.

1924   *27.5in (70cm) high*

$20,000-30,000   DRA

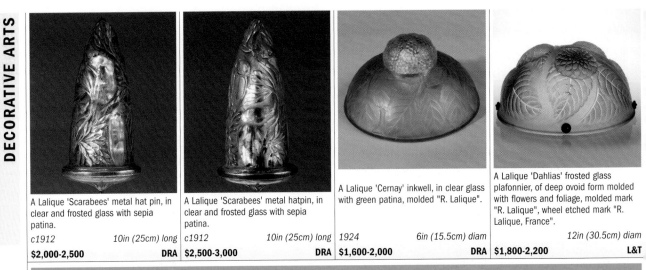

A Lalique 'Scarabees' metal hat pin, in clear and frosted glass with sepia patina.

c1912   10in (25cm) long

$2,000-2,500   DRA

A Lalique 'Scarabees' metal hatpin, in clear and frosted glass with sepia patina.

c1912   10in (25cm) long

$2,500-3,000   DRA

A Lalique 'Cernay' inkwell, in clear glass with green patina, molded "R. Lalique".

1924   6in (15.5cm) diam

$1,600-2,000   DRA

A Lalique 'Dahlias' frosted glass plafonnier, of deep ovoid form molded with flowers and foliage, molded mark "R. Lalique", wheel etched mark "R. Lalique, France".

12in (30.5cm) diam

$1,800-2,200   L&T

Loetz

Originally founded in 1836 by Johann Baptist Eisner, the glass factory at Klostermühle in South West Bohemia was taken over by Susanna Gerstner (neé Witwe) in 1852. Susanna was the widow of glassmaker Johann Loetz and she renamed the company "Glasfabrik Johann Loetz Witwe" (shortened to Loetz). The company's truly successful period was marked by the arrival of

Max Ritter von Spaun (d.1909) who took over the firm in 1879. He worked with his technical director Eduard Prochaskato to develop innovative production methods and designs. One of their specialities was papillon or oil-spot glass. The company is recognised as a key contributor to the Art Nouveau glass movement. The Loetz factory closed in 1948.

A Loetz double gourd-shaped vase, with impressed oilspots on an iridescent ground, small nicks to rim, unmarked.

7in (18cm) high

$1,500-2,000   CR

A Loetz bulbous glass vase, with bubbles under a lustred silver finish, unmarked.

7in (18cm) high

$800-1,000   CR

A Loetz 'Diaspora' iridescent glass vase, of double-gourd form with overall dimpled surface.

7in (18cm) high

$400-500   DN

A Loetz 'Cabinet' blown glass vase, chip to interior of rim.

4.25in (11cm) high

$350-500   FRE

A Loetz Art Deco vase, designed by Friedrich Adler, signed ORION, model-no.315.

c1905   6 .25in (16cm) high

$4,000-4,500   BMN

A Loetz iridescent glass bowl, the body covered with pulled iridescent bands and decorated with applied prunts.

5in (12.5cm) high

$1,500-2,000   L&T

A Loetz Art Nouveau vase, unsigned, coloured glass with applied decoration.

c1900/05 6in (15cm) high

$1,200-1,600   BMN

A Loetz Art Nouveau iridescent glass vase.

c1910   H 30 cm (11.75 inch)

$900-1,200   BMN

A Loetz tapering vase, of green lustred glass with a serpent wrapped around its dimpled neck, small nicks around rim, unmarked.

9in (23cm) high

$400-600　　　　**CR**

A Loetz iridescent glass vase, designed by Robert Holubetz, having an underlying lustrous opalescence and randomly flecked with apple-green iridescence.

11.5in (29.5cm) high

$900-1,200　　　　**DN**

A Loetz glass fan vase, with seven openings in amber oilspot, unmarked.

10in (25.5cm) high

$1,300-1,600　　　　**CR**

A Loetz glass inkwell, of pyramid form etched with pattern in iridescent blue and red on a bottle-green ground, with bronze hinged lid, unmarked.

2.75in (7cm) high

$500-600　　　　**CR**

A Loetz ceiling light marked "Genre Gallé", etched multi-coloured glass, fitted for electricity, signed.

1925　　　*16in (40cm) diam*

$3,000-3,500　　　　**Qu**

Monart

A Monart glass bowl, in mottled pink with mottled blue and aventurine speckling around the rim.

8in (20.5cm) diam

$400-500　　　　**DN**

A Monart-style baluster vase, with inverted rim and mottled turquoise, blue and amethyst inclusions.

12.25in (31cm) high

$250-300　　　　**L&T**

A Monart glass vase, of shouldered oviform tapering to a broad cylindrical neck, of pale blue tone on the lower section, the neck speckled with aventurine and fine amethyst veining.

7.75in (20cm) high

$250-300　　　　**DN**

A Monart glass broad oviform vase, the lower section in bright mottled orange and yellow shading through brown, green, copper-coloured aventurine and veins of black on the shoulders.

9.75in (24.5cm) high

$600-800　　　　**DN**

A Monart glass straight-sided small bowl, of rich mottled green, the area around the neck-rim with black and aventurine speckling.

3.5in (8.5cm) high

$75-115　　　　**DN**

A Monart glass broad oviform vase, of mottled orange tone shading to brownish tones on the shoulders and neck, internal burst bubble.

6.75in (17cm) high

$120-160　　　　**DN**

Tiffany

A Tiffany Favrile floriform vase, with green heart-shaped leaves on a gold lustred ground, etched "L.C Tiffany/Favrile/6427G", re-glued crack in base.

Charles Tiffany (1812-1902) began the Tiffany & Co. manufacturing business in New York in 1837 and opened a store on Broadway. His son Louis Comfort (1848-1933) had trained as an artist and brought a new perspective when he took over the running of the business at his father's death. In 1880 he founded the Tiffany studios, Louis C Tiffany & Associated Artists, and designed his own specialized wares in glass, jewellery, stained glass, silver, metal and ceramics to much critical acclaim. The studios closed in 1932, but the original company still exists today.

Favrile is the trade name of Louis Tiffany's patented glasswares, which have an iridescent finish. The name comes from the Old English word 'Fabrile' which means 'belonging to a craftsman or his craft'.

12in (30.5cm)

$1,200-1,600　　　　　　　　　　CR

A tall Tiffany Favrile floriform glass vase, with ribs and a 'pulled' motif in yellow and green, etched "L.C Tiffany/Favrile/9042J".

11.75in (30cm) high

$2,500-3,000　　　　　　　　　　CR

A Tiffany Favrile two-handled ovoid vase, of lustred gold and purple glass, marked "L.C Tiffany/Favrile/9388J".

8.5in (21.5cm) high

$1,800-2,200　　　　　　　　　　CR

A glass vase, probably Tiffany Studios, unsigned, of baluster form in cased green and iridescent glass with internal gold striped decoration.

c1900　　　　　8.25in (21cm) high

$500-700　　　　　　　　　　　　SI

A pair of Tiffany Favrile glass light shades, of tulip form, covered in peacock iridescence, etched marks, also another similar Tiffany shade.

5.25in (13.5cm) high

$1,200-1,500　　　　　　　　　　L&T

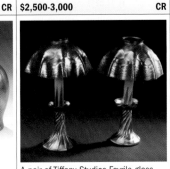

A pair of Tiffany Studios Favrile glass candlesticks, bases inscribed "L.C.T.", one shade "L.C.T. Favrile", the other "L.C. Tiffany-Favrile",

1899-1928　　　　　　13in (33cm)

$4,000-6,000　　　　　　　　　　SI

A Tiffany Favrile iridescent glass finger bowl and stand, each with a golden sheen with peacock-blue and mauve tones, both signed "LCT".

Stand 6in (15.5cm) diam

$450-650　　　　　　　　　　　　DN

A Tiffany Favrile glass plate with scalloped edge, signed "L.C.T/213".

c1899-1928　　　6.25in (16cm) diam

$400-500　　　　　　　　　　　　SI

A pair of Tiffany twisted candlesticks, with cupped bobeches, of gold lustred glass, marked "LCT".

5in (12.5cm) high

$1,400-1,800　　　　　　　　　　CR

A Tiffany Favrile glass floriform vase, signed "L.C. Tiffany, Favrille 6121G".

c1912　　　　　　4.25in (11cm) high

$1,000-1,400　　　　　　　　　　SI

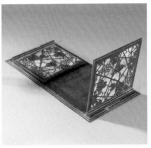

An early 20thC Tiffany Art Nouveau bronze and slag glass book stand, bearing "TIFFANY STUDIOS/NEWYORK/1027" mark, pierced grapevine pattern backed with caramel glass.

14in (35.5cm) long

$1,000-1,400　　　　　　　　　　SI

Whitefriars

A Whitefriars glass large 'tear' vase, designed by Barnaby Powell, the pale green transparent body applied around the lower half with six blue teardrops that extend to the base.

10.5in (25.5cm) high

$850-950　　　　　　　**DN**

A Whitefriars clear glass vase, internally decorated with horizontal wavy bands of green.

8.5in (21.5cm) high

$400-600　　　　　　　**DN**

An opalescent glass vase, attributed to Whitefriars, the oviform vessel with vertical ribbing, dimpled sides and a circular cup-shaped neck, with a milky opalescence.

6in (15cm) high

$100-150　　　　　　　**DN**

A Whitefriars glass 'ribbon-trailed' vase, of broad cylindrical shape with horizontal wreathed bands, the glass of rich amethyst colour.

10in (25.5cm) high

$150-200　　　　　　　**DN**

A Whitefriars large 'Cloudy' tumbler vase, designed by Marriott Powell, the body milky-green and suffused with large bubbles.

11.75in (30cm) high

$400-500　　　　　　　**DN**

A Whitefriars 'Cloudy' oviform vase, the body milky-green and suffused with large bubbles.

9in (23cm) high

$150-200　　　　　　　**DN**

A Whitefriars glass 'Knobbly' vase, designed by William Wilson and Harry Dyer, in deep turquoise with random organic protrusions on the outer surface.

7in (18cm) high

$75-125　　　　　　　**DN**

A Whitefriars 'Knobbly' lampbase, of tapering form, the clear glass with internal smoky-brown streaks.

9.75in (25cm) high

$120-160　　　　　　　**DN**

A Whitefriars 'Textured' vase, designed by Geoffrey Baxter, smoky-grey cased in clear glass and molded on one side with an abstract spiral motif.

10.5in (26.5cm) high

$150-200　　　　　　　**DN**

A Powell Vaseline glass vase, flattened tapering form with frilled rim, slender stem and spreading base, the body decorated with opalescent flower heads, covered with iridescent wash.

6in (15.5cm) high

$700-900　　　　　　　**L&T**

Miscellaneous

A clear glass claret jug with a tin mounting, designed by Friedrich Adler, manufactured by Kunstgewerbliche Werkstätten for Zinnguss Jacob Reinemann & Lichtinger, Munich.

c1904

$800-1,000　　　　　　　**Qu**

A Garbriel Argy-Rousseau pâte-de-verre mask lamp, in smoky glass with six amethyst masks in red on an amethyst band with floral rosettes above, bronze mount, signed "G. ARGY-ROUSSEAU".

21in (53.5cm) high

$2,000-2,500　　　　　　　**FRE**

An Art glass vase, with lobed rim in lustred gold with amber oilspots, unmarked.

6.5in (16.5cm)

$450-550 CR

A set of twelve wine glasses by Peter Behrens, made by Kristallglas-fabrik Benedikt von Poschinger.

c1899

$600-700 (set) Qu

A French Art Nouveau iridescent glass vase, by Duc Amedee de Caranza, signed, chips on neck.

c1890 *5in (12.5cm) high*

$300-400 DN

A Charles Catteau molded glass bowl, with molded signature "Ch. Catteau F-20".

Although Catteau was known primarily for his ceramic work, he also designed some glass, examples of which are relatively rare.

10.5in (26.5cm) diam

$200-300 FRE

A D'Argental cameo glass bottle, carved with stylized flowers in deep red on a pale yellow ground, signed "D'Argental".

8in (20cm) high

$2,000-2,500 CR

A D'Argental squat cameo glass vessel, decorated with branches of bamboo and fruit , signed "D'Argental".

7.75in (19.5cm) wide

$1,800-2,200 CR

A D'Argental cameo glass vase, with smoky glass blossoms on yellow ground, marked "D'Argental".

6in (15cm) high

$600-800 CR

A 1920s French Art Deco acid-etched glass vase, signed "Daum, Nancy France".

13.75in (35cm) high

$2,000-2,500 TDG

A DeLatte cameo glass vase, decorated with orchids and leaves on a pink ground, marked "A DeLatte/Nancy".

8in (20cm) high

$1,600-2,000 CR

A Fachschule Haida glass bowl and cover, painted in silhouette with a frieze of children.

7.5in (19cm) high

$150-200 DN

A vase by Harrach, Neuwelt, with enamelled flower decoration.

$600-900 Qu

An Art Nouveau glass vase, possibly by Fritz Heckert, enamel decoration, marked on the base with a gilt "R".

7.25in (18.5cm) high

$150-200 DN

A footed glass bowl by Josef Hoffmann, Vienna, manufactured by Ludwig Moser & Söhne, Karlsbad.

c1920 *5.5in (13.75cm) high*

$1,000-1,400 FIS

A glass bowl, design attributed to Josef Hoffmann, possibly manufactured by Moser of Karlsbad.

9in (23cm) diam

$300-400 DN

A Marie Kirschner vase, bark-like embossed surface, gold and pearl matt finish.

c1904 *4.5in(11cm) high*

$1,200-1,500 Qu

A pair of Art Nouveau glass vases, probably by Pallme Konig, the bodies with splashes of golden iridescence and horizontal wavy amethyst banding.

8in (20cm) high

$500-600 DN

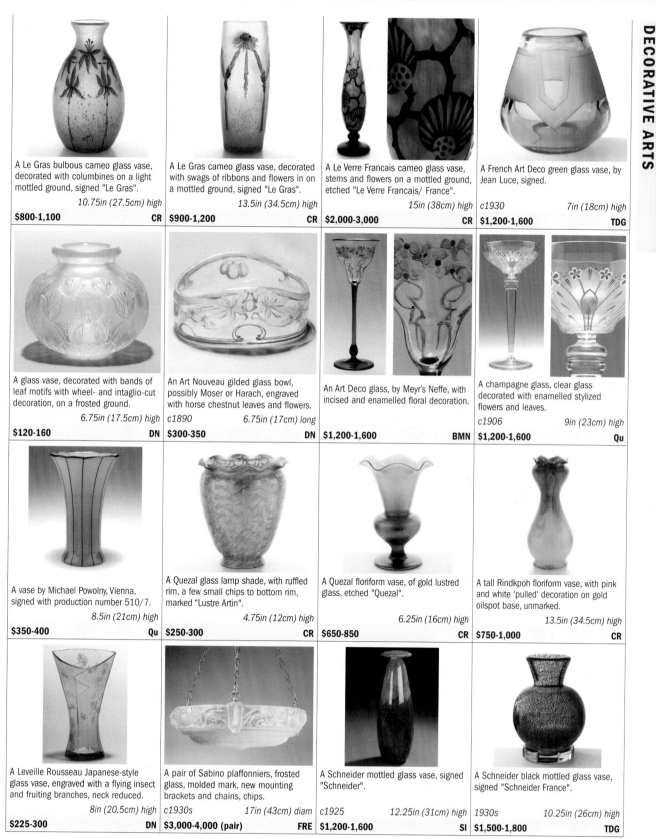

A Le Gras bulbous cameo glass vase, decorated with columbines on a light mottled ground, signed "Le Gras".

10.75in (27.5cm) high

$800-1,100 CR

A Le Gras cameo glass vase, decorated with swags of ribbons and flowers in on a mottled ground, signed "Le Gras".

13.5in (34.5cm) high

$900-1,200 CR

A Le Verre Francais cameo glass vase, stems and flowers on a mottled ground, etched "Le Verre Francais/ France".

15in (38cm) high

$2,000-3,000 CR

A French Art Deco green glass vase, by Jean Luce, signed.

c1930 *7in (18cm) high*

$1,200-1,600 TDG

A glass vase, decorated with bands of leaf motifs with wheel- and intaglio-cut decoration, on a frosted ground.

6.75in (17.5cm) high

$120-160 DN

An Art Nouveau gilded glass bowl, possibly Moser or Harach, engraved with horse chestnut leaves and flowers.

c1890 *6.75in (17cm) long*

$300-350 DN

An Art Deco glass, by Meyr's Neffe, with incised and enamelled floral decoration.

$1,200-1,600 BMN

A champagne glass, clear glass decorated with enamelled stylized flowers and leaves.

c1906 *9in (23cm) high*

$1,200-1,600 Qu

A vase by Michael Powolny, Vienna, signed with production number 510/7.

8.5in (21cm) high

$350-400 Qu

A Quezal glass lamp shade, with ruffled rim, a few small chips to bottom rim, marked "Lustre Artin".

4.75in (12cm) high

$250-300 CR

A Quezal floriform vase, of gold lustred glass, etched "Quezal".

6.25in (16cm) high

$650-850 CR

A tall Rindkpoh floriform vase, with pink and white 'pulled' decoration on gold oilspot base, unmarked.

13.5in (34.5cm) high

$750-1,000 CR

A Leveille Rousseau Japanese-style glass vase, engraved with a flying insect and fruiting branches, neck reduced.

8in (20.5cm) high

$225-300 DN

A pair of Sabino plaffonniers, frosted glass, molded mark, new mounting brackets and chains, chips.

c1930s *17in (43cm) diam*

$3,000-4,000 (pair) FRE

A Schneider mottled glass vase, signed "Schneider".

c1925 *12.25in (31cm) high*

$1,200-1,600 SI

A Schneider black mottled glass vase, signed "Schneider France".

1930s *10.25in (26cm) high*

$1,500-1,800 TDG

Steuben

The Steuben Glassworks were founded in Steuben, New York, in 1903, as a division of Corning Glassworks. The company's founder and first director was Frederick Carder (1863-1963), an English glassmaker and chemist. Before 1933 Carder designed much of the company's wares, which comprised an impressive array of artistic lines influenced by other contemporary glassmakers in the Art Nouveau style.

Popular ranges included: Aurene, an iridescent glass made from 1904 to 1930 is similar to, but brighter than, Tiffany's Favrile glass. Cluthra, inspired by Scottish Clutha glass is characterized by a bubbled interior. Intarsia, similar to Orrefors Graal glass had a boldly colored design sandwiched between two layers of clear glass.

From the 1930s Steuben concentrated on clear glass with a high lead content. Its elegant and distinctive Art Deco wares were mainly designed by John Monteith gates (b1905-) and Sidney Waugh (1904-1963). Cocktail and wine glasses from this period are popular with collectors. During the 1930s and 1940s Steuben produced a range of clear crystal animal-shaped bookends and paperweights which are highly collectible today.

The company is still active and is considered to be the most prestigious and highly regarded in America. Pieces made before 1932 are marked with a fleur-de-lis. Later pieces are engraved or acid-etched with 'Steuben' or a small 'S'.

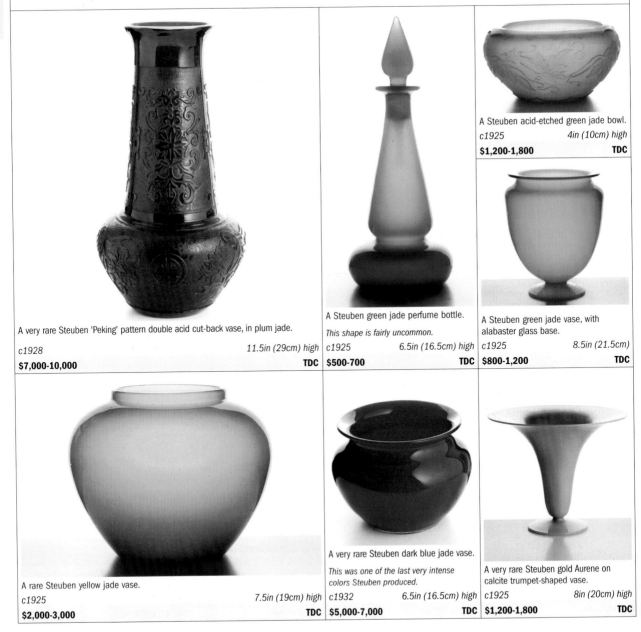

A very rare Steuben 'Peking' pattern double acid cut-back vase, in plum jade.

c1928   11.5in (29cm) high

$7,000-10,000   TDC

A Steuben green jade perfume bottle.

This shape is fairly uncommon.

c1925   6.5in (16.5cm) high

$500-700   TDC

A Steuben acid-etched green jade bowl.

c1925   4in (10cm) high

$1,200-1,800   TDC

A Steuben green jade vase, with alabaster glass base.

c1925   8.5in (21.5cm)

$800-1,200   TDC

A rare Steuben yellow jade vase.

c1925   7.5in (19cm) high

$2,000-3,000   TDC

A very rare Steuben dark blue jade vase.

This was one of the last very intense colors Steuben produced.

c1932   6.5in (16.5cm) high

$5,000-7,000   TDC

A very rare Steuben gold Aurene on calcite trumpet-shaped vase.

c1925   8in (20cm) high

$1,200-1,800   TDC

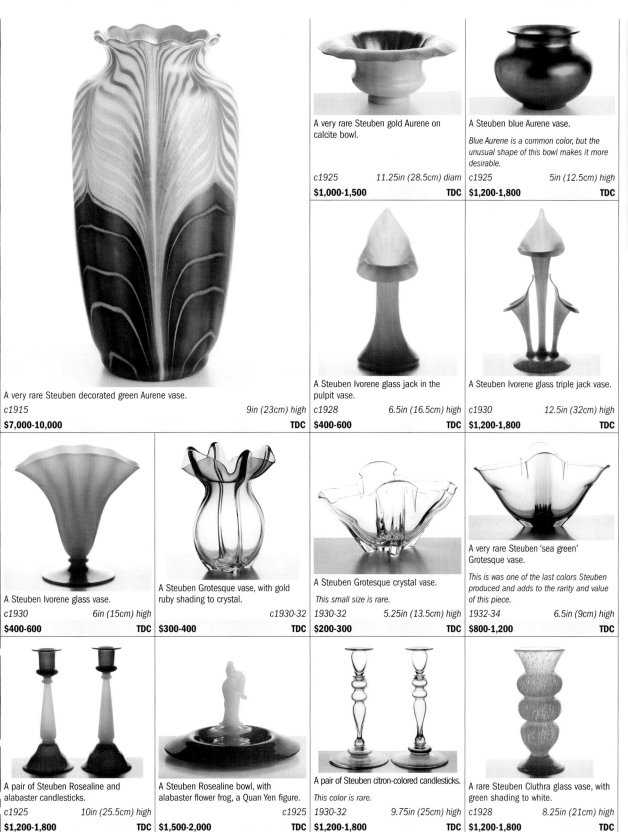

A very rare Steuben decorated green Aurene vase.

c1915   9in (23cm) high

$7,000-10,000   **TDC**

A very rare Steuben gold Aurene on calcite bowl.

c1925   11.25in (28.5cm) diam

$1,000-1,500   **TDC**

A Steuben blue Aurene vase.

Blue Aurene is a common color, but the unusual shape of this bowl makes it more desirable.

c1925   5in (12.5cm) high

$1,200-1,800   **TDC**

A Steuben Ivorene glass jack in the pulpit vase.

c1928   6.5in (16.5cm) high

$400-600   **TDC**

A Steuben Ivorene glass triple jack vase.

c1930   12.5in (32cm) high

$1,200-1,800   **TDC**

A Steuben Ivorene glass vase.

c1930   6in (15cm) high

$400-600   **TDC**

A Steuben Grotesque vase, with gold ruby shading to crystal.

c1930-32

$300-400   **TDC**

A Steuben Grotesque crystal vase.

This small size is rare.

1930-32   5.25in (13.5cm) high

$200-300   **TDC**

A very rare Steuben 'sea green' Grotesque vase.

This is was one of the last colors Steuben produced and adds to the rarity and value of this piece.

1932-34   6.5in (9cm) high

$800-1,200   **TDC**

A pair of Steuben Rosealine and alabaster candlesticks.

c1925   10in (25.5cm) high

$1,200-1,800   **TDC**

A Steuben Rosealine bowl, with alabaster flower frog, a Quan Yen figure.

c1925

$1,500-2,000   **TDC**

A pair of Steuben citron-colored candlesticks.

This color is rare.

1930-32   9.75in (25cm) high

$1,200-1,800   **TDC**

A rare Steuben Cluthra glass vase, with green shading to white.

c1928   8.25in (21cm) high

$1,200-1,800   **TDC**

A CLOSER LOOK AT A PAIR OF STEUBEN CANDLESTICKS

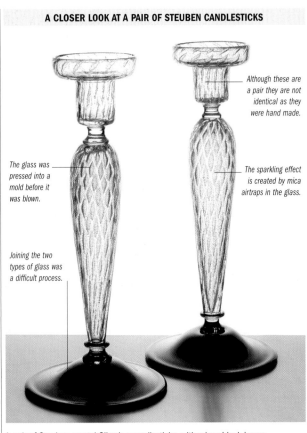

Although these are a pair they are not identical as they were hand made.

The glass was pressed into a mold before it was blown.

The sparkling effect is created by mica airtraps in the glass.

Joining the two types of glass was a difficult process.

A pair of Steuben crystal Silverina candlesticks, with mirror black bases.

This model went out of production in 1929 due to the Wall Street stock market crash.

c1928   12in (30.5cm) high

$4,000-5,000   **TDC**

A Steuben Cluthra glass vase, with pink shading to white.

c1928   8in (20cm) high

$1,000-1,500   **TDC**

A Steuben Pomona glass vase.

This is a fairly common color and shape, but is usually found in Aurene glass, rather than transparent glass.

c1925   6in (15cm) high

$200-300   **TDC**

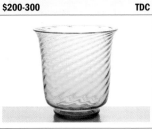

A rare Steuben wisteria-colored glass vase, with swirl optic.

This is a late, pale color for Steuben.

c1930   6.75in (17cm) high

$500-700   **TDC**

A Steuben verre de soie pinched bowl.

c1915-20   7in (18cm) high

$400-600   **TDC**

A very rare Steuben smoke-colored vase.

This was not a popular color and so it is now rarely seen.

c1928   8in (20cm) high

$120-180   **TDC**

A Steuben verre de soie cup or tulip-shaped vase.

This glass is an iridized crystal.

c1910-15   8.25in (21cm) high

$400-600   **TDC**

A rare Steuben crystal quartz glass vase, with applied Mat-su-no-ke acid-etched flowers and leaves.

This vase is known in other colors, including rose quartz, but this is the only one known in cyrstal quartz.

1930-32   11.5in (29cm) high

$8,000-12,000   **TDC**

Amberina

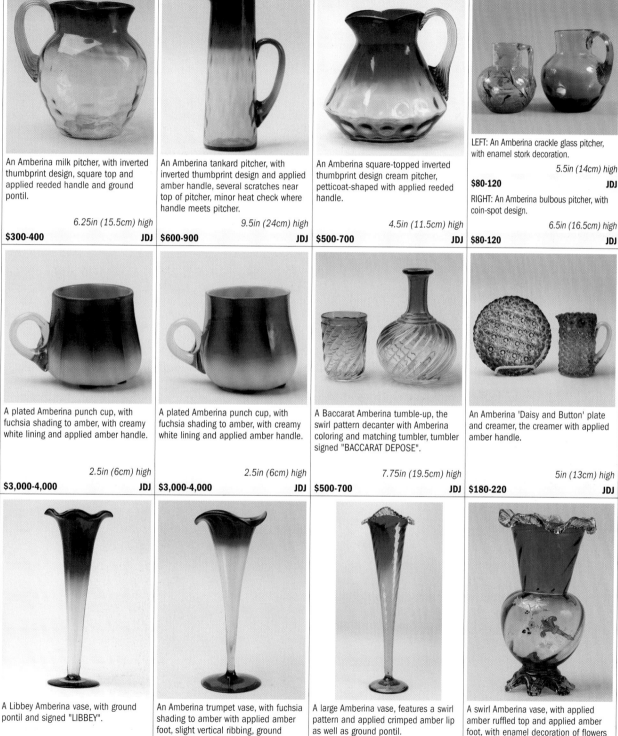

An Amberina milk pitcher, with inverted thumbprint design, square top and applied reeded handle and ground pontil.

6.25in (15.5cm) high

$300-400 **JDJ**

An Amberina tankard pitcher, with inverted thumbprint design and applied amber handle, several scratches near top of pitcher, minor heat check where handle meets pitcher.

9.5in (24cm) high

$600-900 **JDJ**

An Amberina square-topped inverted thumbprint design cream pitcher, petticoat-shaped with applied reeded handle.

4.5in (11.5cm) high

$500-700 **JDJ**

LEFT: An Amberina crackle glass pitcher, with enamel stork decoration.

5.5in (14cm) high

$80-120 **JDJ**

RIGHT: An Amberina bulbous pitcher, with coin-spot design.

6.5in (16.5cm) high

$80-120 **JDJ**

A plated Amberina punch cup, with fuchsia shading to amber, with creamy white lining and applied amber handle.

2.5in (6cm) high

$3,000-4,000 **JDJ**

A plated Amberina punch cup, with fuchsia shading to amber, with creamy white lining and applied amber handle.

2.5in (6cm) high

$3,000-4,000 **JDJ**

A Baccarat Amberina tumble-up, the swirl pattern decanter with Amberina coloring and matching tumbler, tumbler signed "BACCARAT DEPOSE".

7.75in (19.5cm) high

$500-700 **JDJ**

An Amberina 'Daisy and Button' plate and creamer, the creamer with applied amber handle.

5in (13cm) high

$180-220 **JDJ**

A Libbey Amberina vase, with ground pontil and signed "LIBBEY".

10.75in (27cm) high

$600-900 **JDJ**

An Amberina trumpet vase, with fuchsia shading to amber with applied amber foot, slight vertical ribbing, ground pontil.

10.25in (26cm) high

$280-320 **JDJ**

A large Amberina vase, features a swirl pattern and applied crimped amber lip as well as ground pontil.

23in (58.5cm) high

$800-1,200 **JDJ**

A swirl Amberina vase, with applied amber ruffled top and applied amber foot, with enamel decoration of flowers and a bird.

9.5in (24cm) high

$300-400 **JDJ**

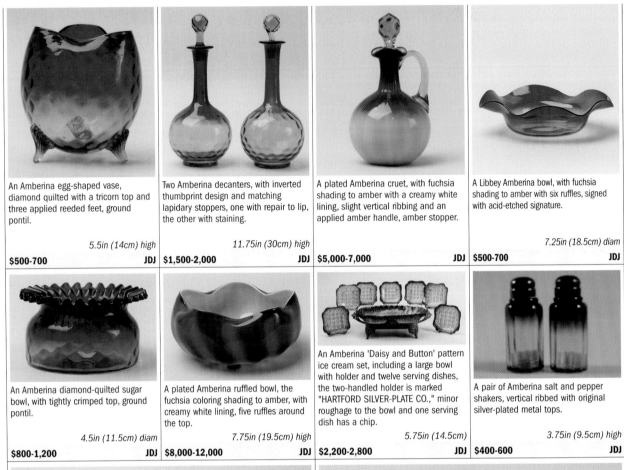

An Amberina egg-shaped vase, diamond quilted with a tricorn top and three applied reeded feet, ground pontil.

5.5in (14cm) high

$500-700 JDJ

Two Amberina decanters, with inverted thumbprint design and matching lapidary stoppers, one with repair to lip, the other with staining.

11.75in (30cm) high

$1,500-2,000 JDJ

A plated Amberina cruet, with fuchsia shading to amber with a creamy white lining, slight vertical ribbing and an applied amber handle, amber stopper.

$5,000-7,000 JDJ

A Libbey Amberina bowl, with fuchsia shading to amber with six ruffles, signed with acid-etched signature.

7.25in (18.5cm) diam

$500-700 JDJ

An Amberina diamond-quilted sugar bowl, with tightly crimped top, ground pontil.

4.5in (11.5cm) diam

$800-1,200 JDJ

A plated Amberina ruffled bowl, the fuchsia coloring shading to amber, with creamy white lining, five ruffles around the top.

7.75in (19.5cm) high

$8,000-12,000 JDJ

An Amberina 'Daisy and Button' pattern ice cream set, including a large bowl with holder and twelve serving dishes, the two-handled holder is marked "HARTFORD SILVER-PLATE CO.," minor roughage to the bowl and one serving dish has a chip.

5.75in (14.5cm)

$2,200-2,800 JDJ

A pair of Amberina salt and pepper shakers, vertical ribbed with original silver-plated metal tops.

3.75in (9.5cm) high

$400-600 JDJ

An Amberina punch set, including a covered punch bowl and eight punch cups, each piece has etched decoration of leaves birds and eight paneled and featured applied amber handles, the punchbowl lid has matching etched design and applied amber handle, small flake to underside of lid, chip to inside rim and one cup has open air bubble at lip.

$2,000-3,000 JDJ

An Amberina water set, the pitcher with applied amber handle and decorated with enameled flowers, butterflies, bees, grasshopper and dragonfly, the center cartouche features two enameled birds standing in a pond, gold decoration swirls from the top, five water tumblers feature matching enamel decoration, dome wear to gold trim on tumblers and pitcher.

4.5in (11.5cm) high

$600-900 JDJ

Peachblow

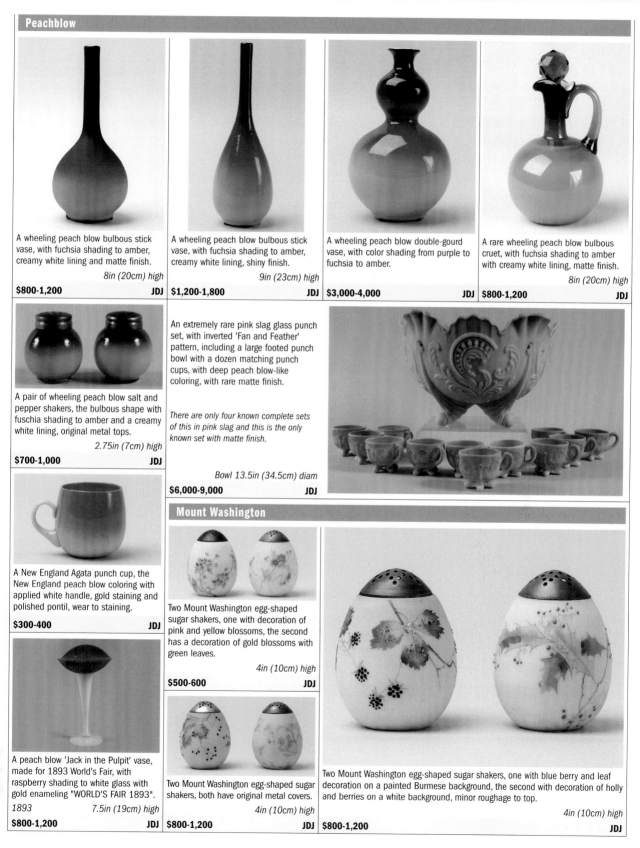

A wheeling peach blow bulbous stick vase, with fuchsia shading to amber, creamy white lining and matte finish.

8in (20cm) high

$800-1,200   **JDJ**

A wheeling peach blow bulbous stick vase, with fuchsia shading to amber, creamy white lining, shiny finish.

9in (23cm) high

$1,200-1,800   **JDJ**

A wheeling peach blow double-gourd vase, with color shading from purple to fuchsia to amber.

$3,000-4,000   **JDJ**

A rare wheeling peach blow bulbous cruet, with fuchsia shading to amber with creamy white lining, matte finish.

8in (20cm) high

$800-1,200   **JDJ**

A pair of wheeling peach blow salt and pepper shakers, the bulbous shape with fuschia shading to amber and a creamy white lining, original metal tops.

2.75in (7cm) high

$700-1,000   **JDJ**

An extremely rare pink slag glass punch set, with inverted 'Fan and Feather' pattern, including a large footed punch bowl with a dozen matching punch cups, with deep peach blow-like coloring, with rare matte finish.

There are only four known complete sets of this in pink slag and this is the only known set with matte finish.

Bowl 13.5in (34.5cm) diam

$6,000-9,000   **JDJ**

A New England Agata punch cup, the New England peach blow coloring with applied white handle, gold staining and polished pontil, wear to staining.

$300-400   **JDJ**

A peach blow 'Jack in the Pulpit' vase, made for 1893 World's Fair, with raspberry shading to white glass with gold enameling "WORLD'S FAIR 1893".

1893   *7.5in (19cm) high*

$800-1,200   **JDJ**

Mount Washington

Two Mount Washington egg-shaped sugar shakers, one with decoration of pink and yellow blossoms, the second has a decoration of gold blossoms with green leaves.

4in (10cm) high

$500-600   **JDJ**

Two Mount Washington egg-shaped sugar shakers, both have original metal covers.

4in (10cm) high

$800-1,200   **JDJ**

Two Mount Washington egg-shaped sugar shakers, one with blue berry and leaf decoration on a painted Burmese background, the second with decoration of holly and berries on a white background, minor roughage to top.

4in (10cm) high

$800-1,200   **JDJ**

A Mount Washington fig-shaped sugar, in unfired Burmese glass with decoration of blue, pink and yellow blossoms, original metal cover.

4in (10cm) high

$2,200-2,800 JDJ

A Mount Washington egg-shaped sugar shaker, in unfired Burmese glass with decoration of daisies, green leaves and stems, original metal cover.

4in high

$600-900 JDJ

A Mount Washington egg-shaped perfume, with decoration of amethyst and blue irises on a beige background.

4in (10cm) high

$600-900 JDJ

A Mount Washington Crown Milano biscuit jar, with heavily gold enameled decoration on a painted Burmese background, original metal hardware is signed "MW 4404", the base is signed and numbered "2585".

7in high

$700-1,000 JDJ

A Mount Washington Burmese water pitcher, with verse decoration and enameled pansies and butterflies, extensive repairs.

9in (23cm) high

$600-900 JDJ

Other Factories

An Alexandrite compote, with blue shading to amber coloring, ruffled top, ground pontil.

4.5in (11.5cm) diam

$2,000-2,500 JDJ

A Victorian Art Glass vase, in cranberry glass with applied crystal decoration of pink and white blossom and bud with clear crystal drippings and applied thorn feet.

11.25in (28.5cm) high

$300-400 JDJ

A cranberry pickle castor, the inverted thumbprint design has enameled white and yellow daisies, in silver-plated frame marked "BROOKLYN SILVER CO. QUADRUPLE PLATE".

11in (28cm) high

$400-600 JDJ

A Findlay onyx-covered sugar shaker, with silver onyx staining and original metal top.

5.5in (14cm) high

$400-600 JDJ

A Wave Crest cracker jar, with decorated opal glass and decoration of irises and green leaves with gold and purple highlights, original metal hardware with gold wash finish, unsigned, some wear to gold finish.

7.5in (19cm) high

$300-500 JDJ

A satin glass vase and metal holder, with yellow satin shading to white with white and blue blossoms and branches, crimped top, the silver plated holder with ribbon handles, minor wear to silver plating.

9in (23cm) high

$500-700 JDJ

A Pairpoint biscuit jar, the blown out mold with decoration of pansies and gold scrolls, original metal hardware, cover is signed "PAIRPOINT 3930", base is numbered "3930/17".

6in (15cm) high

$500-700 JDJ

Leaded

A leaded and jeweled hanging shade, of white leaded panels with a border of red faceted jewels in a Greek key design, a few cracked panels.

22in (55.5cm) diam

$200-300 JDJ

A leaded hanging shade, eight bent panels, with a wide floral leaded border with blown out pears, plums and grapes, a few cracked panels.

18in (20.5cm) diam

$180-225 JDJ

A leaded glass table lamp, leaded bamboo design shade with all over leaves and bamboo stocks against a light purple slag background (possibly Suess), base features relief flowers, vines and leaves at the foot.

25in (63.5cm) high

$1,800-2,250 JDJ

A large leaded lamp on tree trunk base, the shade, probably Suess, features white daisies with an all over green leaf background, shade rests on a bronze tree trunk base.

31in (78.5cm) high

$9,000-11,000 JDJ

A large leaded green floral table lamp, with flowers and berries, the lengthened bronze tree trunk base with three-socket fixture, with small repair to foot.

29.5in (75cm) high

$3,000-4,000 JDJ

A cherry table lamp, with cherries and leaves, attributed to Chicago Mosaic, three socket sculpted metal base, cracks on some tiles and stem.

22in (56cm) high

$900-1,100 JDJ

A Chicago mosaic leaded glass table lamp, with two bands of pink flowers with green leaves against a light green geometric background, simple bronze tone three-socket base, several cracked panels, base has minor wear to finish.

24in (61cm) high

$1,500-2,000 JDJ

A leaded glass table lamp, attributed to Suess, an unusual step-back design, geometric background with a red floral border, the base stands on four tall sweeping legs with a floral design cap.

22in (56cm) high

$2,000-3,000 JDJ

A leaded floral table lamp, shade attributed to Wilkinson, with lavender and white background glass with all over red, yellow and pink flowers, several cracked panels.

27in (68.5cm) high

$4,000-5,000 JDJ

A Duffner and Kimberly geometric leaded glass lamp, with long narrow caramel slag panels with a geometric Arts and Crafts design border, the three-socket base has sculpted stem and heart cut-out shade cap, shade has some cracked panels.

22in (56cm) high

$2,200-2,800 JDJ

A bent glass panel overlay table lamp, the panels white when off, caramel when lit, wear to gilding on both base and shade.

29.75in (76cm) high

$1,500-2,000 JDJ

A leaded bent panel ball ceiling fixture, attributed to Duffner & Kimberly, six sections with bent panels, green and purple slag glass, two cracked panels.

22in (55.5cm) high

$1,200-1,800 JDJ

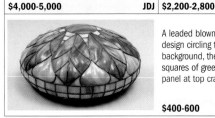

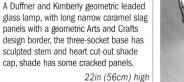

A leaded blown out shade, the leaf design circling top of shade on pink background, the border with leaded squares of green slag glass, center green panel at top cracked.

14in (35.5cm) diam

$400-600 JDJ

Handel

In 1885 Philip J. Handel founded the Handel glass factory in Meriden, Connecticut in the United States. Handel made both gas and electric lamps and the shades are typically hemispherical and painted on the interior with scenic views. The frosting on the outside of the shade has the appearance of chipped ice.

Most are signed on the shade border and on the metalwork. While other designers of this style often focused on floral designs, Handel branched out using a range of scenes from the natural world. The rarer designs of this factory can today compete with Tiffany lamps in price.

A Handel lamp with leaded slag glass shade, the paneled shade with ruby glass accents, resting on a bronze verdigris finish, hexagonal base, signed "Handel 5031", repaired/replaced glass.

19in (48.5cm) high

$2,000-3,000   **AAC**

A reverse-painted Handel table lamp, the chipped ice shade with landscape of ruins and palm trees, signed "Handel 6641" on rim and on smoke ring, supported by a trumpet form base in a bronze verdigris finish hexagonal base.

27in (69cm) high

$4,000-6,000   **AAC**

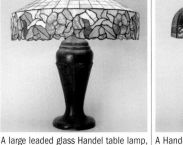

A large leaded glass Handel table lamp, with pink and green border, shade signed "Handel", base with leaf design with three light sockets and signed "Handel", several damaged panels.

24in (61cm) high

$2,800-3,200   **JDJ**

A Handel Hawaiian sunset table lamp, metal overlay, nine bent slag glass panels with palm trees and tropical vegetation against orange and green, shade signed on the rim "Handel".

24.5in (62cm) high

$15,000-20,000   **JDJ**

A Handel table lamp, the bronzed base with three sockets and acorn pulls, the glass painted with blossoms, leaves and berries, small nicks to rim, original base patina, shade painted "Handel 6332", base with cloth tag.

23.5in (59.5cm) high

$4,000-6,000   **DRA**

A Handel table lamp, embossed with Oriental style cherry blossom branches, with three sockets and acorn pulls, the shade reverse-painted with yellow daffodils, painted "Handel 5857", the bronzed base unmarked.

23in (58.5cm) high

$9,000-11,000   **DRA**

A Handel boudoir lamp base, bronze finish, base has molded trees and foliage around the bulbous body, pull chain has acorn knob.

14in (35.5cm) high

$400-600   **JDJ**

A Handel tree trunk lamp base, the three socket tree trunk base with good patina, original chains with acorn pulls, small bit of corrosion on the foot.

25in (63.5cm) high

$1,800-2,200   **JDJ**

A Handel leaded floral border table lamp, with deep red poppies on striated green and white, with rippled glass leaves, impressed signature on the rim "HANDEL 1837-20", four socket base, applied "HANDEL", tag inside base, four panels on shade are cracked and glued, several cracked tiles to border.

22in (56cm) high

$3,000-4,000   **JDJ**

A Handel lamp base, three socket, bronze finish, open work foot extending to a ribbed body and slender chest, some minor blistering and bad original wiring.

23.5in (59.5cm) high

$600-900   **JDJ**

A Handel tropical painted table lamp, with obverse painted palm trees and sand and reverse painted sunset colors and setting sun, shade signed "HANDEL 6322" plus "R" in a diamond, copper finish completely worn on base.

$7,000-10,000   **JDJ**

Tiffany

A Tiffany oil candlelamp, with gold lustered glass candlestick base, corked white glass stem, oil lantern, and gold lustered ruffled shade, base and shade marked "LCT/Favrile".

12in (30.5cm) high

$2,200-2,800 CR

A Tiffany blue iridescent candle lamp, swirl ribbed base, white with green pulled feather riser, electric socket, shade and base signed "LCT", two tiny flakes to top rim of shade.

12.5in (30.5cm) high

$4,000-6,000 JDJ

A Tiffany oil candlelamp, with gold lustered candlestick base and Tiffany Studios pierced pine needle shade with silver-beaded trim, base marked "LCT", shade marked "Tiffany Studios".

9in (23cm) high

$5,000-7,000 CR

A Tiffany Studios bronze harp desk lamp, with acid-etched finish, gold Favrile glass shade, base marked "Tiffany Studios", shade marked "L.C.T./Favrile", knob missing at top.

17.5in (44.5cm) high

$5,000-7,000 CR

A signed Tiffany harp desk lamp, the gold iridescent pulled feather shade with bronze, plain harp shape base, shade signed "LCT" and base signed "TIFFANY STUDIOS NEW YORK 419", shade has large chip to fitter rim.

13.5in (34.5cm) high

$1,800-2,200 JDJ

A gilt bronze table lamp with a Tiffany Favrile glass shade, the trumpet-form shade, a cut down vase, of amber iridescent glass fitted into a pierced base with circular foot cast with roses.

8in (20.5cm) high

$300-500 SI

A signed Tiffany floorlamp, the damascene shade with green and orange iridescence, shade is signed "LC TIFFANY FAVRILE" and sets in a gold finish three footed harp base, signed "TIFFANY STUDIOS NEW YORK", base shows minor wear to finish.

55in (134cm) high

$12,000-18,000 JDJ

A Tiffany metal floorlamp, the brown colored metal shade with an engraved design around the edge, suspended within a harp shaped holder on a molded tall base with scrolled feet, some wear to the patina.

55in (139.5cm) high

$4,000-6,000 JDJ

A Tiffany Favrile lamp base, blue and green iridescence with blue and green swirls encircling the base, signed on the bottom "LOUIS C TIFFANY 04542", original bronze patinated oil font signed on the bottom "TIFFANY STUDIOS NEW YORK D890", burner has been electrified (font not drilled), original bronze patina spider for 6in (15cm) shade, base would be with glass or even a silk shade.

14.5in (37cm) high

$15,000-20,000 JDJ

A Tiffany Studios leaded glass dome lamp shade, with squares and triangles of mottled green and yellow glass verdigris patination to lead, breaks to a few pieces on outer layers, stamped "Tiffany Studios".

16in (40.5cm) diam

$7,000-10,000 DRA

Glass Lamps

A bronze lamp, a figure of a woman with raised arms holding a glass ball.

c1930

$400-600   **TDG**

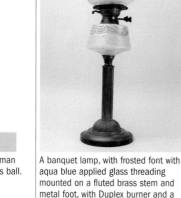

A banquet lamp, with frosted font with aqua blue applied glass threading mounted on a fluted brass stem and metal foot, with Duplex burner and a frosted and cut ball shade.

22in (56cm) high

$400-600   **JDJ**

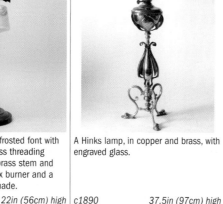

A Hinks lamp, in copper and brass, with engraved glass.

c1890   37.5in (97cm) high

$1,000-1,500   **TDG**

A marriage or wedding lamp, with blue fonts connected by a white clambroth match holder, zero burners with slightly worn transfer decorated chimneys with zero fitters, match holder lid missing.

20.5in (52cm) high

$2,200-2,800   **JDJ**

A brass double student lamp, electrified Duplex burners, 10in lithophane shades, four shade panels showing a hunter and maiden, signed "B&H DUPLEX", "DARDONVILLE NEW YORK".

25in (63.5cm) high

$7,000-10,000   **JDJ**

A Pittsburgh hanging Art Deco fixture, the gold iridescent shade with six panels with geometric and stylized exotic birds design, on a gold tone metal fixture, an Art Deco parrot in the center, minor wear to paint on metal.

29in (73.5cm) high

$300-500   **JDJ**

An Art Deco table light, cast in pewter with opposed and stylized figures of Pierrot and Pierrette, seated on a frosted orb shade and raised on a marble plinth.

11.5in (29.5cm) high

$1,500-2,000   **L&T**

An Art Deco patinated spelter figured table lamp, cast as the figure of a seated girl holding an ivorine ball with adjacent light fitting and pink glass shade, the whole raised on marble and onyx base with gilt sphere feet.

19.75in (50cm) wide

$400-600   **L&T**

A rare Austrian bronze peacock lamp, shaped as a peacock holding the shade ring, the eyes of the tail feathers set with iridescent glass, with Loetz type art glass shade, one chip to shade.

19.5in (49.5cm) high

$5,000-7,000   **JDJ**

A Dolphin base cut overlaid lamp, white cut and pink font, clambroth/alabaster base, triple dolphin figures on stepped base, No. 2 collar, chips to foot.

12.5in (32cm) high

$1,800-2,200   **JDJ**

A red satin GWTW lamp, with blown-out red satin glass shade and base, with drapery-type design in eight panels, base sits on a filigree brass foot with matching collar around font, electrified.

10in (25cm) high

$600-900   **JDJ**

A blue hobnail hall light, the shade set in a brass pull down frame.

11in (28cm) high

$300-400   **JDJ**

Miscellaneous

A Gothic Revival brass candelabra.

18.5in (47cm) high

$150-200　　　　　　　**TDG**

An Art Deco candelabra, one of a pair.

12.5in (32cm) high

$400-600 (pair)　　　　　**TGD**

A pair of Arts and Crafts copper and brass candlesticks, by Benham & Froud, designed by C. Dresser.

c1900　　　　　*7.5in (19cm) high*

$600-900　　　　　　　**TDG**

One of a pair of Arts and Crafts oak twin-light candelabra, each with simple curved arms of square section supporting square copper sconces and raised on stepped rectangular bases.

5.75in (14.5cm) high

$200-300 (pair)　　　　　**DN**

A pair of 1930s chromium plated table lamps, each with domed mushroom shades raised on turned stepped columns with spreading bases.

c1930　　　　*16.25in (41cm) high*

$600-900　　　　　　　**L&T**

A Goldscheider lamp, with shade signed "Dakon".

c1920　　　*26.75in (68cm) high*

$1,500-2,000　　　　　　**TDG**

A Continental Secessionist style brass table lamp, domed shade with beaded frieze, pierced with apertures for molded green flaws rock cabochons, base with central cylindrical reservoir.

21.25in (54cm) high

$1,800-2,200　　　　　　**L&T**

An Arts & Crafts extending brass and copper table lamp, the ovoid reservoir supported on a patented extending ratchet column with copper knops and applied scrolling brackets, the whole raised on a tripod base.

$220-280　　　　　　　**L&T**

A rare shell lamp by Gustav Gurschner, Vienna, a figure of a silver-plated girl, carrying a snail-shell on her shoulders, the snail is decorated with glass stones, on a black marble base.

23in (57cm) high

$5,000-7,000　　　　　　**JDJ**

A 19thC Aesthetic movement hexagonal brass hall lantern, the beveled glass plates enclosed within a frame surmounted by leafy crestings and sunflower rosettes and with six curved arms supporting scalloped finial fixing.

32in (81cm) high

$3,000-5,000　　　　　　**L&T**

A French Art Deco brass and frosted glass chandelier, the shade with eight small fixtures with original bulbs, hanging from four posts, from the Chateau de Grenany in Lyons, France, one missing bobeche, unmarked.

16.5in (42cm) high

$600-900　　　　　　　**DRA**

Pairpoint

A Pairpoint Puffy lamp with roses and butterflies, signed "Pairpoint", puffy shade has red and yellow roses, the gold finished base is signed "Pairpoint", the base shows slight wear to finish.

16in (40.5cm) high

$3,000-4,000   **JDJ**

A Pairpoint Puffy boudoir lamp, the shade with puffy roses in pink and yellow, set on original tree trunk base in a silver finish, base signed "PAIRPOINT".

10.5in (26.5cm) high

$6,000-9,000   **JDJ**

A Pairpoint Puffy boudoir reverse painted lamp with roses on a blue and white background, base signed "Pairpoint", chips and several other minor flakes, wear to finish on base.

15in (38cm) high

$400-600   **JDJ**

A Pairpoint Puffy boudoir lamp, the shade reverse painted with flowers, leaves and a lattice work background, base signed "PAIRPOINT", chip to rim of shade, base finish worn.

14.5in high

$1,000-1,500   **JDJ**

A Pairpoint reverse painted Florence lamp, the obverse of the shade is highlighted with gold trim, silver plated base signed "Pairpoint", base shows some wear to plating.

21in (53.5cm) high

$7,000-10,000   **JDJ**

A Pairpoint reverse painted Florence lamp, the obverse of shade with gold trimmings, the silver colored base signed "PAIRPOINT", small spot on bottom of shade, wear to the finish.

19.5in (49.5cm) high

$3,000-5,000   **JDJ**

A Livorino pink and white vertical stripped table lamp, with medallions of white flowers and gold accented exterior, signed "Pairpoint", original signed wooden base.

15.5in (39.5cm) diam

$1,500-2,000   **JDJ**

A Pairpoint Portsmouth boudoir lamp, reverse painted shade, stems and leaves outlined on the obverse with enamel, the shade is signed "PAIRPOINT CORP'n", some wear to the finish.

8in (20.5cm) high

$3,000-5,000   **JDJ**

A Pairpoint scenic boudoir lamp, the setting with trees, grounds and stairway, signed "PAIRPOINT CORP", original Pairpoint brass finished base, marked "Pairpoint" on the bottom, some scratching to the paint at top rim of shade where shade rests on support.

14in (35.5cm) high

$2,000-3,000   **JDJ**

A reverse painted figural wildlife lamp, the reverse painted shade features three bull elk grazing in a meadow, the black metal tree trunk base with figure of a moose standing in the front, on a green onyx foot, signed "A FREDERICK", moose horns repainted.

$5,000-7,000   **JDJ**

A Pairpoint reverse painted table lamp, chipped ice shade, artist signed "A FOX", turned wooden base with brass trim at foot.

24in (61cm) high

$2,000-2,500   **JDJ**

DECORATIVE ARTS

Other Factories

A signed Jefferson reverse painted table lamp, with textured exterior and reverse painted scene of farmhouse, trees and landscape, signed "1378R JEFFERSON R", shade has one minor chip to rim, base has some wear to finish.

$1,800-2,200   JDJ

A Jefferson reverse painted boudoir lamp, signed "JEFFERSON CO. 1520" with artist signature, cream colored base, flake to the bottom rim of shade and two small flakes at the top edge (covered by cap).

$600-900   JDJ

A signed Bradley & Hubbard overlay desk lamp shade, the metal overlay design depicting trees, an arched bridge and mountains, set against slag glass panels, double socket base features geometric design on the foot and is signed "B & H", some minor corrosion to metal overlay.

19in (48.5cm) high

$800-1,200   JDJ

A GWTW painted milk glass lamp, with green ground and burgundy, yellow and green floral decoration, the lamp has been electrified.

23.5in (60cm) high

$600-900   JDJ

A Phoenix reverse painted table lamp, shade has small chip to rim, wear to finish on base.

25in (63.5cm) high

$1,000-1,500   JDJ

A decorated milk glass mini lamp, with shade, shade spider is a replacement and fits poorly, flake to inside shade rim, roughness to shade rims.

8.5in (21.5cm) high

$250-300   JDJ

A slag glass table lamp, with filigree metal shade comprising eight panels of bent caramel colored slag glass with vasiform base.

18in (45.75cm) diam

$700-1,000   AAC

Miniatures

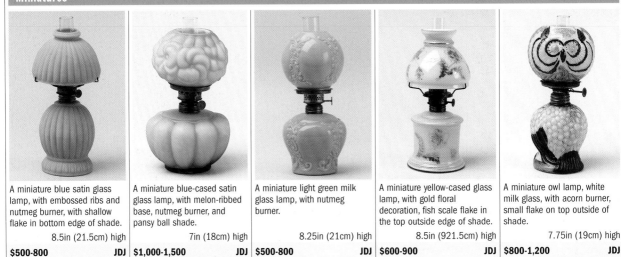

A miniature blue satin glass lamp, with embossed ribs and nutmeg burner, with shallow flake in bottom edge of shade.

8.5in (21.5cm) high

$500-800   JDJ

A miniature blue-cased satin glass lamp, with melon-ribbed base, nutmeg burner, and pansy ball shade.

7in (18cm) high

$1,000-1,500   JDJ

A miniature light green milk glass lamp, with nutmeg burner.

8.25in (21cm) high

$500-800   JDJ

A miniature yellow-cased glass lamp, with gold floral decoration, fish scale flake in the top outside edge of shade.

8.5in (921.5cm) high

$600-900   JDJ

A miniature owl lamp, white milk glass, with acorn burner, small flake on top outside of shade.

7.75in (19cm) high

$800-1,200   JDJ

Other Factories

A pair of Roycroft brass-washed hammered copper Princess candlesticks, with pyramid base, original patina, orb and cross mark.

7.5in (19cm) high

$800-1,200   DRA

A pair of Roycroft hammered copper candlesticks, with floriform base, original dark patina, unmarked.

8in (20.5cm) high

$600-900   DRA

A Roycroft hammered copper table lamp, with dome shade, bell-shaped harp and candlestick base, original patina, shade has areas of verdigris near rim, and narrow dent, orb and cross mark.

15.75in (40cm) high

$2,500-3,500   DRA

A Roycroft boudoir lamp, with pink glass stem on acid-etched, silver-washed base and single socket, topped by a ribbed parchment shade, tear and paint losses to shade, orb and cross mark and "ROYCROFT".

Base 10.75in (27.5cm) high

$800-1,200   DRA

A Heintz Sterling-on-bronze boudoir lamp, with waterlily overlay on base and cut-out waterlily motif to shade, with fine verdigris patina, shade missing silk lining, foil label.

9.5in (24cm) high

$2,500-3,000   DRA

A hammered copper table lamp, with shaft of three wrought spiral ribbons, complete with Arts & Crafts wicker shade.

30in (76.5cm) high

$300-400   DRA

A table lamp with Roseville Pauleo baluster base, complete with filigree base mount, bakelite finial and fringed silk shade.

22in (56cm)

$300-400   DRA

An Arts & Crafts wrought-iron lantern, attributed to Gustav Stickley, with vented four-sided cap on a faceted base with hammered amber glass, unmarked.

27.5in (70cm) high

$400-600   DRA

A Dirk Van Erp hammered copper table lamp, with large drum shade pierced with quatrefoils over mica panels, on a riveted trumpet base with three arms and three original sockets, new patina and mica, windmill mark with open box and "San Francisco".

19in (48.5cm) diam

$10,000-15,000   DRA

An Arts & Crafts hammered copper hanging fixture, with four pendant lanterns with small squares over yellow slag glass, suspended by hanging chains from a square ceiling plate, original patina, unmarked.

30in (76cm) long

$1,500-2,000   DRA

A pair of Arts and Crafts copper two-light sconces, mounted with iridescent yellow glass shades.

c1900   *10in (25.5cm) high*

$400-600   SI

583

Clocks

An Orivit Arts and Crafts silvered pewter clock, from an Albin Muller design.

c1900   9.25in (23.5cm) high

$2,500-3,500   TDG

An Arts and Crafts mantel clock, by Hamburg American Clock Co., with half hour strike.

c1900

$1,000-1,500   TDG

A Scottish School copper wall clock, by James Peddie, Kilbarchan, repoussé decorated with the legend "Time and Tide", above Roman chapters and a galleon in full sail.

18.5in (47cm) high

$300-400   L&T

A Liberty & Co. 'English' pewter timepiece, with hammer-textured surface, swing handle, blue enameled center, maker's marks on base with "0581", not in working order.

3.5in (9cm) high

$400-600   DN

A Liberty tudric pewter and enamel clock.

c1905   5in (13cm) high

$1,500-2,000   TDG

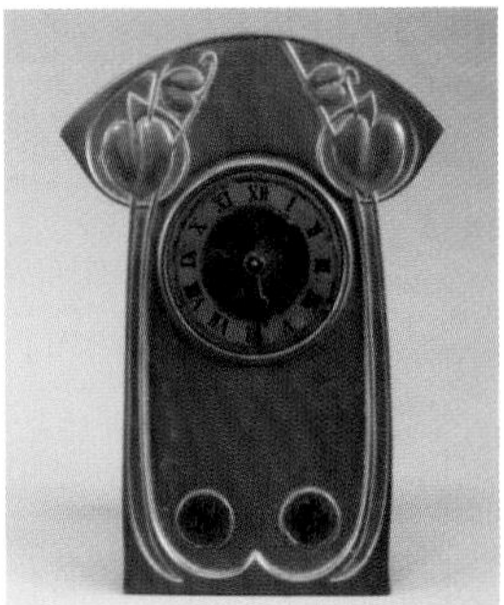

A Liberty & Co. pewter desk clock, embossed with leaves and enameled with dots and clock face in blue and green, stamped "Made in England/0370/English Pewter".

8in (20.5cm) high

$4,500-6,500   DRA

An Art Nouveau silver clock, hallmarked Birmingham.

c1910   14in (36cm) high

$400-600   OACC

An Art Nouveau patinated mantel clock, by A. de Ranier, the circular enamel dial painted with flowers, the case molded with leaves and dragonflies with a figure of a girl, signed on the base.

22.75in (58cm) high

$1,000-1,500   L&T

An Art Deco white onyx and coral inlaid part desk set, comprising a clock and a cigarette box with silver gilt hinges inlaid with carved coral floral medallions.

6.25in (16cm) high

$80-120   L&T

A Continental Art Deco 8-day chiming wall clock, the plain walnut panels flanked by fluted bands, with triple-train movement, anchor escapement, striking the hours and chiming the quarters.

28.75in (73cm) high

$300-400   DN

An Art Deco marble and metal mantel clock, the girl signed "Geo Maxim", clock works signed "DUPLAHIL SAINT ETIENNE," some damage to marble.

14in (35.5cm) wide

$280-320   FRE

An Art Deco clock, with "Cartier" name on a mother-of-pearl dial, on a mirrored ground with an enameled case, loss to case.

6.5in (16.5cm) high

$1,500-2,000　　　　　**OAAC**

A Lalique 'Moineaux' clock, for ATO, in clear and frosted glass with sepia patina, original Art Deco face and modern quartz movement, molded "R LALIQUE".

c1924　　　　6in (15.5cm) high

$8,000-12,000　　　　　**DRA**

A French Art Deco gilt metal-mounted marble three-piece clock garniture, by Japy Freres, the circular white enamel clock face with black Arabic numerals in a hexagonal taupe marble surround flanked by rouge marble triangles mounted with stylized flower baskets, on a rectangular plinth and domed feet, the pair of compotes with conforming decoration.

c1925　　Clock 12.5in (32cm) wide

$1,000-1,500　　　　　**SI**

A Tiffany and Co.-style mahogany tall case clock, with an 8-day striking movement, and moon face silvered dial.

c1925　　77.5in (197cm) high

$2,200-2,800　　　　　**SI**

A 1920s Art Deco 8-day clock, with enameled brass and Swiss movement "Rosemont".

$400-600　　　　　**TDG**

A Lalique 'Inseparables' clock, in opalescent glass, fitted into an Art Deco blue and white hardstone mount of the period, molded "R. LALIQUE".

c1926　　　　4in (10cm) high

$1,800-2,200　　　　　**DRA**

A 1930s walnut-veneered Art Deco-style mantel clock.

$40-60　　　　　**D**

A 1930s mirrored clock, the arched beveled plate with circular clock face to the arch, flanked by smaller pink sections.

c1930　　40.5in (103cm) high

$280-320　　　　　**L&T**

A 1930s Arts Deco clock, in shagreen and ivory.

7in (18cm) high

$1,500-2,000　　　　　**TDG**

A Henry Dreyfuss wafer clock, manufactured by E. Ingraham Co., Bristol, Connecticut, with working electric motor, mild abrasions to copper surround.

Henry Dreyfuss (American, 1904-1972) was a noted industrial designer, most famous for the Bell Model 302 telephone and the luxury locomotive 'Twentieth Century Limited'. Dreyfuss' use of a large red dot on the second hand turns the otherwise functional axis into an interesting design element.

7in (17.5cm) diam

$120-180　　　　　**FRE**

A Tiffany gold dore 8-day desk clock, signed on back of stand "Tiffany & Co", marked on face "Tiffany & Co".

4.5in (11.5cm) high

$600-900　　　　　**JDJ**

A mid-20thC leather-cased travel alarm clock, the white enamel dial inscribed "Harrods" and within blue bassetaille enamel frame.

3in (8cm) diam

$150-200　　　　　**Chef**

Liberty Tudric & Cymric

A Tudric circular pewter charger, decorated to the rim with seven applied cast buds set with heart shaped abalone shell pieces, stamped mark "Tudric 0113".

13in (33cm) diam

$400-600　　　**L&T**

A Liberty & Co. English pewter tray, designed by Archibald Knox, rounded rectangular form, cast in low relief with entrelac motif stamped marks, model no. "0309".

17.75in (45cm) wide

$700-1,000　　　**WW**

A Liberty & Co. Tudric pewter tray, designed by Archibald Knox, rounded rectangular form, cast in low relief, Art Nouveau heart-shaped stamped marks.

19.75in (50cm) wide

$1,200-1,800　　　**WW**

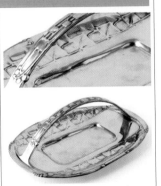

A Liberty & Co. English pewter cake tray, designed by Archibald Knox, the central handle cast in low relief with stylized ivy foliage, stamped marks, model no. "0357".

11.75in (30cm) wide

$300-400　　　**WW**

A Liberty & Co. Tudric pewter tray, designed by Archibald Knox, model no. "0359", with central spanning handle, cast in low relief, with ivy motif stamped marks.

9.25in (23.5cm) wide

$300-400　　　**WW**

A pair of Liberty & Co. Tudric pewter candlesticks, with tapering cylindrical stems, with drop-in sconces, all with hammer-textured surfaces, stamped "Tudric" and "Solketts", and numbered "0871".

6.5in (16.5cm) high

$400-600　　　**DN**

A pair of Liberty & Co. Tudric pewter candlesticks, cast in low relief with interlocking foliate motif, stamped marks, model no. "022".

5in (13cm) high

$400-600　　　**WW**

A Tudric pewter three-piece tea service, designed by Archibald Knox, comprising a tea pot, a milk jug and a sucrier, each of flattened ovoid form cast with Celtic whiplash budding foliage, stamped marks "0231".

4in (10cm) high

$400-600　　　**L&T**

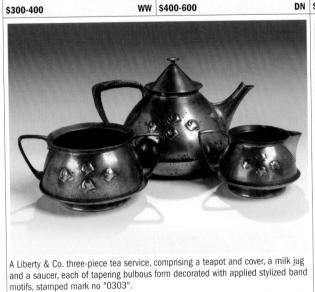

A Liberty & Co. three-piece tea service, comprising a teapot and cover, a milk jug and a saucer, each of tapering bulbous form decorated with applied stylized band motifs, stamped mark no "0303".

Teapot 5.5in (14cm) high

$300-500　　　**L&T**

A Liberty & Co. Tudric pewter hot water jug, designed by Archibald Knox, embellished with sinuous plant forms, with a sloping hinged lid and short thumbpiece and wicker-covered loop handle, stamped "Tudric" and numbered "0305", several small repairs.

8in (20.5cm) high

$80-120　　　**DN**

A Tudric two-handled pewter trophy, embossed with stylized trees and "For Old Times Sakein," and incised "Dominion of Canada/Track Shooting Association/1910", a few small dents, stamped "Tudric/010/4".

8in (20cm) high

$280-320　　　**CR**

A Liberty & Co. Tudric pewter four-piece tea set, designed by Archibald Knox, comprising a compressed teapot with wicker handle, a similar hot water jug, a milk jug and a sugar bowl, with maker's marks and numbered "0231", with a repair to base of hot water jug.

Teapot 4in (10cm) high

$400-600   **DN**

A Liberty & Co. Tudric pewter faceted vase with embossed band of ovals, some enameled in blue and green, on four buttressed claw feet supports mounted to a circular base, stamped "Tudric/01004/4".

8in (20.5cm) high

$1,500-2,000   **DRA**

A Tudric bullet-shaped pewter vase, designed by Archibald Knox, cast with panels of stylized buds and entwined foliage with three applied bracket supports, stamped marks "Tudric 0927".

11.5in (29cm) high

$800-1,200   **L&T**

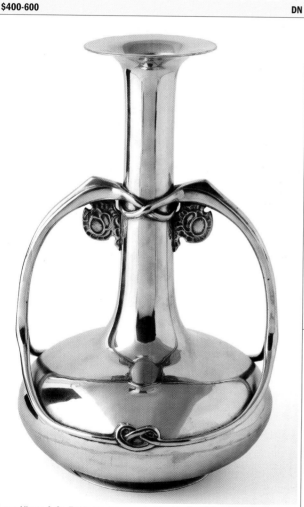

A rare Liberty & Co. Tudric pewter vase, designed by David Veazey, of compressed form with cylindrical neck, applied with twin-handles and honesty roundels, stamped marks, model no. "0214".

13.25in (34cm) high

$1,500-2,000   **WW**

A Liberty & Co. Tudric pewter vase, designed by Archibald Knox, with green glass liner, in bombé form cast in low relief with interlocking foliate motif, stamped marks, model no. "0312", replacement liner.

5.75in (14.5cm) high

$350-450   **WW**

A Tudric squat pewter vessel, with two pairs of 'riveted' strap handles, a few small dents, stamped "Tudric/05".

8in (20cm) wide

$300-500   **CR**

A Liberty & Co. English pewter preserve pot, cover and spoon, designed by Archibald Knox, cast in low relief with stylized bramble motif, stamped marks, model number "0700".

5.75in (14.5cm) high

$1,800-2,200   **WW**

A Liberty & Co. Solkets English pewter jam dish and cover, with clear glass liner, designed by Archibald Knox, cast in low relief with stylized honesty stamped marks.

5in (13cm) diam

$400-600   **WW**

A Liberty & Co. Tudric pewter slop bowl, designed by Archibald Knox, cast in low relief with stylized honesty stamped marks, model number "0231".

6.25in (16cm) wide

$500-800 **WW**

A Tudric bowl stand, designed by Archibald Knox, of printed ovoid form, pierced and cast with berries on finned supports and circular base, stamped marks "0276".

5.25in (13cm) high

$350-450 **L&T**

A Liberty & Co. pewter biscuit box designed by Archibald Knox, embossed with stylized flowers and squares, stamped "Made in England/English Pewter".

4.5in (11.5cm) high

$1,500-2,000 **DRA**

A Liberty & Co. electroplated rose bowl, with three applied handles and slightly lobed circular form raised on a corresponding foot, stamped marks.

10.75in (27.5cm) diam

$180-220 **L&T**

A Liberty & Co. silver sugar basin, decorated with simple ropetwist band, stamped marks "Birmingham 1914", minor scratch.

4.5in (11.5cm) diam

$300-500 **WW**

A Liberty & Co. silver two-piece condiment set, comprising a salt and pepper dish, with circular embossed and lobed bowls, Birmingham mark 1924.

1.5in (3.5cm) high

$80-120 **L&T**

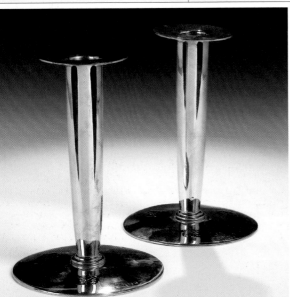

A pair of Liberty & Co. Cymric silver and enamel candlesticks, each with broad detachable drip and nozzles, bases inset with enameled Celtic knots, marks for Birmingham 1903.

6.25in (16.2cm) high

$3,000-5,000 **L&T**

A Liberty & Co. three-piece silver cruet set, comprising a mustard pot with hinged lid and blue glass liner, a salt pot with blue glass liner, a pepper pot, each set with turquoise cabochons, marks for Birmingham 1917.

2in (5cm) high

$400-600 **L&T**

A Liberty & Co. Art Nouveau silver four handled cup or vase, of spun baluster shape, Birmingham 1902, stamped "Cymric".

4.5in (11.25cm) high

$700-1,000 **Chef**

A Liberty & Co. Cymric silver spoon, designed by Archibald Knox , the bowl cast with Celtic knotwork and bearing initials "AC" and "ER", the pointed terminal with knotwork design, stamped mark Birmingham.

4.75in (12.5cm) high

$180-220 **L&T**

WMF

The Württemberg Metalwork Factory, known as WMF, was originally established in 1853 in Deislingen, Germany. It began producing pieces in the Renaissance and Rococo styles, but became particularly well known for its Art Nouveau metalware. WMF also produced glass from 1883. Art Nouveau elements of design were popular, eg. flowers and trailing foliage and women with flowing, long hair. Pieces were mass-produced in an electroplated metal alloy known as Continental pewter. The company achieved great success and the WMF Art Nouveau style inspired the design of the popular 'Tudric' pewter range at Liberty in London. WMF specialized in decorative items including vases, trophies and picture frames. The factory is still in operation, but stopped producing glass in 1984.

A WMF Art Nouveau twin handled tray, the white metal gallery with a glazed earthenware panel printed and painted with a moonlit scene with lily, starfish and wave border, stamped mark, earthenware marked "2024/137" verso.

22.25in (56.5cm) diam

$1,000-1,500   **L&T**

A German WMF Jugendstil plated brass and glazed ceramic tray, ink-stamped mark, stamp to pewter.

c1905   *17in (43cm) long*

$1,000-1,500   **FRE**

A large WMF Art Nouveau plated tray, embellished at the edges with ivy leaves and berries and sinuous interwoven bands, marked "WMF" and "plated".

24.75in (63cm) wide

$800-1,200   **DN**

A WMF Art Nouveau electroplated tray, cast the naked figure of a crouching child, studying a snail, with a cast mark "210".

10.75in (27.5cm) diam

$220-280   **L&T**

A WMF Art Nouveau electroplated card tray, cast with a naked child wearing a hat and staring at a frog, stamped and cast mark "349".

8.75in (22cm) diam

$100-150   **L&T**

A WMF Art Nouveau electroplated comport on a stand, the dish with pierced rim embossed with flowers, the column cast as a maiden in diaphanous robes, the pierced domed base raised on bracket feet, stamped marks.

14.5in (37cm) high

$400-600   **L&T**

A WMF Art Nouveau electroplated comport stand, the base with dished panels with void for comport lacking, the handle cast as entwined tendrils, the base with similar casting, stamped mark.

19.75in (50cm) diam

$100-150   **L&T**

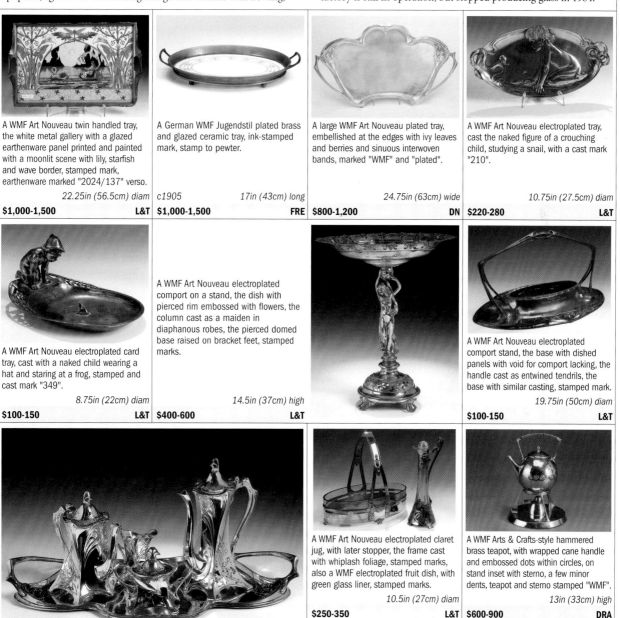

A WMF Art Nouveau electroplated comport stand, the base with dished panels with void for comport lacking, the handle cast as entwined tendrils, the base with similar casting, stamped mark.

19.75in (50cm) diam

$100-150   **L&T**

A WMF Art Nouveau electroplated claret jug, with later stopper, the frame cast with whiplash foliage, stamped marks, also a WMF electroplated fruit dish, with green glass liner, stamped marks.

10.5in (27cm) diam

$250-350   **L&T**

A WMF Art Nouveau electroplated sugar and cream set, comprising a tray, a cream jug and a sucrier, stamped marks.

11.5in (29.5cm) long

$400-600   **L&T**

A WMF Arts & Crafts-style hammered brass teapot, with wrapped cane handle and embossed dots within circles, on stand inset with sterno, a few minor dents, teapot and sterno stamped "WMF".

13in (33cm) high

$600-900   **DRA**

A WMF silver plated pewter jug, with hinged cover, embossed with a maiden and sinuous foliage in Art Nouveau style, impressed marks.

c1910   8.75in (22.5cm) high

$80-120   GorL

A WMF electroplated and etched glass claret jug, of tall tapered cylindrical form, the domed hinged lid above collar and handle cast with panels of deer above an incised clear glass body, stamped marks.

15in (38cm) high

$350-450   L&T

A WMF ewer, of tapering cylindrical form, with an angular handle, a hinged domed cover and embellished with geometric plant form motifs, stamped marks on base.

12.5in (32cm) high

$350-450   DN

A WMF silver-plated ice bucket, of broad cylindrical shape with vertical ribbing and applied with shaped and solid ebonized handles, stamped "WMF" on base.

8in (20cm) high

$220-280   DN

A large WMF plated metal and clear glass punch bowl, engraved with sinuous bands and geometric motifs, the geometric base with elliptical loop handles, the domed cover having an openwork finial, the ladle embellished, all with stamped maker's marks.

14.25in (36cm) high

$1,500-2,000   DN

A WMF fruit bowl & glass liner.

8.75in (22.5cm) diam

$220-280   TDG

A WMF Art Nouveau electroplated twin-handled jardinière, cast with opposed butterflies and whiplash foliage, stamped marks.

11.5in (29.5cm) diam

$220-280   L&T

A WMF silver-plated flower dish with crystal glass lining.

21.25in (54cm) wide

$3,500-4,500   TDG

A pair of WMF pewter candlesticks, the flared square bases pierced with tendrils and rising to a foliate motif below the circular drip-pan and sconce.

10.75in (27.5cm) high

$1,200-1,800   DN

A large WMF chalice, silver plated, stamped.

c1910

$220-280   TDG

A WMF silver-plated easel mirror, surmounted with an oval panel, a band of Classical foliate motifs at the base, on foliate feet, stamped marks on edge.

18.5in (47cm) high

$400-600   DN

A WMF small, silver-plated handbag mirror, in the Secessionist style, embellished with a flower and foliate motif, marked on handle.

4.75in (12cm) long

$60-90   DN

Georg Jensen

A Georg Jensen sterling pin, of circular form with applied leaf and flower design, stamped marks "Georg Jensen, Sterling, Denmark 127".

2in (4cm) diam

$300-400   **L&T**

A Georg Jensen sterling silver oval pin, with deer, stamped "Georg Jensen/sterling/Denmark/256".

1.75in wide

$300-500   **DRA**

A Georg Jensen circular silver pin, with an openwork butterfly design, Danish maker's mark, numbered "283" with London import marks.

c1967   *2in (5.5cm) diam*

$400-600   **DN**

A Georg Jensen sterling pin, cast as a tendril with fruits and buds, stamped marks "Georg Jensen, Sterling, Denmark, 100A".

$220-280   **L&T**

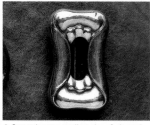

A Georg Jensen sterling pin, of pierced rectangular outline depicting an abstract flower head form, stamped marks, "Georg Jensen, Sterling, Denmark 33".

$70-100   **L&T**

A Georg Jensen sterling silver pin of a stylized flower with inverted triangular petals, stamped "Georg Jensen/Sterling/Denmark/308".

1.75in (4.5cm) long

$400-600   **DRA**

A Georg Jensen silver and rutilated-quartz necklace and pendant, designed by Torun Bulow-Hube, rock-crystal drop pendant, maker's marks "Torun", "167".

17in (43cm) long

$400-600   **DN**

A Georg Jensen silver sauce ladle, the curved stem with a stylized leaf and berry terminal, import marks for London.

c1966

$150-200   **BonS**

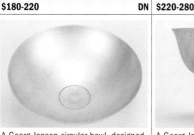

A Georg Jensen serving spoon, with broad oval bowl, reeded handle and foliate top, oval maker's mark, Copenhagen town mark for 1930 and assay master's mark for Heisse.

8in (20.5cm) long

$180-220   **DN**

A Georg Jensen 'Acorn' pattern tea strainer and resting bowl, the strainer with pierced center and notched and beaded edge, makers' marks on both, the bowl numbered "363B".

Strainer 5in (12.5cm) long

$220-280   **DN**

A Georg Jensen 'Acorn' pattern sterling silver and stainless steel cheese set, including cheese knife and cutter, in original Georg Jensen Inc. case, handles with stamped oval mark and "DENMARK STERLING".

$300-500   **FRE**

An early 20thC Danish Jensen-style silver three-piece tea service with tray, comprising a teapot, a two-handled sugar with cover, a creamer and an oval tray, maker's mark "DGS".

Tray 16in (40.5cm) wide

$1,000-1,500   **SI**

A Georg Jensen circular bowl, designed by Sigvard Bernadotte, decorated in the center with a floret motif, on a fluted circular foot, maker's marks on foot-rim, designer facsimile signature and "823".

6.25in (16cm) diam

$500-800   **DN**

A Georg Jensen silver bowl, stamped with maker's mark, "925S", Copenhagen town mark for 1923, assay master's mark for C.F. Heisse, numbered "197A", London import marks for 1923.

6in (15.5cm) high

$2,200-2,800   **DN**

A Georg Jensen beaker, designed by Harald Nielsen, with a horizontally fluted foot, and engraved with the name "Hanne", maker's marks "Dessin HN" and numbered "600A".

3in (7.5cm) high

$150-200   **DN**

A Georg Jensen small candlestick, designed by Sigvard Bernadotte, the base with a milled edge, maker's marks, designer's facsimile signature, and numbered "711A".

2.5in (6.5cm) high

$300-400   **DN**

DECORATIVE ARTS

A James Dixon & Sons silver-plated wine jug, designed by Dr Christopher Dresser, marks include the designer's facsimile signature and numbered "2546" also on handle "patent 529".

8.5in (21.5cm) high

$18,000-20,000　　　　**DN**

A Heath & Middleton silver-mounted claret jug, the design attributed to Christopher Dresser, with oriental-inspired rod handle, marked "JTH / JHM" for Birmingham 1887.

9.75in (25cm) high

$1,200-1,800　　　　**DN**

An Aesthetic Movement plated metal jug, engraved with foliate garlands and bright-cut banding, swivelling cover and branch-like handle, spreading circular foot, Britannia metal marks on base.

8in (20cm) high

$120-180　　　　**DN**

An Aesthetic Movement silver-plated teapot, in the manner of Christopher Dresser, with a faceted spout, ebonized handle and bun feet, flush hinged cover, knop in the form of a ball.

8.75in (22.5cm) long

$600-900　　　　**DN**

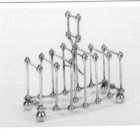

An Elkington & Co. silver-plated toast rack, in the manner of Christopher Dresser, supported on four ball feet, maker's marks on one of the rods.

6.5in (16.5cm) long

$100-150　　　　**DN**

An Aesthetic Movement silver card case, engraved with an oriental fan, similar detail on back, maker's mark for 'S. Mordon, London' hallmarks.

c1880　　　*4in (10.5cm) high*

$220-280　　　　**DN**

An Arts & Crafts silver goblet and cover, by Charles Boyton, the bowl with applied lion and shield handles, lid with crown surmount, stamped marks for "London 1936", with maker's signature and initials.

c1936　　　*10in (25cm) high*

$500-800　　　　**L&T**

A Charles Boyton silver-covered chalice, to commemorate the coronation of George VI, foliate handles with lion holding a shield, the drop-in cover with crown finial, marked "CB" with facsimile signature, London hallmarks for 1936.

10.75in (27cm) high

$600-900　　　　**DN**

An English sterling silver salt and pepper shakers, with turquoise enameled cabochons, a few chips to enamel, stamped "AEB", with lion and shield.

2.25in (5.5cm) high

$350-450　　　　**DRA**

An Arts & Crafts electroplated jug, with a domed hinged lid and applied angular handle, the whole on flared base, stamped marks "G. U. Epns 5665".

7.75in (20cm) high

$120-180　　　　**L&T**

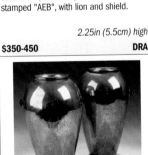

A pair of Arts & Crafts electroplated vases, of ovoid form, set with polished blue cabochon.

7.5in (19cm) high

$220-280　　　　**L&T**

An Articifers Guild Ltd. silver four-piece tea and coffee set, designed by Edward Spencer, comprising a teapot, a sugar bowl, a milk jug and a coffee pot, the pouring vessels with ivory handles, maker's marks for London 1932, the milk jug also marked 'Edward Spencer Del'.

Teapot 4.75in (12cm) high

$4,000-6,000　　　　**DN**

A pair of Arts & Crafts silver bonbon dishes, with hammered finish, each of the dishes oval form with four pierced and curved supports in a domed oval base, maker's mark "J. W.", hallmarked "Glasgow 1904".

5in (12.5cm) high

$280-320　　　　**L&T**

A Ramsden & Carr silver goblet, with a double foliate knop with wirework scroll embellishment above a spreading circular foot, marked "Rn & Cr" for London 1910, and engraved on the underside of base "Omar Ramsden et Alwyn Carr me fecerunt".

5.75in (14.5cm) high

$1,800-2,200   **DN**

An Arts and Crafts planished silver bowl, by Alwyn Carr, the twin handles each cast with a Tudor rose, centered with a green-stained chalcedony cabochon amid foliage, with inscription (dated 5th of July 1928, Shanghai), engraved on base "Alwyn Carr Me Fecit", with maker's mark and London hallmarks for 1921 and a spoon of similar design, maker's mark and London hallmark for 1929.

Bowl 8.25in (21cm) wide

$2,200-2,800   **DN**

An Arts & Crafts circular silver dish, of circular form with rope edging, embossed with a frieze of bulls and centered with an agate cabochon, retailer's mark and marks for Chester 1909.

6in (15.5cm) diam

$280-320   **L&T**

An Arts and Crafts oval copper tray, by Hugh Wallis of Altrincham, with a flowering spray heightened with a silvered patination in the center, with a raised rim with chequered border, marked "HW" in square.

17in (43cm) long

$180-220   **DN**

An Edwardian Arts & Crafts inkwell, of square tapering outline, with 'riveted' corner supports, texturing and flared feet, the hinged cover set with a vivid blue, foiled enamel boss, by the Guild of Handicrafts Ltd, London 1906, glass liner chipped.

2.5in (6.5cm) high

$2,200-2,800   **WW**

A silver and enameled cigarette box, by Omar Ramsden, with a pierced and chased plaque of a full-rigged galleon, within ropework borders and cedar-lined interior, marked "OR" with London hallmarks for 1929 and signed "Omar Ramsden me fecit"; and also enclosing a silver matchbox as a later addition, marked "OR" for London 1932.

5.25in (13.5cm) wide

$4,000-6,000   **DN**

An Arts and Crafts caddy spoon, possibly by Amy Sandheim, with oval, hammer-textured bowl and shaped handle centered with a carnelian cabochon set within an open rope-twist wirework mount.

c1860   *3in (7.5cm) long*

$700-900   **DN**

A Guild of Handicraft Ltd. silver butter knife, probably designed by Charles Robert Ashbee, with a shaped blade and slender, turned ivory handle surmounted by a silver collar set with a chrysoprase cabochon, marked "GofH Ltd", with London hallmarks for 1900.

7.25in (18.5cm) long

$600-900   **DN**

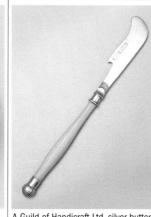

A Kayserzinn electroplated three branch candelabrum, the nozzles and drip trays cast with stylized plant forms, the supports and central column cast in the form of bats with wings outstretched, raised on a triform base cast with leaves, cast marks.

11.75in (30cm) high

$1,800-2,200   **L&T**

A pair of Kayserzinn electroplated candlesticks, each with removable triform drip trays and nozzles, on triform tapered columns and bases, cast with stylized tendrils and leaves, cast marks "4321".

11.5in (29.5cm) high

$800-1,200   **L&T**

Copper

An Arts and Crafts copper coal box, the hinged sloping cover and sides embossed with domed panels of stylized flowering plants, with twin brass handles.

18in (45.5cm) high

$280-320   **DN**

An Arts & Crafts copper jardinière, the sides embossed with stylized plant forms.

9.5in (24cm) high

$220-280   **L&T**

A Newlyn school copper repoussé tea caddy.

c1905   *6in (15.5cm) high*

$800-1,200   **TDG**

A large Arts and Crafts copper and wrought-iron coal box and cover, embossed, with loop handles in wrought iron, with spring-like wire finial.

20.75in (53cm) high

$350-450   **DN**

A pair of Arts and Crafts Cornish copper vases, handmade with sea serpent design.

c1900   *11in (28cm) high*

$180-220   **TDG**

A Benham & Froud copper jardinière, embossed with a panel of blackberries, blossom and leaves, stamped with St. Paul's finial mark and "Made in London".

7.75in (19.5cm) high

$100-150   **DN**

An Arts and Crafts copper coal hod.

24.5in (62cm) high

$220-280   **TDG**

An Arts and Crafts brass and copper jug.

c1900   *13.5in (34.5cm) high*

$400-600   **TDG**

An Arts and Crafts copper octagonal dish, embossed on the everted rim with foliate bands and four stylized floral motifs, each enclosing a Ruskin-style heart-shaped ceramic plaque of shaded blue tone.

13.25in (33.5cm) wide

$800-1,200   **DN**

An Arts and Crafts copper octagonal dish, with ruskin-style ceramic plaques.

c1890   *13.5in (34cm) wide*

$800-1,200   **TDG**

A rare Arts and Crafts copper rosewater dish, designed by Robert Hilton executed by Matthew Armstrong for the Keswick School Of Industrial Arts.

c1907   *18.5in (47cm) diam*

$3,000-4,000   **TDG**

A copper and brass flowerform dish, with a sunken circular center and embossed with radiating petal-like bands and supported on a short brass tripod base.

9.75in (24.5cm) diam

$40-60   **DN**

Brass

A pair of Gothic brass candlesticks, each with a simple sconce and a flared pierced drip-pan with a fleur-de-lys rim, on triple knopped stem and turned base, resting on three foliate feet.

10.75in (27cm) high

$220-280   **DN**

A Gothic Revival brass box, embossed with a dove carrying an olive branch.

5.5in (13.5cm) high

$150-200   **TDG**

An Aesthetic Movement brass square jardinière, embossed with panels resembling tile designs of florets, fruiting boughs and foliage, two ring handles, supported on ball feet, marked on each panel with a design kite mark for 6th October 1879.

8in (20.5cm) high

$150-200   **DN**

An Aesthetic Movement brass trivet, the design attributed to Thomas Jekyll, cast with panels of prunus blossom, alternating with a floral 'mons', against a diaper ground, supported on cast-iron feet.

18in (46cm) wide

$100-150   **DN**

An Aesthetic Movement copper and wrought iron coal hod, cover repoussé decorated with water lilies and sunburst, with attached brass shovel, the wrought iron handle with open twist decoration above scrolling base.

24.5in (62cm) high

$220-280   **L&T**

A Scottish Arts & Crafts brass jardinière, repoussé decorated with a band of Celtic entrelac decoration.

3.25in (8cm) high

$150-200   **L&T**

A brass jardinière, repoussé decorated with panels of stylized flowering branches.

5in (13cm) high

$350-400   **L&T**

A Scottish Arts & Crafts brass jardinière, repoussé decorated with panels of Glasgow roses.

5in (12.5cm) high

$600-900   **L&T**

A Scottish School Arts & Crafts brass coal hod, repoussé decorated with stylized plant forms.

23.25in (59cm) high

$220-280   **L&T**

A Scottish School Arts & Crafts brass jardinière, with broad rim, repoussé decorated with panels of flowering roses, on bracket feet.

26in (66cm) wide

$400-600   **L&T**

A large Glasgow-style charger, by Margaret Gilmour, the broad rim repoussé decorated with a band of entwined tendrils set with turquoise enamel roundels encircling a dished central panel with repoussé knotwork roundel.

23in (58.5cm) diam

$3,500-4,500   **L&T**

A Scottish School Arts & Crafts brass charger, repoussé decorated with stylized plant form.

17.25in (44cm) diam

$220-280   **L&T**

DECORATIVE ARTS

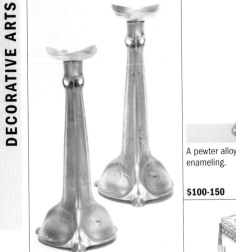

A pair of Kayserzinn candlesticks, probably designed by Hugo Leven, embellished with foliage and with a tapering triangular stem supporting drop-in sconces, marked "Kayserzinn 4521" in oval.

From 1896 a range of pewter was mass-produced by the German firm Kayser & Sohne at Krefeld-Bochum, near Dusseldorf.

11.5in (29.5cm) high

$700-1,000 DN

A pewter alloy candlestick, with green enameling.

11.75in (30cm) high

$100-150 TDG

An 'Osiris' pewter and glass box and cover, with open sides revealing the clear glass liner within, the drop-on cover with a cruciform shaped handle-finial, marked on base "Osiris", "1114" and "Isis" in an oval, also "Gg Leykauf Nuernberg".

5.75in (14.5cm) high

$800-1,000 DN

A Bohemian pewter and iridescent glass centerpiece, the glass probably by Pallme Konig, the glass bowl with a golden, green and mauve silky lusterous sheen, the spreading foliate base on six sinuous stems, indistinct marks on lower stem near base.

9.25in (23.5cm) high

$1,000-1,500 DN

A Kayserzinn double inkwell, probably designed by Hugo Leven, organically modeled extending to form two square-sectioned wells with hinged covers, marked "Kayserzinn 4604" in oval.

12.25in (31cm) wide

$400-600 DN

A Kayerzinn pewter twin-handled jardinière, of tapering form, cast with stylized plant forms, cast mark "4400".

$120-180 L&T

Iron & Bronze

A Falkirk Ironworks cast iron hallstand, in the manner of Christopher Dresser, ornately cast with stylized foliage, with a central mirror surrounded by hooks for coats and with stick stand below, registered 25th March 1872.

74.5in (189cm) high

$1,500-2,000 L&T

An Arts and Crafts wrought iron smoking stand, with matchbox holder and removable hammered copper ashtray on an elaborate pedestal with scrolls and rings, ball and rod supports, snake feet.

33.5in (85cm) high

$400-600 FRE

An Articifers Guild plated-metal sanctuary lamp, the design attributed to Edward Spencer, suspended from a dished ceiling rose by heavy chains, inscribed, "In his temple, everything sayeth Glory".

15in (38cm) diam

$600-900 DN

A Scottish School Arts & Crafts tin charger, of circular form, repoussé decorated with a central panel depicting a galleon in full sail.

20in (51cm) diam

$280-320 L&T

A cast spoon, by Omar Ramsden, the stem decorated with a three leaf clover overlapping tendrils and terminating at a hammered bowl.

c1922   6.25in (16cm) long

$350-400 Bons

Tiffany

A Tiffany bronze floormodel ashtray, removable copper ashtray insert, attached matchbox holder signed on the bottom "Tiffany Studios New York 1649", slender straight stem and slightly swirled base.

26in (66cm) high

$1,000-1,500 JDJ

A Tiffany silver hot-water kettle, the spherical body and domed lid chased with scrolling and flowering foliage, the base with central burner over four bracket feet, each piece marked "Tiffany & Co., Sterling silver 925-1000" and with model numbers.

c1910 *10.75in (27.5cm) high*

$2,200-2,800 FRE

A Tiffany & Co. four-piece silver tea set, comprising a teapot, cream jug, covered sugar bowl and waste bowl, each oval body with reeded rims rising toward the end and chased with lobes on the lower part, on a spreading oval foot with a reeded rim, each engraved with a crest and initials, engraved underfoot "December 4th 1889", marked under base "Tiffany & Co., 8897 M7714, Sterling silver".

1889 *7in (18cm) high*

$3,000-4,000 FRE

A Tiffany & Co. silver bowl with handle, on a short foot with hinged handle, acid-etched with flowers on scrolling vines.

1907 *6.75in (17cm) diam*

$350-400 SI

A Tiffany & Co. sterling silver porringer, of cylindrical form with applied bone handle and riveted decoration, stamped marks "925-1000, 21/4 gills".

7in (18cm) long

$600-900 L&T

A Tiffany & Co. stationery rack, the three shaped dividers in pierced gilt metal enclosing opaque glass panels, stamped marks "Tiffany Studios, New York 1008".

10in (25cm) wide

$600-900 L&T

A pair of Tiffany Studios bronze bookends, in the Zodiac pattern in acid-etched Dore finish, stamped "Tiffany Studios New York, 1091".

5.75in (14.5cm) high

$500-700 DRA

A Tiffany Studios 'Venerian' box, with Dore finished bronze surface.

c1915 *5in (12.5cm) wide*

$800-1,200 TDG

Roycroft

Two Roycroft hammered copper pieces, a brass-washed letter holder and an ovoid vase, slight damage to rim, both with an orb and cross mark.

Vase 4.75in (12cm) high

$150-200 (each) DRA

A pair of Roycroft brass-washed hammered copper bookends, with embossed rope and ship medallion, with an orb and cross mark, minor wear to original patina.

5.5in (14cm) wide

$250-350 DRA

A pair of Roycroft brass-washed hammered copper bookends, with an embossed trefoil motif and an orb and cross mark, minor wear to brass wash and patina.

5.25in (13.5cm) high

$150-250 DRA

Two pairs of Roycroft hammered copper bookends, one with a stamped motif, the other with a cut-out scroll top, both with dark patina and orb and cross mark.

Taller 8.5in (21.5cm) high

$150-200 (a pair) DRA

A pair of Roycroft brass-washed hammered copper bookends, with an owl design embossed leather medallion, one cracked, orb and cross mark.

4in (10cm) high

$250-350   **DRA**

A pair of Roycroft brass-washed hammered copper candlesticks, each with a cup-shaped bobeche, orb and cross mark, slight wear to finish.

6.75in (17cm) high

$400-600   **DRA**

Two Roycroft bud vases, with tubular glass inserts, orb and cross mark, and "Roycroft" stamp.

8.25in (17cm) high

$350-450 (pair)   **DRA**

Two Roycroft hammered copper bowls, each with a crimped rim and orb and cross mark.

4.25in (11cm) diam

$350-400   **DRA**

A pair of Roycroft hammered copper low candlesticks, with circular base and flaring bobeche, original patina, with an orb and cross mark.

4in (10cm) diam

$600-900   **DRA**

A hammered copper vase, in the style of Roycroft, all handles hammered in woodgrain pattern with three applied nickel silver faceted squares, original patina, marked "M".

8in (20cm) high

$400-600   **DRA**

A Roycroft brass-washed hammered copper bud vase, holder with pyramidal base, orb and cross mark.

7.5in (19cm) high

$180-220   **DRA**

A Roycroft hammered copper bud vase, designed by Karl Kipp, with four silver squares affixed to a cylindrical shaft hammered in woodgrain pattern, orb and cross mark.

8in (20.5cm) high

$4,000-6,000   **DRA**

A rare Roycroft hammered copper hinged box designed by Dard Hunter with an overhanging lid and applied nickel silver squares, original suede liner, complete with its original heart-shaped lock and key, orb and cross mark.

6.5in (16.5cm) wide

$15,000-20,000   **DRA**

Heintz

A Heintz sterling-on-bronze cylindrical vase, with rolled rim and cattail overlay on original verdigris patina, stamped mark and patent.

6in (15cm) high

$400-500   **DRA**

A Heintz sterling-on-bronze cabinet vase, with rolled rim and violet overlay on original dark patina, stamped mark and patent.

4in (10cm) high

$280-320   **DRA**

A Heintz sterling-on-bronze vase with a flaring neck and jonquil design overlay, on bright polished ground, stamped mark and patent, minor damage to the rim and base.

6.5in (16.5cm) high

$120-150   **DRA**

A Heintz sterling-on-bronze cylindrical vase, overlaid with leaves and inscribed "Winner Hotel Endicott Dance Contest", verdigris around rim, original patina, stamped "HAMS" with patent.

10in (25.5cm) high

$600-900   **DRA**

A Heintz sterling-on-bronze trophy cup with overlay of trailing vines, separation to one handle at base, repainted finish, stamped "HAMS" with patent.

11.25in (28.5cm) high

$150-250   **DRA**

A Heintz sterling-on-bronze rectangular hinged humidor, complete with cedar lining and removable mesh, the box overlaid with floral swags on a dark bronzed patina, stamped "HAMS" with patent.

10in (25.5cm) long

$280-320   **DRA**

Other Makers

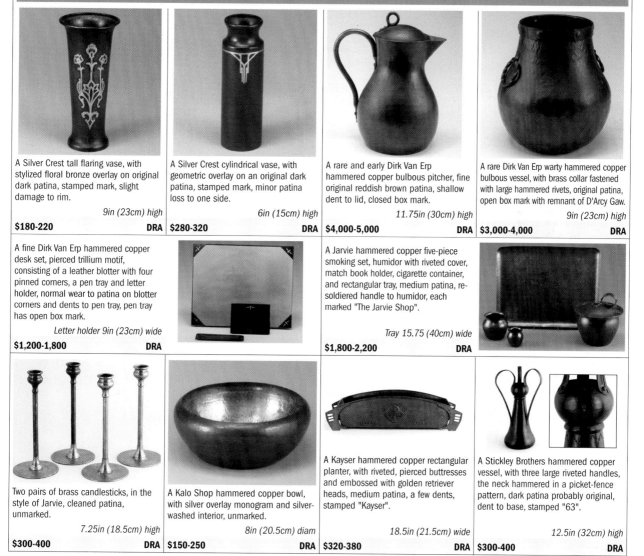

A Silver Crest tall flaring vase, with stylized floral bronze overlay on original dark patina, stamped mark, slight damage to rim.

9in (23cm) high

$180-220   **DRA**

A Silver Crest cylindrical vase, with geometric overlay on an original dark patina, stamped mark, minor patina loss to one side.

6in (15cm) high

$280-320   **DRA**

A rare and early Dirk Van Erp hammered copper bulbous pitcher, fine original reddish brown patina, shallow dent to lid, closed box mark.

11.75in (30cm) high

$4,000-5,000   **DRA**

A rare Dirk Van Erp warty hammered copper bulbous vessel, with brass collar fastened with large hammered rivets, original patina, open box mark with remnant of D'Arcy Gaw.

9in (23cm) high

$3,000-4,000   **DRA**

A fine Dirk Van Erp hammered copper desk set, pierced trillium motif, consisting of a leather blotter with four pinned corners, a pen tray and letter holder, normal wear to patina on blotter corners and dents to pen tray, pen tray has open box mark.

Letter holder 9in (23cm) wide

$1,200-1,800   **DRA**

A Jarvie hammered copper five-piece smoking set, humidor with riveted cover, match book holder, cigarette container, and rectangular tray, medium patina, re-soldiered handle to humidor, each marked "The Jarvie Shop".

Tray 15.75 (40cm) wide

$1,800-2,200   **DRA**

Two pairs of brass candlesticks, in the style of Jarvie, cleaned patina, unmarked.

7.25in (18.5cm) high

$300-400   **DRA**

A Kalo Shop hammered copper bowl, with silver overlay monogram and silver-washed interior, unmarked.

8in (20.5cm) diam

$150-250   **DRA**

A Kayser hammered copper rectangular planter, with riveted, pierced buttresses and embossed with golden retriever heads, medium patina, a few dents, stamped "Kayser".

18.5in (21.5cm) wide

$320-380   **DRA**

A Stickley Brothers hammered copper vessel, with three large riveted handles, the neck hammered in a picket-fence pattern, dark patina probably original, dent to base, stamped "63".

12.5in (32cm) high

$300-400   **DRA**

BRONZES

Bronze and Ivory Figures

An Art Deco carved ivory and bronze figure, by Ferdinand Preiss, modeled as a slender young woman wearing a short and clinging costume with a frilled skirt, golden tights and a plumed skullcap, in tones of copper, on a shaped marble base, signed on bronze support "F. Preiss", losses to two fingers.

c1920   8.5in (21.5cm) high

$5,000-7,000   DN

An early 20thC ivory and gilt bronze figure of a ballerina, modeled as a little girl doing a pirouette, base signed "F. Preiss", bronze with impressed monogram.

7in (18cm) high

$2,200-2,800   SI

An Art Deco bronze and ivory figure, by Demetri Chiparus.

$30,000-35,000   AH

DIMITRI CHIPARUS

Dimitri Chiparus (1888-1950) was born in Romania, but moved to Paris to study under Anonin Mercier and Jean Boucher. He worked in either bronze or bronze with ivory and sometimes produced the same piece in more than one size. Some pieces were made with white metals and then cold painted in the same way as bronze. His Art Deco style female figures and dancers are extremely popular, but he also produced a number of more sentimental pieces of children and some religious sculptures.

A Chiparus bronze 'Starfish Girl' statuette with ivory face and hands, wearing a close-fitting green cold-painted costume with polished bronze starfish and jellyfish decoration, on brown and black marble and green onyx base, signed "D. H. Chiparus", hands have been reaffixed the wrong way round and the tips of three fingers are chipped.

14.75in (37.5cm) high

$20,000-25,000   GorL

CLOSER LOOK AT A PREISS SCULPTURE

The dramatic, life-like movement of this figure is characteristic of Preiss's work.

Preiss sculptures are often Aryan figures with tinted naturalistic faces and stained hair, the clothes have a metallic finish. Female figures are the most desirable and are often modeled on sporting figures or actresses.

The bases are generally simple in design in a green, black or green and black onyx. Sometimes they also have slate banding. Copies may be identified by an elaborately styled base.

Figures mounted on ashtrays or dishes are less sought after.

A rare bronze and ivory figure of the 'Flame Leaper', cast from a model by Ferdinand Preiss, on a stepped black marble base incised "F Preiss", "Les Annees Folle".

13.75in (35cm) high

$26,000-30,000   WW

A gilt bronze and ivory boy in winter clothes, signed "Buhner", the boy depicted standing in a hat, scarf, mittens, boots and holding an umbrella, marble base.

c1925   9in (23cm) high

$600-800   SI

A gilt bronze and ivory skier, Raymond, signed "Buhner".

c1925   7.25in (18.5cm) high

$700-900   SI

An early 20thC gilt bronze and ivory figure of a clown, signed "Amerth", modeled as a little boy in a clown outfit, mounted on an onyx ashtray.

7.25in (18.5cm) high

$1,000-1,500   **SI**

A bronze and ivory figure of St Joan, by Louis-Ernest Barrias, signed, foundry mark, inscription, realistic patination, hairline cracks to ivory, no losses.

c1890   *20.5in (52cm) high*

$6,000-8,000   **FRE**

A carved ivory figure, by Joe Descombs, of a naked girl, the model posed with roses, the whole raised on turned rouge marble base, signed in the ivory base.

8.5in (21.5cm) high

$2,200-2,800   **L&T**

A late19thC/early 20thC French patinated and parcel gilt and ivory figure of a cavalier, signed "P. D'Oure", missing object from hand, onyx base.

10.25in (26cm) high

$1,500-2,000   **SI**

A French Art Deco silvered and gilt bronze and marble figural lamp, marble base inscribed "P. Laurel", alabaster screen inscribed "Lorenzi".

c1925   *14in (35.5cm) high*

$1,800-2,200   **SI**

A cold-painted bronze and ivory figure of Mephistopheles, base inscribed "Roland Paris", the red cloaked figure standing on a black triangular base.

c1925   *5.5in (14cm) high*

$700-900   **SI**

An early 20thC patinated bronze and ivory skier, base signed "L. Sosson", depicting a lady in her ski wear with her skis strapped to her back, marble base.

8.75in (21.5cm) high

$600-900   **SI**

A cold-painted and carved ivory figure, by Titze, the belt with glass studs simulating jewels, on a circular marble base, signed "Titze" on edge of skirt.

8.75in (22.5cm) high

$1,500-2,000   **DN**

A bronze, ormolu and ivory figure of Britannia, by George Lucien Vacossin, in a lion-drawn chariot attended by putti, on a marble base.

25in (64cm) wide

$12,000-15,000   **DN**

An Austrian bronze and ivory figure, with carved ivory head and hands, modeled as a young Pierrot holding a fan, marble base, signed "Luguth", foundry mark for Arthur Rosenberg and "Austria".

7.25in (18.5cm) high

$450-550   **DN**

A dark brown patina bronze of Salome, with white marble body and feet, headdress with pearls, by Ernst Seger, designed by R. Ksionsek & Co of Berlin, on red marble base, , signed "E. Seger".

13.5in (34.5cm) high

$4,000-5,000   **Qu**

A patinated bronze and ivory figure of Salammbo in the presence of Matho, after Theodore-Riviere, inscribed "Theodore-Riviere" "Susse Fres Paris".

14in (36cm) high

$5,500-6,500   **SI**

A bronze and ivory figure of a young girl in late Victorian dress, reading and standing on a circular green onyx dished base.

6in (15cm) high

$300-500   **L&T**

A 1920s female dancer, by Josef Lorenzl, oval green onyx base enhanced to form a bowl, standing on four ball-shaped feet, the plinth signed "Lorenzl".

15.5in (39.5cm) high

$1,000-1,500   **Qu**

A 1920s bronze female runner in dancing position, by Josef Lorenzl, with a green onyx base, the vaulted plinth signed "Lorenzl".

9in (23cm) high

$1,000-1,500   **Qu**

A French plated bronze "Diane Attendric", by Suzanne Bizard, plated bronze, signature to base.

16.5in (42cm) high

$1,200-1,800   **FRE**

A flying bronze male figure, by Peter Breuer, on a quadrangular signed plinth, stamped Lauchhammer, model number "28".

20in (51cm) high

$1,800-2,200   **HERR**

A bronze figure of a male manual worker, entitled 'Rude Labeur' by H. Charcescue, on a rectangular base, signed on one edge and dated "1904", also with foundry marks "E.V 1115".

$750-850   **DN**

A patinated bronze figure, entitled "Weeping Girl", by Demetri H. Chiparus, marble base signed "DH. Chiparus".

12in (30.5cm) high

$3,500-4,500   **SI**

A bronze group entitled "Reaper", by Jules Dalou, with dark brown patina, inscribed "Dalou" and "Susse Fres. Edtr. Paris Cire Perdue".

4in (10cm) high

$1,000-1,500   **SI**

A green patinated figure of a faun playing the cymbals, by Duchemin, raised on an oval plinth, with foundry mark "1.0.BUSC..BERLIN", signed on the bronze.

23.25in (59cm) high

$1,500-2,000   **L&T**

A 'Knight of the Ounce' bronze, by George Frampton R.A., marked on the bronze "Geo. Frampton R.A. 1918", on an ebonised plinth.

This figure seems to be taken from Walter Scott's novel The Talisman, published in 1825 as part of his Tales of the Crusades series. It is clearly indebted to Alfred Gilbert's celebrated figure of St George. The Knight of the Ounce was a Scottish Crusader known as Sir Kenneth who engaged in combat with a Saracen emir, who turned out to be Saladin. After being taken as Saladin's slave, Sir Kenneth's honor was restored in combat and he was revealed to be Prince David of Scotland. A bronze of this figure was exhibited at the Royal Academy, 1918. The only other recorded version of this bronze is in the Imperial War Museum and has traditionally been identified as St George.

28.5in (72cm) high

$10,000-15,000   **L&T**

A patinated bronze figure entitled "Orpheus", by Adrien-Etienne Gandez, with a lyre in one hand and standing above Cerberus, on naturalistic circular socle, with inscription cartouche.

23.5in (60cm) high

$1,000-1,500   **L&T**

A small bronze 'Victory' figure, cast from a model by Sir Alfred Gilbert, a winged Classical female figure, with laurel frond and trumpet, on agate sphere, bronze and green marble base, some losses.

9.5in (24cm) high

$1,200-1,800   **DN**

An Art Nouveau bronze ashtray, by Gustav Gurschner, the figure of a young woman clutching a large scallop shell on a 'wave' base, signed on one edge "Gurschner".

3.5in (9cm) high

$800-1,200   **DN**

A 20thC bronze group entitled "Lovers", by Frans Henin, with brown patina, inscribed "Frans Henin" and "Usines Vojave / Ste. Ame? Bruxelles".

23in (58.5cm) high

$2,800-2,800   **SI**

A 20thC bronze entitled "Blacksmith", by O. Hertel, with dark drown and light brown patinas on a marble base.

8in (20.5cm) high

$500-700   **SI**

A bronze female nude, by Erich Kiemlen, on a marble base, signed "E.KIEMLEN 1903", marked "P. Stotz, Stuttgart".

1903   *23in (58.5cm) high*

$500-700   **FIS**

A bronze bust of a faun, by Hugo Klugt, on a cubic marble base, signed "Hugo Klugt".

11.5in (29.5cm) high

$800-1,200   **HERR**

A Muller Kolms patinated bronze archer, signed, the man depicted nude, lacking bow and arrow, on rectangular green marble plinth.

c1925   *18in (46cm) high*

$2,200-2,800   **SI**

A Lorenzl bronze figure of a female dancer, the body covered with diaphanous-effect veil, square onyx base, signed on metal "Lorenzl".

7.25in (18.5cm) high

$600-900   **DN**

A Lorenzl Art Deco patinated bronze figure, the semi-naked girl dancing and holding a drape, raised on stepped onyx plinth, signed on the bronze.

13.5in (34cm) high

$1,200-1,800   **L&T**

A bronze figure of an Art Nouveau maiden, after Louchet, stamped "PARIS/LOUCHET/CISELEUR", quatrefoil base cast with Queen Anne's lace.

13in (33cm) high

$800-1,200   **SI**

A Negro fisherman bronze, by Arsene Matton, signed in the bronze, foundry mark "LN, Paris JN".

19.75in (50.5cm) high

$3,000-4,000   **L&T**

A bronze group, entitled "Ecossaise Montrant Un Renard A Un Chien" by Pierre Jules Mene, inscribed "P. J. Mene" (1810-1879), with brown and light brown patinas.

19.75in (50cm) high

$3,000-4,000   **SI**

A patinated plaster maquette of a bust of a young woman, by James Pittendrigh Macgillivray, raised on a square tapering plinth, signed.

c1890   *22.75in (58cm) high*

$600-900   **L&T**

A bronze figure of a javelin thrower, by Karl Mobius, raised on a rectangular plinth, signed in the bronze.

A reduction of the original in Berlin.

23.5in (60cm) high

$2,200-2,800   **L&T**

A bronze figure of Madonna and Child, by Pierre Auguste Moreau, on an ebonized base.

16.25in (41cm) high

$3,000-4,000   **DN**

Two recumbent nudes, by Costanzo Mongini, with blackish brown patina on marble bases, each inscribed "Mongini" and numbered in editions of 199.

46in (117cm) long

$1,800-2,200   **FRE**

An early 20thC bronze figure group, signed "S. Moselio", modeled as a fawn and nude female, on a moulded base.

14in (35.5cm) high

$1,000-1,500   **SI**

A bronze bust of a woman sleeping, by H. Müller, with poppy seed blossoms and buds in her hair, signed by the artist "H. Müller".

5in (13cm) high

$220-280   **HERR**

A Nammini bronze head and shoulders of a girl, signed in the bronze.

7in (18cm) high

$150-200   **L&T**

An Art Deco silvered bronze figure of Diana, signed "G. None", on an onyx base.

c1925   *14.5in (37cm) long*

$1,800-2,200   **SI**

A bronze figure of a Classical young woman, by Jessie M. Lawson Peacey, modeled standing naked but for sandals and a robe draped over one arm, her hair arranged in braided bands, she poses above a waisted oval base, signed "J Lawson Peacey".

13.5in (34.5cm) high

$300-500   **DN**

A bronze figure of the Pharaoh's Gift, by Emile Lewis Picault, rectangular plinth and a red griotte-type and ebonized base, centered with a bronze tablet with Egyptian figures, flanked by male figures holding trumpets and papyrus flowers, inscribed "E PICAULT".

37in (94cm) high

$8,000-10,000   **DN**

A female bronze nude, by Edmund Thomas Quinn, inscribed "c Quinn 1913" and "B. ZOPPO. FOUNDRY, N.Y."

72in (183cm) high

$2,800-3,200　　　　**FRE**

A Symbolist patinated bronze 'La Nuit' figure, by H. Sorensen Ringi, the gilded body beneath a silvered 'cloak of night', titled on base "La Nuit", signed "H. Soresen Ringi, Paris", separate stand.

26.5in (67cm) high

$9,000-12,000　　　　**DN**

A bronze bust entitled "Neapolitan Fisherman", by Francois Rude, silver patina, mounted on a seal, on socle, inscribed "Rude" and with "Susse Freres, editeurs, Paris" foundry seal.

4in (10cm) high

$220-280　　　　**SI**

A bronze of Gerhard Hauptmann, by Rudolf Saudeck, a larger-than-life head with a high forehead and distinctive head of hair, marked "Lauchhammer Bildguss", signed "R. Saudeck".

13in (33cm) high

$300-500　　　　**HERR**

A bronze of a faun, by Victor Heinrich Seifert, on a naturalistic plinth, the faun trying to escape with two geese tucked under his arms, the mother goose chasing him, signature on the plinth "V. Seifert".

15in high (38.5cm)

$1,000-1,500　　　　**HERR**

A bronze figure of a naked girl, with overall golden patination, on marble column and base, signed on metal "D. Simon".

11in (28cm) high

$280-320　　　　**DN**

Two bronze female nudes, by Paul Stotz, on round moulded marble bases, one looking at a rose, signed "P. Stotz", marked "Stuttgart" on the back of one statue.

13.25in (33.5cm) & 14.25in (36.5cm)

$2,000-3,000　　　　**HERR**

A bronze spear-throwing Amazon on a stallion, by Franz von Stuck, on a rectangular plinth with a high oblong stepped base, base signed "Franz von Stuck", marked "C. Leyrer Munich".

c1906　　　　*25.5in (65cm)*

$17,000-20,000　　　　**HERR**

A large bronze figure 'Melodie', by Emanuel Villanis, modeled as a Classical girl wearing long robes edged with key-fret borders and supported against rockwork, she rests her lyre on a bent leg, bearing the title, "E. Villanis".

29.5in (75cm) high

$4,500-5,500　　　　**DN**

An Austrian cold-painted bronze statuette of a semi-nude lady dancing with a coiled snake, on circular onyx plinth.

10in (25.5cm) high

$1,000-1,500　　　　**GorL**

A late 19thC Austrian bronze desk set, entitled "Veritas", indistinctly signed and stamped "Geschutzt", brown and gold patination, sienna marble base.

12.5in (32cm) high

$1,000-1,500　　　　**FRE**

An Austrian 'Argentor' bronze table lamp, an Arabic snake charmer, bulb fitments, traces of the original colors, signed on edge "Argentor Vienna".

3.25in (33.5cm) high

$800-1,200　　　　**DN**

A pair of late 19thC French bronze figures of knights, entitled "Duc de Guise" and "Comte De Herford DT".

26in (66cm) high

$4,000-5,000   **SI**

A bronze figure of a naked man, after the antique, raised on a square plinth.

22.75in (57.5cm) high

$600-900   **L&T**

A silvered bronze, by "***Easton", entitled "Art Nouveau Lady", inscribed and numbered "9/10".

20.75in (52.5cm) high

$2,200-2,800   **SI**

A contemporary patinated bronze roundel, by "B*L*F*", "Daughters of Frederick and Elizabeth Shattuck, Clara and Lizzie", inscribed verso "Plowden P. Smith 1991 1/10".

22.5in (57cm) diam

$800-1,200   **L&T**

A Barthelome ivory and giltmetal mounted figure, carved as the head and shoulders of a young boy, mounted with a quiver of arms and raised on a canted onyx base, stamped marks.

6in (15cm) high

$500-700   **L&T**

A late 19thC Goldscheider terracotta figure of a girl walking with baskets, by J Caniroff, incised and impressed marks, some damage.

29.5in (75cm) high

$150-200   **Chef**

A Continental terracotta figure of a boy, possibly Goldscheider, modeled seated, holding a metal flute, some damage and repair.

c1900   *31.5in (80cm) high*

$2,200-2,800   **DN**

A Goldsheider Art Nouveau terracotta bust, of the head and shoulders of a girl, garlanded with flowers and raised on a rocky naturalistic base, moulded marks emboszed "2090/125/32".

23.5in (60cm) high

$1,200-1,800   **L&T**

A terracotta bust of Jean Mermoz, by H. Orresto, with green bronzed patination on a later rectangular base.

Jean Mermoz pioneered the North African to Brazil South Atlantic airmail route and was lost in 1937 in the flying boat 'Croix du Sud'.

18in (49cm) wide

$280-320   **DN**

A pair of painted terracotta busts of female Moors, one inscribed "Pagana 1889", on ebonized socle bases.

27.5in (70cm) high

$4,500–5,500   **L&T**

A late 19thC terracotta figure of a seated pug dog, naturalistically cold painted with brindle coat and tan collar, with glass eyes.

14.25in (36cm) high

$600-900   **CH**

Arts & Crafts

A large Arts and Crafts moonstone and amethyst brooch, the design attributed to John Paul Cooper, with wirework borders, set with five large oval moonstone cabochons and three round amethysts, flanked by golden foliage and punctuated with florets, in a fitted case.

4in (10.5cm) long

$2,500-3,000 **DN**

An Arts and Crafts silver brooch, by Arthur J. Gaskin, of circular form set with opals and pink and green stones within a setting of flying birds and flower-heads, with a stamped "G" monogram.

1.5in (4cm) wide

$1,500-2,000 **L&T**

An Arts and Crafts clip brooch, in the manner of George Hunt, with an oval lapis lazuli cabochon flanked by golden beading, two leaves with wirework stems and a pearl cabochon.

1.5in (3.5cm) long

$220-280 **DN**

An Arts and Crafts heart-shaped pendant, converted to a brooch, with a central carnelian cabochon flanked by dense foliage, lilies and scrolls, punctuated by two smaller carnelian cabochons and a stud of mother-of-pearl, signed on a small metal tag "Minns".

1.75in (4.5cm) long

$800-1,200 **DN**

An Arts and Crafts brooch, with a central carnelian rectangular cabochon, within an octagonal mount, embellished with studs and wirework scrolls.

1.5in (3.5cm) wide

$60-90 **DN**

An Arts and Crafts citrine brooch, possibly by Dorrie Nossiter, centered with a faceted citrine, flanked by golden leaves and wirework tendrils.

1.5in (3.5cm) wide

$300-400 **DN**

An Arts and Crafts enameled gold, garnet and pearl brooch, designed by Harold Stabler for the Morton family, formed as an oval wreath with enameled green leaves, tied at the top with a blue ribbon and punctuated with pearl and garnet berries on golden stems, converted from a pendant, engraved on the reverse "From 24 GR Children 1863-1913", in the original fitted case, marked "Harold Stabler, 34 Upper Mall, Hammersmith, London, W."

In Arts and Crafts circles, the Mortons are best known for their wonderful Donegal carpets made at Killybegs in Ireland, some of which were designed by C.F.A. Voysey, and for their close trading links with Liberty & Co. in London's Regent Street.

2in (5cm) long

$1,800-2,200 **DN**

An Arts and Crafts moonstone pendant, of cruciform with a central oval cabochon, flanked by four further moonstones, held within a fine wirework scroll and beaded mount, suspended on a fine chain.

1.5in (4cm) long

$300-400 **DN**

An Arts and Crafts necklace, attributed stylistically to The Articifers' Guild, the fan-shaped pendant set with green and white pastes and applied with foliate motifs, with a paste drop and paste-set foliate loop above, suspended on a fine chain.

2in (5cm) long

$600-900 **DN**

An Arts and Crafts pendant, in the manner of H.G. Murphy, of pentagonal shape, centered with an oval cabochon of green-stained chalcedony, flanked by heart-shaped leaves and berries.

1.5in (4cm) long

$280-320 **DN**

An Arts and Crafts carnelian necklace, attributed stylistically to Omar Ramsden, with foliate drops graduating in size and having carnelian cabochon 'buds', suspended from an intricate chain.

15.25in (38.5cm) long

$400-600 **DN**

DECORATIVE ARTS

An Arts and Crafts guard chain, attributed to Bernard Instone, the chain with lozenge-shaped plaques, centered with foliate motifs, alternating with pebbles of Swiss lapis.

57in (145cm) long

$280-320   **DN**

An Arts and Crafts ring, with a pale, faceted amethyst flanked on the shoulders with thistles and foliage.

$70-100   **DN**

An Arts and Crafts amethyst ring, with a central circular stone within a cast band of foliage and beading, stamped "Silver".

$70-100   **DN**

An Arts and Crafts citrine ring, the central oval and faceted stone held within an openwork foliate mount, punctuated with florets.

c1860

$300-400   **DN**

Art Nouveau

An Arts and Crafts ring, with an agate gundog intaglio.

1.25in (3cm) wide

$800-1,200   **NBlm**

An Art Nouveau silver and enamel brooch, by Queensway, with a central oval water pearl enclosed by enamel leaves with a seed-pearl drop, with a stamped mark.

2in (5cm) wide

$120-180   **L&T**

An Art Nouveau enameled brooch, of almost circular openwork shape, formed by interwoven foliate stems heightened with blue-green enameling, marked "Sterling Silver".

This design is also found bearing Charles Horner's marks.

1.75in (4.5cm) wide

$100-150   **DN**

A Ramsden and Carr silver and enamel buckle, with a hammer-textured surface and an enameled panel depicting a glade scene, backed with a soft metal panel, possibly aluminium, marked "Rn & Cr" for London 1905.

2.5in (6.5cm) long

$600-900   **DN**

A Charles Horner enameled brooch, of interwoven elliptical shape, heightened with green enameling and terminating with a thistle, with a citrine-colored paste top, marked "CH" for Chester 1907.

1.25in (3cm) wide

$100-150   **DN**

An early 20thC Skonvirke brooch, by Bernhard Hertz, of oval pierced form, worked with leaves and buds and set with green cabochons, stamped mark "BH. S828".

1.75in (4.5cm) wide

$320-380   **L&T**

An Art Nouveau circular silver-plated brooch, designed by Josef Hoffmann, embellished in shallow relief with a bell-shaped flower and stylized foliate branches.

A similar design for a gold-plated brass box and cover is shown as no. 274 in the Wiener Werkstätte records by Waultraud Neuwirth, where it also states that this motif appears on other objects in various materials.

c1890   *2in (5cm) wide*

$1,200-1,800   **DN**

An early 20thC French platinum and diamond brooch, naturalistically modeled as a humming-bird in flight, set with small rose diamonds in openwork millegrain settings to resemble the feathers and a black onyx eye, French marks, the maker's mark mis-struck.

$2,200-2,800   **DN**

A Murrle Bennett enameled pendant, with interwoven loops picked out in yellow, orange and green enamels, edged with beaded wirework and a similarly enameled drop, marked with an "MB&Co." monogram and "950".

Pendant 1.75in (4.5cm) long

$400-600   **DN**

A Murrle Bennett enameled pendant, with a central panel of shaded yellow enamel, the edges pierced, hammer-textured and applied with beading, maker's monogram and "950".

$150-200   **DN**

An enameled pendant of almost heart shape, with an open center, punctuated with a green paste, the outer edges picked out with green enameled leaf shapes, marked "CP" and a partial Birmingham hallmark removed during manufacture.

1in (2.5cm) long

$70-100   **DN**

An Art Nouveau-style silver and enameled pendant, by Norman Grant, of stylized flower-head form with a seed-pearl pendant drop, indistinct hallmarks for Edinburgh.

2in (5cm) long

$300-350   **L&T**

An Art Nouveau enameled pendant, of curved flower-head form, inset with an oval pearl above three graduated pendant drops.

1.5in (4cm) wide

$400-600   **L&T**

An English Art Nouveau silver pendant, in the German style, with a central teardrop-shaped paste cabochon simulating turquois, flanked by winged flanges punctuated with two half pearls, marked "CV & Co" and marks for Birmingham 1904.

0.75in (2cm) wide

$70-100   **DN**

An English Art Nouveau silver pendant, of German appearance, the oval shape with a textured surface and bands of fine scrolls and centered with a row of pale-blue glass beads with similar beads on chains below, marked with possibly "C.H Co", with Chester hallmarks for 1911.

2.25in (6cm) long

$220-280   **DN**

A Murrle Bennett gold and turquois necklace, the shaped pendant centered with an oval plaque of turquois matrix, with a freshwater pearl drop below it and an openwork foliate motif above, suspended from two pierced plaques and two turquois plaques on a fine chain, marked "15ct" and "MB&Co".

2in (5cm) long

$1,200-1,800   **DN**

A gold and opal necklace, with an oval opal cabochon within a golden hoop, with a further opal drop suspended from an elliptical loop, on a fine chain.

$300-400   **DN**

A Murrle Bennett gold and peridot necklace, the pendant centered with a faceted peridot, flanked by three ivy leaves within a wirework mount, punctuated by seed-pearls and having a baroque pearl drop, the chain having further leaves and peridots, stamped with a "MB&Co" monogram and "15ct".

Pendant 1.75in (4.5cm) long

$1,500-2,000   **DN**

An Art Nouveau peridot and seed pearl-set gold pendant, of stylized linear form with a peridot drop, stamped "9ct".

2in (5cm) long

$300-400   **L&T**

An Austro-Hungarian carnelian necklace, the pendant with a central oval plaque of carnelian ringed by seed pearls and small carnelian cabochons, the back engraved with scrolls, suspended from three similarly fashioned plaques, on a chain with further small cabochons.

Pendant 2in (5cm) long

$220-280   **DN**

An unusual London blue topaz, diamond and gold lady's ring, the articulated band composed of alternating heart-shaped plaques, centrally set with a heart-shaped blue gemstone and flanked on the shoulders with diamond-set, heart-shaped panels, with maker's mark "G" in a square and "750".

$1,000-1,500   **DN**

An Austrian Art Nouveau gold ring, with simple interwoven stems, set with a green-stained chalcedony cabochon and a tiny half-pearl, stamped "A.K." and with a dog's head standard poincon.

$80-120   **DN**

An Art Nouveau pearl ring, with a central cultured pearl held within a foliate mount that extends on to the shanks, with an indistinct mark, possibly Scandinavian.

c1890

$180-220   **DN**

An Art Nouveau pink tourmaline ring, set with a central, faceted stone and foliate detail on the shanks.

c1890

$320-380   **DN**

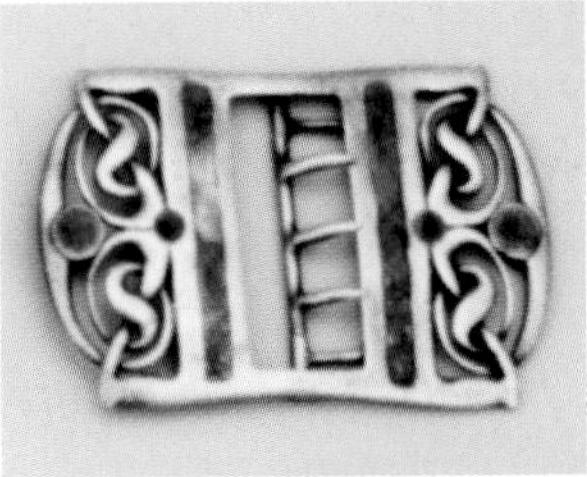

A Liberty & Co. enameled silver buckle, designed by Archibald Knox, of almost rectangular shape, the ends embellished with interwoven entrelacs and punctuated with colored enamels, marked "L&Co", "Cymric" and with Birmingham hallmarks.

c1901   *3in (8cm) long*

$600-900   **DN**

A pair of Art Nouveau diamond and ruby-set cufflinks, with Rhys flags.

c1890   *0.75in (2cm) long*

$4,000-6,000   **NBlm**

Art Deco

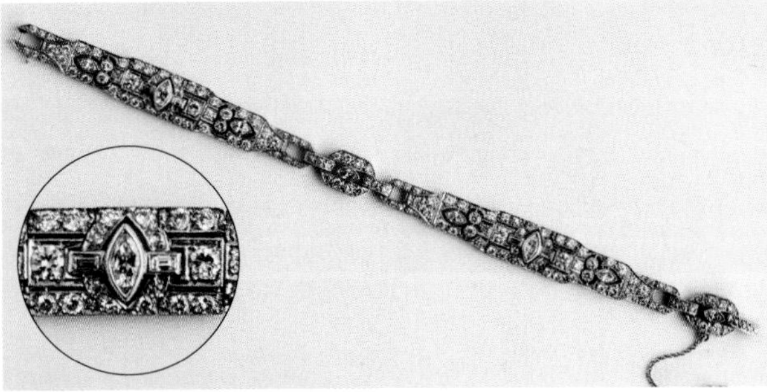

An Art Deco diamond bracelet, with marquise, baguette and round cut diamonds weighing approximately 7cts.

9.25in (23.5cm) long

$15,000-20,000   **NBlm**

An Art Deco platinum and diamond openwork panel bracelet, possibly Dutch.

8in (20cm) long

$7,000-10,000   **NBlm**

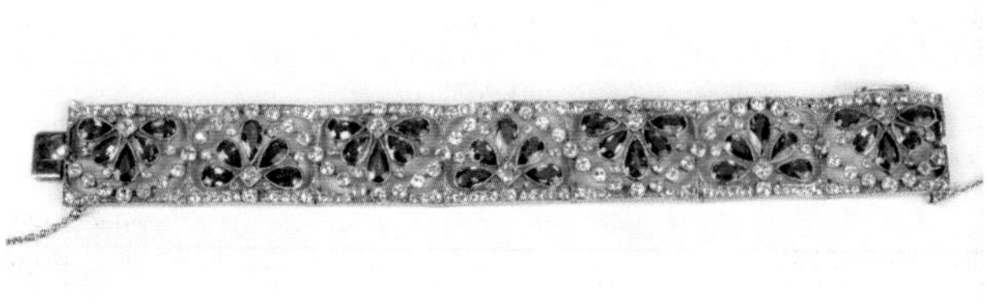

An Art Deco platinum bracelet, set with aquamarine and diamonds.

$12,000-18,000   **JP**

An Art Deco platinum bracelet, set with aquamarine and diamonds.

$12,000-18,000   **JP**

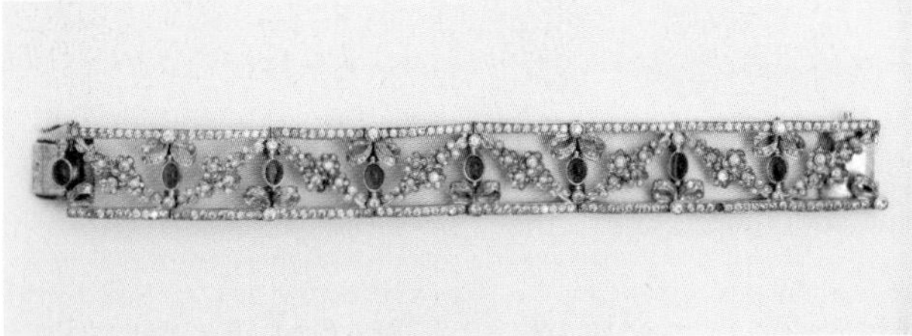

A 1920s English Art Deco silver bracelet, marked "925".

7in (18cm) long

$300-400   **RG**

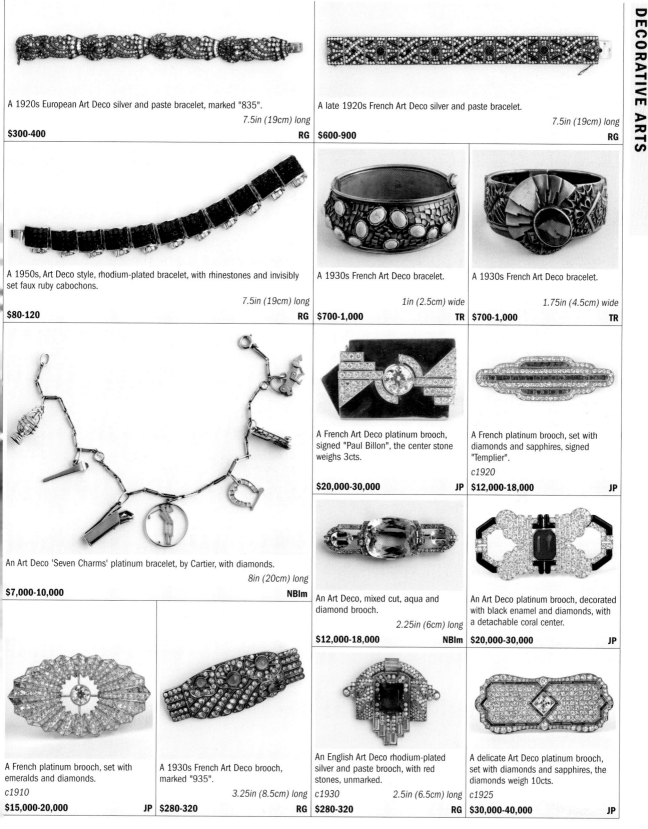

A 1920s European Art Deco silver and paste bracelet, marked "835".

7.5in (19cm) long

$300-400 RG

A late 1920s French Art Deco silver and paste bracelet.

7.5in (19cm) long

$600-900 RG

A 1950s, Art Deco style, rhodium-plated bracelet, with rhinestones and invisibly set faux ruby cabochons.

7.5in (19cm) long

$80-120 RG

A 1930s French Art Deco bracelet.

1in (2.5cm) wide

$700-1,000 TR

A 1930s French Art Deco bracelet.

1.75in (4.5cm) wide

$700-1,000 TR

An Art Deco 'Seven Charms' platinum bracelet, by Cartier, with diamonds.

8in (20cm) long

$7,000-10,000 NBlm

A French Art Deco platinum brooch, signed "Paul Billon", the center stone weighs 3cts.

$20,000-30,000 JP

A French platinum brooch, set with diamonds and sapphires, signed "Templier".

c1920

$12,000-18,000 JP

An Art Deco, mixed cut, aqua and diamond brooch.

2.25in (6cm) long

$12,000-18,000 NBlm

An Art Deco platinum brooch, decorated with black enamel and diamonds, with a detachable coral center.

$20,000-30,000 JP

A French platinum brooch, set with emeralds and diamonds.

c1910

$15,000-20,000 JP

A 1930s French Art Deco brooch, marked "935".

3.25in (8.5cm) long

$280-320 RG

An English Art Deco rhodium-plated silver and paste brooch, with red stones, unmarked.

c1930   *2.5in (6.5cm) long*

$280-320 RG

A delicate Art Deco platinum brooch, set with diamonds and sapphires, the diamonds weigh 10cts.

c1925

$30,000-40,000 JP

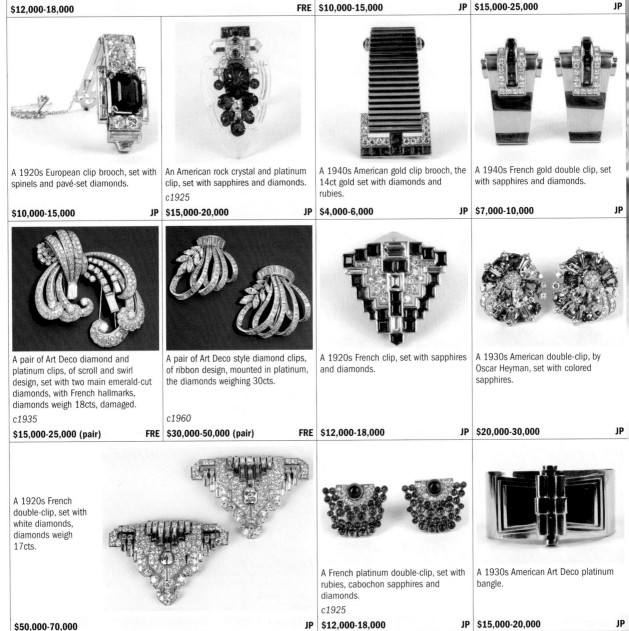

A sapphire and diamond interlocking circle brooch, made by Bonnet, Paris, for Van Cleef and Arpels, the 14 calibre-cut Burma sapphires weigh 4cts and 84 round-cut diamonds weigh 6cts, all mounted in platinum.

c1932

$12,000-18,000　　　　　　　　　　　　　**FRE**

A French platinum bow brooch, set with diamonds and onyx.

c1930

$10,000-15,000　　　　　　　　　**JP**

An American watch brooch, set with onyx, emeralds, sapphires and diamonds.

c1925

$15,000-25,000　　　　　　　　　**JP**

A 1920s European clip brooch, set with spinels and pavé-set diamonds.

$10,000-15,000　　　　**JP**

An American rock crystal and platinum clip, set with sapphires and diamonds.

c1925

$15,000-20,000　　　　**JP**

A 1940s American gold clip brooch, the 14ct gold set with diamonds and rubies.

$4,000-6,000　　　　**JP**

A 1940s French gold double clip, set with sapphires and diamonds.

$7,000-10,000　　　　**JP**

A pair of Art Deco diamond and platinum clips, of scroll and swirl design, set with two main emerald-cut diamonds, with French hallmarks, diamonds weigh 18cts, damaged.

c1935

$15,000-25,000 (pair)　　**FRE**

A pair of Art Deco style diamond clips, of ribbon design, mounted in platinum, the diamonds weighing 30cts.

c1960

$30,000-50,000 (pair)　　**FRE**

A 1920s French clip, set with sapphires and diamonds.

$12,000-18,000　　　　**JP**

A 1930s American double-clip, by Oscar Heyman, set with colored sapphires.

$20,000-30,000　　　　**JP**

A 1920s French double-clip, set with white diamonds, diamonds weigh 17cts.

$50,000-70,000　　　　**JP**

A French platinum double-clip, set with rubies, cabochon sapphires and diamonds.

c1925

$12,000-18,000　　　　**JP**

A 1930s American Art Deco platinum bangle.

$15,000-20,000　　　　**JP**

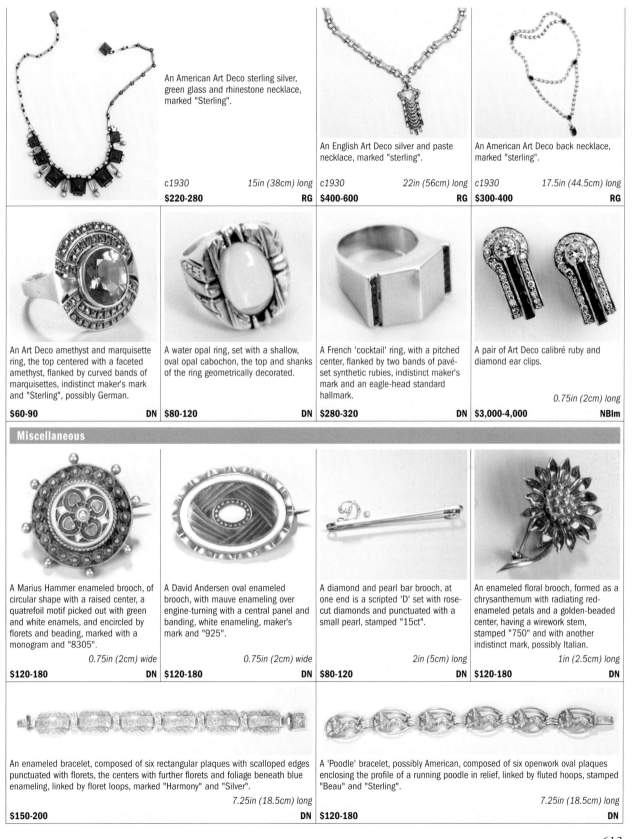

An American Art Deco sterling silver, green glass and rhinestone necklace, marked "Sterling".

c1930   15in (38cm) long
$220-280   **RG**

An English Art Deco silver and paste necklace, marked "sterling".

c1930   22in (56cm) long
$400-600   **RG**

An American Art Deco back necklace, marked "sterling".

c1930   17.5in (44.5cm) long
$300-400   **RG**

An Art Deco amethyst and marquisette ring, the top centered with a faceted amethyst, flanked by curved bands of marquisettes, indistinct maker's mark and "Sterling", possibly German.

$60-90   **DN**

A water opal ring, set with a shallow, oval opal cabochon, the top and shanks of the ring geometrically decorated.

$80-120   **DN**

A French 'cocktail' ring, with a pitched center, flanked by two bands of pavé-set synthetic rubies, indistinct maker's mark and an eagle-head standard hallmark.

$280-320   **DN**

A pair of Art Deco calibré ruby and diamond ear clips.

0.75in (2cm) long
$3,000-4,000   **NBlm**

Miscellaneous

A Marius Hammer enameled brooch, of circular shape with a raised center, a quatrefoil motif picked out with green and white enamels, and encircled by florets and beading, marked with a monogram and "8305".

0.75in (2cm) wide
$120-180   **DN**

A David Andersen oval enameled brooch, with mauve enameling over engine-turning with a central panel and banding, white enameling, maker's mark and "925".

0.75in (2cm) wide
$120-180   **DN**

A diamond and pearl bar brooch, at one end is a scripted 'D' set with rose-cut diamonds and punctuated with a small pearl, stamped "15ct".

2in (5cm) long
$80-120   **DN**

An enameled floral brooch, formed as a chrysanthemum with radiating red-enameled petals and a golden-beaded center, having a wirework stem, stamped "750" and with another indistinct mark, possibly Italian.

1in (2.5cm) long
$120-180   **DN**

An enameled bracelet, composed of six rectangular plaques with scalloped edges punctuated with florets, the centers with further florets and foliage beneath blue enameling, linked by floret loops, marked "Harmony" and "Silver".

7.25in (18.5cm) long
$150-200   **DN**

A 'Poodle' bracelet, possibly American, composed of six openwork oval plaques enclosing the profile of a running poodle in relief, linked by fluted hoops, stamped "Beau" and "Sterling".

7.25in (18.5cm) long
$120-180   **DN**

A Danish necklace, designed by Gertrude Engel for A. Michelsen, composed of 15 linked units, each fashioned as a lily with a golden wirework stamen, and a pair of clip earrings, maker's marks and facsimile signature of designer.

17in (43cm) long

$180-220　　　　　**DN**

A square pendant necklace, by Hans Hansen, with a partially opened cut flap on the upper section and a gilded ball suspended on simple plain chain, bearing facsimile signature and "925S Denmark".

Pendant 1.5in (3.5cm) wide

$150-200　　　　　**DN**

A W.H. Haseler circular pendant, possibly retailed through Liberty & Co., centered with a mother-of-pearl plaque, flanked by interwoven stems and berries, punctuated with three turquoise-colored paste studs, stamped "WHH" and "925".

1in (2.5cm) diam

$150-200　　　　　**DN**

An unusual Polish coral ring, with two oviform beads separated by a ridged band and flanked by interwoven wirework stems, marked "WS" and with a standard mark.

$100-150　　　　　**DN**

A Gothic Revival gold and enameled broad band ring, probably made in the workshops of John Hardman in Birmingham, with six quatrefoil panels of colored champlevé enamels, showing a cupid, a falconer, a maiden, a spray of lilies, a spray of blue flowers and a memento mori motif of a winged skull and crossbones with a serpent, each panel flanked by engraved gargoyle-like masks.

$12,000-18,000　　　　　**DN**

A pair of cufflinks by Alexander Ritchie, each with two linked oval terminals, cast with Norse sailing ships, with stamped mark "Iona AR".

$180-220　　　　　**L&T**

An unusual 'Elephants' ring, with a revolving band applied with five elephants in relief, bearing a 'G' in a square mark and "750".

$400-400　　　　　**DN**

A stylish pair of gold and diamond cuff links, by Boucheron, each with two oval plaques set with diamonds and attached by rods to a plain, L-shaped band, signed on the edge "Boucheron" and with French standard poincons.

1.25in (3cm) wide

$1,500-2,000　　　　　**DN**

A Bernard Instone circular silver enameled box and cover, the push-on cover is set with a blue enameled plaque simulating turquois, edged with a rope-twist border, with an interior mirror, marked "BI" with Birmingham hallmarks for 1923.

2in (5cm) diam

$320-380　　　　　**DN**

An American gold tie-clip, formed by two rows of ropework, set at one end with an oval sapphire cabochon, stamped "14k".

1.75in (4.5cm) long

$120-180　　　　　**DN**

Gothic revival

A Gothic Revival oak upright chair, after a design by A. W. N. Pugin, with a broad horizontal back rail supported by two shaped and chamfered uprights, a stuff-over seat on four square knopped and chamfered supports, united by stretchers, with brass feet at the front.

$700-1,000 **DN**

A small mahogany chair, with a back resembling the tracery of a gothic window, a central rectangular wooden panel carved with St Cecilia standing in a landscape, flanked by two stringed instruments with further instruments on the back, on tapering and beaded front supports, united by stretchers.

$300-400 **DN**

A small mahogany chair, with an openwork arched beaded back, inlaid with pale wooden panels, carved on the front with the figure of St George beneath a flowering bough, the reverse carved with roses and a crown, flanked by smaller floral panels, on tapering beaded supports united by stretchers.

$150-200 **DN**

A Gothic Revival ash stick stand, with ebonized decoration, the divided top with turned and fluted supports on blocked feet with shaped supports.

35.75in (91cm) wide

$700-1,000 **L&T**

A Gothic Revival mahogany adjustable armchair, attributed to Charles Bevan, the turned top above a leaf and berry frieze and chamfered uplifts, supporting a slung button-upholstered leather back and seat, above curved arms pierced with trefoils and adjustable, continuing to curved front legs, the seat support with incised spiral terminals continuing to form shaped supports to the rear linked by a chamfered stretcher.

42.5in (108cm) high

$4,500-5,500 **L&T**

A Gothic Revival oak dressing mirror, of rectangular shape, held between turned uprights with pointed finials supported on T-shaped black feet, with flanges pierced with trefoils.

29.25in (74.5cm) high

$220-280 **DN**

A pair of Gothic Revival brass candelabrum, made for Stockport Town Hall by Sir Arthur Brumwell Thomas, each with pierced coronets supported by leafy scrolling brackets with molded glass fruits raised on a wrythen column, with molded knops with scrolling brackets and raised above an octagonal molded and ebonized base with incised gilded leafy decoration.

c1904 *86.5in (220cm) high*

$4,500-5,500 **L&T**

A Gothic Revival pedestal dressing table, the rectangular top with a raised back, drawers and open shelves with dentilated back rail, each pedestal with three short drawers, with brass handles.

54.25in (138cm) wide

$1,500-2,000 **DN**

Aesthetic Movement

A large Aesthetic Movement oak bookcase, surmounted with a spindle gallery and a carved floral panel, three shelving units behind glazed doors, the base with fielded paneled doors, two of which are carved with roundels depicting scenes from the fable of the stork and the fox.

126in (320cm) wide

$7,000-10,000 DN

An Aesthetic Movement pollard oak dresser, by Boswell of Norwich, with an oval brass plaque on back, reading "Boswell Maker Norwich".

67.75in (172cm) high

$700-1,000 DN

An Aesthetic Movement walnut sideboard, by Maple and Co., with a raised back, the top with a molded edge, three drawers with brass handles and three doors with shaped panels carved centrally with an urn and foliate scrolls, pierced brass strap hinges on turned feet, the top right drawer stamped "Maple and Co. Ltd".

71.25in (181cm) wide

$450-550 DN

An Aesthetic Movement walnut buffet sideboard, by Maple & Co. London, the top with galleried ledge back and central pad carved in relief with pomegranates, the molded top with arcaded panel of sunbursts and sunflowers, on turned and reeded supports, the lower section into twin paneled doors carved with pomegranates on turned feet with brass caps and casters.

60.25in (153cm) wide

$700-1,000 L&T

A Collinson & Lock rosewood and calamander cabinet, designed by T. E. Collcutt, with a top gallery pierced with trefoils, a vaulted top and side sections, the base with a central cupboard with fielded panel doors with 'aesthetic' brass door furniture, flanked by open shelving.

62.25in (158cm) wide

$7,500-8,500 DN

An Aesthetic Movement oak sideboard, in the manner of Bruce Talbert, with a mirrored back, central roundel carved with a songbird on a branch of holly, a short frieze drawer and two cupboards with paneled doors and carved with sunflower motifs.

72in (183cm) wide

$150-200 DN

A CLOSER LOOK AT AN AESTHETIC MOVEMENT CABINET

The carved sunflowers are typically naturalistic, aesthetic movement motifs.

The elegant proportions of this cabinet reflect the Aesthetic Movement's followers' belief in the cult of the beautiful and the pleasure beauty could bring.

Ebonized wood was frequently used for furniture of this style.

The turned legs and supports on this cabinet are relatively simple. Many pieces were carved to resemble bamboo.

An Aesthetic Movement ebonized cabinet, in the manner of Cottier, the top having a carved band of stylized flowers and foliage, the open alcoves with turned pillars, a vaulted back to the central area above bevelled mirrors, between intaglio-carved floral panels, with a glazed display area below, flanked by shelving, the cupboard with spindle-paneled doors and further alcoves on turned legs.

71.75in (182cm) high

$900-1,100 DN

An Aesthetic Movement buffet, ebonized, parcel gilt and marquetry, in the manner of Herter Brothers, New York, the foliate carved panel cupboard doors enclosing shelves.

1880-1890   *69in (175.5cm) wide*

$3,000-4,000 SI

An Aesthetic Movement ebonized bonheur-du-jour, the top rail with a gallery of turned spindles, egg-shaped finials and with panels on all four sides carved with stylized sunflowers and fruiting vines, the drop front reveals pigeon holes and two drawers within.

21in (53.5cm) wide

$300-400 DN

A late Victorian ebonized and parcel gilt Aesthetic Movement kneehole desk, the top with a molded edge above nine mahogany-lined drawers with brass handles arranged around a kneehole with shaped brackets, on turned feet, some damage to top.

Provenance: Chawton House, Alton, Hampshire, the home of Edward Austen Knight (1767-1852) brother of the novelist Jane Austen (1775-1817). Edward was adopted by his childless cousins, the Knights, taking their name and inheriting their estate at Chawton.

48in (122cm) wide

$600-800   **DN**

One of a pair of Aesthetic Movement oak upright chairs, in the manner of Godwin, each with a top rail carved with a frieze of stylized sunflowers and foliage.

$150-200 (pair)   **DN**

One of a set of four Aesthetic Movement ebonized chairs, attributed to Gillows and Bruce Talbert, with beaded top rail and stylized foliate tops to the fluted uprights, upholstered back and seat, the front supports with wreathed and turned banding.

$600-900 (set)   **DN**

An Aesthetic Movement ebonized upright chair, in the manner of Godwin, with a diaper back, a stuff-over seat, on square-section supports united by stretchers.

$60-100   **DN**

An Aesthetic Movement stained beech folding chair, by James Shoolbred & Co., designed in the manner of E. W. Godwin, stamped marks.

Versions of this chair have been attributed to the manufacturer William Watt who executed many of Godwins' designs. Godwins "Old English" or "Jacobean" chair of 1867, based on earlier Sheraton and Regency traditions, was much copied by other manufacturers, in particular Collier and Plucknett of Warwick. This chair by Shoolbred & Co. of London, takes elements from the "Old English" design and adds the folding 'steamer chair' feature, which resembles other attributed examples.

31.5in (80cm) high

$300-400   **L&T**

An Aesthetic Movement turned walnut and upholstered armchair.

c1890

$450-550   **SI**

A late 19thC ebonized Aesthetic Movement table, with octagonal top inlaid with calamander, supported on six curved legs united by a wheel-like system of stretchers, with a central wreathed column, raised on casters.

28.5in (72.5cm) high

$12,000-18,000   **DN**

An Aesthetic Movement small ebonized table, in the manner of Godwin, with an octagonal top on turned supports, a central tier and splayed legs united by pierced and carved cross-stretchers, with gilded detailing.

26.75in (68cm) high

$100-150   **DN**

An Aesthetic Movement small ebonized table, in the manner of Godwin, with a square top, on turned supports with an undertier, further supported by fine rods extending from the stretchers.

25.75in (65.5cm) high

$150-200   **DN**

An Aesthetic Movement ebonized stick stand, unusually long.

71.75in (182cm) long

$250-350   **DN**

An Aesthetic Movement cast iron and brass mounted fire grate.

35.75in (91cm) wide,

$3,000-4,000   **L&T**

A pair of Victorian Aesthetic manner walnut and parcel gilt jardinère stands, the molded square tops raised on turned and paneled columns inset with foliate painted, mirrored and silkwork panels, raised on step block feet.

c1890   *51.5in (131cm) high*

$2,800-3,200   **SI**

FURNITURE

Arts and Crafts

An Arts & Crafts oak wardrobe, in the Gothic style, the projecting cornice above chequer moldings and frieze carved in relief with luxuriant leaves on a blind fretwork ground.

78in (198cm) high

$2,500-3,000   **L&T**

A large Arts and Crafts oak wardrobe, the central section with twin paneled doors, pierced with squares and with copper backing, with separate mirrored door cupboards either side of the main section, each flanked by leaded glass panels.

122in (310cm) wide

$1,000-1,500   **L&T**

An Arts and Crafts mahogany wardrobe, by Shapland & Petter of Barnstaple, with an open compartment at the top and a cupboard below, the door inlaid with Art Nouveau foliate motifs, marked "S.P.B" on locks.

82.75in (210cm) high

$600-900   **DN**

An Arts & Crafts oak wardrobe, the broad projecting cornice above a single mirrored door flanked by embossed copper panels, depicting galleons in full sail, each stamped "Rd. 420976".

81in (206cm) high

$500-700   **L&T**

An Arts and Crafts oak bedroom suite, comprising a dressing table and a wardrobe, only dressing table shown.

Wardrobe 81in (206cm) high

$600-1,000 (set)   **L&T**

A CLOSER LOOK AT AN ARTS AND CRAFTS CABINET

Woods used in this period were those associated with country furniture such as oak and ash.

The hinges used in construction play an important part in the decoration of the piece.

The cabinet is handcrafted and based largely on a traditional country design - most arts and crafts pieces are very sturdily made.

The decoration is restrained and symmetrical.

A Liberty & Co. Arts and Crafts oak chest of drawers, designed by Leonard Wyburd, with a short back rail and sides pierced with heart motifs, four graduated drawers with block and rod vertical handles, the plank sides form the feet.

c1860   *36in (91.5cm) wide*

$1,500-2,000   **DN**

An early 20thC pair of tall oak Arts and Crafts cabinets, the molded cornices above a pair of glazed panel doors carved with stylized plant forms, opening to reveal adjustable shelves, raised on stile feet.

94in (239cm) high

$2,500-3,000 (pair)   **SI**

An Arts and Crafts oak bookcase cabinet, the projecting cornice above an embossed brass plaque bearing inscription "Studies serve for Delight" above two doors with stained and leaded glass panels with stylized floral design, enclosing adjustable shelves, the lower section with sliding shelf above twin paneled doors on square section legs with block feet.

83.75in (213cm) high

$7,500-8,500   **L&T**

An Arts and Crafts mahogany bookcase, the projecting later cornice above twin leaded glass doors enclosing shelves above two paneled doors with incised Art Nouveau floral motifs on bracket feet.

43in (109cm) high

$600-1,000   **L&T**

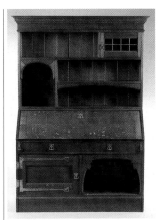

A Liberty & Co. oak bureau bookcase, the lower section with sloping fall, interior fitted with pigeonholes, above a single drawer with cupboard below flanked by open void, the whole with decorative brass work.

80.25in (204cm) high

$3,000-4,000   **L&T**

An Arts and Crafts oak hall stand, the projecting cornice above central panel door with decorative hinges flanked by fluted panels, above a mirror and stepped open shelf, the sides with waved slats, molded feet.

82in (208cm) high

$1,500-2,000   **L&T**

An Arts and Crafts oak sideboard, the overhanging cornice with bracket supports above twin tongue and groove doors flanked by open shelves, the top above two drawers and two tongue and groove doors with bracket feet.

72in (183cm) high

$1,800-2,200   **L&T**

An Arts and Crafts dark-stained oak buffet, probably retailed through Liberty and Co., fitted with wrought iron and copper door and drawer furniture.

69.25in (176cm) high

$600-1,000   **DN**

A Liberty & Co. Arts and Crafts dark oak sideboard, with broad galleried back, a central frieze drawer with drop handle, paneled doors with pierced brass escutcheons, hinged lock plate, bracket feet, "Liberty & Co. Ltd" retail plaque.

c1860   *67.75in (172cm) wide*

$4,500-5,500   **DN**

LIBERTY & CO

One of the leading retail outlets for Arts and Crafts furniture was Liberty & Co, founded by Sir Arthur Lasenby Liberty (1843-1917). The company opened in London in 1875 and sold an extremely successful range of Arts and Crafts furniture, including pieces by such notable designers as Walton. Well known for his interest in and support of new artistic ventures, Liberty commissioned work from his artistic friends. However, he concealed the designer's identity in favour of the Liberty name and this tradition continues to this day. It was not until the 1960's that the identities of the key designers were discovered. The pieces were simply marked 'Liberty & Co.'

A Morris & Co. dark-colored walnut sideboard, designed by Philip Webb, fielded paneled back, short recessed shelf on spindle supports, the base with three frieze drawers and cupboards, block feet, with original brass drop pulls with chased quatrefoil back plates.

c1890   *61.5in (156cm) wide*

$22,000-28,000   **DN**

An Arts & Crafts oak sideboard, the cornice above twin astragal glazed doors and open shelf, the lower section with two drawers and a central door flanked by two smaller doors.

76.25in (194cm) high

$2,500-3,500   **L&T**

A George Walton oak sideboard, the ledge back centered with an oval panel of stained and leaded glass centered by a brass heart, the top with two hinged panels each enclosing a void above a central frieze drawer flanked by two cupboards and each with cut out handles with brass concave backplates, raised on square section tapering legs, possibly adapted from a dressing table, bears ivorine label "George Walton & Co Ltd, Designers, Manufacturers and Decorators 150 & 152 Wellington Street, Glasgow".

The label attached to the rear of this sideboard dates it to c1900. The design demonstrates the influence of the Arts and Crafts movement as well as the simplicity and restraint characteristic of Walton's work. The addition of applied decoration in stained glass and metal are also characteristic of his work from 1890.

c1900   *53in (135cm) wide*

$3,800-4,200   **L&T**

A Scottish School of Arts & Crafts cabinet, with repoussé decorated brass panels in the manner of Alexander Ritchie, Iona, the panels depicting fantastical birds holding brambles in their beaks.

18in (45.5cm) high

$1,500-2,000   **L&T**

An Arts and Crafts oak desk, the rectangular top with raised superstructure pierced with spade motifs and enclosed by cupboard with convex glazing, above three paneled drawers and twin pedestals of three graduated drawers on plinth base.

$500-700   **L&T**

Left: An Arts and Crafts oak coffer, of rectangular section, carved in low relief with Celtic motifs.

28.75in (73cm) wide

Right: An oak Art & Crafts coffer, of rectangular form carved in low relief with Celtic motifs and bearing inscription.

33.75in (86cm) wide

$450-550   **L&T**   **$600-1,000**   **L&T**

An Arts & Crafts carved mahogany spinning stool, with all over relief foliate carving.

33.25in (84.5cm) high

$150-200   **L&T**

An English Arts and Crafts oak armchair, oak ears, woven cane back and oak arms on turned legs with arched stretcher, all supporting a trapezoidal caned slipseat, seat rail stamped "J. H. H.".

29in (73.5cm) high

$2,200-2,800   **FRE**

An English Arts and Crafts oak armchair, with tall carved and paneled back, flat curved arms, trapezoidal seat and turned legs, retains an upholstered seat pad and original finish.

c1900   *51.5in (130.5cm) high*

$1,000-1,500   **FRE**

A Rossetti ebonized armchair by Morris & Co., with waisted spindle splat above curved arms, the rush seat raised above turned legs linked by stretchers, also a single chair with upholstered seat to match.

$350-450 (set)   **L&T**

An Arts and Crafts mahogany elbow chair, possibly by Shapland & Petter or retailed through Liberty & Co., curved top-rail and two back splats simply inlaid with stylized flowering plants.

$450-550   **DN**

One of a pair of Arts and Crafts oak upright chairs, possibly retailed through Liberty & Co., the shaped top-rail inlaid with pewter and fruitwood flowering plant motif and chequered banding, the two back splats similarly inlaid.

$450-550 (pair)   **DN**

One of a set of eight Arts and Crafts oak upright chairs, each with geometric piercing on the top rails, four chairs have pewter inlaid as an arrow with inlay of black squares, the other four have the arrow but with triangular motifs, otherwise identical.

$1,000-1,500 (set)   **DN**

One of a pair of elm Arts & Crafts armchairs, each with slatted rectangular backs above open arms with upholstered rests, the drop-in seats raised on square tapered legs linked by stretchers.

$500-700 (pair)   **L&T**

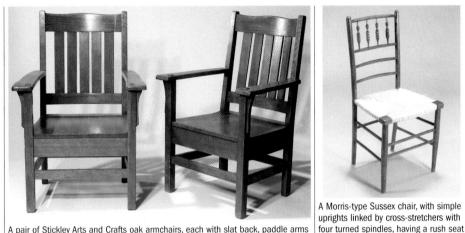

A pair of Stickley Arts and Crafts oak armchairs, each with slat back, paddle arms with through-tenons, rectilinear legs and stretchers, unmarked.

39in (99cm) high

$500-700   **FRE**

A Morris-type Sussex chair, with simple uprights linked by cross-stretchers with four turned spindles, having a rush seat and plain tapering supports united by stretchers.

$100-150   **DN**

One of a pair of 'Clisset' type oak ladder-back chairs, by Edward Gardine, each having three shaped back splats linking simple uprights, with rush seats and the supports united by stretchers.

$250-350 (pair)   **DN**

One of a set of eight oak Arts and Crafts elbow chairs, of 'Clisset' type but probably from High Wycombe, each with a shaped ladder back, curved arm rests and simple tapering supports united by stretchers, with rush seats.

$900-1,100 (set)   **DN**

A pair of oak Arts and Crafts side chairs, the broad top rails with yin and yang piercings raised above drop-in seats on square legs linked by stretchers.

$450-550 (pair)   **L&T**

An Arts & Crafts oak dining chair, the broad rectangular back pierced with yin and yang roundel above further rail on rush seat and square tapered legs linked by stretchers.

$250-350   **L&T**

Two of a set of four oak dining chairs by William Birch, High Wycombe, each with broad slightly arched back with ring turned uprights on rushed seats and turned tapering legs united by stretchers, with ring turning to the feet.

$700-1,000 (set)   **L&T**

One of a harlequin set of four oak Arts and Crafts chairs, by William Birch of High Wycombe, comprising one elbow chair and three uprights, with solid shaped backs, turned uprights and legs, united by stretchers and with rush seats.

$250-350 (set)   **DN**

A set of six oak dining chairs by William Birch, High Wycombe, each with broad back rails supported by ring turned and tapering uprights with finial surmount, above rush seat on ring turned and tapering legs united by stretchers and terminating in pad feet.

$1,800-2,200   **L&T**

One of a pair of ebonized easy chairs, with caned backs and seats, curved arms with spindle supports, with splayed back legs and turned front supports.

$220-280 (pair)   **DN**

A pair of Arts & Crafts lady's and gentleman's oak reclining armchairs, in the manner of Gustav Stickley, each with the slatted and adjustable rectangular back above broad open arms raised above a cushioned seat on square tapering legs linked by an undertier.

35.75in (91cm) long

$500-700 (pair)   **L&T**

An Arts & Crafts oak hall settle, the back with open shelf and heart piercings to the gallery, above an embossed copper panel of a galleon in full sail and slatted panel, enclosed by solid sides forming the arms and enclosing hinged solid seat.

373.25in (186cm) high

$2,500-3,500   **L&T**

An Arts & Crafts mahogany hall settle, the rectangular slatted back with panel below, above slatted open arms and a solid hinged seat above paneled front on disc feet.

43.75in (111cm) wide

$350-450   **L&T**

An Arts & Crafts oak settle, the rectangular slatted back carved with flowering plants, above slatted open arms and hinged solid seat, the paneled front and sides on square supports and block feet.

43.75in (111cm) wide

$700-1,000   **L&T**

An Arts & Crafts oak hall settle, the rectangular back molded top above a pierced gallery carved with seed heads and twin panels of flowering foliage, the open arms above solid hinged seat.

51.5in (131cm) wide

$1,000-1,500   **L&T**

An Arts and Crafts oak settle, the tall paneled back with tapering supports and curved arms with shaped supports above solid seat with exposed pegs on stile supports.

73.25in (186cm wide)

$1,500-2,000   **L&T**

A Scottish school Arts and Crafts stained beech settle by Sir Robert Lorimer (1864-1929), the rectangular back carved with five roundels and bearing inscription "Blessit be simple life without end Reid", the supporting uprights with similar carving bearing initials "WWQ" and "EAJ", the rectangular solid seat raised on carved supports.

59.75in (152cm) wide

$700-1,000   **L&T**

An Arts and Crafts dark oak settle, retailed through Liberty & Co., the back has a broad top rail and plain back splats, flanking two panels with pierced heart motifs, a plain rectangular seat with molded front edge and curved arm rests.

74in (188cm) wide

$1,500-2,000   **DN**

An Arts & Crafts oak window seat, the twin dished solid seat enclosed by slatted open arms on square section supports linked by stretchers.

41.75in (106cm) wide

$1,800-2,200   **L&T**

A mahogany framed sofa, designed by E. A. Taylor (1874-1951) for Wylie and Lochhead, Glasgow, the slatted rectangular back with serpentine slatted arms, above a square cushioned seat raised on square tapering legs, with molded block feet.

71.75in (182cm) wide

$3,000-4,000   **L&T**

An Arts & Crafts white overpainted corner seat, the top rail with reeded molding above upholstered back and solid seat with loose squab cushion, flanked by a tongue and groove arm pierced with hearts to one end and to the other with vertically waved splats.

56in (142cm) high

$3,800-4,200   **L&T**

A small Arts & Crafts oak framed settee, the rectangular back with central upholstered panel and inlaid roundel, above open arms and upholstered seat on square tapering legs.

51.25in (130cm) wide

$300-400   **L&T**

An oak Arts and Crafts 'Thebes' stool, possibly English, with bowed and slatted footrest on turned legs joined by simple stretchers, original finish.

c1900   *16in (40.5cm) high*

$600-900   **FRE**

A Liberty & Co. oak 'Thebes' stool, the dished seat layer carved with a highlander with a foliate border, on three splayed legs.

15in (38cm) high

$120-180   **L&T**

A Liberty & Co mahogany 'Thebes' stool, the molded horseshoe shaped seat on square carved legs terminating in pointed pad feet.

14.5in (36.5cm) high

$700-1,000   **L&T**

One of a pair of Liberty & Co. mahogany 'Thebes' stools, each with a solid dished seat supported on three splayed legs.

13.75in (35cm) high

$500-700 (pair)   **DN**

An Arts and Crafts oak shelf stand, probably English, molded-edge top over four shelves, each with whiplash carving and wooden screws, the canted sides with similar screws and whiplash-carved base, original finish.

c1900   *36in (91.5cm) high*

$600-900   **FRE**

An Arts and Crafts oak etagere, the five square tiers on shaped feet, the sides carved with stylized flower-forms.

c1900   *43.5in (110.5cm) high*

$1,200-1,800   **SI**

An Arts and Crafts oak standing bookshelf, with three shelves and incorporating at the base a magazine or newspaper rack, the front pierced with a foliate motif, on fluted supports, the top side panels pierced with quatrefoils.

50.5in (128cm) high

$250-350   **DN**

An Arts & Crafts oak stick stand, by Wylie & Lochhead, Glasgow, the back with embossed copper panel of stylized flower heads, above divided frame for sticks, raised on square supports.

43in (109cm) high

$1,800-2,200   **L&T**

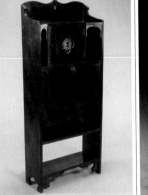

An Arts and Crafts dark oak bureau, probably retailed through Liberty & Co., with a simple curved and pierced top with a shelf, a cupboard below with quatrefoil glazed panel in door, flanked by alcoves, the drop front reveals pigeon-holes within and open shelving beneath.

61.5in (156cm) high

$150-200 DN

An Arts and Crafts oak bureau, the fall front enclosing a fitted interior, flanked by two lateral frieze drawers, raised on chamfered square legs.

c1900 *47in (119.5cm) high*

$700-1,000 SI

A Cotswold School teak cabinet on a stand, the plain top and sides having twin doors with carved bar pulls, having frieze drawers below and a shaped apron, raised on square supports united by stretchers.

49.5in (125.5cm) high

$100-150 DN

A Scottish-style Arts and Crafts mahogany and stained glass firescreen, by Shapland & Petter of Barnstaple, the central glazed panel with a detail of buds in marbled glass against a textured ground, with blue borders flanked by copper panels, each embossed with a heart and roundel with shaped rods above and an overhanging top.

39in (99cm) high

$1,500-2,000 DN

A Morris & Co. mahogany and embroidered fire-screen, the frame, upright stretcher and arched supports inlaid with boxed ebony stringing, the panel embroidered with the 'Rosebush' pattern in pale silks, stamped on the underside with "Morris & Co., 449 Oxford St." and numbered "1259".

41.5in (105cm) high

$900-1,100 DN

A pair of Arts and Crafts oak plant stands, each with a square top raised on stylized foliate arms above a small shelf, with an apron pierced with foliate motifs and supported on slender turned legs united by an undertier.

45.25in (115cm) high

$300-400 DN

An oak Arts and Crafts drop leaf dining table, the rectangular top above rectangular supports pierced with stylized plant forms and linked by square section stretchers.

40.5in (103cm) long

$600-1,000 L&T

An Arts & Crafts oak desk, refinished.

46in (117cm) wide

$1,800-2,200 FRE

An Arts and Crafts oak hall table, with rectangular top on square supports.

36.75in (93.5cm) long

$300-400 DN

A Liberty & Co. walnut and parcel gilt draw-leaf table, the rectangular top with a patera-carved edge, the frieze with ripple-molded borders, on turned legs carved with palmettes, stamped "Liberty".

125.25in (318cm) wide

$6,000-8,000 DN

An Arts and Crafts mahogany jardinière stand, the circular top with beaten copper insert above shaped apron on cabriole legs, linked by a brass stretcher, the whole raised on painted pad feet.

21.25in (54cm) high

$1,000-1,500   **L&T**

An Arts and Crafts oak occasional table, the circular top with red and green tiled insert above three tapered pierced supports linked by a platform stretcher.

24in (61cm) high

$450-550   **L&T**

A Scottish school Arts and Crafts oak stool, the circular concave seat carved with Celtic knotwork above four shaped supports, linked by a circular stretcher with similar carved panels.

12.25in (31cm) high

$180-220   **L&T**

An Arts and Crafts oak table, the circular molded top on four tapering supports with heart piercings linked by cross stretchers with exposed pegs.

26.5in (67cm) high

$700-1,000   **L&T**

An oak center table, by Sir Robert Lorimer (1864-1929) the paneled octagonal top with exposed peg joints and adzed surface, above a shaped frieze on wrythen column supports linked by pegged curved stretchers on shaped block feet.

33.75in (86cm) diam

$7,500-8,500   **L&T**

An Arts & Crafts oak hall table by Wylie & Lochhead, Glasgow, the concave back with open shelf and embossed copper panel depicting stylized flower heads, the sides with heart piercing above a serpentine top and single drawer.

45.75in (116cm) high

$1,800-2,200   **L&T**

An Arts and Crafts oak reading table, the narrow rectangular top with a hinged flap which can be propped to support a book, on tapering square supports, the sides united by stretchers and pierced panels.

27.25in (69.5cm) high

$220-280   **DN**

An oak Arts and Crafts standing lantern, after a design by Charles Rennie Macintosh, recent manufacture, with rectilinear stand and arm, having pierced square design suspending a lantern with slag glass panels and similarly pierced decoration, break to attachment.

64in high

$150-200   **FRE**

An Arts & Crafts oak marquetry screen, with mixed woods, silk and brass, wear to silk.

68in (172.5cm) high

$500-700   **FRE**

This design was exhibited at the Arts and Crafts Exhibition of 1893.

c1900

A mahogany framed upright piano for C. Bechstein, Walter Cave (fl. 1890s), fitted with decorative brass hinges, overstrung with frame no. "81119' above a keyboard of seven octaves.

40in (124.5cm) high

$3,000-4,000   **L&T**

One of a pair of Arts & Crafts oak single beds, attributed to W. R. Lethaby, each with spindle filled rectangular head and foot boards supported by square canted uprights.

Provenance: Melsetter House, Orkney. The majority of this house was built in 1898 by famous architect William Lethaby. It has one of the oldest gardens in Orkney.

37in (94cm) high

$1,500-2,000 (pair)   **L&T**

An Arts & Crafts oak wall mounted coat rack by Wylie & Lochhead, Glasgow, of rectangular outline with turned embossed copper panels depicting stylized flower-heads.

48in (122cm) wide

$1,000-1,500   **L&T**

An Arts & Crafts oak box, of rectangular form with hinged lid, carved to the sides in shallow relief with stylized entwined foliage.

12in (30.5cm) wide

$150-200   **L&T**

An Arts and Crafts penwork framed mirror, of shaped oval outline, the applied oval plate within penwork frame decorated with dragons.

37in (94cm) wide

$150-200   **L&T**

MOUSEMAN

Robert Thompson (1876-1955), of Kilburn, is often known as the 'Mouseman' as his work is signed with a carved figure of a mouse. Early in his career, Thompson carved a mouse into the large piece he was working on, as his companion talked of how he was as 'poor as a church mouse'. When he had finished, Thompson decided to keep the carving as part of the piece and established this feature as a trademark for his work. This tradition continued and each craftsman at his workshop developed their own personalised mouse with different features as their trademark.

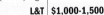

A 'Mouseman' oak side table, the rectangular top with rounded corners on octagonal end supports with splayed feet and a canted stretcher.

36.25in (92cm) wide

$1,200-1,800   **DN**

A 'Mouseman' oak sideboard from the workshops of Robert Thompson of Kilburn, Yorkshire, the rectangular top having an adzed surface, two short and three long drawers flanked by cupboards with paneled doors and wrought iron hinges, latches and drawer pulls, with paneled sides and back, with carved signature mouse on one edge.

60in (152cm) long

$9,000-11,000   **DN**

A 'Mouseman' oak nest of three small tables, with rectangular tops, all slightly adzed, on chamfered supports united by stretchers, each carved with a signature mouse.

Largest 15in (38cm) wide

$1,200-1,800   **DN**

A pair of 'Mouseman' oak stools, by Robert Thompson, each with kidney-shaped seats carved to the edge with a mouse, on tapered and faceted legs.

14.25in (36cm) high

$700-1,000   **L&T**

A 'Mouseman' oak refectory-type dining table, with rectangular top formed from three planks joined by dowels with an adzed surface, carved with a signature mouse on one leg.

72in (183cm) long

$6,000-8,000   **DN**

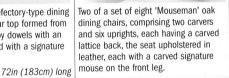

Two of a set of eight 'Mouseman' oak dining chairs, comprising two carvers and six uprights, each having a carved lattice back, the seat upholstered in leather, each with a carved signature mouse on the front leg.

$4,500-5,500 (set)   **DN**

Art Nouveau

An Art Nouveau mahogany wardrobe, attributed to James Salmon, the projecting molded cornice above a central mirror door flanked by paneled doors with decorative brass hinges, enclosed by fluted pilasters, raised on a plinth with square section shaped legs.

The architect and designer James Salmon (1873-1924) was a friend and direct contemporary of Charles Rennie Mackintosh. In common with other Glasgow designers at the time, Salmon's work emulates Mackintosh's, particularly with reference to his best known buildings in Glasgow, amongst them 142 St. Vincent Street (the "Hatrack"), and Lion Chambers in Hope Street. It is likely this influence extended to his design work as this wardrobe demonstrates, particularly with regard to the decorative hinges and the individuality of its design.

77in (196cm) wide

$2,500-3,500 **L&T**

A Glasgow School oak display cabinet, in the manner of E. A. Taylor for Wylie and Lochhead, Glasgow, the overhanging cornice above a central glazed door enclosing shelves, flanked by open shelves and doors, inlaid with marquetry panels of stylized rose trees, the whole raised on square section tapering legs with block feet.

59.75in (151.5cm) high

$3,000-4,000 **L&T**

An Art Nouveau stained mahogany and beech display cabinet, with arched mirror and open shelf supported by inlaid uprights, the molded top above inlaid frieze of fruits, highlighted with pokerwork above two stained and leaded glass doors enclosing shelves.

70in (178cm) high

$3,200-3,800 **L&T**

An Edwardian mahogany line-inlaid and satinwood display cabinet, with two central glazed cupboards, the doors decorated with leaded foliate motifs, flanked by shelves and cupboards, the doors of which are inlaid with urns and foliage.

80in (203cm) high

$1,000-1,500 **DN**

An Austrian Secessionist inlaid mahogany bedroom suite, probably Vienna, comprising an armoire, bed including headboard, footboard and rails, and two nightstands, all inlaid with exotic woods and mother-of-pearl, some losses and repairs, refinished.

c1900 *Armoire 70in (177.5cm) high*

$6,000-8,000 **FRE**

A late 19thC rosewood side cabinet, marquetry and boxwood strung, the back with a swan neck pediment, flanked by two panels inlaid with a roundel, ribbons and garrya (an American ornamental catkin).

60.25in (153cm) high

$700-1,000   **DN**

An early 20thC Art Nouveau walnut etagère vitrine, the dipped cavetto molded cornice over a sunken tapering panel opening to a shelf and with a similarly molded skirt, all with molded stiles terminating in scroll feet.

88in (223.5cm) high

$3,000-4,000   **SI**

A CLOSER LOOK AT A FRENCH ART NOUVEAU VITRINE

The use of elements from the natural world form the main source of inspiration in this period.

Sinuous floral designs are a recurring motif in Art Nouveau designs.

Additional floral decoration is produced by pyrography – the art of creating designs on wood using heated tools that burn away some of the surface.

Organically fashioned carving provides a naturalistic form to the piece.

A French Art Nouveau vitrine, with carved sunflower pediment surmounting an oak pyrography frieze and marble top, the mahogany case with organically carved strapwork and sides with oak pyrography floral decoration, twin glass doors, each with stylized floral decoration in wrought iron and enclosing a series of adjustable shelves.

c1900   *62in (157.5cm) high*

$5,000-6,000   **FRE**

A Liberty & Co. mahogany bureau, the top with turned finials, a gallery and a shelf, with curtains below in Morris and Co. 'Willow' pattern, having a drop front with leather writing surface and pigeon holes, an apron drawer with brass ring-pulls above an open shelf, recessed shelving also at the back.

52.25in (133cm) high

$1,500-2,000   **DN**

An Art Nouveau satin mahogany fall-front desk, the three-quarter serpentine gallery with tapered finials above open shelf and two drawers above a sloping fall, opening to reveal a fitted interior above further single drawer and twin doors.

4.5in (138.5cm) high

$1,500-2,000   **L&T**

A Charles Rennie Mackintosh stained pine cabinet, designed for Scotland Street School, Glasgow, the rectangular top with chamfered edge above one long and two short drawers, each with pierced crescent-shaped handles with brass backing, over three paneled doors, enclosing shelves on stile supports.

The School Board of Glasgow probably commissioned these cabinets from architects Honeyman Keppie Mackintosh in 1904. Six other cabinets of this type remain in situ at the school. The cabinets were presumably commissioned along with a dresser in the cookery room (which is built into the fabric of the building) as the paneling and handle detailing are matched. The School Board had strict regulations as to how many drawers and doors were required for cabinets, which were designed to hold classroom effects. The design of the cabinets reflect these stipulations. There are two sets of drawings for the school, dated 1903 and 1904, although neither shows details of the interior.

c1905   *61in (155cm) wide*

$4,500-5,500   **L&T**

An Art Nouveau mahogany writing desk, the back with pierced gallery enclosed by open shelves backed with embossed copper panels of stylized plant forms and an owl, above two short drawers, the top inset with skiver above two short drawers.

46.5in (118cm) high

$2,500-3,500   **L&T**

An Art Nouveau mahogany and inlaid cupboard, possibly by J. S. Henry, the cornice above a paneled door profusely inlaid with stylized plant forms and flanked by similarly inlaid panels.

82.75in (210cm) high

$2,200-2,800   **L&T**

An Art Nouveau Waddington & Sons mahogany cased upright piano, with over-strung iron frame No.480, above a keyboard of seven octaves.

58.25in (148cm) wide

$700-1,000   **L&T**

An Art Nouveau mahogany coal bin, the square molded top with shaped ledge back above hinged fall-front coal bin, the front with repoussé panel of stylized leaves and flower-heads.

28.25in (72cm) high

$150-200   **L&T**

A Wylie & Lochhead walnut bedroom suite, comprising a three-door wardrobe (pictured), the molded cornice above central mirrored door flanked by two doors inlaid with panels of stylized flower-heads and buds, the base with three drawers, a dressing table, with rectangular mirror flanked by pedestals with doors inlaid with panels of birds and flowers, also a pair of single beds comprising two head boards and two foot boards, and a bedroom chair.

$3,200-3,800 (suite)   **L&T**

A Wylie & Lochhead stained beech tub armchair, the double curved top rail with lozenge inlaid disc dividers and turned spindles above upholstered panel seat, raised on turned and tapering supports with finial terminals linked by stretchers.

$450-550   **L&T**

A Scottish Art Nouveau stained beech armchair, of cacateuse style, the tall and narrow rectangular back inlaid with stylized plant forms, above broad curving arms with horizontal slats, the upholstered panel seat on square tapering legs linked by stretchers.

$1,500-2,000   **L&T**

An Art Nouveau stained mahogany open armchair, the rectangular paneled back with horizontal waved splats and curved uprights above down-swept open arms and upholstered panel seat raised on turned tapered legs linked by stretchers.

$300-400   **L&T**

An Art Nouveau mahogany armchair, the rectangular back with upholstered pad, the top rail inlaid with stylized seed pods above horizontally slatted open arms and drop in seat on square section legs inlaid by stretchers.

$1,000-1,500   **L&T**

An Art Nouveau mahogany single armchair, by G. M. Ellwood, the back of tapering rectangular outline with oval upholstered panel, above open arms and upholstered panel seat on turned legs with tassle carved feet.

$900-1,100   **L&T**

An Art Nouveau mahogany armchair, English or Continental, upholstered crest, slat back and arm supports, carved arms, upholstered seat and bun feet.

c1900   *37in (94cm) high*

$450-550   **FRE**

A pair of Austrian oak side chairs, designed by Hans Ofner, each with pierced lozenge panel backs above rush seats on square section legs linked by stretchers.

c1910

$900-1,100   **L&T**

A pair of Art Nouveau mahogany side chairs, each with shaped top rails inlaid with leafy tendrils above central splat inlaid with mother of pearl and specimen woods and carved in the form of a stylized plant.

$220-280   **L&T**

A pair of Art Nouveau oak side chairs, the backs with curvilinear rails and tapering uprights above drop-in seats on square section tapering legs terminating in pad feet.

$450-550   **L&T**

A Marjorelle-style Art Nouveau desk, the raised back with an open shelf and two small drawers, the lower section with one frieze drawer, raised on openwork splayed legs ending in pointed pad feet.

43in (109cm) high

$6,000-8,000   **SI**

An Austrian ebonized table, in the Secessionist style, the top above four slatted supports with sphere spacers and X-panels, joined by molded cross stretchers on sphere feet.

36.25in (92cm) diam

$300-400   **L&T**

An ebonized Scottish School Art Nouveau hall stand, the arched rectangular mirror set in a shaped and pierced oval frame fitted with coat pegs above a shelf with glove drawer below and with shaped foliate upright supporting a stick stand with drip tray.

75.5in (192cm) high

$1,000-1,500   **L&T**

A Scottish School stained pine artist's work box, the rectangular top with twin hinged lid opening to reveal an interior fitted with compartments for materials.

30.75in (78cm) high

$700-1,000   **L&T**

A stained beech bijouterie table cabinet, by James Herbert MacNair (1868-1953), the square glazed hinged top flanked by sliding demi-lune glazed boxes for display, supported by pegs, the sides with arched glazed panels, the base velvet lined, the whole raised on square section tapering legs.

This cabinet, originally one of a pair, formed part of a scheme for a Writing Room for the Turin Exhibition of 1902. The room was designed jointly by Herbert MacNair and Frances MacNair as part of the Scottish Section of the exhibition under the directorship of Frances Newberry. Charles Rennie Mackinosh was chosen as overall architect to the project and his 'Rose Boudoir' ,which he designed with Margaret MacDonald Mackintosh, formed part of the exhibit. The enthusiastic reaction to the Scottish section at Turin is reflected in the report of the Studio Magazine of July that year where the MacNairs' and Mackintoshes' schemes are illustrated and described in lavish detail. The reviewer writes "...utmost credit is due to the McNairs for this object lesson, showing in what manner the necessities and beauties of life can be brought together in one harmonious whole."

c1901   *30.35in (77cm) high*

$12,000-15,000   **L&T**

An Austrian bentwood hall-stand, attributed to Thonet, the open framework having curved coat and hat hooks at the top, a rectangular space for a mirror, now missing, above a shelf.

74.75in (190cm) high

$300-400   **DN**

An Austrian small bentwood table, with rounded square top on splayed supports united by two undertiers with wooden balls at the joints.

29.5in (75cm) high

$150-200   **DN**

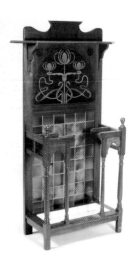

An English Art Nouveau mahogany inlaid and tiled hall stand, possibly retailed through Liberty & Co., the panel inlaid with stylized plants and sinuous stems in colored woods, the back panel below inset with green and olive tiles.

c1890   *50.5in (128cm) high*

$1,000-1,500   **DN**

A Thonet small circular-topped table with two undertiers, on splayed supports, bearing original retail paper label.

29.5in (75cm) high

$150-200   **DN**

A Caplans Art Deco mahogany bedroom suite, with mahogany cases and burlwood veneer, a full-size bed with footboard and attached nightstands, a vanity with mirror, a small armoire, another armoire in two parts, with celluloid label.

c1930

$300-400

Headboard 85in (216cm) wide

FRE

An Art Deco coromandel veneered twin door wardrobe, by Whytock and Reid, Edinburgh, raised on red overpainted and shaped bracket feet.

71.75in (182cm) high

$450-550   L&T

A John Widdicomb Art Deco commode, with a geometrically inlaid top above a single long drawer with stylized inlay, above twin inlaid and figured panel doors enclosing three drawers, on an inlaid frieze upon tapered reeded legs, label to drawer.

44in (111.5cm) wide

$1,500-2,000   FRE

An Art Deco burlwood chest, probably English, cabinet section over three drawers.

c1930   *46.75in (118.5cm) high*

$220-280   FRE

An Art Deco mahogany server and buffet, the server (shown) with carved and arched mirror above a marble top, two cabinet doors either side of glazed door, the matching buffet identical except for the central section which has a drawer above a cabinet door.

c1930   *Server 78in (198cm) wide*

$600-900 (set)   FRE

A CLOSER LOOK AT AN ART DECO COCKTAIL CABINET

A mirrored display shelf with a light. Many cabinets open to show an illuminated interior, the action of the door raising internal fixtures containing glasses and accessories.

Cocktail cabinets are emblematic of the jazz age.

The pale wood is a classic feature of Art Deco furniture.

The design is simple and angular giving a clean form.

An Italian Art Deco bar cabinet, in burlwood and painted wood, chromium, some losses and repairs.

54in (137cm) wide

$300-400   FRE

A Continental Art Deco bar cabinet, in mahogany, nickeled brass, steel, marble and glass, lacks shelves.

A Continental Art Deco bar, in olivewood, mahogany, glass and metal, water stain to top.

23.5in (59.5cm) wide

$600-900   FRE

48in (122cm) wide

$300-400   FRE

A teak sideboard by Russell of Broadway, the rectangular top above twin doors, with raised decoration enclosing a fitted interior, raised on square section legs, bears label.

c1950   *47.75in (121.5cm) wide*

$700-1,000   **L&T**

An Art Deco coromandel veneered side cabinet, by Whytock and Reid, Edinburgh, the stepped top above a central drawer with two doors below and with two doors at the sides, each with red overpainted handles and raised on bracket feet.

55in (140cm) wide

$450-550   **L&T**

An Art Deco inlaid mahogany buffet, the case with molded edge of darker wood, bowed in the middle above a floral inlaid panel, flanked by two sets of cabinet doors with line inlay, all on square tapered legs.

91in (231cm) wide

$600-900   **FRE**

An Italian Art Deco burlwood buffet, with mirror and asymmetrical shelf structure on a case with four small drawers and twin cabinet door enclosing an adjustable shelf.

70in (177.5cm) wide

$1,800-2,200   **FRE**

A Continental Art Deco burled maple console, with nickeled brass rattan, added knobs.

47in (119.5cm) wide

$500-700   **FRE**

A Scottish Art Deco coromandel wood box, of rectangular form, the hinged lid above plain sides on a plinth with block feet, stamped mark to base "R & J Price makers, Scotland, 1925".

12.25in (31cm) wide

$220-280   **L&T**

An Art Deco burr maple desk, the rectangular top above a simple frieze drawer flanked by a single pedestal of one drawer and one cupboard enclosing a shelf, each with ebonized burr handles, the whole raised on ebonized plinths.

38in (96.5cm) wide

$1,200-1,800   **L&T**

An Art Deco walnut veneered display cabinet, of circular form with twin glazed doors enclosing a glazed shelf raised on a paneled base.

73.5in (187cm) high

$700-1,000   **L&T**

An Art Deco inlaid walnut display cabinet 'Gaylayde', designed by Ritcher for the Bath Cabinetmakers, the frame inlaid with mother-of-pearl plaques, a frieze drawer veneered with ebony plaques, the single door inlaid in colored woods and mother-of-pearl with a floral frieze, framed with inlaid leaf motifs, on block feet.

68.5in (174cm) high

$900-1,100   **DN**

An Art Deco oak and ash veneered open bookcase, by Whytock and Reid, Edinburgh, the rectangular top over two drawers and an arrangement of open shelves, the sides inlaid with marquetry roundels depicting entwined fish.

48.5in (123cm) wide

$500-700   **L&T**

An Eavestaff Art Deco "Minipiano", with ebonized case, the iron frame above a keyboard of six octaves, the case with chrome fittings, also a matching stool.

Piano 50.75in (129cm) wide

$450-550   **L&T**

A Lloyd Art Deco chrome sofa, tubular chrome frame, black painted wood arms and brown leatherette cushions, labeled, wear to arms, two small tears to cushions.

64in (162.5cm) wide

$600-900   **FRE**

An Art Deco burlwood Cloud three-piece parlour suite, including a couch and two armchairs, each with bentwood shell and cream leather upholstery.

Chair 32.5in (82.5cm) high

$3,000-4,000   **FRE**

An Art Deco oak veneered tub chair, of curved form with upholstered back and loose cushioned seat, the curved back and arms veneered to the base, and another slightly taller chair similar.

$600-900   **L&T**

A Continental Art Deco upholstered walnut easy chair, with broad curved arm rests, each on three vertical fluted rods, with molded sled-like block feet.

$450-550   **DN**

From left to right:
One of three Heals Arts and Crafts oak lattice-back upright chairs, each having a drop-in rush seat, raised on square supports united by stretchers.

$320-380 (set)   **DN**

An Art Deco satinwood upright chair, with carved top rail and angled uprights, enclosing four carved and fanned splats united by a central semi-circular splat.

$220-280   **DN**

One of a pair of Cotswold School walnut upright chairs, with chamfered top rail and central horizontal splat united by spindles and slightly tapered uprights.

$450-550 (pair)   **DN**

Two of a set of four Dynamique Art Deco dining chairs, designed by David Robertson for Johnson Furniture Co., each with mahogany frame, upholstered seat and back, stepped front legs, blue "DYNAMIQUE CREATIONS" label, wear to original finish.

c1930   *32in (81.5cm) high*

$320-380 (set)   **FRE**

An Art Deco console table, with maple top and molded mahogany edge, single drawer, U-form supports and stretcher beneath.

37in (94cm) wide

$700-1,000   **FRE**

An Art Deco inlaid mahogany console table, rectangular top with reeded ends and inlaid panels.

42in (106.5cm) wide

$1,000-1,500   **FRE**

A mahogany center table designed by Betty Joel, the canted rectangular top with stepped edge above a single drawer of fluted rectangular section supports with fluted trestle ends, bears label, "Token Hand Made Furniture, designed by Betty Joel, made by N.R. Hamilton at Token Works Portsmouth 1929".

48.25in (122.5cm) wide

$600-900   **L&T**

A Lloyd Art Deco chrome stand, continuous tubular chrome base with ebonized wood surface, paper tag.

30.25in (76.5cm) high

$220-280   **FRE**

A 1930s mirrored occasional table, the twelve-sided top on square legs.

20in (51cm) wide

$300-400   **L&T**

An Art Deco mahogany dining table and chairs, the table with simple rectangular top with pullout extensions on a pedestal base with two C-supports, with two of eight chairs with solid backs and upholstered seats.

Table 61.5in (156cm) wide

$3,000-4,000 (set)   **FRE**

A 1950s novelty cocktail cabinet, in the form of an iron safe, the interior fitted with fridge and shelves.

57.5in (146cm) high

$900-1,100   **L&T**

An Art Deco lacquered mirror, by Whytock and Reid, Edinburgh.

39.75in (101cm) high

$450-550   **L&T**

An Art Deco tubular chrome and glass double cheval mirror, possibly by Pel, the rounded upright rectangular frame held between two columns with nulled-edge locking nuts, the base of openwork, almost square shape.

69.5in (176.5cm) high

$500-700   **DN**

An Art Deco wrought-iron stick stand, fashioned in the manner of Edgar Brandt, formed as three openwork towers of square section, with scrollwork embellishment, the center and taller tower capped with a plaque of marble, painted in silver tones.

26.5in (67cm) high

$450-550   **DN**

A CLOSER LOOK AT THE ART DECO STYLE

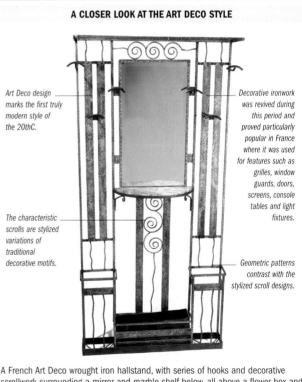

Art Deco design marks the first truly modern style of the 20thC.

Decorative ironwork was revived during this period and proved particularly popular in France where it was used for features such as grilles, window guards, doors, screens, console tables and light fixtures.

The characteristic scrolls are stylized variations of traditional decorative motifs.

Geometric patterns contrast with the stylized scroll designs.

A French Art Deco wrought iron hallstand, with series of hooks and decorative scrollwork surrounding a mirror and marble shelf below, all above a flower box and umbrella stands, break to rod on top shelf.

73in (185.5cm) high

$1,500-2,000   **FRE**

Marble

An early 19thC French marble and alabaster bust of a young woman, wearing a scarf, signed "A. Aurili".

10in (25cm) high

$380-420　　　　**L&T**

A marble bust of a young boy, signed and inscribed "W. Tweed F. co Roma 1831", raised on a socle plinth.

19in (48cm) high

$1,800-2,200　　　　**L&T**

A 19thC marble figure group, by Professor G. Lazzerini, depicting a pair of young lovers, on a rocaille work base.

40in (103cm) high

$15,000-20,000　　　　**L&T**

A 19thC marble figure of a 'Bacchus', on a turned mahogany column with a square marble plinth.

42.5in (108cm) high

$6,000-8,000　　　　**L&T**

A 19thC alabaster sculpture of a shepherdess, depicted standing with three sheep, restorations.

31in (78.5cm) high

$1,500-2,000　　　　**SI**

A 19thC marble sculpture of a girl, depicted testing the water with her toe, together with a marble pedestal.

Sculpture 23.5in (60cm) high

$1,200-1,800　　　　**SI**

A 19thC marble sculpture of a Classical nude, reclining on a lion's pelt, on a gray marble plinth, signed "Jalconet".

$1,200-1,800　　　　**SI**

A late 19thC Continental white marble figure of a classical maiden, in draped robes, on a gray marble base.

26in (66cm) high

$1,500-2,000　　　　**FRE**

A late 19thC Continental marble bust of a young girl, shown wearing a hat, with restorations and some damage.

17.5in (44.5cm) high

$600-900　　　　**FRE**

A late 19thC Victorian white marble bust of a young girl and dove, on a white marble socle, damage to bust.

24in (61cm) high

$450-550　　　　**FRE**

An Art Nouveau marble sculpture of a maiden, depicted standing in a swirling gown, losses.

c1900　　　32in (81.5cm) high

$1,800-2,200　　　　**SI**

An Art Nouveau white marble figure, of a naked maiden, with diaphanous robes, standing on a square base.

19in (48cm) high

$1,200-1,800　　　　**L&T**

An early 20thC Italian mixed marble bust of 'Beatrice', signed "Prof. G. Besli/Made in Italy".

12in (30.5cm) high

$900-1,100　　　　**SI**

An Art Deco white marble figure of a 'Pierrot', depicted playing a mandolin.

24in (61cm) high

$1,500-2,000　　　　**SI**

A marble figure of 'Phryne', by Paul Campagne, signed and inscribed "Campagne (Sculpteur) Phryne".

33.75in (86cm) high

$6,000-8,000　　　　**L&T**

A carved ivory and pink marble female figure, attributed to Maurice Bouraine, the figure with a mandolin hanging by her side.

8in (20cm) high

$450-550　　　　**DN**

Miscellaneous

A Morris & Co. embroidered panel, printed in the 'Honeysuckle' pattern and woven in colored wools, printed maker's mark to the selvedge "Morris & Co., 26 Queen Square, Bloomsbury".

59in (150cm) wide

$700-1,000 L&T

A pair of Arts & Crafts wool hangings, woven with colored threads in a repeating pattern of flowering rose branches on a puckered unbleached ground, also a further piece of the same fabric.

96.75in (246cm) high

$450-550 L&T

A pair of Morris & Co. 'Strawberry Thief' pattern printed cotton curtains.

112.5in (286cm) high

$300-400 L&T

Two Arts & Crafts-style wool throw rugs, each with stylized oak leaf decoration on buff ground.

Larger 69in (175.5cm) long

$250-350 FRE

A Scottish Arts & Crafts table runner, in the manner of Ann McBeth, of rectangular form worked in colored wools with geometric plant form and checker design on an unbleached hessian ground.

56in (142cm) long

$500-700 L&T

Maxwell Ashby Armfield R.W.S. (1881-1972), 'The Minstrel, a little Dance - Play composed by Maxwell Armfield', ink, watercolor and bodycolor, initialled with monogram in pencil and dated.

1916 *12in (30cm) wide*

$500-700 L&T

Alphonse Maria Mucha, Czech (1860-1939), "Zodiac, La Plume", a color lithograph, sheet size.

c1896 *25.5in (64.75cm) long*

$4,500-5,500 SI

An Alphonse Mucha 'Biscuits Lefevre-Utile' colored lithographic calendar, published F. Champenois, Paris.

c1897 *23.5in (60cm) high*

$4,500-5,500 L&T

A René Lalique original design for a necklace, pencil, ink and watercolor on B.H.K. Rives parchment paper.

11in (28cm) wide

$2,000-3,000 DRA

An Art Nouveau oak frame, of shaped outline, carved in base relief with lilies and fruiting berries amongst whiplash foliage.

41.75in (106cm) high

$800-1,200 L&T

A pair of Arts & Crafts carved walnut plaques by Samuel Goldberg, Philadelphia, carved "S. G. 1936".

Samuel Goldberg was a master draftsman in Samuel Yellin's metalworking studio.

1936 *10in (25.5cm) diam*

$450-550 FRE

A Robert Thompson of Kilburn 'Mouseman' oak cheeseboard, of oval shape with a curved handle at one end and carved in relief with a mouse.

14.5in (36.5cm) long

$350-450 DN

A 1930s carved hardwood brooch, depicting the head and shoulders of a woman with flowing hair and large hoop earrings, initialled verso "NF".

c1930 *3.25in (8cm) long*

$150-200 L&T

An unusual ivory stained as tortoiseshell Art Deco lady's box, with engraved Oriental motif, diamond set band and clip.

$2,000-3,000 NBlm

Modern Furniture

An Alvar Aalto 'Model 37' lounge chair, produced by Artek, Finland, designed 1935-36 with broad cantilevered birch arms, the seat upholstered in a putty fabric.

34in (86cm) wide

$2,000-2,500   **FRE**

A pair of Alvar Aalto bent plywood fan leg stools with circular oak veneer top, crackling to varnish on tops, unmarked.

15.25in (39cm) wide

$600-900   **DRA**

A pair of Alvar Aalto bentwood children's chairs, each with squared back and red-enameled plank seat, wear to red paint on seats, and wear to edges, stamped "Aalto Design/Made in Sweden".

25.5in (65cm) high

$550-750   **DRA**

An Alvar Aalto 'Paimio No. 4' chair, designed 1931/1932, manufactured by Artek, laminated birch frame with white lacquered plywood seat.

$900-1,200   **BonE**

An Alvar Aalto 'Model No. 406' chair, designed 1938/1939, manufactured by Artek, laminated birch cantilever frame with black webbed seat.

$225-275   **BonE**

An Alvar Aalto 'Model No. 45' chair, designed 1947, manufactured by Artek, laminated birch frame with woven cane back and seat.

$90-120   **BonE**

A Le Corbusier 'LC2' sofa, produced by Cassina, Italy, polished chromed steel frame with Cassina burgundy leather cushions, Cassina tag.

66in (167.5cm) wide

$2,000-3,000   **FRE**

Left: A Le Corbusier 'LC2' club chair, produced by Cassina, in chromium, leather and nylon, with etched Cassina mark, LC2 and serial number.

30in (76cm) wide

$2,000-2,500   **FRE**

Right: A Le Corbusier 'LC2' club chair, produced by Cassina, in chromium, leather, and nylon, stamped Cassina mark, LC2, serial number and Corbusier's signature.

30in (76cm) wide

$2,000-2,500   **FRE**

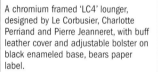

A chromium framed 'LC4' lounger, designed by Le Corbusier, Charlotte Perriand and Pierre Jeanneret, with buff leather cover and adjustable bolster on black enameled base, bears paper label.

65.5in (166cm) long

$1,500-2,000   **L&T**

A Le Corbusier 'LC5' canape, produced by Cassina, Italy, designed 1935, with tubular nickel-plated steel back and legs on a rectangular steel frame woven with Pirelli rubber, Cassina stamp with number 91, lacking cushions.

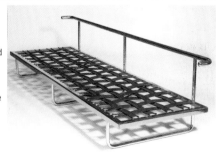

This daybed was designed for Le Corbusier's home in Rue Nungesser et Coli, Paris and first produced by Cassina in 1974 as a very limited edition, of which this was number 91. The current Cassina production is in a smaller scale.

101in (256.5cm) wide

$3,500-5,000   **FRE**

A pair of Le Corbusier 'Basculant' armchairs, tubular chrome frame, taupe leather, spring fasteners, black leather arms, signed "Le Corbusier/LCM 989 and 975" with "Made In Italy" label.

25in (63.5cm) high

$1,200-1,800   **DRA**

A Charles Eames for Herman Miller fibreglass shell armrocker, in chocolate brown, on zinc cat's cradle base with birch runners, embossed mark and paper label.

24.5in (62cm) wide

$1,000-1,300   **DRA**

An Eames fibreglass shell desk chair, produced by Herman Miller, with yellow shell on an aluminum base with casters, molded mark.

32in (81cm) high

$180-220   **FRE**

An Eames desk chair, manufactured by Herman Miller, USA, in aluminum, steel and vinyl.

32in (81.5cm) high

$300-400   **FRE**

Two of a set of six Charles Eames designed molded plywood chairs, the undersides with silvered labels "Evans Products Co.".

$3,500-4,500 (set)   **SI**

A set of six 'DSR' chairs designed by Charles Eames, for Vitra, the molded yellow fibreglass shell raised on chromium plated cross framed supports, bears makers labels.

$300-400 (set)   **L&T**

An Eames dowel-leg swivelling barstool, enameled steel, vinyl and maple, with cloth label, new production base.

44.5in (113cm) high

$200-300   **FRE**

An early Charles Eames for Zenith yellow fibreglass shell armchair, with rope edge and X-leg base, some discolouration to shell and pitting to metal, Zenith label.

29.5in (75cm) high

$150-200   **DRA**

A Charles and Ray Eames 'Aluminum Group' chair, designed 1958, manufactured by Herman Miller, aluminum swivel frame with four prong base with piped fabric upholstery.

$600-800   **BonE**

Two of four Eames 'Aluminum Group' office chairs, manufactured by Herman Miller, USA, in leather, aluminum, steel and plastic, with labels, 1992 production date.

31.5in (80cm) high

$3,500-4,500 (set)   **FRE**

An Eames 670 lounge chair and 671 ottoman, manufactured by Herman Miller, USA, rosewood, aluminum, leather and down, labelled, minor wear.

$3,000-4,000   **FRE**

A Charles Eames for Herman Miller 'Aluminum Group' armchair with original channelled fabric in purple, on swivelling base, die-stamped mark.

34in (86.5cm) high

$400-600　　　　　　　　**DRA**

A pair of Charles Eames for Herman Miller 'Time-Life' armchairs, with tufted seat and back re-upholstered in green polyester, on polished aluminum frame and swivel base, minor stains to upholstery, Herman Miller tags.

30in (76cm) high

$600-900　　　　　　　　**DRA**

A Charles Eames for Herman Miller plywood 'LCW' chair, with red aniline-dye finish, Herman Miller foil label.

26in (66cm) high

$700-900　　　　　　　　**DRA**

A Charles Eames rosewood conference table, produced by Herman Miller, large ovoid top with rosewood laminate and plastic edge on a cast aluminum base, circular metal tag.

95in (241cm) wide

$700-900　　　　　　　　**FRE**

A Charles Eames for Herman Miller 'CTW' table, with molded ash plywood circular tray top on bent plywood legs, original finish and some scratches to top and chips to legs, unmarked.

34in (86.5cm) wide

$800-1,000　　　　　　　　**DRA**

A Charles Eames for Herman Miller 'Aluminum Group' cafe table, with circular white and grey marble top, on pedestal base with black enameled shaft and white plastic feet, black Herman Miller tag.

36in (91.5cm) diam

$400-600　　　　　　　　**DRA**

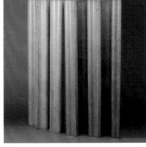

Two Charles Eames for Herman Miller folding plywood screens, one five-panel and one four (was originally one screen), unmarked, each section including fabric.

68in (172.5cm) high

$2,500-3,000　　　　　　　　**DRA**

Two of a set of six Paul Frankl mahogany dining chairs, produced by Johnson Furniture Co., USA, two armchairs and four side chairs, with mahogany legs, arms and upholstered seats and backs.

31in (33.5cm) high

$1,000-1,400 (set)　　　　　　　　**FRE**

A Paul Frankl extension dining table, produced by Johnson Furniture Co., USA, with rectangular gesso top having bowed edges and two 12in (30.5cm) leaves on twin mahogany supports, bowed with V-pattern slats.

29in (73.5cm) high

$2,000-2,500　　　　　　　　**FRE**

A Paul Frankl coffee table, produced by Johnson Furniture Co., biomorphic top in cork on four splayed mahogany legs.

14in (35.5cm) high

$1,000-1,500　　　　　　　　**FRE**

A Paul Frankl cocktail table with circular laminated cork top on four square cut-out legs, stenciled number.

48in (122cm) diam

$1,500-2,000　　　　　　　　**DRA**

A Paul Frankl side table, with cork veneer triangular top over oblong mahogany veneer lower shelf and four tapered legs, non original buff paint to top, and new finish to base, stenciled number.

25in (63.5cm) high

$500-700　　　　　　　　**DRA**

A Paul Frankl mahogany china closet, produced by Johnson Furniture Co., USA, the top with gesso frame surrounding an open space of three glass shelves, the lower case with gesso top on a series of six drawers and two doors with brass hardware, crazing to gesso, base only shown.

48in (122cm) wide

$1,100-1,400   **FRE**

A Paul Frankl china cabinet with limed slate grey base with three ivory doors with semi-circular brass pulls, topped by a china cabinet in limed ivory finish with two sliding glass doors, unmarked.

72in (183cm) wide

$700-1,000   **DRA**

A Norman Bel Geddes for Simmons two-tone enameled metal dresser in pink and beige with four graduated drawers and chrome button pulls with recessed circular back plates, Simmons decal.

41in 104cm) high

$600-900   **DRA**

A Norman Bel Geddes for Simmons black-lacquered metal bedroom suite, comprising double-bed, pair of single drawer nightstands, dressing table with rectangular wall mirror, and chrome stool, with horizontal chrome pulls, Simmons tags and paper labels, with stenciled numbers.

Dressing table: 44in (112cm) wide

$1,200-1,600 (set)   **DRA**

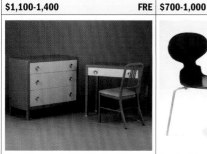

Three Norman Bel Geddes for Simmons enameled metal pieces in rose, comprising a three-drawer chest and single drawer desk with light grey drawer fronts and chrome cupcake pulls, accompanied by a desk chair, minor scratches, chipping, and discolouration to enamel, two marked.

Chest 38.5in (98cm) wide

$800-1,200   **DRA**

A pair of Arne Jacobsen 'Ant' chairs, produced by Fritz Hansen, Denmark, each of molded plywood in black finish on three steel legs, "FH" circle mark, legs with spotting and missing rubber glides.

30in (76cm) high

$400-600   **FRE**

One of a set of three Arne Jacobsen 'Ant' chairs, designed 1952 and a '3107' chair designed 1955, manufactured by Fritz Hansen, one piece lacquered plywood back and seat on tubular supports.

$450-650 (set)   **BonE**

Two of a set of four Arne Jacobsen armchairs, for Fritz Hansen, each with curved black enameled crest rail on chromed steel frame, and circular seat pad upholstered in original black and chartreuse fabric, Fritz Hansen factory tags.

1964   *27.25in (69cm) high*

$1,500-2,500 (set)   **DRA**

An Arne Jacobsen 'Oxford' chair, designed 1965, manufactured by Fritz Hansen, black upholstered plywood back and seat on swivel aluminum base.

$750-1,000   **BonE**

An Arne Jacobsen for Fritz Hansen 'Swan' sofa, upholstered in original taupe wool fabric, on a cast aluminum base, some minor petrification to foam, unmarked.

57in (145cm) wide

$3,000-4,500   **DRA**

An Arne Jacobsen for Fritz Hansen settee, brown leather upholstery on a tubular frame, unmarked.

49in (124cm) wide

$2,000-2,500   **DRA**

An Arne Jacobsen 'Egg' table, manufactured by Fritz Hansen.

45in (114cm) wide

$600-800   **BonE**

A pair of Florence Knoll lounge chairs, each of square form upholstered in silvery blue leather on a chromed steel base.

31in (78.5cm) high

$2,500-3,000   **FRE**

A Florence Knoll sofa, produced by Knoll Associates, rectilinear orange velour upholstered frame with loose cushions on six tapered wood dowel legs, some discolouration to fabric.

90in (228.5cm) wide

$1,200-1,800   **FRE**

FLORENCE KNOLL

Florence Knoll (born 1917) married Hans Knoll (1914-1955) in 1946 and in the same year they formed the company Knoll Associates. Their focus was to provide modern design products that "represented design excellence, technological innovation and mass production". Essential to the success of the company was their policy of crediting and paying royalties to individual designers. This created strong, long lasting working relationships with designers such as Harry Bertoia, Eero Saarinen and Mies Van Der Rohe.

A pair of Florence Knoll for Knoll dressers, each with woodgrain laminate top and three louvre-front drawers, on tubular black metal legs, normal wear, unmarked.

36in (91.5cm) high

$1,500-2,000   **DRA**

A Florence Knoll for Knoll square occasional table, with reddish-brown marble top on angular bright chrome base, Knoll International label.

27in (68.5cm) wide

$500-700   **DRA**

A Florence Knoll for Knoll L-shaped desk, with rectangular woodgrain laminate top, three blind drawers, and cabinet with three pull-out cubbied shelves, on angular black metal frame, unmarked.

66in (167.5cm) wide

$1,000-1,500   **DRA**

A Frank Gehry 'Powerplay' chair, designed 1990/1992, manufactured by Knoll International, laminated plywood construction.

Frank Gehry (born 1929) has established himself as one of the foremost contemporary architects in America and across the world. The acclaim for his buildings, such as the Guggenheim Museum in Bilbao, Spain, and Maggie's Center in Dundee, Scotland, have meant that his furniture is sometimes overlooked. From the 1960s he has pioneered affordable, environmentally responsible furniture. The 'Easy Edges' and the 'Beaver' series were produced using corrugated cardboard. In the 1980s he designed the 'Bentwood' series for Knoll that utilises the wood used to make crates for shipping vegetables. Each piece is named after an ice hockey move, like 'Powerplay' and 'Cross Check'.

$450-550   **BonE**

A rare Pierre Jeanneret for Knoll end table, with white formica top and metal frame, single black fibreglass drawer, wooden sides, back and bottom, unmarked.

18.25in (44cm) wide

$1,400-1,800   **DRA**

A rare Isamu Noguchi (1904-1988) for Knoll teak rocking stool, with chrome-plated wire shaft, some minor pitting to metal, unmarked.

11.5in (29.5cm) high

$10,000-14,000   **DRA**

An Isamu Noguchi for Knoll 'Cyclone' dining table, with circular white laminate top, chrome-plated steel wire column and black enameled cast-iron base, Knoll Associates label.

48in (122cm) diam

$1,500-2,000   **DRA**

A large Richard Knoll work/drafting table with grey laminate top, fuschia laminated top, five fuschia enameled drawers, and blue and red enameled metal base with disc feet, unmarked.

78.25in (199cm) wide

$600-800   **DRA**

A pair of Warren Platner chromium framed armchairs, designed for Knoll International, each of tub form with white leather padded back and arms with mesh support and loose white leather cushion on a tapering mesh support.

These were removed from Brian Drumm hairdressers, George Street, Edinburgh.

c1966

$350-450   **L&T**

A Tobia Scarpa Bastiano sofa, made in Italy for Knoll, hand-woven German wool cushions in a rosewood frame.

83in (211cm) wide

$800-1,000 **FRE**

A William Stephens for Knoll lounge chair, with bent oak frame and hidden fibreglass shell.

28in (71cm) high

$350-450 **FRE**

A Richard Schultz for Knoll 'Petal' side table, with white enameled eight section top on pedestal base, with Knoll Associates label.

This piece was in original pristine condition.

19in (48.5cm) high

$4,000-5,000 **DRA**

Two of a set of eight William Stephens for Knoll dining chairs, each with bent oak frame and upholstered turquoise vinyl seat, needs re-upholstering, Knoll International labels.

Born in Media, Pennsylvania, Stephens was a graduate of the Philadelphia College of Art where he majored in industrial design. He worked as co-director of Knoll's design Development Group when he designed these chairs.

31in (78.5cm) high

$350-450 (set) **FRE**

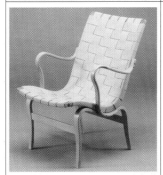

A Bruno Mathsson for Dux 'Eva' bentwood armchair, with oatmeal-coloured webbed seat support, signed "Bruno Mathsson for Dux".

32in (81cm) high

$600-800 **DRA**

A Bruno Mathsson 'Eva' chair, designed 1934, manufactured by Dux, bent plywood and birch frame with hemp webbing and detachable headrest.

$300-400 **BonE**

A Bruno Mathsson for Dux 'Pernilla' lounge chair and ottoman, each with bentwood frame upholstered in tufted beige canvas, the chair also having beige vinyl head and armrest, signed "Bruno Mathsson".

Chair 26in (66cm) wide

$1,000-1,400 **DRA**

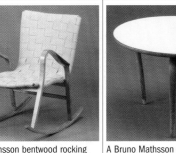

A Bruno Mathsson bentwood rocking chair, with oatmeal-coloured webbed seat support, stamped mark.

31.5in (80cm) high

$1,000-1,500 **DRA**

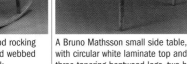

A Bruno Mathsson small side table, with circular white laminate top and three tapering bentwood legs, two have re-glued breaks, unmarked.

17.5in (44.5cm) diam

$2,500-3,000 **DRA**

A set of seven Paul McCobb dining chairs, manufactured by Calvin Furniture, USA, in walnut, includes two arm chairs, cloth tags.

35in (89cm) high

$300-500 (set) **FRE**

A set of eight Paul McCobb Planner Group dining chairs, cherry-finish wood, with labels.

30in (76cm) high

$500-700 **FRE**

MODERN CLASSICS

A Paul McCobb for Calvin coffee table, rectangular birch top with three drawers on brass legs joined by brass stretchers, metal tag.

66in (167.5cm) wide

$800-1,000   **FRE**

A Paul McCobb Planner Group drop-leaf table, blond finish wood, with early decal, water rings to top.

36in (91.5cm) wide

$300-500   **FRE**

A Paul McCobb sideboard, manufactured by Calvin Furniture, USA, in walnut, oak and aluminum, with metal tag.

66in (167.5cm) wide

$500-800   **FRE**

A Paul McCobb Planner Group chest of drawers, blond finish wood and metal, with label.

36in (91.5cm) wide

$300-400   **FRE**

A Paul McCobb Planner Group wide chest of drawers, blond finish wood and brass, with label to drawer.

60in (152.5cm) wide

$700-900   **FRE**

A Paul McCobb Planner Group desk, blond finish wood and brass, label to drawer, some wear.

53in (134.5cm) wide

$400-600   **FRE**

A Paul McCobb Planner Group desk, maple, cherrywood, brass, with branded mark, wear to top, together with a desk chair, wear.

29.5in (75cm) high

$350-450   **FRE**

A Paul McCobb console, manufactured by Calvin Furniture, USA, in walnut, aluminum and glass, with a metal tag.

64in (162.5cm) high

$350-550   **FRE**

A James Mont designed two-door cabinet with black lacquered case, patchwork wood veneer door front with large circular brass pulls, and two adjustable interior shelves, signed "James Mont Design".

40in (101.5cm) wide

$2,500-3,500   **DRA**

An unusual and early James Mont tiger maple chest, four drawers with cylindrical brass pulls, on flaring legs, a few small veneer chips, stamped "James Mont Design".

48in (122cm) wide

$1,500-2,000   **DRA**

A James Mont three drawer nightstand, in tiger maple veneer with cylindrical brass pulls, minor chips to veneer and edges, wear to finish on tops, stamped "James Mont Design".

24in (61cm) high

$400-600   **DRA**

A pair of lounge chairs attributed to James Mont, each fully upholstered in white leather with cut-out back and tufted trim, on wooden legs, each has minor slit to upholstery near back, unmarked.

31in (79cm) high

$4,000-5,000   **DRA**

A James Mont chaise longue with pickled oak veneer platform frame, upholstered in green velvet with loose seat cushions and single pillow, marked "James Mont Design".

112in (284cm) long

$5,000-6,000   **DRA**

A James Mont pickled oak-veneer twin pedestal desk, with seven drawers and kidney-shaped top, the back and sides inset with silver and green striped vinyl, on brass legs, some wear to finish, and veneer loss, marked "James Mont Design".

65in (165cm) wide

$1,000-1,200   **DRA**

A James Mont pickled oak-veneer vanity table, with raised plate glass top, four drawers and single cabinet door with circular pulls, glass glued down, with some minor chips, and some veneer loss, branded "James Mont Design".

46in (117cm) wide

$800-1,000   DRA

A pair of James Mont pickled oak-veneer nightstands, each with raised plate glass top, single drawer and cabinet door with circular pulls, glass glued down, with some chips and some veneer loss, branded "James Mont Design".

25.5in (65cm) high

$500-800   DRA

A James Mont oversized square mirror, with 4in (10cm) beaded-edge moulding covered with gold leaf on a textured gessoed base, a few flecks to gold leaf, unmarked.

56in (142cm) wide

$800-1,000   DRA

A George Nakashima Conoid walnut lounge chair, with hickory spindles, original webbed seat support, with black cushions, light wear to one outer edge of seat, unmarked.

33.75in (85.5cm) wide

$9,000-11,000   DRA

A George Nakashima walnut right-arm settee, with loose cushions.

Provenance: *Tom Takubo commission, NYC, 1966.*

76in (193cm) wide

$4,000-5,000   FRE

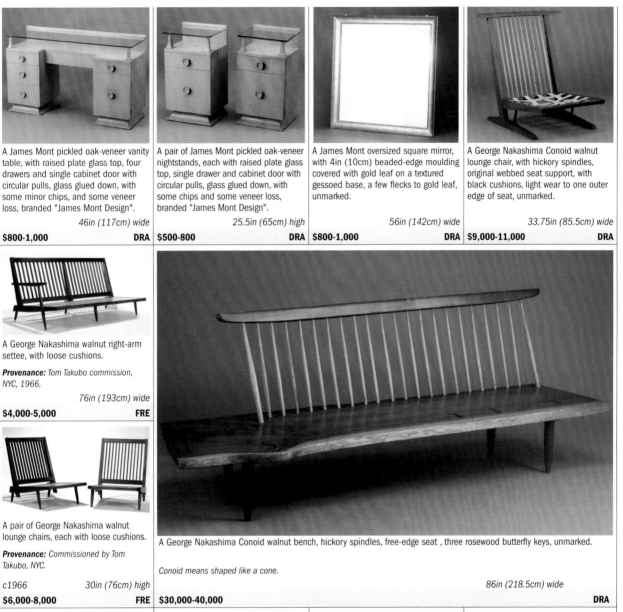

A George Nakashima Conoid walnut bench, hickory spindles, free-edge seat , three rosewood butterfly keys, unmarked.

Conoid means shaped like a cone.

86in (218.5cm) wide

$30,000-40,000   DRA

A pair of George Nakashima walnut lounge chairs, each with loose cushions.

Provenance: *Commissioned by Tom Takubo, NYC.*

c1966   *30in (76cm) high*

$6,000-8,000   FRE

A set of ten walnut and oak dining chairs, by George Nakashima, including two armchairs.

Provenance: *These were sold by the family who commissioned them from Nakashima in the early 1960s.*

36.5in (92.5cm) high

$15,000-20,000 (set)   FRE

A 1960s George Nakashima walnut free-edge dining table, with two 13in (33cm) add-on leaves, client name on leaf.

54in (137cm) long

$7,000-9,000   FRE

A George Nakashima walnut conoid dining table, with double-plank, free-edge top joined by three rosewood butterfly keys, and two 13in (33cm) free-edge leaves for either end, on trestle base.

28.5in (72cm) high

$12,000-15,000   DRA

A George Nakashima walnut Minguren II dining table, the top with single rosewood butterfly key, two free-edges and two V-shaped ends, on trestle base, signed "George Nakashima/ May 1980".

73in (185cm) wide

$30,000-40,000   DRA

A George Nakashima large walnut dining table, with boat-shaped double-plank top with four rosewood butterfly keys, on trestle base with through-tenon stretcher, marked with original owner's name on bottom.

1962   84in (213cm) wide

$12,000-15,000   **DRA**

A George Nakashima walnut cross-legged desk, with free-edge top and single pedestal with three graduated drawers, two with recessed horizontal pulls, unmarked.

50.5in (128.5cm) wide

$10,000-12,000   **DRA**

A George Nakashima single pedestal cherry desk, with three drawers, cantilevered rectangular top and two flaring dowel legs.

48in (122cm) wide

$5,000-6,000   **DRA**

A George Nakashima walnut coffee table, free-edge top on pedestal and canted leg base.

70in (177.5cm) wide

$8,000-10,000   **FRE**

A George Nakashima walnut occasional table, in English burr walnut and black walnut, signed in marker "George Nakashima 1983".

29.5in (75cm) long

$12,000-15,000   **FRE**

A George Nakashima English walnut coffee table.

c1966   48in (122cm) long

$18,000-22,000   **FRE**

A 1960s George Nakashima walnut coffee table.

75in (190.5cm) long

$18,000-22,000   **FRE**

An early George Nakashima walnut coffee table, the client's name "Armstrong" is written underneath.

Provenance: Mr Donald Armstrong commissioned this table from Nakashima in 1956.

52in (132cm) long

$14,000-16,000   **FRE**

A fine George Nakashima walnut Minguren II coffee table, with free-edge burr wood top with two rosewood butterfly keys, signed "George Nakashima. March 1980".

65in (165cm) wide

$25,000-30,000   **DRA**

A George Nakashima walnut slab coffee table, with split-knot free-edge top, marked with owner's name.

1965   50in (127cm) wide

$10,000-12,000   **DRA**

A George Nakashima walnut coffee table, with naturally occluded free-edge top on plank base with two tapering dowel legs, small chips to underside of free-edge, marked "Original Lubowitz".

63.5in (161.5cm) wide

$7,000-10,000   **DRA**

An unusual George Nakashima walnut coffee table, with free-form burr wood top with single butterfly key, on three tapering dowel legs, marked with owner's name on bottom.

40.5in (103cm) wide

$9,000-11,000   **DRA**

A George Nakashima walnut side table, with wedge-shaped top with one free-edge, on three tapering dowel legs mortised through the top, unmarked.

26.75 in (68cm) wide

$9,000-11,000   **DRA**

A CLOSER LOOK AT A NAKASHIMA TABLE

George Nakashima (1905-1990) was an internationally acclaimed artisan whose works are represented in some of the most important collections in the world. Furniture from the Nakashima woodworking concern in New Hope, Pennsylvania, invariably generates a large amount of international interest when it comes up for sale. Collectors are looking for the finest figured cuts of the more unusual timbers with documented provenance.

The first step in Nakashima's furniture production process was the choice of wood. The most commonly found timber in his work is American black walnut and cherry. The more unusual the wood, the more commercial the value will be. This example is executed from a finely burred section of Buckeye, the state tree of Ohio. Other woods to look for are rosewood, English and Persian walnut, myrtle, maple, teak and rosewood.

With Nakashima's work, the design highlights and features the natural qualities of the wood as with British craftsmen such as Tim Stead. For tables the natural or 'free' edge of the cut profile of timber is left unfinished, untouched. The unique, individual edge is an essential part of the overall appeal and look of the chosen wood. His seating furniture often has a more finished quality since the wood is worked into more specific predetermined shapes.

Nakashima wrote that "in dealing with solid wood almost each piece becomes a personal problem and the nature of the slab is used to its fullest capacity". Each piece was hand made, usually to commission and the buyer often chose the specific cut of wood that they wished to be used.

The provenance can be relatively easy to determine since if a collector knows the name of the original buyer of the piece, its details and documentation can be verified at the Nakashima office that retains full records from 1954.

A fine George Nakashima Minguren I coffee table, with free form Buckeye burr wood top with extensive grain pattern and natural occlusions, on walnut base, signed and dated on the bottom, also marked with owner's name.

1980   37in (94cm) wide

$20,000-30,000   **DRA**

A good George Nakashima 'Kornblut' cabinet, Persian walnut, rosewood and curly maple, signed in black marker "George Nakashima, April 1984".

Provenance: Commissioned by Tom Takubo, NYC. This cabinet is detailed in an original Nakashima Studios furniture drawing, signed "Mira Nakashima" and dated "October 16, 1982", which sold along with the original receipt for this cabinet for $650.

28in (71cm) wide

$30,000-40,000   **FRE**

A George Nakashima walnut side table, with triangular top on three tapering dowel legs, unmarked.

13.5 in (34.5cm) wide

$1,500-2,000   **DRA**

A George Nakashima rosewood side table, with free-form top on three tapering dowel legs, unmarked.

18in (45.5cm) wide

$2,000-2,500   **DRA**

A Mira Nakashima walnut side table, with triangular top with one free-edge, on three tapering dowel legs, signed "Mira, 6/6/81".

1981   13.25in (33.5cm) wide

$1,500-2,000   **DRA**

A George Nakashima black walnut and grass cloth credenza, with a finished back.

Provenance: Commissioned by Tom Takubo, NYC.

c1966   84in (213.5cm) wide

$15,000-20,000   **FRE**

An early 1960s George Nakashima walnut double chest of drawers.

60in (152.5cm) wide

$12,000-14,000   **FRE**

An early 1960s George Nakashima walnut console.

72in (183cm) wide

$12,000-15,000   **FRE**

A pair of matching George Nakashima cherrywood and oak chest of drawers.

These chests were commissioned by Ms Ernestine Chamberlain of Ambler, PA. Both were sold with their original receipts together with a letter from Nakashima apologising for a natural split in the wood of the second chest.

1967   36in (91.5cm) wide

$9,000-14,000 (each)   **FRE**

MODERN CLASSICS

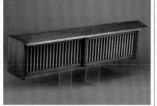

A George Nakashima walnut wall-hanging shelf/cabinet, with free-edge top over two spindle-front doors with pandanus cloth backing, and one interior shelf, marked with owner's name on back.

71in (180cm) wide

$10,000-12,000   DRA

A George Nakashima cherry night stand, with lined drawer and open shelf on flaring dowel legs, unmarked.

21in (53.5cm) high

$2,500-3,000   DRA

A 1960s matching pair of George Nakashima cabinets, in walnut and linen, the client's name is on the back.

36in (91.5cm) wide

$9,000-11,000 (each)   FRE

A George Nakashima walnut double-shelf unit, with open back with two adjustable shelves.

60in (152.5cm) wide

$4,000-6,000   DRA

A George Nakashima walnut ottoman, on flaring dowel legs, with tufted black leather-upholstered cushion, unmarked.

24.25in (61.5cm)

$1,500-2,000   DRA

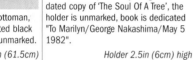

A George Nakashima walnut pen/pencil holder, accompanied by a signed and dated copy of 'The Soul Of A Tree', the holder is unmarked, book is dedicated "To Marilyn/George Nakashima/May 5 1982".

Holder 2.5in (6cm) high

$300-500   DRA

A Gilbert Rhode lounge chair, on an angular wood frame, unmarked.

31.5in (80cm) high

$2,500-3,000   DRA

GILBERT RHODE

Gilbert Rhode (1894-1944) was born and raised in New York, the son of a cabinetmaker. In 1930 he moved to Grand Rapids, Michigan where companies such as John Widdicomb and Herman Miller were active in producing traditional pieces of furniture as well as expanding into contemporary design items. Rhode designed furniture which used the existing conventional production methods at Herman Miller and convinced them to develop new processes to make furniture in the Modernist style using chrome, Bakelite and tubular steel.

A set of six Gilbert Rhode channel-back dining chairs, two arm and four side, the armchairs upholstered in blue-grey vinyl with light blue piping, the side chairs upholstered in reverse color scheme, unmarked.

Armchairs 31.5in (80cm) high

$2,000-2,500   DRA

A Gilbert Rhode armchair, on cantilevered bright chrome base, unmarked.

37in (94cm) high

$400-600   DRA

A rare Gilbert Rhode ottoman, circular top and tufted mid-section on a green enameled wood base, unmarked.

18in (45.5cm) diam

$800-1,000   DRA

A Gilbert Rhode extension dining table, with rectangular top and two pull-out leaves concealed underneath, on trestle base with tubular metal stretchers and bracket feet, unmarked.

Closed 60in (152.5cm) long

$2,000-2,500   DRA

A Gilbert Rhode for Herman Miller 'Paldao' flip-top console/dining table, on tapering legs, with two leaves and a fifth leg, re-glued crack to one rear leg, stenciled "4166".

36in (91.5cm) wide

$900-1,100   **DRA**

A pair of Gilbert Rhode for Troy 'Sunshade' two-tiered end tables, with chrome trimmed black laminate surface on tubular chrome base, unmarked.

17.75in (45.5cm) wide

$600-900   **DRA**

A Gilbert Rhode black lacquered serving/bar cart, with utensil holder and lower shelf, on tubular chrome frame, some chipping to lacquer around edges, missing several screws, unmarked.

33in (84cm) high

$1,000-1,500   **DRA**

A Gilbert Rhode for Herman Miller four drawer rosewood veneer chest, with ivory laminate case and tubular black metal horizontal pulls, on black laminate base, Herman Miller metal tag.

45in (114.5cm) wide

$2,500-3,000   **DRA**

A Gilbert Rhode for Herman Miller burr wood and mahogany veneer china cabinet, with illuminated and mirrored top with two sliding glass doors over two door cabinet with recessed pulls, stenciled "3725".

36in (91.5cm) wide

$2,000-2,500   **DRA**

A pair of Ludwig Mies van der Rohe MR10 chairs, designed 1927, produced in Italy for Stendig, each with continuous chromed tubular steel frame and slung silvery-blue leather seat, Stendig sticker to one.

33in (84cm) high

$500-700   **FRE**

A pair of Mies van der Rohe MR10 armchairs, manufactured by Knoll, USA, in chromium and leather, with Knoll sticker.

31in (78.5cm) high

$1,000-1,200   **FRE**

A set of four Mies van der Rohe for Knoll 'Brno' armchairs, each upholstered in burgundy velvet on a cantilevered flat steel base, a few minor stains to upholstery, unmarked.

32in (81.25cm) high

$2,000-2,500   **DRA**

A Mies van der Rohe 'Barcelona' chair, with tufted brown leather seat and back cushions, on a flat steel X-base, tears and cracking to leather on seat cushion, back cushion missing connector straps, Knoll Associates factory tag.

$600-1,000   **DRA**

A pair of Mies van der Rohe 'Barcelona' chairs, the cross framed chromium frame with black leather upholstered buttoned cushions, for Knoll International.

$2,500-3,000 (pair)   **L&T**

A Hans Wegner for Getama teak daybed with rear shelf, upholstered in textured green wool fabric on tapering cylindrical legs, minor wear overall, branded mark.

77in (196cm) long

$1,800-2,200   **DRA**

A set of eight Hans Wegner for Fritz Hansen oak and teak three legged stacking chairs, each with curved crest rail and spade shaped seat with through tenon detail, marked "FH-Made in Denmark", with chalk numbers.

$1,800-2,200   **DRA**

A Hans Wegner for Johannes Hansen folding chair, with original woven reed back and seat, with front grips, branded mark.

30in (76cm) high

$1,400-1,800   **DRA**

A set of seven teak armchairs, probably by Hans Wegner, with black leather-upholstered seats, wear and tears to leather, Illums-Bolignus metal tag, and incised "HN" or "NH" under each arm.

28.25in (72cm) high

$1,000-1,500   **DRA**

A Hans Wegner 'Peacock' chair, designed 1947, manufactured by Johannes Hansen, Soeborg, ash construction.

$1,000-1,300   **BonE**

One of a pair of Hans Wegner 'JH701' chairs, designed 1965, manufactured by Johannes Hansen Mobeisneakeri, veneered hoop shaped back with tan leather seats.

$750-950 (pair)   **BonE**

One of a pair of Hans Wegner 'PP63' chairs, designed 1975, manufactured by PP Mobler, inlaid oak frame with rope seats.

$600-800 (pair)   **BonE**

A Hans Wegner 'Chinese' chair, designed 1943, manufactured by Fritz Hansen, light oak and plywood frame with woven rope seat.

$450-600   **BonE**

A Hans Wegner drop-leaf dining table, manufactured by Andreas Tuck, Denmark, in oak, teak and brass, with branded marks.

94in (239cm) long

$1,800-2,200   **FRE**

A Hans Wegner teak cabinet, Ry Mobler, Denmark, top section with twin sliding doors enclosing open compartments, the case beneath with six long drawers, two lined for silverware, stamped mark.

71in (180.5cm) wide

$1,200-1,800   **FRE**

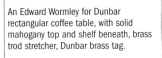

An Edward Wormley for Dunbar rectangular coffee table, with solid mahogany top and shelf beneath, brass trod stretcher, Dunbar brass tag.

48in (122cm) wide

$350-450   **FRE**

A pair of Edward Wormley slipper chairs, upholstered with original striped silk fabric, over bleached mahogany legs, complete with throw pillows, Dunbar metal tags.

30in (76cm) high

$2,500-3,500   **DRA**

An Edward Wormley for Dunbar table, with circular top hand painted and signed by Elizabeth Gross, the turned base on four geometrically conceived legs, gold Dunbar label, paper tag.

39.5in (100cm) wide

$550-750   **FRE**

An Edward Wormley for Dunbar mahogany bookstand, circular top covered in chocolate brown leather with swivel base, each side with an open bookshelf, Dunbar factory tag.

35.5in (90cm) diam

$2,000-2,500   **DRA**

An Edward Wormley for Dunbar bentply occasional table, ebonised oak veneer with two rings, joined by three legs and topped by a circular smoked glass top, unmarked.

23.25in (59cm) diam

$600-900   **DRA**

An Edward Wormley for Dunbar nine-drawer buffet with rosewood drawer fronts, ebonised oak frame, and brass ring pulls, excellent original condition, brass "D" tag.

69.25in (176cm) wide

$2,000-3,000   **DRA**

An Edward Wormley for Dunbar mahogany cabinet, two small drawers over two woven slat sliding doors enclosing drawers and storage space, on a leather wrapped plinth base, Dunbar factory tag on bottom.

42.5in (108cm) wide

$1,800-2,200   **DRA**

An Edward Wormley for Dunbar mahogany chest, with two small drawers over three large ones, all with recessed pulls, on a leather wrapped plinth base, unmarked.

41.5in (105cm) wide

$1,000-1,500   **DRA**

An Edward Wormley for Dunbar executive desk and chair (not shown), in walnut, mahogany, brass, the desk with a Dunbar brass tag.

75in (193cm) wide

$600-800   **FRE**

Other influential designers

An Asko orange ball chair designed by Eero Aarnio, the ovoid swivelling unit with upholstered orange Dakron fabric and loose cushion on a pedestal base, molded marks to base.

1965

7.25in (120cm) high

$3,000-3,500   **L&T**

A Guy Aulenti 'Kartell' armchair, black injection molded plastic frame.

$120-160   **BonE**

An Allesandro Becchi for Giovanetti foam sofabed, with internal steel frame, brown leather upholstery and mattress covered in synthetic sheepskin, unmarked.

93in (236cm) wide

$2,000-2,500   **DRA**

A Giandomenico Belotti 'Spaghetti' chair, designed 1979, manufactured by Alias, Grumello del Monte, Bergamo, polished tubular steel with stitched tan leather slings.

$400-500   **BonE**

A set of four Harry Bertoia wire chairs, produced by Knoll, USA, each with white enameled steel seat, blue vinyl cushion and black steel base, Knoll International tags.

30in (76cm) high

$800-1,200 **FRE**

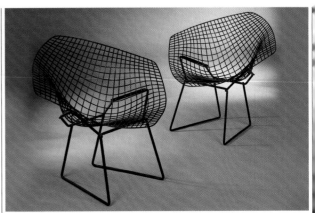

A pair of 'Diamond' chairs by Harry Bertoia, designed for Knoll International 1952, each with black vinyl coated seats on black enameled supports.

$500-700 **L&T**

A Harry Bertoia 'Model No. 420C' chair, designed 1950/1952, manufactured by Knoll International, vinyl coated steel lattice frame with white leather seat.

$220-280 **BonE**

One of a pair of 'Boex 591' chairs, flattened steel frame with leather bound boot-lace back rest and black leather seats.

$2,800-3,200 (pair) **BonE**

A 'Pipe' chair, circa 1985, manufactured by Botium, tubular steel painted in limited edition launch colours of red and blue.

$600-900 **BonE**

One of a set of six Hans Brattrud for Hove Mobler dining chairs, each having a continuous seat and back in slatted rosewood and supported on chromium-plated steel rod legs.

$1,800-2,200 (set) **DN**

One of a pair of Wassily B3 chromium armchairs, designed by Marcel Breuer, each with tubular frames and black leather strap upholstery.

$800-1,200 (pair) **L&T**

A Marcel Breuer B3 club chair, in chromium, leather and chrome, with "Made In Italy" sticker.

31in (78.5cm) wide

$320-380 **FRE**

A Calvin Modernist mahogany dining table, by Calvin Furniture Co., Grand Rapids, includes two leaves.

62in (157.5cm) long

$600-900 **FRE**

A set of four Calvin Modernist upholstered mahogany dining chairs, Calvin Furniture Co., Grand Rapids, American Design Foundation and Calvin tags.

$300-380 **FRE**

One of a pair of Paul Cadovious '291-00' chairs, manufactured by Cado, white fibre-glass shell, detachable seat.

c1969

$150-200 (pair) **BonE**

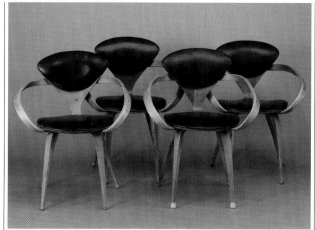

A set of four Norman Chener for Plycraft bentwood armchairs, each with black leather upholstered seat and back, small slit to one seat, Plycraft label.

$2,800-3,200   **DRA**

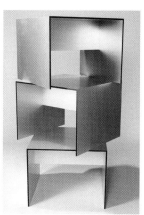

A set of three Antonio Citterio 'T60' tables, produced by B and B Italia, square forms of aluminum laminate.

c1998   *23.5in (59.5cm) wide*

$600-900   **FRE**

A Joe Colombo white lacquer laminated armchair, the slightly arched curved back with continuous downswept arms issuing a curved and shaped backrest and seat and continuing into a U-shaped base.

$2,800-3,200   **SI**

A Michael Coffey 'Variations' sculptural wall hanging bar, in Mozambique and white oak, with dovetail construction, drop front door and interior lined in white laminate, illuminated compartment on one side, sliding double shelf and small drawer on the other, unmarked.

36in (91.5cm) wide

$4,000-5,000   **DRA**

One of a pair of Dr Hans Coray 'Landi' chairs, designed 1938, manufactured by Zanotta, aluminum frame with perforated back and seat.

$300-500 (pair)   **BonE**

One of a pair of Robin Day 'Polyprop' chairs, designed 1962/1963, manufactured by Hille, white injection molded shell, tubular steel supports.

$60-90 (pair)   **BonE**

A Swiss De Sede leather lounge chair and ottoman, with black leather upholstered seat, back and arms on a stainless steel pedestal base.

Chair 30in (76cm) high

$500-700   **FRE**

Three Swiss DeSede nesting tables, in ebonised oak, with brass label.

Largest 22.5in 957cm) wide

$1,000-1,500   **FRE**

A Dunbar coffee table, with patinated bronze cruciform base and rectangular 0.5in (1cm) thick smoked glass top, unmarked.

1965   *46.25in (117cm) wide*

$1,500-2,000   **DRA**

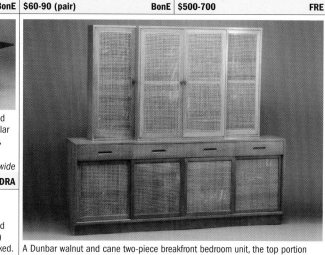

A Dunbar coffee table, with patinated bronze ribbon base and 0.5in (1cm) thick clear glass circular top, unmarked.

c1965   *42in (107cm) wide*

$1,500-2,000   **DRA**

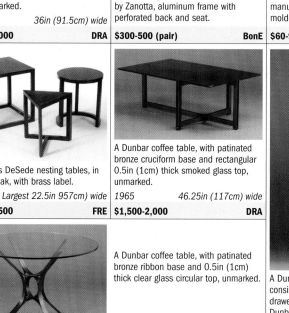

A Dunbar walnut and cane two-piece breakfront bedroom unit, the top portion consisting of a four-door unit with shelved interior, the bottom portion with three drawers and recessed oval pulls over four sliding doors, on plinth base, Dunbar/Berne, IN metal tag.

81.5in (207cm) wide

$2,200-2,800   **DRA**

A Dunbar settee, with wooden frame caned back and side panels, on castered base, unmarked.

60in (152cm) wide

$2,800-3,200   **DRA**

An Yngve Ekstrom oak and teak armchair, upholstered in brown leather, branded mark.

40in (102cm) high

$1,500-2,000   **DRA**

A Paul Evens 'PE11' single-door cube cabinet, with rivetted copper, bronze and pewter patchwork case with slate top, red and black painted interior with single shelf, unmarked.

20in (51cm) wide

$1,000-1,500   **DRA**

A Reuter Produkts egg chair designed by Peter Ghyczy, of flattened ovoid form with hinged lid enclosing blue upholstered seat.

32.25in (82cm) long

$800-1,200   **L&T**

A Jeremy Harvey 'Hello' chair, designed in 1979, manufactured by Artifact, polished steel frame incised with letters.

$500-700   **BonE**

A Robert Heritage 'Apollo 1235' chair, designed 1969 for the QE2 liner, manufactured by Ernest Race, aluminum frame with plywood shell upholstered in black fabric.

$120-180   **BonE**

A Wolfgang Hoffmann three-piece sectional sofa, with tubular chrome frame, upholstered in slunskskin and black leather, unmarked.

c1936   *79.5in (202cm) long*

$3,500-4,500   **DRA**

A pair of Howell lounge chairs, each with tubular chrome frame, seat and black cushions and black enameled armrests, nicks, Howell decals.

34in (86.5cm) high

$1,000-1,500   **DRA**

A Wolfgang Hoffmann for Howell circular dining table, with layered black laminate top of tubular chrome support mounted on cast iron base, Howell decal.

60in (152.5cm) diam

$800-1,200   **DRA**

A Peter Hvidt and Orla Molgaard-Nielsen settee, manufactured by France & Son, Denmark, in teak, chromium, rubber and fabric, with metal manufacturer's tag and John Stuart NYC retailers' tag.

53in (134.5cm) wide

$600-900   **FRE**

A Wolfgang Hoffmann for Howell dining table, with black enameled rectangular top on bright chrome tubular base, Howell decal.

58in (147.5cm) wide

$600-900   **DRA**

A 'Table Table' contemporary center table by Clementine Hope, printed MDF.

63in (160cm) wide

$150-200   **L&T**

A Jorgen Hovelskov 'Harp' chair, designed 1968, manufactured by Christensen and Larsen, ebonised frame with synthetic string flag back.

$1,200-1,800   **BonE**

A Grete Jalk Danish coffee table, rectangular top with dished sides on tapered dowel legs joined by a stretcher shelf with nine slats, unmarked.

63.5in (161cm) wide

$500-700   **FRE**

A 'Jason' laminated plywood chair, designed by Carl Jacobs for Kandya, Middlesex, the single piece seat and back veneered with beech, with a black covered pad, and supported on black painted rod legs.

$220-280   **DN**

A rare Vladimir Kagan biomorphic 'Cloud' sofa, fully upholstered in finely woven fabric with undulating pattern in red, pink and grey, with three matching throw pillows, unmarked.

116in (294.5cm) wide

$13,000-15,000   **DRA**

A Vladimir Kagan for Grosfeld House cherry two-door cabinet, with contoured door fronts with ebony inlay, its interior fitted with a mirror, four shelves, and four small drawers with ivory enameled pulls, on black cylindrical feet, Grosfeld House metal tag.

34in (86.5cm) high

$3,000-4,000   **DRA**

A pair of Vladimir Kagan for Grosfeld House cherry nightstands, each with contoured cabinet door with ebony inlay, and two adjustable shelves on a sculpted whalebone base, unmarked.

28in (71cm) wide

$2,200-1,800   **DRA**

A Vladimir Kagan for Grosfeld House cherry bench, channelled surface on a sculpted whalebone base, Grosfeld House factory tag.

$2,800-3,200   **DRA**

A pair of Vladimir Kagan cantilevered nesting maple end tables, with black laminate tops, some scratches to top and lifting of laminate, unmarked.

Tallest 28in (71cm) wide

$800-1,200   **DRA**

A Vladimir Kagan L-shaped sofa, on plexiglass base, Vladimir Kagan Designs, Inc., factory tag.

88in (223.5cm) wide

$3,200-3,800   **DRA**

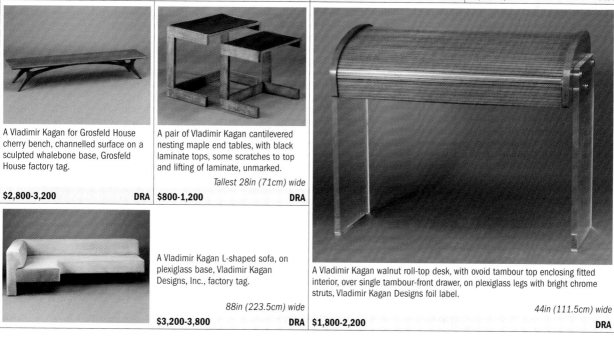

A Vladimir Kagan walnut roll-top desk, with ovoid tambour top enclosing fitted interior, over single tambour-front drawer, on plexiglass legs with bright chrome struts, Vladimir Kagan Designs foil label.

44in (111.5cm) wide

$1,800-2,200   **DRA**

MODERN FURNITURE

A set of four Rodney Kinsman 'Omkstack' chairs, designed 1972, manufactured by OMK, perforated steel back and seat, one polished finish, one white and two epoxy coated black.

$100-150 BonE

A Poul Kjaerholm 'PK22' chair, brown leather sling seat on a stainless steel base.

28in (71cm) high

$1,000-1,500 FRE

A Poul Kjaerholm 'PK24' chaise longue, hammock model, designed 1965, manufactured by Fritz Hansen, polished steel frame, woven cane and black leather headrest.

$2,800-3,200 BonE

A Poul Kjaerholm 'PK22' chair, designed 1955, manufactured by Fritz Hansen, flattened steel frame, black leather seat with stitched detail.

$1,000-1,500 BonE

A Yrjo Kokkapuro 'Fysio' chair, designed 1978, manufactured by Asko, birch and laminated plywood frame, black fabric upholstery.

$600-900 BonE

A Yrjo Kokkapuro 'Karuselli' chair, designed 1965, manufactured by Haimi, fibre-glass shell with tan leather upholstery, swivel arc, steel and fibre-glass base.

$1,500-2,000 BonE

A LaVerne bronze coffee table, its elliptical top acid-etched with scenes of Chinese warriors and landscapes, signed "Philip/Kevin LaVerne".

65.5in (166cm) wide

$1,800-2,200 DRA

A pair of IB Kofod Larsen for Selig armchairs, with thin brass arms and white vinyl upholstered seat and back pads, on tapering dowel legs with arched aprons, unmarked.

c1956 *28in (71cm) high*

$1,500-2,000 DRA

One of a pair of Vico Magistretti 'Golem' chairs, designed 1970, manufactured by Trannaker, black lacquered frame with leather cushion seat.

$1,000-1,500 (pair) BonE

One of a pair of Vico Magistretti 'Vicario' chairs, designed 1971, manufactured by Artemide, white compression molded plastic frame.

$280-320 (pair) BonE

A Modernist chair, attributed to Robert Mallet-Stevens, of strict rectangular construction, with prominent feature screws, ebonised wood seat panel, back panel, arms and four floor level stretchers, figured oak panel legs/upright supports.

c1930

$2,200-2,800 BonBay

A Francis McCarthy tiled table, Philadelphia, mixed woods frame, with tile top, signed "McCarthy 83".

1983 *22in (56cm) high*

$1,500-2,000 FRE

An Arne Norell 'Ari' chair, designed 1966, flattened steel frame with ribbed black leather cover.

$1,000-1,500   **BonE**

A Verner Panton 'Cone' chair, with black wire frame on swivel base, and loose seat pad upholstered in purple fabric, unmarked.

32in (81cm) high

$1,000-1,500   **DRA**

A Verner Panton 'Cone' chair, upholstered in crimson chenille on a swivelling bright chrome star shaped base, unmarked.

34.25in high

$1,800-2,200   **DRA**

A good Tommi Parzinger ivory lacquered buffet, with five doors concealing interior drawers and shelves, with large brass ring pulls and brass studs applied to front and sides, branded "Parzinger Original".

82in (208.25cm) wide

$9,000-12,000   **DRA**

A Tommi Parzinger inlaid cabinet, rectangular case of burr birch with macassar ebony inlay, four cabinet doors enclosing a series of shelves and drawers, brass arrow keys, "Parzinger Originals" branded mark, lacks feet and rings to side.

72in (182.5cm) wide

$2,800-3,200   **FRE**

A set of four Pierre Paulin for Artifort 'Tulip' chairs, each upholstered in teal blue snakeskin vinyl on swivelling aluminum star shaped base, foil label.

30in (76cm) high

$2,800-3,200   **DRA**

A set of 12 Giancarlo Piretti Plia chairs, produced by Castelli, Italy, designed in 1969, each with stainless steel folding frame and clear plastic seat/back.

c1969   *29in (73.5cm) wide*

$1,500-2,000 (set)   **FRE**

A Harvey Probber server, ebonised wood case with black laminate surface, single long drawer above twin cabinet doors on dowel legs with brass caps.

36in (91.5cm) wide

$180-220   **FRE**

A Harvey Probber jewellery chest, with rosewood veneer case on plinth base, original finish, stencilled number.

36in (91cm) high

$3,800-4,200   **DRA**

A set of three Jens Risom stacking tables, each with circular mahogany top on blackened steel base, stickers.

20.5in (52cm) high

$800-1,200   **FRE**

A Gerrit Rietveld 'Zigzag' chair, designed 1934, manufactured by Cassina, oak construction.

$600-900   **BonE**

A T. H. Robsjohn-Gibbings for Widdicomb armchair, on blond wood dowel frame.

35.5in (90cm) high

$420-480   **DRA**

A Roma safari chair, with collapsible wood frame, brass and copper hardware, hard leather seat, unmarked.

1in (104cm) high

$600-900   **DRA**

A china cabinet designed by Count Sahknoffsky for the 1933 Chicago World's Fair, with two sliding glass doors enclosing two fixed shelves, over three bowed drawers with recessed circular pulls, a few small veneer chips to one side, unmarked.

37.75in (96cm) wide

$600-900　　　　　　　　　**DRA**

Two of a set of four Eero Saarinen for Knoll 'Tulip' chairs, designed 1956, two armchairs and two side, each in molded white fibreglass on an enameled white base, original red woven slip seats, Knoll International label.

c1956　　　　　　*32in (81cm) high*

$600-900 (set)　　　　　　　**FRE**

One of a pair of Gigi Sabadin 'Fiora' chairs, designed 1979, manufactured by Crasserig, light oak frame with three piece oval back and leather seats.

$420-480 (pair)　　　　　　**BonE**

One of a pair of Gigi Sabadin 'Canossa' chairs, light oak frame with hemp cover and leather seats.

c1979

$500-700 (pair)　　　　　　**BonE**

A 1970's Arkana 'Mushroom' dining room set, comprising a table with circular laminated top on waisted resin columnar base, and six molded resin chairs to match each with upholstered pads woven red fabric with original care instructions.

$1,200-1,800　　　　　　　**L&T**

A Bertha Schaeffer for M. Singer & Sons walnut two tier occasional table, with white laminate surface on tapering dowel leg frame, M. Singer & Sons tag.

28in (71cm) wide

$1,000-1,500　　　　　　　**DRA**

One of a pair of Tobia and Afra Scarpa 'Africa' chairs, designed 1975, made by Maxalto, two piece cherrywood back, leather upholstered seat.

$800-1,200 (pair)　　　　　**BonE**

One of a pair of Fred Scott folding chairs, designed 1974, manufactured by Hille, polished steel frame with plastic back and seat rests.

$180-220 (pair)　　　　　　**BonE**

A Fred Scott 'Supporto' chair, Limited Edition No. 14/20 to celebrate 10th Anniversary, designed 1979, made by Hille, polished aluminum frame.

$500-700　　　　　　　　　**BonE**

One of a pair of Ettore Sottsass 'Eastside' chairs, designed 1982/1983, manufactured by Knoll International, tubular steel frame upholstered in blue fabric with red seat.

$500-700 (pair)　　　　　　**BonE**

ETTORE SOTTSASS

Ettore Sottsass (born 1917) made his international reputation through his work for the design department of the Olivetti electronics department in the 1960s and 1970s, designing typewriters and office furniture. Integral to his work is the use of bright colours applied to functional everyday equipment and furnishings. In 1981 he founded the influential Memphis group in Italy that included designers such as Mario Bellini, Michael Graves and Arata Isozaki.

An Ettore Sottsass 'Westside' chair, designed 1982/1983, steel frame upholstered in blue, red and yellow on square section supports.

$800-1,200　　　　　　　　**BonE**

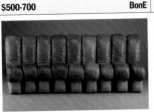

A Stendig 'Non-stop' sofa, comprising nine individual foam sections upholstered in brown leather, on reinforced molded foam base, Stendig label.

87.5in (222.25cm) wide

$1,000-1,500　　　　　　　**DRA**

A Stow-Davis mahogany veneer credenza, on bright chrome frame with white marble top, tab hardware and two cabinets, flanking five center drawers, metal tag.

76in (193cm) wide

$1,500-2,000　　　　　　　**DRA**

A pair of Thaden-Jordan molded plywood telephone tables, with elliptical lower tier, on bentwood legs, paper label.

29.75in (75.5cm) wide

$1,000-1,500   **DRA**

A Rud Thygesen and Johnny Sorensen 'Duet' chair, circa 1986, manufactured by Magnus Olesen, plywood frame with red fabric seat.

$220-280   **BonE**

A Rud Thygesen and Johnny Sorensen 'Kings' chair and stool, c1985, made by Botium, oak frame, cane back and seat.

This was originally designed for the King of Sweden.

$150-200   **BonE**

A Heywood Wakefield 'Champagne' dining suite, comprising six chairs, dining table and three leaves.

Table 56in (142cm) wide

$1,800-2,200 (suite)   **FRE**

A Shizuhiko Watanabe walnut single pedestal long desk, with free-edge top, three drawers with overhanging horizontal pulls and tapering dowel legs, unmarked.

72in (183cm) wide

$2,200-2,800   **DRA**

A Shizuhiko Watanabe walnut credenza, with free-edge top, two sliding doors with recessed rectangular pulls, unmarked.

72in (183cm) wide

$1,000-1,500   **DRA**

A Shizuhiko Watanabe walnut dresser, with free-edge top and overhanging horizontal pulls, on platform base, unmarked.

73.5in (187cm) wide

$600-900   **DRA**

A Shizuhiko Watanabe king-size bed, with bench-supported headboard with four sliding doors and circular pulls (two missing), rectangular mattress frame and platform base, unmarked.

81in (205.75cm) wide

$600-900   **DRA**

A set of six Kem Weber for Lloyd tubular chrome armchairs, each with seat cushion and back pad upholstered in a dark brown brushed fabric, unmarked.

31in (78.5cm) high

$500-700   **DRA**

A pair of Kem Weber for Lloyd tubular chrome armchairs, each with seat cushions and black pad upholstered in a rose-coloured brushed fabric, unmarked.

31.5in (79cm) high

$220-280   **DRA**

Two of a suite of Russell Woodard 1950s patio furniture, including six wire armchairs painted light blue with circular vinyl seats, and two tables with octagonal slate tops and steel legs.

Table 48in (122cm) wide

$2,200-2,800 (suite)   **FRE**

A 1960s upholstered chrome seating set, two chairs, each cylindrical, upholstered in a blue paisley silk, on rotating chrome base, together with a matching ottoman.

Chairs 33in (84cm) high

$300-500 (suite)   **FRE**

A plywood 'Floor' chair, in laminated and molded plywood.

15in (38cm) high

$150-200   **FRE**

A large, unusual wall-hanging console mirror, possibly Italian, with geometric forms in gilt and polychrome wood, the bevelled glass flanked by two tubular holders, signed "A.D.63", on reverse.

67in (170.25cm) high

$1,000-1,500   **DRA**

A groovy foam settee, with stretch fabric cover in yellow, black, green and white psychedelic pattern, unmarked.

c1975   *60in (152.5cm) wide*

$500-700   **DRA**

A 1960s wicker hanging chair, the egg shaped lattice seat suspended by a spring on a tubular steel support and hoop base.

69.25in (176cm) high

$220-280   **L&T**

A pair of Niels Joergen Haugesen 'X-line' stacking chairs, designed in 1977, manufactured by Zon International, steel rod X-frame with black perforated steel back and seat.

$70-100 (pair)   **BonE**

A pair of Bonacina 'Cisk' chairs, manufactured by Bonacina, black steel folding X-frame, canvas sling seat and adjustable back rest.

$120-180 (pair)   **BonE**

A set of four Rodney Kinsman 'Omkstack' chairs, designed in 1972, manufactured by OMK, perforated steel back and seat, one polished finish, one white and two epoxy-coated black.

$80-120 (set)   **BonE**

A Giandomenico Belotti 'Spaghetti' chair, designed in 1976, manufactured by Alias, Grumello del Monte, Bergamo, polished tubular steel with PVC spaghetti strips.

$400-600   **BonE**

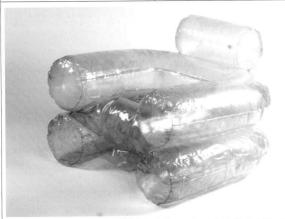

A Gionatan de Pas, Donato D'Urbino, Paolo Lomazzi and Carla Scolari 'Blow' chair, designed in 1967, manufactured by Zanotta, inflatable radio-frequency welded PVC.

$70-100   **BonE**

A Pierre Paulin tulip stool, manufactured by Artifort, Holland, in vinyl and steel, molded.

29in (73.5cm) wide

$350-400   **FRE**

An Erwin and Estelle Laverne lucite 'Lily' chair from the Invisible Group series, with fuzzy white seat pad, unmarked.

37.25in (94.5cm) wide

$3,000-4,000   **DRA**

A Danish teak and leather lounge chair, with heavy teak frame, bentwood back and black leather upholstered cushions.

36in (91.5cm) wide

$180-220   **FRE**

A 1960s leather lounge chair and ottoman, each over-upholstered in brown leather on bentwood frame and circular base.

Chair 38in (96.5cm) high

$600-900   **FRE**

A blond-wood daybed with two horizontal backslats, spring seat support and loose foam cushions, upholstered in crimson velvet, on tubular black metal base, minor wear to upholstery, unmarked.

$600-900   **DRA**

A Swiss DeSede leather sectional sofa.

$4,000-6,000 FRE

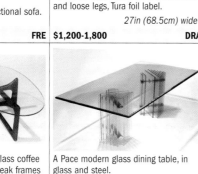

A set of six Aldo Tura nesting tables with green-dyed parchment tops on tapering burlwood legs, scratches to parchment and loose legs, Tura foil label.

27in (68.5cm) wide

$1,200-1,800 DRA

An Amoebic coffee table, by Lawrence Kelley, Media, Pa., with free-form top in thick laminated wood on four screw-in black dowel legs, signed.

1973 *64.5in (163.5cm) wide*

$120-180 FRE

A 1960s Danish teak and glass coffee table, base with conjoined teak frames supporting a free-form glass top.

15.5in (39cm) high

$400-600 FRE

A Pace modern glass dining table, in glass and steel.

96in (244cm) long

$1,200-1,800 FRE

A Modernist birchwood tea cart, the top with three retractable surfaces, brass handles on an organically streamlined frame with single drawer and two shelves, on casters.

42.5in (108cm) wide

$400-600 FRE

A blond mahogany modern buffet, rectangular case in bleached mahogany with three veneered doors, one enclosing adjustable shelves, the others with a series of drawers, on a simple bracket base, partial label.

$400-600 FRE

A Danish rosewood veneer credenza with nine graduated drawers and black laminated tab pulls, on ebonized wood base, stencilled number.

77.5in (197cm) long

$400-600 DRA

A Danish teak and pine wardrobe, from Falster, with metal tag, some wear.

48in (122cm) wide

$1,200-1,800 FRE

A 1960s Pop Art desk white laminate top and sides, three molded yellow plastic drawers.

47.25in (120cm) wide

$300-400 FRE

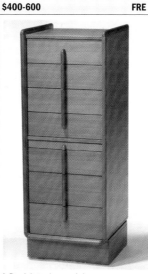

A Danish teak semainier.

20in (51cm) wide

$800-1,200 FRE

A pair of Modernist folding room screens, each having four folding panels with ebonized oak frames and canework body, hinged together.

80in (203cm) high

$800-1,200 (pair) FRE

MODERN GLASS

Scandinavian

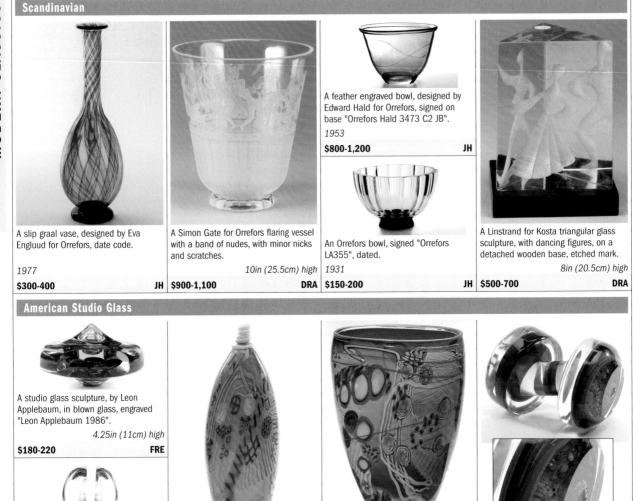

A slip graal vase, designed by Eva Engluud for Orrefors, date code.

1977

$300-400　　　　　　**JH**

A Simon Gate for Orrefors flaring vessel with a band of nudes, with minor nicks and scratches.

10in (25.5cm) high

$900-1,100　　　　　　**DRA**

A feather engraved bowl, designed by Edward Hald for Orrefors, signed on base "Orrefors Hald 3473 C2 JB".

1953

$800-1,200　　　　　　**JH**

An Orrefors bowl, signed "Orrefors LA355", dated.

1931

$150-200　　　　　　**JH**

A Linstrand for Kosta triangular glass sculpture, with dancing figures, on a detached wooden base, etched mark.

8in (20.5cm) high

$500-700　　　　　　**DRA**

American Studio Glass

A studio glass sculpture, by Leon Applebaum, in blown glass, engraved "Leon Applebaum 1986".

4.25in (11cm) high

$180-220　　　　　　**FRE**

A studio glass sculpture, by Michael David and Kit Karbler, in blown glass, with Plexiglas, steel and granite, unsigned.

10in (25.5cm) high

$700-1,000　　　　　　**FRE**

A studio glass vase, by Wes Hunting, in blown and cased glass, engraved "WS Hunting", detached piece to coil at top.

19in (48.5cm) high

$320-380　　　　　　**FRE**

A studio glass vase, by Wes Hunting, in blown glass, engraved "Wes Hunting", on a Plexiglas base.

16in (40.5cm) high

$700-1,000　　　　　　**FRE**

A studio glass sculpture, by Michael Pavlik, in blown glass, engraved "Michael Pavlik 83 1767", few scratches near base, chip to one side.

13.5in (34.5cm) long

$1,800-2,200　　　　　　**FRE**

British Glass

An Art Deco cut vase, by Thomas Webb, marked "Webb. Made in England for the Rembrandt Guild", Birmingham.

c1935

$380-420　　　　　　**JH**

A late 1930s Stuart Stourbridge jug and two tumblers, with gold-amber feet, cut with circles.

Tumbler 4.5in high

$500-700　　　　　　**JH**

A Whitefriars 'Drunken Bricklayer' vase, designed 1966.

8.5in (21.5cm) high

$300-400　　　　　　**JH**

A Whitefriars 'Kingfisher' hoop vase, designed 1966.

c1967-73　　*11.25in (28.5cm) high*

$320-380　　　　　　**JH**

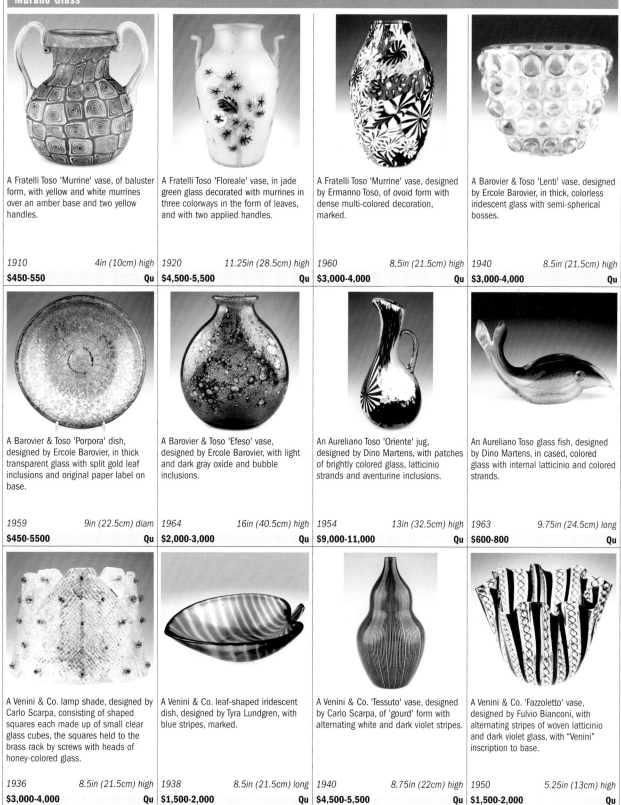

Murano Glass

A Fratelli Toso 'Murrine' vase, of baluster form, with yellow and white murrines over an amber base and two yellow handles.

1910　　　*4in (10cm) high*
$450-550　　　**Qu**

A Fratelli Toso 'Floreale' vase, in jade green glass decorated with murrines in three colorways in the form of leaves, and with two applied handles.

1920　　　*11.25in (28.5cm) high*
$4,500-5,500　　　**Qu**

A Fratelli Toso 'Murrine' vase, designed by Ermanno Toso, of ovoid form with dense multi-colored decoration, marked.

1960　　　*8.5in (21.5cm) high*
$3,000-4,000　　　**Qu**

A Barovier & Toso 'Lenti' vase, designed by Ercole Barovier, in thick, colorless iridescent glass with semi-spherical bosses.

1940　　　*8.5in (21.5cm) high*
$3,000-4,000　　　**Qu**

A Barovier & Toso 'Porpora' dish, designed by Ercole Barovier, in thick transparent glass with split gold leaf inclusions and original paper label on base.

1959　　　*9in (22.5cm) diam*
$450-5500　　　**Qu**

A Barovier & Toso 'Efeso' vase, designed by Ercole Barovier, with light and dark gray oxide and bubble inclusions.

1964　　　*16in (40.5cm) high*
$2,000-3,000　　　**Qu**

An Aureliano Toso 'Oriente' jug, designed by Dino Martens, with patches of brightly colored glass, latticinio strands and aventurine inclusions.

1954　　　*13in (32.5cm) high*
$9,000-11,000　　　**Qu**

An Aureliano Toso glass fish, designed by Dino Martens, in cased, colored glass with internal latticinio and colored strands.

1963　　　*9.75in (24.5cm) long*
$600-800　　　**Qu**

A Venini & Co. lamp shade, designed by Carlo Scarpa, consisting of shaped squares each made up of small clear glass cubes, the squares held to the brass rack by screws with heads of honey-colored glass.

1936　　　*8.5in (21.5cm) high*
$3,000-4,000　　　**Qu**

A Venini & Co. leaf-shaped iridescent dish, designed by Tyra Lundgren, with blue stripes, marked.

1938　　　*8.5in (21.5cm) long*
$1,500-2,000　　　**Qu**

A Venini & Co. 'Tessuto' vase, designed by Carlo Scarpa, of 'gourd' form with alternating white and dark violet stripes.

1940　　　*8.75in (22cm) high*
$4,500-5,500　　　**Qu**

A Venini & Co. 'Fazzoletto' vase, designed by Fulvio Bianconi, with alternating stripes of woven latticinio and dark violet glass, with "Venini" inscription to base.

1950　　　*5.25in (13cm) high*
$1,500-2,000　　　**Qu**

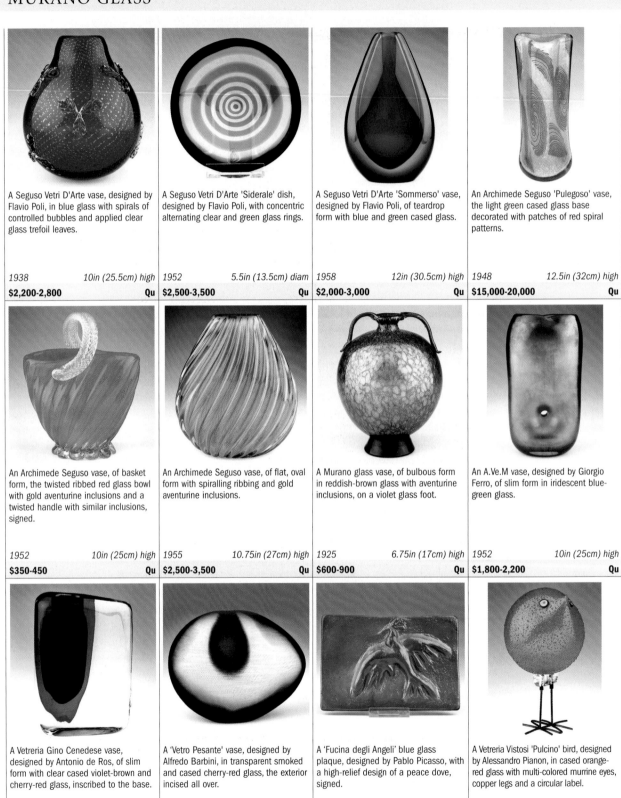

A Seguso Vetri D'Arte vase, designed by Flavio Poli, in blue glass with spirals of controlled bubbles and applied clear glass trefoil leaves.

1938   10in (25.5cm) high
$2,200-2,800   **Qu**

A Seguso Vetri D'Arte 'Siderale' dish, designed by Flavio Poli, with concentric alternating clear and green glass rings.

1952   5.5in (13.5cm) diam
$2,500-3,500   **Qu**

A Seguso Vetri D'Arte 'Sommerso' vase, designed by Flavio Poli, of teardrop form with blue and green cased glass.

1958   12in (30.5cm) high
$2,000-3,000   **Qu**

An Archimede Seguso 'Pulegoso' vase, the light green cased glass base decorated with patches of red spiral patterns.

1948   12.5in (32cm) high
$15,000-20,000   **Qu**

An Archimede Seguso vase, of basket form, the twisted ribbed red glass bowl with gold aventurine inclusions and a twisted handle with similar inclusions, signed.

1952   10in (25cm) high
$350-450   **Qu**

An Archimede Seguso vase, of flat, oval form with spiralling ribbing and gold aventurine inclusions.

1955   10.75in (27cm) high
$2,500-3,500   **Qu**

A Murano glass vase, of bulbous form in reddish-brown glass with aventurine inclusions, on a violet glass foot.

1925   6.75in (17cm) high
$600-900   **Qu**

An A.Ve.M vase, designed by Giorgio Ferro, of slim form in iridescent blue-green glass.

1952   10in (25cm) high
$1,800-2,200   **Qu**

A Vetreria Gino Cenedese vase, designed by Antonio de Ros, of slim form with clear cased violet-brown and cherry-red glass, inscribed to the base.

1960   9in (22.5cm) high
$2,200-2,800   **Qu**

A 'Vetro Pesante' vase, designed by Alfredo Barbini, in transparent smoked and cased cherry-red glass, the exterior incised all over.

1962   7in (17.5cm) high
$3,000-4,000   **Qu**

A 'Fucina degli Angeli' blue glass plaque, designed by Pablo Picasso, with a high-relief design of a peace dove, signed.

1962   8in (20.5cm) wide
$1,800-2,200   **Qu**

A Vetreria Vistosi 'Pulcino' bird, designed by Alessandro Pianon, in cased orange-red glass with multi-colored murrine eyes, copper legs and a circular label.

1962   8.5in (22cm) high
$3,800-4,200   **Qu**

Modern Ceramics

A huge jug 'Pichet gothique aux oiseaux', designed by Pablo Picasso, made by Madoura, Vallauris, interior glazed, partially incised, marked.

1953   *11in (28cm) high*
$5,000-7,000   **Qu**

A jug 'Têtes', designed by Pablo Picasso, made by Madoura, Vallauris, depicting two heads of a Faun, signed.

1956   *5in (13cm) high*
$1,500-2,000   **Qu**

A jug 'Bearded man', designed by Pablo Picasso, made by Madoura, Vallauris, partially incised, depicting a bearded head of man, marked.

1953   *13in (32cm) high*
$6,000-8,000   **HERR**

A tea service "TAC 1", designed by Walter Gropius, made by Rosenthal, signed.

1968   *Jug 5in (12.5cm) high*
$200-300   **Qu**

A tea service 'TAC 1', designed by Walter Gropius, made by Rosenthal, nineteen pieces, signed.

1968   *Jug 5in (12.5cm) high*
$200-300   **HERR**

A plate by the Lomonosov Porcelain Factory, Leningrad (St. Petersburg), by Kazimir S. Malevich.

This plate realised a very high price because of the original design by Kazimir S. Malevich. The painting "Dynamic Suprematism" of 1916 from the Ludwig collection in Cologne functioned as a model. Another plate from the same series no. 660/21 is to be found in the Lomonosov Porcelain museum in St. Petersburg.

1925   *9.5in (23.5cm) diam*
$30,000-35,000   **HERR**

Twelve wall plates 'Eva', by Piero Fornasetti, made by Thomas, Selb, signed.

1990   *10.5in (26cm) diam*
$2,000-3,000   **Qu**

A KPM, Berlin 'Tête-à-Tête Urbino' set of eight pieces, by Trude Petri, two espresso cups, two saucers, two bowls, a cream jug, and one espresso jug, partly painted in black, marked.

1950   *Jug 6in (15cm) high*
$600-900   **HERR**

A Marcello Fantoni vase, an amorphe cubic double vase, signed on base.

1955   *16in (41cm) high*
$2,000-3,000   **Qu**

A plate 'Amour totale', by Jean Tinguely, Bernardaud, Limoges, packed in original box.

1990   *15.5in (39.5cm) high*
$1,500-2,000   **HERR**

Modern Ceramics

A Japanese Bizen pottery turnip, modelled as a realistic oversized turnip in brown clay, character signature to base.

18in (45.5cm) high

$600-800   **FRE**

A late 20thC Santodio Paz Juarez art pottery vase, from Chulucanas, Peru, with an etched signature.

9.5in (24cm) high

$220-280   **FRE**

A Raymond Loewy Rosenthal-form coffee pot, marks to underside.

$60-80   **MHT**

A Rosenthal plate with white molded decoration, designed by Martin Freyer.

c1970   *12.75in (32.5cm) diam*

$80-120   **Ren**

A Colin Pearson studio pottery bowl, the interior scratched in black with a stylized face in black on a white and green tinged ground.

9.75in (25cm) diam

$50-80   **Chef**

A Picasso pottery jug, with a strap handle, painted in brick red and black with a girl's face on a cream unglazed ground, impressed "Edition Picasso, Madoura" and inscribed in black.

c1955   *12.25in (31cm) high*

$3,000-4,000   **WW**

LUCIE RIE

Lucie Rie (1902-1985) was born in Vienna and studied pottery there. Four years after leaving college, her work had been exhibited in Austria, Italy and France, where she won a silver medal at the Paris International Exhibition in 1937. Her simple, often burnished, earthenware pots were very different to the decorative, complex styles of the time.

She fled to London in 1938, where she earned a living making buttons. Her style was not appreciated, and her work did not pick up until after the war when a young potter named Hans Coper, also a fugitive from the Nazi regime, started working for her. He had been employed to cast buttons for her to glaze, but when she spotted his talent she was inspired. Coper's influence on her work lasted until his death in 1981.

In 1946, Rie began working in stoneware and porcelain and in the late 1950s she extended the use of 'sgraffito' to her pots. She was awarded the OBE in 1968. She trained some of the best-known British Studio potters, notably Ewen Henderson and John Ward, and her status as an artist increased during her last years. She was active until her death, producing the delicate yet functional pots that characterized her style from the start.

A Lucie Rie and Hans Coper stoneware bowl, the flared rounded form on a turned foot, covered with a muted green glaze but of more greyish tone on the interior, impressed seal mark for each potter.

5.75in (14.5cm) diam

$400-600   **DN**

A Lucie Rie stoneware bowl, with steep sides flaring slightly at the rim, supported on a turned foot and covered with a streaked and mottled oatmeal glaze, impressed with seal mark and with old label showing the price "12/-".

5in (12.5cm) diam

$380-420   **DN**

A Scheier Studio pottery bowl, of flaring form under a bluish glossy glaze, incised "Scheier".

8.5in (21.5cm) diam

$500-700   **FRE**

A Winchcombe plate by Sidney Tustin, pupil to Michael Cardew, impressed marks "Winchcombe & S.T".

c1950   *9in (23cm) wide*

$150-200   **MHT**

A Frans Wildenhain studio pot, hand-thrown with crumpled top, the bottom with an earthy brown glaze, top with an organic green glaze, hash mark signature.

Born in Germany, Frans enrolled at the Bauhaus in 1924, studying under Josef Albers, Paul Klee and Max Krehan, among others. Conscripted to fight for Germany during World War II, Frans relocated to America in 1947 and joined his wife Marguerite, a Bauhaus-trained potter.

8in (20.5cm) high

$600-900   **FRE**

A Jim Adamson slab-built earthware sculpture, "cal-cutta", incised across the front, and an open back exposing genital "components".

15.5in (39cm) high

$2,500-3,000 DRA

A Clayton Bailey Funk sculpture, "corrosive", of a biohazardous materials container with brown substance oozing from rim and fissures at base, covered in white, grey and colbalt glazes, signed Clayton Bailey/1994 on bottom.

1994 *19.5in (49cm) high*

$1,500-2,000 DRA

A Clayton Bailey Funk sculpture, "corrosive", of a biohazardous materials container with brown substance oozing from rim and fissures at base, covered in white, grey and colbalt glazes, signed Clayton Bailey/1994 on bottom.

1994 *19.5in (49cm) high*

$1,500-2,000 DRA

A Clayton Bailey earthenware Funk sculpture, "Gargoyle Nose", with highly exaggerated features, three-section triangle on back re-glued by the artist, signed and dated.

1968 *14.5in (37cm) high*

$1,500-2,000 DRA

A Ken Ferguson earthenware vase with three large lobes, mermaid handle, and twisted spout, covered in a verdigris and grey dead-matte volcanic glaze, no visible mark.

17.5in (19cm) high

$4,000-5,000 DRA

A Howard Kottler glazed earthware sculpture, "Hustler's Delight", with parts composed of male and female genitalia covered in lustered and bright polychrome glazes, two firing lines from base, one runs up side, and a few small nicks, incised.

1967 *15.25in (39cm) high*

$6,500-7,500 DRA

A Lietzke stoneware four-sided planter with deeply modeled and excised abstact designs, its rim covered in mottled dark brown glaze, a few small chips, unmarked.

12.5in (32cm) high

$500-700 DRA

A fine Natzler straight-walled vessel covered in indigo, ivory and brown volcanic glaze, signed Natzler in ink, and paper label.

1/2in (10cm) high

$4,000-5,000 DRA

A fine Natzler straight-walled vessel covered in indigo, ivory and brown volcanic glaze, signed Natzler in ink, and paper label.

1/2in (10cm) high

$4,000-5,000 DRA

A fine Natzler straight-walled vessel covered in indigo, ivory and brown volcanic glaze, signed Natzler in ink, and paper label.

7 1/2in (10cm) high

$4,000-5,000 DRA

A fine Natzler hemispherical bowl covered in a grey and amber microcrystalline glaze, Natzler, in ink.

3.25in (9cm) high

$1,200-1,500 DRA

A Chris Unterseher Funk ceramic sculpture, "Champion Surfer Mike Doyle Teachers Dave's Frogs a Few Tricks," with surfing frogs and title inscription, one surfboard and one frog's arm re-glued, unmarked.

1969 *14in (36cm) wide*

$800-1,200 DRA

Lighting

An unusual Arredoluce brass easel-lamp, with tall tubular shaft, swing-arm light and three-footed base, without wiring, Arredoluce/Monza label.

82in (208cm) high

$3,000-4,000   **DRA**

An Arredoluce torchère, its base composed of six rods enameled in teal and topped by flaring hammered brass fronds with green interiors, and pierced conical shade, embossed Arredoluce/Monza/ Italy.

89in (226cm) high

$2,500-3,500   **DRA**

An Arteluce chrome floor lamp, with three pivoting arms with black enameled handles, and black conical shades, also six additional shades in various colors, "Made in Italy" label.

80.5in (204cm) high

$3,800-4,200   **DRA**

An Achille Castiglioni/Pier Giacomo Castiglioni for Flos 'Taccia' table lamp, its reflector comprised of a concave white enameled spun aluminum disc over clear hand-blown glass bowl, resting on a fluted steel base, unmarked.

21.5in (55cm) high

$1,500-2,000   **DRA**

A Kartell-Columbo table lamp, designed by Joe Columbo, the bulbous opaque plastic shade on silvered spreading plastic base.

16in (41cm) high

$250-350   **L&T**

A Greta Grossman 'Grasshopper' floor lamp, red enamel dome shade and built-in magazine rack on tubular tripod base, minor wear, unmarked.

53in (135cm) high

$700-1,000   **DRA**

An Elino Martinelli table lamp, with bulbous opaque plastic shade and base, factory marks.

15.75in (40cm) high

$250-350   **L&T**

A Gianfranco Frattini 'Megaron' floor lamp, produced by Artemide, Italy, red enameled shaft on a black base, halogen light to top, losses to enamel.

71.25in (181cm) high

$380-420   **FRE**

A pair of Modaluce bright chrome and clear glass floor lamps with hemi-spherical milk glass shades, Modulace labels.

67in (170cm) high

$500-700   **DRA**

A pair of Chase 'Taurex' bright chrome asymmetrical double candlesticks, designed by Altyer von Nessen, on fluted circular bases, die-stamped mark.

9.75in (25cm) high

$120-180   **DRA**

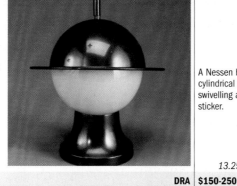

A Chase 'Constellation' accent lamp, designed by Walter von Nessen, in English bronze finish with helmet shade pierced with stars and white milk glass dome on a flared base, some chipping around rim of glass, stamped 'Chase'.

$500-700   DRA

A Nessen brass table lamp, cylindrical shade on swivelling arm, Nessen sticker.

13.25in (33.5cm) high

$150-250   FRE

A Nessen chrome floor lamp, with unusual dome-shaped spun aluminium shade on pivoting chrome arm, pole shaft and circular base, stamped "NESSEN LAMPS N.Y.C."

49in (124.5cm) high

$600-900   FRE

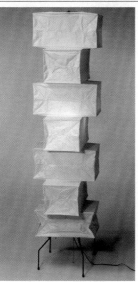

An Isamu Noguchi light sculpture, collapsible paper cubes on metal stand with adjustable legs, Noguchi signature with "Japan".

76in (193cm) high

$900-1,100   FRE

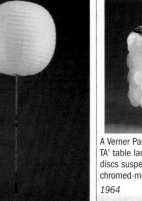

An Isamu Noguchi for Akari floor lamp, with spherical mulberry paper shade on bamboo shaft with weighted black metal base, a few small tears to shade, marked on shade.

76.5in (194cm) high

$380-420   DRA

A Verner Panton for J. Luber AG, 'Fun 2 TA' table lamp, with a series of shell discs suspended from a tiered chromed-metal frame, unmarked.

1964   *17in (43cm) high*

$1,200-1,800   DRA

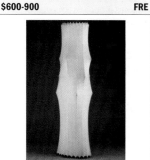

A rare 'Phantasma' floor lamp with ivory spun fiberglass covering stretched over a wire shell, professional repair to one minor split, unmarked.

76in (193cm) high

$1,200-1,800   DRA

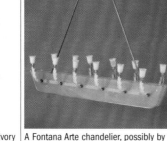

A Fontana Arte chandelier, possibly by Gio Ponti, with two frosted glass shades suspended from tubular brass rods, and ten acanthus leaf fixtures in white enameled metal, unmarked.

49in (124cm) long

$2,000-3,000   DRA

A Frederick Ramond Atomic lamp, in the form of an atom with alternating bentwood, green and blue Lucite strips around a plastic cylinder, chain suspension, Fredrick Ramond label.

21in (53.5cm) diam

$180-220   FRE

A Concetta Scaravaglione bronze cylindrical table lamp base, adjustable height shaft, embossed with mother and child on one side, father and child on the other, deep patina, signed "C. Scaravaglione", socket repaired.

1945   *34.25in (87cm) high*

$1,500-2,000   DRA

A pair of Ernesto Gismondi Sintesi lamps, produced by Artemide, Italy, designed 1979, each with white enameled metal base, black shaft, white light frame and black guard for special 'hammer' bulb, some wear to metal.

69.5in (176.5cm) high

$500-700 **FRE**

A Stemlite mushroom table lamp, with white glass mushroom shade on a black enameled tulip base, stickered.

11.75in (29.5cm) high

$350-450 **FRE**

A set of three Machine Age aluminum wall sconces, produced by Visa Lighting, USA, of recent manufacture, each half-cylinder form with aluminum frame encasing a white plastic shade.

16in (40.5cm) high

$500-700 **FRE**

A Danish floor lamp, black enameled metal shade, white enameled steel shaft and tripod base.

64.5in (163.5cm) high

$450-550 **FRE**

A 1960s Modernist chrome floor lamp with chrome base, shaft and light brackets holding three circular plastic shades.

55in (139.5cm) high

$220-280 **FRE**

A Laurel 'Mushroom' floor lamp, white frosted glass shade on black metal tulip base, blue "Laurel" sticker.

56.5in (143.5cm) high

$600-900 **FRE**

A 'Cobra' desk lamp with shallow dome shade, reflector, and three-sided shaft with applied boomerangs, on a circular base, break to rim of reflector, unmarked.

12.5in (32cm) high

$380-420 **DRA**

An Italian architectural lamp, stainless steel wall mount and pivoting arm with a black enameled metal shade, stamped "REGOLABILE", scratches to shade.

$300-400 **FRE**

Two Chase bright chrome lighting pieces, one lamp base with semi-circular ribbed shaft and one with a pivoting socket on ribbed 'O' shaft and pyramid.

13in (33cm) high

$80-120 **DRA**

A pair of Machine Age aluminum plaffoniers, by Edwin F. Guth. Co., USA, each with ink mark.
1940

35in (89cm) diam

$600-900 **FRE**

Sculpture

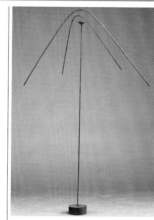

An early and rare Harry Bertoia brass washed wire mobile, comprised of twelve interlocking ovals forming a helix, unmarked.

c1950   28in (71cm) high
$12,000-15,000   **DRA**

An early and rare Harry Bertoia welded outdoor sculpture, with flaring geometric forms arranged along a narrow shaft, five counterweights, new matching base, rusting and pitting, unmarked.

120in (305cm) high
$12,000-15,000   **DRA**

A large and rare Harry Bertoia steel and bronze floor sculpture, with a series of interconnected rods fitted with rectangular, triangular, and diamond shaped forms, unmarked.

c1952   44.5in (113cm) high
$18,000-22,000   **DRA**

An early Harry Bertoia welded outdoor sculpture, on circular base comprised of a narrow shaft with conical tip, and two balancing arcs, new matching base, rusting and pitting, unmarked.

72in (183cm) high
$5,000-6,000   **DRA**

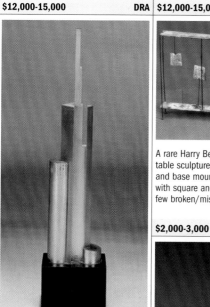

A rare Harry Bertoia wire and metal table sculpture, with rectangular top and base mounted with a series of rods with square and trapezoidal elements, a few broken/missing pieces, unmarked.

12in (31.5cm) wide
$2,000-3,000   **DRA**

A cement sculpture of a stylized horse head, after an original work by George Braque, unmarked.

c1940
$2,000-3,000   **DRA**

Richard Hunt, (American, born 1953) "Hybrid Form", welded steel.

c1964   30in (76cm) high
$3,000-4,000   **SI**

John Bradley Storrs, (American 1885-1956), 'Study In Pure Form (Forms in Space No. 4)', in stainless steel, copper, brass, signed with etched initials "J.S" on base of sculpture, indistinctly numbered, on a black slate base.

Born in Chicago, John Storrs studied in Germany, Boston, Philadelphia and with Auguste Rodin in Paris. He collaborated on many projects with Lois Sullivan and Frank Lloyd Wright.

14.75in (37.5cm) high overall
$120,000-180,000   **FRE**

An acrylic sculpture, by Hivo G. Van Teal, segmented pyramids on a diamond shaped base, signed.

17in (43cm) high
$300-400   **FRE**

An abstract wood sculpture, comprised of six pieces of wood laminated together, then carved.

19.5in (49.5cm) high
$200-300   **FRE**

An abstract iron sculpture wood base, signed "BM 1960".

c1960   18in (45.5cm) high
$180-220   **FRE**

Miscellaneous

A pair of John Piper large 'Chiesa Della Salute' curtains, produced by Sanderson Fabrics Ltd.

c1965   78.75in (200cm) long

$450-550   **BonBay**

A contemporary Modernist carpet, in mixed fabrics.

144in (366cm) long

$500-700   **FRE**

A Constructivist wool-weave shag rug.

109in (277cm) long

$220-280   **FRE**

An HMV 'Lincoln Model F3' electric fire, having curved flanges radiating from within a folded canopy with chromed ends and supported on a grey enameled domed base.

10.75in (27cm) high

$50-70   **DN**

A Richard Galef for Raven Ware wall shelf and coat hanger, with polychrome balls on coated wire, in the style of Charles Eames, original manufacturers tag.

24in (61cm) wide

$100-150   **DRA**

A ten piece novelty cocktail set, comprising a shaker with monogrammed cap and vessel transfer printed with drink recipes, eight clear wire glass tumblers, and a spherical bright chrome stand with pivoting ring holders and clearwire glass panels, unmarked.

24.5in (62cm) high

$700-1,000   **DRA**

A Howard Miller ball clock, with blonde wood balls on brass spokes, enameled hands, red second hand, gold label.

13.5 in (34.5cm) diam

$500-700   **DRA**

A Howard Miller wall clock, with brass tone roman numerals on oak blocks, plastic label.

11.5 in (29cm) diam

$300-400   **DRA**

A George Nelson ball clock, produced by Vitra, recent manufacture, with orange balls and black hands, new in box.

$150-200   **FRE**

An unusual glass-fronted wall mirror, possibly made by Orrefors in Sweden, surrounded by frosted panels.

28in (71cm) high

$700-1,000   **DN**

Two contemporary Italian silver centerpieces, signed "G. Vavassori," each realistically modeled as a woven bag.

Larger 12in (30.5cm) wide

$2,000-2,500   **SI**

Two pairs of contemporary Italian silver salt and pepper shakers, by Pampaloni, each of asymmetric pyramidal form.

Peppers 4.25in (10.5cm) high

$450-550   **SI**

A pair of figural enameled glass decanters and stoppers, one a Prussian officer, the other a woman.

Larger 7.75in (19.5cm) high

$150-200   **DN**

Posters

'New York World's Fair / American Airlines', designed Henry K. Bencathy.

1964   *40in (101.5cm) high*

$550-650   **Swa**

'Red Star Line', designed by Henri Cassiers, produced by O. de Rycker, Brussels, repaired along vertical and horizontal folds, matted and framed.

A mother and her daughter are eagerly awaiting an incoming liner. The young girl, peering through binoculars held by her mother, can see the ship so clearly that she is trying to touch it. This is one of the most tender images in a genre renowned for its hard-edged, Machine Age images.

1899   *49.75in (126cm) wide*

$12,000-14,000   **Swa**

'Cruise the Saguenay and St Lawrence Rivers / Canada Steamship Lines', designed by Roger Couillard, screen print, tears at edges, tears and abrasions in image.

c1952   *36.5in (92.5cm) high*

$650-750   **Swa**

'Sail White Empress to Europe', designed by Roger Couillard, restored losses in lower margin, creases.

1950   *35in (89cm) high*

$900-1,000   **Swa**

'Tadoussac', designed by Roger Couillard, screen print dry-mounted on on foam-core, minor tears and losses at edge.

c1950   *36in (91.5cm) high*

$1,200-1,700   **Swa**

'Canadian Pacific', designed by Cyrus Cuneo, produced by W. H. Smith, London, light vertical and horizontal folds, restoration and restored losses in top and bottom margins.

39.75in (101cm) high

$700-800   **Swa**

'Trans World Airlines', designed by James Cutter, produced by Stan Ramsay, Oklahoma City, in two-sheets, restoration, repaired tears and creases.

c1946   *68in (173cm) wide*

$1,800-2,300   **Swa**

'Atlantic City / Pennsylvania Railroad', designed by Eggleston, produced by O. Co., Clifton, New Jersey. Footnote: One in a series of posters Eggleston created for the Pennsylvania Railroad featuring beautiful, elegant women. Here, accompanied by a well-dressed suitor, the woman is looking out over the hustle and bustle of the famous Atlantic City Boardwalk, with the ocean and the Steel Pier in the distance.

c1935   *40.75in (103.5cm) high*

$14,000-16,000   **Swa**

'Amerika / Hamburg-Amerika Linie', designed by Theodore Etbauer, Petermann, Hamburg, sharp creases along top and bottom margins.

1934   *33in (83.5cm) high*

$550-650   **Swa**

'Hawaii / United Air Lines', designed by Feher, restored losses in corners.

c1960   *40in (101.5cm) high*

$1,300-1,800   **Swa**

'Go Pullman To America's Great Fairs', produced by Charles Daniel Frey, Chicago, creases and tears in corners and margins, abrasions in image, matted and framed.

1939   27.5in (70cm) high

$1,000-2,000   **Swa**

'Hamburg-Amerika Linie Nach New York', designed by Hugo Koeke, Muhlmeister & Johler, tears in margins, tape on verso.

1930   47in (119cm) high

$1,500-2,000   **Swa**

'Rainier National Park / The New Yakima Gateway', by Sydney Laurence, minor restoration and overpainting in margins.

c1935   40in (101.5cm) wide

$1,000-1,500   **Swa**

'Flying Down To Rio / Pan American', designed by Paul George Lawler, tear in image, creases in margins, pinholes in corners.

c1938   41in (104cm) high

$1,300-1,700   **Swa**

'Across the Pacific / Five Days', designed by Paul George Lawler.

1938   41.5in (105.5cm) high

$4,500-5,000   **Swa**

'American Railway Express / Our Service at Your Call', designed by Robert E. Lee , produced by Seitter & Kappes, New York, vertical and horizontal folds, repaired tears and creases in margins and image, overpainting and restoration in image.

1925   56in (142cm) wide

$2,000-3,000   **Swa**

'Bermuda', designed by Lesnon, produced by Mardon, Son and Hall, Bristol, creases and tears in margins, some affecting image, paper tape on verso.

38in (96.5cm) high

$1,300-1,800   **Swa**

'Bermuda', designed by Lesnon, produced by Mardon, Son and Hall, Bristol, wrinkles and creases in margins and image, paper.

37.75in (95.5cm) high

$700-800   **Swa**

One of a group of six 'Southern Pacific' posters, designed by Maurice Logan, stains, pinholes and creases in corners.

1928-1929   23in (58.5cm) high

$4,500-5,500 (set)   **Swa**

'Cunard to Canada', designed by Frank Newbould, produced by Thomas Forman & Sons, Nottingham, restoration and creases in corners and margins.

40in (101.5cm) high

$400-500   **Swa**

'American Airlines to New York', designed by Weimer Pursell, paper, minor tears and wrinkles in margins, creases in image.

c1950   *40in (101.5cm) high*
$1,700-2,300   **Swa**

'Chicago World's Fair', designed by Weimer Pursell, produced by Neely Printing Co., repaired tears in margins and image, repaired loss in left margin affecting image.

c1933   *41in (104cm) high*
$1,400-1,900   **Swa**

'Chicago World's Fair', by Weimer Pursell, Neely Printing Co, expertly restored losses in margins affecting image, repaired tears in image.

This is the most dramatic of Pursell's Chicago world's fair posters and depicts the three towers of the Federal Building - representing the branches of government - jutting up into the text.

c1933   *41.5in (105.5cm) high*
$2,000-2,500   **Swa**

'We Shall Not Fail', designed by Leslie Ragan, produced by Brett Lithographing Company, expertly recreated text at bottom, restoration in margins, creases in image.

This rare poster was produced by the New York Central System railroad company during World War II to show their commitment to the war effort. Ragan is best known for his graphic depictions of trains and prominent destinations along the New York Central Line system.

1943   *41in (104cm) high*
$7,000-8,000   **Swa**

'French Line', designed by Richard Rummell, Albert J Leon, New York, creases and abrasions in image, restoration in corners.

c1920   *27in 68.5cm) wide*
$1,500-2,000   **Swa**

'World's Fair/ Chicago/ 1933', designed by Glen C. Sheffer, produced by Goes Litho Co, repaired tears through margins into image, restoration in margins and corners.

1933   *41.75in (106cm) high*
$5,500-6,500   **Swa**

'National and State Parks', designed by Dorothy Waugh, produced by U.S. Government Printing Office, expertly restored losses and overpainting in margins and corners, some affecting image.

c1934   *40in (101.5cm) high*
$1,200-1,700   **Swa**

'Speed to Winter Playgrounds', designed by William P Welsh, produced by Charles Daniel Frey, Chicago, card, creases, wrinkles and overpainting in corners, abrasions in image.

1935   *27in (68.5cm) high*
$1,000-1,500   **Swa**

'Royal Mail', designed by Kenneth Shoesmith, restoration along vertical and horizontal folds in margins.

c1932   *39in (99cm) high*
$1,300-1,800   **Swa**

'Historic National Parks and Monuments', designed by Dorothy Waugh, repaired tear through top margin into image.

40in (101.5cm) high
$900-1,000   **Swa**

'A Pleasant Trip to Germany', designed by Jupp Wiertz, produced by Reichsbahnzentrale fur den Deutschen Reiseverkehr, tear in image.

This Art Deco image features the Hindenburg, a Lufthansa Foker airplane and a Hapag Line ship and a visual travelogue - taking the traveler from the skyscrapers of Manhattan past the mountains and palm trees of South America to the silhouetted sights of Germany.

c1935   39.75in (101cm) high

$6,500-7,500   **Swa**

'Express', from the famous Russian film, 'Pojezd idjot na vostok' (The Train to the East), minor restoration in margins, pinhole and crease in right bottom corner.

1954   33.5in (85cm) high

$750-850 Swa

'Montana's Gift / Great Northern Railway', produced by Rand, McNally & Co., Chicago, horizontal folds, tears in margins.

c1892   28in (71cm) high

$1,500-2,000   **Swa**

One of a group of six 'Santa Fe Railroad' posters, titles include 'Mission Churches', 'Carlsbad Caverns', 'Yosemite', 'Streamliners' and 'Indian Detours'.

c1940   36in (91.5cm) high

$850-950 (set)   **Swa**

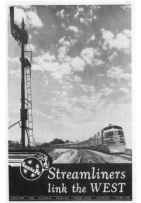
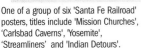
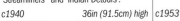

'Train Travel / New York', repaired tears and creases in image.

c1953   0.75in (103.5cm) high

$650-750   **Swa**

'Mexico Via Pan American', creases in margins and text, horizontal folds, minor abrasions in image, pinholes and losses in corners.

1940   41in (104cm) high

$1,000-1,500   **Swa**

'Nach Canada / White Star Line', produced by Muhlmeister & Johler, Hamburg, restoration and overpainting in margins.

c1930   38.25in (97cm) high

$700-800   **Swa**

'Canadian Pacific Great Atlantic Fleet', restoration and repaired tear in image.

c1932   35.75in (91cm) high

$800-900   **Swa**

'Murray Bay', produced by Brigdens Limited, Canada, dry-mounted on foam-core, pinholes and staining in corners, minor losses in margins and corners.

An elegant couple is keeping track of their score as they follow their caddy around a stunning course. Murray Bay is the third oldest golf course in the Americas. Founded in 1876, it is also the oldest one still in its original location.

c1935   38in (96.5cm) wide

$3,000-4,000   **Swa**

'See Boulder Dam Enroute To California', produced by Amalgamated Lithographers, Chicago, tears, wrinkles and slight paper loss at edges.

c1936   41in (104cm) high

$2,000-3,000   **Swa**

Portraits

A pair of portraits of Mary Shipley Pell and William Ferris Pell (1779-1840), pastel on paper, each identified and inscribed "Howland Pell" on reverse.

17.5 x 13.75in (44.5 x 35cm)

$1,500-2,000   NA

A portrait of American seaman James Hall (b. c1786) of Portsmouth, New Hampshire, pastel on paper, in eglomise and gilt frame, on the reverse a document signed and dated 1811 by James Whipple, Collector of Portsmouth, describing Hall's appearance and verifying his American citizenship in accordance with "The Act of Relief and Protection of American Seamen".

$8,000-12,000   NA

A portrait of Mrs Ruben Folger and her son, Timothy of Nantucket, oil on canvas, in a frame carved in the Chinese taste by Helen Ellis, signed bottom right.

16 x 16in (40.5 x 40.5cm)

$12,000-18,000   NA

A woman seated in Federal interior, oil on canvas.

10 x 8in (25.5 x 20.5cm)

$2,500-3,000   NA

Chester Harding (1792-1866), portrait of Miss Biddle of Philadelphia, oil on canvas, signed and inscribed on reverse.

32 x 24in (81 x 61cm)

$2,200-2,800   NA

A pair of American School portraits of a young lady and a gentleman, unsigned, oil on panel, some paint loss to lady, framed.

c1830   28in (71cm) high

$3,000-4,000   FRE

A 19thC American School portrait of George Washington after Gilbert Stuart, unsigned, oil on canvas, lined, some retouching.

30.25in (77cm) high

$5,000-7,000   FRE

An early 19thC portrait of George Washington after Gilbert Stuart, reverse painted on glass, framed, old crack upper right corner.

31 x 38in (79 x 96.5cm)

$4,000-6,000   FRE

Emanuel Leutze (1816-1868), portrait of George Washington, unsigned, oil on canvas, framed, mounted on Masonite panel, restored, soiled.

Provenance: The Free Library of Philadelphia Foundation, this portrait hung for many years in Pepper Hall.

117 x 80in (297 x 203cm)

$4,000-6,000   FRE

Emanuel Leutze (1816-1868), portrait of the Marquis de Lafayette, unsigned, oil on canvas, framed, mounted on Masonite panel, paint loss, repairs unstable areas.

Provenance: The Free Library of Philadelphia Foundation, this portrait hung for many years in Pepper Hall.

105 x 74in (267 x 188cm)

$2,500-3,000   FRE

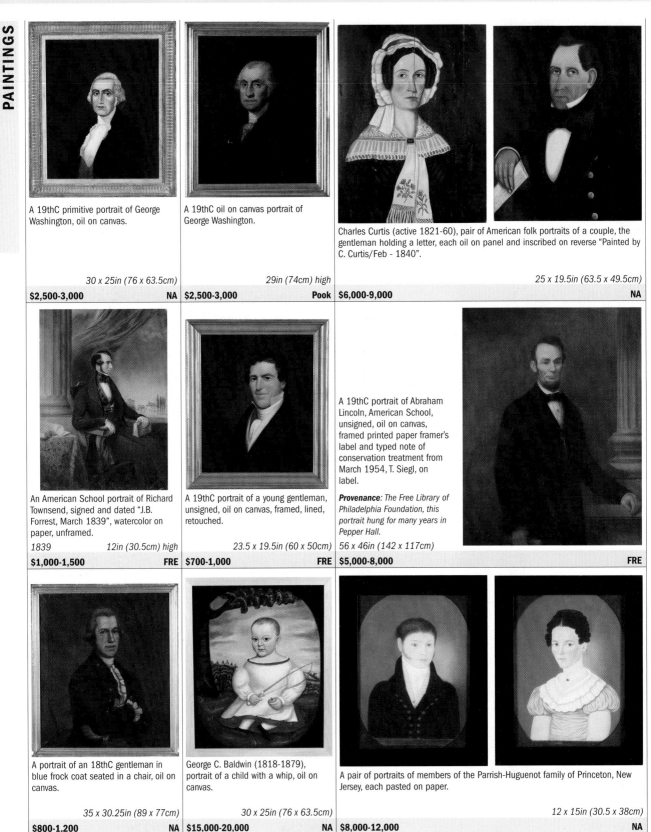

A 19thC primitive portrait of George Washington, oil on canvas.

30 x 25in (76 x 63.5cm)

$2,500-3,000 NA

A 19thC oil on canvas portrait of George Washington.

29in (74cm) high

$2,500-3,000 Pook

Charles Curtis (active 1821-60), pair of American folk portraits of a couple, the gentleman holding a letter, each oil on panel and inscribed on reverse "Painted by C. Curtis/Feb - 1840".

25 x 19.5in (63.5 x 49.5cm)

$6,000-9,000 NA

An American School portrait of Richard Townsend, signed and dated "J.B. Forrest, March 1839", watercolor on paper, unframed.

1839 *12in (30.5cm) high*

$1,000-1,500 FRE

A 19thC portrait of a young gentleman, unsigned, oil on canvas, framed, lined, retouched.

23.5 x 19.5in (60 x 50cm)

$700-1,000 FRE

A 19thC portrait of Abraham Lincoln, American School, unsigned, oil on canvas, framed printed paper framer's label and typed note of conservation treatment from March 1954, T. Siegl, on label.

Provenance: *The Free Library of Philadelphia Foundation, this portrait hung for many years in Pepper Hall.*

56 x 46in (142 x 117cm)

$5,000-8,000 FRE

A portrait of an 18thC gentleman in blue frock coat seated in a chair, oil on canvas.

35 x 30.25in (89 x 77cm)

$800-1,200 NA

George C. Baldwin (1818-1879), portrait of a child with a whip, oil on canvas.

30 x 25in (76 x 63.5cm)

$15,000-20,000 NA

A pair of portraits of members of the Parrish-Huguenot family of Princeton, New Jersey, each pasted on paper.

12 x 15in (30.5 x 38cm)

$8,000-12,000 NA

A portrait of Mrs Catherine Arnold Hummelo, holding a bible, oil on canvas.

Provenance: Maxim Karolilk Collection of American Paintings.

36 x 29in (91.5 x 73.5cm)

$10,000-15,000   **NA**

A portrait of young boy, with a leatherbound book, oil on canvas, inscribed "l.l. 'P... Greco 1851'".

1851   23.5 x 18in (60cm x 46cm)

$2,000-2,500   **NA**

FRANCIS MARTIN DREXEL

This painting was shown at Pennsylvania Academy of Fine Art in 1825. Drexel was born in Dornbin, Austrian Tyrol. He studied fine arts in Turin, Italy and then sailed for the United States in 1817 to avoid conscription in Austria, and settled in Philadelphia. He traveled to South America, painting portraits in Peru and Chile – including that of General Simon Bolivar, who became a friend. Once permanently settled back in Philadelphia in 1837, he founded the banking house Drexel & Co. The Paris house Drexel, Harjes & Co was founded in 1868 and the New York house Drexel, Morgan & Co three years later.

Francis Martin Drexel (1792-1863), portrait of Mary Johanna Drexel as a child, oil on canvas retains old paper label verso.

Provenance; Mary J. Drexel home, Gladwyne, PA.

24.5in (62.5cm) high

$3,500-4,500   **Pook**

Francis Martin Drexel (1792-1863), self portrait of the artist, oil on canvas.

Provenance: Mary J. Drexel home, Gladwyne, PA.

19.5in (49.5cm) high

$3,000-4,000   **Pook**

Francis Martin Drexel (1792-1863), Drexel family portrait of the artist holding a palette at his easel beside Federal stand containing artist's pigments, with his wife, Catherine Hookey Drexel, and daughter Mary Johanna Drexel, oil on canvas.

Provenance: Mary J. Drexel home, Gladwyne, PA. This is a world record price for a work by Drexel.

54.5in (138cm) high

$250,000-300,000   **Pook**

George Hartwell (1815-1901), a half-length folk portrait of young woman holding a rose seated in scroll-back chair with patterned upholstery, oil on canvas.

27 x 21.25in (68.5 x 54cm)

$12,000-18,000   **NA**

A portrait of a young boy in regimental gray uniform, with drum, oil on canvas.

40in (101.5cm) high

$6,000-9,000   **NA**

A portrait of a 19thC gentleman, oil on canvas, with ink monogram "SPL" on reverse.

27 x 24in (68.5 x 61cm)

$2,500-3,000   **NA**

PAINTINGS

A pair of 19thC Canadian School portraits of a lady and a gentleman, seated in landscapes, pair of oils on panel, unframed.

9 x 7.25in (23 x 18.5cm)

$500-700 **WAD**

A pair of 19thC Anglo-American School portraits of a 'Lady' and a 'Gentleman', unsigned, watercolor and ink on paper, framed, minor discoloration.

7.5in (19cm) high

$4,000-6,000 **FRE**

A 19thC American School portrait of a young gentleman, unsigned, oil on canvas, lined, framed.

25in (63.5cm) wide

$500-700 **FRE**

A late 19thC watercolor, of a boy with a bird.

$500-800 **BCAC**

A late 19thC portrait of a lady, oil on canvas, wearing a white lace bonnet and collar, holding a letter.

28.5in (73cm) high

$800-1,200 **Pook**

Henry Walton, watercolour portrait painting of Julia Jane Chambers, aged 13 years, on paper, signed and dated.

This is unusually large for his work. Henry Walton is a little-known artist from the Finger Lakes or Ithaca areas of New York State.

Frame 16.75in (42.5cm) high

$20,000-30,000 **SG**

A primitive painting of a white dog with puppies, oil on canvas, initialled "L R" and dated.

1888 *26 x 18in (66 x 46cm)*

$3,000-4,000 **NA**

A 19thC American School painting, the Boston Railroad at Cottage Farm Bridge, oil on canvas.

14 x 22in (35.5 x 56cm)

$3,500-4,500 **NA**

A Hudson River primitive painting, with steam and sidewheel riverboat and townscape in distance, oil on board.

23.5 x 31.5in (60 x 80cm)

$1,500-2,000 **NA**

Landscapes

A set of four primitive paintings of the voyage of life, each with angel-form skiff or gondola on fanciful riverscape, two with face-filled moons, oil on canvas.

24 x 36in (61cm x 91.5cm)

$7,000-10,000 NA

An American School painting, 'Western Mountain Landscape with Rushing River', oil on canvas.

22.75 x 29.5in (58 x 75cm)

$1,500-2,000 SI

A Primitive School painting of a wood chopper near a log cabin, oil on canvas.

18 x 22in (45.5 x 56cm)

$2,000-3,000 NA

A 19thC primitive school painting, Hudson River near the palisades, oil on canvas laid down masonite, titled verso.

24 x 30in (61 x 76cm)

£250-300 WAD

A 19thC view of the 1794 eruption of Mount Vesuvius, American School, signed on reverse "painted about 1817 by ... Mel Bingham when he was 14 years old", watercolor on paper, framed, losses to margin and image, professionally conserved.

15.5in x 21in (39.5 x 53.5cm)

$1,500-2,000 FRE

A 19thC American School portrait of a house, oil on canvas, unsigned, printed paper label, "Albert L. Calder Apothecary No. 151 Westminster St., Providence".

12in (30.5cm) wide

$1,000-1,500 FRE

A 20thC American School country landscape, unsigned, oil on maple veneer panel, slight warping to panel, minor abrasion.

23 x 33.5in (58.5 x 85cm)

$700-1,000 FRE

A 19thC American School view of East River Drive, inscribed "Fairmount", signed T. B. Schell and dated, watercolor on paper, framed.

1876 *9.5in (24cm) diam*

$1,200-1,800 FRE

A 19thC American School 'Young Girl with Basket of Flowers', unsigned, inscription at lower margin, "An old picture of my mother's, found among her relics S.L. Wister 1883", watercolor and ink on paper, unframed.

1883 *7.25in (18.5cm)*

$1,500-2,000 FRE

One of a pair of American School sketches of the 'Belfield Prints Works, Philadelphia', unsigned, together with an engraving of the 'Wakefield Mills', pencil and ink on paper, unframed.

Provenance: The Belfield Print Works in Germantown was owned by William Logan Fisher (1781-1862) and operated by his son-in-law William Wister, husband of Sarah Logan Fisher.

c1830

$1,500-2,000 (pair)   FRE

One of a pair of American School 'Views of Duncannon House at the iron works, Clarks Ferry, PA', signed Ellicott Fisher, pencil on paper, unframed.

Provenance: These drawings descended in the Fisher family until 1972 when they were sold.

c1835   13.5in (34.5cm) wide

$700-1,000 (pair)   FRE

One of a pair of American School sketches of 'Philadelphia Bridges', unsigned, indecipherable notations in the upper left-hand corner, pencil on paper.

Provenance: Descended in the Fisher family's belongings at Wakefield, to Mrs Wister Wurts, and purchased from her in 1972.

c1835   11.5in (29cm)

$350-400 (pair)   FRE

John Richards, 'The Residence of John Hancock and the Statehouse', 19thC American School Boston sketches, unsigned, ink on paper, discoloration and abrasions.

Provenance: These sketches are by Swedish immigrant and well-known Germantown character John Richards, and were produced while he was convalescing after injuries sustained in the Civil War. They were found in a trunk from Wakefield, purchased in 1972 from a Fisher descendant, Mrs Wister Wurts.

c1835   11.5in (29cm) wide

$250-300 (set)   FRE

John Richards 'Four Views of Stenton, Philadelphia', 19thC American School pen and ink on paper, signed "J. Richard", unframed.

Provenance: Stenton was built by James Logan, agent to William Penn 1720-1730. It is now one of the best preserved colonial homes in the country. These John Richards sketches were found in a trunk from Wakefield, purchased in 1972 from a Fisher descendant, Mrs Wister Wurts.

c1835   11in (28cm) wide

$800-1,200 (set)   FRE

A 19thC American School romantic landscape, signed by "Miss Caroline F. Simpson", ink on paper, framed, a note on the back reads "Presented to E.A. Kirk by Mrs. David Stevenson 1846".

5.25in (13.5cm) wide

$150-200   FRE

A 19thC American School drawing of two young girls feeding chickens, signed "drawn by Sally Johnson, daughter", pencil on tinted paper, unframed.

Provenance: Descended in the Fisher family's belongings at Wakefield, to Mrs Wister Wurts, and purchased from her in 1972.

13.5in (34.5cm) wide

$600-900   FRE

A 19thC American School romantic landscape, unsigned, charcoal and chalk on sandpaper, framed.

8.5 x 11.25in (21.5 x 28.5cm)

$500-800   FRE

A 19thC American School Hudson River scene with sailboats, unsigned, charcoal and chalk on sandpaper, in a rosewood grain-painted frame.

13 x 17in (33 x 43cm)

$800-1,200   FRE

Marine

A folk art watercolor, of Liberty holding an American flag, being drawn in a sea chariot by two horses with an American frigate to the side, ink and watercolor on paper.

9.75 x 17in (24 x 43.5cm)

$10,000-15,000 NA

A marine scene, of the War of 1812, Naval engagement between the 'Constitution' and 'Guerriere', oil on canvas.

18 x 23.5in (45.5 x 59.5cm)

$6,000-9,000 NA

A marine scene, 'Ohio of Salem, Samuel Hill, Master', in the style of George Ropes, oil on canvas, titled and dated August 1851.

18 x 24in (46 x 61cm)

$12,000-18,000 NA

A 19thC American School marine scene, 'View of Lock Haven, Pennsylvania', oil on canvas.

14 x 26in (35.5 x 66cm)

$3,500-4,500 NA

A Vespian of Boston marine scene, Benjamin C. Green, Commander 1842, attributed to Petrus C. Weyts (Belgian 1799-1855), reverse painted on glass with caption "l.c".

19 x 26in (48 x 66cm)

$20,000-30,000 NA

A late 19th/early 20thC American School whaling scene, signed "Thos. Balchen"(?), oil on canvas, craquelure, framed.

33in (84cm) wide

$800-1,200 FRE

A Canadian Brigantine in artic waters, attributed to Joseph Heard (British 1799-1859), oil on canvas.

21 x 29in (53.5 x 73cm)

$1,800-2,200 WAD

A 19thC American School marine scene, 'Southern Railway at Niagara Falls', oil on canvas in a black and gilt frame with incised decoration.

30 x 48in (76 x 122cm)

$8,000-12,000 NA

A 19thC American School river scene, 'Hudson River Landscape', oil on canvas.

17.5 x 24in (44.5 x 61cm)

$1,800-2,200 SI

A 19thC American School marine scene, 'The Breakers', signed with initials, "S.W." and dated "87" lower left, also inscribed indistinctly on portion of old label on reverse, oil on panel, unframed.

5.75in x 12.25in (14.5 x 31cm)

$250-300 SI

A 19thC American School river scene, 'Entrance to Highlands on Hudson, New York', inscribed on reverse, oil on board.

14 x 10.5in (35.6 x 27cm)

$500-700 SI

Still life

A still life, a fire board of flowers in a vase on a marble plinth, oil on canvas.

25 x 36in (63.5 x 91.5cm)

$3,500-4,500 NA

A 19thC American School still life, with fruit and an insect, oil on panel, unsigned, cracks to panel.

14.25in (36cm) wide

$3,500-4,500 FRE

A 19thC American School still life, 'Tabletop Still Life with Basket of Grapes', oil on canvas.

10 x 16.5in (26 x 42cm)

$1,000-1,500 SI

A 19thC American School still life, 'Still Life of Pears and Plums', oil on board.

8in (20cm) wide

$4,000-6,000 FRE

A 19th/20thC American School still life, 'A Spilled Basket of Cherries', oil on canvas, laid on masonite.

14 x 18in (35.5 x 46cm)

$500-800 SI

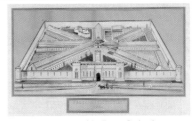

A 19th/20thC American School still life, 'Tabletop Still Life', oil on canvas laid on artist board.

18 x 23in (45.5 x 58.5cm)

$400-500 SI

An American School watercolor on paper, 'The Hall and Front Door of School, Old Academy of Germantown', signed "drawn by Lindley Fisher" (1818-1852), unframed, tears to margins, some discoloration.

PROVENANCE: *From a loose page in a scrap book found in a trunk from Wakefield, purchased in 1972 from Mrs Wister Wurts, a Fisher descendant*

c1835 *12.25in (31cm) wide*

$20,000-30,000 FRE

A Quebec folk art school interior study, oil on cardboard, initialled "G.E.T.Y" lower right.

18 x 22.5in (45.5 x 56.5cm)

$1,500-2,000 WAD

An American School view of the Eastern Penitentiary, Pennsylvania, dated, unsigned, view identified in margin, watercolor on paper, lot includes prison book of laws, a typed note suggests the painter was inmate Samuel Couperthwaite.

1855 *18in (45.5cm) wide*

$3,500-4,500 FRE

A 19thC American School amusing drawing, 'Piggy's father applies the cane', dated "Jan 7, 1871", pencil and watercolor on lined paper, framed, some discoloration.

1871 *7in (18cm) high*

$250-300 FRE

A 19th/20thC Latin American School painting 'Figures Before a Shop Window', oil on panel.

7.75in x 9.5in (20 x 24cm)

$800-1,200 SI

An amusing 20thC American fishing scene, unsigned, oil on canvas, cut down, paint loss.

7 x 9 in (18 x 23cm)

$350-400 FRE

Landscapes

David B. Bechtel (b. 1895), barnyard landscape with chickens, oil on canvas.

16 x 21in (40.5 x 53.5cm)

$1,000-1,500   **AAC**

Harry G. Bergman (1900-1932), 'Winter Landscape', oil on canvas, signed "H.G. Berman" bottom right, indistinctly inscribed verso.

20in (51cm) wide

$4,000-5,000   **FRE**

John E. Berninger (1897-1981), autumn landscape with corn shucks and country road, oil on board.

16 x 20in (40.5 x 50.5cm)

$1,500-2,000   **AAC**

George Louis Berg (1868-1941), 'Autumn view of a mountain through birches', oil on canvas, signed lower right.

27 x 36in (68.5 x 91.5cm)

$1,800-2,200   **NA**

Franz Arthur Bischoff (1864-1929), 'Hilly Landscape', oil on canvas, signed "Franz A. Bischoff" bottom left.

20in (51cm) wide

$4,000-6,000   **FRE**

Thomas Doughty, Hudson River valley landscape with house, figures and animals, oil on canvas on panel, restoration note from "Sept '36".

13.5 x 18in (34.5 x 46cm)

$12,000-18,000   **AAC**

John J. Enneking (1841-1916), 'Mountain Vista with Pines', oil on canvas, signed lower right.

25 x 30in (63.5 x 76.5cm)

$15,000-20,000   **NA**

Daniel Charles Grose (1838-1890), 'Fisherman in a Landscape', signed "D. C. Grose" lower left, oil on canvas.

25 x 37.25in (63.5 x 94.5cm)

$3,000-5,000   **SI**

Peter A. Gross (1849-1914), landscape with pond and children sailing pond boat, oil on canvas.

22.5 x 32in (57.25 x 81.25cm)

$2,500-3,000   **AAC**

Harry Horn, landscape with house and covered bridge with children on country road, oil on canvas.

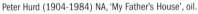

Peter Hurd (1904-1984) NA, 'My Father's House', oil.

Peter Hurd (1904-1984) NA, 'Exhibition, Chester County Art Association', ink.

20 x 24in (51 x 70cm)

$5,000-7,000   **AAC**

16 x 20in (41 x 22cm)

$15,000-20,000   **Alt**

10.25 x 15.25in (26 x 39cm)

$2,500-3,000   **Alt**

Alfred Jansson (Swedish/American 1862-1931), 'View Along the River, Spring', oil on canvas, signed and dated "Alfred Jansson 1915" bottom right.

Louis Aston Knight (French/American 1873-1948), 'Setting Sun, Diane's Cottage', oil on canvas, signed and inscribed "Aston Knight Paris" bottom right, inscribed on label verso (now detached).

30.25in (76.5cm) high

$5,000-8,000   **FRE**

27.75 x 60in (66 x 152.5cm)

$30,000-40,000   **FRE**

Louis Aston Knight (1873-1948), 'Garden On The Riviera', oil on canvas, signed lower right.

Francois Koch, 'Patterns of Gold', oil on canvas, signed lower right.

Sydney Laurence (1865-1940), 'The Lower Suisana', oil on canvas laid on board, signed lower right.

22 x 18in (56 x 46cm)

$2,500-3,000   **NA**

32 x 56in (81 x 142cm)

$40,000-50,000   **RENO**

8 x 10in (20 x 25.5cm)

$10,000-15,000   **RENO**

Richard Hayley Lever (1876-1958), 'Horsecart', oil on panel, signed "H. Lever" lower left.

Raphael Lillywhite (1891-1958), 'Lone Pine Ranch, Colorado', signed lower left, also pencil titled on reverse, oil on masonite.

Luigi Lucioni (1900-1988), 'Vermont Classic', oil on panel, signed and dated "L. Lucioni '27", exhibited at Dallas Museum of Fine Arts June 6 - November 29, 1936.

28in (71cm) wide	*25 x 30in (63.5 x 76cm)*	*24 x 20in (61 x 51cm)*
$2,500-3,000 FRE	**$4,000-6,000** SI	**$4,000-6,000** NA

William Rickarby Miller (1818-1893), 'Figures Resting by a Riverbank', oil on board, signed and dated "W.R. Miller 1877", bottom left, unframed.

P. Buckley Moos (b.1933), 'The Ride Home, Winter', signed and dated "Moss '80" and copyrighted lower centre right, ink and watercolour on paper.

Forrest K. Moses (1893-1974), 'Yellow Straw: Winter snow scene', oil on board, signed lower right, with artist's label on reverse inscribed "Eagle bridge" with title, no 27 and dated March 1966.

Forrest K. Moses, son of 'Grandma' Moses, was a farmer who began painting at the age of 56 in a style similar to his mother's.

10in (25.5cm) high	*20 x 20in (51 x 51cm)*	*16 x 24in (40.5 x 61cm)*
$4,000-6,000 FRE	**£3,000-4,000** SI	**$2,500-3,000** NA

Sheldon Parsons (1866-1943), 'Headwaters of the Rio Grande', oil.

Parsons studied at the National Academy of Design with William Merritt Chase among others. While in New York he became a celebrity portrait painter but due to tuberculosis he moved to Santa Fe in 1913.

Ogden M. Pleissner (1905-1983), 'Vermont farm with view of Mt. Equinox and the Manchester Valley', oil on canvas, signed lower left, with gallery label on reverse.

24 x 36in (61 x 91.5cm)	*26 x 38in (71 x 96.5cm)*
$20,000-30,000 Alt	**$60,000-90,000** NA

James Reynolds (b 1926), CAA, NAWA, 'Near Wilcox', oil.

18 x 24in (45.5 x 61cm)

$8,000-12,000   **Alt**

Porfirio Salinas (1910-1973), 'Autumn Hill Country Landscape', oil.

16 x 20in (41 x 51cm)

$5,000-7,000   **Alt**

Porfirio Salinas (1910-1973), 'Hill County Landscape' oil.

25 x 30in (63.5 x 76cm)

$8,000-12,000   **Alt**

Albert F. Schmitt (b.1873), 'Gloucester Marsh and Dunes', oil on canvas, carved gilt frame by Thulin, signed, marked Number 141 and indistinctly dated "191_ " lower right.

24.25 x 29in (62.5 x 73.5cm)

$12,000-18,000   **NA**

Richard Schmidt, 'Dogwood', oil on canvas, signed lower right.

20 x 30in (51 x 76cm)

$20,000-30,000   **RENO**

Conrad Schwiering (1916-1986), NAWA 'Tetons', oil.

12 x 18in (30.5 x 46cm)

$3,500-4,500   **Alt**

Christopher H. Shearer (1840-1926), impressionist landscape with house and stone bridge, oil on canvas.

24 x 36in (61 x 91.5cm)

$3,000-5,000   **AAC**

Carol Sirak (1906-1976), 'Overlooking the Delaware River', winter landscape, oil on canvas, relined and restored.

25 x 30in (63.5 x 7.5cm)

$6,000-9,000   **AAC**

William Lester Stevens (1888-1969), landscape, oil on canvas.

20 x 24in (51cm x 61cm)

$1,800-2,200   **AAC**

Tod Lindenmuth (1885-1976), 'A Mountain Farm', oil on board.

8.5 x 10.5in (22 x 27cm)

$1,200-1,500   **AAC**

Florence Tricker, impressionist landscape, oil on canvas.

12 x 12in (30.5 x 30.5cm)

$2,000-3,000   **AAC**

Curt Walters (b. 1950) AOA, 'Statelines', oil.

Curt Walters is the official artist of the Grand Canyon Trust.

36 x 36in (91.5 x 91.5cm)

$12,000-18,000   **Alt**

Max Weyl (1837-1914), 'Washington, DC, Landscape with U.S. Capitol', oil on canvas, signed and dated "Max Weyl 1911".

24in (61cm) wide

$5,000-8,000   **FRE**

Guy Carleton Wiggins (1883-1962), 'Indian Summer', oil on canvas, signed lower right and inscribed "Indian Summer, Guy Wiggins" on reverse, with label of the Lyme Art Association on the stretcher.

21.75 x 28.75in (55.5 x 73cm)

$5,000-7,000   **NA**

Edmund Aylburnon Willis (1808-1899), 'Haying time - the first load', oil on canvas, signed and dated "A.V. Willis, 1884" lower right.

22 x 36in (56 x 91.5cm)

$3,000-4,000   **NA**

Robert Wood (1889-1979), 'Grand Tetons', oil.

20in (51cm) wide

$3,500-4,500   **ALT**

Robert Wood (1889-1979), 'Field of Bluebonnets', oil.

16 x 20in (40.5 x 51cm)

$5,000-7,000   **Alt**

Joseph E. Yoakum (1886-1972), 'Mt. Siple in Elsworth Highland Distric (sic) of Antarctica, Island of South Pole', signed "Joseph E. Yoakum" and titled upper left, also stamped "SEP 1 - 1970", colored pencil, pen and ink on paper.

12 x 19in (30.5 x 48.5cm)

$5,000-7,000   **SI**

TOWNSCAPES

Johann Berthelsen (1883-1969), '42nd Street Looking East from Vanderbilt Avenue, New York City', oil on canvas, signed.

16in (40.5cm) high

$6,000-9,000   **FRE**

Johann Berthelsen (1883-1969), 'New York City in Winter', oil on canvas, signed bottom right.

16in (40.5cm) high

$5,000-8,000   **FRE**

Hattie K. Brunner (1890-1982), 'The Country Auction', watercolor on paper, signed and dated, framed.

Purchased from the artist in Reinholds, Pennsylvania.

1966   *14.5in (37cm) wide*

$4,000-6,000   **FRE**

Hattie K. Brunner (1890-1982), 'An Autumn Harvest Scene', watercolor on paper, signed and dated, framed.

1965   *14.5in (37cm) wide*

$3,500-4,500   **FRE**

Hattie K. Brunner (1890-1982), 'A Winter Scene: Skating and a Sleigh Ride', watercolor on paper, signed and dated, framed.

1965   *14.5in (37cm) wide*

$3,000-4,000   **FRE**

Paul Cornoyer (1864-1923), 'Flower Market, San Sulspice', oil on canvas, signed and inscribed verso.

12in (30.5cm) high

$7,000-10,000   **FRE**

George Wharton Edwards (1869-1950), 'Pont Neuf, Paris', oil on canvas laid down on panel, signed bottom right.

24in (61cm) wide

$5,000-7,000   **FRE**

Earle Horter (1880-1940), 'Pennsylvania Farm House', watercolor on paper, signed bottom left.

17in (43cm) wide

$2,000-3,000   **FRE**

Jonas Lie (1880-1940), 'New York Street Scene', oil on canvasboard, signed "Jonas Lie" bottom left and signed and dated verso.

1917   *12in (30.5cm) high*

$10,000-15,000   **FRE**

Frederick J. Mulhaupt (1871-1938), 'Market at Moret, France', oil on board, signed "Mulhaupt" bottom right.

10in (25.5cm) wide

$10,000-15,000   **FRE**

Jane Peterson (1876-1965), 'Beach Scene', oil on canvas.

16in (40.5cm) wide

$15,000-20,000   **FRE**

George J. Stengel (1872-1937), 'On the Canal', signed, located and dated "G. J. Stengel / Mexico 1932" lower left, also signed on reverse, oil on canvas.

32 x 36in (81.5 x 91.5cm)

$3,000-4,000   **SI**

George J Stengel (1872-1937), 'Tepotzopian Village Scene', signed, dated lower left, also on reverse, oil on canvas.

1932   *32 x 36in (81.5 x 91.5cm)*

$3,500-4,500   **SI**

Guy Carleton Wiggins (1883-1962), '5th Ave from 57th Street', oil on artist board, signed lower left and inscribed on reverse.

10 x 8.25in (25.5 x 21cm)

$7,000-10,000   **NA**

Guy Carleton Wiggins (1883-1962), 'Church of the Ascension', oil on canvas, signed "Guy Wiggins" bottom left, signed, titled and dated verso.

1937   *24in (61cm) high*

$30,000-50,000   **FRE**

MARINE

Montague Dawson (British 1895-1973), 'The Torrens in Californian Water', oil on canvas, signed lower left.

28 x 42in (71 x 106.5cm)

$40,000-60,000 RENO

Emil Gelhaar (1862-1934), 'Boats at Sea', signed "E. Gelhaar" lower left, oil on canvas.

26 x 32in (66 x 81.5cm)

$1,000-1,500 SI

Walter Granville-Smith (1870-1938), 'Mending the Nets', oil on board, signed "Granville-Smith" bottom left, with artist's estate stamp verso.

10in (25.5cm) wide

$5,000-8,000 FRE

Gordon Grant (1875-1962), 'Lobsterman in a dory', watercolor on paper, signed and dated lower right.

1938   *12.25 x 17.75in (31 x 45cm)*

$8,000-12,000 NA

Emile Jacques (Belgian/American 1874-1937), 'Peaceful Hour (High Water)', oil on canvas, signed "Em Jacques" bottom right.

30in (76cm) wide

$8,000-12,000 FRE

Marshall Johnson (1850-1921), clipper ship under sail, oil on canvas, signed lower left.

36 x 29in (91.5 x 73.5cm)

$5,000-7,000 NA

Richard Hayley Lever (1876-1958), 'Masts, Gloucester Harbor', oil on canvas, signed lower right, inscribed "Gloucester, Mass. Masts" on stretcher.

24in (61cm) wide

$12,000-18,000 FRE

Edward Moran (1829-1901), 'Moonlight Sail', signed "Moran" lower left, oil on canvas.

12 x 18in (30.5 x 45.5cm)

$2,500-3,000 SI

Henry Pember Smith (1854-1907), 'Coast of New England', oil on canvas, signed and dated "Henry P. Smith, 1883" bottom left.

28in (71cm) wide

$3,500-4,500 FRE

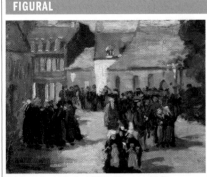

Harriette Bowdoin (b. 1947), 'Figures and Nuns on a Village Street', oil on canvasboard, signed "Harriette Bowdoin" bottom left.

8.5in (21.5cm) wide

$2,000-3,000　　　　**FRE**

Abbott Fuller Graves (1859-1936), 'Luxembourg Garden, Paris', oil on board, inscribed in pencil "Luxembourg Garden/Paris/by Abbott Graves" verso.

9.5in (24cm) high

$8,000-12,000　　　　**FRE**

Howard Logan Hildebrandt (1872-1958), 'Portrait of a Lady with Plumed Hat', oil on canvas, signed "H.L. Hildebrandt" bottom right.

27in (68.5cm) high

$6,000-9,000　　　　**FRE**

Edward Cucuel (1879-1951), 'East Wind', oil on canvas, signed "Cucuel" bottom right, signed twice verso.

27.75in (70.5cm) high

$70,000-100,000　　　　**FRE**

Hy Hintermeister (1897-1972), 'Gramps', oil on canvas, signed lower right.

30 x 22in (76 x 56cm)

$7,000-10,000　　　　**RENO**

Ben Kamihira (b. 1925), 'The Card Players', oil on canvas, signed "KAMIHIRA" bottom right.

35in (89cm) wide

$3,000-4,000　　　　**FRE**

William McGregor Paxton (1869-1941), portrait of a seated woman in a white dress, oil on board, signed lower right.

30 x 25in (76 x 63.5cm)

$2,500-3,500   **NA**

Pino, 'The Country Girl', oil on canvas, signed lower left.

40 x 26in (101.5 x 66cm)

$30,000-40,000   **RENO**

Robert Riggs (1896-1970), 'Out for the Count', watercolor and pencil, signed "Robert Riggs".

28.25in (72cm) wide

$2,500-3,000   **FRE**

F. Humphrey Woolrych (1868-1941), portrait of a woman seated amid flowers, oil on board, signed lower left.

40 x 30in (101.5 x 76cm)

$2,500-3,000   **NA**

M. J. Ward (1799-1874), 'Coursing', oil on canvas, signed lower right.

***Provenance**: The Estate of Molly Flagg Knuddtsen, New York-Reno, Nevada.*

12 x 18.5in (30.5 x 47cm)

$2,500-3,000   **RENO**

Frank B. Hoffman (1888-1958), 'Fox Hunt', oil.

Hoffman worked at his family-owned racing stable in Ohio where he jockeyed while studying the subjects that would dominate his art. He was then educated at the Art Institute of Chicago where he met and worked for Leon Gaspard.

34.25 x 42.25in (87 x 107cm)

$20,000-30,000   **Alt**

STILL LIFE

Cora S. Brooks (1885-1930), 'Zinnias and Marigolds', floral still life with glass bottle, oil on canvas board.

12 x 16in (30.5 x 40.75cm)

$3,500-4,500   **AAC**

David Y. Ellinger, theorem of basket of strawberries, watermelon, various fruit, bird, bees and butterfly, oil on velvet.

19.5 x 23.5in (49.5 x 60cm)

$3,500-4,500   **AAC**

David Y. Ellinger, theorem of fruit in basket with yellow bird, oil on velvet, minor foxing.

13.75 x 17in (35 x 43.25cm)

$2,000-3,000   **AAC**

Arthur C. Goodwin (1864-1929), still life of roses and chrysanthemums in an orange vase, pastel on paper.

23 x 18.75in (58.5 x 47.5cm)

$2,500-3,000   **NA**

George Harvey (1800-1878), 'Still Life of Peaches', signed "G. Harvey" lower right, oil on canvas.

9.5 x 13in (24.5 x 33cm)

$1,500-2,000   **SI**

Jimmy Lueders (1927-1997), 'Zinias on a Pink Tablecloth', oil on canvas, signed and inscribed "J C Lueders/6819 Greene St./Phila. Penna" verso, also signed on stretcher.

60in (152.5cm) wide

$5,000-7,000   **FRE**

Lillian B. Meeser (1864-1942), 'The Chinese Vase', oil on canvas, signed lower left, with a letter written by the artist to the owner of the painting, exhibited Pennsylvania Academy of the Fine Arts, Annual Exhibition, 1936.

30 x 25in (76 x 63.5cm)

$3,000-5,000   **NA**

Joseph Sacks (1887-1974), 'Still Life', oil on canvas, signed and dated "Joseph Sacks 1932" bottom left.

40in (101.5cm) wide

$7,000-10,000   **AAC**

Loran Speck (b. 1943), 'Indian pottery with Pears', oil.

16 x 20in (41 x 51cm)

$10,000-15,000   **Alt**

Loran Speck (b. 1943), 'Chile Peppers on a Ledge', oil.

6 x 11in (15.5 x 28cm)

$6,000-9,000   **Alt**

ABSTRACT

Alexander Calder (1898-1967), 'Loops and Grids', gouache, signed and dated "Calder 63" bottom right.

41.25in (105cm) wide

$10,000-15,000   **FRE**

Joseph Meierhans (1890-1980), abstract composition, oil on masonite, in an artist-made frame.

32 x 24in (81.25 x 101.5cm)

$600-1,000   **AAC**

Joseph Meierhans (1890-1980), abstract composition, oil on masonite, in an artist made frame.

32 x 24in (81.25 x 101.5cm)

$1,000-1,500   **AAC**

George L.K. Morris (1905-1975), abstract composition, oil on panel, signed "Morris" lower right, with artist's monogram, dated, gallery label on reverse.

1937   *18 x 14in (45.75 x 35.5cm)*

$10,000-15,000   **NA**

Kim Wiggins (b. 1960), SAI, 'Cycle of Life #12', oil.

24 x 30in (61 x 76cm)

$7,000-10,000   **Alt**

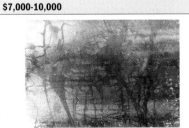

Richard Dempsey (20thC), 'North Carolina (Search for Shells) 1965', signed and located "Dempsey / North Carolina" lower left, watercolor on paper.

22 x 30.5in (56 x 77.5cm)

$2,500-3,000   **SI**

Kim Wiggins (b. 1960), SAI, 'All the Stars of April', oil.

36 x 36in (91.5 x 91.5cm)

$10,000-15,000   **Alt**

George Biddle (1885-1973), 'Cuban Landscape', oil on canvas, unframed, signed and dated "Biddle 1925" bottom right, signed, tilted and numbered "125" verso.

40in (101.5cm) wide

$20,000-30,000   **FRE**

Everett Lloyd Bryant (1864-1945), 'Yellow and White Flowers in a White Vase', oil on canvas, signed "E.L. Bryant" bottom left.

27in (56cm) wide

$10,000-15,000   **FRE**

Everett Lloyd Bryant (1864-1945), 'Still Life on a Demi-Lune Table by a Garden Window', oil on canvas, signed "E L Bryant" bottom left.

30in (76cm) wide

$3,500-4,500   **FRE**

Maude Drein Bryant (1880-1946), still life of flowers and ceramics on desk, oil on canvas.

36 x 30in (91.5 x 76cm)

$2,500-3,500   **AAC**

Circle of Arthur Carles (1882-1952), 'Still Life of Flowers', oil on canvas.

36.25in (92cm) high

$1,500-2,000   **FRE**

Frank F. English (1854-1922), 'Horsecart in the Fields', watercolor on paper, signed "F.F. English" bottom left.

29.5in (74.5cm) high

$3,000-4,000   **FRE**

Nancy Maybin Ferguson (1872-1967), 'Church, Provincetown', oil on board, signed with monogram "NMF" lower left, signed "Nancy Maybin Ferguson" verso.

13.5in (34.5cm) wide

$7,000-10,000   **FRE**

Leslie Henderson (b.1895), 'A Wissahickon Winter', oil on canvasboard, signed and dated "Leslie Henderson 3-17-56" bottom right, signed and inscribed with title verso, also inscribed "from Rittenhouse town to Park Manor painted by Leslie Henderson" verso.

20in (51cm) wide

$2,000-3,000   **FRE**

Laura D. Stroud Ladd (1863-1943), 'Harbor Scene', oil on board, signed "Laura D.S. Ladd" bottom left.

20in (51cm) wide

$6,000-9,000   **FRE**

Edmund Darch Lewis (1835-1910), 'Nebraska Notch', oil on canvas, signed and dated "Edmund D. Lewis 1875" and inscribed "Nebraska Notch" bottom right, unframed.

60in (152.5cm) wide

$8,000-12,000   **FRE**

Lance Ray Lauffer, 'Peaches', oil on board, signed and dated "Lance Ray Lauffer 1979" bottom right, signed, titled and dated verso.

24in (61cm) high

$3,500-4,500   **FRE**

Edmund Darch Lewis (1835-1910), 'Sailboats in an Estuary', oil on canvas, signed and dated "Edmund D. Lewis 1884" bottom right.

50in (127cm) wide

$7,000-10,000   **FRE**

Edmund Darch Lewis (1835-1910), 'Derasago Falls', oil on canvas, signed and dated "Edmund D. Lewis 1892" bottom right, inscribed on stretcher label.

37in (94cm) wide

$4,000-6,000   **FRE**

Attributed to Edmund Darch Lewis (1835-1910), 'Waterfall in a Tropical Landscape', oil on canvas.

50in (127cm) wide

$6,000-9,000   **FRE**

Edmund Darch Lewis (1835-1910), Rhode Island coastline, watercolor on paper in gilt period frame, signed and dated lower right.

1905   *8.75 x 19.75in (22 x 50cm)*

$5,000-7,000   **NA**

Jimmy Lueders (1927-1994), 'Landscape, 1977', oil on canvas, signed and inscribed "Lueders/Landscape" on stretcher verso.

66in (167.5cm) high

$4,000-6,000   **FRE**

Jean McGrath, 'Still Life with Flowers and Apples', oil on canvas, signed "Jean McGrath" bottom left.

24in (61cm) wide

$1,800-2,200   **FRE**

Olaf Moller (b.1903), 'Impressionist Landscape', oil on canvas, signed "O. Moller" lower right.

36in (91.5cm) high

$3,000-4,000   **FRE**

PAINTINGS

Hobson Pittman (1898-1972), 'Late Afternoon', oil on canvas, signed "Hobson Pittman" bottom right, inscribed on stretcher label.

30in (76cm) wide

$1,500-2,000   **FRE**

Hobson Pittman (1898-1972), 'Pennsylvanian Landscape with Cat on front porch', oil on canvas, signed "Hobson Pittman" bottom right.

30in (76cm) wide

$3,500-4,500   **FRE**

Joseph Sacks (1887-1974), 'Atlantic City', oil on canvas.

20in (51cm) wide

$3,000-5,000   **FRE**

Nelson Shanks (b. 1937), 'Scott', oil on board, portrait of the artist's son, signed "Nelson Shanks" upper left, titled and dated "1970" upper right.

16in (40.5cm) high

$1,800-2,200   **FRE**

Russell Smith (1812-1896), 'Pennypack Park', oil on canvas, signed with initials "R S" bottom right, inscribed "Russell Smith 1881 Pennypack" verso.

18in (45.5cm) wide

$8,000-12,000   **FRE**

Jessie Willcox Smith (1863-1935), 'Mother and Child', signed "Jessie Willcox Smith" lower right, oil and charcoal on board.

14 x 16.25in (35.5 x 41.5cm)

$12,000-18,000   **SI**

Walter Stuempfig (1914-1970), 'Sea Shells', oil on canvas.

30in (76cm) wide

$7,000-10,000   **FRE**

William Trego (1859-1909), portrait of weary soldier standing outside house, oil on canvas.

21 x 17in (53.25 x 43.25cm)

$10,000-15,000   **AAC**

Eugene Paul Ullman (1877-1953), 'Lady in Interior', oil on canvas, signed "Eugene Paul Ullman" bottom left.

21.75in (55cm) wide

$1,800-2,200   **FRE**

PENNSYLVANIA IMPRESSIONISM

Walter Emerson Baum (1884-1956), 'Hill City', oil on masonite, signed bottom left, inscribed "Sellersville, PA", titled and inscribed verso.

39.75in (101cm) wide

$30,000-40,000   **FRE**

Walter Emerson Baum (1884-1956), 'A Winter Landscape', oil on board, signed "Baum" bottom right.

16.75in (42.5cm) wide

$4,000-6,000   **FRE**

Walter Emerson Baum (1884-1956), 'Easton, Pennsylvania', oil on canvas, signed "W E BAUM" bottom left.

36in (91.5cm) wide

$4,000-6,000   **FRE**

Walter Emerson Baum (1884-1956), 'Autumn', oil on board, signed "W E BAUM" bottom right, signed and inscribed with title verso.

20in (51cm) wide

$7,000-10,000   **FRE**

Walter Emerson Baum (1884-1956), 'Roadside Houses', oil on board, signed "W E BAUM" lower right.

36in (91.5cm) wide

$6,000-9,000   **FRE**

Walter Emerson Baum (1884-1956), oil on canvas, signed "Baum" bottom right, inscribed and dated "Spring 1934" verso.

36in (91.5cm) high

$8,000-10,000   **FRE**

Walter Emerson Baum (1884-1956), 'Autumn Creek, Bucks County', oil on board, signed "W E BAUM" lower left, and another by the same hand verso, "Center Bridge", signed "BAUM" lower right.

29.75in (75.5cm) wide

$20,000-30,000   **FRE**

Walter Emerson Baum (1884-1956), 'The Brook-Zero', oil on board.

20 x 24in (50.75 x 60cm)

$30,000-50,000   **AAC**

Walter Emerson Baum (1884-1956), 'The River', miniature winter landscape, oil on board.

6 x 8in (15.5 x 20.5cm)

$3,500-4,500   **AAC**

Walter Emerson Baum (1884-1956), 'Berks Co. Brook', oil on board.

8 x 10in (20.5 x 25.5cm)

$5,000-8,000   **AAC**

Walter Emerson Baum (1884-1956), mill by stream oil on board.

12 x 24in (30.5 x 70cm)

$15,000-20,000   AAC

Walter Emerson Baum (1884-1956), 'Wile Ave., Souderton, PA', autumn landscape of village street, oil on board.

10 x 14in (25.5 x 35.5cm)

$2,500-3,000   AAC

Walter Emerson Baum (1884-1956), pastoral landscape with winding stream through meadow lined by trees, oil on board, minor flaking.

16 x 20in (40.5 x 51cm)

$2,500-3,000   AAC

Walter Emerson Baum (1884-1956), landscape with farmhouse and barn, watercolor.

10 x 14in (25.5 x 35.5cm)

$1,200-1,800   AAC

Walter Emerson Baum (1884-1956), 'The White House', lithograph, pencil signed and dated 1943.

12 x 16.5 (30.5 x 42cm)

$220-280   AAC

John E. Berninger (1897-1981), winter landscape with village houses with figures sledding on street, oil on canvas.

30 x 36in (76.5 x 91.5cm)

$20,000-30,000   AAC

John E. Berninger (1897-1981), village scene with boy and dog walking on road, oil on canvas board.

20 x 24in (51 x 70cm)

$2,500-3,000   AAC

Fern Isabel Coppedge (1888-1951), 'New Hope - Early Spring', oil on canvas, signed "Fern I. Coppedge" bottom right.

20in (51cm) wide

$70,000-100,000   FRE

Fern Isabel Coppedge (1888-1951), 'After Christmas (Near Carversville, PA)', oil on board, signed "Fern I Coppedge" bottom left.

Fern Isabel Coppedge (1888-1951), 'Skytop', oil on canvasboard, signed "Fern I. Coppedge" bottom right.

Frank F. English (1854-1922), 'Midday Rest', watercolor and gouache.

24in (61cm) wide

$60,000-90,000   **FRE**

12in (31cm) wide

$12,000-18,000   **FRE**

17.5 x 26.75in (44.5 x 68cm)

$2,000-3,000   **AAC**

Frank F. English (1854-1922), 'Haying Time', watercolor and gouache.

John Fulton Folinsbee (1892-1972), 'October Showers', oil on canvas, signed "John F. Folinsbee" bottom left, titled on stretcher.

Daniel Garber (1880-1958), 'Frog Hollow' , oil on canvas, signed "Daniel Garber" bottom right.

16 x 31in (40.5 x 79cm)

$3,000-4,000   **AAC**

20in (51cm) high

$60,000-90,000   **FRE**

19.5in (49.5cm) wide

$200,000-400,000   **FRE**

Daniel Garber (1880-1958), 'Portrait of Roy Lynde', oil on canvas, in a signed Harer frame.

Albert Van Nesse Greene (1887-1971), 'Riverscape', oil on board, signed "A.V. Greene" bottom left.

Antonio Pietro Martino (1902-1989), 'The Bridge and Creek', oil on canvas, signed and dated "A P Martino 1929" bottom left, signed and titled on the stretcher.

30in (76cm) high

$10,000-15,000   **FRE**

22.75in (58cm) wide

$7,000-10,000   **FRE**

40in (101.5cm) wide

$8,000-12,000   **FRE**

Antonio Pietro Martino (1902-1989), 'Rocky Shoreline', oil on canvas, signed "A P Martino" bottom left.

30in (76cm) wide

$4,000-6,000   **FRE**

Antonio Pietro Martino (1902-1989), 'Manayunk', oil on canvas, signed "Antonio P. Martino" bottom right, signed, titled and inscribed "16 So. Broad St. Phila, 2 Pa."

36in (91.5cm) wide

$5,000-8,000   **FRE**

Antonio Pietro Martino (1902-1989), 'The Corner House', oil on canvas, signed "Antonio P. Martino" bottom right, signed on verso.

40in (101.5cm) wide

$6,000-9,000   **FRE**

Antonio Pietro Martino (1902-1989), 'The Canal, New Hope', oil on canvas, signed "A P Martino" lower left.

30in (76cm) wide

$20,000-30,000   **FRE**

Antonio Pietro Martino (1902-1989), 'Harbor Scene', oil on board, signed "A P Martino" bottom left.

20in (51cm) wide

$5,000-7,000   **FRE**

Antonio Pietro Martino (1902-1989), 'Morning Light', Manayunk landscape, oil on canvas.

36 x 40 (91.5 x 101.5cm)

$12,000-18,000   **AAC**

Antonio Pietro Martino (1902-1989), 'Manayunk Country', oil on canvas.

35 x 40in (90 x 101.5cm)

$12,000-18,000   **AAC**

Antonio Pietro Martino (1902-1989), 'Stonington, Maine', oil on canvas.

30 x 40in (76 x101.5cm)

$3,500-4,500   **AAC**

Antonio Pietro Martino (1902-1989), 'Leo Carillo Coast', oil on canvas.

24 x 30in (61 x 76cm)

$3,000-4,000   **AAC**

Antonio Pietro Martino (1902-1989), Manayunk winter landscape, oil on board.

10 x 20in (25.5 x 51cm)

$600-750   **AAC**

Giovanni Martino (1908-1998), 'Reflections', oil on board, signed and dated "M. Giovanni '31" bottom right, inscribed with title on stretcher verso.

30in (76cm) wide

$5,000-7,000   **FRE**

Arthur Meltzer (1893-1989), 'The Yellow Lemon', oil on board, signed "Arthur Meltzer" bottom right.

20in (51cm) wide

$2,000-2,500   **FRE**

Arthur Meltzer (1893-1989), 'Golden Quarry', oil on board, signed "Arthur Meltzer" bottom left, signed and inscribed with title on label verso, inscribed with title verso.

14in (35.5cm) wide

$50,000-70,000   **FRE**

Arthur Meltzer (1893-1989), 'Silver Springs Nevada', oil on canvas, signed "Arthur Meltzer" bottom left, signed verso.

20in (51cm) wide

$5,000-7,000   **FRE**

Arthur Meltzer (1893-1989), 'Bygone Era', oil on canvas, signed "Arthur Meltzer" bottom right, inscribed on stretcher label.

20in (51cm) wide

$800-1,200   **FRE**

Arthur Meltzer (1893-1989), 'Gladiolas', oil on board, signed "Arthur Meltzer" bottom left.

20in (51cm) high

$2,200-2,800   **FRE**

Arthur Meltzer (1893-1989), impressionist landscape with house and stone bridge, oil on canvas.

18 x 24in (46 x 61cm)

$40,000-60,000   **AAC**

Arthur Meltzer (1893-1989), 'Pennsylvania Farm', oil on canvas in a hand-carved and painted frame by the artist, with artist note, "Stone barns are part of the landscape of Bucks Co. Penn".

12 x 14in (30.5 x 35.5cm)

$8,000-12,000   **AAC**

Mary Elizabeth Price (1888-1973), 'Mixed Flowers', oil on canvas, signed "M. Elizabeth Price" bottom left.

33.75in (85.5cm) high

$5,000-8,000   FRE

Edward Willis A. Redfield (1869-1965), 'Sunny Brook', oil on canvas winter landscape, with a meandering brook, trees, and a house, signed lower left "E.W. A Redfield".

32in (81.5cm) wide

$125,000-150,000   Pook

Paulette Van Roekens (1896-1988), 'Village in Winter', oil on canvas, signed and dated "P. Van Roekens 25(?)" bottom left.

30in (76cm) wide

$20,000-30,000   FRE

Paulette Van Roekens (1896-1988), 'The Mirror', oil on canvas, signed "P. Van Roekens" bottom left, titled and dated on stretcher.

c1960   *14in (35.5cm) wide*

$10,000-15,000   FRE

Paulette Van Roekens (1896-1988), 'Little Girl with Pink', oil on canvas, signed "P Van Roekens" bottom left.

20in (51cm) high

$3,000-4,000   FRE

Paulette Van Roekens (1896-1988), 'May Day', oil on board with artist label in a hand-carved and painted frame by Arthur Meltzer.

8 x 10in (20.5 x 25.4cm)

$3,000-4,000   AAC

Melville F. Stark (1904-1987), 'Autumn Landscape', oil on canvasboard, signed and indistinctly dated "M. Stark *4" bottom right.

20in (51cm) wide

$3,500-4,500   FRE

Ethel A. Wallace (1885-1968), 'Still Life of Mixed Flowers in a Vase', oil on canvas, laid down, in a Newcomb Macklin frame designed by Stanford White.

Much of the value of this painting can be attributed to the exceptional frame.

30in (76cm) high

$20,000-30,000   FRE

Martha Walter (1875-1976), 'Spring Landscape with Figure', oil on canvas, with "David David Art Gallery Philadelphia, Estate of Martha Walter" stamp verso, estate stamp on stretcher twice.

24in (61cm) high

$12,000-18,000   FRE

Western Art

William Acheff (b. 1947) AOA, NAWA, 'Acoma Corn', oil.

14 x 10in (35.5 x 25.5cm)

$20,000-30,000   **Alt**

William Acheff (b. 1947) AOA, NAWA, 'Saints and Santero', oil.

28 x 14in (71 x 35.5cm)

$20,000-30,000   **Alt**

Roy Andersen (b.1930) CAA, NAWA, 'Apache', oil.

7 x 5in (18 x 13cm)

$2,500-3,000   **Alt**

Roy Andersen (b.1930) CAA, NAWA, 'It Speaks Good Medicine', oil on canvas, signed lower right.

48 x 60in (122 x 154cm)

$60,000-90,000   **RENO**

Roy Andersen (b.1930) 'The Warrior's Greeting', oil on canvas, signed lower left

 Provenance: *The Estate of James Conte.*

48 x 30in (122 x 76cm)

$40,000-60,000   **RENO**

Clyde Aspevig, 'High in the Wind River Range', oil on canvas, signed lower left.

30 x 36in (76 x 91.5cm)

$50,000-70,000   **RENO**

Henry Balink (1882-1963), 'A Taos Indian', oil on canvas, signed lower right.

24 x 20in (61 x 51cm)

$15,000-20,000   **RENO**

James Bama (b.1926) NAWA, 'Faith Sings Good in Profile', watercolor.

19 x 13in (48 x 33cm)

$20,000-30,000   **Alt**

James Bama, 'Confederate Stars and Bars', oil on board, signed lower left.

24 x 14in (61 x 35.5cm)

$20,000-30,000   **RENO**

Eliza Barchus (1857-1959), 'Mount Hood', oil on canvas, signed lower right.

22 x 36in (56 x 91.5cm)

$6,000-9,000   **RENO**

Robert Bateman, 'Stretching Canada Goose', oil on board, signed lower right.

36 x 28in (91.5 x 71cm)

$70,000-100,000   **RENO**

Tom Beecham (1926-2000), 'Black Bear', oil on board, signed lower right.

24 x 30in (61 x 76cm)

$7,000-10,000   **RENO**

Tom Beecham (1926-2000), 'Pronghorns', oil on board signed lower right.

24 x 30in (61 x 76cm)

$10,000-15,000   **RENO**

Oscar E. Berninghaus (1874-1952) ANA, Taos SA, 'Taos Indians and the Sangre Cristos', oil on board, signed lower left "O. E. Berninghaus 1915 TAOS, N.M".

1915   *20 x 16in (51 x 40.5cm)*

$150,000-200,000   **Alt**

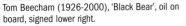

Oscar E. Berninghaus (1874-1952), 'Harvest Season', oil on canvas, signed lower left.

A founder of the Taos Society of Artists, Oscar Edmund Berninghaus was born in St. Louis, Missouri and developed an interest in art through his family's lithography business. He depicted Indians in a realistic, unromaticised way, going about their lives as they actually did in 20thC New Mexico.

25 x 30in (63.5 x 76cm)

$100,000-150,000   **RENO**

Oscar E. Berninghaus (1874-1952) ANA, Taos SA, 'Around Taos', oil on board, signed lower left.

9 x 12.75in (23 x 32cm)

$15,000-20,000   **RENO**

Oscar E. Berninghaus (1874-1952) ANA, Taos SA, 'Stagecoach', oil on board, unsigned study.

4.25 x 15.5in (11 x 39cm)

$7,000-10,000   **RENO**

Albert Bierstadt (1830-1902), 'Grazing Antelope', oil on paper, laid on canvas, signed lower right.

1859   *11 x 15in (28 x 38cm)*

$150,000-200,000   **RENO**

Carl Oscar Borg (1879-1947), 'Shepherd at Sunset', gouache, watercolor and graphite.

10.25in (26cm) wide

$3,500-4,500   **Alt**

Carl Oscar Borg (1879-1947), 'Wagon Camp', gouache, watercolor and graphite.

15.5in (40cm) wide

$2,500-3,000   **Alt**

James Boren (1921-1990) AOA, CAA, NAWA, 'Old Abilene', watercolor,

29in (74cm) wide

$3,500-4,500 Alt

James Boren (1921-1990) AOA, CAA, NAWA, 'Waiting for the Late Train', oil.

28 x 40in (71 x 101.5cm)

$12,000-18,000 Alt

James Boren (1921-1990) AOA, CAA, NAWA, 'Acoma', watercolor.

15 x 20in (38 x 51cm)

$4,000-6,000 Alt

James Boren (1921-1990) AOA, CAA, NAWA, 'South of Laredo', oil.

28 x 40in (71 x 101.5cm)

$12,000-18,000 Alt

Nelson Boren (b. 1952) 'Old Arizona Boots', watercolor.

58 x 37in (47 x 94cm)

$15,000-20,000 Alt

Harley Brown (b 1939) NAWA, NWR, 'Dyane', pastel.

12 x 9in (30.5 x 23cm)

$4,000-6,000 Alt

Harley Brown (b 1939) NAWA, NWR, 'Yellowknife', pastel, signed lower left.

21 x 16in (53 x 40.5cm)

$15,000-25,000 RENO

Belmore Browne (1880-1954), 'Mt Rundle', oil on canvas, signed lower right.

18 x 24in (45.5 x 61cm)

$5,000-10,000 RENO

Ken Carlson, 'Called from Cover', oil on board, signed lower right.

24 x 36in (61 x 91.5cm)

$30,000-40,000 RENO

William de la Montagne Cary (1840-1922), 'Evening Sunset', oil on board, signed lower right.

10 x 16in (25.5 x 40.5cm)

$12,000-18,000 RENO

John Clymer (1907-1989), 'Pony Soldier*2', oil.

36in (91.5cm) wide

$15,000-20,000 Alt

John Clymer (1907-1989) CAA, NAWA, 'Long Ago Winter', oil.

24 x 40in (61 x 102cm)

$150,000-200,000　　　　　　　**Alt**

Nicholas Coleman (b.1980), 'Woodland Fire', oil.

30in (76.5cm) wide

$7,000-10,000　　　　　　　**Alt**

Michael Coleman (b.1946), 'Golden Moment Indian Encampment', oil.

48 x 36in (122 x 91.5cm)

$40,000-60,000　　　　　　　**Alt**

Michael Coleman (b.1946), Guest Artist NAWA, 'In the Woods', oil.

12 x 7.5in (30.5 x 19cm)

$6,000-9,000　　　　　　　**Alt**

Michael Coleman (b. 1946), Guest Artist NAWA, 'Canadian Sunset', oil.

20 x 30in (51 x 76cm)

$15,000-20,000　　　　　　　**Alt**

Eanger Irving Couse (1866-1936) NA, Taos SA, 'Mountain Birds', oil.

E. I. Couse painted this at his Taos home which still contains the artist's collection of Indian artifacts and costumes. The beaded moccasins, loin cloth, belt and hair ornament worn by the model, Jerry Mirabal, are preserved in this collection.

36 x 30in (91.5 x 76cm)

$100,000-150,000　　　　　　　**Alt**

Eanger Irving Couse (1866-1936) NA, Taos SA, 'The Ambush', soil on canvas, signed lower right.

12 x 16in (30.5 x 40.5cm)

$50,000-70,000　　　　　　　**RENO**

Eanger Irving Couse (1866-1936) NA, Taos SA, 'Across the Dunes', watercolor.

21in (53.5cm) wide

$6,000-9,000　　　　　　　**Alt**

Donald Crowley (1926) CAA, 'Firewood', oil.

40 x 30in (101.5 x 76cm)

$5,000-8,000　　　　　　　**Alt**

Henry Herman Cross (1837-1918), 'E-Tey-Hoo-Taey, Face' oil.

36 x 29in (91.5 x 74cm)

$5,000-7,000　　　　　　　**Alt**

Henry Herman Cross (1837-1918),
'Ran-In-Yak-Kan', oil.

36 x 29in (91.5 x 74cm)

$2,500-3,000   Alt

Don Crowley (b. 1926), 'Jingle Dancer',
pencil.

16 x 20in (40.5 x 51cm)

$4,500-6,000   Alt

Henry Herman Cross (1837-1918),
'Buffalo by River', oil.

28 x 46in (71 x 117cm)

$4,000-6,000   Alt

Stan Davis (b 1942), 'Autumn
Morning', oil.

42 x 60in (107 x 152.5cm)

$40,000-60,000   Alt

Gerard Curtis Delano (1890-1972), CAA, 'Peace or War', oil.

22 x 40in (56 x 102cm)

$100,000-150,000   Alt

Mike Desatnick (b. 1943), 'Deer Dancers', oil.

40in (101.5cm) wide

$7,000-10,000   Alt

Steve Devenyns (b. 1953), 'Tough Trip Thru Paradise', oil.

16 x 30in (40.5 x 76cm)

$3,000-4,000   Alt

Steve Devenyns (b. 1953), 'Yellowstone Straggler', oil.

24 x 42in (61 x 107cm)

$8,000-12,000   Alt

MAYNARD DIXON

According to Larry Len Peterson, "When the Great Northern Railway offered Maynard Dixon a commission to come to Glacier National Park to paint, he jumped at the opportunity, although this 1917 trip proved to be his last visit to Glacier Country, he continued to paint memorable scenes of the area for the rest of his life".

He camped at Cutbank Green with Curly Bear, Owen Heavy Breast, Two Guns White Calf, Old Beaver Woman and Lazy Bear. He thought they were "the best Indians I have seen yet". The crisp September days were appealing and he watched the "smoke-tanned cones of teepees stand sharp in the sun, sending their blue-white breath into the breathless morning". Going on to Browning, he saw Grass and Scalp Dances and the opening of a sacred Beaver Medicine Bundle.

Donald J. Hagerty notes that Dixon's "Montana paintings show Maynard moving into a post impressionist painting style, with vigorous, bold brushstrokes and virile, forceful presentation ... (they) have a raw vitality, capturing the picturesque and colorful elements of their subject, there is a physical vigor, even a gusto in the paintings with the paint anchored by strong composition". 'Home of the Half Breed' exemplifies one of the finest paintings of Dixon's Montana period.

Maynard Dixon (1875-1946), 'Home of the Half Breed', oil on canvas, signed lower left.

Provenance: Fred Rosenstock, Denver, Colorado, Eric J. Myhre, Great Falls, Montana, Property of the Eric J. Myhre Testamentary Trust.

26 x 30in (66 x 76cm)

$800,000-1,000,000   **RENO**

Maynard Dixon (1875-1946), 'Montana Plains', oil on board, signed lower left.

1922   6 x 20in (15 x 51cm)

$60,000-90,000   **RENO**

Maynard Dixon (1875-1946), 'Carson (Valley) Nev- Nov 1907', watercolor, initialled lower left.

7 x 9in (18 x 23cm)

$5,000-8,000   **RENO**

Robert Duncan (b. 1952) CAA, 'After Lost Horses', oil.

W. Herbert Dunton (1878-1936) Taos SA, 'The Orange Bonnet', oil.

W. Herbert Dunton (1878-1936) Taos SA, 'High Country', oil on canvas, signed lower left.

Charlie Dye (1906-1972) CAA, 'Navajo Trading Post', oil.

Charlie Dye was one of the founders of the Cowboy Artists of America. He was born in the cow town of Canon City, CO and rode for ranches in Colorado, Arizona and California before at age 21 deciding he wanted to become a commercial artist. He studied at the Art Institute of Chicago and the American Academy.

20 x 40in (51 x 101cm)   c1912-1918   16in (41cm)   36 x 25in (91.5 x 63.5cm)   24 x 36in (61 x 91.5cm)

$15,000-20,000   **Alt**   **$200,000-300,000**   **Alt**   **$40,000-60,000**   **RENO**   **$40,000-60,000**   **Alt**

Charlie Dye (1906-1972), 'Pancho Villa at Zacatecas', oil on board, signed lower right.

Provenance: O'Briens Art Emporium, Scottsdale, Arizona, The Jennings Survivors Trust.

30 x 48in (76 x 122cm)

$40,000-60,000   RENO

Valoy Eaton, 'Ranch Kids', oil on board, signed lower right.

30 x 40in (76 x 101.5cm)

$12,000-18,000   RENO

Nick Eggenhofer (1897-1985), CAA, NAWA, 'Putting Out the Fire', illustration and watercolor.

8.5 x 9.5in (22 x 24.5cm)

$2,500-3,000   Alt

Nick Eggenhofer (1897-1985), 'Last Mile', gouache.

28in (72.5cm) wide

$7,000-10,000   Alt

Robert Farrington Elwell (1874-1962), 'The Link that Closed the Gap between East and West', oil on canvas, signed lower right.

30 x 40in (76 x 101cm)

$12,000-18,000   RENO

Tony Eubanks (b. 1939) OPA PSA, 'From Where the Sun Now Stands', oil.

30 x 50in (76 x 127cm)

$15,000-20,000   Alt

Henry Farny (1847-1916), 'Red Horse Nez Perce Scout', gouache.

Henry Farny was born in France and studied throughout Europe before settling in Cincinnati in the late 1870s. From there he made various trips West to gather sketches and ideas for his illustration work for magazines such as Harpers Weekly and century. It is likely that he met Red Horse in 1883/1884.

5.5in (14cm) wide

$80,000-100,000   Alt

John Fawcett (b. 1952), 'Sagebrush Stories', watercolor.

20.5 x 28.5in (52 x72cm)

$7,000-10,000   Alt

Nicolai Fechin (1881-1955), 'Indian Girl with Flower Basket', oil on canvas, signed lower corner.

Provenance: The Robert and Virginia Caldwell Trust.

12 x 10in (30.5 x 25.5cm)

$100,000-150,000   RENO

Nicolai Fechin (1881-1955), 'Indian Girl with Kachina Doll', oil on canvas, signed upper right.

Provenance: The Robert and Virginia Caldwell Trust.

24 x 20in (61 x 51cm)

$250,000-350,000   RENO

711

Nicolai Fechin (1881-1955), 'Taos in Winter', oil on canvas, signed lower right.

Provenance: *The Robert and Virginia Caldwell Trust.*

13 x 14in (33 x 35.5cm)

$60,000-90,000   **RENO**

Nicolai Fechin (1881-1955), 'Virginia Caldwell', oil on canvas, signed upper left.

Provenance: *The Robert and Virginia Caldwell Trust.*

15.5 x 12.5in (39.5 x 32cm)

$30,000-40,000   **RENO**

Nicolai Fechin (1881-1955), 'Cabin in Wooded Area', oil on canvas, unsigned.

17 x 14.5in (43 x 37cm)

$50,000-70,000   **RENO**

John Fery (1859-1934), 'Grossley Lake, Mt. Cleveland, Glacier National Park', oil on canvas, signed lower right.

40 x 60in (101.5 x 152cm)

$12,000-18,000   **RENO**

Eugene C. Frank (1845-1914), 'Grazing Buffalo at Sunset', oil.

Eugene Frank was born in Stuttgart, Germany. As a teenager he went to New York just as the Civil War broke out and became an engraver for the Heliographic Engraving Company. In 1874 he began formal art studies.

24 x 36in (61 x 91.5cm)

$30,000-40,000   **Alt**

Arnold Friberg, 'In the Land of the Shining Mountains'.

Provenance: *The Estate of James Conte.*

32 x 26in (81 x 66cm)

$30,000-50,000   **RENO**

Philip R. Goodwin (1882-1935), 'Blazing the Trail', oil on canvas, signed lower right.

Provenance: *Manley-McLennan Agency 1911; Liston B. Manley bequeathed to; Rollin S. Manley, bequeathed to; James R. Manley, 1949 donated to; Church of the Holy Cross, Belmont, CA.*

24 x 33in (61 x 84cm)

$120,000-150,000   **RENO**

Philip R. Goodwin (1882-1935), 'Time for Action', oil on canvas, signed lower left.

24 x 33in (61 x 84cm)

$70,000-100,000   **RENO**

Philip R. Goodwin (1882-1935), 'Porcupine in Camp', oil on canvas, signed lower right.

24 x 33in (61 x 84cm)

$80,000-120,000   **RENO**

Joe Grandee (b. 1929), 'His Last Hunt', oil.

31 x 41in (79 x 104cm)

$7,000-10,000   **Alt**

Martin Grelle (B. 1954), CAA, 'Lords of the Land', oil.

16 x 30in (40.5 x 76cm)

$4,000-6,000   **Alt**

Bruce Greene (b. 1953), 'Matters of Philosophy', oil.

28 x 40in (71 x101cm)

$20,000-30,000   **Alt**

Robert Griffing, 'We dined in a Hollow Cottonwood Tree', oil on canvas, signed lower right.

34 x 52in (86 x 132cm)

$100,000-150,000   **RENO**

Herman W. Hansen (1854-1924), 'Buffalo Hunt', watercolor.

17ins (43cm) wide

$20,000-30,000   **Alt**

G. Harvey (b. 1933), 'Softness of Winter', oil.

16 x 24in (40.5 x 61cm)

$20,000-25,000   **Alt**

Martin Hennings (1886-1956), 'Winter Stream', oil on canvas, signed lower left.

14 x 20in (35.5 x 51cm)

$10,000-15,000   **RENO**

Thomas Hill (1829-1908), 'Yosemite Valley from Inspiration Point', on the reverse in pencil 'Thomas Hill/Wawona/Ca', this refers to Yosemite's Wawona Hotel, where Hill's daughter married the hotel's proprietor John Washburn, oil on canvas, signed lower right.

1897   *20 x 24in (51 x 61cm)*

$30,000-40,000   **RENO**

Frank B. Hoffman (1888-1958), 'Disputed Prize', published in the 1949 Brown & Bigelow's "The Hunting and Fishing Calendar", oil on board, signed lower left.

Provenance: *Private Collection, Mexico City, Mexico.*

18 x 24in (45.5 x 61cm)

$30,000-50,000   **RENO**

Frank B. Hoffman (1888-1958), 'Ambush', oil on board, signed lower right, published in the 1949 Brown & Bigelow's "The Hunting and Fishing Calendar".

18 x 24in (45.5 x 61cm)

$15,000-20,000   **RENO**

Frank B. Hoffman (1888-1958), 'Honking Canadas', oil on board, signed lower left.

18 x 24in (45.5 x 61cm)

$15,000-20,000   **RENO**

Clark Hulings, 'Old Man of Mexico', oil on canvas, signed lower left.

16 x 20in (40.5 x 51cm)

$40,000-60,000   RENO

Ned Jacob, 'Taos Indian - Winter', oil on canvas, signed lower right.

26 x 16in (66 x 61cm)

$4,000- 6,000   RENO

Gary Knapp (b. 1942), NWR, 'Nez Perce Sunset'.

30 x 40in (76 x 101.5cm)

$12,000-18,000   Alt

W. H. D. Koerner (1878-1938), 'The Trapper's Daughter', oil on canvas, signed lower right.

27.5 x 35in (70 x 89cm)

$10,000-15,000   RENO

Bob Kuhn, 'Above the Plains', acrylic on board, signed centre left.

24 x 36in (61 x 91.5cm)

$30,000-50,000   RENO

Sydney Laurence (1865-1940), 'Mt McKingley', oil on canvas laid on board, signed lower left.

Provenance: Mr & Mrs George S. Hiddleston, Private Collection, Montana.

12 x 16in (30.5 x 40.5cm)

$12,000-18,000   RENO

William Robinson Leigh (1866-1955), NA, AAA, 'Sioux Family Escaping - Escape from Wounded Knee', oil.

22 x 28in (56 x 71cm)

$120,000-150,000   Alt

William Robinson Leigh (1866-1955), NA, AAA, 'The Old Family Mare', oil.

40.25 x 60in (102 x 152cm)

$140,000-180,000   Alt

William Robinson Leigh (1866-1955), NA, AAA, 'The Right of Way', oil on board, signed lower right.

Provenance: Kennedy Galleries Inc, NYC, Period Gallery West, Scottsdale, Arizona, Sydney Shoenberg, St. Loius Missouri, Private Collection, St. Louis Missouri.

24 x 18in (61 x 45.5cm)

$150,000-250,000   RENO

William Robinson Leigh (1866-1955), NA, AAA, 'Papago Weaving Grain Basket', oil.

18 x 20in (46 x 51cm)

$60,000-90,000   Alt

Robert Lougheed (1910-1982), CAA, NAWA ,
'Crossing Yellowstone Country', oil on board, signed
lower left.

12 x 24in (30.5 x 61cm)

$12,000-18,000 **RENO**

Robert Lougheed (1910-1982), CAA, NAWA,
'In the Valley of Eire', oil on board, signed lower right.

12 x 24in (30.5 x 61cm)

$8,000-12,000 **RENO**

Robert Lougheed (1910-1982), CAA, NAWA, 'Scouting
Deep in Snow Country', oil.

12 x 24in (30.5 x 61cm)

$20,000-30,000 **Alt**

Robert Lougheed (1910-1982), CAA, NAWA,
'In the Valley of the Rio Chama', oil.

24ins (61cm) wide

$7,000-10,000 **Alt**

Robert Lougheed (1910-1982), CAA, NAWA ,
'Black Mesa Country', oil on board, signed lower right.

12 x 16in (30.5 x 41cm)

$5,000-7,000 **RENO**

Tom Lovell (1909-1997), 'No Room at the Inn', oil on
canvas, signed lower left.

34 x 26in (86 x 66cm)

$70,000-100,000 **RENO**

David Maass, 'Heading for Shelter', oil on board,
signed lower left, illustrated in the 1995 Brown &
Bigelow calendar.

Provenance: *Archives of Brown & Bigelow Inc, St. Paul,
Minnesota.*

24 x 32in (61 x 81cm)

$10,000-15,000 **RENO**

David Maass, 'Morning Exercise', oil on board, signed
lower right, illustrated in the 1995 Brown & Bigelow
calendar.

Provenance: *Archives of Brown & Bigelow Inc, St. Paul,
Minnesota.*

$12,000-18,000 **RENO**

Grant Macdonald (b. 1944), 'Cottonwoods on the
Rio Grande', oil.

30 x 24in (76 x 61cm)

$7,000-10,000 **Alt**

PAINTINGS

David Mann (b. 1948), ' The Healer's Art' , oil.

24 x 36in (61 x 91.5cm)

$12,000-18,000   Alt

David Mann (b. 1948) 'Cheyenne Summer', oil.

48 x 36in (122 x 91.5cm)

$30,000-50,000   Alt

David Mann (b. 1948), 'Thunderbird Shield', oil.

36 x 48in (91.5 x 122cm)

$20,000-30,000   Alt

David Mann (b. 1948), 'Commanche Ridge', oil on canvas, signed lower left.

1907   *30 x 40in (76 x 101.5cm)*

$8,000-12,000   RENO

Frank C. McCarthy (b. 1924), CAA, 'Cheyenne Scout', oil.

18 x 30in (45.5 x 76cm)

$20,000-30,000   Alt

Frank C. McCarthy (b. 1924), CAA, 'Kiowa on the Southern Plains', oil.

20 x 40in (51 x 101.5cm)

$30,000-40,000   Alt

Frank C. McCarthy (1924), CAA, 'Shoot Out (desc)', oil.

16 x 29in (40.5 x 74cm)

$8,000-12,000   Alt

Frank McCarthy (b. 1924), AAA, AOA, CAA, NAWA, NWR, 'Chiefs', oil on canvas, signed lower right.

Provenance: *The Estate of James Conte.*

32 x 50in (81 x 112cm)

$50,000-70,000   RENO

Frank McCarthy (b. 1924), AAA, AOA, CAA, NAWA, NWR, 'The Hostile Threat', oil.

28 x 30in (71 x 76cm)

$30,000-40,000   Alt

Frank McCarthy (b. 1924), AAA, AOA, CAA, NAWA, NWR, 'Apaches', oil.

18 x 24in (45.5 x 61cm)

$30,000-40,000   Alt

Frank McCarthy (b. 1924), AAA, AOA, CAA, NAWA, NWR, 'The Circle - Sioux', oil.

24 x 36in (61 x 91.5cm)

$40,000-60,000   **Alt**

Frank McCarthy (b. 1924), AAA, AOA, CAA, NAWA, NWR, 'Hostiles', oil on board, signed lower right.

24 x 36in (61 x 91cm)

$50,000-70,000   **RENO**

R. Brownell McGrew (1916-1994), CAA, NAWA, 'Lure of the Canyon', oil.

28 x 36in (71 x 91.5cm)

$20,000-30,000   **Alt**

R. Brownell McGrew (1916-1994), CAA, NAWA, 'Under the Flying Clouds', oil, signed lower bottom right indistinctly.

17.5 x 14in (44.5 x 35.5cm)

$3,500-4,500   **Alt**

R. Brownell McGrew (1916-1994), CAA, NAWA, 'Wizhoni Bessie', oil.

15.75 x 20in (40 x 51cm)

$20,000-30,000   **Alt**

R. Brownell McGrew (1916-1994), 'Duggai Kleh', oil on board, signed lower left.

Provenance: *The Estate of James Conte.*

18 x 14in (45.5 x 35.5cm)

$15,000-20,000   **RENO**

R. Brownell McGrew (1916-1994), CAA, NAWA, 'Siyah Nez Navajo', oil.

17.5 x 13.5in (44.5 x 34.5cm)

$20,000-30,000   **Alt**

R. Brownell McGrew (1916-1994), CAA, NAWA, 'Jimmie Yazzie', oil.

14 x 10in (35.5 x 25.5cm)

$6,000-9,000   **Alt**

R. Brownell McGrew (1916-1994), CAA, NAWA, 'Hasti in Cowshirt', oil.

18 x 24in (46 x 61cm)

$40,000-60,000   **Alt**

R. Brownell McGrew (1916-1994), CAA, NAWA, 'Jimmie Yellow Shirt', oil.

20 x 16in (51 x 40.5cm)

$15,000-20,000   **Alt**

R. F. Morgan, 'Sundown for the Red Man', oil on canvas, signed lower right.

30 x 40in (76 x 101cm)

$3,500-4,500   **RENO**

Terri Kelly Moyers (b.1953), 'Santa Fe Style', oil.

40 x 38in (101.5 x 96.5cm)

$30,000-40,000   **Alt**

Terri Kelly Moyers (b. 1953), 'The Road Not Taken', oil.

20 x 24in (51 x 61cm)

$6,000-9,000   **Alt**

John Moyers (b. 1958), CAA, 'Winter Above Taos', oil.

48 x 34in (122 x 86.5cm)

$20,000-30,000   **Alt**

Newman Myrah, 'Going on Day Herd', oil on canvas, signed lower right.

30 x 40in (76 x 101cm)

$10,000-15,000   **RENO**

Robert Jenkins Onderdonk (1852-1917), 'Cattle in Pasture with Wagon in Background', pastel.

11.5 x 17.5in (29 x 44.5cm)

$12,000-18,000   **Alt**

Edmund H. Osthaus (1858-1928), 'On Point', oil on canvas, signed lower right.

24 x 32in (61 x 81cm)

$20,000-30,000   **RENO**

Orrin Sheldon Parsons (1866-1943), 'Adobe in Winter Landscape', oil on canvas, signed lower left.

28 x 36in (71 x 91.5cm)

$20,000-30,000   **RENO**

Edgar S. Paxson (1852-1919), 'Custer's Last Buffalo Hunt, Little Missouri River, Dakota Badlands (1897)', oil on canvas.

54in (137.5cm) wide

$150,000-200,000   **RENO**

Edgar S. Paxson (1852-1919), 'Portrait of Custer', watercolor, signed lower right.

1908   *13 x 9in (33 x 23cm)*

$20,000-30,000   **RENO**

Edgar S. Paxson (1852-1919), 'Indian Portrait', watercolor, signed centre right.

1904   *16 x 9in (40.5 x 23cm)*

$20,000-30,000   **RENO**

Edgar S. Paxson (1852-1919), 'Sacajawea and Her Dog Scammon', oil on canvas, signed lower right.

Provenance: *Dr & Mrs Franz Stenzel, John F. Eyulich Collection, Dallas, Texas, Private Collection, Idaho.*

24 x 16in (61 x 40.5cm)

$15,000-20,000   **RENO**

Edgar S. Paxson (1852-1919), 'The Backwoods Swain', watercolor, signed lower right.

Provenance: Dr Alfred A. Wallner, Kalispell, Montana, property from the Lola and Otha D. Wearin Collection, May 1965.

1905   *21.5 x 17.5in (31.5 x 44.5cm)*
$20,000-30,000   RENO

Edgar S. Paxson (1852-1919), 'Saving Scalp', gouache, signed lower right.

21.5 x 17in (55 x 43cm)
$40,000-60,000   RENO

Edgar S. Paxson (1852-1919), 'Ruler of the Plains', watercolor, signed lower right.

16.5 x 13in (42 x 33cm)
$20,000-30,000   RENO

Edgar S. Paxson (1852-1919), 'Medicine Crow', oil on canvas, signed lower right.

14 x 11in (35.5 x 28cm)
$10,000-15,000   RENO

Edgar S. Paxson (1852-1919), 'Paxson Artefacts', beaded buckskin shirt (signed by Paxson), quilled buckskin pants, quilled vest, shot pouch, felt hat and a photograph of Paxson wearing hat.

$30,000-40,000   RENO

Edgar Payne (1882-1947), 'Desert Clouds', oil on canvas, signed lower left.

28 x 34in (71 x 86cm)
$150,00-200,000   RENO

Edgar Payne (1882-1947), 'Towering Peaks', oil on board, signed lower right.

12 x 15.25in (30.5 x 39cm)
$10,000-15,000   RENO

George Phippen (1916-1966), CAA, 'Quarter Horse', oil.

16 x 20in (41 x 51cm)
$7,000-10,000   Alt

George Phippen (1916-1966), CAA, 'When There's Time to Talk', oil.

24 x 30in (61 x 76cm)
$40,000-60,000   Alt

PAINTINGS

Robert Pummill (b. 1936), CAA, 'The Troopers Warning', oil.

30 x 40in (76 x 101.5cm)

$12,000-18,000   **Alt**

James Reynolds (b. 1926), CAA, NAWA, 'Cold Night Watch', oil on board.

18 x 24in (45.5 x 61cm)

$30,000-40,000   **Alt**

Frederic Remington (1861-1909), ANA, NIAL, 'You Know This Thing Chief? The Indian Nodded Slightly', gouache.

19 x 27in (48 x 68.5cm)

$200,000-300,000   **Alt**

Theodore Richardson (1855-1914), 'Taku Glacier', watercolor, signed lower right.

13.25 x 21.25in (34 x 54cm)

$6,000-9,000   **RENO**

Diego Rivera (1886-1957), 'The Yellow Horse', watercolor.

Diego Rivera is considered one of the greatest muralists of the 20thC. At the time 'The Yellow Horse' was painted, Rivera was married to Frida Kahlo and was working on some his most important work in San Francisco and California.

15in (38cm) wide

Gary Lynn Roberts (b. 1953), 'No Immediate Danger', oil.

Alfredo Rodriguez, 'French Trapper', oil on canvas, signed.

Kenneth Riley (b. 1919), CAA, NAWA, 'Canyon Scout', oil.

40 x 34in (101.5 x 86cm)

$70,000-100,000   **Alt**

$40,000-60,000   **Alt**

24 x 30in (61 x 76cm)

$6,000-9,000   **Alt**

22 x 28in (56 x 71cm)

$12,000-18,000   **RENO**

Carl Rungius (1869-1959), 'Mt Moran from Near Jenny Lake', oil on canvas board, signed lower right.

Provenance: *The Artist, gifted to Dr Robert Bickley, New York 1920 Private Collection, Colorado, 2001.*

9 x 11in (23 x 28cm)

$15,000-20,000   **RENO**

Charles M. Russell (1864-1926), 'The Vaquero', oil on board, signed lower right, together with a letter from Russell to Alex Leggat of Butte Montana, explaining where it was painted dated 19 January 1918.

11.5in (29cm) diam

$30,000-40,000   **RENO**

Tom Ryan (b. 1922), CAA, NAWA, 'Big Enough', oil.

24 x 36in (61 x 91.5cm)

$70,000-100,000   **Alt**

Tom Ryan (b.1922), CAA, NAWA, 'Ghost Town', oil.

24 x 36in (61 x 91.5cm)

$100,000-150,000   **Alt**

Tom Ryan (b. 1922), CAA, NAWA, 'Henry, 6666 Ranch', pastel.

19 x 17in (48 x 43cm)

$6,000-9,000   **Alt**

BIRGER SANDZEN

Birger Sandzen was born in the village of Blidsberg, Sweden, in 1871. He studied at Lund University and then went to Stockholm where he joined a group of young artists who became the first students of the Artist's League, an organisation which introduced the modern art movement to Sweden. He was strongly influenced by the French Impressionists use of light, color, and visible brushwork. In 1894 he was invited to join the faculty of Bethany College in Lindsborg, Kansas and taught for 52 years, retiring in 1946. He was declared Professor Emeritus in art and continued as Bethany's official Artist in Residence. He died at his home in 1954.

Birger Sandzen (1871-1954), 'Mountain Cabins, Logan Utah', oil on canvas, signed lower left.

Provenance: *The Artist, Private Collection, Eugene, Missouri.*

1929   *36 x 48in (91.5 x 122cm)*

$250,000-350,000   **RENO**

John Scott (1907-1987), 'The Deer Hunter', oil on canvas, signed lower right.

Provenance: *Period Gallery, Scottsdale, Arizona, The General Mills Collection, Minneapolis, Minnesota.*

$15,000-20,000   **RENO**

Olaf C. Seltzer (1877-1957), 'Indian Rider', watercolor, signed lower right.

10 x 15in (25.5 x 38cm)

$20,000-30,000   **RENO**

Joseph Henry Sharp (1859-1953), Taos SA, 'The Drummer', oil.

20 x 24in (51 x 61cm)

$150,000-200,000   **Alt**

Joseph Henry Sharp (1859-1953), Taos SA, 'Summer Clouds, Taos Valley', oil on board, signed lower left.

12 x 16in (30.5 x 40.5cm)

$40,000-60,000   **RENO**

Joseph Henry Sharp (1859-1953), Taos SA, 'Cotton woods', oil on canvas, signed lower right.

30 x 40in (76 x 101cm)

$70,000-100,000   **RENO**

Joseph Henry Sharp (1859-1953), Taos SA, 'Path Along the Cottonwoods-Taos', oil on canvas, signed lower right.

16 x 24in (40.5 x 61cm)

$10,000-15,000   **RENO**

PAINTINGS

Joseph Henry Sharp (1859-1953), Taos SA, 'Taos Valley from my Studio Yard', oil.

10 x 14.75in (25.5 x 37.5cm)

$20,000-30,000   Alt

Brett Smith, 'Summer Canvas', oil on canvas, signed lower right.

24 x 36in (61cm x 91.5cm)

$15,000-20,000   RENO

Will Sparks (1862-1937), 'Old Mexican House near San Antonio Mission', oil on canvas, signed lower right.

12.25 x 18.25in (31 x 46cm)

$6,000-9,000   RENO

Oleg Stavrowsky (b. 1927), 'As I Git Older This ____ Gits Heavier', oil.

30 x 24in (76 x 61cm)

$6,000-9,000   Alt

Michael Stack (b. 1947), AOA, 'Evening Storm in the Mountains', oil.

24 x 30in (61 x 76cm)

$12,000-18,000   Alt

Ray Swanson (b 1937), AOA, AWA, CAA, NAWA, 'Her First Baby Girl', oil.

20,000-30,000   Alt

Ray Swanson (b 1937), AOA, AWS, CAA, NAWA, 'Shearing the Churro Sheep', oil.

52 x 62in (133 x 157.5cm)

$40,000-60,000   Alt

John Swatsley, 'Hunters Moon', oil on canvas, signed lower left.

28 x 40in (71 x101.5cm)

$10,000-15,000   RENO

Arthur F. Tait (1819-1905), 'The Forest', oil on canvas, signed lower right.

12 x 10in (30.5 x 25.5cm)

$20,000-30,000   RENO

Howard Terpning (b. 1927), CAA, NAWA, 'Time stood still', oil.

18 x 26in (45.5 x 66cm)

$180,000-220,000   Alt

Howard Terpning (b. 1927), CAA, NAWA, 'Chiracahua Apache', oil.

16 x 10in (40.5 x 25.5cm)

$70,000-100,000   Alt

Howard Terpning (b. 1927), CAA, NAWA, 'Badger Medicine', oil on board, signed lower right.

38.5 x 24in (98 x 61cm)

$180,000-220,000   RENO

Susan Terpning (b.1953), AOA, NWS, 'Lame Pony', oil.

18 x 24in (45.5 x 61cm)

$6,000-9,000   Alt

Richard Thomas (b. 1935), 'Passage Through Winter's Bite', oil.

Melvin Warren (1920-1995), CAA, 'Run for the Pass', oil on canvas.

Olaf Wieghorst (1899-1988), 'Moonlight and Shadows', oil.

Olaf Wieghorst (1899-1988), 'The Wood Gatherers', oil.

20 x 32in (51 x 81.5cm)

$8,000-12,000   Alt

24 x 36in (61 x 91.5cm)

$15,000-20,000   Alt

28 x 36in (71 x 91.5cm)

$60,000-90,000   Alt

25 x 30in (63.5 x 76cm)

$25,000-30,000   Alt

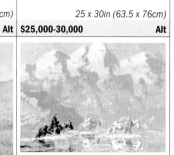

Kim Wiggins (b. 1960), SAI, 'Tale of Don Wray', oil.

Loran Wilford (1895-1972), 'Indian with Horses', oil on canvas, signed lower left.

Provenance: *Vose Galleries, Boston, Massachusetts, Private Collection, Newburyport, Massachusetts.*

Byron Wolfe (1904-1973), CAA, 'First Snow on the Peaks', oil.

Eustace Ziegler (1881-1969), 'Horses crossing a stream', oil on board, signed on the reverse.

24 x 36in (61 x 91.5cm)

$5,000-7,000   Alt

25 x 29in (63.5 x 73.5cm)

$8,000-12,000   RENO

20 x 23in (51 x 58.5cm)

$4,000-6,000   Alt

5 x 7in (13 x 18cm)

$5,000-8,000   REN

EVERY ANTIQUE ILLUSTRATED in *DK Antiques Price Guide 2004* by Judith Miller has a letter code which identifies the dealer or auction house that sold it. The list below is a key to these codes. In the list, auction houses are shown by the letter Ⓐ and dealers by the letter Ⓓ. Some items may have come from a private collection, in which case the code in the list is accompanied by the letter Ⓟ. Inclusion in this book in no way constitutes or implies a contract or a binding offer on the part of any of our contributors to supply or sell the goods illustrated, or similar items, at the prices stated.

AAC Ⓐ
Sanford Alderfer Auction Company
501 Fairgrounds Road, Hatfield, PA 19440
Tel: 215 393 3000
info@alderferauction.com
www.alderferauction.com

AC Ⓓ
Ambre Congo 17 Impasse Saint Jacques,
B-1000 Brussels, Belgium
Tel: 00 32 2 514 02 09
Fax : 00 32 2 514 02 09
info@bruneaf.com
www.bruneaf.com

ACM Ⓓ
Antiques of Cape May
Tel: 800 224 1687

AD Ⓓ
Andrew Dando 34 Market Street,
Bradford on Avon BA15 1LL UK
Tel: 00 44 (0)1225 865 444
andrew@andrewdando.co.uk
www.andrewdando.co.uk

AH Ⓐ
Andrew Hartley Fine Arts Victoria Hall
Salerooms, Little Lane, Ilkley
West Yorkshire LS29 8EA UK
Tel: 00 44 (0)1943 816 363
Fax: 00 44 (0)1943 817 610
info@andrewhartleyfinearts.co.uk
www.andrewhartleyfinearts.co.uk

AL Ⓓ
Andrew Lineham Fine Glass The Mall,
Camden Passage, London N1 8ED UK
Tel: 00 44 (0)20 7704 0195
Fax: 00 44 (0)20 7704 0195
Mob: 00 44 (0)7767 702 722
Andrew@AndrewLineham.co.uk
www.andrewlineham.co.uk

Alt Ⓐ
Altermann Galleries
Santa Fe Galleries, 203 Canyon Road,
Santa Fe, New Mexico 87501
info@altermann.com
www.altermann.com

AM Ⓓ
Arthur Millner 2 Campden Street, Off
Kensington Church Street, London W8 7EP UK
Tel: 00 44 (0)20 7229 3268
Mob: 00 44 (0)7900 248 390
info@arthurmillner.com
www.arthurmillner.com

AnA Ⓓ
Ancient Art 85 The Vale, Southgate,
London N14 6AT UK
Tel: 00 44 (0)20 8882 1509
Fax: 00 44 (0)20 8886 5235
ancient.art@btinternet.com
www.ancientart.co.uk

AOY Ⓓ
All Our Yesterdays 6 Park Road,
Kelvinbridge, Glasgow G4 9JG UK
Tel: 00 44 (0)141 334 7788
Fax: 00 44 (0)141 339 8994
antiques@allouryesterdays.fsnet.co.uk

ATK Ⓐ
Auction Team Köln Postfach 50 11 19, Bonner
Str. 528-530, D-50971 Köln, Germany
Tel: 00 49 (0) 221 38 70 49
Fax: 00 49 (0) 221 37 48 78
Auction@Breker.com
www.Breker.com

ATL Ⓓ
Antique Textiles and Lighting 34 Belvedere,
Lansdowne Road, Bath BA1 5HR UK
Tel: 00 44 (0)1225 310 795
Fax: 00 44 (0)1225 443 884
joannaproops@aol.co.uk

B Ⓐ
Bracketts Fine Art Auctioneers
Auction Hall, The Pantiles, Tunbridge Wells,
Kent TN2 5QL UK
Tel: 00 44 (0)1892 544 500
Fax: 00 44 (0)1892 515 191
sales@bfaa.co.uk
www.bfaa.co.uk

BA Ⓓ
Branksome Antiques
370 Poole Road, Branksome, Poole,
Dorset BH12 1AW UK
Tel: 00 44 (0)1202 763 324
Fax: 00 44 (0)1202 763 643

BAntC Ⓓ
Bath Antiquities Centre 4 Bladud Buildings,
Bath, BA1 5LS UK
Tel: 00 44 (0)1225 460 408
Fax: 00 44 (0)1225 316889
artefacts@bathantiquities.freeserve.co.uk

BCAC Ⓓ
Bucks County Antique Center Route 202,
Lahaska PA 18931
Tel: 215 794 9180

BMN Ⓐ
Auktionshaus Bergmann Möhrendorfer Str. 4,
91056, Erlangen, Germany
Tel: 00 49 (0)9131 45 06 66
Fax: 00 49 (0)9131 45 02 04
www.auction-bergmann.de

BonBay Ⓐ
Bonhams Bayswater
10 Salem Road, London W2 4DL UK
Tel: 00 44 (0)20 7313 2727
Fax: 00 44 (0)20 7313 2701
info@bonhams.com
www.bonhams.com

BonC Ⓐ
Bonhams Knightsbridge
Monpelier Street,
London SW7 1HH UK
toys@bonhams.com
www.bonhams.com

BonE Ⓐ
Bonhams Edinburgh
65 George Street, Edinburgh, EH2 2JL UK
Tel: 00 44 (0)131 225 2266
Fax: 00 44 (0)131 220 2547
info@bonhams.com
www.bonhams.com

BonL Ⓐ
Bonhams Leeds Hepper House,
17A East Parade, Leeds, LS1 2BH UK
Tel: 00 44 (0)113 244 8011
Fax: 00 44 (0)113 242 9875
info@bonhams.com
www.bonhams.com

BonS Ⓐ
Bonhams
101 New Bond Street, London W1S 1SR UK
Tel: 00 44 (0)20 7629 6602
Fax: 00 44 (0)20 7629 8876
info@bonhams.com
www.bonhams.com

BP Ⓓ
The Blue Pump 178 Davenport Road,
Toronto ON Canada
Tel: 414 944 1673

BS Ⓓ
Below Stairs of Hungerford 103 High Street,
Hungerford, Berkshire RG17 0NB UK
Tel: 00 44 (0)1488 682 317
Fax: 00 44 (0)1488 684 294
hofgartner@belowstairs.co.uk
www.belowstairs.co.uk

CamA (D)
Camelot Antiques 7871 Ocean Gateway
Easton, Maryland 21601
Tel: 410 820 4396
camelot@goeastern.net
www.about-antiques.com

CBe (P)
Christina Bertrand Collection
tineke@rcn.com

Chef (A)
Cheffins The Cambridge Saleroom,
2 Clifton Road, Cambridge CB1 4BW UK
Tel: 00 44 (0)1223 213 343
Fax: 00 44 (0)1223 413 396
fine.art@cheffins.co.uk
www.cheffins.co.uk

Clv (A)
Clevedon Salerooms The Auction Centre,
Kenn Road, Clevedon, Bristol BS21 6TT UK
Tel: 00 44 (0)1934 830 111
Fax: 00 44 (0)1934 832 538
info@clevedon-salerooms.com
www.clevedon-salerooms.com

CO (A)
Cooper Owen 10 Denmark Street,
London WC2H 8LS UK
Tel: 00 44 (0)20 7240 4132
Fax: 00 44 (0)20 7240 4339
info@cooperowen.com
www.cooperowen.com

CR (A)
Craftsman Auctions 333 North Main Street,
Lambertville, NJ 08530 UK
Tel: 609 397 9374
Fax: 609 397 9377
info@ragoarts.com
www.ragoarts.com

Cris (D)
Cristobal 26 Church Street,
London NW8 8EP UK
Tel/Fax: 00 44 (0)20 7724 7230
steven@cristobal.co.uk
www.cristobal.co.uk

D (A)
Dickins Auctioneers The Claydon Saleroom,
Claydon House Park, Calvert Rd,
Middle Claydon,
Bucks MK18 2EZ UK
Tel: 00 44 (0)1296 714 434
Fax: 00 44 (0)1296 714 492
info@dickins-auctioneers.com
www.dickins-auctioneers.com

DN (A)
Dreweatt Neate Donnington Priory Salerooms,
Donnington, Newbury, Berkshire RG14 2JE UK
Tel: 00 44 (0)1635 553 553
Fax: 00 44 (0)1635 553 599
fineart@dreweatt-neate.co.uk
www.auctions.dreweatt-neate.co.uk

DRA (A)
David Rago Auctions 333 North Main Street,
Lambertville, NJ 08530
Tel: 609 397 9374
Fax: 609 397 9377
info@ragoarts.com
www.ragoarts.com

ET (D)
Early Technology Monkton House, Old
Craighall, East Lothian, Scotland
Tel: 00 44 (0)131 665 5753
www.earlytech.com

FIS (A)
Dr Fischer Trappensee-Schlösschen,
D-74074 Heilbronn, Germany
Tel: 00 49 (0)7131 15 55 7 0
Fax: 00 49 (0)7131 15 55 7 20
kunstauktionenDr.Fischer@t-online.de
www.auctions-fischer.de

FRE (A)
Freemans 1808 Chestnut Street,
Philadelphia, PA 19103
Tel: 215 563 9275
Fax: 215 563 8236
info@freemansauction.com
www.freemansauction.com

G (A)
Guernsey's Auctions Guernsey's
New York Office, 108 East 73rd Street,
New York, NY 10021
Tel: 212 794 2280
Fax: 212 744 3638
guernsey@guernseys.com
www.guernseys.com

GG (D)
Guest & Gray 1-7 Davies Mews,
London W1K 5AB UK
Tel: 00 44 (0)20 7408 1252
Fax: 00 44 (0)20 7499 1445
info@chinese-porcelain-art.com
www.chinese-porcelain-art.com

GN (D)
Gillian Neale Antiques
P.O. Box 247, Aylesbury, HP20 1JZ UK
Tel : 00 44 (0)1296 423754
Fax : 00 44 (0)1296 334601
Mob: 00 44 (0)7860 638700
gillianneale@aol.com
www.gilliannealeantiques.co.uk

GorL (A)
Gorringes
15 North Street, Lewes, BN7 2PD UK
Tel: 00 44 (0)1273 472 503
Fax: 00 44 (0)1273 479 559
auctions@gorringes.co.uk
www.gorringes.co.uk

Gro (D)
Mary Wise and Grosvenor Antiques
27 Holland Street, London W8 4NA UK
Tel: 00 44 (0)20 7937 8649
Fax: 00 44 (0)20 7937 7179

GS (D)
Goodwins Antiques Ltd
15 & 16 Queensferry Street,
Edinburgh EH2 4QW UK
Tel: 00 44 (0)131 225 4717
Fax: 00 44 (0)131 220 1412

H&G (D)
Hope and Glory
131A Kensington Church Street,
London W8 7LP UK
Tel: 00 44 (0)20 7727 8424

HA (A)
Hunt Auctions 75E. Uwchlan Ave.
Suite 130, Exton, PA 19341
Tel: 610 524 0822
Fax: 610 524 0826
info@huntauctions
www.huntauctions.com

HamG (A)
Hamptons Baverstock House,
93 High Street, Godalming, Surrey GU7 1AL UK
Tel: 00 44 (0)1483 423 567
Fax: 00 44 (0)1483 426 392
fineart@hamptons-int.com
www.hamptons.co.uk

HB (D)
Victoriana Dolls 101 Portobello Rd,
London W11 2BQ UK
Tel: 00 44 (0)1737 249 525
Fax: 00 44 (0)1737 226 254
heather.bond@totalserve.co.uk

HD (D)
Halcyon Days 14 Brook Street,
London W1S 1BD UK
Tel: 00 44 (0)20 7629 8811
Fax: 00 44 (0)20 7409 7901
info@halcyondays.co.uk
www.halcyondays.co.uk

HERR (A)
Auktionshaus W. G. Herr Friesenwall 35,
D-50672 Köln, Germany
Tel: 00 49 (0)221 25 45 48
Fax: 00 49 (0)221 270 67 42
kunst@herr-auktionen.de
www.herr-auktionen.de

HG (D)
Helios Gallery 292 Westbourne Grove,
London W11 2PS UK
Tel: 00 44 (0)7711 955 997
Fax: 00 44 (0)1225 336 097
mail@heliosgallery.com
www.heliosgallery.com

HGS
Harper General Store
10482 Jonestown Road, Annville,
PA, 17003
Tel: 717 865 3456
Fax: 717 865 3813
lauver5@comcast.net
www.harpergeneralstore.com

IHB
Imperial Half Bushel
831 N Howard Street,
Baltimore, MD 21201
Tel: 410 462 1192
ihb@imperialhalfbushel.com
www.imperialhalfbushel.com

JBB ⓓ
Jean-Baptiste Bacquart
www.AfricanAndOceanicArt.com

JDB ⓓ
Jo De Buck
43 Rue Des Minimes,
1000 Brussels, Belgium
Tel/Fax: 00 32 2 512 5516
jdb-tribalart@belgacom.net

JDJ Ⓐ
James D Julia Inc
PO Box 830, Fairfield,
Maine 04937
Tel: 207 453 7125
Fax: 207 453 2502
jjulia@juliaauctions.com
www.juliaauctions.com

JF ⓓ
Jill Fenichell 305 East 61st Street,
New York, NY
Tel: 212 980 9346
jfenichell@yahoo.com

JH ⓓ
Jeanette Hayhurst Fine Glass
32A Kensington Church St.,
London W8 4HA
Tel: 00 44 (0)20 7938 1539

JP ⓓ
Juwelier Pütz St-Apern-Str. 17-21,
50667 Köln, Germany
Tel: 00 49 221 257 49 95

JSC Ⓟ
Jean Scott Collection
Stanhope Collectors' Club,
42 Frankland Crescent, Parkstone,
Poole, Dorset BH14 9PX UK
jean@stanhopes.info
www.stanhopes.info

JW ⓓ
Wadsworth's Marehill, Pulborough,
West Sussex, RH20 2DY UK
Tel: 00 44 (0)1798 873 555
Fax: 00 44 (0)1798 839 017
Mob: 00 44 (0)7770 942 489

JYP ⓓ
JYP Tribal Art Avenue Jean Van Horenbeek,
258b, 1160 Brussels, Belgium
Tel: 00 32 2 (0) 660 09 18
Fax: 00 32 2 (0) 660 12 67
info@jyp-art.com
www.jyp-art.com

KBon Ⓐ
Bonhams Knowle The Old House,
Station Road, Knowle, Solihull,
West Midlands, B93 0HT UK
Tel: 00 44 (0)1564 776 151
Fax: 00 44 (0)1564 778 069
info@bonhams.com
www.bonhams.com

KC ⓓ
Kevin Conru 8a Rue Bodenbroek,
B-1000 Brussels, Belgium
Tel/Fax: 00 32 2 512 7635
Mob: 0478 566 459
kevinconru@yahoo.com

L&T Ⓐ
Lyon and Turnbull Ltd.
33 Broughton Place, Edinburgh EH1 3RR UK
Tel: 00 44 (0)131 557 8844
Fax: 00 44 (0)131 557 8668
info@lyonandturnbull.com
www.lyonandturnbull.com

LC Ⓐ
Lawrence's Fine Art Auctioneers
South Street, Crewkerne,
Somerset TA18 8AB UK
Tel: 00 44 (0)1460 73041
Fax: 00 44 (0)1460 74627
enquiries@lawrences.co.uk
www.lawrences.co.uk

LFA Ⓐ
Law Fine Art Ltd.
Firs Cottage, Church Lane,
Brimpton, Berkshire RG7 4TJ UK
Tel: 00 44 (0)118 971 0353
Fax: 00 44 (0)118 971 3741
info@lawfineart.co.uk
www.lawfineart.co.uk

LHS
L.H. Selman Ltd 123 Locust Street,
Santa Cruz, CA 95060
Tel: 800 538 0766
www.selman.com/pwauction/

LPZ Ⓐ
Lempertz Neumarkt
350667, Köln, Germany
Tel 00 49 (0) 221 925 72 9 0
Fax: 00 49 (0) 221 925 72 9 6
www.lempertz.com

MB ⓓ
Mostly Boxes 93 High Street,
Eton, Windsor, Berkshire SL4 6AF UK
Tel: 00 44 (0)1753 858 470
Fax: 00 44 (0)1753 857 212

MHT ⓓ
Mum Had That
info@mumhadthat.com
www.mumhadthat.com

MP Ⓟ
Marie Penman
Private Collector

NA Ⓐ
Northeast Auctions
93 Pleasant Street, Portsmouth,
NH 03801
Tel: 603 433 8400
Fax: 603 433 0415
neainfo@ttic.net
www.northeastauctions.com

NAG Ⓐ
Nagel D-70030 Stuttgart,
Postfach 10 35 54, Adlerstrasse 31-33,
70199 Stuttgart, Germany
Tel: 00 49 (0)341 26151 61
Fax: 00 49 (0)341 26151 62
www.auction.de

NB Ⓐ
Noel Barrett Antiques & Auctions Ltd
P.O. Box 300, Carversville,
Pennsylvania, 18913
Tel: 215 297 5109
toys@noelbarrett.com
www.noelbarrett.com

NBlm ⓓ
N. Bloom & Son Ltd. 12 Piccadilly Arcade,
London, SW1Y 6NH UK
Tel: 00 44 (0)20 7629 5060
Fax: 00 44 (0)20 7493 2528
nbloom@nbloom.com
www.nbloom.com

OACC ⓓ
Otford Antiques and Collectors Centre
26-28 High Street, Otford, Kent TN15 9DF UK
Tel: 00 44 (0)1959 522 025
www.otfordantiques.co.uk

OG ⓓ
Ormonde Gallery
156 Portobello Road,
London W11 2EB UK
Tel: 00 44 (0)20 7229 9800

PC Ⓟ
Private Collection

Pen ⓓ
Pendulum of Mayfair
51 Maddox Street, London W1 UK
Tel: 00 44 (0)20 7629 6606
Fax: 00 44 (0)20 7629 6616
pendulumclocks@aol.com
www.pendulumofmayfair.co.uk

PM Ⓟ
P. Mestdagh Private collector

Pook Ⓐ
Pook and Pook PO Box 268,
Downington PA 19335
Tel: 610 269 4040/
610 269 0695
Fax: 610 269 9274
info@pookandpook.com
www.pookandpook.com

PW Ⓐ
Peter Wilson
Victoria Gallery, Market Street,
Nantwich, Cheshire,
CW5 5DG UK
Tel: 00 44 (0)1270 623 878
Fax: 00 44 (0)1270 610 508
auctions@peterwilson.co.uk
www.peterwilson.co.uk

Qu Ⓐ
Quittenbaum Kunstauktionen München
Hohenstaufenstraße 1, D-80801,
München, Germany
Tel: 00 49 (0)89 33 00 75 6
Fax: 00 49 (0)89 33 00 75 77

R&GM Ⓓ
R & G McPherson Antiques
40 Kensington Church Street,
London W8 4BX UK
Tel: 00 44 (0)20 7937 0812
Fax: 00 44 (0)20 7938 2032
Mob: 00 44 (0)7768 432 630
rmcpherson@orientalceramics.com
www.orientalceramics.com

RAA Ⓓ
Axtell Antiques 1 River Street,
Deposit, New York 13754
Tel: 607 467 2353
Fax: 607 467 4316
rsaxtell@msn.com
www.axtellantiques.com

RB Ⓓ
Roger Bradbury Church Street,
Coltishall, Norwich, Norfolk,
NR12 7DJ UK
Tel: 00 44 (0)1603 737 444

RdeR Ⓓ
Rogers de Rin 76 Royal Hospital Road,
Paradise Walk, Chelsea,
London SW3 4HN UK
Tel: 00 44 (0)20 7352 9007
Fax: 00 44 (0)20 7351 9407
rogersderin@rogersderin.co.uk
www.rogersderin.co.uk

Ren Ⓓ
Rennies 13 Rugby Street,
London WC1 3QT UK
Tel: 00 44 (0)20 7405 0220
info@rennart.co.uk

RENO Ⓐ
The Coeur d'Alene Art Auction
PO Box 310, Hayden, ID 83835
Tel: 208 772 9009
Fax: 208 772 8294
drumgallery@nidlink.com
www.cdaartauction.com

RG Ⓓ
Richard Gibbon
34/34a Islington Green,
London N1 8DU UK
Tel: 00 44 (0)20 7354 2852
neljeweluk@aol.com

RGA Ⓓ
Richard Gardner Antiques
Swan House, Market Square,
Petworth, West Sussex GU28 0AN UK
Tel: 00 44 (0)1798 343 411
rg@richardgardenerantiques.co.uk
www.richardgardenerantiques.co.uk

Rox Ⓓ
Roxanne Stuart
gemfairy@aol.com

RTC Ⓐ
Ritchies Auctioneers & Appraisers
288 King Street East, Toronto, Ontario,
Canada M5A 1KA
Tel: 416 364 1864
Fax: 416 364 0704
auction@ritchies.com
www.ritchies.com

SA Ⓓ
Stockspring Antiques
114 Kensington Church Street,
London W8 4BH UK
Tel/Fax: 00 44 (0)20 7727 7995
stockspring@antique-porcelain.co.uk
www.antique-porcelain.co.ukgemfairy@aol.com

SAS Ⓐ
Special Auction Services
Kennetholme, Midgham,
Reading, RG7 5UX UK
Tel: 00 44 (0)118 971 2949
Fax: 00 44 (0)118 971 2420
commemorative@aol.com
www.invaluable.com/sas/

SCG Ⓓ
**Gallery 1930 Susie Cooper Ceramics Art
Deco** 18 Church Street, Marylebone,
London NW8 8EP UK
Tel: 00 44 (0)20 7723 1555
Fax: 00 44 (0)20 7735 8309
gallery1930@aol.com
www.susiecooperceramics.com

SG Ⓓ
Sidney Gecker 226 West 21st Street,
New York, NY 10011
Tel: 212 929 8769

SJH Ⓐ
S. J. Hales Auctioneers Tracey House
Salerooms, Newton Road, Bovey Tracey,
Newton Abbot, Devon TQ13 9AZ UK
Tel: 00 44 (0)1626 836 684
Fax: 00 44 (0)1626 836 318
info@sjhales.com
www.sjhales.com

SI Ⓐ
Sloans
No longer trading

Som Ⓓ
Somlo Antiques 7 Piccadilly Arcade,
London SW1Y 6NH UK
Tel: 00 44 (0)20 7499 6526
Fax: 00 44 (0)20 7499 0603
www.somloantiques.com

SS Ⓓ
Spencer Swaffer Antiques,
30 High Street, Arundle,
West Sussex BN18 9AB UK
Tel: 00 44 (0)1903 882 132
Fax: 00 44 (0)1903 884 564
spencerswaffer@btconnect.com

SvA Ⓓ
Somervale Antiques
6 Radstock Road, Midsomer Norton,
Somerset, BA3 2AJ UK
Tel/Fax: 00 44 (0)1761 412 686
Mob: 07885 088 022
ronthomas@somervaleantiquesglass.co.uk
www.somervaleantiquesglass.co.uk

Swa Ⓐ
Swann Galleries Inc
104 East 25th Street
New York, New York 10010
Tel: 212 254 4710
Fax: 212 979 1017

TBk Ⓓ
T.C.S. Brooke The Grange,
Wroxham, Norfolk NR12 8RX UK
Tel: 00 44 (0)1603 782 644

TDC Ⓟ
Thomas Dreiling Collection

TDG Ⓓ
The Design Gallery
5 The Green, Westerham
Kent TN16 1AS UK
Tel: 00 44 (0)1959 561 234
Mob: 00 44 (0)7974 322 858
sales@thedesigngallery.uk.com
www.thedesigngallery.uk.com

TR Ⓓ
Terry Rodgers & Melody
30 & 31 Manhattan Art and Antique Center,
1050 2nd Avenue, New York,
NY 10022
Tel: 212 758 3164
Fax: 212 935 6365
melodyjewelnyc@aol.com

TWC Ⓓ
T W Conroy 36 Oswego St.,
Baldwinsville, NY 13027
Tel: 315 638 6434
Fax: 315 638 7039
www.twconroy.com

Vec Ⓐ
Vectis Auctions Limited, Fleck Way,
Thornaby, Stockton on Tees TS17 9JZ UK
Tel: 00 44 (0)1642 750 616
Fax: 00 44 (0)1642 769 478
enquiries@vectis.co.uk
www.vectis.co.uk

VV Ⓓ
Vintage to Vogue 28 Milsom Street,
Bath BA1 1DG UK
Tel: 00 44 (0)1225 337 323
www.vintagetovoguebath.com

W&W Ⓐ
Wallis and Wallis West Steet Auction Galleries, Lewes, East Sussex BN7 2NJ UK
Tel: 00 44 (0)1273 480 208
Fax: 00 44 (0)1273 476 562
grb@wallisandwallis.co.uk
www.wallisandwallis.co.uk

WAD Ⓐ
Waddington's 111 Bathurst Street, Toronto, Ontario, Canada M5V 2R1
Tel: 416 504 9100
Fax: 416 504 0033
info@waddingtonsauctions.com
www.waddingtonsauctions.com

Wain Ⓓ
William Wain at Antiquarius
Stand J6, Antiquarius,
135 King's Road, Chelsea,
London SW3 4PW UK
Tel: 00 44 (0)20 7351 4905

WG Ⓓ
The Watch Gallery
129 Fulham Road, London, SW3 6RT UK
Tel: 00 44 (0)20 7581 3239
Fax: 00 44 (0)20 7584 6497

WHA Ⓐ
Willis Henry Auctions Inc
22 Main Street, Marshfield, MA 02050
Tel: 781 834 7774
Fax: 781 826 3520
wha@willishenry.com
www.willishenry.com

WW Ⓐ
Woolley and Wallis 51-61 Castle Street, Salisbury, Wiltshire SP1 3SU UK
Tel: 00 44 (0)1722 424 500
Fax: 00 44 (0)1722 424 508
enquiries@woolleyandwallis.co.uk
www.woolleyandwallis.co.uk

NOTE

For valuations, it is advisable to contact the dealer in advance to confirm that they will perform this service and whether any charge is involved. Telephone valuations are not possible, so it will be necessary to send details, including a photograph, of the object to the dealer, along with a stamped addressed envelope for response. While most dealers will be happy to help you with an enquiry, do remember that they are busy people. Please mention *DK Antiques Price Guide 2004* by Judith Miller when making an enquiry.

KEY TO ADVERTISERS

CLIENT	PAGE NO
North East Auctions	17
Bergmann	75
Quittenbaum	146
Freemans	216, 535
L H Selman Ltd	310

CLIENT	PAGE NO
Hermann Historica	474
David Rago	517
James D Julia	573
Van Ham	639

DIRECTORY OF AUCTIONEERS

This is a list of auctioneers that conduct regular sales. Auction houses that would like to be included in the next edition should contact us by February 2004.

Alabama

Flomaton Antique Auction
P.O. Box 1017, 320 Palafox Street, Flomaton 36441
Tel: 334 296 3059
Fax: 334 296 3710
www.flomatonantiqueauction.com

Jim Norman Auctions 201 East Main St, Hartselle, 35640
Tel: 205 773 6878

Vintage Auctions Star Rte Box 650, Blountsville, 35031
Tel: 205 668 0204
Fax: 205 429 2457

Arizona

Dan May & Associates 4110 North Scottsdale Road, Scottsdale, 85251
Tel: 602 941 4200

Old World Mail Auctions
671 Highway 179, St 2C, Sedona, 86334
Tel: 928 282 3944
marti@oldworldauctions.com
www.oldworldauctions.com

Star Auction Inc P. O. Box 1232, Dolan Springs, 86441-1232
Tel: 602 767 4774
Fax: 602 767 3900

Arkansas

Hanna-Whysel Auctions 3403 Bella Vista Way, Bella Vista, 72714
Tel: 501 855 9600

Ponders Auctions 1504 South Leslie, Stuttgart, 72160
Tel: 501 673 6551

California

Bonhams & Butterfields
7601 Sunset Blvd, Los Angeles, 90046-2714
Tel: 323 850 7500
Fax: 323 850 5843
info@butterfields.com
www.butterfields.com

Bonhams & Butterfields
220 San Bruno Ave, San Francisco, CA 94103
Tel: 415 861 7500
Fax: 415 861 8951
info@butterfields.com
www.butterfields.com

I.M. Chait Gallery 9330 Civic Center Drive, Beverly Hills 90210
Tel: 310 285 0182
Fax: 310 285 9740
imchait@aol.com
www.chait.com

Cuschieri's Auctioneers & Appraisers 863 Main Street, Redwood City, 94063
Tel: 650 556 1793
Fax: 650 556 9805
peter@cuschieris.com
www.cuschieris.com

eBay, Inc 2005 Hamilton Ave, Ste 350, San Jose 95125
Tel: 408 369 4839
staff@ebay.com
www.ebay.com

San Rafael Auction Gallery 634 Fifth Avenue, San Rafael, San Rafael, 9490
Tel: 415 457 4488
Fax: 415 457 4899
srauction@aol.com
www.sanrafael-auction.com

L. H. Selman Ltd 123 Locust St, Santa Cruz, 95060
Tel: 800 538 0766
Fax: 408 427 0111
lselman@got.net
www.paperweight.com

Slawinski Auction Co 6192 Hwy 9, Felton, 95018
Tel: 831 335 9000
wjantqs@znet.com
www.slawinski.com

North Carolina

Robert S. Brunk Auction Services Inc P. O. Box 2135, Asheville, 28802
Tel: 828 254 6846
auction@brunkauctions.com
www.brunkauctions.com

Historical Collectible Auctions P. O. Box 975, Burlington, 27215
Tel: 336 570 2803
info@hcaauctions.com
www.hcaauctions.com

South Carolina

Charlton Hall Galleries, Inc 912 Gervais St, Columbia, 29201
Tel: 803 799 5678
info@charltonhallauctions.com
www.charltonhallauctions.com

Colorado

Pacific Auction 9138 North 95th, Longmont, 80501
Tel: 303 772 9401

Pettigrew Auction Company 1645 South Tejon Street, Colorado Springs, 80906
Tel: 719 633 7963

Priddy's Auction Galleries 5411 Leetsdale Drive, Denver, 80222
Tel: 800 380 4411

Stanley & Co Auction Room, 395 Corona Street, Denver
Tel: 303 355 0506

Connecticut

Norman C. Heckler & Company 79 Bradford Corner Rd, Woodstock Valley, 06282-2002
Tel: 860 974 1634
heckler@neca.com
www.hecklerauction.com

Lloyd Ralston Toys 350 Long Beach Blvd, Stratford, 06615
Tel: 203 386 9399
www.lloydralstontoys.com

Winter Associates, Inc Auctioneers & Appraisers, 21 Cooke St, P. O. Box 823, Plainville, 06062
Tel: 860 793 0288

North Dakota

Curt D. Johnson Auction Company RR1 Box 135, Grand Forks, 58201
Tel: 701 746 1378
merfeld@rrv.net
www.curtdjohnson.com

South Dakota

Fischer Auction Company 238 Haywire Ave, P. O. Box 667, Long Lake, 57457-0667
Tel: 800 888 1766/
605 577 6600
gofish@valleytel.net
www.fischerauction.com

Delaware

Remember When Auctions, Inc 42 Sea Gull Rd, Swann Estates, Selbyville, 19975
Tel: 302-436-8869
sales@history-attic.com
www.history-attic.com

Florida

Auctions Neapolitan 995 Central Avenue, Naples 34102
Tel: 941 262 7333
www.auctionsneapolitan.com

Burchard Galleries/Auctioneers 2528 30th Ave North, St Petersburg, 33713
Tel: 727 821 11667/
727 823 4156
burchard@atlantic.net
www.burchardgalleries.com

Dawson's P.O. Box 646, Palm Beach, 33480
Tel: 561 835 6930
info@dawsons.org www.dawsons.org

Arthur James Galleries 615 E. Atlantic Ave, Delray Beach
Tel: 561 278 2373

Kincaid Auction Company 3214 East Hwy 92, Lakeland, 33801
Tel: 800 970 1977
kincaid@kincaid.com
www.kincaid.com

Albert Post Galleries 809 Lucerne Ave, Lake Worth, 33460
Tel: 561 582 4477
a.postgallery@juno.com
www.albertpostgallery.com

Sloan's Auction Galleries 8861 NW 18th Terrace, Ste 100, Miami, 33172
Tel: 305 751 4770/800 660 4524
sloans@sloansauction.com
www.sloansauction.com

Georgia

Arwood Auctions 26 Ayers Ave, Marietta, 30060
Tel: 770 423 0110

Great Gatsby's 5070 Peachtree Industrial Blvd, Atlanta,
Tel: 770 457 1905/
800 428 7297

My Hart Auctions Inc P. O. Box 2511, Cumming, 30028
Tel: 770 888 9006

Red Baron's Auction Gallery 6450 Roswell Rd, Atlanta, 30328
Tel: 404 252 3770
rbarons@onramp.net

Southland Auction Inc 3350 Riverwood Parkway, Atlanta
Tel: 770 818 2418

Idaho

The Coeur d'Alene Art Auction P. O. Box 310, Hayden, 83835
Tel: 208 772 9009

Indiana

Kruse International P. O. Box 190, Auburn, 46706
Tel: 219 925 5600/
800 968 4444

Lawson Auction Service 923 Fourth St, Columbus, 47265
Tel: 812 372 2571
dlawson@lawson-auction.com
www.lawson-auction.com

Majolica Auctions Michael G. Strawser, 200 North Main, P. O. Box 332, Wolcottville, 46795
Tel: 219 854 285
michael@strawserauctions.com
www.strawserauctions.com

Curran Miller Auction & Realty, Inc 4424 Vogel Rd, Ste. 400, Evansville, 47715
Tel: 800 264 0601/
812 474 6100
auctionx@evansville.net
www.cmillerauctions.com

Schrader Auction 209 West Van Buren St, Columbia City, 46725
Tel: 219 244 7606

Slater's Americana 5335 North Tacoma Ave, Suite 24, Indianapolis, 46220
Tel: 317 257 0863

Stout Auctions 11 West Third St, Williamsport, 47993-1119
Tel: 765 764 6901

Illinois

Butterfield & Dunning 755 Church Rd, Elgin, 60123
Tel: 847 741 3483
info@butterfields.com
www.butterfields.com

Hack's Auction Center Box 296, Pecatonica, 61063
Tel: 815 239 1436

Hanzel Galleries 1120 South Michigan Ave, Chicago, 60605-2301
Tel: 312 922 6247

Joy Luke Auction Gallery 300 East Grove St, Bloomington, 61701-5232
Tel: 309 828 5533
robert@joyluke.com
www.joyluke.com

Susanin's Auction 228 Merchandise Mart, Chicago, 60654
Tel: 888 787 2646/
312 832 9800
info@susanins.com
www.susanins.com

Iowa

Gene Harris Antique Auction Center 2035 18th Ave, P. O. Box 476, Marshalltown, 50158
Tel: 641 752 0600/
800 862 6674
ghaac@marshallnet.com
www.geneharrisauctions.com

Jackson's Auctioneers & Appraisers 2229 Lincoln St, P. O. Box 50613, Cedar Falls, 50613
Tel: 319 277 2256
jacksons@jacksonsauction.com
www.jacksonsauction.com

Tubaugh Auctions 1702 8th Ave, Belle Plaine, 52208
Tel: 319 444 2413/
800 368 1292
www.tubaughauctions.com

Kansas

AAA Historical Auction Service P. O. Box 12214, Kansas City, 66112
www.manions.com

CC Auction 416 Court, Clay Center, 67432
Tel: 913 632 6511

Spielman Auction 2259 Homestead Rd, Lebo, 66856
Tel: 316 256 6558

Kentucky

Hays & Associates, Inc 120 South Spring St, Louisville, 40206-1953
Tel: 502 584 4297

Steffen's Historical Militaria
P. O. Box 280, Newport, 41072
Tel: 606 431 4499

Louisiana

Estate Auction Gallery 3374
Government St, Baton Rouge,
70806
Tel: 504 383 7706

Morton M. Goldberg Auction
Galleries, 547 Baronne St, New
Orleans, 70113
Tel: 504 592 2300

New Orleans Auction Galleries,
Inc, 801 Magazine St,
New Orleans, 70130
Tel: 504 566 1849

Maine

James D Julia Auctioneers Inc Rte
201, Skowhegan Rd, P. O. Box 830,
Fairfield, 04937
Tel: 207 453 7125
jjulia@juliaauctions.com
www.juliaauctions.com

**Thomaston Place Auction
Galleries** P. O. Box 300, Business
Rt 1, Thomaston, 04861
Tel: 207 354 8141
johnh@kajav.com
www.kagav.com

Maryland

DeCaro Auction Sales, Inc 8133
Elliott Rd, Easton, 21601-7184
Tel: 410 820 4000
info@decaroauctions.com
www.decaroauctions.com

**Hantman's Auctioneers &
Appraisers** P. O. Box 59366,
Potomac, 20859-9366
Tel: 301 770 3720
hantman@hantmans.com
www.hantmans.com

**Isennock Auctions & Appraisals,
Inc** 4203 Norrisville Rd, White Hall,
21161-9306,
Tel: 410 557 8052
isennock@starix.net
www.isennockauction.com

Richard Opfer Auctioneering, Inc
1919 Greenspring Dr, Lutherville,
Timonium, 21093-4113
Tel: 410 252 5035
info@opferauction.com
www.opferauction.com

Sloans & Kenyon
4605 Bradley Boulevard
Bethesda, Maryland 20815
Tel: 301 634-2330
Fax: 301 656-7074

Massachusetts

Douglas Auctioneers Rte 5,
South Deerfield, 01373
Tel: 413 665 3530
www.douglasauctioneers.com

Eldred's P. O. Box 796, East Dennis,
02641-0796
Tel: 508 385 3116
info@eldreds.com
www.eldreds.com

Grogan & Company Auctioneers
22 Harris St, Dedham, 02026
Tel: 781 461 9500
grogans@groganco.com
www.groganco.com

Shute Auction Gallery 850 West
Chestnut St, Brockton, 02401
Tel: 508 588 0022/
508 588 7833

Skinner, Inc 357 Main St, Bolton,
01740-1104
Tel: 978 779 6241
info@skinnerinc.com
www.skinnerinc.com

Willis Henry Auctions, Inc 22 Main
St, Marshfield, 02050
Tel: 781 834 7774/
800 244 8466
wha@willishenry.com
www.willishenry.com

Michigan

DuMouchelle Art Galleries Co 409
East Jefferson Ave, Detroit, 48226
Tel: 313 963 6255
info@dumouchelles.com
www.dumouchelles.com

Minnesota

Buffalo Bay Auction Co 5244
Quam Circle, Rogers, 55374
Tel: 612 428 8480
buffalobay@aol.com

Tracy Luther Auctions 2548 East
7th Ave, St. Paul, 55109
Tel: 612 770 6175

Rose Auction Galleries 2717
Lincoln Dr, Roseville, 55113
Tel: 612 484 1415
www.rosegalleries.com

Missouri

Ivey-Selkirk 7447 Forsyth Blvd,
Saint Louis, 63105
Tel: 314 726 5515
www.iveyselkirk.com

Simmons & Company Auctioneers
40706 East 144th St, Richmond,
64085
Tel: 816 776 2936/800 646 2936

simmons_auction@raycounty.com
www.raycounty.com/simmons

Montana

Stan Howe & Associates 4433
Red Fox Dr, Helena, 59601-7561
Tel: 406 443 5658/
800 443 5658

New Hampshire

Northeast Auction 694 Lafayette
Rd, P. O. Box 363, Hampton, 03483
Tel: 603 926 9800

New Jersey

Bertoia Auctions 2141 Demarco
Dr, Vineland, 08360
Tel: 856 692 1881
bill@bertoiaauctions.com
www.bertoiaauctions.com

Craftsman Auctions 333 North
Main Street, Lambertville, 08530
Tel: 609-397-9374
mtucker@ragoarts.com
www.ragoarts.com

Dawson's 128 American Rd, Morris
Plains, 07950
Tel: 973 984 6900
info@dawsons.org www.dawsons.org

Greg Manning Auctions, Inc 775
Passaic Ave, West Caldwell, 07006
Tel: 973 883 0004/800 221 0243
info@gregmanning.com
www.gregmanning.com

Rago Modern Auctions, LLP 333
North Main Street, Lambertville,
08530
Tel: 609-397-9374
mtucker@ragoarts.com
www.ragoarts.com

New York

Christie's 502 Park Ave, New York,
10022
Tel: 212 546 1000
info@christies.com
www.christies.com

Christie's East 219 East 67th St,
New York, 10021
Tel: 212 606 0400
info@christies.com
www.christies.com

Samuel Cottone Auctions 15
Genesee St, Mount Morris, 14510
Tel: 716 658 3119

William Doyle Galleries 175 East
87th St, New York, 10128-2205
Tel: 212 427 2730
info@doylegalleries.com
www.doylegalleries.com

Framefinders 454 East 84th
Street, New York 10028
Tel: 212 396 3896
framefinders@aol.com
www.framefinders.com

Guernsey's Auction 108 East 73rd
St, New York, 10021
Tel: 212 794 2280
catalogues@guernseys.com
www.guernseys.com

Mapes Auction Gallery 1729
Vestal Parkway, West Vestal, 13850
Tel: 607 754 9193
davidmapes@compuserve.com
www.mapesauction.com

Phillip's, De Pury & Luxemburg 23
West 57th Street, New York, 10019
Tel: 212 940 1200
carole.bellidora@phillips-dpl.com
www.phillips-dpl.com

Sotheby's 1334 York Ave, New York,
10021
Tel: 212 606 7000
info@sothebys.com
www.sothebys.com

Swann Galleries, Inc 104 East
25th St, New York, 10010-2977
Tel: 212 254 4710
swann@swanngalleries.com
www.swanngalleries.com

New Mexico

Altermann Galleries
Santa Fe Galleries,
203 Canyon Road,
Santa Fe, New Mexico 87501
info@altermann.com
www.altermann.com

Ohio

**Cowan's Historic Americana
Auctions** 673 Wilmer Avenue,
Cincinnati, 45226
Tel: 513 871 1670
info@historicamericana.com
www.historicamericana.com

DeFina Auctions 1591 State Route
45, Austinburg, 44010
Tel: 440 275 6674
info@definaauctions.com
www.definaauctions.com

Garth's Auction, Inc 2690
Stratford Rd, P. O. Box 369,
Delaware, 43015
Tel: 614 362 4771/614 369 5085
info@garths.com www.garths.com

Oklahoma

C & C The Auction Company 4801
MacKelman Dr, Oklahoma City,
73135-4135
Tel: 405 670 1705

Pennsylvania

Alderfer Auction Company 501 Fairground Rd, P. O. Box 640, Hatfield, 19440-0640
Tel: 215 393 3000
auction@alderfercompany.com
www.alderfercompany.com

Noel Barrett P.O. Box 300, Carversville, 18913
Tel: 215 297 5109
toys@noelbarrett.com
www.noelbarrett.com

Dargate Auction Galleries 5607 Baum Blvd, Pittsburgh, 15206
Tel: 412 362 3558
dargate@dargate.com
www.dargate.com

Freeman's 1808 Chestnut St, Philadelphia, 19103
Tel: 610 563 9275/
610 563 9453
info@freemansauction.com
www.freemansauction.com
Hunt Auctions 75E. Uwchlan Ave. Suite 130, Exton, Pa 19341
Tel: 610 524 0822
Fax: 610 524 0826
info@huntauctions
www.huntauctions.com

Pook & Pook, Inc P. O. Box 268, Downington, 19335-0268
Tel: 610 269 0695/
610 269 4040
info@pookandpook.com
www.pookandpook.com

Skinner's Auction Company 3807 Margate Rd, Bethlehem, 18020
Tel: 610 868 985
skinnauct@aol.com www.skinner-auct.baweb.com

Stephenson's Auction 1005 Industrial Blvd, Southampton, 18966-4006
Tel: 215 322 6182
info@stephensonsauction.com
www.stephensonsauction.com

Rhode Island

Gustave White Auctioneers 37 Bellevue, Newport, 02840-3207
Tel: 401 841 5780

Tennessee

Berenice Denton Estates 4403 Murphy Road, Nashville, 37209
Tel: 615 292 5765
lnichols66@home.com

Kimball M Sterling Inc 125 West Market St, Johnson City, 37601,
Tel: 423 928 1471
kimsold@tricon.net
www.sterlingsold.com

Texas

Austin Auctions 8414 Anderson Mill Road, Austin, 78729-5479
Tel: 512 258 5479
austinauction@cs.com
www.austinauction.com

Utah

America West Archives P. O. Box 100, Cedar City, 84721-0100
Tel: 435 586 9497/
435 586 7323
awa@netutah.com
www.americawestarchives.com

Vermont

Eaton Auction Service RR 1, Box 333, Fairlee, 05045
Tel: 802 333 9717

Virginia

The Auction Gallery 3140 West Cary St, Richmond, 23221
Tel: 804 358 0500/
804 359 0688
knightm@mindspring.com

Ken Farmer Auctions & Estates 105A Harrison Street, Radford, 24141
Tel: 540 639 0939
info@kfauctions.com
www.kenfarmer.com

Phoebus Auction Gallery 14-16 East Mellen St, Hampton, 23663
Tel: 757 722 9210
bwelch@phoebusauction.com
www.phoebusauction.com

Washington DC

Weschler's 909 East St NW, Washington, 20004-2006
Tel: 202 628 1281/
800 331 1430
www.weschlers.com

Wisconsin

Krueger Auctions P. O. Box 275, Iola, 54945-0275
Tel: 715 445 3845

Milwaukee Auction Galleries 1919 North Summit Ave, Milwaukee, 53202
Tel: 414 271 1105

Schrager Auction Galleries, Ltd P. O. Box 10390, 2915 North Sherman Blvd, Milwaukee, 53210
Tel: 414 873 3738

DIRECTORY OF SPECIALISTS

SPECIALISTS WHO WOULD LIKE TO BE INCLUDED in the next edition, or have a change of address or telephone number, should contact us by February 2004.

Readers should contact dealers by telephone before visiting them to avoid a wasted journey.

American Paintings

James R Bakker Antiques Inc 248 Bradford Street, Provincetown, MA 02657
Tel: 508 487 9081

Jeffrey W. Cooley The Cooley Gallery Inc, 25 Lyme Street, Old Lyme, CT 06371
Tel: 860 434 8807
cooleygallery@snet.net

Richard York Gallery 21 East Street, New York, NY 10021
Tel: 212 772 9155
www.richardyorkgallery.com

Americana and Folk Art

Augustus Decorative Arts Ltd, Box 700, New York, NY 10101
Tel: 212 333 7888
elle@portrait minatures.com

Thomas and Julia Barringer 26 South Main Street, Stockton, NJ 08559
Tel: 609 397 4474
Fax: 609 397 4474
tandjb@voicenet.com

Bucks County Antique Center Route 202, Lahaska, PA 18931
Tel: 215 794 9180

J M Flanigan American Antiques 1607 Park Avenue, Baltimore, MD 21217
Tel: 800 280 9308
jmf745i@aol.com

Frank Gaglio, Inc 56 Market St., Suite B, Rhinebeck NY 12572
Tel: 845 876 0616

Sidney Gecker 226 West 21st Street, New York, NY 10011
Tel: 212 929 8769

Pat and Rich Garthoeffner Antiques 122 East Main Street, Lititz, PA 17543
Tel: 717 627 7998
Fax: 717 627 3259
patgarth@voicenet.com

Allan Katz Americana 25 Old Still Road, Woodbridge, CT 06525
Tel: 203 393 9356
alkatze@concentric.net

Nathan Liverant and Son 168 South Main Street, P.O. Box 103, Colchester, CT 06415
Tel: 860 537 2409
nliverantandson@biz.ctol.net

Judith and James Milne Inc 506 East 74th Street, New York IL 60035
Tel: 847 433 2213
FPollack@compuserve.com

Monkey Hill 6465 Route 202, New Hope, PA 18938
Tel: 215 862 0118
Fax: 215 862 3436
info@monkeyhillantiques.com

Olde Hope Antiques Inc P.O. Box 718, New Hope, PA 18938
Tel: 215 297 0200
Fax: 215 297 0300
info@oldehopeantiques.com
www.oldehopeantiques.com

Pantry & Hearth 121 East 35th Street, New York, NY 10016
Tel: 212 532 0535
gail.lettick@prodigy.net

Sharon Platt 1347 Rustic View, Manchester, MO 63011
Tel: 636 227 5304
sharonplatt@postnet.com

Raccoon Creek Antiques P.O. Box 457, 20 Main Street Bridgeport, NJ 08014
Tel: 856 467 3197

J. B. Richardson 6 Partrick Lane, Westport, CT 06880
Tel: 203 226 0358

Marion Robertshaw Antiques P.O. Box 435, Route 202, Lahaska, PA 18931
Tel: 215 295 0648

Cheryl and Paul Scott P.O. Box 835, 232 Bear Hill Road, Hillsborough, NH 03244
Tel: 603 464 3617

The Splendid Peasant Route 23 and Sheffield Road, P. O. Box 536, South Egremont, MA 01258
Tel: 413 528 5755
folkart@splendidpeasant.com
www.splendidpeasant.com

The Stradlings 1225 Park Avenue, New York, NY 10028
Tel: 212 534 8135

Jeffrey Tillou Antiques 33 West Street & 7 East Street, P.O. Box 1609, Litchfield, CT 06759
Tel: 860 567 9693
webmaster@tillouantiques.com

Paul and Karen Wendhiser P.O. Box 155, Ellington, CT 06029

Antiquities

Frank & Barbara Pollack 1214 Green Bay Road, Highland Park, IL 60035
Tel: 847 433 2213
FPollack@compuserve.com

Architectural Antiques

Garden Antiques Katonah, NY 10536
Tel: 212 744 6281
gardenantiques@pipeline.com
www.bi gardenantiques.com

Cecilia B Williams 12 West Main Street, New Market, MD 21774
Tel: 301 865 0777

Canadiana

The Blue Pump 178 Davenport Road, Toronto ON Canada
Tel: 414 944 1673

Carpets and Rugs

John J Collins Jr Gallery, P.O. Box 958, 11 Market Square, Newburyport, MA 01950
Tel: 978 462 7276
bijars@att.net

Karen and Ralph Disaia Oriental Rugs Ltd, 23 Lyme Street, Old Lyme, CT 06371
Tel: 860 434 1167
orientalrugs@snet
www.orientalrugsltd.com

D B Stock Antique Carpets 464 Washington Street, Wellesley, MA 02482
Tel: 781 237 5859

Ceramics

Charles & Barbara Adams 289 Old Main St, South Yarmouth, 02664
Tel: 508 760 3290
adams_2430@msn.com

Jill Fenichell 305 East 61st Street, New York, NY
Tel: 212 980 9346
jfenichell@yahoo.com

Mark & Marjorie Allen 6 Highland Drive, Amherst, NH 03031
Tel: 603 672 8989
mandmallen@antiquedelft.com
www.antiquedelft.com

Mellin's Antiques P.O. Box 1115, Redding, CT 06875
Tel: 203 938 9538
remellin@aol.com

Philip Suval, Inc 1501 Caroline Street, Fredericksburg, VA 22401
Tel: 540 373 9851

Clocks

Kirtland H Crump 387 Boston Post Road, Madison, 06443
Tel: 203 245 7573
kirt@crumpclocks.com

Decorative Arts

Sumpty Priddy 601 South Washington Street, Alexandria, 22314 4109
Tel: 703 299 0800
sumpterpriddy@sumpterpriddy.com

Leah Gordon Antiques Gallery 18, Manhattan Art and Antiques Center, 1050 Second Avenue, New York, NY 10022
Tel: 212 872 1422

Lillian Nassau 220 East 57th Street New York, NY 10022
Tel: 212 759 6062
lilnassau@aol.com
www.lilliannassau.com

Furniture

American Antiques 161 Main Street, P.O. Box 368, Thomaston, ME 04861
Tel: 207 354 6033
acm@midcoast.com

American Spirit Antiques P.O. Box 11152, Shawnee Mission, KS 66207
Tel: 913 345 9494
Tedatiii@aol.com

Barbara Ardizone P.O. Box 433, 62 Main Street, Salisbury, CT 06068
Tel: 860 435 3057

DIRECTORY OF SPECIALISTS

Artemis Gallery Wallace Road, North Salem, NY 10560
Tel: 914 669 5971
artemis@optonline.net
www.artemisantiques.com

Carswell Rush Berlin, Inc P.O. Box 0210, Planetarium Station, New York, NY 0024 0210
Tel: 212 721 0330
carswellberlin@msn.com
www.americanantiques.net

Joanne and Jack Boardman 522 Joanne Lane, DeKalb, IL 06115
Tel: 815 756 359
boardmanantiques@aol.com

Joan R Browstein Daniel Hightower, 2068 Ellis Hollow Road, Ithaca, NY

Susie Burmann 23 Burpee Lane, New London, NH 03257
Tel: 603 526 5934
rsburmann@tds.net

H L Chalfant Antiques 1352 Paoli Pike, West Chester, PA 19380
Tel: 610 696 1862
chalfant@gateway.net

Brian Cullity 18 Plesant Street, P.O. Box 595, Sagamore, MA 02561
Tel: 508 888 8409
bcullity@capecod.net

Gordon and Marjorie Davenport Inc 4250 Manitou Way, Madison, WI 53711
Tel: 608 271 2348
GMDaven@aol.com

Ron and Penny Dionne 55 Fisher Hill Road, Willington, CT 06279
Tel: 860 487 0741

Peter H Eaton Antiques Inc 39 State Street, Newburyport, MA 01950
Tel: 978 465 2754
peter@petereaton.com
www.petereaton.com

Stephen H Garner Antiques P.O. Box 136, Yarmouthport, MA 02675
Tel: 508 362 8424

Samuel Herrup Antiques 35 Sheffield Plain Road (Route 7), Sheffield, MA 01257
Tel: 413 229 0424
ssher@ben.net

R Jorgensen Antiques 502 Post Road (US Route 1), Wells, ME 04090
Tel: 207 646 9444
rja@cybertours.com

Leigh Keno American Antiques 127 East 69th Street, New York, NY 10021
Tel: 212 734 2381
leigh@leighkeno.com
www.leighkeno.com

Bettina Krainin 289 Main Street, Woodbury, CT 06798
Tel: 203 263 7669

William E Lohrman 248 Route 208, New Paltz, NY 12561
Tel: 845 255 6762

Gart and Martha Ludlow Inc 5284 Golfway Lane, Lyndhurst, OH 44124,
Tel: 440 449 3475,

Milly McGehee P.O. Box 666, Riderwood, 21139 MD 0666
Tel: 410 653 3977
millymcgehee@home.com

Jackson Mitchell Inc 5718 Kennett Pike, Wilmington, DE 19807
Tel: 302 656 0110
JacMitch@aol.com

James L Price Antiques 831 Alexander Spring Rd, Carlisle, PA 17013
Tel: 717 243 0501
jlpriceantiques@earthlink.net

RJG Antiques P.O. Box 60, Rye, NH 03870
Tel: 603 433 1770
antiques@rjgantiques.com
www.rjgantiques.com

John Keith Russell Antiques Inc 110 Spring Street, P.O. Box 414, South Salem, NY 10590
Tel: 914 763 8144
jkrantique@aol.com

Israel Sack 730 Fifth Avenue, Suite 605, New York, NY 109
Tel: 212 399 6562

Lincoln and Jean Sander 235 Redding Road, Redding, CT 06896
Tel: 203 938 2981
sanderlr@aol.com

Kathy Schoemer American Antiques P.O. Box 429, 12 McMorrow Lane, North Salem, NY 10560
Tel: 914 277 8464

Thomas Schwenke Inc 50 Main Street North, Woodbury, CT 06798
Tel: 203 266 0303
tgs@schwenke.com
www.schwenke.com

Jack and Ray Van Gelder Conway House, 468 Ashfield Road, Conway, MA 01341
Tel: 413 369 4660

Van Tassel/Baumann American Antiques, 690 Sugartown Road, Malvern, PA 19355
Tel: 610 647 3339

Glass

L.H. Selman Ltd 123 Locust Street, Santa Cruz, CA 95060
Tel: 800 538 0766
www.selman.com/pwauction/

Paul Reichwein 2321 Hershey Avenune, East Petersburg, PA 17520
Tel: 717 569 7637

Jewelry

Arthur Guy Kaplan P.O. Box 1942, Baltimore, MD 21203
Tel: 410 752 2090

Marine Antiques

Hyland Granby Antiques P.O. Box 457, Hyannis Port, MA 02647
Tel: 508 771 3070
gmarine@capecod.net

Metalware

Wayne and Phyllis Hilt RR 1, Haddam Neck, CT 06424 3022
Tel: 860 267 2146
philt@snet.net

Toys

Harper General Store 10482 Jonestown Road, Annville, PA, 17003
Tel: 717 865 3456
Fax: 717 865 3813
lauver5@comcast.net
www.harpergeneralstore.com

Silver

Jonathan Trace P.O. Box 418, 31 Church Hill Road, Rifton, NY 12471
Tel: 914 658 7336

Imperial Half Bushel 831 N Howard Street, Baltimore, MD 21201
Tel: 410 462 1192
ihb@imperialhalfbushel.com
www.imperialhalfbushel.com

Textiles

Colette Donovan 98 River Road, Merrimacport, MA 01860
Tel: 978 346 0614

M Finkel & Daughter 936 Pine Street, Philadelphia, PA 19107 6128
Tel: 215 627 7797
mailbox@finkelantiques.com
www.samplings.com

Cora Ginsburg 19 East 74th Street New York, NY 10021
Tel: 212 744 1352

Stephen & Carol Huber 40 Ferry Road, Old Saybrook, CT 06475
Tel: 860 388 6809
hubers@antiquesamplers.com
www.antiquesamplers.com

Fayne Landes Antiques 593 Hansell Road, Wynnewood, PA 19096
Tel: 610 658 0566

Tribal Art

Marcy Burns American Indian Arts P.O. Box 181 Glenside, PA 19038
Tel: 215 576 1559
mbindianart@home.com

Elliot & Grace Snyder P.O. Box 598, South Egremont, MA 01258
Tel: 413 528 3581

A

acanthus A popular leaf motif found carved and inlaid.

acid etching A technique using acid to decorate glass to produce a matt or frosted effect.

appliqué Decoration that is formed separately and then applied to a piece. In textiles, decoration that is made from a different material and then applied to the main ground, often with braids or decorative stitching.

apron/skirt The piece of wood underneath the seat rail of a chair or settee, or beneath the legs of a table or chest.

architrave The molding around a door or aperture on a piece of furniture.

articulated A doll or figure's body with jointed limbs.

astragal Small architectural molding with a semi-circular section.

B

bakelite An early form of plastic which was popular in the 1920s and 1930s.

balance A type of escape mechanism that is used in clocks without pendulums.

ball-jointed Limbs that are attached to a doll's body with a ball and socket.

baluster A curved form with a bulbous base and a slender neck.

beading A type of decoration, usually in a band or border, and in the shape of small beads.

bébé The French term for a doll that represents a baby rather than an adult.

bergère The French term for an armchair with an upholstered back and sides, and a deep seat.

bezel The groove or rim on the inside of the cover or lid on vessels such as coffeepots or teapots.

biscuit Porcelain that has been fired once and has a characteristic matt white body.

bisque A type of unglazed porcelain used for making dolls' heads from 1860 to 1925.

blowing A method of shaping glass by blowing a blob of molten glass through a tube.

bob The metal weight at the end of a pendulum rod.

body The material from which ceramics are made, such as pottery, porcelain, earthenware, or stoneware.

bombé A swollen curving form.

bone china A type of porcelain which has dried ox bone added to the body to produce a very white china. Produced extensively in Britain from 1820.

boulle case A type of marquetry that includes tortoiseshell and metal.

bow front An outwardly curving shape typically found on case furniture.

bracket clock A spring-driven clock originally designed to stand on a wall bracket and later on a shelf or table.

bracket foot A square-shaped foot often found on case furniture from the 18thC.

break/broken arch The arch at the top of longcase and bracket clocks.

C

cabriole leg A leg formed of two slight curves that create an S-shape.

cameo Hardstone, coral, or shell that has been carved in relief to show a design in a contrasting color.

cameo glass Decorative glass made from two or more differently colored layers, which are then carved or etched to reveal the color beneath.

cannetille Filgree formed from silver or gold wire coiled into scrolls or rosettes.

canterbury A small stand with dividers for storing sheet music.

capital The end of a column on the hood or trunk of a longcase clock.

carriage clock A small, spring-driven clock, designed for traveling.

cartouche A framed panel, often in the shape of a paper scroll, the side of which can be inscribed.

caryatid An architechtural column in the form of a woman, also found on 17th and 18thC furniture.

cast metal Metalware formed by pouring molten metal into a cast or mold.

celluloid An early plastic invented in 1869 and used for making dolls heads and bodies.

centre seconds hand A seconds hand that is pivoted at the centre of the dial.

champlevé A type of decoration where enamel is applied to stamped hollows in metal.

chapter ring The ring of hour and minute numbers applied to a clock dial.

character doll A doll with a face that resembles a real child rather than an idealised one.

chassis The base of a toy vehicle including the wheels and fender.

chinoiserie Oriental-style lacquered or painted decoration featuring figures, buildings, and fauna.

chronometer Precision timekeeper designed for use at sea to calculate longitude.

clock garniture A matching set comprising of a clock and candelabra.

closed back A jewelry setting where the back of the gem is covered with metal.

collet setting A jewelry setting where the gem sits on a circular mount.

commode A decorated low chest of drawers with a bombé or serpentine shape.

composition A mixture including wood pulp, plaster, and glue and used as a cheaper alternative to bisque in the production of dolls' heads and bodies.

core forming An early form of glass-making where trails of molten glass are wound around a mud or clay core.

cornice The projecting molding on the top of tall furniture.

crackle A deliberate crazed effect found in the glaze of Chinese Song dynasty and later porcelain.

craze A network of fine cracks in the glaze caused by uneven shrinking during firing.

creamware A cream-colored earthenware with a lead glaze. Produced by Wedgwood in the 1760s and then by other factories.

credenza The Italian term for a side cabinet with display shelves at both ends.

crewelwork An embroidery technique using wool thread on a linen ground.

cultured pearl A pearl formed when an irritant is artifically introduced to the mollusc.

D

damask Fabric woven from silk, linen, or cotton with the decoration formed from the contrasting warp and weft threads.

davenport A large parlour sofa and, in the UK, a small writing desk with drawers.

dentils Small teeth-like blocks that form a border under a cornice.

diaper A repeating pattern of diamond or other geometric shapes.

diecast Objects made by pouring molten metal into a closed metal die or mold.

drop-in seat/slip-in A removable, usually upholstered seat.

E

earthenware A type of porous pottery that requires a glaze to make it waterproof.

épergne A metal or glass centerpiece with a bowl at the center and other detachable bowls.

escapement The mechanical part of a clock that regulates the transfer of energy from the weights or spring to the movement.

escucheon The protective shield-shaped plates fixed over keyholes.

excelsior A stuffing for teddy bears made from wood shavings.

F

faïence The French name for tin-glazed earthenware.

fashion doll A mid- to late-19thC French doll, usually with a bisque head and elaborate, fashionable clothing.

finial A decorative knob at the end of a terminal or on the cover of silver or ceramic vessels.

firing The baking of ceramics in a kiln.

flashing The covering of a glass vessel with a thin layer of differently colored glass which can then be carved.

flatware A general term of any type of cutlery.

flirty eyes Dolls' eyes that move from left to right as well as open and close.

foliate Leaf and flower motifs.

footrim The projecting circular support at the base of a plate or vessel.

fretwork Geometric pierced decoration.

frieze A long ornamental piece of wood underneath table top or cornice.

frit Powdered glass added to white clay to produce a type of soft-paste porcelain.

fusee A grooved metal cone that offsets the force of the spring as it runs down to ensure accurate timekeeping.

G

gadroon A decorative border of flutes or reeds.

gesso A plaster-like base applied to timber and then carved and gilded.

gilding Applying a gold coating to silver or other metals or materials.

gimbals The rotating rings attached to a chronometer to keep it level in its case.

glaze The glassy coating applied to porous ceramics to make them stronger and waterproof.

googly eyes Dolls' eyes that are large and round and glance to one side.

grosse point A needlepoint stitch that crosses two warp and two weft threads.

ground The base or background color of ceramics on which decoration is applied.

growler A mechanism found in teddy bears from the early to mid 20thC that makes a growling noise.

guilloché enamel Translucent enamel applied over engraved metal.

H

hard-paste porcelain Porcelain made from kaolin, petuntse, and quartz.

hyalith Opaque black or sealing-wax red glass produced in Bohemia from c1818.

I

inclusion Naturally occuring flaw within a gemstone.

intaglio Cut or engraved decoration on glass.

J

jasperware A hard and refined stoneware produced by Wedgwood c1775. Can be colored blue, green, yellow, or claret.

K

kaolin A fine white china clay used as the main ingredient in hard-paste porcelain.

kapok A lightweight fiber made from the seeds of the kapok tree and used to stuff teddy bears.

knop The decorative knob on lids and covers and also the bulge on the stem of a candlestick or glass.

L

lamé Silk or synthetic woven fabric shot through with metal threads.

lantern clock A mostly brass weight-driven wall clock shaped like a lantern.

lead glass or crystal A particularly clear type of glass with a high lead oxide content.

lead glaze A clear glaze that includes a lead based component.

lithography A method of printing where a design is drawn in ink on to a stone surface and then transferred to the object.

longcase clock A weight-driven, free-standing clock.

lustre An iridescent finish found on pottery and produced using metallic oxides.

M

maiolica Italian tin-glazed earthenware produced from the 14thC.

majolica 19thC heavily modeled earthenware with thick lead glazes.

mantel clock A small bracket or table clock designed to stand on a shelf or mantlepiece.

marquetry A decorative veneer with the design made up from colored woods and other materials.

mohair plush Used to make teddy bear fur and produced from angora fleece.

monochrome Single color decoration.

mold blowing A method of shaping glass objects by blowing molten glass in a mold.

molding Geometric decoration formed as strips from wood, metal, or plaster.

movement The entire time-keeping mechanism of a clock or watch.

N

niello A black alloy of lead, silver, sulphur, and copper, which is applied to metal and engraved.

O

ogee An S-shaped shallow curve.

opaline glass A translucent white glass made with the addition of oxides and bone ash.

open back A jewelry setting where the back of the gemstone is exposed.

open work Pierced decoration.

ormolu Bronze gilded by the mercury or fine gilding processes, and used in 18thC and early 19thC France as decorative mounts.

overglaze Enamel or transfer-printed decoration on porcelain, which is applied after the glaze has been fired.

ovolo A quarter-circle shaped molding.

P

paisley A soft woollen fabric with a stylized design based on pinecones.

palette The range of colors used in the decoration of ceramics.

parian A semi-matt type of porcelain produced with feldspar, and that does not require a glaze.

parure/demi-parure A jewelry set usually comprising a matching necklace, earrings, a pair of bracelets, and a brooch. A demi-parure is typically just two items such as a necklace and earrings.

pashmina A fine shawl made from the fine underbelly hair of a Himalayan mountain goat.

paste The mixture of ingredients that make up porcelain. Also a compound of glass used to make imitation gemstones.

patera An oval or circular motif often with a floral or fluted center.

pâte-sur-pâte A form of cameo-like low relief decoration produced by carving through layered slip.

pearlware Fine English earthenware developed by Wedgwood. Identified by its blue tinted glaze.

pedestal clock A large bracket clock designed to stand on a matching pedestal.

pediment The gabled form on top of a cornice.

pembroke table A small table with two flaps and four legs.

pendulum A wood or metal rod with a weighted end that controls the timekeeping of a clock.

penny toys Small and simple toys made from a variety of materials and designed to be sold for a penny.

petit point Finely worked embroidery with stiches that only cross one warp or weft thread.

petuntse The Chinese name for china stone. A feldspar that is mixed with kaolin to form hard-paste porcelain.

pinion A small toothed wheel that acts a gear within a clock movement.

piqué Form of decoration where metal is inlaid into tortoiseshell or ivory.

plique-à-jour Technique where translucent enamel is set into an openwork metal frame to create an effect similar to stained glass.

plush A fabric with a long cut pile used to make teddy bear fur.

polychrome Decoration in more than two colors.

prattware A type of creamware decorated with a high-fired palette of blue, green, and yellow.

press-molded Ceramics formed by pressing clay into a mold. Press-molded glass is made by pouring molten glass into a mold and pressing it with a plunger.

Q

quatrefoil A motif incorporating four lobes or leaves.

R

regulator A precision timekeeper used to regulate other clocks.

repoussé Embossed relief decoration on metal.

S

sabot The metal "shoe" on the end of cabriole legs.

sabre leg A leg shaped like the curved blade of a sabre.

salt glaze A thin glaze used on stonewares and made with the addition of salt during firing.

sautoir A long chain with gems or pearls set at intervals along the length.

seat rail The horizontal bar that joins the chair legs directly below a chair seat.

serpentine A curved form with a projecting middle used in case furniture.

silver gilt Silver with a thin layer of gold.

skiver The sheepskin leather inset found in the top of writing tables and desks.

slip A smooth mixture of clay and water used to decorate pottery and in the production of slip-cast wares.

slip-casting Method of manufacturing thin-bodied vessels by pouring slip into a mold.

socle A plain block that forms the base of a sculpture, vase, or column.

soda glass Formed by the addition of soda to the batch to produce a light glass with a yellow or brown tint.

soft-paste porcelain Porcelain made from kaolin, powdered glass, soapstone, and clay.

spandrel The triangular bracket found at the top of legs.

splat The central upright in a chair back.

sprigged ware Pottery decorated with ornaments applied with slip.

staining (glass) A method of coloring glass with metal oxides which are painted on and then fired.

stoneware A type of ceramic similar to earthenware and porcelain and made of high-fired clay mixed with stone, such as feldspar, which makes it non-porous.

stretchers The bar between two legs on tables and chairs used to stablise the structure.

stuff-over seat A chair with an upholstered seat rail.

stumpwork Raised embroidered needlework.

subsidiary dial A secondary dial set in the main dial that indicates seconds or the date.

swags Decorative ornaments similar to a festoon made up of fruit, flowers, husks, or nuts, or a loop of cloth.

swan-neck cresting or pediment Formed when two S-shaped curves almost meet.

T

tallcase clock See longcase clock

tantulus A lockable frame holding cut-glass spirit decanters.

tazza A shallow bowl or cup on a pedestal foot.

terracotta A red earthenware that is lightly fired and usually unglazed.

thrown ware Hollow vessels made by hand on a wheel.

tin-glaze An opaque, white glaze used on earthenware such as delftware, faïence, and maiolica and produced using tin oxide.

tinplate Toys made from thin steel covered with a coating of tin to guard against rust, which could then be painted or decorated with lithography.

toile Cotton fabric printed with a monochrome design.

torchère A portable stand with a table top to support a candle or lamp.

train A set of interconnected wheels and pinions that transfers energy from the spring or wheel to the escape mechanism.

transfer printing A method of decorating ceramic objects. An image is transferred to paper from an inked engraving and then to the vessel.

trefoil A motif incorporating three lobes or leaves.

U

underglaze The color or decoration painted on to a biscuit body before the glazing and firing.

W

wax doll Dolls with heads and occasionally bodies made from either molded or carved wax.

INDEX

INDEX

PUBLISHER'S ACKNOWLEDGEMENTS

Dorling Kindersley would like to thank Paula Regan, Anna Plucinska
and Cecilia Patterson for their assistance in producing this book.